The American Promise

A HISTORY OF THE UNITED STATES

Fourth Edition

J.-YVES MOUGIN, *CHARLIE PARKER,* **OIL ON CANVAS**
jymo@net2000.ch.

The American Promise

A HISTORY OF THE UNITED STATES

Fourth Edition

Volume II: From 1865

James L. Roark
Emory University

Michael P. Johnson
Johns Hopkins University

Patricia Cline Cohen
University of California, Santa Barbara

Sarah Stage
Arizona State University

Alan Lawson
Boston College

Susan M. Hartmann
The Ohio State University

BEDFORD/ST. MARTIN'S
Boston ◆ New York

FOR BEDFORD/ST. MARTIN'S

Publisher for History: Mary Dougherty
Director of Development for History: Jane Knetzger
Developmental Editor: Laura Arcari
Senior Production Editor: Rosemary R. Jaffe
Senior Production Supervisor: Joe Ford
Executive Marketing Manager: Jenna Bookin Barry
Editorial Assistants: Daniel Cole, Marissa Zanetti
Production Assistants: David Ayers, Katherine Caruana, Lidia MacDonald-Carr, Nicholas McCarthy
Copyeditor: Barbara Jatkola
Text Design: Wanda Kossak, Joan O'Connor
Page Layout: DeNee Reiton Skipper
Photo Research: Pembroke Hebert/Sandi Rygiel, Picture Research Consultants & Archives, Inc.
Indexer: Lois Oster
Cover Design: Billy Boardman
Cover Art: J.-Yves Mougin, *Charlie Parker,* oil on canvas. jymo@net2000.ch.
Cartography: Mapping Specialists Limited
Composition: Aptara
Printing and Binding: R.R. Donnelley & Sons Company

President: Joan E. Feinberg
Editorial Director: Denise B. Wydra
Director of Marketing: Karen Melton Soeltz
Director of Editing, Design, and Production: Marcia Cohen
Assistant Director of Editing, Design, and Production: Elise S. Kaiser
Managing Editor: Elizabeth M. Schaaf

Library of Congress Control Number: 2007927233

Manufactured in the United States of America.

1   0   9   8
f   e   d   c   b

For information, write: Bedford/St. Martin's, 75 Arlington Street, Boston, MA 02116 (617-399-4000)

ISBN–10: 0–312–45291–8   ISBN–13: 978–0–312–45291–9 (combined edition)
ISBN–10: 0–312–45292–6   ISBN–13: 978–0–312–45292–6 (Vol. I)
ISBN–10: 0–312–45293–4   ISBN–13: 978–0–312–45293–3 (Vol. II)
ISBN–10: 0–312–46999–3   ISBN–13: 978–0–312–46999–3 (Vol. A)
ISBN–10: 0–312–47000–2   ISBN–13: 978–0–312–47000–5 (Vol. B)
ISBN–10: 0–312–47001–0   ISBN–13: 978–0–312–47001–2 (Vol. C)

BRIEF CONTENTS

CONTENTS

CHAPTER 16

Reconstruction,
1863–1877   553

CHAPTER 23

From New Era to Great Depression, 1920–1932   825

CHAPTER 24

The New Deal Experiment, 1932–1939   863

(continued)

Maps

MAPS, FIGURES, AND TABLES

SPECIAL FEATURES

SPECIAL FEATURES

THE PROMISE OF TECHNOLOGY

SEEKING THE AMERICAN PROMISE

As authors, we are deeply gratified that *The American Promise* has become one of the most widely adopted texts for the U.S. history survey. This fourth edition has caused us to reflect on the evolution of the book over the years. It rests solidly on our original goals and premises, but it also has changed significantly, in large part because of the crucial suggestions made by adopters who cared enough to help us make the book better. From edition to edition, our revisions have consistently conformed to our goal to make this book the most teachable and readable introductory American history textbook available. In developing the new edition, we were gratified to learn how actively instructors teach from this book, and in response we sought in our revisions to provide instructors with even more flexibility in the classroom. Thus, for example, we've provided a greater array of special features—including new features on America's role in the world and a new biographical feature—from which teachers can construct effective classroom experiences. To engage students more fully in the American story, we've created a more vivid and compelling art program, increased the "voices" of real Americans actively shaping history, and found new ways to position American history in the global world in which students live. Finally, in our quest to make this book even easier to study from, we've created a host of imaginative pedagogical aids that provide students with greater guidance in reading, understanding, and remembering American history. Like America itself over the centuries, the fourth edition of *The American Promise* is both recognizable and new.

From the beginning, *The American Promise* has been shaped by our firsthand knowledge that the survey course is the most difficult to teach and the most difficult to take. Collectively, we have logged considerably more than a century in introductory American history classrooms in institutions that range from small community colleges to large research institutions. Our experience as teachers informs every aspect of our text, beginning with its framework. In our classrooms, we have found that students need **both** the structure a political narrative provides **and** the insights gained from examining social and cultural experience. To write a comprehensive, balanced account of American history, we focused on the public arena—the place where politics intersects social and cultural developments—to show how Americans confronted the major issues of their day and created far-reaching historical change.

We also thought hard about the concerns most frequently voiced by instructors: that students often find history boring, unfocused, and difficult and their textbooks lifeless and overwhelming. Getting students to open the book is one of the biggest hurdles instructors face. We asked ourselves how our text could address these concerns and engage students in ways that would help them understand and remember the main developments in American history. To make the political, social, economic, and cultural changes vivid and memorable and to portray fully the diversity of the American experience, we stitched into our narrative the voices of hundreds of contemporaries—from presidents to pipefitters, sharecroppers to suffragists—whose ideas and actions shaped their times and whose efforts still affect our lives. By incorporating a rich selection of authentic American voices, we seek to capture history as it happened and to create a compelling narrative that captures students' interests and sparks their historical imagination.

Our title, *The American Promise*, reflects our emphasis on human agency and our conviction that American history is an unfinished story. For millions, the nation has held out the promise of a better life, unfettered worship, representative government, democratic politics, and other freedoms seldom found elsewhere. But none of these promises has come with guarantees. As we see it, much of American history is a continuing struggle over the definition and realization of the nation's promise. Abraham Lincoln, in the midst of what he termed the "fiery trial" of the Civil War, pronounced the nation "the last best hope of Earth." Kept alive by countless sacrifices, that hope has been marred by compromises, disappointments, and denials, but it lives still. We believe that *The American Promise*, Fourth Edition, with its increased attention to making history come alive, will help students become aware of the legacy of hope bequeathed to them by previous generations of Americans stretching back nearly four centuries, a legacy that is theirs to preserve and build on.

Features

From the beginning, readers have proclaimed this textbook a visual feast, richly illustrated in ways that extend and reinforce the narrative. The fourth edition offers more than 775 contemporaneous **illustrations**. In our effort to make history tangible, we include over 300 **artifacts**—from boots and political buttons to guns and sewing machines—that emphasize the importance of material culture in the study of the past and enrich the historical account. **Comprehensive captions** for the illustrations in the book entice students to delve deeper into the text itself, and two **new visual activities** per chapter encourage students to assess visual evidence.

Our highly regarded **map program**, with over 170 maps in all, rests on the old truth that "History is not intelligible without geography." Each chapter offers, on average, four **full-size maps** showing major developments in the narrative and two to three **spot maps** embedded in the narrative that emphasize an area of detail from the discussion. To help students think critically about the role of geography in American history, we include **two critical-thinking map exercises** per chapter. New maps in the fourth edition highlight such topics as the Treaty of Fort Stanwix, Zululand and Cape Colony in 1878, worldwide oil reserves in 1980, and the recent conflict in Iraq. Another unique feature is our brief **Atlas of the Territorial Growth of the United States**, a series of full-color maps at the end of each volume that reveal the changing cartography of the nation.

As part of our ongoing efforts to make this the most teachable and readable survey text available, we paid renewed attention to imaginative and effective pedagogy. Thus, this fourth edition has increased its reach, lending greater in-text help to all levels of students. Chapters are constructed to preview, reinforce, and review the narrative in the most memorable and engaging means possible. To prepare students for the reading to come, each chapter begins with a **chapter outline** to accompany the colorful **opening vignette** that invites students into the narrative with lively accounts of individuals or groups who embody the central themes of the chapter. New vignettes in this edition include, among others, Queen Isabella supporting Columbus's expedition to the New World, the Robin Johns' experiences in the Atlantic slave trade, Deborah Sampson masquerading as a man to join the Continental army, Alexander Hamilton as a polarizing figure, James T. Rapier emerging in the early 1870s as Alabama's most prominent black leader, Frances Willard participating in the creation of the Populist Party in 1892, and Congresswoman Helen Gahagan Douglas during the cold war. Each vignette ends with a **narrative overview** of all of the chapter's main topics. Major sections within each chapter have **introductory paragraphs** that preview the subsections that follow and conclude with **new review questions** to help students check their comprehension of main ideas. **Two-tiered runningheads** with dates and topical headings remind students of chronology, and **call-outs** draw attention to interesting quotes. In addition, **thematic chronologies** reinforce points in the narrative, and **Glossary terms**, set in boldface type at first use, make historical terms accessible. At the end of each chapter, a **conclusion** reexamines central ideas and provides a bridge to the next chapter, and a **Selected Bibliography** lists important books to jump-start student research.

Perhaps the most notable new way this edition reaches out to students is through a substantial **new Reviewing the Chapter** section at the end of each chapter that provides step-by-step study plans to ensure student success. These two-page chapter review guides start with clear **study instructions** for reviewing the chapter. Lists of **Key Terms** highlight important people, events, and concepts, while illustrated chapter **Timelines** give clear chronological overviews of key events. Two sets of questions prompt students to think critically and make use of the facts they have mastered: **Review Questions** repeated from within the narrative and **Making Connections** questions that prompt students to think about broad developments. **Online Study Guide cross-references** at the end of the review section point students to free self-assessment quizzes and other study aids.

An enriched array of special features reinforces the narrative and offers teachers more points of departure for assignments and discussion. We've developed two additional options for this edition. To support our increased emphasis on the global context of U.S. history, we include sixteen **new Global Comparison figures** that showcase data visually with an emphasis on global connections. These figures introduce students to both the methods of quantitative analysis and the interesting stories behind the numbers. Features are focused on a wide range of topics, from comparing "Nineteenth-Century School Enrollment and Literacy Rates" worldwide to "Energy Consumption per Capita" in 1980. In addition, we've added seven new **Beyond America's Borders** features. These essays seek to widen students' perspectives and help students see that this country did not develop in isolation. New essays as varied as "Prisoners of War in the Eighteenth Century" and "Imperialism, Colonialism, and the Treatment of the Sioux and the Zulu" consider the reciprocal connections between the United States and the wider world and challenge students to think about the effects of transnational connections over time.

This edition also introduces fifteen **new Seeking the American Promise essays**. Each essay explores a different promise of America—from the promise of home ownership to the promise of higher education, for example—while recognizing that the promises fulfilled for some have meant promises denied to others. Biographical in nature, these features seek to inform students about how ordinary Americans have striven over the centuries to create better, richer, and happier lives for themselves. Students connect to the broader themes through the stories of Americans such as Ebenezer Mackintosh, a little-known Boston shoemaker who pursued liberty during the colonial crisis, and paraplegic Beverly Jones, who sued for access under the American with Disabilities Act in her home state of Tennessee.

Fresh topics in our three enduring special features further enrich this edition. Each **Documenting the American Promise** feature juxtaposes three or four primary documents to dramatize the human dimension of major events and show varying perspectives on a topic or issue. Feature introductions and document headnotes contextualize the sources, and Questions for Analysis and Debate promote crit-

ical thinking about primary sources. New topics in this edition include "Virginia Laws Governing Servants and Slaves," "How News of the Powder Alarm Traveled," "Defending Slavery," and "The Final Push for Woman Suffrage." **Historical Questions** essays pose and interpret specific questions of continuing interest so as to demonstrate the depth and variety of possible answers, thereby countering the belief of many beginning students that historians simply gather facts and string them together in a chronological narrative. Students recognize that history is an interpretive enterprise by joining in the questioning, arguing about, and wrestling with the past. New questions in this edition include "Who Were the First Americans?" and "Was There a Sexual Revolution in the 1920s?" The **Promise of Technology** essays examine the ramifications—positive and negative—of technological developments in American society and culture. New topics in this edition include "Electrifying America: The War of the Currents," "Household Appliances: Laborsaving Devices for Women?" and "The Pill."

Textual Changes

Because students live in an increasingly global world and need help making connections with the world outside the United States, we have substantially increased our attention to the global context of American history in the fourth edition. In addition to the two global features—Beyond America's Borders and Global Comparison figures—the transnational context of American history has been integrated throughout the narrative as appropriate, including a new section on international diplomacy during the Civil War and a comparison of the welfare state in the United States and Europe during the cold war. These additions contribute to a broader notion of American history and help students understand more fully the complex development of their nation's history and help prepare them to live in the twenty-first century.

In our ongoing effort to offer a comprehensive text that braids all Americans into the national narrative, we have increased our attention to women's history in the fourth edition. In addition to enhancing our coverage of women in the narrative—including a new section on women's education in the early republic and more on woman's suffrage—we've added thirteen new features and vignettes focused around women. Features such as a new Promise of Technology essay on laborsaving devices for women and a new Global Comparison figure on the average age of marriage in the nineteenth century place women firmly in the national narrative. Other features introduce students in more depth to many of the women who've contributed to this nation's story. Some of the extraordinary women profiled in this edition include Queen Liliuokalani in a Beyond America's Borders feature on regime change in Hawaii, Ernestine Rose in a new Seeking the American Promise feature on married women's rights to own property, and Frances Willard and Helen Gahagan Douglas in new chapter-opening vignettes.

To strengthen coverage and increase clarity and accessibility, we reorganized certain chapters. In particular, reorganization in Chapter 11, "The Expanding Republic, 1815–1840," and Chapter 12, "The New West and Free North, 1840–1860," provides clearer themes with smoother transitions. Chapter 17—newly titled "The Contested West, 1870–1900"—has also been reorganized to incorporate the latest scholarship on the colonization of the West and to accommodate an expanded treatment of the struggles of Native Americans.

Staying abreast of current scholarship is a primary concern of ours, and this edition reflects that keen interest. We incorporated a wealth of new scholarship into the fourth edition in myriad ways to benefit students. Readers will note that we made good use of the latest works on a number of topics, such as the French and Indian borderlands, the education of women in the early republic, the Barbary Wars, Denmark Vesey, black soldiers in the Civil War, the colonization of the West and the struggles of Native Americans in response to it, and American imperialism in Hawaii, as well as providing up-to-date coverage of the George W. Bush administration, the Middle East, Hurricane Katrina, and the war on terrorism.

Supplements

Developed with our guidance and thoroughly revised to reflect the changes in the fourth edition, the comprehensive collection of free and premium resources accompanying the textbook provides a host of practical learning and teaching aids. Again, we learned much from the book's community of adopters, and we broadened the scope of the supplements to create a learning package that responds to the real needs of instructors and students. Many of the new media options can not only save you and your students time and money but also add sound to the voices, movement to the images, and interactivity to the documents that help bring history to life. Cross-references in the textbook to the Online Study Guide and to the primary source reader signal the tight integration of the core text with the supplements.

For Students

Print Resources

Reading the American Past: Selected Historical Documents, Fourth Edition. Edited by Michael P. Johnson (Johns Hopkins University), one of the authors of *The American Promise*, and designed to complement the textbook, *Reading the American Past* provides a broad selection of over 150 primary source documents, as well as editorial apparatus to help students understand the sources. Emphasizing the important social, political, and economic themes of U.S. history courses, thirty-two new documents (at least one per chapter) were added to provide a multiplicity of perspectives on environmental, western, ethnic, and gender history and to bring a global dimension to the anthology. Available free when packaged with the text and now available as an e-book (see below).

Maps in Context: A Workbook for American History. Written by historical cartography expert Gerald A. Danzer (University of Illinois, Chicago), this skill-building workbook helps students comprehend essential connections between geographic literacy and historical understanding. Organized to correspond to the typical U.S. history survey course, *Maps in Context* presents a wealth of map-centered projects and convenient pop quizzes that give students hands-on experience working with maps. Available free when packaged with the text.

Student Guide for *Shaping America: U.S. History to 1877* and *Transforming America: U.S. History since 1877*. This guide by Kenneth G.

Alfers (Dallas County Community College District) is designed for students using *The American Promise* in conjunction with the Dallas TeleLearning telecourse *Shaping America* and *Transforming America*. Lesson overviews, assignments, objectives, and focus points provide structure for distance learners, while enrichment ideas, suggested readings, and brief primary sources extend the unit lessons. Practice tests help students evaluate their mastery of the material.

NEW Trade Books. Titles published by sister companies Farrar, Straus and Giroux; Henry Holt and Company; Hill and Wang; Picador; and St. Martin's Press are available at a 50 percent discount when packaged with Bedford/St. Martin's textbooks. For more information, visit bedfordstmartins.com/tradeup.

NEW *The Bedford Glossary for U.S. History.* This handy supplement for the survey course gives students clear, concise definitions of the political, economic, social, and cultural terms used by historians and contemporary media alike. The terms are historically contextualized to aid comprehension. Available free when packaged with the text.

History Matters: A Student Guide to U.S. History Online. This resource, written by Alan Gevinson, Kelly Schrum, and Roy Rosenzweig (all of George Mason University), provides an illustrated and annotated guide to 250 of the most useful Web sites for student research in U.S. history as well as advice on evaluating and using Internet sources. This essential guide is based on the acclaimed "History Matters" Web site developed by the American History Social Project and the Center for History and New Media. Available free when packaged with the text.

Bedford Series in History and Culture. Over one hundred titles in this highly praised series combine first-rate scholarship, historical narrative, and important primary documents for undergraduate courses. Each book is brief, inexpensive, and focused on a specific topic or period. Package discounts are available.

Historians at Work Series. Brief enough for a single assignment yet meaty enough to provoke thoughtful discussion, each volume in this series examines a single historical question by combining unabridged selections by distinguished historians, each with a different perspective on the issue, with helpful learning aids. Package discounts are available.

New Media Resources

NEW e-Book integrating *The American Promise* **with its companion sourcebook and Online Study Guide.** Not your usual e-book, this one-of-a-kind online resource integrates the text of *The American Promise*, with the 150 additional written sources of the companion sourcebook, *Reading the American Past*, and the self-testing and activities of the Online Study Guide into one easy-to-use e-book. With search functions stronger than in any competing text, this e-book is an ideal study and reference tool for students. Instructors can easily add documents, images, and other material to customize the text, making this e-book perfect for instructors who wish to build dynamic online courses or use electronic texts and documents. **Can be packaged FREE with the print text or purchased stand-alone for about half the price.**

Online Study Guide at bedfordstmartins.com/roark. The popular Online Study Guide for *The American Promise* is a free and uniquely personalized learning tool to help students master themes and information presented in the textbook and improve their historical skills. Assessment quizzes let students evaluate their comprehension and provide them with customized plans for further study through a variety of activities. Instructors can monitor students' progress through the online Quiz Gradebook or receive e-mail updates.

NEW Audio Reviews for *The American Promise*, **Fourth Edition, at** bedfordstmartins.com/roark. Audio Reviews are a new tool that fits easily into students' lifestyles and provides a practical new way for them to study. These twenty-five-to thirty-minute summaries of each chapter in *The American Promise* highlight the major themes of the text and help reinforce student learning.

Online Bibliography at bedfordstmartins.com/roark. Organized by book chapter and topic, the online bibliography provides an authoritative and comprehensive list of references to jump-start student research.

A Student's Online Guide to History Reference Sources at bedfordstmartins.com/roark. This Web site provides links to history-related databases, indexes, and journals, plus contact information for state, provincial, local, and professional history organizations.

The Bedford Research Room at bedfordstmartins .com/roark. The Research Room, drawn from Mike Palmquist's *The Bedford Researcher*, offers a wealth of resources—including interactive tutorials, research activities, student writing samples, and links to hundreds of other places online—to support students in courses across the disciplines. The site also offers instructors a library of helpful instructional tools.

The Bedford Bibliographer at bedfordstmartins .com/roark. *The Bedford Bibliographer*, a simple but powerful Web-based tool, assists students with the process of collecting sources and generates bibliographies in four commonly used documentation styles.

Research and Documentation Online at bedfordstmartins.com/roark. This Web site provides clear advice on how to integrate primary and secondary sources into research papers, how to cite sources correctly, and how to format in MLA, APA, *Chicago*, or CBE style.

The St. Martin's Tutorial on Avoiding Plagiarism at bedfordstmartins.com/roark. This online tutorial reviews the consequences of plagiarism and explains what sources to acknowledge, how to keep good notes, how to organize research, and how to integrate sources appropriately. The tutorial includes exercises to help students practice integrating sources and recognize acceptable summaries.

Critical Thinking Modules at bedfordstmartins .com/roark. This Web site offers over two dozen online modules for interpreting maps, audio, visual, and textual sources, centered on events covered in the U.S. history survey.

For Instructors

Print Resources

Instructor's Resource Manual. This popular manual by Sarah E. Gardner (Mercer University) and Catherine A. Jones (Johns Hopkins University) offers both experienced and first-time instructors tools for presenting textbook material in exciting and engaging ways—learning objectives, annotated chapter outlines, lecture strategies, tips for helping students with common misconceptions and difficult topics, and suggestions for in-class activities, including using film and video, ways to start discussions, topics for debate, and analyzing primary sources. The new edition includes model answers for the questions in the book as well as a chapter-by-chapter guide to all of the supplements available with *The American Promise*. An extensive guide for first-time teaching assistants and sample syllabi are also included.

Transparencies. This set of over 160 full-color acetate transparencies includes all full-size maps and many other images from the textbook to help instructors present lectures and teach students important map-reading skills.

Using the Bedford Series in History and Culture in the U.S. History Survey at bedfordstmartins .com/usingseries. This online guide helps instructors integrate volumes from the highly regarded Bedford Series in History and Culture into their U.S. history survey course. The guide not only correlates themes from each series book with the survey course but also provides ideas for classroom discussions.

New Media Resources

NEW HistoryClass. Bedford/St. Martin's course management system for the history classroom provides a complete online learning solution by integrating our e-books and the rich content of our book companion sites.

Instructor's Resource CD-ROM. This disc provides instructors with ready-made and customizable PowerPoint multimedia presentations built around chapter outlines, maps, figures, and selected images from the textbook, plus jpeg versions of all maps, figures, and selected images.

Computerized Test Bank. Written by Bradford Wood (Eastern Kentucky University), Peter Lau (University of Rhode Island), and Sondra Cosgrove (Community College of Northern Nevada), the test bank provides over eighty exercises per chapter, including multiple-choice, fill-in-the-blank, map analysis, short essay, and full-length essay questions. Instructors can customize quizzes, add or edit both questions and answers, and export questions and answers to a variety of formats, including WebCT and Blackboard. The disc includes correct answers and essay outlines as well as separate test banks for the associated telecourses *Shaping America* and *Transforming America*.

Book Companion Site at bedfordstmartins .com/roark. The companion Web site gathers all the electronic resources for *The American Promise*, including the Online Study Guide and related Quiz Gradebook, at a single Web address, providing convenient links to lecture, assignment, and research materials such as PowerPoint chapter outlines and the digital libraries at Make History.

Make History at bedfordstmartins.com/roark. Comprising the content of our five acclaimed on-line libraries — Map Central, the Bedford History Image Library, DocLinks, HistoryLinks, and PlaceLinks — Make History provides one-stop access to relevant digital content, including maps, images, documents, and Web links. Students and instructors alike can search this free, easy-to-use database by keyword, topic, date, or specific chapter of *The American Promise* and download the content they find. Instructors can also create entire collections of content and store them online for later use or post their collections to the Web to share with students.

Content for Course Management Systems. A variety of student and instructor resources de-veloped for this textbook is ready for use in course management systems such as Blackboard, WebCT, and other platforms. This e-content in-cludes nearly all of the offerings from the book's Online Study Guide as well as the book's test bank and the test banks from the associated tele-courses *Shaping America* and *Transforming America*.

NEW Reel Teaching. A valuable tool for enhanc-ing media-rich lectures, short segments in VHS and DVD format are available to qualified adopters from the award-winning telecourses *Shaping America* and *Transforming America* by Dallas TeleLearning at the LeCroy Center for Educational Telecommunications.

The American Promise **via Telecourse.** We are pleased to announce that *The American Promise* has been selected as the textbook for the award-winning U.S. history telecourses *Shaping America: U.S. History to 1877* and *Transforming America: U.S. History since 1877* by Dallas TeleLearning at the LeCroy Center for Educational Telecommunications, Dallas County Community College District. Guides for students and instructors fully integrate the narrative of *The American Promise* into each telecourse. For more information on these distance-learning opportunities, visit the Dallas TeleLearning Web site at http://telelearning .dcccd.edu, e-mail tlearn@dcccd.edu, or call 972-669-6650.

Videos and Multimedia. A wide assortment of videos and multimedia CD-ROMs on various topics in American history is available to quali-fied adopters.

Acknowledgments

We gratefully acknowledge all of the helpful suggestions from those who have read and taught from the previous editions of *The American Promise*, and we hope that our many classroom collaborators will be pleased to see their influence in the fourth edition. In particular, we wish to thank the talented scholars and teachers who gave generously of their time and knowledge to review this book; their critiques and suggestions contributed greatly to the published work: Kathryn Abbot, *Western Kentucky University*; Carol Anderson, *University of Missouri, Columbia*; Melissa Anyiwo, *University of Tennessee, Chattanooga*; Janis Appier, *University of Tennessee*; Marjorie Berman, *Red Rocks Community College*; Bill Bush, *University of Nevada, Las Vegas*; Charles Byler, *Carroll College*; Dominic Carrillo, *Grossmont College*; Stephanie Cole, *University of Texas, Arlington*; Barak Cook, *University of Missouri*; Sheri David, *North Virginia Community College, Manassas*; Tracy Davis, *Victor Valley College*; Thomas Dicke, *Missouri State University*; Don Doyle, *University of South Carolina*; Bill G. Dykes, *Temple Baptist College*; John Elder, *University of Central Oklahoma*; Karen Enloe, *Glendale Community College*; Amy Essington, *California State University, Long Beach*; Dana Frank, *University of California, Santa Cruz*; Hal Friedman, *Henry Ford Community College*; Steven Gargo, *Appleton Area Schools*; Michael Garcia, *Arapahoe Community College*; David Gerleman, *George Mason University*; Gina Estep Gompert, *Sierra College*; Larry Grubbs, *University of Georgia*; Allen Hamilton, *St. Phillips College*; Paul Hudson, *Georgia Perimeter College*; Jeffrey Irvin, *Monroe County Community College*; Frances M. Jacobson, *Tidewater Community College*; Jeanette Keith, *Bloomsburg University*; Daniel P. Kotzin, *Kutztown University*; Lou LaGrande, *St. Petersburg College*; Brad Lookingbill, *Columbia College*; Robert Martin, *University of Northern Iowa*; Suzanne Summers McFadden, *Austin Community College*; Rebecca Mead, *Northern Michigan University*; Warren Metcalf, *University of Oklahoma*; Carlos Mujal, *De Anza College*; William Murphy, *SUNY Oswego*; Cassandra Newby-Alexander, *Old Dominion*; Cynthia Clark Northrup, *University of Texas, Arlington*; Carla Pestana, *Miami University*; Caroline Pruden, *North Carolina State*; Kimber Quinney, *California State San Marcos*; Akin Reinhardt, *Towson University*; Rob Risko, *Trinity Valley Community College*; Jere Roberson, *University of Central Oklahoma*; Horacia Salinas Jr., *Laredo Community College*; Sharon Salinger, *University of California, Irvine*; Ken Shafer, *Cerritos College*; Donald R. Shaffer, *University of Northern Colorado*; John Simpson, *Pierce College*; Tiwanna Simpson, *Louisiana State University*; Sherry Smith, *Southern Methodist University*; Melissa Soto-Schwartz, *Cuyahoga Community College*; Mark Stephens, *Los Positas College*; Thomas Summerhill, *Michigan State University*; Wesley Swanson, *San Joaquin Delta College*; Stacy L. Tanner, *Georgia Southern University*; Pat Thompson, *University of Texas, San Antonio*; Stephen Tootle, *University of Northern Colorado*; Kenneth Townsend, *Coastal University*; David White, *McHenry Community College*; LeeAnn Whites, *University of Missouri, Columbia*; and Rosemary Zagarri, *George Mason University*.

A project as complex as this requires the talents of many individuals. First, we would like to acknowledge our families for their support, forbearance, and toleration of our textbook responsibilities. Pembroke Herbert and Sandi Rygiel of Picture Research Consultants, Inc., contributed their unparalleled knowledge, soaring imagination, and diligent research to make possible the extraordinary illustration program.

We would also like to thank the many people at Bedford/St. Martin's who have been crucial to this project. No one contributed more than developmental editor Laura Arcari, who managed the entire revision and oversaw the development of each chapter. The results of her dedication to excellence and commitment to creating the best textbook imaginable are evident on every page. We greatly appreciate the acute intelligence and indomitable good humor that Laura brought to this revision. We thank freelance editors Jan Fitter, Michelle McSweeney, and Terri Wise for their help with the manuscript. Thanks also go to editorial assistant Daniel Cole for his assistance managing the reviews and associate editor Marissa Zanetti, who provided unflagging assistance and who coordinated the supplements. We are also grateful to Jane Knetzger, director of development for history, and Mary Dougherty, publisher for history, for their support and guidance. For their imaginative and tireless efforts to promote the book, we want to thank Jenna Bookin Barry, executive marketing manager; John Hunger, senior history specialist; and Amanda Byrnes, senior marketing associate. With great skill and professionalism, Rosemary Jaffe, senior production editor, pulled together the many pieces related to copyediting, design, and typesetting, with the able assistance of David Ayers, Katherine Caruana, Lidia MacDonald-Carr, and Nicholas McCarthy and the guidance of managing editor Elizabeth Schaaf and assistant managing editor John Amburg. Senior production supervisor Joe Ford oversaw the manufacturing of the book. Designers Wanda Kossak and Joan O'Connor and page makeup artist DeNee Reiton Skipper, copyeditor Barbara Jatkola, and proofreaders Linda McLatchie and Stella Gelboin attended to the myriad details that help make the book shine. Lois Oster provided an outstanding index. The book's gorgeous covers were designed by Billy Boardman. Editor Danielle Slevens and associate editor Marissa Zanetti made sure that *The American Promise* remains at the forefront of technological support for students and instructors. Editorial director Denise Wydra provided helpful advice throughout the course of the project. Finally, Charles H. Christensen, former president, took a personal interest in *The American Promise* from the start, and Joan E. Feinberg, president, guided all editions through every stage of development.

JAMES L. ROARK

Born in Eunice, Louisiana, and raised in the West, James L. Roark received his B.A. from the University of California, Davis, in 1963 and his Ph.D. from Stanford University in 1973. His dissertation won the Allan Nevins Prize. He has taught at the University of Nigeria, Nsukka; the University of Nairobi, Kenya; the University of Missouri, St. Louis; and, since 1983, Emory University, where he is Samuel Candler Dobbs Professor of American History. In 1993, he received the Emory Williams Distinguished Teaching Award, and in 2001–2002 he was Pitt Professor of American Institutions at Cambridge University. He has written *Masters without Slaves: Southern Planters in the Civil War and Reconstruction* (1977). With Michael P. Johnson, he is author of *Black Masters: A Free Family of Color in the Old South* (1984) and editor of *No Chariot Let Down: Charleston's Free People of Color on the Eve of the Civil War* (1984). He has received research assistance from the American Philosophical Society, the National Endowment for the Humanities, and the Gilder Lehrman Institute of American History. Active in the Organization of American Historians and the Southern Historical Association, he is also a fellow of the Society of American Historians.

MICHAEL P. JOHNSON

Born and raised in Ponca City, Oklahoma, Michael P. Johnson studied at Knox College in Galesburg, Illinois, where he received a B.A. in 1963, and at Stanford University in Palo Alto, California, earning a Ph.D. in 1973. He is currently professor of history at Johns Hopkins University in Baltimore, having previously taught at the University of California, Irvine; San Jose State University; and LeMoyne (now LeMoyne-Owen) College in Memphis. His publications include *Toward a Patriarchal Republic: The Secession of Georgia* (1977); with James L. Roark, *Black Masters: A Free Family of Color in the Old South* (1984) and *No Chariot Let Down:*

Charleston's Free People of Color on the Eve of the Civil War (1984); *Abraham Lincoln, Slavery, and the Civil War: Selected Speeches and Writings* (2001); *Reading the American Past: Selected Historical Documents*, the documents reader for *The American Promise*; and articles that have appeared in the *William and Mary Quarterly*, the *Journal of Southern History, Labor History*, the *New York Review of Books*, the *New Republic*, the *Nation*, and other journals. Johnson has been awarded research fellowships by the American Council of Learned Societies, the National Endowment for the Humanities, the Center for Advanced Study in the Behavioral Sciences and Stanford University, and the Times Mirror Foundation Distinguished Research Fellowship at the Huntington Library. He has directed a National Endowment for the Humanities Summer Seminar for College Teachers and has been honored with the University of California, Irvine, Academic Senate Distinguished Teaching Award and the University of California, Irvine, Alumni Association Outstanding Teaching Award. He won the *William and Mary Quarterly* award for best article in 2002 and the Organization of American Historians ABC-CLIO *America: History and Life* Award for best American history article in 2002. He is an active member of the American Historical Association, the Organization of American Historians, and the Southern Historical Association.

PATRICIA CLINE COHEN

Born in Ann Arbor, Michigan, and raised in Palo Alto, California, Patricia Cline Cohen earned a B.A. at the University of Chicago in 1968 and a Ph.D. at the University of California, Berkeley, in 1977. In 1976, she joined the history faculty at the University of California, Santa Barbara. In 2005–2006, she received the university's Distinguished Teaching Award. Cohen has written *A Calculating People: The Spread of Numeracy in Early America* (1982; reissued 1999) and *The Murder of Helen Jewett: The Life and Death of a*

Prostitute in Nineteenth-Century New York (1998). She has also published articles on quantitative literacy, mathematics education, prostitution, and murder in journals including the *Journal of Women's History, Radical History Review,* the *William and Mary Quarterly,* and the *NWSA Journal.* Her scholarly work has received support from the National Endowment for the Humanities, the National Humanities Center, the University of California President's Fellowship in the Humanities, the Mellon Foundation, the American Antiquarian Society, the Schlesinger Library, and the Newberry Library. She is an active associate of the Omohundro Institute of Early American History and Culture, sits on the advisory council of the Society for the History of the Early American Republic, and is past president of the Western Association of Women Historians. She has served as chair of the history department, as chair of the Women's Studies Program, and as acting dean of the humanities and fine arts at the University of California at Santa Barbara. In 2001–2002, she was the Distinguished Senior Mellon Fellow at the American Antiquarian Society. Currently she is working on a book about women's health advocate Mary Gove Nichols.

SARAH STAGE

Sarah Stage was born in Davenport, Iowa, and received a B.A. from the University of Iowa in 1966 and a Ph.D. in American studies from Yale University in 1975. She has taught U.S. history for more than twenty-five years at Williams College and the University of California, Riverside. Currently she is professor of Women's Studies at Arizona State University at the West campus in Phoenix. Her books include *Female Complaints: Lydia Pinkham and the Business of Women's Medicine* (1979) and *Rethinking Home Economics: Women and the History of a Profession* (1997), which has been translated for a Japanese edition. Among the fellowships she has received are the Rockefeller Foundation Humanities Fellowship, the American Association of University Women dissertation fellowship, a fellowship from the Charles Warren Center for the Study of History at Harvard University, and the University of California President's Fellowship in the Humanities. She is at work on a book entitled *Women and the Progressive Impulse in American Politics, 1890–1914.*

ALAN LAWSON

Born in Providence, Rhode Island, Alan Lawson received his B.A. from Brown University in 1955 and his M.A. from the University of Wisconsin in 1956. After Army service and experience as a high school teacher, he earned his Ph.D. from the University of Michigan in 1967. Since winning the Allan Nevins Prize for his dissertation, Lawson has served on the faculties of the University of California, Irvine; Smith College; and, currently, Boston College. He has written *The Failure of Independent Liberalism* (1971) and coedited *From Revolution to Republic* (1976). While completing the forthcoming *Ideas in Crisis: The New Deal and the Mobilization of Progressive Experience,* he has published book chapters and essays on political economy, the cultural legacy of the New Deal, multiculturalism, and the arts in public life. He has served as editor of the *Review of Education* and the *Intellectual History Newsletter* and contributed articles to those journals as well as to the *History of Education Quarterly.* He has been active in the field of American studies as director of the Boston College American studies program and as a contributor to the *American Quarterly.* Under the auspices of the United States Information Agency, Lawson has been coordinator and lecturer for programs to instruct faculty from foreign nations in the state of American historical scholarship and teaching.

SUSAN M. HARTMANN

Professor of history at Ohio State University, Susan M. Hartmann received her B.A. from Washington University and her Ph.D. from the University of Missouri. After specializing in the political economy of the post–World War II period and publishing *Truman and the 80th Congress* (1971), she expanded her interests to the field of women's history, publishing many articles and three books: *The Home Front and Beyond: American Women in the 1940s* (1982); *From Margin to Mainstream: American Women and Politics since 1960* (1989); and *The Other Feminists: Activists in the Liberal Establishment* (1998). Her work has been supported by the Truman Library Institute, the Rockefeller Foundation, the National Endowment for the Humanities, and the American Council of

Learned Societies. At Ohio State, she has served as director of women's studies, and in 1995 she won the Exemplary Faculty Award in the College of Humanities. Hartmann has taught at the University of Missouri, St. Louis, and Boston University, and she has lectured on American history in Australia, Austria, France, Germany, Greece, Japan, Nepal, and New Zealand. She is a fellow of the Society of American Historians; has served on award committees of the American Historical Association, the Organization of American Historians, the American Studies Association, and the National Women's Studies Association; and currently is on the Board of Directors at the Truman Library Institute. Her current research is on gender and the transformation of politics since 1945.

The
American
Promise

A HISTORY OF THE UNITED STATES

Fourth Edition

CARPETBAG

A carpetbag was a nineteenth-
century suitcase made from carpet, often brightly
colored. Applied first to wildcat bankers on the western frontier,
"carpetbagger" was a derogatory name for rootless and penniless adventurers who
could carry everything they owned in a single bag. Critics of Republican administrations
in the South hurled the name "carpetbaggers" at white Northerners who moved South
during Reconstruction and became active in politics. According to white Southerners,
carpetbaggers exploited gullible ex-slaves to gain power and wealth. In fact, many
Northerners who came to the South joined with blacks and some southern whites to
form Republican state and local governments that were among the most progressive
anywhere in the nineteenth century.

Reconstruction

1863–1877

I N 1856, JOHN RAPIER, a free black barber in Florence, Alabama, urged his four freeborn sons to flee the increasingly repressive and dangerous South. Searching for a color-blind society, three of the brothers scattered to New York, California, and Panama. The fourth, James T. Rapier, chose Canada, where he went to live with his uncle in a largely black community and studied Greek and Latin in a log schoolhouse. After his conversion at a Methodist revival, James wrote to his father: "I have not thrown a card in 3 years[,] touched a woman in 2 years[,] smoked nor drunk any Liquor in going on 2 years." And he vowed, "I will endeavor to do my part in solving the problems [of African Americans] in my native land."

The approaching Union victory in the Civil War gave James Rapier the opportunity to redeem his pledge. Defeat promised to turn the South upside down. With the Confederacy dead and slavery gone, blacks could push for equality. A few months before the war ended, after eight years of exile, the twenty-seven-year-old Rapier returned to the South. He participated in a freedmen's convention in Tennessee and then went home to Alabama, where he presided over the first political gathering of former slaves in the state. The Alabama freedmen produced a petition that called on the federal government to thoroughly reconstruct the South, to grant blacks the vote, and to guarantee free speech, free press, free schools, and equal rights for all men, regardless of color.

Rapier soon discovered that Alabama's whites found it agonizingly difficult to accept defeat and black freedom. They responded to the revolutionary changes under the banner "White Man—Right or Wrong—Still the White Man!" In 1868, when Rapier and other Alabama blacks vigorously supported the Republican presidential candidate, former Union general Ulysses S. Grant, the recently organized Ku Klux Klan went on a bloody rampage of whipping, burning, and shooting. In September, a mob of 150 outraged whites scoured Rapier's neighborhood seeking four black politicians they claimed were trying to "Africanize Alabama." They caught and hanged three, but the "nigger carpetbagger from Canada" escaped. Badly shaken, Rapier considered fleeing the state, but he decided to stay and fight.

Tall, handsome, knowledgeable, and quick-witted, Rapier emerged in the early 1870s as Alabama's most prominent black leader. He demanded that the federal government end the violence against ex-slaves and guarantee their civil rights. He called for debt relief for black sharecroppers and tenant farmers, the end of racial segregation in public places, and land for freedmen. In 1872, he won election to the House of Representatives and joined six other black congressmen in Washington, D.C. Even those who sought to destroy him and overthrow so-called "Negro rule" admitted that Rapier was "the

J. T. Rapier

Only two years after emancipation, ex-slaves in the United States gained full political rights and wielded far more political power than former bondsmen anywhere else in the New World. Black suffrage sent fourteen African American congressmen to Washington, D.C., during Reconstruction, among them James T. Rapier of Alabama. Temporarily at least, he and his black colleagues helped shape post-emancipation society. In 1874, Rapier spoke passionately in favor of a civil rights bill. He described the humiliation of being denied service at inns all along his route from Montgomery to Washington. Elsewhere in the world, he said, class and religion were invoked to defend discrimination. In Europe, "they have princes, dukes, lords"; in India, "brahmans or priests, who rank above the sudras or laborers." But in America, "our distinction is color."
Alabama Department of Archives and History.

best intellect under a colored skin in Alabama." Defeated for reelection in 1874 in a fraudulent campaign of violence and ballot box stuffing, Rapier turned to cotton farming, generously giving thousands of dollars of his profits to black schools and churches.

Rapier's black constituents celebrated him as a hero, but in the eyes of dominant whites, he was "nothing but a nigger." Embittered by persistent black poverty and illiteracy, demoralized by continuing racial violence and a federal government that refused to stop it, Rapier again chose exile. Kansas attracted him because of its millions of acres of cheap land and because it was, before the war, home to that fiery enemy of slavery John

Brown. After more than a dozen trips scouting the possibilities in Kansas, Rapier purchased land and urged Alabama's blacks to escape with him. Buoyant and confident when he returned to Alabama in 1865, he had over the years grown profoundly pessimistic that blacks could ever achieve equality and prosperity in the South. In 1883, however, before he could leave Alabama, Rapier died of tuberculosis at the age of forty-five.

In 1865, Carl Schurz had foreseen many of the troubles Rapier would encounter in the postwar South. A Union general who undertook a fact-finding mission to the former Confederate states immediately after the war, Schurz concluded that the Civil War was "a revolution but half accomplished." Northern victory had freed the slaves, but it had not changed former slaveholders' minds about blacks' unfitness for freedom. Left to themselves, Schurz believed, whites would "introduce some new system of forced labor, not perhaps exactly slavery in its old form but something similar to it." To defend their freedom, Schurz concluded, blacks would need federal protection, land of their own, and voting rights. Until whites "cut loose from the past, it will be a dangerous experiment to put Southern society upon its own legs."

As Schurz discovered, the end of the war did not mean peace. The United States was one of only two societies in the New World in which slavery ended in bloody war. (The other was Haiti, where a slave revolt that began in 1791 eventually swept slavery away.) Not surprisingly, racial turmoil continued in the South after the armies quit fighting in 1865. The nation entered one of its most chaotic and conflicted eras—Reconstruction, a violent period that would define the defeated South's status within the Union and the meaning of freedom for ex-slaves.

The place of the South within the nation and the extent of black freedom were determined not only in Washington, D.C., where the federal government played an active role, but also in the state legislatures and county seats of the South, where blacks participated in the process. Moreover, on farms and plantations from Virginia to Texas, ex-slaves struggled to become free people while ex-slaveholders clung to the Old South.

In the midst of Reconstruction's racial flux and economic chaos, a small band of crusading women sought to achieve gender equality. Their attempts to secure voting rights for women as well as blacks were blunted, and they soon turned their attention solely to the feminist cause.

Reconstruction witnessed a gigantic struggle to determine the consequences of Confederate defeat and **emancipation**. In the end, white Southerners prevailed. Their **New South** was a different South from the one to which most whites wished to return but also vastly unlike the one of which James Rapier dreamed.

Wartime Reconstruction

Reconstruction did not wait for the end of war. As the odds of a northern victory increased, thinking about reunification quickened. Immediately, a question arose: Who had authority to devise a plan for reconstructing the Union? President Abraham Lincoln believed firmly that reconstruction was a matter of executive responsibility. Congress just as firmly asserted its jurisdiction. Fueling the argument about who had the authority to set the terms of reconstruction were significant differences about the terms themselves. Lincoln's primary aim was the restoration of national unity, which he sought through a program of speedy, forgiving political reconciliation. Congress feared that the president's program amounted to restoring the old southern ruling class to power. It wanted greater assurances of white loyalty and greater guarantees of black rights.

In their eagerness to formulate a plan for political reunification, neither Lincoln nor Congress gave much attention to the South's land and labor problems. But as the war rapidly eroded slavery and traditional plantation agriculture, Yankee military commanders in the Union-occupied areas of the Confederacy had no choice but to oversee the emergence of a new labor system.

"To Bind Up the Nation's Wounds"

On March 4, 1865, President Lincoln delivered his second inaugural address. He surveyed the history of the long, deadly war and then looked ahead to peace. "With malice toward none; with charity for all; with firmness in the right, as God gives us to see the right," Lincoln said, "let us strive on to finish the work we are in; to bind up the nation's wounds . . . to do all which may achieve and cherish a just, and a lasting peace." Lincoln had contemplated reunion for nearly two years. While deep compassion for the enemy guided his thinking about peace, his plan

for reconstruction aimed primarily at shortening the war and ending slavery.

In his Proclamation of Amnesty and Reconstruction, issued in December 1863, Lincoln offered a full pardon to rebels willing to renounce secession and to accept emancipation. (Pardons were valuable because they restored all property, except slaves, and full political rights.) His offer excluded only high-ranking Confederate military and political officers and a few other groups. When merely 10 percent of a state's voting population had taken an oath of allegiance, the state could organize a new government. Lincoln's plan did not require ex-rebels to extend social or political rights to ex-slaves, nor did it anticipate a program of long-term federal assistance to freedmen. Clearly, the president looked forward to the speedy restoration of the broken Union.

Lincoln's easy terms enraged abolitionists such as Wendell Phillips of Boston, who charged that the president "makes the negro's freedom a mere sham." He "is willing that the negro should be free but seeks nothing else for him," Phillips declared. He compared Lincoln to the most passive of the Civil War generals: "What McClellan was on the battlefield— 'Do as little hurt as possible!'— Lincoln is in civil affairs—'Make as little change as possible!' " Phillips and other northern radicals called instead for a thorough

> Lincoln "is willing that the negro should be free but seeks nothing else for him," Wendell Phillips declared.

overhaul of southern society. Their ideas proved to be too drastic for most Republicans during the war years, but Congress agreed that Lincoln's plan was inadequate. In July 1864, Congress put forward a plan of its own.

Congressman Henry Winter Davis of Maryland and Senator Benjamin Wade of Ohio jointly sponsored a bill that demanded that at least half of the voters in a conquered rebel state take the oath of allegiance before reconstruction could begin. Moreover, the Wade-Davis bill banned all ex-Confederates from participating in the drafting of new state constitutions. Finally, the bill guaranteed the equality of freedmen before the law. Congress's reconstruction would be neither as quick nor as forgiving as Lincoln's. When Lincoln exercised his right not to sign the bill and let it die instead, Wade and Davis charged the president with usurpation of power. They warned Lincoln to confine himself to "his executive duties—to obey and execute, not make the laws—to suppress by arms armed rebellion, and leave political organization to Congress."

Military Auction of Condemned Property, Beaufort, South Carolina, 1865
During the war, thousands of acres of land in the South came into federal hands as abandoned property or as a result of seizures due to nonpayment of taxes. The government authorized the sale of some of this land at public auction. This rare photograph shows expectant blacks (and a few whites) gathered in Beaufort, South Carolina, for a sale. Very few former slaves could raise enough money to purchase land, and even when they pooled their resources, they usually lost out to northern army officers, government officials, or speculators with deeper pockets. Several of the individuals here are wearing Union army caps, strong affirmation of their political loyalties.
The Huntington Library, San Marino, California.

Undeterred, Lincoln continued to nurture the formation of loyal state governments under his own plan. Four states—Louisiana, Arkansas, Tennessee, and Virginia—fulfilled the president's requirements, but Congress refused to seat representatives from the "Lincoln states." In his last public address in April 1865, Lincoln defended his plan but for the first time expressed publicly his endorsement of **suffrage** for southern blacks, at least "the very intelligent, and . . . those who serve our cause as soldiers." The announcement demonstrated that Lincoln's thinking about reconstruction was still evolving. Four days later, he was dead.

Land and Labor

Of all the problems raised by the North's victory in the war, none proved more critical than the South's transition from slavery to **free labor**. As federal armies invaded and occupied the Confederacy, hundreds of thousands of slaves became free workers. Union armies controlled vast territories in the South where legal title to land had become unclear. The wartime Confiscation Acts punished "traitors" by taking away their property. The question of what to do with federally occupied land and how to organize labor on it engaged former slaves, former slaveholders, Union military commanders, and federal government officials long before the war ended.

Up and down the Mississippi valley, occupying federal troops announced a new labor code. The code required slaveholders to sign contracts with ex-slaves and to pay wages. It obligated employers to provide food, housing, and medical care. It outlawed whipping, but it reserved to the army the right to discipline blacks who refused to work. The code required black laborers to enter into contracts, work diligently, and remain subordinate and obedient. Military leaders clearly had no intention of promoting a social or economic revolution. Instead, they sought to restore plantation agriculture with wage labor. The effort resulted in a hybrid system that one contemporary called "compulsory free labor," something that satisfied no one. Depending on one's point of view, it provided either too little or too much of a break with the past.

Planters complained because the new system fell short of slavery. Blacks could not be "transformed by proclamation," a Louisiana sugar planter warned. Yet under the new system, blacks "are expected to perform their new obligations without coercion, & without the fear of punishment which is essential to stimulate the idle and correct the vicious." Without the right to whip, he argued, the new labor system did not have a chance.

African Americans found the new regime too reminiscent of slavery to be called free labor. Its chief deficiency, they believed, was the failure to provide them with land of their own. "What's the use of being free if you don't own land enough to be buried in?" one man asked. Freedmen believed they had a moral right to land because they and their ancestors had worked it without compensation for more than two centuries. Moreover, several wartime developments led them to believe that the federal government planned to undergird black freedom with land-ownership.

In January 1865, General William Tecumseh Sherman set aside part of the coast south of Charleston for black settlement. He devised the plan to relieve himself of the burden of thousands of impoverished blacks who trailed desperately after his army. By June 1865, some 40,000 freedmen sat on 400,000 acres of "Sherman land." In addition, in March 1865, Congress passed a bill establishing the Bureau of Refugees, Freedmen, and Abandoned Lands. The Freedmen's Bureau, as it was called, distributed food and clothing to destitute Southerners and eased the transition of blacks from slaves to free persons. Congress also authorized the agency to divide abandoned and confiscated land into 40-acre plots, to rent them to freedmen, and eventually to sell them "with such title as the United States can convey." By June 1865, the bureau had situated nearly 10,000 black families on a half million acres abandoned by fleeing planters. Hundreds of thousands of other ex-slaves eagerly anticipated farms of their own.

Despite the flurry of activity, wartime reconstruction failed to produce agreement about whether the president or Congress had the authority to devise and direct policy or what proper policy should be. As Lincoln anticipated, the nation faced postwar dilemmas almost as trying as those of the war.

The African American Quest for Autonomy

Ex-slaves never had any doubt about what they wanted from freedom. They had only to contemplate what they had been denied as slaves. (See "Documenting the American Promise," page 558.) Slaves had to remain on their plantations; freedom allowed blacks to go wherever they pleased. Thus, in the first heady weeks after emancipation, freedmen often abandoned their plantations just to see what was on the other side of the hill. Slaves had to be at work in the fields by dawn; freedom permitted blacks to taste the formerly forbidden pleasure of sleeping through a sunrise. Freedmen also tested the etiquette of racial subordination. "Lizzie's maid passed me today when I was coming from church *without speaking to me*," huffed one plantation mistress.

> "The way we can best take care of ourselves is to have land," one former slave declared in 1865, "and turn it and till it by our own labor."

To whites, emancipation looked like pure anarchy. Blacks, they said, had reverted to their natural condition: lazy, irresponsible, and wild. Without the discipline of slavery, whites predicted, blacks would go the way of "the Indian and the buffalo." Actually, former slaves were experimenting with freedom, but they could not long afford to roam the countryside, neglect work, and casually provoke whites. Soon, most were back at work in whites' kitchens and fields.

But other items on ex-slaves' agenda of freedom endured. They continued to dream of land and economic independence. "The way we can best take care of ourselves is to have land," one former slave declared in 1865, "and turn it and till it by our own labor." Another explained that he wanted land, "not a Master or owner[,] Neither a driver with his Whip."

Antebellum southern whites had deliberately kept blacks illiterate, and freedmen wanted to learn to read and write. Many black soldiers had become literate in the Union army, and they understood the value of the pen and book. "I wishes the Childern all in School," one black veteran asserted. "It is beter for them then to be their Surveing a mistes [mistress]."

Moreover, bondage had denied slaves secure family lives, and the restoration of their families became a persistent black aspiration. Thousands of black men and women took to the roads in 1865 to look for kin who had been sold away or to free those who were being held illegally as slaves. A black soldier from Missouri

The Meaning of Freedom

On New Year's Day 1863, President Abraham Lincoln issued the Emancipation Proclamation. It states that "all persons held as slaves" within the states still in rebellion "are, and henceforward shall be, free." Although the Proclamation in and of itself did not free any slaves, it transformed the character of the war. Despite often intolerable conditions, black people focused on the possibilities of freedom.

DOCUMENT 1
Letter from John Q. A. Dennis to Edwin M. Stanton, July 26, 1864

John Q. A. Dennis, formerly a slave in Maryland, wrote to ask Secretary of War Edwin M. Stanton for help in reuniting his family.

Boston
Dear Sir I am Glad that I have the Honour to Write you afew line I have been in troble for about four yars my Dear wife was taken from me Nov 19th 1859 and left me with three Children and I being a Slave At the time Could Not do Anny thing for the poor little Children for my master it was took me Carry me some forty mile from them So I Could Not do for them and the man that they live with half feed them and half Cloth them & beat them like dogs & when I was admitted to go to see them it use to brake my heart & Now I say again I am Glad to have the honour to write to you to see if you Can Do Anny thing for me or for my poor little Children I was keap in Slavy untell last Novr 1863. then the Good lord sent the Cornel borne [federal Colonel William Birney?] Down their in Marland in worsester Co So as I have been recently freed I have but letle to live on but I am Striveing Dear Sir but what I went too know of you Sir is it possible for me to go & take my Children from those men that keep them in Savery if it is possible will you pleas give me a permit from your hand then I think they would let them go. . . .

Hon sir will you please excuse my Miserable writeing & answer me as soon as you can I want get the little Children out of Slavery, I being Criple would like to know of you also if I Cant be permited to rase a Shool Down there & on what turm I Could be admited to Do so No more At present Dear Hon Sir

SOURCE: *Freedom: A Documentary History of Emancipation, 1861–1867*, ser. 1, vol. 1, *The Destruction of Slavery*, 386, by Ira Berlin, Joseph P. Reidy, and Leslie S. Rowland, eds. Copyright © 1985. Reprinted with the permission of Cambridge University Press.

DOCUMENT 2
Report from Reverend A. B. Randall, February 28, 1865

Freedom prompted ex-slaves to seek legal marriages, which under slavery had been impossible. Writing from Little Rock, Arkansas, to the adjutant general of the Union army, A. B. Randall, the white chaplain of a black regiment, affirmed the importance of marriage to freed slaves and emphasized their conviction that emancipation was only the first step toward full freedom.

Weddings, just now, are very popular, and abundant among the Colored People. They have just learned, of the Special Order No. 15. of Gen Thomas [Adjutant General Lorenzo Thomas] by which, they may not only be lawfully married, but have their Marriage Certificates, Recorded; in a book furnished by the Government. This is most desirable. . . . Those who were captured . . . at Ivy's Ford, on the 17th of January, by Col Brooks, had their Marriage Certificates, taken from them; and destroyed; and then were roundly cursed, for having such papers in their posession. I have married, during the month, at this Post; Twenty five couples; mostly, those, who have families; & have been living together for years. I try to dissuade single men, who are soldiers, from marrying, till their time of enlistment is out: as that course seems to me, to be most judicious.

The Colord People here, generally consider, this war not only; their exodus, from bondage; but the road, to Responsibility; Competency; and an honorable Citizenship—God grant that their hopes and expectations may be fully realized.

SOURCE: *Freedom: A Documentary History of Emancipation, 1861–1867*, ser. 2, vol. 1, *The Black Military Experience*, 712, by Ira Berlin, Joseph P. Reidy, and Leslie S. Rowland, eds. Copyright © 1982. Reprinted with the permission of Cambridge University Press.

DOCUMENT 3
Petition "to the Union Convention of Tennessee Assembled in the Capitol at Nashville," January 9, 1865

Early efforts at political reconstruction prompted petitions from former slaves demanding civil and political rights.

In January 1865, black Tennesseans petitioned a convention of white Unionists debating the reorganization of state government.

We the undersigned petitioners, American citizens of African descent, natives and residents of Tennessee, and devoted friends of the great National cause, do most respectfully ask a patient hearing of your honorable body in regard to matters deeply affecting the future condition of our unfortunate and long suffering race.

First of all, however, we would say that words are too weak to tell how profoundly grateful we are to the Federal Government for the good work of freedom which it is gradually carrying forward; and for the Emancipation Proclamation which has set free all the slaves in some of the rebellious States, as well as many of the slaves in Tennessee. . . .

We claim freedom, as our natural right, and ask that in harmony and co-operation with the nation at large, you should cut up by the roots the system of slavery, which is not only a wrong to us, but the source of all the evil which at present afflicts the State. For slavery, corrupt itself, corrupted nearly all, also, around it, so that it has influenced nearly all the slave States to rebel against the Federal Government, in order to set up a government of pirates under which slavery might be perpetrated.

In the contest between the nation and slavery, our unfortunate people have sided, by instinct, with the former. We have little fortune to devote to the national cause, for a hard fate has hitherto forced us to live in poverty, but we do devote to its success, our hopes, our toils, our whole heart, our sacred honor, and our lives. We will work, pray, live, and, if need be, die for the Union, as cheerfully as ever a white patriot died for his country. The color of our skin does not lessen in the least degree, our love either for God or for the land of our birth. . . .

We know the burdens of citizenship, and are ready to bear them. We know the duties of the good citizen, and are ready to perform them cheerfully, and would ask to be put in a position in which we can discharge them more effectually. . . .

This is a democracy—a government of the people. It should aim to make every man, without regard to the color of his skin, the amount of his wealth, or the character of his religious faith, feel personally interested in its welfare. Every man who lives under the Government should feel that it is his property, his treasure, the bulwark and defence of himself and his family, his pearl of great price, which he must preserve, protect, and defend faithfully at all times, on all occasions, in every possible manner.

This is not a Democratic Government if a numerous, law-abiding, industrious, and useful class of citizens, born and bred on the soil, are to be treated as aliens and enemies, as an inferior degraded class, who must have no voice in the Government which they support, protect and defend, with all their heart, soul, mind, and body, both in peace and war. . . .

The possibility that the negro suffrage proposition may shock popular prejudice at first sight, is not a conclusive argument against its wisdom and policy. No proposition ever met with more furious or general opposition than the one to enlist colored soldiers in the United States army. The opponents of the measure exclaimed on all hands that the negro was a coward; that he would not fight; that one white man, with a whip in his hand could put to flight a regiment of them; that the experiment would end in the utter rout and ruin of the Federal army. Yet the colored man has fought so well, on almost every occasion, that the rebel government is prevented, only by its fears and distrust of being able to force him to fight for slavery as well as he fights against it, from putting half a million of negroes into its ranks.

The Government has asked the colored man to fight for its preservation and gladly has he done it. It can afford to trust him with a vote as safely as it trusted him with a bayonet.

SOURCE: *Freedom: A Documentary History of Emancipation, 1861–1867*, ser. 2, vol. 1, *The Black Military Experience*, 811–16, by Ira Berlin, Joseph P. Reidy, and Leslie S. Rowland, eds. Copyright © 1982. Reprinted with the permission of Cambridge University Press.

QUESTIONS FOR ANALYSIS AND DEBATE

1. How does John Q. A. Dennis interpret his responsibility as a father?

2. Why do you think ex-slaves wanted their marriages legalized?

3. Why, according to petitioners to the Union Convention of Tennessee, did blacks deserve voting rights?

Samuel Dove Ad, 1865, and Harry Stephens and Family, 1866
Dressed in their Sunday best, this Virginia family sits proudly for a photograph. Many black families were not as fortunate as the Stephens family. Separated by slavery or war, former slaves desperately sought news of missing family members through newspaper advertisements like the one posted by Samuel Dove in August 1865. We do not know whether he succeeded in locating his mother, brother, and sisters.

Ad: Chicago Historical Society; Family: The Metropolitan Museum of Art, Gilman Collection, Purchase, The Horace W. Goldsmith Foundation Gift, 2005 (2005.100.277)

SAML. DOVE wishes to know of the whereabouts of his mother, Areno, his sisters Maria, Neziah, and Peggy, and his brother Edmond, who were owned by Geo. Dove, of Rockingham county, Shenandoah Valley, Va. Sold in Richmond, after which Saml. and Edmond were taken to Nashville, Tenn., by Joe Mick; Areno was left at the Eagle Tavern, Richmond

Respectfully yours,
SAML. DOVE.

Utica, New York, Aug. 5, 1865–3m
U. S. CHRISTIAN COMMISSION, NASHVILLE, TENN., July 19, 1865.

wrote his daughters that he was coming for them. "I will have you if it cost me my life," he declared. "Your Miss Kitty said that I tried to steal you," he told them. "But I'll let her know that god never intended for a man to steal his own flesh and blood." And he swore that "if she meets me with ten thousand soldiers, she [will] meet her enemy."

Another hunger was for independent worship. African Americans greeted freedom with a mass exodus from white churches, where they had been required to worship when slaves. Some joined the newly established southern branches of all-black northern churches, such as the African Methodist Episcopal Church. Others formed black versions of the major southern denominations, Baptists and Methodists. Slaves

had comprehended their tribulations through the lens of their deeply felt Christian faith, and freedmen continued to interpret the events of the Civil War and reconstruction as people of faith. One black woman thanked Lincoln for the Emancipation Proclamation, declaring, "When you are dead and in Heaven, in a thousand years that action of yours will make the Angels sing your praises I know it."

REVIEW Why did Congress object to Lincoln's wartime plan for reconstruction?

Presidential Reconstruction

Abraham Lincoln died on April 15, 1865, just hours after John Wilkes Booth shot him at a Washington, D.C., theater. Chief Justice Salmon P. Chase immediately administered the oath of office to Vice President Andrew Johnson of Tennessee. Congress had adjourned in March, which meant that legislators were away from Washington when Lincoln was killed. They would not reconvene until December. Throughout the summer and fall, therefore, the "accidental president" made critical decisions about the future of the South without congressional advice. Like Lincoln, Johnson believed that responsibility for restoring the Union lay with the president. With dizzying speed, he drew up and executed a plan of reconstruction.

Congress returned to the capital in December to find that, as far as the president and former Confederates were concerned, reconstruction was already decided. Most Republicans, however, thought Johnson's modest demands of ex-rebels

made a mockery of the sacrifice of Union soldiers. Instead of honoring the dead by insisting on "a new birth of freedom," as Lincoln had promised in his 1863 speech at Gettysburg, Johnson had acted as midwife to the rebirth of the Old South and the stillbirth of black **liberty**. To let his program stand, Republican legislators said, would mean that the North's dead had indeed died in vain. They proceeded to dismantle it and substitute a program of their own, one that southern whites found ways to resist.

Johnson's Program of Reconciliation

Born in 1808 in Raleigh, North Carolina, Andrew Johnson was the son of illiterate parents. Self-educated and ambitious, Johnson moved to Tennessee, where he worked as a tailor, accumulated a fortune in land, acquired five slaves, and built a career in politics championing the South's common white people and assailing its "illegitimate, swaggering, bastard, scrub aristocracy." The only senator from a Confederate state to remain loyal to the Union, Johnson held the planter class

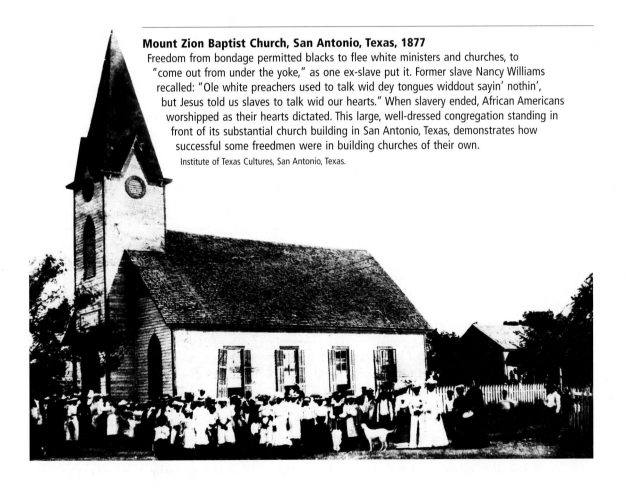

Mount Zion Baptist Church, San Antonio, Texas, 1877
Freedom from bondage permitted blacks to flee white ministers and churches, to "come out from under the yoke," as one ex-slave put it. Former slave Nancy Williams recalled: "Ole white preachers used to talk wid dey tongues widdout sayin' nothin', but Jesus told us slaves to talk wid our hearts." When slavery ended, African Americans worshipped as their hearts dictated. This large, well-dressed congregation standing in front of its substantial church building in San Antonio, Texas, demonstrates how successful some freedmen were in building churches of their own.
Institute of Texas Cultures, San Antonio, Texas.

responsible for secession. Less than two weeks before he became president, he made it clear what he would do to planters if he ever had the chance: "I would arrest them—I would try them—I would convict them and I would hang them."

Despite such statements, Johnson was no friend of the Republicans. A southern Democrat all his life, Johnson occupied the White House only because the Republican Party in 1864 had needed a vice presidential candidate who would appeal to loyal, Union-supporting Democrats. Johnson favored traditional Democratic causes, vigorously defending **states' rights** (but not secession) and opposing Republican efforts to expand the power of the federal government. A steadfast defender of slavery, Johnson had owned slaves until 1862, when Tennessee rebels, angry at his Unionism, confiscated them. He only grudgingly accepted emancipation. When he did, it was more because he hated planters than sympathized with slaves. "Damn the negroes," he said. "I am fighting those traitorous aristocrats, their masters." At a time when the nation confronted the future of black Americans, the new president harbored unshakable racist convictions. Africans, Johnson said, were "inferior to the white man in point of intellect—better calculated in physical structure to undergo drudgery and hardship."

Like Lincoln, Johnson stressed reconciliation between the Union and the defeated Confederacy and rapid restoration of civil government in the South. Like Lincoln, he promised to pardon most, but not all, ex-rebels. Johnson recognized the state governments created by Lincoln but set out his own requirements for restoring the other rebel states to the Union. All that the citizens of a state had to do was to renounce the right of secession, deny that the debts of the Confederacy were legal and binding, and ratify the Thirteenth Amendment abolishing slavery, which became part of the Constitution in December 1865. Johnson's plan ignored Lincoln's acceptance near the end of his life of some form of limited black voting.

Johnson's eagerness to restore relations with southern states and his lack of sympathy for blacks also led him to return to pardoned ex-Confederates all confiscated and abandoned land, even if it was in the hands of freedmen. Reformers were shocked. They had expected the president's hatred of planters to mean the permanent confiscation of the South's plantations and the distribution of the land to loyal freed-

> Not a single southern state granted any black—no matter how educated, wealthy, or refined—the right to vote.

men. Instead, his instructions canceled the promising beginnings made by General Sherman and the Freedmen's Bureau to settle blacks on land of their own. As one freedman observed, "Things was hurt by Mr. Lincoln getting killed."

White Southern Resistance and Black Codes

In the summer of 1865, delegates across the South gathered to draw up the new state constitutions required by Johnson's plan of reconstruction. Rather than take their medicine, delegates choked on even the president's mild requirements. Refusing to renounce secession, the South Carolina and Georgia conventions merely "repudiated" their secession ordinances, preserving in principle their right to secede. South Carolina and Mississippi refused to disown their Confederate war debts. Mississippi rejected the Thirteenth Amendment outright, and Alabama rejected it in part. Despite these defiant acts, Johnson did nothing. By failing to draw a hard line, he rekindled southern resistance. White Southerners began to think that by standing up for themselves they—not victorious Northerners—would shape reconstruction. In the fall of 1865, newly elected southern legislators set out to reverse what they considered the "retreat into barbarism" that followed emancipation.

State governments across the South adopted a series of laws known as *black codes*, which made a travesty of black freedom. The codes sought to keep ex-slaves subordinate to whites by subjecting them to every sort of discrimination. Several states made it illegal for blacks to own a gun. Mississippi made insulting gestures and language by blacks a criminal offense. The codes barred blacks from jury duty. Not a single southern state granted any black—no matter how educated, wealthy, or refined—the right to vote.

At the core of the black codes, however, lay the matter of labor. Faced with the death of slavery, legislators sought to hustle freedmen back to the plantations. South Carolina attempted to limit blacks to either farmwork or domestic service by requiring them to pay annual taxes of $10 to $100 to work in any other occupation. Mississippi declared that blacks who did not possess written evidence of employment could be declared vagrants and be subject to involuntary plantation labor. Most states allowed judges to bind black children—orphans and others whose parents they deemed unable to support them—to white employers. Under these so-

The Black Codes
Titled "Selling a Freeman to Pay His Fine at Monticello, Florida," this 1867 drawing from a northern magazine equates black codes with the reinstitution of slavery. The laws stopped short of reenslavement but sharply restricted blacks' freedom. In Florida, as in other southern states, certain acts, such as breaking a labor contract, were made criminal offenses, the penalty for which could be involuntary plantation labor for a year.
Granger Collection.

called apprenticeship laws, courts bound thousands of black children to work for planter "guardians."

Johnson refused to intervene. A staunch defender of states' rights, he believed that the citizens of every state, even those who attempted to destroy the Union, should be free to write their own constitutions and laws. Moreover, since Johnson was as eager as other white Southerners to restore white supremacy and black subordination, the black codes did not offend him.

But Johnson also followed the path that he believed would offer him the greatest political return. A **conservative** Tennessee Democrat at the head of a northern Republican Party, he began to look southward for political allies.

Despite tough talk about punishing traitors, he personally pardoned fourteen thousand wealthy or high-ranking ex-Confederates. By pardoning powerful whites, by acquiescing in the black codes, and by accepting governments even when they failed to satisfy his minimal demands, he won useful southern friends.

In the fall elections of 1865, white Southerners dramatically expressed their mood. To represent them in Congress, they chose former Confederates, not loyal Unionists. Of the eighty senators and representatives they sent to Washington, fifteen had served in the Confederate army, ten of them as generals. Another sixteen had served in civil and judicial posts in the Confederacy. Nine others had served in the Confederate Congress.

One—Alexander Stephens—had been vice president of the Confederacy. In December, this remarkable group arrived on the steps of the nation's Capitol building to be seated in Congress. As one Georgian remarked, "It looked as though Richmond had moved to Washington."

Expansion of Federal Authority and Black Rights

Southerners had blundered monumentally. They had assumed that what Andrew Johnson was willing to accept, Republicans would accept as well. But southern intransigence compelled even moderates to conclude that ex-rebels were a "generation of vipers," still untrustworthy and dangerous. So angry were Republicans with the rebels that the federal government refused to supply artificial limbs to disabled Southerners, as they did for Union veterans. (See "The Promise of Technology," page 566.)

> The *Chicago Tribune* roared, "The men of the North will convert the State of Mississippi into a frog pond before they will allow [black codes] to disgrace one foot of the soil in which the bones of our soldiers sleep."

The black codes became a symbol of southern intentions to "restore all of slavery but its name." Northerners were hardly saints when it came to racial justice, but black freedom had become a hallowed war aim. "We tell the white men of Mississippi," the *Chicago Tribune* roared, "that the men of the North will convert the State of Mississippi into a frog pond before they will allow such laws to disgrace one foot of the soil in which the bones of our soldiers sleep and over which the flag of freedom waves."

The moderate majority of the Republican Party wanted only assurance that slavery and treason were dead. They did not champion black equality or the confiscation of plantations or black voting, as did the radicals, a minority within the party. But southern obstinacy had succeeded in forging unity (at least temporarily) among Republican factions. In December 1865, exercising Congress's right to determine

the qualifications of its members, Republicans refused to seat the southern representatives. Rather than accept Johnson's claim that the "work of restoration" was done, Congress challenged his executive power. Congressional Republicans enjoyed a three-to-one majority over the Democrats, and if they could agree on a program of reconstruction, they could easily pass legislation and even override presidential vetoes.

Senator Lyman Trumbull of Illinois declared that the president's policy meant that the ex-slave would "be tyrannized over, abused, and virtually reenslaved without some legislation by the nation for his protection." Early in 1866, the moderates produced two bills that strengthened the federal shield. The first, the Freedmen's Bureau bill, prolonged the life of the agency established by the previous Congress. Since the end of the war, it had distributed food, supervised labor contracts, and sponsored schools for freedmen. Arguing that the Constitution never contemplated a "system for the support of indigent persons," President Andrew Johnson vetoed the bill. Congress failed by a narrow margin to override the president's veto.

The moderates designed their second measure, the Civil Rights Act, to nullify the black codes by

Confederate Flag Dress
While politicians in Washington, D.C., debated the future of the South, white Southerners were coming to grips with the reality of Confederate defeat. They began to refer to their failure to secede from the Union as the "Lost Cause." They enshrined the memory of certain former Confederates, especially Robert E. Lee, whose nobility and courage represented the white South's image of itself, and they made a fetish of the Confederate flag. White Southerners incorporated symbols of the Lost Cause into their daily lives. This dress, made from material embossed with the rebel flag, did double duty. It both memorialized the Confederacy and, through the sale of the cloth, raised funds for the Confederate Soldiers' Home in Richmond, Virginia.
Valentine Museum, Cook Collection.

affirming African Americans' rights to "full and equal benefit of all laws and proceedings for the security of person and property as is enjoyed by white citizens." The act boldly required the end of legal discrimination in state laws and represented an extraordinary expansion of black rights and federal authority. The president argued that the civil rights bill amounted to "unconstitutional invasion of states' rights" and vetoed it. In essence, he denied that the federal government possessed the authority to protect the civil rights of blacks.

In April 1866, an incensed Republican Party again pushed the civil rights bill through Congress and overrode the presidential veto. In July, it passed another Freedmen's Bureau bill and overrode Johnson's veto. For the first time in American history, Congress had overridden presidential vetoes of major legislation. As a worried South Carolinian observed, Johnson had succeeded in uniting the Republicans and probably touched off "a fight this fall such as has never been seen."

> **REVIEW**   How did the North respond to the passage of black codes in the southern states?

Congressional Reconstruction

By the summer of 1866, President Andrew Johnson and Congress had dropped their gloves and stood toe-to-toe in a bare-knuckle contest unprecedented in American history. Johnson made it clear that he would not budge on either constitutional issues or policy. Moderate Republicans responded by amending the Constitution. But the obstinacy of Johnson and white Southerners pushed Republican moderates ever closer to the radicals and to acceptance of additional federal intervention in the South. In time, Congress debated whether to give the ballot to black men. Congress also voted to impeach the president. Outside of Congress, blacks championed color-blind voting rights, while women sought to make voting sex-blind as well.

The Fourteenth Amendment and Escalating Violence

In June 1866, Congress passed the Fourteenth Amendment to the Constitution, and two years later it gained the necessary ratification of three-fourths of the states. The most important provisions of this complex amendment made all native-born or naturalized persons American citizens and prohibited states from abridging the "privileges and immunities" of citizens, depriving them of "life, liberty, or property without due process of law," and denying them "equal protection of the laws." By making blacks national citizens, the amendment provided a national guarantee of equality before the law. In essence, it protected blacks against violation by southern state governments.

The Fourteenth Amendment also dealt with voting rights. It gave Congress the right to reduce the congressional representation of states that withheld suffrage from some of its adult male population. In other words, white Southerners could either allow black men to vote or see their representation in Washington slashed.

Whatever happened, Republicans stood to benefit from the Fourteenth Amendment. If southern whites granted voting rights to freedmen, Republicans, entirely a northern party, would gain valuable black votes, establish a wing in the South, and secure their national power. If whites refused, representation of southern Democrats would plunge, and Republicans would still gain political power.

The Fourteenth Amendment's suffrage provisions completely ignored the small band of politicized and energized women who had emerged from the war demanding "the ballot for the two disenfranchised classes, negroes and women." Founding the American Equal Rights Association in 1866, Susan B. Anthony and Elizabeth Cady Stanton lobbied for "a government by the people, and the whole people; for the people and the whole people." They felt betrayed when their old anti-slavery allies, who now occupied positions of national power, proved to be fickle and refused to work for their goals. "It was the Negro's hour," Frederick Douglass later explained. Senator Charles Sumner suggested that woman suffrage could be "the great question of the future."

> Susan B. Anthony and Elizabeth Cady Stanton lobbied for "a government by the people, and the whole people; for the people and the whole people."

The Fourteenth Amendment dashed women's expectations. It provided for punishment of any state that excluded voters on the basis of race but not on the basis of sex. The amendment also introduced the word *male* into the Constitution when it referred to a citizen's right to vote. Stanton predicted that "if that word 'male' be inserted, it will take us a century at least to get it out."

Filling the "Empty Sleeve": Artificial Limbs

Industrial and technological developments that had made the war so destructive also came to the aid of maimed veterans during national reconstruction. A new kind of ammunition used in the war, the minié ball, proved extremely destructive to human flesh. In attempts to save lives, northern and southern surgeons performed approximately 60,000 amputations. Confederate nurse Kate Cummings observed that amputations were so common in her hospital that they were "scarcely noticed." Approximately 45,000 of the amputees survived, and as the nation began reconstructing the Union, it also sought the literal reconstruction of disabled veterans.

Once their wounds had healed, most amputees were eager to fill an empty sleeve or pant leg with an artificial limb. The federal government provided limbs to those who had fought for the Union, and individual southern states provided limbs for Confederate veterans. Innovations in design and production began during the war and accelerated sharply as the enormous demand produced a surge of interest in prosthetic technology. In the fifteen years before the war, 34 patents were issued for artificial limbs and assisting devices; in the twelve years from the beginning of the war to 1873, 133 patents for limbs were issued, nearly a 300 percent increase. As Oliver Wendell Holmes Jr., an army veteran and future Supreme Court justice, observed, if "war unmakes legs," then "human skill must supply their places."

The search for a functional, lightweight, artificial limb drew on a number of advancing fields, including photography, physiology, physics, mathematics, and psychology. For example, in 1859 photographers in Edinburgh and New York succeeded in taking a rapid succession of fast-speed pictures of pedestrians and breaking their strides down into minute parts. Photographs of individuals frozen in mid-step provided new information about human movement that helped make better artificial limbs. The application of photography is but one example of the growing application of science and technology to the alleviation of human suffering in the late nineteenth century.

As excited designers sought to overcome problems of noise, weight, appearance, and discomfort, artificial limbs advanced quickly from crude peg legs to hollow willow legs with movable ankles that simulated the natural motions of the foot. Newly invented vulcanized rubber (called India rubber) increased strength and flexibility and allowed disabled veterans to dispense with metal bolts and springs in their new limbs. Limb makers sought to erase the line between nature and technology, to merge "bodies with machines," as one manufacturer promised. One doctor boasted: "In our time, limb-making has been carried to such a state of perfection that both in form and function they so completely resemble the natural extremity that those who wear them pass unobserved and unrecognized in walks of business and pleasure." He exaggerated, for the artificial limbs of the 1860s were crude by today's standards, but they did represent significant technological advances.

Less than two years after the war, the manufacture of artificial limbs had become, according to Oliver Wendell Holmes Jr., "a great and active branch of history." Before the war, locksmiths, gunsmiths, toolmakers, harness makers, and cabinetmakers made peg legs and artificial arms individually as sidelines to their principal tasks. After the war, the great demand for artificial limbs prompted businesses to apply industrial manufacturing processes to limbs. Soon American factories—high-volume, mechanized, uniform—were producing untold numbers of sewing machines, bicycles, typewriters, and artificial limbs.

The postwar business of prosthetics was highly competitive. With the federal and state governments placing large, lucrative orders, dozens of manufacturers entered the market. Very quickly, buyers could choose from English, French, German, and American models. With so many choices, men had to be persuaded that one leg was better than another. Aggressive advertising campaigns announced the new products. Northern manufacturers used government military and pension registration rolls to mail brochures directly to the homes of Union veterans. Manufacturers in New York, Philadelphia, and Boston established dazzling showrooms on major shopping streets. They also sponsored "cripple races" to test and promote their products.

Politics sometimes entered into decisions. Southern manufacturers proclaimed that they were "home manufacturers" and deserved contracts from former Confederate states more than their northern competitors did. Confederate general John B. Hood made a controversial admission when he declared that his "Yankee leg was the best of all." Another disabled Southerner, however, disliked his northern-manufactured leg, which, he concluded, "like the majority of Yankee inventions proved to be a 'humbug.'"

Disabled veterans sometimes found their postwar struggle to find work, to overcome the stigma of being disabled, and to regain confidence as difficult as their battlefield experiences. To help them, some prosthetic manu-facturers dabbled in medicine that wedded technological and psycho-logical efforts to renew wholeness. New York, for example, was host to an annual left-handed penman-ship contest to encourage men who had lost their right hands to learn to write with their left. Well into the twentieth century, a veteran's "empty sleeve" remained both a badge of courage and a sign of permanent loss—a wound that national reconstruction could never heal.

"Before and After"
These photographic images, one showing a veteran with two amputations and the other showing him wearing his artificial legs, come from the back of an A. A. Marks business card in about 1878. This manufacturer of artificial limbs sent a clear message: Marks legs make maimed men whole again. Marks promised that, thus restored, the wounded man would be the "equal of his fellowmen in every employment of life."
Warshaw Collection, National Museum of American History, Smithsonian Institution.

Susan B. Anthony
Like many outspoken suffragists, Anthony, depicted here in 1852, began her public career working on behalf of temperance and abolition. But she grew tired of laboring under the direction of male clergymen—"white orthodox little saints," she called them—who controlled the reform movements and routinely dismissed the opinions of women. Anthony's continued passion for other causes—improving working conditions for labor, for example—led some conservatives to oppose women's political rights because they equated the suffragist cause with radicalism in general. Women could not easily overcome such views, and the long struggle for the vote eventually drew millions of women into public life.
Susan B. Anthony House, Inc.

Tennessee approved the Fourteenth Amendment in July, and Congress promptly welcomed the state's representatives and senators back. Had President Johnson counseled other southern states to ratify this relatively mild amendment and warned them that they faced the fury of an outraged Republican Party if they refused, they might have listened. Instead, Johnson advised Southerners to reject the Fourteenth Amendment and to rely on him to trounce the Republicans in the fall congressional elections.

Johnson had decided to make the Fourteenth Amendment the overriding issue of the 1866 congressional elections and to gather its white opponents into a new conservative party, the National Union Party. The president's strategy suffered a setback when whites in several southern cities went on rampages against blacks—an escalation of the violence that had never really ceased. When a mob in New Orleans assaulted delegates to a black suffrage convention, thirty-four blacks died. In Memphis, white mobs crashed through the black sections of town, killing at least forty-six people. The slaughter shocked Northerners and renewed skepticism about Johnson's claim that southern whites could be trusted. "Who doubts that the Freedmen's Bureau ought to be abolished forthwith," a New Yorker observed sarcastically, "and the blacks remitted to the paternal care of their old masters, who 'understand the nigger, you know, a great deal better than the Yankees can.'"

The 1866 elections resulted in an overwhelming Republican victory in which the party retained its three-to-one congressional majority. Johnson had bet that Northerners would not support federal protection of black rights and that a racist backlash would blast the Republican Party. But the war was still fresh in northern minds, and as one Republican explained, southern whites "with all their intelligence were traitors, the blacks with all their ignorance were loyal."

Radical Reconstruction and Military Rule

The 1866 election should have taught southern whites the folly of relying on Andrew Johnson to guide them through reconstruction. But when Johnson continued to urge Southerners to reject the Fourteenth Amendment, every southern state except Tennessee voted it down. "The last one of the sinful ten," thundered Representative James A. Garfield of Ohio, "has flung back into our teeth the magnanimous offer of a generous nation." After the South rejected the moderates' program, the radicals seized the initiative.

Each act of defiance by southern whites had boosted the standing of the radicals within the Republican Party. Except for freedmen themselves, no one did more to make freedom the "mighty moral question of the age." Radicals such as Massachusetts senator Charles Sumner and Pennsylvania representative Thaddeus Stevens did not speak with a single voice, but they united in demanding civil and political equality. They insisted on extending to ex-slaves the same opportunities that northern working people enjoyed under the free-labor system. Southern states were "like clay in the

Reconstruction Military Districts, 1867

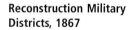

hands of the potter," Stevens declared in January 1867, and he called on Congress to begin reconstruction all over again.

In March 1867, Congress overturned the Johnson state governments and initiated military rule of the South. The Military Reconstruction Act (and three subsequent acts) divided the ten unreconstructed Confederate states into five military districts. Congress placed a Union general in charge of each district and instructed him to "suppress insurrection, disorder, and violence" and to begin political reform. After the military had completed voter registration, which would include black men, voters in each state would elect delegates to conventions that would draw up new state constitutions. Each constitution would guarantee black suffrage. When the voters of each state had approved the constitution and the

state legislature had ratified the Fourteenth Amendment, the state could submit its work to Congress. If Congress approved, the state's senators and representatives could be seated, and political reunification would be accomplished.

Radicals proclaimed the provision for black suffrage "a prodigious triumph," for it extended far beyond the limited suffrage provisions of the Fourteenth Amendment. Republicans united in the conviction that only the voting power of ex-slaves could bring about a permanent revolution in the South. Indeed, suffrage provided blacks with a powerful instrument of change and self-protection. When combined with the **disfranchisement** of thousands of ex-rebels, it promised to cripple any neo-Confederate resurgence and guarantee Republican state governments in the South.

Memphis Riots, May 1866
On May 1, 1866, two carriages, one driven by a white man and the other by a black man, collided on a busy street in Memphis, Tennessee. This minor incident led to three days of bloody racial violence in which dozens of blacks and two whites died. Racial friction was common in postwar Memphis, and white newspapers routinely heaped abuse on black citizens. "Would to God they were back in Africa, or some other seaport town," the *Memphis Argus* shouted two days before the riot erupted, "anywhere but here." South Memphis, pictured in this lithograph from *Harper's Weekly*, was a shantytown where the families of black soldiers stationed at nearby Fort Pickering lived. The army commander refused to send troops to protect soldiers' families and property, and white mobs ran wild.
Granger Collection.

THIS LITTLE BOY WOULD PERSIST IN HANDLING BOOKS ABOVE HIS CAPACITY.

AND THIS WAS THE DISASTROUS RESULT.

Andrew Johnson Cartoon
Appearing in 1868 during President Andrew Johnson's impeachment trial, this cartoon includes captions that read: "This little boy would persist in handling books above his capacity" and "And this was the disastrous result." The cartoonist's portrait of Johnson being crushed by the Constitution refers to the president's flouting of the Tenure of Office Act, which caused Republicans to vote for his impeachment. The cartoon's celebration of Johnson's destruction proved premature, however.
Granger Collection.

Despite its bold suffrage provision, the Military Reconstruction Act of 1867 disappointed those who advocated the confiscation and redistribution of southern plantations to ex-slaves. Thaddeus Stevens, who believed that at bottom reconstruction was an economic problem, agreed with the freedman who said, "Give us our own land and we take care of ourselves, but without land, the old masters can hire us or starve us, as they please." But most Republicans believed they had already provided blacks with what they needed: equal legal rights and the ballot. If blacks were to get forty acres, as some freedmen had in 1865 when Sherman distributed forty-acre lots, they would have to gain the land themselves.

Declaring that he would rather sever his right arm than sign such a formula for "anarchy and chaos," Andrew Johnson vetoed the Military Reconstruction Act. Congress overrode his veto the very same day, dramatizing the shift in power from the executive to the legislative branch of government. With the passage of the Reconstruction Acts of 1867, congressional reconstruction was virtually completed. Congress left whites owning most of the South's land but, in a departure that justified the term "radical reconstruction," had given black men the ballot. In 1867, the nation began an unprecedented experiment in interracial **democracy**—at least in the South, for Congress's plan did not touch the North. But before the spotlight swung away from Washington to the South, the president and Congress had one more scene to play.

Impeaching a President

Despite his defeats, Andrew Johnson had no intention of yielding control of reconstruction. In a dozen ways, he sabotaged Congress's will and encouraged southern whites to resist. He issued a flood of pardons to undermine efforts at political and economic change. He waged war against the Freedmen's Bureau by removing officers who sympathized too much with ex-slaves. And he replaced Union generals eager to enforce Congress's Reconstruction Acts with conservative men eager to defeat them. Johnson claimed that he was merely defending the "violated Constitution." At bottom, however, the president subverted congressional reconstruction to protect southern whites from what he considered the horrors of "Negro domination."

When Congress realized that overriding Johnson's vetoes did not ensure that it got its way, it looked for other ways to exert its will. According to the Constitution, the House of Representatives can impeach and the Senate can try any federal official for "treason, bribery, or other high crimes and misdemeanors." Radicals argued that Johnson's abuse of constitutional powers and his failure to fulfill constitutional obligations to enforce the law were impeachable offenses. Moderates interpreted the constitutional provision to mean violation of criminal statutes. As long as Johnson refrained from breaking the law, **impeachment** remained a faint hope.

Then, in August 1867, Johnson suspended Secretary of War Edwin M. Stanton from office. As required by the Tenure of Office Act, which demanded the approval of the Senate for the removal of any government official who had been appointed with Senate approval, the president requested the Senate to consent to the dismissal. When the Senate balked, Johnson removed Stanton anyway. "Is the President crazy, or only drunk?" asked a dumbfounded Republican moderate. "I'm afraid his doings will make us all favor impeachment."

News of Johnson's open defiance of the law convinced every Republican in the House to vote for a resolution impeaching the president. Supreme Court chief justice Salmon Chase presided over the Senate trial, which lasted from March until May 1868. Chase refused to allow Johnson's opponents to raise broad issues of misuse of power and forced them to argue their case exclusively on the narrow legal grounds of Johnson's removal of Stanton. Johnson's lawyers argued that the president had not committed a criminal offense, that the Tenure of Office Act was unconstitutional, and that in any case it did not apply to Stanton, who had been appointed by Lincoln. When the critical vote came, 35 senators voted guilty and 19 not guilty. The impeachment forces fell one vote short of the two-thirds needed to convict.

Although Johnson survived, he did not come through the ordeal unscathed. After his trial, he called a truce, and for the remaining ten months of his term, congressional reconstruction proceeded unhindered by presidential interference. Without interference from Johnson, Congress revisited the suffrage issue.

The Fifteenth Amendment and Women's Demands

In February 1869, Republicans passed the Fifteenth Amendment to the Constitution, which prohibited states from depriving any citizen of the right to vote because of "race, color, or previous condition of servitude." The Reconstruction Acts of 1867 already required black suffrage in

Major Reconstruction Legislation, 1865–1875

1865	
Thirteenth Amendment (ratified 1865)	Abolishes slavery.
1865 and 1866	
Freedmen's Bureau Acts	Establish the Freedmen's Bureau to distribute food and clothing to destitute Southerners and help freedmen with labor contracts and schooling.
Civil Rights Act of 1866	Affirms the rights of blacks to enjoy "full and equal benefit of all laws and proceedings for the security of person and property as is enjoyed by white citizens" and effectively requires the end of legal discrimination in state laws.
Fourteenth Amendment (ratified 1868)	Makes native-born blacks citizens and guarantees all citizens "equal protection of the laws." Threatens to reduce representatives of a state that denies suffrage to any of its male inhabitants.
1867	
Military Reconstruction Acts	Impose military rule in the South, establish rules for readmission of ex-Confederate states to the Union, and require those states to guarantee the vote to black men.
1869	
Fifteenth Amendment (ratified 1870)	Prohibits racial discrimination in voting rights in all states in the nation.
1875	
Civil Rights Act of 1875	Outlaws racial discrimination in transportation, public accommodations, and juries.

the South; the Fifteenth Amendment extended black voting nationwide. Partisan advantage played an important role in the amendment's passage. Gains by northern Democrats in the 1868 elections worried Republicans, and black voters now represented the balance of power in several northern states. By giving the ballot to northern blacks, Republicans could lessen their political vulnerability. As one Republican congressman observed, "Party expediency and exact justice coincide for once."

Some Republicans, however, found the final wording of the Fifteenth Amendment "lame and halting." Rather than absolutely guaranteeing the right to vote, the amendment merely prohibited exclusion on grounds of race. The distinction would prove to be significant. In time, inventive white Southerners would devise tests of literacy and property and other apparently nonracial measures that would effectively disfranchise blacks yet not violate the Fifteenth Amendment. But an amendment that fully guaranteed the right to vote courted defeat outside the South. Rising antiforeign sentiment—against the Chinese in California and European immigrants in the Northeast—caused states to resist giving up total control of suffrage requirements. (Because the vast majority of Native Americans became citizens only in 1924, the Fifteenth Amendment had little immediate impact on Indian voting.) In March 1870, after three-fourths of the states had ratified it, the Fifteenth Amendment became part of the Constitution. Republicans generally breathed a sigh of relief, confident that black suffrage was "the last great point that remained to be settled of the issues of the war."

Woman suffrage advocates, however, were sorely disappointed with the Fifteenth Amendment's failure to extend voting rights to women. Although women fought hard to include the word *sex* (as they had fought hard to keep the word *male* out of the Fourteenth Amendment), the amendment denied states the right to forbid suffrage only on the basis of race. Elizabeth Cady Stanton and Susan B. Anthony condemned the Republicans' "negro first" strategy and pointed out that women remained "the only class of citizens wholly unrepresented in the government." Black enfranchisement provoked racist statements from Stanton, who wondered aloud why ignorant black men should legislate for educated and cultured white women. Increasingly, activist

> Wendell Phillips concluded that the black man now held "sufficient shield in his own hands. . . . Whatever he suffers will be largely now, and in future, his own fault."

women concluded that woman "must not put her trust in man." The Fifteenth Amendment severed the early **feminist** movement from its abolitionist roots. Over the next several decades, women would establish an independent suffrage crusade that drew millions of women into political life.

Republicans took enough satisfaction in the Fifteenth Amendment to promptly scratch the "Negro question" from the agenda of national politics. Even that steadfast crusader for equality Wendell Phillips concluded that the black man now held "sufficient shield in his own hands. . . . Whatever he suffers will be largely now, and in future, his own fault." Northerners had no idea of the violent struggles that lay ahead.

REVIEW Why did Johnson urge the southern states to reject the Fourteenth Amendment?

The Struggle in the South

Northerners believed they had discharged their responsibilities with the Reconstruction Acts and the amendments to the Constitution, but Southerners knew that the battle had just begun. Black suffrage established the foundation for the rise of the Republican Party in the South. Gathering together outsiders and outcasts, southern Republicans won elections, wrote new state constitutions, and formed new state governments.

Challenging the established class for political control was dangerous business. Equally dangerous were the confrontations that took place on farms and plantations in the southern countryside, where blacks sought to give practical, everyday meaning to their newly won legal and political equality. Ex-masters had their own ideas about the social and economic arrangements that should replace slavery. Freedom remained contested territory, and Southerners fought pitched battles with one another to determine the contours of their new world.

Freedmen, Yankees, and Yeomen

African Americans made up the majority of southern Republicans. After gaining voting rights in 1867, nearly every eligible black man registered to vote. Almost all black men registered as Republicans, grateful to the party that had freed them and granted them the **franchise**. In Monroe,

Alabama, black men participating in their first political meeting pressed toward the speaker, crying "God bless you" and "Bless God for this." Black women, like white women, remained disfranchised but mobilized along with black men. In the 1868 presidential election, they bravely wore buttons supporting the Republican candidate, Ulysses S. Grant. Southern blacks did not have identical political priorities, but they united in their desire for education and equal treatment before the law.

Northern whites who made the South their home after the war were a second element of the South's Republican Party. Conservative white Southerners called them "carpetbaggers," men so poor that they could stuff all their earthly belongings in a single carpet-sided suitcase and swoop southward like buzzards to "fatten on our misfortunes." But most Northerners who moved south were restless, relatively well-educated young men who looked upon the South as they did the West—as a promising place to make a living. They expected that the South without slavery would prosper, and they wanted to be part of it. Northerners in the southern Republican Party consistently supported programs that encouraged vigorous economic development along the lines of the northern free-labor model.

Southern whites made up the third element of the South's Republican Party. Approximately one out of four white Southerners voted Republican. The other three condemned the one who did as a traitor to his region and his race and called him a "scalawag," a term for runty horses and low-down, good-for-nothing rascals. **Yeoman** farmers accounted for the majority of southern white Republicans. Some were Unionists who emerged from the war with bitter memories of Confederate persecution. Others were small farmers who wanted to end state governments' favoritism toward plantation owners. Yeomen usually supported initiatives for public schools and for expanding economic opportunity in the South.

The South's Republican Party, then, was made up of freedmen, Yankees, and yeomen—an improbable coalition. The mix of races, regions, and classes inevitably meant friction as each group maneuvered to define the party. But Reconstruction represents an extraordinary moment in American politics: Blacks and whites joined together in the Republican Party to pursue political change. Formally, of course, only men participated in politics—casting ballots and holding offices—but women also played a part in the political struggle by joining in parades and rallies, attending stump speeches, and even campaigning.

Reconstruction politics was not for cowards. Activity on behalf of Republicans in particular took courage. Most whites in the South condemned reconstruction politics as illegitimate and felt justified in doing whatever they could to stamp out Republicanism. Violence against blacks—the "white terror"—took brutal institutional form in 1866 with the formation in Tennessee of the Ku Klux Klan, a social club of Confederate veterans that quickly developed into a paramilitary organization supporting Democrats. The Klan went on a rampage of whipping, hanging, shooting, burning, and throat-cutting to defeat Republicans and restore white supremacy. (See "Historical Question," page 574.) Rapid demobilization of the Union army after the war left only twenty thousand troops to patrol the entire South, a vast territory. Without effective military protection, southern Republicans had to take care of themselves.

Republican Rule

In the fall of 1867, southern states held elections for delegates to state constitutional conventions, as required by the Reconstruction Acts. About 40 percent of the white electorate stayed home because they had been disfranchised or because they had decided to boycott politics. Republicans won three-fourths of the seats. About 15 percent of the Republican delegates to the conventions were Northerners who had moved south, 25 percent were African Americans, and 60 percent were white Southerners. As a British visitor observed, the delegate elections reflected "the mighty revolution that had taken place in America." But Democrats described the state conventions as zoos of "baboons, monkeys, mules . . . and other jackasses." In fact, the conventions brought together serious, purposeful men who hammered out the legal framework for a new order.

The reconstruction constitutions introduced two broad categories of changes in the South: those that reduced aristocratic privilege and increased democratic equality and those that expanded the state's responsibility for the general welfare. In the first category, the constitutions adopted universal male suffrage, abolished property qualifications for holding office, and

> Conservative white Southerners called them "carpetbaggers," men so poor that they could stuff all their earthly belongings in a single carpet-sided suitcase and swoop southward like buzzards to "fatten on our misfortunes."

What Did the Ku Klux Klan Really Want?

In the summer of 1866, six Confederate veterans in Pulaski, Tennessee, founded the Ku Klux Klan. Borrowing oaths and rituals from a college fraternity, the young men innocently sought fun and fellowship in a social club. But they quickly tired of playing pranks on one another and shifted to more serious matters. By the spring of 1868, when congressional reconstruction went into effect, new groups, or "dens," of the Ku Klux Klan had sprouted throughout the South.

According to former Confederate general and Georgia Democratic politician John B. Gordon, the Klan owed its popularity to the "instinct of self-preservation . . . the sense of insecurity and danger, particularly in those neighborhoods where the Negro population largely predominated." Everywhere whites looked, he said, they saw "great crime." Republican politicians organized ignorant freedmen and marched them to the polls, where they blighted honest government. Ex-slaves drove overseers from plantations and claimed the land for themselves. Black robbers and rapists made white women cower behind barred doors. It was necessary, Gordon declared, "in order to protect our families from outrage and preserve our own lives, to have something that we could regard as a brotherhood—a combination of the best men of the country, to act purely in self-defense." According to Gordon and other conservative white Southerners, Klansmen were good men who stepped forward to do their duty, men who

wanted nothing more than to guard their families and defend decent society from the assaults of degraded ex-slaves and a vindictive Republican Party.

Behind the Klan's high-minded and self-justifying rhetoric, however, lay another agenda. It was revealed in their actions, not their words. Klansmen embarked on a campaign to reverse history. Garbed in robes and hoods, they engaged in hit-and-run **guerrilla warfare** against free labor, civil equality, and political democracy. They aimed to terrorize their enemies—ex-slaves and white Republicans—into submission. As the South's chief terrorist organization between 1868 and 1871, the Klan whipped, burned, and shot in the name of white supremacy. Changes in four particular areas of southern life proved flash points for Klan violence: racial etiquette, education, labor, and politics.

The Klan punished those blacks and whites whom they deemed guilty of breaking the Old South's racial code. The Klan considered "impudence" a punishable offense. Asked to define "impudence" before a congressional investigating committee, one white opponent of the Klan responded: "Well, it is considered impudence for a negro not to be polite to a white man—not to pull off his hat and bow and scrape to a white man, as was done formerly." Klansmen whipped blacks for crimes that ranged from speaking disrespectfully and refusing to yield the sidewalk to raising a good crop and dressing well. Black women who "dress up and fix up like ladies"

risked a midnight visit from the Klan. The Ku Klux Klan sought to restore racial subordination in every aspect of private and public life.

Klansmen also took aim at black education. White men, especially those with little schooling, found the sight of blacks in classrooms hard to stomach. Schools were easy targets, and scores of them went up in flames. Teachers, male and female, were flogged, or worse. Klansmen drove northern-born teacher Alonzo B. Corliss from North Carolina for "teaching niggers and making them like white men." In Cross Plains, Alabama, the Klan hanged an Irish-born teacher along with four black men. But not just ill-educated whites opposed black education. Planters wanted ex-slaves back in the fields, not at desks. Each student meant one less laborer. In 1869, an Alabama newspaper reported the burning of a black school and observed that it should be "a warning for them to stick hereafter to 'de shovel and de hoe,' and let their dirty-backed primers go."

Planters turned to the Klan as part of their effort to preserve plantation agriculture and restore labor discipline. An Alabama white admitted that in his area, the Klan was "intended principally for the negroes who failed to work." Masked bands "punished Negroes whose landlords had complained of them." Sharecroppers who disputed their share at "settling up time" risked a visit from the night riders. Klansmen murdered a Georgia blacksmith who refused to do additional work for a white man until he was paid for a previous job. It was dangerous for freedmen to consider changing employers. "If we got out looking for some other place to go," an ex-slave from Texas remembered, "them KKK they would

Ku Klux Klan Rider in Tennessee about 1868 and Klan Banner

The white robes that we associate with the Ku Klux Klan are a twentieth-century phenomenon. During Reconstruction, Klansmen wore robes of various designs and colors. This robe's fancy trim and the man's elaborate hat make it highly unlikely that the rider sewed the costume himself. Women did not participate in midnight raids, but they often shared the Klan's reactionary vision and did what they could to help the cause. Hooded horses added another element to the Klan's terror. The Klansman holds a flag that looks very much like the satanic dragon on the colorful Klan banner shown here, which contains a Latin motto from Saint Augustine's definition of Catholic truth: "that which [has been believed] always, everywhere, by all." Among Klansmen, this motto was likely to refer to the truth of white supremacy.

Rider: Tennessee State Museum Collection; Banner: Chicago Historical Society.

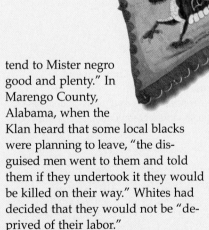

tend to Mister negro good and plenty." In Marengo County, Alabama, when the Klan heard that some local blacks were planning to leave, "the disguised men went to them and told them if they undertook it they would be killed on their way." Whites had decided that they would not be "deprived of their labor."

Above all, the Klan terrorized Republican leaders and voters. Klansmen became the military arm of the Democratic Party. They drove blacks from the polls on election day and terrorized black officeholders. Klansmen gave Andrew Flowers, a black politician in Chattanooga, a brutal beating and told him that they "did not intend any nigger to hold office

in the United States." Jack Dupree, president of the Republican Club in Monroe County, Mississippi, a man known to "speak his mind," had his throat cut and was disemboweled while his wife was forced to watch.

Between 1868 and 1871, political violence reached astounding levels. Arkansas experienced nearly three hundred political killings in the three months before the fall elections in 1868, including Little Rock's U.S. congressman, J. M. Hinds. Louisiana was even bloodier. Between the local elections in the spring of 1868 and the presidential election in the fall, Louisiana experienced more than one thousand killings. Political violence often proved effective. In Georgia, Republican presidential candidate Ulysses S. Grant received no votes at

all in 1868 in eleven counties, despite black majorities. The Klan murdered three scalawag members of the Georgia legislature and drove ten others from their homes. As one Georgia Republican commented after a Klan attack: "We don't call them [D]emocrats, we call them southern murderers."

It proved hard to arrest Klansmen and harder still to convict them. "If a white man kills a colored man in any of the counties of this State," observed a Florida sheriff, "you cannot convict him." By 1871, the death toll had reached thousands. Federal intervention—in the Ku Klux Klan Acts of 1870 and 1871—signaled an end to much of the Klan's power but not to counterrevolutionary violence in the South. Other groups continued the terror.

Republican Rule Cartoon, California, 1867

This racist Democratic cartoon from California ridicules Republican support of black suffrage, and it links black voting with the enfranchisement of Chinese immigrants and Native Americans, topics of some urgency to westerners. Uncle Sam, on the left, admonishes George C. Gorham, Republican candidate for governor: "Young Man! Read the history of your Country, and learn that this ballot box was dedicated to the white race alone. The load you are carrying will sink you in perdition, where you belong." The black man, Chinese man, and Indian all speak in thick dialects that confirm white racial stereotypes. On the right, a man in a top hat, holding a monkey on a leash, calls out mockingly, "Say, Gorham! Put this Brother up."

Library of Congress.

Unionists that unless all former Confederates were banned from politics they would storm back and wreck reconstruction, no state constitution disfranchised ex-rebels wholesale.

Democrats, however, were blind to the limits of the Republican program. They thought they faced wild revolution. According to Democrats, Republican victories initiated "black and tan" (ex-slave and mulatto) governments across the South. But the claims of "Negro domination" had almost no validity. Although four out of five Republican voters were black men, more than four out of five Republican officeholders were white. Southerners sent fourteen black congressmen and two black senators to Washington, but only 6 percent of Southerners in Congress during Reconstruction were black (Figure 16.1). With the exception of South Carolina, where blacks briefly held a majority in one house of the legislature, no state experienced "Negro rule," despite black majorities in the populations of some states.

In almost every state, voters ratified the new constitutions and swept Republicans into power. When the former Confederate states ratified the Fourteenth Amendment, Congress readmitted them. Southern Republicans then turned to a staggering array of problems. Wartime destruction—burned cities, shattered bridges, broken levees—still littered the landscape. The South's

made more offices elective and fewer appointed. In the second category, they enacted prison reform; made the state responsible for caring for orphans, the insane, and the deaf and mute; and exempted debtors' homes from seizure.

These forward-looking state constitutions provided blueprints for a new South but stopped short of the specific reforms advocated by some. Despite the wishes of virtually every former slave, no southern constitution confiscated and redistributed land. And despite the prediction of

FIGURE 16.1   Southern Congressional Delegations, 1865–1877

The statistics contradict the myth of black domination of congressional representation during Reconstruction.

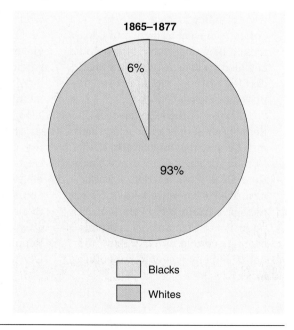

1865–1877

6%

93%

☐ Blacks
☐ Whites

share of the nation's wealth had fallen from 30 percent to only 12 percent. Manufacturing limped along at a fraction of prewar levels, agricultural production remained anemic, and the region's railroads lay devastated. Without the efforts of the Freedmen's Bureau, black and white Southerners would have starved. Making matters worse, racial harassment and reactionary violence dogged Southerners who sought reform. In this desperate context, Republicans struggled to breathe life into their new state governments.

Republican activity focused on three areas—education, civil rights, and economic development. Every state inaugurated a system of public education. Before the Civil War, whites had deliberately kept slaves illiterate, and planter-dominated governments rarely spent tax money to educate the children of yeomen. By 1875, half of Mississippi's and South Carolina's eligible children (the majority of whom were black) were attending school. Despite underfunding and dilapidated facilities, literacy rates rose sharply. Although public schools were racially segregated, education remained for many blacks a tangible, deeply satisfying benefit of freedom and Republican rule.

State legislatures also attacked racial discrimination and defended civil rights. Republicans especially resisted efforts to segregate blacks from whites in public transportation. Mississippi levied fines of up to $1,000 and three

---

Students at a Freedmen's School in Virginia, circa 1870s, and a One-Cent Primer
"The people are hungry and thirsty after knowledge," a former slave observed immediately after the Civil War. African American leader Booker T. Washington remembered "a whole race trying to go to school." The students at this Virginia school stand in front of their log-cabin classroom reading books, but more common were eight-page primers that cost a penny. These simple readers offered ex-slaves the elements of literacy. For people long forbidden to learn to read and write, literacy symbolized freedom. Literacy also allowed those who were deeply religious to experience the joy of reading the Bible for themselves and those who were merely practical to understand labor contracts and participate knowledgeably in politics.

Primer: Gladstone Collection; Students: Valentine Museum, Cook Collection.

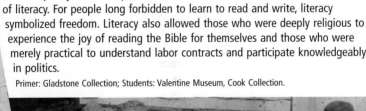

years in jail for railroads and steamboats that pushed blacks, regardless of their ability to pay, into "smoking cars" or to lower decks. Refined, well-off blacks took particular aim at hotels and theaters that denied "full and equal rights." An exasperated Mississippian complained: "Education amounts to nothing, good behavior counts for nothing, even money cannot buy for a colored man or woman decent treatment and the comforts that white people claim and can obtain." But passing color-blind laws was one thing; enforcing them was another. Despite the laws, segregation—later called **Jim Crow**—developed at white insistence and became a feature of southern life long before the end of the Reconstruction era.

Republican governments also launched ambitious programs of economic development. They envisioned a South of diversified agriculture, roaring factories, and booming towns. Republican legislatures chartered scores of banks and industrial companies, appropriated funds to fix ruined levees and drain swamps, and went on a railroad-building binge. These efforts fell far short of solving the South's economic troubles, however. Republican spending to stimulate economic growth also meant rising taxes and enormous debt that drained funds from schools and other programs.

The southern Republicans' record, then, was mixed. To their credit, the biracial party took up under trying circumstances an ambitious agenda to change the South. Money was scarce, the Democrats continued their harassment, and factionalism threatened the Republican Party from within. However, corruption infected Republican governments in the South. Public morality reached new lows everywhere in the nation after the Civil War, and the chaos and disruption of the postwar South proved fertile soil for bribery, fraud, and influence peddling. Despite problems and shortcomings, however, the Republican Party made headway in its efforts to purge the South of aristocratic privilege and racist oppression. Republican governments had less success in overthrowing the long-established white oppression of black farm laborers in the rural South.

White Landlords, Black Sharecroppers

In the countryside, clashes occurred daily between ex-slaves who wished to escape slave labor and ex-masters who wanted to reinstitute old ways. Except for having to put down the whip and pay subsistence wages, planters had not been required to offer many concessions to

Black Woman in Cotton Fields, Thomasville, Georgia
Few images of everyday black women during the Reconstruction era survive. This photograph was taken in 1895, but it nevertheless goes to the heart of the labor struggle after the Civil War. Before emancipation, black women worked in the fields; after emancipation, white landlords wanted them to continue working there. Freedom allowed some women to escape field labor, but not this Georgian, who probably worked to survive. The photograph reveals a strong person with a clear sense of who she is. Though worn to protect her head and body from the fierce heat, her intricately wrapped headdress dramatically expresses her individuality. Her bare feet also reveal something about her life.
Courtesy, Georgia Department of Archives and History, Atlanta, Georgia.

emancipation. They continued to believe that African Americans were inherently lazy and would not work without coercion. Whites moved quickly to restore the antebellum world of work gangs, white overseers, field labor for black women and children, clustered cabins, minimal personal freedom, and even whipping whenever they could get away with it.

Ex-slaves resisted every effort to turn back the clock. They argued that if any class could be described as "lazy," it was the planters, who, as one ex-slave noted, "lived in idleness all their lives on stolen labor." Land of their own would anchor their economic independence, they believed, and end planters' interference in their personal lives. They could then, for example, make their own decisions about whether women and children would labor in the fields. Indeed, within months after the war, perhaps one-third of black women abandoned field labor to work on chores in their own cabins just as poor white women did. With freedom to decide how to use family time, hundreds of thousands of black children enrolled in school. But landownership proved to be beyond the reach of most blacks once the federal government abandoned plans to redistribute Confederate property. Without land, ex-slaves had little choice but to work on plantations.

Although they were forced to return to the planters' fields, freedmen resisted efforts to restore slavelike conditions. In his South Carolina neighborhood, David Golightly Harris discovered that few freedmen were "willing to hire by the day, month or year." Instead of working for wages, "the negroes all seem disposed to rent land," which would increase their independence from whites. By rejecting wage labor, by striking, and by abandoning the most reactionary employers, blacks sought to force concessions. Out of this tug-of-war between white landlords and black laborers emerged a new system of southern agriculture.

Sharecropping was a compromise that offered both ex-masters and ex-slaves something but satisfied neither. Under the new system, planters divided their cotton plantations into small farms of twenty-five to thirty acres that freedmen rented, paying with a share of each year's crop, usually half. Sharecropping gave blacks more freedom than the system of wages and labor gangs and released them from the day-to-day supervision of whites. Black families abandoned the old slave quarters and scattered over plantations, building separate cabins for themselves on the patches of land they rented (Map 16.1, page 580). Black families now decided who would work, for how long, and how hard. Still, most blacks remained dependent on white landlords, who had the power to expel them at the end of each growing season. For planters, sharecropping offered a way to resume agricultural production, but it did not allow them to restore the old slave plantation.

Sharecropping introduced a new figure— the country merchant—into the agricultural equation. Landlords supplied sharecroppers with land, mules, seeds, and tools, but blacks also needed credit to obtain essential food and clothing before they harvested their crops. Thousands of small crossroads stores sprang up to offer credit. Under an arrangement called a crop lien, a merchant would advance goods to a sharecropper in exchange for a *lien*, or legal claim, on the farmer's future crop. Some merchants charged exorbitant rates of interest, as much as 60 percent, on the goods they sold. At the end of the growing season, after the landlord had taken half of the farmer's crop for rent, the merchant took most of the rest. Sometimes, the farmer's debt to the merchant exceeded the income he received from his remaining half of the crop, and the farmer would have no choice but to borrow more from the merchant and begin the cycle all over again.

An experiment at first, sharecropping spread quickly and soon dominated the cotton South. Lien merchants forced tenants to plant cotton, which was easy to sell, instead of food crops. The result was excessive production of cotton and falling cotton prices, developments that cost thousands of small white farmers their land and pushed them into the great army of sharecroppers. The new sharecropping system of agriculture took shape just as the political power of Republicans in the South began to buckle under Democratic pressure.

> **REVIEW**   Why was the Republican Party in the South a coalition party?

Reconstruction Collapses

By 1870, after a decade of war and reconstruction, Northerners wanted to turn to their own affairs and put "the southern problem" behind them. Increasingly, practical, business-minded men came to the forefront of the Republican Party, replacing the band of reformers and idealists who had been prominent in the 1860s. While northern commitment to defend black freedom eroded, southern commitment to white supremacy intensified. Without northern protection, southern Republicans were no match for the Democrats' economic coercion, political corruption, and bloody violence. One

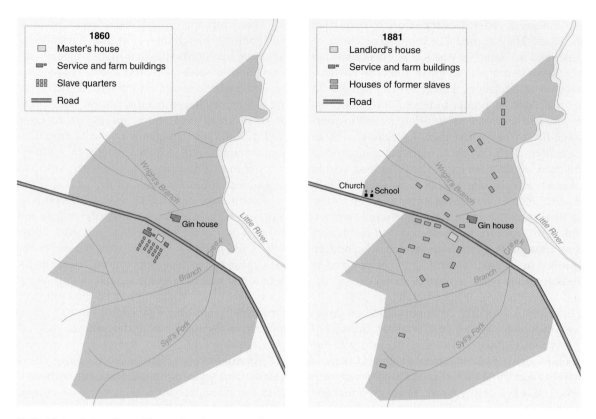

MAP 16.1   A Southern Plantation in 1860 and 1881

These maps of the Barrow plantation in Georgia illustrate some of the ways in which ex-slaves expressed their freedom. Freedmen and freedwomen deserted the clustered living quarters behind the master's house, scattered over the plantation, built family cabins, and farmed rented land. The former Barrow slaves also worked together to build a school and a church.

READING THE MAP: Compare the number and size of the slave quarters in 1860 with the homes of the former slaves in 1881. How do they differ? Which buildings were prominently located along the road in 1860, and which could be found along the road in 1881?

CONNECTIONS: How might the former master feel about the new configuration of buildings on the plantation in 1881? In what ways did the new system of sharecropping replicate the old system of plantation agriculture? In what ways was it different?

FOR MORE HELP ANALYZING THIS MAP, see the map activity for this chapter in the Online Study Guide at bedfordstmartins.com/roark.

by one, Republican state governments fell in the South. The election of 1876 both confirmed and completed the collapse of reconstruction.

Grant's Troubled Presidency

In 1868, the Republican Party's presidential nomination went to Ulysses S. Grant, the North's favorite general. Hero of the Civil War and a supporter of congressional reconstruction, Grant was the obvious choice. His Democratic opponent, Horatio Seymour of New York, ran on a platform that blasted congressional reconstruction as "a flagrant usurpation of power . . . unconstitu-

tional, revolutionary, and void." The Republicans answered by "waving the **bloody shirt**"— that is, they reminded voters that the Democrats were "the party of rebellion." During the campaign, the Ku Klux Klan erupted in a reign of terror, murdering hundreds of southern Republicans. Violence in the South cost Grant votes, but he gained a narrow 309,000-vote margin in the popular vote and a substantial victory (214 votes to 80) in the electoral college (Map 16.2).

Grant hoped to forge a policy that secured both justice for blacks and sectional reconciliation. But he

took office at a time when a majority of white Northerners had grown weary of the "Southern Question" and were increasingly willing to let southern whites manage their own affairs. Moreover, Grant had doubts about his preparation for the White House. "To go into the Presidency opens altogether a new field to me, in which there is to be a new strife to which I am not trained," he admitted. Indeed, Grant was not as good a president as he was a general. The talents he had demonstrated on the battlefield—decisiveness, clarity, and resolution—were less obvious in the White House. Able advisers might have helped, but he surrounded himself with fumbling kinfolk and old cronies from his army days. He also made a string of dubious appointments that led to a series of damaging scandals. Charges of corruption tainted his vice president, Schuyler Colfax, and brought down two of his cabinet officers. Grant's dogged loyalty to liars and cheats only compounded the damage. Though never personally implicated in any scandal, Grant was aggravatingly naive and blind to the rot that filled his administration. Congressman James A. Garfield declared: "His imperturbability is amazing. I am in doubt whether to call it greatness or stupidity."

In 1872, anti-Grant Republicans bolted and launched the Liberal Party. To clean up the graft and corruption, Liberals proposed ending the **spoils system**, by which victorious parties rewarded loyal workers with public office, and replacing it with a nonpartisan **civil service** com-

Grant and Scandal

This anti-Grant cartoon by Thomas Nast, the nation's most celebrated political cartoonist, shows the president falling headfirst into the barrel of fraud and corruption that tainted his administration. During Grant's eight years in the White House, many members of his administration failed him. Sometimes duped, sometimes merely loyal, Grant stubbornly defended wrongdoers, even to the point of perjuring himself to keep an aide out of jail. Library of Congress.

READING THE IMAGE: How does Thomas Nast portray President Grant's role in corruption? According to this cartoon, what caused the problems?
CONNECTIONS: How responsible was President Grant for the corruption that plagued his administration?

FOR MORE HELP ANALYZING THIS IMAGE, see the visual activity for this chapter in the Online Study Guide at bedfordstmartins.com/roark.

MAP 16.2 The Election of 1868

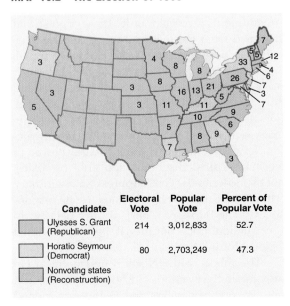

Candidate	Electoral Vote	Popular Vote	Percent of Popular Vote
Ulysses S. Grant (Republican)	214	3,012,833	52.7
Horatio Seymour (Democrat)	80	2,703,249	47.3
Nonvoting states (Reconstruction)			

mission that would oversee competitive examinations for appointment to office. Moreover, they demanded that the federal government remove its troops from the South and restore "home rule" (southern white control). Democrats liked the Liberals' southern policy and endorsed the Liberal presidential candidate, Horace Greeley, the longtime editor of the *New York Tribune*. However, the nation still felt enormous affection for the man who had saved the Union and reelected Grant with 56 percent of the popular vote.

Grant's ambitions for his administration extended beyond reconstruction, but not even foreign affairs could escape the problems of the

Grant's Proposed Annexation of Santo Domingo

South. The annexation of Santo Domingo in the Caribbean was Grant's greatest passion. He argued that the acquisition of this tropical land would permit the United States to expand its trade and also provide a new home for the South's blacks, who were so desperately harassed by the Klan. Aggressive foreign policy had not originated with the Grant administration. Lincoln's and Johnson's secretary of state, William H. Seward, had thwarted French efforts to set up a puppet empire under Maximilian in Mexico, and his purchase of Alaska ("Seward's Ice Box") from Russia in 1867 for only $7 million fired Grant's **imperialist** ambition. But in the end, Grant could not convince Congress to approve the treaty annexing Santo Domingo. The South preoccupied Congress and undermined Grant's initiatives.

Northern Resolve Withers

Although Grant genuinely wanted to see blacks' civil and political rights protected, he understood that most Northerners had grown weary of reconstruction. Average citizens wanted to shift their attention to other issues, especially after the nation slipped into a devastating economic depression in 1873. More than eighteen thousand businesses collapsed, leaving more than a million workers without jobs. Northern businessmen who wanted to invest in the South believed that recurrent federal intrusion was itself a major cause of instability in the region. Republican leaders began to question the wisdom of their party's alliance with the South's lower classes—its small farmers and sharecroppers. Grant's secretary of the interior, Jacob D. Cox of Ohio, proposed allying with the "thinking and influential native southerners . . . the intelligent, well-to-do, and controlling class."

Congress, too, wanted to leave reconstruction behind, but southern Republicans made that difficult. When the South's Republicans begged for federal protection from Klan violence, Congress enacted three laws in 1870 and 1871 that were intended to break the back of white terrorism. The severest of the three, the Ku Klux Klan Act (1871), made interference with voting rights a felony and authorized the use of the army to enforce it. Intrepid federal marshals arrested thousands of Klansmen, and the govern-

ment came close to destroying the Klan but did not end terrorism against blacks. Congress also passed the Civil Rights Act of 1875, which boldly outlawed racial discrimination in transportation, public accommodations, and juries. But federal authorities never enforced the law aggressively, and segregated facilities remained the rule throughout the South.

By the early 1870s, the Republican Party had lost its principal spokesmen for African American rights to death or defeat at the polls. Others in Congress concluded that the quest for black equality was mistaken or hopelessly naive. In May 1872, Congress restored the right of office-holding to all but three hundred ex-rebels. In the opinion of many, traditional white leaders offered the best hope for honesty, order, and prosperity in the South.

Underlying the North's abandonment of reconstruction was unyielding racial prejudice. During the war, Northerners had learned to accept black freedom, but deep-seated prejudice prevented many from following freedom with equality. Even the actions they took on behalf of blacks often served partisan political advantage. Northerners generally supported Indiana senator Thomas A. Hendricks's harsh declaration that "this is a white man's Government, made by the white man for the white man."

The U.S. Supreme Court also did its part to undermine reconstruction. The Court issued a series of decisions that significantly weakened the federal government's ability to protect black Southerners under the Fourteenth and Fifteenth Amendments. In the *Slaughterhouse* cases (1873), the Court distinguished between national and state citizenship and ruled that the Fourteenth Amendment protected only those rights that stemmed from the federal government, such as voting in federal elections and interstate travel. Since the Court decided that most rights derived from the states, it sharply curtailed the federal government's authority to protect black citizens. Even more devastating, the *United States v. Cruikshank* ruling (1876) said that the reconstruction amendments gave Congress the power to legislate against discrimination only by states, not by individuals. The "suppression of ordinary crime," such as assault, remained a state responsibility. The Supreme Court did not declare reconstruction unconstitutional but undermined its legal foundation.

The mood of the North found political expression in the election of 1874, when for the first time in eighteen years the Democrats gained control of the House of Representatives. As one Republican observed, the people had grown tired of the "negro question, with all its complications, and the reconstruction of Southern States, with all its interminable embroilments." Reconstruction had come apart. The people were tired of it. Grant grew increasingly unwilling to enforce it. Congress gradually abandoned it. The Supreme Court busily denied the constitutionality of significant parts of it. Rather than defend reconstruction from its southern enemies, Northerners steadily backed away from the challenge. After the early 1870s, southern blacks faced the forces of reaction largely on their own.

White Supremacy Triumphs

Republican state and local governments in the South attracted more bitterness and hatred than any other political regimes in American history. In the eyes of the majority of whites, Republican rule meant intolerable insults: Black militiamen patrolled town streets, black laborers negotiated contracts with former masters, black maids stood up to former mistresses, black voters cast ballots, and black legislators such as James T. Rapier enacted laws. The northern retreat from reconstruction permitted southern Democrats to harness this white rage to politics. Taking the name "Redeemers," they promised to replace "bayonet rule" (some federal troops continued to be stationed in the South) with "home rule." They branded Republican governments a carnival of extravagance, waste, and fraud and promised that honest, thrifty Democrats would supplant the irresponsible tax-and-spend Republicans. Above all, Redeemers swore to save southern civilization from a descent into African "barbarism" and "Negro rule." As one man put it, "We must render this either a white man's government, or convert the land into a Negro man's cemetery."

Southern Democrats adopted a two-pronged racial strategy to

"White Man's Country"

White supremacy emerged as a central tenet of the Democratic Party before the Civil War, and Democrats kept up a vicious racist attack on Republicans throughout Reconstruction. This silk ribbon from the 1868 presidential campaign between Republican Ulysses S. Grant and his Democratic opponent, New York governor Horatio Seymour, openly declares the Democrats' racial goal. During the campaign, Democratic vice presidential nominee Francis P. Blair Jr. promised that a Seymour victory would restore "white people" to power by declaring the reconstruction governments in the South "null and void." The Democrats' promotion of white supremacy reached new levels of shrillness in the 1870s, when northern support for reconstruction began to waver.
Collection of Janice L. and David J. Frent.

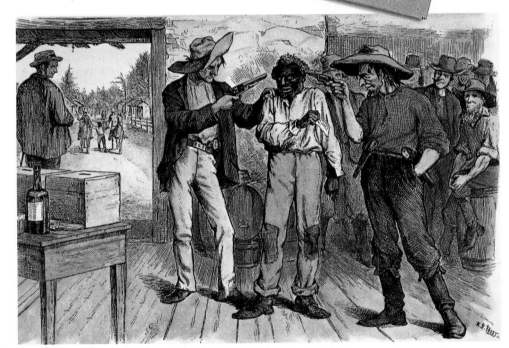

"Of Course He Wants to Vote the Democratic Ticket"

This Republican cartoon from the October 21, 1876, issue of *Harper's Weekly* comments sarcastically on the possibility of honest elections in the South. The caption reads, "You're free as air, ain't you? Say you are or I'll blow yer black head off." The cartoon demonstrates not only some Northerners' concern that violence would deliver the election to the Democrats but also the perception that white Southerners were crude, drunken, ignorant brutes.
Granger Collection.

READING THE IMAGE: What does the cartoon reveal about the cartoonist's political stance? How does the cartoonist demonstrate his view of white Southerners?
CONNECTIONS: Was the cartoonist's outrage about southern violence against blacks typical of white northern opinion in 1876?

FOR MORE HELP ANALYZING THIS IMAGE, see the visual activity for this chapter in the Online Study Guide at bedfordstmartins.com/roark.

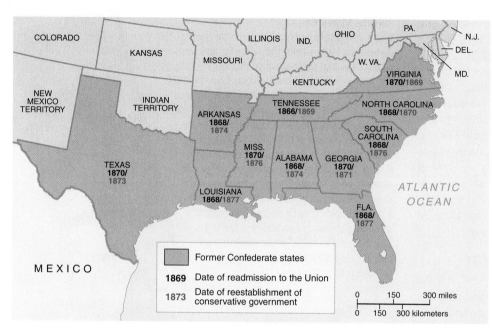

MAP 16.3   The Reconstruction of the South
Myth has it that Republican rule of the former Confederacy was not only harsh but long. In most states, however, conservative southern whites stormed back into power in months or just a few years. By the election of 1876, Republican governments could be found in only three states, and they soon fell.

READING THE MAP: List in chronological order the readmission of the former Confederate states to the Union. Which states reestablished conservative governments most quickly?
CONNECTIONS: What did the former Confederate states need to do in order to be readmitted to the Union? How did reestablished conservative governments react to reconstruction?

FOR MORE HELP ANALYZING THIS MAP, see the map activity for this chapter in the Online Study Guide at bedfordstmartins.com/roark.

overthrow Republican governments. First, they sought to polarize the parties around color. They went about gathering all the South's white voters into the Democratic Party, leaving the Republicans to depend on blacks. The "straight-out" appeal to whites promised great advantage because whites made up a majority of the population in every southern state except Mississippi, South Carolina, and Louisiana.

To dislodge whites from the Republican Party, Democrats fanned the flames of racial prejudice. A South Carolina Democrat crowed that his party appealed to the "proud Caucasian race, whose sovereignty on earth God has proclaimed." Ostracism also proved effective. Local newspapers published the names of whites who kept company with blacks. So complete was the ostracism that one of its victims said, "No white man can live in the South in the future and act with any other than the Democratic party unless he is willing and prepared to live a life of social isolation."

Democrats also exploited the severe economic plight of small white farmers by blaming

it on Republican financial policy. Government spending soared during reconstruction, and small farmers saw their tax burden skyrocket. "This is tax time," South Carolinian David Golightly Harris observed. "We are nearly all on our head about them. They are so high & so little money to pay with." Farmers without enough cash to pay their taxes began "selling every egg and chicken they can get." In 1871, Mississippi reported that one-seventh of the state's land—3.3 million acres—had been forfeited for nonpayment of taxes. The small farmers' economic distress had a racial dimension. Because few freedmen succeeded in acquiring land, they rarely paid taxes. In Georgia in 1874, blacks made up 45 percent of the population but paid only 2 percent of the taxes. From the perspective of a small white farmer, Republican rule meant that he was paying more taxes and paying them to aid blacks. Democrats asked whether it was not time for hard-pressed yeomen to join the white man's party.

If racial pride, social isolation, and Republican financial policies proved insufficient to drive yeomen from the Republican Party, Democrats turned to terrorism. "Night riders" targeted white Republicans as well as blacks for murder and assassination. "A dead Radical is very harmless," South Carolina Democratic leader Martin Gary told his followers. By the 1870s, only a handful of white Republicans remained.

The second prong of Democratic strategy aimed at the complete intimidation of black Republicans, especially local leaders. Emanuel Fortune, whom the Klan drove from Jackson County, Florida, declared: "The object of it is to kill out the leading men of the republican party . . . men who have taken a prominent stand." Violence expanded to all black voters and escalated to unprecedented levels. In 1873, a clash between black militiamen and gun-toting whites killed two white men and an estimated seventy black men in Louisiana. The whites slaughtered half of the black men after they surrendered. Although the federal government indicted more than one hundred of the white men, local juries failed to convict even one.

Even before adopting the all-out white supremacist tactics of the 1870s, Democrats had already taken control of the governments of Virginia, Tennessee, and North Carolina. The new campaign brought fresh gains. The Redeemers retook Georgia in 1871, Texas in 1873, and Arkansas and Alabama in 1874. Mississippi became a scene of open, unrelenting, and often savage intimidation of black voters and their few remaining white allies. As the state election approached in 1876, Governor Adelbert Ames appealed to Washington for federal troops to control the violence, only to hear from the attorney general that the "whole public are tired of these annual autumnal outbreaks in the South." Abandoned, Mississippi Republicans succumbed to the Democratic onslaught in the fall elections. By the election of 1876, only three Republican state governments—in Florida, Louisiana, and South Carolina—survived in the South (Map 16.3).

An Election and a Compromise

The centennial year of 1876 witnessed one of the most tumultuous elections in American history. Its chaos and confusion provided a fitting conclusion to the experiment known as reconstruction. The election took place in November, but not until March 2 of the following year did the nation know who would be inaugurated president on March 4. The Democrats nominated New York's governor, Samuel J. Tilden, who immediately targeted the corruption of the Grant administration and the despotism of Republican reconstruction. The Republicans put forward Rutherford B. Hayes, governor of Ohio. Privately, Hayes considered "bayonet rule" a mistake but concluded that waving the "bloody shirt"—reminding voters that the Democrats were the "party of rebellion"—remained the Republicans' best political strategy.

On election day, Tilden tallied 4,288,590 votes to Hayes's 4,036,000. But in the all-important electoral college, Tilden fell one vote short of the majority required for victory. The electoral votes of three states—South Carolina, Louisiana, and Florida, the only remaining Republican governments in the South—remained in doubt because both Republicans and Democrats in those states claimed victory. To win, Tilden needed only one of the nineteen contested votes. Hayes had to have all of them.

Congress had to decide who had actually won the elections in the three southern states and thus who would be president. The Constitution provided no guidance for this situation. Moreover, Democrats controlled the House, and Republicans controlled the Senate. Congress created a special electoral commission to arbitrate the disputed returns. All of the commissioners voted their party affiliation, giving every state to the Republican Hayes and putting him over the top in electoral votes (Map 16.4).

Some outraged Democrats vowed to resist Hayes's victory. Rumors flew of an impending coup and renewed civil war. But the impasse was broken when negotiations behind the scenes between Hayes's lieutenants and some moderate southern Democrats resulted in an informal understanding known as the Compromise of 1877. In exchange for a Democratic promise not to block Hayes's inauguration and to deal fairly with the freedmen, Hayes vowed to refrain from using the army to uphold the remaining Republican regimes in the South and to provide the South with substantial federal subsidies for internal improvements. Two days later, the nation celebrated Hayes's peaceful inauguration.

Stubborn Tilden supporters bemoaned the "stolen election" and damned "His Fraudulency," Rutherford B. Hayes. Old-guard radicals such as William Lloyd Garrison denounced Hayes's bargain as a "policy of compromise, of credulity, of weakness, of subserviency, of surrender." But the

MAP 16.4 The Election of 1876

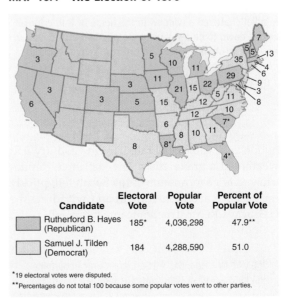

Candidate	Electoral Vote	Popular Vote	Percent of Popular Vote
Rutherford B. Hayes (Republican)	185*	4,036,298	47.9**
Samuel J. Tilden (Democrat)	184	4,288,590	51.0

*19 electoral votes were disputed.

**Percentages do not total 100 because some popular votes went to other parties.

"Reading Election Bulletin by Gaslight"
Throughout the nation in November 1876, eager citizens gathered on street corners at night to catch the latest news about the presidential election. When Democrats and Republicans disputed the returns, anxiety and anger mounted. With Samuel J. Tilden well ahead in the popular count, some Democrats began chanting "Tilden or War." Tilden received letters declaring that thousands of "well armed men" stood ready to march on Washington. In Columbia, Ohio, a bullet shattered a window in the home of Rutherford B. Hayes as his family sat down to dinner. Violent rhetoric and actions badly frightened a nation with fresh memories of a disastrous civil war, and for four long months, it was unclear whether the nation would peacefully inaugurate a new president.
Granger Collection.

nation as a whole celebrated, for the country had weathered a grave crisis. The last three Republican state governments in the South fell quickly once Hayes abandoned them and withdrew the U.S. army. Reconstruction came to an end.

> **REVIEW**   How did the Supreme Court undermine the Fourteenth and Fifteenth Amendments?

Conclusion: "A Revolution But Half Accomplished"

In 1865, when General Carl Schurz visited the South, he discovered "a revolution but half accomplished." White Southerners resisted the passage from slavery to free labor, from white racial despotism to equal justice, and from white political **monopoly** to biracial democracy. The old elite wanted to get "things back as near to slavery as possible," Schurz reported, while African Americans such as James T. Rapier and some whites were eager to exploit the revolutionary implications of defeat and emancipation.

The northern-dominated Republican Congress pushed the revolution along. Although it refused to provide for blacks' economic welfare, Congress employed constitutional amendments to require ex-Confederates to accept legal equality and share political power with black men. Congress was not willing to extend such power to women. Conservative southern whites fought ferociously to recover their power and privilege. When Democrats regained control of politics, whites used both state power and private violence to wipe out many of the gains of Reconstruction, leading one observer to conclude that the North had won the war but the South had won the peace.

The Redeemer counterrevolution, however, did not mean a return to slavery. Northern victory in the Civil War ensured abolition, and ex-slaves gained the freedom to not be whipped or sold, to send their children to school, to worship in their own churches, and to work independently on their own rented farms. Even sharecropping, with all its hardships, provided more autonomy and economic welfare than bondage had. It was limited freedom, to be sure, but it was not slavery.

The Civil War and emancipation set in motion the most profound upheaval in the nation's history, and nothing whites did entirely erased its revolutionary impact. War destroyed the largest slave society in the New World. The world of masters and slaves succumbed to that of landlords and sharecroppers, a world in which old lines of racial dominance continued, though with greater freedom for blacks. War also gave birth to a modern nation-state. For the first time, sovereignty rested uncontested in the federal government, and Washington increased its role in national affairs. When the South returned to the Union, it did so as a junior partner. The victorious North now possessed the power to establish the nation's direction, and it set the nation's compass toward the expansion of industrial capitalism and the final conquest of the West.

Despite massive changes, the Civil War remained only a "half accomplished" revolution. By not fulfilling the promises the nation seemed to hold out to black Americans at war's end, Reconstruction represents a tragedy of enormous proportions. The failure to protect blacks and guarantee their rights had enduring consequences. Almost a century after Reconstruction, the nation would embark on what one observer called a "second reconstruction." The solid achievements of the Thirteenth, Fourteenth, and Fifteenth Amendments to the Constitution would provide a legal foundation for the renewed commitment. It is worth remembering, though, that it was only the failure of the first reconstruction that made the modern civil rights movement necessary.

Selected Bibliography

General Works

Eric Foner, *Reconstruction: America's Unfinished Revolution* (1988).

James M. McPherson, *Ordeal by Fire: The Civil War and Reconstruction* (3rd ed., 2000).

The Meaning of Freedom

Ira Berlin et al., eds., *Freedom: A Documentary History of Emancipation, 1861–1867*, 4 vols. to date (1982–).

Michael W. Fitzgerald, *The Union League Movement in the Deep South: Politics and Agricultural Change during Reconstruction* (1989).

John Hope Franklin and Loren Schweninger, *In Search of the Promised Land: A Slave Family in the Old South* (2006).

Leon F. Litwack, *Been in the Storm So Long: The Aftermath of Slavery* (1979).

Howard N. Rabinowitz, *Race Relations in the Urban South, 1865–1890* (1978).

Roger L. Ransom and Richard Sutch, *One Kind of Freedom: The Economic Consequences of Emancipation* (1977).

Loren Schweninger, *James T. Rapier and Reconstruction* (1978).

Clarence E. Walker, *A Rock in a Weary Land: The African Methodist Episcopal Church during the Civil War and Reconstruction* (1982).

The Politics of Reconstruction

Michael Les Benedict, *The Impeachment and Trial of Andrew Johnson* (1973).

Richard F. Bensel, *Yankee Leviathan: The Origins of Central State Authority in America, 1859–1877* (1990).

Ellen Carol DuBois, *Feminism and Suffrage: The Emergence of an Independent Women's Movement in America, 1848–1869* (1978).

Victor B. Howard, *Religion and the Radical Republican Movement, 1860–1870* (1990).

Heather Cox Richardson, *The Death of Reconstruction: Race, Labor, and Politics in the Post–Civil War North, 1865–1901* (2001).

Terry L. Seip, *The South Returns to Congress: Men, Economic Measures, and Intersectional Relationships, 1868–1879* (1983).

Brooks D. Simpson, *The Reconstruction Presidents* (1998).

Mark W. Summers, *The Era of Good Stealings* (1993).

C. Vann Woodward, *Reunion and Reaction: The Compromise of 1877 and the End of Reconstruction* (1951).

The Struggle in the South

James Alex Baggett, *The Scalawags: Southern Dissenters in the Civil War and Reconstruction* (2003).

Nancy D. Bercaw, *Gendered Freedoms: Race, Rights, and the Politics of Household in the Delta, 1861–1875* (2003).

Jane Turner Censer, *The Reconstruction of White Southern Womanhood, 1865–1895* (2003).

Paul A. Cimbala, *Under the Guardianship of the Nation: The Freedmen's Bureau and the Reconstruction of Georgia, 1865–1870* (1997).

Jane E. Dailey, *Before Jim Crow: The Politics of Race in Post-emancipation Virginia* (2000).

Laura F. Edwards, *Gendered Strife and Confusion: The Political Culture of Reconstruction* (1997).

Sarah E. Gardner, *Blood and Irony: Southern White Women's Narratives of the Civil War, 1861–1937* (2004).

Stephen Kantrowitz, *Ben Tillman and the Reconstruction of White Supremacy* (2000).

Robert C. Kenzer, *Kinship and Neighborhood in a Southern Community: Orange County, North Carolina, 1849–1881* (1987).

Scott Reynolds Nelson, *Iron Confederacies: Southern Railways, Klan Violence, and Reconstruction* (1999).

George C. Rable, *But There Was No Peace: The Role of Violence in the Politics of Reconstruction* (1984).

James L. Roark, *Masters without Slaves: Southern Planters in the Civil War and Reconstruction* (1977).

Hyman Rubin III, *South Carolina Scalawags* (2006).

Allen Trelease, *White Terror: The Ku Klux Klan Conspiracy and Southern Reconstruction* (1971).

Peter Wallenstein, *From Slave South to New South: Public Policy in Nineteenth-Century Georgia* (1987).

▶ **FOR MORE BOOKS ABOUT TOPICS IN THIS CHAPTER,** see the Online Bibliography at bedfordstmartins.com/roark.

▶ **FOR ADDITIONAL FIRSTHAND ACCOUNTS OF THIS PERIOD,** see Chapter 16 in Michael Johnson, ed., *Reading the American Past*, Fourth Edition.

▶ **FOR WEB SITES, IMAGES, AND DOCUMENTS RELATED TO TOPICS AND PLACES IN THIS CHAPTER,** visit bedfordstmartins.com/makehistory.

REVIEWING THE CHAPTER

Follow these steps to review and strengthen your understanding of the chapter.

STEP 1: *Study the* **Key Terms** *and* **Timeline** *to identify the significance of each item listed.*

STEP 2: *Answer the* **Review Questions***, drawing on key terms and dates to support your answers.*

STEP 3: *Drawing on the Key Terms, Timeline, and Review Questions, answer the broader* **Making Connections** *questions.*

KEY TERMS

Who

James T. Rapier (p. 553)
Carl Schurz (p. 554)
Abraham Lincoln (p. 555)
Wendell Phillips (p. 555)
William Tecumseh Sherman (p. 557)
John Wilkes Booth (p. 561)
Andrew Johnson (p. 561)
Susan B. Anthony (p. 565)
Elizabeth Cady Stanton (p. 565)
Charles Sumner (p. 565)
Thaddeus Stevens (p. 568)
Edwin M. Stanton (p. 571)
Ulysses S. Grant (p. 573)
Horace Greeley (p. 581)
William H. Seward (p. 582)
Redeemers (p. 583)
night riders (p. 584)

Samuel J. Tilden (p. 585)
Rutherford B. Hayes (p. 585)

What

Proclamation of Amnesty and Reconstruction (p. 555)
Wade-Davis bill (p. 555)
suffrage (p. 556)
Confiscation Acts (p. 556)
Freedmen's Bureau (p. 557)
black codes (p. 562)
apprenticeship laws (p. 563)
Civil Rights Act of 1866 (p. 564)
radicals (p. 565)
Fourteenth Amendment (p. 565)
American Equal Rights Association (p. 565)
National Union Party (p. 568)
Memphis riots (p. 568)

Military Reconstruction Act (p. 569)
Reconstruction Acts of 1867 (p. 570)
impeachment (p. 571)
Tenure of Office Act (p. 571)
Fifteenth Amendment (p. 572)
carpetbagger (p. 573)
scalawag (p. 573)
Ku Klux Klan (p. 573)
sharecropping (p. 579)
country merchant (p. 579)
crop lien (p. 579)
waving the bloody shirt (p. 580)
Liberal Party (p. 581)
civil service commission (p. 581)
Ku Klux Klan Act (p. 582)
Civil Rights Act of 1875 (p. 582)
Slaughterhouse cases (p. 582)
United States v. Cruikshank (p. 582)
Compromise of 1877 (p. 585)

TIMELINE

1863 • Proclamation of Amnesty and Reconstruction.

    1864 • Wade-Davis bill.

        1865 • Freedmen's Bureau established.
             • President Abraham Lincoln shot; dies on April 15; succeeded by Andrew Johnson.
             • Black codes enacted.
             • Thirteenth Amendment becomes part of Constitution.

            1866 • Congress approves Fourteenth Amendment.
                 • Civil Rights Act.
                 • American Equal Rights Association founded.
                 • Ku Klux Klan founded.

                1867 • Military Reconstruction Act.
                     • Tenure of Office Act.

                    1868 • Impeachment trial of President Johnson.
                         • Republican Ulysses S. Grant elected president.

                        1869 • Congress approves Fifteenth Amendment.

REVIEW QUESTIONS

1. Why did Congress object to Lincoln's wartime plan for reconstruction? (pp. 555–60)

2. How did the North respond to the passage of black codes in the southern states? (pp. 561–65)

3. Why did Johnson urge the southern states to reject the Fourteenth Amendment? (pp. 565–72)

4. Why was the Republican Party in the South a coalition party? (pp. 572–79)

5. How did the Supreme Court undermine the Fourteenth and Fifteenth Amendments? (pp. 579–86)

MAKING CONNECTIONS

1. Reconstruction succeeded in advancing black civil rights but failed to secure them over the long term. Why and how did the federal government retreat from defending African Americans' civil rights in the 1870s? In your answer, cite specific actions by Congress and the Supreme Court.

2. Why was distributing plantation land to former slaves such a controversial policy? In your answer, discuss why landownership was important to freedmen and why Congress rejected redistribution as a general policy.

3. At the end of the Civil War, it remained to be seen exactly how emancipation would transform the South. How did emancipation change political and labor organization in the region? In your answer, discuss how ex-slaves exercised their new freedoms and how white Southerners attempted to limit them.

4. The Republican Party shaped Reconstruction through its control of Congress and state legislatures in the South. How did the identification of the Republican Party with Reconstruction policy affect the party's political fortunes in the 1870s? In your answer, be sure to address developments on the federal and state levels.

▶ FOR PRACTICE QUIZZES, A CUSTOMIZED STUDY PLAN, AND OTHER STUDY TOOLS, see the Online Study Guide at bedfordstmartins.com/roark.

1871 • Ku Klux Klan Act.
1872 • Liberal Party formed; calls for end of government corruption.
• President Grant reelected.
1873 • Economic depression sets in for remainder of decade.
• *Slaughterhouse* cases.
1874 • Democrats win majority in House of Representatives.
1875 • Civil Rights Act.
1876 • *United States v. Cruikshank.*
1877 • Republican Rutherford B. Hayes assumes presidency; Reconstruction era ends.

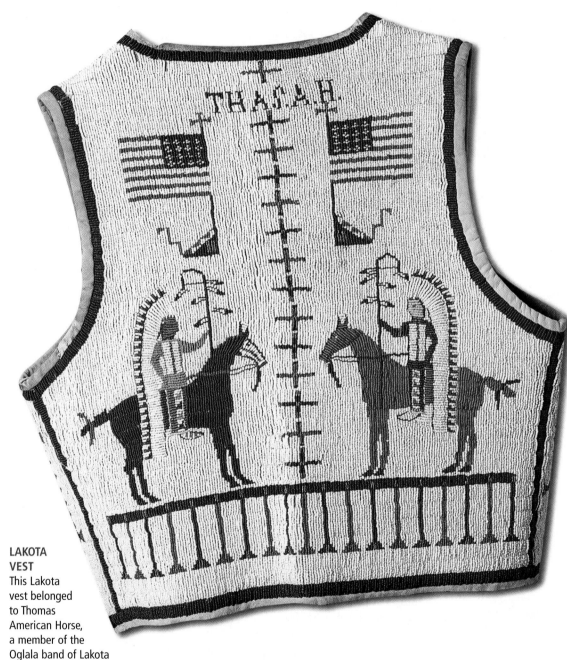

LAKOTA VEST
This Lakota vest belonged to Thomas American Horse, a member of the Oglala band of Lakota Sioux who lived on the Pine Ridge Reservation in South Dakota at the end of the nineteenth century. His initials are worked in beads across the shoulders. Made of tanned hide, with glass beads and tanned leather binding and lining, the vest shows how Native Americans adopted Euro-American articles of clothing and decorative motifs while employing materials that perpetuated native traditions. On the vest, two mounted Indians in feathered headdresses face each other under American flags. The American flag appeared frequently as a decorative motif in Indian bead art and testifies to some of the great changes taking place in the American West.

Private Collection, Photograph American Hurrah Archive, NYC.

17

The Contested West
1870–1900

To celebrate Indian Citizenship Day in 1892, students at Hampton Institute's Indian boarding school in Virginia staged a pageant honoring the four hundredth anniversary of the "discovery" of the New World. Students appeared dressed as the nation's heroes—among them Christopher Columbus, Miles Standish, and George Washington. Halfway through the program, the pageant finally honored some Native American heroes, but the Indians selected—Samoset, Pocahontas—all came from the distant past in lands east of the Appalachians. There was no mention of Crazy Horse, Sitting Bull, or Geronimo—Indians who resisted white encroachment and appropriation of their land in the West. Only two years earlier, the massacre of more than two hundred Miniconjou Sioux at Wounded Knee, South Dakota, marked the end of three decades of war against the Indians in the trans-Mississippi West. The Indian wars left the Native American population in the continental United States at 250,000 according to the census of 1900 (admittedly an undercount), down from estimates as high as 15 million at the time of first contact with Europeans. Not only had the population been decimated by war and disease, but Indian lands had shrunk so much that by 1890 Euro-Americans controlled 97.5 percent of the territory formerly occupied by Native Americans.

The Hampton pageant could not entirely ignore a catastrophe of this magnitude. Yet it managed to end on a note of reconciliation with a student proclaiming:

> You have taken our rivers and fountains
>   And the plains where we loved to roam,—
> Banish us not to the mountains
>   And the lonely wastes for home!
> Our clans that were strongest and bravest,
>   Are Broken and powerless through you:
> Let us join the great tribe of the white men,
>   As brothers to dare and to do!

How the actors felt about the lines they spoke we cannot know. But the pageant clearly reflected the values and beliefs that Indian boarding schools hoped to inculcate in their pupils at the end of the nineteenth century.

Indian schools constituted the cultural battleground of the Indian wars in the West, their avowed purpose "to destroy the Indian in him and save the man." In 1877, Congress appropriated funds for Indian education, reasoning "it was less expensive to educate Indians than to kill them." Hampton Institute, created in 1868 to school newly freed slaves, accepted its first Indian students in 1878. Although many Indian schools operated on the reservations, authorities much preferred boarding facilities that isolated students from the "contamination" of tribal values.

Hampton Pageant, 1892
The Indian students in this picture are dressed for Columbia's Roll Call, a pageant at Hampton Institute honoring the nation's heroes on Indian Citizenship Day, 1892. Among those portrayed are Christopher Columbus, Pocahontas, George Washington, and, in the center, a student dressed as Columbia, symbol of the Republic, draped in the American flag.
Courtesy of Hampton University Archives.

Many Native American parents resisted sending their children away. When all else failed, the military kidnapped the children and sent them off to school. An agent at the Mescalero Apache Agency in Arizona Territory reported in 1886 how "it became necessary to visit the camps unexpectedly with a detachment of police, and seize such children as were proper and take them away to school, willing or unwilling." The parents put up a struggle. "Some hurried their children off to the mountains or hid them away in camp, and the police had to chase and capture them like so many wild rabbits," the agent observed. "This unusual proceeding created quite an outcry. The men were sullen and muttering, the women loud in their lamentations, and the children almost out of their wits with fright."

Once at school, the children were stripped and scrubbed, their clothing and belongings confiscated, their hair hacked off and doused with kerosene to kill lice. Issued stiff new uniforms, shoes, and what one boy recalled as the "torture" of woolen long underwear, the children often lost not only their possessions but also their names:

Hehakaavita (Yellow Elk) became Thomas Goodwood; Polingaysi Qoyawayma became Elizabeth White.

The curriculum featured agricultural and manual arts for boys and domestic skills for girls, training designed to make Indians "willing workers" who would no longer be a burden to the government. The Carlisle Indian School in Pennsylvania, founded in 1879, became the model for later institutions. To encourage assimilation, Carlisle pioneered the "outing system"— sending students to live with white families during summer vacations. The policy reflected the school's slogan, "To civilize the Indian, get him into civilization. To keep him civilized, let him stay." Some graduates, like the two Omaha sisters Susan and Suzette LaFlesche, put their education to work to champion Indian rights. But many entered a dismal netherworld—never accepted in white society as equals but no longer at home on the reservation.

Merrill Gates, a member of the Board of Indian Commissioners, summed up the goal of Indian education: "To get the Indian out of the blanket and into trousers,—and trousers with a pocket in them, *and with a pocket that aches to be filled with dollars!*" Gates's faith in the "civilizing" power of the dollar reflected the unabashed materialism of his age. In 1871, author Mark Twain published *Roughing It*, a chronicle of his days spent in mining towns in California and Nevada. There he found the same corrupt politics, vulgar display, and mania for speculation that he later skewered in *The Gilded Age* (1873), a biting satire of greed and corruption in the nation's capital. Far from being an antidote to the meretricious values of the East—an innocent idyll out of place and time—the American West, with its get-rich-quick ethos and its addiction to gambling and speculation, played an integral part in the politics and economics of the Gilded Age.

"West" has always been a relative term. Until the gold rush of 1849 focused attention on California, the West for settlers lay beyond the Appalachians, east of the Mississippi in the area drained by the Ohio River. But by 1860, "West" increasingly referred to the land across the Mississippi, from the Great Plains to the Pacific Ocean. The expansion of U.S. domination into the trans-Mississippi West and the displacement of Native Americans and their **culture** point to the cruel paradox that the promise that drew miners and settlers into the West meant conquest and subjugation for Indian peoples. With its rich natural resources and land, the West became fiercely contested terrain, not only for the Indians who struggled to preserve their sovereignty and their cultural identity but also among competing groups of Anglos, Hispanics, and a host of others who followed the promise of land and riches into the West.

All the major themes of U.S. history in the era following the Civil War played themselves out under western skies. The expansion of U.S. empire; the consolidation of business in mining, ranching, and commercial farming; corruption and cupidity in territorial government; vicious ethnic and racial animosity whether in the form of Chinese exclusion or prejudice against Mexicans and Mormons; and the exploitation of natural resources that led to the decimation of the great bison herds, the despoliation of the landscape and the pollution of rivers with mining wastes, and pitched battles between workers and bosses—all marked western variants of the major currents in American political, social, and economic history in the period from 1860 to 1900.

Conquest and Empire in the West

While the European powers expanded their authority and wealth through *imperialism* and *colonialism*, establishing far-flung empires abroad, the United States focused its attention on the West. American *exceptionalism* has stressed how the history of the United States differs from that of western European nations, and America's preoccupation with its western **frontier** has often been cited as a case in point. Yet recent historians have argued that the process by which the United States expanded its borders in the nineteenth century can best be understood in terms of imperialism and colonialism—language applied to European powers in this period that makes explicit how expansion in the American West involved the conquest, displacement, and rule over native peoples. (See "Beyond America's Borders," page 598.) The federal government, through chicanery and conquest, pushed the Indians off their land (Map 17.1, page 594). Removed to Indian Territory or confined on reservations, Indians became wards of the federal government, their culture assaulted by policies designed to force assimilation. Through the lens of colonialism, we can see how the United States' commitment to an imperialist, expansionist ideology resulted in the displacement of Native Americans and the establishment of new territories and eventually states. The colonizing of the West was a dynamic process in which Native Americans actively resisted, contested, and adapted to colonial rule.

Indian Removal and the Reservation System

From the first encounter, when Christopher Columbus mistakenly identified Native Americans as "Indians," Euro-Americans have used the term as if it designated a homogeneous race, disregarding the fact that Native Americans once included more than five hundred distinct tribal entities with different languages, myths, religions, and physical appearance. Beginning in the early days of the Republic, Americans advocated a policy of Indian removal. With plenty of land open in the West, the government removed eastern tribes—often against their will—to territory west of the Mississippi. In the 1830s, President Andrew Jackson pushed the Five Civilized Tribes—the Cherokee, Choctaw, Chickasaw, Creek, and Seminole peoples—off their land in the southern United States. Jackson's Indian removal forced thousands of men, women, and children to leave their homes in Georgia and Tennessee and walk hundreds of miles west. So many died of hunger, exhaustion, and disease along the way that the Cherokees called their path "the trail on which we cried." At the end of this trail of tears stood land set aside as Indian Territory (present-day Oklahoma). Here, the government promised, the Indians could remain "as long as grass shall grow" (see chapter 11). But hunger for western land soon negated that promise.

Manifest destiny—the belief that the United States had a "God-given" right to aggressively spread the values of white civilization and expand the nation from ocean to ocean—dictated U.S. policy. In the name of manifest destiny, Americans forced the removal of the Five Civilized Tribes to Oklahoma; colonized Texas and won its independence from Mexico in 1836; conquered California, Arizona, New Mexico, and parts of Utah and Colorado in the Mexican-American War of 1846–1848; and invaded Oregon in the 1840s (see chapter 12). But by the mid-nineteenth century, western land no longer seemed inexhaustible, and instead of removing Indians to the west, the government sought control of Indian lands and promised in return to pay annuities and put the Indians on lands reserved for their use—*reservations*. This policy won the support of both friends of the

MAP 17.1 **The Loss of Indian Lands, 1850–1890**

By 1890, western Indians were isolated on small, scattered reservations. Native Americans had struggled to retain their land in major battles, from the Santee Uprising in Minnesota in 1862 to the massacre at Wounded Knee, South Dakota, in 1890.

READING THE MAP: Where was the largest reservation located in 1890? Which states on this map show no reservations in 1890? Compare this map to Map 17.3, Federal Land Grants to Railroads and the Development of the West.

CONNECTIONS: Why did the federal government force Native Americans onto reservations? What developments prompted these changes?

FOR MORE HELP ANALYZING THIS MAP, see the map activity for this chapter in the Online Study Guide at bedfordstmartins.com/roark.

Indians, who feared for their survival, and Indian haters, who coveted their land and wished to confine them to the least desirable areas in the West. The Navajo, like the Cherokee, endured a forced march, called the "Long Walk," from their homeland to the desolate Bosque Redondo Reservation in New Mexico in 1864. "This ground we were brought on, it is not productive," complained the Navajo leader Barboncito. "We plant but it does not yield. All the stock we brought here have nearly all died."

By midcentury, settlers in unprecedented numbers crossed the Great Plains on their way to the goldfields of California or the rich farm land of Washington and Oregon. In their path stood a solid wall of Indian land, stretching from

Minnesota to Texas, much of it granted through the policy of Indian removal. As the *United States Magazine* observed, "Now the removed tribes are precisely in the center of this path." The "Indian problem" needed to be solved—through treaties if possible or coercion if necessary. In 1851, some ten thousand Plains Indians came together at Fort Laramie in Wyoming to negotiate a treaty that ceded a wide swath of their land to allow passage of the wagon trains. In return, the government promised that the rest of the Indian land would remain inviolate. It was yet another promise the government would not keep.

The Indians who "touched the pen" to the Treaty of Fort Laramie hoped to preserve their culture in the face of the white onslaught, which already had decimated their population and despoiled their environment. White invaders cut down trees, miners polluted streams, and hunters killed off bison and small game. Whites brought alcohol, guns, and something even more deadly—disease. Smallpox was the biggest killer of Native Americans in the West. Epidemics spread from Mexico up to Canada. Between 1780 and 1870, the population of the Plains tribes declined by half. Cholera, diphtheria, measles, scarlet fever, and other contagious diseases also took their toll. "If I could see this thing, if I knew where it came from, I would go there and fight it," a Cheyenne warrior anguished. Disease shifted the balance of power on the plains from Woodland agrarian tribes like the Mandan and Hidatsa (who died at the rate of 79 percent) to the Lakota Sioux, who fled the contagion of villages to take up life as equestrian (horse-riding) nomads on the western plains. As the Sioux pushed west, they displaced weaker tribes.

The Indian wars in the West marked the last resistance of a Native American population devastated by disease and demoralized by the removal policy pursued by the federal government. More accurately called "settlers' wars" (since they began with "peaceful settlers," often miners, overrunning Native American land), the wars flared up again only a few years after the signing of the Fort Laramie treaty. The Dakota Sioux in Minnesota went to war in 1862. For years, under the leadership of Chief Little Crow, the Dakota, also known as the Santee, had pursued a policy of accommodation, ceding land in return for the promise of annuities. But with his people on the verge of starvation (the local Indian agent told the hungry Dakota, "Go and eat grass"), Little Crow reluctantly led his angry warriors in a desperate campaign against the intruders, killing

more than 1,000 settlers. American troops quelled what was called the Great Sioux Uprising (also called the Santee Uprising) and marched 1,700 Sioux to Fort Snelling, where 400 Indians were put on trial for murder and 38 died in the largest mass execution in American history.

On the southern plains, the conflict reached its nadir in November 1864 at the Sand Creek massacre in Colorado Territory. There Colonel John M. Chivington and his Colorado militia descended on a village of Cheyenne, mostly women and children. Their leader, Black Kettle, raised a white flag and an American flag to signal surrender, but the charging cavalry ignored his signal and butchered 270 Indians. Chivington watched as his men scalped and mutilated their victims and later justified the killing of Indian children with the terse remark, "Nits make lice." The city of Denver treated Chivington and his men as heroes, but a congressional inquiry castigated the soldiers for their "fiendish malignity" and condemned the "savage cruelty" of the massacre. To escape court-martial, Chivington resigned his commission and left the army. To Americans like Chivington, fed theories of racial superiority, the Indians constituted, in the words of one Colorado militia major, "an obstacle to civilization . . . [and] should be exterminated."

After the Civil War, President Ulysses S. Grant faced the prospect of an Indian war on the Great Plains. Reluctant to spend more money and sacrifice more lives in battle, Grant adopted a "peace policy," advocating reservations as a way to segregate and control the Indians while opening up land to white settlers. General William Tecumseh Sherman summed up the new Indian policy succinctly: "Remove all to a safe place and then reduce them to a helpless condition." The army herded the Indians onto reservations (see Map 17.1), where the U.S. Bureau of Indian Affairs—a badly managed, weak agency, often acting through corrupt agents—supposedly ministered to their needs. When Indians refused to give up their hunting grounds and move onto reservations, the army launched military campaigns to "bring in" bands who would not accept confinement.

Poverty and starvation stalked the reservations. Confined by armed force, the Indians eked out an existence on stingy government rations. These once proud peoples found themselves dependent on government handouts and the assistance of Indian agents who, in the words of Paiute

> General William Tecumseh Sherman summed up the new Indian policy succinctly: "Remove all to a safe place and then reduce them to a helpless condition."

"Slaughtered for the Hide"

Harper's Weekly in 1874 featured this cover with its illustration of a buffalo hide hunter skinning a carcass on the southwestern plains. By 1872, the Santa Fe railroad reached Kansas, making Dodge City the center for the shipment of buffalo hides to the East, where they were made into leather belting used to run the nation's machinery. In a matter of months, hunters decimated the great southern bison herds. City father Colonel Richard Dodge wrote of the carnage, "The air was foul with sickening stench, and the vast plain which only a short twelve months before teemed with animal life, was a dead, solitary putrid desert." Dodge estimated that hunters slaughtered more than three million bison between 1872 and 1874. The grim reality of the trade makes the magazine's subtitle, "A Journal of Civilization," highly ironic.

Library of Congress.

READING THE IMAGE: What virtues and stereotypes of the West does this magazine cover extol?

CONNECTIONS: How might the notion of "civilization" have differed according to the Native American perspective?

FOR MORE HELP ANALYZING THIS IMAGE, see the visual activity for this chapter in the Online Study Guide at bedfordstmartins.com/roark.

Sarah Winnemucca, did "nothing but fill their pockets." Winnemucca launched a lecture campaign in the United States and Europe, denouncing the government's reservation policy.

Indian reservations became cultural battlegrounds. Styled as stepping-stones on the road to "civilization," they closely resembled colonial societies where native populations, ruled by outside bureaucrats, saw their culture assaulted, their religious practices outlawed, their children sent away to school, and their way of life attacked in the name of progress and civilization. Even the most well-meaning reformers, the self-styled "friends of the Indians," championed reservations as the best route to assimilation. These reformers, many of them easterners with little experience in the West, held the romantic notion that the Indians, if given a chance, would settle down peacefully and become farmers. Reservations would provide a classroom of civilization where Indians could be taught to speak English, to worship a Christian god, to give up hunting for farming, and to reject tribal ways. In the face of this assault, Indians found ways to resist and hold on to their cultural identity.

The Decimation of the Great Bison Herds and the Fight for the Black Hills

By the nineteenth century, more than two hundred years of contact with whites had utterly transformed Native American societies. Indians had been pushed off their lands east of the Mississippi and moved west. Through trade with the Spanish and French, Indians had acquired horses and guns. The Sioux, hunting on horseback, staked their survival on the buffalo (American bison). But the great herds, once numbering as many as thirty million, fell into decline. A host of environmental and human factors contributed to the destruction of the bison. The dynamic ecology of the Great Plains, with its drought, fires, and blizzards, combined with the ecological imperialism of humans (Indian buffalo robe traders as well as whites and their cattle) put increasing pressure on the bison. By the 1850s, a combination of drought and commerce had driven the great herds onto the far western plains.

After the Civil War, the accelerating pace of industrial expansion brought about the near extinction of the bison. Industrial demand for heavy leather belting used in machinery and the development of larger, more accurate rifles contributed to the slaughter of the bison. The nation's growing transcontinental rail system cut the range in two and divided the herds. For the nomadic tribes of the plains, the buffalo constituted a way of life—a source of food, fuel, and shelter and a central part of their religion and rituals. To the railroads, the bison were a nuisance, at best a cheap source of meat for their workers and a target for sport. Buffalo hunters hired by the railroads, joined by sport hunters, fired from railroad cars just for the thrill of the kill. "It will not be long before all the buffaloes are extinct near and between the railroads," Ohio senator John Sherman prophesied in 1868. The army took credit for the conquest of the Plains Indians, but victory came about largely as a result of the decimation of the great bison herds. General Philip Sheridan acknowledged as much when he applauded white hide hunters for "destroying the Indians' commissary." With their food supply gone, Indians had to choose between starvation and the reservation. "A cold wind blew across the prairie when the last buffalo fell," the great Sioux leader Sitting Bull lamented, "a death wind for my people."

On the southern plains in 1867, more than five thousand warring Comanches, Kiowas, and Southern Arapahos gathered at Medicine Lodge Creek in Kansas to negotiate a treaty. Satak, or Sitting Bear, a prominent Kiowa chief and medicine man, explained why the Indians sought peace: "In the far-distant past . . . the world seemed large enough for both the red man and the white man." But, he observed, "its broad plains seem now to contract, and the white man grows jealous of his red brother." To preserve their land from white encroachment, the Indians signed the Treaty of Medicine Lodge, agreeing to move to a reservation. But after 1870, hide hunters poured into the region, and within a decade, they had nearly exterminated the southern bison herds. Luther Standing Bear recounted the sight and stench: "I saw the bodies of hundreds of dead buffalo lying about, just wasting, and the odor was terrible. . . . They were letting our food lie on the plains to rot."

On the northern plains, the fever for gold fueled the conflict between Indians and Euro-Americans. In 1866, the Cheyenne united with the Sioux in Wyoming to protect their hunting grounds in the Powder River valley, which were threatened by the construction of the Bozeman Trail connecting Fort Laramie with the goldfields in Montana. Captain William Fetterman, who had boasted that with eighty men he could ride

through the Sioux nation, was killed along with all of his troops in an Indian attack. The Sioux's impressive victories led to the second Treaty of Fort Laramie in 1868, in which the United States agreed to abandon the Bozeman Trail and guaranteed the Indians control of the Black Hills, land sacred to the Lakota Sioux. The treaty was full of contradictions—in one breath promising to preserve Indian land and in the next forcing the tribes to relinquish all territory outside their reservations. A controversial provision of the treaty guaranteed the Indians access to their traditional hunting grounds "so long as the buffalo may range thereon in such numbers as to justify the chase." With the bison facing extermination, the provision was ominous. Yet the government's fork-tongued promises induced some of the tribes to accept the treaty. The great Sioux chief Red Cloud led many of his people onto the reservation. Red Cloud soon regretted his decision. "Think of it!" he told a visitor to the Pine Ridge Reservation. "I, who used to own . . . country so extensive that I could not ride through it in a week . . . must tell Washington when I am hungry. I must beg for that which I own." Several Sioux chiefs, among them Crazy Horse of the Oglala band and Sitting Bull of the Hunkpapa, refused to sign the treaty. Crazy Horse said that he wanted no part of the "piecemeal penning" of his people.

In 1874, the discovery of gold in the Black Hills of the Dakotas led the government to break its promise to Red Cloud. Miners began pouring into the region, and the Northern Pacific Railroad made plans to lay track. Lieutenant Colonel George Armstrong Custer, whose troopers found gold in the area, trumpeted news of the strike. At first, the government offered to purchase the Black Hills. But to the Lakota Sioux the Black Hills were sacred—"the heart of everything that is." They refused to sell. The army responded by issuing an ultimatum ordering all Lakota Sioux and Northern Cheyenne bands onto the Pine Ridge Reservation and threatening to hunt down those who refused.

In the summer of 1876, the army launched a three-pronged attack led by Custer, General George Crook, and Colonel John Gibbon. Crazy Horse stopped Crook at the Battle of the Rosebud. Custer, leading the second prong of the army's offensive, divided his troops and ordered an attack. On June 25, he spotted signs of the Indians' camp and crying "Hurrah Boys, we've got them," led 265 men of the Seventh Cavalry into the largest Indian camp ever assembled on

Imperialism, Colonialism, and the Treatment of the Sioux and the Zulu

Viewed through the lens of colonialism, the British war with the Zulu in South Africa offers a compelling contrast to the United States' war against the Lakota Sioux. Comparing the subjugation of the Zulu and the Sioux points to the escalation of conflict between white imperialist powers and indigenous peoples of color over land, labor, and resources in the context of the global economic expansion of the nineteenth century.

The Zulu, like the Sioux, came to power as a result of devastating intertribal warfare. In the area that is today the KwaZulu-Natal province of the Republic of South Africa, Shaka, the Zulu king, united his empire by 1826 with an army of more than twenty thousand. And like the Sioux, the Zulu earned a formidable reputation as brave warriors who fought to protect their land from white encroachment.

The British and the Boers made up the two dominant European groups in South Africa. Dutch-speaking white settlers came to the Cape of Good Hope, at the southernmost tip of Africa, in the seventeenth century, when the place was little more than a way station for the Dutch East India Company on the long sea route to the East Indies. They stayed and took up land, becoming farmers and mingling with French and German settlers to create a tough new breed known as Afrikaners, or Boers. By the nineteenth century, the Cape Colony consisted of a community of more than ten thousand settlers

stretching six hundred miles inland from Cape Town.

The British seized the Cape in 1806 to protect their sea route to India, and land-hungry British settlers poured into the colony in the wake of the agricultural depression that followed the long Napoleonic Wars in Europe. The British settlers and the Boers soon clashed over land and labor. The Boers relied on slave labor to work their vast farmlands. When the British passed the Act of Emancipation in 1834, the Boers rebelled. Clashes between Britons and Boers resulted in the Great Trek, the migration of nearly twelve thousand Boers to the northeast beginning in 1835. There they claimed land and established the South African Republic (the Transvaal) in 1853 and the Orange Free State in 1854 both independent of British rule. But the Great Trek brought the Boers into Zululand, where they met with bold and bloody resistance.

The Zulu lived in a highly complex society, with all the young men organized into *amabutho*, regiments of warriors arranged by age and bound to local chiefs and under the supreme command of the Zulu king, who demanded obedience and bravery. During Shaka's bloodthirsty reign, he inspected his regiments after each battle, picking out cowards and putting them to death on the spot. Young men could not start their own households without the local chief's permission, thus ensuring an ample stock of warriors and making the Zulu army, in the words

of one English observer, "a celibate, man-slaying machine."

The Boer settlers repeatedly faced the wrath of the Zulu, who slaughtered the first trekkers to arrive in Zululand after promising them permission to settle and luring them to a feast. But it was the Zulu's dependence on cattle that put them in permanent conflict with the Boers. To pay for a wife, a Zulu man had to acquire an *ilobolo*, a dowry payment of cattle. The more cattle a man owned the more wives he could buy. The Zulu regarded the Boer herds as theirs for the taking and repeatedly raided settlements to steal cattle.

To restore order, the British entered the fray in 1879, sparking the Anglo-Zulu War, which a recent historian has condemned "as unnecessary as it was unjust." Britain issued an ultimatum to the Zulu king Cetshwayo, a former British ally who ruled with Queen Victoria's blessing. Sir Theophilus Shepstone, British secretary for native affairs, hinted at a motive for the invasion when he wrote in 1878, "Had Cetshwayo's 30,000 warriors been in time changed to labourers working for wages, Zululand would have been a prosperous peaceful country instead of what it is now, a source of perpetual danger to itself and its neighbors." Clearly, the incen-

Zululand and Cape Colony, 1878

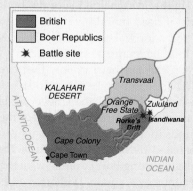

tive for invasion came not only from a desire to placate the Boers but also from the desire to secure a source of labor for British economic expansion, made paramount by the discovery of diamonds in the region.

Crack British troops under Lord Chelmsford, armed with the latest rifles and artillery, expected to subdue the Zulu easily. With a confidence reminiscent of that of George Armstrong Custer, the British commander wrote, "I am inclined to think that the first experience of the power of the Martini-Henrys [rifles] will be such a surprise to the Zulus, that they will not be formidable after the first effort." But in January 1879, at the battle of Isandhlwana, the Zulu army of more than 25,000 surprised a British encampment. The battle lasted less than two hours, but when it was over, more than 4,000 Zulu and British bodies lay indiscriminately piled on top of one another across the British position. Only a handful of British soldiers managed to escape. Chelmsford lost 1,300 officers and men—the biggest single defeat of British troops since the Crimean War.

When news of Isandhlwana reached London, commentators compared the massacre to Custer's defeat at the Little Big Horn three years earlier, and noted that native forces armed with spears had defeated a modern army. The military disaster shocked and outraged the nation, damaging the British military's reputation of invincibility.

Vowing that the Zulu would "pay dearly for their triumph of a day," the British immediately launched unconditional war against the Zulu. In the ensuing battles, neither side took prisoners. The Zulu beat the British twice more, but the tide turned at Rorke's Drift, and after seven months of battle, the British defeated the Zulu. After routing the Zulu army, the

Zulu Warriors
Chief Ngoza (center) poses with Zulu men in full war dress. Their distinctive cowhide shields date to the reign of King Shaka. Each warrior also carried two or three throwing spears and an *ikwa*, or flat-bladed stabbing spear used in close combat. Zulu warriors marched at the double and could cover up to fifty miles a day.
Campbell Collections of the University of KwaZulu-Natal.

British marched away, imprisoning Cetshwayo on Robben Island and abandoning Zululand to its fate—partition, starvation, and civil war.

Historians would later compare the British victory at Rorke's Drift to the U.S. army's defeat of the Sioux at Wounded Knee. But the Zulu and the Sioux met different economic fates. As Shepstone hinted in 1878, the British goal had been to subdue the Zulu and turn them into a reservoir of plentiful, cheap labor. In 1887, the British formally annexed Zululand, and in 1902 they defeated their white rivals in the Anglo-Boer War and gained dominance in the region. The Zulu ended up laboring on the estates and in the mines of the white colonialists in a condition little better than slavery. Compared to the naked economic exploitation of the Zulu, the U.S. policy toward the Sioux with its forced assimilation on reservations and its misguided attempts to turn the nomadic tribes

into sedentary, God-fearing farmers, may seem less exploitative if no less ruthless in its cultural imperialism.

Both the Little Big Horn and Isandhlwana became legends that spawned a romantic image of the "noble savage": fierce in battle, honored in defeat. Describing this myth, historian James Gump, who has chronicled the subjugation of the Sioux and the Zulu, observed, "Each western culture simultaneously dehumanized and glamorized the Sioux and Zulu," and noted that the noble savage mythology marked "a product of the racist ideologies of the late nineteenth century as well as the guilt and compassion associated with the bloody costs of empire building." Imperial powers, both Britain and the United States defeated indigenous rivals and came to dominate their lands (and in the case of the Zulu, their labor) in the global expansion that marked the nineteenth century.

599

the Great Plains. Nomadic bands of Sioux, Cheyenne, and Arapaho had come together for a summer buffalo hunt and camped along the banks of the Greasy Grass River (whites called it the Little Big Horn). Indian warriors led by Sitting Bull and Crazy Horse set upon Custer and his men and quickly annihilated them. "It took us about as long as a hungry man to eat his dinner," the Cheyenne chief Two Moons recalled. Gibbon arrived two days later to discover the carnage. "Custer's Last Stand," as the Battle of the Little Big Horn was styled in myth, turned out to be the last stand for the Sioux. The Indians' nomadic way of life meant they could not remain a combined force for long. The bands that had massed at the Little Big Horn scattered, and the army hunted them down. "Wherever we went," wrote the Oglala holy man Black Elk, "the soldiers came to kill us." Crazy Horse was killed in 1877, and Sitting Bull surrendered four years later, in 1881. The government took the Black Hills and confined the Lakota to the Great Sioux Reservation. The Sioux never accepted the loss of the Black Hills. In 1923, they filed suit, demanding the return of the land taken illegally from them. After a protracted court battle lasting nearly sixty years, the U.S. Supreme Court ruled in 1980 that the government had illegally abrogated the Treaty of Fort Laramie and upheld an award of $122.5 million in compensation to the tribes. The Sioux refused the settlement and continue to press for the return of the Black Hills.

The Dawes Act and Indian Land Allotment

In the 1880s, the practice of rounding up Indians and herding them onto reservations lost momentum in favor of allotment—a new policy designed to encourage assimilation through farming and the ownership of private property. Americans vowing to avenge Custer urged the government to get tough with the Indians. Reservations, they argued, took up too much good land that white settlers could put to better use. At the same time, those sympathetic to the Indians were appalled at the desperate poverty on the reservations and feared for the Indians' survival. Helen Hunt Jackson, in her classic work *A Century of Dishonor* (1881), convinced many readers that the Indians had been treated unfairly. "Our Indian policy," the *New York Times* concluded, "is usually spoliation behind the mask of benevolence."

Reformers pressed for change. The Indian Rights Association, a group of mainly white east-erners formed in 1882, campaigned for the dismantling of the reservations, now viewed as obstacles to progress. To "cease to treat the Indian as a red man and treat him as a man" meant putting an end to tribal communalism and fostering individualism. "Selfishness," declared Senator Henry Dawes of Massachusetts, "is at the bottom of civilization." The solution to the "Indian problem" called for "allotment in severalty"—the institution of private property. Dawes promised to grant Indians full citizenship and promote economic self-sufficiency by making them trade their tribal lands for individual farms.

In 1887, Congress passed the Dawes Allotment Act, dividing up reservations and allotting parcels of land to individual Indians as private property. Each Indian household was eligible to receive 160 acres of land from reservation property. Only those Indians who took allotments earned citizenship. Since Indian land far surpassed the acreage needed for allotments, the government reserved the right to sell the "surplus" to white settlers—a goal those less benevolent in their attitudes toward the Indians had no trouble supporting. The Dawes Act effectively reduced Indian land from 138 million acres to a scant 48 million. The legislation, in the words of one critic, worked "to despoil the Indians of their lands and to make them vagabonds on the face of the earth." Sitting Bull put it bluntly: "The life of white men is slavery. They are prisoners in towns or farms." He concluded, "I have seen nothing that a white man has, houses or railways or clothing or food, that is as good as the right to move in open country, and live in our own fashion." The Dawes Act completed the dispossession of the western Indian peoples and dealt a crippling blow to traditional tribal culture. It remained in effect until 1934, when the United States restored the right of Native Americans to own land communally (see chapter 24).

Indian Resistance and Survival

Faced with the extinction of their entire way of life, different groups of Indians responded in different ways in the waning decades of the nineteenth century. Some tribes, including the Crow, Arikara, Pawnee, and Shoshoni, fought alongside the U.S. army against their old enemies the Sioux. The Crow chief Plenty Coups explained why he allied with the United States: "Not because we loved the white man . . . or because we hated the Sioux . . . but because we plainly saw that this course was the only one which might

Chief Joseph

Chief Joseph came to symbolize the heroic resistance of the Nez Percé, whose epic trek to escape the U.S. army won them the sympathy of many Americans. General Nelson Miles promised the Nez Percé that they could return to their homeland if they surrendered. But he betrayed them, as he would betray the Apache people seven years later. The Nez Percé were shipped off to Indian Territory (Oklahoma). In 1879, Chief Joseph traveled to Washington, D.C., to speak for his people. "Let me be a free man," he pleaded, "free to travel, free to stop, free to work, free to trade where I choose, free to choose my own teachers, free to follow the religion of my fathers, free to think and talk and act for myself—and I will obey every law." His speech lasted for two hours, and when it was over, he received a standing ovation. But despite his eloquence, Joseph did not live to return to his homeland. He died in 1904.

National Anthropological Archives, Smithsonian Institution, Washington, D.C. (#2906).

save our beautiful country for us." The Crow and Shoshoni got to stay in their homelands and avoided the fate of other tribes shipped to reservations far away.

Indians who refused to stay on reservations risked being hunted down—a clear indication that reservations were intended to keep Indians in, not to keep whites out, as the friends of the Indians had intended. The Nez Percé war of 1877 is perhaps the most harrowing example of the army's policy. In 1863, the government dictated a treaty drastically reducing Nez Percé land. Most of the chiefs refused to sign the treaty and did not move to the reservation. In 1877, the army issued an ultimatum—come in to the reservation or be hunted down. Some eight hundred Nez Percé people, many of them women and children, fled across the mountains of Idaho, Wyoming, and Montana, heading for the safety of Canada. At the end of their 1,300-mile trek, 50 miles from freedom, they stopped to rest in the snow. The army's Indian scouts spotted their tepees, and the soldiers attacked. Yellow Wolf recalled their plight: "Children crying with cold. No fire. There could be no light. Everywhere the crying, the death wail." After a five-day siege, the Nez Percé leader, Chief Joseph, surrendered. His speech, reported by a white soldier, would become famous. "I am tired of fighting," he said as he surrendered his rifle. "Our chiefs are killed. It is cold and we have no blankets. The little children are freezing to death. . . . I am tired. My heart is sick and sad. From where the sun now stands, I will fight no more forever."

In the Southwest, the Apaches resorted to armed resistance. They roamed the Sonoran Desert of southern Arizona and northern Mexico, perfecting a hit-and-run **guerrilla warfare** that terrorized white settlers and bedeviled the army in the 1870s and 1880s. General George Crook combined a policy of dogged pursuit with judicious diplomacy. Crook relied on Indian scouts to track the raiding parties, recruiting nearly two hundred, including Apaches along with Navajos and Paiutes. By 1882, Crook had succeeded in persuading most of the Apaches to settle on the San Carlos Reservation in Arizona Territory. A desolate piece of desert inhabited by scorpions and rattlesnakes, San Carlos, in the words of one Apache, was "the worst place in all the great territory stolen from the Apaches."

Geronimo, a respected shaman (medicine man) of the Chiricahua Apache, refused to stay at San Carlos and repeatedly led raiding parties in the early 1880s. His warriors attacked ranches to obtain ammunition and horses. Among Geronimo's band was Lozen, a woman who rode with the warriors, armed with a rifle and a cartridge belt. The sister of a great chief who described her as being as "strong as a man, braver than most, and cunning in strategy," Lozen never married and remained a warrior in Geronimo's band even after her brother's death. In the spring of 1885, Geronimo and his followers, including Lozen, went on a ten-month offensive, moving from the Apache sanctuary in the Sierra Madre to raid and burn ranches and towns on both sides of the Mexican border. General Crook caught up with Geronimo in the fall and persuaded him to return to San Carlos, only to have him slip away on the way back to the reservation. Chagrined, Crook resigned his post. General Nelson Miles, Crook's replacement, adopted a policy of hunt and destroy.

Geronimo's band of thirty-three Apaches, including women and children, managed to elude Miles's troops for more than five months. In the end, this small band fought two thousand soldiers to a stalemate. After months of pursuit, Lieutenant Leonard Wood, a member of Miles's spit-and-polish cavalry, discarded his horse and most of his clothes until he was reduced to wearing nothing "but a pair of canton flannel drawers, and an old blue blouse, a pair of moccasins and a hat without a crown."

Eventually, Miles's scouts cornered Geronimo in 1886. Caught between Mexican regulars and the U.S. army, Geronimo agreed to march north with the soldiers and negotiate a settlement. "We have not slept for six months," he admitted, "and we are worn out." Although fewer than three dozen Apaches had been considered "hostile," when General Miles induced them to surrender, the government rounded up nearly five hundred Apaches, including the scouts who had helped track Geronimo, and sent them as prisoners to Florida. By 1889, more than a quarter of them had died, some due to illnesses contracted in the damp lowland climate and some by suicide. Their plight roused public opinion, and in 1892 they were moved to Fort Sill in Oklahoma and later to New Mexico.

Geronimo lived to become something of a celebrity. He appeared at the St. Louis Exposition in 1904, and he rode in President Theodore Roosevelt's inaugural parade in 1905. In a newspaper interview, he confessed, "I want to go to my old home before I die. . . . Want to go back to the mountains again. I asked the Great White Father to allow me to go back, but he said no." None of the Apaches were permitted to return to Arizona; when Geronimo died in 1909, he was buried in Oklahoma.

On the plains, many tribes turned to a nonviolent form of resistance—a compelling new religion called the Ghost Dance. The Paiute shaman Wovoka, drawing on a cult that had developed in the 1870s, combined elements of Christianity and traditional Indian religion to found the Ghost Dance religion in 1889. Wovoka claimed that he had received a vision in which the Great Spirit spoke through him to all Indians, prophesying that if they would unite in the Ghost Dance ritual, whites would be destroyed in an apocalypse. The shaman promised that Indian warriors slain in battle would return to life and that buffalo once again would roam the land unimpeded. This religion, born of despair with its message of hope, spread like wildfire over the plains. The Ghost Dance was performed in Idaho, Montana, Utah, Wyoming, Colorado, Nebraska, Kansas, the Dakotas, and Indian Territory by tribes as diverse as the Sioux, Arapaho, Cheyenne, Pawnee, and Shoshoni. Dancers often went into hypnotic trances, dancing until they dropped from exhaustion.

The Ghost Dance was nonviolent, but it frightened whites, especially when the Sioux taught that wearing a white ghost shirt made Indians immune to soldiers' bullets. Soon whites began to fear an uprising. "Indians are dancing in the snow and are wild and crazy," wrote the Bureau of Indian Affairs agent at the Pine Ridge Reservation in South Dakota. Frantic, he pleaded for reinforcements. "We are at the mercy of these dancers. We need protection, and we need it now." President Benjamin Harrison dispatched several thousand federal troops to Sioux country to handle any outbreak.

In December 1890, when Sitting Bull joined the Ghost Dance, he was killed by Indian police as they tried to arrest him at his cabin on the Standing Rock Reservation. His people, fleeing the scene, joined with a larger group of Miniconjou Sioux, who were apprehended by the Seventh Cavalry, Custer's old regiment, near Wounded Knee Creek, South Dakota. As the Indians laid down their arms, a shot rang out, and the soldiers opened fire. In the ensuing melee, Indian men, women, and children were mowed down in minutes by the army's brutally efficient Hotchkiss rapid-fire guns. More than

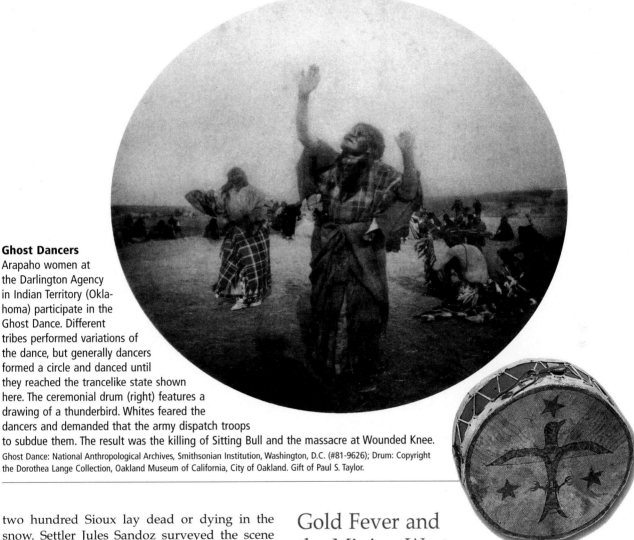

Ghost Dancers
Arapaho women at the Darlington Agency in Indian Territory (Oklahoma) participate in the Ghost Dance. Different tribes performed variations of the dance, but generally dancers formed a circle and danced until they reached the trancelike state shown here. The ceremonial drum (right) features a drawing of a thunderbird. Whites feared the dancers and demanded that the army dispatch troops to subdue them. The result was the killing of Sitting Bull and the massacre at Wounded Knee.
Ghost Dance: National Anthropological Archives, Smithsonian Institution, Washington, D.C. (#81-9626); Drum: Copyright the Dorothea Lange Collection, Oakland Museum of California, City of Oakland. Gift of Paul S. Taylor.

two hundred Sioux lay dead or dying in the snow. Settler Jules Sandoz surveyed the scene the day after the massacre at Wounded Knee. "Here in ten minutes an entire community was as the buffalo that bleached on the plains," he wrote. "There was something loose in the world that hated joy and happiness as it hated brightness and color, reducing everything to drab agony and gray."

It had taken Euro-Americans 250 years to wrest control of the eastern half of the United States from the Indians. It took them less than forty years to take the western half. The subjugation of the American Indians marked the first chapter in a national mission of empire that would later lead to overseas imperialistic adventures in Asia, Latin America, the Caribbean, and the Pacific Islands.

REVIEW How did the slaughter of the bison contribute to the Plains Indians' removal to reservations?

Gold Fever and the Mining West

Mining stood at the center of the United States' quest for empire in the West. The California gold rush of 1849 touched off the frenzy. The four decades following witnessed equally frenetic rushes for gold and other metals, most notably on the Comstock Lode in Nevada and later in New Mexico, Colorado, the Dakotas, Montana, Idaho, Arizona, and Utah. Each rush built on the last, producing new technologies and innovations in financing as hordes of miners, eager to strike it rich, moved from one boomtown to the next. (See "The Promise of Technology," page 604.) Mining in the West, however, was a story not only of boom and bust but also of community building and the development of territories into states (Map. 17.2, page 606). At first glance, the mining West may seem much different from the East, but by the 1870s, the term "urban industrialism" described Virginia City, Nevada,

Hydraulic Mining

Individual prospectors who made the first gold strikes in California in 1849 employed a simple process known as placer mining. "No capital is required to obtain this gold, as the laboring man wants nothing but his pick and shovel and tin pan with which to dig and wash the gravel." But when the easy pickings along the rivers and streams gave out, a good deal of gold still remained trapped in quartz or buried deep in the earth, extractable only by methods far beyond the means and capacity of the average prospector.

Soon technology and capital invaded the diggings. As early as 1853, a French Canadian sailmaker, Antoine Chabot, hoping to avoid the cost and labor of digging a long feeder ditch to get water to his claim, stitched together heavy strips of canvas and made a 100-foot length of hose. Building on this invention, a Connecticut forty-niner named Edward Matteson marveled at the power of the new technology he called "hydraulicking": "Ten men who own a claim are en-abled . . . by directing streams of water against the base of a high bank to cut away such an extent as to cause immense slides of earth which often bring with them large trees and heavy boulders." Tons of fallen earth "are carried away through the sluices with almost as much rapidity as if they were a bank of [melting] snow."

The speed and efficiency of hydraulic mining promised more gold in less time for less work. With water doing the labor formerly provided by pick and shovel, prospectors who came to the goldfields to make a fortune often ended up working for the big mines for $3 a day, a decent wage for the time but no way to get rich quick.

Hydraulic mining industrialized gold mining, introducing what amounted to a form of mass production that involved all the features of modern, capital-intensive industry: corporations trading shares on an international market, engineers installing large and expensive works and equipment, and wage laborers replacing prospectors. By the 1880s, the Army Corps of Engineers estimated that some $100 million had been spent to build California's hydraulic mining system. The results proved worthwhile for the mine owners. Hydraulic mining produced 90 percent of California's gold.

Eager to make a quick profit, the purveyors of this new technology gave little thought to its impact on the environment. Hydraulic mining used prodigious amounts of water—two large nozzles could shoot out 1.7 million gallons a day. These huge water cannons washed away entire mountains, clogging streambeds and creating heaps of rubble. Thomas Starr King, a young Unitarian minister visiting hydraulic mining operations near Nevada City, California, was appalled by the sight that greeted him. Enormous nozzles blasted water, "tearing all the beauty out of the landscape and setting up 'the abomination of desolation' in its place." He grimly predicted, "If the hydraulic mining method is to be infinitely used, without restraint, upon all the surface that will yield a good return, then California of the future will be a waste more repulsive than any denounced in prophecy."

as accurately as it did Pittsburgh or Cleveland. And the diverse peoples drawn to the West by the promise of mining riches made the region the most cosmopolitan in the nation. A close look at mining on the Comstock Lode indicates some of the patterns and paradoxes of western mining. And a look at territorial government uncovers striking parallels with corruption and cupidity in politics east of the Mississippi.

Mining on the Comstock Lode

By 1859, refugees from California's played-out goldfields flocked to the Washoe basin in Nevada. There prospectors found the gold they sought mired in blackish sand they called "that blasted blue stuff." Eventually, an enterprising miner had the stuff assayed, and it turned out the Washoe miners had stumbled on the richest vein of silver ore on the continent—the legendary Comstock Lode, named for prospector Henry Comstock.

To exploit even potentially valuable silver claims required capital and expensive technology well beyond the means of the prospector. An active San Francisco stock market sprang up to finance operations on the Comstock. Shrewd businessmen soon recognized that the easiest way to get rich was not to mine at all but to sell their claims or to form mining companies and sell shares of stock. The most unscrupulous mined

Angry farmers protested that hydraulic mines discharged tailings (debris) that filled channels and forced rivers out of their banks, causing devastating floods. Farms were swept away and cattle drowned. Millions of cubic yards of silt from the hydraulic tailings washed down and covered farms with a muddy sand (slickens)

two to seven feet deep, destroying all hopes of vegetation. Orchards and fields disappeared each year under new layers of mining debris.

In 1875, farmers organized to stop the destruction. But after four years of litigation, the California Supreme Court ruled in favor of the miners. Gold remained king in California.

Not until the mid-1880s, when California's economy tilted from mining to agriculture and wheat became California's new gold, did farmers finally succeed in winning a court injunction against hydraulic mining. Renegade miners continued to use hydraulic methods until the 1890s, when more aggressive enforcement finally silenced the great hoses. The sounds of nature eventually returned to the California foothills, and the rivers once again ran clear.

Hydraulic Mining and the Environment
Hydraulic mining of California's gold ripped up the landscape, creating waterfalls, as seen in this picture. The pipes connected to huge hoses capable of washing away entire hillsides. The debris clogged rivers and caused devastating floods that wiped out local farms.
California History Section, California State Library.

the wallets of gullible investors by selling shares in bogus mines to stockholders to whom the very word *Comstock* conjured up images of riches. Speculation, misrepresentation, and outright thievery ran rampant. In twenty years, more than $300 million poured from the earth in Nevada alone. A little stayed in Virginia City, but a great deal more went to speculators in California, some of whom got rich without ever leaving San Francisco.

The promise of gold and silver drew thousands to the mines of the West, the honest as well as the unprincipled. As Mark Twain observed, the Comstock attracted an international array of immigrants. "All the peoples of the earth had representative adventures in the Silverland," he wrote.

Irish, Chinese, Germans, English, Scots, Welsh, Canadians, Mexicans, Italians, Scandinavians, French, Swiss, Chileans, and other South and Central Americans came to share in the bonanza. With them came a sprinkling of Russians, Poles, Greeks, Japanese, Spaniards, Hungarians, Portuguese, Turks, Pacific Islanders, and Moroccans, as well as other North Americans, African Americans, and American Indians. This polyglot population, typical of mining boomtowns, made Virginia City in the 1870s more cosmopolitan than New York or Boston. In the part of Utah Territory that eventually became Nevada, as many as 30 percent of the people came from outside the United States, compared to 25 percent in New York and 21 percent in Massachusetts.

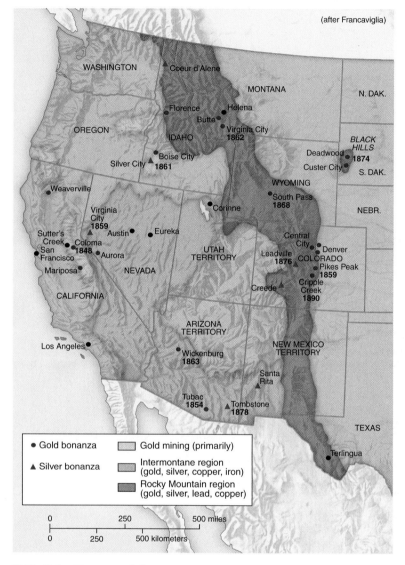

(after Francaviglia)

MAP 17.2 Western Mining, 1848–1890

Rich deposits of gold, silver, copper, lead, and iron larded the mountains of the West, from the Sierra Nevada of California to the Rockies of Colorado and the Black Hills of South Dakota. Beginning with the gold strike on Sutter's Creek in California in 1848 and continuing through the rush for gold in Cripple Creek, Colorado, in 1890, miners from all over the world flocked to the West. Few struck it rich, but many stayed on as paid workers in the increasingly mechanized corporate mines.

Irish immigrants formed the largest ethnic group in the mining district. In Virginia City, fully one-third of the population claimed at least one parent from Ireland. Irish and Irish American women constituted the largest group of women on the Comstock. As servants, boardinghouse owners, and washerwomen, they made up a significant part of the workforce. In contrast, the Chinese community, composed of 642 men in 1870, remained overwhelmingly male. Virulent anti-Chinese sentiment barred the men

from work in the mines, but despite the violent anti-Asian rhetoric, the mining community came to depend on Chinese labor. Many boardinghouses and affluent homes employed a Chinese cook or servant along with an Irish parlor maid.

As was so often the case in the West, where Euro-American ambitions clashed with Native American ways, the discovery of precious metals on the Comstock spelled disaster for the Indians. No sooner had the miners struck pay dirt than they demanded army troops to "hunt Indians" and establish forts to protect transportation to and from the diggings. This sudden and dramatic intrusion left Nevada's native tribes— the Northern Paiute and Bannock Shoshoni— exiles in their own land. At first they resisted, but over time they made peace with the invaders and proved resourceful in finding ways to adapt and preserve their culture and identity despite the havoc wrought by western mining and settlement.

In 1873, Comstock miners uncovered a new vein of ore, a veritable cavern of gold and silver. This "Big Bonanza" speeded the transition from small-scale industry to corporate **oligopoly**, creating a radically new social and economic environment. The Comstock became a laboratory for new mining technology, a place of industry and engineers. Huge stamping mills pulverized rock with pistonlike hammers driven by steam engines. Enormous engines known as Cornish pumps sucked water from the mine shafts, and huge ventilators circulated air in the underground chambers. No backwoods mining camp, Virginia City was an industrial center, with more than 1,200 stamping mills working on average a ton of ore every day. Almost 400 men worked in milling, nearly 300 labored in manufacturing industries, and roughly 3,000 toiled in the mines. The Gould and Curry mine covered sixty acres. Most of the miners who came to the Comstock ended up as laborers for the big companies, although they sometimes worked their own small "rat hole" mines on their time off, still hoping to strike it rich.

The miner's job was filled with peril. Descending deep into the earth, down 1,500 to 3,000 feet where temperatures rose to 120 degrees, stripped-down miners on the Comstock Lode retreated to "cooling-off rooms" where the company provided barrels of ice water to bring down the miners' body temperature. Death stalked the mines and came in many forms—fires, floods, cave-ins, bad air, falling timbers, and misfired explosives.

New technology eliminated some of the dangers of mining but often created new ones. In the hard-rock mines of the West, accidents in the 1870s disabled one out of every thirty miners and killed one in eighty. Ross Moudy, who worked as a miner in Cripple Creek, Colorado, recalled how a stockholder visiting the mine nearly fell to his death. The terrified visitor told the miner next to him that "instead of being paid $3 a day, they ought to have all the gold they could take out." Moudy's biggest worry was carbon dioxide, which often filled the tunnels because of poor ventilation. "Many times," he confessed, "I have been carried out unconscious." Those who avoided accidents still breathed air so dangerous that respiratory diseases eventually disabled them. After a year on the job, Moudy joined a labor union "because I saw it would help me to keep in work and for protection in case of accident or sickness." The union provided good sick benefits and hired nurses, "so if one is alone and sick he is sure to be taken care of." On the Comstock Lode, because of the difficulty of obtaining

skilled labor, the richness of the ore, and the need for a stable workforce, labor unions formed early and held considerable bargaining power. Comstock miners commanded $4 a day, the highest wage in the mining West.

The mining towns of the "Wild West" are often portrayed as lawless outposts, filled with saloons and rough gambling dens and populated almost exclusively by men, except for the occasional dance-hall floozy. The truth is more complex, as Virginia City's development attests. An established urban community built to serve an industrial giant, Virginia City in its first decade boasted churches, schools, theaters, an opera house, and hundreds of families. By 1870, women composed 30 percent of the population, and 75 percent of the women listed their occupation in the census as housekeeper. Many of them made money on the side by providing lodging and by cooking or sewing and doing laundry for bachelor miners. Mary McNair Mathews, a widow

"Mining on the Comstock"

This illustration, made at Gold Hill, Nevada, in 1876, shows a sectional view of a mine, including the tunnels, incline, cooling-off room, blower, and air shaft, along with a collection of miner's tools. Mines like the one pictured here honeycombed the hills of Gold City and neighboring Virginia City on the Comstock Lode in Nevada.

University of California at Berkeley, Bancroft Library.

from Buffalo, New York, who lived on the Comstock in the 1870s, worked as a teacher, nurse, seamstress, laundress, and lodging-house operator. She later published a book on her adventures.

By 1875, Virginia City boasted a population of 25,000 people, making it one of the largest cities between St. Louis and San Francisco. A must-see stop on the way west, the Queen of the Comstock hosted American presidents as well as legions of lesser dignitaries. No rough outpost of the Wild West, Virginia City represented, in the words of a recent chronicler, "the distilled essence of America's newly established course—urban, industrial, acquisitive, and materialistic, on the move, 'a living polyglot' of cultures that collided and converged." In short, Virginia City formed an integral part of a new urban, industrial America.

> Virginia City represented, in the words of a recent chronicler, "the distilled essence of America's newly established course—urban, industrial, acquisitive, and materialistic, on the move, 'a living polyglot' of cultures that collided and converged."

Territorial Government

The federal government practiced a policy of benign neglect when it came to territorial government in the West. The president appointed a governor, a secretary, and two to four judges, along with an attorney and a marshal. In Nevada Territory, that meant that a handful of officials governed an area the size of New England. Originally a part of the larger Utah Territory, Nevada, propelled by mining interests, moved on the fast track to statehood, entering the Union in 1864, long before its population or its development merited statehood.

More typical were the territories extant in 1870—New Mexico, Utah, Washington, Colorado, Dakota, Arizona, Idaho, Montana, and Wyoming. These areas remained territories for inordinately long periods ranging from twenty-three to sixty-two years. While awaiting statehood, they were subject to territorial governors who were underpaid, often unqualified, and largely ignored in Washington. The vast majority of territorial appointments were given to men because of their party loyalty. Most governors had no knowledge of the areas they served, little notion of their duties, and limited ability to perform them.

In theory, territorial governors received adequate salaries, as high as $3,500 in an era when the average workingman earned less than $500 a year. In practice, the funds rarely arrived in a timely fashion, and more than one governor found that he had to pay government expenses out of his own pocket. As one cynic observed, "Only the rich or those having 'no visible means of support,' can afford to accept office." John C. Frémont, the governor of Arizona Territory, was so poor he complained to Washington that he could not inspect the Grand Canyon because he didn't have enough money to keep a horse.

Territorial governors with fewer scruples accepted money from special-interest groups such as mine owners or ranchers. Nearly all territorial appointees tried to make ends meet by maintaining business connections with the East or by taking advantage of investment opportunities in the West. Distance and the lack of funds made it difficult to summon officers from Washington to investigate charges of corruption. Officials who ventured west to look into malfeasance often felt intimidated by gun-packing westerners. One judge sent to New Mexico Territory in 1871 reported that he "stayed three days, made up his mind that it would be dangerous to do any investigating, . . . and returned to his home without any action." Underfunded

Norwegian Immigrant and Sod House

Norwegian immigrant Beret Olesdater sits in front of her sod house in Lac qui Parle, Minnesota, in 1896. On the plains, where trees were scarce and lumber was often prohibitively expensive, settlers built with the materials at hand. The dugout was the most primitive dwelling, carved into a hillside. Huts cut from blocks of sod, like the one pictured here, marked a step up. Life for women on the plains proved especially lonely and hard. "Each day brought new, unexpected challenges and at times I wondered if I would be able to stay with it," one female homesteader wrote. "Could any land be worth the lonely hours and hardships? The howling wind and driving snow, the mournful wail of the coyotes . . . did nothing to make the winter any more pleasant."
© Minnesota Historical Society/Corbis.

and overlooked, victims of political cronyism and prey to local interests, territorial governments were rife with conflicts of interest and corruption, mirroring the self-serving political and economic values of the country as a whole in the rush for riches that followed the Civil War.

The Diverse Peoples of the West

The West of the late nineteenth century was a polyglot place, as much so as the big cities of the East. The parade of peoples who came to the West included immigrants from Europe, Asia, and Canada, not to mention New Englanders, Mormons, African Americans, Mexicans, and Latinos. The sheer number of peoples who mingled in the West produced a complex blend of racism and prejudice. One historian has noted, not entirely facetiously, that there were at least eight oppressed "races" in the West—Indians, Latinos, Chinese, Japanese, blacks, Mormons, strikers, and radicals.

African Americans who ventured out to the territories faced hostile settlers determined to keep the West "for whites only." In response, they formed all-black communities such as Nicodemas, Kansas. That settlement, founded by thirty black Kentuckians in 1877, grew to a community of seven hundred by 1880. Isolated and often separated by great distances, small black settlements grew up throughout the West, in Nevada, Utah, and the Pacific Northwest as well as in Kansas. Black soldiers who served in the West during the Indian wars often stayed on as settlers. Called "buffalo soldiers" because Native Americans thought their hair resembled that of the buffalo, these black troops numbered up to 25,000. The army pitted people of color against one another, using black soldiers to fight the Apaches in Arizona Territory and to help subdue the Sioux in the Dakotas.

Hispanic peoples had lived in Texas and the Southwest since Juan de Oñate led pioneer settlers up the Rio Grande in 1598. Hispanics had occupied the Pacific coast since San Diego was founded in 1769. Overnight, they were reduced to a "minority" after the United States annexed Texas in 1845 and took land stretching to California after the Mexican-American War ended in 1848. At first, the Hispanic owners of large *ranchos* in California, New Mexico, and Texas greeted conquest as an economic opportunity—new markets for their livestock and buyers for their lands. But racial prejudice soon ended their optimism. Californios (Mexican residents of California), who

Buffalo Soldiers
Members of the African American Tenth Cavalry are shown here near St. Mary's, Montana, in 1894. The army formed two cavalry regiments of African American soldiers under white officers to serve in the Indian wars beginning in 1866. Called "buffalo soldiers" by the Comanche and Cheyenne, the soldiers adopted the title and wore it proudly. More than 25,000 African American soldiers fought in the West. In the face of discrimination, poor treatment, and harsh conditions, the buffalo soldiers served with distinction and boasted the lowest desertion rate in the army. Twenty members of the Ninth and Tenth Cavalry regiments received the coveted Congressional Medal of Honor.
Hayes Foundation Collection, Montana Historical Society.

had been granted American citizenship by the Treaty of Guadalupe Hidalgo (1848), faced discrimination by Anglos who sought to keep them out of California's mines and commerce. Whites illegally squatted on *rancho* land while protracted litigation over Spanish and Mexican **land grants** forced the Californios into court. Although the U.S. Supreme Court eventually validated most of their claims, it took so long—seventeen years on average—that many Californios sold their property to pay taxes and legal bills. The city of Oakland, California, sits on what was once a 19,000-acre ranch owned by the Peralta family, who lost the land to Anglos. Swindles, chicanery, and intimidation dispossessed scores of Californios. Many ended up segregated in urban barrios (neighborhoods) in their own homeland. Their percentage of California's population declined from 82 percent in 1850 to 19 percent in 1880 as Anglos migrated to the state. In New

Peralta Family

Don Antonio Peralta, grandson of Don Luis Peralta, whose vast landholdings once included most of Alameda County, California, is shown here in an 1870 photograph with his two sons, Nelson (left) and Vicente (right). The Peraltas and many other Californio families lost their land in protracted legal proceedings trying to prove the validity of their ancestors' Spanish land grants, which had gone unchallenged when Mexico ruled Alta California. The city of Oakland now sits on what was once the Peralta *rancho*.

The Oakland Tribune.

Mexico and Texas, Mexicans remained a majority of the population but became increasingly impoverished as Anglos dominated business and took the best jobs. Skirmishes between Hispanics and whites in northern New Mexico over the fencing of the open range lasted for decades. Groups of Hispanics with names such as *Las Manos Negras* (the Black Hands) cut fences and burned barns. In Texas, violence along the Rio Grande pitted Tejanos (Mexican residents of Texas) against the Texas Rangers, who saw their role as "keeping Mexicans in their place."

Like the Mexicans, the Mormons faced prejudice and hostility. The followers of Joseph Smith,

> Miners determined to keep "California for Americans" succeeded in passing prohibitive foreign license laws to keep the Chinese out of the mines.

the founder and prophet of the Church of Jesus Christ of Latter-Day Saints, fled west to avoid religious persecution. They believed that they had a divine right to the land, and their messianic militancy contributed to making them outcasts. The Mormon practice of polygamy (a man taking more than one wife) became a convenient point of attack for those who hated and feared the group. After Smith was killed by an Illinois mob in 1844, Brigham Young led the flock, which numbered more than 20,000, over the Rockies to the valley of the Great Salt Lake in Utah Territory. The Mormons quickly set to work irrigating the desert. They relied on cooperation and communalism, a strategy that excluded competition from those outside the faith. The church controlled water supplies, stores, insurance companies, and later factories and mining smelters. By 1882, the Mormons had built Salt Lake City, a thriving metropolis of more than 150,000 residents.

The Mormon practice of polygamy (Brigham Young had twenty-seven wives) had come under attack as early as 1857, when U.S. troops occupied Salt Lake City (see chapter 12). To counter criticism of polygamy, the Utah territorial legislature gave women the right to vote in 1870, the first universal woman suffrage act in the nation. (Wyoming had granted suffrage to white women in 1869.) Although woman's rights advocates argued that the newly enfranchised women would "do away with the horrible institution of polygamy," it remained in force. Not until 1890 did the church hierarchy give in to pressure to renounce polygamy. The fierce controversy over polygamy postponed statehood for Utah until 1896.

The Chinese suffered brutal treatment at the hands of employers and other laborers. Drawn by the promise of gold, more than 20,000 Chinese had joined the rush to California by 1852. Miners determined to keep "California for Americans" succeeded in passing prohibitive foreign license laws to keep the Chinese out of the mines. But Chinese immigration continued. In the 1860s, when white workers moved on to find riches in the bonanza mines of Nevada, Chinese laborers took jobs abandoned by the whites. Railroad magnate Charles Crocker hired Chinese gangs to work on the Central Pacific, reasoning that the race that built the Great Wall could lay tracks across the treacherous Sierra Nevada. Some 12,000 Chinese, representing 90 percent of Crocker's workforce, completed America's first transcontinental railroad in 1869.

By 1870, more than 63,000 Chinese immigrants lived in America, 77 percent of them in

California. A 1790 federal statute that limited naturalization to "white persons" was modified after the Civil War to extend naturalization to blacks ("persons of African descent"). But the Chinese and other Asians continued to be denied access to citizenship. As perpetual aliens, they constituted a reserve army of transnational industrial laborers that many saw as a threat to American labor. For the most part, the Chinese did not displace white workers but instead found work as railroad laborers, cooks, servants, and farmhands while white workers sought out more lucrative fields. In the 1870s, when California and the rest of the nation weathered a major economic depression, the Chinese became easy scapegoats. California workingmen rioted and fought to keep Chinese workers out of the state, claiming they were "coolie labor"—involuntary contract laborers recruited by business interests determined to keep wages at rock bottom.

In 1876, the Workingmen's Party formed to fight for Chinese exclusion. Racial and cultural animosities stood at the heart of anti-Chinese agitation. Denis Kearney, the fiery San Francisco leader of the movement, made clear this racist bent when he urged legislation to "expel every one of the moon-eyed lepers." Nor was California alone in its anti-immigrant **nativism**. As the country confronted growing ethnic and racial diversity with the rising tide of global immigration in the decades following the Civil War, many questioned the principle of racial equality at the same time they argued against the assimilation of "nonwhite" groups. In this climate, Congress passed the Chinese Exclusion Act in 1882, effectively barring Chinese immigration and becoming a precedent for further immigration restrictions. The Chinese Exclusion Act led to a sharp drop in the Chinese population—from 105,465 in 1880 to 89,863 in 1900—because Chinese immigrants, overwhelmingly male, did not have families to sustain their population. Eventually, Japanese immigrants, including women as well as men, replaced the Chinese, particularly in agriculture. As "nonwhite" immigrants, they could not become naturalized citizens, but their children

Chinese Workers
Chinese section hands, wearing their distinctive conical hats, are shown here in 1898 shoveling dirt for the North Pacific Coast Railroad in Corte Madera, California. Charles Crocker was the first railroad executive to hire Chinese laborers to work on the Central Pacific railroad in the 1860s, reasoning that the race that built the Great Wall could build tracks through the Sierra Nevada.
California Historical Society, FN-25345.

born in the United States claimed the rights of citizenship. Japanese parents, seeking to own land, purchased it in their children's names. Although anti-Asian prejudice remained strong in California and elsewhere in the West, Asian immigrants formed an important part of the economic fabric of the western United States.

The American West in the nineteenth century witnessed more than its share of conflict and bloodshed. Violent prejudice against the Chinese and other Asian immigrants remained common. But violence also broke out between cattle ranchers and sheep ranchers, between ranchers and farmers, between striking miners and their bosses, among rival Indian groups, and between whites and Indians. At issue was who would control the vast resources of the emerging region.

REVIEW How did industrial technology change mining in Nevada?

Land Fever

After the Civil War, Americans by the hundreds of thousands packed up and moved west, goaded if not by the hope of striking gold, then by the promise of owning land. In the three decades following 1870, more land was settled than in all the previous history of the country. Between 1876 and 1900, eight new western states entered the Union—Colorado, Montana, North and South Dakota, Washington, Idaho, Wyoming, and Utah—leaving only three territories— Oklahoma, New Mexico, and Arizona. The agrarian West shared with the mining West a persistent restlessness, an equally pervasive addiction to speculation, and a penchant for exploiting natural resources and labor.

Two factors stimulated the land rush in the trans-Mississippi West. The Homestead Act of 1862 promised 160 acres free to any citizen or prospective citizen, male or female, who settled on the land for five years. Even more important, transcontinental railroads opened up new areas and actively recruited settlers. After the completion of the first transcontinental railroad in 1869, homesteaders abandoned the covered wagon, and by the 1880s they could choose from four competing rail lines and make the trip in a matter of days.

Although the country was rich in land and resources, not all who wanted to own land achieved their goal. A growing number of Americans found themselves forced to work for wages on land they would never own. During the transition from the family farm to large commercial farming, small farms gave way to vast spreads worked by migrant labor or paid farmworkers. Just as industry corporatized and consolidated in the East, the period from 1870 to 1900 witnessed corporate consolidation in mining, ranching, and agriculture.

Moving West: Homesteaders and Speculators

A Missouri homesteader remembered packing as her family pulled up stakes and headed west to Oklahoma in 1890. "We were going to God's Country," she wrote. "You had to work hard on that rocky country in Missouri. I was glad to be leaving it. . . . We were going to a new land and get rich."

People who ventured west searching for "God's Country" faced hardship, loneliness, and deprivation. To carve a farm from the raw prairie of Iowa, the plains of Nebraska, or the forests of the Pacific Northwest took more than fortitude and backbreaking toil. It took luck. Blizzards, tornadoes, grasshoppers, hailstorms, drought, prairie fires, accidental death, and disease were only a few of the catastrophes that could befall even the best farmer. Homesteaders on free land still needed as much as $1,000 for a house, a team of farm animals, a well, fencing, and seed. Poor farmers called "sodbusters" did without even these basics, living in dugouts carved into hillsides and using muscle instead of machinery.

"Father made a dugout and covered it with willows and grass," one Kansas girl recounted. When it rained, the dugout flooded, and "we carried the water out in buckets, then waded around in the mud until it dried." Rain wasn't the only problem. "Sometimes the bull snakes would get in the roof and now and then one would lose his hold and fall down on the bed. . . . Mother would grab the hoe . . . and after the fight was over Mr. Bull Snake was dragged outside." The sod house, a step up from the dugout, had walls cut from blocks of sod and a roof of sod, lumber, or tin. In requiring that homesteaders "settle" on the land for five years to achieve ownership, the government did not stipulate a specific size or manner of construction for homesteads. In the Dakotas, homesteaders often erected claim shacks, some as small as eight by ten feet. (See "Documenting the American Promise," page 616.)

For women on the frontier, obtaining simple daily necessities such as water and fuel meant backbreaking labor. Out on the plains, where

Admission of States in the Trans-Mississippi West

Year	State	Year	State
1821	Missouri	1889	North Dakota
1836	Arkansas	1889	South Dakota
1845	Texas	1889	Montana
1846	Iowa	1889	Washington
1850	California	1890	Idaho
1858	Minnesota	1890	Wyoming
1859	Oregon	1896	Utah
1861	Kansas	1907	Oklahoma
1864	Nevada	1912	New Mexico
1867	Nebraska	1912	Arizona
1876	Colorado		

water was scarce, women often had to trudge to the nearest creek or spring. "A yoke was made to place across [Mother's] shoulders, so as to carry at each end a bucket of water," one daughter recollected, "and then water was brought a half mile from spring to house." Gathering fuel was another heavy chore. Without ready sources of coal or firewood, settlers on the plains turned to what substitutes they could scavenge—twigs, tufts of grass, corncobs, sunflower stalks. But by far the most prevalent fuel was "chips"—chunks of dried cattle and buffalo dung, found in abundance on the plains.

Despite the hardships, some homesteaders succeeded in building comfortable lives. The sod hut made way for a more substantial house; the log cabin yielded to a white clapboard home with a porch and a rocking chair. And the type and quality of the family diet improved. "Our living at first was very scanty," recalled one Kansas woman, "mostly corn coarsely ground and made into hominy." Then the family raised a crop of wheat and ground it into flour. "We would invite the neighbors proudly telling them we have 'flour doings.'" When the farm wife began to raise chickens, the family added "chicken fixings" to its diet, "and when we could have 'flour doings' and 'chicken fixings' at the same meal we felt we were on the road to prosperity."

For others, the promise of the West failed to materialize. Already by the 1870s, much of the best land had been taken. Too often, homesteaders found that only the least desirable tracts were left—poor land, far from markets, transportation, and society. Speculators held the lion's share of the land. "There is plenty of land for sale in California," one migrant complained in 1870, but "the majority of the available lands are held by speculators, at prices far beyond the reach of a poor man."

The railroads, flush from land grants provided by the state and federal governments, owned huge swaths of land in the West and actively recruited settlers. Altogether, the land grants totaled approximately 180 million acres—an area almost one-tenth the size of the United States (Map 17.3, page 614). Many farmers who went west ended up buying land from the railroads or from the speculators and land companies that quickly followed the railroads into the West. Of the 2.5 million farms established between 1860 and 1900, homesteading accounted for only one in five; the vast majority of farmland sold for a profit.

Railroad Locomotive
In the years following the Civil War, the locomotive replaced the covered wagon, enabling settlers to travel from Chicago or St. Louis to the West Coast in two days. By the 1890s, more than 72,000 miles of track stretched west of the Mississippi River. The first transcontinental railroad, completed in 1869, soon led to the creation of competing systems, so that by the 1880s, travelers going west could choose from four railroad lines. In this photograph, men and women perched on a locomotive celebrate the completion of a section of track.
Library of Congress.

As land grew scarce on the prairie in the 1870s, farmers began to push farther west, moving into western Kansas, Nebraska, and eastern Colorado—the region called the Great American Desert by settlers who had passed over it on their way to California and Oregon. Many agricultural experts warned that the semiarid land (where less than twenty inches of rain fell annually) would not support a farm on the 160 acres allotted to homesteaders, but their words of caution were drowned out by the extravagant claims of western promoters, many employed by the railroads to sell off their land grants. "Rain follows the plow" became the slogan of western boosters, who insisted that cultivation would alter the climate of the region and bring more rainfall.

Midwestern Settlement before 1862

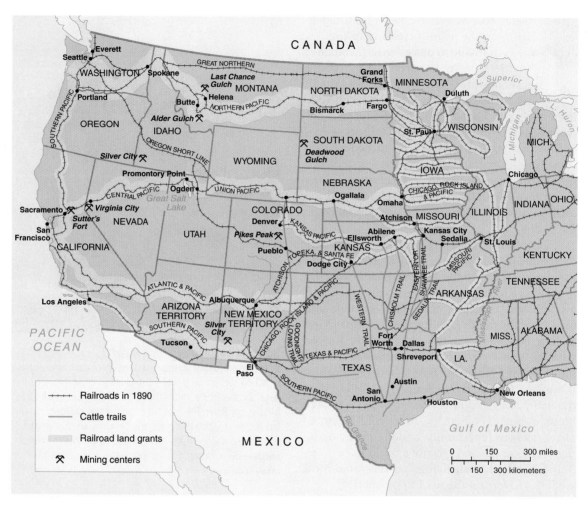

MAP 17.3   Federal Land Grants to Railroads and the Development of the West, 1850–1900
Generous federal land grants meant that railroads could sell the desirable land next to the track at a profit
or hold it for speculation. Railroads received more than 180 million acres, an area as large as Texas. Notice
how the cattle trails connect with major railheads in Dodge City, Abilene, and Kansas City and to mining
towns in Montana, Nevada, Colorado, and New Mexico.

READING THE MAP: Which mining cities and towns were located directly on a railroad line? Which towns
were located at the junction of more than one line or railroad branch?
CONNECTIONS: In what ways did the growth of the railroad affect the population of the West? What western
goods and products did the railroads help bring east and to ports for shipping around the world?

FOR MORE HELP ANALYZING THIS MAP, see the map activity for this chapter in the Online Study Guide at
bedfordstmartins.com/roark.

Instead, drought followed the plow. Droughts
were a cyclical fact of life on the Great Plains.
Plowed up, the dry topsoil blew away in the
wind. A period of relatively good rainfall in the
early 1880s encouraged farming; then a protracted
drought in the late 1880s and early 1890s sent
starving farmers reeling back from the plains.
Thousands left, some in wagons carrying the slogan "In God we trusted, in Kansas we busted." A
popular ballad bitterly summed up the plight of
the worst off, those too poor to leave.

But here I am stuck and here I must stay
My money's all gone and I can't get away;
There's nothing will make a man hard and
    profane
Like starving to death on a government claim.

Fever for fertile land set off a series of spectacular land runs in Oklahoma. When two million acres of land in former Indian Territory
opened for settlement in 1889, thousands of
homesteaders massed on the border. At the
opening pistol shot, "with a shout and a yell the

swift riders shot out, then followed the light buggies or wagons," a reporter wrote. "Above all, a great cloud of dust hover[ed] like smoke over a battlefield." By nightfall, Oklahoma boasted two tent cities with more than ten thousand residents. In the last frenzied land rush on Oklahoma's Cherokee strip in 1893, several settlers were killed in the stampede, and nervous men guarded their claims with rifles. As public land grew scarce, the hunger for land grew fiercer for both farmers and ranchers.

Ranchers and Cowboys

Cattle ranchers followed the railroads onto the plains, establishing between 1865 and 1885 a cattle kingdom from Texas to Wyoming. Cowboys drove huge herds, as many as three thousand head of cattle, that grazed on public lands as they followed cattle tracks like the Chisholm Trail from Texas to railheads in Kansas. From there, the cattle traveled by boxcar to Chicago, where they sold for as much as $45 a head. More than a million and a half Texas longhorns went to market before the range began to close in the 1880s.

Barbed wire revolutionized the cattle business and sounded the death knell for the open range. In 1874, Joseph F. Glidden, an Illinois sheriff, invented and patented barbed wire. Gambler and promoter John "Bet a Million" Gates made his fortune by corralling a herd of Texas longhorns in downtown San Antonio, proving the merit of the flimsy-looking wire

he went on to market profitably. As the largest ranches in Texas began to fence, nasty fights broke out between big ranchers and "fence cutters," who resented the end of the free range. One old-timer observed, "Those persons, Mexicans and Americans, without land but who had cattle were put out of business by fencing." Fencing forced small-time ranchers who owned land but could not afford to buy barbed wire or sink wells to sell out for the best price they could get. The displaced ranchers, many of them Mexicans, ended up as wageworkers on the huge spreads owned by Anglos or by European syndicates.

On the range, the cowboy gave way to the cattle king and, like the miner, became a wage laborer. Many cowboys were African Americans (as many as five thousand in Texas alone). Writers of western literature chose to ignore the presence of black cowboys like Deadwood Dick (Nat Love), who was portrayed as a white man in the dime novels of the era. Cowboy life was hard, and like many other dissatisfied workers in the East, cowboys organized labor unions in the 1880s and mounted strikes in both Texas and Wyoming.

By 1886, cattle overcrowded the range. Severe blizzards during the winters of 1886–87

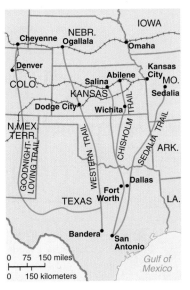

Cattle Trails, 1860–1890

Barbed Wire Machine and Soothing Liniment

The original working model of Joseph Glidden's barbing machine, patented in 1874, consisted of an old-fashioned coffee mill with its casing cut away and its grinder altered to cut and coil small lengths of wire. The barbs were strung by hand between strands of plain wire. Despite its flimsiness, barbed wire could contain cattle, as master promoter John "Bet a Million" Gates demonstrated by corralling a herd of Texas longhorns in downtown San Antonio in 1879. With the invention of barbed wire, medicine makers cashed in by marketing products such as Perrigo's Barb Wire Liniment to soothe the cuts and scrapes suffered by man and beast after coming in contact with the barbs.

Barbed wire machine: Ellwood House Museum, De Kalb, Illinois; Liniment: Kansas Barbed Wire Museum.

Young Women Homesteaders and the Promise of the West

"**Y**oung men! Poor men! Widows! Resolve to have a home of your own!" urged New York editor Horace Greeley. "If you are able to buy and pay for one in the East, very well; if not, make one in the broad and fertile West!" In his exhortation to go west, Greeley did not speak to men alone. Many women, and not just widows, heeded the call. The Homestead Act of 1862 allowed unmarried women and female heads of households to claim free land. Many did. The number of women establishing homesteads in the West ranged from 5 percent of homesteaders in the early settlements to more than 20 percent after 1900.

Among the women homesteaders were Clara and Mary Troska and their two cousins Helen and Christine Sonnek, who headed to North Dakota. "Mary, Helen, Christine and I packed our suitcases," Clara wrote. "I took my mandolin, Christine took hers and her rifle. . . . We were on our way to Minot." Young women like Clara between the ages of twenty-one and twenty-five constituted the largest percentage of women (53 percent) taking up claims in the Dakotas. Like Christine Sonnek, who took her mandolin along with her rifle, homesteading women prepared to enjoy their new environment despite its challenges. Their letters, diaries, and reminiscences reveal not only the hardships they faced but also the sense of promise that lured them west. Adventurous, resourceful, and exuberant, many of these young homesteading women seemed to relish their experiences.

DOCUMENT 1
The Varied Activities of a Woman Homesteader

Dakota homesteader Bess Cobb's letter to a friend reveals the optimism and high spirits that energized the young women who filed homesteading claims.

Suppose you girls are saying "poor Bess" and feeling dreadfully sorry for me out here in the wild and wooly uncivilized regions of America. But really time just seems to fly. I haven't done half I had planned and I am afraid winter will be here before we are ready for it. I've sewed some, done a little fancy-work and lots of darning and mending but most of my time has been spent out of doors digging in the garden and riding. . . . You can see a team miles away—up one valley we can see ten miles, up to the Cannon Ball river—so when any one starts to our shack, if we see them in time we can comb our hair, change our gowns and get a good meal in running order before they arrive. You see Dakota has some redeeming qualities. Wish you could come out, but I suppose you think I am too far away. I have the neatest little shack I've ever seen and "my crops" are tip top. I know you would enjoy our camp life for a short time.

SOURCE: "Excerpts from a letter written by Bess Cobb, Guide to Manuscripts

1364, State Historical Society, North Dakota Heritage Center, Bismarck," from pages 140–41 in *Land in Her Own Name: Women as Homesteaders in North Dakota* by H. Elaine Lindgren. Copyright © 1996. Reprinted with permission of University of Oklahoma Press.

DOCUMENT 2
A Hard Winter

Lucy Goldthorpe, a young schoolteacher, came from Iowa to Dakota in 1905. Here she describes to a reporter her survival during the winter and contrasts her childhood fantasies with homestead reality.

There were many long, cold days and nights in my little homestead shack that winter! The walls were only single board thickness, covered with tar paper on the outside. I'd spent money sparingly, because I didn't have much, but I had worked hard all during summer and fall in an effort to winterize the structure. Following the pattern used by many of the settlers, I covered the interior walls with a blue building paper. Everything was covered, including the ceiling, and the floor. To help seal out the cold I'd added layers of gunny sacks over the paper on the floor and then the homemade wool rugs I'd shipped from home.

Regardless of what I did the cold crept in through the thin walls. With no storm entry at the door and only single windows my little two-lid laundry stove with oven attached to the pipe had a real struggle to keep the place livable. . . .

A neighbor family returning to their claim "from the outside" brought me fresh vegetables. They were such a prized addition to my meals that I put the bag in bed with me at night to keep them from freezing. Night after night I stored food and my little alarm clock in the stove pipe oven; that was the only way I could keep the clock running and be sure of a non-frozen breakfast.

Each day brought new, unexpected challenges and at times I wondered if I would be able to stay with it until the land was mine. Could any land be worth the lonely hours and hardships? The howling wind and driving snow, the mournful wail of coyotes searching the tormented land for food did nothing to make the winter any more pleasant. . . .

As a child I had enjoyed hearing my father tell of the hardships of the early days. They seemed so exciting to me as I listened in the warmth and security of our well built, fully winterized Iowa home. Like most youngsters I'd wished for the thrill of those other days. Little did I think that an opportunity for just that would come through homesteading alone, far out in the windswept, unsettled land. Believe me, it wasn't nearly as glamorous as the imagination would have it!

SOURCE: Roberta M. Starry, "Petticoat Pioneer." Excerpt from page 48 in *The West* 7, no. 5, October 1967. Copyright © 1967. Reprinted with permission.

DOCUMENT 3
Socializing and Entertainment

Homesteading wasn't all hard times. Young, single homesteaders found time for fun. Here Effie Vivian Smith describes a "shack party" during the winter of 1906 on her Dakota claim.

I never enjoyed myself better in my life than I have this winter. We go some place or some one is here from 1 to 4 times a week. A week ago last Fri. a load of 7 drove out to my claim. Cliff, Clara, David, and I had gone out the Wed. before and such a time as we had. My shack is 10 feet 3 inches by 16 feet and I have only 2 chairs and a long bench for seats, a table large enough for 6, a single bed, and only 3 knives so 2 of them ate with paring knives & 1 with the butcher knife. We had two of them sit on the bed and moved the table up to them. . . . We played all the games we could think of both quiet and noisy and once all but Clara went out & snowballed. They brought a bu[shel] of apples, & a lot of nuts, candy, & gum & we ate all night. . . .

We have just started a literary society in our neighborhood. Had our first debate last Fri. The question was Resolved that city life is better than country life. All the judges decided in the negative. . . . Tomorrow our crowd is going to a literary [society] 6 or 7 miles from here, and the next night to a dance at the home of one of our bachelor boys. We always all go in our sleigh. I am learning to dance this winter but don't attend any except the ones we get up ourselves and they are just as nice & just as respectable as the parties we used to have at Ruthven [Iowa]. I just love to dance. . . .

SOURCE: H. Elaine Lindgren, "Letter to her cousin, written on January 9, 1906." From pages 177–78 in *Land in Her Own Name: Women as Homesteaders in North Dakota.* Copyright © 1996 University of Oklahoma Press. Reprinted with permission.

DOCUMENT 4
Homesteading Pays Off

Homesteading proved rewarding for many women, not only economically but also because of the sense of accomplishment they experienced. Here Theona Carkin tells how the sale of her Dakota homestead helped finance her university degree.

Life in general was dotted with hardships but there were many good times also. I have always felt that my efforts on my homestead were very worthwhile and very rewarding, and I have always been proud of myself for doing it all.

By teaching off and on . . . and upon selling the homestead, I was able to pay all my own college expenses.

SOURCE: "99-Year-Old U Graduate Recalls Early Childhood." From page 5 in *Alumni Review*, June 1985. Published by the University of North Dakota, Grand Forks.

QUESTIONS FOR ANALYSIS AND DEBATE

1. What sorts of hardships did the young women homesteaders encounter in the Dakotas?
2. How did their youth affect how they reacted to hardship?
3. What did the young women find particularly appealing about their experiences as homesteaders?
4. What did they wish to convey about their experiences?
5. How did homesteading benefit women who chose not to remain on the land?

and 1887–88 decimated the herds. "A whole generation of cowmen," wrote one chronicler, "went dead broke." Fencing worsened the situation. During blizzards, cattle stayed alive by keeping on the move. But when they ran up against barbed wire fences, they froze to death. In the aftermath of the "Great Die Up," new labor-intensive forms of cattle ranching replaced the open-range model.

Tenants, Sharecroppers, and Migrants

Many who followed the American promise into the West prospered, but landownership proved an elusive goal for many others—among them freed slaves, immigrants from Europe and Asia, and Mexicans in California and on the Texas border. In the post–Civil War period, as agriculture became a big business tied to national and global markets, an increasing number of laborers worked land that they would never own.

In the southern United States, farmers labored under particularly heavy burdens (see chapter 16). The Civil War wiped out much of the region's capital, which had been invested in slaves, and crippled the plantation economy. Newly freed slaves rarely obtained land of their own and often ended up as farm laborers. "The colored folks stayed with the old boss man and farmed and worked on the plantations," a black Alabama sharecropper observed bitterly. "They were still slaves, but they were free slaves." Some freed people did manage to pull together enough resources to go west. In 1879, more than fifteen thousand black "Exodusters" moved from Mississippi and Louisiana to take up land in Kansas.

Many Mexicans who held land grants from the former Spanish or Mexican governments found themselves in the aftermath of the Mexican-American War in the new state of California (1850), which demanded that they prove their claims in court. The protracted legal battles over their land claims drove many *rancheros* (Mexican ranchers), discouraged by the wait, to sell out to Anglos.

California's Mexican cowboys, or *vaqueros*, commanded decent wages throughout the Southwest. Skilled horsemen, the vaqueros boasted that five of them could do the work of thirty Anglo cowboys. The vocabulary of ranch-

> Severe blizzards during the winters of 1886–87 and 1887–88 decimated the herds. "A whole generation of cowmen," wrote one chronicler, "went dead broke."

ing, with words such as *rodeo, lasso, lariat,* and *rancho,* testified to the centrality of the vaqueros' place in the cattle industry. But in the 1870s, when the coming of the railroads ended the long cattle drives and large feedlots began to replace the open range, the value of their skills declined. Many vaqueros ended up as migrant laborers, often on land their families had once owned. Similarly, in Texas, Tejanos found themselves displaced. After the heyday of cattle ranching ended in the late 1880s, cotton production rose in the southeastern regions of the state. Ranchers turned their pastures into sharecroppers' plots and hired displaced cowboys, most of them Mexicans, as seasonal laborers for as little as seventy-five cents a day. Within ten years, ranch life in southern Texas gave way to a growing army of agricultural wageworkers.

Land **monopoly** and large-scale farming fostered tenancy and migratory labor on the West Coast. By the 1870s, less than 1 percent of California's population owned half the state's available agricultural land. The rigid economics of large-scale commercial agriculture and the seasonal nature of the crops spawned a ragged army of migratory agricultural laborers. Derisively labeled "blanket men" or "bindle stiffs," these transients worked the fields in the growing

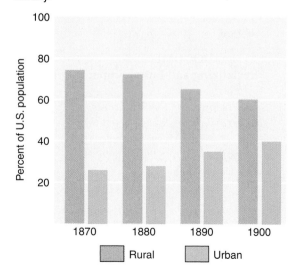

FIGURE 17.1   Changes in Rural and Urban Populations, 1870–1900
Between 1870 and 1900, not only did the number of urban dwellers increase, but, even as the number of rural inhabitants fell, the number of farms increased. Mechanization made it possible to farm with fewer hands, fueling the exodus from farm to city throughout the second half of the nineteenth century.

season and wintered in the flophouses of San Francisco. Wheat farming in California in the 1870s and 1880s exhausted the land and was replaced, with the introduction of irrigation, by fruit and sugar beet farming. Most of the California farm laborers were Chinese immigrants until the Chinese Exclusion Act of 1882 forced big growers to look to other groups, primarily Mexicans, Filipinos, and Japanese, for farm labor.

Commercial Farming and Industrial Cowboys

In the late nineteenth century, America's population remained overwhelmingly rural. The 1870 census showed that nearly 80 percent of the nation's people lived on farms and in villages of fewer than 8,000 inhabitants. By 1900, the figure had dropped to 66 percent (Figure 17.1). At the same time, the number of farms rose. Rapid growth in the West increased the number of the nation's farms from 2 million in 1860 to more than 5.7 million in 1900.

Despite the hardships individual farmers experienced on the plains, new technology and farming techniques revolutionized American farm life. Mechanized plows and reapers halved the time and labor cost of production and made it possible to cultivate vast tracts of land. Urbanization provided farmers with expanding markets for their produce, and railroads carried crops to markets thousands of miles away. Even before the opening of the twentieth century, American agriculture had entered the era of what would come to be called **agribusiness**—farming as a big business—with the advent of huge commercial farms.

As farming moved onto the prairies and plains, mechanization took command. Steel plows, reapers, mowers, harrows, seed drills, combines, and threshers replaced human muscle. Horse-drawn implements gave way to steam-powered machinery. By 1880, a single combine could do the work of twenty men, vastly increasing the acreage a farmer could cultivate. Mechanization spurred the growth of bonanza wheat farms, some more than 100,000 acres, in California and the Red River Valley of North Dakota and Minnesota. This agricultural revolution meant that Americans raised more than four times the corn, five times the hay, and seven times the wheat and oats they had before the Civil War. Much of this new production went to feed people as far away as England and Germany.

Mechanical Corn Planter
Mechanical planters came into use in the 1860s. The Farmers Friend Manufacturing Company of Dayton, Ohio, advertised its lever and treadle corn planter in the early 1880s. Although this planter, which featured attachments for grain drilling and fertilizing, appears to have been designed to be drawn by farm animals, steam-powered farm implements would soon replace animal power. Notice how the female figure on the left, symbolizing the bucolic farm life, is offset by the company's impressive factory in Dayton on the right.
Ohio Historical Society.

Like cotton farmers in the South, western grain and livestock farmers increasingly depended on foreign markets for their livelihood. A fall in global market prices meant that a farmer's entire harvest went to pay off debts. In the depression that followed the panic of 1893, many heavily mortgaged farmers lost their land to creditors. As a Texas cotton farmer complained, "By the time the World Gets their Liveing out of the Farmer as we have to Feed the World, we the Farmer has nothing Left but a Bear Hard Liveing."

Commercial farming, along with mining, represented another way in which the West developed its own brand of industrialism. The far

West's industrial economy sprang initially from California gold and the vast territory that came under American control following the Mexican-American War. In the ensuing rush on land and resources, environmental factors interacted with economic and social forces to produce enterprises as vast in scale and scope as anything found in the East. Two Alsatian immigrants, Henry Miller and Charles Lux, pioneered the West's mix of agriculture and industrialism.

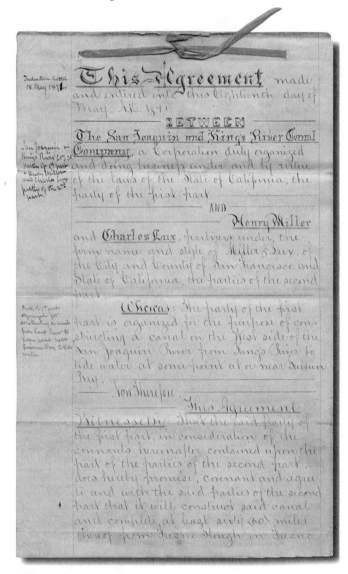

Miller & Lux Contract

This handwritten agreement dated May 18, 1871, provides for the construction of a canal in California's San Joaquin Valley. Reclamation projects such as canals and irrigation systems constituted one branch of business for the firm of Miller & Lux, which industrialized agriculture and eventually controlled 1.25 million acres of land in California, Nevada, and Oregon. Canals and irrigation ditches transformed the landscape, making vast tracts available for huge bonanza wheat farms.
University of California at Berkeley, Bancroft Library.

Beginning as meat wholesalers, Miller and Lux quickly expanded their business to encompass cattle, land, and land reclamation projects such as dams and irrigation systems. With a labor force of migrant workers, a highly coordinated corporate system, and large sums of investment capital, the firm of Miller & Lux became one of America's industrial behemoths. Already by 1870, Miller & Lux owned well over 300,000 acres of grazing land in California's central San Joaquin Valley, over half of it derived from former Mexican land grants. Its industrial-sized wheat operations in California bore little resemblance to any previous form of agriculture. Eventually, these "industrial cowboys" grazed a herd of 100,000 cattle on 1.25 million acres of company land in three western states (California, Oregon, and Nevada) and employed more than 1,200 migrant laborers on their corporate ranches. By 1900, Miller & Lux controlled capital and labor to a degree far surpassing that of most eastern manufacturing firms.

Miller & Lux developed remarkably dynamic investment strategies and corporate structures to control not only California land but water rights as well. The state's largest land speculators, Miller & Lux employed an army of lobbyists to serve its interests in Sacramento. Although the specific components of the Miller & Lux business may have differed from those of industries in the East, the company nonetheless shared the main characteristics of other modern enterprises: corporate consolidation, ownership of resources and raw materials, and schemes to minimize labor costs and stabilize the workforce. Miller & Lux dealt with the labor problem by offering free meals to migratory workers, thus keeping wages low while winning goodwill among an army of unemployed who competed for the work. When the company's Chinese cooks rebelled at washing the dishes resulting from the free meals, the migrant laborers were forced to eat after the ranch hands and use their dirty plates. By the 1890s, more than eight hundred migrants followed what came to be known as the "Dirty Plate Route" on Miller & Lux ranches throughout California.

Since the days of Thomas Jefferson, agrarian life had been linked with the highest ideals of a democratic society. Now agrarianism itself had been transformed. The farmer was no longer a self-sufficient **yeoman** but often a businessman or a wage laborer tied to a global market. And even as farm production soared, industrializa-

Buffalo Bill Poster

Buffalo Bill Cody used colorful posters to publicize his Wild West show during the 1880s and 1890s. One of his most popular features was the reenactment of Custer's Last Stand, which he performed for Queen Victoria in London and at the World's Columbian Exposition in Chicago. Sitting Bull, who fought at the Battle of the Little Big Horn, toured with the company in 1885 and traveled to England with the show. Cody's romantic depictions of western history helped create the myth of the Old West.

Buffalo Bill Historical Center, Cody, Wyoming.

READING THE IMAGE: What did the phrase "as Presented by" in the banner "Custer's Last Stand, as Presented by Buffalo Bill's Wild West," suggest to the audience?

CONNECTIONS: What were viewers supposed to understand about Custer from this poster?

FOR MORE HELP ANALYZING THIS IMAGE, see the visual activity for this chapter in the Online Study Guide at bedfordstmartins.com/roark.

tion outstripped it. More and more farmers left the fields for urban factories or found work in the "factories in the fields" of the new industrialized agribusiness. Now that the future seemed to lie not with the small farmer but with industrial enterprises, was democracy itself at risk? This question would ignite a farmers' revolt in the 1880s and dominate political debate in the 1890s.

REVIEW   Why did many homesteaders find it difficult to acquire good land in the West?

Conclusion: The Mythic West

Even as the Old West was changing, the mythic West was being born. The prince of the dime novel, Buffalo Bill, became its icon. Born William F. Cody, the real-life Buffalo Bill had panned for gold, ridden for the Pony Express, scouted for the army, and earned his nickname hunting buffalo for the railroad. The masterful showman formed a touring Wild West company in 1883. Part circus, part theater, the Wild West extravaganza featured exhibitions of riding, shooting, and roping and presented dramatic reenactments of great moments in western lore. The star of the show, Annie Oakley (Phoebe Moses), dubbed "Little Miss Sure Shot," delighted the crowd by shooting a dime out of her husband's hand. For years, the centerpiece of Buffalo Bill's Wild West show was a reenactment of Custer's Last Stand featuring real Indians wearing war paint and feathered headdresses. Some of them, including Sitting Bull, who traveled with the show in 1885, had fought at Little Big Horn. At the end of the mock battle, Buffalo Bill galloped in through a cloud of dust and dramatically mouthed the words "Too late!" Highly dubious as history, as spectacle the Wild West show was unbeatable. At the World's Columbian Exposition in 1893, crowds numbering tens of thousands packed the bleachers to cheer. By the turn of the twentieth century, the high drama of the struggle for the West had become little more than a thrilling but harmless entertainment.

While Buffalo Bill's show entertained the crowds on the Midway, across the fairgrounds historian Frederick Jackson Turner addressed the American Historical Association on "The Significance of the Frontier in American History." Turner noted that by 1890, the census could no longer discern a clear frontier line. His tone was elegiac: "The existence of an area of free land, its continuous recession, and the advance of settlement westward," he observed, "explained American development" and was inextricably linked to what was best and unique in America. Of course, land in the West had never been empty or free; nor were the whites who moved westward its only inhabitants. The pastoral agrarianism Turner celebrated belied the urban, industrial West found on the Comstock and in the commercial farms of California. Nevertheless, Turner's "frontier thesis" became one of the most enduring myths of the American West.

The real West was no less dramatic than the mythic West. Between 1860 and 1900, the United States developed an empire in the West that filled the map of the continent with states and territories all the way to the Pacific. Native Americans ended up dispossessed, forced onto reservations, and later put out to farm on 160-acre plots. At the same time, whites sought to erase tribal identity and force assimilation. As miners poured into the West, giant mining operations like those on the Comstock replaced the

prospector with his burro and pan. Agriculture, too, became increasingly mechanized and commercial; huge farms totaling thousands of acres were tilled by machine and the muscle of hired workers. With its consolidated mining companies and burgeoning agribusiness, the West developed its own brand of urban industrialism.

In the decades following the Civil War, as the United States pursued empire in the American West, new problems replaced the old issues of slavery and sectionalism. The growing power of big business, the exploitation of labor and natural resources, corruption in politics, and ethnic and racial tensions exacerbated by colonial expansion and unparalleled immigration dominated the debates of the day in both East and West. As the nineteenth century ended, Americans had more questions than answers. Could the American promise survive in the new world of corporations, wage labor, and mushrooming cities? Neither out of place nor out of time, the West contributed its share to both the promise and the problems of the era Mark Twain would brand the Gilded Age.

Selected Bibliography

General Works

Najia Aarin-Heriot, *Chinese Immigrants, African Americans, and Racial Anxiety in the United States, 1848–1882* (2003).

Robert V. Hine and John Mack Faragher, *The American West: A New Interpretive History* (2000).

Patricia Nelson Limerick, *Something in the Soil: Legacies and Reckonings in the New West* (2000).

Valerie Matsumoto and Blake Allmendinger, eds., *Over the Edge: Remapping the American West* (1999).

Louis S. Warren, *Buffalo Bill's America: William Cody and the Wild West Show* (2005).

Richard White, *"It's Your Misfortune and None of My Own": A New History of the American West* (1991).

David M. Wrobel, *Promised Lands: Promotion, Memory, and the Creation of the American West* (2002).

Indians

David Wallace Adams, *Education for Extinction: American Indians and the Boarding School Experience, 1875–1928* (1995).

Gary Clayton Anderson, *The Conquest of Texas: Ethnic Cleansing in the Promised Land, 1820–1875* (2005).

Stuart Banner, *How the Indians Lost Their Land: Law and Power on the Frontier* (2005).

Colin G. Calloway, *First Peoples: A Documentary Survey of American Indian History* (3rd ed., 2008).

Adrian Greaves, *Crossing the Buffalo: The Zulu War of 1879* (2005).

James O. Gump, *The Dust Rose Like Smoke: The Subjugation of the Zulu and the Sioux* (1994).

Andrew C. Isenberg, *The Destruction of the Bison: An Environmental History, 1730–1920* (2000).

Edward Lazarus, *Black Hills, White Justice: The Sioux Nation versus the United States, 1775 to the Present* (1991).

Jeffrey Ostler, *The Plains Sioux and U.S. Colonialism from Lewis and Clark to Wounded Knee* (2004).

Francis Paul Prucha, *The Great Father: The United States Government and the American Indian* (1986).

Charles M. Robinson III, *A Good Year to Die: The Story of the Great Sioux War* (1995).

Alan Trachtenberg, *Shades of Hiawatha: Staging Indians, Making Americans, 1880–1930* (2004).

Mining, Ranching, and Farming

Suchen Chan, *This Bittersweet Soil: The Chinese in American Agriculture, 1860–1919* (1986).

Suchen Chan, Douglas Henry Daniels, Mario T. Garcia, and Terry P. Wilson, *Peoples of Color in the American West* (1994).

Roger Daniels, *Asian American: Chinese and Japanese in the United States since 1850* (1997).

Deborah Fitzgerald, *Every Farm a Factory: The Industrial Ideal in American Agriculture* (2003).

Manuel G. Gonzales, *Mexicanos: A History of Mexicans in the United States* (1999).

J. S. Holliday, *Rush for Riches: Gold Fever and the Making of California* (1999).

David Igler, *Industrial Cowboys: Miller & Lux and the Transformation of the Far West, 1850–1920* (2001).

Andrew C. Isenberg, *Mining California: An Ecological History* (2005).

Ronald M. James, *The Roar and the Silence: The History of Virginia City and the Comstock Lode* (1998).

William Loren Katz, *Black West: A Documentary and Pictorial History of the African American Role in the Westward Expansion of the United States* (2005).

H. Helen Lindgren, *Land in Her Own Name: Women as Homesteaders in North Dakota* (1996).

Karen R. Merrill, *Public Lands and Political Meaning: Ranchers, the Government, and the Property between Them* (2002).

Rodman Wilson Paul, *Mining Frontiers of the Far West, 1848–1880* (rev. ed., 2001).

Paula Petrik, *No Step Backward: Women and Family on the Rocky Mountain Mining Frontier* (1987).

William G. Robbins, *Colony and Empire: The Capitalist Transformation of the American West* (1994).

Steven Stoll, *Larding the Lean Earth: Soil and Society in Nineteenth-Century America* (2002).

► For more books about topics in this chapter, see the Online Bibliography at bedfordstmartins.com/roark.

► For additional firsthand accounts of this period, see Chapter 17 in Michael Johnson, ed., *Reading the American Past*, Fourth Edition.

► For Web sites, images, and documents related to topics and places in this chapter, visit bedfordstmartins.com/makehistory.

REVIEWING THE CHAPTER

Follow these steps to review and strengthen your understanding of the chapter.
STEP 1: *Study the* **Key Terms** *and* **Timeline** *to identify the significance of each item listed.*
STEP 2: *Answer the* **Review Questions**, *drawing on key terms and dates to support your answers.*
STEP 3: *Drawing on the Key Terms, Timeline, and Review Questions, answer the broader* **Making Connections** *questions.*

KEY TERMS

Who

John M. Chivington (p. 595)
William Tecumseh Sherman (p. 595)
Philip Sheridan (p. 597)
Red Cloud (p. 597)
Crazy Horse (p. 597)
Sitting Bull (p. 597)
George Armstrong Custer (p. 597)
Plenty Coups (p. 600)
Chief Joseph (p. 601)
George Crook (p. 601)
Geronimo (p. 601)
Lozen (p. 602)
Nelson Miles (p. 602)
Wovoka (p. 602)
buffalo soldiers (p. 609)

Brigham Young (p. 610)
Exodusters (p. 618)
William F. Cody (p. 621)
Frederick Jackson Turner (p. 622)

What

Carlisle Indian School (p. 592)
Indian removal (p. 593)
Treaty of Fort Laramie (1851) (p. 595)
Great Sioux Uprising (Santee Uprising) (p. 595)
Sand Creek Massacre (p. 595)
U.S. Bureau of Indian Affairs (p. 595)
Treaty of Medicine Lodge (p. 597)
Bozeman Trail (p. 597)
Treaty of Fort Laramie (1868) (p. 597)
Black Hills (p. 597)

Pine Ridge Reservation (p. 597)
Battle of the Little Big Horn (p. 600)
Dawes Allotment Act (p. 600)
Ghost Dance (p. 602)
massacre at Wounded Knee (p. 603)
California gold rush (p. 603)
Comstock Lode (p. 603)
Workingmen's Party (p. 611)
Chinese Exclusion Act (p. 611)
Homestead Act of 1862 (p. 612)
Great American Desert (p. 613)
Chisholm Trail (p. 615)
barbed wire (p. 615)
free range (p. 615)
agribusiness (p. 619)
Miller & Lux (p. 620)
Buffalo Bill's Wild West show (p. 621)
frontier thesis (p. 622)

TIMELINE

◀ **1851** • First Treaty of Fort Laramie.

1862 • Homestead Act.
• Great Sioux Uprising (Santee Uprising).

1864 • Sand Creek Massacre.

1867 • Treaty of Medicine Lodge.

1868 • Second Treaty of Fort Laramie.

1869 • First transcontinental railroad completed.

1870 • Hunters begin to decimate bison herds.
• Henry Miller and Charles Lux develop agricultural empire in California.

1873 • "Big Bonanza" on Comstock Lode.

1874 • Discovery of gold in Black Hills.

1876 • Battle of the Little Big Horn.

1877 • Chief Joseph surrenders.
• Crazy Horse surrenders and is later arrested and killed.

1878 • Indian students enroll at Hampton Institute in Virginia.

1879 • Carlisle Indian School opens in Pennsylvania.
• More than fifteen thousand Exodusters move to Kansas.

REVIEW QUESTIONS

1. How did the slaughter of the bison contribute to the Plains Indians' removal to reservations? (pp. 593–603)

2. How did industrial technology change mining in Nevada? (pp. 603–11)

3. Why did many homesteaders find it difficult to acquire good land in the West? (pp. 612–21)

MAKING CONNECTIONS

1. Westward migration brought settlers into conflict with Native Americans. What was the U.S. government's policy toward Indians in the West, and how did it evolve over time? How did the Indians resist and survive white encroachment? In your answer, discuss the cultural and military features of the conflict.

2. The economic and industrial developments characteristic of the East after the Civil War also made their mark on the West. How did innovations in business and technology transform mining and agriculture in the West? In your answer, be sure to consider effects on production and the consequences for the lives of miners and agricultural laborers.

3. Settlers from all over the world came to the American West seeking their fortunes but found that opportunity was not equally available to all. In competition for work and land, why did Anglo-American settlers usually have the upper hand? How did legal developments contribute to this circumstance?

▶ For practice quizzes, a customized study plan, and other study tools, see the Online Study Guide at bedfordstmartins.com/roark.

1881 • Sitting Bull surrenders.

1882 • Chinese Exclusion Act.
• Indian Rights Association formed.

1883 • Buffalo Bill Cody begins touring.

1886 • Geronimo surrenders.

1886–1888 • Severe blizzards decimate cattle herds.

1887 • Dawes Allotment Act.

1889 • Rise of Ghost Dance.
• 2 million acres in Oklahoma opened for settlement.

1890 • Sitting Bull killed.
• Massacre at Wounded Knee, South Dakota.
• Gold discovered in Cripple Creek, Colorado.

1893 • Last land rush takes place in Oklahoma Territory.

1900 • Census finds 66 percent of population lives in rural areas, compared to 80 percent in 1870.

CAMPAIGN PINS, 1884
These gilt campaign pins from the election of 1884 show
Republican candidate James G. Blaine, on the right, thumbing his nose at Democratic candidate Grover Cleveland.
Styled by a contemporary journalist as "the vilest campaign ever waged," the 1884 race pitted Cleveland, who
had made his political reputation on his honest dealings,
against Blaine, who was tainted with charges of corruption. However, when the
Buffalo Telegraph revealed that the bachelor Cleveland had fathered an illegitimate
child, the tables turned, and Cleveland and his followers lost the high moral ground.
Perhaps this is why Blaine is portrayed in this mechanical pin as thumbing his nose
at Cleveland. His gesture proved premature; Cleveland squeaked past Blaine in a
close race. The gilt pins are a good symbol for Gilded Age politics—an era characterized by corruption and party strife.
Collection of Janice L. and David J. Frent.

Business and Politics in the Gilded Age

1870–1895

ONE NIGHT OVER DINNER, humorist and author Mark Twain and his friend Charles Dudley Warner teased their wives about the popular novels they read. When the two women challenged them to write something better, they set to work. Warner supplied the sentimental melodrama, while Twain "hurled in the facts." The result was a runaway best seller, uneven as fiction but offering a savage satire of the "get-rich-quick" era that forever after would be known by the book's title, *The Gilded Age* (1873).

Twain left no one unscathed in the novel—political hacks, Washington lobbyists, Wall Street financiers, small-town boosters, wildcat miners, and the "great putty-hearted public" that tolerated the plunder. Underneath the glitter of the Gilded Age, as Twain's title implied, lurked baser stuff. Twain had witnessed up close the corrupt partnership of business and politics in the administration of Ulysses S. Grant. Drawing on this experience, he described how a lobbyist could get an appropriation bill through Congress:

> Why the matter is simple enough. A Congressional appropriation costs money. Just reflect, for instance. A majority of the House Committee, say $10,000 apiece—$40,000; a majority of the Senate Committee, the same each—say $40,000; a little extra to one or two chairmen of one or two such committees, say $10,000 each—$20,000; and there's $100,000 of the money gone, to begin with. Then, seven male lobbyists, at $3,000 each—$21,000; one female lobbyist, $3,000; a high moral Congressman or Senator here and there—the high moral ones cost more, because they give tone to a measure—say ten of these at $3,000 each, is $30,000; then a lot of small fry country members who won't vote for anything whatever without pay—say twenty at $500 apiece, is $10,000 altogether; lot of jimcracks for Congressmen's wives and children—those go a long way—you can't spend too much money in that line—well, those things cost in a lump, say $10,000—along there somewhere;—and then comes your printed documents. . . . Oh, my dear sir, printing bills are destruction itself. Ours, so far amount to—let me see—. . . well, never mind the details, the total in clean numbers foots up $118,254.42 thus far!

In Twain's satire, Congress is for sale to the highest bidder. The unseemly intimacy between government and business meant that more often than not, senators, representatives, and even members of the executive branch were on the payroll of business interests, if not in their pockets. The corrupt interplay of business and politics raised serious questions about the health of American **democracy**.

The Gilded Age seemed to tarnish all who touched it. No one would learn that lesson better than Twain, who, even as he attacked it as an "era of

Mark Twain and *The Gilded Age*
Popular author Mark Twain (Samuel Langhorne Clemens) wrote acerbically about the excesses of the Gilded Age in his novel of that name written with Charles Dudley Warner and published in 1873. No one knew the meretricious lure of the era better than Twain, who succumbed to a get-rich-quick scheme that left him bankrupt.
Book: Beinecke Rare Book and Manuscript Library, Yale University; Photo: Newberry Library.

incredible rottenness," fell prey to its enticements. Born Samuel Langhorne Clemens, he grew up in a rough Mississippi River town, where he first became a journeyman printer and then a riverboat pilot. Taking the pen name Mark Twain, he moved west and gained fame chronicling mining booms in California and Nevada. In 1866, he came east to launch a career as an author, public speaker, and itinerant humorist. Twain played to packed houses, but his work was judged too vulgar for the genteel tastes of the time because he wrote about common people and used common language. His masterpiece, *The Adventures of Huckleberry Finn*, was banned in Boston when it appeared in 1884.

Huck Finn's creator eventually stormed the citadels of polite society, hobnobbing with the wealthy and living in increasingly expensive and elegant style. Succumbing to the money fever of his age, Twain plunged into one scheme after another in the hope of making millions. The Paige typesetting machine proved his downfall. Twain invested heavily in this elaborate invention that promised to mechanize typesetting. The idea was a good one; a competing invention, the Linotype,

eventually replaced hand type. The Paige machine, however, proved too complicated and temperamental to be practical. By the 1890s, Twain faced bankruptcy. Only the help of his friend Standard Oil millionaire Henry H. Rogers enabled him to begin his dogged climb out of debt.

Twain's tale was common in an age when the promise of wealth led as many to ruin as to riches. In the Gilded Age, fortunes were made and lost with dizzying frequency. Wall Street panics, like those in 1873 and 1893, periodically interrupted the boom times and plunged the country into economic depression. But with railroads and cities to be built and industry expanding on every level, the mood of the country remained buoyant.

The rise of industrialism in the United States and the interplay of business and politics strike the key themes in the Gilded Age. In the decades from 1870 to 1890, the transition from a rural, agricultural economy to urban industrialism, global in its reach, transformed American society. The growth of old industries and the creation of new ones, along with the rise of big business, signaled the coming of age of industrial capitalism. With new times came new economic and political issues. Old divisions engendered by sectionalism and slavery still influenced politics. But increasingly, economic issues such as the tariff and monetary policy shaped party politics. And as concern grew over the power of big business and the growing chasm between the rich and the poor, many Americans looked to the government for solutions.

Perhaps nowhere were the hopes and fears that industrialism inspired more evident than in the public's attitude toward the great business moguls of the day, men like Jay Gould, Andrew Carnegie, John D. Rockefeller, and J. P. Morgan. These larger-than-life figures not only dominated business but also sparked the popular imagination as the heroes and villains in the high drama of industrialization. At no other period in U.S. history would the industrial giants and the businesses they built (and sometimes wrecked) loom so large in American life.

Old Industries Transformed, New Industries Born

In the years following the Civil War, the scale and scope of American industry expanded dramatically. Old industries like iron transformed into modern industries typified by the behemoth U.S.

Steel. Discovery and invention stimulated new industries from oil refining to electric light and power. The expansion of the nation's rail system in the decades after the Civil War played the key role in the transformation of the American economy. New rail lines created a national market and fueled a new **consumer culture** that enabled businesses to expand from a regional to a nationwide scale. The railroads became America's first big business.

Jay Gould, Andrew Carnegie, John D. Rockefeller, and other business leaders pioneered new strategies to seize markets and consolidate power in the rising railroad, steel, and oil industries. Always with an eye to the main chance, these business tycoons set the tone in the get-rich-quick era of freewheeling capitalism that came to be called the Gilded Age.

Railroads: America's First Big Business

In the decades following the Civil War, the United States built the greatest railroad network in the world. The first transcontinental railroad was completed in 1869 when the tracks of the Union Pacific and Central Pacific railroads came together at Promontory Point, Utah, linking new markets in the West to the nation's economy. Between 1870 and 1880, the amount of track in the country doubled, and it nearly doubled again in the following decade. By 1900, the nation boasted more than 193,000 miles of railroad track—more than in all of Europe and Russia combined (Map 18.1, page 630).

To understand how the railroads developed and came to dominate American life, there is no better place to start than with the career of Jay Gould, who pioneered the expansion of America's railway system and became the era's most notorious speculator. Jason "Jay" Gould bought his first railroad before he turned twenty-five. It was only sixty-two miles long, in bad repair, and on the brink of failure, but within two years, he sold it at a profit of $130,000.

Gould, by his own account, knew little about railroads and cared less about their operation. The secretive Gould operated in the stock market like a shark, looking for vulnerable railroads, buying enough stock to take control, and threatening to undercut his competitors until they bought him out at a high profit. The railroads that fell into his hands fared badly and often went bankrupt. Gould's genius lay in cleverly buying and selling railroad stock, not in providing trans-

portation. In the 1880s, he moved to put together a second transcontinental railroad. To defend their interests, his competitors had little choice but to adopt his strategy of expansion and consolidation, which in turn encouraged railroad building and stimulated a national market.

The dramatic growth of the railroads created the country's first big business. Before the Civil War, even the largest textile mill in New England employed no more than 800 workers. In contrast, the Pennsylvania Railroad by the 1870s boasted a payroll of more than 55,000 workers. Capitalized at more than $400 million, the Pennsylvania Railroad constituted the largest private enterprise in the world.

The Republican Party, firmly entrenched in Washington in the wake of the Civil War, worked closely with business interests, subsidizing the transcontinental railroad system with **land grants** of a staggering 100 million acres of public land and $64 million in tax incentives and direct

Jay Gould as a Spider

In this 1885 political cartoon titled "Justice in the Web," artist Fredrick Burr Opper portrays Jay Gould as a hideous spider whose web, formed by Western Union telegraph lines, has entrapped "justice" through its monopoly of the telegraph industry. The telegraph, by transmitting coded messages across electric wire, formed the nervous system of the new industrial order. Gould, who controlled Western Union as well as the Erie Railroad, made his fortune by stock speculation. Images like this one fueled the public's distaste for Gould and made him, in his own words, "the most hated man in America."

Granger Collection.

JUSTICE IN THE WEB.

aid. (See "Global Comparison.") States and local communities joined the railroad boom, knowing that only those towns and villages along the tracks would grow and flourish. The combined federal and state giveaway amounted to more than 180 million acres, an area larger than Texas. The land grants diminished the amount of public land available to homesteaders and allowed the railroads to increase their profits by selling excess land to the settlers who followed the railroads west.

A revolution in communication accompanied and supported the growth of the railroads. The telegraph, developed by Samuel F. B. Morse,

marched across the continent alongside the railroad. By transmitting coded messages along electrical wire, the telegraph formed the "nervous system" of the new industrial order. Telegraph service quickly replaced Pony Express mail carriers in the West and transformed business by providing instantaneous communication. Again Jay Gould took the lead. In 1879, through stock manipulation, he seized control of Western Union, the company that monopolized the telegraph industry. By the end of the century, the telegraph carried 63 million messages a year and made it increasingly easy to move money around the world. Financiers in London and New York, Paris and

MAP 18.1   Railroad Expansion, 1870–1890

Railroad mileage nearly quadrupled between 1870 and 1890, with the greatest growth occurring in the trans-Mississippi West. New transcontinental lines—the Great Northern, Northern Pacific, Southern Pacific, and Atlantic and Pacific—were completed in the 1880s. Small feeder lines such as the Oregon Short Line and the Atchison, Topeka, and Santa Fe fed into the great transcontinental systems, knitting the nation together.

READING THE MAP: Where were most of the railroad lines located in 1870? What cities were the major railroad centers? What was the end point of the only western route?

CONNECTIONS: Why were so many rails laid between 1870 and 1890? How did the railroads affect the nation's economy?

FOR MORE HELP ANALYZING THIS MAP, see the map activity for this chapter in the Online Study Guide at bedfordstmartins.com/roark.

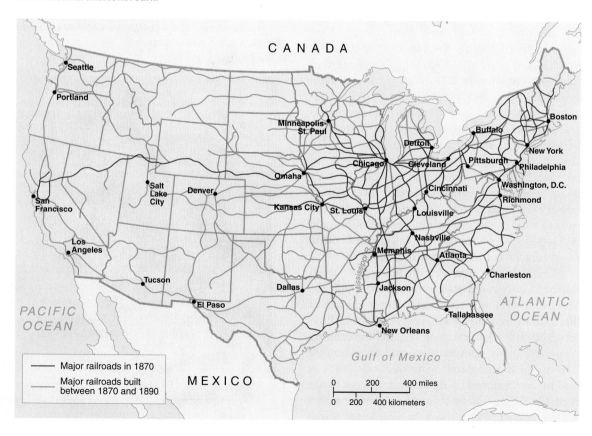

GLOBAL COMPARISON

Railroad Track Mileage, 1890

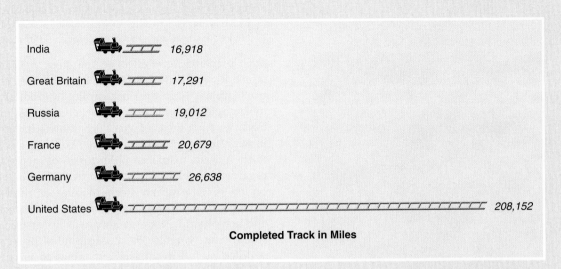

		Completed Track in Miles
India		16,918
Great Britain		17,291
Russia		19,012
France		20,679
Germany		26,638
United States		208,152

By 1850, the railway network in Great Britain was already well established, and most of the main lines in Germany had been built. France was slower to invest in railroads, but during the period 1850 to 1860, the government invested heavily in laying track, and the French soon caught up with, and then bypassed, their European neighbors. Russia's railway development experienced its greatest growth in the late nineteenth century. This growth was driven by the country's need to access its newly developing industrial regions and the vast natural resources of its far-flung territories in Asia. Like Russia, most of India's railroad growth occurred late in the century. This development was financed by the British, who were eager to tap the economic potential of their profitable overseas colony. By 1890, the United States had laid more railroad track than Britain, Germany, France, Russia, and India combined. Most of this growth occurred in the period 1870 to 1890, when railroad mileage in the United States almost quadrupled. The vast area of the United States and its western territories accounted for some of the disparity between railroad mileage here and that in Europe. After all, England, France, and Germany combined contained less land than the states east of the Mississippi River.

Brussels, could follow the markets on ticker tape and transfer funds by wire.

The railroads soon fell on hard times. Already by the 1870s, lack of planning led to overbuilding. On the eastern seaboard, railroads competed fiercely for business. A manufacturer in an area served by competing railroads could get substantially reduced shipping rates in return for promises of steady business. Because railroad owners lost money through this kind of competition, they tried to set up agreements, or "pools," to end cutthroat competition by dividing up territory and setting rates. But these informal gentlemen's agreements invariably failed because men like Jay Gould, intent on undercutting all competitors, refused to play by the rules.

Not all the early railroad builders proved as unscrupulous as Gould. James J. Hill built the

Great Northern Railroad and built it well. Entering the railroad business too late to benefit from land grants or subsidies, Hill had to plan carefully to maximize returns to his investors. As a result, the Great Northern, completed in 1893, became one of the few major railroads able to weather the depression that began that same year. In contrast, speculators like Gould could more accurately be called wreckers rather than builders. Through speculation, they ruined the Erie Railroad by gambling with its stock on Wall Street to line their own pockets. Novelist Charles Dudley Warner described how they operated:

> [They fasten upon] some railway that is prosperous, pays dividends, pays a liberal interest on its bonds, and has a surplus. They contrive to buy, no matter at what cost, a controlling interest in it, either in its stock or its management. Then

"The Curse of California"
Even when unprincipled magnates did not wreck the railroads, their enormous power made them a menace. In the West, the "Big Four" railroad builders—Collis P. Huntington, Charles Crocker, Leland Stanford, and Mark Hopkins—grew so powerful that critics claimed, not without justification, that the Southern Pacific Railroad held California in the grip of an "octopus." This political cartoon drawn by G. Frederick Keller appeared in 1882. Here the railroad trust is pictured as an octopus with its many tentacles controlling such financial interests as San Francisco's Nob Hill elite, farmers, the lumber industry, shipping, fruit growers, stage lines, mining, and the wine industry. Novelist Frank Norris later expanded on the theme in his 1901 best-selling novel, *The Octopus*.
University of California at Berkeley, Bancroft Library.

they absorb its surplus; they let it run down so that it pays no dividends and by-and-by cannot even pay its interest; then they squeeze the bondholders, who may be glad to accept anything that is offered out the wreck, and perhaps then they throw the property into the hands of a receiver, or consolidate it with some other road at a value enormously greater than it cost them in stealing it. Having in one way or another sucked it dry, they look around for another road.

Such machinations relied on the stock market, which played a key role in the growth of industrial capitalism. In the past, capital traditionally took tangible form in property, whether in land or in slaves. After the Civil War, corporate capitalism, in which companies incorporated and sold stock to the public, displaced older forms of business organization such as partnerships. Increasingly, capital took the form of stocks in railroads, mines, or ranches. The relationship between shares of stock and actual value, then as now, was never clear-cut. In the worst cases, unscrupulous brokers peddled stocks in nonexistent mines to buyers looking to get rich quick. But the volatility of the market and the manipulations of speculators meant that even shareholders in solid companies fell prey to boom-and-bust cycles in the stock market. As the scale and complexity of the financial system increased, the line between investment and speculation blurred, leading to the exuberant era of risk and speculation Twain skewered as the Gilded Age.

Discomfort with this new state of affairs, in which the nation's financial markets seemed more concerned with paper profits than with building tangible wealth, colored the public's reaction to speculators like Jay Gould. When he died in 1892, the press described Gould as "the world's richest man," estimating his fortune at more than $100 million. His competitor "Commodore" Cornelius Vanderbilt, who built the New York Central Railroad, judged Gould "the smartest man in America." But to the public, he was, as he himself admitted shortly before his death, "the most hated man in America."

Andrew Carnegie, Steel, and Vertical Integration

If Jay Gould was the man Americans loved to hate, Andrew Carnegie became one of America's heroes. Unlike Gould, for whom speculation was the game and wealth the goal, Carnegie turned his back on speculation and worked to build something enduring—Carnegie Steel, the biggest steel business in the world during the Gilded Age.

The growth of the steel industry proceeded directly from railroad building. The first railroads ran on iron rails, which cracked and broke with alarming frequency. Steel, both stronger and more flexible than iron, remained too expensive for use in rails until Englishman Henry Bessemer developed a way to make steel more cheaply from pig iron. Andrew Carnegie, among the first to champion the new "King Steel," came to dominate the emerging industry.

Carnegie, a Scottish immigrant, landed in New York in 1848 at the age of twelve. He rose from a job cleaning bobbins in a textile factory to become one of the richest men in America. Before he died, he gave away more than $300 million, most notably to public libraries. His generosity, combined with his own rise from poverty, burnished his public image. But Carnegie had a darker side: He was a harsh taskmaster who made nearly inhuman demands on his employees.

When Carnegie was a teenager, his skill as a telegraph operator caught the attention of Tom Scott, superintendent of the Pennsylvania Railroad. Scott hired Carnegie, soon promoted him, and lent him the money for his first foray into Wall Street investment. A millionaire before his thirtieth birthday, Carnegie turned away from speculation and struck out on his own to reshape the iron and steel industry. "My preference was always manufacturing," he wrote. "I wished to make something tangible." By applying the lessons of cost accounting and efficiency that he had learned from twelve years with the Pennsylvania Railroad, Carnegie turned steel into the nation's first manufacturing big business.

In 1872, Andrew Carnegie acquired one hundred acres in Braddock, Pennsylvania, on the outskirts of Pittsburgh, convenient to two railroad lines and fronted by the Monongahela River, a natural highway to Pittsburgh and the Ohio River and to the coal and iron mines farther north. There Carnegie built the largest, most up-to-date Bessemer steel plant in the world and began turning out steel at a furious rate. At that time, steelmakers produced about 70 tons a week. Within two decades, Carnegie's blast furnaces poured out an incredible 10,000 tons a week (Figure 18.1). He soon cut the cost of making rails by more than half, from $58 to $25 a ton. His formula for success was simple: "Cut the prices, scoop the market, run the mills full; watch the costs and profits will take care of themselves." And they did. By 1900, Carnegie Steel earned $40 million a year.

To guarantee the lowest costs and the maximum output, Carnegie pioneered a system of business organization called **vertical integration**. All aspects of the business were under Carnegie's control—from the mining of iron ore, to its transport on the Great Lakes, to the production of steel. Vertical integration, in the words of one observer, meant that "from the moment these crude stuffs were dug out of the earth until they flowed in a stream of liquid steel in the ladles, there was never a price, profit, or royalty paid to any outsider."

> When he died in 1892, the press described Gould as "the world's richest man," estimating his fortune at more than $100 million. But to the public, he was, as he himself admitted shortly before his death, "the most hated man in America."

FIGURE 18.1 Iron and Steel Production, 1870–1900

Iron and steel production in the United States grew from nearly none in 1870 to 10 million tons a year by 1900. The secrets to the great increase in steel production were the use of the Bessemer process and vertical integration, pioneered by Andrew Carnegie. By 1900, Carnegie's mills alone produced more steel than all of Great Britain. With corporate consolidation after 1900, the rate of growth in steel proved even more spectacular.

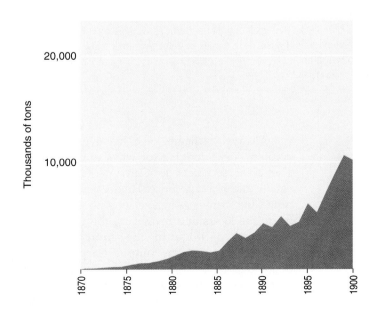

Andrew Carnegie
"The man who dies rich . . . dies disgraced," Andrew Carnegie asserted. Carnegie gave away more than $300 million before he died in 1919. Convinced that the rich would spend money more wisely than the poor (who might squander it on beer or meat), he argued in his "Gospel of Wealth" that the wealthy should act as stewards for the poor. Public libraries were among his favorite philanthropies; he contributed to the building of nearly 2,500. This cartoon from *Harper's Weekly* shows him playing with building blocks that spell out "library." But as workers complained, after working twelve hours a day, six days a week in Carnegie's steel mills, they had little time to visit a library.
Harper's Weekly, April 11, 1903.

Always Carnegie kept his eyes on the account books, looking for ways to cut costs. The great productivity Carnegie encouraged came at a high price. He deliberately pitted his managers against one another, firing the losers and rewarding the winners with a share in the company. Workers achieved the output Carnegie demanded by enduring low wages, dangerous working conditions, and twelve-hour days six days a week. One worker,

commenting on the contradiction between Carnegie's generous philanthropy in endowing public libraries and his tightfisted labor policy, observed, "After working twelve hours, how can a man go to a library?"

By 1900, Andrew Carnegie had become the best-known manufacturer in the nation, and the age of iron had yielded to an age of steel. Steel from Carnegie's mills supported the elevated trains in New York and Chicago, formed the skeleton of the Washington Monument, supported the first steel bridge to span the Mississippi, and girded America's first skyscrapers. Carnegie steel armored the naval fleet that helped make the United States a world power. As a captain of industry, Carnegie's only rival was the titan of the oil industry, John D. Rockefeller.

John D. Rockefeller, Standard Oil, and the Trust

Edwin Drake's discovery of oil in Pennsylvania in 1859 sent thousands rushing to the oil fields in search of "black gold." In the days before the automobile and gasoline, crude oil was refined into lubricating oil for machinery and kerosene for lamps, the major source of lighting in nineteenth-century houses before the invention of gas lamps or electric lighting. The amount of capital needed to buy or build an oil refinery in the 1860s and 1870s remained relatively low—less than $25,000, or roughly what it cost to lay one mile of railroad track. With start-up costs so low, the new petroleum industry experienced riotous competition among many small refineries. Ultimately, John D. Rockefeller and his Standard Oil Company succeeded in controlling nine-tenths of the oil-refining business.

Rockefeller grew up the son of a shrewd Yankee who peddled quack cures for cancer. Under his father's rough tutelage, he learned how to drive a hard bargain. "I trade with the boys and skin 'em and just beat 'em every time I can," "Big Bill" Rockefeller boasted. "I want to make 'em sharp." John D. learned his lessons well. In 1865, at the age of twenty-five, he controlled the largest oil refinery in Cleveland. Like a growing number of business owners, Rockefeller abandoned partnership or single proprietorship to embrace the corporation as the business structure best suited to maximize profit and minimize personal liability. In 1870, he incorporated his oil business, founding the Standard Oil Company, a behemoth so huge it served as the precursor not only of today's ExxonMobil but also of Amoco, Chevron, Sunoco, and Conoco.

As the largest refiner in Cleveland, Rockefeller demanded secret rebates from the railroads in exchange for his steady business. Rebates enabled Rockefeller to drive out his competitors through predatory pricing. The railroads, facing the pressures of cutthroat competition, needed Rockefeller's business so badly that they gave him a share of the rates that his competitors paid. A Pennsylvania Railroad official later confessed that Rockefeller extracted such huge rebates that the railroad, which could not risk losing his business, sometimes ended up paying him to transport Standard's oil. Secret deals, predatory pricing, and rebates enabled Rockefeller to undercut his competitors and pressure competing refiners to sell out or face ruin. Because Rockefeller operated under the cloak of secrecy, the unsuspecting public knew nothing about the extent of Standard Oil's holdings until a New York State inquiry in 1888 revealed the reach of Rockefeller's oil empire.

To gain legal standing for Standard Oil's secret deals, Rockefeller in 1882 pioneered a new form of corporate structure—the **trust**. The trust differed markedly from Carnegie's vertical approach in steel. Instead of attempting to control all aspects of the oil business, from the well to the consumer, Rockefeller used **horizontal integration** to control the refining process. Several trustees held stock in various refinery companies "in trust" for Standard's stockholders. This elaborate stock

---

"What a Funny Little Government"

The power wielded by John D. Rockefeller and the Standard Oil Company is captured in this political cartoon by Horace Taylor, which appeared in the January 22, 1900, issue of the *Verdict*. Rockefeller is pictured holding the White House and the Treasury Department in the palm of his hand, while in the background the U.S. Capitol has been converted into an oil refinery. Rockefeller and the company he ran held so much power that many feared democracy itself was threatened in the Gilded Age.
Collection of The New-York Historical Society.

READING THE IMAGE: According to Horace Taylor, what kind of relationship did John D. Rockefeller have with the federal government? What benefits did he accrue from it?

CONNECTIONS: How much influence did industrialists such as Rockefeller exert over the national government in the late nineteenth century?

FOR MORE HELP ANALYZING THIS IMAGE, see the visual activity for this chapter in the Online Study Guide at bedfordstmartins.com/roark.

Ida M. Tarbell

Ida M. Tarbell, shown at her desk in 1898, served as managing editor at *McClure's Magazine*, where her "History of the Standard Oil Company" ran in serial form for three years. A copy of one of the magazine's covers is shown in the inset. Tarbell grew up in the Pennsylvania oil region and knew firsthand how Standard Oil forced out competitors. Her revelations of the ruthless practices that Rockefeller used to seize control of the oil-refining industry convinced readers that it was time for economic and political reforms to curb the power of big business.

Tarbell: Courtesy of The Ida Tarbell Collection, Pelletier Library, Allegheny College; Magazine: Special Collections, The Ida Tarbell Collection, Pelletier Library, Allegheny College.

swap allowed the trustees to coordinate policy among the refineries, giving Rockefeller a virtual **monopoly** on the oil-refining business. The Standard Oil trust, valued at more than $70 million, paved the way for trusts in sugar, whiskey, matches, and many other products.

When the federal government responded to public pressure to outlaw the trust as a violation of free trade, Standard Oil changed tactics and reorganized as a **holding company**. Instead of stockholders in competing companies acting through trustees to set prices and determine territories, the holding company simply brought competing companies under one central administration. No longer technically separate businesses, they could act in concert without violating antitrust laws that forbade companies from forming "combinations in restraint of trade."

As Standard Oil's empire grew, Rockefeller ended the independence of the refinery operators and closed inefficient plants. Next he moved to control sources of crude oil and took charge of the transportation and marketing of petroleum products. By the 1890s, Standard Oil ruled more than 90 percent of the oil business, employed 100,000 people, and was the biggest, richest, most feared, and most admired business organization in the world.

John D. Rockefeller enjoyed enormous success in business, but he was not well liked by the public. Before he died in 1937 at the age of ninety-eight, Rockefeller had become the country's first billionaire. But despite his modest habits, his pious Baptist faith, and his many charitable gifts, he never shared in the public affection that Carnegie enjoyed. Editor and journalist Ida M. Tarbell's "History of the Standard Oil Company," which ran for three years (1902–1905) in serial form in *McClure's Magazine*, largely shaped the public's harsh view of Rockefeller. Tarbell had grown up in the Pennsylvania oil region, and her father had owned one of the small refineries gobbled up by Standard Oil. Her devastatingly thorough history chronicled the methods Rockefeller had used to take over the oil industry. Publicly, Rockefeller refused to respond to her allegations, although in private he dubbed her "Miss Tarball." "If I step on that worm I will call attention to it," he explained. "If I ignore it, it will disappear." Yet by the time Tarbell finished publishing her story, Rockefeller slept with a loaded revolver by his bed in fear of would-be assassins. Standard Oil and the man who created it had become the symbol of heartless monopoly. (See "Documenting the American Promise," page 638.)

Mass Marketing, Advertising, and Consumer Culture

By the 1880s, the railroad made possible a national market for consumer goods. Manufacturers integrated methods of mass production with mass distribution to achieve the first large-scale consumer businesses in the United States. These enterprises came to dominate many of the nation's most vital industries. Successful organizational changes in the meatpacking and food processing industries enabled manufacturers to reap huge profits from products like hot dogs and ketchup.

What Carnegie did for steel, Gustavus Swift did for meatpacking. Until well after the Civil

War, cattle moved out of the West on the hoof to be slaughtered by local butchers. Swift, who first visited Chicago in 1875 to buy beef for a Boston company, realized that it would be more efficient to slaughter cattle in the Midwest and transport the meat to the East in refrigerated railway cars. He put together a vertically integrated meatpacking business that controlled the entire process—from the purchase of cattle for slaughter to the mass distribution of meat to retailers and consumers. Through high quality, low prices, and effective advertising, Swift won over consumers who at first worried about buying meat from anyone but the local butcher. The success of Swift & Company led the older meatpackers, including Philip Armour, to build similarly integrated businesses to compete.

Swift's transformation of the beef industry had far-reaching consequences. In the West, it stimulated the rise of commercial cattle ranching, which in turn led to overgrazing and contributed to the near extinction of the bison and the ultimate conquest of Native American tribes (see chapter 17). A national market created a complicated web, an intricate tangle of competition and dependency.

Just as Swift combined mass production with mass distribution in meatpacking, Henry John Heinz transformed the processed food industry. In 1880, Heinz, struggling to recover from bankruptcy after the depression of the 1870s, produced pickles, sauces, and condiments in his factory outside Pittsburgh. By adopting new, more efficient methods of canning and bottling, he built a network of sales offices to advertise his

Heinz Company Advertisement
Trading cards were an important form of early advertising. Agents handed them out to retailers and customers. In this early card advertising the H. J. Heinz Company, women wearing aprons and caps bottle pickles.
Picture Research Consultants & Archives.

READING THE IMAGE: How accurately do you think the ad portrays the Heinz plant?
CONNECTIONS: How did ads like this one work to create demand for a product?

FOR MORE HELP ANALYZING THIS IMAGE, see the visual activity for this chapter in the Online Study Guide at bedfordstmartins.com/roark.

Rockefeller and His Critics

No one inspired the nation's fear of industrial consolidation more than John D. Rockefeller, creator of the Standard Oil trust. To many Americans, Rockefeller and "the sovereign state of Standard Oil" came to represent a danger to democracy itself because of the secretive methods and enormous political influence of the corporation and its founder.

DOCUMENT 1
"The Smokeless Rebate," from Henry Demarest Lloyd's *Wealth against Commonwealth*, 1894

As early as 1881, Henry Demarest Lloyd introduced Rockefeller to a national audience by attacking Standard Oil and its founder in "The Story of a Great Monopoly," published in the February issue of Atlantic Monthly. *The public snapped up the exposé—the issue went through six printings. In 1894, Lloyd published* Wealth against Commonwealth, *a full-scale exposé of the company. To avoid charges of libel, Lloyd*

used no names, but readers knew he referred to Rockefeller and Standard Oil. Here Lloyd describes how Rockefeller used illegal railroad rebates to best his competitors.

That entirely modern social arrangement—the private ownership of [railroads]—has introduced a new weapon into business warfare which means universal dominion to him who will use it with an iron hand.

This weapon is the rebate, smokeless, noiseless, invisible, of extraordinary range, and the deadliest gun known to commercial warfare. It is not a lawful weapon. . . . It has to be used secretly. All the rates [Rockefeller] . . . got were a secret between himself and the railroads. "It has never been otherwise," testified one of the oil combination.

The smokeless rebate makes the secret of success in business to be not manufacture, but manufracture—breaking down with a strong hand the true makers of things. To those who can get the rebate it makes no difference who does the digging,

building, mining, making, producing the million forms of wealth they covet for themselves. They need only get control of the roads. . . . Builders, not of manufactories, but of privileges; inventors only of schemes . . . , contrivers, not of competition, but of ways to tax the property of their competitors into their pockets. They need not make money; they can take it from those who have made it.

SOURCE: Henry Demarest Lloyd, *Wealth against Commonwealth* (New York: Harper & Brothers, 1894), 474–75, 488.

DOCUMENT 2
Ida M. Tarbell, "The Oil War of 1872"

Editor and journalist Ida Minerva Tarbell, whose "History of the Standard Oil Company" ran for three years (1902–1905) in serial form in McClure's Magazine, *proved Rockefeller's most damaging critic. Tarbell grew up in the Pennsylvania oil region; her father had owned a small refinery gobbled up by Standard Oil. In a devastatingly thorough history, she chronicled the underhanded methods Rockefeller used to gain control of the oil-refining industry. Here she portrays a critical chapter in the history of Standard Oil: In 1879, Rockefeller's first attempt to consolidate*

fifty-seven varieties and sell them across the nation. To ensure a steady flow of vegetables and other foodstuffs, he created a large buying and storing organization to contract with local farmers. By 1888, Heinz was rich, and ketchup had become an American staple. Using similar methods, other food processors, including Quaker Oats, Campbell Soup, and Borden, coordinated mass production with mass distribution to produce low-priced, packaged consumer goods for the national market.

The Gilded Age witnessed the rise of a mass consumer culture. The same economic transfor-

mations that made life difficult for ordinary workers paradoxically helped them as consumers. Mass production slashed prices and made available a wide array of new products, from Coca-Cola to kerosene. Although the meager pay of many workers meant a struggle to make ends meet, the more comfortable middle class could choose from a wide array of goods, including new products such as Gillette safety razors, Duke cigarettes, and Kodak cameras.

Advertising played a vital role. Just as the railroad made possible a national market, advertising stimulated the rise of a new consumer culture. Ad-

the oil industry through the use of illegal rebates had failed.

If Mr. Rockefeller had been an ordinary man the outburst of popular contempt and suspicion which suddenly poured on his head would have thwarted and crushed him. But he was no ordinary man. He had the powerful imagination to see what might be done with the oil business if it could be centered in his hands—the intelligence to analyze the problem into its elements and to find the key to control. He had the essential element to all great achievement, a steadfastness to a purpose once conceived which nothing can crush. The Oil Regions might rage, call him a conspirator and those who sold to him traitors; the railroads might withdraw their contracts and the legislature annul his charter; undisturbed and unresting he kept at this great purpose. . . .

He got a rebate. . . . How much less a rate than $1.25 Mr. Rockefeller had before the end of April the writer does not know. Of course the rate was secret and he probably understood now, as he had not two months before, how essential it was that he keep it secret. His task was more difficult now, for he had an enemy active, clamorous, contemptuous, whose suspicions had reached that acute point where they could believe nothing but evil of him—the producers and independents of the Oil Regions. . . .

They believed in independent effort—every man for himself and fair play for all. They wanted competition, loved open fight. They considered that all business should be done openly—that railways were bound as public carriers to give equal rates—that any combination which favored one firm or one locality at the expense of another was unjust and illegal. . . .

Those theories which the body of oil men held as vital and fundamental Mr. Rockefeller and his associates either did not comprehend or were deaf to. This lack of comprehension by many men of what seems to other men to be the most obvious principles of justice is not rare. Many men who are widely known as good, share it. Mr. Rockefeller was "good." There was no more faithful Baptist in Cleveland than he. Every enterprise of that church he had supported liberally from youth. He gave to its poor. He visited its sick. He wept with its suffering. Moreover, he gave unostentatiously to many outside charities of whose worthiness he was satisfied. He was simple and frugal in his habits. He never went to the theater, never drank wine. He was a devoted husband, and he gave much time to the training of his children. . . . Yet he was willing to strain every nerve to obtain for himself special and illegal privileges from the railroads which were bound to ruin every man in the oil business not sharing them with him. Religious emotion and sentiments of charity, propriety and self-denial seem to have taken the place in him of notions of justice and regard for the rights of others.

SOURCE: From pages 77–79 in *Muckraking: Three Landmark Articles* by Ellen F. Fitzpatrick, ed. Copyright © 1994. Reprinted with permission of St. Martin's Press. Originally published in *McClure's Magazine*, January 1903.

QUESTIONS FOR ANALYSIS AND DEBATE

1. Henry Demarest Lloyd and Ida Tarbell agree that Rockefeller gained control of the oil industry through illegal methods. What was his primary weapon, and how did it operate?

2. Compare Lloyd's style to that of Tarbell. Which is more effective and why? Was either one of these journalists an impartial observer?

3. Rockefeller never responded to his critics. Do you think Rockefeller's silence was a good strategy? Why or why not?

vances in printing enabled magazines and newspapers to subsidize their costs by selling advertising. By the 1870s, more than eight thousand newspapers circulated in the United States, and many magazines reached a nationwide audience at the cost of just five cents an issue. The *Ladies' Home Journal* boasted half a million subscribers in the 1880s. In its pages, advertisements, sprinkled among the articles and advice, tempted readers to buy new products such as Jell-O, Uneeda biscuits, and Hershey chocolate bars. An essential part of the consumer culture, advertising turned the old law of supply and demand on its head by enticing people to buy things they did not need or had never needed before. Electric lights and telephones soon numbered among the new products Americans demanded.

New Inventions: The Telephone and Electricity

Although many Americans disliked and distrusted industrial giants such as Gould and Rockefeller, they admired inventors. The second half of the nineteenth century was an age of invention. Men like Thomas Alva Edison and

Alexander Graham Bell became folk heroes. But no matter how dramatic the inventors or the inventions, the new electric and telephone industries pioneered by Edison and Bell soon eclipsed their inventors and fell under the control of bankers and industrialists.

Alexander Graham Bell came to America from Scotland at the age of twenty-four with a passion to find a way to teach the deaf to speak (his wife and mother were deaf). Instead, he developed a way to transmit voice over wire—the telephone. Bell's invention astounded the world when he demonstrated it at the Philadelphia Centennial Exposition in 1876. Dumbfounded by the display, the emperor of Brazil cried out, "My God, it talks!" In 1880, Bell's company, American Bell, pioneered "long lines" (long-distance telephone service), creating American Telephone and Telegraph (AT&T) as a subsidiary. In 1900, AT&T became the parent company of the system as a whole, controlling Western Electric, which manufactured and installed the equipment, and coordinating the Bell regional divisions. This complicated organizational structure meant that Americans could communicate not only locally but also across the country. And unlike a telegraph message, which had to be written out and taken to a telegraph station, sent over the wire, and then delivered by hand to the recipient, the telephone connected both parties immediately and privately. Bell's invention proved a boon to business, contributing to speed and efficiency. The number of telephones soared, reaching 310,000 in 1895 and more than 1.5 million in 1900.

Even more than Alexander Graham Bell, inventor Thomas Alva Edison embodied the old-fashioned virtues of Yankee ingenuity and rugged individualism that Americans most admired. A self-educated dynamo, he worked twenty hours a day in his laboratory in Menlo Park, New Jersey, vowing to turn out "a minor invention every ten days and a big thing every six months or so." He almost made good on his promise. At the height of his career, he averaged a patent every eleven days and invented such "big things" as the phonograph, the motion picture camera, and the filament for the incandescent lightbulb.

Edison, in competition with George W. Westinghouse, pioneered the use of electricity as an energy source. (See "The Promise of Technology," page 642.) By the late nineteenth century, electricity had become a part of American urban life. It powered trolley cars and lighted factories, homes, and office buildings. Indeed, electricity became so prevalent in urban life that it symbolized the city, whose bright lights contrasted with rural America, left largely in the dark because private enterprise judged it not profitable enough to run electric lines to outlying farms and ranches.

While Americans thrilled to the new electric cities and the changes wrought by inventors, the day of the inventor quietly yielded to the heyday of the corporation. In 1892, the electric industry consolidated. Reflecting a nationwide trend in business, Edison General Electric dropped the name of its inventor, becoming simply General Electric (GE). For years, an embittered Edison refused to set foot inside a GE building. General Electric could afford to overlook the slight. A prime example of the trend toward business consolidation taking place in the 1890s, GE soon dominated the market.

Notable American Inventions 1865–1899

1865	Railroad sleeping car
1867	Typewriter
1868	Railroad refrigerator car
1870	Stock ticker
1874	Barbed wire
1876	Telephone
1877	Phonograph
1879	Electric lightbulb
1882	Electric fan
1885	Adding machine
1886	Coca-Cola
1888	Kodak camera
1890	Electric chair
1891	Zipper
1895	Safety razor
1896	Electric stove
1899	Tape recorder

REVIEW   How did John D. Rockefeller gain control of 90 percent of the oil-refining business by 1890?

From Competition to Consolidation

Even as Rockefeller and Carnegie built their empires, the era of the "robber barons," as they were dubbed by their detractors, was drawing to a close. Increasingly, businesses replaced partnerships and sole proprietorships with the anonymous corporate structure that would come to dominate the twentieth century. At the same time, mergers led to the creation of huge new corporations.

Banks and financiers played a key role in this consolidation, so much so that the decades at the turn of the twentieth century can be characterized as a period of **finance capitalism**— investment sponsored by banks and bankers. When the depression that followed the panic of 1893 bankrupted many businesses, bankers stepped in to bring order and to reorganize major industries. During these years, a new social philosophy based on the theories of naturalist Charles Darwin helped to justify consolidation and to inhibit state or federal regulation of business. A **conservative** Supreme Court further frustrated attempts to control business by consistently declaring unconstitutional legislation designed to regulate railroads or to outlaw trusts and monopolies.

J. P. Morgan and Finance Capitalism

John Pierpont Morgan, the preeminent finance capitalist of the late nineteenth century, loathed competition and sought whenever possible to eliminate it by substituting consolidation and central control. Morgan's passion for order made him the architect of business mergers. The son of a prominent banker, J. P. Morgan inherited along with his wealth the stern business code of the old-fashioned merchant bankers, men who valued character and reputation. Aloof and silent, Morgan looked down on the climbers and the speculators with a haughtiness that led his rivals to call him "Jupiter," after the ruler of the Roman gods. At the turn of the twentieth century, he dominated American banking, exerting an influence so powerful that his critics charged he controlled a vast "money trust."

Morgan acted as a power broker in the reorganization of the railroads and the creation of industrial giants such as General Electric and U.S. Steel. When the railroads fell on hard times in the 1890s, he used his access to capital to rescue embattled, wrecked, and ruined companies. Morgan quickly took over the struggling railroads and moved to eliminate competition by creating what he called "a community of interest" among the managers he handpicked. By the time he finished reorganizing the railroads, Morgan had concentrated the nation's rail lines in the hands of a few directors who controlled two-thirds of the nation's track.

Banker control of the railroads rationalized, or coordinated, the industry. But stability came at a high price. To keep investors happy and to guarantee huge profits from the sale of stock, Morgan heavily "watered" the stock of the railroads, issuing more shares than the assets of the company warranted. J. P. Morgan & Co. made millions of dollars from commissions and from blocks of stock acquired through reorganization. The flagrant overcapitalization created by the watered stock hurt the railroads in the long run, saddling them with enormous debt. Equally harmful was the management style of the Morgan directors. Bankers, not railroad men, they aimed at short-term profit and discouraged the continued technological and organizational innovation needed to run the railroads effectively.

In 1898, Morgan moved into the steel industry, directly challenging Andrew Carnegie. Morgan supervised the mergers of several smaller steel companies, which soon expanded from the manufacture of finished goods to compete head-to-head with Carnegie in steel production. The pugnacious Carnegie cabled his partners in the summer of 1900: "Action essential: crisis has arrived . . . have no fear as to the result; victory certain."

The press trumpeted news of the impending fight between the feisty Scot and the haughty Wall Street banker, but what the papers called the "battle of the giants" in the end proved little more than the wily maneuvering of two businessmen so adept that even today it is difficult to say who won. For all his belligerence, the sixty-six-year-old Carnegie yearned to retire to Skibo Castle, his home in Scotland. He may well have welcomed Morgan's bid for power. Morgan, who disdained haggling, agreed to pay Carnegie's asking price, $480 million (the equivalent of about $9.6 billion in today's currency). According to legend, when Carnegie later teased Morgan, saying that he should have asked $100 million more, Morgan replied, "You would have got it if you had."

Morgan's acquisition of Carnegie Steel signaled the passing of one age and the arrival of

> Aloof and silent, Morgan looked down on the climbers and the speculators with a haughtiness that led his rivals to call him "Jupiter," after the ruler of the Roman gods.

Electrifying America: The War of the Currents

In the summer of 1882, J. P. Morgan's brownstone at 219 Madison Avenue in New York City blazed with light, from the servants' quarters to Morgan's sumptuous paneled library. An early convert to electricity, Morgan had hired inventor Thomas Alva Edison to wire his home with 385 electric lightbulbs, making it the first private residence in the nation to boast electric lighting. An engineer visited daily to start the generator housed in the basement. When the lamp in Morgan's library short-circuited and set his desk on fire, the engineer promptly fixed the problem. Morgan, his faith in electricity restored, invested heavily in Edison's company and later consolidated the industry, forming General Electric in 1892.

No industry that developed in the years following the Civil War faced a more difficult set of problems than electric light and power. Edison patented a filament for the incandescent lightbulb in 1879, ushering in the age of electricity. But how was he to sell his wonderful invention? "Customers did not exist," one electrical manager confessed. "They had to be created." And before Edison could begin electrifying the nation's homes, he faced the enormous task of developing an integrated system of conductors, power stations, generators, lamps, and electric machines to service and make use of the new technology. Because electricity was so technically complex, it created new skilled jobs for electricians and linemen and a new profession—electrical engineer.

Despite the hurdles Edison faced in marketing electricity, the public quickly recognized the superiority of his product. Incandescent bulbs gave a clear, even light—not flickering like candles, not smoking like kerosene lamps, not emitting odor or eating up oxygen like gas lamps. With no wick to trim or smoky globes to clean, electricity promised, in Edison's words, "the healthiest lights possible." At first, businesses and wealthy customers who wanted electric lighting had to install stand-alone generators, like the one in Morgan's basement. To bring electric lighting to the nation's homes and offices, Edison worked steadily to build power stations to provide electric current, opening a station on Pearl Street in lower Manhattan in 1882 that soon lighted Wall Street and newspaper row. By 1887, he had 121 central stations built or in the works. But Edison's system had one major flaw: It relied on direct current (DC), which could reach only a square mile from the power station. To overcome this obstacle, George W. Westinghouse, the inventor and manufacturer of the air brake for trains, experimented with alternating current (AC), which could travel much greater distances. Alternating current already powered the huge outdoor arc lights that lit up Broadway, making it the Great White Way. Westinghouse determined to use AC for indoor lighting, and in 1886 he formed his own electric company, which soon challenged Edison's.

The competition touched off the "war of the electric currents." Edison fired the first salvo in 1888 when he published a pamphlet bearing the ominous title *WARNING!* Alternating current, he claimed, "jeopardizes life." He went on to detail the gruesome deaths of workers killed by high-voltage AC. Low-voltage DC wires, Edison pointed out, "may be grasped by the naked hand." Edison declared war on Westinghouse, arguing that low-voltage, copper DC wires buried underground provided the only safe electricity for consumers.

A month after Edison published his *WARNING!* pamphlet, a young boy died after he playfully grabbed an electric wire swinging from a pole on East Broadway in New York City. The next month witnessed the death of a lineman for an arc light company who failed to wear heavy gloves when handling a wire. The tangle of wires that festooned the streets of the city's commercial districts provided electricity for telegraphs and telephones and powered the high-voltage arc lights used for outdoor lighting. In the legendary blizzard of 1888, New York City's electric lines collapsed under the weight of ice and snow, sparking and causing fires. In the months that followed, the tabloid press trumpeted accounts of "death by wire," and readers who warily looked up at the web of wires overhead suddenly saw not simply an eyesore but a peril to public safety.

Not content merely to attack AC, Edison worked to get it outlawed, launching a massive public relations campaign to discredit Westinghouse. He found an eager ally in Harold Brown, an obscure scientist who demonstrated the deadly effects of AC in grisly public experiments on dogs, horses, and most infamously a wayward circus elephant. The press dubbed the deaths *electrocution*.

In his zeal to attack Westinghouse and his "deadly current," Edison agreed to provide an "electric chair" to the New York State prison system as a modern alternative to the gallows. Westinghouse, appalled by the invention, refused to have anything to do with the "horrible experiment." Edison finagled a secondhand Westinghouse AC alternator to power the chair and quipped that criminals would be "Westinghoused." In 1890, New York conducted its first execution at Auburn Prison using the electric chair. The *New York Times* described the death as "an awful botch" (the condemned man had to be given a second jolt, and the stench of burning flesh sickened the reporter). "It has been a brutal affair," Westinghouse wrote to a friend. "They could have done it better with an axe." But Edison gloated. Once customers associated electrocution with Westinghouse, he reasoned, they would think twice before installing AC current in their homes.

Despite his campaign to discredit Westinghouse, Edison lost the war of the currents. Cities clamoring for electricity found that Westinghouse's AC, with its longer range and expandable capacity, served their needs much better than Edison's DC. Unfazed by Edison's bad publicity, Westinghouse steadily continued to expand his market. By 1891, more than 1,000 AC central stations had been built, compared to only 202 DC stations. Cities including New Orleans, Birmingham, Grand Rapids, Richmond, and Buffalo contracted for electric light and power, and increasingly Westinghouse captured the market. In a major coup, he beat out Edison winning the contract to electrify the

AN UNRESTRAINED DEMON.

Fears of Electricity

Published at the height of the "war of the currents," which Thomas Edison waged against George Westinghouse's use of alternating current (AC), this 1889 cartoon shows the dangers of high-voltage alternating current used in outdoor arc lights in the nation's cities. Innocent pedestrians are electrocuted by the tangle of wires; a woman swoons, presumably as a result of the buzzing current; a horse and driver have collapsed; and a policeman runs for help. The skull in the wires attached to the electric lightbulb warns that this new technology is deadly. Both an urban sophisticate in a top hat and a cowboy in boots have succumbed to the deadly wires. Edison's attempt to frighten users away from Westinghouse did not work. Although the direct current Edison championed was less deadly to handle, it could reach only a one-mile radius from a power station. Cities that wanted electric lighting found Westinghouse's system less expensive and better suited to their needs. Granger Collection.

World's Columbian Exposition in Chicago in 1893.

Edison belatedly admitted the superiority of AC, and in the 1890s General Electric converted to high-voltage current. The American Institute of Electrical Engineers in 1912 awarded George Westinghouse its highest honor, the Edison Medal for meritorious achievement, without a trace of irony. The award acknowledged that both Westinghouse, the businessman, and Edison, the inventor, played a key role in developing the nation's electric light and power industry.

another. Carnegie represented the old entrepreneurial order, Morgan the new corporate world. The banker quickly moved to pull together Carnegie's chief competitors to form a huge new corporation, United States Steel, known today as USX. Created in 1901 and capitalized at $1.4 billion, U.S. Steel was the largest corporation in the world. Yet for all its size, it did not hold a monopoly in the steel industry. Significant small competitors, such as Bethlehem Steel, remained independent, creating a competitive system called an **oligopoly**, in which several companies control production. The smaller manufacturers simply followed the lead of U.S. Steel in setting prices and dividing the market so that each company held a comfortable share. Many other industries, such as meatpacking, also functioned as oligopolies. Although oligopoly did not entirely eliminate competition, it did effectively blunt it.

When J. P. Morgan died in 1913, his estate totaled $68 million, not counting an estimated $50 million in art treasures. Andrew Carnegie, who gave away more than $300 million before his death six years later, is said to have quipped, "And to think he was not a rich man!" But Carnegie's gibe missed the mark. The quest for power, not wealth, had motivated J. P. Morgan, and his power could best be measured not in the millions he owned but in the billions he controlled. Even more than Carnegie or Rockefeller, Morgan left his stamp on the twentieth century and formed the model for corporate consolidation that economists and social scientists soon justified with a new social theory known as **social Darwinism**.

Social Darwinism and the Gospel of Wealth

John D. Rockefeller Jr., the son of the founder of Standard Oil, once remarked to his Baptist Bible class that the Standard Oil Company, like the American Beauty rose, resulted from "pruning the early buds that grew up around it." The elimination of smaller, inefficient units, he said, was "merely the working out of a law of nature and a law of God." The comparison of the business world to the natural world gave rise to a theory of society based on the law of evolution formulated by British naturalist Charles Darwin. In his monumental work *On the Origin of Species* (1859), Darwin theorized that in the struggle for survival, adaptation to the environment triggered among species a natural selection process that led to evolution. Drawing on Darwin's work, Herbert Spencer in Britain and William Graham Sumner in the United States developed the theory of social Darwinism. Crudely applying Darwin's theory to human society, the social Darwinists concluded that progress came about as a result of relentless competition in which the strong survived and the weak died out.

In social terms, the idea of the "survival of the fittest" had profound significance, as Sumner, a professor of political economy at Yale University, made clear in his 1883 book, *What Social Classes Owe to Each Other*. "The drunkard in the gutter is just where he ought to be, according to the fitness and tendency of things," Sumner insisted. Conversely, "millionaires are the product of natural selection," and although "they get high wages and live in luxury," Sumner claimed, "the bargain is a good one for society."

Social Darwinists equated wealth and power with "fitness" and believed that the unfit should be allowed to die off to advance the

J. P. Morgan, Photograph by Edward Steichen
Few photographs of J. P. Morgan exist. Morgan, who suffered from a skin condition that left him with a misshapen strawberry of a nose, rarely allowed his picture to be taken. But it was his eyes that people remembered—eyes so piercing that Edward Steichen, who took this photograph, observed that "meeting his gaze was a little like confronting the headlights of an express train."
George Eastman House. Reprinted with permission of Joanna T. Steichen.

Homestead Steelworks
The Homestead steelworks, outside Pittsburgh, is pictured shortly after J. P. Morgan bought out Andrew
Carnegie and created U.S. Steel, the precursor of today's USX. Try to count the smokestacks in the picture.
Air pollution on this scale posed a threat to the health of citizens and made for a dismal landscape. Workers
complained that trees would not grow in Homestead.
Hagley Museum & Library.

progress of humanity. Any efforts by the rich to
aid the poor would only tamper with the rigid
laws of nature and slow down evolution. Social
Darwinism acted to curb social reform while at
the same time glorifying great wealth. In an age
when Rockefeller and Carnegie amassed hundreds of millions of dollars (billions in today's
currency) and the average worker earned $500
a year (about $8,800 today), social Darwinism
justified economic inequality. (See "Historical
Question," page 646.)

Andrew Carnegie softened some of the harsh-
ness of social Darwinism in his essay "The Gospel
of Wealth," published in 1889. The millionaire,
Carnegie wrote, acted as a "mere trustee and agent
for his poorer brethren, bringing to their service
his superior wisdom, experience, and ability to
administer, doing for them better than they could
or would do for themselves." Carnegie preached
philanthropy and urged the rich to "live un-
ostentatious lives" and "administer surplus wealth
for the good of the people." His **gospel of wealth**
earned much praise but won few converts. Most
millionaires followed the lead of J. P. Morgan,
who contributed to charity but ostentatiously
amassed private treasures in his marble library.

Social Darwinism nicely suited an age in
which the gross inequalities accompanying industrialization seemed to cry out for action.
Assuaging the nation's conscience, social
Darwinism justified neglect of the poor in the
name of "race progress." With so many of the
poor coming from different races and ethnicities,
social Darwinism fueled racism. A new "scientific racism" purported to prove "Anglo-Saxons"
superior to all other groups. In an era noted for
greed and crass materialism, social Darwinism
buttressed the status quo and provided reassurance to comfortable, white Americans that all
was as it should be. Even the gospel of wealth,
which mitigated the harshest dictates of social
Darwinism, insisted that Americans lived in the
best of all possible worlds and that the rich were
the natural rulers.

Laissez-Faire and the Supreme Court

Social Darwinism, with its emphasis on the free
play of competition and the survival of the fittest,
encouraged the economic theory of **laissez-faire**
(French for "let it alone"). Business argued that government should not meddle in economic affairs,

Social Darwinism: Did Wealthy Industrialists Practice What They Preached?

Darwinism, with its emphasis on tooth-and-claw competition, seemed ideally suited to the get-rich-quick mentality of the Gilded Age. By placing the theory of evolution in an economic context, social Darwinism argued against government intervention in business while at the same time insisting that reforms to ameliorate the evils of urban industrialism would only slow evolutionary progress. Most of the wealthy industrialists of the day probably never read Charles Darwin or the exponents of social Darwinism. Nevertheless, the catchphrases of social Darwinism larded the rhetoric of business in the Gilded Age.

Andrew Carnegie, alone among the American business moguls, not only championed social Darwinism but also avidly read the works of its primary exponent, the British social philosopher Herbert Spencer. Significantly, Spencer, not Darwin, coined the phrase "survival of the fittest." Carnegie spoke of his indebtedness to Spencer in terms usually reserved for religious conversion: "Before Spencer, all for me had been darkness, after him, all had become light—and right." In his autobiography, Carnegie wrote: "I had found the truth of evolution. 'All is well since all grows better' became my motto, my true source of comfort."

Not content to worship Spencer from afar, Carnegie assiduously worked to make his acquaintance and then would not rest until he had convinced the reluctant Spencer to come to America. In Pittsburgh, Carnegie promised, Spencer could best view his evolutionary theories at work in the world of industry. Clearly, Carnegie viewed his steelworks as the apex of America's new industrial order, a testimony to the playing out of evolutionary theory in the economic world.

In 1882, Spencer undertook an American tour. Carnegie personally invited him to Pittsburgh, squiring him through the Braddock steel mills. But Spencer failed to appreciate Carnegie's achievement. The heat, noise, and pollution of Pittsburgh reduced Spencer to near collapse, and he could only choke out, "Six months' residence here would justify suicide." Carnegie must have been devastated by Spencer's reaction to America's new industrial order, but he never let on.

How well Carnegie actually understood the principles of social Darwinism is debatable. In his 1900 essay "Popular Illusions about Trusts," Carnegie spoke of the "law of evolution that moves from the heterogeneous to the homogeneous," citing Spencer as his source. Spencer, however, had written of the movement "from an indefinite incoherent homogeneity to a definite coherent heterogeneity." Instead of acknowledging that the history of human evolution moved from the simple to the more complex, Carnegie seemed

except to protect private property. A conservative Supreme Court agreed. During the 1880s and 1890s, the Court increasingly reinterpreted the Constitution to protect business from taxation, regulation, labor organization, and antitrust legislation.

In a series of landmark decisions, the Court used the Fourteenth Amendment, originally intended to protect freed slaves from state laws violating their rights, to protect corporations. The Fourteenth Amendment declares that no state can "deprive any person of life, liberty, or property, without due process of law." In 1886, in *Santa Clara County v. Southern Pacific Railroad*, the Court insisted that corporations be considered "persons." Reasoning that legislation designed to regulate corporations deprived them of "due process," the Court struck down state laws regulating railroad rates, declared income tax unconstitutional, and judged labor unions a "conspiracy in restraint of trade." The Court insisted on elevating the rights of property over all other rights. According to Justice Stephen J. Field, the Constitution "allows no impediments to the acquisition of property." Field, born into a wealthy New England family, to insist that evolution moved from the complex to the simple. This confusion of the most basic evolutionary theory calls into question Carnegie's grasp of Spencer's ideas or indeed of Darwin's. Other business leaders too busy making money to read no doubt understood even less about the working of evolutionary theory and social Darwinism, which they nevertheless often claimed as their own.

The distance between preachment and practice is boldly evident in the example of William Graham Sumner, America's foremost social Darwinist. Ironically, Sumner, who so often sounded like an apologist for the rich, aroused the wrath of the very group he championed. The problem was that strict social Darwinists like Sumner insisted absolutely that the government ought not to meddle in the economy. The purity of Sumner's commitment to laissez-faire led him to adamantly oppose the protective tariffs the pro-business Republicans enacted to inflate the prices of manufactured goods produced abroad so that U.S. businesses could compete against foreign rivals. Sumner outspokenly attacked the tariff and firmly advocated free trade from his chair in political economy at Yale University. In

Herbert Spencer
The British writer and philosopher Herbert Spencer became a hero to industrialist Andrew Carnegie, who orchestrated Spencer's trip to America in 1882. The sage of social Darwinism proved a great disappointment to Carnegie. A cautious hypochondriac, Spencer guarded himself zealously against any painful contact with that teeming competitive world that he extolled. Once on American soil, Spencer spurned Carnegie's offer of hospitality during his visit to Pittsburgh and insisted on staying in a hotel. And when Carnegie eagerly demonstrated the wonders of the world's most modern steel mill to his guest, the tour reduced Spencer to a state of near collapse.
Hulton Archives/Getty Images.

1890, the same year Congress passed the McKinley tariff, Sumner's fulminations against this highest tariff in the nation's history so outraged Yale's wealthy alumni that they mounted a campaign (unsuccessful) to have him fired.

Sumner's theoretical consistency did not seem to trouble Andrew Carnegie, who never acknowledged a contradiction between his worship of Spencer and his strong support for the tariff. The comparison of

Carnegie's position and Sumner's underscores the reality that although in theory laissez-faire constrained the government from playing an active role in business affairs, in practice industrialists fought for government favors—whether tariffs, land grants, or subsidies—that worked to their benefit. Only when legislatures proposed taxes or regulation did business leaders cry foul and invoke the "natural laws" of social Darwinism and its corollary laissez-faire.

spoke with the bias of the privileged class to whom property rights were sacrosanct. Imbued with this ideology, the Court refused to impede corporate consolidation and did nothing to curb the excesses of big business. Only in the arena of politics did Americans tackle the issues raised by corporate capitalism.

REVIEW Why did the ideas of social Darwinism appeal to many Americans in the late nineteenth century?

Politics and Culture

One could easily argue that politics, not baseball, constituted America's pastime in the Gilded Age. For many Americans, politics provided a source of identity, a means of livelihood, and a ready form of entertainment. No wonder voter turnout averaged a hefty 77 percent (compared to 60 percent in the 2004 presidential election; Figure 18.2, page 648). A variety of factors contributed to the complicated interplay of politics and **culture**. Patronage provided an economic

648   CHAPTER 18 • BUSINESS AND POLITICS IN THE GILDED AGE

1870–1895

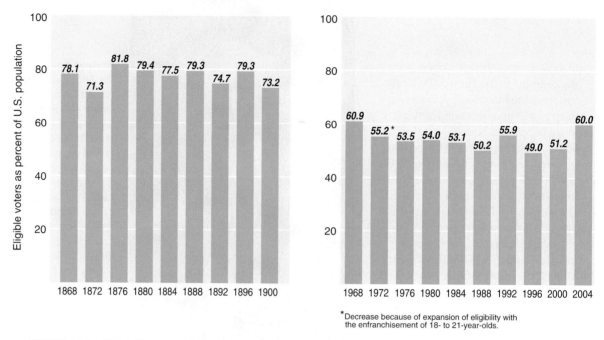

FIGURE 18.2   Voter Turnout, 1868–1900 and 1968–2004
Despite the weakness of the presidency and the largely undistinguished men who filled the office, people turned out in record numbers to vote in late-nineteenth-century elections. Compare the robust rate of voter participation then to the anemic turnout in more recent elections. What factors do you think accounted for the change?

incentive for voter participation, but ethnicity, religion, sectional loyalty, race, and gender all influenced the political life of the period.

Political Participation and Party Loyalty

Patronage—the **spoils system**—proved a strong motivation for party loyalty among many voters. Political parties in power doled out federal, state, and local government jobs to their loyal supporters. With hundreds of thousands of jobs to be filled, the choice of party affiliation could mean the difference between a paycheck and an empty pocket. Money greased the wheels of this system of patronage, dubbed the spoils system from the adage "to the victor go the spoils." Party bosses expected jobholders to kick back from 2 to 4 percent of their salaries to support the party's electoral campaigns. With their livelihoods tied to their party identity, government employees in particular had an incentive to vote in great numbers during the Gilded Age.

Political affiliation provided a powerful sense of group identity for many voters proud of their loyalty to the Democrats or the Republicans. Democrats, who traced the party's roots back to

Thomas Jefferson, called theirs "the party of the fathers." The Republican Party, founded in the 1850s, still claimed strong loyalties as a result of its alignment with the Union during the Civil War. Noting the power of old sectional loyalties, one of the party faithful observed, "Iowa will go Democratic when Hell goes Methodist." Both Republicans in the North and Democrats in the South employed a tactic called "waving the **bloody shirt**"—reminding voters which side they had fought for in the Civil War.

Politics also provided entertainment and spectacle for voters and nonvoters alike in an age before mass recreation and amusement, particularly in rural areas. Political parties sponsored parades, rallies, speeches, picnics, torchlight processions, and Fourth of July fireworks, attracting millions of Americans. Outside the big cities, only religious revivals and traveling shows could compete.

Religion and ethnicity also played a significant role in politics. In the North, **Protestants** from the old-line denominations, particularly Presbyterians and Methodists, flocked to the Republican Party, which championed a series of moral reforms, including local laws requiring businesses to close in observance of the Sabbath.

In the burgeoning cities, the Democratic Party courted immigrants and working-class Catholic and Jewish voters charging, rightly, that Republican moral crusades often masked attacks on immigrant culture.

Sectionalism and the New South

After the end of Reconstruction, most white voters in the former Confederate states remained loyal Democrats, voting for Democratic candidates in every presidential election for the next seventy years. Labeling the Republican Party the agent of "Negro rule," Democrats urged white southerners to "vote the way you shot." Yet the so-called solid South proved far from solid on the state and local levels. The economic plight of the South led to shifting political alliances and to third-party movements that challenged Democratic attempts to define politics along race lines and maintain the Democratic Party as the white man's party.

The South's economy, devastated by the war, foundered at the same time the North experienced an unprecedented industrial boom. Soon an influential group of southerners called for a **New South** modeled on the industrial North. Henry Grady, the ebullient young editor of the *Atlanta Constitution*, used his paper's substantial influence (it boasted the largest circulation of any weekly in the country) to extol the virtues of a new industrial South. Part bully, part booster, Grady exhorted the South to use its natural advantages—cheap labor and abundant natural resources—to go head-to-head in competition with northern industry.

Grady's message fell on receptive ears. Many southerners, men and women, black and white, joined the national migration from farm to city, leaving the old plantations to molder and decay. With the end of military rule in 1877, southern Democrats took back state governments, calling themselves "Redeemers." Yet rather than restore the economy of the old **planter** class, they embraced northern promoters who promised prosperity and profits.

The railroads came first, opening up the region for industrial development. Southern railroad mileage grew fourfold from 1865 to 1890 (see Map 18.1). The number of cotton spindles also soared, as textile mill owners abandoned New England in search of the cheap labor and proximity to raw materials promised in the South. By 1900, the South had become the nation's leading producer of cloth, and more than

Hayes Campaign Lantern, 1876
Republicans carried this lantern in the presidential campaign of 1876. Designed for nighttime rallies, the lantern featured paper transparencies that allowed light to shine through the stars and illuminate the portrait of the candidate, Rutherford B. Hayes. Marching men with lighted lanterns held aloft must have been a dramatic sight in small towns across the country, where politics constituted a major form of entertainment in the nineteenth century.
Collection of Janice L. and David J. Frent.

100,000 southerners, many of them women and children, worked in the region's textile mills.

The New South prided itself most on its iron and steel industry, which grew up in the area surrounding Birmingham, Alabama. During this period, the smokestack replaced the white-pillared plantation as the symbol of the New South. Andrew Carnegie toured the region in 1889 and observed, "The South is Pennsylvania's most formidable industrial enemy." But southern industry remained controlled by northern investors, who had no intention of letting the South beat the North at its own game. Elaborate mechanisms rigged the price of southern steel, inflating it, as one northern insider confessed, "for the purpose of protecting the Pittsburgh mills and in turn the Pittsburgh steel users." Similarly, in the extractive industries—lumber and mining—investors in the North and abroad, not southerners, reaped the lion's share of the profits.

In only one industry did the South truly dominate—tobacco. Capitalizing on the invention of a machine for rolling cigarettes, the American Tobacco Company, founded by the Duke family of North Carolina, eventually dominated the industry. As cigarettes replaced chewing tobacco in popularity at the turn of the twentieth century, a booming market developed for Duke's "ready mades." Soon the company sold 400,000 cigarettes a day.

In practical terms, the industrialized New South proved an illusion. Much of the South remained agricultural, caught in

the grip of the insidious crop lien system (see chapter 16). White southern farmers, desperate to get out of debt, sometimes joined with African Americans to pursue their goals politically. Southerners used this strategy in a variety of ways. Between 1865 and 1900, voters in every state south of the Mason-Dixon line experimented with political alliances that crossed the color line. In Virginia, the "Readjusters," a coalition of blacks and whites determined to "readjust" (lower) the state debt and spend more money on public education, captured state offices from 1879 to 1883. In southern politics, the interplay of race and gender made coalitions like the Readjusters a potent threat to the status quo.

Gender, Race, and Politics

Gender—society's notion of what constitutes acceptable masculine or feminine behavior—influenced politics throughout the nineteenth century. From the early days of the Republic, citizenship had been defined in male terms. Citizenship and its prerogatives (voting and officeholding) served as a badge of manliness and rested on its corollary, patriarchy—the power and authority men exerted over their wives and families. With the advent of universal (white) male **suffrage** in the early nineteenth century, gender eclipsed class as the defining feature of citizenship; men's dominance over women provided the common thread that knit all white men together politically. The concept of **separate spheres** dictated political participation for men only. Once the public sphere of political participation became equated with manhood, women found themselves increasingly restricted to the private sphere of home and hearth.

Gender permeated politics in other ways, especially in the tangled skein of the New South. Cross-racial alliances like the Readjusters rested on the belief that universal political rights (voting, officeholding, patronage) could be extended to black males in the public sphere without eliminating racial barriers in the private sphere. Democrats, for their part, fought back by trying to convince voters that black voting would inevitably lead to **miscegenation** (racial mixing). Black male political power and sexual power, they warned, went hand in hand. Ultimately, their arguments prevailed, and many whites returned to the Democratic fold to protect "white womanhood" and with it white supremacy.

The notion that black men threatened white southern womanhood reached its most vicious form in the practice of lynching—the killing and mutilation of black men by white mobs. By 1892, the practice had become so prevalent that a courageous black woman, Ida B. Wells, launched an antilynching movement. That year, a white mob lynched a friend of Wells's whose grocery store competed too successfully with a white-owned store. Wells shrewdly concluded that lynching served "as an excuse to get rid of Negroes who were acquiring wealth and property and thus keep the race terrorized." She began to collect data on lynching and discovered that in the decade between 1882 and 1892, lynching rose in the South by an overwhelming 200 percent, with more than 241 people killed. The vast increase in lynching testified to the retreat of the federal government following Reconstruction and to white southerners' determination to maintain supremacy through terrorism and intimidation. Wells struck back.

As the first salvo in her attack, Wells put to rest the "old threadbare lie that Negro men assault white women." As she pointed out, violations of black women by white men, which were much more frequent than black attacks on white women, went unnoticed and unpunished. Wells articulated lynching as a problem of race and gender. She insisted that the myth of black attacks on white southern women masked the reality that mob violence had more to do with economics and the shifting social structure of the South than with rape. She demonstrated in a sophisticated way how the southern patriarchal system, having lost its control over blacks with the end of slavery, used its control over women to circumscribe the liberty of black men.

Wells's strong stance immediately resulted in reprisal. While she was traveling in the North, vandals ransacked her office in Tennessee and destroyed her printing equipment. Yet the warning that she would be killed on sight if she ever returned to Memphis only stiffened her resolve. As she wrote in her autobiography, *Crusade for Justice* (1928), "Having lost my paper, had a price put on my life and been made an exile . . . , I felt that I owed it to myself and to my race to tell the whole truth now that I was where I could do so freely."

Antilynching became a lifelong commitment that took Wells twice to Britain, where she placed lynching on the international agenda. As a reporter, first for the *New York Age* and later for the *Chicago Inter-Ocean*, she used every opportunity to hammer home her message. Wells's activities mobilized other black women, including Victoria

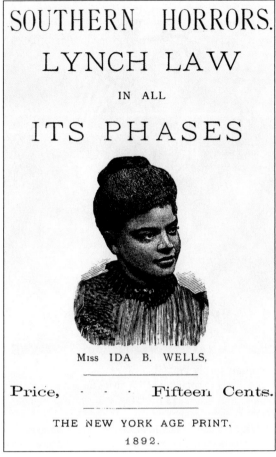

SOUTHERN HORRORS.

LYNCH LAW

IN ALL

ITS PHASES

Miss IDA B. WELLS,

Price, - - - Fifteen Cents.

THE NEW YORK AGE PRINT,
1892.

Ida B. Wells
Ida B. Wells began her antilynching campaign in 1892 after a friend's murder led her to examine the problem of lynching in the South. She spread her message in lectures and pamphlets like this one, distributed for fifteen cents. Wells brought the horror of lynching to a national and international audience and mobilized other African American women to undertake social action under the auspices of the National Association of Colored Women. She later became a founding member of the National Association for the Advancement of Colored People (NAACP).
Manuscript, Archives and Rare Books Division, Schomburg Center for Research in Black Culture, The New York Public Library, Astor, Lenox, and Tilden.

Earle Matthews and Maritcha Lyons, who were already engaged in social reform and self-improvement. They hosted a testimonial dinner for Wells in New York in 1892 that led to the organization of a black women's club, the Women's Loyal Union. The club became the spearhead for the creation of the National Association of Colored Women (NACW) in 1896. The organization's first president, Mary Church Terrell of Washington, D.C., urged her followers to "promote the welfare of our race, along all the lines that tend to its development and advancement."

Taking as their motto "Lifting as we climb," the women of the NACW attacked myriad issues, including health care, housing, education, and the promotion of a positive image of the race. The NACW played a critical role in Wells's antilynching campaign by lobbying for legislation to make lynching a federal crime. Beginning in 1894 and continuing for decades, antilynching bills were introduced in Congress only to be defeated by southern opposition.

Lynching did not end during Ida B. Wells's lifetime, but Wells's forceful voice brought the issue to national prominence. At her funeral in 1931, black leader W. E. B. Du Bois eulogized Wells as the woman who "began the awakening of the conscience of the nation." Wells's determined campaign against lynching provided just one example of women's political activism during the Gilded Age. The suffrage and **temperance movements**, along with the growing popularity of women's clubs, dramatized how women refused to be relegated to a separate sphere that kept them out of politics.

Women's Activism

No one better recognized the potency of the gendered notion of political rights than Elizabeth Cady Stanton, who lamented the introduction of the word *male* into the Fourteenth Amendment (see chapter 16). The explicit linking of manhood with citizenship and voting rights in the Constitution marked a major setback for reformers who supported the vote for women. In 1869, Stanton along with Susan B. Anthony formed the National Woman Suffrage Association (NWSA), the first independent woman's rights organization in the United States (see chapter 20).

Women found ways to act politically long before they voted and cleverly used their moral authority as wives and mothers to move from the domestic sphere into the realm of politics. The extraordinary activity of women's clubs in the period following the Civil War provides just one example. Women's clubs proliferated from the 1860s to the 1890s, often in response to the exclusionary policies of men's organizations. In 1868, newspaper reporter Jane Cunningham Croly (pen name Jennie June) founded the Sorosis Club in New York City after the New York Press Club denied entry to women journalists wishing to attend a banquet honoring the British author Charles Dickens. In 1890, Croly brought state and local clubs together under the umbrella of the General Federation of Women's Clubs (GFWC).

Not wanting to alienate southern women, the GFWC barred black women's clubs from joining, despite their vehement objections. Women's clubs soon turned from literary pursuits to politics and reform. "Very early," wrote an officer of the GFWC, "club women became unwilling to discuss Dante and Browning over the teacups in some ladies' drawing room . . . while unsightly heaps of rubbish flanked the paths over which they had passed." Women's clubs resolved to devote themselves to "civic usefulness," endorsing an end to child labor, supporting the eight-hour workday, and helping pass pure food and drug legislation.

The temperance movement (the movement to end drunkenness) attracted by far the largest number of organized women in the late nineteenth century. By the late 1860s and 1870s, the liquor business flourished, with about one saloon for every fifty males over the age of fifteen. During the winter of 1873–74, temperance women adopted a radical new tactic. Armed with Bibles and singing hymns, they marched on taverns and saloons and refused to leave until the proprietors signed a pledge to quit selling liquor. Known as the Woman's Crusade, the movement spread like a prairie fire through small towns in Ohio, Indiana, Michigan, and Illinois and soon moved east into New York, New England, and Pennsylvania. Before it was over, more than 100,000 women had marched in more than 450 cities and towns.

> "Very early," wrote an officer of the General Federation of Women's Clubs, "club women became unwilling to discuss Dante and Browning over the teacups in some ladies' drawing room . . . while unsightly heaps of rubbish flanked the paths over which they had passed."

The women's tactics may have been new, but the temperance movement dated back to the 1820s. Originally, the movement was led by Protestant men who organized clubs to pledge voluntary abstinence from liquor. By the 1850s, temperance advocates won significant victories when states, starting with Maine, passed laws to prohibit the sale of liquor (known as "Maine laws"). The Woman's Crusade dramatically brought the issue of temperance back into the national spotlight and led to the formation of a new organization, the Woman's Christian Temperance Union (WCTU) in 1874. Composed entirely of women, the WCTU advocated total abstinence from alcohol. The drunken, abusive husband and father epitomized the evils of a society in which women remained second-class citizens, dependent on men for their livelihood. Temperance provided women with a respect-

"Woman's Holy War"
This political cartoon from 1874 styles the temperance campaign as "Woman's Holy War" and shows a woman knight in armor demurely seated sidesaddle on her charger, wielding a battle-ax and trampling on barrels of liquor. The temperance movement experienced a resurgence in the 1870s after Bible-toting women marched to shut down saloons from New York to Michigan. Their activism led to the creation of the Woman's Christian Temperance Union in 1874.
Picture Research Consultants & Archives.

able outlet for their increasing resentment of women's inferior status and their growing recognition of women's capabilities. In its first five years, the WCTU relied on education and moral suasion, but when Frances Willard became president in 1879, she politicized the organization (see chapter 20). When the women of the WCTU joined with the Prohibition Party (formed in 1869 by a group of **evangelical** clergymen), one wag observed, "Politics is a man's game, an' women, childhern, and prohyibitionists do well to keep out iv it." By sharing power with women, the Prohibitionist men violated the old political rules and risked attacks on their honor and manhood.

Temperance, club work, antilynching, and suffrage constituted only a few of women's political causes. Even though they could not yet vote, women found ways to affect the political process. Like men, they displayed strong party loyalties and rallied around traditional Republican and Democratic candidates. Third parties courted women, recognizing that their volunteer labor and support could be key assets in party building. Nevertheless, despite growing political awareness among women, politics, particularly presidential politics, remained—like chewing tobacco—an exclusively male prerogative.

REVIEW   How did race and gender influence politics?

Presidential Politics

Why do the great industrialists—Rockefeller, Morgan, Carnegie—jump vividly from the pages of the past while the presidents of that period remain so pallid? The presidents from Rutherford B. Hayes (1877–1881) to William McKinley (1897–1901) are indeed forgotten men, largely because little was expected of them. Until the 1890s, few Americans thought the president or the national government had any role to play in addressing the problems accompanying the nation's industrial transformation. The dominant creed of laissez-faire, coupled with the dictates of social Darwinism, warned government to leave business alone (except to encourage it with tariffs and subsidies). Still, presidents in the Gilded Age grappled with corruption and party strife and struggled toward the creation of new political ethics designed to replace patronage with a **civil service** system that promised to award jobs on the basis of merit, not party loyalty.

Corruption and Party Strife

The political corruption and party factionalism that characterized the administration of Ulysses S. Grant (1869–1877) continued to trouble the nation in the 1880s. The spoils system—awarding jobs for political purposes—remained the driving force in party politics at all levels of government in the Gilded Age. Pro-business Republicans generally held a firm grip on the White House, while Democrats had better luck in Congress. Both parties relied on patronage to cement party loyalty. Reformers eager to replace the spoils system with civil service faced an uphill battle.

A small but determined group of reformers championed a new ethics that would preclude politicians from getting rich from public office. The selection of U.S. senators particularly concerned them. Under the Constitution, senators were selected by state legislatures, not directly elected by the voters. Powerful business interests often contrived to control state legislatures and through them U.S. senators. As journalist Henry Demarest Lloyd quipped, Standard Oil "had done everything to the Pennsylvania legislature except to refine it." The "oil combination," he charged, virtually owned Pennsylvania's two senators. Nothing prevented a senator from collecting a paycheck from any of the great corporations. So many did so that political cartoonists often portrayed senators as huge money bags labeled with the names of the corporations they served. Nelson Aldrich, the powerful Republican senator from Rhode Island (whose daughter married John D. Rockefeller Jr.), did not object to being called "the senator from Standard Oil." In this climate, a constitutional amendment calling for the direct election of senators faced stiff opposition from entrenched interests.

> As journalist Henry Demarest Lloyd quipped, Standard Oil "had done everything to the Pennsylvania legislature except to refine it."

Republican president Rutherford B. Hayes, whose disputed election in 1876 signaled the end of Reconstruction in the South, tried to steer a middle course between spoilsmen and reformers. Although the Democratic press ridiculed him as "Rutherfraud" because he had not been popularly elected (see chapter 16), Hayes proved a hardworking, well-informed executive who wanted peace, prosperity, and an end to party strife. Yet the Republican Party remained divided into factions led by strong party bosses who boasted that they could make or break any president.

Fiery and dynamic party bosses who harbored their own presidential ambitions dominated politics on the national scene. Foremost among the Republicans stood Senator Roscoe Conkling of New York, a master spoilsman who ridiculed civil service as "snivel service." He and his followers, called the "Stalwarts," represented the Grant faction of the party. Conkling's archrival, Senator James G. Blaine of Maine, led the "Half Breeds." Not as openly corrupt as the Grant wing of the party, the Half Breeds and their champion were nevertheless tainted with charges of corruption. A third group, called the "Mugwumps," consisted primarily of reform-minded Republicans from Massachusetts and New York who deplored the spoils system and advocated civil service reform. The name "Mugwump" came from the Algonquian word for chief, but critics used the term derisively, punning that the Mugwumps straddled the fence on issues of party loyalty, "with their mug on one side and wump on the other."

President Hayes's middle course pleased no one, and he soon managed to alienate all factions of his party. No one was surprised when he announced that he would not seek reelection in 1880. To avoid choosing among its factions, the Republican Party in 1880 nominated a dark-horse candidate, Representative James A. Garfield from Ohio. To appease Conkling, they picked Stalwart Chester A. Arthur as the vice presidential candidate. The Democrats made an attempt to overcome sectionalism and establish a national party by selecting as their presidential standard-bearer an old Union general,

> "Assassination," Garfield told a friend, "can no more be guarded against than death by lightning, and it is best not to worry about either."

Winfield Scott Hancock. But as one observer noted, "It is a peculiarly constituted party that sends rebel brigadiers to Congress because of their rebellion, and then nominates a Union General as its candidate for president because of his loyalty." Hancock garnered only lukewarm support, receiving just 155 electoral votes to Garfield's 214, although the popular vote was less lopsided.

Garfield's Assassination and Civil Service Reform

"My God," Garfield swore after only a few months in office, "what is there in this place that a man should ever want to get into it?" Garfield, like Hayes, faced the difficult task of remaining independent while pacifying the party bosses and placating the reformers. As the federal bureaucracy grew to nearly 150,000 jobs, thousands of office seekers swarmed to the nation's capital, each clamoring for a position. In the days before Secret Service protection, the White House door stood open to all comers. Garfield took a fatalistic view. "Assassination," he told a friend, "can no more be guarded against than death by lightning, and it is best not to worry about either."

On July 2, 1881, less than four months after taking office, Garfield was shot. His assailant, Charles Guiteau, though clearly insane, turned out to be a disappointed office seeker who claimed to be motivated by political partisanship. He told the police officer who arrested him, "I did it; I will go to jail for it; Arthur is president, and I am a Stalwart." Throughout the hot summer, the country kept a deathwatch as Garfield lingered. When he died in September, Chester A. Arthur became president.

The press almost universally condemned Republican factionalism for creating the political climate that produced Guiteau and led to the second political assassination in a generation. Stalwart Roscoe Conkling saw his hopes for the White House dashed. Attacks on the spoils system increased, and the public joined the chorus calling for reform. But reformers faced stiff opposition from those who recognized that civil service had class and ethnic biases. At a time when few men achieved more than a grammar school education, written civil service examinations threatened to undo political advances made by Irish Americans and return government to an educated Yankee elite. As one opponent pointed out, "George Washington could not have passed examination for a clerkship," noting that

Civil Service Exams

In this 1890s photograph, prospective police officers in Chicago take the written civil service exam. Civil service meant that politicians and party bosses could no longer use jobs in the government to reward the party faithful. Many people worried that merit examinations would favor the educated elite at the expense of immigrant groups such as the Irish, who had made a place for themselves in the political system by the late nineteenth century.

Chicago Historical Society.

"in his will written by his own hand, he spells clothes, cloathes."

Reform came with the passage of the Pendleton Civil Service Act in 1883. Both parties claimed credit for the act, which established a permanent Civil Service Commission consisting of three members appointed by the president. Some fourteen thousand jobs came under a merit system that required examinations for office and made it impossible to remove jobholders for political reasons. Half of the postal jobs and most of the customhouse jobs, the largest share of the spoilsmen's bounty, passed to the control of the Civil Service Commission. The new law also prohibited federal jobholders from contributing to political campaigns, thus drying up the major source of the party bosses' revenue. Soon business interests stepped in to replace officeholders as the nation's chief political contributors. Ironically, civil service reform thus gave business an even greater influence in political life.

Reform and Scandal: The Campaign of 1884

With Conkling's downfall, James G. Blaine assumed leadership of the Republican Party and at long last captured the presidential nomination in 1884. A magnetic Irish American politician, Blaine inspired such devotion that his supporters called themselves Blainiacs. But Mugwumps like editor Carl Schurz insisted that Blaine "wallowed in spoils like a rhinoceros in an African pool." They bolted the party and embraced the Democrats' presidential nominee, the stolid Grover Cleveland, reform governor of New York. The burly, beer-drinking Cleveland distinguished himself from an entire generation of politicians by the simple motto "A public office is a public trust." First as mayor of Buffalo and later as governor of New York, he built a reputation for honesty, economy, and administrative efficiency. The Democrats, who had not won the presidency since 1856, had high hopes for his candidacy, especially after the Mugwumps threw their support to Cleveland, insisting that "the paramount issue this year is moral rather than political."

The Mugwumps soon regretted their words. The 1884 contest degenerated so far into scandal and nasty mudslinging that one disgusted journalist styled it "the vilest campaign ever waged." In July, Cleveland's hometown paper, the *Buffalo Telegraph*, dropped the bombshell that the candidate had fathered an illegitimate child in an af-

"Another Voice for Cleveland"
This political cartoon ran in the magazine *Judge* in the fall of 1884 during the presidential campaign. Grover Cleveland, the Democratic candidate, is pictured cringing from the cries of a babe in arms—an allusion to his admission that he had fathered an illegitimate child. Despite the lurid publicity, Cleveland won the election.
Library of Congress.

fair with a local widow. Cleveland, a bachelor, stoically accepted responsibility for the child, perhaps to save the reputation of his married law partner, who may have been the actual father (and whose daughter Cleveland later married). Crushed by the scandal, the Mugwumps tried to argue the difference between public and private morality. But robbed of their moral righteousness, they lost much of their enthusiasm. "Now I fear it has resolved itself into a choice of two evils," one weary reformer confessed. At public rallies, Blaine's partisans taunted Cleveland, chanting, "Ma, Ma, where's my Pa?" Silent but fuming, Cleveland waged his campaign in the traditional fashion by staying home.

While Cleveland sat at home, Blaine launched a whirlwind national tour. On a last-minute stop in New York City, the exhausted candidate committed a misstep that may have cost him the election. He overlooked a remark by a supporter, a local clergyman who cast a slur on Catholic voters by styling the Democrats as the party of "Rum, Romanism, and Rebellion." Linking drinking (rum) and Catholicism (Romanism)

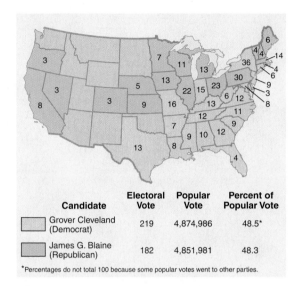

Candidate	Electoral Vote	Popular Vote	Percent of Popular Vote
Grover Cleveland (Democrat)	219	4,874,986	48.5*
James G. Blaine (Republican)	182	4,851,981	48.3

*Percentages do not total 100 because some popular votes went to other parties.

MAP 18.2   The Election of 1884

offended Irish Catholic voters, whom Blaine had counted on to desert the Democratic Party and support him because of his Irish background.

With less than a week to go until the election, Blaine had no chance to recover from the negative publicity. He lost New York State by fewer than 1,200 votes and with it the election. In the final tally, Cleveland defeated Blaine by a scant 23,005 votes nationwide but won with 219 electoral votes to Blaine's 182 (Map 18.2), ending twenty-five years of Republican control of the presidency. Cleveland's followers had the last word. To the chorus of "Ma, Ma, where's my Pa?" they retorted, "Going to the White House, ha, ha, ha."

REVIEW   How did the question of civil service reform contribute to divisions within the Republican Party?

Economic Issues and Party Realignment

Four years later, in the election of 1888, fickle voters turned Cleveland out, electing Republican Benjamin Harrison, the grandson of President William Henry Harrison. Then, in the only instance in America's history when a president once defeated at the polls returned to office, the

voters brought Cleveland back in the election of 1892. What factors account for such a surprising turnaround? Personalities played a part. The stubborn Cleveland, newly married, refused to campaign in 1888. Although he won more popular votes than Harrison, he lost in the electoral college. Once in office, Harrison proved to be a cold and distant leader, prompting critics to call him "the human iceberg." But new issues as well as personalities increasingly swayed the voters. The 1880s witnessed a remarkable political realignment as a set of economic concerns replaced appeals to Civil War sectional loyalties. The tariff, federal regulation of the railroads and trusts, and the campaign for **free silver** restructured American politics.

The Tariff and the Politics of Protection

The tariff became a potent political issue in the 1880s. The concept of a protective tariff to raise the price of imported goods and stimulate American industry dated back to Alexander Hamilton in the founding days of the Republic. Congress enacted the first tariff following the War of 1812. The Republicans turned the tariff to political ends in 1861 by enacting a measure that both raised revenues for the Civil War and rewarded their industrial supporters, who wanted protection from foreign competition. After the war, the pro-business Republicans continued to revise and enlarge the tariff. Manufactured goods such as steel and textiles, and some agricultural products, including sugar and wool, benefited from protection. Most farm products, notably wheat and cotton, did not. By the 1880s, the tariff produced more than $2.1 billion in revenue. The high tariff not only paid off the nation's Civil War debt and funded pensions for Union soldiers, but it also created a huge surplus that sat idly in the Treasury's vaults while the government argued about how (or even whether) to spend it.

To many Americans, particularly southern and midwestern farmers who sold their crops in a world market but had to buy goods priced artificially high because of the protective tariff, the answer was simple: Reduce the tariff. Advocates of free trade and moderates agitated for tariff reform. But those who benefited from the tariff—industrialists insisting that America's "infant industries" needed protection and some westerners producing protected raw materials such as wool, hides, and lumber—firmly opposed lowering the tariff. Many argued that workers, too, benefited from high tariffs that protected American wages by giving American products an edge over imported goods.

The Republican Party seized on the tariff question to forge a new national coalition. "Fold up the bloody shirt and lay it away," Blaine advised a colleague in 1880. "It's of no use to us. You want to shift the main issue to protection." By encouraging an alliance among industrialists, labor, and western producers of raw materials—groups seen to benefit from the tariff—Blaine hoped to solidify the North, Midwest, and West against the solidly Democratic South. Although the tactic failed for Blaine in the presidential election of 1884, it worked for the Republicans four years later. Cleveland, who had straddled the tariff issue in the election of 1884, startled the nation in 1887 by calling for tariff reform. Cleveland attacked the tariff as a tax levied on American consumers by powerful industries. And he pointed out that high tariffs impeded the expansion of American markets abroad at a time when American industries needed to expand if they were to keep growing. The Republicans countered by arguing that "tariff tinkering" would only unsettle prosperous industries, drive down wages, and shrink the farmers' home market. Republican Benjamin Harrison, who supported the high tariff, ousted Cleveland from the White House in 1888, carrying all the western and northern states except Connecticut and New Jersey.

Back in power, the Republicans brazenly passed the highest tariff in the nation's history in 1890. The new tariff, sponsored by Republican representative William McKinley of Ohio and signed into law by Harrison, stirred up a hornet's nest of protest across the United States. The American people had elected Harrison to preserve protection but not to enact a higher tariff. Democrats condemned the McKinley tariff and labeled the Republican Congress that passed it the "Billion Dollar Congress" for its carnival of spending, which depleted the nation's surplus by enacting a series of pork barrel programs shamelessly designed to bring federal money to congressmen's own constituents. In the congressional election of 1890, angry voters swept the hapless Republicans, including tariff sponsor McKinley, out of office. Two years later, Harrison himself was defeated. Grover Cleveland, whose call for tariff revision had cost him the election in

1888, triumphantly returned to the White House vowing to lower the tariff. Such were the changes in the political winds whipped up by the tariff issue.

However real the contest between Republicans and Democrats over the economic advantages of the tariff, the debate masked deeper divisions in American society. Conflict between workers and farmers on the one side and bankers and corporate giants on the other erupted throughout the 1880s and came to a head in the 1890s. Both sides of the tariff debate spoke to concern over class conflict when they insisted that their respective plans, whether McKinley's high tariff or Cleveland's tariff reform, would bring prosperity and harmony. For their part, many working people shared the sentiment voiced by one labor leader that the tariff was "only a scheme devised by the old parties to throw dust in the eyes of laboring men."

Railroads, Trusts, and the Federal Government

American voters may have divided on the tariff, but increasingly they agreed on the need for federal regulation of the railroads and federal legislation to curb the power of the "trusts" (a term loosely applied to all large business combinations). As early as the 1870s, angry farmers in the Midwest who suffered from the unfair shipping practices of the railroads organized to fight for railroad regulation. The Patrons of Husbandry, or the Grange, founded in 1867 as a social and educational organization for farmers, soon became an independent political movement. By electing Grangers to state office, farmers made it possible for several midwestern states to pass laws in the 1870s and 1880s regulating the railroads. At first the Supreme Court ruled in favor of state regulation (*Munn v. Illinois*, 1877). But in 1886, the Court reversed itself, ruling that because railroads crossed state boundaries, they fell outside state jurisdiction (*Wabash v. Illinois*). With more than three-fourths of railroads crossing state lines, the Supreme Court's decision effectively quashed the states' attempts at railroad regulation.

Anger at the *Wabash* decision finally led to the first federal law regulating the railroads, the Interstate Commerce Act, passed in 1887

> American voters may have divided on the tariff, but increasingly they agreed on the need for federal regulation of the railroads and federal legislation to curb the power of the "trusts."

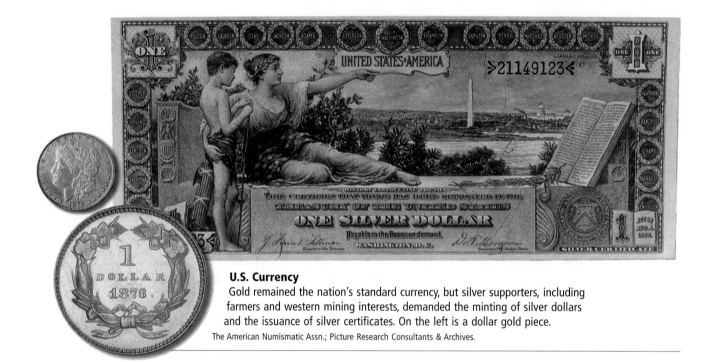

U.S. Currency
Gold remained the nation's standard currency, but silver supporters, including
farmers and western mining interests, demanded the minting of silver dollars
and the issuance of silver certificates. On the left is a dollar gold piece.
The American Numismatic Assn.; Picture Research Consultants & Archives.

during Cleveland's first administration. The act established the nation's first federal regulatory agency, the Interstate Commerce Commission (ICC), to oversee the railroad industry. In its early years, the ICC was never strong enough to pose a serious threat to the railroads. It could not, for example, end rebates to big shippers. In its early decades, the ICC proved more important as a precedent than effective as a watchdog.

Concern over the growing power of the trusts led Congress to pass the Sherman Antitrust Act in 1890. The act outlawed pools and trusts, ruling that businesses could no longer enter into agreements to restrict competition. It did nothing to restrict huge holding companies such as Standard Oil, however, and proved to be a weak sword against the trusts. In the following decade, the government successfully struck down only six trusts but used the law four times against labor by outlawing unions as a "conspiracy in restraint of trade." In 1895, the Supreme Court dealt the antitrust law a crippling blow in *United States v. E. C. Knight Company*. In its decision, the Court ruled that "manufacture" did not constitute "trade." This semantic quibble drastically narrowed the law, in this case allowing the American Sugar Refining Company, which had bought out a number of other sugar companies (including E. C. Knight) and controlled 98 percent of the production of sugar, to continue its virtual monopoly.

Both the ICC and the Sherman Antitrust Act testified to the nation's concern about corporate abuses of power and to a growing willingness to use federal measures to intervene on behalf of the public interest. As corporate capitalism became more and more powerful, public pressure toward government intervention grew. Yet not until the twentieth century would more active presidents sharpen and use these weapons effectively against the large corporations.

The Fight for Free Silver

While the tariff and regulation of the trusts gained many backers, the silver issue stirred passions like no other issue of the day. On one side stood those who believed that gold constituted the only honest money. Although other forms of currency circulated, notably paper money such as banknotes and greenbacks, the government's support of the **gold standard** meant that anyone could redeem paper money for gold. Many who supported the gold standard were eastern creditors who did not wish to be paid in devalued dollars. On the opposite side stood a coalition of western silver barons and poor farmers from the West and South who called for free silver. The mining interests, who had seen the silver bonanza in the West drive down the price of the precious metal, wanted the government to buy silver and mint silver dollars. Farmers from the West and South who had suffered from deflation during the 1870s and 1880s hoped that increasing the money supply with silver dollars, thus causing inflation, would give them some relief by enabling them to pay off their debts with cheaper dollars.

During the depression following the panic of 1873, critics of hard money organized the Greenback Labor Party, an alliance of farmers and urban wage laborers. The Greenbackers favored issuing paper currency not tied to the gold supply, citing the precedent of the greenbacks issued during the Civil War. The government had the right to define what constituted legal tender, the Greenbackers reasoned: "Paper is equally money, when . . . issued according to law." They proposed that the nation's currency be based on its wealth—land, labor, and capital—and not simply on its reserves of gold. The Greenback Labor Party captured more than a million votes and elected fourteen members to Congress in 1878. Although conservatives considered the Greenbackers dangerous cranks, their views eventually prevailed in the 1930s, when the country abandoned the gold standard.

After the Greenback Labor Party collapsed, proponents of free silver came to dominate the monetary debate in the 1890s. Advocates of free silver pointed out that until 1873, the country had enjoyed a system of bimetallism—the minting of both silver and gold into coins. In that year, at the behest of those who favored gold, the Republican Congress had voted to stop buying and minting silver, an act silver supporters denounced as the "crime of '73." By sharply contracting the money supply at a time when the nation's economy was burgeoning, the Republicans had enriched bankers and investors at the expense of cotton and wheat farmers and industrial wage workers. In 1878 and again in 1890, with the Sherman Silver Purchase Act, Congress took steps to ease the tight money policy and appease advocates of silver by passing legislation requiring the government to buy silver and issue silver certificates. Though good for the mining interests, the laws did little to promote the inflation desired by farmers. Soon they began to call for "the free and unlimited coinage of silver," a plan whereby nearly all the silver mined in the West would be minted into coins circulated at the rate of sixteen ounces of silver to one ounce of gold.

By the 1890s, the silver issue crossed party lines. The Democrats hoped to use it to achieve a union between western and southern voters. Unfortunately for them, Democratic president Grover Cleveland remained a staunch conservative in money matters and supported the gold standard as vehemently as any Republican. After a panic on Wall Street in the spring of 1893, Cleveland called a special session of Congress and bullied the legislature into repealing the Silver Purchase Act because he believed it threatened economic confidence. Repeal proved disastrous for Cleveland, not only economically but also politically. It did nothing to bring prosperity and dangerously divided the country. Angry farmers, furious at the president's harsh monetary policy, warned Cleveland not to travel west of the Mississippi River if he valued his life.

> Angry farmers, furious at the president's harsh monetary policy, warned Cleveland not to travel west of the Mississippi River if he valued his life.

Panic and Depression

President Cleveland had scarcely begun his second term in office in 1893 when he faced a deep economic depression, the worst the country had yet seen. In the face of economic disaster, Cleveland clung to the economic orthodoxy of the gold standard. In the winter of 1894–95, the president walked the floor of the White House, sleepless over the prospect that the United States might go bankrupt. Individuals and investors, rushing to trade in their banknotes for gold, strained the country's monetary system. The Treasury's gold reserves dipped so low that unless they could be buttressed, the unthinkable might happen: The U.S. Treasury might not be able to meet its obligations.

At this juncture, J. P. Morgan stepped in and suggested a plan. A group of bankers would purchase gold abroad and supply it to the Treasury. Cleveland knew that such a scheme would unleash a thunder of protest, yet to save the gold standard, the president had no choice but to turn to Morgan for help. A storm of controversy erupted over the deal. The press claimed that Cleveland had lined his own pockets and rumored that Morgan had made $8.9 million. Neither allegation was true. Cleveland had not profited a penny, and Morgan made far less than the millions his critics claimed.

But if President Cleveland's action managed to salvage the gold standard, it did not save the country from hardship. The winter of 1894–95 was one of the worst times in American history. People faced unemployment, cold, and hunger. A firm believer in limited government, Cleveland insisted that nothing could be done to help.

"I do not believe that the power and duty of the General Government ought to be extended to the relief of individual suffering which is in no manner properly related to the public service or benefit." Nor did it occur to Cleveland that his great faith in the gold standard prolonged the depression, favored creditors over debtors, and caused immense hardship for millions of Americans.

> **REVIEW** Why were Americans split on the question of the tariff and currency?

Conclusion: Business Dominates an Era

The gold deal between J. P. Morgan and Grover Cleveland underscored a dangerous reality: The federal government was so weak that its solvency depended on a private banker. This lopsided power relationship signaled the dominance of business in the era Mark Twain satirically but accurately characterized as the Gilded Age. Perhaps no other era in American history spawned greed, corruption, and vulgarity on so grand a scale—an era when speculators like Jay Gould not only built but wrecked businesses to turn paper profits; an era when business boasted openly of buying politicians, who in turn lined their pockets at the public's expense.

Nevertheless, the Gilded Age was not without its share of solid achievements. In these years, America made the leap into the industrial age. Factories and refineries poured out American steel and oil at unprecedented rates. Businessmen like Carnegie, Rockefeller, and Morgan developed new strategies to consolidate American industry. New inventions, including the telephone and electric light and power, changed Americans' everyday lives. And the rise of mass marketing and advertising created a new consumer culture. By the end of the nineteenth century, the country had achieved industrial maturity. It boasted the largest, most innovative, most productive economy in the world. Its citizens enjoyed the

Cleveland insisted that nothing could be done to help save the country from hardship. "I do not believe that the power and duty of the General Government ought to be extended to the relief of individual suffering."

highest standard of living on the globe. No other era in the nation's history witnessed such a transformation.

Yet the changes that came with these developments worried many Americans and gave rise to the era's political turmoil. Race and gender profoundly influenced American politics, leading to new political alliances. Fearless activist Ida B. Wells fought racism in its most brutal form—lynching. Women's organizations championed causes, notably suffrage and temperance, and challenged prevailing views of woman's proper sphere. Reformers fought corruption by instituting civil service. And new issues—the tariff, the regulation of the trusts, and currency reform—restructured the nation's politics.

The Gilded Age witnessed a nation transformed. Where dusty roads and cattle trails once sprawled across the continent, steel rails now bound the country together. Cities grew exponentially, not only with new inhabitants from around the globe but also with new bridges, subways, and skyscrapers. The nation's workers and the great cities they labored to build are the focus of Chapter 19.

Selected Bibliography

General Works

Charles W. Calhoun, ed., *The Gilded Age: Essays on the Origins of Modern America* (1996).
Sean Dennis Cashman, *America in the Gilded Age: From the Death of Lincoln to the Rise of Theodore Roosevelt* (1993).
Rebecca Edwards, *New Spirits: Americans in the Gilded Age, 1865–1905* (2006).

Business

Kathleen Brady, *Ida Tarbell: Portrait of a Muckraker* (1984).
Edward Chancellor, *Devil Take the Hindmost: A History of Financial Speculation* (1999).
Ron Chernow, *Titan: The Life of John D. Rockefeller, Sr.* (1998).
Theresa M. Collins and Lisa Gitelman, *Thomas Edison and Modern America* (2002).
Morton J. Horowitz, *The Transformation of American Law, 1870–1960* (1992).
Walter Licht, *Industrializing America* (1995).
Carol Marvin, *When Technologies Were New* (1988).
David Nasaw, *Andrew Carnegie* (2006).
Jean Strouse, *Morgan: American Financier* (1999).
Viviana A. Zelizer, *The Social Meaning of Money* (1994).

Politics

Paula Baker, *The Moral Framework of Public Life* (1991).

Richard F. Bensel, *The Political Economy of American Industrialization, 1877–1900* (2000).

Ruth Bordin, *Women and Temperance: The Quest for Power and Liberty, 1873–1900* (1990).

Alyn Brodsky, *Grover Cleveland: A Study in Character* (2000).

Robert W. Cherny, *American Politics in the Gilded Age, 1868–1900* (1997).

Jane Dailey, Glenda Elizabeth Gilmore, and Bryant Simon, eds., *Jumpin' Jim Crow: Southern Politics from the Civil War to Civil Rights* (2000).

Laura F. Edwards, *Gendered Strife and Confusion: The Political Culture of Reconstruction* (1997).

Rebecca Edwards, *Angels in the Machinery: Gender in American Party Politics from the Civil War to the Progressive Era* (1997).

Dana Frank, *Buy American: The Untold Story of Economic Nationalism* (1999).

Steven Hahn, *A Nation under Our Feet: Black Political Struggles in the Rural South from Slavery to the Great Migration* (2003).

Darlene Clark Hine and Kathleen Thompson, *A Shining Thread of Hope: The History of Black Women in America* (1998).

Ari Hoogenboom, *Rutherford B. Hayes: Warrior and President* (1995).

H. Paul Jeffers, *An Honest President: The Life and Presidencies of Grover Cleveland* (2000).

Ross Evans Paulson, *Liberty, Equality and Justice: Civil Rights, Women's Rights and the Regulation of Business, 1865–1932* (1997).

Jacqueline Jones Royster, *Southern Horrors and Other Writings: The Anti-Lynching Campaign of Ida B. Wells, 1892–1900* (1996).

Dorothy Salem, *To Better Our World: Black Women in Organized Reform, 1890–1920* (1990).

Ian Tyrell, *Woman's World, Woman's Empire: The Woman's Christian Temperance Union in International Perspective, 1880–1930* (1991).

LeeAnn Whites, *Gender Matters: Civil War, Reconstruction, and the Making of the New South* (2005).

Culture

Ellen Gruber Garvey, *The Adman in the Parlor: Magazines and the Gendering of Consumer Culture, 1880s to 1910s* (1996).

Judy Arlene Hilkey, *Character Is Capital: Success Manuals and Manhood in Gilded Age America* (1997).

Jane H. Hunter, *How Young Ladies Became Girls: The Victorian Origins of American Girlhood* (2002).

Jill Jonnes, *Empires of Light: Edison, Tesla, Westinghouse, and the Race to Electrify the World* (2003).

Paulette D. Kilmer, *The Fear of Sinking: The American Success Formula in the Gilded Age* (1996).

▶ For more books about topics in this chapter, see the Online Bibliography at bedfordstmartins.com/roark.

▶ For additional firsthand accounts of this period, see Chapter 18 in Michael Johnson, ed., *Reading the American Past*, Fourth Edition.

▶ For Web sites, images, and documents related to topics and places in this chapter, visit bedfordstmartins.com/makehistory.

REVIEWING THE CHAPTER

Follow these steps to review and strengthen your understanding of the chapter.
STEP 1: *Study the* **Key Terms** *and* **Timeline** *to identify the significance of each item listed.*
STEP 2: *Answer the* **Review Questions**, *drawing on key terms and dates to support your answers.*
STEP 3: *Drawing on the Key Terms, Timeline, and Review Questions, answer the broader* **Making Connections** *questions.*

KEY TERMS

Who
Mark Twain (p. 627)
Jay Gould (p. 628)
Andrew Carnegie (p. 628)
John D. Rockefeller (p. 634)
Ida M. Tarbell (p. 636)
Gustavus Swift (p. 636)
Henry John Heinz (p. 637)
Alexander Graham Bell (p. 640)
Thomas Alva Edison (p. 640)
George W. Westinghouse (p. 640)
John Pierpont Morgan (p. 641)
William Graham Sumner (p. 644)
Ida B. Wells (p. 650)
Elizabeth Cady Stanton (p. 651)
Susan B. Anthony (p. 651)
Jane Cunningham Croly (Jennie June)
   (p. 651)
Frances Willard (p. 652)
Rutherford B. Hayes (p. 653)
Roscoe Conkling (p. 653)

James G. Blaine (p. 653)
James A. Garfield (p. 654)
Grover Cleveland (p. 655)
Benjamin Harrison (p. 656)
William McKinley (p. 657)

What
The Gilded Age (p. 627)
Carnegie Steel (p. 632)
vertical integration (p. 633)
Standard Oil Company (p. 634)
trust (p. 635)
horizontal integration (p. 635)
holding company (p. 636)
finance capitalism (p. 641)
United States Steel (p. 644)
oligopoly (p. 644)
social Darwinism (p. 644)
"The Gospel of Wealth" (p. 645)
laissez-faire (p. 645)
spoils system (p. 648)

New South (p. 649)
Redeemers (p. 649)
Readjusters (p. 650)
antilynching movement (p. 650)
National Woman Suffrage Association
   (NWSA) (p. 651)
General Federation of Women's Clubs
   (GFWC) (p. 651)
Woman's Crusade (p. 652)
Woman's Christian Temperance Union
   (WCTU) (p. 652)
Stalwarts (p. 653)
Half Breeds (p. 653)
Mugwumps (p. 653)
civil service reform (p. 655)
Grange (p. 657)
Interstate Commerce Act (p. 657)
Sherman Antitrust Act (p. 658)
gold standard (p. 658)
Greenback Labor Party (p. 659)
free silver (p. 659)

TIMELINE

◀ **1869** • First transcontinental railroad completed.
    • National Woman Suffrage Association (NWSA) founded.
  1870 • John D. Rockefeller incorporates Standard Oil Company.
    1872 • Andrew Carnegie builds the largest, most up-to-date Bessemer steel plant in the world.
      1873 • U.S. government stops minting silver.
        • Wall Street panic leads to major economic depression.
        • Woman's Crusade begins.

        1874 • Woman's Christian Temperance Union (WCTU) founded.
          1876 • Alexander Graham Bell demonstrates telephone.

            1877 • Republican Rutherford B. Hayes sworn in as president.
              • "Redeemers" come to power in South.
              • *Munn v. Illinois*.
                1879 • Thomas Alva Edison perfects lightbulb.
                  1880 • Republican James A. Garfield elected president.
                    1881 • Garfield assassinated; Vice President Chester A. Arthur becomes president.

REVIEW QUESTIONS

1. How did John D. Rockefeller gain control of 90 percent of the oil-refining business by 1890? (pp. 628–40)

2. Why did the ideas of social Darwinism appeal to many Americans in the late nineteenth century? (pp. 641–47)

3. How did race and gender influence politics? (pp. 647–53)

4. How did the question of civil service reform contribute to divisions within the Republican Party? (pp. 653–56)

5. Why were Americans split on the question of the tariff and currency? (pp. 656–60)

MAKING CONNECTIONS

1. Late-nineteenth-century industrialization depended on developments in technology and business strategy. What were some of the key innovations in both arenas? How did they facilitate the maturation of American industry? How did the railroads contribute to the growth of American industry? In your answer, discuss the drawbacks and benefits of these developments.

2. By the 1870s, several new concerns had displaced slavery as the defining question of American politics. What were these new issues, and how did they shape new regional, economic, and racial alliances and rivalries? In your answer, consider the part political parties played in this process.

3. Energetic political activity characterized Gilded Age America, both within formal party politics and beyond. How did the activism of women denied the vote contribute to the era's electoral politics? In your answer, be sure to cite specific examples of political action.

4. The U.S. Congress and the Supreme Court facilitated the concentration of power in the hands of private business concerns during the Gilded Age. Citing specific policies and court decisions, discuss how government helped augment the power of big business in the late nineteenth century.

▶ FOR PRACTICE QUIZZES, A CUSTOMIZED STUDY PLAN, AND OTHER STUDY TOOLS, see the Online Study Guide at bedfordstmartins.com/roark.

1882 • John D. Rockefeller develops the trust.

1883 • Pendleton Civil Service Act.

1884 • Democrat Grover Cleveland elected president.

1886 • *Wabash v. Illinois.*

1887 • Interstate Commerce Act.

1888 • Republican Benjamin Harrison elected president.

1890 • McKinley tariff.
• General Federation of Women's Clubs (GFWC) founded.
• Sherman Antitrust Act.

1892 • Ida B. Wells launches antilynching campaign.

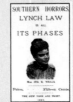

1893 • Wall Street panic touches off national depression.

1895 • J. P. Morgan bails out U.S. Treasury.

1901 • U.S. Steel incorporated for $1.4 billion.

BROOKLYN BRIDGE FAN

This commemorative fan celebrates the opening of the Great East River Bridge on May 24, 1883. A testament in stone and steel to the growing importance of urban America, the Brooklyn Bridge stood as a symbol not only of New York but of the era. Conceived amid the corruption of Boss Tweed's regime and inaugurated at a ceremony that pointedly excluded the workers who had risked their lives to build it, the bridge evoked all the contradictions of the Gilded Age. In an age of enterprise and hucksterism, the bridge became a popular motif in advertising. The lithograph on the fan depicts a view of the bridge over the East River with ships in the foreground and the Manhattan skyline, as well as commerce along the quays illustrated in detail in the background. On the back is an advertisement for the Cowperthwaits Furniture Company. The firm's sign is visible among the buildings in the lithograph, and an image of the company's building, along with its address and telephone number, is printed on the back.

Museum of the City of New York.

The City and Its Workers

1870–1900

"**A** TOWN THAT CRAWLED now stands erect, and we whose backs were bent above the hearths know how it got its spine," boasted a steelworker surveying New York City. Where once wooden buildings stood rooted in the mire of unpaved streets, cities of stone and steel sprang up in the last decades of the nineteenth century. The labor of millions of workers, many of them immigrants, laid the foundations for urban America.

No symbol better represented the new urban landscape than the Brooklyn Bridge, opened in May 1883 and quickly hailed as "one of the wonders of the world." The great bridge soared over the East River in a single mile-long span. Begun in 1869, the bridge was the dream of builder John Roebling, who died in a freak accident almost as soon as construction began.

The building of the Brooklyn Bridge took fourteen years and cost the lives of thirty men. Nearly three hundred workers labored around the clock in three shifts, six days a week, most for $2 a day. To sink the foundation deep into the riverbed, common laborers tunneled down through mud and debris, working in reinforced wooden boxes called caissons, which were open at the bottom and pressurized to keep the water from flooding in. Before long, the workers experienced a mysterious malady they called "bends" because it left them doubled over in pain after they came to the surface. (Scientists later discovered that nitrogen bubbles trapped in the bloodstream caused the condition and that it could be prevented if the men came up slowly to allow for decompression.)

The first death occurred when the caisson reached a depth of seventy-one feet. On April 22, 1872, a heavyset German immigrant named John Meyers complained that he did not feel well and headed home to his boardinghouse. Before he could reach his bed, he collapsed and died. Eight days later, another man dropped dead, and the entire workforce in the caissons went out on strike. Conditions had become so hazardous, so terrifying that the workers demanded a higher wage for fewer hours of work.

One worker, Frank Harris, remembered the men's fear of working in the caissons. As a scrawny sixteen-year-old from Ireland, Harris started to work a few days after landing in America. He described how the men went into a coffin-like "air-lock" to acclimate to the pressure of the compressed air in the caissons:

> When the air was fully compressed, the door of the air-lock opened at a touch and we all went down to work with pick and shovel on the gravelly bottom. My headaches soon became acute. The six of us were working naked to the

Construction of the Brooklyn Bridge
This photograph shows the giant cables of the Brooklyn Bridge being put in place.
The sloping wooden footpath that leads to the gothic tower provided access for
the workers. The massive bridge took fourteen years to build and cost the lives
of thirty men.
© Bettmann/Corbis.

waist in the small iron chamber with the temperature of about 80 degrees Fahrenheit: In five minutes the sweat was pouring from us, and all the while we were standing in icy water that was only kept from rising by the terrific pressure. No wonder the headaches were blinding.

Harris recalled the big Swede who headed the work gang telling him that "I could stay as long as I liked, but he advised me to leave at the end of a month: It was too unhealthy." By the fifth day, Harris experienced terrible shooting pains in his ears, and fearing he might go deaf, he quit. Like Harris, many immigrant workers walked off the job, often as many as a hundred a week. But a ready supply of immigrants meant that the work never slowed or stopped; new workers eagerly entered the caissons, where they could earn in a day more than they made in a week in Ireland or Italy.

Washington Roebling, who took over as chief engineer after his father's death, routinely worked twelve to fourteen hours six days a week. Soon he, too, fell victim to the bends and ended up an invalid, directing the completion of the bridge through a telescope from his window in Brooklyn Heights. His wife, Emily Warren Roebling, acted as site superintendent and general engineer of the project. At the dedication of the bridge, Roebling turned to his wife and said, "I want the world to know that you, too, are one of the Builders of the Bridge."

Arching 130 feet above the East River, the bridge carried a roadway for vehicles and above it a pedestrian walkway. Together, they pierced massive granite towers at each end through two huge Gothic arches. Roebling intended the bridge to stand as "a great work of art" as well as "a successful specimen of advanced Bridge engineering." Generations of artists and poets have testified to his success.

At the end of the nineteenth century, the Brooklyn Bridge stood as a symbol of many things: the industrial might of the United States; the labor of the nation's immigrants; the ingenuity and genius of its engineers and inventors; the rise of iron and steel; and most of all, the ascendancy of urban America. Poised on the brink of the twentieth century, the nation was shifting inexorably from a rural, agricultural society to an urban, industrial nation. In the nation's cities, tensions would erupt into conflict as workers squared off to fight for their rights to organize into labor unions and demand safer working conditions, shorter hours, and better pay. And the explosive growth of the cities would foster political corruption as unscrupulous bosses and entrepreneurs cashed in on the building boom. Immigrants, political bosses, middle-class managers, poor laborers, and the very rich populated the burgeoning cities, crowding the streets, laboring in the stores and factories, and taking their leisure at the new ballparks, amusement parks, dance halls, and municipal parks that dotted the urban landscape. As the new century dawned, the city and its workers moved to center stage in American life.

The Rise of the City

"We cannot all live in cities, yet nearly all seem determined to do so," New York editor Horace Greeley complained. The last three decades of the nineteenth century witnessed an urban explosion. Cities and towns grew more than twice as rapidly as the total population. Among the fastest-growing cities, Chicago expanded at a meteoric rate, from 100,000 in 1860 to over a million by 1890, doubling its population each decade. By 1900, the number of cities with more than 100,000 inhabitants had jumped from eighteen in 1870 to thirty-eight. Most of the nation's largest cities were east of the Mississippi, although St. Louis and San Francisco both ranked among the top ten urban areas in 1900. And in the far West, Los Angeles mushroomed from a sleepy village of 5,000 in 1870 to a metropolis of more than 100,000 a scant thirty years later. By 1900, the United States boasted three cities with more than a million inhabitants—New York, Chicago, and Philadelphia.

Patterns of global migration contributed to the rise of the city. In the port cities of the East Coast, more than fourteen million people arrived, many from southern and eastern Europe, and huddled together in dense urban ghettos. The word *slum* entered the American vocabulary and with it growing concern over the rising tide of newcomers. In the city, the widening gap between rich and poor became more visible, exacerbated by changes in the city landscape brought about by advances in transportation and technology.

The Urban Explosion, a Global Migration

The United States grew up in the country and moved to the city, or so it seemed by the end of the nineteenth century. Between 1870 and 1900, eleven million people moved into cities. Burgeoning industrial centers such as Pittsburgh, Chicago, New York, and Cleveland acted as giant magnets, attracting workers from the countryside. But migrants to the cities were by no means limited to rural Americans. Worldwide in scope, the movement from rural areas to urban industrial centers attracted millions of immigrants to American shores in the waning decades of the nineteenth century.

By the 1870s, the world could be conceptualized as three interconnected geographic regions (Map 19.1, page 668). At the center stood an industrial core bounded by Chicago and St. Louis in the west; Toronto, Glasgow, and Berlin in the north; Warsaw in the east; and Milan, Barcelona, Richmond, and Louisville in the south. Surrounding this industrial core lay a vast agricultural domain encompassing Canada, much of Scandinavia, Russia and Poland, Hungary, Greece, Italy and Sicily, southern Spain, the South and the western plains of America, central and northern Mexico, the hinterlands of northern China, and the southern islands of Japan. Capitalist development in the late nineteenth century shattered traditional patterns of economic activity in this rural periphery.

As old patterns broke down, these rural areas exported, along with other raw materials, new recruits for the industrial labor force.

Beyond this second circle lay an even larger third world including the Caribbean, Central and South America, the Middle East, Africa, India, and most of Asia. Ties between this part of the world and the industrial core strengthened in the late nineteenth century, but most of the people living there stayed put. They worked on plantations and railroads, in mines and ports, as part of a huge export network managed by foreign powers that staked out spheres of influence and colonies in this vast region.

Russian Immigrant Family

A Russian immigrant family is shown leaving Ellis Island in 1900. Notice the white slips of paper pinned to their coats indicating that they have been processed. The couple is well dressed, she in a dark dress and scarf and he in a suit and tie. But the paucity of their possessions testifies to the struggles they would face in their new country. She carries her belongings in a white cloth sack, and he has a suitcase in one hand and bedding draped over his arm. An immigration official in uniform stands on the left. Ellis Island opened the year this photograph was taken, replacing the old immigration station at Castle Garden in lower Manhattan.

Keystone-Mast Collection, UCR/California Museum of Photography, University of California, Riverside.

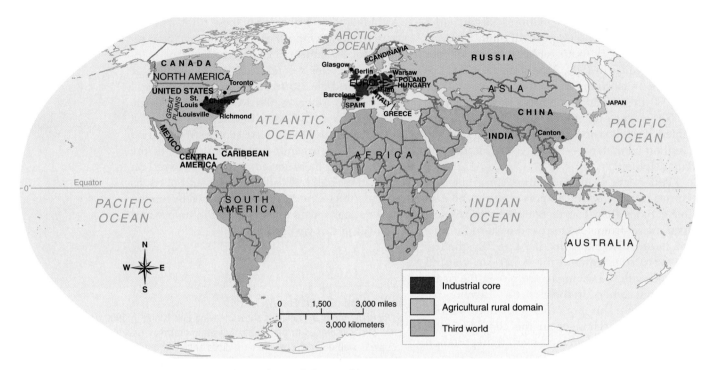

MAP 19.1   **Economic Regions of the World, 1890s**
The global nature of the world economy at the turn of the twentieth century is indicated by three inter-connected geographic regions. At the center stands the industrial core—western Europe and the north-eastern United States. The second region—the agricultural periphery—supplied immigrant laborers to the industries in the core. Beyond these two regions lay a vast area tied economically to the industrial core by colonialism.

READING THE MAP: What types of economic regions were contained in the United States in this period? Which held most of the industrial core—the Northern or the Southern Hemisphere? Which hemisphere held most of the agricultural rural domain? Which held the greatest portion of the third world?
CONNECTIONS: Which of these three areas provided the bulk of immigrant workers to the United States? What major changes prompted the global migration at the end of the nineteenth century?

FOR MORE HELP ANALYZING THIS MAP, see the map activity for this chapter in the Online Study Guide at
bedfordstmartins.com/roark.

In the 1870s, railroad expansion and low steamship fares gave the world's peoples a new-found mobility that enabled industrialists to draw on a global population for cheap labor. When Andrew Carnegie opened his first steel mill in 1872, his superintendent hired workers he called "buckwheats"—young American boys just off the farm. By the 1890s, however, Carnegie's workforce was liberally sprinkled with other rural boys—Hungarians and Slavs who had migrated to the United States, willing to work for low wages.

Altogether, more than 25 million immigrants came to the United States between 1850 and 1920. They came from all directions: east from Asia, south from Canada, north from Latin

America, and west from Europe (Map 19.2). Part of a worldwide migration, immigrants traveled to South America and Australia as well as to the United States. Yet more than 70 percent of all European immigrants chose North America as their destination.

The largest number of immigrants to the United States came from the British Isles and from German-speaking lands. (See "Global Comparison," page 670.) The vast majority of immigrants were white; Asians accounted for fewer than one million immigrants, and other people of color numbered even fewer. Yet ingrained racial prejudices increasingly influenced the country's perception of immigration patterns. One of the classic formulations of the history of European immigration divided immigrants into two distinct waves that have been called the "old" and the "new" immigration. According to this formulation, before 1880 the majority of immigrants came from northern and western Europe, with Germans, Irish, English, and Scandinavians making up approximately 85 percent of the newcomers. After 1880, the pattern shifted, with more and more ships carrying passengers from southern and eastern Europe. Italians, Hungarians, eastern European Jews, Turks, Armenians, Poles, Russians, and other Slavic peoples accounted for more than 80 percent of all immigrants by 1896 (Figure 19.1, page 671). Implicit in the distinction

was an invidious comparison between "old" pioneer settlers and "new" unskilled proletarians. Yet this sweeping generalization spoke more to perception than to reality. In fact, many of the earlier immigrants from Ireland, Germany, and Scandinavia came not as settlers or farmers, but as wage laborers, much like the Italians and Slavs who followed them.

The "new" immigration resulted from a number of factors. Improved economic conditions in western Europe coupled with increased immigration to Australia and Canada slowed the flow of immigrants coming into the United States from northern and western Europe. At the same

---

MAP 19.2   The Impact of Immigration, to 1910

Immigration flowed in all directions—south from Canada, north from Mexico and Latin America, east from Asia to Seattle and San Francisco, and west from Europe to East Coast port cities including Boston and New York.

READING THE MAP: Which states had high percentages of immigrants? Which cities attracted the most immigrants? Which cities the fewest?

CONNECTIONS: Why did most immigrants gravitate toward the cities? Why do you think the South drew such a low percentage of immigrants?

FOR MORE HELP ANALYZING THIS MAP, see the map activity for this chapter in the Online Study Guide at bedfordstmartins.com/roark.

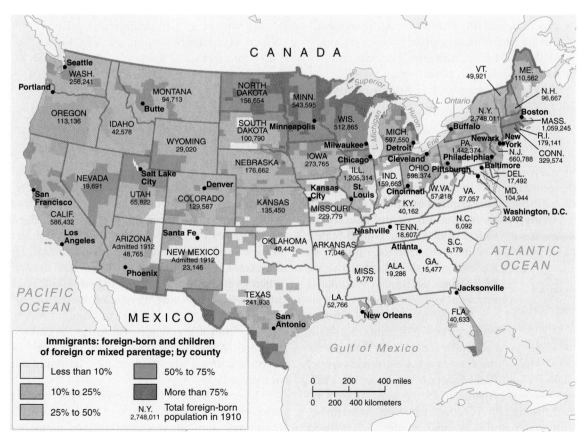

GLOBAL COMPARISON

European Emigration, 1870–1890

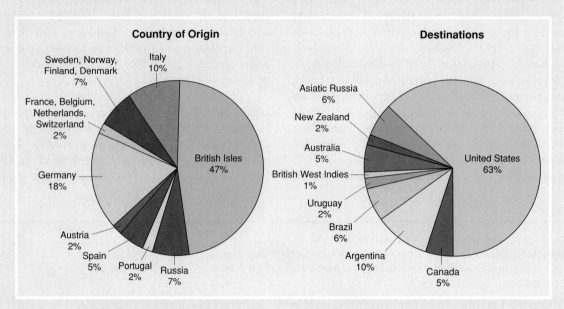

Country of Origin

- Sweden, Norway, Finland, Denmark 7%
- Italy 10%
- France, Belgium, Netherlands, Switzerland 2%
- Germany 18%
- Austria 2%
- Spain 5%
- Portugal 2%
- Russia 7%
- British Isles 47%

Destinations

- Asiatic Russia 6%
- New Zealand 2%
- Australia 5%
- British West Indies 1%
- Uruguay 2%
- Brazil 6%
- Argentina 10%
- Canada 5%
- United States 63%

A comparison of European emigrants and their destinations between 1870 and 1890 shows that emigrants from Germany and the British Isles (including England, Ireland, Scotland, and Wales) formed the largest group of out-migrants. The United States, which took in 63 percent of these emigrants, was by far the most popular destination, with Argentina, Brazil, Australia, Canada, and Asiatic Russia also attracting a share of the European immigrants. After 1890, the origin of European emigrants would tilt south and east, with Italians and eastern Europeans growing in number. Argentina proved a particularly popular destination among Italian emigrants, who found the climate and geography to their liking. In the United States, the number of German and British immigrants declined. What factors might account for why Europeans immigrated to the port cities of the eastern United States rather than to South America or Australia?

time, economic depression in southern Italy, the persecution of Jews in eastern Europe, and a general desire to avoid **conscription** into the Russian army led many people from southern and eastern Europe to move to the United States. The need of America's industries for cheap, unskilled labor during prosperous years also stimulated immigration.

Steamship companies courted immigrants—a highly profitable, self-loading cargo. By the 1880s, the price of a ticket from Liverpool had dropped to less than $25. Agents from the large lines traveled throughout Europe drumming up business. Colorful pamphlets and posters advertised America as the land of promise. Would-be immi-

> People left Europe for the United States believing, as one Italian immigrant observed, "that if they were ever fortunate enough to reach America, they would fall into a pile of manure and get up brushing the diamonds out of their hair."

grants eager for information about the United States relied on letters from friends and relatives, advertisements, and word of mouth—sources that were not always dependable or truthful. Even photographs proved deceptive: Workers dressed in their Sunday best looked more prosperous than they actually were to relatives in the old country, where only the very wealthy wore white collars or silk dresses. No wonder people left for the United States believing, as one Italian immigrant observed, "that if they were ever fortunate enough to reach America, they would fall into a pile of manure and get up brushing the diamonds out of their hair."

Most of the newcomers stayed in the nation's cities. By 1900, almost two-thirds of the country's immigrant population resided in cities, many too poor to move on. (The average laborer immigrat-

Rags to Riches

Popular author Horatio Alger's formulaic novels feature fatherless young men who, through the right combination of "pluck and luck," move ahead in the world. Alger's message of rags to riches fueled the dreams of countless young people in the late nineteenth century. Yet despite the myth, few Americans rose from rags to riches. Even Alger's heroes, such as his popular character Ragged Dick, pictured here, more often traded their rags for respectability, not for great wealth.

Private Collection.

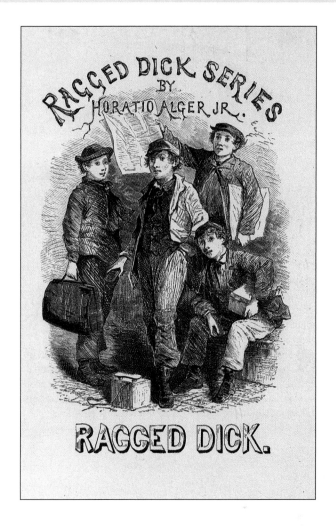

ing to the United States carried only about $21.50.) Although the foreign-born population rarely outnumbered the native-born population, taken together immigrants and their American-born children did constitute a majority, particularly in the nation's largest cities: Philadelphia, 55 percent; Boston, 66 percent; Chicago, 75 percent; and New York City, an amazing 80 percent in 1900.

Not all the newcomers came to stay. Perhaps eight million European immigrants—most of them young men—worked for a year or a season and then returned to their homelands. Immigration officers called these young male immigrants, many of them Italians, "birds of passage" because they followed a regular pattern of migration to and from the United States. By 1900, almost 75 percent of the new immigrants were young, single men.

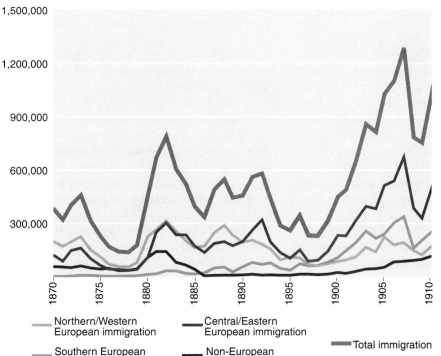

FIGURE 19.1 European Immigration, 1870–1910
Before 1880, more than 85 percent of U.S. immigrants came from northern and western Europe—Germany, Ireland, England, and the Scandinavian countries. After 1880, 80 percent of the "new" immigrants came from Italy, Turkey, Hungary, Armenia, Poland, Russia, and other Slavic countries.

Knife and Scissors Sharpener Pushcart
Joseph Antonucci, an Italian immigrant, used this knife and scissors sharpener cart on Chicago's West Side in 1900. After a day's work, Antonucci usually parked the cart in a fire station or a customer's stable, then took the train home. Sometimes he pushed his cart for miles to ply his trade beyond the city limits in towns such as Hammond, Indiana. For poor immigrants who could not afford rent, pushcarts provided a cheap and portable means of livelihood. The cries of street peddlers, vendors, and scissors sharpeners like Antonucci added to the cacophony of the urban streets.
Chicago Historical Society.

York City's Lower East Side rang with the calls of pushcart peddlers and vendors hawking their wares, from pickles to feather beds.

Racism and the Cry for Immigration Restriction

Ethnic diversity and racism played a role in dividing skilled workers (those with a craft or specialized ability) from the globe-hopping proletariat of unskilled workers (those who supplied muscle or tended machines). As industrialists mechanized to replace skilled workers with lower-paid, unskilled labor, they drew on immigrants, particularly those from southern and eastern Europe, who had come to the United States in the hope of bettering their lives. Skilled workers, frequently members of older immigrant groups from northern or western Europe, criticized the newcomers. One Irish worker complained, "There should be a law . . . to keep all the Italians from comin' in and takin' the bread out of the mouths of honest people."

The Irish worker's resentment of the new Italian immigrants brings into focus the impact of racism on America's immigrant laborers. Throughout the nineteenth century and into the twentieth, members of the educated elite as well as the uneducated viewed ethnic and even religious differences as racial characteristics, referring to the Polish or the Jewish "race." Americans judged "new" immigrants of southern and eastern European "races" as inferior to those of Anglo-Teutonic "stock." Each wave of newcomers was deemed somehow inferior to the established residents. The Irish who criticized the Italians so harshly had themselves been stigmatized as a lesser "race" a generation earlier.

Immigrants not only brought their own religious and racial prejudices to the United States but also absorbed the popular prejudices of American culture. **Social Darwinism**, with its strongly racist overtones, decreed that whites stood at the top of the evolutionary ladder. But who was "white"? Skin color supposedly served as a marker for the "new" immigrants — "swarthy" Italians; dark-haired, olive-skinned Jews. But even blond, blue-eyed Poles were not considered white. The social construction of "race" is nowhere more apparent than in the testimony of an Irish dockworker who boasted that he hired only "white men" to load cargo, a category that he insisted excluded "Poles and Italians." For the new immigrants, Americanization and assimilation would prove inextricably part of becoming "white."

Women generally had less access to funds for travel and faced tighter family control. Because they stood to make less money than men, their prospective wages rarely merited the expense of long-distance travel. The traditional sexual division of labor relied on women's unpaid domestic labor and care of the very young and the very old. For these reasons, women most often came to the United States as wives, mothers, or daughters, not as single wage laborers. Only among the Irish did women immigrants outnumber men by a small margin from 1871 to 1891.

> "To die from the bite of frost is far more glorious than at the hands of a mob," proclaimed the *Defender*, Chicago's largest African American newspaper.

Jews from eastern Europe most often came with their families and came to stay. Beginning in the 1880s, a wave of violent **pogroms**, or persecutions, in Russia and Poland prompted the departure of more than a million Jews in the next two decades. (See "Seeking the American Promise," page 674.) Most of the Jewish immigrants settled in the port cities of the East, creating distinct ethnic enclaves. Hester Street in the heart of New

Racism took its most blatant form in the treatment of African Americans and Asians. Like other migrants from the rural periphery, African American men in the South—former slaves and the children of slaves—found work as "human machines." The labor gang system used in many industries reached brutal extremes in the South, where private employers contracted prison labor, mostly African Americans jailed for such minor crimes as vagrancy. Shackled together in chains as they worked under the watchful eyes of armed guards, these men stood on the bottom rung of labor's ladder. A Georgia man who escaped the brutal chain gang system remarked, "Call it slavery, peonage, or what not, the truth is we lived in a hell on earth." Eager to escape bigotry and poverty, many African Americans fled to the North.

For African Americans, the cities of the North promised not just economic opportunity but also an end to institutionalized segregation and persecution. **Jim Crow** laws—restrictions that segregated blacks—became common throughout the South in the decades following Reconstruction. Intimidation and lynching (essentially pogroms against black people) terrorized blacks throughout the South (see chapter 18). "To die from the bite of frost is far more glorious than at the hands of a mob," proclaimed the *Defender*, Chicago's largest African American newspaper. In the 1890s, many blacks moved north, settling for the most part in the growing cities. Racism relegated them to poor jobs and substandard living conditions, but by 1900 New York, Philadelphia, and Chicago had the largest black communities in the nation. Although the most significant African American migration out of the South would occur during and after World War I, the great exodus was already under way.

On the West Coast, Asian immigrants became scapegoats of the changing economy. After California's gold rush of the mid-1800s, many Chinese who had come to work "on the gold mountain" found jobs on the country's transcontinental railroads. When the railroad work ended, they most often took work other groups shunned, including domestic service. But hard times in the 1870s made them a target for disgruntled workers. Prohibited from owning land, the Chinese migrated to the cities. In 1870, San Francisco housed a Chinese population estimated at 12,022, and it continued to grow until passage of the Chinese Exclusion Act in 1882 (see chapter 17). For the first time in the nation's history, U.S. law excluded an immigrant group on the basis of race. Some Chinese managed to come to America using a loophole that allowed relatives to join their families. In contrast, the nation's small Japanese community of about 3,000 expanded rapidly after 1890, until pressures to keep out all Asians led in 1910 to the creation of an immigration station at Angel Island in San Francisco Bay. Asian immigrants were detained there, sometimes for months, and many were deported as "undesirables." Their sad stories can be read in the graffiti on the barracks walls. One immigrant from Heungshan (Macao) wrote:

> There are tens of thousands of poems
> on these walls.
> They are all cries of suffering
> and sadness.

> "These people are not Americans," editorialized the popular journal *Public Opinion*, "they are the very scum and offal of Europe."

On the East Coast, the volume of immigration from Europe in the last two decades of the century proved unprecedented. In 1888 alone, more than half a million Europeans landed in America, 75 percent of them in New York City. The Statue of Liberty, a gift from the people of France erected in 1886, stood sentinel in the harbor. The nation's response to the new immigrants was best summed up in the verse inscribed at Liberty's base, penned by a young Jewish girl named Emma Lazarus:

> Give me your tired, your poor,
> Your huddled masses yearning to breathe free,
> The wretched refuse of your teeming shore,
> Send these, the homeless, tempest-tost to me,
> I lift my lamp beside the golden door!

The tide of immigrants to New York City soon swamped the immigration office at Castle Garden in lower Manhattan. An imposing new brick facility opened on Ellis Island in New York harbor in 1900. Its overcrowded halls became the gateway to the United States for millions.

To many Americans, the "new" immigrants seemed uneducated, backward, and uncouth—impossible to assimilate. "These people are not Americans," editorialized the popular journal *Public Opinion*, "they are the very scum and offal of Europe." Terence V. Powderly, head of the broadly inclusive Knights of Labor, complained that the newcomers "herded together like animals and lived like beasts."

Blue-blooded Yankees led by Senator Henry Cabot Lodge of Massachusetts formed an unlikely alliance with organized labor to press for

Seeking Refuge: A Russian Jew Flees the Pogroms

Religious refugees have sought haven on America's shores since the Pilgrims first landed at Plymouth Rock in 1620. The Founding Fathers affirmed the tradition of religious tolerance in the **Bill of Rights**, making the United States a haven for people fleeing religious persecution. To Jews caught up in the deadly pogroms (anti-Jewish riots) of czarist Russia, the United States promised a refuge and a new beginning at the turn of the twentieth century. Goldie Stone, who immigrated as a young girl in 1889, remembered the awe the Statue of Liberty inspired in her as she steamed into New York harbor. "In some mystical way it seemed to me," she wrote, "that the ship was entering a cathedral, a vast cathedral that was the land itself, a sanctuary."

The horrors of the pogroms that swept Russia beginning in the 1880s remained vivid in the minds of the refugees. Fifteen-year-old Abraham Bisno recalled running for his life. "I hid myself in a clay hole in an old brickyard on a hillside," he remembered. "I witnessed the mob coming down the hill to assault the Jewish settlement. I saw children and old people beaten—buildings burned— I heard women screaming."

Years of anti-Semitic policies pursued by the czarist government had forced the Jews into the Pale of Settlement—an area that included the territory of present-day Latvia, Lithuania, Ukraine, and Belorussia.

More than 90 percent of Russian Jews—five million by the end of the nineteenth century—lived in the Pale. There Jews faced further discrimination; they were denied legal rights, prohibited from leasing land, and charged exorbitant taxes. At the same time, Jewish men faced conscription into the Russian army— forced to serve a country that denied them basic rights and refused to allow Jewish soldiers to practice their religion.

Violent pogroms erupted in 1881 in the wake of the assassination of Czar Alexander II, sparked by rumors that he had been murdered by Jews. (One of the eight terrorists convicted of plotting the assassination proved to be Jewish.) Kiev, where Abraham Bisno lived with his parents, became the scene of a pogrom in late April. "For days on end," Bisno wrote, "entire neighborhoods were looted and largely destroyed by crowds estimated at over four thousand." Fanatical priests fed the flames by denouncing the Jews as heartless "Christ-killers" who used the blood of Christian children in their rituals. The government failed to move quickly to put down the violence, fueling the perception that the pogroms had state sanction.

Bands of Russians swarmed through the Jewish quarters, breaking down doors and smashing windows, looting or destroying all the furnishings. They ripped to shreds feather beds and feather pillows,

sending the white down into the breeze until it settled like snow over the scenes of violence and mayhem. No one knows precisely how many Jews died at the hands of the mob, but estimates range as high as five hundred.

"The building we lived in and the place we worked in were assaulted at the same time," Bisno recalled. "Mother ran for her life while we struggled for ours; we were all separated by the mob—the shop was destroyed, the goods carried away." Eventually reunited with his family, Bisno, along with some ten thousand Jews, sought sanctuary in a Christian church in Kiev, where they huddled for weeks. "There was famine, after these riots, among the Jews," Bisno reported. "No work, no food, and very poor shelter. We lay around on dirt floors with not even necessities available." In the wake of the pogroms, the Russian government issued the May Laws, placing further restrictions on Jews.

These and subsequent pogroms and persecutions prompted a great wave of Jewish emigration. Between 1880 and 1914, more than 2.7 million Jews sought refuge from religious persecution, the vast majority of them heading to the United States. Mary Antin recalled the emigration fever in her native village of Plotzk. "'America' was in everybody's mouth," she wrote. "Businessmen talked of it over their accounts; the market women . . . discuss[ed] it from stall to stall; . . . children played at emigrating. . . . All talked of it, but scarcely anybody knew one true fact about this magic land."

Among the first to emigrate were Abraham Bisno and his family. When the Bisnos learned that Jewish groups in Europe and America had raised money to help Russian Jews emigrate, they scraped together forty rubles to get from Kiev to Brody, in Galicia, where the refugees gathered. "Our family sold a sewing machine and whatever clothing could be spared—some from our very backs," he wrote. Once in Brody, the Bisnos had to wait six weeks, begging for bread on the streets, before they received money to pay for their passage overland to Hamburg and from there to Liverpool and on to the United States.

The trip was long and arduous. Crowded in steerage, the immigrants suffered seasickness in the crossing, which took two to three weeks by steamer. Once in the United States, the Bisno family was sent to Atlanta by an American committee formed to help the immigrants. The men quickly found work as tailors. Abraham struck out on his own, moving to Chattanooga, where he apprenticed to an English-speaking tailor and quickly learned the language by reading signs and advertisements. But the Bisnos were unhappy in the South. Abraham's mother complained that she could not find a butcher who sold kosher meat, and his father fretted that there was no Orthodox synagogue in the neighborhood. So after nine months, the family moved to a larger Jewish community in Chicago.

The slums of the nation's big cities, where many of the Jewish immigrants ended up, were far from a "promised land." The Bisnos lived in a dilapidated shack above a stable with a yard "full of rags, junk, rats, and vermin." Other Jewish immigrants voiced their disappointment at the conditions they encountered in the United States. "The dirt, the noise, the confusion, the swarming hurrying crowds!" Goldie Stone exclaimed. "My heart sank. This was all so different from what I had expected or dreamed."

Jewish Refugees from the Pogroms
In this colorful depiction, Liberty, dressed in the Stars and Stripes, opens the gates of the country to a Jewish immigrant couple and their children fleeing the pogroms in Russia. Abraham Bisno and his family were among the first group of immigrants to flee Kiev after the pogroms of 1881 and to seek refuge in the United States.
Yivo Institute for Jewish Research.

Bad as conditions were, the immigrant Jews appreciated the safe haven the United States afforded. And although the sweatshops where Abraham Bisno and other Jewish immigrants labored were dark and bleak, for most Jews the slums and the sweatshops proved a temporary prison. The United States provided not only a refuge but also a chance to start over and prosper. Bisno watched as many of his friends and relatives, after saving or borrowing a little money, opened small businesses of their own. "All had to begin in a very small way," he recalled. "With a hundred or two hundred dollars they were able to start grocery stores, markets, cigar stores." Bisno quickly moved up in his trade, becoming a contractor in a sweatshop by the time he reached the age of sixteen. But then his life took a different turn. In 1886, moved by the Haymarket martyrs, he converted to socialism, joined the Knights of Labor, and went on to become a labor organizer. The first president of the Chicago Cloak Makers Union, he worked until his death in 1929 to improve the lot of garment workers.

immigration restrictions. Lodge and his old-stock followers championed a literacy test, knowing that the vast majority of Italian and Slavic peasants were unable to read. In 1896, Congress approved a literacy test for immigrants, but President Grover Cleveland promptly vetoed it. "It is said," the president reminded Congress, "that the quality of recent immigration is undesirable. The time is quite within recent memory when the same thing was said of immigrants, who, with their descendants, are now numbered among our best citizens." Cleveland's veto forestalled immigration restriction but did not stop anti-immigrant forces from seeking to close the gates. They would continue to press for restrictions until they achieved their goal in the 1920s (see chapter 23).

The Social Geography of the City

During the Gilded Age, cities experienced demographic and technological changes that greatly altered the social geography of the city. Cleveland, Ohio, provides a good example. In the 1870s, Cleveland was a small city, in both population and area. Oil magnate John D. Rockefeller could, and often did, walk from his large brick house on Euclid Avenue to his office downtown. On his way, he passed the small homes of his clerks and other middle-class families. Behind these homes ran miles of alleys crowded with the dwellings of Cleveland's working class. Farther out, on the shores of Lake Erie, close to the factories and foundries, clustered the shanties of the city's poorest laborers.

Within two decades, the Cleveland that Rockefeller knew no longer existed. The coming of mass transit transformed the walking city. In its place emerged a central business district surrounded by concentric rings of residences organized by ethnicity and income. First the horsecar in the 1870s and then the electric streetcar in the 1880s made it possible for those who could afford the five-cent fare to work downtown and flee after work to the "cool green rim" of the city, with its single-family homes, lawns, gardens, and trees. By the early twentieth century, more than half of Cleveland's residents rode streetcars to work. Unable to afford even a few cents for streetcar fare, the city's poor crowded into the inner city or lived "back of the yards" near the factories where they worked. This pattern of development repeated throughout the country as urban congestion and suburban sprawl forever altered the social geography of the city. Social segregation—the separation of rich and poor, and of ethnic and old-stock Americans—was one of the major social changes engendered by the rise of the industrial metropolis, evident not only in Cleveland but in cities across the nation.

Race and ethnicity affected the way cities evolved. Newcomers to the burgeoning cities faced hostility and not surprisingly sought out their kin and country folk as they struggled to survive. Distinct ethnic neighborhoods often formed around a synagogue or church. Blacks typically experienced the greatest residential segregation, but every large city had its ethnic enclaves—Little Italy, Chinatown, Bohemia Flats, Germantown—where English was rarely spoken.

In 1890, Jacob Riis, a young police reporter, took his notebook and camera into the tenements of New York City. (See chapter 21, "The Promise of Technology," page 762.) The result was the best-selling book *How the Other Half Lives* (1890). Riis invited his readers into a Bottle Alley tenement:

> Here is a "flat" [made up] of "parlor" and two pitch-dark coops called bedrooms. Truly the bed is all there is room for. The family tea-kettle is on the stove, doing duty for the time being as a wash-boiler. . . . One, two, three beds are there, if the old boxes and heaps of foul straw can be called by that name; a broken stove with a crazy pipe from which the smoke leaks at every joint, a table of rough boards propped up on boxes, piles of rubbish in the corner. The closeness and smell are appalling.

Poverty, crowding, dirt, and disease constituted the daily reality of New York City's immigrant poor. Riis's book, like his photographs, presented a world of black and white. There were many layers to the population Riis labeled the "other half," distinctions deepened by ethnicity, religion, race, and gender. *How the Other Half Lives* is best read as a social reformer's call to action rather than as an accurate portrayal of the city's poor. But by taking his camera into the hovels of the poor, Riis opened the nation's eyes to conditions in the tenements.

Riis's audience shivered at his revelations about the "other half." But middle-class Americans worried equally about the excesses of the wealthy. They feared the class antagonism fueled by the growing chasm between rich and poor so visible in the nation's cities. Many people shared Riis's view that "the real danger to society comes not only from the tenements, but from the ill-spent wealth which reared them."

The excesses of the Gilded Age's newly minted millionaires were nowhere more visible than in the lifestyle of the Vanderbilts. "Commodore" Cornelius Vanderbilt, the uncouth ferryman who built the New York Central Railroad, died in 1877, leaving his son $90 million. William Vanderbilt doubled that sum, and his two sons proceeded to spend it on Fifth Avenue mansions and "cottages" in Newport, Rhode Island, which, with their marble and gold leaf, sought to rival the palaces of Europe. In 1883, Alva Vanderbilt (Mrs. William Vanderbilt) launched herself into New York society by throwing a costume party so lavish that not even old New York society, which turned up its nose at the nouveau riche, could resist an invitation. Dressed as a Venetian princess, the hostess greeted her twelve hundred guests. But her sister-in-law Alice Vanderbilt stole the show by appearing as that miraculous new invention, the electric light, resplendent in a white satin evening dress studded with diamonds. The *New York World* speculated that Alva Vanderbilt's party cost more than a quarter of a million dollars (more than $4 million today).

Such ostentatious displays of wealth became especially alarming when they were coupled with disdain for the well-being of ordinary people. When a reporter in 1882 asked William Vanderbilt whether he considered the public good when running his railroads, he shot back, "The public be damned." The fear that America had become a **plutocracy**—a society ruled by the rich—gained credence from the fact that the wealthiest 1 percent of the population owned more than half the real and personal property in the country. (A century later, the top 1 percent controlled less than a quarter.) As the new century dawned, reformers would form a **progressive movement** to address the problems of urban industrialism and the substandard living and working conditions it produced.

> **REVIEW** Why did American cities experience explosive growth in the late nineteenth century?

The Vanderbilt Costume Ball, 1884
Alice Vanderbilt appeared at her sister-in-law Alva Vanderbilt's costume ball in 1883 dressed as the "Spirit of Electricity." Her costume, by the French design house of Worth, was no doubt inspired by Thomas Edison's triumphant lighting of lower Manhattan six months earlier. Made of silk and satin and trimmed with velvet, gilt metallic bullion, and real diamonds, the gown epitomized what political economist Thorstein Veblen would brand "conspicuous consumption."
Collection of the New York Historical Society.

READING THE IMAGE: In what ways does the visual image represent what Thorstein Veblen called conspicuous consumption?
CONNECTIONS: What does the image of Alice Vanderbilt imply about life in the nation's cities in the late nineteenth century?

FOR MORE HELP ANALYZING THIS IMAGE, see the visual activity for this chapter in the Online Study Guide at
bedfordstmartins.com/roark.

At Work in Industrial America

The number of industrial wageworkers in the United States exploded in the second half of the nineteenth century, more than tripling from 5.3 million in 1860 to 17.4 million in 1900. These workers toiled in a variety of settings. Many skilled workers and **artisans** still earned a living in small workshops. But with the rise of corporate capitalism, large factories, mills, and mines increasingly dotted the landscape. Sweatshops and outwork, the contracting of piecework to be performed in the home, provided work experiences different from those of factory operatives (machine tenders) and industrial workers. Pick-and-shovel labor, whether on the railroads or in the building trades, constituted yet another kind of work. Managers and other white-collar employees, as well as women "typewriters" and salesclerks, formed a new white-collar segment of America's workforce. The best way to get a sense of the diversity of workers and workplaces is to look at the industrial nation at work.

America's Diverse Workers

Common laborers formed the backbone of the American labor force. They built the railroads and subways, tunneled under New York's East River to anchor the Brooklyn Bridge, and helped lay the foundation of industrial America. These "human machines" stood at the bottom of the country's economic ladder and generally came from the most recent immigrant groups. Initially, the Irish wielded the picks and shovels that built American cities, but by the turn of the century, as the Irish bettered their lot, Slavs and Italians took up their tools.

At the opposite end of labor's hierarchy stood skilled craftsmen like iron puddler James J. Davis, a Welsh immigrant. Using brains along with brawn, puddlers took the melted pig iron in the heat of the furnace and, with long poles, formed the cooling metal into 200-pound balls, relying on eye and intuition to make each ball uniform. Davis compared the task to baking bread: "I am like some frantic baker in the inferno kneading a batch of iron bread for the devil's breakfast. My spoon weighs twenty-five pounds, my porridge is pasty iron, and the heat of my kitchen is so great that if my body was not hardened to it, the ordeal would drop me in my tracks."

Possessing such a skill meant earning good wages, up to $7 a day, when there was work. But often no work could be found. Much industry and manufacturing in the nineteenth century remained seasonal; few workers could count on year-round pay. In addition, two major depressions only twenty years apart, beginning in 1873 and 1893, spelled unemployment and hardship for all workers. In an era before unemployment insurance, workers' compensation, or old-age pensions, even the best worker could not guarantee security for his family. "The fear of ending in the poor-house is one of the terrors that dog a man through life," Davis confessed.

Skilled workers like Davis wielded power on the shop floor. Employers attempted to limit workers' control by replacing people with machines, breaking down skilled work into ever smaller tasks that could be performed by unskilled factory operatives. New England's textile mills provide a classic example of the effects of mechanized factory labor in the nineteenth century. Mary, a weaver at the mills in Fall River, Massachusetts, told her story to the *Independent* magazine. She went to work in the 1880s at the age of twelve. By then, mechanization of the looms had reduced the job of the weaver to watching for breaks in the thread. "At first the noise is fierce, and you have to breathe the cotton all the time, but you get used to it," Mary told her interviewer. "When the bobbin flies out and a girl gets hurt, you can't hear her shout—not if she just screams, you can't. She's got to wait, 'till you see her. . . . Lots of us is deaf."

During the 1880s, the number of foreign-born mill workers almost doubled. At the

Sweatshop Worker

Sweatshop workers endured crowded and often dangerous conditions. Most were young women, like the one shown here sewing pants in New York City. Young working girls earned little money but prided themselves on their independence. Notice the young woman's stylish hairdo, white shirtwaist, and necklace (an indication that she did not turn over all the money in her pay envelope to her father, as was often the case).
George Eastman House.

Amoskeag textile mill in New Hampshire, foreign-born workers, many French Canadians, constituted more than half of the workforce. At Fall River, Mary and her Scots-Irish family resented the new immigrants. "The Polaks learn weavin' quick," she remarked, using a common derogatory term to identify a rival group. "They just as soon live on nothin' and work like that. But it won't do 'em much good for all they'll make out of it." Employers encouraged racial and ethnic antagonism because it inhibited labor organization.

The majority of factory operatives in the textile mills were young, unmarried women like Mary. They worked from six in the morning to six at night six days a week, and they took home about $1 a day. The seasonal nature of the work also drove wages down. "Like as not your mill will 'shut down' three months," and "some weeks you only get two or three days' work," Mary recounted. After twenty years of working in the mill, Mary's family had not been able to scrape together enough money to buy a house: "We saved some, but something always comes."

Mechanization transformed the garment industry as well. With the introduction of the foot-pedaled sewing machine in the 1850s and the use of mechanical cloth-cutting knives in the 1870s, independent tailors were replaced with workers hired by contractors to sew pieces of cloth into clothing. Working in sweatshops, small rooms hired for the season or even in the contractor's own tenement, women and children formed an important segment of garment workers. Discriminated against in the marketplace, where they earned less than men, women generally worked for wages only eight to ten years, until they married.

Sadie Frowne, a sixteen-year-old Polish Jew, went to work in a Brooklyn sweatshop in the 1890s. Frowne sewed for eleven hours a day in a room twenty feet long and fourteen feet wide containing fourteen machines. "The machines go like mad all day, because the faster you work the more money you get," she recalled. Paid by the piece, she earned about $4.50 a week and, by rigid economy, tried to save $2. Young and single, Frowne typified the woman wage earner in the late nineteenth century. In 1890, the average workingwoman was twenty-two and had been working since the age of fifteen, laboring twelve hours a day six days a week and earning less than $6 a week.

The Family Economy: Women and Children

In 1890, the average male worker earned $500 a year, about $8,000 in today's dollars. Many working-class families, whether native-born or immigrant, lived in or near poverty, their economic survival dependent on the contributions of all family members, regardless of sex or age. One statistician estimated that in 1900, as many as 64 percent of working-class families relied on income other than the husband's wages to make ends meet. The paid and unpaid work of women and children proved essential for family survival and economic advancement.

In the cities, boys as young as six years old plied their trades as bootblacks and newsboys. Often working under an adult contractor, these children earned as little as fifty cents a day. Many of them were homeless—orphaned or cast off by their families. "We wuz six, and we ain't got no father," a child of twelve told reporter Jacob Riis. "Some of us had to go." So out he went to work on his own. In New York City, the Children's Aid Society tried to better the situation of the city's youngest workers by establishing lodging houses. To encourage "self sufficiency and self respect," the boys were expected to pay their way—six cents for a bed, six for a breakfast of bread and coffee, and six for a supper of pork and beans. Lodged in dormitories that sometimes held more than a hundred berths, the boys had to be on good behavior. A sign at the entrance admonished, "Boys who swear and chew tobacco cannot sleep here."

> Sadie Frowne, a sixteen-year-old Polish Jew, sewed for eleven hours a day. "The machines go like mad all day, because the faster you work the more money you get."

Child labor increased decade by decade after 1870. The percentage of children under fifteen engaged in paid labor did not drop until after World War I. The 1900 census estimated that 1,750,178 children ages ten to fifteen were employed, an increase of more than a million over thirty years. Children in this age range constituted more than 18 percent of the industrial labor force. Many younger children not counted by the census worked in mills, in factories, and on the streets.

In the late nineteenth century, the number of women workers also rose sharply, with their most common occupation changing slowly from domestic service to factory work and then to office work. In 1870, the census listed 1.5 million women working for wages in nonagricultural

Bootblacks

The faces and hands of the two bootblacks shown here with a third boy on a New York City street in 1896 testify to their grimy trade. Boys as young as six years old found work on city streets as bootblacks and newsboys. Often they worked for contractors who took a cut of their meager earnings. When families could no longer afford to feed their children, boys often headed out on their own at a young age. For these child workers, education was a luxury they could not afford.

Alice Austin photo, Staten Island Historical Society.

occupations. By 1890, the number had more than doubled, with 3.7 million women working for pay (Figure 19.2). Women's working patterns varied considerably according to race and ethnicity. White married women, even among the working class, rarely worked for wages outside the home. In 1890, only 3 percent were employed. Nevertheless, married women found ways to contribute to the family economy. Families often took in boarders or lodgers, which meant extra housework. In many Italian families, piecework such as making artificial flowers allowed married women to contribute to the family economy without leaving their homes. Black women, married and unmarried, worked for wages in much greater numbers than white women. The 1890 census showed that 25 percent of married

> Working-class families joined together in the struggle to make ends meet. Women's labor, paid and unpaid, and children's meager wages could mean the difference between eating and going hungry.

African American women were employed, often as domestics in the houses of white families.

Working-class families joined together in the struggle to make ends meet. Women's labor, paid and unpaid, and children's meager wages could mean the difference between eating and going hungry. Meanwhile, industrial capitalism created new "white-collar" jobs in management, offices, and department stores.

Managers and White Collars

In the late nineteenth century, business expansion and consolidation led to a managerial revolution, creating a new class of managers. As skilled workers saw their crafts replaced by mechanization, some moved into management positions. "The middle class is becoming a salaried class," a writer for the *Independent* magazine observed, "and is rapidly losing the economic and moral independence of former days." As large business organizations consolidated, corporate development separated management from ownership, and the job of directing the firm became the province of salaried executives and managers,

FIGURE 19.2   Women and Work, 1870–1890

In 1870, close to 1.5 million women worked in nonagricultural occupations. By 1890, that number had more than doubled to 3.7 million. More and more women sought work in manufacturing and mechanical industries, although domestic service still constituted the largest employment arena for women.

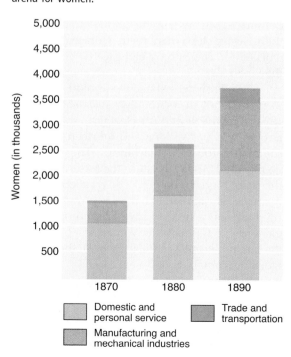

the majority of whom were white men drawn from the 8 percent of Americans who held high school diplomas. In 1880, the middle managers at the Chicago, Burlington, and Quincy Railroad earned between $1,500 and $4,000 a year; senior executives, generally recruited from the college-educated elite, took home $4,000 or more; and the company's general manager made $15,000 a year, approximately thirty times what the average worker earned. (Today's top CEOs earn as much as 411 times more than the average worker.) At the top of the economic pyramid, the great industrialists like Andrew Carnegie and John D. Rockefeller amassed fortunes calculated today in the billions.

Until late in the century, when engineering schools began to supply recruits, many skilled workers moved from the shop floor to positions of considerable responsibility. The career of William "Billy" Jones provides a glimpse of a skilled ironworker turned manager. Jones, the son of a Welsh immigrant, grew up in the heat of the blast furnaces, where he started working as an apprentice at the age of ten. When Andrew Carnegie opened his steelworks on the outskirts of Pittsburgh in 1872, he hired Jones as his plant superintendent. By all accounts, Jones was the best steel man in the industry. "Good wages and good workmen" was his motto. Carnegie constantly tried to force down workers' pay, but Jones succeeded in shortening the shift from twelve to eight hours a day by convincing Carnegie that shorter hours would reduce absenteeism and accidents. Jones himself demanded and received a "hell of a big salary." Carnegie paid him $25,000—the same salary as the president of the United States—a stupendous sum in the 1870s, which made Jones perhaps the most successful manager to move up from the shop floor. He did not have long to enjoy his newfound wealth. Jones died in 1889 when a blast furnace exploded, adding his name to the estimated 35,000 killed each year in industrial accidents.

"Typewriters" and Salesclerks

In the decades after the Civil War, as businesses became larger and more far-flung, the need for more elaborate and exact records, as well as the greater volume of correspondence, led to the hiring of more office workers. Mechanization transformed business as it had industry and manufacturing. The adding machine, the cash register, and

the typewriter came into general use in the 1880s. Employers seeking literate workers soon turned to nimble-fingered women. Educated men had many other career choices, but for middle-class white women, secretarial work constituted one of very few areas where they could put their literacy to use for wages.

Clerical Worker

A stenographer takes dictation in an 1890s office. Notice that the apron, a symbol of feminine domesticity, has accompanied women into the workplace. In the 1880s, with the invention of the typewriter, many women put their literacy skills to use in the nation's offices.
Brown Brothers.

Macy's Christmas Windows
In this 1884 engraving, a crowd of fashionably dressed New Yorkers stands three deep to look at the Christmas decorations in the window of the R. H. Macy Company on Sixth Avenue and Fourteenth Street. Department stores became monuments to mass consumption in the late 1800s. Occupying entire city blocks, big department stores such as Macy's in New York and Marshall Field in Chicago boasted up to ten floors overflowing with goods, not counting the main floor and the bargain basement. Department stores used lavishly decorated windows to attract shoppers. Here men in top hats and derbies and women in hats and bustles press forward to see the elaborate displays, indulging in a favorite new pastime—window-shopping.
Granger Collection.

Sylvie Thygeson was typical of the young women who went to work as secretaries. Thygeson grew up in an Illinois prairie town. When her father died in 1884, she went to work as a country schoolteacher at the age of sixteen, immediately after graduating high school. Quickly learning that teaching school did not pay a living wage, she mastered typing and stenography and found work as a secretary to help support her family. According to her account, she made "a fabulous sum of money." Nevertheless, she gave up her job after a few years when she met and married her husband.

Called "typewriters," women workers like Thygeson were seen as indistinguishable from the machines they operated. Far from viewing their jobs as dehumanizing, women typewriters took pride in their work and relished the economic independence it afforded them. By the 1890s, secretarial work was the overwhelming choice of white, native-born women, who constituted more than 90 percent of the female clerical force. Not only considered more genteel than factory work or domestic labor, office work also meant more money for shorter hours. Boston's clerical workers made more than $6 a week in 1883, compared with less than $5 for women working in manufacturing.

As a new **consumer culture** came to dominate American urban life in the late nineteenth century, department stores offered another employment opportunity for women in the cities. Boasting ornate facades, large plate-glass display windows, and marble and brass fixtures, stores such as Macy's in New York, Wanamaker's in Philadelphia, and Marshall Field in Chicago stood as monuments to the material promise of the era. Within these palaces of consumption, cash girls, stock clerks, and wrappers earned as little as $3 a week, while at the top of the scale, buyers like Belle Cushman of the fancy goods department at Macy's earned $25 a week, an unusually high salary for a woman in the 1870s.

In all stores, saleswomen were subject to harsh and arbitrary discipline. Sitting was forbidden, and conversation with other clerks led to instant dismissal. The women worked under the watchful eyes of male supervisors called floorwalkers, who commanded salaries twice as high as the typical saleswoman. Yet salesclerks counted themselves a cut above factory workers. Their work was neither dirty nor dangerous, and even when they earned less than factory workers, they felt a sense of superiority.

> **REVIEW** How did business expansion and consolidation change workers' occupations in the late nineteenth century?

Workers Organize

By the late nineteenth century, industrial workers were losing ground in the workplace. In the fierce competition to lower prices and cut costs, industrialists like Andrew Carnegie invested heavily in new machinery that enabled managers to replace skilled workers with unskilled labor. The erosion of skills and the redefinition of labor as mere "machine tending" left the worker with a growing sense of individual helplessness that served as a spur to collective action. In the 1870s and 1880s, labor organizations grew, and the Knights of Labor and the American Federation of Labor attracted workers. Convinced of the inequity of the wage-labor system, labor organizers spoke eloquently of abolishing class privileges and monopoly. The rhetoric frightened many middle-class Americans and led them to equate the labor movement with the specter of violence and **anarchism**. Strikes particularly underscored the tensions produced by rapid indus-

trialization. In 1877, in the midst of a depression that left many workers destitute, labor flexed its muscle in the Great Railroad Strike and showed the power of collective action.

The Great Railroad Strike of 1877

Economic depression following the panic of 1873 threw as many as three million people out of work. Those who were lucky enough to keep their jobs watched as pay cuts eroded their wages until they could no longer feed their families. In the summer of 1877, the Baltimore and Ohio (B&O) Railroad announced a 10 percent wage reduction and at the same time declared a 10 percent dividend to its stockholders. Angry brakemen in West Virginia, whose wages had already fallen from $70 to $30 a month, walked out on strike. One B&O worker described the hardship that drove him to take such desperate action: "We eat our hard bread and tainted meat two days old on the sooty cars up the road, and when we come home, find our children gnawing bones and our wives complaining that they cannot even buy hominy and molasses for food."

> One B&O worker described the hardship that drove him to strike: "We eat our hard bread and tainted meat two days old on the sooty cars up the road, and when we come home, find our children gnawing bones."

The West Virginia brakemen's strike touched off the Great Railroad Strike of 1877, a nationwide uprising that spread rapidly to Pittsburgh and Chicago, St. Louis and San Francisco (Map 19.3, page 684). Within a few days, nearly 100,000 railroad workers walked off the job. The spark of rebellion soon led an estimated 500,000 laborers to join the train workers. In Reading, Pennsylvania, militiamen refused to fire on the strikers, saying, "We may be militiamen, but we are workmen first." Rail traffic ground to a halt; the nation lay paralyzed.

Violence erupted as the strike spread. In Pittsburgh, strikers clashed with militia brought in from Philadelphia, who arrogantly boasted they would clean up "the workingmen's town." Opening fire on the crowd, the militia killed twenty people. Angry workers retaliated by reducing an area two miles long beside the tracks to smoldering rubble. Before the day ended, twenty more workers had been shot, and the railroad had sustained property damage totaling $2 million.

Within eight days, the governors of nine states, acting at the prompting of the railroad owners and managers, defined the strike as an "insurrection" and called for federal troops. President Rutherford B. Hayes, after hesitating briefly, called out the army. By the time the troops arrived, the violence had run its course. Federal troops did not shoot a single striker in 1877. But they struck a blow against labor by acting as strikebreakers—opening rail traffic, protecting nonstriking "scab" train crews, and maintaining peace along the line. In three weeks, the strike was over.

Although the Great Railroad Strike was spontaneous and unorganized, it frightened the authorities and upper classes like nothing before in U.S. labor history, fueling their hostility toward labor organization. They quickly tried to blame the tiny, radical Workingman's Party for the strike and predicted a bloody uprising. "Any hour the mob chooses it can destroy any city in the country—that is the simple truth," wrote future secretary of state John Hay to his wealthy father-in-law.

Although many middle-class Americans initially sympathized with the conditions that led to the strike, they condemned the strikers for the

violence and property damage that occurred. The *New York Times* editorialized about the "dangerous classes," and the *Independent* magazine offered the following advice on how to deal with "rioters":

> If the club of a policeman, knocking out the brains of the rioter, will answer then well and good; but if it does not promptly meet the exigency, then bullets and bayonets . . . constitutes [*sic*] the one remedy and one duty of the hour.

"The strikes have been put down by force," President Hayes noted in his diary on August 5. "But now for the real remedy. Can't something be done by education of the strikers, by judicious control of the capitalists, by wise general policy to end or diminish the evil? The railroad strikers, as a rule, are good men, sober, intelligent, and industrious." While Hayes acknowledged the workers' grievances, most businessmen and industrialists did not and fought the idea of labor unions, arguing that workers and employers entered into contracts as individuals and denying the right of unions to bargain collectively for their workers. For their part, workers quickly recognized that they held little power individually

MAP 19.3 The Great Railroad Strike of 1877
Starting in West Virginia and Pennsylvania, the strike spread as far north as Albany, New York, and as far west as San Francisco, bringing rail traffic to a standstill. Called the Great Uprising, the strike heralded the beginning of a new era of working-class protest and trade union organization.

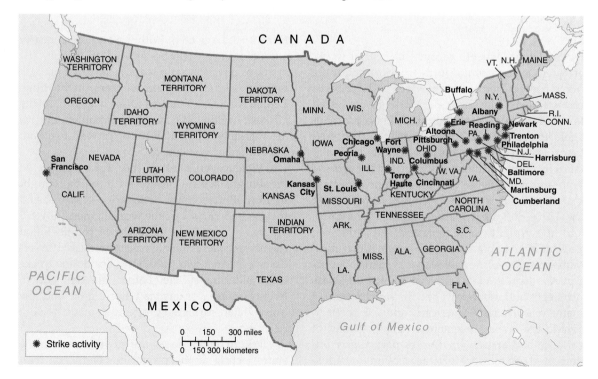

Destruction from the Great Railroad Strike of 1877
Pictures of the devastation caused in Pittsburgh during the strike shocked many Americans. When militia-men fired on striking workers, killing more than twenty strikers, the mob retaliated by destroying a two-mile area along the track, reducing it to a smoldering rubble. Property damage totaled $2 million. Curious pedestrians came out to view the destruction.
Carnegie Library of Pittsburgh.

and flocked to join unions. As labor leader Samuel Gompers noted, the strike served as an alarm bell to labor "that sounded a ringing message of hope to us all."

The Knights of Labor and the American Federation of Labor

The Knights of Labor, the first mass organization of America's working class, proved the chief beneficiary of labor's newfound consciousness. The Noble and Holy Order of the Knights of Labor had been founded in 1869 by Uriah Stephens, a Philadelphia garment cutter. A secret society of workers, the Knights envisioned a "universal brotherhood" of all workers, from common laborers to master craftsmen. The organization's secrecy and ritual served to bind Knights together at the same time that it discouraged company spies and protected members from reprisals.

Although the Knights played no active role in the 1877 railroad strike, membership swelled as a result of the growing interest in labor organizing that accompanied the strike. In 1878, the Knights abandoned secrecy and launched an ambitious campaign to organize workers regardless of skill, sex, race, or nationality. The Knights of Labor attempted to bridge the boundaries of ethnicity, gender, ideology, race, and occupation in a badly fragmented society. Under the leadership of Leonora Barry, who served as general investigator for women's work from 1886 to 1890, the Knights recruited teachers, waitresses, housewives, and domestics along with factory and sweatshop workers. Women composed perhaps 20 percent of the membership. The Knights also made good on its vow to include African Americans, organizing more than 95,000 black workers. That the Knights of Labor often fell short of its goals to unify the working class proved less surprising than the scope of its efforts.

Under the direction of Grand Master Workman Terence V. Powderly, the Knights became the dominant force in labor during the 1880s. The organization advocated a kind of workers' **democracy** that embraced reforms such as public ownership of the railroads, an income tax, equal pay for women workers, and the abolition of child labor. A loose mix of ideology, unionism, culture, fraternalism, and mysticism, the Knights called for one big union to create a cooperative commonwealth that would supplant the wage system and remove class distinctions. Only the "parasitic" members of society—gamblers, stockbrokers, lawyers, bankers, and liquor dealers—were denied membership.

In theory, the Knights of Labor opposed strikes. Powderly championed arbitration and preferred to use boycotts. But in practice, much of the organization's appeal came from a successful strike the Knights mounted in 1885 against railroads controlled by Jay Gould. The Knights won a sweeping victory, including the revocation of a 15 percent pay cut. Despite the reservations of its leadership, the Knights became a militant labor organization that won passionate support from working people with the slogan "An injury to one is the concern of all."

The Knights of Labor was not without rivals. Many skilled workers belonged to craft unions organized by trade. Among the largest and richest of these unions stood the Amalgamated Association of Iron and Steel Workers, founded in 1876 and counting twenty thousand skilled workers as members. Trade unionists spurned the broad reform goals of the Knights and focused on workplace issues. Samuel Gompers, a cigar maker born in London of Dutch Jewish ancestry, promoted what he called "pure and simple" unionism. More hardheaded than Powderly, Gompers embraced class struggle—the implacable enmity between workers and employers posited by European **socialist** Karl

Marx—and wielded the strike as the workers' most effective weapon. Gompers founded the Organized Trades and Labor Unions in 1881 and reorganized it in 1886 into the American Federation of Labor (AFL), which coordinated the activities of craft unions throughout the United States. His plan was simple: organize skilled workers such as machinists and locomotive engineers—those with the most bargaining power—and use strikes to gain immediate objectives such as higher pay and better working conditions. Gompers at first drew few converts. The AFL had only 138,000 members in 1886, compared with 730,000 for the Knights of Labor. But events soon brought down the Knights, and Gompers's brand of unionism came to prevail.

Haymarket and the Specter of Labor Radicalism

While the AFL and the Knights of Labor competed for members, more radical labor groups, including socialists and anarchists, believed that reform was futile and called instead for social revolution. Both groups, sensitive to criticism that they preferred revolution in theory to improvements here and now, rallied around the popular issue of the eight-hour day.

Since the 1840s, labor had sought to end the twelve-hour workday, which was standard in industry and manufacturing. By the mid-1880s, it seemed clear to many workers that labor shared too little in the new prosperity of the decade, and pressure mounted for the eight-hour day. Labor rallied to the popular issue and launched major rallies in cities across the nation. Supporters of the movement set May 1, 1886, as the date for a nationwide general strike in support of the eight-hour workday.

All factions of the nascent labor movement came together in Chicago on May Day for what was billed as the largest demonstration to date. A group of labor radicals led by anarchist Albert Parsons, a *Mayflower* descendant, and August Spies, a German socialist, spearheaded the eight-hour movement in Chicago. Chicago's Knights of Labor rallied to the cause even though Terence Powderly and the union's national leadership, worried about the increasing activism of the rank and file, refused to endorse the movement for shorter hours. Samuel Gompers was on hand, too, to lead the city's trade unionists, although he privately urged the AFL assemblies not to participate in the general strike.

Despite the reservations of its leadership, the Knights of Labor became a militant labor organization that won passionate support from working people with the slogan "An injury to one is the concern of all."

Gompers's skilled workers were labor's elite. Many still worked in small shops where negotiations between workers and employers took place in an environment tempered by personal relationships. Well dressed in their frock coats and starched shirts, the AFL's skilled workers stood in sharp contrast to the dispossessed workers out on strike across town at Chicago's huge McCormick reaper works. There strikers watched helplessly as the company brought in strikebreakers to take their jobs and marched the "scabs" to work under the protection of the Chicago police and security guards supplied by the Pinkerton Detective Agency. Cyrus McCormick Jr., son of the inventor of the mechanical reaper, viewed labor organization as a threat to his power as well as to his profits; he was determined to smash the union.

During the May Day rally, 45,000 workers paraded peacefully down Michigan Avenue in support of the eight-hour day, many singing the song that had become the movement's anthem:

> We mean to make things over;
>   we're tired of toil for naught
> But bare enough to live on: never
>   an hour for thought.
> We want to feel the sunshine; we
>   want to smell the flowers;
> We're sure that God has willed it,
>   and we mean to have eight hours.
> Eight hours for work, eight hours for rest,
>   eight hours for what we will!

Trouble came two days later, when strikers attacked scabs outside the McCormick works and police opened fire, killing or wounding six men. Angry radicals rushed out a circular urging workers to "arm yourselves and appear in full force" at a rally in Haymarket Square.

On the evening of May 4, the turnout at Haymarket was disappointing. No more than two or three thousand gathered in the drizzle to hear Spies, Parsons, and the other speakers. Mayor Carter Harrison, known as a friend of labor, mingled conspicuously in the crowd, pronounced the meeting peaceable, and went home to bed. A short time later, police captain John "Blackjack" Bonfield, who had made his reputation cracking skulls, marched his men into the crowd, by now fewer than three hundred people, and demanded that it disperse. Suddenly, someone threw a bomb into the police ranks. After a moment of stunned silence, the police drew their revolvers. "Fire and kill all you can," shouted a police lieutenant. When the melee ended, seven policemen and an unknown number of others lay dead. An additional sixty policemen and thirty or forty civilians suffered injuries.

News of the "Haymarket riot" provoked a nationwide convulsion of fear, followed by blind rage directed at anarchists, labor unions, strikers, immigrants, and the working class in general. Eight men, including Parsons and Spies, went on trial in Chicago, although witnesses testified that none of them had thrown the bomb. "Convict these men," thundered the state's attorney,

---

"The Chicago Riot"
Inflammatory pamphlets like this one published in the wake of the Haymarket bombing presented a one-sided view of the incident and stirred public passion. In this charged atmosphere, the anarchist speakers at the rally were tried and convicted for the bombing even though witnesses testified that none of them had thrown the bomb. The identity of the bomb thrower remains uncertain. Chicago Historical Society.

READING THE IMAGE: What does the cover suggest about the views of the author of the pamphlet?
CONNECTIONS: In what ways does this pamphlet reflect the public climate following the Haymarket bombing?

FOR MORE HELP ANALYZING THIS IMAGE, see the visual activity for this chapter in the Online Study Guide at bedfordstmartins.com/roark.

Julius S. Grinnell, "make examples of them, hang them, and you save our institutions." Although the state could not link any of the defendants to the Haymarket bombing, the jury nevertheless found them all guilty. Four were executed, one committed suicide, and three received prison sentences. On the gallows, August Spies spoke for the Haymarket martyrs: "The time will come when our silence will be more powerful than the voices you throttle today."

In 1893, Governor John Peter Altgeld, after a thorough investigation, pardoned the three remaining Haymarket anarchists. He denounced the trial as a shameless travesty of justice. The governor's action brought on a storm of protest and cost him his political career.

The bomb blast at Haymarket had lasting repercussions. To commemorate the death of the Haymarket martyrs, labor made May 1 an annual international celebration of the worker. But the Haymarket bomb, in the eyes of one observer, proved "a godsend to all enemies of the labor movement." It effectively scotched the eight-hour-day movement and dealt a blow to the Knights of Labor, already wracked by internal divisions.

With the labor movement everywhere under attack, many skilled workers turned to the American Federation of Labor. Gompers's narrow economic strategy made sense at the time and enabled one segment of the workforce—the skilled—to organize effectively and achieve tangible gains. But the nation's unskilled workers remained untouched by the AFL's brand of trade unionism. The vast majority of America's workers would have to wait another forty years before a mainstream labor union, the Congress of Industrial Organizations (CIO), moved to organize the unskilled (see chapter 24).

> On the gallows, August Spies spoke for the Haymarket martyrs: "The time will come when our silence will be more powerful than the voices you throttle today."

REVIEW Why did the fortunes of the Knights of Labor rise in the late 1870s and decline in the 1890s?

At Home and at Play

The growth of urban industrialism not only dramatically altered the workplace but also transformed home and family life and gave rise to new forms of commercialized leisure. Industrialization redefined the very concepts of work and home. Increasingly, men went out to work for wages, while most white married women stayed home, either working in the home without pay—cleaning, cooking, and rearing children—or supervising paid domestic servants who did the housework.

Domesticity and "Domestics"

The separation of the workplace and the home that marked the shift to industrial society redefined the home as a "haven in the heartless world," presided over by a wife and mother who made the household her **separate sphere**. The growing separation of workplace and home led to a new ideology, one that sentimentalized the home and women's role in it. The cultural ideology that dictated woman's place in the home has been called the **cult of domesticity**, a phrase used to prescribe an ideal of middle-class, white womanhood that dominated the period from 1820 to the end of the nineteenth century (see chapter 11).

The cult of domesticity and the elaboration of the middle-class home led to a major change in patterns of hiring household help. The live-in servant, or domestic, became a fixture in the North, replacing the hired girl of the previous century. (The South continued to rely on black female labor, first slave and later free.) In American cities by 1870, 15 to 30 percent of all households included live-in domestic servants, more than 90 percent of them women. By the mid-nineteenth century, native-born women increasingly took up other work and left domestic service to immigrants. In the East, the maid was so often Irish that "Bridget" became a generic term for female domestics.

Servants by all accounts resented the long hours and lack of privacy. "She is liable to be rung up at all hours," one study reported. "Her very meals are not secure from interruption, and even her sleep is not sacred." No wonder tension between domestic servants and their female employers proved endemic. Furthermore, going into service carried a social stigma. As one young woman observed, "If a girl goes into the kitchen she is sneered at and called 'the Bridget,' but if she goes behind the counter she is escorted by gentlemen." Domestic service became the occupation of last resort, a "hard and lonely life" in the words of one servant girl.

For women of the white middle class, domestics were a boon, freeing them from household drudgery and giving them more time to spend with their children or to pursue club work or reform. Thus, while domestic service supported the cult of domesticity, it created for those women who could afford it opportunities that expanded their horizons outside the home in areas such as women's clubs and the temperance and suffrage movements.

As if to emphasize the new role of the home as a refuge and a haven in the decades after the Civil War, the typical middle-class dwelling itself became more embellished architecturally and its interior more cluttered. Possession of such a home, indeed of any home, marked the gulf between the working poor and the middle class. Homeowners constituted only 36 percent of the U.S. housing population in 1900, compared with 69 percent today.

The gap between working-class austerity and the trappings associated with middle-class respectability becomes apparent in the comparison of two households. Margaret Byington, a reformer who undertook a scientific survey of Homestead, the Carnegie mill town outside Pittsburgh, recounted her visit with the family of a Slavic worker. The family lived in a two-room tenement, and Byington found the young mother doing the family laundry in a big washtub set on a chair in the middle of the room, struggling to keep her two babies from tumbling into the scalding water. Byington noted the sparse furnishings:

> On one side of the room was a huge puffy bed, with one feather tick to sleep on and another for covering; near the window stood a sewing machine; in the corner, an organ,—all these, besides the inevitable cook stove upon which in the place of honor was simmering the evening's soup. Upstairs in a second room, a boarder and the man of the house were asleep. Soon they would get up and turn their beds over to two more boarders, who were out at work.

Compare the Slavic family's household with the description of a middle-class home taken from *The Gilded Age*, the 1873 novel by Mark Twain and Charles Dudley Warner:

> Every room has its book-cases or book-shelves, and was more or less a library; upon every table was liable to be a litter of new books, fresh periodicals and daily newspapers. There were plants in the sunny windows and some choice engravings on the walls, with bits of color in oil or watercolors; the piano was sure to be open and strewn with music; and there were photographs and little souvenirs here and there of foreign travels.

In the eyes of Byington and many middle-class reformers, the Slavs' crowded tenement, with its boarders and its lack of privacy, scarcely qualified as a "home." Yet for all the obvious differences between the households, one can see in the workers' two feather ticks, sewing machine, and organ the same urge for sociability and impulse toward comfort apparent in the middle-class home.

Mill Towns and Company Towns

Mill towns like the one Byington studied became a feature of the industrial landscape in the nineteenth century. Many, like Homestead, grew up haphazardly. By 1892, eight thousand people lived in Homestead, transforming a rural village into a bustling mill town that belied its pastoral name. As the steelworks expanded, they encroached on the residential area, pushing the homes out of the flatlands along the Monongahela River. Workers moved into the hills and ravines. In an area called the Hollow, shanties hung precariously on the hillsides. These small, boxlike dwellings—many no larger than two rooms—housed the unskilled laborers from the mills.

Servants by all accounts resented the long hours and lack of privacy. "She is liable to be rung up at all hours," one study reported. "Her very meals are not secure from interruption, and even her sleep is not sacred."

Elsewhere, particularly in New England and the South, the company itself planned and built the town. The Amoskeag textile mill in Manchester, New Hampshire, was a self-contained world laid out according to a master plan conceived in the 1830s. Such planned communities rested on the notion of benevolent corporate paternalism. Viewing the workers as the "corporation's children," Amoskeag's owners sought to socialize their increasingly immigrant workforce to the patterns of industrial work and to instill loyalty to the company, curb labor unrest, and prevent unionization.

By the 1880s, Amoskeag employed tens of thousands of workers, housing 35 percent of them in corporation tenements. "The corporations," as workers called them, were three- to five-story attached brick houses. Workers paid the equivalent of $1 per month for company housing. To qualify, families had to have more than one member working in the mill, a requirement that encouraged child labor. The substantial brick row houses with high ceilings and hardwood floors offered a striking contrast to the ramshackle shanties of Homestead. But

690 CHAPTER 19 • THE CITY AND ITS WORKERS

through its housing, the mill exerted a powerful hold over the lives of its workers. "If you told the boss to go to hell, you might as well move out of the city," one mill worker acknowledged.

In western mining towns, companies exerted control not only over the housing of employees but over their religious and social lives as well. In Ludlow, a mining town in Colorado controlled by the Rockefeller family, the local minister was hired and supported by the company. Such ironfisted control was designed to prevent labor unions from gaining a foothold. Rockefeller hired spies to infiltrate the town, hang out at the local saloons, and report on any union activity.

Control by the mill owners reached its height in company towns south of the Mason-Dixon line. "Practically speaking," a federal investigator observed, "the company owns everything and controls everybody in the mill village." These largely nameless company towns, with their company-controlled stores, churches, schools, and houses, offer a classic example of social control over workers. Paid in company currency, or scrip, workers had no choice but to patronize the company store, where high prices led to a mounting spiral of debt that reduced the workers to virtual captives of the company. At the turn of the century, 92 percent of southern textile workers' families lived in company towns.

The mill towns and company towns of the United States provide only the most dramatic examples of the ways in which industrialization and the rise of corporate capitalism changed the landscape of the country and altered traditional patterns of work and home life.

Cheap Amusements

Growing class divisions manifested themselves in patterns of leisure as well as in work and home life. The poor and working class took their leisure, when they had any, not in the crowded tenements that housed their families, but increasingly in the cities' new dance halls, music houses, ballparks, and amusement arcades, which by the 1890s formed a familiar part of the urban landscape.

Saloons played a central role in workers' lives, often serving informally as political headquarters, employment agencies, and union halls.

But not all the working class thronged to saloons. Recreation varied according to ethnicity, religion, gender, and age. For many immigrants, social life revolved around the family. Weddings, baptisms, birthdays, and bar mitzvahs constituted the chief celebrations. Men spent more time away from home in neighborhood clubs, saloons, and fraternal orders than did women, who were largely barred from these establishments. An exception was the German beer garden, which welcomed the entire family.

The growing anonymity of urban industrial society posed a challenge to traditional rituals of courtship. Adolescent working girls no longer met prospective husbands only through their families. Fleeing crowded tenements, the young sought each other's company in dance halls and other commercial retreats. Scorning proper introductions, working-class youths "picked up" partners at dance halls, where drinking was part of the evening's entertainment. Young working-women, who rarely could afford more than trolley fare when they went out, counted on being "treated" by men, a transaction that often implied sexual payback. Young women's need to negotiate sexual encounters if they wished to participate in commercial amusements blurred the line between respectability and promiscuity and made the dance halls a favorite target of reformers who feared they lured girls into prostitution.

For men, baseball became a national pastime in the 1870s—then, as now, one force in urban life capable of uniting a city across class lines. Cincinnati mounted the first entirely paid team, the Red Stockings, in 1869. Soon professional teams proliferated in cities across the nation, and Mark Twain hailed baseball as "the very symbol, the outward and visible expression, of the drive and push and rush and struggle of the raging, tearing, booming nineteenth century."

The increasing commercialization of entertainment in the late nineteenth century can best be seen at Coney Island. A two-mile stretch of sand nine miles from Manhattan by trolley or steamship, Coney Island in the 1870s and 1880s attracted visitors to its beaches, dance pavilions, and penny arcades, where they consumed treats ranging from oysters to saltwater taffy. In the 1890s, Coney Island was transformed into the site of some of the largest and most elaborate amusement parks in the country. Promoter George Tilyou built Steeplechase Park in 1897,

Beach Scene at Coney Island

Opened in the 1870s, Coney Island came into its own at the turn of the twentieth century with the development of elaborate amusement parks. Coney Island became a symbol of commercialized leisure and mechanical excitement. This fanciful rendering captures the frenetic goings-on. Men and women, along with costumed clowns, frolic in the waves. Notice the women's bathing outfits, with their leggings, modest skirts and blouses, and bathing hats. Men box and play ball, while a uniformed policeman wades into the fray, brandishing his billy club. On the shore are the rides—with the Ferris wheel dominating the skyline—and the famous hotel in the shape of an elephant. Sunday crowds on the island reportedly reached 100,000.

Beach scene: Library of Congress; Sand pail: Private Collection.

advertising "10 hours of fun for 10 cents." With its mechanical thrills and fun-house laughs, the amusement park encouraged behavior that one schoolteacher aptly described as "everyone with the brakes off." By 1900, as many as a million New Yorkers flocked to Coney Island on any given weekend, making the amusement park the unofficial capital of a new mass culture.

REVIEW How did urban industrialism shape the world of leisure?

City Growth and City Government

Private enterprise, not planners, built the cities of the United States. Boosters, builders, businessmen, and politicians all had a hand in creating the modern metropolis. With a few notable exceptions, such as Washington, D.C., and Savannah, Georgia, there was no such thing as a comprehensive city plan. Cities simply mush-roomed, formed by the dictates of private enterprise and the exigencies of local politics. With the rise of the city came the need for public facilities, transportation, and services that would tax the imaginations of America's architects and engineers and set the scene for the rough-and-tumble of big-city government, politics, and politicians.

Building Cities of Stone and Steel

Skyscrapers and mighty bridges dominated the imagination and the urban landscape. Less imposing but no less significant were the paved streets, the parks and public libraries, and the subways and sewers. In the late nineteenth century, Americans rushed to embrace new technology of all kinds, making their cities the most modern in the world.

Structural steel made enormous advances in building possible. A decade after the completion of the Brooklyn Bridge, engineers used the new technology to construct the Williamsburg Bridge three miles to the north. More prosaic and utilitarian than its neighbor, the new bridge was never as acclaimed, but it was longer by four feet

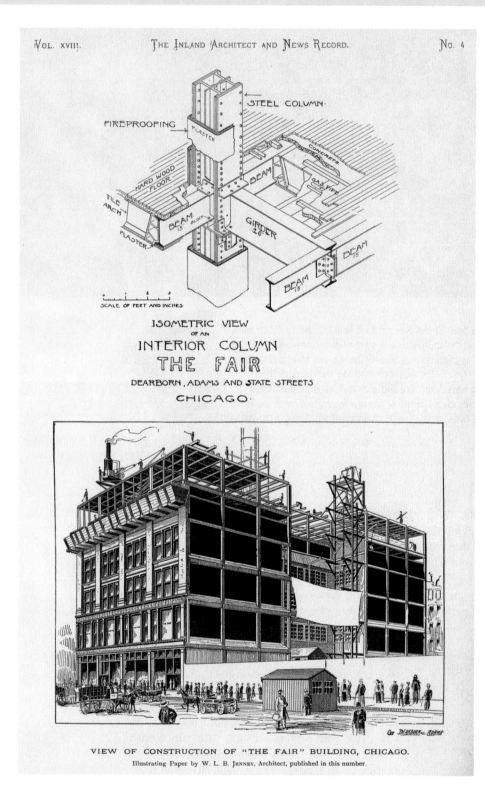

VIEW OF CONSTRUCTION OF "THE FAIR" BUILDING, CHICAGO.
Illustrating Paper by W. L. B. JENNEY, Architect, published in this number.

Chicago Skyscraper Going Up

With the advent of structural steel, skyscrapers like this one in progress in Chicago in 1891 became prominent features of the American urban landscape. This architect's rendering of the Fair Building, a department store designed by William Le Baron Jenney, shows the foundations, the structural steel skeleton, and the way the walls could simply "hang" on the outside of the building, because they no longer had to support the structure.

Newberry Library (Inland Architect, Nov. 1891).

and completed in half the time. It became the model for future building as the age of steel supplanted the age of stone and iron.

Skyscrapers forever changed the cityscape. Competition for space in Manhattan pushed the city up into the air even before the use of steel. The invention of Elisha Otis's elevator (called a "safety hoister") in the 1850s led to the construction of cast-iron buildings with elevators that carried passengers as high as ten stories. But until the advent of structural steel in the 1880s, no building in Manhattan topped the spire of Wall Street's Trinity Church.

Chicago, not New York, gave birth to the modern skyscraper. Rising from the ashes of the Great Fire of 1871, which destroyed three square miles and left eighteen thousand people homeless, Chicago offered a generation of skilled architects and engineers the chance to experiment with new technologies. Commercial architecture became an art form at the hands of a skilled group of architects who together constituted the "Chicago school." Men of genius such as Louis Sullivan and John Wellborn Root gave Chicago some of the world's finest commercial buildings. Employing the dictum "Form follows function," they built startlingly modern structures. A fitting symbol of modern America, the skyscraper expressed the domination of corporate power.

Alongside the skyscrapers rose new residential apartments for the rich and middle class. The "French flat"—apartments with the latest plumbing and electricity—gained popularity in the 1880s as affluent city dwellers overcame their distaste for multi-family housing (which carried the stigma of the tenement) and gave in to "flat fever." Fashionable new apartments boasted modern luxuries such as telephones, central heating, and elevators. The convenience of apartment living appealed particularly to women. "Housekeeping isn't fun," cried one New York woman. "Give us flats!" In 1883 alone, more than one thousand new apartments went up in Chicago.

The flush toilets, bathtubs, and lavatories of the new apartments would not have been possible without major improvements in city sewers and water mains. In the absence of proper sewage disposal, contaminated water wreaked havoc in big cities. In 1882, an outbreak of typhoid fever caused by the city's polluted water killed more than twenty thousand people in Chicago. To end this scourge, enlightened city engineers created and expanded municipal sewage systems and devised ingenious ways to bring clean water to the urban population. By the 1890s, the residents

of U.S. cities demanded and received, at the twist of a faucet, water for their bathtubs, toilets, and even their lawn sprinklers. Those who could afford it enjoyed a standard of living that was the envy of civilization.

Across the United States, municipal governments undertook public works on a scale never before seen. They paved streets, built sewers and water mains, replaced gas lamps with electric lights, ran trolley tracks on the old horsecar lines, and dug underground to build subways, tearing down the unsightly elevated tracks that had clogged city streets. In San Francisco, Andrew Smith Hallidie mastered the city's hills, building a system of cable cars in 1873. Boston completed the nation's first subway system in 1897, and New York and Philadelphia soon followed.

Cities became more beautiful with the creation of urban public parks to complement

Central Park Lake, 1896
Looking south across Central Park Lake, this photograph shows boaters and well-dressed New Yorkers with their bowler hats and parasols taking their leisure on Bethesda Terrace. Its centerpiece, the bronze figure *Angel of the Waters*, was the work of sculptor Emma Stebbins. Calvert Vaux, who along with Frederick Law Olmsted designed the landscaping, considered Bethesda Terrace the "drawing room of the park." By the 1870s, the broad plaza had become one of the most popular gathering places in the city, especially on Sundays. People of all ages, from children floating toy sailboats (inset) on the pond to grandparents out for a stroll and young couples boating, found something to enjoy in the park.
Photo: Culver Pictures; Boat: Picture Research Consultants & Archives.

the new buildings that quickly filled city lots. Much of the credit for America's greatest parks goes to one man—landscape architect Frederick Law Olmsted. The indefatigable Olmsted designed parks in Atlanta, Boston, Brooklyn, Hartford, Detroit, Chicago, and Louisville, as well as the grounds for the U.S. Capitol. But he is best remembered for the creation of New York City's Central Park. Completed in 1873, it became the first landscaped public park in the United States. Olmsted and his partner, Calvert Vaux, directed the planting of more than five million trees, shrubs, and vines to transform the eight hundred acres between 59th and 110th streets into an oasis for urban dwellers. We want a place, he wrote, where people "may stroll for an hour, seeing, hearing, and feeling nothing of the bustle and jar of the streets."

American cities did not overlook the mind in their efforts at improvement. They created a comprehensive free public school system that educated everyone from the children of the middle class to the sons and daughters of immigrant workers. The exploding urban population strained the system and led to crowded and inadequate facilities. In 1899, more than 544,000 pupils attended school in New York's five boroughs. Schools in Boston, New York, Chicago, and San Francisco, as well as those in other cities and towns, provided the only classrooms in the world where students could attend secondary school free of charge.

In addition to schools, the cities built libraries to educate their citizens. In the late nineteenth century, American cities created the most extensive free public library system in the world. In 1895, the Boston Public Library opened its bronze doors under the inscription "Free to All." Designed in the style of a Renaissance palazzo, with more than 700,000 books on the shelves ready to be checked out, the library earned the description "a palace of the people."

Despite the Boston Public Library's legend "Free to All," the poor did not share equally in the advantages of city life. The parks, the libraries, and even the subways and sewers benefited some city dwellers more than others. Few library cards were held by Boston's laborers, who worked six days a week and found the library closed on Sunday. And in the 1890s, there was nothing central about New York's Central Park. It was a four-mile walk from the tenements of Hester Street to the park's entrance at 59th Street and Fifth Avenue. Cities spent more money on plumbing improvements for affluent apartment dwellers than on public baths and lodging houses for the down-and-out. Even the uniform subway fare, which enabled Boston and New York riders to travel anywhere in the system for five cents, worked to the advantage of middle-class commuters but not the downtown poor. Then, as now, the comfortable majority, not the indigent minority, reaped a disproportionate share of the benefits in the nation's big cities.

Any story of the American city, it seems, must be a tale of two cities—or, given the cities' great diversity, a tale of many cities within each metropolis. At the turn of the twentieth century, a central paradox emerged: The enduring monuments of America's cities—the bridges, skyscrapers, parks, and libraries—stood as the undeniable achievements of the same system of municipal government that reformers dismissed as boss-ridden, criminal, and corrupt.

City Government and the "Bosses"

The physical growth of the cities required the expansion of public services and the creation of entirely new facilities: streets, subways, elevated trains, bridges, docks, sewers, and public utilities. There was work to be done and money to be made. The professional politician—the colorful big-city boss—became a phenomenon of urban growth. Though corrupt and often criminal, the boss saw to the building of the city and provided needed social services for the new residents. Yet not even the big-city boss could be said to rule the unruly city. The governing of America's cities resembled more a tug-of-war than boss rule.

The most notorious of all the city bosses was William Marcy Tweed of New York. At midcentury, Boss Tweed's Democratic Party "machine" held sway. A machine was really no more than a political party organized at the grassroots level. Its purpose was to win elections and reward its followers, often with jobs on the city's payroll. New York's citywide Democratic machine, Tammany Hall, commanded an army of party functionaries. At the bottom were district captains. In return for votes, they provided services for their constituents, everything from a scuttle of coal in the winter to housing for an evicted family. At the top were powerful ward bosses who distributed lucrative franchises for subways and streetcars. They formed a shadow government, more powerful than the city's elected officials. The only elected office Tweed ever held was alderman. But as chairman of the Tammany general committee, he wielded more power than the mayor. Through the use of bribery and graft, he kept the Democratic Party together and ran the city. "As long as I count the votes," he shamelessly boasted, "what are you going to do about it?"

The cost of Tweed's rule was staggering. The construction of New York City's courthouse, budgeted at $250,000, ended up costing the taxpayers $14 million. The inflated sum represented bribery, kickbacks, and the greasing of many palms. The excesses of the Tweed ring soon led to a clamor for reform and cries of "Throw the rascals out." Cartoonist Thomas Nast pilloried Tweed in the pages of *Harper's Weekly*. His cartoons, easily understood even by those who could not read, did the boss more harm than hundreds of outraged editorials. Tweed's rule ended in 1871. Eventually, he was tried and convicted and later died in jail.

New York was not the only city to experience bossism and corruption. The British visitor James Bryce concluded in 1888, "There is no denying that the government of cities is the one conspicuous failure of the United States." More than 80 percent of the nation's thirty largest cities experienced some form of boss rule in the decades around the turn of the twentieth century. However, infighting among powerful ward bosses often meant that no single boss enjoyed exclusive power in the big cities.

Urban reformers and proponents of good government (derisively called "goo goos" by their rivals) challenged machine rule and sometimes succeeded in electing reform mayors. But the reformers rarely managed to stay in office for long. Their detractors called them "mornin' glories," observing that they "looked lovely in the mornin' and withered up in a short time." The bosses enjoyed continued success largely because the urban political machines helped the cities' immigrants and poor, who remained its staunchest allies. "What tells in holding your district," a Tammany ward boss observed, "is to go right down among the poor and help them in the different ways they need help. It's philanthropy, but it's politics, too— mighty good politics."

A few reform mayors managed to achieve success and longevity by following

the bosses' model. Hazen S. Pingree of Detroit exemplified the successful reform mayor. A businessman who went into politics in the 1890s, Pingree, like most good-government candidates, promised to root out dishonesty and inefficiency. But when the depression of 1893 struck, Pingree emerged as a champion of the working class and the poor. He hired the unemployed to build schools, parks, and public baths. By providing jobs and needed services, he built a powerful political organization based on working-class support. Detroit's voters kept him in the mayor's office for four terms and then helped elect him governor twice.

While most good-government candidates harped on the Sunday closing of saloons and attacked vice and crime, Pingree demurred: "The most dangerous enemies to good government are not the saloons, the dives, the dens of iniquity and the criminals," but "the temptations which are offered to city officials when franchises are sought by wealthy corporations, or contracts are to be let for public works." Through the skillful orchestration of rewards, an astute political operator could exert powerful leverage and line up support for his party from a broad range of constituents, from the urban poor to wealthy industrialists. In 1902, when journalist Lincoln Steffens began "The Shame of the Cities," a series of articles exposing city corruption, he found that

Tammany Bank
This cast-iron bank, a campaign novelty, bears the name of the New York City Democratic machine. It conveys its political reform message graphically: When you put a penny in the politician's hand, he puts it in his pocket. Tammany Hall dominated city politics for more than a century, dispensing contracts and franchises worth millions of dollars. Some of those dollars invariably found their way into the pockets of Tammany politicians.
Collection of Janice L. and David J. Frent.

business leaders who fastidiously refused to mingle socially with the bosses nevertheless struck deals with them. "He is a self-righteous fraud, this big businessman," Steffens concluded. "I found him buying boodlers [bribers] in St. Louis, defending grafters in Minneapolis, originating corruption in Pittsburgh, sharing with bosses in Philadelphia, deploring reform in Chicago, and beating good government with corruption funds in New York."

The complexity of big-city government, apparent in the many levels of corruption that

Steffens uncovered, pointed to one conclusion: For all the color and flamboyance of the big-city boss, he was simply one of many actors in the drama of municipal government. The successful boss was not an autocratic ruler but a power broker. Old-stock aristocrats, new professionals, saloonkeepers, pushcart peddlers, and politicians all fought for their interests in the hurly-burly of city government. They didn't much like each other, and they sometimes fought savagely. But they learned to live with one another. Compromise and accommodation—not boss

Chicago's White City

This painting by H. D. Nichols captures the monumental architecture of the White City built for the World's Columbian Exposition in 1893. It shows the Court of Honor as viewed from the balcony of the Administration Building, with Frederick MacMonnies's fountain featuring Columbus at the prow of his ship in the foreground. To the left is the huge Manufacturers and Liberal Arts Building—at more than one million square feet, the largest building in the world. To the right stands the Agriculture Building. In the distance, Daniel Chester French's sixty-foot gilded statue *Republic* raises her arms in front of the columned Peristyle. Monumental, harmonious, and pristine, the White City was designed by its creators, Daniel Burnham and Frederick Law Olmsted, to awe and overwhelm fairgoers. And so it did, drawing millions of visitors from America and abroad, who eagerly snapped up souvenirs, such as the playing cards pictured here, to commemorate their visit.

Painting: Chicago Historical Society; Cards: Compliments of Columbus Antique Mall & Museum.

rule—best characterized big-city government by the turn of the twentieth century, although the cities' reputation for corruption left an indelible mark on the consciousness of the American public.

White City or City of Sin?

Americans in the late nineteenth century, like Americans today, were of two minds about the city. They liked to boast of its skyscrapers and bridges, its culture and sophistication, and they prided themselves on its bigness and bustle. At the same time, they feared it as the city of sin, the home of immigrant slums, the center of vice and crime. Nowhere did the divided view of the American city take form more graphically than in Chicago in 1893.

In that year, Chicago hosted the World's Columbian Exposition, the grandest world's fair in the nation's history. The fairground, called the White City and built on the shores of Lake Michigan, offered a lesson in what Americans on the eve of the twentieth century imagined a city might be. Only five miles down the shore from Chicago, the White City seemed light-years away. Its very name celebrated a harmony and pristine beauty unknown in Chicago, with its stockyards, slums, and bustling terminals. Frederick Law Olmsted and architect Daniel Burnham supervised the transformation of a swampy wasteland into a paradise of lagoons, fountains, wooded islands, gardens, and imposing buildings.

"Sell the cookstove and come," novelist Hamlin Garland wrote to his parents on the farm. And come they did, in spite of the panic and depression that broke out only weeks after the fair opened in May 1893. In six months, fairgoers purchased more than 27 million tickets, turning a profit of nearly a half million dollars for promoters. Visitors from home and abroad strolled the elaborate grounds, visited the exhibits—everything from a model of the Brooklyn Bridge carved in soap to the latest goods and inventions. (See "Beyond America's Borders," page 698.) Half carnival, half culture, the great fair offered something for everyone. On the Midway Plaisance, crowds thrilled to the massive wheel built by Mr. Ferris and watched agog as Little Egypt danced the hootchy-kootchy.

In October, the fair closed its doors in the midst of the worst depression the country had yet seen. During the winter of 1894, Chicago's unemployed and homeless took over the grounds, vandalized the buildings, and frightened the city's comfortable citizens out of their wits. When reporters asked Daniel Burnham what should be done with the moldering remains of the White City, he responded, "It should be torched." And it was. In July 1894, in a clash between federal troops and striking railway workers, incendiaries set fires that leveled the fairgrounds.

In the end, the White City remained what it had always been, a dreamscape. Buildings that looked like marble were actually constructed of staff, a plaster of paris substance that began to crumble even before fire destroyed the fairgrounds. The White City was a fantasy never destined to last. Perhaps it was not so strange, after all, that the legacy of the White City could be found on Coney Island, where two new amusement parks, Luna and Dreamland, sought to combine, albeit in a more tawdry form, the beauty of the White City and the thrill of the Midway Plaisance. More enduring than the White City itself was what it represented: the emergent industrial might of the United States, at home and abroad, with its inventions, manufactured goods, and growing consumer culture.

> "Sell the cookstove and come," novelist Hamlin Garland wrote to his parents on the farm. And come they did, in spite of the panic and depression that broke out only weeks after the Columbian Exposition opened in May 1893.

REVIEW How did municipal governments respond to the challenges of urban expansion?

Conclusion: Who Built the Cities?

As much as the great industrialists and financiers, as much as eminent engineers like John and Washington Roebling, common workers, most of them immigrants, built the nation's cities. The unprecedented growth of urban, industrial America resulted from the labor of millions of men, women, and children who toiled in workshops and factories, in sweatshops and mines, on railroads and construction sites across America.

America's cities in the late nineteenth century teemed with life. Immigrants and blue

The World's Columbian Exposition and Nineteenth-Century World's Fairs

Dedicated more to commerce than to culture, the 1893 World's Columbian Exposition in Chicago and the other great world's fairs of the nineteenth century represented a unique phenomenon of industrial capitalism and a testament to the expanding global market economy. The Chicago fair, named to celebrate the four hundredth anniversary of Columbus's arrival in the New World, offered a cornucopia of international exhibits testifying to growing international influences ranging from cultural to technological exchange. Such a celebration of global commerce and influence seemed an appropriate way to honor Columbus, whose voyage in 1492, after all, initiated one of the world's most significant international exchanges.

Beginning with London's Great Exhibition in 1851, with its famous Crystal Palace, and continuing through the age of commercial and cultural expansion in the late nineteenth century, international exhibitions proliferated and flourished. By the time Chicago secured the right to host its celebration, world's fairs had evolved into monumental extravaganzas that showcased the products of the host country and city along with impressive international displays. Great cities vied to play host to world's fairs, as much to promote commercial growth as to demonstrate their cultural refinement. Each

successive fair sought to outdo its predecessor. Chicago's fair followed on the great success of the 1889 Universal Exposition in Paris, commissioned to celebrate the one hundredth anniversary of the French Revolution. The Paris Exposition featured as its crowning glory the 900-foot steel tower constructed by Alexander Gustav Eiffel. What could Chicago, a prairie upstart, do to top that?

The answer was the creation of the White City, with its monumental architecture, landscaped grounds, and first Ferris wheel. Itself a tribute to the international style of architecture, the White City celebrated the classicism of the French Beaux Arts school, which borrowed heavily from the massive geometric styling and elaborate detailing of Greek and Renaissance architecture. With the exception of Louis Sullivan's Transportation Building, nothing hinted of the clean and simple lines of indigenous American design soon to be celebrated with the advent of Frank Lloyd Wright.

Beneath its Renaissance facade, the White City acted as an enormous emporium dedicated to the unabashed materialism of the Gilded Age. Participants from more than one hundred states, territories, countries, and colonies, as well as thousands of concessionaires—from small businesses to the largest corporations—mounted exhibits to demonstrate

their wares and compete for international attention. Fairgoers could view virtually every kind of manufactured product in the world inside the imposing Manufactures and Liberal Arts Building: Swiss glassware and clocks, Japanese lacquerware and bamboo, British woolen products, and French perfumes and linens. The German pavilion included fine wooden furniture as well as tapestries, porcelain, and jewelry belonging to the ruling family. As suited an industrial age, manufactured products and heavy machinery received privileged status, drawing the largest crowds. Displays introduced visitors to the latest mechanical and technological innovations, many the result of international influences. For five cents, fairgoers could put two hard rubber tubes into their ears and listen for the first time to a Gramophone playing the popular tune "The Cat Came Back." The Gramophone, which signaled the beginning of the recorded music industry, was itself the work of a German immigrant, Emile Berliner (although Thomas Edison later claimed credit for a similar invention, calling it the phonograph).

Such international influences were evident throughout the Columbian Exposition. At the Tiffany pavilion, one of the most popular venues at the fair, visitors oohed and aahed over the display of lamps, ornamental metalwork, and fine jewelry that Louis Comfort Tiffany credited to the influence of Japanese art forms. Juxtaposed with Tiffany's finery stood a display of firearms in the Colt gallery. Colt had been an international company since 1851, when it opened a factory in England. The company's revolvers enjoyed an international reputation— the best-known firearms not only in America but also in Canada, Mexico, and many European countries. And Colt's new automatic weapon, the machine gun, would soon play a

"All Nations Are Welcome"
Uncle Sam, flanked by the city of Chicago, welcomes representatives carrying the flags of many nations to the World's Columbian Exposition in 1893. In the background are the fairgrounds on the shores of Lake Michigan. More than one hundred nations participated in the fair by sending exhibits and mounting pavilions to showcase their cultures and products.
Chicago Historical Society.

major role on the world stage in both the Boxer uprising in China and the Spanish-American War.

All manner of foodstuffs—teas from India, Irish whiskey, and pastries and other confectionery from Germany and France—tempted fairgoers. American food products such as Shredded Wheat, Aunt Jemima syrup, and Juicy Fruit gum debuted at the fair, where they competed for ribbons. Winners such as Pabst "Blue Ribbon" Beer used the award in advertisements. And the fair introduced two new foods—carbonated soda and the hamburger—destined to become America's best-known contributions to international cuisine.

The Columbian Exposition also served as a testimony to American technological achievement and progress. By displaying technology

in action, the White City tamed it and made it accessible to American and world consumers. The fair helped develop positive reactions to new technology, particularly electric light and power. With 90,000 electric lights, 5,100 arc lamps, electric fountains, an electric elevated railroad, and electric launches plying the lagoons, the White City provided a glowing advertisement for electricity. Indeed, an entire building was devoted to it. In the Electricity Building, fairgoers visited the Bell Telephone Company exhibit, marveled at General Electric's huge dynamo (electric generator), and gazed into the future at the all-electric home and model demonstration kitchen.

Consumer culture received its first major expression and celebration at the Columbian Exposition. Not

only did this world's fair anticipate the mass marketing, packaging, and advertising of the twentieth century, but the vast array of products on display also cultivated the urge to consume. Thousands of concessionaires with products for sale sent a message that tied enjoyment inextricably to spending money and purchasing goods, both domestic and foreign. The Columbian Exposition set a pattern for the twentieth-century world's fairs that followed, making a powerful statement about the possibilities of urban life in an industrial age and encouraging the rise of a new middle-class consumer culture. As G. Brown Goode, head of the Smithsonian Institution in 1893, observed, the Columbian Exposition was in many ways "an illustrated encyclopedia of civilization."

bloods, poor laborers and millionaires, middle-class managers and corporate moguls, secretaries, salesgirls, sweatshop laborers, and society matrons lived in the cities and contributed to their growth. Town houses, tenements, and new apartment buildings jostled for space with skyscrapers and great department stores, while parks, ball fields, amusement arcades, and public libraries provided the city masses with recreation and entertainment.

Municipal governments, straining to build the new cities, experienced the rough-and-tumble of machine politics as bosses and their constituents looked to profit from city growth. Reformers deplored the graft and corruption that accompanied the rise of the cities. But they were rarely able to oust the party bosses for long because they failed to understand the services the political machines provided for their largely immigrant and poor constituents, as well as the ties between the politicians and wealthy businessmen who sought to benefit from franchises and contracts.

For America's workers, urban industrialism along with the rise of big business and corporate consolidation drastically changed the workplace. Industrialists replaced skilled workers with new machines that could be operated by cheaper, unskilled labor. And during hard times, employers did not hesitate to cut workers' already meager wages. As the Great Railroad Strike of 1877 demonstrated, when labor united, it could bring the nation to attention. Organization held out the best hope for the workers; first the Knights of Labor and later the American Federation of Labor won converts among the nation's working class.

The rise of urban industrialism challenged the American promise, which for decades had been dominated by Jeffersonian agrarian ideals. Could such a promise exist in the changing world of cities, tenements, immigrants, and huge corporations? In the great depression that came in the 1890s, mounting anger and frustration would lead workers and farmers to join forces and create a grassroots movement to fight for change under the banner of a new People's Party.

Selected Bibliography

Immigration

Mary Antin, *From Plotzk to Boston* (1899).
Stephen M. Berk, *Year of Crisis, Year of Hope: Russian Jewry and the Pogroms of 1881–1882* (1985).
Abraham Bisno, *Abraham Bisno: Union Pioneer*, with a foreword by Joel Seidman (1967).
John Bodnar, *The Transplanted: A History of Immigration in Urban America* (1985).
Roger Daniels, *Coming to America: A History of Immigration and Ethnicity in American Life* (1991).
Roger Daniels, *Guarding the Golden Door: American Immigration Policy and Immigrants since 1882* (2004).
Donna Gabaccia, *From the Other Side: Women, Gender, and Immigrant Life in the U.S., 1820–1990* (1994).
Martha Gardner, *The Qualities of a Citizen: Women, Immigration, and Citizenship, 1870–1965* (2005).
Dirk Hoerder, *Cultures in Contact: World Migrations in the Second Millennium* (2002).
Matthew Frye Jacobson, *Whiteness of a Different Color: European Immigrants and the Alchemy of Race* (1998).
Edward H. Judge, *Easter in Kishinev: Anatomy of a Pogrom* (1992).
Hilda Satt Polachek, *I Came a Stranger: The Story of a Hull-House Girl* (1989).
David M. Reimers, *Unwelcome Strangers* (1998).
David R. Roediger, *Working toward Whiteness: How America's Immigrants Became White* (2005).
Ronald Takaki, *Strangers from a Different Shore: A History of Asian Americans* (1998).
Mark Wyman, *Round-Trip to America: The Immigrants Return to Europe, 1880–1930* (1993).

Workers and Unions

Susan Porter Benson, *Counter Cultures: Saleswomen, Managers, and Customers in American Department Stores, 1890–1940* (1986).
Ileen A. DeVault, *United Apart: Gender and the Rise of Craft Unionism* (2004).
Nan Enstad, *Ladies of Labor, Girls of Adventure: Working Women, Popular Culture, and Labor Politics at the Turn of the Twentieth Century* (1999).
Leon Fink, *Workingman's Democracy: The Knights of Labor and American Politics* (1983).
James Green, *Death in the Haymarket: A Story of Chicago, the First Labor Movement and the Bombing That Divided Gilded Age America* (2006).
Hamilton Hold, ed., *The Life Stories of Undistinguished Americans as Told by Themselves* (2000).

Jacqueline Jones, *American Work: Four Centuries of Black and White Labor* (1998).

Alice Kessler-Harris, *Out to Work: A History of Wage-Earning Women in the United States* (20th anniv. ed., 2003).

Susan Levine, *Labor's True Women: Carpet Weavers, Industrialization, and Labor Reform in the Gilded Age* (1984).

David Montgomery, *The Fall of the House of Labor: The Workplace, the State, and American Labor Activism, 1865–1925* (1987).

Roy Rosenzweig, *Eight Hours for What We Will: Workers and Leisure in an Industrial City, 1870–1920* (1983).

Sharon Hartman Strom, *Beyond the Typewriter: Gender, Class, and the Origins of Modern American Office Work, 1900–1930* (1992).

Robert E. Weir, *Knights Unhorsed: Internal Conflict in a Gilded Age Social Movement* (2000).

The City and Its Amusements

Gary S. Cross and John K. Walton, *The Playful Crowd: Pleasure Places in the Twentieth Century* (2005).

Margaret Garb, *City of American Dreams: A History of Home Ownership and Housing Reform in Chicago, 1871–1919* (2005).

Richard Haw, *The Brooklyn Bridge: A Cultural History* (2005).

Kathy Peiss, *Cheap Amusements: Working Women and Leisure in Turn-of-the-Century New York* (1986).

Roy Rosenzweig and Elizabeth Blackmar, *The Park and the People: A History of Central Park* (1992).

Witold Rybczynski, *A Clearing in the Distance: Frederick Law Olmsted and America in the Nineteenth Century* (1999).

Julies Tygiel, *Past Time: Baseball as History* (2000).

► **FOR MORE BOOKS ABOUT TOPICS IN THIS CHAPTER,** see the Online Bibliography at bedfordstmartins.com/roark.

► **FOR ADDITIONAL FIRSTHAND ACCOUNTS OF THIS PERIOD,** see Chapter 19 in Michael Johnson, ed., *Reading the American Past*, Fourth Edition.

► **FOR WEB SITES, IMAGES, AND DOCUMENTS RELATED TO TOPICS AND PLACES IN THIS CHAPTER,** visit bedfordstmartins.com/makehistory.

REVIEWING THE CHAPTER

Follow these steps to review and strengthen your understanding of the chapter.

STEP 1: *Study the* **Key Terms** *and* **Timeline** *to identify the significance of each item listed.*

STEP 2: *Answer the* **Review Questions**, *drawing on key terms and dates to support your answers.*

STEP 3: *Drawing on the Key Terms, Timeline, and Review Questions, answer the broader* **Making Connections** *questions.*

KEY TERMS

Who

Washington Roebling (p. 666)
Henry Cabot Lodge (p. 673)
Grover Cleveland (p. 676)
Jacob Riis (p. 676)
the Vanderbilts (p. 677)
Leonora Barry (p. 685)
Terence V. Powderly (p. 686)
Samuel Gompers (p. 686)
Albert Parsons (p. 686)
August Spies (p. 686)
John Peter Altgeld (p. 688)
Margaret Byington (p. 689)
Louis Sullivan (p. 692)

Frederick Law Olmsted (p. 694)
Calvert Vaux (p. 694)
William Marcy "Boss" Tweed (p. 694)
Thomas Nast (p. 695)
Hazen S. Pingree (p. 695)
Lincoln Steffens (p. 695)

What

global migration (p. 667)
industrial core (p. 667)
rural periphery (p. 667)
pogroms (p. 672)
Lower East Side (p. 672)
Angel Island (p. 673)

Ellis Island (p. 673)
Great Railroad Strike of 1877 (p. 683)
Workingman's Party (p. 684)
Knights of Labor (p. 685)
American Federation of Labor (AFL) (p. 685)
May Day rally (p. 687)
Haymarket bombing (p. 687)
Coney Island (p. 690)
Great Fire of 1871 (p. 692)
Central Park (p. 694)
Tammany Hall (p. 694)
bossism (p. 695)
World's Columbian Exposition (p. 697)
White City (p. 697)

TIMELINE

◄ 1869 • Knights of Labor founded.
• Cincinnati mounts first paid baseball team, the Red Stockings.

1871 • Boss Tweed's rule in New York ends.
• Chicago's Great Fire.

1873 • Panic on Wall Street touches off depression.
• San Francisco's cable car system opens.

1877 • Great Railroad Strike.

1878 • Knights of Labor organizes workers.

1880s • Immigration from southern and eastern Europe rises.

1882 • Chinese Exclusion Act.

1883 • Brooklyn Bridge opens.

REVIEW QUESTIONS

1. Why did American cities experience explosive growth in the late nineteenth century? (pp. 666–77)

2. How did business expansion and consolidation change workers' occupations in the late nineteenth century? (pp. 677–83)

3. Why did the fortunes of the Knights of Labor rise in the late 1870s and decline in the 1890s? (pp. 683–88)

4. How did urban industrialism shape the world of leisure? (pp. 688–91)

5. How did municipal governments respond to the challenges of urban expansion? (pp. 691–97)

MAKING CONNECTIONS

1. Americans expressed both wonder and concern at the nation's mushrooming cities. Why did cities provoke such divergent responses? In your answer, discuss the dramatic demographic, environmental, and political developments associated with urbanization.

2. Why did patterns of immigration to the United States in the late nineteenth century change? How did Americans respond to the immigrants who arrived late in the century? In your answer, consider how industrial capitalism, nationally and globally, contributed to these developments.

3. How did urban industrialization affect Americans' lives outside of work? Describe the impact late-nineteenth-century economic developments had on home life and leisure. In your answer, consider how class, race, gender, and ethnicity contributed to diverse urban experiences.

4. When workers began to embrace organization in the late 1870s, what did they hope to accomplish? Were they successful? Why or why not? In your answer, discuss both general conditions and specific events that shaped these developments.

▶ **FOR PRACTICE QUIZZES, A CUSTOMIZED STUDY PLAN, AND OTHER STUDY TOOLS,** see the Online Study Guide at bedfordstmartins.com/roark.

1886 • American Federation of Labor (AFL) founded.
     • Haymarket bombing.

    1890s • African American migration from the South begins.
    1890 • Jacob Riis publishes *How the Other Half Lives*.

       1893 • World's Columbian Exposition.
       • Panic on Wall Street touches off major economic depression.

        1895 • Boston Public Library opens.

         1896 • President Grover Cleveland vetoes immigrant literacy test.

          1897 • Steeplechase Park opens on Coney Island.
          • Nation's first subway system opens in Boston.

           1900 • Ellis Island opens.

BUFFALO BANNER FROM THE 1892 POPULIST CONVENTION
This flag graphically declares the frustration with the Democratic and Republican parties that led angry Americans, particularly farmers, to gather in St. Louis in 1892 to create a new People's Party. Featuring the buffalo (American bison) as a symbol, the flag urged the election of "honest men" and proclaimed as its motto "Down with Monopoly." The buffalo was perhaps a poor choice as a mascot, for just as the great herds on the western plains had been decimated during the 1880s, the People's (or Populist) Party would not survive the '90s.
Nebraska State Historical Society.

20

Dissent, Depression, and War

1890–1900

FRANCES WILLARD TRAVELED to St. Louis in February 1892 with high hopes. She was not alone. Farmers, laborers, and reformers of all stripes flocked to Missouri to attend a meeting, in the words of one reporter, "different from any other political meeting ever witnessed in St. Louis." The cigar-chomping politicians who generally worked the convention circuit were nowhere to be seen. In their place, "mostly gray-haired, sunburned and roughly clothed men" assembled under a banner that proclaimed, "We do not ask for sympathy or pity. We ask for justice."

Political change was in the air, and Willard was there to help fashion a new reform party, one that she hoped would embrace her two passions—temperance and woman **suffrage**. As head of the Woman's Christian Temperance Union, an organization with members in every state and territory in the nation, Willard wielded considerable clout. At her invitation, twenty-eight of the country's leading reformers had already met in Chicago to draft a set of principles to bring to St. Louis. Always expedient, Willard had settled for a statement condemning the saloon rather than an endorsement for a stronger measure to prohibit the sale of alcohol. But at the convention she hoped to press the case for woman suffrage and prohibition. Willard knew it would not be easy, but in the heady atmosphere of 1892, she determined to try. No American woman before her had played such a central role in a political movement. At the height of her political power, Willard took her place among the leaders on the podium in St. Louis.

Exposition Music Hall presented a colorful spectacle. "The banners of the different states rose above the delegates throughout the hall, fluttering like the flags over an army encamped," wrote one reporter. The fiery orator Ignatius Donnelly attacked the money kings of Wall Street. Mary Elizabeth Lease, a veteran campaigner from Kansas known for exhorting farmers to "raise less corn and more hell," added her powerful voice to the cause. Terence V. Powderly, head of the Knights of Labor, called on workers to join hands with farmers against the "nonproducing classes." Frances Willard exhorted the crowd to outlaw the liquor traffic and give the vote to women. Between speeches, the crowd sang labor songs like "Hurrah for the Toiler" and "All Hail the Power of Laboring Men."

In the course of the next few days, delegates hammered out a series of demands, breathtaking in their scope. They tackled the tough questions of the day—the regulation of business, the need for banking and currency reform, the right of labor to organize and bargain collectively, and the role of the

Frances Willard

Frances Willard, the forward-thinking leader of the
Woman's Christian Temperance Union, learned to
ride a bicycle at age fifty-three. The bicycle became
hugely popular in the 1890s, even though traditionalists fulminated that it was unladylike for women to straddle a bike and immodest
for them to wear the divided skirts that allowed them to pedal. Willard, shown
here in 1895, wears a cycling costume typical of the period: "a skirt and blouse
of tweed, with belt, rolling collar, and loose cravat, the skirt three inches from
the ground; a round straw hat, and walking-shoes with gaiters." She declared
bicycling a "harmless pleasure" that encouraged "clear heads and steady hands."
Willard brought her progressive ideas to the People's Party convention in 1892.
A ribbon from that meeting depicts the party's nominees, James Weaver, a former
Union general, and ex-Confederate James Field. The Populists hoped that the issues
proclaimed on the ribbon—"money, land, and transportation"—would trump
sectional loyalties, and symbolized their wish by portraying the Blue (Union) and
Gray (Confederate) hands shaking.

Photo: Courtesy of the Frances E. Willard Memorial Library and Archives (WCTU); Ribbon: Collection of
Janice L. and David J. Frent.

federal government in regulating business, curbing **monopoly**, and guaranteeing **democracy**.
But the new party determined to stick to economic issues and resisted endorsing either temperance or woman suffrage. As a member of the

platform committee, Willard fought for both and
complained of the "crooked methods . . . employed to scuttle these planks." Outmaneuvered
in committee, she brought the issues to the floor
of the convention, only to go down to defeat by
a vote of 352 to 238.

Despite Willard's disappointment, the convention ended its work amid a chorus of cheers.
According to one eyewitness, "Hats, paper,
handkerchiefs, etc., were thrown into the air; . . .
cheer after cheer thundered and reverberated
through the vast hall reaching the outside of the
building where thousands who had been waiting the outcome joined in the applause till for
blocks in every direction the exultation
made the din indescribable."

What was all the shouting about?
The cheering crowd celebrated the
birth of a new political party, officially
named the People's Party. Fed up with
the Democrats and Republicans, a broad
coalition of groups came together in St.
Louis to fight for change. They resolved to
reconvene in Omaha in July to nominate
candidates for the upcoming presidential
election. Defeated but not willing to abandon
the new party, Willard urged the nomination of
a presidential candidate committed to temperance and suffrage.

The St. Louis gathering marked a milestone in
one of the most turbulent decades in U.S. history.
Unrest, agitation, agrarian revolt, labor strikes, a
severe financial panic and depression, and a war
of expansion shook the 1890s. While the two major
political parties continued to do business as usual,
Americans flocked to organizations including the
Farmers' Alliance, the American Federation of
Labor, and the Woman's Christian Temperance
Union, and they worked together to create the political alliance that gave birth to the People's (or
Populist) Party. In a decade of unrest and uncertainty, the People's Party challenged **laissez-faire**
economics by insisting that the federal government play a more active role to ensure greater economic equity in industrial America. This challenge
to the status quo culminated in 1896 in one of the
most hotly contested presidential elections in the
nation's history. At the close of the tumultuous
decade, the Spanish-American War helped to
bring the country together as Americans rallied to
support the troops. But disagreement over
American **imperialism** and overseas expansion
raised questions about the nation's role on the
world stage as the United States stood poised to
enter the twentieth century.

The Farmers' Revolt

Hard times in the 1880s and 1890s created a groundswell of agrarian revolt. A bitter farmer wrote from Minnesota, "I settled on this Land in good Faith Built House and Barn. Broken up Part of the Land. Spent years of hard Labor in grubbing fencing and Improving." About to lose his farm to foreclosure, he lamented, "Are they going to drive us out like trespassers . . . and give us away to the Corporations?"

Farm prices fell decade after decade, even as American farmers' share of the world market grew. (See "Global Comparison," page 708.) Wheat that sold for a dollar a bushel in 1870 dropped to sixty cents in the 1890s. Cotton plummeted from fifteen cents to five cents a pound. Corn started at forty-five cents and fell to thirty cents a bushel. In parts of Kansas, it sold for as little as ten cents, and angry farmers burned their corn for fuel rather than market it at that price. At the same time, consumer prices soared (Figure 20.1, page 709). By 1894, in Kansas alone almost half the farms had fallen into the hands of the banks because poor farmers could no longer afford to pay their mortgages.

At the heart of the problem stood a banking system dominated by eastern commercial banks committed to the **gold standard**, a railroad rate system that was capricious and unfair, and rampant speculation that drove up the price of land. In the West, farmers rankled under a system that allowed railroads to charge them exorbitant freight rates while granting rebates to large shippers (see chapter 18). The railroads' policy of charging higher rates for short hauls meant that large grain elevator companies could ship their wheat from Chicago to New York for less money than it cost a Dakota farmer to send his crop to nearby Minneapolis. In the South, lack of currency and credit drove farmers to the stopgap credit system of the crop lien, turning the entire region into "a vast pawn shop." To pay for seed and supplies, farmers had to pledge their crops to local creditors, called "furnishing merchants," whose exorbitant prices meant chronic debt and destitution for southern farmers. Determined to do something, farmers banded together to fight for change.

The Farmers' Alliance

Farm protest was not new. In the 1870s, farmers had supported the Grange and the Greenback Labor Party. And as the farmers' situation grew more desperate, they organized, forming regional alliances. The first Farmers' Alliance

Nebraska Farm Family
A Nebraska farm family posed in front of their sod hut in Custer County, Nebraska, in 1889. The house is formed of blocks of sod cut from the prairie. The wife stands in the doorway, wearing a hat, while the husband stands with a team of horses and the family dog keeps a vigilant eye on the photographer. The photo testifies to the hard, lonely life of farmers on the Great Plains. Drought and falling crop prices devastated farmers in the 1880s, and many lost their land to bank foreclosures when they could not make their mortgage payments. Growing discontent among farmers in the Midwest and South led to the growth of the Farmers' Alliance in the 1880s and the creation of the People's Party in the 1890s.

Nebraska State Historical Society.

GLOBAL COMPARISON

Share of the World Wheat Market, 1860–1900

Although many countries produced wheat for home use, Britain, Germany, and the United States were among the largest wheat exporters. Exporting wheat worldwide became viable in the United States only after the completion of the transcontinental railroad in 1869. The resulting growth of the railroads, coupled with the development of improved mechanical reapers throughout the second half of the century, led to the mechanization of U.S. agriculture, allowing wheat farmers to harvest ever-larger crops. From 1860 to 1900, the United States' percentage of world wheat production more than doubled, while Germany's declined and Britain's was cut in half as a result of its growing emphasis on industrialization.

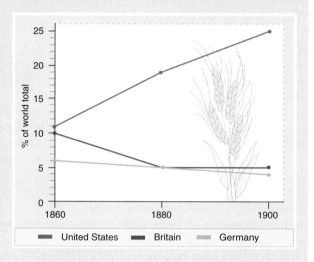

% of world total

■ United States   ■ Britain   ■ Germany

---

came together in Lampasas County, Texas, to fight "landsharks and horse thieves." During the 1880s, the movement spread rapidly. In **frontier** farmhouses in Texas, in log cabins in the backwoods of Arkansas, and in the rural parishes of Louisiana, separate groups of farmers formed similar alliances for self-help.

The First Farmers' Alliance Flag

In 1878, the Grand State Farmers' Alliance formed in Texas as a self-help organization. Growing out of a meeting in Lampasas County a year earlier, the group was part of a spontaneous Farmers' Alliance movement that spread rapidly during the 1880s. By 1890, the Southern Farmers' Alliance boasted more than three million members. This flag commemorates the organization's founding and spells out what the Alliance stood for: "Free Trade," "The Most Good for the Most People," and "Wisdom, Justice & Moderation." Many viewed the last claim skeptically, seeing the Alliance not as a moderate group, but as a force for sweeping change.
Torreyson Library, University of Central Arkansas.

As the movement grew, farmers' groups consolidated into two regional alliances. The Northwestern Farmers' Alliance was active in Kansas, Nebraska, and other midwestern Granger states. The more radical Southern Farmers' Alliance got its start in Texas and spread rapidly. In the 1880s, traveling lecturers preached the Alliance message. Worn-out men and careworn women did not need to be convinced that something was wrong. Overnight, scores of local alliances sprang up, each with its own lecturer, who in turn carried the word to every crossroads in the South.

The Southern Alliance soon spread from Texas to Louisiana and Arkansas, recruiting at the amazing rate of 20,000 a month in the autumn of 1886. "The farmers seem like unto ripe fruit—you can gather them by a gentle shake of the bush," an Alliance lecturer gloated. By 1887, the Southern Farmers' Alliance had grown to more than 200,000 members, and by 1890 it counted more than 3 million members.

Determined to reach blacks as well as whites, the Southern Alliance worked with the Colored Farmers' Alliance, an African American group founded in Texas in the 1880s. Although the Colored Alliance did not always agree with the Southern Alliance, blacks and whites attempted to make common cause. As Georgia's Tom Watson, a Southern Alliance stalwart,

---

pointed out, "The colored tenant is in the same boat as the white tenant, . . . and . . . the accident of color can make no difference in the interests of farmers, croppers, and laborers."

The Farmers' Alliance reached out to workers as well as to farmers. During the Great Southwestern Strike against Jay Gould's Texas and Pacific Railroad in 1886, the Alliance supported the strikers. The Southern Farmers' Alliance rushed food and supplies to the striking workers and issued a proclamation in support of the Knights of Labor, calling on farmers to boycott Gould's railroad.

Women rallied to the Alliance banner along with their menfolk. In Kansas, more than 30 percent of Alliance members were women. "I am going to work for prohibition, the Alliance, and for Jesus as long as I live," swore one woman. The political culture of the Alliance encouraged the inclusion of women and children and used the family as its defining symbol. As journalist Elizabeth Barr wrote, "Women with skins tanned to parchment . . . with bony hands of toil and clad in faded calico, could talk in meeting, and could talk straight to the point."

Alliance meetings combined picnic, parade, revival, country fair, and political convention into a day of socializing, eating (no drinking— the Alliance banned alcohol), playing, and edu-

cation. In wagon trains a thousand strong, men and women thronged to the meetings to listen to speeches and to debate and discuss the issues raised by the prophets of the movement. Alliance lecturers aimed to do more than exhort their followers; they worked to educate them. The Alliance produced and distributed "a perfect avalanche of literature"—speeches, newspapers, books, and tracts—full of damning details about the political collusion between business and politics, along with detailed analyses of the securities and commodities markets, the tariff and international trade, and credit and currency. Secular preachers, the Alliance lecturers reached out to the illiterate, often speaking for hours under the broiling sun to educate their rapt audiences on the fine points of economics and politics.

At the heart of the Alliance movement stood a series of farmers' cooperatives. By "bulking" their cotton—that is, selling it together—farmers could negotiate a better price. And by setting up trade stores and exchanges, they sought to escape the grasp of the merchant/creditor. Through the cooperatives, the Farmers' Alliance promised to change the way farmers lived. "We are going to get out of debt and be free and independent people once more," exulted one Georgia farmer.

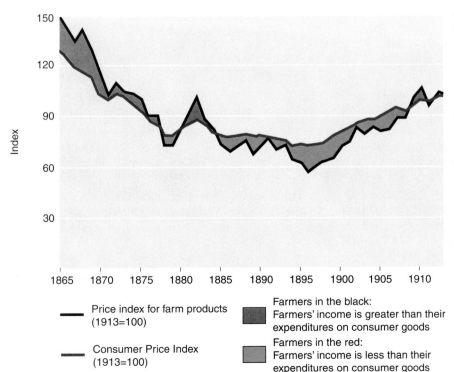

FIGURE 20.1
Consumer Prices and Farm Income, 1865–1910
Around 1870, consumer prices and farm income were about equal. During the 1880s and 1890s, however, farmers suffered great hardships as prices for their crops steadily declined and the cost of consumer goods continued to rise.

Price index for farm products (1913=100)

Consumer Price Index (1913=100)

Farmers in the black: Farmers' income is greater than their expenditures on consumer goods

Farmers in the red: Farmers' income is less than their expenditures on consumer goods

Cooperatives flowered throughout the South and West. In 1888, farmers scored a major victory when they defeated the jute-bagging trust in its scheme to double the price of the bags used to bale cotton. But the Alliance could not succeed in its attempts to run cooperative stores. Opposition by merchants, bankers, wholesalers, and manufacturers made it impossible for the cooperatives to get credit.

As the cooperative movement died, the Farmers' Alliance moved toward direct political action. Texas farmers drafted a set of demands in 1886 and pressured political candidates to endorse them. In 1890, the Southern Farmers' Alliance called for railroad regulation, laws against land speculation, and currency and credit reform. The Alliance urged farmers to use the platform as a "yardstick," warning that candidates must "stand up and be measured." Confounded by the failure of the Democrats and Republicans to break with commercial interests and support the farmers, Alliance leaders moved, often reluctantly, toward the formation of a third party.

The Populist Movement

In the earliest days of the Alliance movement, C. W. Macune, a leader of the Southern Farmers' Alliance, insisted, "The Alliance is a strictly white man's nonpolitical, secret business association." But by 1892, it was none of those things. Although some white southern leaders, including Macune, made it clear that they would never threaten the unity of the white vote in the South by leaving the Democratic Party, advocates of a third party carried the day at the convention of laborers, farmers, and common folk in St. Louis in 1892. There, the Farmers' Alliance gave birth to the People's Party and launched the Populist movement. "There is something at the back of all this turmoil more than the failure of crops or the scarcity of ready cash," a journalist observed in 1892.

Populism was indeed more than a set of demands and a list of economic grievances. The same spirit of religious revival that animated the Farmers' Alliance infused the People's Party. The Populists built on the work of the Farmers' Alliance to mount a critique of industrial society

On the Way to a Populist Meeting in Kansas
Populism was more than a political movement; it was a culture unto itself. For farmers in sparsely settled regions, the movement provided reassurance that they were not alone, that others shared their problems, and that solutions could be found. When the Populists called a meeting, wagons came from miles around. This photograph shows a gathering in Dickinson County, Kansas.
Kansas State Historical Society.

Mary Elizabeth Lease
This photograph of Lease, taken in 1895 at the height of her political activities in Kansas, shows a well-dressed, mild-eyed woman—belying her reputation as a hell-raiser who supposedly exhorted Kansas farmers to "raise less corn and more hell." Lease brought her considerable oratorical skills to the causes of temperance, suffrage, and the Populist Party. Her admirers styled her "The People's Joan of Arc." But in the eyes of her detractors, who attacked not only her speeches but the propriety of a woman who dared to pursue a career as a public speaker, she was "a lantern-jawed, google-eyed nightmare" and "a petticoated smut-mill." Kansas State Historical Society.

and a call for action. Far from being backward-looking romantics, they articulated a rational and sophisticated program that called on the government to mediate between the interests of business and agriculture.

Convinced that the money and banking systems worked to the advantage of the wealthy few, they demanded economic democracy. To help farmers get the credit they needed at reasonable rates, southern farmers hit on the ingenious idea of a subtreasury—a plan that would allow farmers to store nonperishable crops in government store-houses until market prices rose. At the same time, borrowing against their crops, farmers would receive commodity credit from the federal government to enable them to purchase needed supplies and seed for the coming year. In the South, the subtreasury promised to get rid of the crop lien system once and for all. Although the idea

would be enacted piecemeal in **progressive** and **New Deal** legislation in the twentieth century, **conservatives** in the 1890s dismissed it as far-fetched "corn tassel communism."

To the western farmer, the Populists promised land reform, championing a plan that would reclaim excessive land granted to railroads or sold to foreign investors. The Populists' boldest proposal called for government ownership of the railroads and the telegraph system to put an end to discriminatory rates. Citing examples of how the powerful railroads had corrupted the political system, the Populists did not shrink from advocating what their opponents branded state **socialism**.

In addition to economic democracy and land reform, the Populists demanded currency reform. Farmers in all sections rallied to the cry for cheaper currency, endorsing platform planks calling for **free silver** and greenbacks—attempts to increase the nation's tight money supply and thus make credit easier to obtain.

To empower the common people, the Populist platform called for the direct election of senators and for other electoral reforms, including the secret ballot and the right to initiate legislation, to recall elected officials, and to submit issues to the people by means of a referendum. Because the Populists shared common cause with labor against corporate interests, they also supported the eight-hour workday and an end to contract labor.

Missing from the Populist platform were the moral reforms championed by the Farmers' Alliance. Prohibition was judged too divisive an issue by a party hoping to win votes from urban workers. Frances Willard speculated that party leaders kept suffrage off their platform in a desire to court more traditional southern voters. A political party and not a grassroots movement like the Alliance, Populism looked to a male electorate for support. Since women didn't vote, their power within the party was circumscribed, although women like Mary Elizabeth Lease participated actively in the Populist movement.

Yet the sweeping array of Populist reforms enacted in the Populist platform changed the agenda of politics for decades to come. More than just a response to hard times, Populism presented an alternative vision of American economic democracy. (See "Documenting the American Promise," page 712.)

> **REVIEW** Why did American farmers organize alliances in the late nineteenth century?

Populist Voices of Protest

Populists spoke with passion and fire, documenting the plight of farmers, workers, and the nation's dispossessed. Intending to educate as well as to agitate, Populist speakers larded their speeches with statistics, but the speeches were never dull. The sense of a new day dawning when the people would rule brought apocalyptic vision and religious fervor to their rhetoric.

DOCUMENT 1
Mary Elizabeth Lease, Address to the WCTU, 1890

Populist orator Mary Elizabeth Lease, born in Pennsylvania in 1850, moved to Kansas in 1868, where she became a schoolteacher, studied law, and gained admittance to the bar. Lease spent ten years trying to make a living farming, then gave up and moved with her husband, a pharmacist, to Wichita in 1883. She lent her voice to many causes, including temperance, and spoke in support of the Knights of Labor and the Farmers' Alliance. She earned her greatest fame in the 1890s when she spoke in support of Populist causes. Her charismatic speaking style led the Kansas newspaper editor William Allen White to observe, "She could recite the multiplication table and set a crowd hooting and harrahing at her will." In a speech given before the Woman's Christian Temperance Union in 1890, Lease explained why women supported the Farmers' Alliance.

You wonder, perhaps, at the zeal and enthusiasm of the Western woman in this reform movement.

Let me tell you why they are interested. Turn to your school-maps and books of a quarter of a century ago, and you will find that what is now a teeming and fruitful West was then known as the Treeless Plain, the Great American Desert. To this sterile and remote region, infested by savage beasts and still more savage men, the women of the New England states, the women of the cultured East, came with husbands, sons and brothers to help them build up a home upon the broad and vernal prairies of the West. We came with roses of health on our cheek, the light of hope in our eyes, the fire of youth and hope burning in our hearts. . . . We endured hardships, dangers and privations; hours of loneliness, fear and sorrow; our little babes were born upon these wide, unsheltered prairies; and there, upon the sweeping prairies beneath the cedar trees our hands have planted to mark the sacred place, our little ones lie buried. We toiled in the cabin and in the field; we planted trees and orchards; we helped our loved ones to make the prairie blossom as the rose. The neat cottage took the place of the sod shanty, the log-cabin and the humble dug-out.

Yet, after all our years of toil and privation, dangers and hardships upon the Western frontier, monopoly is taking our homes from us by the infamous system of mortgage foreclosure, the most infamous that has ever disgraced the statutes of a civilized nation. It takes from us at the rate of five hundred a month the homes

that represent the best years of our life, our toil, our hopes, our happiness. How did it happen? The government, at the bid of Wall Street, repudiated its contracts with the people; the circulating medium was contracted . . . from $54 per capita to less than $8 per capita; or, . . . as grand Senator [William Morris] Stewart [of Nevada] put it, "For twenty years the market value of the dollar has gone up and the market value of labor has gone down, till to-day the American laborer, in bitterness and wrath, asks which is the worst—the black slavery that has gone or the white slavery that has come?"

Do you wonder the women are joining the [Farmers'] Alliance? I wonder if there is a woman in all the broad land who can afford to stay out of the Alliance.

SOURCE: Joan M. Jensen. Excerpt from pp. 154–160 in *With These Hands: Women Working on the Land*. Copyright © 1981 by Joan M. Jensen.

DOCUMENT 2
Ignatius Donnelly, Address to the People's Party Convention, 1892

An Irish immigrant, Ignatius Donnelly practiced law in Philadelphia before moving to St. Paul in Minnesota Territory in 1856. By turns a liberal Republican and a member of the Greenback Party, Donnelly became a leader in the midwestern Populist movement in the 1890s. His hellfire rhetoric earned him the spot as keynote speaker at the 1892 Populist convention in St. Louis, where he delivered a speech that later became the preamble to the People's Party platform.

We meet in the midst of a nation brought to the verge of moral, political, and material ruin. Corruption dominates the ballot-box, the legislatures, the Congress, and touches even the ermine of the bench. The people are demoralized; most of the States have been compelled to isolate the voters at the polling-places to prevent universal intimidation or bribery. The newspapers are largely subsidized or muzzled; public opinion silenced; business prostrated; our homes covered with mortgages; labor impoverished; and the land concentrating in the hands of the capitalists. The urban workmen are denied the right of organization for self-protection; imported pauperized labor beats down their wages; a hireling standing army, unrecognized by our laws, is established to shoot them down, and they are rapidly degenerating into European conditions. The fruits of the toil of millions are boldly stolen to build up colossal fortunes for a few, unprecedented in the history of mankind; and the possessors of these, in turn, despise the republic and endanger liberty. From the same prolific womb of governmental injustice we breed the two great classes— tramps and millionaires.

SOURCE: Excerpt from pp. 51–54 in *The Populist Mind* by Norman Pollock, ed. Copyright © 1967 by Norman Pollock. Reprinted with permission of Pearson Education.

DOCUMENT 3
Lorenzo Lewelling,
Inaugural Address, 1893

By turns a schoolteacher, a newspaper reporter, and a farmer, Lorenzo Lewelling moved to Wichita, Kansas, in 1887 and soon became active in the Farmers' Alliance and later the Populist movement. Elected governor on the People's Party ticket in 1893, he used his inaugural address to attack social Darwinism and define a new role for government as the champion of the people.

The survival of the fittest is the government of brutes and reptiles, and such philosophy must give place to a government which recognizes human brotherhood. It is the province of government to protect the weak, but the government of to-day is resolved into a struggle of the masses with the classes for supremacy and bread, until business, home, and personal integrity are trembling in the face of possible want in the family. Feed a tiger regularly and you tame and make him harmless, but hunger makes tigers of men. If it be true that the poor have no right to the property of the rich let it also be declared that the rich have no right to the property of the poor. . . .

The problem of to-day is how to make the State subservient to the individual, rather than to become his master. . . . What is the State to him who toils, if labor is denied him and his children cry for bread? What is the State to the farmer, who wearily drags himself from dawn till dark to meet the stern necessities of the mortgage on the farm? What is the State to him if it sanctions usury and other legal forms by which his home is destroyed and his innocent ones become a prey to the fiends who lurk in the shadow of civilization? What is the State to the business man, early grown gray, broken in health and spirit by successive failures; anxiety like a boding owl his constant companion by day and the disturber of his dreams by night? How is life to be sustained, how is liberty to be pursued under such adverse conditions as the State permits if it does not sanction? Is the State powerless against these conditions?

This is the generation which has come to the rescue. Those in distress who cry out from the darkness shall not be heard in vain. Conscience is in the saddle. We have leaped the bloody chasm and entered a contest for the protection of home, humanity, and the dignity of labor.

SOURCE: Excerpt from pp. 51–54 in *The Populist Mind* by Norman Pollock, ed. Copyright © 1967 by Norman Pollock. Reprinted with permission.

QUESTIONS FOR ANALYSIS AND DEBATE

1. According to Mary Elizabeth Lease, what accounted for the high rate of foreclosures on Kansas farms?

2. When Ignatius Donnelly spoke of "a hireling standing army, unrecognized by our laws," what current event was he referring to?

3. Kansas governor Lorenzo Lewelling said, "If it be true that the poor have no right to the property of the rich let it also be declared that the rich have no right to the property of the poor." What did he mean by the "property of the poor"? What did he want the state to do?

The Labor Wars

While farmers united to fight for change, industrial laborers fought their own battles in a series of bloody strikes so fiercely waged on both sides that historians have called them the "labor wars." Coal miners struck to fight the use of convict labor in the mines of eastern Tennessee. Miners in Coeur d'Alene, Idaho, battled the bosses and founded the militant Western Federation of Miners. Railroad switchmen went on strike in Buffalo, New York, and black and white workers mounted a general strike that closed down the port of New Orleans. Industrial workers felt increasingly threatened as businesses combined into huge corporations, and in the 1890s labor took a stand. At issue was the right of workers to organize and speak through unions to bargain collectively and fight for better working conditions, higher wages, shorter hours, and greater worker control in the face of increased mechanization.

Three major conflicts of the period, the lockout of steelworkers in Homestead, Pennsylvania, in 1892; the miners' strike in Cripple Creek, Colorado, in 1894; and the Pullman strike in Illinois that same year, raised fundamental questions about the rights of labor and the sanctity of private property.

The Homestead Lockout

In 1892, steelworkers in Pennsylvania squared off against Andrew Carnegie in a decisive struggle over the right to organize in the Homestead steel mills. At first glance, it seemed ironic that Carnegie became the adversary in the workers' fight for the right to unionize. Andrew Carnegie was unusual among industrialists as a self-styled friend of labor. In 1886, he had written, "The right of the workingmen to combine and to form trade unions is no less sacred than the right of the manufacturer to enter into associations and conferences with his fellows."

Yet as much as he cherished his **liberal** beliefs, Carnegie cherished his profits more. Labor unions had worked to his advantage during the years when he was building his empire. Labor strife at Homestead during the 1870s had enabled Carnegie to buy the plant from his competitors at cost and to take over the steel industry. But by the 1890s, Carnegie had beat out his competitors, and the only thing standing in the way of his control of the industry was the Amalgamated Association of Iron and Steel Workers, one of the largest and richest of the craft unions that made up the American Federation of Labor (AFL).

In 1892, when the Amalgamated attempted to renew its contract at Carnegie's Homestead mill, its leaders were told that since "the vast majority of our employees are Non union, the Firm has decided that the minority must give place to the majority." While it was true that only 800 skilled workers belonged to the elite Amalgamated, the union had long enjoyed the support of the plant's 3,000 nonunion workers. Slavs, who did much of the unskilled work, made common cause with the Welsh, Scots, and Irish skilled workers who belonged to the union. Never before had the Amalgamated been denied a contract.

Carnegie preferred not to be directly involved in the union busting that lay on the horizon, so that spring he sailed to Scotland and left Henry Clay Frick, the toughest antilabor man in the industry, in charge of the Homestead plant. By summer, a strike looked inevitable. Frick prepared by erecting a fifteen-foot fence around the plant and topping it with barbed wire. Workers aptly dubbed it "Fort Frick." To defend his fort and protect strikebreakers, Frick hired 316 mercenaries from the Pinkerton National Detective Agency at the rate of $5 per day, more than double the wage of the average Homestead worker.

The Pinkerton Agency, founded before the Civil War, came into its own in the 1880s as businessmen like Frick used Pinkerton agents as a private security force. The agents were a motley crew, recruited from all levels of society, from urban thugs to college boys. The "Pinks" earned the hatred of workers by protecting strikebreakers and acting as company spies.

On June 28, Frick locked the workers out of the mills and prepared to bring in scab workers. Hugh O'Donnell, the young Irishman who led the union, vowed to prevent strikebreakers from entering the plant. On July 6 at four in the morning, a lookout spotted two barges moving up the Monongahela River in the fog. Frick was attempting to smuggle Pinkertons into Homestead. Workers sounded the alarm, and within minutes a crowd of more than a thousand, hastily armed with rifles, hoes, and fence posts, rushed to the riverbank to meet the enemy. When the Pinkertons

> One Homestead worker complained bitterly, "We have stood idly by and let the town be occupied by soldiers. . . . If we undertake to resist the seizure of our jobs, we will be shot down like dogs."

attempted to come ashore, gunfire broke out, and more than a dozen Pinkertons and some thirty strikers fell, killed or wounded. The Pinkertons retreated to the barges.

For twelve hours, the workers, joined by their family members, threw everything they had at the barges, from fireworks to dynamite. Finally, the Pinkertons hoisted a white flag and arranged with O'Donnell to surrender. With three workers dead and scores wounded, the crowd, numbering perhaps ten thousand, was in no mood for conciliation. As the hated "Pinks" came up the hill, they were forced to run a gantlet of screaming, cursing men, women, and children. When a young guard dropped to his knees, weeping for mercy, a woman used her umbrella to poke out his eye. One Pinkerton had been killed in the siege on the barges. In the grim rout that followed their surrender, not one avoided injury.

The "battle of Fort Frick" ended in a dubious victory for the workers. They took control of the plant and elected a council to run the community. At first, public opinion favored their cause. Newspapers urged Frick to negotiate or submit to arbitration. A congressman castigated Carnegie for "skulking in his castle in Scotland." Populists, meeting in St. Louis, condemned the use of "hireling armies."

But the action of the Homestead workers struck at the heart of the capitalist system, pitting the workers' right to their jobs against the rights of private property. The workers' insistence that "we are not destroying the property of the company—merely protecting our rights" did not prove as compelling to the courts and the state as the property rights of the mill owners. Four days after the confrontation, Pennsylvania's governor, who sympathized with the workers, nonetheless yielded to pressure from Frick and ordered eight thousand National Guard troops into Homestead to protect Carnegie's property. The strikers, thinking they had nothing to fear from the militia, welcomed the troops with a brass band. But they soon understood the reality. The troops' ninety-five-day occupation not only protected Carnegie's property but also enabled Frick to reopen the mills and bring in strikebreakers. "We have been deceived," one worker complained bitterly. "We have stood idly by and let the town be occupied by soldiers who come here, not as our protectors, but as the protectors of non-union men. . . . If we undertake to resist the seizure of our jobs, we will be shot down like dogs."

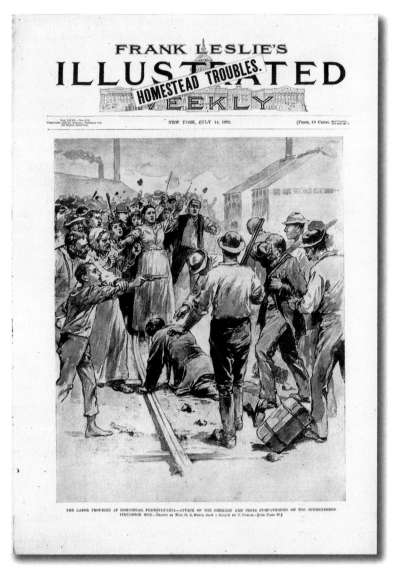

Homestead Workers Attack the Pinkertons
The nation's attention was riveted on labor strife at the Homestead steel mill in the summer of 1892. *Frank Leslie's Illustrated Weekly* ran a cover story on the violence that Pinkerton agents faced from a crowd of men, women, and children armed with clubs, guns, and ax handles. The workers, who had been locked out by Henry Clay Frick, were enraged that Frick had hired the Pinkertons to bring in strikebreakers. In a standoff with workers, the Pinkertons fired into the crowd, killing three men and wounding scores. A truce was negotiated, but the crowd could not contain its rage and viciously attacked the hated "Pinks." The illustration shows a boy with a gun in the foreground. Although the mob was armed, not one of the Pinkertons was shot as they ran the gantlet. All, however, were beaten.
The New-York Society Library.

READING THE IMAGE: How does the illustration portray the crowd?
CONNECTIONS: Public opinion turned against the workers over the course of the lockout. Can you tell whose side the magazine was on?

FOR MORE HELP ANALYZING THIS IMAGE, see the visual activity for this chapter in the Online Study Guide at bedfordstmartins.com/roark.

Then, in a misguided effort to ignite a general uprising, Alexander Berkman, a Russian immigrant and **anarchist**, attempted to assassinate Frick. Berkman bungled his attempt. Shot twice and stabbed with a dagger, Frick survived and showed considerable courage, allowing a doctor to remove the bullets but refusing to leave his desk until the day's work was completed. "I do not think that I shall die," Frick remarked coolly, "but whether I do or not, the Company will pursue the same policy and it will win."

After the assassination attempt, public opinion turned against the workers. Berkman was quickly tried and sentenced to prison. Although the Amalgamated and the AFL denounced his action, the incident linked anarchism and unionism, already associated in the public mind as a result of the Haymarket bombing in 1886 (see chapter 19). Hugh O'Donnell later wrote, "The bullet from Berkman's pistol, failing in its foul intent, went straight through the heart of the Homestead strike."

In the end, the workers capitulated after four and a half months. The Homestead mill reopened in November, and the men returned to work, except for the union leaders, now blacklisted in every steel mill in the country. With the owners firmly in charge, the company slashed wages, reinstated the twelve-hour day, and eliminated five hundred jobs.

In the drama of events at Homestead, the significance of what occurred often remained obscured: The workers at Homestead had been taught a lesson. They would never again, in the words of the National Guard commander, "believe the works are their's [sic] quite as much as Carnegie's." Another forty-five years would pass before steelworkers, unskilled as well as skilled, successfully unionized. In the meantime, Carnegie's production tripled, even in the midst of a depression. "Ashamed to tell you profits these days," Carnegie wrote a friend in 1899. And no wonder: Carnegie's profits had grown from $4 million in 1892 to $40 million in 1900.

The Cripple Creek Miners' Strike of 1894

Less than a year after the Homestead lockout, a panic on Wall Street in the spring of 1893 touched off a bitter economic depression. In the West, silver mines fell on hard times. Looking for work, many miners left for the goldfields of Cripple Creek, Colorado, where miners enjoyed relatively high wages—$3 a day. When conservative mine owners moved to lengthen the workday from eight to ten hours, the newly formed Western Federation of Miners (WFM) vowed to hold the line. In February 1894, the WFM threatened to strike all mines working more than eight-hour shifts. The mine owners divided: Some quickly settled with the WFM; others continued to demand ten hours, provoking a strike.

The striking miners received help from many quarters. Working miners paid $15 a month to a strike fund, and miners in neighboring districts sent substantial contributions. Because so many of the mine owners lived in nearby Colorado Springs, Cripple Creek styled itself a workers' town. The miners enjoyed the support and assistance of local businesses and grocers, who provided credit to the strikers. With these advantages, the Cripple Creek strikers could afford to hold out for their demands.

Even more significant was the solidarity of local officials. The mine owners controlled the county sheriff, but when he called up deputies to put down the strike, local officials intervened. In nearby Altman, Colorado, the mayor, city marshal, and police magistrate all belonged to the WFM. When sheriff's deputies arrived in Altman, the mayor ordered them arrested for disturbing the peace and carrying concealed weapons. The sheriff then appealed to Governor Davis H. Waite to send troops. But Waite, a Populist elected in 1892, also had strong ties to the miners and refused to use the power of the state against the peaceful strikers. Desperate, the sheriff deputized more than a thousand men and in May sent them to occupy the mines. The strikers, entrenched on Bull Hill outside of Cripple Creek, prepared for a showdown. Kathleen Welch Chapman recalled her mother's story of one confrontation where the miners managed to trick the militia and avoid bloodshed: "The men took their coats off, and their hats, and put them up in a tree and put the guns up in there . . . and oh, they just thought that the world was up there, this militia [sheriff's deputies] did, when they saw them."

After several confrontations at Bull Hill, pressure mounted for a settlement. Governor Waite asked the strikers to lay down their arms and demanded that the mine owners disperse their hired deputies. The miners agreed to arbitration and selected Waite as their sole arbitrator. By May, the recalcitrant mine owners capitulated, and the union won an eight-hour day.

Governor Waite's intervention demonstrated the pivotal power of the state in the nation's labor wars. At Cripple Creek, the WFM's union organization, divisions among the mine owners, and support from local officials combined with the restraint of Governor Waite to bring about the strike's success. Having a Populist in power made a difference. A decade later, in 1904, with Waite out of office, mine owners relied on state troops to take back control of the mines, defeating the WFM and blacklisting all of its members. In retrospect, the Cripple Creek miners' strike of 1894 proved the exception to the rule of state intervention on the side of private property. More typical was the outcome of another strike in 1894 in Pullman, Illinois.

Eugene V. Debs and the Pullman Strike

The economic depression that began in 1893 swelled the ranks of the unemployed to three million, almost half of the working population. "A fearful crisis is upon us," wrote a labor publication. "Countless thousands of our fellow men are unemployed; men, women and children are suffering the pangs of hunger." Nowhere were workers more demoralized than in the model town of Pullman, on the outskirts of Chicago.

In the wake of the Great Railroad Strike of 1877, George M. Pullman, the builder of Pullman railroad cars, had moved his plant and workers away from the "snares of the great city." In 1880, he purchased 4,300 acres nine miles south of Chicago on the shores of Lake Calumet and built a model town. He intended the company town to be orderly, clean, and with the appearance of luxury, like the Pullman Palace cars that had made his fortune. The town of Pullman boasted parks, fountains, playgrounds, an auditorium, a library, a hotel, shops, and markets, along with 1,800 units of housing. Noticeably absent was a saloon.

The housing in Pullman was clearly superior to that in neighboring areas, but workers paid a high price to live in the model town. George M. Pullman expected a 6 percent return on his investment. As a result, Pullman's rents ran 10 to 20 percent higher than housing costs in nearby communities. And a family in Pullman could never own its own home. George Pullman refused to "sell an acre under any circumstances." As long as he controlled the town absolutely, he held the powerful whip of eviction over his employees and could quickly get rid of "troublemakers." Although observers at first

A Pullman Craftsworker
Pullman Palace cars were known for their luxurious details. Here, a painter working in the 1890s applies elaborate decoration to the exterior of a Pullman car. In the foreground is an intricately carved door, an example of fine hand-detailing. The Pullman workers' strike in 1894 stemmed in part from the company's efforts to undermine the status of craftsworkers by reducing them to low-paid piecework. Control of the workplace, as much as issues related to wages and hours, fueled the labor wars of the 1890s.
Chicago Historical Society.

praised the beauty and orderliness of the town, critics by the 1890s compared Pullman's model town to a "gilded cage" for workers.

The depression brought hard times to Pullman. Workers saw their wages slashed five times between May and December 1893, with cuts totaling at least 28 percent. At the same time, Pullman refused to lower the rents in his model town, insisting that "the renting of the dwellings and the employment of workmen at Pullman are in no way tied together." When workers went to the bank to cash their paychecks, they found the rent had been taken out. One worker discovered only forty-seven cents in his pay envelope for two weeks' work. When the bank teller asked him whether he wanted to apply it to his back rent, he retorted, "If Mr. Pullman needs that forty-seven cents worse than I do, let him have it." At the same time, Pullman continued to pay his stockholders an 8 percent dividend, and the company accumulated a $25 million surplus.

At the heart of the labor problems at Pullman lay not only economic inequity but also the company's attempt to control the work process, substituting piecework for day wages and undermining skilled craftsworkers. The Pullman workers rebelled. During the spring of 1894, Pullman's desperate workers, seeking help, flocked to the ranks of the American Railway Union (ARU), led by the charismatic Eugene V. Debs. The ARU, unlike the skilled craft unions of the AFL, pledged to organize all railway workers—from engineers to engine wipers.

George Pullman responded to union organization at his plant by firing three of the union's leaders the day after they led a delegation to protest wage cuts. Angry men and women walked off the job in disgust. What began as a spontaneous protest in May 1894 quickly blossomed into a strike that involved more than 90 percent of Pullman's 3,300 workers. "We do not know what the outcome will be, and in fact we do not much care," one worker confessed. "We do know that we are working for less wages than will maintain ourselves and families in the necessaries of life, and on that proposition we refuse to work any longer." Pullman countered by shutting down the plant.

In June, the Pullman strikers appealed to the ARU to come to their aid. Debs hesitated to commit his fledgling union to a major strike in the midst of a depression. He pleaded with the workers to find another solution. When George Pullman adamantly refused arbitration, the ARU membership voted to boycott all Pullman cars. Beginning on June 29, switchmen across the United States refused to handle any train that carried Pullman cars.

The conflict escalated quickly. The General Managers Association (GMA), an organization of managers from twenty-four different railroads, acted in concert to quash the boycott. Determined to kill the ARU, they recruited strikebreakers and fired all the protesting switchmen. Their tactics set off a chain reaction. Entire train crews walked off the job in a show of solidarity with the Pullman workers. In a matter of days, the boycott/strike spread to more than fifteen railroads and affected twenty-seven states and territories. By July 2, rail lines from New York to California lay paralyzed. Even the GMA was forced to concede that the railroads had been "fought to a standstill."

The boycott remained surprisingly peaceful. Mobs stopped trains carrying Pullman cars and forced train crews to uncouple the cars and leave them on the sidings. In contrast to the Great Railroad Strike of 1877, no major riots broke out, and no serious property damage occurred. Debs, in a whirlwind of activity, fired off telegrams to all parts of the country advising his followers to avoid violence and respect law and order. But the nation's newspapers, fed press releases by the GMA, distorted the issues and misrepresented the strike. Across the country, papers ran headlines like "Wild Riot in Chicago" and "Mob Is in Control."

In Washington, Attorney General Richard B. Olney, a lawyer with strong ties to the railroads, determined to put down the strike. In his way stood the governor of Illinois, John Peter Altgeld, who, observing that the boycott remained peaceful, refused to call out troops. To get around Altgeld, Olney convinced President Grover Cleveland that federal troops had to intervene to protect the mails. To further cripple the boycott, two conservative Chicago judges issued an injunction so sweeping that it prohibited Debs from speaking in public. By issuing the injunction, the court made the boycott a crime punishable by a jail sentence for contempt of court, a civil process that did not require a jury trial. Even the conservative *Chicago Tribune* judged the injunction "a menace to liberty . . . a weapon ever ready for the capitalist." Furious, Debs risked jail by refusing to honor it.

Olney's strategy worked. With the strikers violating a federal injunction and with the mails in jeopardy (the GMA made sure that Pullman cars were put on every mail train), Cleveland called out the army. On July 5, nearly 8,000 troops marched into Chicago. Violence immediately erupted. In one day, troops killed 25 workers and wounded more than 60. In the face of bullets and bayonets, the strikers held firm.

"Troops cannot move trains," Debs reminded his followers, a fact that was borne out as the railroads remained paralyzed despite the military intervention. But if the army could not put down the boycott, the injunction could and did. Debs was arrested and imprisoned for contempt of court. With its leader in jail, its headquarters raided and ransacked, and its members demoralized, the ARU was defeated along with the boycott. Pullman reopened his factory, hiring new workers to replace many of the strikers and leaving 1,600 workers without jobs.

In the aftermath of the strike, a special commission investigated the events at Pullman, taking testimony from 107 witnesses, from the lowliest workers to George M. Pullman himself. Stubborn and self-righteous, Pullman spoke for the business orthodoxy of his era, steadfastly affirming the right of business to safeguard its interests through confederacies such as the GMA and at the same time denying labor's right to organize. "If we were to receive these men as representatives of the union," he stated, "they could probably force us to pay any wages which they saw fit."

From his jail cell, Eugene Debs reviewed the events of the Pullman strike. With the courts and the government ready to side with industrialists in the interest of defending private property, Debs realized that labor had little recourse. Strikes seemed futile, and unions remained helpless; workers would have to take control of the state itself. Debs went into jail a trade unionist and came out six months later a socialist. At first, he turned to the Populist Party, but after its demise, he formed the Socialist Party in 1900 and ran for president on its ticket five times. Debs's dissatisfaction with the status quo was shared by another group even more alienated from the political process—women.

REVIEW   Why did the strikes of the 1890s fail to produce permanent gains for workers?

National Guard Occupying Pullman, Illinois
After President Grover Cleveland called out the troops to put down the Pullman strike in 1894, the National Guard occupied the town of Pullman to protect George M. Pullman's property. Here, guardsmen ring the Arcade building, the town shopping center, while curious men and women look on. The intervention of troops at Homestead and Pullman enabled the owners to bring in strikebreakers and defeat the unions. In Cripple Creek, Colorado, where a Populist governor used the militia only to keep the peace and not against the strikers, the miners won the day in 1894.
Chicago Historical Society.

Woman's Christian Temperance Union Postcards
The Woman's Christian Temperance Union distributed postcards like these to attack the liquor trade. These cards are typical in their portrayal of saloon backers as traitors to the nation. In the first card, notice the man trampling on the American flag as he casts his ballot—a sly allusion to the need for woman suffrage. The second card shows a saloon keeper recruiting an "army of drunkards." The third one illustrates the WCTU's support of total abstinence, urging youths to sign "the pledge" and promise never to "touch, taste, or handle intoxicating drink." Collection of Joyce M. Tice.

Women's Activism

"Do everything," Frances Willard urged her followers in 1881. The new president of the Woman's Christian Temperance Union (WCTU) meant what she said. The WCTU followed a trajectory that was common for women in the late nineteenth century. As women organized to deal with issues that touched their homes and families, they moved into politics, lending new urgency to the cause of woman suffrage. Urban industrialism dislocated women's lives no less than men's. Like men, women sought political change and organized to promote issues central to their lives, from temperance and suffrage to antilynching (see chapter 18).

Frances Willard and the Woman's Christian Temperance Union

Frances Willard, the visionary leader of the WCTU, spoke for a group left almost entirely out of the U.S. electoral process—women. In 1890, only one state, Wyoming, allowed women to vote in national elections. But lack of the **franchise** did not mean that women were apolitical. The WCTU demonstrated the breadth of women's political activity in the late nineteenth century.

Women supported the **temperance movement** because they felt particularly vulnerable to the effects of drunkenness. Dependent on men's wages, women and children suffered when money went for drink. The drunken, abusive husband epitomized the evils of a nation in which women remained second-class citizens. Composed entirely of women, the WCTU viewed all women's interests as essentially the same—crossing class, ethnic, and racial lines—and therefore did not hesitate to use the singular *woman* to emphasize gender solidarity. Although mostly white and middle-class, WCTU members resolved to speak for their entire sex.

When Frances Willard became president in 1879, she radically changed the direction of the organization. Moving away from a religious approach, the WCTU began to view alcoholism as a disease rather than a sin, and poverty as a cause rather than a result of drink. Accordingly, social action replaced prayer as women's answer to the threat of drunkenness. By the 1890s, the WCTU worked to establish women's reformatories, promoted the hiring of female police officers, and sponsored day nurseries, industrial training schools for women, missions for the homeless, medical dispensaries, and lodging houses for the poor. At the same time, the WCTU became involved in labor issues, joining with the Knights of Labor to press for better working conditions for women workers. Describing workers in a textile mill, a WCTU member wrote in the *Union Signal*, the WCTU monthly magazine, "It is dreadful to see these girls, stripped almost to the skin . . . and running like racehorses from the beginning to the end of the day." She concluded, "The hard slavish work is drawing the girls into the saloon."

Willard capitalized on the **cult of domesticity** as a shrewd political tactic to move women into public life and gain power to ameliorate social problems. Using "home protection" as her watchword, she argued as early as 1884 that women needed the vote to protect home and family. By the 1890s, the WCTU's grassroots network of local unions had spread to all but the most isolated rural areas of the country. Strong and rich, with more than 200,000 dues-paying members, the WCTU was a formidable group.

Willard worked to create a broad reform coalition in the 1890s, embracing the Knights of Labor, the People's Party, and the Prohibition Party. Until her death in 1898, she led, if not a women's rights movement, then the first organized mass movement of women united around a women's issue. By 1900, thanks largely to the WCTU, women could claim a generation of experience in political action—speaking, lobbying, organizing, drafting legislation, and running private charitable institutions. As Willard observed, "All this work has tended more toward the liberation of women than it has toward the extinction of the saloon."

Elizabeth Cady Stanton, Susan B. Anthony, and the Movement for Woman Suffrage

Unlike the WCTU, the organized movement for woman suffrage remained small and relatively weak in the late nineteenth century. The woman's rights movement, begun by Elizabeth Cady Stanton at Seneca Falls in 1848 (see chapter 12), split in 1867 over whether the Fourteenth and Fifteenth Amendments, which granted voting rights to African American men, should have extended the vote to women as well. Stanton and her ally, Susan B. Anthony,

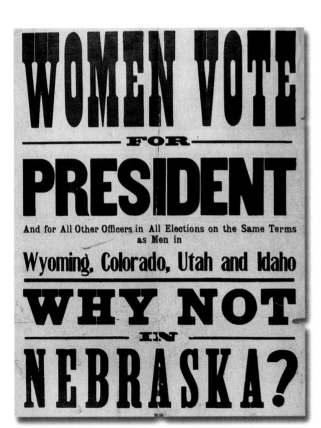

Campaigning for Woman Suffrage

In 1896, women voted in only four states—Wyoming, Colorado, Idaho, and Utah. The West led the way in the campaign for woman suffrage, with Wyoming Territory granting women the vote as early as 1869. Sparse population meant that only sixteen votes were needed in the state's territorial legislature to obtain passage of woman suffrage. The poster calls on Nebraska to join the suffrage column, while the flag illustrates the number of states where women could vote.

Poster: Nebraska State Historical Society; Flag: Smithsonian Institution, Washington, D.C.

launched the National Woman Suffrage Association (NWSA) in 1869, demanding the vote for women (see chapter 18). A more conservative group, the American Woman Suffrage Association (AWSA), formed the same year. Composed of men as well as women, the AWSA believed that women should vote in local but not national elections.

By 1890, the split had healed, and the newly united National American Woman Suffrage Association (NAWSA) launched campaigns on the state level to gain the vote for women. Twenty years had made a great change. Woman suffrage, though not yet generally supported, was no longer considered a crackpot idea. Thanks to the WCTU's support of the "home protection" ballot, suffrage had become accepted as a means to an end even when it was not embraced as a woman's natural right. The NAWSA honored Elizabeth Cady Stanton by electing her its first president, but Susan B. Anthony, who took the helm in 1892, emerged as the leading figure in the new united organization.

Stanton and Anthony, both in their seventies, were coming to the end of their public careers. Since the days of the Seneca Falls woman's rights convention, they had worked for reforms for their sex, including property rights, custody rights, and the right to education and gainful employment. But the prize of woman suffrage still eluded them. Suffragists won victories in Colorado in 1893 and Idaho in 1896. One more state joined the suffrage column in 1896 when Utah entered the Union. But women suffered a bitter defeat in a California referendum on woman suffrage that same year. Never losing faith, Susan B. Anthony remarked in her last public appearance, in 1906, "Failure is impossible." Although it would take until 1920 for all women to gain the vote with the ratification of the Nineteenth Amendment, the unification of the two woman suffrage groups in 1890 signaled a new era in women's fight for the vote just as Frances Willard's place on the platform in 1892 at the founding of the People's Party in St. Louis symbolized women's growing role in politics and reform.

> Never losing faith, Susan B. Anthony remarked in her last public appearance, in 1906, "Failure is impossible."

REVIEW How did women's temperance activism contribute to the cause of woman suffrage?

Depression Politics

The depression that began in the spring of 1893 and lasted for more than four years put nearly half of the labor force out of work, a higher percentage than during the Great Depression of the 1930s. The country swarmed with people looking for jobs. The human cost of the depression was staggering. "I Take my pen in hand to let you know that we are Starving to death," a Kansas farm woman wrote to the governor in 1894. "Last cent gone," wrote a young widow in her diary. "Children went to work without their breakfasts." The burden of feeding and sheltering the unemployed and their families fell to private charity, city government, and some of the stronger trade unions. Following the harsh dictates of **social Darwinism** and laissez-faire, the majority of America's elected officials believed that it was inappropriate for the government to intervene. But the scope of the depression made it impossible for local agencies to supply sufficient relief, and increasingly Americans called on the federal government to take action. Armies of the unemployed marched on Washington to demand relief, and the Populist Party experienced a surge of support as the election of 1896 approached.

Coxey's Army

Masses of unemployed Americans marched to Washington, D.C., in the spring of 1894 to call attention to their plight and to urge Congress to enact a public works program to end unemployment. From as far away as Seattle, San Francisco, Los Angeles, and Denver, hundreds joined the march. Jacob S. Coxey of Massilon, Ohio, led the most publicized contingent. Coxey, a millionaire with a penchant for racehorses and high living, seemed an unlikely champion of the unemployed. Convinced that men could be put to work building badly needed roads for the nation, Coxey proposed a scheme to finance public works through non-interest-bearing bonds. "What I am after," he maintained, "is to try to put this country in a condition so that no man who wants work shall be obliged to remain idle." His plan won support from the AFL and the Populists.

Starting out from Ohio with one hundred men, "Coxey's army," as it was dubbed by journalists, swelled as it marched east through the spring snows of the Alleghenies. In Pennsylvania, Coxey recruited several hundred from the ranks

Coxey's Army
A contingent of Coxey's army stops to rest on its way to Washington, D.C. A "petition in boots," Coxey's followers were well dressed, as evidenced by the men in this photo wearing white shirts, vests, neckties, and bowler hats. Music was an important component of the march, including the anthem "Marching with Coxey," sung to the tune of "Marching through Georgia." Band members are pictured on the right with their instruments. Despite their peaceful pose, the marchers stirred the fears of many conservative Americans, who predicted an uprising of the unemployed. Only a few Populist members of Congress—notably Senator William V. Allen of Nebraska—supported them and urged Congress to hear their grievances. Instead, Coxey and a contingent of his marchers were arrested and jailed for "walking on the grass" when they reached the nation's capital.
Ohio Historical Society.

of those left unemployed by the Homestead lockout. Called by Coxey the Commonweal of Christ, the army advanced to the tune of "Marching through Georgia":

> We are not tramps nor vagabonds,
>   that's shirking honest toil,
> But miners, clerks, skilled artisans,
>   and tillers of the soil
> Now forced to beg our brother worms
>   to give us leave to toil,
> While we are marching with Coxey.
> Hurrah! hurrah! for the unemployed's appeal
> Hurrah! hurrah! for the marching commonweal!

On May 1, Coxey's army arrived in Washington. When Coxey defiantly marched his men onto the Capitol grounds, police set upon the demonstrators with nightsticks, cracking skulls and arresting Coxey and his lieutenants. Coxey went to jail for twenty days and was fined $5 for "walking on the grass."

Those who had trembled for the safety of the Republic heaved a sigh of relief after Coxey's arrest, hoping that it would halt the march on Washington. But other armies of the unemployed, totaling possibly as many as five thousand people, were still on their way. Too poor to pay for railway tickets, they rode the rails as "freeloaders." The more daring contingents commandeered entire trains, stirring fears of revolution. Journalists who covered the march did little to quiet the nation's fears. They delighted in military terminology, describing themselves as "war correspondents." To boost newspaper sales, they gave to the episode a tone of urgency and heightened the sense of a nation imperiled.

By August, the leaderless, tattered armies dissolved. Although the "On to Washington" movement proved ineffective in forcing federal relief legislation, Coxey's army dramatized the plight of the unemployed and acted, in the words of one participant, as a "living, moving object lesson." Like the Populists, Coxey's army called into question the underlying values of the new industrial order and demonstrated how ordinary citizens turned to means outside the regular party system to influence politics in the 1890s.

The People's Party and the Election of 1896

Even before the depression of 1893 gave added impetus to their cause, the Populists had railed against the status quo. "We meet in the midst of a nation brought to the verge of moral, political, and material ruin," Ignatius Donnelly had declared in his keynote address at the creation of the People's Party in St. Louis in 1892. "The fruits of the toil of millions are boldly stolen to build up colossal fortunes for a few. . . . From the same prolific womb of governmental injustice we breed the two great classes—tramps and millionaires."

The fiery rhetoric frightened many who saw in the People's Party a call not to reform but to revolution. Throughout the country, the press denounced the Populists as "cranks, lunatics, and idiots." When one self-righteous editor dismissed them as "calamity howlers," Populist governor Lorenzo Lewelling of Kansas shot back, "If that is so I want to continue to howl until those conditions are improved."

The People's Party captured more than a million votes in the presidential election of 1892, a respectable showing for a new party (Map 20.1). The Populists might have done better, but on the eve of the convention, they lost their standard-bearer when Leonidis L. Polk, president of the Southern Farmers' Alliance, died suddenly. Scrambling to find a replacement, the convention nominated General James B. Weaver of Iowa, a former Union general who had run for president on the Greenback Labor ticket in 1880. To balance the ticket, they selected an ex-Confederate as his running mate. But many southern Populists could not bring themselves to vote for a Yankee general and stayed away from the polls.

Increasingly, sectional and racial animosities threatened the unity of the People's Party. More than their alliance with the Yankee North, it was the Populists' willingness to form common cause with black farmers that made them anathema in the white South. Tom Watson of Georgia had tackled the "Negro question" head-on in 1892. Realizing that race prejudice obscured the common economic interests of black and white

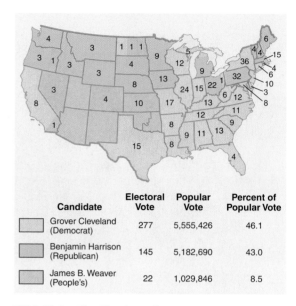

Candidate	Electoral Vote	Popular Vote	Percent of Popular Vote
Grover Cleveland (Democrat)	277	5,555,426	46.1
Benjamin Harrison (Republican)	145	5,182,690	43.0
James B. Weaver (People's)	22	1,029,846	8.5

MAP 20.1   The Election of 1892

farmers, Watson openly courted African Americans, appearing on platforms with black speakers and promising "to wipe out the color line." When angry Georgia whites threatened to lynch a black Populist preacher, Watson rallied two thousand gun-toting Populists to the man's defense. Although many Populists remained racist in their attitudes toward African Americans, the spectacle of white Georgians riding through the night to protect a black man from lynching was symbolic of the enormous changes the Populist Party promised in the South.

The People's Party fared better in the 1894 congressional election, when, unencumbered by a Union general, the Populists added half a million voters to their column. With the depression swelling the ranks of the disaffected, the Populists looked forward to the election of 1896.

As the presidential election approached, the depression intensified cries for reform not only from the Populists but also throughout the electorate. Depression worsened the tight money problem caused by the deflationary pressures of the gold standard. Once again, proponents of free silver (the unlimited coinage of silver in addition to gold) stirred rebellion in the ranks of both the Democratic and the Republican parties. When the Republicans nominated Ohio governor William McKinley on a platform pledging the preservation of the gold standard, western advocates of free silver representing miners and farmers walked out of the convention. Open rebellion also split the Democratic Party as vast segments in the West and South repudiated President Grover Cleveland because of his support for gold. In South Carolina, Benjamin Tillman won his race for Congress by promising, "Send me to Washington and I'll stick my pitchfork into [Cleveland's] old ribs!"

The spirit of revolt animated the Democratic National Convention in Chicago in the summer of 1896. "Pitchfork Ben" Tillman set the tone by attacking the party's president, denouncing the Cleveland administration as "undemocratic and tyrannical." But the man of the hour was William Jennings Bryan of Nebraska, the thirty-six-year-old "boy orator from the Platte," who whipped the convention into a frenzy with his passionate call for free silver. In his keynote address, Bryan masterfully cataloged the grievances of farmers and laborers, closing his dramatic speech with a ringing exhortation: "Do not crucify mankind upon a cross of gold." Pandemonium broke loose as delegates stampeded to nominate Bryan, the youngest candidate ever to run for the presidency.

The juggernaut of free silver rolled out of Chicago and on to St. Louis, where the People's Party met a week after the Democrats adjourned. Smelling victory, many western Populists urged the party to ally with the Democrats and endorse Bryan. A major obstacle in the path of fusion, however, was Bryan's running mate, Arthur M. Sewall. A Maine railway director and bank president, Sewall, who had been placed on the ticket to appease conservative Democrats, embodied everything the Populists opposed.

Populism's regional constituencies remained as divided on tactics as they were uniform in their call for change. Western Populists, including a strong coalition of farmers and miners in states such as Idaho and Colorado, championed free silver as a way to put the ailing Rocky Mountain silver industry back on its feet and restore prosperity to the region. In these largely Republican states, Populists had joined forces with Democrats in previous elections and saw no problem with becoming "Popocrats" once Bryan led the Democratic ticket on a free-silver platform. Similarly in the

Midwest, a Republican stronghold, Populists who had used fusion with the Democrats as a tactic to win elections had little trouble backing Bryan. But in the South, where Democrats had resorted to fraud and violence to steal elections from the Populists in 1892 and 1894, support for a Democratic ticket proved especially hard to swallow. Die-hard southern Populists wanted no part of fusion.

All of these tactical differences emerged as the Populists met in St. Louis in 1896 to nominate a candidate for president. To show that they remained true to their principles, delegates first voted to support all the planks of the 1892 platform, added to it a call for public works projects for the unemployed, and only narrowly defeated a plank for woman suffrage. To deal with the problem of fusion, the convention selected the vice presidential candidate first. The nomination of Tom Watson undercut opposition to Bryan's candidacy. And although Bryan quickly sent a telegram to protest that he would not drop Sewall as his running mate, mysteriously his message never reached the convention floor. Fusion triumphed. Watson's vice presidential

Gold Elephant Campaign Button and Silver Ribbon from St. Louis, 1896

Mechanical elephant badges that opened to show portraits of William McKinley and his running mate, Garret Hobart, were popular campaign novelties in the election of 1896. The elephant, the mascot of the Republican Party, is gilded to indicate the party's support of the gold standard. In contrast, the delegate ribbon from the St. Louis National Silver Convention in 1896 features a silver eagle testifying to the power of free silver as a campaign issue. The Democrats nominated William Jennings Bryan on a free-silver platform, and the Populists put him on their ticket as well.

Pin: Collection of Janice L. and David J. Frent; Ribbon: Nebraska State Historical Society.

nomination paved the way for the selection of Bryan by a lopsided vote. The Populists did not know it, but their cheers for Bryan signaled not a chorus of victory but the death knell of the People's Party.

Few contests in the nation's history have been as fiercely fought and as full of emotion as the presidential election of 1896. On one side stood Republican William McKinley, backed by the wealthy industrialist and party boss Mark Hanna. Hanna played on the business community's fears of Populism to raise more than $4 million for the Republican war chest, double the amount of any previous campaign. On the other side, William Jennings Bryan, with few assets beyond his silver tongue, struggled to make up in energy and eloquence what his party lacked in campaign funds.

> The Populists did not know it, but their cheers for Bryan in St. Louis signaled not a chorus of victory but the death knell of the People's Party.

He set a new style for presidential campaigning, crisscrossing the country in a whirlwind tour, traveling more than eighteen thousand miles and delivering more than six hundred speeches in three months. According to his own reckoning, he visited twenty-seven states and spoke to more than five million Americans.

As election day approached, the silver states of the Rocky Mountains lined up solidly for Bryan. The Northeast stood solidly for McKinley. Much of the South, with the exception of the border states, abandoned the Populists and returned to the Democratic fold, leaving Tom Watson to lament that "[Populists] play Jonah while [Democrats] play the whale." The Midwest hung in the balance. Bryan intensified his campaign in Illinois, Michigan, Ohio, and Indiana. But midwestern farmers proved less receptive than western voters to the blandishments of free silver.

In the cities, Democrats charged the Republicans with mass intimidation. "Men, vote as you please," the head of New York's Steinway Piano Company reportedly announced to his workers on the eve of the election, "but if Bryan is elected tomorrow the whistle will not blow Wednesday morning." Intimidation alone did not explain the failure of urban labor to rally to Bryan. Republicans repeatedly warned workers that if the Democrats won, the inflated silver dollar would be worth only fifty cents. However much farmers and laborers might insist that they were united as producers against the nonproducing bosses, it was equally true that inflation did not offer the boon to urban laborers that it

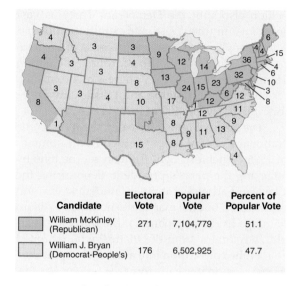

Candidate	Electoral Vote	Popular Vote	Percent of Popular Vote
William McKinley (Republican)	271	7,104,779	51.1
William J. Bryan (Democrat-People's)	176	6,502,925	47.7

MAP 20.2   The Election of 1896

did to western farmers. For while debtors benefited from the inflated currency, which allowed them to pay off their debts with cheaper, more plentiful dollars, inflation promised no real gain to city workers and in fact might worsen their situation by leading to higher prices for food and rent. Although industrial workers in the West and South, particularly miners, voted Populist, eastern workers failed to rally to Bryan.

On election day, four out of five voters went to the polls in an unprecedented turnout. In the critical midwestern states, as many as 95 percent of the eligible voters cast their ballots. In the end, the election hinged on between 100 and 1,000 votes in several key states, including Wisconsin, Iowa, and Minnesota. Although McKinley won twenty-three states to Bryan's twenty-two, the electoral vote showed a lopsided 271 to 176 in McKinley's favor (Map 20.2).

The biggest losers in 1896 turned out to be the Populists. On the national level, they polled fewer than 300,000 votes, a million less than in 1894. In the clamor to support Bryan, Populists in the South had drifted back to the Democratic Party. The People's Party was crushed, and with it the agrarian revolt.

But if Populism proved unsuccessful at the polls, it nevertheless set the domestic political agenda for the United States in the next decades, highlighting issues such as banking and currency reform, electoral reforms, and an enlarged role for the federal government in the economy. Meanwhile, as the decade ended, the bugle call to arms turned America's attention to foreign affairs and effectively drowned out the trumpet of reform. The struggle for social justice gave way to a war for empire as the United States asserted its power on the world stage.

REVIEW Why was the People's Party unable to translate national support into victory in the 1896 election?

The United States and the World

Throughout much of the second half of the nineteenth century, U.S. interest in foreign policy took a backseat to domestic developments. Intent on its own continental expansion, the United States stood aloof while Great Britain, France, Germany, Spain, Belgium, and the increasingly powerful Japan competed for empires in Asia, Africa, Latin America, and the Pacific. Between 1870 and 1900, European nations **colonized** more than 20 percent of the world's landmass and 10 percent of the world's population.

At the turn of the twentieth century, American foreign policy consisted of two currents—**isolationism** and expansionism. Although the determination to remain aloof from European politics had been a hallmark of U.S. foreign policy since the nation's founding, Americans simultaneously believed in **manifest destiny**—the "obvious" right to expand the nation from ocean to ocean. The United States' determination to protect its sphere of influence in the Western Hemisphere at the same time it expanded its trading in Asia moved the nation away from isolationism and toward a more active role on the world stage. The push for commercial expansion joined with a sense of Christian mission to refocus the nation's attention abroad and led both to the strengthening of the **Monroe Doctrine** in the Western Hemisphere and to a new Open Door policy in Asia.

Markets and Missionaries

The depression of the 1890s provided a powerful impetus to American commercial expansion. As markets weakened at home, American businesses looked abroad for profits. As early as 1890, Captain Alfred Thayer Mahan, leader of a growing group of American expansionists, prophesied, "Whether they will or not, Americans must now begin to look outward. The growing production of the country requires it." Although not all U.S. business leaders thought it advantageous to undertake adventures abroad, the logic of acquiring new markets to absorb the nation's growing capacity for production proved convincing to many. As the depression deepened, one diplomat warned that Americans "must turn [their] eyes abroad, or they will soon look inward upon discontent."

Exports constituted a small but significant percentage of the profits of American business in the 1890s (Figure 20.2). And where American

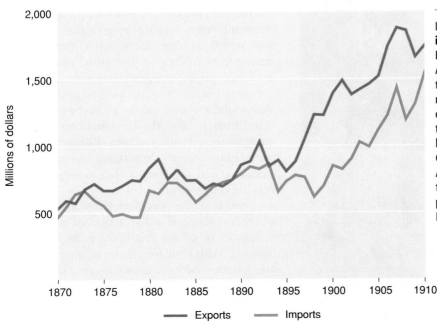

FIGURE 20.2 Expansion in U.S. Trade, 1870–1910 Between 1870 and 1910, American exports more than tripled. Imports generally rose, but they were held in check by the high protective tariffs championed by Republican presidents from Ulysses S. Grant to William Howard Taft. A decline in imports is particularly noticeable after the passage of the prohibitive McKinley tariff in 1890.

Exports Imports

interests led, businessmen expected the government's power and influence to follow to protect their investments. America's foreign policy often appeared to be little more than a sidelight to business development. Companies like Standard Oil actively sought to use the U.S. government as their agent, often putting foreign service employees on the payroll. "Our ambassadors and ministers and consuls," wrote John D. Rockefeller appreciatively, "have aided to push our way into new markets and to the utmost corners of the world." Whether "our" referred to the United States or to Standard Oil remained ambiguous; in practice, the distinction was of little importance in late-nineteenth-century foreign policy.

Mei Foo Lamp

The Standard Oil Company sold more than a million *Mei Foo* ("beautiful companion") lamps in China during the 1890s to promote the sale of kerosene in the China market. The first oil tankers were square-rigged kerosene clipper ships that plied the Pacific beginning in 1892 as the petroleum industry rushed to capture the China trade. Standard Oil ads admonished, "If a person wishes to have luck, longevity, health and peace, he or she must live in a world of light."
Courtesy of Exxon Mobil Corporation.

America's foreign policy often appeared little more than a sidelight to business development. In Hawaii (first called the Sandwich Islands), American sugar interests fomented a rebellion in 1893, toppling the increasingly independent Queen Liliuokalani. (See "Beyond America's Borders," page 730.) They pushed Congress to annex the islands, which would allow planters to avoid the high McKinley tariff on sugar. When President Cleveland learned that Hawaiians opposed annexation, he withdrew the proposal from Congress. But expansionists still coveted the islands and continued to look for an excuse to push through annexation.

However compelling the economic arguments about overseas markets proved, business interests alone did not account for the new expansionism that seized the nation during the 1890s. As Mahan confessed, "Even when material interests are the original exciting cause, it is the sentiment to which they give rise, the moral tone which emotion takes that constitutes the greater force." Much of that moral tone was set by American missionaries intent on spreading the gospel of Christianity to the "heathen." No area on the globe constituted a greater challenge than China. In 1858, the Tientsin treaty admitted foreign missionaries to China. Roman Catholics from France and Protestants from Britain, Germany, and the United States rushed to convert the Chinese.

Increased missionary activity and Western enterprise touched off a series of antiforeign outbreaks in China culminating in the Boxer uprising. Although for the most part Christian missionaries proved unsuccessful, converting only 100,000 in a population of 400 million, the Chinese nevertheless resented the interference of missionaries in village life and the preference

Women Missionaries

Methodist women missionaries in China's Szechuan Province relied on traditional means of transportation, in this case "back chairs." The independence enjoyed by women missionaries stood in marked contrast to the restrictions placed on young, unmarried women of their class at home. Perhaps the opportunity for autonomy, as well as missionary zeal, explains why women constituted 60 percent of America's foreign missionaries by 1890.
Special Collections, Yale Divinity School Library.

and protection they afforded their Christian converts. Opposition to foreign missionaries took the form of antiforeign secret societies, most notably the Boxers, whose Chinese name translated to "Righteous Harmonious Fist." No simple boxing club, in 1899 the Boxers began to terrorize Chinese Christians and missionaries in northwestern Shandong Province. Men and women were hacked to death with swords, burned alive in their houses, and dragged by howling mobs to their execution. With the tacit support of China's Dowager Empress, the Boxers became bolder. Under the slogan "Uphold the Ch'ing Dynasty, Exterminate the Foreigners," they marched on the cities. Their rampage eventually led to the massacre of some 30,000 Chinese converts and 250 foreign nuns, priests, and missionaries along with their families.

As the Boxers spread terror throughout northern China, some 800 Americans and Europeans sought refuge in the foreign legation buildings in Beijing (then called Peking). Along with missionaries from the countryside came thousands of their Chinese converts, fleeing the Boxers. Unable to escape and cut off from outside aid and communication, the Americans and Europeans in Beijing mounted a defense to face the Boxer onslaught. For two months, they held out under siege, eating mule and horse meat and losing 76 men in battle. American missionary Luella Miner wrote sadly, "We are isolated here as if we were on a desert island. . . . Are our Christians everywhere being slaughtered?"

Americans back home who learned of the fate of their compatriots at the hands of the Chinese showed little toleration for the cautious diplomatic approach favored by Secretary of State John Hay. In August 1900, 2,500 U.S. troops joined an international force sent to rescue the foreigners besieged in Beijing. After routing the Boxers, the troops looted the Forbidden City, home of the imperial court, forcing the Dowager Empress to flee disguised as a peasant. In 1901, the European powers imposed the humiliating Boxer Protocol, giving them the right to maintain military forces in the Chinese capital and requiring the Chinese government to pay an indemnity of $333 million for the loss of life and property resulting from the Boxer uprising.

In the aftermath of the uprising, missionaries voiced no concern at the paradox of bringing Christianity to China at gunpoint. "It is worth any cost in money, worth any cost in blood-

shed," argued one bishop, "if we can make millions of Chinese true and intelligent Christians." Merchants and missionaries alike shared such moralistic reasoning. Indeed, they worked hand in hand; trade and Christianity marched into Asia together. "Missionaries," admitted the American clergyman Charles Denby, "are the pioneers of trade and commerce. . . . The missionary, inspired by holy zeal, goes everywhere and by degrees foreign commerce and trade follow."

The Monroe Doctrine and the Open Door Policy

The emergence of the United States as a world power pitted the nation against the colonial powers, particularly Germany and Japan, which posed a threat to the twin pillars of America's expansionist foreign policy—one dating back to President James Monroe in the 1820s, the other formalized in 1900 under President William McKinley. The first, the Monroe Doctrine, came to be interpreted as establishing the Western Hemisphere as an American "sphere of influence" and warned European powers to stay away or risk war. The second, the Open Door, dealt with maintaining market access to China.

American diplomacy actively worked to buttress the Monroe Doctrine, with its assertion of American hegemony (domination) in the Western Hemisphere. In the 1880s, Republican secretary of state James G. Blaine promoted hemispheric peace and trade through Pan-American cooperation but at the same time used American troops to intervene in Latin American border disputes. In 1895, Americans risked war with Great Britain to enforce the Monroe Doctrine when a conflict developed between Venezuela and British Guiana. President Cleveland asserted the U.S. prerogative to step in and mediate, reducing Venezuela to the role of mere onlooker in its own affairs. At first, Britain refused to accept U.S. mediation, and conflict seemed imminent. "Let the fight come if it must," wrote rising Republican neophyte Theodore Roosevelt, always itching to do battle. Seeing an opportunity to extend manifest destiny to the north, Roosevelt vowed, "We [will] take Canada." But the British, who feared the possibility of war in Europe and as a consequence wished to avoid conflict in Latin America, accepted the terms of U.S. mediation, resolving the Venezuelan crisis.

Regime Change in Hawaii

Queen Liliuokalani came to the throne in Hawaii in 1891 determined to take back power for her monarchy and her people. As a member of Hawaii's native royalty, or *alii*, she had received a first-rate education in missionary school. A convert to Christianity, she had taken the English name Lydia and married the *haole* (white) governor of Maui. Yet she maintained a reverence for traditional Hawaiian ways and resented the treatment of her people by the white minority.

Her brother, King Kalakaua, had proved to be a weak and compliant leader. In 1876, he signed a treaty that turned Hawaii essentially into an American protectorate. And in 1887, while Liliuokalani was traveling in Europe, the white elite coerced Kalakaua to sign the "Bayonet Constitution," which leased Pearl Harbor to the United States and put the government squarely in the hands of the white minority. When Liliuokalani learned of the power grab, she bluntly styled it "a revolutionary movement inaugurated by those of foreign blood, or American blood." After the death of her brother, Liliuokalani assumed the throne resolved to institute a new constitution that would restore power to the Hawaiian people by making only native Hawaiians eligible to vote.

Her task would not be easy. She had already been warned by a member of the haole elite, "You will live longer and happier and be more popular by not trying to do too much." Yet determined to rule, not simply to reign, Liliuokalani moved ahead with plans to wrest power from the minority she referred to as Hawaii's "guests."

For Hawaiians, contact with whites had followed a course very similar to that of Native Americans on the mainland—death, disease, and dispossession. Not long after Captain James Cook sailed into the islands in 1778, things turned deadly. Cook killed one of the chiefs, and the Hawaiians retaliated by hacking Cook to pieces. But more deadly than armed conflict were the diseases carried by the sailors who soon made Hawaii a Pacific port of call. Lacking immunity, the native Hawaiian population shrank over the next century from more than 300,000 to just 50,000.

American missionaries first came to Hawaii in 1820 and soon intermarried with their Christian converts, creating a group of *hapa haole* (half whites), as well as a growing number of children born in Hawaii to white parents. The temptations of wealth led many missionaries, like Amos Starr Cooke, to acquire land and try their hand at sugar planting. In 1851, he founded Castle & Cooke, which became one of the world's largest sugar producers. By the end of the century, missionaries and planters had blended into one ruling class and gained control of extensive tracts of land. Thanks to the Bayonet Constitution, they controlled the islands, even though native Hawaiians and the Japanese and Chinese "coolie" laborers imported to work on the sugar plantations outnumbered the whites ten to one.

Sugar became a booming business in Hawaii as a result of favorable reciprocity treaties with the United States. Exports grew from 21 million pounds in 1876 to 225 million pounds by 1890. But hard times came to the islands with the passage of the McKinley tariff in 1890. The tariff wiped out the advantage Hawaiian sugar had enjoyed in the American market, with devastating results. Within two years, the value of Hawaiian sugar exports plummeted from $13 million to $8 million.

One way to avoid the tariff was by incorporating Hawaii into the United States through annexation. Foremost among those who championed this scheme was Lorrin Thurston, the thirty-five-year-old grandson of American missionaries. Thurston, born in Hawaii and educated in the United States, was zealous in his belief that Hawaii should be ruled by "the intelligent part of the community"—white Americans and their children. In 1892, he founded the secret Annexation Club and traveled to Washington, D.C., where he won the support of Republican secretary of state James G. Blaine, an enthusiastic supporter of American expansion. Blaine went so far as to suggest that Thurston bribe Queen Liliuokalani, offering her $250,000 to abdicate and assign the sovereignty of Hawaii to the United States. Unfortunately, Thurston replied, there was "no probability" that the independent-minded queen would accept such an offer. But he returned to Hawaii armed with the knowledge that annexation had influential friends in Washington.

Queen Liliuokalani picked Saturday, January 14, 1893, as the day to promulgate her new constitution. She dressed with care in a lavender silk gown and a diamond coronet and called her cabinet to meet at the Iolani Palace. Learning of her intentions, Thurston quickly sprang into action. He persuaded four of the cabinet ministers to oppose the constitution, stalling for time while he plotted to overthrow the monarchy. Thurston's daring plan could work only with the cooperation of the United States. So late that night, he knocked on the door of John L. Stevens, the American minister to Hawaii. Laying out his plan, he urged Stevens, a staunch annexationist, to support the overthrow of the queen and to pledge U.S. support for his actions. Without hesitating, Stevens promised to land marines from the USS *Boston* "to protect American lives and property."

Two days later, 162 American marines and sailors marched into Honolulu armed with carbines, and dragging howitzers (small cannons) and Gatling guns. The next day, Thurston and 17 of his confederates seized control of a government building across the street from the palace and proclaimed themselves a "provisional government." Minister Stevens promptly recognized the revolutionaries as the legitimate government of Hawaii.

To avoid bloodshed, Queen Liliuokalani bowed to the inevitable and agreed to step aside. But in a masterstroke, she sat down and composed a letter addressed not to her enemies in the provisional government, but to the U.S. government. Protesting her overthrow, she yielded her authority "until such time as the Government of the United States, shall, upon the facts being presented to it, undo the action of its representatives and reinstate me in the authority which I claim as the constitutional sovereign of the Hawaiian Islands."

The action now shifted to Washington, where Grover Cleveland, a Democrat skeptical of America's adventures abroad, came to the presidency in March 1893. Cleveland quickly squelched plans for annexation and called for an inquiry. When his investigation concluded that the Hawaiian people did not support the takeover, Cleveland admonished Stevens for his role in the overthrow and called for the restoration of the monarchy. The provisional government, however, enjoyed the support of Republicans in Congress and refused to step down. In a bid to gain American sympathy, Hawaii's white government declared itself a republic on July 4, 1894, and then bided its time, waiting for the Republicans to take back the White House.

In 1898, as the taste for empire swept the United States in the wake of the Spanish-American War, President William McKinley quietly signed a treaty annexing Hawaii. His action pleased not only Hawaii's sugar growers but also American expansionists, who judged Hawaii strategically important in expanding U.S. trade with China.

"Hawaii is ours," Grover Cleveland wrote sadly. "As I look back upon the first steps in this miserable business, and as I contemplate the means used to complete the outrage, I am ashamed of the whole affair."

Queen Liliuokalani (1838–1917)

An accomplished woman who straddled two cultures, Lydia Kamakaeha Dominis, or Queen Liliuokalani, spoke English as easily as her native Hawaiian and was fluent in French and German as well. She traveled widely in Europe and the United States. Despite President Cleveland's belief that the monarchy should be restored, Liliuokalani never regained her throne. In 1898, she published *Hawaii's Story by Hawaii's Queen* outlining her version of the events that had led to her downfall. In 1993, on the one hundredth anniversary of the revolution that deposed her, Congress passed and President Bill Clinton signed a resolution offering an apology to native Hawaiians for the overthrow of their queen.

Courtesy of the Liliuokalani Trust.

731

The Open Door
The trade advantage gained by the United States through the Open Door policy, enunciated by Secretary of State John Hay in 1900, is portrayed graphically in this political cartoon. Uncle Sam stands prominently in the "open door," while representatives of the other great powers seek admittance to the "Flowery Kingdom" of China. Uncle Sam holds the golden key of "American diplomacy," while the Chinese man on the other side of the door beams with pleasure. In fact, the Open Door policy promised equal access for all powers to the China trade, not U.S. preeminence as the cartoon implies.
Culver Pictures.

READING THE IMAGE: How does the cartoon portray the United States' role in international diplomacy?
CONNECTIONS: In what ways does this image misrepresent the reality of American and European involvement in China and the Open Door policy?

FOR MORE HELP ANALYZING THIS IMAGE, see the visual activity for this chapter in the Online Study Guide at
bedfordstmartins.com/roark.

In Central America, where the United States kept a watchful eye on European adventures, American business triumphed in a bloodless takeover that saw French and British interests routed by behemoths such as the United Fruit Company of Boston. United Fruit virtually dominated the Central American nations of Costa Rica and Guatemala, while an importer from New Orleans turned Honduras into a "banana republic" (a country run by U.S. business interests). Thus, by 1895, the United States, through business as well as diplomacy, had successfully achieved hegemony in Latin America and the

Caribbean, forcing even the British to concur with the secretary of state that "the infinite resources [of the United States] combined with its isolated position render it master of the situation and practically invulnerable as against any or all other powers."

At the same time that American foreign policy warned European powers to stay out of the Western Hemisphere, the United States competed with the colonial powers for trade in the Eastern Hemisphere. As American interests in China grew, the United States became more aggressive in defending its presence in Asia and the Pacific. The United States risked war with Germany in 1889 to guarantee the U.S. navy access to a port for refueling on the way to Asia. The U.S. held treaty rights to the harbor at Pago Pago in the Samoan Islands. Germany, seeking dominance over the islands, challenged the United States by sending warships to the region. But before fighting broke out, a great typhoon destroyed the German and American ships. Acceding to the will of nature, the potential combatants later divided the islands amicably in the 1899 Treaty of Berlin.

The biggest prize in Asia remained the China market. In the 1890s, China, weakened by years of internal warfare, was beginning to be partitioned into spheres of influence by Britain, Japan, Germany, France, and Russia. Concerned about the integrity of China and no less about American trade, Secretary of State John Hay in 1899–1900 wrote a series of notes calling for an "open door" policy that would ensure trade access to all and maintain Chinese sovereignty. The notes—sent to Britain, Germany, and Russia and later to France, Japan, and Italy—were greeted by the major powers with polite evasion. Nevertheless, Hay skillfully managed to maneuver the major powers into doing his bidding, and in 1900 he boldly announced the Open Door as international policy. The United States, by insisting on the Open Door policy, managed to secure access to Chinese markets, expanding its economic power while avoiding the problems of maintaining a far-flung colonial empire on the Asian mainland. But as the Spanish-American War soon demonstrated, Americans found it hard to resist the temptations of empire.

> **REVIEW** Why did the United States largely abandon its isolationist foreign policy in the 1890s?

War and Empire

The Spanish-American War began as a humanitarian effort to free Cuba from Spain's colonial grasp and ended with the United States itself becoming a colonial power and fighting a dirty **guerrilla war** with Filipino nationalists, who, like the Cubans, sought independence. Behind the contradiction stood the twin pillars of American foreign policy: The Monroe Doctrine made Spain's presence in Cuba unacceptable, and U.S. determination to keep open the door to

Asia made the Philippines attractive as a stepping-stone to China.

"A Splendid Little War"

Looking back on the Spanish-American War of 1898, Secretary of State John Hay judged it "a splendid little war; begun with the highest motives, carried on with magnificent intelligence and spirit, favored by that fortune which loves the brave." At the close of a decade marred by bitter depression, social unrest, and political upheaval, the war offered Americans a chance to wave the flag and march in unison. War fever proved as infectious as the tune of a John Philip Sousa march. Few argued the merits of the conflict until it was over and the time came to divide the spoils.

The war began with moral outrage over the treatment of Cuban revolutionaries, who had launched a fight for independence against the Spanish colonial regime in 1895. In an attempt to isolate the guerrillas, the Spanish general Valeriano Weyler herded Cubans into crowded and unsanitary concentration camps, where thousands died of hunger, disease, and exposure. Starvation soon spread to the cities. Tens of thousands of Cubans died, and countless others were left without food, clothing, or shelter. By 1898, fully a quarter of the island's population had perished in the Cuban revolution.

As the Cuban rebellion dragged on, pressure for American intervention mounted. American newspapers fueled public outrage at Spain. A fierce circulation war raged in New York City between William Randolph Hearst's *Journal* and Joseph Pulitzer's *World*. Their competition provoked what came to be called "yellow journalism," named for the colored ink used in a popular comic strip. Practitioners of yellow journalism pandered to the public's appetite for sensationalism. The Cuban war provided a wealth of dramatic copy. Newspapers fed the American people a daily diet of "Butcher" Weyler and Spanish atrocities. Hearst sent artist Frederic Remington to document the horror, and when Remington wired home, "There is no trouble here. There will be no war," Hearst shot back, "You furnish the pictures and I'll furnish the war."

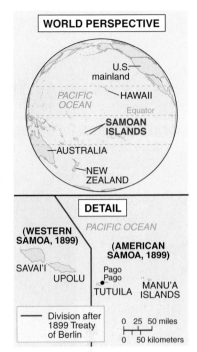

The Samoan Islands, 1889

Yellow Journalism

Most cartoonists followed the lead of Hearst and Pulitzer in promoting war with Spain. Cartoonist Grant Hamilton drew this cartoon for *Judge* magazine in March 1898. It shows a brutish Spain (the "Devil's Deputy") with bloody hands trampling on a sailor from the *Maine*. Cuba is prostrate, and a pile of skulls represents civilians "starved to death by Spain." Such vicious representations of Spain became common in the American press in the weeks leading up to the Spanish-American War. What does the cartoon say about American attitudes toward race?

Collection of the New-York Historical Society.

American interests in Cuba were, in the words of the U.S. minister to Spain, more than "merely theoretical or sentimental." American business had more than $50 million invested in Cuban sugar, and American trade with Cuba, a brisk $100 million a year before the rebellion, had dropped to near zero. Nevertheless, the business community balked, wary of a war with Spain. When industrialist Mark Hanna, the Republican kingmaker and senator from Ohio, urged restraint, a hotheaded Theodore Roosevelt exploded, "We will have this war for the freedom of Cuba, Senator Hanna, in spite of the timidity of commercial interests."

To expansionists like Roosevelt, more than Cuban independence was at stake. War with Spain

opened up the prospect of expansion into Asia as well, since Spain controlled not only Cuba and Puerto Rico but also Guam and the Philippine Islands. Appointed assistant secretary of the navy in April 1897, Roosevelt worked for preparedness whenever his boss's back was turned. During the hot summer while the navy secretary vacationed, Roosevelt took the helm in his absence and audaciously ordered the U.S. fleet to Manila in the Philippines. In the event of conflict with Spain, Roosevelt put the navy in a position to capture the islands and gain an entry point to China.

President McKinley slowly moved toward intervention. In a show of American force, he dispatched the battleship *Maine* to Cuba. On the night of February 15, 1898, a mysterious explosion destroyed the *Maine*, killing 267 crew members. The source of the explosion remained unclear, but inflammatory stories in the press enraged Americans, who immediately blamed the Spanish government. (See "Historical Question," page 736.) Rallying to the cry "Remember the *Maine*," Congress declared war on Spain in April. In a surge of patriotism, more than 235,000 men enlisted. War brought with it a unity of purpose and national harmony that ended a decade of political dissent and strife. "In April, everywhere over this good fair land, flags were flying," wrote Kansas editor William Allen White. "At the stations, crowds gathered to hurrah for the soldiers, and to throw hats into the air, and to unfurl flags."

Soon they had something to cheer about. Five days after McKinley signed the war resolution, a U.S. navy squadron commanded by Admiral George Dewey destroyed the Spanish fleet in Manila Bay (Map 20.3). Dewey's stunning victory caught the United States by surprise. Although naval strategists including Theodore Roosevelt had been orchestrating the move for some time, few Americans had ever heard of the Philippines. Even McKinley confessed that he could not immediately locate the archipelago on the map. He nevertheless recognized the strategic importance of the Philippines and dispatched U.S. troops to secure the islands.

The war in Cuba ended almost as quickly as it began. The first troops landed on June 22, and after a handful of battles, the Spanish surrendered on July 17. The war lasted just long enough to elevate Theodore Roosevelt to the status of bona fide war hero. Roosevelt resigned his navy post and formed the Rough Riders, a regiment composed about equally of Ivy League polo players and cowboys Roosevelt knew from his stint as a cattle rancher in the Dakotas. While the troops languished in Tampa awaiting their orders, Roosevelt and his men staged daily rodeos for the press, with the likes of New York blue blood William Tiffany busting broncs in competition with Dakota cowboy Jim "Dead Shot" Simpson. When the Rough Riders shipped out to Cuba, journalists fought for a berth with the colorful regiment. Roosevelt's charge up Kettle Hill and his role in the decisive battle of San Juan Hill made front-page news. Overnight, Roosevelt became the most famous man in America. By the time he sailed home from Cuba, a coalition of independent Republicans was already plotting his political future.

The Debate over American Imperialism

After a few brief campaigns in Cuba and Puerto Rico brought the Spanish-American War to an end, the American people woke up in possession of an empire that stretched halfway around the globe. As part of the spoils of war, the United States acquired Cuba, Puerto Rico, Guam, and the Philippines. Yielding to pressure from American sugar growers, President McKinley expanded the empire further, annexing Hawaii in July 1898. (See "Beyond America's Borders," page 730.)

Cuba, freed from Spanish rule, failed to gain full autonomy. Contemptuous of the Cubans, whom General William Shafter declared "no more fit for self-government than gun-powder is

---

MAP 20.3   The Spanish-American War, 1898

The Spanish-American War was fought in two theaters, the Philippine Islands and Cuba. Five days after President William McKinley called for a declaration of war, Admiral George Dewey captured Manila without the loss of a single American sailor. The war lasted only eight months. Troops landed in Cuba in mid-June and by mid-July had taken Santiago and Havana and destroyed the Spanish fleet.

READING THE MAP: Which countries held imperial control over countries and territories immediately surrounding the Philippine Islands and Cuba?

CONNECTIONS: What role did American newspapers play in the start of the war? How did the results of the war serve American aims in both Asia and the Western Hemisphere?

FOR MORE HELP ANALYZING THIS MAP, see the map activity for this chapter in the Online Study Guide at bedfordstmartins.com/roark.

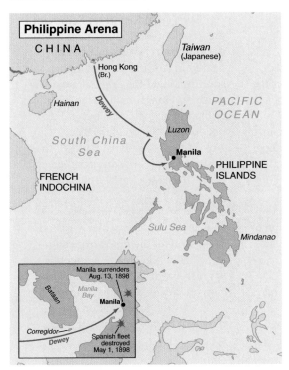

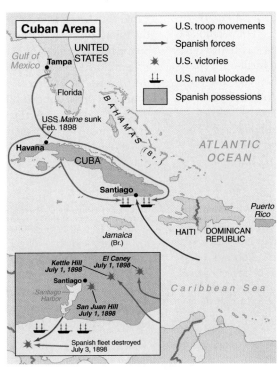

Did Terrorists Sink the *Maine*?

At 9:40 p.m. on the evening of February 15, 1898, the U.S. battleship *Maine* blew up in Havana harbor. Eyewitness accounts differed, but most reported hearing a small concussion followed by a ferocious blast. An American who witnessed the explosion from the wharf reported, "The shock threw us backward. From the deck forward of amidships shot a streak of fire as high as the tall buildings on Broadway. Then the glare of light widened out like a funnel at the top, and down through this bright circle fell showers of wreckage and mangled sailors." Two hundred sixty-seven sailors drowned or burned to death in one of the worst naval catastrophes to occur during peacetime.

Captain Charles Dwight Sigsbee, the last man to leave the burning ship, filed a terse report saying that the *Maine* had blown up and "urging [that] public opinion should be suspended until further report." Within two days, however, the yellow press, led by William Randolph Hearst's *New York Journal*, carried banner headlines announcing, "The War Ship *Maine* Was Split in Two by an Enemy's Secret Infernal Machine!" Such sensational headlines more than doubled the *Journal*'s circulation in the weeks following the disaster.

Public opinion quickly divided between those who suspected foul play and those who believed the explosion had been an accident. Foremost among the accident theorists was the Spanish government,

but U.S. business interests who hoped to avoid war with Spain also favored this view. Among the jingoes, as proponents of war were called, there was no doubt who was to blame. Assistant Secretary of the Navy Theodore Roosevelt wrote even before the details were known, "The *Maine* was sunk by an act of dirty treachery on the part of the Spaniards I believe; though we shall never find out definitely, and officially it will go down as an accident."

In less than a week, the navy formed a court of inquiry, and divers inspected the wreckage. The panel reported on March 25, 1898, that a mine had exploded under the bottom of the ship, igniting gunpowder in the forward magazine. The navy named no guilty party since the panel could not determine whether the mine had been planted by the Spanish government or by recalcitrant followers of Valeriano Weyler, the Spanish general recalled after the American press dubbed him "the Butcher" for his harsh treatment of the Cubans. The U.S. Senate carried on its own investigation, concluding that whether by intent or by negligence, the Spanish government bore responsibility for the catastrophe.

As time passed, however, more people came to view the explosion of the *Maine* as an accident. European naval authorities analyzed the U.S. naval court inquiry and concluded that it had made a gross error: The explosion had not occurred at the location named in the report. The

European experts concluded that the *Maine* had exploded accidentally, from a fire in the coal bunker adjacent to the reserve gunpowder and shell magazine. Many came to believe that poor design, not treachery, had sunk the *Maine*.

In 1910, the *Maine* still lay in the mud of Havana harbor, a sunken tomb containing the remains of many sailors. The Cuban government asked for the removal of the wreck, and veterans demanded a decent burial for the sailors. With so many questions about the naval court of inquiry's report, American public opinion urged further investigation. New York congressman William Sultzer put it succinctly, "The day after the ship was sunk, you could hardly find an American who did not believe that she had been foully done to death by a treacherous enemy. Today you can hardly find an American who believes Spain had anything to do with it." So in March 1910, Congress voted to raise the *Maine* and reinvestigate.

The "Final Report on Removing the Wreck of Battleship *Maine* from the Harbor of Habana, Cuba" appeared in April 1913. This report confirmed that the original naval inquiry was in error about the location of the initial explosion, but it did not endorse the accident theory. According to the "Final Report," the destruction of the *Maine* resulted from "the explosion of a charge of a low form of explosive exterior to the ship," which led to a massive explosion as the ship's magazine ignited. The nature of the initial explosion indicated a homemade bomb, not a Spanish naval mine—casting suspicion on Weyler's fanatic followers.

After the investigation and removal of human remains, the wreckage of the *Maine* was towed out to sea and, with full funeral honors, sunk in six hundred fathoms of water.

But the controversy over the *Maine* proved harder to sink. In the Vietnam era, when faith in the "military establishment" reached an all-time low, Admiral Hyman Rickover launched yet another investigation. Many critics had come to believe that the 1913 "Final Report" was little more than a cover-up; they complained that the ship had been sunk so deep "that there will be no chance of the true facts being revealed." Rickover, a maverick who held the naval brass in low esteem, hired experts to pore over the evidence from previous investigations. He noted that "the warlike atmosphere in Congress and the press, and the natural tendency to look for reasons for the loss that did not reflect on the Navy," made the earlier findings highly suspect. Self-ignition in the coal bunker, he concluded, had triggered an explosion in the reserve magazine. Reading the past in the jaundiced light of the early 1970s, Rickover warned, "We must make sure that those in 'high places' do not without more careful consideration of the consequences, exert our prestige and might," presumably in unnecessary and immoral wars. Published in book form in 1976, Rickover's report, titled *How the Battleship* Maine *Was Destroyed*, became for a time the accepted version of the event.

Nearly twenty years later, the pendulum swung back. A 1995 study of the *Maine* published by the Smithsonian Institution concluded that zealot followers of General Weyler sank the battleship. "They had the opportunity, the means, and the motivation, and they blew up the *Maine* with a small low-strength mine they made themselves." According to this theory, the terrorists' homemade bomb burst the *Maine*'s hull, triggering a massive explosion.

Today, only one thing seems certain: The lessons of the *Maine* have changed with the times and may continue to be redrawn as each new generation questions history.

"Maine Explosion Caused by Bomb or Torpedo"

The yellow press wasted no time claiming foul play in the explosion of the *Maine*. The front page of the *New York World* on February 17, 1898, two days after the blast, trumpeted the news and graphically portrayed the destruction of the ship. The text hinted at a plot to blow up the *Maine* and insisted that the explosion was not accidental, although there was no evidence to back up the assertion. The extent of the destruction and the deaths of 267 sailors fueled war fever.

© Collection of the New-York Historical Society.

The Battle of San Juan Hill
This 1898 lithograph portrays a highly romantic version of the battle of San Juan Hill. The famous charge was much less glamorous than pictured here. Theodore Roosevelt, whose Rough Riders had taken nearby Kettle Hill, called to his men to charge the next line of Spanish trenches in the San Juan hills. But in the excitement of battle, they didn't hear him, and Roosevelt found himself charging virtually alone. He had to go back and rally the Rough Riders, who then charged the hill on foot. The illustration does get one thing right: The nearsighted Roosevelt led the charge wearing his spectacles. Fearing that he might lose his glasses in battle, he insisted that Brooks Brothers custom-make his uniforms to include a dozen pockets for extra eyeglasses.
Library of Congress.

for hell," the U.S. government dictated a Cuban constitution in 1898. It included the so-called Platt Amendment—a series of provisions that granted the United States the right to intervene to protect Cuba's "independence," as well as the power to oversee Cuban debt so that European creditors would not find an excuse for intervention. For good measure, the United States gave itself a ninety-nine-year lease on a naval base at Guantánamo. In return, McKinley promised to implement an extensive sanitation program to clean up the island, making it more attractive to American investors.

In the formal Treaty of Paris (1898), Spain ceded the Philippines to the United States along with its former colonies of Puerto Rico and Guam (Map 20.4). Empire did not come cheap. When Spain initially balked at these terms, the United States agreed to pay an indemnity of $20 million for the islands. Nor was the cost measured in money alone. Filipino revolutionaries under Emilio Aguinaldo, who had greeted U.S. troops as liberators, bitterly fought the new masters. It would take seven years and 4,000 American dead—almost ten times the number killed in Cuba—not to mention an estimated 20,000 Filipino casualties, to defeat Aguinaldo and secure American control of the Philippines, America's coveted stepping-stone to China.

At home, a vocal minority, mostly Democrats and former Populists, resisted the country's foray into overseas empire, judging it unwise, immoral, and unconstitutional. William Jennings Bryan, who enlisted in the army but never saw action, concluded that American expansionism only distracted the nation from problems at home.

What did imperialism offer the ordinary American, Bryan asked, except "heavier taxes, Asiatic emigration and an opportunity to furnish more sons for the army." Pointing to the central paradox of the war, Representative Bourke Cockran of New York admonished, "We who have been the destroyers of oppression are asked now to become its agents." Mark Twain, lending his bitter eloquence to the cause of anti-imperialism, lamented that the United States had indeed become "yet another Civilized Power, with its banner of the Prince of Peace in one hand and its loot-basket and its butcher-knife in the other."

The anti-imperialists were soon drowned out by cries for empire. As Senator Knute Nelson of Minnesota assured his colleagues, "We come as ministering angels, not as despots." The moral tone of the age, set by social Darwinism, with its

MAP 20.4   U.S. Overseas Expansion through 1900

The United States extended its interests abroad with a series of territorial acquisitions. Although Cuba was granted independence, the Platt Amendment kept the new nation firmly under U.S. control. In the wake of the Spanish-American War, the United States woke up to find that it held an empire extending halfway around the globe.

READING THE MAP: Does the map indicate that more territory was acquired by purchase or by war, occupation, or unilateral decision? How many purchases of land outside the continental United States did the government make?

CONNECTIONS: What foreign policy developments occurred in the 1890s? How did American political leaders react to them? Where was U.S. expansion headed and why?

FOR MORE HELP ANALYZING THIS MAP, see the map activity for this chapter in the Online Study Guide at bedfordstmartins.com/roark.

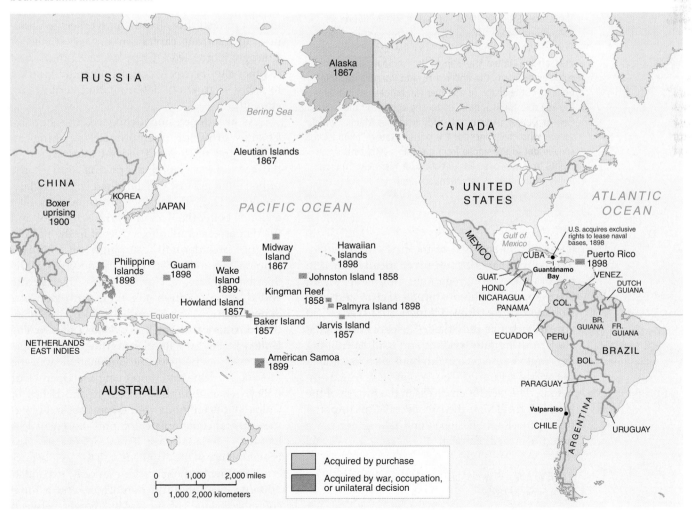

Conclusion: Rallying around the Flag

Columbia's Easter Bonnet

The United States, symbolized by the female figure of Columbia, tries on "World Power" in this cartoon from *Puck*, which appeared in 1901 after the Spanish-American War left the United States in control of Spain's former colonies in Guam, the Philippines, and Puerto Rico. The bonnet, in the shape of an American battleship, indicates the key role the U.S. navy, under the command of Admiral George Dewey, played in the U.S. victory at Manila, which secured the Philippines for the United States. "Expansion," spelled out in the smoke from the ship's smokestack, points to a new overseas direction for American foreign policy at the turn of the twentieth century.
Library of Congress.

emphasis on survival of the fittest and Anglo-Saxon racial superiority, proved ideally suited to imperialism. Congregational minister Josiah Strong revealed the mixture of racism and missionary zeal that fueled American adventurism abroad when he remarked, "It seems to me that God, with infinite wisdom and skill, is training the Anglo Saxon race for an hour sure to come in the world's future." The *Washington Post* trumpeted, "The taste of empire is in the mouth of the people," thrilled at the prospect of "an imperial policy, the Republic renascent, taking her place with the armed nations."

> **REVIEW** Why did the United States declare war on Spain in 1898?

A decade of domestic strife ended amid the blare of martial music and the waving of flags. The Spanish-American War drowned out the calls for social reform that had fueled the Populist politics of the 1890s. During that decade, angry farmers facing hard times looked to the Farmers' Alliance to fight for their vision of economic democracy, workers staged bloody battles across the country to assert their rights, and women attacked drunkenness and the conditions that fostered it and mounted a suffrage movement to secure their basic political rights. In St. Louis in 1892, Frances Willard joined with other disaffected Americans to form a new People's Party to fight for change.

The bitter depression that began in 1893 led to increased labor strife. The Pullman boycott brutally dramatized the power of property and the conservatism of the laissez-faire state. Even the miners' victory in Cripple Creek, Colorado, in 1894 proved short-lived. But workers' willingness to confront capitalism on the streets of Chicago, Homestead, Cripple Creek, and a host of other sites across America eloquently testified to labor's growing determination, unity, and strength.

As the depression deepened, the sight of Coxey's army of unemployed marching on Washington to demand federal intervention in the economy signaled a growing shift in the public mind against the stand-pat politics of laissez-faire. The call for the government to take action to better the lives of workers, farmers, and the dispossessed manifested itself in the fiercely fought presidential campaign of William Jennings Bryan in 1896. With the outbreak of the Spanish-American War in 1898, the decade ended on a harmonious note with patriotic Americans rallying around the flag. Few questioned America's foray into overseas empire. The United States took its place on the world stage, buttressing its hemispheric domination with the Monroe Doctrine and employing the Open Door policy, which promised access to the riches of China. But even though Americans basked in patriotism and contemplated empire, old grievances had not been laid to rest. The People's Party had been beaten, but the Populists' call for greater government involvement in the economy, expanded opportunities for direct democracy, and a more equitable balance of profits and power between the people and the big corporations sounded the themes that would be taken up by a new generation of progressive reformers in the first decades of the twentieth century.

Selected Bibliography

The Farmers' Alliance, the Labor Wars, and Militant Women

Peter H. Argersinger, *The Limits of Agrarian Radicalism: Western Populism and American Politics* (1995).

Jean H. Baker, *Sisters: The Lives of America's Suffragists* (2005).

Ruth Bordin, *Frances Willard: A Biography* (1986).

Alan Dawley, *Struggles for Justice: Social Responsibility and the Liberal State* (1991).

Ellen Carol DuBois, *Woman Suffrage and Women's Rights* (1998).

Michael Lewis Goldberg, *An Army of Women: Gender and Politics in Gilded Age Kansas* (1997).

Steven Hahn, *A Nation under Our Feet: Black Political Struggles in the Rural South from Slavery to the Great Migration* (2003).

Elizabeth Jameson, *All That Glitters: Class, Conflict, and Community in Cripple Creek* (1998).

Michael Kazin, *The Populist Persuasion: An American History* (rev. ed., 1998).

Paul Krause, *The Battle for Homestead, 1880–1892* (1992).

Connie L. Lester, *Up from the Mudsills of Hell: The Farmers' Alliance, Populism, and Progressive Agriculture in Tennessee, 1870–1915* (2006).

Theodore R. Mitchell, *Political Education in the Southern Farmers' Alliance, 1887–1900* (1987).

David Nasaw, *Andrew Carnegie* (2006).

Nick Salvatore, *Eugene V. Debs: Citizen and Socialist* (1982).

Depression and the Election of 1896

Louis L. Gould, *The Presidency of William McKinley* (1981).

Stephen Kantrowitz, *Ben Tillman and the Reconstruction of White Supremacy* (2000).

Michael Kazin, *A Godly Hero: The Life of William Jennings Bryan* (2006).

Kenneth L. Kusmer, *Down and Out, on the Road: The Homeless in American History* (2002).

Gretchen Ritter, *Goldbugs and Greenbacks: The Antimonopoly Tradition in the Politics of Finance in America* (1997).

Carol A. Schwantes, *Coxey's Army: An American Odyssey* (1985).

Douglas Steeples and David O. Whitten, *Democracy in Desperation: The Depression of 1892* (1998).

War and Foreign Policy

Edward P. Crapol, *James G. Blaine: Architect of Empire* (1999).

Kristin Hoganson, *Fighting for American Manhood: How Gender Politics Provoked the Spanish-American and Philippine-American Wars* (1998).

Matthew Frye Jacobson, *Special Sorrows: The Diasporic Imagination of Irish, Polish, and Jewish Immigrants in the United States* (1995).

Matthew Frye Jacobson, *Barbarian Virtues: The United States Encounters Foreign Peoples at Home and Abroad, 1876–1917* (2000).

Stephen Kinzer, *Overthrow: America's Century of Regime Change from Hawaii to Iraq* (2006).

Walter LaFeber, *The American Search for Opportunity, 1865–1913* (1993).

Brian Linn, *The Philippine War, 1899–1902* (2000).

Paul T. McCartney, *Power and Progress: American National Identity, the War of 1898, and the Rise of American Imperialism* (2006).

Ivan Musicant, *Empire by Default: The Spanish-American War and the Dawn of the American Century* (1998).

Thomas J. Osborne, *Annexation Hawaii* (1998).

Louis A. Perez Jr., *The War of 1898: The United States and Cuba in History and Historiography* (1998).

Diana Preston, *Besieged in Peking: The Story of the 1900 Boxer Uprising* (1999).

Lars Shoultz, *Beneath the United States* (1998).

Margaret Strobel, *Gender, Sex, and Empire* (1993).

David Traxel, *1898: The Birth of the American Century* (1999).

Walter Zimmerman, *First Great Triumph: How Five Americans Made Their Country a World Power* (2002).

▶ For more books about topics in this chapter, see the Online Bibliography at bedfordstmartins.com/roark.

▶ For additional firsthand accounts of this period, see Chapter 20 in Michael Johnson, ed., *Reading the American Past*, Fourth Edition.

▶ For Web sites, images, and documents related to topics and places in this chapter, visit bedfordstmartins.com/makehistory.

REVIEWING THE CHAPTER

Follow these steps to review and strengthen your understanding of the chapter.

STEP 1: *Study the **Key Terms** and **Timeline** to identify the significance of each item listed.*

STEP 2: *Answer the **Review Questions**, drawing on key terms and dates to support your answers.*

STEP 3: *Drawing on the Key Terms, Timeline, and Review Questions, answer the broader **Making Connections** questions.*

KEY TERMS

Who

Frances Willard (pp. 705, 711)
Mary Elizabeth Lease (p. 705)
Andrew Carnegie (p. 714)
Henry Clay Frick (p. 714)
Alexander Berkman (p. 716)
Davis H. Waite (p. 716)
George M. Pullman (p. 717)
Eugene V. Debs (p. 718)
Grover Cleveland (p. 718)
Elizabeth Cady Stanton (p. 721)
Susan B. Anthony (p. 721)
Jacob S. Coxey (p. 722)
James B. Weaver (p. 724)
Tom Watson (p. 724)
William McKinley (p. 724)
William Jennings Bryan (p. 725)
Mark Hanna (p. 726)
Queen Liliuokalani (p. 728)
John Hay (p. 729)
Valeriano Weyler (p. 733)
William Randolph Hearst (p. 733)
Joseph Pulitzer (p. 733)
Theodore Roosevelt (p. 734)

George Dewey (p. 734)
Emilio Aguinaldo (p. 738)

What

People's Party (Populist Party) (p. 704)
agrarian revolt (p. 707)
crop lien (p. 707)
Farmers' Alliance (p. 707)
Colored Farmers' Alliance (p. 708)
subtreasury (p. 711)
Homestead lockout (p. 714)
Amalgamated Association of Iron and Steel Workers (p. 714)
Pinkerton National Detective Agency (p. 714)
panic and depression of 1893 (p. 716)
Western Federation of Miners (WFM) (p. 716)
Cripple Creek miners' strike of 1894 (p. 716)
American Railway Union (ARU) (p. 718)
Pullman boycott (p. 718)
General Managers Association (GMA) (p. 718)

Woman's Christian Temperance Union (WCTU) (p. 720)
National American Woman Suffrage Association (NAWSA) (p. 722)
Coxey's army (p. 722)
gold standard (p. 724)
free silver (p. 725)
expansionism (p. 727)
manifest destiny (p. 727)
annexation of Hawaii (pp. 728, 730)
Boxer uprising (p. 728)
Monroe Doctrine (p. 729)
Venezuelan crisis (p. 729)
Samoan Islands (p. 733)
Open Door policy (p. 733)
Spanish-American War (p. 733)
Maine (p. 734)
Rough Riders (p. 734)
battle of San Juan Hill (p. 735)
imperialism (p. 735)
Platt Amendment (p. 738)
Treaty of Paris (p. 738)

TIMELINE

◄ **1884** • Woman's Christian Temperance Union, headed by Frances Willard, calls for woman suffrage.

   1889 • Typhoon averts hostilities between German and U.S. ships in Samoan Islands.

      1890 • National American Woman Suffrage Association (NAWSA) formed.

• Wyoming enters Union with woman suffrage.
• Southern Farmers' Alliance numbers three million members.

         1892 • People's (Populist) Party founded.
            • Homestead lockout.

            1893 • Stock market crash touches off severe economic depression.
               • President Grover Cleveland nixes attempt to annex Hawaii.

               1894 • Miners strike in Cripple Creek, Colorado.
                  • Coxey's army marches to Washington, D.C.
                  • Federal troops and court injunction crush Pullman boycott.

REVIEW QUESTIONS

1. Why did American farmers organize alliances in the late nineteenth century? (pp. 707–11)

2. Why did the strikes of the 1890s fail to produce permanent gains for workers? (pp. 714–19)

3. How did women's temperance activism contribute to the cause of woman suffrage? (pp. 720–22)

4. Why was the People's Party unable to translate national support into victory in the 1896 election? (pp. 722–27)

5. Why did the United States largely abandon its isolationist foreign policy in the 1890s? (pp. 727–33)

6. Why did the United States declare war on Spain in 1898? (pp. 733–40)

MAKING CONNECTIONS

1. In the late nineteenth century, Americans clashed over the disparity of power brought about by industrial capitalism. Why did many working Americans look to the government to help advance their vision of economic justice? In your answer, discuss specific reforms working-class Americans pursued and the strategies they employed.

2. In the 1890s, workers mounted labor protests and strikes. What circumstances gave rise to these actions? How did they differ from earlier strikes, such as the Great Railroad Strike of 1877? In your answer, discuss specific actions, being sure to consider how local and national circumstances contributed to their ultimate resolution.

3. How did women's activism in the late nineteenth century help advance the cause of woman suffrage? How did women activists in the late nineteenth century differ from their predecessors? In your answer, discuss specific gains made in the late nineteenth century, as well as shifts in reformers' strategies.

4. How did the conquest of Native Americans in the West foreshadow U.S. expansion abroad? In what ways did assumptions of racial superiority evident in U.S. Indian policy affect the treatment of Cubans and Filipinos?

▶ For practice quizzes, a customized study plan, and other study tools, see the Online Study Guide at bedfordstmartins.com/roark.

1895 • President Grover Cleveland defends Monroe Doctrine in border dispute between British Guiana and Venezuela.

1896 • Democrats and Populists support William Jennings Bryan for president.
• Republican William McKinley elected president.

1898 • U.S. battleship *Maine* explodes in Havana harbor.
• Congress declares war on Spain.
• Admiral George Dewey destroys Spanish fleet in Manila Bay, the Philippines.
• U.S. troops defeat Spanish forces in Cuba.
• Treaty of Paris ends war with Spain and cedes Philippines, Puerto Rico, and Guam to the United States.
• United States annexes Hawaii.

1899–1900 • Secretary of State John Hay enunciates Open Door policy in China.
• Boxer uprising in China.

1901 • Boxer Protocol imposed on Chinese government.

THE PROGRESSIVE PARTY

BORN 1912

PROGRESSIVE PARTY CAMPAIGN SOUVENIR BANDANA

This colorful cotton bandana, a campaign novelty from the 1912 presidential race, celebrates the Progressive Party and its candidate, Theodore Roosevelt. The progressive reform movement grew out of the crises of the 1890s to emerge full-blown in the first decades of the twentieth century. Progressives challenged laissez-faire liberalism and argued for government action to counter the power of big business and ensure greater social justice. Theodore Roosevelt, whose presidency set the tone for the era, became so closely associated with progressivism that when he failed to win the Republican nomination in 1912, his followers formed a new Progressive Party proclaiming, as the bandana notes, "We Want Our Teddy Back." The red bandana became the symbol of the new party. Roosevelt, brandishing one, led the crowd in a rousing verse of "Onward, Christian Soldiers." But progressivism was more than one man or one party. A movement that ran from the grass roots to the White House, it included not only members of the short-lived Progressive Party but also insurgent Democrats and Republicans whose belief in government activism would reshape the liberal state of the twentieth century.

Collection of Janice L. and David J. Frent.

21

Progressivism from the Grass Roots to the White House

1890–1916

I N THE SUMMER OF 1889, a young woman leased the upper floor of a dilapidated mansion on Chicago's West Side in the heart of a burgeoning immigrant population. Watching as she prepared to move in, neighbors scratched their heads, wondering why the well-dressed woman, who surely could afford a better house in a better neighborhood, chose to live on South Halsted Street. Yet the house, built by Charles Hull, precisely suited the needs of Jane Addams.

For Addams, personal action marked the first step in the search for solutions to the social problems fostered by urban industrialism. Her object was twofold: She wanted to help her immigrant neighbors, and she wanted to offer an opportunity for educated women like herself to find meaningful work. As she later wrote in her autobiography, *Twenty Years at Hull-House* (1910), "I gradually became convinced that it would be a good thing to rent a house in a part of the city where many primitive and actual needs are found, in which young women who had been given over too exclusively to study might restore a balance of activity along traditional lines and learn of life from life itself." Addams's emphasis on the reciprocal relationship between the social classes made Hull House different from other philanthropic enterprises. She wished to do things with, not just for, Chicago's poor.

In the next decade, Hull House expanded from one rented floor in the old brick mansion to some thirteen buildings housing a remarkable variety of activities. Addams converted the bathrooms in the basement into public baths, opened a coffee shop and restaurant to sell take-out food to workingwomen too tired to cook after their long shifts, and sponsored a nursery and kindergarten for neighborhood children. Hull House offered classes, lectures, art exhibits, musical instruction, and college extension courses. It boasted a gymnasium, a theater, a manual training workshop, a labor museum, and the first public playground in Chicago.

But Hull House was more than a group of buildings. From the first, it attracted an extraordinary set of reformers. Some stayed for decades, as did Julia Lathrop before she went to Washington, D.C., in 1912 to head the Children's Bureau. Others, like Gerard Swope, who later became president of the General Electric Company, came for only a short time. Hull House residents pioneered the scientific investigation of urban ills. Armed with statistics, they launched campaigns to improve housing, end child labor, fund playgrounds, mediate between labor and management, and lobby for laws to protect workers.

Addams quickly learned that it was impossible to deal with urban problems without becoming involved in political action. Her determination to clean up the garbage on Halsted Street led her into politics. Piles of decaying garbage overflowed the street's wooden trash bins, breeding flies and disease. Investigation revealed that the local ward boss awarded the contract to pick up the trash as a political plum to one of his henchmen, who felt under no obligation to provide adequate service. To end the graft, Addams got herself appointed garbage inspector. Out on the streets at six in the morning, she rode atop the garbage wagon to make sure it made its rounds. Addams mounted several unsuccessful political campaigns to oust the corrupt

Jane Addams

Jane Addams was twenty-nine years old when she founded Hull House on South Halsted Street in Chicago. She and her college roommate, Ellen Gates Starr, established America's premier social settlement. Her desire to live among the poor and her insistence that settlement house work benefited educated women such as herself as well as her immigrant neighbors separated her from the charity workers who had come before her and marked the distance from philanthropy to progressive reform. Her autobiographical *Twenty Years at Hull-House*, published in 1910, is shown in the inset.

Photo: Jane Addams Memorial Collection, (JAMC neg. 14) Special Collections, University of Illinois at Chicago, photographer: Max Platz. Book: Newberry Library.

ward boss but eventually realized that bossism was a symptom and not the cause of urban blight. Recognizing that bosses stayed in power by providing jobs and services to their constituents, she moved instead to sponsor legislation to help her neighbors. Eventually, her struggle to aid the urban poor led her not only to city hall but on to the state capitol and to Washington, D.C.

Under Jane Addams's leadership, Hull House became a "spearhead for reform," part of a broader movement that contemporaries called **progressivism**. The transition from personal action to political activism that Addams personified became one of the hallmarks of this reform period, which lasted from the 1890s to World War I.

By the 1890s, it had become clear to many Americans that the **laissez-faire** approach of government toward business no longer worked. The classical **liberalism** of the nation's Founders, with its emphasis on opposition to the tyranny of centralized government, had not reckoned on the enormous private wealth and power of the Gilded Age's business giants. As the gap between rich and poor widened in the 1890s, issues of social justice challenged traditional notions of laissez-faire liberalism. The violence and militancy of the 1890s—labor strikes, farmers' revolt, **suffrage** and antilynching movements—eloquently testified to the growing polarities in society. Yet a laissez-faire state only exacerbated the inequalities of class, race, and gender. A generation of progressive reformers demanded government intervention to guarantee a more equitable society. The willingness to use the government to promote change and to counterbalance the power of private interests redefined liberalism in the twentieth century.

Faith in activism in both the political and the private realms formed a common thread that united an otherwise diverse group of progressive reformers. A sense of Christian mission inspired some. Others, fearing social upheaval, sought to remove some of the worst evils of urban industrialism—tenements, child labor, and harsh working conditions. Progressives shared a growing concern about the power of wealthy individuals and corporations and a strong dislike of the **trusts**. But often they feared the immigrant poor and sought to control and Americanize them. Along with moral fervor, a belief in technical expertise and scientific management infused progressivism and made the cult of efficiency part and parcel of the movement. All of these elements—uplift and efficiency, social justice and social control—came together in the Progressive

Children Playing at Hull House

A young settlement house worker leads neighborhood children in a circle game in this photograph taken at Hull House at the turn of the twentieth century. Jane Addams recognized early on that Chicago's working mothers needed safe, reliable child care. Hull House filled the need by providing day nurseries. Older children, like the boys and girls pictured here in their short pants and pinafores, could find at Hull House a snack and a place to play after school.

Jane Addams Memorial Collection, Special Collection, University Library, University of Illinois at Chicago.

Era and characterized the progressive movement both at the grassroots level in the cities and states and in the presidencies of Theodore Roosevelt and Woodrow Wilson.

Grassroots Progressivism

Much of progressive reform began at the grassroots level and percolated upward into local, state, and eventually national politics as reformers attacked the social problems fostered by urban industrialism. Although reform flourished in many different settings across the country, urban problems inspired the progressives' greatest efforts. In their zeal to "civilize the city," reformers founded settlement houses, professed a new Christian **social gospel**, and campaigned against vice and crime in the name of "social purity." Allying with the working class, they sought to better the lot of sweatshop garment workers and to end child labor. Their reform efforts often began on the local level but ended up being debated in state legislatures and in the U.S. Congress.

Civilizing the City

Progressives attacked the problems of the city on many fronts. The settlement house movement attempted to bridge the distance between the classes. The social gospel called for the churches to play a new role in social reformation. And the **social purity movement** campaigned to clean up vice, particularly prostitution.

The settlement house movement that began in England came to the United States in 1886 with the opening of the University Settlement House in New York City. The needs of poor urban neighborhoods provided the impetus for these social settlements. In 1893, Lillian Wald, a nurse attending medical school in New York, went to care for a woman living in a dilapidated tenement. The experience led Wald to leave medical school and recruit several other nurses to move to New York City's Lower East Side "to live in the neighborhood as nurses, identify ourselves with it socially, and . . . contribute to it our citizenship." Wald's Henry Street settlement expanded in 1895, pioneering public health nursing. Although Wald herself was Jewish, she insisted that the settlement remain independent of religious ties, making it different from the avowedly religious settlements in England.

Women, particularly college-educated women like Jane Addams and Lillian Wald, formed the backbone of the settlement house movement and stood in the vanguard of the progressive movement. Eager to use their knowledge, they often found themselves blocked from careers in medicine, law, and the clergy. (Fewer than fifteen hundred women practiced law in 1900, and women constituted only 6 percent of the medical profession.) Settlement houses gave college-educated women a place to put their talents to work in the service of society and to champion progressive reform. Largely due to women's efforts, settlements like Hull House grew in number from six in 1891 to more than four hundred in 1911. In the process, settlement house women created a new profession—social work—and stimulated a new reform movement—progressivism.

For their part, churches confronted urban social problems by enunciating a new social gospel, one that saw its mission not simply to reform individuals but to reform society. The social gospel offered a powerful corrective to **social Darwinism** and the **gospel of wealth**, which fostered the belief that riches somehow signaled divine favor. Washington Gladden, a prominent social gospel minister, challenged that view when he urged Congregationalists to turn down a gift from John D. Rockefeller, arguing that it was "tainted money." In place of the gospel of wealth, progressive clergy exhorted their congregations to put Christ's teachings to work in their daily lives. Charles M. Sheldon's popular book *In His Steps* (1898) called on men and women to Christianize capitalism by asking the question "What would Jesus do?"

For Walter Rauschenbusch, a Baptist minister working in New York's tough Hell's Kitchen neighborhood, the social gospel grew out of the depression of the 1890s, which left hundreds of thousands of people unemployed. "They wore down our threshold and they wore away our hearts," he later wrote. "One could hear human virtue cracking and crumbling all around." In *Christianity and the Social Crisis* (1907), Rauschenbusch called for churches to play a new role in promoting social justice, and many congregations across the country heeded the call.

Ministers also played an active role in the social purity movement, the campaign to attack vice. The Reverend Charles H. Parkhurst shocked his Madison Square congregation in the 1890s by donning a disguise and touring New York City's brothels to uncover the links between political corruption and urban vice. Armed with eyewitness accounts and affidavits, he demanded reform. To end the "social evil," as reformers euphemistically called prostitution, the social purity movement brought together ministers who wished to stamp out sin, doctors concerned about the spread of venereal disease, and women reformers determined to fight the double standard that made it acceptable for men to engage in premarital and extramarital sex but demanded chastity of women. Advanced progressive reformers linked prostitution to poverty and championed higher wages for women. "Is it any wonder," asked the Chicago vice commission, "that a tempted girl who receives only six dollars per week working with her hands sells her body for twenty-five dollars per week when she learns there is a demand for it and men are willing to pay the price?"

Together, social purity reformers of all stripes waged campaigns to close red-light districts in cities across the country and lobbied for the Mann Act, passed in 1910, which made it illegal to transport women across state lines for "immoral purposes." On the state level, they struck at venereal disease by securing legislation to require a blood test for syphilis before marriage.

Attacks on alcohol went hand in hand with the push for social purity. The **temperance** campaign launched by the Woman's Christian Temperance Union (WCTU) heated up in the early twentieth century. The Anti-Saloon League, formed in 1895 under the leadership of **Protestant** clergy, campaigned for an end to the sale of liquor. Reformers pointed to links between drinking, prostitution, wife and child abuse, unemployment, and industrial accidents. The powerful liquor lobby fought back, spending liberally in election campaigns, fueling the charge that liquor corrupted the political process.

An element of **nativism** (dislike of foreigners) ran through the movement for prohibition, as it did in a number of progressive reforms. The Irish, the Italians, and the Germans were among the groups stigmatized by temperance reformers for their drinking. Progressives often failed to see the important role the tavern played in many ethnic communities. Unlike the American saloon, an almost exclusively male domain, the tavern often provided a family retreat. German Americans of all ages socialized at beer gardens after church on Sunday. Even though most workers toiled six days a week and had only Sunday for recreation and relaxation, some progressives campaigned on the local level to enforce the Sunday closing of taverns, stores, and other commercial establishments. To deny the working class access to alcohol, these progressives pushed for state legislation to outlaw the sale of liquor. By 1912, seven states were "dry."

Progressives' efforts to civilize the city demonstrated their willingness to take action; their belief that environment, not heredity alone, determined human behavior; and their optimism that conditions could be corrected through government action without radically altering America's economy or institutions. All of these attitudes characterized the progressive movement.

Progressives and the Working Class

Day-to-day contact with their neighbors made settlement house workers particularly sympathetic to labor unions. When Mary Kenney O'Sullivan complained that her bookbinders' union met in a dirty, noisy saloon, Jane Addams invited the union to meet at Hull House. And during the Pullman strike in 1894, Hull House residents organized strike relief. "Hull-House has been so unionized," grumbled one Chicago businessman, "that it has lost its usefulness and become a detri-

ment and harm to the community." But to the working class, the support of middle-class reformers marked a significant gain.

Attempts to forge a cross-class alliance became institutionalized in 1903 with the creation of the Women's Trade Union League (WTUL). The WTUL brought together women workers and middle-class "allies." Its goal was to organize workingwomen into unions under the auspices of the American Federation of Labor (AFL). However, the AFL paid little more than lip service to unionizing women. As one workingwoman confided, "The men think that the girls should not get as good work as the men and should not make half as much money as a man." Samuel Gompers, president of the AFL, endorsed the principle of equal pay for equal work, shrewdly observing that it would help male workers more than women, since many employers hired women precisely because they could be paid less.

Although the alliance between workingwomen, primarily immigrants and daughters of immigrants, and their middle-class allies was not without tension, the WTUL helped workingwomen achieve significant gains. Its most notable success came in 1909 in the

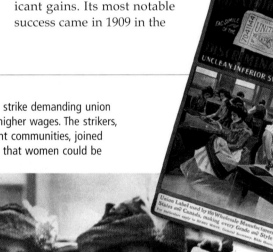

Women Strikers

Throughout the bitter winter of 1909, garment workers led a strike demanding union representation, shorter hours, better working conditions, and higher wages. The strikers, primarily young women from the Jewish and Italian immigrant communities, joined the International Ladies' Garment Workers Union and proved that women could be unionized and mount an effective strike. The Women's Trade Union League, a cross-class alliance of working women and middle-class "allies," contributed money and offered moral support to the strikers. The women pictured here claim 30,000 are on strike, but historically the strike has been called the "uprising of the 20,000." One strategy used by the Women's Trade Union League to promote better working conditions in the garment industry was to sew a union label into clothing made in shops where workers were unionized. Urging consumers to buy only merchandise with the union label, an 1891 ad from the United Garment Workers of America warns against "unclean inferior sweatshop clothing."

Strikers: Brown Brothers; Ad: Picture Research Consultants & Archives.

"uprising of the twenty thousand." In November, hundreds of women employees of the Triangle Shirtwaist Company in New York City went on strike to protest low wages, dangerous and demeaning working conditions, and management's refusal to recognize their union, the International Ladies' Garment Workers Union (ILGWU). In support of the walkout, the ILGWU called for a general strike of all garment workers. An estimated twenty thousand workers, most of them teenage girls and many of them Jewish and Italian immigrants, stayed out on strike through the winter, picketing in the bitter cold. More than six hundred were arrested, and many were sent to jail for "streetwalking," a move by the authorities to try to break the spirit and impugn the morals of the striking women. By the time the strike ended in February 1910, the workers had won important demands in many shops. But they lost their bid to gain recognition for their union. The solidarity shown by the women workers proved to be the strike's greatest achievement. As Clara Lemlich, one of the strike's leaders, exclaimed, "They used to say that you couldn't even organize women. They wouldn't come to union meetings. They were 'temporary' workers. Well we showed them!"

> Clara Lemlich, one of the garment strike's leaders, exclaimed, "They used to say that you couldn't even organize women. They wouldn't come to union meetings. They were 'temporary' workers. Well we showed them!"

The WTUL made enormous contributions to the strike. It provided volunteers for the picket lines, posted more than $29,000 in bail, protested police brutality, organized a parade of ten thousand strikers, took part in the arbitration conference, appealed for funds, and generated publicity for the strike. Under the leadership of the WTUL, women from every class of society, from J. P. Morgan's daughter Anne to **socialists** on New York's Lower East Side, joined the strikers in a dramatic display of cross-class alliance.

But for all its success, the uprising of the twenty thousand failed fundamentally to change conditions for women workers, as the tragic Triangle fire dramatized in 1911. A little over a year after the shirtwaist makers' strike ended, fire alarms sounded at the Triangle Shirtwaist factory. The ramshackle building, full of lint and combustible cloth, burned to rubble in half an hour. A WTUL member described the scene below on the street: "Two young girls whom I knew to be working in the vicinity came rushing toward me, tears were running from their eyes and they were white and shaking as they caught me by the arm.

'Oh,' shrieked one of them, 'they are jumping. Jumping from ten stories up! They are going through the air like bundles of clothes.'"

The terrified Triangle workers had little choice but to jump. Flames blocked one exit, and the other door had been locked to prevent workers from pilfering. The flimsy, rusted fire escape collapsed under the weight of fleeing workers, killing dozens. Trapped, 54 workers jumped from the ninth-floor windows, only to smash to their deaths on the sidewalk. Of 500 workers, 146 died and scores of others were injured. The owners of the Triangle firm went to trial for negligence, but they avoided conviction when authorities determined that the fire had been started by a careless smoker. The Triangle Shirtwaist Company reopened in another firetrap within a matter of weeks.

Outrage and a sense of futility overwhelmed Rose Schneiderman, a leading WTUL organizer, who made a bitter speech at the memorial service for the dead Triangle workers. "I would be a traitor to those poor burned bodies if I came here to talk good fellowship," she told her audience. "We have tried you good people of the public and we have found you wanting. . . . I know from my experience it is up to the working people to save themselves . . . by a strong working class movement."

The Triangle fire tested severely the bonds of the cross-class alliance. Along with Rose Schneiderman, WTUL leaders experienced a growing sense of futility. It seemed not enough to organize and to strike, particularly when the AFL paid so little attention to women workers. Increasingly, the WTUL turned its efforts to lobbying for protective legislation—laws that would limit hours and regulate working conditions for women workers.

Advocates of protective legislation won a major victory in 1908 when the U.S. Supreme Court, in *Muller v. Oregon*, reversed its previous rulings and upheld an Oregon law that limited to ten the hours women could work in a day. A mass of sociological evidence put together by Florence Kelley of the National Consumers' League and Josephine Goldmark of the WTUL demonstrated the ill effects of long hours on the health and safety of women. The data convinced the Court that long hours endangered women and therefore the entire human race. The Court's ruling set a precedent, but one that separated the well-being of women workers from that of men by arguing that women's reproductive role justified special treat-

14. Viewing the unfortunates at the Morgue

Triangle Fire Morgue
After the Triangle fire on March 26, 1911, New York City set up a makeshift morgue at the end of Manhattan's Charities Pier. There, the remains of more than a hundred young women and two dozen young men were laid out in coffins for their friends and relatives to identify. Victims who had jumped to their deaths from the ninth-floor windows or leaped down the elevator shaft could be easily recognized. Those trapped in the building were burned beyond recognition. A ring, a charred shoe, a melted hair comb often provided the only clues to the identity of a sister, a daughter, or a sweetheart. Artist John Sloan created this illustration to commemorate those who died in the fire. The striking image, with its dark triangle representing the capitalist triumvirate of Rent, Profit, and Interest, features a bloated businessman weeping over his lost profits while a young woman worker lies burning on the pavement and a leering skeleton poses on the left. In the trial that followed the fire, the owners of the Triangle Shirtwaist Company avoided penalty when their skillful lawyer challenged the credibility of witnesses.
Photo: United Archives, Kheel Center, Cornell University, Ithaca, NY; Illustration: Granger Collection.

ment. Later generations of women fighting for equality would question the effectiveness of this strategy and argue that it ultimately closed good jobs to women. The WTUL, however, greeted protective legislation as a first step in the attempt to ensure the safety of all workers.

The National Consumers' League (NCL), like the WTUL, fostered cross-class alliance. When Florence Kelley took over the leadership of the NCL in 1899, she urged middle-class women to boycott stores and exert pressure for decent wages and working conditions for women employees, primarily saleswomen. The league published a "white list" of stores that met its standards. The NCL's tactics were widely copied abroad. (See "Beyond America's Borders," page 752.) Like the WTUL, the National Consumers' League increasingly promoted protective legislation to

better working conditions for working women. Frustrated by the reluctance of the private sector to respond to the need for reform, progressives turned to government at all levels. Critics would later charge that the progressives assumed too easily that government regulation could best solve social problems.

Reform also fueled the fight for woman suffrage. For women like Jane Addams and Florence Kelley, involvement in social reform led inevitably to support for woman suffrage. These new suffragists emphasized the reforms that could be accomplished if women had the vote. When they talked of the need for the ballot, they often compared it to the broom. Addams insisted that in an urban, industrial society, a good housekeeper could not be sure the food she fed her family or the water and milk they drank were

Protecting the World's Workers: The National Consumers' League

The United States was not alone in wrestling with the problems accompanying urban industrialism. In western Europe, particularly Germany and England, where industrial development occurred even more rapidly than in the United States, concern for the welfare of the industrial workforce led in the 1890s to the elaboration of statutes designed to protect workers' safety and general welfare. America lagged behind. "In no country of the first rank is this legislation so weak as in the United States," observed John Graham Brooks, the first president of the National Consumers' League (NCL). Compared to European workers, he concluded, American workers' lives were barely touched by protective legislation. But progressive associations in the United States slowly began to work on issues of protection, and with the help of their transatlantic connections, they eventually inspired the formation of additional groups in Europe to fight for similar measures.

The National Consumers' League drew on European models of factory inspection and legislation that sought to promote better working conditions for laborers. Like the social settlement movement, another significant European import, the consumers' league movement in the United States soon outstripped its European counterparts, largely thanks to the college-educated women who also gave the American settlement house movement its unique stamp. Although Brooks and other men served as the league's officers (largely honorific posts), women formed the backbone of the NCL.

The league began on the grassroots level. In 1888, New York City garment worker and union organizer Leonora O'Reilly invited some of the city's prominent women to a meeting of the New York Working Women's Society, where they heard an appeal to help their "toiling and down-trodden sisters." The group appointed a committee to make and circulate a list of "such shops as deal justly with their employees" so that women consumers could patronize establishments that met minimum standards. Begun as a genteel boycott among New York City women alarmed at the conditions of women in the garment trades, the Consumers' League of New York took shape in 1891, led by philanthropist Josephine Shaw Lowell. Lowell liked to portray the league's

work as part of a historical continuum in women's activism, tracing its roots back to colonial women's patriotic refusal to buy British goods in the Revolutionary War era.

Taking as its motto "Investigate, agitate, legislate," the New York league affixed a "white label" to goods made in shops that met its standards for wages, working hours, and safety. Women shoppers were urged to "look for the white label" before buying. To determine which shops merited the label, league inspectors explored working conditions in cramped sweatshops, canneries, laundries, and department stores. They collected masses of data on women's wages, budgets, health, employment, and living standards. And they used the tactics of exposure and muckraking to bring to the nation's attention the grim realities of women's working conditions.

The movement spread rapidly. By 1896, sixty-four consumers' leagues had formed in twenty states, primarily in the Northeast and Midwest. In 1898, the national scope of the movement was recognized with the founding of the National Consumers' League. Membership in the NCL peaked in 1916, when it claimed fifteen thousand members in forty-three states.

The most prominent woman in the NCL was Florence Kelley, who left Hull House in 1899 to become the salaried executive secretary of the newly formed NCL, a post she held for two decades. Kelley grew up in Philadelphia, the daughter of a Republican congressman nicknamed William "Pig Iron" Kelley because of his support for the protective tariff benefiting Pennsylvania's iron and steel industry.

When she was a young girl, her father reportedly told her, "My generation has created industry, and your generation must humanize it." Kelley, along with other highly educated and public-spirited women of the Progressive Era, eagerly took on the task of civilizing capitalism.

After graduating from Cornell University in 1882, Kelley traveled to Europe to study law and government at the University of Zurich. There, she became an ardent socialist, married a Russian medical student, and had three children. In 1891, she left her abusive husband and moved into Chicago's Hull House. She soon established herself as an expert on tenement labor. In 1893, reform governor John Peter Altgeld named Kelley Illinois's chief factory inspector, making her the first woman in the United States to head a state labor department. Kelley developed a formidable reputation as a champion of better working conditions. And, as an active member of Chicago's consumers' league, she spearheaded the campaign against sweatshops.

At the NCL, Kelley helped propel the league from consumer pressure tactics to political action, sometimes with influence from abroad. By 1902, the league maintained a separate lobbying agency to fight for an end to child labor. After hearing convincing arguments from British delegates at the 1908 international consumers' league congress in Geneva, Kelley led the NCL to push for minimum wage legislation. Working with women such as Maud Nathan (a prominent figure in international women's circles), Mary Kingsbury Simkhovitch of New York's Greenwich House, and Pauline and Josephine Goldmark

Florence Kelley, 1905
Florence Kelley left Hull House in 1899 to become the salaried executive secretary of the National Consumers' League, headquartered in New York City. Although men held higher offices in the organization, Kelley and other highly educated women made up the backbone of the NCL, demonstrating the significant role women played in international progressive reform. Until her death in 1932, Kelley used the NCL to campaign for shorter hours and better working conditions for America's workingwomen.
Rare Books & Manuscripts, Columbia University in the City of New York.

and their brother-in-law Louis Brandeis, the NCL also mounted a legal defense campaign on behalf of state statutes limiting the maximum hours of women wage earners. Their efforts paid off in 1908 when in *Muller v. Oregon*, the Supreme Court ruled constitutional the regulation of women's working hours—a landmark decision in which, for the first time, the Court acknowledged that an individual's right to form contracts did not rule out setting limits on working hours.

Such successes, along with the international ties of many NCL activists, helped the league spin off a number of European sister organizations. By 1910, league-inspired affiliates had formed in France, Belgium, Germany, and Switzerland. Reversing the trend for progressive reform measures to cross the Atlantic from Europe to America, the National Consumers' League reached beyond America's borders as European consumer organizations borrowed American tactics to help protect workers.

pure unless she became involved in politics and wielded the ballot—and not just the broom—to protect her family. The concept of municipal housekeeping encouraged women to put their talents to work in the service of society.

> **REVIEW** What types of people were drawn to the progressive movement, and what motivated them?

Progressivism: Theory and Practice

Progressive reformers developed a theoretical basis for their activist approach by countering social Darwinism with a dynamic new **reform Darwinism** and by championing the uniquely American philosophy of **pragmatism**. The progressives emphasized action and experimentation. Dismissing the view that humans should leave progress to the dictates of natural selection, progressive reform Darwinists argued that human intelligence could shape change and improve society. In their zeal for action, progressives often showed an unchecked admiration for speed and efficiency that promoted **scientific management** and a new cult of efficiency. These varied strands of progressive theory found practical application in state and local politics, where reformers challenged traditional laissez-faire government.

Reform Darwinism and Social Engineering

The active, interventionist approach of the progressives directly challenged social Darwinism, with its insistence that the world operated on the principle of survival of the fittest and that human beings stood powerless in the face of the law of natural selection. Without abandoning the evolutionary framework of Darwinism, a new group of sociologists argued that evolution could be advanced more rapidly if men and women used their intellects to alter the environment. Sociologist Lester Frank Ward put it clearly in his book *Dynamic Sociology* (1883). "I insist that the time must soon come," he wrote, "when control of blind natural forces in society

> "I insist that the time must soon come," sociologist Lester Frank Ward wrote, "when control of blind natural forces in society must give way to human foresight."

must give way to human foresight." Dubbed "reform Darwinism," the new sociological theory condemned the laissez-faire approach, insisting that the liberal state should play a more active role in solving social problems.

In their pursuit of reform, progressives were influenced by the work of two philosophers, William James and John Dewey, who argued for a new test for truth. They insisted that there were no eternal truths and that the real worth of any idea lay in its consequences. They called their pluralistic, relativistic philosophy "pragmatism." Dewey put his theories to the test in the classroom of his laboratory school at the University of Chicago. A pioneer in American education, he emphasized process rather than content and encouraged students to learn by doing. By championing social experimentation, the American pragmatists provided an important impetus for progressive reform.

Efficiency and *expertise* became watchwords in the progressive vocabulary. In *Drift and Mastery* (1914), journalist and critic Walter Lippmann called for skilled "technocrats" to use scientific techniques to control social change, substituting social engineering for aimless drift. Progressive reformers' emphasis on expertise inevitably fostered a kind of elitism. Unlike the **Populists**, who advocated a greater voice for the masses, progressives, for all their interest in social justice, insisted that experts be put in charge.

At its extreme, the application of expertise and social engineering took the form of scientific management, which by elevating productivity and efficiency alienated the working class. Frederick Winslow Taylor pioneered "systematized shop management." After dropping out of Harvard, Taylor went to work as a machinist at Midvale Steel in Philadelphia in the 1880s. Obsessed with making humans and machines produce more and faster, he earned a master of engineering degree in 1885 and went back to Midvale to restructure the workplace. With his stopwatch, he carefully timed workers and attempted to break down their work into its simplest components, one repetitive action after another, on the theory that productivity would increase if tasks could be simplified. An advocate of piecework, quotas, and pay incentives for productivity, Taylor insisted that unions were unnecessary. As a consulting engineer, he spread his gospel of efficiency and won many converts among corporate managers. Workers hated the monotony of systematized shop management and argued that it

Tom Johnson

Tom Johnson, the reform mayor of Cleveland from 1901 to 1909, is shown here campaigning in Cleveland's Wade Park in 1908. For more than seven years, Mayor Johnson fought for a three-cent streetcar fare, winning the support of the working class and angering the businessmen who ran the city's streetcars. To get this low fare, Johnson finally instituted municipal ownership of the transit system.

The Western Reserve Historical Society, Cleveland, Ohio.

led to the speedup—pushing workers to produce more in less time and for less pay. But many progressives applauded the increased productivity and efficiency of Taylor's system.

Progressive Government: City and State

The politicians who became premier progressives were generally the followers, not the leaders, in a movement already well advanced at the grassroots level. Yet they left their stamp on the movement. Tom Johnson made Cleveland a model of progressive reform, Robert M. La Follette turned Wisconsin into a laboratory for progressivism, and Hiram Johnson ended the domination of the Southern Pacific Railroad in California politics.

Progressivism burst forth at every level of government in 1900, but nowhere more forcefully than in Cleveland, with the election of Thomas Loftin Johnson as mayor. A self-made millionaire by age forty, Johnson made his money in the street railroad business in Detroit. A flamboyant man who craved power and acclaim, Johnson turned his back on business and moved to Cleveland in 1899, where he began his career in politics. During his mayoral campaign, he pledged to reduce the streetcar fare from five cents to three cents. His election touched off a seven-year war between advocates of the lower fare, who believed that

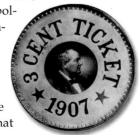

workers paid a disproportionate share of their meager earnings for transportation, and the streetcar moguls, who argued that they couldn't meet costs with the lower fare. When Johnson responded by building his own streetcar line, his foes tore up the tracks and blocked him with court injunctions and legal delays. At the prompting of his opponents, the Ohio legislature sought to limit Johnson's mayoral power by revoking the charter of every city in the state, replacing home rule with central control from the state capitol in Columbus.

When news of President McKinley's assassination reached his friend and political mentor Mark Hanna, Hanna is said to have growled, "Now that damned cowboy is president."

Reelected four times, Johnson fought for fair taxation and championed greater **democracy** through the use of the initiative, referendum, and recall—devices that allowed voters to have a direct say in legislative and judicial matters. Frustrated in his attempt to bring the streetcar industry to heel, he had the city buy the streetcar system and institute the three-cent fare. He also championed the municipal ownership of public utilities, a tactic that progressives called "gas and water socialism." Under Johnson's administration, Cleveland became, in the words of journalist Lincoln Steffens, the "best governed city in America."

In Wisconsin, Robert M. La Follette, who as a young congressional representative had supported William McKinley, converted to the progressive cause early in the 1900s. An astute politician, La Follette capitalized on the grassroots movement for reform to launch his long political career, first as governor (1901–1905) and later as a U.S. senator (1906–1925). A graduate of the University of Wisconsin, La Follette brought scientists and professors into his administration and used the university, just down the street from the statehouse in Madison, as a resource in drafting legislation. As governor, he lowered railroad rates, raised railroad taxes, improved education, preached conservation, established factory regulation and workers' compensation, instituted the first direct primary in the country, and inaugurated the first state income tax. Under his leadership, Wisconsin earned the title "laboratory of democracy."

A fiery orator, "Fighting Bob" La Follette united his supporters around issues that transcended party loyalties. This emphasis on reform characterized progressivism, which attracted followers from both major parties. Democrats like Tom Johnson and Republicans like Robert La Follette could lay equal claim to the label "pro-gressive." When La Follette moved to the U.S. Senate in 1906, he joined a coalition of insurgent progressives, Democrats and Republicans alike, who crossed party lines to work for reform.

West of the Rockies, progressivism arrived somewhat later and found a champion in Hiram Johnson of California, who served as governor from 1911 to 1917 and later as a U.S. senator. Since the 1870s, California politics had been dominated by the Southern Pacific Railroad, a corporation so rapacious that novelist Frank Norris styled it *The Octopus* (1901). Johnson ran for governor in 1910 on the promise to "kick the Southern Pacific out of politics." With the support of the reform wing of the Republican Party and the promise "to return the government to the people," he handily won. As governor, he introduced the direct primary; supported the initiative, referendum, and recall; strengthened the state's railroad commission; supported conservation; and signed an employer's liability law.

Who benefited most from Johnson's progressivism? California's entrepreneurs—large farmers, independent oil producers, and other rising businessmen who could make money more easily once Johnson curtailed the influence of the Southern Pacific. A vigorous, compelling personality with a reputation for a towering temper, Hiram Johnson proved an able governor. In 1912, he could boast that by regulating the Southern Pacific Railroad, he had saved shippers more than $2 million.

> **REVIEW** How did progressives justify their demand for more activist government?

Progressivism Finds a President: Theodore Roosevelt

On September 6, 1901, President William McKinley was shot by Leon Czolgosz, an **anarchist**, while attending the Pan-American Exposition in Buffalo, New York. Eight days later, McKinley died. When news of his assassination reached his friend and political mentor Mark Hanna, Hanna is said to have growled, "Now that damned cowboy is president." He was speaking of Vice President Theodore Roosevelt, the colorful hero of the battle of San Juan Hill, who had indeed punched cattle in the

Dakotas in the 1880s. Roosevelt's status as a Spanish-American War hero had propelled him to the governorship of New York in 1898. A moderate reformer, he had clashed with New York's Republican "Easy Boss" Tom Platt. To get rid of Roosevelt, the boss finagled to get him "kicked upstairs" as a candidate for the vice presidency in 1900. His energy and popularity added luster to the Republican ticket and helped President McKinley win a second term. As vice president, Platt and the party bosses reasoned, Roosevelt could do little harm. But one bullet proved the error of their logic.

In the first hours of his presidency, Roosevelt reassured the shocked nation that he intended "to continue absolutely unbroken" the policies of McKinley. But Roosevelt was as different from McKinley as the twentieth century was from the nineteenth. An activist and a moralist, imbued with the progressive spirit, Roosevelt would turn the White House into a "bully pulpit" advocating reforms like conservation and championing the nation's emergence as a world power. In the process, Roosevelt would work to shift the nation's center of power from Wall Street to Washington.

The Square Deal

At age forty-two, Theodore Roosevelt became the youngest man ever to move into the White House. A patrician by birth and an activist by temperament, Roosevelt brought to the job enormous talent and energy. By the time he graduated from Harvard, he was already an accomplished naturalist, an enthusiastic historian, and a naval strategist. He could have chosen from any of those promising careers. Instead, he chose politics, not a bad choice for a man who relished competition and craved power.

Roosevelt was shrewd enough to realize that the path to power did not lie in the good-government leagues formed by his well-bred friends. Instead, he apprenticed himself to the local ward boss, who held court in a grimy, smoke-filled Republican club above a Manhattan saloon. Roosevelt's rise in politics was swift and sure. He went from the New York assembly at the age of twenty-three to the presidency in less than twenty years, with time out as a cowboy in the Dakotas, police commissioner of New York City, assistant secretary of the navy, colonel of the Rough Riders, and governor of New York.

As president, Roosevelt would harness his explosive energy to strengthen the power of the federal government, putting business on notice that it could no longer count on a laissez-faire government to give it free rein. The "absolutely vital question" facing the country, Roosevelt wrote to a friend in 1901, was "whether or not the government has the power to control the trusts." The Sherman Antitrust Act of 1890 had been badly weakened by a conservative Supreme Court and by attorneys general more willing to use it against labor unions than against **monopolies**. To determine whether the law had any teeth left, Roosevelt, in one of his first acts as president, ordered his attorney general to begin a secret antitrust investigation of the Northern Securities Company.

Roosevelt trained his sights on a good target. Northern Securities had resulted from one of the most controversial mergers of the era. When Edward H. Harriman, who controlled the Union Pacific and Southern Pacific railroads, attempted to add the Northern Pacific to his holdings, James J. Hill of the Great Northern squared off against

Theodore Roosevelt
Described aptly by a contemporary observer as "a steam engine in trousers," Theodore Roosevelt, at forty-two, was the youngest president ever to occupy the White House. He brought to the office energy, intellect, and activism in equal measure. Roosevelt boasted that he used the presidency as a "bully pulpit"—a forum from which he advocated reforms ranging from trust-busting to conservation.
Library of Congress.

Roosevelt and the Trusts
This political cartoon drawn by Clifford Berryman depicts Roosevelt on a bear hunt, slaying a "bad trust" while restraining on a leash a "good trust." The cartoon alludes to an actual hunt during which Roosevelt refused to shoot an orphaned bear cub. His highly publicized act of mercy gave birth to the "teddy bear" and led to the marketing of many plush children's toys.
Granger Collection.

him. The result was a ruinous rate war that precipitated a panic on Wall Street, bankrupting thousands of small investors. To bring peace to the warring factions, financier J. P. Morgan stepped in and created the Northern Securities Company in 1901, linking under one management three competing railroads. This new behemoth monopolized railroad traffic in the Northwest. Small investors, still smarting from their losses, farmers worried about freight rates, and the public in general saw in Northern Securities the symbol of corporate high-handedness.

In February 1902, just five months after Roosevelt took office, Wall Street rocked with the

news that the government had filed an antitrust suit against Northern Securities. As one newspaper editor sarcastically observed, "Wall Street is paralyzed at the thought that a President of the United States would sink so low as to try to enforce the law." An indignant J. P. Morgan demanded to know why he had not been consulted. "If we have done anything wrong," he told the attorney general, "send your man to my man and they can fix it up." Roosevelt, amused, later noted that Morgan "could not help regarding me as a big rival operator." In a sense, that was just what he intended. Roosevelt's thunderbolt put Wall Street on notice that the new president expected to be treated as an equal and was willing to use government as a weapon to curb business excesses. Perhaps sensing the new mood, the Supreme Court, in a significant turnaround, upheld the Sherman Act and called for the dissolution of Northern Securities in 1904.

"Hurrah for Teddy the Trustbuster," cheered the papers. Roosevelt went on to use the Sherman Act against forty-three trusts, including such giants as American Tobacco, Du Pont, and Standard Oil. Always the moralist, he insisted on a "rule of reason." He would punish "bad" trusts (those that broke the law) and leave "good" ones alone. In practice, he preferred regulation to antitrust suits. In 1903, he pressured Congress to pass the Elkins Act, outlawing railroad rebates. And he created the new cabinet-level Department of Commerce and Labor with the subsidiary Bureau of Corporations to act as a corporate watchdog.

Observing Roosevelt in action, journalist Joseph Pulitzer remarked, "He has subjugated Wall Street." Pulitzer exaggerated, but Roosevelt had masterfully asserted the moral and political authority of the executive, underscoring, in his words, the "duty of the President to act upon the theory that he is the steward of the people."

In his handling of the anthracite coal strike in 1902, Roosevelt again demonstrated his willingness to assert the authority of the presidency, this time to mediate between labor and management. In May, 147,000 coal miners in Pennsylvania went on strike. The United Mine Workers (UMW) demanded a reduction in the workday from twelve to ten hours, an equitable system of weighing each miner's output, and a 10 percent wage increase, along with recognition of the union.

When asked about the appalling conditions in the mines that led to the strike, George Baer, the mine operators' spokesman, scoffed, "The miners don't suffer, why they can't even speak English." Buttressed by social Darwinism, Baer observed that "God in his infinite wisdom" had placed "the rights and interests of the laboring man" in the hands of the capitalists, not "the labor agitators." His Olympian confidence rested on the fact that six eastern railroads owned more than 70 percent of the anthracite mines. With the power of the railroads behind them, Baer and the mine owners refused to budge.

The strike dragged on through the summer and into the fall. Hoarding and profiteering drove the price of coal from $2.50 to $6.00 a ton. Coal heated nearly every house, school, and hospital in the Northeast, and as winter approached, coal shortages touched off near riots in the nation's big cities. Labor's sympathizers called for national ownership of the coal mines. Business leaders urged Roosevelt to follow President Grover Cleveland's example in 1894 and call out federal troops to break the strike. In the face of mounting tension, Roosevelt steered a middle course by doing what no president had ever done. He stepped in to mediate, issuing a personal invitation to representatives from both sides to meet in Washington in October. His unprecedented intervention served notice that gov-

ernment counted itself an independent force in business and labor disputes. At the same time, it gave unionism a boost by granting the UMW a place at the table. At the meeting, Baer and the mine owners arrogantly refused to talk with the union representative—a move that angered the attorney general and insulted the president. The meeting ended in an impasse.

Beside himself with anger over the "wooden-headed obstinacy and stupidity" of management, Roosevelt threatened to seize the mines and run them with federal troops. It was a powerful bluff, one that called into question not only the supremacy of private property but also the rule of law. But the specter of federal troops being used to operate the mines quickly brought management around. At the prompting of J. P. Morgan, the mine owners agreed to arbitration ending the strike. In the end, the miners won a reduction in hours and a wage increase, but the owners succeeded in preventing formal recognition of the UMW.

Taken together, Roosevelt's actions in the Northern Securities case and the anthracite coal strike marked a dramatic departure from the

Breaker Boys
Child labor in America's mines and mills was common at the turn of the twentieth century, despite state laws that tried to restrict it. Here, "breaker boys," some as young as seven years old, pick over coal in a Pennsylvania mine. Their unsmiling faces bear witness to the difficulty and danger of their work. A committee investigating child labor found more than ten thousand children illegally employed in the Pennsylvania coalfields.
Brown Brothers.

presidential passivity of his predecessors in the Gilded Age. Roosevelt's actions demonstrated conclusively that government intended to act as a countervailing force to the power of the big corporations. Pleased with his role in the anthracite strike, he announced that all he had tried to do was give labor and capital a "square deal."

The phrase "Square Deal" became Roosevelt's campaign slogan in the 1904 election. But to win the presidency in his own right, Roosevelt needed to wrest control of the Republican Party from kingmaker and party boss Mark Hanna. Roosevelt adroitly used patronage to win supporters and weaken Hanna's power. The standoff never reached a climax. Hanna died of typhoid fever in 1904, leaving Roosevelt the undisputed leader of the party.

In the presidential election of 1904, Roosevelt easily defeated the Democrats, who abandoned their perennial candidate, William Jennings Bryan, to support Judge Alton B. Parker, a "safe" candidate they hoped would lure business votes away from Roosevelt. In the months before the election, the president prudently toned down his criticism of big business. Wealthy Republicans like J. P. Morgan may have grumbled privately, branding Roosevelt a class traitor, but they remained loyal to the party. Roosevelt swept into office with the largest popular majority—57.9 percent—any candidate had polled up to that time.

Roosevelt the Reformer

"Tomorrow I shall come into my office in my own right," Roosevelt is said to have remarked on the eve of his election. "Then watch out for me!" Roosevelt's stunning victory gave him a mandate for reform. He would need all the popularity and political savvy he could muster, however, to guide his reform measures through Congress. The Senate remained controlled by a staunchly **conservative** Republican "old guard," with many senators on the payrolls of the corporations Roosevelt sought to curb. Roosevelt's pet project remained railroad regulation. The Elkins Act prohibiting rebates had not worked. No one could stop big shippers like Standard Oil from wringing concessions from the railroads. Roosevelt determined that the only solution lay in giving the Interstate Commerce Commission (ICC) real power to set rates and prevent discriminatory practices. But the right to determine the price of goods or services was an age-old prerogative of private enterprise, and one that business had no intention of yielding to government.

To ensure passage of the Hepburn Act, which would increase the power of the ICC, Roosevelt worked skillfully behind the scenes. In its final form, the Hepburn Act, passed in May 1906, gave the ICC the power to set rates subject to court review. Committed progressives like La Follette judged the law a defeat for reform. Diehard conservatives branded it a "piece of populism." Both sides exaggerated. The law left the courts too much power and failed to provide adequate means for the ICC to determine rates, but its passage proved a landmark in federal control of private industry. For the first time, a government commission had the power to investigate private business records and to set rates.

Passage of the Hepburn Act marked the high point of Roosevelt's presidency. In a serious political blunder, Roosevelt had announced on the eve of his election in 1904 that he would not run again. By 1906, he had become a "lame duck" at the very moment he enjoyed his greatest public popularity.

Always an apt reader of the public temper, Roosevelt witnessed a growing appetite for reform fed by the revelations of corporate and political wrongdoing and social injustice that filled the papers and boosted the sales of popular periodicals. (See "The Promise of Technology," page 762.) Roosevelt, who wielded publicity like a weapon in his pursuit of reform, counted many of the new investigative journalists, including Jacob Riis, among his friends. But he warned them against going too far, citing the allegorical character in *Pilgrim's Progress* who was so busy raking muck that he took no notice of higher things. Roosevelt's criticism gave the American vocabulary a new word, *muckraker*, which journalists soon appropriated as a title of honor.

Muckraking, as Roosevelt well knew, provided enormous help in securing progressive legislation. In the spring of 1906, publicity generated by the muckrakers about poisons in patent medicines goaded the Senate, with Roosevelt's backing, into passing a pure food and drug bill. Opponents in the House of Representatives hoped to keep the legislation locked up in committee. There it would have died, were it not for publication of Upton Sinclair's novel *The Jungle* (1906), with its sensational account of filthy conditions in meatpacking plants. A massive public outcry led to the passage of the Pure Food and Drug Act and the Meat Inspection Act in 1906.

In the waning years of his administration, Roosevelt allied with the more progressive elements of the Republican Party. In speech after speech, he attacked "malefactors of great wealth." Styling himself a "radical," he claimed credit for leading the "ultra conservative" party of McKinley to a position of "progressive conservatism and conservative radicalism."

When an economic panic developed in the fall of 1907, business interests quickly blamed the president. The panic of 1907 proved severe but short. Once again, J. P. Morgan stepped in to avert disaster, this time switching funds from one bank to another to prop up weak institutions. For his services, he claimed the Tennessee Coal

The Jungle

Novelist Upton Sinclair, a lifelong socialist, wrote *The Jungle* to expose the evils of capitalism. But readers were more horrified by the unsanitary conditions he described in the meatpacking industry, where the novel's hapless hero sees rats, filth, and diseased animals processed into meat products. It was rumored that after reading the book, President Theodore Roosevelt could no longer stomach sausage for breakfast. The president immediately ordered a thorough study of conditions in the meatpacking industry. The public outcry surrounding *The Jungle* contributed to the enactment of pure food and drug legislation and a federal meat inspection law. Sinclair ruefully remarked, "I aimed at the public's heart, but I hit them in the stomach."

Picture Research Consultants, Inc.

and Iron Company, an independent steel business that had long been coveted by the U.S. Steel Corporation. Morgan dispatched his lieutenants to Washington, where they told Roosevelt that the sale of the company would aid the economy "but little benefit" U.S. Steel. Willing to take the word of a gentleman, Roosevelt tacitly agreed not to institute antitrust proceedings against U.S. Steel over the acquisition. Roosevelt later learned that Morgan had been less than candid. U.S. Steel acquired Tennessee Coal and Iron for a price well below market value, doing away with a competitor and undercutting the economy of the Southeast. Roosevelt's promise not to institute antitrust proceedings against U.S. Steel would give rise to the charge that he acted as a tool of the Morgan interests.

The charge of collusion between business and government underscored the extent to which corporate leaders like Morgan found federal regulation preferable to unbridled competition or harsher state measures. During the Progressive Era, enlightened business leaders cooperated with government in the hope of avoiding antitrust prosecution. Convinced that regulation and not trust-busting offered the best way to deal with big business, Roosevelt never acknowledged that his regulatory policies fostered an alliance between business and government that today is called corporate liberalism. Despite his harsh attacks on "malefactors of great wealth," Roosevelt's actions in the panic of 1907 demonstrated his indebtedness to Morgan, who still functioned informally as the national bank and would continue to do so until the passage of the Federal Reserve Act six years later.

Roosevelt and Conservation

In one area, Roosevelt proved indisputably ahead of his time. Robert La Follette, who thought Roosevelt a lukewarm progressive and found much to criticize in his presidency, hailed as Roosevelt's "greatest work" his efforts in the conservation of natural resources. When Roosevelt took office, some 45 million acres of land remained as government reserves. He more than tripled that number to 150 million acres, buying land and creating national parks and wildlife preserves by executive order. To conserve natural resources, he fought western cattle barons, lumber kings, mining interests, and powerful leaders in Congress, including Speaker of the House Joseph Cannon, who was determined to spend "not one cent for scenery."

Flash Photography and the Birth of Photojournalism

The camera was not new at the turn of the twentieth century. As early as the 1840s, Americans had eagerly imported the technology developed by the Frenchman L. J. M. Daguerre to make portraits known as daguerreotypes. By the 1880s, the invention of dry plates had simplified photography, and by the 1890s, Americans could purchase a Kodak camera marketed by George Eastman. But for Jacob Riis, who wished to document the horrors of tenement life, photography was useless because it required daylight or careful studio lighting. Riis, a progressive reformer and journalist who covered the police beat for the *New York Tribune*, never thought of buying a camera. He could only rudely sketch the dim hovels, the criminal nightlife, and the windowless tenement rooms of New York. Then came the breakthrough. "One morning scanning my newspaper at the breakfast table," he wrote, "I put it down with an outcry. . . . There it was, the thing I had been looking for all these years. . . . A way had been discovered . . . to take pictures by flashlight. The darkest corner might be photographed that way."

The new technology involved a pistol lamp that fired magnesium cartridges to provide light for instantaneous photography. Armed with the new flash pistols, Riis and a band of amateur photographers soon set out to shine light in the dark corners of New York. "Our party carried terror wherever it went," Riis later recounted. "The spectacle of strange men invading a house in the midnight hours armed with [flash] pistols which they shot off recklessly was hardly reassuring . . . and it was not to be wondered at if the tenants bolted through the windows and down fire-escapes."

Unhappy with the photographers he hired to follow him on his nighttime forays into the slums, Riis determined to try his own hand at taking pictures and laid out $25 for his first photographic equipment in 1888. It consisted of a 4-by-5-inch wooden box camera, glass plates, a tripod, a safety lantern, flash pistols, developing trays, and a printing frame. He soon replaced the pistols with a newer flash technology developed in 1887 that used magnesium powder blown through an alcohol flame. Riis carried a frying pan in which to ignite the powder, observing, "It seemed more homelike."

Flash photography was dangerous. The pistol lamp cartridges contained highly explosive chemicals that could seriously burn the photographer. The newer technology employing magnesium powder also proved risky. Riis once blew the flash into his own eyes, and only his glasses saved him from being blinded. Nor was Riis the only one in peril. When he photographed the residents of a tenement on "Blind Man's Alley," he set the place on fire when he ignited the flash. He later claimed the tenement, nicknamed the "Dirty Spoon," was so filthy it wouldn't burn. He was able to douse the flames without his blind subjects ever realizing their danger.

Riis turned his photographs into slides that he used to illustrate his lectures on tenement life. They helped spread his message, but not until *Scribner's* magazine printed his story titled "How the Other Half Lives" in December 1889 did he begin to develop a mass audience. The article, illustrated with line drawings of Riis's photographs, became the basis for his best-selling book of the same title published in 1890.

How the Other Half Lives made photographic history. It contained, along with Riis's text and the line drawings that had appeared in *Scribner's*, seventeen halftone prints of Riis's photographs. Riis's text and pictures shined the light on New York's darkest corners: vagrants in filthy lodging houses; "street arabs," homeless boys who lived by their wits on the streets; the saloons and dives of lower New York; evil-smelling tenement yards; stifling sweatshops. For the first time, unposed action pictures taken with a flash documented social conditions. Riis's pioneering photojournalism shocked the nation and led not only to tenement reform but also to the development of city playgrounds, neighborhood parks, and child labor laws.

Jacob Riis and Baxter Street Courtyard

Jacob Riis (to the right), a Danish immigrant who knew the squalor of New York's lodging houses and slums from his early days in the city, vigorously campaigned for tenement reform. He warned slumlords (some of them prominent New Yorkers) that their greed bred crime and disease and might provoke class warfare. Flash photography enabled Riis to expose the dark alleys and tenements of New York. He took his camera (much like the one pictured in the inset) into Baxter Street courtyard, then recorded these observations: "I counted the other day the little ones, up to ten years old in a . . . tenement that for a yard has a . . . space in the center with sides fourteen or fifteen feet long, just enough for a row of ill-smelling [water] closets . . . and a hydrant. . . . There was about as much light in the 'yard' as in the average cellar. . . . I counted one hundred twenty eight [children] in forty families."

Riis portrait: National Portrait Gallery, Smithsonian Institution/Art Resource, NY; Baxter Street courtyard: The Jacob A. Riis Collection, #108 Museum of the City of New York; Camera: George Eastman House.

As the first president to have lived and worked in the West, Roosevelt came to the White House convinced of the need for better management of the nation's rivers and forests. During the 1890s, concern for the wanton exploitation of natural resources had led Congress to pass legislation giving the president the power to "reserve" forest land from commercial development by executive proclamation. During his presidency, Roosevelt did not hesitate to wield that power. He placed the nation's conservation policy in the hands of scientifically trained experts like his chief forester, Gifford Pinchot. Pinchot fought for the principle of managed use. He desired not so much to remove land from commercial use, but to use the power of the federal government to effect long-term planning and the rational management of the nation's resources.

> Roosevelt created twenty-one new reserves and enlarged eleven more, saving sixteen million acres for posterity. "Opponents of the forest service turned handsprings in their wrath," he wrote, "but the threats . . . were really only a tribute to the efficiency of our action."

Roosevelt and Pinchot preached conservation—the efficient use of natural resources. Willing to permit grazing, lumbering, and the development of hydroelectric power, conservationists fought private interests only when they felt business acted irresponsibly or threatened to monopolize water and electric power.

Roosevelt's conservation policies drew criticism from many quarters. Preservationists like John Muir, founder of the Sierra Club, believed the wilderness needed to be protected from all commercial exploitation. Muir soon clashed with Roosevelt, whose policy of managed use led to the destruction of the Hetch Hetchy valley in California's Yosemite National Park. (See "Historical Question," page 766.) Progressives also criticized the Newlands Reclamation Act of 1902, arguing that the legislation encouraged the growth of large-scale farming at the expense of small farmers. The law established the Reclamation Bureau within the Department of the Interior and provided federal funding for irrigation projects. The growing in-

MAP 21.1 National Parks and Forests

The national park system in the West began with Yellowstone in 1872. Grand Canyon, Yosemite, Kings Canyon, and Sequoia followed in the 1890s. During his presidency, Theodore Roosevelt added six parks—Crater Lake, Wind Cave, Petrified Forest, Lassen Volcanic, Mesa Verde, and Zion.

READING THE MAP: Collectively, do national parks or national forests encompass more land? According to the map, how many national parks were created before 1910? How many were created after 1910? CONNECTIONS: How do conservation and preservation differ? Why did Roosevelt believe that conservation was important? What principle guided the national land use policy of the Roosevelt administration?

FOR MORE HELP ANALYZING THIS MAP, see the map activity for this chapter in the Online Study Guide at bedfordstmartins.com/roark.

THE WORLD'S CONSTABLE.

"The World's Constable"
In this political cartoon from 1905, President Theodore Roosevelt, dressed as a constable, wields the club of "The New Diplomacy" in one hand with "Arbitration" tucked under his arm. The Roosevelt Corollary to the Monroe Doctrine made the United States the Western Hemisphere's policeman, a role Roosevelt relished.
Granger Collection.

READING THE IMAGE: How does this political cartoon visually represent Roosevelt's foreign policy? Does it appear to be supportive or critical of his policies? How does it treat the other peoples of the world?
CONNECTIONS: What aspects of Roosevelt's foreign policy ideas and actions are depicted in the cartoon?

FOR MORE HELP ANALYZING THIS IMAGE, see the visual activity for this chapter in the Online Study Guide at
bedfordstmartins.com/roark.

volvement of the federal government in the management of water resources, a critical issue in the West, marked another victory for the policy of federal intervention that characterized progressivism and marked the end of laissez-faire liberalism.

In 1907, Congress put the brakes on Roosevelt's conservation program by passing a law limiting his power to create forest reserves in six western states. In the days leading up to the law's enactment, Roosevelt feverishly created twenty-one new reserves and enlarged eleven more, saving sixteen million acres for posterity. Once again, Roosevelt had outwitted his adversaries. "Opponents of the forest service turned handsprings in their wrath," he wrote, "but the threats . . . were really only a tribute to the efficiency of our action." Worried that private utilities were gobbling up waterpower sites and

creating a monopoly of hydroelectric power, he authorized Pinchot to withdraw 2,565 power sites from private use by designating them "ranger stations." Firm in his commitment to conservation, Roosevelt proved willing to stretch the law when it served his ends. Today, the six national parks, sixteen national monuments, and fifty-one wildlife refuges that he created bear witness to his substantial accomplishments as a conservationist (Map 21.1).

The Big Stick

Roosevelt's activism extended to his foreign policy, where he worked to buttress the nation's newly won place among world leaders. A fierce proponent of America's interests abroad, he believed that Congress was inept in foreign

Progressives and Conservation: Should Hetch Hetchy Be Dammed or Saved?

In 1890, President Benjamin Harrison signed into law an act setting aside two million acres in California's Yosemite Valley and designating Yosemite a national park. For naturalist John Muir, the founder of the Sierra Club, the act marked a victory in his crusade to guarantee that "incomparable Yosemite" would be preserved for posterity. But Muir's fight was not yet over.

The growing city of San Francisco needed water and power, and Mayor James Phelan soon sought to obtain water rights in Hetch Hetchy, a spectacular mountain valley within Yosemite's borders. There, the Tuolumne River could easily be dammed and the valley flooded to create a reservoir large enough to ensure the city's water supply for one hundred years.

When Muir heard of the plan, he sprang into action to save Hetch Hetchy. "That any one would try to destroy such a place seems incredible," he wrote, describing the valley as "one of Nature's rarest and most precious mountain temples." All of Yosemite National Park, he argued, should remain sacrosanct. In 1903, the secretary of the interior concurred, denying San Francisco supervisors commercial use of Hetch

Hetchy on the grounds that it lay within the national park.

But the San Francisco earthquake and resulting fire in 1906 created a groundswell of sympathy for the devastated city. In this climate, San Francisco renewed its efforts to obtain Hetch Hetchy and in 1907 succeeded in gaining authorization to proceed with plans to dam the river and flood the valley.

Given President Theodore Roosevelt's commitment to conservation, how could his administration have agreed to the destruction of the Hetch Hetchy valley? Historians traditionally have styled the struggle as one that pitted conservationists against preservationists. Roosevelt and his chief forester, Gifford Pinchot, represented the forces of conservation, or managed use. To them, the battle was not over preservation but over public versus private control of water and power. California progressives, who swept into office with the election of Hiram Johnson as governor in 1910, argued that if Congress did not grant the city of San Francisco the right to control Hetch Hetchy, the powerful Pacific Gas and Electric Company (PG&E) would monopolize the city's light and power industry. These progressives dismissed Muir and his fol-

lowers as "nature fakers" and judged them little more than dupes in the machinations of PG&E.

For their part, Muir and the preservationists, although they fought for the integrity of the national parks, did not champion the preservation of wilderness for its own sake. The urban professional men and women who joined the Sierra Club saw nature as a retreat and restorative for city dwellers. The club hosted an annual camping trip to popularize Yosemite and spoke in glowing terms of plans to build new roads and hotels that would make the "healing power of Nature" accessible to "thousands of tired, nerve-shaken, over-civilized people." As historian Robert Righter has pointed out, the battle over Hetch Hetchy represented not so much conservation versus preservation or managed use versus wilderness as it did the victory of water and power over tourism and recreation.

Nevertheless, the engineers and irrigation men who dammed Hetch Hetchy demonstrated a breathtaking arrogance. Speaking for them, Franklin Lane, President Woodrow Wilson's secretary of the interior, proclaimed, "Every tree is a challenge to use, and every pool of water and every foot of soil." Certain of humans' right to dominate nature and bend it to their will, Lane concluded, "The mountains are our enemy. We must pierce them and make them serve. The sinful rivers we must curb."

Lane and the conservationists won the day. In 1913, Congress passed the Raker Act authorizing the building of the O'Shaughnessy Dam, completed a decade later. To build the dam, the Hetch Hetchy valley was first denuded of its trees, then flooded under two hundred feet of

Roosevelt and Muir in Yosemite
This 1903 photograph shows President Theodore Roosevelt on a camping trip in Yosemite National Park with John Muir. Roosevelt and Muir later clashed over the flooding of the Hetch Hetchy valley in Yosemite. Roosevelt and his chief forester, Gifford Pinchot, favored giving San Francisco the right to dam the valley to supply water and power. Muir bitterly noted that Pinchot had never bothered to visit the valley he condemned to a watery grave.

Theodore Roosevelt Collection, Harvard College Library.

water. Muir did not live to see the destruction of Hetch Hetchy. He died in 1914, cursing the "dark damn-dam-damnation." But his fight to save Hetch Hetchy galvanized the preservation movement and led to the passage of the National Park Service Act in 1916 creating a federal agency to protect the nation's parks.

The last chapter in the battle over Hetch Hetchy may yet be written. In 1987, President Ronald Reagan's secretary of the interior, Donald Hodel, shocked San Francisco by suggesting the removal of the O'Shaughnessy Dam and the restoration of the Hetch Hetchy valley. Although it is unlikely that the dam will be demolished (it supplies San Francisco not only with water but also with revenue from electric power), advocates for the restoration of the Hetch Hetchy valley continue to rally to the cause. As Ken Browner of the Sierra Club wrote, "Waiting in Yosemite National Park, under water, is a potential masterpiece of restoration" and a chance "to correct the biggest environmental mistake ever committed against the National Park System."

affairs, and he relied on executive power to pursue a vigorous foreign policy, sometimes stretching the powers of the presidency beyond legal limits. A man who relished military discipline and viewed life as a constant conflict for supremacy, Roosevelt believed that "civilized nations" should police the world and hold "backward" countries in line. In his relations with the European powers, he relied on military strength and diplomacy, a combination he aptly described with the aphorism "Speak softly but carry a big stick."

The Roosevelt Corollary in Action

In the Caribbean, Roosevelt jealously guarded the U.S. sphere of influence defined in the **Monroe Doctrine**. In 1902, he risked war to keep Germany from intervening in Venezuela when that country's dictator borrowed money in Europe and could not repay it. Roosevelt issued an ultimatum to the German kaiser, warning him not to intervene in Venezuela to secure payment of the debt. Roosevelt's message was blunt—stay out of Latin America or face war with the United States. Both sides eventually backed down and agreed to arbitration.

Roosevelt's proprietary attitude toward the Western Hemisphere became evident in the case of the Panama Canal. A firm advocate of naval power and an astute naval strategist, Roosevelt had long been a supporter of a canal linking the Caribbean and the Pacific. By enabling ships to move quickly from the Atlantic to the Pacific, a canal could effectively double the U.S. navy's power. Having decided on a route across the Panamanian isthmus (a narrow strip of land connecting North and South America), then part of Colombia, Roosevelt in 1902 offered the Colombian government a one-time sum of $10 million and an annual rent of $250,000. When the government in Bogotá refused to accept the offer, Roosevelt became incensed at what he called the "homicidal corruptionists" in Colombia for trying to "blackmail" the United States. At the prompting of a group of New York investors, the Panamanians staged an uprising in 1903, and with unseemly haste the U.S. government recognized the new government within twenty-four hours. The Panamanians promptly accepted the $10 million, and the building got under way. The canal would take eleven years and $375 million to complete; it opened in 1914 (Map 21.2).

In the wake of the Panama affair, the confrontation with Germany over Venezuela, and yet another default on a European debt, this time in the Dominican Republic, Roosevelt announced in 1904 what became known as the Roosevelt Corollary to the Monroe Doctrine. Couched in the moralistic rhetoric typical of Roosevelt, the corollary declared that the United States would not intervene in Latin America as long as nations there conducted their affairs with "decency." But the United States would step in if any Latin American nation proved guilty of "brutal wrongdoing." The Roosevelt Corollary in effect made the United States the policeman of the Western Hemisphere and served notice to the European powers to keep out. To ensure the payment of debts, Roosevelt immediately put the corollary into practice by intervening in Costa Rica and by taking over the customhouse in the Dominican Republic to ensure the repayment of European debt.

In Asia, Roosevelt inherited the Open Door policy initiated by Secretary of State John Hay in 1899, designed to ensure U.S. commercial entry into China. As Britain, France, Russia, Japan, and Germany raced to secure Chinese trade and territory, Roosevelt was tempted to use force to enter the fray and gain economic or possibly territorial concessions. As a result of victory in the Spanish-American War, the United States already enjoyed a foothold in the region by virtue of its control of the Philippines. Realizing that Americans would not support an aggressive Asian policy, Roosevelt sensibly held back.

In his relations with Europe, Roosevelt sought to establish the United States, fresh from its victory over Spain, as a rising force in world affairs. When tensions flared between France and Germany in Morocco in 1905, Roosevelt mediated at a conference in Algeciras, Spain, where he worked to maintain a balance of power that helped neutralize German ambitions. His skillful mediation gained him a reputation as an astute

In his relations with the European powers, Roosevelt relied on military strength and diplomacy, a combination he aptly described with the aphorism "Speak softly but carry a big stick."

player on the world stage and demonstrated the nation's new presence in world affairs.

Roosevelt earned the Nobel Peace Prize in 1906 for his role in negotiating an end to the Russo-Japanese War, which had broken out when the Japanese invaded Chinese Manchuria, threatening Russia's sphere of influence in the area. Once again, Roosevelt sought to maintain a balance of power, in this case working to curb Japanese expansionism. Roosevelt admired the Japanese, judging them "the most dashing fighters in the world," but he did not want Japan to become too strong in Asia. He presided over the peace conference at Portsmouth, New Hampshire, where he was able to prevent Japan from dominating Manchuria. He had no qualms, however, about initiating the Taft-Katsura agreement, which granted Japan control of the sovereign nation of Korea in exchange for a pledge that Japan would not threaten the Philippines.

When good relations with Japan were jeopardized by discriminatory legislation in California calling for segregated public schools for "Orientals," Roosevelt smoothed over the incident and negotiated the "Gentlemen's Agreement" in 1907, which allowed the Japanese to save face by voluntarily restricting immigration to the United States. To demonstrate America's naval power and counter Japan's growing bellicosity, Roosevelt dispatched the Great White Fleet, sixteen of the navy's most up-to-date battleships, on a "goodwill mission" around the world. U.S. relations with Japan improved, and in the 1908 Root-Takahira agreement, the two nations pledged to maintain the Open Door and support the status quo in the Pacific. Roosevelt's show of American force constituted a classic example of his dictum "Speak softly but carry a big stick." Political cartoonists delighted in caricaturing the president wielding a cudgel in foreign affairs, and the American public relished the image.

REVIEW How did Roosevelt's foreign policy move the United States onto the world stage?

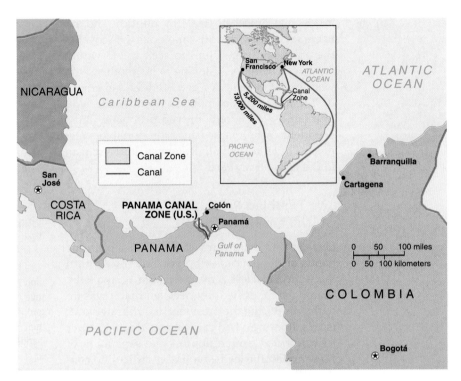

MAP 21.2 The Panama Canal, 1914
The Panama Canal, completed in 1914, bisects the isthmus in a series of massive locks and dams. As Theodore Roosevelt had planned, the canal greatly strengthened the U.S. navy by allowing ships to move from the Atlantic to the Pacific in a matter of days.

READING THE MAP: How long was the trip from New York to San Francisco before and after the Panama Canal was built?
CONNECTIONS: How did Roosevelt's desire for a canal lead to independence for Panama? How did the canal benefit the U.S. navy?

FOR MORE HELP ANALYZING THIS MAP, see the map activity for this chapter in the Online Study Guide at bedfordstmartins.com/roark.

Progressivism Stalled

Roosevelt retired from the presidency in 1909 at age fifty and removed himself from the political scene by going on safari in Africa. He turned the White House over to his handpicked successor, William Howard Taft, a lawyer who had served as governor-general of the Philippines. In the presidential election of 1908, Taft soundly defeated the perennial Democratic candidate, William Jennings Bryan. But Taft's popular majority amounted to only half of Roosevelt's record win in 1904.

Any man would have found it difficult to follow in Roosevelt's footsteps, but Taft proved hopelessly ill suited to the task. A genial man with a talent for law, Taft had no experience in elective office, no feel for politics, and no nerve for controversy. His ambitious wife coveted the office and urged him to seek it. He would have been better off listening to his mother, who warned, "Roosevelt is a good fighter and enjoys it, but the malice of politics would make you miserable." Her words proved prophetic. Taft's presidency was marked by a progressive stalemate, a bitter break with Roosevelt, and a schism in the Republican Party.

The Troubled Presidency of William Howard Taft

Once in office, Taft proved a perfect tool in the hands of Republicans who yearned for a return to the days of a less active executive. A lawyer by training and instinct, Taft believed that it was up to the courts, not the president, to arbitrate social issues. Roosevelt had carried presidential power to a new level, often flouting the separation of powers. Taft the legalist found it difficult to condone Roosevelt's actions. Wary of the progressive insurgents in Congress, Taft relied increasingly on conservatives in the Republican Party. As a progressive senator lamented, "Taft is a ponderous and amiable man completely surrounded by men who know exactly what they want."

Taft's troubles began on the eve of his inaugural, when he called a special session of Congress to deal with the tariff, which had grown inordinately high under Republican rule. Roosevelt had been too politically astute to tackle the troublesome tariff issue, even though he knew that rates needed to be lowered. Taft blundered into the fray. The House of Representatives passed a modest downward revision and, to make up for lost revenue, imposed a small inheritance tax. Led by Senator Nelson Aldrich of Rhode Island, the conservative Senate struck down the tax and added more than eight hundred crippling amendments to the tariff. The Payne-Aldrich bill that emerged actually raised the tariff, benefiting big business and the trusts at the expense of consumers. As if paralyzed, Taft neither fought for changes nor vetoed the measure. On a tour of the Midwest in 1909, he was greeted with jeers when he claimed, "I think the Payne bill is the best bill that the Republican Party ever passed." In the eyes of a growing number of Americans, Taft's praise of the tariff made him either a fool or a liar.

> A progressive senator lamented, "Taft is a ponderous and amiable man completely surrounded by men who know exactly what they want."

Taft's legalism soon got him into hot water in the area of conservation. He undid Roosevelt's work to preserve hydroelectric power sites when he learned that they had been improperly designated as ranger stations. And when Gifford Pinchot publicly denounced Taft's secretary of the interior as a tool of western land-grabbers, Taft fired Pinchot, touching off a storm of controversy that damaged Taft and alienated Roosevelt.

William Howard Taft
William Howard Taft had little aptitude for politics. When Theodore Roosevelt tapped him as his successor in 1908, Taft had never held an elected office. A legalist by training and temperament, Taft moved congenially in the conservative circles of the Republican Party. His actions dismayed progressives and eventually led Roosevelt to challenge him for the presidency in 1912. The break with Roosevelt saddened and embittered Taft, who heartily disliked the presidency and was glad to leave it. One symptom of his unhappiness was his weight. Already a hefty 320 pounds when he was elected, Taft ballooned to more than 355 pounds by the time he left office.
Library of Congress.

When Roosevelt returned to the United States in June 1910, he received a hero's welcome and attracted a stream of visitors and reporters seeking his advice and opinions. Hurt, Taft kept his distance. By late summer, Roosevelt had taken sides with the progressive insurgents in his party. "Taft is utterly hopeless as a leader," Roosevelt confided to his son as he set out on a speaking tour of the West. Reading the mood of the country, Roosevelt began to sound more and more like a candidate.

With the Republican Party divided, the Democrats swept the congressional elections of 1910. Branding the Payne-Aldrich tariff "the mother of trusts," they captured a majority in the House of Representatives and won several key governorships. The revitalized Democratic Party could look to new leaders, among them the progressive governor of New Jersey, Woodrow Wilson.

The new Democratic majority in the House, working with progressive Republicans in the Senate, achieved a number of key reforms, including legislation to regulate mine and railroad safety, to create the Children's Bureau in the Department of Labor, and to establish an eight-hour day for federal workers. Two significant constitutional amendments—the Sixteenth Amendment, which provided for a modest graduated income tax, and the Seventeenth Amendment, which called for the direct election of senators (formerly chosen by state legislatures)—went to the states, where they would win ratification in 1913. While Congress rode the high tide of progressive reform, Taft sat on the sidelines.

In foreign policy, Taft continued Roosevelt's policy of extending U.S. influence abroad, but here, too, Taft had a difficult time following in Roosevelt's footsteps. His policy of "dollar diplomacy" championed commercial goals rather than the strategic aims Roosevelt had pursued. Taft naively assumed he could substitute "dollars for bullets." In the Caribbean, he provoked anti-American feeling by attempting to force commercial treaties on Nicaragua and Honduras and by dispatching U.S. marines to Nicaragua and the Dominican Republic in 1912 pursuant to the Roosevelt Corollary. In Asia, he openly avowed his intent to promote in China "active intervention to secure for . . . our capitalists opportunity for profitable investment." Lacking Roosevelt's understanding of power politics, Taft never recognized that an aggressive commercial policy could not exist without the willingness to use military might to back it up.

Taft faced the limits of dollar diplomacy when revolution broke out in Mexico in 1911. Under pressure to protect American investments, which amounted to more than $4 billion, he mobilized troops along the border. In the end, however, with no popular support for a war with Mexico, he had to fall back on diplomatic pressure to salvage American interests.

Taft's "Dollar Diplomacy"

Taft hoped to encourage world peace through the use of a world court and arbitration. He unsuccessfully sponsored a series of arbitration treaties that Roosevelt, who prized national honor more than international law, vehemently opposed as weak and cowardly. By 1910, Roosevelt had become a vocal critic of Taft's foreign policy, which he dismissed as "maudlin folly."

The final breach between Taft and Roosevelt came in 1911, when Taft's attorney general filed an antitrust suit against U.S. Steel. In its brief against the corporation, the government cited Roosevelt's agreement with the Morgan interests in the 1907 acquisition of Tennessee Coal and Iron. The incident greatly embarrassed Roosevelt. Thoroughly enraged, he lambasted Taft's "archaic" antitrust policy and hinted that he might be persuaded to run for president again.

Progressive Insurgency and the Election of 1912

In February 1912, Roosevelt challenged Taft for the Republican nomination, announcing, "My hat is in the ring." But for all his popularity, Roosevelt no longer controlled the party machinery. Taft, with uncharacteristic strength, refused to step aside. As he bitterly told a journalist, "Even a rat in a corner will fight." Roosevelt took advantage of newly passed primary election laws and ran in thirteen states, winning 278 delegates to Taft's 48. But at the Chicago convention, Taft's bosses refused to seat the Roosevelt delegates. Fistfights broke out on the convention floor as Taft won nomination on the first ballot. Crying robbery, Roosevelt's supporters bolted the party.

Seven weeks later, in the same Chicago auditorium, the hastily organized Progressive Party met to nominate Roosevelt. Amid a thunder of applause, Jane Addams seconded Roosevelt's

Wilson Ribbon

Woodrow Wilson's political career was meteoric, propelling him from the presidency of Princeton University to the White House in three years. As governor of New Jersey from 1910 to 1912, Wilson turned against the Democratic political machine that had backed him and made a reputation as a champion of progressive reform. With the Republicans divided in 1912, the Democrats turned to Wilson to lead the party, nominating him on the forty-sixth ballot. In those days, prospective candidates generally did not attend the nominating convention. The ribbon in the photograph belonged to a member of the Democratic National Committee, who traveled to Wilson's summer home in Sea Girt, New Jersey, on August 7, 1912, to inform Wilson officially of his nomination.

Collection of Janice L. and David J. Frent.

nomination. Full of reforming zeal, the delegates chose Roosevelt and Hiram Johnson to head the new party and approved the most ambitious platform since the Populists'. Planks called for woman suffrage, presidential primaries, conservation of natural resources, an end to child labor, a minimum wage that would include women workers, workers' compensation, social security, and a federal income tax.

Roosevelt arrived in Chicago to accept the nomination and announced that he felt "as strong as a bull moose," giving the new party a nickname and a mascot. But for all the excitement and the cheering, the new Progressive Party was doomed, and the candidate knew it. The people may have supported the party, but the politicians, even progressives like La Follette, stayed within the Republican fold. "I am under no illusion about it," Roosevelt confessed to a friend. "It is a forlorn hope." But he had gone too far to turn back. He led the Bull Moose Party into the fray, exhorting his followers in ringing biblical tones, "We shall not falter, we stand at Armageddon and do battle for the Lord."

The Democrats, delighted at the split in the Republican ranks, smelled victory. Their convention turned into a bitter fight for the nomination. After forty-six ballots, Woodrow Wilson became the party's nominee. Wilson's career in politics was nothing short of meteoric. He was elected governor of New Jersey in 1910, and after only

eighteen months in office, the former professor of political science and president of Princeton University found himself running for president of the United States.

Voters in 1912 could choose among four candidates who claimed to be progressives. Taft, Roosevelt, and Wilson each embraced the label, and even the Socialist candidate, Eugene V. Debs, styled himself a progressive. That the term *progressive* could stretch to cover these diverse candidates underscored major disagreements in progressive thinking about the relationship between business and government. Taft, in spite of his trust-busting, was generally viewed as the candidate of the old guard. The real contest for the presidency was between Roosevelt and Wilson and the two political philosophies summed up in their respective campaign slogans: "The New Nationalism" and "The New Freedom."

The New Nationalism expressed Roosevelt's belief in federal planning and regulation. He accepted the inevitability of big business but demanded that government act as "a steward of the people" to regulate the giant corporations. Roosevelt called for an increase in the power of the federal government, a decrease in the power of the courts, and an active role for the president. He hoped to use an active federal government to promote social justice and democracy, replacing the laissez-faire policies of the old liberal state with a new form of liberalism.

MAP 21.3   The Election of 1912

Candidate	Electoral Vote	Popular Vote	Percent of Popular Vote
Woodrow Wilson (Democrat)	435	6,293,454	41.9
Theodore Roosevelt (Progressive)	88	4,119,538	27.4
William H. Taft (Republican)	8	3,484,980	23.2
Eugene V. Debs (Socialist)	0	900,672	6.1

Wilson, schooled in the Democratic principles of limited government and **states' rights**, set a markedly different course with his New Freedom. Wilson promised to use antitrust legislation to get rid of big corporations and to give small businesses and farmers better opportunities in the marketplace.

Wilson and Roosevelt fought it out, and the energy and enthusiasm of the Bull Moosers made the race seem closer than it really was. In the end, the Republican vote split, while the Democrats remained united. No candidate claimed a majority in the race. Wilson captured a bare 42 percent of the popular vote. Roosevelt and his Bull Moose Party won 27 percent, an unprecedented tally for a new party. Taft came in third with 23 percent. The Socialist Party, led by Debs, captured 6 percent. In the electoral college, however, Wilson won a decisive 435 votes, with 88 going to Roosevelt and only 8 to Taft (Map 21.3). The Progressive Party essentially collapsed after Roosevelt's defeat. It had always been, in the words of one astute observer, "a house divided against itself and already mortgaged."

1912 Election Cartoon
In this 1912 political cartoon, an elephant—the mascot of the Republican Party (the Grand Old Party, or GOP)—and a donkey—representing the Democratic Party—react in alarm as a bull moose charges into the fray. The bull moose, with its spectacles and gleaming teeth, caricatures Theodore Roosevelt, the new Progressive Party's presidential candidate.
Granger Collection.

REVIEW   Why did Roosevelt become the presidential nominee of the Progressive Party in 1912?

Woodrow Wilson and Progressivism at High Tide

Born in Virginia and raised in Georgia, Woodrow Wilson became the first southerner to be elected president since 1844 and only the second Democrat to occupy the White House since Reconstruction. Democrats who anticipated a wild celebration when Wilson took office had their hopes dashed. The son of a Presbyterian minister, Wilson was a teetotaler more given to Scripture than to celebration. He called instead for a day of prayer.

This lean, ascetic scholar was, as one biographer conceded, a man whose "political convictions were never as fixed as his ambition." Although he owed his governorship to the Democratic machine, he quickly turned his back on the bosses and put New Jersey in the vanguard of progressivism. A year into his term, Wilson had his eye on the presidency. Always able to equivocate, Wilson proved rarely able to compromise. He brought to the White House a gift for oratory, a stern will, and a set of fixed beliefs. His tendency to turn differences of opinion into personal hatreds would impair his leadership and damage his presidency. Fortunately for Wilson, he came to power with a Democratic Congress eager to do his bidding.

Although he opposed big government in his campaign, Wilson was prepared to work on the base built by Roosevelt to strengthen presidential power, exerting leadership to achieve banking reform and working through his party in Congress to accomplish the Democratic agenda. Before he was finished, Wilson presided over progressivism at high tide and lent his support not only to the platform of the Democratic Party but to many of the Progressive Party's social reforms as well.

Wilson's Reforms: Tariff, Banking, and the Trusts

In March 1913, Wilson showed off his oratorical ability by becoming the first president since John Adams to go to Capitol Hill and speak directly to Congress. With the Democratic Party firmly in control, he called for tariff reform. "The object of the tariff," Wilson told Congress, "must be effective competition." Eager to topple the high tariff, the Democratic House of Representatives hastily passed the Underwood tariff, which lowered rates by 15 percent. To compensate for lost revenue, the House approved a moderate federal income tax, made possible by ratification of the Sixteenth Amendment a month earlier. In the Senate, lobbyists for industries quietly went to work to get the tariff raised, but Wilson rallied public opinion by attacking the "industrious and insidious lobby." In the harsh glare of publicity, the Senate passed the Underwood tariff, which earned praise as "the most honest tariff since the Civil War."

Wilson next turned his attention to banking. The panic of 1907 dramatically testified to the failure of the banking system. That year, Roosevelt, like President Grover Cleveland before him, had to turn to J. P. Morgan to avoid economic catastrophe. But by the time Wilson came to office, Morgan's legendary power had come under close scrutiny. In 1913, a Senate committee investigated the "money trust," calling J. P. Morgan himself to testify. The committee uncovered an alarming concentration of banking power. J. P. Morgan and Company and its affiliates held 341 directorships in 112 corporations, controlling assets of more than $22 billion ($457 billion in today's dollars). The sensational findings created a mandate for banking reform.

> With the Democratic Party firmly in control, Wilson called for tariff reform. "The object of the tariff," he told Congress, "must be effective competition."

The Federal Reserve Act of 1913 marked the most significant piece of domestic legislation of Wilson's presidency. It established a national banking system composed of twelve regional banks, privately controlled but regulated and supervised by the Federal Reserve Board, appointed by the president. It gave the United States its first efficient banking and currency system and, at the same time, provided for a greater degree of government control over banking. The new system made currency more elastic and credit adequate for the needs of business and agriculture. It did not, however, attempt to take control of the boom and bust cycles in the U.S. economy, which would produce the Great Depression of the 1930s.

Wilson, flushed with success, tackled the trust issue next. When Congress reconvened in January 1914, he supported the introduction of the Clayton Antitrust Act to outlaw "unfair competition"—practices such as price discrimination and interlocking directorates (directors from one corporation sitting on the board of another). By spelling out unfair practices, Wilson hoped to guide business activity back to healthy competition without resorting to regulation. Despite a grandiose preamble that stated, "The labor of human beings is not a commodity or article of commerce," the Clayton Act did not improve labor's position. Although AFL president Samuel Gompers hailed the act as the "Magna Carta of labor," the conservative courts continued to issue injunctions and to use antitrust legislation against labor unions.

In the midst of the fight for the Clayton Act, Wilson changed course and threw his support behind the creation of the Federal Trade Commission (FTC), precisely the kind of federal regulatory agency that Roosevelt had advocated in his New Nationalism platform. The FTC, created in 1914, had not only wide investigatory powers but the authority to prosecute corporations for "unfair trade practices" and to enforce its judgments by issuing "cease and desist" orders. Despite his campaign promises, Wilson's antitrust program worked to regulate rather than to break up big business.

By the fall of 1914, Wilson had exhausted the stock of ideas that made up the New Freedom. He alarmed progressives by declaring that the progressive movement had fulfilled its mission and that the country needed "a time of healing." Disgruntled progressives also disapproved of Wilson's conservative appointments. Having fought provisions in the Federal Reserve Act that would give bankers control, Wilson promptly named a banker as the first chief of the Federal Reserve Board. Appointments to the new FTC also went to conservative businessmen. The progressive penchant for expertise helps explain Wilson's choices. Believing that experts in the field could best understand the complex issues at stake, Wilson appointed bankers to oversee the banks and businessmen to regulate business.

Wilson, Reluctant Progressive

Progressives watched in dismay as Wilson repeatedly obstructed or obstinately refused to endorse further progressive reforms. He failed to support labor's demand for an end to court injunctions against labor unions. He twice threatened to veto legislation providing farm credits for nonperishable crops. He refused to support child labor legislation or woman suffrage. Wilson used the rhetoric of the New Freedom to justify his actions, claiming that his administration would condone "special privileges to none." But, in fact, his stance often reflected the interests of his small-business constituency.

In the face of Wilson's obstinacy, reform might have ended in 1913 had not politics intruded. In the congressional elections of 1914, the Republican Party, no longer split by Roosevelt's Bull Moose faction, won substantial gains. Democratic strategists, with their eyes on the 1916 presidential race, recognized that Wilson needed to pick up support in the Midwest and the West by capturing votes from former Bull Moose progressives.

Wilson responded belatedly by lending his support to reform in the months leading up to the election of 1916. In a sharp about-face, he cultivated union labor, farmers, and social reformers. To please labor, he appointed progressive Louis Brandeis to the Supreme Court. To woo farmers, he threw his support behind legislation to obtain rural credits. And he won praise from labor by supporting workers' compensation and the Keating-Owen child labor law (1916), which outlawed the regular employment of children younger than sixteen. When a railroad strike threatened in the months before the election, Wilson practically ordered Congress to establish an eight-hour day on the railroads. He had moved a long way from his position in 1912 to embrace many of the social reforms championed by Theodore Roosevelt. As Wilson boasted, the Democrats had "opened their hearts to the demands of social justice" and had "come very near to carrying out the platform of the Progressive Party." Wilson's shift toward reform, along with his claim that he had kept the United States out of the war in Europe (see chapter 22), helped him win reelection in 1916.

REVIEW   How and why did Wilson's reform program evolve during his first term?

Progressive Poster Condemning Child Labor
This poster attacks child labor, borrowing the convention of the business flowchart to portray graphically how industries employing children were "making human junk." Progressives' concern for the plight of poor children won them the label "child savers." Although activists worked hard to pass the Keating-Owen Act prohibiting child labor in 1916, the Supreme Court declared the law unconstitutional two years later on the grounds that Congress had no right to regulate manufacturing within states. What does this poster emphasize more in its appeal to end child labor—concern for children or concern for society?
Library of Congress.

The Limits of Progressive Reform

While progressivism called for a more active role for the liberal state, at heart it was a movement that sought reforms designed to preserve American institutions and stem the tide of more radical change. Its basic conservatism can be seen by comparing it to more radical movements of the era—

Eugene V. Debs
Eugene Victor Debs, shown here campaigning in 1912, argued that the Socialist Party offered the only real hope for change for the working class. More than 900,000 voters agreed and cast their ballots for him. This photo is striking to today's audience because of the hats and suits worn by the working-class candidate and his supporters. Note that there is not a woman in sight, evidence of the predominately male electorate in the era before passage of the Nineteenth Amendment extended the vote to women. Debs, whose fiery style is captured well in this picture, argued that there was no difference between the Republican and Democratic candidates when it came to their support of capitalism, which Debs styled "wage slavery."
Photo: Brown Brothers; Button: Collection of Janice L. and David J. Frent.

socialism, radical labor, and birth control—and by looking at the groups progressive reform left behind, including women and African Americans.

Radical Alternatives

The year 1900 marked the birth of the Social Democratic Party in America, later called simply the Socialist Party. Like the progressives, the socialists were middle-class and native-born. They had broken with the older, more militant Socialist Labor Party precisely because of its dogmatic approach and immigrant constituency. The new group of socialists proved eager to appeal to a broad mass of disaffected Americans. Socialists elected mayors in Schenectady and Milwaukee, and by 1912 the party counted more than 100,000 members.

The Socialist Party chose as its presidential standard-bearer Eugene V. Debs, whose experience in the Pullman strike of 1894 convinced him that "there is no hope for the toiling masses of my countrymen, except by the pathways mapped out by Socialism." Debs would run for president five times, in every election (except 1916) from 1900 to 1920. The socialism Debs advocated preached cooperation over competition and urged men and women to liberate themselves from "the barbarism of private ownership and wage slavery." Roosevelt labeled Debs a "mere inciter to murder and preacher of applied anarchy." Debs, for his part, pointed to the conservatism that underlay Roosevelt's rhetoric. In the 1912 election, Debs indicted both old parties as "Tweedledee and Tweedledum," each dedicated to the preservation of capitalism and the continuation of the wage system. Only through socialism, he argued, could democracy exist. Styling the Socialist Party the "revolutionary party of the working class," he urged voters to rally to his standard. Debs's best showing came in 1912, when he polled 6 percent of the popular vote, capturing more than 900,000 votes.

Farther to the left of the socialists stood the Industrial Workers of the World (IWW), nicknamed the Wobblies. In 1905, Debs, along with Western Federation of Miners leader William Dudley "Big Bill" Haywood, created the IWW, "one big union" dedicated to organizing the most destitute segment of the workforce, the unskilled workers disdained by Samuel Gompers's AFL: western miners, migrant farmworkers, lumbermen, and immigrant textile workers. Haywood, a craggy-faced miner with one eye (he had lost the other in a childhood accident), was a charismatic leader and a proletarian intellectual. Seeing workers on the lowest rung of the social ladder as the victims of violent repression, the IWW un-

hesitatingly advocated direct action, sabotage, and the general strike—tactics designed to trigger a workers' uprising. The IWW never had more than 10,000 members at any one time, although possibly as many as 100,000 workers belonged to the union at one time or another in the early twentieth century. Nevertheless, the IWW's influence on the country extended far beyond its numbers.

In contrast to political radicals like Debs and Haywood, Margaret Sanger promoted birth control as a movement for social change. Sanger, a nurse who had worked among the poor on New York's Lower East Side, coined the term *birth control* in 1915 and launched a movement with broad social implications. Sanger and her followers saw birth control not only as a sexual and

Margaret Sanger's Brownsville Birth Control Clinic
Margaret Sanger opened the first birth control clinic in the United States in the Brownsville section of Brooklyn in 1916. During the nine days it operated before police shut it down, more than four hundred women visited the clinic. Here, they are shown waiting patiently in line with their baby carriages. Sanger published her fliers in English, Yiddish, and Italian. Her clinic, located in the heart of an immigrant neighborhood, proved that immigrant women—including Italian Catholics and Russian Jews—wanted information about birth control as much as their middle- and upper-class Protestant counterparts did.
Sophia Smith Collection, Smith College.

READING THE IMAGE: What does the picture and flier say about which women—married or single—sought birth control?
CONNECTIONS: What does the high number of women who visited the clinic in the few days before it was shut down suggest about the social implications of access to birth control?

FOR MORE HELP ANALYZING THIS IMAGE, see the visual activity for this chapter in the Online Study Guide at bedfordstmartins.com/roark.

medical reform but also as a means to alter social and political power relationships and to alleviate human misery.

The desire for family limitation was widespread, and in this sense, birth control was nothing new. The birthrate in the United States had been falling consistently throughout the nineteenth century. The average number of children per family dropped from 7.0 in 1800 to 3.6 by 1900. But the open advocacy of *contraception*, the use of artificial means to prevent pregnancy, struck many people as both new and shocking. And it was illegal. Anthony Comstock, New York City's commissioner of vice, promoted laws in the 1870s making it a felony not only to sell contraceptive devices like condoms and cervical caps but also to publish information on how to prevent pregnancy. Labeling birth control "obscene matter" meant the Post Office could seize and censor any article or pamphlet promoting birth control. Theodore Roosevelt was among those who fulminated against birth control as "race suicide," warning that the "white" population was declining while immigrants and "undesirables" continued to breed.

Convinced that women needed to be able to control their pregnancies but unsure of the best methods to do so, Sanger traveled to Europe in 1913 to learn more about contraceptive techniques. On her return, she promoted birth control in her militant **feminist** newspaper, the *Woman Rebel.* On the masthead in bold letters she proclaimed her motto: "No Gods, No Masters." The Post Office confiscated Sanger's publication and brought charges against her. Facing arrest, she fled to Europe, only to return in 1916 something of a national celebrity. In her absence, birth control had become linked with free speech and had been taken up as a liberal cause. Under public pressure, the government dropped the charges against Sanger, who undertook a nationwide tour to publicize the birth control cause.

Sanger then turned to direct action, opening the nation's first birth control clinic in the Brownsville section of Brooklyn in October 1916. Located in the heart of a Jewish and Italian immigrant neighborhood, the clinic attracted 464 clients in the nine days it remained open. On the tenth day, police shut down the clinic and threw Sanger in jail. By then, she had become a national figure, and the cause she championed had gained legitimacy, if not legality. After World War I, the birth control movement would become much less radical as Sanger turned to medical doctors

for support and mouthed the racist theories of the eugenics movement. But in its infancy, the movement Sanger led was part of a radical vision for reforming the world that made common cause with the socialists and the IWW in challenging the limits of progressive reform.

Progressivism for White Men Only

The day before President Woodrow Wilson's inauguration in March 1913, the largest mass march to date in the nation's history took place as more than five thousand demonstrators took to the streets in Washington to demand the vote for women. A rowdy crowd on hand to celebrate the Democrats' triumph attacked the marchers. Men spat at the suffragists and threw lighted cigarettes and matches at their clothing. "If my wife were where you are," a burly cop told one suffragist, "I'd break her head." But for all the marching, Wilson, who didn't believe that a "lady" should vote, pointedly ignored woman suffrage in his inaugural address the next day.

The march served as a reminder that the political gains of progressivism were not spread equally throughout the population. As the twentieth century dawned, women still could not vote in most states, although they had won major victories in the West. Increasingly, however, woman suffrage had become an international movement. In Great Britain, Emmeline Pankhurst and her daughters Cristabel and Sylvia promoted a new, militant suffragism. They seized the spotlight in a series of marches, mass meetings, and acts of **civil disobedience**, which sometimes escalated into riots, violence, and arson.

Alice Paul, a Quaker social worker who had visited England and participated in suffrage activism there, returned to the United States in 1910 in time to plan the mass march on the eve of Wilson's inauguration and to lobby for a federal amendment to give women the vote. Paul's dramatic tactics alienated many in the National American Woman Suffrage Association (NAWSA). In 1916, Paul founded the militant National Woman's Party (NWP), which became the radical voice of the suffrage movement, advocating direct action such as mass marches and civil disobedience.

The NAWSA, spurred by the actions of Paul and her followers, gained new direction after Carrie Chapman Catt became president in 1915. Catt revitalized the organization with a carefully crafted "winning plan" designed to achieve suffrage in six years. While Paul and her NWP held a six-

month vigil outside the White House—holding banners that read "Mr. Wilson, What Will You Do for Woman Suffrage?"—Catt led a centrally directed effort that worked on several levels. Catt's strategy was to "keep so much 'suffrage noise' going all over the country that neither the enemy [n]or friends will discover where the real battle is." Catt's "winning plan" worked. It took only four years instead of the six Catt had predicted to obtain ratification of the Nineteenth Amendment granting woman suffrage.

Women weren't the only group left out in progressive reform. Progressivism, as it was practiced in the West and South, was tainted with racism and sought to limit the rights of African and Asian Americans. Anti-Asian bigotry in the West led to a renewal of the Chinese Exclusion Act in 1902. At first, California governor Hiram Johnson stood against the strong anti-Asian prejudice of his state. Then, in 1913, he caved in to near-unanimous pressure and signed the Alien Land Law, which barred Japanese immigrants from purchasing land in California. The law was largely symbolic—ineffectual in practice because Japanese children born in the United States were U.S. citizens and property could be purchased in their names.

South of the Mason-Dixon line, the progressives' racism targeted African Americans. Progressives preached the **disfranchisement** of black voters as a "reform." During the bitter electoral fights that had pitted Populists against Democrats in the 1890s, the party of white supremacy held its power by votes purchased or coerced from African Americans. Southern progressives proposed to "reform" the electoral system by eliminating black voters. Beginning in 1890 with Mississippi, southern states curtailed the African American vote through devices such as poll taxes (fees required for voting) and literacy tests. The racist intent of southern voting legislation became especially clear after 1900 when states resorted to the grandfather clause, a legal provision that allowed men who failed a literacy test to vote if their grandfathers had cast a ballot. Grandfathering permitted southern white men to vote while excluding blacks.

The Progressive Era also witnessed the rise of **Jim Crow** laws to segregate public facilities. The new railroads precipitated segregation in the

Inez Milholland Leads the Washington Suffrage Parade

In 1913, when women marched on Washington, D.C., to demand the vote, the mass march was a novel tactic. Many worried that women would not be physically able to march the full distance. Ambulances stood by to tend to any who fainted along the way. Led by Inez Hayes Milholland, riding her horse Grey Dawn, the women proved neither faint nor fainthearted. They had to fend off angry crowds that attacked them and tried to break up the parade. Surrounded by one nasty mob, Milholland, spurring her horse into the crowd, shouted, "You men ought to be ashamed of yourselves." The men fell back, some of them raising a cheer for suffrage's "white knight." Despite the publicity surrounding the march, incoming president Woodrow Wilson refused even to acknowledge the suffragists' protest in his inaugural address the following day. Sophia Smith Collection, Smith College.

DINNER GIVEN AT THE WHITE HOUSE BY PRESIDENT ROOSEVELT TO BOOKER T. WASHINGTON, OCTOBER 17th, 1901

Booker T. Washington and Theodore Roosevelt Dine at the White House
When Theodore Roosevelt invited Booker T. Washington to the White House in 1901, he stirred up
a hornet's nest of controversy that continued into the election of 1904. This Republican campaign
piece gives the meeting a positive slant, showing Roosevelt and a light-skinned Washington sitting
under a portrait of Abraham Lincoln, a symbol of the party's historic commitment to African Americans.
Democrats portrayed the meeting in a very different light; their campaign buttons pictured Washington
with darker skin and implied that Roosevelt favored "race mingling."
Collection of Janice L. and David J. Frent.

South where it had rarely existed before, at least on paper. Blacks traveling by train found themselves restricted to Jim Crow coaches even when they paid the first-class fare. Soon, separate waiting rooms, separate bathrooms, and separate dining facilities for blacks sprang up across the South. In courtrooms in Mississippi, blacks were even required to swear on a separate Bible.

In the face of this growing repression, Booker T. Washington, the preeminent black leader of the day, urged caution and restraint. A former slave, Washington had opened the Tuskegee Institute in Alabama in 1881 to teach vocational skills to African Americans. He emphasized education and economic progress for his race and urged African Americans to put aside issues of political and social equality. In an 1895 speech in Atlanta, which came to be known as the "Atlanta Compromise," he stated, "In all things that are purely social we can be as separate as the fingers, yet one as the hand in all things essential to mutual progress." Washington's accommodationist policy appealed to whites and elevated "the wizard of Tuskegee" to the role of national spokesman for African Americans.

The year after Washington proclaimed the Atlanta Compromise, the Supreme Court upheld the legality of racial segregation, affirming in *Plessy v. Ferguson* (1896) the constitutionality of the doctrine of "separate but equal." Blacks could be segregated in separate schools, restrooms, and other facilities, as long as the facilities were "equal" to those provided for whites. In actuality, facilities for blacks rarely proved equal. In the North, where racism of a different sort led to a clamor for legislation to restrict immigration, support for African American equality found few advocates. And with anti-Asian bigotry strong in the West, the doctrine of "white supremacy" found increasing support in all sections of the country.

When Theodore Roosevelt invited Booker T. Washington to dine at the White House in 1901, a storm of racist criticism erupted. One southern editor fumed that the White House "had been painted black." But Roosevelt summoned Washington to talk politics and patronage, not African American rights. Roosevelt's unquestioned racial prejudice became obvious in the Brownsville incident in 1906, when he dishonorably discharged an entire battalion of 167 black soldiers because he suspected (although there was no proof) that they were shielding the murderer of a white saloon-keeper killed in a shoot-out in the Texas town.

Woodrow Wilson brought to the White House southern attitudes toward race and racial segregation. He instituted segregation in the federal workforce, especially the Post Office, and approved segregated drinking fountains and restrooms in the nation's capital. When critics attacked the policy, Wilson insisted that segregation was "in the interest of the Negro."

A major race riot in Atlanta in 1906 called into question Booker T. Washington's strategy of up-lift and accommodation. For three days in September, the streets of Atlanta ran red with blood as angry white mobs chased and cornered any blacks they happened upon, pulling passengers from streetcars and invading black neighborhoods to kill and loot. An estimated 250 African Americans died in the riots—members of Atlanta's black middle class along with the poor and derelict. Professor William Crogman of Clark College noted the central irony of the riot: "Here we have worked and prayed and tried to make good men and women of our colored population," he observed, "and at our very doorstep the whites kill these good men." In Dark Town, a working-class neighborhood, blacks fought back to defend their homes, shooting into the white mob and driving off the attackers. In the aftermath of the riot, the city's leaders, black and white, managed to quash any nascent black unity by falling back on the old strategy of allying "the best white people and the best colored people" in the interest of peace and prosperity. But the riot caused many African Americans to question Washington's strategy of gradualism and accommodation.

Foremost among Washington's critics stood W. E. B. Du Bois, a Harvard graduate who urged African Americans to fight for civil rights and racial justice. In *The Souls of Black Folk* (1903), Du Bois attacked the "Tuskegee Machine," comparing Washington to a political boss who used his

W. E. B. Du Bois
W. E. B. Du Bois grew up in Great Barrington, Massachusetts, and attended Fisk University. In 1895, he became the first African American to earn a doctorate from Harvard. Throughout his life, he urged African Americans not only to focus on their own education and economic prospects but also to work politically for racial equality. In *The Souls of Black Folk* (1903), he wrote that he wished "to make it possible for a man to be both a Negro and an American, without being cursed and spit upon by his fellows, without having the doors of Opportunity closed roughly in his face."
Photo: Special Collections Department, W. E. B. Du Bois Library, University of Massachusetts Amherst; Book: Newberry Library.

influence to silence his critics and reward his followers. Du Bois founded the Niagara movement in 1905, calling for universal male suffrage, civil rights, and leadership by a black intellectual elite. The Atlanta riot only bolstered his resolve. In 1909, the Niagara movement helped found the National Association for the Advancement of Colored People (NAACP), a coalition of blacks and whites that sought legal and political rights for African Americans through the courts. Like many progressive reform coalitions, the NAACP attracted a diverse group—social workers, socialists, and black intellectuals. In the decades that followed, the NAACP came to represent the future for African Americans, while Booker T. Washington, who died in 1915, represented the past.

> **REVIEW** How did race, class, and gender shape the limits of progressive reform?

Conclusion: The Transformation of the Liberal State

Progressivism was never a radical movement. Its goal remained to reform the existing system—by government intervention if necessary, but without uprooting any of the traditional American political, economic, or social institutions. As Theodore Roosevelt, the bellwether of the movement, insisted, "The only true conservative is the man who resolutely sets his face toward the future." Roosevelt was such a man, and progressivism was such a movement. But although progressivism was never radical, neither was it the laissez-faire liberalism of the previous century. Progressives' willingness to use the power of government to regulate business and achieve a measure of social justice redefined liberalism in the twentieth century, tying it to the expanded power of the state.

Progressivism contained many paradoxes. A diverse coalition of individuals and interests, the progressive movement began at the grass roots but left as its legacy a stronger presidency and unprecedented federal involvement in the economy and social welfare. A movement that believed in social justice, progressivism often promoted social control. And while progressives called for greater democracy, they fostered elitism with their worship of experts and efficiency.

Whatever its inconsistencies and limitations, progressivism took action to deal with the problems posed by urban industrialism. Progressivism saw grassroots activists address social problems on the local and state levels and search for national solutions. By increasing the power of the presidency and expanding the power of the state, progressives worked to bring about greater social justice and to achieve a better balance between government and business. Jane Addams and Theodore Roosevelt could lay equal claim to the movement that redefined liberalism and launched the liberal state of the twentieth century. War on a global scale would provide progressivism with yet another challenge even before it had completed its ambitious agenda.

Selected Bibliography

Grassroots Progressivism

Victoria Bissell Brown, *The Education of Jane Addams* (2004).
Ellen Fitzpatrick, *Endless Crusade: Women, Social Scientists, and Progressive Reform* (1990).
Robert Kanigel, *The One Best Way: Frederick Winslow Taylor* (1997).
Louise W. Knight, *Citizen: Jane Addams and the Struggle for Democracy* (2005).
Seth Koven and Sonya Michel, eds., *Mothers of a New World: Maternalist Politics and the Origins of the Welfare State* (1993).
Robyn Muncy, *Creating a Female Dominion in American Reform* (1991).
Kathryn Kish Sklar, *Florence Kelley and the Nation's Work: The Rise of Women's Political Culture, 1830–1900* (1995).
Landon R. Y. Storre, *Civilizing Capitalism: The National Consumers' League, Women's Activism, and Labor Standards in the New Deal Era* (2000).
David Straddling, *Smokestacks and Progressives: Environmentalists, Engineers, and Air Quality in America, 1881–1951* (1999).
Nancy C. Unger, *Fighting Bob La Follette: The Righteous Reformer* (2000).
David Von Drehle, *Triangle: The Fire That Changed America* (2003).
Michael A. Weatherson and Hal W. Bochin, *Hiram Johnson, Political Revivalist* (1995).

Progressive Politics and Diplomacy

James Chace, *1912: Wilson, Roosevelt, Taft and Debs—The Election That Changed the Country* (2004).
Alan Dawley, *Struggles for Justice: Social Responsibility and the Liberal State* (1991).
Alan Dawley, *Changing the World: American Progressives in War and Revolution* (2003).

Steven Diner, *A Very Different Age: Americans of the Progressive Era* (1998).

Brett Flehinger, *The 1912 Election and the Power of Progressivism* (2003).

Matthew Frye Jacobson, *Barbarian Virtues: The United States Encounters Foreign Peoples at Home and Abroad, 1876–1917* (2000).

Richard Coke Lower, *A Bloc of One: The Political Career of Hiram W. Johnson* (1993).

Michael McGerr, *A Fierce Discontent: The Rise and Fall of the Progressive Movement in America, 1870–1920* (2003).

Robert W. Righter, *The Battle over Hetch Hetchy: America's Most Controversial Dam and the Birth of Modern Environmentalism* (2005).

Daniel T. Rodgers, *Atlantic Crossings: Social Politics in a Progressive Age* (1998).

Radicals, Race Relations, and Woman Suffrage

Mary Jo Buhle, *Women and American Socialism, 1870–1920* (1981).

Ellen Chesler, *Woman of Valor: Margaret Sanger and the Birth Control Movement in America* (1993).

Melvyn Dubofsky, *"Big Bill" Haywood* (1987).

Gary Gerstle, *American Crucible: Race and Nation in the Twentieth Century* (2002).

Glenda Elizabeth Gilmore, *Gender and Jim Crow: Women and the Politics of White Supremacy in North Carolina, 1896–1920* (1996).

David Fort Godshalk, *Veiled Visions: The 1906 Atlanta Race Riot and the Reshaping of American Race Relations* (2005).

Evelyn Higginbotham, *Righteous Discontent: The Women's Movement in the Black Baptist Church, 1880–1920* (1993).

David Levering Lewis, *W. E. B. Du Bois: Biography of a Race, 1868–1919* (1993).

Linda J. Lumsden, *Inez: The Life and Times of Inez Milholland* (2004).

Suzanne M. Mari, *Woman Suffrage and the Origins of Liberal Feminism in the United States, 1820–1920* (1996).

Rebecca J. Mead, *How the Vote Was Won: Woman Suffrage in the Western United States, 1868–1914* (2004).

Nick Salvatore, *Eugene V. Debs: Citizen and Socialist* (1982).

▶ FOR MORE BOOKS ABOUT TOPICS IN THIS CHAPTER, see the Online Bibliography at bedfordstmartins.com/roark.

▶ FOR ADDITIONAL FIRSTHAND ACCOUNTS OF THIS PERIOD, see Chapter 21 in Michael Johnson, ed., *Reading the American Past*, Fourth Edition.

▶ FOR WEB SITES, IMAGES, AND DOCUMENTS RELATED TO TOPICS AND PLACES IN THIS CHAPTER, visit bedfordstmartins.com/makehistory.

REVIEWING THE CHAPTER

Follow these steps to review and strengthen your understanding of the chapter.

STEP 1: Study the **Key Terms** and **Timeline** to identify the significance of each item listed.

STEP 2: Answer the **Review Questions**, drawing on key terms and dates to support your answers.

STEP 3: Drawing on the Key Terms, Timeline, and Review Questions, answer the broader **Making Connections** questions.

KEY TERMS

Who

Jane Addams (p. 745)
Lillian Wald (p. 747)
Walter Rauschenbusch (p. 748)
Florence Kelley (p. 753)
John Dewey (p. 754)
Frederick Winslow Taylor (p. 754)
Thomas Loftin Johnson (p. 755)
Robert M. La Follette (p. 755)
Hiram Johnson (p. 755)
William McKinley (p. 756)
Leon Czolgosz (p. 756)
Theodore Roosevelt (p. 756)
J. P. Morgan (p. 758)
Upton Sinclair (p. 760)
Gifford Pinchot (p. 764)
John Muir (p. 764)
William Howard Taft (p. 769)
Woodrow Wilson (p. 771)
Eugene V. Debs (p. 772)
William Dudley "Big Bill" Haywood
   (p. 777)
Margaret Sanger (p. 777)

Alice Paul (p. 778)
Carrie Chapman Catt (p. 778)
Booker T. Washington (p. 780)
W. E. B. Du Bois (p. 781)

What

social gospel (p. 747)
social purity movement (p. 747)
Women's Trade Union League (WTUL)
   (p. 749)
Triangle fire (p. 750)
Muller v. Oregon (p. 750)
National Consumers' League (NCL) (p. 752)
reform Darwinism (p. 754)
pragmatism (p. 754)
scientific management (p. 754)
Square Deal (p. 757)
Interstate Commerce Commission (ICC)
   (p. 760)
Hepburn Act (p. 760)
Pure Food and Drug Act (p. 760)
panic of 1907 (p. 761)
Hetch Hetchy valley (p. 764)

Newlands Reclamation Act (p. 764)
Panama Canal (p. 768)
Roosevelt Corollary (p. 768)
Payne-Aldrich tariff (p. 771)
dollar diplomacy (p. 771)
Progressive Party (Bull Moose Party)
   (p. 772)
"The New Nationalism" (p. 772)
"The New Freedom" (p. 772)
Underwood tariff (p. 774)
Federal Reserve Act of 1913 (p. 774)
Clayton Antitrust Act (p. 774)
Federal Trade Commission (FTC) (p. 774)
Socialist Party (p. 776)
Industrial Workers of the World (IWW;
   Wobblies) (p. 777)
National Woman's Party (NWP) (p. 778)
Atlanta Compromise (p. 780)
Plessy v. Ferguson (p. 780)
Atlanta race riot (p. 781)
National Association for the
   Advancement of Colored People
   (NAACP) (p. 782)

TIMELINE

◀ **1889** • Jane Addams opens Hull House.

1895 • Booker T. Washington enunciates Atlanta Compromise.

1896 • *Plessy v. Ferguson.*

1900 • Socialist Party founded.

1901 • William McKinley assassinated; Theodore Roosevelt becomes president.

1902 • Antitrust lawsuit filed against Northern Securities Company.
• Roosevelt mediates anthracite coal strike.
• Newlands Reclamation Act.

1903 • Women's Trade Union League founded.
• United States begins construction of Panama Canal.
• Elkins Act.

1904 • Roosevelt Corollary to Monroe Doctrine.

1905 • Industrial Workers of the World founded.
• W. E. B. Du Bois founds Niagara movement.
• Roosevelt mediates at Algeciras conference.

1906 • Pure Food and Drug Act and Meat Inspection Act.
• Atlanta race riot.
• Hepburn Act.

REVIEW QUESTIONS

1. What types of people were drawn to the progressive movement, and what motivated them? (pp. 747–54)

2. How did progressives justify their demand for more activist government? (pp. 754–56)

3. How did Roosevelt's foreign policy move the United States onto the world stage? (pp. 756–69)

4. Why did Roosevelt become the presidential nominee of the Progressive Party in 1912? (pp. 769–73)

5. How and why did Wilson's reform program evolve during his first term? (pp. 773–75)

6. How did race, class, and gender shape the limits of progressive reform? (pp. 775–82)

MAKING CONNECTIONS

1. Diverse approaches to reform came under the umbrella of progressivism. Discuss the work of three progressive reformers working at the grassroots or local government level. What do your examples reveal about progressivism? What characteristics connected their reform efforts? What separated them?

2. During the Gilded Age, industrial capitalism concentrated power in the hands of corporations. Americans searched for ways to shift the balance, including strikes, antitrust actions, and regulation. How did Theodore Roosevelt attempt to respond to this problem? How did his approach differ from earlier efforts? Was it effective?

3. Opponents on the campaign stump, Theodore Roosevelt and Woodrow Wilson shared a commitment to domestic reform. Compare their legislative programs, including the evolution of their policies over time and their ability to respond to shifting political circumstances. What do their policies reveal about their understandings of the roles of the executive and the federal government?

4. What contemporary movements lay beyond the limits of progressive reform? Why did progressive reform coincide with the restriction of minority rights? In your answer, discuss how radical movements provide insights into the character of progressivism itself.

▶ **FOR PRACTICE QUIZZES, A CUSTOMIZED STUDY PLAN, AND OTHER STUDY TOOLS,** see the Online Study Guide at bedfordstmartins.com/roark.

1907 • Panic on Wall Street.
    • Roosevelt signs "Gentlemen's Agreement" with Japan restricting immigration.
  1908 • *Muller v. Oregon.*
      • Republican William Howard Taft elected president.
    1909 • Garment workers' strike in New York City.
        • National Association for the Advancement of Colored People (NAACP) formed.
      1910 • Hiram Johnson elected governor of California.

        1911 • Triangle fire in New York City.
          • Taft launches antitrust suit against U.S. Steel.
          1912 • Roosevelt runs for president on Progressive Party ticket.
            • Democrat Woodrow Wilson elected president.
            1913 • Suffragists march in Washington, D.C.
              • Federal Reserve Act.
              1914 • Federal Trade Commission (FTC) created.
                • Clayton Antitrust Act.
                1916 • Alice Paul launches National Woman's Party.
                  • Margaret Sanger opens first U.S. birth control clinic.
                  • Keating-Owen child labor law.
                    1918 • Supreme Court declares Keating-Owen unconstitutional.

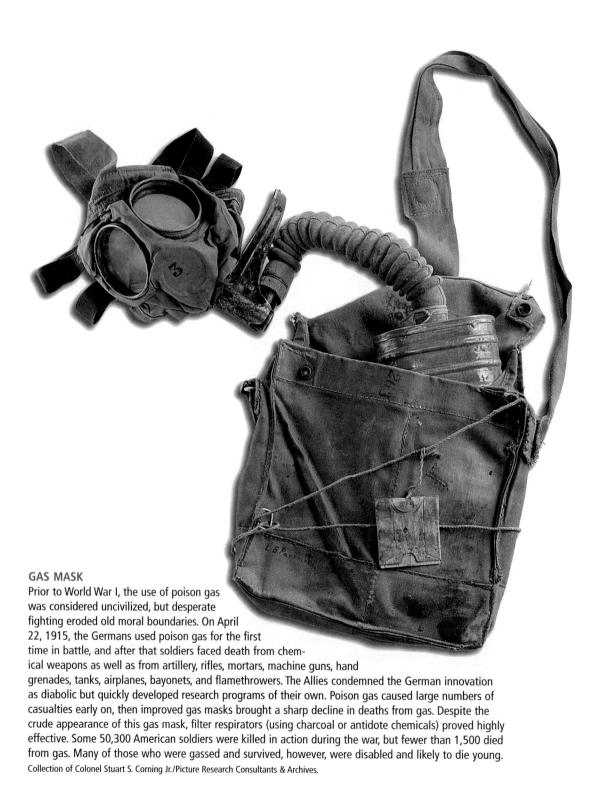

GAS MASK

Prior to World War I, the use of poison gas
was considered uncivilized, but desperate
fighting eroded old moral boundaries. On April
22, 1915, the Germans used poison gas for the first
time in battle, and after that soldiers faced death from chemical weapons as well as from artillery, rifles, mortars, machine guns, hand
grenades, tanks, airplanes, bayonets, and flamethrowers. The Allies condemned the German innovation
as diabolic but quickly developed research programs of their own. Poison gas caused large numbers of
casualties early on, then improved gas masks brought a sharp decline in deaths from gas. Despite the
crude appearance of this gas mask, filter respirators (using charcoal or antidote chemicals) proved highly
effective. Some 50,300 American soldiers were killed in action during the war, but fewer than 1,500 died
from gas. Many of those who were gassed and survived, however, were disabled and likely to die young.

22

World War I: The Progressive Crusade at Home and Abroad

1914–1920

WHEN THE UNITED STATES entered World War I against Germany and its allies in 1917, it had neither a grand army nor a commander to lead one. But President Woodrow Wilson quickly tapped Major General John "Black Jack" Pershing, a ramrod-straight West Point graduate, to command the American Expeditionary Force (AEF) on the battlefields of France. Pershing had much to recommend him: He fought Apaches in the West in the 1880s, led a company of African American soldiers up San Juan Hill in Cuba in 1898 (hence his nickname "Black Jack"), overcame fierce resistance in the Philippine jungles in the first decade of the twentieth century, and headed Wilson's Punitive Expedition into Mexico in 1916 and 1917 in pursuit of the revolutionary bandit Pancho Villa. Pershing's courage and resilience had been severely tested in 1915 when he suffered the devastating loss of his wife and three daughters in a fire at their home in San Francisco.

On June 13, 1917, Pershing and his officer corps arrived in war-weary France, where huge crowds shouted "Vive l'Amérique!" and greeted the Americans as saviors. But Pershing knew that it would be months before America's disorganized war effort succeeded in supplying a steady stream of "doughboys," as American troops would be called. Pershing, who was responsible for organizing, training, and supplying this inexperienced force that eventually numbered two million, put his own stamp on the AEF. "The standards for the American Army will be those of West Point," he announced. "The upright bearing, attention to detail, uncomplaining obedience to instruction required of the cadet will be required of every officer and soldier of our armies in France." Hard and relentless, Pershing more than once chewed out an exhausted soldier for having mud on his boots and his collar unbuttoned.

Pershing found himself waging two wars, one against the Germans and the other against America's allies, as he constantly rebuffed French and British efforts to feed his fresh soldiers into their decimated and demoralized armies. Having seen too much of Europe's trench warfare, where enemies dug in, pounded one another with artillery, and squandered thousands of lives in hopeless assaults, Pershing insisted on keeping U.S. soldiers under his own command. He believed that the Americans could break the impasse by relying on the rifle and rapid-movement tactics taught at West Point to create "open

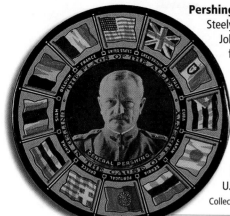

Pershing Button
Steely-eyed and determined, General John J. Pershing, surrounded by the flags of the Allied nations, stares out at the viewer. The words circling the button declare that the Allies are "united in the cause of liberty," echoing President Woodrow Wilson's insistence that American democratic ideals were universal and could be achieved internationally through U.S. participation in the war.
Collection of Janice L. and David J. Frent.

warfare," an American style of warfare. But as a disgusted British journalist observed, "After eight months . . . you haven't really fired a damned shot!"

By the summer of 1918, when the Allied armies began preparing a massive attack against the Germans, Ferdinand Foch, head of the French army, rushed to Pershing's headquarters to "insist" once again that U.S. troops merge with his depleted divisions. Pershing responded: "Marshal Foch, you may insist all you please, but . . . our army will fight . . . only as an independent American Army." Foch stormed out, and Pershing readied his army to strike at the German forces dug in at St.-Mihiel and to begin what he was certain would be a victory march to Berlin. Assembling his officers, Pershing praised them for what they were about to do—break the stalemate of trench warfare. But U.S. troops met a storm of machine-gun and artillery fire, and it took forty days and 100,000 casualties for the Americans to reach the German border, something Pershing had thought his soldiers could do in a few days. Nevertheless, fresh American troops helped destroy the German will to continue the war. In November 1918, Berlin asked for an immediate armistice, and the "Great War," as participants called the conflict, ended.

Pershing's stubborn effort to protect the autonomy of his army was only part of the United States' tortuous struggle to identify its interests in World War I and to maintain its national independence. When Wilson entered the White House, he believed that war was an affliction that modern diplomacy would eventually eradicate. He proclaimed America's absolute neutrality when war erupted in Europe in 1914. By standing apart, Wilson explained, America could

offer "impartial mediation" and broker a healing peace. But trade and principle soon entangled the United States in Europe's troubles. When the nation was finally drawn into the war in 1917, Wilson sought to maintain America's grand purpose. Clinging to his battered ideals, he hoped that America's participation would uplift both the United States and the entire world.

At home, the war helped reformers finally achieve their goals of national prohibition and woman **suffrage**, but it also promoted a vicious attack on Americans' civil liberties. Hyperpatriotism meant intolerance, repression, and vigilante violence. Overseas, Pershing's troops helped win the war in 1918, and in 1919 Wilson sailed for Europe to secure a just peace. Unable to dictate a settlement to the victors, Wilson accepted disappointing compromises. Upon his return to the United States, he met a crushing defeat that marked the end of Wilsonian internationalism. Crackdowns on dissenters, immigrants, racial and ethnic minorities, and unions signaled the end of the **Progressive** Era at home.

Woodrow Wilson and the World

Shortly after winning election to the presidency in 1912, Woodrow Wilson confided to a friend: "It would be an irony of fate if my administration had to deal with foreign affairs." Indeed, Wilson had focused his life and career on domestic concerns, seldom venturing far from home and traveling abroad only on brief vacations. As president of Princeton University and then governor of New Jersey, he had remained rooted in local affairs. In his campaign for the presidency, Wilson spoke passionately about domestic reform but hardly mentioned foreign affairs.

But Wilson could not avoid the world and the rising tide of militarism, **nationalism**, and violence that beat against American shores. Economic interests compelled the nation outward. Moreover, Wilson was drawn abroad by his own progressive political principles. He believed that the United States had a moral duty to champion national self-determination, peaceful free trade, and political **democracy**. "We have no selfish ends to serve," he proclaimed. "We desire no conquest, no dominion. . . . We are but one of the champions of the rights of mankind." Yet as president, Wilson revealed he was as ready as any American president to apply military solutions to problems of foreign policy.

Taming the Americas

When he took office, Wilson sought to distinguish his foreign policy from that of his Republican predecessors. To Wilson, Theodore Roosevelt's "big stick" and William Howard Taft's "dollar diplomacy" appeared a crude flexing of military and economic muscle. To signal a new direction, Wilson appointed William Jennings Bryan as secretary of state. A pacifist on religious grounds, Bryan immediately turned his attention to making agreements with thirty nations for the peaceful settlement of disputes.

But Wilson and Bryan, like Roosevelt and Taft, also believed that the **Monroe Doctrine** gave the United States special rights and respon-

sibilities in the Western Hemisphere. Issued in 1823 to warn Europeans not to attempt to **colonize** the New World again, the doctrine had become a cloak for U.S. domination. Wilson thus authorized the 1912 occupation of Nicaragua by U.S. marines to thwart a radical revolution that threatened property owned by U.S. businesses. In 1915, he sent marines into Haiti to quell lawlessness and to protect U.S. interests, and in 1916 he followed a similar course in the Dominican Republic. Throughout the Western Hemisphere, U.S. military intervention paved the way for the financial domination of stateside banks and corporations. All the while, Wilson believed that U.S. actions were promoting order and democracy. "I am going to teach the South American Republics to elect good men!" he declared. He did not mention protecting the Panama Canal and U.S. investments (Map 22.1).

Wilson's most serious involvement in Latin America came in Mexico. When General Victoriano

---

MAP 22.1   U.S. Involvement in Latin America and the Caribbean, 1895–1941
Victory against Spain in 1898 made Puerto Rico an American possession and Cuba a protectorate. The United States later gained control of the Panama Canal Zone. The nation was quick to protect expanding economic interests with military force by propping up friendly, though not necessarily democratic, governments.

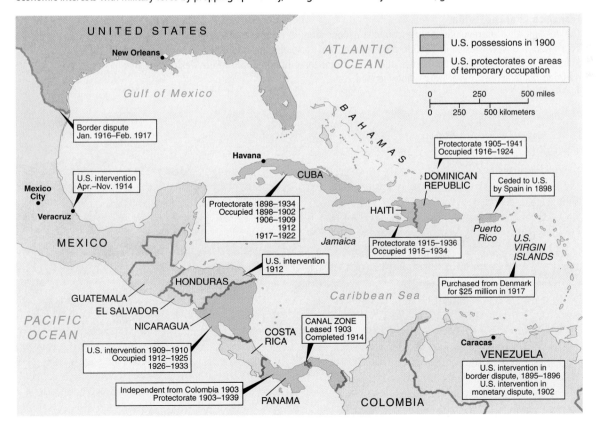

U.S. Intervention in Mexico, 1916–1917

Huerta seized power by violent means, most European nations promptly recognized Mexico's new government, but Wilson refused, declaring that he would not support a "government of butchers." In April 1914, when Huerta refused to apologize for briefly detaining American sailors in Tampico, Wilson sent 800 marines to seize the port of Veracruz to prevent the unloading of a large shipment of arms for Huerta, who was by then involved in a civil war of his own. Huerta fled to Spain, and the United States welcomed a more compliant government.

Wilson was not able to subdue Mexico that easily, however. A rebellion erupted among desperately poor farmers who believed that the new government of Venustiano Carranza, aided by U.S. business interests, had betrayed the revolution's promise to help the common people. In January 1916, the rebel army, commanded by Francisco "Pancho" Villa, seized a train carrying gold to Texas from an American-owned mine in Mexico and killed the 17 American engineers aboard. On March 9, a band of some 400 to 500 of Villa's men crossed the border for a predawn raid on Columbus, New Mexico. They stayed for less than two hours, but they burned much of Columbus and killed 18 Americans. Wilson promptly dispatched 12,000 troops, led by General John J. Pershing. The wily Villa avoided capture, and in January 1917, Wilson recalled Pershing so that he might prepare the army for the possibility of fighting in the Great War.

The European Crisis

Before 1914, Europe had enjoyed decades of peace, but just beneath the surface lay the potentially destructive forces of nationalism and **imperialism**. The consolidation of the German and Italian states into unified nations and the similar ambition of Russia to create a "Pan-Slavic" union initiated new rivalries throughout Europe. As the conviction spread that colonial possessions were a mark of national greatness, competition expanded onto the world stage. Most ominously, Germany's efforts under Kaiser Wilhelm II to challenge Great

Francisco "Pancho" Villa

The dashing Mexican revolutionary Pancho Villa gallops along a column of his soldiers in 1914. After Villa's raid into New Mexico in 1916 to punish Americans for aiding his revolutionary rivals, General John J. Pershing dove across the border, pursued Villa for three hundred miles into Mexico, and then returned home almost a year later empty-handed.

Brown Brothers.

Britain's world supremacy by creating industrial muscle at home, an empire abroad, and a mighty navy threatened the balance of power and thus the peace.

European nations sought to avoid an explosion with a complex web of military and diplomatic alliances. By 1914, Germany, Austria-Hungary, and Italy (the Triple Alliance) stood opposed to Great Britain, France, and Russia (the Triple Entente, also known as "the Allies"). But in their effort to prevent war through a balance of power, Europeans had actually magnified the possibility of large-scale conflict by creating trip wires along the boundaries of two heavily armed power blocs (Map 22.2). Treaties, some of them secret, obligated members of the alliances to come to the aid of another member if attacked.

The fatal sequence began on June 28, 1914, in the Bosnian city of Sarajevo, when a Bosnian Serb terrorist assassinated Archduke Franz Ferdinand, heir to the Austro-Hungarian throne. On July 18, Austria-Hungary declared war on Serbia, holding it accountable for the killing. The elaborate **alliance system** meant that the war could not remain local. Russia announced that it would back the Serbs. Compelled by treaty to support Austria-Hungary, Germany on August 3 attacked Russia and France. In response, on August 4, Great Britain, upholding its pact with France, declared war on Germany. Within weeks, Europe was engulfed in war. The conflict became a world war when Japan, seeing an opportunity to rid itself of European competition in China, joined the cause against Germany.

Recognizing that war would devastate the civilization he knew, Britain's foreign secretary, Edward Grey, announced sadly: "The lamps are going out all over Europe. We shall not see them lit again in our lifetime." Indeed, the evenly matched alliances would fight a long and bloody war lasting more than four years, at a cost of 8.5 million soldiers' lives—an entire generation of young men. A war that started with a solitary murder proved impossible to stop.

The Ordeal of American Neutrality

Woodrow Wilson promptly announced that the war was purely a European matter. Because it engaged no vital American interest and involved no significant principle, he said, the United States

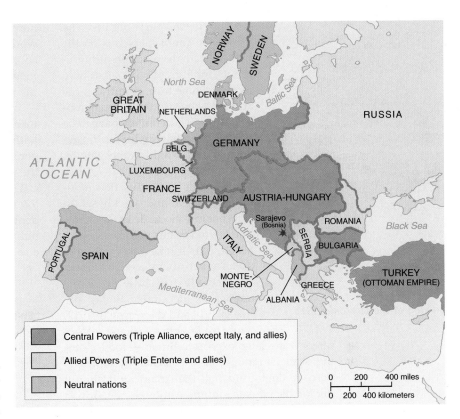

MAP 22.2   European Alliances after the Outbreak of World War I
With Germany and Austria-Hungary wedged between their Entente rivals and all parties fully armed, Europe was poised for war when Archduke Franz Ferdinand of Austria-Hungary was assassinated in Sarajevo in June 1914.

would remain neutral and continue normal relations with the warring nations. America had traditionally insisted that "free ships made free goods"—that neutral nations were entitled to trade safely with all nations at war and to demand the safe passage of their citizens on the merchant and passenger ships of all belligerents. But more was involved than lofty principle. In the year before Europe went to war, the U.S. economy had slipped into a recession that wartime disruption of European trade could drastically worsen.

Although Wilson proclaimed neutrality, his sympathies, like those of many Americans, lay with Great Britain and France. Americans remembered gratefully crucial French assistance in the American Revolution. And they shared with the British a language, a **culture**, and a commitment to **liberty**. Germany, in contrast, was a monarchy with strong militaristic traditions. The British portrayed the German ruler, Kaiser Wilhelm II, as personally responsible for the war's atrocities, and before long American newspapers were labeling him "the Mad Dog of Europe" and "the Beast of Berlin." Still, Wilson insisted on

German submarine blockade

NOR.

North Sea

DEN.

GREAT BRITAIN   NETH.

Lusitania sunk

BELG.

ATLANTIC OCEAN

LUX.

GERMANY

FRANCE   SWITZ.

ITALY

PORT.   SPAIN

Sinking of the *Lusitania*, 1915

neutrality, in part because he feared the conflict's effects on the United States as a nation of immigrants, millions of whom had only recently come from countries now at war. As he told the German ambassador, "We definitely have to be neutral, since otherwise our mixed populations would wage war on each other."

Britain's powerful fleet controlled the seas and quickly set up an economic blockade of Germany. The United States vigorously protested, but Britain refused to give up its naval advantage. The blockade actually had little economic impact on the United States. Between 1914 and the spring of 1917, while trade with Germany evaporated, war-related exports to Britain—food, clothing, steel, and munitions—escalated by some 400 percent, enough to pull the American economy out of its prewar slump. Although the British blockade bruised American feelings and clearly violated American neutrality, the Wilson administration gradually and reluctantly acquiesced, thus beginning the fateful process of alienation from Germany.

Germany retaliated with a submarine blockade of British ports. This terrifying new form of combat by *Unterseebooten*, or U-boats, threatened traditional rules of war. Unlike surface warships that could harmlessly stop freighters and prevent them from entering a war zone, submarines relied on surprising and sinking their quarry. And once they sank a ship, the tiny U-boats could not possibly pick up survivors. Britain portrayed the submarine as an outlaw weapon that violated notions of "civilized" warfare. Nevertheless, in February 1915, Germany announced that it intended to sink on sight enemy ships en route to the British Isles. On May 7, 1915, a German U-boat torpedoed the British passenger liner *Lusitania*, killing 1,198 passengers, 128 of them U.S. citizens.

Front pages of American newspapers featured drawings of drowning women and children, and some demanded war. Others pointed out that Germany had warned prospective passengers and that the *Lusitania* carried millions of rounds of ammunition and so was a legitimate target. Secretary of State Bryan resisted the hysteria and declared that a ship carrying war materiel "should not rely on passengers to protect

her from attack—it would be like putting women and children in front of an army." He counseled Wilson to warn American citizens that they traveled on ships of belligerent countries at their own risk.

Wilson sought a middle course that would retain his commitment to peace and neutrality without condoning German attacks on passenger ships. On May 10, he distanced himself from the proponents of American intervention by declaring that "there is such a thing as a man being too proud to fight," which caused former president Theodore Roosevelt, who urged war, to label him a "flub dub and mollycoddle." But Wilson also rejected Bryan's position. Any further de-

---

"Enlist"

This poster depicting a young mother and her baby sinking beneath the cold waters of the Atlantic Ocean brought home the terrible cost of Germany's sinking of the British passenger liner *Lusitania* in 1915. When a German propagandist in the United States sought to defend the sinking, the American response was so ferocious that the German ambassador was forced to send him back to Germany. Burned into American memory, the *Lusitania* remained a compelling reason to enlist in the armed forces after the United States entered the war in 1917. Library of Congress.

ENLIST

struction of ships, Wilson declared, would be regarded as "deliberately unfriendly" and might lead the United States to break diplomatic relations with Germany. Wilson essentially demanded that Germany abandon unrestricted submarine warfare. Bryan resigned, predicting that the president had placed the United States on a collision course with Germany. Wilson's replacement for Bryan, Robert Lansing, was far from neutral. He announced that "the German Government is utterly hostile to all nations with democratic institutions." Because of Germany's "ambition for world dominance," it "must not be permitted to win this war or even to break even."

After Germany apologized for the civilian deaths on the *Lusitania*, tensions subsided. But in 1916, a German U-boat captain sank the British steamer *Sussex*, at the cost of two more American lives. To ensure continued U.S. neutrality, Germany went further, promising no more submarine attacks without warning and without provisions for the safety of civilians. Wilson's supporters celebrated the success of his middle-of-the-road strategy, which steered a course between belligerence and pacificism.

Wilson's diplomacy proved helpful in his bid for reelection in 1916. In the contest against Republican Charles Evans Hughes, the Democratic Party ran Wilson under the slogan "He kept us out of war." Wilson felt uneasy with the claim, recognizing that any "little German lieutenant can push us into the war at any time by some calculated outrage." But the Democrats' case for Wilson's neutrality appealed to enough of those in favor of peace to eke out a majority. Wilson won, but only by the razor-thin margins of 600,000 popular and 23 electoral votes.

The United States Enters the War

Step by step, the United States backed away from "absolute neutrality" and more forthrightly sided with the Allies (that is, with the Triple Entente). The consequence of protesting the German blockade of Great Britain but accepting the British blockade of Germany was that by 1916, the United States was supplying the Allies with 40 percent of their war materiel. When France and Britain ran short of money to pay for U.S. goods and asked for loans, Wilson argued that "loans by American bankers to any foreign government which is at war are inconsistent with the true spirit of neutrality." But rather than jeopardize America's wartime prosperity, Wilson relaxed his objections, and billions of dollars in loans kept American goods flowing to Britain and France.

In January 1917, Germany decided that it could no longer afford to allow neutral shipping to reach Great Britain while Britain's blockade gradually starved Germany. The German government announced that its navy would resume unrestricted submarine warfare and sink without warning any ship, enemy and neutral, found in the waters off Great Britain. Germany understood that the decision would probably bring the United States into the war but gambled that the submarines would strangle the British economy and allow German armies to win a military victory in France before American troops arrived in Europe.

Resisting demands for war, Wilson continued to hope for a negotiated peace and only broke off diplomatic relations with Germany. Then on February 25, 1917, British authorities informed Wilson of a secret telegram sent by the German foreign secretary, Arthur Zimmermann, to the German minister in Mexico. It promised that in the event of war between Germany and the United States, Germany would see that Mexico regained its "lost provinces" of Texas, New Mexico, and Arizona if Mexico would declare war against the United States. Wilson angrily responded to the Zimmermann telegram by asking Congress to approve a policy of "armed neutrality" that would allow merchant ships to fight back against any attackers. Germany's overture to Mexico convinced Wilson that the war was, indeed, a defense of democracy against German aggression.

In March, German submarines sank five American vessels off Britain, killing 66 Americans. On April 2, the president asked Congress to issue a declaration of war. No longer too proud to fight, he accused Germany of "warfare against all mankind." Still, he called for a "war without hate" and insisted that the destruction of Germany was not the goal of the United States. Rather, America fought to "vindicate the principles of peace and justice." He promised a world made "safe for democracy." On April 6, 1917, by majorities of 373 to 50 in the House and 82 to 6 in the Senate, Congress voted to declare war. Among those voting no was Representative Jeannette Rankin of Montana, the first woman elected to Congress.

Wilson continued to fear how the war would affect the nation at home. He said despairingly, "Once lead this people into war, and they'll forget there ever was such a thing as tolerance. To fight you must be brutal and ruthless, and the spirit of ruthless brutality will infect Congress, the courts, the policeman on the beat, the man in the street."

> REVIEW   Why did President Wilson authorize repeated military interventions in the Americas?

"Over There"

American soldiers sailed for France with songwriter George M. Cohan's rousing "Over There" ringing in their ears:

> Over there, over there
> Send the word, send the word over there,
> That the Yanks are coming, the Yanks are coming
> The drums rum-tumming ev'rywhere.

Two million American troops eventually reached Europe, by far the largest military venture the United States had ever undertaken on foreign soil. Filled with a sense of democratic mission and trained to be morally upright as well as fiercely effective, some doughboys found the adventure exhilarating and maintained their idealism to the end. The majority, however, saw little that was gallant in rats, lice, and poison gas, and—despite the progressives' hopes—little to elevate the human soul in a landscape of utter destruction and death.

The Call to Arms

When America entered the war, Britain and France were nearly exhausted after almost three years of conflict. Hundreds of thousands of soldiers had perished; food and morale were dangerously low. Another Allied power, Russia, was in turmoil. In March 1917, a revolution had forced Czar Nicholas II to abdicate, and eight months later, in a separate peace with Germany, the Bolshevik revolutionary government withdrew Russia from the war.

On May 18, 1917, to meet the demand for fighting men, Wilson signed a sweeping Selective Service Act, authorizing a **draft** of all young men into the armed forces. **Conscription** soon transformed a tiny volunteer armed force into a vast army and navy. Although almost 350,000 inductees either failed to report or claimed conscientious objector status, draft boards eventually inducted 2.8 million men into the armed services, in addition to the 2 million who volunteered.

Among the 4.8 million men under arms, 370,000 were black Americans. Although African Americans remained understandably skeptical about President Wilson's war for democracy, most followed W. E. B. Du Bois's advice to "close ranks" and to temporarily "forget our special grievances" until the nation had won the war. During training, black recruits suffered the same prejudices that they encountered in civilian life. Rigidly segregated, they faced crude abuse and miserable conditions, and they were usually assigned to labor battalions, where they shouldered shovels more often than rifles.

Training camps sought to transform raw white recruits into fighting men. Progressives in the government were determined that American fighting men would emerge from training with the highest moral and civic values. Secretary of War Newton D. Baker, whose outlook had been shaped by his reform crusades as the progressive mayor of Cleveland, created the Commission on Training Camp Activities, staffed by YMCA workers and veterans of the settlement house and playground movements. Military training included games, singing, and college extension courses. The army asked soldiers to stop thinking about sex, explaining that a "man who is thinking below the belt is not efficient." The Military Draft Act of 1917 prohibited prostitution and alcohol near training camps. Wilson's choice to command the American Expeditionary Force (AEF), Major General John "Black Jack" Pershing, was as morally upright as he was militarily uncompromising. Described by one observer as "lean, clean, keen," he gave progressives perfect confidence.

The War in France

At the front, the AEF discovered a desperate situation. By mid-1917, the war had degenerated into a stalemate of armies dug defensively into hundreds of miles of trenches across France. Huddling in the mud among the corpses and rats, soldiers were separated from the enemy by only a few hundred yards of "no-man's-land." When ordered "over the top," troops raced desperately toward the enemy's trenches, only to be entangled in barbed wire, enveloped in poison gas, and mowed down by machine guns. (See "Historical Question," page 796.) The three-day battle of the Somme in 1916 cost the French and British forces 600,000 dead and wounded and the Germans 500,000. The

"Men Wanted for the United States Army"
The exuberant soldiers swarming over this truck were so thrilled with their task of recruiting new men that they managed to display the flag backward. Their urgency reflects the fact that when America declared war on Germany in April 1917, its army numbered only 127,000, roughly the size of the army of Chile. Unwilling to trust voluntary enlistments, Wilson included in his war message to Congress an endorsement of "the principle of universal liability to service"—in other words, a draft. Congress quickly obliged with a conscription bill, and within months, nearly 10 million American men had registered for the draft. When the war ended, 2 million men had volunteered for military service and 2.8 million had been drafted. The navy was as desperate for men as the army. This heroic poster helped attract thousands of volunteers.

Photo: Brown Brothers; Poster: Image by © Swim Ink 2, LLC/Corbis.

FOLLOW THE FLAG

ENLIST IN THE NAVY
U.S. NAVY RECRUITING STATION
34 East 23rd Street, New York

deadliest battle of the war allowed the Allies to advance their trenches only a few meaningless miles across devastated land.

Still, U.S. troops saw almost no combat in 1917. The only exception was the 92nd Division of black troops. When Pershing received an urgent call for troops from the French, he sent the 92nd to the front to be integrated into the French army because he did not want to lose command over the white troops he valued more. In the 191 days they spent in battle—longer than any other American outfit—the 369th Regiment of the 92nd Division won more medals than any other American combat unit. Black soldiers recognized the irony of having to serve with the French to gain respect. Pershing told the French that their failure to draw the color line threatened Franco-American relations because it risked "spoiling the Negroes." German propagandists raised some painful questions. In a leaflet distributed to black troops, the Germans reminded them of their second-class citizenship and asked, "Why, then, fight the Germans, only for the benefit of the Wall Street robbers and to protect the millions they have loaned to the British, French, and Italians?"

What Did the Doughboys Find in France?

Two million American soldiers crossed the Atlantic with the American Expeditionary Force (AEF) to participate in the Great War in France. No two doughboys (a term whose origins are unclear) had exactly the same experience. Some 200,000 were black; 18 percent were foreign-born. Some were drafted; others volunteered. Two-thirds of the doughboys saw action; one-third did not. France was a huge arena that allowed for diverse experiences, but for almost all American soldiers, going to France was both their first time out of the United States and their first military experience.

A few doughboys saw the war through Woodrow Wilson's eyes—as a noble crusade. But most American soldiers, though dedicated to defeating the "Huns," saw the war early on as an adventure, agreeing with the poet Alan Seeger, who died in France in 1916, that this was "the biggest thing yet . . . the supreme experience."

The doughboys were like fresh air in the sour swamp of wartime France. One French general called the American troops "sturdy, eager, and well-disciplined." They were also brash, inexperienced, and poorly trained for the kind of warfare they were entering. The nearly exhausted French offered the Americans a warm welcome, but everything in rural France—language, food, farmhouses—was strange. French farmers' habit of living with their animals—people upstairs, animals down—revolted Americans. In time, French civilians and American soldiers developed a mutual contempt. The official report of the First Division accused the French of "Profiteering, Ingratitude, and Inhospitality."

Once in France, the Americans received additional training, but they were shocked by the emphasis the French put on trench warfare. General John J. Pershing promoted mobile, open tactics where expert marksmanship prevailed, but the French knew that in the trenches, hand grenades and machine guns counted more. In the spring of 1918, the Allies awoke to a sledgehammer German offensive. The doughboys were pressed into the trenches on the front lines, where their experience proved no different than that of the French and British foot soldiers.

Private Donald Kyler of the First Division was one of the first to enter the front lines. Friend and foe were "deeply dug in," he remembered, "with extensive communication trenches, second line trenches, belts of barbed wire entanglements, dug outs, and protected gun emplacements." For miles around, "the trees had been broken by shell bursts in the past and the land was pitted with shell holes." His platoon followed the zigzagging trench for about a mile, until it was seven feet deep, with wooden shelves on either side on which to stand and fire weapons. "At several places along our trench there were narrow tunnels leading downward into the earth to our sleeping places. To enter, one had to stoop and descend into a dark, damp, smelly hole." The "whole place was infested with rats, body lice, and bed bugs. At the far end of the tunnel was a shaft and ladder to escape by in case the entrance was caved in by shell fire."

At 3 a.m. on Kyler's first night in the trenches, the horizon suddenly became as light as day. "It was the muzzle blasts of the enemies' guns," Kyler recalled. "No sound was heard for a few moments until the sound wave hit us, and then with a mighty roar it came." The bombardment grew so intense that "the explosion of one shell could not be distinguished from another. It was an inferno of crashing, splintering, rending explosions." Another doughboy, Lieutenant Maury Maverick, described the explosion of shells this way: "The intensity of it simply enters your heart and brain, and tears every nerve to pieces."

Friendly fire could be as dangerous as that of the enemy. Artillery officer Raymond Austin, who died in France, described the rolling barrage of big guns that began the attack on Cantigny, the first American offensive. At 6:40 a.m., hundreds of large Allied artillery opened fire, their shells falling just beyond the front-line trenches where the doughboys waited. Each gun adjusted its range "until along the whole front of attack there was a perfect, even, line of bursting shells a mile long." The barrage moved forward at a rate just fast enough for the infantry to keep up with it at a walk. "The infantry suddenly appeared . . . close behind our barrage—a long brown line with bayonets glistening in the sun. They seemed to have sprung from the earth, as in reality they had when they went over the top." They walked steadily along behind the barrage across "no-man's-land" toward the German trenches. As the line reached the crest of a hill "and was silhouetted in the morning sun . . . it looked like a long picket fence. Occasionally a shell would strike among them and a gap would appear among the pickets, then quickly close." The U.S. military found it notoriously difficult to coordinate inexperienced infantry and inexperienced artillery, and the shells that burst among American troops were sometimes fired by their own guns.

Even when shells were not screaming, trench life was a trial. One private listed his enemies: first the officers; then the weather, mules, leaky clothes, lice and fleas (called cooties), loathsome rations, and homesickness; and finally the Germans. Amid the stench of living and dead bodies, rats the size of cats, and constant mud, there was little in the trenches to sustain the sense of war as a great crusade or an innocent adventure. "Mail call and the quality of the mess [food] become of deeper interest than the future of the world," Lieutenant Howard O'Brien declared.

American troops learned the ways of the trenches, got used to the shell fire, and generally hardened themselves to war. On July 25, 1918, an American soldier named Leo Cuthbertson described the transformation: "As we walked along the roads yesterday we could look on either side and see dead Huns. . . . Strange as it may seem, my heart is hardened to a point where such a sight, while pitiful, is a pleasure. For surely that is one way to defeat our enemy—put him in his grave." Doughboys, however, were filling graves, too. In four brutal days in September 1918, during the Meuse-Argonne offensive, the AEF sustained 45,000 casualties.

Occasionally, doughboys left the trenches and enjoyed brief respites behind the lines. Volunteers from the Salvation Army, Red Cross, and YMCA served coffee and doughnuts to thankful soldiers. One volunteer, Mrs. Sidney Walker, remembered that soldiers treated "Red Cross workers as though they were goddesses." After having the chance to shower, delouse their clothes, rest their jangled nerves, and flirt with a few young women, the doughboys returned to the hell of the trenches, where they, through their numbers and courage, tipped the balance toward an Allied victory.

With the armistice in November 1918, the AEF disbanded, and the survivors returned home with a uniform, a pair of shoes, a coat, and $60. For most doughboys, their time in France proved the most significant episode in their lives. Nothing else could match the war's camaraderie, intensity, and horror.

Doughboys in France

Stretched out in the mud in the middle of what used to be a forest, men in the 23rd Infantry of the Second Division fire a 37 mm gun at German positions. The black tree trunks offer dramatic testimony to the devastating power of the massive artillery bombardments. We can only imagine the cost to soldiers who were dug in here when the artillery opened up. National Archives.

Life in the Trenches

One U.S. soldier in a rat-infested trench tensely looks out for danger, another slumps in exhausted sleep, and a third lies flat on his stomach. They offer a glimpse of the reality of the Great War, minus the noise, stench, and danger. This trench is dry for the moment, but with the rains came mud so deep that wounded men drowned in it. By the time American doughboys arrived in Europe, hostile troops had faced each other for more than three years, burrowed into a double line of trenches that were protected by barbed wire, machine-gun nests, and mortars and backed by heavy artillery. Trenches with millions of combatants stretched from French ports on the English Channel all the way to Switzerland. Nothing could make living in such holes anything better than miserable, but a decent shave with a Gillette safety razor, a pair of dry boots, and a set of checkers offered doughboys temporary relief. Inevitably, however, the whistles would blow, sending the young men "over the top" and rushing toward enemy lines.

Photo: Imperial War Museum; Shaving kit and boots: Collection of Colonel Stuart S. Corning Jr./Picture Research Consultants, Inc.

READING THE IMAGE: What do these images suggest about the reality of life for American soldiers during World War I?

CONNECTIONS: How does the photograph of the trench contrast with the larger tactical approach to war employed by the American Expeditionary Force in France?

FOR MORE HELP ANALYZING THIS IMAGE, see the visual activity for this chapter in the Online Study Guide at bedfordstmartins.com/roark.

White troops continued to train and used their free time to explore places that most of them otherwise could never have hoped to see. True to the crusader image, American officials allowed only uplifting tourism. Paris temptations were off-limits, and French premier Georges Clemenceau's offer to supply U.S. troops with licensed prostitutes was declined with the half-serious remark that if Wilson found out, he would stop the war.

The sightseeing ended abruptly in March 1918. The Brest-Litovsk treaty signed that month by Germany and the Bolsheviks officially took Russia out of the war, and the Germans launched a massive offensive aimed at French ports on the Atlantic. After 6,000 cannons unleashed the heaviest barrage in history, a million German soldiers smashed a hole in the Allied lines at a cost of 250,000 casualties on each side. Pershing, who believed the right moment for U.S. action had finally come, visited Foch to ask for the "great honor" of becoming "engaged in the greatest battle in history." Foch agreed to Pershing's terms of a separate American command and in May assigned the Americans to the central sector.

In May and June, at Cantigny and then at Château-Thierry, the eager but green Americans checked the German advance with a series of dashing assaults (Map 22.3). Then they headed toward the forest stronghold of Belleau Wood, moving against streams of retreating Allied soldiers who cried defeat: "La guerre est finie!" (The war is over!). A French officer commanded American soldiers to retreat with them, but the American commander replied sharply, "Retreat, hell. We just got here." After charging through a wheat field against withering machine-gun fire, the marines plunged into hand-to-hand combat. Victory came hard, but a German report praised the enemy's spirit, noting that "the Americans' nerves are not yet worn out." Indeed, it was German morale that was on the verge of cracking.

In the summer of 1918, the Allies launched a massive counteroffensive that would end the war. A quarter of a million U.S. troops joined in the rout of German forces along the Marne River. In September, more than a million Americans took part in the assault that threw the Germans back from positions along the Meuse River. In November, a revolt against the German government sent Kaiser Wilhelm II fleeing to Holland. On November 11, 1918, a delegation from the newly established German republic met with the French high command to sign an armistice that brought the fighting to an end.

The adventure of the AEF was brief, bloody, and victorious. When Germany resumed unrestricted U-boat warfare in 1917, it was gambling that it could defeat Britain and France before the Americans could raise and train an army and ship it to France. The German military had miscalculated badly. By the end, 112,000 AEF soldiers perished from wounds and disease. Another 230,000 Americans suffered casualties but survived, many of them with permanent physical and psychological disabilities. Only the Civil War, which lasted much longer, had been more costly in American lives. European nations,

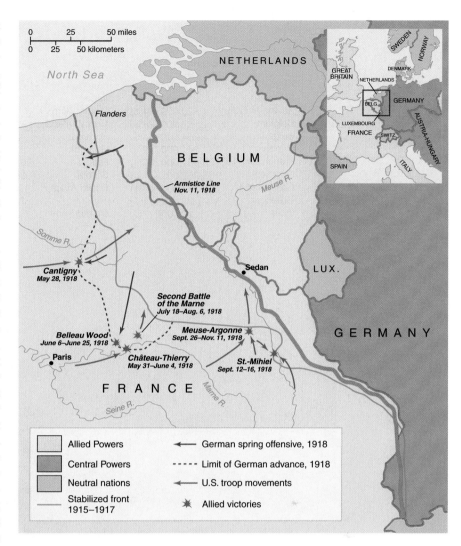

MAP 22.3 The American Expeditionary Force, 1918
In the last year of the war, the AEF joined the French army on the western front to respond to the final German offensive and pursue the retreating enemy until surrender.

READING THE MAP: Across which rivers did the Germans advance in 1918? Where did the armistice line of November 11, 1918, lie in relation to the stabilized front of 1915–1917? Through which countries did the armistice line run?
CONNECTIONS: What events paved the way for the American Expeditionary Force to join the combat effort in 1918? What characteristic(s) differentiated American troops from other Allied forces and helped them achieve victory?

FOR MORE HELP ANALYZING THIS MAP, see the map activity for this chapter in the Online Study Guide at bedfordstmartins.com/roark.

GLOBAL COMPARISON

Casualties of the First World War

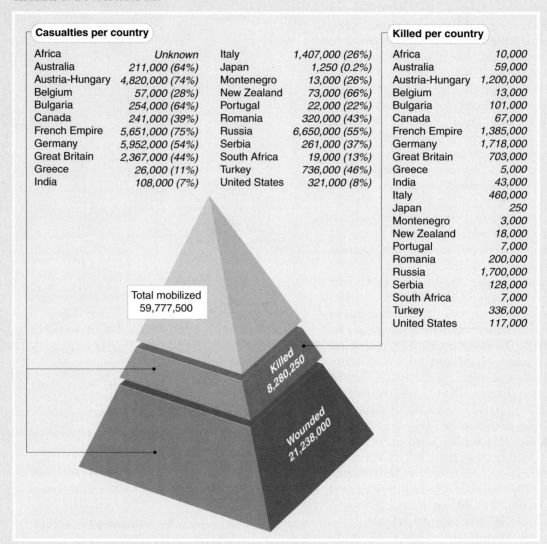

Casualties per country

Africa	*Unknown*	Italy	*1,407,000 (26%)*
Australia	*211,000 (64%)*	Japan	*1,250 (0.2%)*
Austria-Hungary	*4,820,000 (74%)*	Montenegro	*13,000 (26%)*
Belgium	*57,000 (28%)*	New Zealand	*73,000 (66%)*
Bulgaria	*254,000 (64%)*	Portugal	*22,000 (22%)*
Canada	*241,000 (39%)*	Romania	*320,000 (43%)*
French Empire	*5,651,000 (75%)*	Russia	*6,650,000 (55%)*
Germany	*5,952,000 (54%)*	Serbia	*261,000 (37%)*
Great Britain	*2,367,000 (44%)*	South Africa	*19,000 (13%)*
Greece	*26,000 (11%)*	Turkey	*736,000 (46%)*
India	*108,000 (7%)*	United States	*321,000 (8%)*

Killed per country

Africa	*10,000*
Australia	*59,000*
Austria-Hungary	*1,200,000*
Belgium	*13,000*
Bulgaria	*101,000*
Canada	*67,000*
French Empire	*1,385,000*
Germany	*1,718,000*
Great Britain	*703,000*
Greece	*5,000*
India	*43,000*
Italy	*460,000*
Japan	*250*
Montenegro	*3,000*
New Zealand	*18,000*
Portugal	*7,000*
Romania	*200,000*
Russia	*1,700,000*
Serbia	*128,000*
South Africa	*7,000*
Turkey	*336,000*
United States	*117,000*

Total mobilized
59,777,500

Killed
8,280,250

Wounded
21,238,000

There is no agreement about the number of casualties in World War I. Record keeping in many countries was only rudimentary. Moreover, the destructive nature of the war meant that countless soldiers were wholly obliterated or instantly buried. However approximate, these figures make clear that the conflict that raged from 1914 to 1918 was a truly cata-strophic world war. Although soldiers came from almost every part of the globe, the human devastation was not evenly distributed. Which country suffered the most casualties? Which country lost the greatest percentage of its soldiers? What do you think was the principal reason the United States lost a smaller percentage of its soldiers than most other nations lost?

however, suffered much greater losses: 2.2 million Germans, 1.9 million Russians, 1.4 million French, and 900,000 Britons. (See "Global Comparison.") Where they had fought, the landscape was as blasted and barren as the moon.

> **REVIEW** How did the American Expeditionary Force contribute to the defeat of Germany?

The Crusade for Democracy at Home

Many progressives hoped that war would improve the quality of American life as well as free Europe from its bondage to tyranny and militarism. Mobilization helped propel the crusades for woman suffrage and prohibition to success.

Progressives enthusiastically channeled industrial and agricultural production into the war effort. Labor shortages caused by workers entering the military provided new opportunities for women in the booming wartime economy. With labor at a premium, unionized workers gained higher pay and shorter hours. To instill loyalty in Americans whose ancestry was rooted in the belligerent nations, Wilson launched a campaign to foster patriotism. The campaign included the creation of a government agency to promote official propaganda, indoctrination in the schools, and parades, rallies, and films. But boosting patriotism led to suppressing dissent. When the government launched a harsh assault on civil liberties, mobs gained license to attack those whom they considered disloyal. As Wilson feared, the progressive ideals of rational progress and free expression took a beating at home when the nation undertook its foreign crusade for democracy.

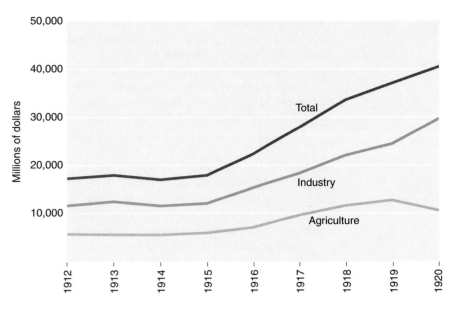

Agriculture: cash receipts.
Industry: includes mining, electric power, manufacturing, construction, and communications.

FIGURE 22.1 Industrial Wages, 1912–1920
With help from unions and progressive reformers, wageworkers gradually improved their economic condition. The entry of millions of young men into the armed forces during World War I caused labor shortages and led to a rapid surge in industrial wages.

The Progressive Stake in the War

The idea of the war as an agent of national improvement fanned the old zeal of the progressive movement. The influential philosopher-educator John Dewey urged Americans to recognize the "social possibilities of war." The Wilson administration realized that the federal government would have to assert greater control to mobilize the nation's human and physical resources. The nation's capital soon bristled with hastily created agencies charged with managing the war effort. Bernard Baruch headed the War Industries Board (WIB), created to stimulate and direct industrial production. At once a wealthy southern gentleman, a Jewish Wall Street stockbroker, and a reform Democrat, Baruch brought industrial management and labor together into a team that produced everything from boots to bullets and made U.S. troops the best-equipped soldiers in the world.

Herbert Hoover, a self-made millionaire engineer, headed the Food Administration. He led remarkably successful "Hooverizing" campaigns for "meatless" Mondays and "wheatless" Wednesdays and other ways of conserving resources. Guaranteed high prices, the American heartland not only supplied the needs of U.S. citizens and armed forces but also became the breadbasket of America's allies. Even Wilson's family

did its part with a White House "victory garden" and sheep put out to graze on the White House lawn when the gardeners took war-related work.

Other wartime agencies abounded. The Railroad Administration directed railroad traffic, the Fuel Administration coordinated the coal industry and other fuel suppliers, the Shipping Board organized the merchant marine, and the National War Labor Policies Board resolved labor disputes. Their successes gave progressives reason to believe that the war promoted harmony between business and labor and progressive reform in general. Some progressives, however, stubbornly refused to accept the argument that war and reform marched together. Wisconsin senator Robert La Follette attacked the war unrelentingly, claiming that Wilson's promises of peace and democracy were a case of "the blind leading the blind," at home and abroad.

Industrial leaders found that wartime agencies and enforced efficiency helped corporate profits triple. Some working people also had cause to celebrate. Mobilization meant high prices for farmers and plentiful jobs at high wages in the new war industries (Figure 22.1). Because increased industrial production required peaceful labor relations, the National War Labor Policies Board enacted the eight-hour day, a living minimum wage, and **collective bargaining** rights in some industries. Wages rose sharply during the war (as did prices), and the American Federation of Labor (AFL) saw its membership soar from 2.7 million to more than 5 million.

The war also provided a huge boost to the stalled moral crusade to ban alcohol. By 1917, prohibitionists had convinced nineteen states to go dry. Liquor's opponents now argued that banning alcohol would make the cause of democracy powerful and pure. At the same time, shutting down the distilleries would save millions of bushels of grain that could feed the United States and its allies. "Shall the many have food or the few drink?" the drys asked. Prohibitionists added a patriotic twist by arguing that closing breweries with German names such as Schlitz, Pabst, and Anheuser-Busch would deal a blow to the German cause. In December 1917, Congress passed the Eighteenth Amendment, which banned the manufacture, transportation, and sale of alcohol. After swift ratification by the states, the amendment went into effect on January 1, 1920.

Women, War, and the Battle for Suffrage

Women had made real strides during the Progressive Era, but war presented new opportunities. More than 25,000 women served in France. About half were nurses. The others drove ambulances; ran canteens for the Salvation Army, Red Cross, and YMCA; worked with French civilians in devastated areas; and acted as telephone operators and war correspondents. Like the men who joined the war effort, they believed that they were taking part in a great national venture. "I am more than willing to live as a soldier and know of the hardships I would have to undergo," one canteen

worker declared when applying to go overseas, "but I want to help my country. . . . I want . . . to do the *real* work." And like men, women struggled against disillusionment and depression in France. One woman explained: "Over in America, we thought we knew something about the war . . . but when you get here the difference is [like the one between] studying the laws of electricity and being struck by lightning."

At home, long-standing barriers against hiring women fell when millions of workingmen became soldiers and few new immigrant workers crossed the Atlantic. The new Women's Bureau of the Department of Labor, along with the Women's Trade Union League (WTUL), helped open jobs to women, sometimes against the opposition of the major trade organization, the AFL. Tens of thousands of women found work in defense plants as welders, metalworkers, and heavy machine operators—jobs traditionally reserved for men—and with the railroads. A black woman who had worked before the war as a domestic explained why she wanted to keep her job as a laborer in a railroad yard: "We are making more money at this than any work we can get, and we do not have to work as hard as at housework which requires us to be on duty from six o'clock in the morning until nine or ten at night, with might[y] little time off and at very poor wages." Other women found white-collar work. Between 1910 and 1920, the number of women clerks doubled. Before the war ended, more than a million women had found work in

U.S. Army Medical Corps Contract Surgeon's Uniform
Before the war ended, some 25,000 American women made it to France, all as volunteers. Ex-president Theodore Roosevelt once proclaimed war the "Great Adventure," and some women were eager to share in it. About half became nurses, who dealt with "a sea of stretchers, a human carpet." Women also drove ambulances, acted as social workers, and ran canteens for the Salvation Army, Red Cross, and YMCA. One YMCA worker, Mary Baldwin, hoped that a few hours in her canteen would "make life, and even death, easier 'out there.'" A handful of female physicians worked as contract surgeons for the U.S. army. Dr. Loy McAfee wore this uniform in France.
National Museum of American History, Smithsonian Institution, Washington, D.C.

MAP 22.4 Women's Voting Rights before the Nineteenth Amendment

The long campaign for women's voting rights reversed the pioneer epic that moved from east to west. From its first successes in the new democratic West, suffrage rolled eastward toward the entrenched, male-dominated public life of the Northeast and South.

READING THE MAP: What was the first state to grant woman suffrage? How many states extended full voting rights to women before 1914? How many extended these rights during World War I (1914–1918)?

CONNECTIONS: Suffragists redirected their focus during the war. What strategies did they use then?

FOR MORE HELP ANALYZING THIS MAP, see the map activity for this chapter in the Online Study Guide at bedfordstmartins.com/roark.

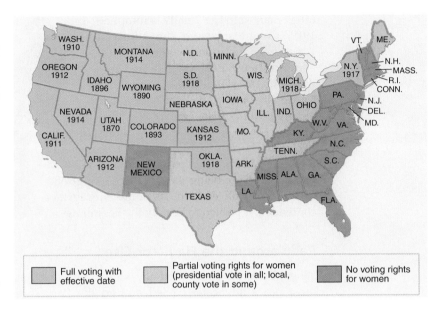

war industries. "This is the women's age," exaggerated Margaret Dreier Robins, president of the WTUL. "At last . . . women are coming into the labor and festival of life on equal terms with men."

The most dramatic advance for women came in the political arena. Since the Seneca Falls convention of 1848, where women voiced their first formal demand for the ballot, the struggle for woman suffrage had inched forward. Adopting a state-by-state approach, suffragists had achieved some success, but before 1910 only four small western states had adopted woman suffrage (Map 22.4). Elsewhere, voting rights for women met strong hostility and defeat. After 1910, suffrage leaders added a federal campaign to amend the Constitution, targeting Congress and the president, to the traditional state-by-state strategy for suffrage.

The radical wing of the suffragists, led by the indomitable Alice Paul, picketed the White House, where they unfurled banners that proclaimed: "America Is Not a Democracy. Twenty Million Women Are Denied the Right to Vote." They chained themselves to fences and went to jail, where many engaged in hunger strikes. "They seem bent on making their cause as obnoxious as possible," Woodrow Wilson declared. His wife, Edith, detested the idea of "masculinized" voting women. But membership in the mainstream organization, the National American Woman Suffrage Association (NAWSA), led by Carrie Chapman Catt, soared to some two million members. The NAWSA even accepted African American women into its ranks, though not on an equal

basis. Seeing the handwriting on the wall, the Republican and Progressive parties endorsed woman suffrage in 1916.

In 1918, Wilson gave his support to suffrage, calling the amendment "vital to the winning of the war." He conceded that it would be wrong not to reward the wartime "partnership of suffering and sacrifice" with a "partnership of privilege and right." By linking their cause to the wartime emphasis on national unity, the advocates

Women's Liberty Bell

Suffragists in Pennsylvania made great efforts to get their message out to rural people. This life-size replica of the Liberty Bell in Philadelphia, which suffragists called the Women's Liberty Bell or the Justice Bell, toured country roads on a specially reinforced truck. When rural folks rushed to see this symbol of freedom, suffragists mounted the truck's raised platform to preach the gospel of voting rights for women. Historical Society of Pennsylvania.

of woman suffrage finally triumphed. In 1919, Congress passed the Nineteenth Amendment, granting women the vote, and by August 1920, the required two-thirds of the states had ratified it. As Carrie Chapman Catt later recalled, "to get that word, male, out of the Constitution, cost the women of the country fifty-two years of campaigning." (See "Documenting the American Promise," page 806.) But rather than woman suffrage being the end of the long road to women's full equality, as some suffragists contended, it proved to be only the beginning.

Rally around the Flag—or Else

When Congress committed the nation to war, most peace advocates rallied around the flag. Several business and civic leaders who had been antiwar created the League to Enforce Peace in support of Wilson's insistence that military force had become the only means to peaceful ends. The Carnegie Endowment for International Peace adopted new stationery with the heading "Peace through Victory" and issued a resolution saying that "the most effectual means of promoting peace is to prosecute the war against the Imperial German Government."

Only a handful of reformers resisted the tide of patriotism. Soon after the guns began booming in 1914, a group of professional women, led by settlement house leader Jane Addams and economics professor Emily Greene Balch, denounced what Addams described as "the pathetic belief in the regenerative results of war." The Women's Peace Party that emerged in 1915 and its foreign affiliates in the Women's International League for Peace and Freedom (WILPF) led the struggle to persuade governments to negotiate peace and spare dissenters from harsh punishment. It proved discouraging, unpopular work, and after America entered the conflict, advocates for peace were routinely labeled cowards and traitors, their efforts crushed by the steamroller of conformity.

To suppress criticism of the war, Wilson stirred up patriotic fervor. In 1917, the president created the Committee on Public Information (CPI) under the direction of George Creel, a muckraking journalist, who became the nation's cheerleader for war. He sent "Four-Minute Men," a squad of 75,000 volunteers, around the country to give brief pep talks that celebrated successes on the battlefields and in the factories. Posters, pamphlets (many written by respected journalists and professors), and cartoons depicted brave American soldiers and sailors defending freedom and democracy against the evil "Huns," the derogatory nickname applied to German soldiers.

America rallied around Creel's campaign. The film industry cranked out reels of melodrama about battle-line and home-front heroes and taught audiences to hiss at the German kaiser. A musical, *The Kaiser: The Beast of Berlin*, opened on Broadway in 1918. Colleges and universities generated war propaganda in the guise of scholarship, and some added courses depicting the war as a culmination of the age-old struggle for civilization. When Professor James McKeen Cattell of Columbia University urged that America seek peace with Germany short of victory, university president Nicholas Murray Butler fired him on the grounds that "what had been folly is now treason."

A firestorm of anti-German passion erupted. Across the nation, "100% American" campaigns enlisted ordinary people to sniff out disloyalty. German, the most widely taught foreign language in 1914, practically disappeared from the nation's schools. Targeting German-born Americans, the *Saturday Evening Post* declared that it was time to rid the country of "the scum of the melting pot." The rabid attempt to punish Germans reached its extreme with the lynching of Robert Prager, a baker in Collinsville, Illinois. In the eyes of the mob, it was enough that Prager was German-born and had **socialist** leanings, even though he had not opposed American participation in the war. Persuaded by the defense lawyer who praised what he called a "patriotic murder," the jury at the trial of the killers took only twenty-five minutes to acquit.

As hysteria increased, the campaign reached absurd levels. In Montana, a school board barred a history text that had good things to say about medieval Germany. Menus across the nation changed German toast to French toast and sauerkraut to liberty cabbage. In Milwaukee, vigilantes mounted a machine gun outside the Pabst Theater to prevent the staging of Schiller's *Wilhelm Tell*, a powerful protest against tyranny. One vigilant citizen claimed to see a periscope in the Great Lakes, and the fiancée of one of the war's leading critics, caught dancing on the dunes of Cape Cod, was held on suspicion of signaling to German submarines.

> When Professor James McKeen Cattell of Columbia University urged that America seek peace with Germany short of victory, university president Nicholas Murray Butler fired him on the grounds that "what had been folly is now treason."

The Wilson administration's zeal in suppressing dissent contrasted sharply with its war aims of defending democracy. In the name of self-defense, the Espionage Act (June 1917), the Trading with the Enemy Act (October 1917), and the Sedition Act (May 1918) gave the government sweeping powers to punish any opinion or activity it considered "disloyal, profane, scurrilous, or abusive." When Postmaster General Albert Burleson blocked mailing privileges for publications he considered disloyal, dozens of dissenting journals were forced to close down, including a leading literary magazine. Of the fifteen hundred individuals eventually charged with sedition, all but a dozen had merely spoken words the government found objectionable. One of them was Eugene V. Debs, the leader of the Socialist Party, who was convicted under the Espionage Act for speeches condemning the war as a capitalist plot and sent to the Atlanta penitentiary.

The president hoped that national commitment to the war would subdue partisan politics, but his Republican rivals used the war as a weapon against the Democrats. The trick was to oppose Wilson's conduct of the war but not the war itself. Republicans outshouted Wilson on the nation's need to mobilize for war but then complained that Wilson's War Industries Board was a tyrannical agency that crushed free enterprise. Such attacks appealed to widely diverse business, labor, and patriotic groups. As the war progressed, Republicans gathered power against the Democrats, who had narrowly reelected Wilson in 1916.

Wilson erred when he attempted to make the off-year congressional elections of 1918 a referendum on his leadership. Instead, amid criticism of the White House for playing politics with the war, Republicans gained a narrow majority in both the House and Senate. The end of Democratic control of Congress not only halted further domestic reform but also meant that the United States would advance toward military victory in Europe with political power divided between a Democratic president and a Republican Congress likely to challenge Wilson's plans for international cooperation.

D. W. Griffith's *Hearts of the World*

Hollywood joined in the government's efforts to stir up rage against the "brutal Huns," as Germans were often called. In a film made for the British and French governments by America's leading filmmaker, D. W. Griffith, a hulking German is about to whip a defenseless farm woman (played by Lillian Gish, one of the nation's favorite actresses) innocently carrying potatoes from a field. When the film premiered in Washington, D.C., in 1918, First Lady Edith Wilson wrote to Griffith, pleading with him to cut or soften the violent whipping scene. Wilson was one of the few people in the nation's capital who sought to moderate the hate campaign.

Library of Congress.

> **REVIEW**   How did progressive ideals fare during wartime?

A Compromised Peace

Wilson decided to reaffirm his noble war ideals by announcing his peace aims before the end of hostilities. He hoped the victorious Allies would adopt his plan for international democracy, but he was sorely disappointed. The leaders of Britain, France, and Italy (which joined the Allies in 1915 in hopes of postwar gains) understood that Wilson's principles jeopardized their own postwar plans for the acquisition of enemy territory, new colonial empires, and reparations. Wilson also faced strong opposition at home from those who feared that his enthusiasm for international cooperation would undermine American sovereignty.

The Final Push for Woman Suffrage

B y the early twentieth century, the women's movement had mobilized millions, who increasingly concentrated on the passage of an amendment to the U.S. Constitution to ensure women's voting rights. Nothing came easily to the suffragists, but in 1920 their passion and courage were rewarded by the ratification of the Nineteenth Amendment.

DOCUMENT 1
Passing the Baton

Elizabeth Cady Stanton and Susan B. Anthony were best friends and close colleagues in the woman suffrage movement. In this October 1902 letter to Stanton, Anthony acknowledges that neither of them would live to see victory, but she nevertheless remains confident that the campaign will succeed. Stanton died days after receiving this letter, and Anthony died four years later.

My dear Mrs. Stanton
. . . It is fifty-one years since first we met and we have been busy through every one of them, stirring up the world to recognize the rights of women. The older we grow, the more keenly we feel the humiliation of disfranchisement and the more vividly we realize its disadvantages in every department of life and most of all in the labor market.

We little dreamed when we began this contest, optimistic with the hope and buoyancy of youth, that half a century later we would be compelled to leave the finish of the battle to another generation of women. But our hearts are filled with joy to know that they enter upon this task equipped with a college education, with business experience, with the fully admitted right to speak in public—all of which were denied to women fifty years ago. They have practically but one point to gain—the suffrage; we had all. These strong, courageous, capable young women will take our place and complete our work. There is an army of them, where we were but a handful. Ancient prejudice has become so softened, public sentiment so liberalized and women have so thoroughly demonstrated their ability as to leave not a shadow of doubt that they will carry our cause to victory. . . .

Ever lovingly yours,
Susan B. Anthony

SOURCE: From *The Elizabeth Cady Stanton–Susan B. Anthony Reader: Correspondence, Writings, Speeches,* 298–99, by Ellen Carol DuBois, ed. By permission of Northeastern University Press, 1992.

DOCUMENT 2
Politicking for Suffrage

While radical suffragists chained themselves to the White House fence and went on hunger strikes, other women followed more traditional political channels—methodically gathering petitions, lobbying legislators, building alliances, and rounding up votes. Mary Garrett Hay, vice president of the National American Woman Suffrage Association (NAWSA), reports her efforts with New York state legislators.

New York City, N.Y.
March 13th, 1919
Mrs. Maud Wood Park
1626 Rhode Island Avenue
Washington, D.C.
Dear Mrs. Park,
. . . I kept in very close touch on the telephone and telegraph wire with New York Congressmen and they reported to me, really twice a day what was going on, as far as Speaker, Floor Leader and Suffrage Committee was concerned. I can do more in the House than in the Senate, and I have asked Mr. Hays on the long distance telephone to try and see that things are perfectly straight for our Cause there.

Things will be all right, I believe, but I have made up my mind not to trust either Democrats or Republicans, until the Suffrage Amendment is passed; however, I do not say this to the men[,] only to you, and I shall keep my eyes and ears open and busy, and on the job all I can.

SOURCE: *Women and Social Movements in the United States, 1600–2000,* "How Did Suffragists Lobby to Obtain Congressional Approval of a Woman Suffrage Amendment to the U.S. Constitution, 1917–1920?" Document #10, http://www.binghampton.edu/homhist/ Schlesinger Library, Radcliffe Institute, Harvard University.

DOCUMENT 3
The President Intervenes

Although some people urged suffragists to muffle their demands during the war so that the nation could concentrate on victory, Carrie Chapman Catt, president of the NAWSA since 1915, pressed on, recognizing that the war offered a special opportunity. Catt prodded President Woodrow Wilson quietly but persistently, and on September 30, 1918, Wilson finally intervened directly, urging the Senate to pass the Nineteenth Amendment. His argument on behalf of democracy mirrored precisely that of radical suffragists who were protesting in front of the White House.

[The Senate's] adoption is, in my judgment, clearly necessary to the successful prosecution of the war and the successful realization of the objects for which the war is being fought.

. . . If we be indeed democrats and wish to lead the world to democracy, we can ask other peoples to accept in proof of our sincerity and our ability to lead them whither they wish to be led, nothing less persuasive and convincing than our actions.

. . . They are looking to the great, powerful, famous democracy of the West to lead them to a new day for which they have so long waited; and they think, in their logical simplicity, that democracy means that women shall play their part in affairs alongside men and upon an equal footing with them.

. . . We have made partners of the women in this war. Shall we admit them only to a partnership of suffering and sacrifice and toil and not to a partnership of privilege and right? This war could not have been fought, either by the other nations engaged or by America, if it had not been for the services of the women—services rendered in every sphere. . . .

. . . I tell you plainly that this measure which I urge upon you is vital to the winning of the war and to the energies alike of preparation and of battle.

. . . And not to winning the war only. It is vital to the right solution of the great problems which we must settle, and settle immediately, when the war is over. We shall need in our vision of affairs, as we have never needed them before, the sympathy and insight and clear moral instinct of the women of the world. . . . We shall need their moral sense to preserve what is right and fine and worthy in our system of life as well as to discover just what it is that ought to be purified and reformed. Without their counsellings we shall be only half wise.

SOURCE: "Appeal of President Wilson to the Senate of the United States to Submit the Federal Amendment for Woman Suffrage Delivered in Person Sept. 20, 1918," in *History of Woman Suffrage*, Vol. 5: 1900–1920, 760–63.

DOCUMENT 4
Reflections on Victory

Carrie Chapman Catt celebrates the passage of the Nineteenth Amendment in this letter to her staff at the NAWSA on Thanksgiving Day 1920. She reflects on the long road to victory and considers the satisfactions of the journey.

I have kept Thanksgiving sacred to reflections upon the long trail behind us, and the triumph which was its inevitable conclusion. John Adams said long after the Revolution that only about one third of the people were for it, a third being against it, and the remaining third utterly indifferent. Perhaps this proportion applies to all movements. At least a third of the women were for our cause at the end. . . . As I look back over the years . . . I realize that the greatest thing in the long campaign for us was not its crowning victory, but the discipline it gave us all. . . . It was a great crusade, the world has seen none more wonderful. . . . My admiration, love and reverence go out to that band which fought and won a revolution . . . with congratulations that we were permitted to establish a new and good thing in the world.

SOURCE: Carrie Chapman Catt to NAWSA Office Staff, Thanksgiving Day 1920, in Elizabeth Frost and Kathryn Cullen-DuPont, *Women's Suffrage in America: An Eyewitness History* (1992), 335–36.

QUESTIONS FOR ANALYSIS AND DEBATE

1. Why was Susan B. Anthony confident that woman suffrage would soon become a reality?

2. Why do you think some legislators in New York and elsewhere were willing to work closely with suffragists such as Mary Garrett Hay?

3. What, according to Woodrow Wilson, would America's rejection of the Nineteenth Amendment have jeopardized?

4. What do you suppose Carrie Chapman Catt meant when she said that the greatest gain for women in the suffrage campaign was "discipline"?

Wilson's Fourteen Points

On January 8, 1918, President Wilson revealed to Congress his vision of a generous peace. Wilson's Fourteen Points provided a blueprint for a new democratic world order. The first five points affirmed basic liberal ideals: "open covenants of peace, openly arrived at"—that is, an end to secret treaties; freedom of the seas; removal of economic barriers to free trade; reduction of weapons of war; and recognition of the rights of colonized peoples. The next eight points supported the right to self-determination of European peoples who had been dominated by Germany or its allies. Wilson's fourteenth point called for a "general association of nations"—a League of Nations—to provide "mutual guarantees of political independence and territorial integrity to great and small states alike." The insistence on a League of Nations reflected Wilson's lifelong dream of a "parliament of man." Only such an organization of "peace-loving nations," he believed, could justify the war and secure a lasting peace. Wilson concluded his speech by pledging that the United States would welcome Germany into the family of "peace-loving nations" if it would renounce its militarism and imperialism.

Citizens of the United States and of every Allied country greeted the Fourteen Points enthusiastically. Wilson felt confident that he could prevail against undemocratic and selfish forces at the peace table. During the final year of the war, he pressured the Allies to accept the Fourteen Points as the basis of the postwar settlement. If necessary, Wilson was willing to speak over the heads of government leaders directly to the people and thus expand his role as spokesman for Americans to be the champion of all the world's people. The Allies had won the war; Wilson would win the peace.

The Paris Peace Conference

From January 18 to June 28, 1919, the eyes of the world focused on Paris. There, powerful men wrestled with difficult problems. Although no other American president had ever gone to Europe while in office, Wilson, inspired by his mission, decided to head the U.S. delegation. He believed he owed it to the American soldiers. "It is now my duty," he announced, "to play my full part in making good what they gave their life's blood to obtain." A dubious British diplomat retorted that Wilson was drawn to Paris "as a debutante is entranced by the prospect of her

Leaders of the Paris Peace Conference
The three leaders in charge of putting the world back together after the Great War—from left to right, David Lloyd George, prime minister of Great Britain; Georges Clemenceau, premier of France; and U.S. president Woodrow Wilson—amiably and confidently stride toward the peace conference at the Versailles palace. Clemenceau is caught offering animated instruction to Wilson, whom he considered naively idealistic. Indeed, in an unguarded moment, Clemenceau expressed his contempt for the entire United States as a country that was unique in having passed directly from barbarism to decadence without an intervening period of civilization. Walking silently alongside, Lloyd George maintains the poker face that helped him keep his views carefully guarded throughout the conference.
Gamma Liaison.

first ball." The decision to leave the country at a time when his political opponents challenged his leadership was risky enough, but his stubborn refusal to include prominent Republicans in the delegation proved foolhardy and eventually cost him his dream of a new world order with the United States at its center.

When Wilson and his entourage arrived on the French coast on Friday, December 13, Wilson joked that thirteen was his lucky number. Two million Parisians cheered the American president's motorcade as it entered France's capital city. After four terrible years of war, the common people of Europe almost worshipped Wilson, believing that he would create a safer, more decent world. When the conference convened at Louis XIV's magnificent palace at Versailles, however, Wilson encountered a different reception. Representing the Allies were the decidedly unidealistic David Lloyd George, prime minister of Britain; Georges Clemenceau, premier of France; and Vittorio Orlando, former prime minister of Italy. To the Allied leaders, Wilson appeared a naive and impractical moralist. His desire to gather former enemies within a new international democratic order showed how little he understood hard European realities. Clemenceau claimed that Wilson "believed you could do everything by formulas" and "empty theory." Disparaging the Fourteen Points, he added, "God himself was content with ten commandments."

The Allies wanted to fasten blame for the war on Germany, totally disarm it, and make it pay so dearly that it would never threaten its neighbors again. The French demanded retribution in the form of territory containing Germany's richest mineral resources. The British made it clear that they were not about to give up the powerful weapon of naval blockade for the vague principle of freedom of the seas.

The Allies forced Wilson to make drastic compromises. In return for France moderating its territorial claims, he agreed to support Article 231 of the peace treaty, assigning war guilt to Germany. Though saved from permanently losing Rhineland territory to the French, Germany was outraged at being singled out as the instigator of the war and saddled with more than $33 billion in damages. Many Germans felt that their nation had been betrayed. After agreeing to an armistice in the belief that peace terms would be based in Wilson's generous Fourteen Points, they faced hardship and humiliation instead.

Wilson had better success in establishing the principle of self-determination. But from the beginning, Secretary of State Robert Lansing knew that the president's concept of self-determination was "simply loaded with dynamite." Lansing wondered, "What unit has he in mind? Does he mean a race, a territorial area, or a community?" Even Wilson was vague about what self-determination actually meant. "When I gave utterance to those words," he admitted, "I said them without the knowledge that nationalities existed, which are coming to us day after day." Lansing suspected that the notion "will raise hopes which can never be realized. It will, I fear, cost thousands of lives. In the end it is bound to be discredited, to be called the dream of an idealist who failed to realize the danger until it was too late."

Yet partly on the basis of self-determination, the conference redrew the map of Europe and parts of the rest of the world. Portions of Austria-Hungary were ceded to Italy, Poland, and Romania, and the remainder was reassembled into Austria, Hungary, Czechoslovakia, and Yugoslavia—independent republics whose boundaries were drawn with attention to concentrations of major ethnic groups but which also included minorities. More arbitrarily, the Ottoman empire was carved up into small mandates (including Palestine) run by local leaders but under the control of France and Great Britain. The conference reserved the mandate system for those regions it deemed insufficiently "civilized" to have full independence. Thus, the reconstructed nations—each beset with ethnic and nationalist rivalries—faced the challenge of making a new democratic government work (Map 22.5, page 810). Many of today's bitterest disputes—in the Balkans and Iraq, between Greece and Turkey, between Arabs and Jews—have roots in the decisions made in Paris in 1919.

> Disparaging Wilson's Fourteen Points, French premier Georges Clemenceau said, "God himself was content with ten commandments."

Wilson hoped that self-determination would also dictate the fate of Germany's colonies in Asia and Africa. But the Allies who had taken over the colonies during the war only allowed the League of Nations a mandate to administer them. Technically, the mandate system rejected imperialism, but in reality it only avoided the formality of imperialism while still allowing Europeans to maintain control. Because of mandates, Britain's empire grew by more than eight million people, while France added more than five million to its empire. Thus, while denying Germany its colonies, the Allies retained and added to their own far-flung territories.

The cause of democratic equality suffered another setback when the peace conference rejected Japan's call for inclusion of a principle of racial equality in the treaty. Wilson's belief in the superiority of whites, as well as his apprehension about how white Americans would respond to such a declaration, led him to oppose the clause. To soothe hurt feelings, Wilson agreed to grant Japan a mandate over the Shantung Peninsula in northern China, which had formerly been controlled by Germany. The gesture mollified Japan's moderate leaders, but the military faction preparing to take over the country used bitterness toward racist Western colonialism to build support for expanding Japanese power throughout Asia.

Closest to Wilson's heart was finding a new way to manage international relations. In Wilson's

MAP 22.5   Europe after World War I
The post–World War I settlement redrew boundaries to create new nations based on ethnic groupings. This outcome left within defeated Germany and Russia bitter peoples who resolved to recover the territory taken from them.

The Fight for the Treaty

The tumultuous reception Wilson received when he arrived home persuaded him, probably correctly, that the American people supported the treaty. When the president submitted the treaty to the Senate in July 1919, he warned that failure to ratify it would "break the heart of the world." By then, however, criticism of the treaty was mounting, especially from Americans convinced that their countries of ethnic origin had not been given fair treatment. Irish Americans raged against the treaty's failure to grant Ireland independence from the British. Italian Americans complained that Italy had not gained all of the territory it deserved. And German Americans condemned the treaty as ferociously unfair to Germany. Others worried that the president's concessions at Versailles had jeopardized the treaty's capacity to provide a generous plan for rebuilding Europe and to guarantee world peace.

Some of the most potent critics were found in the Senate. Bolstered by a slight Republican majority in Congress, a group of Republican "irreconcilables," which included such powerful **isolationist** senators as Hiram Johnson of California and William Borah of Idaho, condemned the treaty for entangling the United States in world affairs. A larger group of Republicans did not object to American participation in world politics but feared that membership in the League of Nations would jeopardize the nation's ability to act independently. No Republican, in any case, was eager to hand Wilson and the Democrats a foreign policy victory with the 1920 presidential election little more than a year away.

At the center of Republican opposition was Wilson's archenemy, Senator Henry Cabot Lodge of Massachusetts. Lodge's hostility was in part personal. "I never thought I could hate a man as much as I hate Wilson," he once admitted. But Lodge also raised cogent objections to the treaty and the league. Lodge was no isolationist, but he thought that much of the Fourteen Points was a "general bleat about virtue being better than vice." Lodge expected the United States' economic and military power to propel the nation into a major role in world affairs. But he insisted that membership in the League of Nations, which would require collective action to main-

view, war had finally discredited the old strategy of balance of power. Instead, he proposed a League of Nations, which would provide **collective security** and order. The league would establish rules of international conduct and resolve conflicts between nations through rational and peaceful means. When the Allies agreed to the league, Wilson was overjoyed. He believed that the league would rectify the errors his colleagues had forced on him in Paris. The league would solidify and extend the noble work he had begun.

To many Europeans and Americans, the Versailles treaty came as a bitter disappointment. Wilson's admirers were shocked that the president dealt in compromise like any other politician. But without Wilson's presence, the treaty that was signed on June 28, 1919, surely would have been more vindictive. Wilson returned home in July 1919 consoled that, despite his frustrations, he had gained what he most wanted—a League of Nations. In Wilson's judgment, "We have completed in the least time possible the greatest work that four men have ever done."

tain peace, threatened the nation's freedom of choice in foreign relations.

Lodge used his position as chairman of the Senate Foreign Relations Committee to air every sort of complaint. Out of the committee hearings came several amendments, or "reservations," that sought to limit the consequences of American membership in the league. For example, several reservations required approval of both the House and Senate before the United States could participate in league-sponsored economic sanctions or military action.

It gradually became clear that ratification of the treaty depended on acceptance of the Lodge reservations. Democratic senators, who overwhelmingly supported the treaty, urged Wilson to accept Lodge's terms, arguing that they left the essentials of the treaty intact. Wilson, however, insisted that the reservations cut "the very heart out of the treaty." He expressed personal hatred as well. "*Lodge* reservations?" he thun-

dered. "Never! I'll never consent to adopt any policy with which that impossible name is so prominently identified."

Wilson decided to take his case directly to the people. On September 3, 1919, still exhausted from the peace conference and against the objections of his doctors, he set out by train on the most ambitious speaking tour ever undertaken by a president. He enjoyed some early success, but on September 25 in Pueblo, Colorado, Wilson collapsed and had to return to Washington. There, he suffered a massive stroke that partially paralyzed him. From his bedroom, Wilson sent messages instructing Democrats in the Senate to hold firm against any and all reservations. If the Senate approved the treaty with reservations, he said, he would not sign it. In the end, Wilson commanded enough loyalty to ensure a vote against the Lodge reservations. But when the treaty without reservations came before the Senate in March 1920, the combined opposition of the Republican irreconcilables and reservationists left Wilson six votes short of the two-thirds majority needed for passage.

The nations of Europe organized the League of Nations at Geneva, Switzerland, but the United States never became a member. Whether American membership could have prevented the world war that would begin in Europe in 1939 is highly unlikely, but the United States' failure to join certainly weakened the league from the start. In refusing to accept relatively minor compromises with Senate moderates, Wilson lost his treaty and American membership in the league. Woodrow Wilson and Henry Cabot Lodge both died in 1924, never seeing international order or security, never knowing the whirlwind of resentment and violence that would eventually follow the Great War's failure to make the world safe for democracy.

> **REVIEW** Why did the Senate fail to ratify the Versailles treaty?

Democracy at Risk

The defeat of Wilson's idealistic plan for international democracy proved the crowning blow to progressives who had hoped that the war could boost reform at home. When the war ended, Americans wanted to demobilize swiftly. In the process, servicemen, defense workers, and farmers lost

"Refusing to Give the Lady a Seat"
Woodrow Wilson promised that the League of Nations would usher in an age of international peace. When stiff opposition to American membership in the league developed in the Unites States, friends of the league mounted a counterattack. This cartoon skewers the three leading Republican opponents of the league—Senators William Borah of Idaho, Henry Cabot Lodge of Massachusetts, and Hiram Johnson of California—who stubbornly refuse to budge an inch for the angel of peace. Clever cartoons could not save the league, however. Only shrewd diplomacy could do that, and Wilson was not able to deliver.
Picture Research Consultants & Archives.

their war-related jobs. The volatile combination—of unemployed veterans returning home, a stalled economy, and leftover wartime patriotism looking for a new cause—threatened to explode. Wartime anti-German passion was quickly followed by antiradicalism, a fevered campaign that ensnared unionists, socialists, dissenters, and African Americans and Mexicans who had committed no offense but to seek to escape rural poverty. The 1920 election marked the end of Wilson's two terms in the White House and his crusades.

Economic Hardship and Labor Upheaval

Americans greeted peace with a demand that the United States return to a peacetime economy. The government abruptly abandoned its wartime controls on the economy and canceled war contracts worth millions of dollars. In a matter of months, more than three million soldiers were mustered out of the military with only $60 and a one-way ticket home. When war production ceased and veterans flooded the job market, unemployment rose sharply. At the same time, consumers went on a postwar spending spree that drove inflation skyward. In 1919, prices rose 75 percent over prewar levels, and in 1920 prices rose another 28 percent.

Most of the gains workers had made during the war evaporated. Freed from wartime controls, business turned against the eight-hour day and attacked labor unions. With inflation eating up their paychecks, workers fought back. The year 1919 witnessed nearly 3,600 strikes involving 4 million workers. The most spectacular strike occurred in February 1919 in Seattle, where shipyard workers had been put out of work by demobilization. When a coalition of the radical International Workers of the World (IWW, called Wobblies) and the moderate American Federation of Labor (AFL) called a general strike, the largest work stoppage in American history shut down the city. Newspapers across the nation claimed that the walkout was "a Bolshevik effort to start a revolution." The suppression of the strike by Seattle officials cost the AFL many of its wartime gains and contributed to the destruction of the IWW soon afterward.

A strike by Boston policemen in the fall of 1919 underscored postwar hostility toward labor militancy. Although the police had received no raise since before the war and were paid less

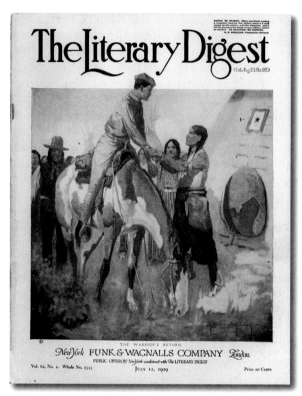

"The Warrior's Return"

About sixteen thousand Native Americans served in the U.S. armed forces during World War I. This magazine cover offers a romanticized reconstruction of one homecoming. The young soldier, still in uniform and presumably fresh from France, rides his pony to the tepee of his parents, who proudly welcome their brave warrior. The tepee is decorated with a star, a national symbol that families with sons in the military displayed on their homes. The painting sought to demonstrate that even Americans on the margins of national life were sufficiently assimilated and loyal to join the national sacrifice to defeat the enemy.
Picture Research Consultants & Archives.

than pick-and-shovel laborers, they won little sympathy. Once the officers stopped walking their beats, looters sacked the city. After two days of near anarchy, only slightly tamed by a volunteer police force of Harvard students and recently discharged soldiers, Massachusetts governor Calvin Coolidge called in the National Guard to restore order. The public, yearning for peace and security in the wake of war, welcomed Coolidge's anti-union assurance that "there is no right to strike against the public safety by anybody, anywhere, any time."

Labor strife climaxed in the grim steel strike of 1919. For decades, the steel industry had succeeded in beating back its workers' efforts to unionize. Faced with the industry's plan to revert

Returning Veterans and Work
After the triumphal parades ended, attention turned to the question of what the heroes would do at home. The Department of Labor poster tries to convey a strong image of purposefulness and prosperity by portraying a soldier in front of a booming industrial landscape. But the U.S. Employment Service had little to offer veterans beyond posters, and unions were unprepared to cope with the massive numbers of former soldiers who needed retraining. As workplace conditions deteriorated, the largest number of strikes in the nation's history broke out in 1919.
Veterans: Library of Congress; Poster: © Bettmann/Corbis.

to seven-day weeks, twelve-hour days, and weekly wages of about $20, the AFL determined to try again. When U.S. Steel and Bethlehem Steel refused to negotiate, Samuel Gompers, head of the AFL, called for a strike. In response, 350,000 workers in fifteen states walked out in September 1919. The steel industry hired 30,000 strikebreakers (many of them African Americans) and convinced the public that the strikers were radicals bent on subverting the Republic. State and federal troops protected scabs who crossed picket lines. In January 1920, after eighteen striking workers had been killed, the strike collapsed. That devastating defeat initiated a sharp decline in the fortunes of the labor movement, a trend that would continue for almost twenty years.

The Red Scare

Suppression of labor strikes was one response to the widespread fear of internal subversion that swept the nation in 1919. The "Red scare" ("Red" referred to the color of the Bolshevik flag), which far outstripped the assault on civil liberties during the war, had homegrown causes: the postwar recession, labor unrest, and the difficulties of reintegrating millions of returning veterans. But unsettling events abroad also added to Americans' anxieties.

Russian bolshevism became even more menacing in March 1919, when the new Soviet leaders created the Comintern, a worldwide association of **Communist** leaders intent on fomenting revolution in capitalist countries. (See "Beyond America's Borders," page 816.) A Communist revolution in the United States was extremely unlikely, but edgy Americans faced with a flurry of terrorist acts, most notably thirty-eight bombs mailed to prominent individuals, believed otherwise. Fear, anger, and uncertainty led swiftly to a hunt for terrorists, led by Attorney General A. Mitchell Palmer. Targeting men and women who harbored what Palmer considered ideas that could lead to violence, even though the individuals may not have done anything illegal, the Justice Department sought to purge the supposed enemies of America.

In January 1920, Palmer ordered a series of raids that netted 6,000 alleged subversives. Finding no revolutionary conspiracies, Palmer nevertheless ordered 500 noncitizen suspects deported. His action came in the wake of a campaign against the most notorious radical alien, Russian-born Emma Goldman. Before the war, Goldman's passionate support of labor strikes, women's rights, and birth control had made her a symbol of radicalism. Finally, after a stay in

Emma Goldman Is Deported

In the fall of 1919, federal agents arrested hundreds of "Bolsheviks" whom they considered a "menace to law and order." On December 6, 1919, anarchist Emma Goldman, seen here hiding her face, was escorted to detention on Ellis Island, which had welcomed millions of immigrants over the years. Two weeks later, Goldman and 248 others were put on the aging troopship *Buford* and deported to Soviet Russia. Some of this crowd (and much of America) was happy to see "Red Emma" and her friends sent, as the State Department said, "whence they came." © Bettmann/Corbis.

prison for attacking military conscription, she was ordered deported by J. Edgar Hoover, the eager director of the Justice Department's Radical Division. In December 1919, as Goldman and 250 others boarded a ship for exile in Russia, the defiant rebel turned on the gangplank to thumb her nose at a jeering crowd.

The effort to rid the country of alien radicals was matched by efforts to crush troublesome citizens. Law enforcement officials and vigilante groups joined hands against so-called Reds. In November 1919 in the rugged lumber town of Centralia, Washington, a menacing crowd gathered in front of the IWW hall. Nervous Wobblies inside opened fire, killing three people. Three IWW members were arrested and later convicted of murder, but another, ex-soldier Wesley Everett, was carried off by the mob, which castrated him, hung him from a bridge, and then riddled his body with bullets. His death was officially ruled a suicide.

Public institutions joined the attack on civil liberties. Local libraries removed dissenting books. Schools fired unorthodox teachers. Police shut down radical newspapers. State legislatures refused to seat elected representatives who professed socialist ideas. And in 1919, Congress removed its lone socialist representative, Victor Berger, on the pretext that he was a threat to national safety.

That same year, the Supreme Court provided a formula for restricting free speech. In upholding the conviction of socialist Charles Schenck for publishing a pamphlet urging resistance to the draft during wartime (*Schenck v. United States*), the Court established a "clear and present danger" test. Such utterances as Schenck's during a time of national peril, Justice Oliver Wendell Holmes wrote, were equivalent to shouting "Fire!" in a crowded theater. But Schenck's pamphlet had little power to provoke a public firmly opposed to its message.

In time, the Red scare lost credibility. The lack of any real radical menace became clear after Attorney General Palmer warned in 1920 that radicals were planning to celebrate the Bolshevik Revolution with a nationwide wave of violence on May 1, international workers' day. Officials called out state militias, fortified public buildings and churches, mobilized bomb squads, and even placed machine-gun nests at major city intersections. When May 1 came and went without a single disturbance, the public mood turned from fear to scorn. The Red scare collapsed as a result of its excesses.

The Great Migrations of African Americans and Mexicans

Before the Red scare lost steam, the government raised alarms about the loyalty of African Americans. A Justice Department investigation concluded that Reds were fomenting racial unrest among blacks. Although the report was wrong about Bolshevik influence, it was correct in notic-ing a new stirring among African Americans, an assertiveness born of participation in the war effort and the massive migration out of the South.

In 1900, nine of every ten blacks still lived in the South, where poverty, **disfranchisement**, segregation, and violence dominated their lives. Thirty-five years after **emancipation**, African Americans had made little progress toward full citizenship. A majority of black men continued to

African Americans Migrate North
This southern family arrived in their new home in an unnamed northern city in 1912.
Wearing their Sunday best, they carried the rest of what they owned in two suitcases.
Several factors, including World War I, combined to prompt the massive African American migration out of the South. In the 1920s, many rural blacks lost work when boll weevils devoured the cotton crop. Then mechanization and government programs to support crop prices by reducing acreage drove many more people off the land.

In Chicago, the League on Urban Conditions among Negroes, which eventually became the Urban League, sought to ease the transition of southern blacks to life in the North by distributing cards such as the one shown here (front and back). Other cards advised hard work, sobriety, cleanliness, finding a church, getting children into school, and speaking softly in public places.

Photo: Photographs and Prints Division, Schomburg Center for Research in Black Culture, New York Public Library, Astor, Lenox and Tilden Foundations; Card: Arthur and Graham Aldis Papers (Aldis neg. 1A + 1B) Special Collections, The University Library, University of Illinois at Chicago.

READING THE IMAGE: What emotions do the faces of this family reveal?
CONNECTIONS: What problems would this family likely have encountered when they reached their destination?
Do you think the cards distributed by the Chicago League on Urban Conditions would have helped?

FOR MORE HELP ANALYZING THIS IMAGE, see the visual activity for this chapter in the Online Study Guide at
bedfordstmartins.com/roark.

Bolshevism

One month before Woodrow Wilson asked Congress for a declaration of war against Germany, revolutionary forces in Russia overthrew Czar Nicholas II and installed a democratic government. The March 1917 revolution removed the last despot among the Allies fighting Germany and bolstered Wilson's confidence that the war really was a clear-cut fight between "democracy and autocracy." The American president embraced the revolution, declaring Russia "a fit partner for a league of honour."

In November 1917, Russia experienced a second revolution. Marxist radicals calling themselves Bolsheviks seized control and made their leader, Vladimir Ilyich Lenin, ruler of Russia. Lenin scoffed at the idea that the Allies were fighting for democracy and insisted that greedy capitalists were waging war for international dominance. In March 1918, he shocked Wilson and the Allies by signing a separate peace with Germany and withdrawing Russia from the war. Still locked in the desperate struggle with Germany, the Allies cried betrayal and feared that vast numbers of German soldiers who had been fighting the Russian army on the eastern front would turn to confront exhausted Allied troops on the western front.

Prodded by British leader Winston Churchill, who declared that "the Bolshevik infant should be strangled in its cradle," Britain and France urged the United States to join them in sending troops to Russia in support of Russian democrats opposing the new revolutionary regime. Wilson hesitated before committing U.S.

troops to a civil war in Russia. He told his trusted adviser Colonel Edward House, "I've been sweating blood over the question of what is right and feasible to do in Russia." Several prominent Americans spoke out against American intervention. Senator William Borah of Idaho declared: "The Russian people have the same right to establish a Socialist state as we have to establish a republic." But Wilson concluded that the Bolsheviks were a dictatorial party that had come to power through a violent coup that denied Russians political choice, and he thought that if anti-Bolshevik forces were successful, Russia might reenter the war against Germany. Thus by September 1918, on the pretext of helping 60,000 trapped Czechoslovakians return to the western front to fight the Germans, Wilson had ordered 14,000 U.S. troops to Russia to join British and French forces there.

After the Allies defeated Germany in November 1918, they could no longer rationalize the continued presence of their troops in Russia as part of the war with Germany. It became clear that the U.S., British, and French troops were fighting to overthrow Lenin and annul the Bolshevik Revolution. But the Bolsheviks (by now calling themselves Communists) prevailed, and U.S. troops withdrew from Russia in June 1919, after the loss of more than 200 American lives.

The Bolshevik regime dedicated itself not only to ending capitalism in Russia (known as the Soviet Union after 1922) but also to overthrowing capitalist and imperialist regimes everywhere. Clearly, Lenin's imagined future was at odds with Wilson's proposed liberal new world order.

Wilson withheld U.S. diplomatic recognition of the Soviet Union (a policy that persisted until 1934) and joined the Allies in an economic boycott to bring down the Bolshevik government. Unbowed, Lenin promised that his party would "incite rebellion among all the peoples now oppressed," and revolutionary agitation became central to Soviet foreign policy. Just after the armistice, Communist revolutions erupted in Bavaria and Hungary. Though short-lived, the Communist regimes there sent shock waves throughout the West. In 1919, moreover, a Russian official bragged that monies being sent to Europe to foment Bolshevik rebellion were "nothing compared to the funds transmitted to New York for the purpose of spreading bolshevism in the United States." American attention shifted from revolutionaries in Europe to revolutionaries at home. The Red scare was on.

Having failed to make the world "safe for democracy," the Wilson administration set out to make democracy safe in America. Rather than looking on the Bolshevik success as monstrous, a few Americans saw Russia as the world's best hope, especially after the Versailles treaty shattered Wilson's grand plans for the peace. Some traveled to Russia and wrote rapturously about the society that promised economic and social justice and the end of capitalist bosses' exploitation of workers. The vast majority of Americans, however, were no more drawn to communism than to czarism.

In 1919, disgruntled socialists founded the American Communist Party, but it attracted only a handful of members, who spent most of their time arguing the fine points of doctrine, not manufacturing bombs. But the few radicals who did resort to bombs prompted near panic in some quarters. One observer warned that "Bolshevism means chaos, wholesale murder, the complete destruction of civilization." Attorney General A. Mitchell Palmer perceived a "blaze of Revolution sweeping over every American institution of law and order . . . licking the altars of churches . . . crawling into the sacred corners of American homes." In 1919, the U.S. government launched an all-out attack on the Communist ("Red") menace. Even mild dissenters faced bullying and threats. Workers seeking better wages and conditions, women and African Americans demanding equal rights, and anyone else pushing for change found the government hurling the epithet "Red" at them. Beatings, jailings, and deportation often followed. After the sailing of the "Soviet Ark," which deported Emma Goldman and other radicals on December 21, 1919, the hysteria began to subside.

The Bolshevik Revolution had endless consequences. In the Soviet Union, it initiated a brutal reign of terror that lasted for more than seven decades. In international politics, it set up a polarity that lasted nearly as long. In a very real sense, the cold war, which set the United States and the Soviet Union at each other's throats after World War II, began in 1917. America's abortive military intervention against the Bolshevik regime and the Bolsheviks' call for worldwide revolution convulsed relations from the very beginning. In the United States, the rabid antiradicalism of the Red scare significantly damaged traditional American values. Commitment to the protection of dissent succumbed to irrational anticommunism. Even mild reform became tarred with the brush of bolshevism. Although the Red scare quickly withered, the habit of crushing dissent in the name of security would live on. Years later, in the 1950s, when Americans' anxiety mounted and their confidence waned once again, witch-hunts against radicalism reemerged to undermine American democracy.

Attorney General A. Mitchell Palmer

On January 2, 1920, Palmer (left) ordered hundreds of federal agents to thirty-three American cities to smash the alleged Bolshevik conspiracy. Led by J. Edgar Hoover, the agents arrested more than six thousand individuals on charges of plotting to overthrow the government. Palmer revealed much more about himself than about those arrested when he said, "Out of the sly and crafty eyes of many of them leap cupidity, cruelty, insanity, and crime; from their lopsided faces, sloping brows, and misshapen features may be recognized the unmistakable criminal type." The agents who carried out Palmer's Red-hunting were not particularly careful about protecting the property of those they targeted. This photograph of the International Workers of the World (IWW) headquarters in New York City shows the results of one raid.

Palmer: Library of Congress; Headquarters: Labadie Collection, University of Michigan.

toil in agriculture as dirt-poor tenants or share-croppers, or they worked for wages of 60 cents a day. Black women worked in the homes of whites as domestics for $2 a week. Whites remained committed to keeping blacks down. "If we own a good farm or horse, or cow, or bird-dog, or yoke of oxen," a black sharecropper in Mississippi observed in 1913, "we are harassed until we are bound to sell, give away, or run away, before we can have any peace in our lives."

The First World War provided African Americans with the opportunity to escape the South's cotton fields and kitchens. War channeled almost 5 million American workers into military service. Moreover, it caused the number of European immigrants to fall from more than a million in 1914 to 31,000 in 1918. Deprived of their traditional sources of laborers just as production demands were increasing, northern industrialists turned to black labor. Lured north by labor recruiters, newspapers, and word of mouth, young black men, who made up the bulk of the early migrants, found work in steel mills, shipyards, munitions plants, railroad yards, automobile factories, and mines. From 1915 to 1920, a half million blacks (approximately 10 percent of the South's black population) boarded trains bound for Philadelphia, Detroit, Cleveland, Chicago, St. Louis, and other industrial cities.

Opportunities differed from city to city. In Detroit, for example, blacks found work in automobile factories. Ford and other companies established strong relations with urban black churches, which acted as recruiters for the labor-strapped industry. Workers at Ford wore badges to get in the gates, and black men were so proud of their jobs that they wore their badges to church on Sunday. Thousands of migrants wrote home to tell family and friends about their experiences in the North. One man announced proudly that he had recently been promoted to "first assistant to the head carpenter." He added, "I should have been here twenty years ago. I just begin to feel like a man. . . . My children are going to the same school with the whites and I don't have to [h]umble to no one. I have registered—will vote the next election and there ain't any 'yes sir'—it's all yes and no and Sam and Bill."

But the North was not the promised land. Black men stood on the lowest rungs of the labor ladder. Jobs of any kind proved scarce for black women. Limited by both race and sex, most worked as domestic servants as they did in the South. The existing black middle class sometimes shunned the less educated, less sophisticated rural southerners crowding into northern cities. Many whites, fearful of losing jobs and status, lashed out against the new migrants. Savage race riots ripped through two dozen northern cities. The worst occurred in July 1917 when a mob of whites invaded a section of East St. Louis, Illinois, crowded with blacks who had been recruited to help break a strike. The mob murdered at least 39 people and left most of the black district in flames. In 1918, the nation witnessed 96 lynchings of blacks, some of them returning war veterans still in uniform.

African Americans in the military also experienced racial violence. The worst episode occurred in August 1917 when a group of armed black soldiers in Houston, Texas, set out to avenge incidents of harassment by the police. In the clash that followed, thirteen whites, including several policemen, and one black soldier were killed. With vengeful swiftness that denied any appeal, a military court had thirteen black soldiers hanged and sentenced forty-one others to life imprisonment.

Still, most black migrants stayed in the North and encouraged friends and family to follow. By 1940, more than one million blacks had left the South, profoundly changing their own lives and the course of the nation's history. Black enclaves such as Harlem in New York and the South Side of Chicago, "cities within cities," emerged in the North. These assertive communities provided a foundation for black protest and political organization in the years ahead.

At nearly the same moment that black Americans streamed into northern cities, another migration was under way in the American Southwest. Between 1910 and 1920, the Mexican-born population in the United States soared from 222,000 to 478,000. Mexican immigration resulted from developments on both sides of the border. At the turn of the twentieth century, the Mexican dictator Porfirio Diaz initiated land policies that decimated poor farmers. When the Mexicans revolted against Diaz in 1910, initiating a ten-year civil war, the trickle of migration became a flood. North of the border, the Chinese Exclusion Act of 1882 and later the disruption of World War I cut off the supply of cheap foreign labor and caused western employers in the expanding rail, mining, construction, and agricultural industries to look south to Mexico for workers.

> One black man who migrated north announced proudly that he had recently been promoted to "first assistant to the head carpenter." He added, "I should have been here twenty years ago. I just begin to feel like a man."

As a result of Americans' racial stereotyping of Mexicans—a U.S. government economist described them as "docile, patient, usually orderly in camp, fairly intelligent under competent supervision, obedient and cheap"—Mexicans were considered excellent prospects for manual labor but not for citizenship. Employers tried to dampen racial fears by stressing that the immigrants were only temporary residents, not a lasting threat. In 1917, when anti-immigration advocates convinced Congress to do something about foreigners coming into the United States, the restrictive legislation bowed to southwestern industry and exempted Mexicans. By 1920, ethnic Mexicans made up about three-fourths of California's farm laborers. They were also crucial to the Texas economy, accounting for three-fourths of laborers in the cotton fields and in construction there.

Like immigrants from Europe and black migrants from the South, Mexicans in the American Southwest dreamed of a better life. And like the others, they found both opportunity and disappointment. Wages were better than in Mexico, but life in the fields, mines, and factories was hard, and living conditions—in boxcars, labor camps, or urban barrios—often were dismal. Signs warning "No Mexicans Allowed" increased rather than declined. Mexican women nurtured families, but many also worked for wages. Thousands of women picked cotton, sometimes dragging hundred-pound cotton sacks with a baby perched on top. Among Mexican Americans, some of whom had lived in the Southwest for a century or more, *los recien llegados* (the recent arrivals) encountered mixed reactions. One Mexican American expressed this ambivalence: "We are all Mexicans anyway because the *gueros* [Anglos] treat us all alike." But he also called for immigration quotas because the recent arrivals drove down wages and incited white prejudice that affected all ethnic Mexicans. *Los recien llegados* also harbored mixed feelings,

Mexican Women Arriving in El Paso, 1911

These Mexican women, carrying bundles and wearing traditional shawls, try to get their bearings upon arriving in El Paso, Texas—the Ellis Island for Mexican immigrants. Perhaps they are looking for a family member who preceded them, or perhaps they are alone and calculating their next step. In any case, they were part of the first modern wave of Mexican immigration to the United States. Women like them found work in the cotton and sugar beet fields, canneries, and restaurants of the Southwest, as well as at home taking in sewing, laundry, and boarders. Whatever their work, their journey across the border was life changing. Courtesy of the Rio Grande Historical Collections, New Mexico State University Library, Las Cruces, New Mexico.

sometimes calling Mexican Americans *pochos* (faded or bleached ones).

Despite friction, large-scale immigration into the Southwest meant a resurgence of the Mexican cultural presence, which became the basis for greater solidarity and political action for the ethnic Mexican population. Shortly after World War I, Mexican Americans began organizing, a development that culminated with the formation of the League of United Latin American Citizens (LULAC) in Texas in 1929.

Postwar Politics and the Election of 1920

A thousand miles away in Washington, D.C., President Woodrow Wilson, bedridden and paralyzed, stubbornly ignored the mountain of domestic troubles—labor strikes, the Red scare, race riots, immigration backlash—and insisted that the 1920 election would be a "solemn referendum" on the League of Nations. Dutifully, the Democratic nominees for president, James M. Cox of Ohio, and for vice president, Franklin Delano Roosevelt of New York, campaigned on Wilson's international ideals. The Republican Party chose the handsome, gregarious Warren Gamaliel Harding, senator from Ohio. Harding's

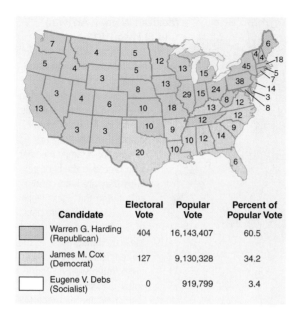

Candidate	Electoral Vote	Popular Vote	Percent of Popular Vote
Warren G. Harding (Republican)	404	16,143,407	60.5
James M. Cox (Democrat)	127	9,130,328	34.2
Eugene V. Debs (Socialist)	0	919,799	3.4

MAP 22.6   The Election of 1920

rise in Ohio politics was a tribute to his amiability, not his mastery of the issues.

Harding found the winning formula when he declared that "America's present need is not heroics, but healing; not nostrums [questionable remedies] but normalcy." But what was "normalcy"? Harding explained: "By 'normalcy' I don't mean the old order but a regular steady order of things. I mean normal procedure, the natural way, without excess." Eager to put wartime crusades and postwar strife behind them, voters responded by giving Harding the largest presidential victory ever: 60.5 percent of the popular vote and 404 out of 531 electoral votes (Map 22.6). Once in office, Harding and his wife, Florence, threw open the White House gates, which had been closed since the declaration of war in 1917. Their welcome brought throngs of visitors and lifted the national pall, signaling a new, more easygoing era.

> **REVIEW**   How did the Red scare contribute to the erosion of civil liberties after the war?

Conclusion: Troubled Crusade

America's experience in World War I was exceptional. For much of the world, the Great War produced great destruction, acres of blackened fields, ruined factories, and millions of casualties. But in the United States, war and prosperity marched hand in hand. America emerged from the war with the strongest economy in the world and a position of international preeminence.

Still, the nation paid a heavy price both at home and abroad. American soldiers and sailors encountered unprecedented horrors—submarines, poison gas, machine guns—and more than 100,000 died. On Memorial Day 1919, at the Argonne Cemetery, where 14,200 Americans lie, General John J. Pershing said: "It is not for us to proclaim what they did, their silence speaks more eloquently than words, but it is for us to uphold the conception of duty, honor and country for which they fought and for which they died. It is for the living to carry forward their purpose and make fruitful their sacrifice." Rather than redeeming their sacrifice, however, as Wilson promised, the peace that followed the armistice tarnished it. At home, rather than permanently improving working conditions, advancing public health, and spreading educational opportunity, as progressives had hoped, the war threatened to undermine the achievements of the previous two decades. Moreover, rather than promoting democracy in the United States, the war bred fear, intolerance, and repression that led to a crackdown on dissent and a demand for conformity. Reformers could count only woman suffrage as a permanent victory.

Woodrow Wilson had promised more than anyone could deliver. Progressive hopes of extending democracy and **liberal** reform nationally and internationally were dashed. In 1920, a bruised and disillusioned society stumbled into a new decade. The era coming to an end had called on Americans to crusade and sacrifice. The new era promised peace, prosperity, and a good time.

Selected Bibliography

General Works

Thomas Fleming, *The Illusion of Victory: America in World War I* (2003).

Robert H. Zieger, *America's Great War: World War I and the American Experience* (2000).

Over There

Gerald Astor, *The Right to Fight: A History of African Americans in the Military* (1998).

Peter Boyle, *American-Soviet Relations: From the Russian Revolution to the Fall of Communism* (1993).

Edward M. Coffman, *The War to End All Wars: The American Military Experience in World War I* (1968).

Byron Farwell, *Over There: The United States in the Great War, 1917–1918* (1999).

Lloyd C. Gardner, *Safe for Democracy: The Anglo-American Response to Revolution, 1913–1923* (1987).

Jennifer D. Keene, *Doughboys, the Great War, and the Remaking of America* (2001).

Lee Kennett, *The First Air War, 1914–1918* (1990).

Thomas Knock, *To End All Wars: Woodrow Wilson and the Quest for a New World Order* (1992).

Margaret Olwen Macmillan, *Paris 1919: Six Months That Changed the World* (2002).

Gary Mead, *The Doughboys: America and the First World War* (2000).

Emily S. Rosenberg, *Financial Missionaries to the World: The Politics and Culture of Dollar Diplomacy, 1890–1930* (1999).

Martin J. Sklar, *The United States as a Developing Country: Studies in U.S. History in the Progressive Era and the 1920s* (1992).

Gene Smith, *Until the Last Trumpet Sounds: The Life of General of the Armies John J. Pershing* (1998).

David F. Trask, *The AEF and Coalition Warmaking, 1917–1918* (1993).

Susan Zeiger, *In Uncle Sam's Service: Women with the AEF, 1917–1919* (1999).

The Home Front

Jean Baker, *Sisters: The Lives of America's Suffragists* (2005).

Nancy Cott, *The Grounding of American Feminism* (1987).

Leslie Midkiff DeBauche, *Reel Patriotism: The Movies and World War I* (1997).

Marc A. Eisner, *From Warfare State to Welfare State: World War I, Compensatory State Building, and the Limits of the Modern Order* (2000).

Elizabeth Frost and Kathryn Cullen-DuPont, eds., *Women's Suffrage in America: An Eyewitness History* (1992).

Maurine Weiner Greenwald, *Women, War, and Work: The Impact of World War I on Women Workers in the United States* (1980).

James N. Gregory, *Southern Diaspora: How the Great Migrations of Black and White Southerners Transformed America* (2005).

James R. Grossman, *Land of Hope: Chicago, Black Southerners, and the Great Migration* (1989).

David Kennedy, *Over Here: The First World War and American Society* (1980).

David Levering Lewis, *W. E. B. Du Bois: Biography of a Race, 1868–1919* (1993).

Robert K. Murray, *Red Scare: A Study in National Hysteria, 1919–1920* (1955).

George J. Sanchez, *Becoming Mexican American: Ethnicity, Culture, and Identity in Chicano Los Angeles, 1900–1945* (1993).

Ronald Schaffer, *America in the Great War: The Rise of the War Welfare System* (1991).

Barbara J. Steinson, *American Women's Activism in World War I* (1982).

Joe William Trotter Jr., ed., *The Great Migration in Historical Perspective* (1991).

▶ FOR MORE BOOKS ABOUT TOPICS IN THIS CHAPTER, see the Online Bibliography at bedfordstmartins.com/roark.

▶ FOR ADDITIONAL FIRSTHAND ACCOUNTS OF THIS PERIOD, see Chapter 22 in Michael Johnson, ed., *Reading the American Past*, Fourth Edition.

▶ FOR WEB SITES, IMAGES, AND DOCUMENTS RELATED TO TOPICS AND PLACES IN THIS CHAPTER, visit bedfordstmartins.com/makehistory.

REVIEWING THE CHAPTER

Follow these steps to review and strengthen your understanding of the chapter.

STEP 1: *Study the* **Key Terms** *and* **Timeline** *to identify the significance of each item listed.*

STEP 2: *Answer the* **Review Questions**, *drawing on key terms and dates to support your answers.*

STEP 3: *Drawing on the Key Terms, Timeline, and Review Questions, answer the broader* **Making Connections** *questions.*

KEY TERMS

Who

Woodrow Wilson (p. 787)
John "Black Jack" Pershing (p. 787)
Ferdinand Foch (p. 788)
William Jennings Bryan (p. 789)
Francisco "Pancho" Villa (p. 790)
Wilhelm II (p. 790)
Archduke Franz Ferdinand (p. 791)
Robert Lansing (p. 793)
Alice Paul (p. 803)
Carrie Chapman Catt (p. 803)
George Creel (p. 804)
David Lloyd George (p. 808)
Georges Clemenceau (p. 808)
Vittorio Orlando (p. 809)
Henry Cabot Lodge (p. 810)
Calvin Coolidge (p. 812)
A. Mitchell Palmer (p. 814)
Emma Goldman (p. 814)
Warren Gamaliel Harding (p. 819)

What

American Expeditionary Force (AEF) (pp. 787, 794)
Triple Alliance (p. 791)
Triple Entente ("the Allies") (p. 791)
U-boats (p. 792)
Lusitania (p. 792)
Zimmermann telegram (p. 793)
Selective Service Act (p. 794)
Brest-Litovsk treaty (p. 798)
War Industries Board (p. 801)
Food Administration (p. 801)
Eighteenth Amendment (p. 802)
Women's Trade Union League (WTUL) (p. 802)
National American Woman Suffrage Association (NAWSA) (p. 803)
Nineteenth Amendment (p. 804)
Women's Peace Party (p. 804)

Committee on Public Information (p. 804)
Sedition Act (p. 805)
Fourteen Points (p. 808)
League of Nations (p. 808)
Paris peace conference (p. 808)
mandate system (p. 809)
Versailles treaty (p. 810)
Seattle general strike of 1919 (p. 812)
Boston police strike of 1919 (p. 812)
steel strike of 1919 (p. 812)
Red scare (p. 813)
Comintern (p. 813)
Schenck v. United States (p. 814)
great migrations (p. 815)
East St. Louis race riot (p. 818)
League of United Latin American Citizens (LULAC) (p. 819)

TIMELINE

1914 • **April.** U.S. marines occupy Veracruz, Mexico.
• **June 28.** Assassination of Archduke Franz Ferdinand.
• **July 18.** Austria-Hungary declares war on Serbia.
• **August 3.** Germany attacks Russia and France.
• **August 4.** Great Britain declares war on Germany.

1915 • *Lusitania* sunk.
• Women's Peace Party formed.
• Italy joins Allies.

1916– • General Pershing pursues Pancho Villa.
1917 • Wilson reelected.

1917 • Zimmermann telegram intercepted.
• **April 6.** United States declares war on Germany.
• Committee on Public Information created.
• Selective Service Act.
• Espionage Act, Trading with the Enemy Act, and Sedition Act.
• East St. Louis, Illinois, race riot.
• Russia arranges separate peace with Germany.

REVIEW QUESTIONS

1. Why did President Wilson authorize repeated military interventions in the Americas? (pp. 788–94)

2. How did the American Expeditionary Force contribute to the defeat of Germany? (pp. 794–800)

3. How did progressive ideals fare during wartime? (pp. 800–805)

4. Why did the Senate fail to ratify the Versailles treaty? (pp. 805–11)

5. How did the Red scare contribute to the erosion of civil liberties after the war? (pp. 811–20)

MAKING CONNECTIONS

1. Why did the United States at first resist intervening in World War I? Why did it later retreat from this policy and send troops? In your answer, discuss whether these decisions revised or reinforced earlier U.S. foreign policy.

2. Some reformers were optimistic that World War I would advance progressive ideals at home. Discuss specific wartime domestic developments that displayed progressivism's influence. How did war contribute to these developments? Did they endure in peacetime? Why or why not?

3. A conservative reaction in American politics followed peace, most vividly in the labor upheaval and Red scare that swept the nation. What factors drove these developments? How did they shape the postwar political spectrum?

4. During World War I, the nation witnessed important demographic changes. What drove African American and Mexican migration north? How did the war facilitate these changes? In your answer, explain the significance of these developments to the migrants and the nation.

▶ FOR PRACTICE QUIZZES, A CUSTOMIZED STUDY PLAN, AND OTHER STUDY TOOLS, see the Online Study Guide at bedfordstmartins.com/roark.

1918 • **January 8.** President Wilson gives Fourteen Points speech.
- **May–June.** U.S. marines see first major combat at Cantigny and Château-Thierry.
- **November 11.** Armistice signed ending World War I.

1919 • **January.** Paris peace conference begins.
- **June.** Treaty of Versailles signed.
- **September.** Wilson undertakes speaking tour.
- Wave of labor strikes.

1920 • **January 1.** Prohibition begins.
- **January.** Palmer raids.
- **March.** Senate votes against ratification of Treaty of Versailles.
- **August 18.** Nineteenth Amendment ratified.
- **November.** Republican Warren G. Harding elected president.

MODEL T FORD
Nothing symbolized the 1920s more than
the automobile. Americans drove millions
of cars—Briscoes, Dodges, Lexingtons,
Cadillacs, Maxwells, and especially Model T Fords.
When Henry Ford introduced the Model T in 1908, Americans thought of automobiles as
toys of the rich, far too costly for average people. By the 1920s, millions of Americans owned
Fords, and their lives were never the same. Oklahoma humorist Will Rogers claimed that Henry
Ford "changed the habits of more people than Caesar, Mussolini, Charlie Chaplin, Clara Bow,
Xerxes, Amos 'n Andy, and Bernard Shaw." One of novelist Booth Tarkington's characters
expressed some reservations about automobiles: "With all their speed forward, they may be
a step backward in civilization." But most Americans loved their automobiles and sped away
into the future.

National Museum of American History, Smithsonian Institution, Behring Center.

23

From New Era to Great Depression
1920–1932

A MERICANS IN THE 1920s cheered Henry Ford as an authentic American hero. When the decade began, he had already produced six million automobiles; by 1927, the figure reached fifteen million. In 1920, one car rolled off the Ford assembly line every minute; in 1925, one appeared every ten seconds. In 1920, a Ford car cost $845; in 1928, the price was less than $300, within range of most of the country's skilled workingmen. Henry Ford put America on wheels, and in the eyes of most Americans, he was an honest man who made an honest car: basic, inexpensive, and reliable. He became the greatest example of free enterprise's promise and achievement. But like the age in which he lived, Henry Ford was many-sided, more complex and contradictory than this simple image suggests.

Born in 1863 on a farm in Dearborn, Michigan, Ford hated the drudgery of farmwork and loved tinkering with machines. At sixteen, he fled rural life for Detroit, where he became a journeyman machinist and experimented with internal combustion engines. In 1893, he put together one of the first successful gasoline-driven carriages in the United States. His ambition, he said, was to "make something in quantity." The product he chose reflected American restlessness, the desire to be on the move. "Everybody wants to be someplace he ain't," Ford declared. "As soon as he gets there he wants to go right back." In 1903, with $28,000 from a few backers, Ford gathered twelve workers in a 250-by-50-foot shed and created the Ford Motor Company.

Ford's early cars were custom-made one at a time. By 1914, his cars were being built along a continuously moving assembly line; workers bolted on parts brought to them by cranes and conveyor belts. Ford made only one kind of car, the Model T, which became synonymous with mass production. A boxlike black vehicle, it was cheap, easy to drive, and simple to repair. The Model T dominated the market. Throughout the rapid expansion of the automotive industry, the Ford Motor Company remained the industry leader, peaking in 1925, when it outsold all its rivals combined (Map 23.1, page 827).

Nobody entertained grander or more contradictory visions of the new America he had helped to create than Henry Ford himself. When he began his rise, **progressive** critics condemned the industrial giants of the nineteenth century as "robber barons" who lived in luxury while reducing their workers to wage slaves. Ford, however, identified with the common folk and saw himself as the benefactor of Americans yearning to be free and mobile.

Ford's automobile plants made him a billionaire, but their highly regimented assembly lines reduced Ford workers to near robots. On the cutting edge

Henry and Edsel Ford
In this 1924 photograph, Henry Ford looks fondly at his first car while his son, Edsel, stands next to the ten millionth Model T. Edsel, the Fords' only child, remained unspoiled by his father's enormous wealth. Forsaking college, he entered the family business out of high school. Serious, disciplined, and an acute observer, Edsel Ford realized by the mid-1920s that General Motors's more advanced Chevrolet was about to surpass the Model T. Henry Ford stubbornly refused to change his automobile, insisting that the "Model T is the most perfect car in the world." Under Edsel's leadership, however, the Ford Motor Company moved beyond the plain, boxy, black, and fabulously successful Model T.
Henry Ford Museum and Greenfield Village.

materialism. A great outpouring of artistic talent led, ironically, to incessant critiques of America's artistic barrenness. The Ku Klux Klan and other champions of an idealized older America resorted to violence as well as words when they chastised the era's "new woman," "New Negro," and surging immigrant populations.

The public, disillusioned with the outcome of World War I, turned from the Christian moralism and idealism of the Progressive Era. In the twenties, Ford and businessmen like him replaced political reformers such as Theodore Roosevelt and Woodrow Wilson as the models of progress. The U.S. Chamber of Commerce crowed, "The American businessman is the most influential person in the nation." Social justice gave way to individual advancement. At the center of it all, President Calvin Coolidge spoke in praise of those in power when he declared, "The business of America is business." The fortunes of the era rose, then crashed, according to the values and practices of the business community.

The New Era

The rejection of progressives' pleas for government intervention and regulation in favor of the revival of free-enterprise individualism helped make the 1920s a time of contradiction and ambivalence. Once Woodrow Wilson left the White House, the energy generated by the crusade in Europe flowed away from civic reform and toward private economic endeavor. The rise of a freewheeling economy and a heightened sense of individualism caused Secretary of Commerce Herbert Hoover to declare that America had entered a "New Era," one of many labels used to describe the complex 1920s. Some terms focus on the decade's high-spirited energy and cultural changes: Roaring Twenties, Jazz Age, Flaming Youth, Age of the Flapper. Others echo the rising importance of money—Dollar Decade, Golden Twenties, Prosperity Decade—or reflect the sinister side of gangster profiteering—Lawless Decade. Still others emphasize the lonely confusion of the Lost Generation and the stress and anxiety of the Aspirin Age.

America in the twenties was many things, but there was no getting around the truth of Calvin Coolidge's insight: The business of America *was* business. Politicians and diplomats proclaimed business the heart of American civilization. Average men and women bought into

of modern technology, Ford nevertheless remained nostalgic about rural values. He sought to revive the past in Greenfield Village, a museum outside Detroit, where he relocated buildings from a bygone era, including his parents' farmhouse. His museum contrasted sharply with the roaring Ford plant farther along the Detroit River at River Rouge. The African American and immigrant workers who worked there found no place in Greenfield Village. Yet all would be well, Ford insisted, if Americans remained true to their agrarian past and somehow managed to be modern and scientific at the same time.

Tension between traditional values and modern conditions lay at the heart of the conflicted 1920s. For the first time, more Americans lived in urban than in rural areas, yet Americans remained nostalgic about farms and small towns. Although the nation generally prospered, the new wealth widened the gap between rich and poor. While millions admired urban America's sophisticated new style and consumer products, others condemned postwar society for its vulgar

MAP 23.1 Auto Manufacturing

By the mid-1920s, the massive coal and steel industries of the Midwest had made that region the center of the new automobile industry. A major road-building program by the federal government carried the thousands of new cars produced each day to every corner of the country.

READING THE MAP: How many states had factories involved with the manufacture of automobiles? In what regions was auto manufacturing concentrated?

CONNECTIONS: On what related industries did auto manufacturing depend? How did the integration of the automobile into everyday life affect American society?

FOR MORE HELP ANALYZING THIS MAP, see the map activity for this chapter in the Online Study Guide at bedfordstmartins.com/roark.

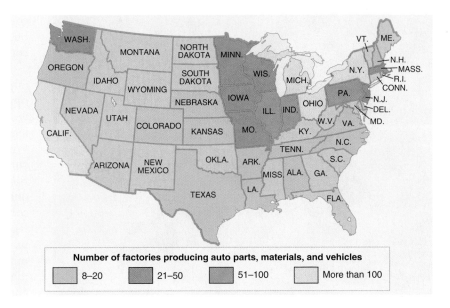

Number of factories producing auto parts, materials, and vehicles

8–20 | 21–50 | 51–100 | More than 100

the idea that business and its wonderful products were what made America great, as they snatched up the unprecedented flood of new consumer items American factories sent forth.

A Business Government

Republicans controlled the White House from 1921 to 1933. The first of the three Republican presidents was Warren Gamaliel Harding, the Ohio senator who in his 1920 campaign called for a "return to normalcy," by which he meant the end of public crusades and a return to private pursuits. Harding, who had few qualifications for the presidency, promised a government run by the best minds, and he appointed to his cabinet a few men of real stature. Herbert Hoover, the self-made millionaire and former head of the wartime Food Administration, became secretary of commerce and, according to one wag who testified to Hoover's ambition and energy, assistant secretary of everything else. But wealth also counted. Most significantly, Harding answered the call of **conservatives** and appointed Andrew Mellon, one of the richest men in America, secretary of the treasury. And friendship counted, too. Harding handed out jobs to his old "Ohio gang," whose only qualification was their friendship. This curious combination of merit and cronyism made for a disjointed administration in which a few "best minds" debated national needs, while much less qualified men looked for ways to advance their own interests.

When Harding was elected in 1920 in a landslide over Democratic opponent James Cox (see

chapter 22, Map 22.6), the unemployment rate hit 20 percent, the highest ever up to that point. Farmers fared the worst, as their bankruptcy rate increased tenfold. Harding pushed measures to aid American enterprise and regain national prosperity—high tariffs to protect American businesses (the Fordney-McCumber tariff in 1922 raised duties to unprecedented heights), price supports for agriculture, and the dismantling of wartime government control over industry in favor of unregulated private business. "Never before, here or anywhere else," the U.S. Chamber of Commerce said proudly, "has a government been so completely fused with business."

Harding's policies to boost American enterprise made him very popular, but ultimately his small-town congeniality and trusting ways did him in. Some of his friends in the "Ohio gang" were up to their necks in lawbreaking. Three of Harding's appointees would go to jail, and others would be indicted. Interior Secretary Albert Fall was convicted of accepting bribes of more than $400,000 for leasing oil reserves on public land in Teapot Dome, Wyoming, and "Teapot Dome" became a synonym for political corruption.

Baffled about how to deal with "my Goddamned friends," Harding in the summer of 1923 set off on a trip to Alaska to escape his troubles. But the president found no rest, and his health declined. On August 2, 1923, a shocked nation learned of the fifty-eight-year-old Harding's death from a heart attack.

Vice President Calvin Coolidge was vacationing at his family's farmhouse in Plymouth Notch, Vermont, when he was awakened during

Warren G. Harding and Babe Ruth
President Warren G. Harding shakes hands with New York Yankee home run king George Herman "Babe" Ruth Jr. during an April 4, 1923, visit to Yankee Stadium. The 1920s were the Golden Age of Sports, and Ruth was the best paid and most highly acclaimed athlete of the decade. In 1920, a man died of excitement when Ruth slugged a ball into the bleachers. Even when he struck out, "the Babe" usually attracted more attention than any politician—even the president of the United States.
© Bettmann/Corbis.

the night with the news of Harding's death. The family gathered in the parlor, where, by the flickering light of an oil lamp, Coolidge's father, a justice of the peace, swore his son in as president. This rustic drama had the intended effect of calming a nation confronting the death of a president and continuing scandal in Washington.

Coolidge once expressed his belief that "the man who builds a factory builds a temple, the man who works there worships there." Reverence for free enterprise meant that Coolidge continued and extended Harding's policies of promoting business and limiting government. With Coolidge's approval, Secretary of the Treasury Andrew Mellon reduced the government's control over the economy. Tax cuts for corporations and wealthy individuals sliced government tax revenue by about half. New rules for the Federal Trade Commission severely limited its power to regulate business. Secretary of Commerce Herbert Hoover limited government authority by en-

> Coolidge once expressed his belief that "the man who builds a factory builds a temple, the man who works there worships there."

couraging trade associations that would keep business honest and efficient through voluntary cooperation.

Coolidge found a staunch ally in the Supreme Court. For many years, the Court had opposed federal regulation of hours, wages, and working conditions on the grounds that such legislation was the proper concern of the states. With Coolidge, the Court also found ways to curtail a state's ability to regulate business. It ruled against **closed shops**—businesses where only union members could be employed—while confirming the right of owners to form exclusive trade associations. In 1923, the Court declared unconstitutional the District of Columbia's minimum-wage law for women, asserting that the law interfered with the freedom of employer and employee to make labor contracts. On a broad front, the Court and the president attacked government intrusion in the free market, even when the prohibition of government regulation threatened the welfare of workers.

The election of 1924 confirmed the defeat of the progressive principle that the state should take a leading role in ensuring the general welfare. To oppose Coolidge, the Democrats nominated John W. Davis, a corporate lawyer whose conservative views differed little from Republican principles. Only the Progressive Party and its presidential nominee, Senator Robert La Follette of Wisconsin, offered a genuine alternative. When La Follette championed labor unions, regulation of business, and protection of civil liberties, Republicans coined the slogan "Coolidge or Chaos." By 1924, most Americans had turned their backs on what they considered labor radicalism and reckless reform, and Coolidge captured more votes than his two opponents put together. The election proved that Coolidge was right when he declared, "This is a business country, and it wants a business government." What was true of the government's relationship to business at home was also true abroad.

Promoting Prosperity and Peace Abroad

After orchestrating the Senate's successful effort to block U.S. membership in the League of Nations, Henry Cabot Lodge boasted, "We have torn Wilsonism up by the roots." But repudiation of Wilsonian internationalism and rejection of **collective security** through the League of Nations did not mean that the United States retreated into **isolationism**. The United States emerged from World War I with its economy intact and enjoyed a decade of stunning growth. Economic involvement in the world and the continuing chaos in Europe made withdrawal impossible. Corporate chieftain Owen Young observed: "Whether the United States will sit in the court of great economic movements throughout the world is not a question which the Senate, or even all of our people combined can decide. We are there . . . inescapably there." New York replaced London as the center of world finance, and the United States became the world's chief creditor. American banks poured billions into war-torn Europe's economic recovery. Europe not only absorbed American loans and products but also encountered a flood of American popular culture in the form of fashion, style, and Hollywood motion pictures.

One of the Republicans' most ambitious foreign policy initiatives was the Washington Disarmament Conference, which convened to establish a global balance of naval power. Secretary of State Charles Evans Hughes shaped the Five-Power Naval Treaty of 1922 committing Britain, France, Japan, Italy, and the United States to a proportional reduction of naval forces. The treaty led to the scrapping of more than two million tons of warships, by far the world's greatest success in disarmament. Americans celebrated President Harding for safeguarding the peace while remaining outside the League of Nations. By fostering international peace, he also helped make the world a safer place for American trade.

A second major effort on behalf of world peace came in 1928, when Secretary of State Frank Kellogg joined French foreign minister Aristide Briand to produce the Kellogg-Briand pact. Nearly fifty nations signed the solemn pledge to renounce war and settle international disputes peacefully. Most Americans considered the nation's signature an affirmation of its commitment to peace rather than to Wilson's foolish notion of a progressive, uplifting war.

But Republican administrations preferred private sector diplomacy to state action. With the blessing of the White House, a team of American financiers led by Chicago banker Charles Dawes swung into action when Germany suspended its war reparation payments in 1923. Impoverished, Germany was staggering under the massive bill of $33 billion presented by the victorious Allies in the Versailles treaty. When Germany failed to meet its annual payment, France sought to enforce the treaty by occupying Germany's industrial Ruhr Valley, creating the worst international

Coolidge Posing as a Farmer
After the labor wars subsided, the image of Calvin Coolidge as the enforcer of law and order gave way to the softer image of "Silent Cal." Although he knew the ways of farming from his youth, the hay and pitchfork here are mere props for playing the political game. Coolidge's gleaming dress shoes and the official car with Secret Service men in the background give the game away. Throughout American society, traditional rural imagery had become nostalgic window dressing for the New Era of wealth and power.
Brown Brothers.

crisis since the war. In 1924, American corporate leaders produced the Dawes Plan, which halved Germany's annual reparation payments, initiated fresh American loans to Germany, caused the French to retreat from the Ruhr, and got money flowing again in Germany's financial markets. Although the United States failed to join the league, it continued to exercise significant economic and diplomatic influence abroad. These Republican successes overseas helped fuel prosperity at home.

Automobiles, Mass Production, and Assembly-Line Progress

The automobile industry emerged as the largest single manufacturing industry in the nation. By the end of the decade, aided by the federal government's decision to spend more on roads than on anything else, cars, trucks, and buses surged past railroads as the primary haulers of passengers and freight. Henry Ford shrewdly located his company in Detroit. Key materials for the automobile were manufactured in nearby states,

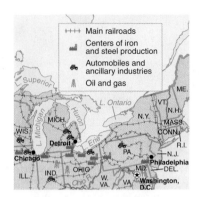

Detroit and the Automobile Industry in the 1920s

making their transport convenient (see Map 23.1). Keystone of the American economy, the automobile industry not only employed hundreds of thousands of workers directly but also brought whole industries into being—filling stations, garages, fast-food restaurants, and "guest cottages" (motels). The need for tires, glass, steel, highways, oil, and refined gasoline for automobiles provided millions of related jobs. By 1929, one American in four found employment directly or indirectly in the automobile industry. "Give us our daily bread" was no longer addressed to the Almighty, one commentator quipped, but to Detroit.

Automobiles altered the face of America. Cars changed where people lived, what work they did, how they spent their leisure, even how they thought. Hundreds of small towns decayed because the automobile enabled rural people to bypass them in favor of more distant cities and towns. The one-room schoolhouse and the crossroads church began to vanish from the landscape. Urban streetcars began to disappear as workers moved from the cities to the suburbs and commuted to work along crowded highways. In Los Angeles, which boasted of the nation's most extensive system of electric trolleys, almost a thousand miles of track suffered a slow death at the hands of the automobile. Nothing shaped modern America more than the automobile, and efficient mass production made the automobile revolution possible.

Mass production by the assembly-line technique had become standard in almost every factory, from automobiles to meatpacking to cigarettes. To improve efficiency, corporations reduced assembly-line work to the simplest, most repetitive tasks. They also established specialized divisions—procurement, production, marketing, and employee relations—each with its own team of professionally trained managers. Changes on the assembly line and in management, along with technological advances, significantly boosted overall efficiency. Between 1922 and 1929, productivity in manufacturing increased 32 percent. Average wages, however, increased only 8 percent. As assembly lines became standard, laborers lost many of the skills in which

> "Give us our daily bread" was no longer addressed to the Almighty, one commentator quipped, but to Detroit.

they had once taken pride, but corporations reaped great profits from these changes.

Industries also developed programs for workers that came to be called **welfare capitalism**. Some businesses improved safety and sanitation inside factories and instituted paid vacations and pension plans. Welfare capitalism purposely encouraged loyalty to the company and discouraged traditional labor unions. Not wanting to relive the chaotic strikes of 1919, industrialists sought to eliminate reasons for workers to join unions. One labor organizer in the steel industry bemoaned the success of welfare capitalism. "So many workmen here had been lulled to sleep by the company union, the welfare plans, the social organizations fostered by the employer," he declared, "that they had come to look upon the employer as their protector, and had believed vigorous trade union organization unnecessary for their welfare."

Consumer Culture

Mass production fueled corporate profits and national economic prosperity. Despite a brief postwar recession, the economy grew spectacularly during the 1920s. Per capita income increased by a third, the cost of living stayed the same, and unemployment remained low. But the rewards of the economic boom were not evenly distributed. Americans who labored with their hands inched ahead, while white-collar workers enjoyed significantly more spending money and more leisure time to spend it. Mass production of a broad range of new products—automobiles, radios, refrigerators, electric irons, washing machines—produced a consumer-goods revolution. (See "The Promise of Technology," page 832.)

In this new era of abundance, more people than ever conceived of the American dream in terms of the things they could acquire. How the business boom and business values of the 1920s affected average Americans is revealed in the classic *Middletown* (1929), an analysis of the lives of the inhabitants of Muncie, Indiana. Muncie was, above all, "a culture in which everything hinges on money." Moreover, faced with technological and organizational change beyond their comprehension, many citizens had lost confidence in their ability to play an effective role in civic affairs. Instead, they deferred to the supposed expertise of leaders in politics and economics and so found themselves relegated to the role of more passive consumers.

The pied piper of these disturbing changes, according to *Middletown*, was the rapidly expanding business of advertising, which stimulated the desire for new products and hammered away at the traditional values of thrift and saving. Newspapers, magazines, radios, and billboards told Americans what they had to have in order to be popular, secure, and successful. Advertising linked material goods to the fulfillment of every spiritual and emotional need. Americans increasingly defined and measured their social status, and indeed their personal worth, on the yardstick of material possessions. Happiness itself rode on owning a car and choosing the right cigarettes and toothpaste.

Colorado Filling Station and Gas Pump
Gulf Oil Company gave away the first free road map in 1914. By 1929, when Conoco (Continental Oil Company) produced this lavish map with Colorado's spectacular mountains looming in the background, nearly every oil company was supplying road maps as part of its campaign to attract the booming tourist trade. This appealing drive-through station is a far cry from the first retail outlets for gas—blacksmith shops and hardware stores, the same places individuals bought kerosene to burn in their lamps. Because motorists did not trust what they could not see, companies in the 1910s introduced glass-cylinder, gravity-flow gas pumps.
Courtesy, Colorado Historical Society.

READING THE IMAGE: What does this road map and accompanying image of a gravity-flow gasoline pump tell us about American consumer culture on the eve of the Great Depression?
CONNECTIONS: Does the road map accurately reflect the economic direction of the U.S. economy in 1929?

FOR MORE HELP ANALYZING THIS IMAGE, see the visual activity for this chapter in the Online Study Guide at bedfordstmartins.com/roark.

Household Appliances: Laborsaving Devices for Women?

In March 1921, Mrs. W. C. Lathrop of Norton, Kansas, wrote a fan letter to her hero, Thomas Edison, America's greatest inventor of electric marvels. She explained that as a mother of four who did all her own housework, she was dependent on Edison's fertile brain "for every pleasure and labor saving device I have." She explained, "I cook on a Westinghouse electric range" and "wash dishes in an electric dish washer." She washed "clothes in an electric machine" and ironed with "an electric iron." She cleaned her floors "with electric [vacuum] cleaners." But Edison had done more than make housework easier, she wrote. "I rest, take an electric massage and curl my hair on an electric iron. Dress in a gown sewed on a machine run by a[n electric] motor. Then start the Victrola and either study Spanish for a while or listen to Kreisler and Cluck and Galli-Curci in almost heavenly strains, forgetting I'm living in a tiny town of two thousand where nothing much ever happens." Her husband came home to "a wife not tired and dissatisfied but a woman waiting who has worked faithfully and . . . is now rested and ready to serve the tired man and discuss affairs of the day." Edison had once cheerfully predicted that electrified homes would free women from household drudgery, and here apparently was dramatic evidence.

By the end of the 1920s, most urban homes in America had electricity, paving the way for appliances. (See chapter 18, "The Promise of Technology," page 642.) Nine out of ten country folk lacked access to electricity, however, and the urban poor could not afford to buy into the promise of a fully wired paradise. Despite these inequities, middle-class urban families began acquiring household appliances that transformed women's daily lives. An advertisement in a leading women's magazine insisted, "Any woman who turns the wringer [on a hand-operated clothes washer]—any woman who irons by hand—any woman who beats a rug—any woman who cooks in a hot, stuffy kitchen is doing work which electricity will do for a few cents per day." The conclusion was clear: "The wise woman delegates to electricity all that electricity can do."

Before electricity, most chores were daylong ordeals. Washing clothes took hours and involved fetching water and fuel, building a fire, boiling the clothes and scrubbing them, boiling more water to rinse, and wringing them out by hand. Early washing machines were not fully automatic. To operate them, women had to stop and start the machine repeatedly to add soap and drain water, then put each item through the wringer. Nevertheless, washing machines saved housewives considerable work formerly spent hauling,

scrubbing, and hand-wringing, and they made "Blue Monday" (wash day) considerably less blue. Ironing had been one of the most dreaded household chores, especially in the summer when the kitchen stove had to be kept hot so that women could return their heavy irons to the stove for frequent reheating. Electric irons eased the burden enormously. Early vacuum cleaners were heavy and cumbersome, but they cleaned better than brooms, and they saved the labor of hauling rugs out of the house to be beaten. The appliances that filled electrified homes transformed the day-to-day work within the home.

Although household appliances relieved women of backbreaking labor, housework did not take less time. Indeed, there was no relationship between the presence of appliances in the home and hours spent doing housework. Several factors explain this ironic outcome of the mechanization of middle-class households. First, with the appearance of appliances, standards of cleanliness rose, and so did the frequency of many household chores. Urban families changed clothes more often, for example, and therefore housewives had to wash and iron more often. Instead of dragging rugs outside once a year for beating, vacuum cleaners allowed housewives to vacuum weekly. Appliances raised the standard of living, but they did not save women time. Second, washing machines, electric irons, vacuum cleaners, and other appliances made it possible for middle-class housewives to dispense with maids and take on the chores themselves. Without servants, the entire job of housekeeping fell to the housewife. Therefore, laborsaving appliances added new chores to the responsibilities of middle-class housewives—chores that in their mothers' day had been performed by others. Finally, if any time was saved in performing one task, it was spent in others, such as child care, education, and oversight of children's social lives.

Technology did not save women time because it was not accompanied by a rearrangement of gender responsibilities at home. Indeed, advertisements in the 1920s reinforced the connection between housework and housewives. Ads assumed that women alone would use the new appliances. In addition, ads suggested that because appliances took the drudgery out of housework, women could find emotional satisfaction in completing their work. Housework among middle-class women became not just a set of chores that had to be done, but a calling, an expression of love for the family. Women's magazines traded in guilt and embarrassment—guilt that a woman didn't eradicate all germs that threatened her family, embarrassment that her whites weren't as white as they could be. Increasingly, a woman's sense of self-worth depended on her performance of housework. The "scientification" of housework obligated middle-class women to buy the latest "laborsaving" devices in order to fulfill their familial duties.

In 1928, the editors of the *Ladies' Home Journal* summarized this new ideology of household technology: "The fact is that the American home was never a more satisfying place than it is today. Science and invention have outfitted it with a great range of conveniences and comforts." Women could have homes "in keeping with their instinctive longings." In the end, household appliances helped to lock married women

Eden Washing Machine Ad
This advertisement attempts to counter critics' claims that washing machines were hard on clothes by portraying a lady admiring her freshly laundered sheer lingerie. The caption points out that the gentle action of the machine avoided the harsh rubbing of hand washing. It claims that washing machines were now "essential" items and reminded prospective buyers that this beautiful Eden could be theirs through an "easy-payment plan." By 1930, nearly one million Americans had responded to advertising like this to buy a washing machine. Manufacturers of washing machines pitched their products as laborsaving devices, but what does this ad suggest about the leisure this machine left for the housewife who washed clothes in it?
Picture Research Consultants & Archives.

more firmly into traditional roles in the home and to create the idea of the full-time homemaker, who employed the latest technology for the good of her family. Edison's promise of an idyllic electrified future that would free women from the drudgery of housework was hard to keep. Despite Mrs. Lathrop's extravagant praise, appliances had not given women greater leisure or freedom.

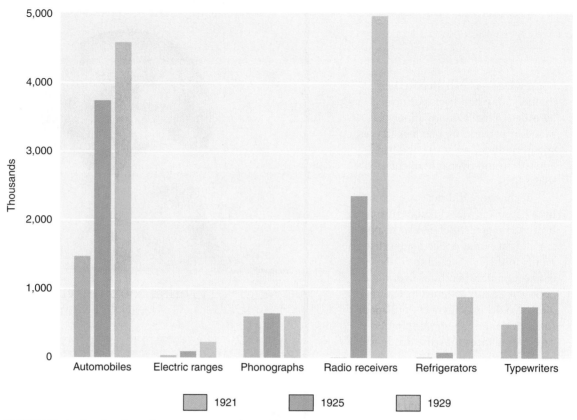

FIGURE 23.1   Production of Consumer Goods, 1920–1930
Transportation, communications, and entertainment changed the lives of consumers in the 1920s.
Laborsaving devices for the home were popular, but the vastly greater sales of automobiles and radios
showed that consumerism was powerful in moving people's attention beyond their homes.

By the 1920s, the United States had achieved the physical capacity to satisfy Americans' material wants (Figure 23.1). The economic problem shifted from production to consumption: Who would buy the goods flying off American assembly lines? One solution was to expand America's markets in foreign countries, and government and business joined in that effort. Another solution to the problem of consumption was to expand the market at home.

Henry Ford realized early on that "mass production requires mass consumption." He understood that automobile workers not only produced cars but would also buy them if they made enough money. "One's own employees ought to be one's own best customers," Ford said. In 1914, he raised wages in his factories to $5 a day, more than twice the going rate. High wages made for workers who were more loyal and more exploitable, and high wages returned as profits when workers bought Fords. Within twenty-four hours of Ford's announcement, ten thousand men had lined up outside his employment office in Detroit.

Not all industrialists were as farseeing as Ford. Because the wages of many workers barely edged upward, many people's incomes were too puny to satisfy the growing desire for consumer goods. Business supplied the solution: Americans could realize their dreams through credit. Installment buying—a little money down, a payment each month—allowed people to purchase expensive items they could not otherwise afford or purchase items before saving the necessary money. As one newspaper announced, "The first responsibility of an American to his country is no longer that of a citizen, but of a consumer." During the 1920s, America's motto became spend, not save. Old values—"Use it up, wear it out, make it do or do without"—seemed about as pertinent as a horse and buggy. American **culture** had shifted.

REVIEW   How did the spread of the automobile transform the United States?

The Roaring Twenties

By the beginning of the decade, psychoanalyst Sigmund Freud had become a household name. Most Americans knew little of the complexity of his pioneering work in the psychology of the unconscious because they learned about his therapies in popular magazines. Still, people realized that Freud offered a way of looking at the world that was as radically different and important to the twentieth century as Charles Darwin's theory of evolution had been to the century before. In the twenties, much to Freud's disgust, the American media turned his therapeutic wisdom about the sexual origins of behavior on its head. If it is wrong to deny that we are sexual beings, some reasoned, then the key to health and fulfillment must lie in following impulse freely. Those who doubted this reasoning were simply "repressed."

The new ethic of personal freedom excited a significant number of Americans to seek pleasure without guilt in a whirl of activity that earned the decade the name "Roaring Twenties." Prohibition made lawbreakers of millions of otherwise decent folk. Flappers and "new women" challenged traditional gender boundaries. Other Americans enjoyed the "Roaring Twenties" at a safe distance through the words and images of vastly expanded mass communication. Motion pictures, radio, and magazines marketed celebrities. In the freedom of America's big cities, particularly New York, a burst of creativity produced the "New Negro," who confounded and disturbed white Americans. The "Lost Generation" of writers, profoundly disillusioned with mainstream America's cultural direction, fled the country.

Prohibition

Republicans generally sought to curb the powers of government and liberate private initiative, but the twenties witnessed a great exception to this rule when the federal government implemented one of the last reforms of the Progressive Era: the Eighteenth Amendment, which banned the manufacture and sale of alcohol and took effect in January 1920 (see chapter 22) and made the United States the world's only society ever to outlaw its most popular intoxicant. Drying up the rivers of liquor that Americans consumed, supporters of prohibition declared, would boost production, eliminate crime, and lift the nation's morality. A powerful coalition supported prohibition, but women were particularly enthusiastic because heavy drinking was closely associated with domestic violence and poverty.

Charged with enforcing prohibition, the Treasury Department put more than 3,000 agents in the field, and in 1925 alone, they smashed more than 172,000 illegal stills. The annual per person consumption of alcoholic beverages declined from 2.60 gallons just before prohibition to less than a gallon in 1934, the year after prohibition ended. But Treasury agents faced a staggering task. Local resistance was intense. In 1929, an agent in Indiana reported, "Conditions in most important cities very bad. Lax and corrupt public officials great handicap . . . prevalence of

Lucky Strike

Cigarette smoking promised instant maturity, sophistication, and worldliness—not to mention, as revealed in this 1929 advertisement for the popular brand Lucky Strike, a svelte figure. Any woman seeking to remain attractive by avoiding matronly weight gain could simply reach for her Luckies. In the 1920s, Americans smoked billions of cigarettes each year, and ads assured them that they could feel confident about Lucky's purity because "it's toasted." How did smokers know that they ran no health risk? Because precisely 20,679 physicians said so! How has cigarette advertising changed? How has it remained the same?
Picture Research Consultants & Archives.

Prohibition Action
Prohibition agents sometimes entertained appreciative audiences. The wastefulness of pouring nine hundred gallons of perfectly good wine down a drain in Los Angeles amused some spectators and troubled others. Of course, those who had an interest in drinking despite the law could witness the disposal of bootleg alcohol serenely confident that they could easily find more.
Corbis.

notorious event came on St. Valentine's Day 1929, when Capone's Italian-dominated mob machine-gunned seven members of a rival Irish gang. Federal authorities finally sent Capone to prison for income tax evasion. "I give the public what the public wants," Capone told a reporter, "and all I get is abuse." Capone was a gangster, but he portrayed himself as a resourceful entrepreneur and successful businessman.

Gang-war slayings prompted demands for the repeal of the Eighteenth Amendment. In 1931, a panel of distinguished experts reported that prohibition, which supporters had defended as "a great social and economic experiment," had failed. The social and political costs of prohibition outweighed the benefits. Prohibition caused ordinary citizens to disrespect the law, corrupted the police, and demoralized the judiciary. In 1933, after thirteen years, the nation ended prohibition, making the Eighteenth Amendment the only constitutional amendment to be subsequently repealed.

The New Woman

Of all the changes in American life in the 1920s, none sparked more heated debate than the alternatives offered to the traditional roles of women. Increasing numbers of women worked and went to college, defying older gender hierarchies and norms. Even mainstream magazines such as the *Saturday Evening Post* began publishing stories about young, college-educated women who drank gin cocktails, smoked cigarettes, wore skimpy dresses and dangly necklaces, daringly rolled their stockings at the knee, and enjoyed sex. Before the Great War, the "new woman" dwelt in New York City's bohemian Greenwich Village, but afterward the mass media brought her into middle-class America's living rooms.

Politically, women entered uncharted territory when the Nineteenth Amendment, ratified in 1920, granted them the vote. **Feminists** felt liberated and expected women to reshape the political landscape. Celebrating enfranchisement, a Kansas woman declared, "I went to bed last night a *slave*[;] I awoke this morning a *free woman*." Women began pressuring Congress to pass laws that especially concerned women, including measures to protect women in factories and grant federal aid to schools. Black women lobbied particularly for federal courts to assume jurisdiction over the crime of lynching. But women's only significant legislative success came in 1921 when Congress enacted the Sheppard-Towner Act, which extended federal assistance to states seeking to reduce shockingly

drinking among minor boys and the . . . middle or better class of adults." The "speakeasy," a place where men (and, increasingly, women) drank publicly, became a common feature of the urban landscape. There, bootleggers, so named a century before because they put bottles in their tall boots to sneak past tax collectors, provided whiskey smuggled from Canada, tequila from Mexico, and liquor concocted in makeshift stills. Otherwise upright people discovered the thrill of breaking the law. One dealer, trading on common knowledge that whiskey still flowed in the White House, distributed cards advertising himself as the "President's Bootlegger."

> "I give the public what the public wants," Al Capone told a reporter, "and all I get is abuse."

Eventually, serious criminals took over the liquor trade. Alphonse "Big Al" Capone became the era's most notorious gang lord by establishing in Chicago a bootlegging empire that reputedly grossed more than $60 million in a single year. During the first four years of prohibition, Chicago witnessed more than two hundred gang-related killings as rival mobs struggled for control of the lucrative liquor trade. The most high infant mortality rates. Rather than the beginning of women's political success, the act marked the high tide of women's influence in the 1920s.

A number of factors helped thwart women's political influence. Male domination of both political parties, the rarity of female candidates, and lack of experience in voting, especially among recent immigrants, kept many women away from the polls. In the South, poll taxes, literacy tests, and outright terrorism continued to decimate the vote of African Americans, men and women alike.

Most important, rather than forming a solid voting bloc, feminists divided. Some argued for women's right to special protection; others demanded equal protection. The radical National Woman's Party fought for an Equal Rights Amendment that stated flatly: "Men and women shall have equal rights throughout the United States." The more moderate League of Women Voters feared that the amendment's wording threatened state laws that provided women special protection, such as barring women from night work and preventing them from working on certain machines. Put before Congress in 1923, the Equal Rights Amendment went down to defeat, and radical women were forced to act within a network of private agencies and reform associations to advance the causes of birth control, legal equality for minorities, and the end of child labor.

Economically, women's relationship to paid work changed. More women worked for pay—approximately one in four by 1930—but they clustered in "women's jobs." The proportion of women working in manufacturing fell, while the number of women working as secretaries, stenographers, and typists skyrocketed. Women almost monopolized the occupations of librarian, nurse, elementary school teacher, and telephone operator. Women also represented 40 percent of salesclerks by 1930. More female white-collar workers meant fewer women were interested in protective legislation for women; new women wanted salaries and opportunities equal to men's.

Increased earnings gave working women more buying power and a special relationship with the new **consumer culture**. A stereotype soon emerged of the flapper, so called because of the short-lived fad of wearing unbuckled galoshes. The flapper had short "bobbed" hair and wore lipstick and rouge. She spent freely on the latest styles—dresses with short skirts and drop waists, bare arms, and no petticoats—and she danced all night to wild jazz.

The new woman both reflected and propelled the modern birth control movement. Mar-

garet Sanger, the crusading pioneer for contraception during the Progressive Era, restated her principal conviction in 1920: "No woman can call herself free until she can choose consciously whether she will or will not be a mother." By shifting strategy in the twenties, Sanger courted the conservative American Medical Association; linked birth control with the eugenics movement, which advocated limiting reproduction among "undesirable" groups; and thus made contraception a respectable subject for discussion.

Flapper style and values spread from coast to coast through films, novels, magazines, and advertisements. New women challenged American convictions about **separate spheres** for women and men, the double standard of sexual conduct, and Victorian ideas of proper female appearance and behavior. (See "Historical Question," page 838.)

"The Girls' Rebellion"
The August 1924 cover of *Redbook*, a popular women's magazine, portrays the kind of postadolescent girl who was making respectable families frantic. Flappers scandalized their middle-class parents by flouting the old moral code. This young woman sports the "badges of flapperhood," including what one critic called an "intoxication of rouge." The cover promises a story inside about girls gone wild. Fictionalized, emotion-packed stories such as this brought the new woman into every woman's home. Picture Research Consultants & Archives.

Was There a Sexual Revolution in the 1920s?

"Cigarette in hand, shimmying to the music of the masses, the New Woman and the New Morality have made their theatric debut upon the modern scene," lamented one commentator in 1926. A moral chasm, the *Atlantic* magazine declared, had opened between the generations. The old and young in America "were as far apart in point of view, codes, and standards as if they belonged to different races." Endless articles appeared in the 1920s with titles such as "These Wild Young People" and "The Uprising of Youth." Settlement house leader Jane Addams objected to the "astounding emphasis upon sex." Charlotte Perkins Gilman represented many older feminists who were disappointed with the outcome of recent advances for women: "It is sickening to see so many of the newly freed abusing that freedom in a mere imitation of masculine weakness and vice." Older Americans wholeheartedly agreed that the younger generation was in full-fledged revolt against traditional standards of morality and that America was in danger of going to hell in a handbasket.

Critics had, it seemed, plenty of evidence. Between newspapers, movies, and magazines, even the small towns of America were "literally saturated with sex," one observer complained. Flappers and college coeds claimed the privileges of men, smoking cigarettes, drinking from hip flasks, and staying out all night. Their skimpy dresses, new dances ("a maximum of motion in the minimum of space"), and public proclamations about sexual emancipation punctuated the revolution. When eight hundred college women met to discuss life on campus and what "nice girls" should do, they concluded, "Learn temperance in petting, not abstinence." The president of the University of Florida bellowed, "The low-cut gowns, the rolled hose and short skirts are born of the Devil and his angels, and are carrying the present and future generations to chaos and destruction." Anxious individuals counseled intervention. The Ohio legislature debated whether to prohibit any "female over fourteen years of age" from wearing a "skirt which does not reach to that part of the foot known as the instep." The *Ladies' Home Journal* urged "legal prohibition" of jazz dancing.

But were the anxious observers correct? Was there really a sexual revolution in the 1920s? The principal movers of the new morality were youths, and without a doubt young, middle-class men and women felt freer than ever to express openly their feelings about sex. Mass media spread sex talk across the nation. But we must separate actual sexual behavior from the new candor in talking about sex. Although solid evidence is difficult to come by, correspondence, diaries, and other personal documents; physicians' records; divorce proceedings; advice literature; and a few early sex surveys provide important clues. It's worth noting that as difficult as it is to reconstruct the sexual lives of the middle class, it is even more difficult to recover the sex lives of working-class Americans, who left even fewer records, and of same-sex relationships, which most sources hardly mention.

But what of middle-class, white Americans; did they walk the walk or just talk the talk? A good place to begin the investigation is where young, middle-class Americans congregated: educational campuses. For the first time in U.S. history, more than half of all young people were enrolled in some sort of educational institution, and women were enrolled at almost the same rate as men. Campus life included a self-conscious ethos of experimentation and innovation, but as students demolished old rules, they also created new ones. One major innovation was "dating"—that is, going out unsupervised rather than receiving callers at home or meeting at church socials. Dating was encouraged by the automobile, that "house of prostitution on wheels," as one juvenile judge in Indiana labeled it. Dating led to a second innovation: "petting," or any sexual activity short of intercourse. One examination of coed behavior at the end of the 1920s found that 92 percent of women admitted engaging in petting.

Like dating, petting represented a significant change in female behavior. But it was not a total rejection of traditional morality because it took place within the search for the ideal marriage partner. There was also a modest increase in premarital sexual intercourse, made possible by the widespread acceptance of contraceptives, especially the diaphragm. But sexual intercourse usually took place between partners who assumed they would marry. Importantly, the marriage they looked forward to was a romantic/sexual union in which both husband and wife had equal rights to sexual satisfaction. Effective contraception transformed sex from a merely "propagative act" to a "spiritual avenue of expression." In this way, the new woman of the 1920s, though freer sexually, continued to focus on romance, marriage, and family.

Did the new sexual behavior mark a drastic change from the past? Evidence of sexual habits before World War I is even more difficult to come by than for the 1920s, but it appears that changes in attitudes and behaviors had been under way for decades. Nineteenth-century Victorian notions of sexless women who felt little or no passion had been eroding since at least the 1890s. A small survey of the sexual practices of middle-class women in the 1890s conducted by Dr. Clelia

Duel Mosher, a physician at Stanford University, found that women were enthusiastic about sex and often found satisfaction. The primary ideologues of the sexual revolution, Havelock Ellis and Sigmund Freud, reached American audiences before World War I. Ellis, an English therapist, celebrated female passion, and Freud stressed the centrality of sex in human endeavor. (His popularizers stressed the dangers of sexual repression.)

Changes in sexual morality, therefore, were evolutionary rather than revolutionary. Still, liberal attitudes and behaviors had their greatest impact in the 1920s. American culture was being remade, and young people, especially women, were at the cutting edge. Now equal at the polling booth, women were also growing more economically independent. When World War I began, two million women worked in business offices. By 1930, the number soared to ten million. Changes in women's political and economic lives were reflected in their sexual attitudes and behaviors. In place of the idea that women were naturally pure, the new morality proclaimed the equality of desire. Only the boldest women rejected a "double standard" (the notion that the sexual behavior of women should be more circumscribed than that of men), but many jettisoned notions of female submission, obedience, and endless childbearing. As traditional controls of family, religion, and communities lessened in the 1920s, the influence of peers grew more important than that of parents, and movies were more influential than community opinion. Charges that the giddy flapper and her partner were bringing down American civilization were overblown, but young women certainly were changing the culture.

Heroes and Heroines

Two kinds of women look up adoringly at two kinds of 1920s heroes. A wholesome image is seen on the left in a 1927 cover of *People's Popular Monthly* magazine. The healthy outdoor girl, smartly turned out in her raccoon coat and pennant, flatters a naive college football hero. On the right, the pale, sensitive Vilma Banky kneels imploringly before the hypnotic gaze of the movies' greatest heartthrob, Rudolph Valentino.

Magazine: Picture Research Consultants & Archives; Poster: Billy Rose Theatre Collection, The New York Public Library at Lincoln Center.

READING THE IMAGE: Is the pale heroine in the movie poster beseeching her kidnapper to release her, or is she swooning with desire? How is the depiction of the college girl similar to the depiction of the movie star, and how is it different?

CONNECTIONS: How do these portrayals of women conform to the social and sexual mores of the 1920s?

FOR MORE HELP ANALYZING THIS IMAGE, see the visual activity for this chapter in the Online Study Guide at bedfordstmartins.com/roark.

Although only a minority of American women became flappers, all women, even those who remained at home, felt the great changes of the era.

The New Negro

The 1920s witnessed the emergence not only of the "new woman" but also of the "New Negro." Both new identities riled conservatives and reactionaries. African Americans who challenged the caste system that confined dark-skinned Americans to the lowest levels of society confronted whites who insisted that race relations would not change. Cheers for black soldiers quickly faded after their return from World War I, and African Americans soon faced grim days of economic hardship and race riots (see chapter 22).

Noah's Ark

Kansas-born painter Aaron Douglas expressed the Harlem Renaissance visually. When Douglas arrived in New York City in 1925, he quickly attracted the attention of W. E. B. Du Bois, who believed that the arts could manifest the African American soul. At Du Bois's urging, Douglas sought ways of integrating the African cultural heritage with American experience. This depiction of an African Noah commanding the loading of the ark displays a technique that became closely associated with African American art: strong silhouetted figures awash in misty color, indicating a connection between Christian faith and the vital, colorful origins of black Americans in a distant, mythologized African past. Fisk University Art Galleries.

During the 1920s, the prominent African American intellectual W. E. B. Du Bois and the National Association for the Advancement of Colored People (NAACP) aggressively pursued the passage of a federal antilynching law to counter mob violence against blacks in the South. Many poor blacks, however, disillusioned with mainstream politics, turned for new leadership to a Jamaican-born visionary named Marcus Garvey. Garvey urged African Americans to rediscover the heritage of Africa, take pride in their own culture and achievements, and maintain racial purity by avoiding **miscegenation**. In 1917, Garvey launched the Universal Negro Improvement Association (UNIA) to help African Americans gain economic and political independence entirely outside white society. In 1919, the UNIA created its own shipping company, the Black Star Line, to support the "Back to Africa" movement among black Americans. Garvey knew how to inspire followers, but he was no businessman, and the enterprise was an economic failure. In 1927, the federal government pinned charges of illegal practices on Garvey and deported him to Jamaica. Nevertheless, the issues Garvey raised about racial pride, black identity, and the search for equality persisted, and his legacy remains at the center of **black nationalist** thought.

Still, most African Americans maintained hope in the American promise. In New York City, hope and talent came together. Poor blacks from the South, as well as sophisticated immigrants from the West Indies, poured into Harlem in uptown Manhattan. New York City's black population increased 115 percent (from 152,000 to 327,000) in the 1920s, while its white population increased only 20 percent. Similar demographic changes occurred on a smaller scale throughout the urban North. Overcrowding and unsanitary housing accompanied this black population explosion, but so too did a new self-consciousness and self-confidence that fed into artistic accomplishment.

The extraordinary mix of black artists, sculptors, novelists, musicians, and poets in Harlem deliberately set out to create a distinctive African American culture that drew on their identities as Americans and Africans. As scholar Alain Locke put it in 1925, they introduced to the world the "New Negro," who rose from the ashes of slavery and segregation to proclaim African Americans' creative genius. The emergence of the New Negro came to be known as the Harlem Renaissance. Building on the independence and pride displayed by black soldiers during the war, black

artists sought to defeat the fresh onslaught of racial discrimination and violence with poems, paintings, and plays. "We younger Negro artists . . . intend to express our individual dark-skinned selves without fear or shame," Langston Hughes, a determined young black poet, said of the Harlem Renaissance. "If white people are pleased, we are glad. If they are not, it doesn't matter. We know we are beautiful. And ugly, too."

The Harlem Renaissance produced dazzling talent. Black writer James Weldon Johnson, who in 1903 had written the Negro national anthem, "Lift Every Voice," wrote "God's Trombones" (1927), in which he expressed the wisdom and beauty of black folktales from the South. The poetry of Langston Hughes, Claude McKay, and Countee Cullen celebrated the vitality of life in Harlem. Zora Neale Hurston's novel *Their Eyes Were Watching God* (1937) explored the complex passions of black people in a southern community. Black painters, led by Aaron Douglas, linked African art, which had recently inspired European modernist artists, to the concept of the New Negro. In bold, colorful scenes, Douglas combined biblical and African myths in ways that expressed a powerful cultural heritage for African Americans.

Despite such vibrancy, Harlem for most whites remained a separate black ghetto known only for its lively nightlife. Fashionable whites crowded into Harlem's nightclubs, the most famous of which was the Cotton Club. There, whites believed they could hear "real" jazz, a relatively new musical form, in its "natural" surroundings. The vigor and optimism of the Harlem Renaissance left a powerful legacy for black Americans, but the creative burst did little in the short run to dissolve the prejudice of a white society not yet prepared to allow African Americans equal opportunities. (See "Seeking the American Promise," page 842.)

Mass Culture

By the late 1920s, jazz had captured the nation. Americans who clung to symphonic music called jazz "jungle music," but jazz giants such as Louis Armstrong, Jelly Roll Morton, and Duke Ellington, accompanied by singers such as Ma Rainey, Bessie Smith, and Ethel Waters, entertained huge audiences. Jazz was only one of the entertainment choices of Americans, however. In the twenties, popular culture, like consumer goods, was mass-produced and mass-consumed. Since politics was undemanding and uninteresting, Americans looked elsewhere for excitement. The proliferation of movies, radios, music, and sports meant that they found plenty to do, and in doing the same things, they helped create a national culture.

Nothing offered escapist delights like the movies (Figure 23.2). Admission was cheap, and in the dark, Americans of all classes could savor the same ideal of the good life. Blacks and whites,

FIGURE 23.2 Movie and Baseball Attendance America's favorite pastimes, movies and baseball, tracked the economy. The rise and fall of weekly movie attendance and seasonal baseball attendance shown here mirrored the rise and fall of prosperity.

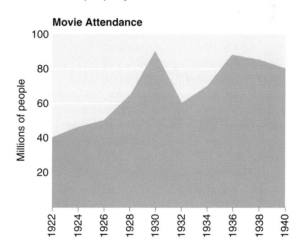
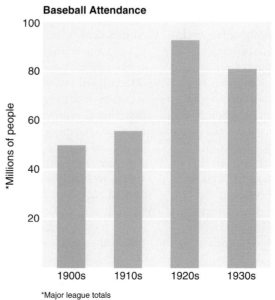

A Place of One's Own: The Quest for Home Ownership

Owning a place of one's own has always been important in America. In the nineteenth century, with the rise of industry and cities, the goal of a family farm gave way to the goal of a single-family house. Home ownership has been widely realized today, with roughly two-thirds of Americans (with the assistance of mortgage companies) owning their own homes. Still, fewer than one-half of African Americans and Hispanics own their own homes. The aspiration of home ownership unites Americans, but efforts to achieve this goal have sometimes set Americans against one another.

In the 1920s, decent housing was in short supply in Detroit, America's great boomtown, as thousands poured in to work in Henry Ford's automobile factories. Arriving before World War I, blue-collar German, Irish, and Polish immigrants found homes in working-class neighborhoods scattered around the city center. Detroit's black population was tiny when the war began, but the great migration out of the South sent the population soaring by 1925. Tens of thousands of black newcomers frightened white property-owners who had worked hard for their modest homes and believed that blacks would drive down property values, cause neighborhood decay, and fill their streets with criminals.

They resolved to keep their neighborhoods all-white by channeling blacks into Black Bottom, the downtown ghetto. Although the U.S. Supreme Court had struck down a law mandating segregated housing in 1917, inventive white homeowners created other means to draw racial boundaries. Real estate agents refused to show blacks houses in white neighborhoods. Banks turned down blacks for mortgages. Whites signed restrictive covenants, promising not to sell their homes to blacks. If a black family managed to slip through their defenses, whites resorted to violence. In Detroit during the 1920s, income, education, occupation, wealth, and respectability meant little compared to race.

Dr. Ossian Sweet, a black physician who had washed dishes and waited tables to pay for his college education at Wilberforce University in Ohio and to attend medical school at Howard University in Washington, D.C., arrived in Detroit in 1921. He set up his medical practice in Black Bottom and prospered. He soon had the down payment for a home, but he refused to settle his wife and baby daughter in the congested, rat-infested ghetto. In 1925, Sweet bought a substantial bungalow at 2905 Garland Avenue, several blocks inside a working-class white neighborhood. His brother said later, "He wasn't looking for trouble. He just wanted to bring up his little girl in good surroundings." But Sweet understood the danger of trying to escape Black Bottom. Whites had recently run other black professionals out of their Detroit neighborhoods. Sweet told a friend, "Well, we have decided we are not going to run. We're not going to look for any trouble, but we're going to be prepared to protect ourselves if trouble arises." When Gladys and Ossian Sweet moved into their home on September 8, 1925, nine friends and family members accompanied them. The moving van that brought their furniture also carried a shotgun, two rifles, six pistols, and four hundred rounds of ammunition.

It did not take long for a crowd to gather. Hundreds of white men filled the streets, greatly outnumbering the few police who hoped to keep the peace. Shouting that they would send the "niggers" back where they belonged, the mob began throwing rocks, breaking windows, and advancing. Suddenly, gunfire erupted from the second story of the Sweet house, and two white men were shot; one was killed. The police kept the mob away long enough for a paddy wagon to haul the eleven blacks to the police station, where they were all indicted for murder.

Asked why he wanted to move to a white neighborhood, where there was likely to be trouble, Sweet said, "Because I bought the house, and it was my house, and I felt I had a right to live in it." The NAACP, which saw the case as a symbol of injustice and an opportunity to strike a legal blow in favor of self-defense against racial violence, hired Clarence Darrow to defend the accused. Darrow was the most celebrated defense lawyer in the

Dr. Ossian Sweet and His House
Dr. Ossian Sweet's substantial two-story brick home is listed on the National Register of Historic Places. In September 1925, Sweet tried to move his family into the then all-white Detroit suburb where the house is located. Residents reacted violently, determined to uphold "the present high standards of the neighborhood."
The Detroit News.

country and fresh from the Scopes trial in Tennessee (see page 848). In the courtroom, Sweet claimed that he had acted in self-defense. Darrow said that the facts were simple: "When they defended their home, they were arrested and charged with murder." He reminded the all-white jury that "every man's home is his castle, which even the king may not enter. Every man has a right to kill to defend himself or his family, or others, either in defense of the home, or in defense of themselves." A split jury caused the judge to declare a mistrial. A second trial ended in not

guilty verdicts for all the defendants. "The verdict meant simply that the doctrine that a man's house is his castle applied to the black man as well as the white man," Darrow concluded optimistically.

Over the next several decades, however, housing discrimination became entrenched throughout the nation. Blacks succeeded in breaking out of the inner cities and moving into the suburbs, where today more than one-third of African Americans live, but breaching city boundaries did not mean leaving residential segregation behind. Of all the na-

tion's segregated cities, none was more segregated than Detroit. As late as 1963, Martin Luther King Jr. declared: "I have a dream this afternoon that one day right here in Detroit Negroes will be able to buy a house or rent a house anywhere their money will carry them."

As for Sweet, he moved back into his home on Garland Avenue in 1928, but without his wife and daughter, who had both died. He stayed in the bungalow for more than twenty-five years, and when he left, the neighborhood around him was still largely white.

however, still entered theaters through separate entrances and sat separately. Hollywood, California, discovered the successful formula of combining opulence, sex, and adventure. By 1929, Hollywood was drawing more than 80 million people to the movies in a single week, as many as lived in the entire country. Rudolph Valentino, described as "catnip to women," and Clara Bow, the "It Girl" (everyone knew what *it* was), became household names. "America's Sweetheart," Mary Pickford, and her real-life husband, Douglas Fairbanks, offered more wholesome adventure. Most loved of all was the comic Charlie Chaplin, whose famous character, the wistful Little Tramp, showed an endearing inability to cope with the rules and complexities of modern life.

Americans also found heroes in sports. Baseball, professionalized since 1869 and segregated into white and black leagues, solidified its place as the national pastime in the 1920s (see Figure 23.2). It remained essentially a game played by and for the working class, an outlet for raw energy with a tinge of rebelliousness. In George Herman "Babe" Ruth, baseball had the most cherished free spirit of the time. The "Sultan of Swat" mixed his record-setting home runs with rowdy escapades, demonstrating to fans that sports offered a way to break out of the ordinariness of everyday life. By "his sheer exuberance," one sportswriter declared, Ruth "has lightened the cares of the world."

The public also fell in love with a young boxer from the grim mining districts of Colorado. As a teenager, Jack Dempsey had made his living hanging around saloons betting he could beat anyone in the house. When he took the heavyweight crown just after World War I, he was revered as the people's champ, an American equalizer who was a stand-in for the average American who felt increasingly confined by bureaucracy and machine-made culture. In Philadelphia in 1926, a crowd of 125,000 fans saw challenger Gene Tunney carve up and defeat the people's champ.

Football, essentially a college sport, held greater sway with the upper classes. The most famous coach, Knute Rockne of Notre Dame, celebrated football for its life lessons of hard work and teamwork. Let the professors make learning as interesting and significant as football, Rockne advised, and the problem of getting young people to learn would disappear. But in keeping with the times, football moved toward a more commercial spectacle. Harold "Red" Grange, "the Galloping Ghost," led the way by going from stardom at the University of Illinois to the Chicago Bears in the new professional football league.

The decade's hero worship reached its zenith in the celebration of Charles Lindbergh, a young pilot who set out on May 20, 1927, from Long Island in his single-engine plane, *The Spirit of St. Louis*, to become the first person to fly nonstop across the Atlantic. Newspapers tagged Lindbergh "the Lone Eagle"— the perfect hero for an age that celebrated individual accomplishment. "Charles Lindbergh," one journalist proclaimed, "is the stuff out of which have been made the pioneers that opened up the wilderness. His are the qualities which we, as a people, must nourish." Lindbergh realized, however, that technical and organizational complexity was fast reducing chances for solitary achievement. Consequently, he titled his book about the flight *We* (1927) to include the machine that had made it all possible.

Another machine—the radio—became important to mass culture in the 1920s. The nation's first licensed radio station, KDKA in Pittsburgh, began broadcasting in 1920, and soon American airwaves buzzed with news, sermons, soap operas, sports, comedy, and music. Americans on the West Coast laughed at the latest jokes from New York. For the first time, citizens were able to listen to the voices of political candidates without leaving home. Because they could now reach prospective customers in their own homes, advertisers bankrolled radio's rapid growth. Between 1922 and 1929, the number of radio stations in the United States increased from 30 to 606. In just seven years, homes with radios jumped from 60,000 to a staggering 10.25 million.

Radio added to the spread of popular music, especially jazz. Jazz—with its energy and freedom—provided the sound track for a new, distinct social class of youths. As the traditional bonds of community, religion, and family loosened, the young felt less pressure to imitate their elders and more freedom to develop their own culture. An increasing number of college students helped the "rah-rah" style of college life become a fad promoted in movies, songs, and advertisements. The collegiate set was the vanguard of the decade's "flaming youth."

Although F. Scott Fitzgerald gained fame and wealth as the chronicler of flaming youth, he spoke sadly in *This Side of Paradise* (1920) of a disillusioned generation "grown up to find all Gods dead, all wars fought, all faiths in man shaken."

The Lost Generation

Some writers and artists felt alienated from America's mass-culture society, which they found shallow, anti-intellectual, and materialistic. Adoration of silly movie stars disgusted them. Moreover, they believed that business culture blighted American life. To their minds, Henry Ford made a poor hero. Young, white, and mostly college educated, these expatriates, as they came to be called, felt embittered by the war and renounced the progressives who had promoted it as a crusade. For them, Europe—not Hollywood or Harlem— seemed the place to seek their renaissance.

The American-born writer Gertrude Stein, long established in Paris, remarked famously as the young exiles gathered around her, "They are the lost generation." Most of the expatriates, however, believed to the contrary that they had finally found themselves. Far from the complications of home, the expatriates helped launch the most creative period in American art and literature in the twentieth century. The novelist whose spare, clean style best exemplified the expatriate efforts to make art mirror basic reality was Ernest Hemingway. Hemingway's experience in the Great War convinced him that the world in which he was raised, with its Christian moralism and belief in progress, was bankrupt. Admirers found the terse language and hard lessons of his novel *The Sun Also Rises* (1926) to be perfect expressions of a world stripped of illusions.

Many writers who remained in America were exiles in spirit. Before the war, intellectuals had eagerly joined progressive reform movements. Afterward, they were more likely to act as lonely critics of American cultural vulgarity. With prose dripping with scorn for conventional values, novelist Sinclair Lewis in *Main Street* (1920) and *Babbitt* (1922) satirized his native Midwest as a cultural wasteland. Humorists such as James Thurber created outlandish characters to poke fun at American stupidity and inhibitions. And southern writers, led by William Faulkner, explored the South's grim class and race heritage. Worries about alienation surfaced as well. Although F. Scott Fitzgerald gained fame and wealth as the chronicler of flaming youth, he spoke sadly in *This Side of Paradise* (1920) of a disillusioned generation "grown up to find all Gods dead, all wars fought, all faiths in man shaken."

REVIEW How did the new freedoms of the 1920s challenge older conceptions of gender and race?

Resistance to Change

Large areas of the country did not share in the wealth of the 1920s and had little confidence that they would anytime soon. By the end of the decade, 40 percent of the nation's farmers were landless, and 90 percent of rural homes had no indoor plumbing, gas, or electricity. Rural America's wariness and distrust of urban America turned to despair in the 1920s when the census reported that the majority of the population had shifted from the country to the city (Map 23.2, page 846). Urban domination over the nation's political and cultural life and sharply rising economic disparity drove rural Americans in often ugly, reactionary directions.

Cities seemed to stand for everything rural areas stood against. Rural America imagined itself as solidly Anglo-Saxon (despite the presence of millions of African Americans in the South and Mexican Americans, Native Americans, and Asian Americans in the West), and the cities seemed to be filled with undesirable immigrants. Rural America was the home of old-time **Protestant** religion, and the cities teemed with Catholics, Jews, liberal Protestants, and atheists. Rural America championed old-fashioned moral standards—abstinence and self-denial—while the cities spawned every imaginable vice. Once the "backbone of the Republic," rural Americans had become poor country cousins. In the 1920s, frustrated rural people sought to recapture their country by helping to push through prohibition, dam the flow of immigrants, revive the Ku Klux Klan, defend the Bible as literal truth, and defeat an urban Roman Catholic for president.

Rejecting the Undesirables

Before the war, when about a million immigrants arrived each year, some Americans warned that unassimilable foreigners were smothering the nation. War against Germany and its allies expanded **nativist** and anti-radical sentiment. After the war, large-scale immigration resumed (another 800,000 immigrants arrived in 1921) at a moment when industrialists no longer needed new factory laborers. African American and Mexican migration had relieved labor shortages. Moreover, union leaders feared that millions of poor immigrants would undercut their efforts to organize American workers. Rural America's God-fearing

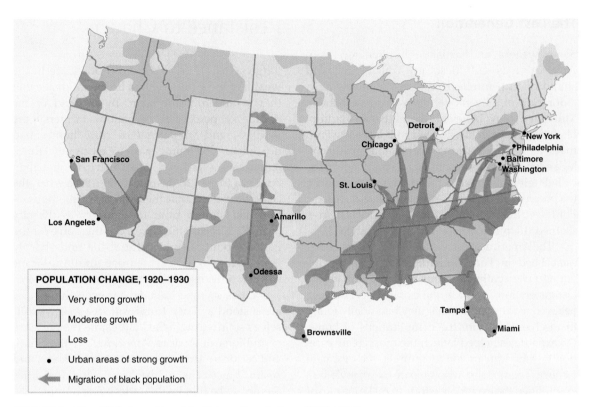

MAP 23.2   The Shift from Rural to Urban Population, 1920–1930
The movement of whites and Hispanics toward urban and agricultural opportunity made Florida, the West, and the Southwest the regions of fastest population growth. In contrast, large numbers of blacks left the rural South to find a better life in the North. Because almost all migrating blacks went from the countryside to cities in distant parts of the nation, while white and Hispanic migrants tended to move shorter distances toward familiar places, the population shift brought more drastic overall change to blacks than to whites and Hispanics.

READING THE MAP: Which states had the strongest growth? To which cities did southern blacks predominantly migrate?
CONNECTIONS: What conditions in the countryside made the migration to urban areas appealing to many rural Americans? In what social and cultural ways did rural America view itself as different from urban America?

FOR MORE HELP ANALYZING THIS MAP, see the map activity for this chapter in the Online Study Guide at bedfordstmartins.com/roark.

Protestants were particularly alarmed that most of the immigrants were Catholic, Jewish, or atheist. In 1921, Congress responded by severely restricting immigration.

In 1924, Congress very nearly slammed the door shut. The Johnson-Reid Act limited the number of immigrants to no more than 161,000 a year and gave each European nation a quota based on 2 percent of the number of people from that country in America in 1890. The act revealed the fear and bigotry that fueled anti-immigration legislation. While it cut immigration by more than 80 percent, it squeezed some nationalities far more than others. Backers of Johnson-Reid

openly declared that America had become the "garbage can and the dumping ground of the world," and they manipulated quotas to ensure entry only to "good" immigrants. By basing quotas on the 1890 census, in which western Europeans predominated, the law effectively reversed the trend toward immigration from southern and eastern Europe, which by 1914 had amounted to 75 percent of the yearly total. For example, the Johnson-Reid Act allowed Great Britain 62,458 entries, but Russia could send only 1,992.

The 1924 law reaffirmed the 1880s legislation barring Chinese immigrants and added Japanese and other Asians to the list of the excluded. But it left open immigration from the Western Hemisphere, and during the 1920s, some 500,000 Mexicans crossed the border. Farm interests preserved Mexican immigration because of Mexicans' value in southwestern agriculture.

Rural Americans, who had most likely never laid eyes on a Polish packinghouse worker, a Slovak coal miner, an Armenian sewing machine operator, or a Chinese laundry worker, strongly supported the 1924 law, as did industrialists and labor leaders. The immigration restriction laws of the 1920s provided the basic framework for immigration policy until the 1960s. They marked the end of an era—the denial of the Statue of Liberty's open-arms welcome to Europe's "huddled masses yearning to breathe free."

Antiforeign hysteria climaxed in the trial of two **anarchist** immigrants from Italy, Nicola Sacco and Bartolomeo Vanzetti. Arrested in 1920 for robbery and murder in South Braintree, Massachusetts, the men were sentenced to death by a judge who openly referred to them as "anarchist bastards." In response to doubts about the fairness of the verdict, the governor of Massachusetts named a blue-ribbon review committee that found the trial judge guilty of a "grave breach of official decorum" but refused to recommend a motion for retrial. When Massachusetts executed Sacco and Vanzetti on August 23, 1927, fifty thousand mourners followed the cas-

kets in the rain, convinced that the men had died because they were immigrants and radicals, not because they were murderers.

The Rebirth of the Ku Klux Klan

The nation's sour, antiforeign mood struck a responsive chord in members of the Ku Klux Klan. The Klan first appeared in the South during Reconstruction to thwart black freedom and expired with the reestablishment of white supremacy. In 1915, the Klan revived soon after D. W. Griffith's blockbuster film *Birth of a Nation* celebrated earlier Klan racist violence as heroic and necessary. Reborn at Stone Mountain, Georgia, the new Klan extended its targets beyond black Americans and quickly spread beyond the South. Under a banner proclaiming "100 percent Americanism," the Klan promised to defend family, morality, and traditional American values against the threats posed by blacks, immigrants, radicals, feminists, Catholics, and Jews.

Building on the frustrations of rural America, the Klan attracted three million to four million members—women as well as men. Women members worked for prohibition, strong public schools, and traditional morality. By the mid-1920s, the Klan had spread throughout the nation, almost controlling Indiana and influencing

Sacco and Vanzetti
After the guilty verdicts were announced, American artist Ben Shahn produced a series of paintings to preserve the memory of Nicola Sacco and Bartolomeo Vanzetti, whom many immigrants, liberals, and civil libertarians believed were falsely accused and unfairly convicted. Even today, the 1927 executions symbolize for some the shortcomings of American justice.
Digital Image © Museum of Modern Art/ Licensed by Scala/Art Resource, NY.

WKKK Badge
Some half a million women were members of the Women of the Ku Klux Klan (WKKK). Young girls could join the female youth auxiliary, the Tri-K for Girls. Klanswomen fit perfectly within the KKK because the organization proclaimed itself the defender of the traditional virtues of pure womanhood and decent homes. This badge from Harrisburg, Pennsylvania, advertises the local WKKK's support for a home for "orphan and dependent children." Klanswomen also joined in boycotts of businesses owned by Jews and others whom they did not consider "100% American."
Collection of Janice L. and David J. Frent.

politics in Illinois, California, Oregon, Texas, Louisiana, Oklahoma, and Kansas. The Klan's uniforms and rituals helped counter a sense of insignificance among people outside the new world of cities and corporations. In 1926, Klan imperial wizard Hiram Wesley Evans described the assault of modernity. "One by one all our traditional moral standards went by the boards or were so disregarded that they ceased to be binding," he explained. "The sacredness of our Sabbath, of our homes, of chastity, and finally even of our right to teach our own children in schools [were] fundamental facts and truth torn away from us." Americans "who maintained the old standards did so only in the face of constant ridicule," he said. The Klan offered a certain counterfeit dignity to old-stock, Protestant, white Americans who felt passed over, and its hoods allowed members to beat and intimidate their victims with little fear of consequences.

> In 1926, Klan imperial wizard Hiram Wesley Evans described the assault of modernity. "One by one all our traditional moral standards went by the boards or were so disregarded that they ceased to be binding," he explained.

Eventually, social changes, along with lawless excess, crippled the Klan. Immigration restrictions eased the worry about invading foreigners, and sensational wrongdoing by Klan leaders cost it the support of traditional moralists. Grand Dragon David Stephenson of Indiana, for example, went to jail for the kidnapping and rape of a woman who subsequently committed suicide. Yet the social grievances, economic problems, and religious anxieties of the countryside and small towns remained, ready to be ignited.

The Scopes Trial

In 1925 in a steamy Tennessee courtroom, old-time religion and the new spirit of science went head-to-head. The confrontation occurred after several southern states passed legislation against the teaching of Charles Darwin's theory of evolution in the public schools. **Fundamentalist** Protestants insisted that the Bible's creation story be taught as the literal truth. In answer to a clamor from scientists and civil liberties organizations for a challenge to the law, John Scopes, a young biology teacher in Dayton, Tennessee, offered to test his state's ban on teaching evolution. When Scopes came to trial in the summer of 1925, Clarence Darrow, a brilliant defense lawyer from Chicago, volunteered to defend him. Darrow, an avowed agnostic, took on the prosecution's William Jennings Bryan, three-time Democratic nominee for president, symbol of rural America, and fervent fundamentalist, who was eager to defeat the proposition that humans had evolved from apes.

The Scopes trial quickly degenerated into a media circus. The first trial to be covered live on radio, it attracted an avid nationwide audience. Most of the reporters from big-city newspapers were hostile to Bryan, none more so than the cynical H. L. Mencken, who painted Bryan as a sort of Darwinian missing link ("a sweating anthropoid" and a "gaping primate"). When, under relentless questioning by Darrow, Bryan declared on the witness stand that he did indeed believe that the world had been created in six days and that Jonah had lived in the belly of a whale, his humiliation in the eyes of most urban observers was complete. Nevertheless, the Tennessee court upheld the law and punished Scopes with a $100 fine. Although fundamentalism won the battle, it lost the war. Mencken had the last word in a merciless obituary for Bryan, who died just a week after the trial ended. Portraying the "monkey trial" as a battle between the country and the city, Mencken flayed Bryan as a "charlatan, a mountebank, a zany without shame or dignity," motivated solely by "hatred of the city men who had laughed at him for so long."

As Mencken's acid prose indicated, Bryan's humiliation was not purely a victory of reason and science. It also revealed the disdain urban people felt for country people and the values they clung to. The Ku Klux Klan revival and the Scopes trial dramatized and inflamed divisions between city and country, intellectuals and the uneducated, the privileged and the poor, the scoffers and the faithful.

Al Smith and the Election of 1928

The presidential election of 1928 brought many of the developments of the 1920s—prohibition, immigration, religion, and the clash of rural and urban values—into sharp focus. Republicans emphasized the economic success of their party's pro-business government. But because both parties generally agreed that the American economy was basically sound, the campaign turned on social issues that divided Americans. Tired of the limelight, Calvin Coolidge chose not to seek reelection, and the Republicans turned to Herbert Hoover, the energetic secretary of commerce and the leading public symbol of 1920s prosperity.

The Democrats nominated four-time governor of New York Alfred E. Smith. Smith adopted "The Sidewalks of New York" as a campaign theme song and seemed to represent all

that rural Americans feared and resented. A child of immigrants, Smith got his start in politics with the help of Tammany Hall, New York City's Irish-dominated political machine and the epitome of big-city corruption in many minds. He believed that immigration quotas were wrong, and he spoke out against restriction. He signed New York State's anti-Klan bill and condemned the decade's growing intolerance. Smith also opposed prohibition, believing that it was a nativist attack on immigrant customs. When Smith supposedly asked reporters in 1922, "Wouldn't you like to have your foot on the rail and blow the foam off some suds?" prohibition forces dubbed him "Alcohol Al."

Smith's greatest vulnerability in the heartland, however, was his religion. He was the first Catholic to run for president. A Methodist bishop in Virginia denounced Roman Catholicism as "the Mother of ignorance, superstition, intolerance and sin" and begged Protestants not to vote for a candidate who represented "the kind of dirty people that you find today on the sidewalks of New York." An editorial in the *Baptist and Commoner* argued that the election of Smith "would be granting the Pope the right to dictate to this government what it should do."

Hoover, who neatly combined the images of morality, efficiency, service, and prosperity, won the election by a landslide (Map 23.3). He received nearly 58 percent of the vote and gained 444 electoral votes to Smith's 87. The Republicans' most notable success came in the previously solid Democratic South, where Smith's religion, views on prohibition, and big-city persona allowed them to take four states. Smith carried the Lower South, where the Democratic Party's identification with white supremacy prevailed. The Republican victory was marred only by the party's reduced support in the cities and among discontented farmers. The nation's largest cities voted Democratic in a striking reversal of 1924, indicating the rising strength of ethnic minorities, including Smith's fellow Catholics.

> Portraying the "monkey trial" as a battle between the country and the city, H. L. Mencken flayed William Jennings Bryan as a "charlatan, a mountebank, a zany without shame or dignity," motivated solely by "hatred of the city men who had laughed at him for so long."

MAP 23.3 The Election of 1928

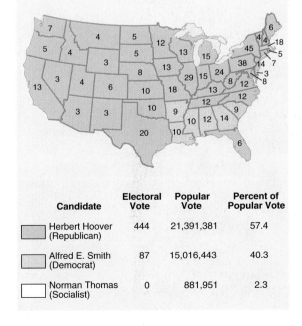

Candidate	Electoral Vote	Popular Vote	Percent of Popular Vote
Herbert Hoover (Republican)	444	21,391,381	57.4
Alfred E. Smith (Democrat)	87	15,016,443	40.3
Norman Thomas (Socialist)	0	881,951	2.3

REVIEW Why did the relationship between urban and rural America deteriorate in the 1920s?

The Great Crash

At his inauguration in 1929, Herbert Hoover told the American people, "Given a chance to go forward with the policies of the last eight years, we shall soon with the help of God be in sight of the day when poverty will be banished from this nation." Those words came back to haunt Hoover, for within eight months, the Roaring Twenties came to a crashing halt. The prosperity Hoover touted collapsed with the stock market, and the nation ended nearly three decades of barely interrupted economic growth. Like much of the world, the United States fell into the most serious economic depression of all time. Hoover and his reputation were among the first casualties, along with the reverence for business that had been the hallmark of the New Era.

Herbert Hoover: The Great Engineer

When Herbert Hoover became president in 1929, he seemed the perfect choice to lead a prosperous business nation. He personified America's rags-to-riches ideal, having risen from poor Iowa orphan to one of the world's most celebrated mining engineers by the time he was thirty. His success in managing efforts to feed civilian victims of the fighting during World War I won him acclaim as the "Great Humanitarian" and led Woodrow Wilson to name him head of the Food Administration once the United States entered the war. Hoover's reputation soared even higher as secretary of commerce in the Harding and Coolidge administrations.

Hoover was no old-fashioned pro-business advocate like most of the men who gathered in Washington during the 1920s. He belonged to the progressive wing of his party, and as early as 1909, he declared, "The time when the employer could ride roughshod over his labor is disappearing with the doctrine of 'laissez-faire' on which it is founded." He urged a limited business-government partnership that would actively manage the sweeping changes Americans experienced. In his thoughtful book *American Individualism* (1922), Hoover sketched a picture of American individualism that was as much cooperative, mutual, and responsible as it was "rugged." When Hoover entered the White House, he brought a reform agenda: "We want to see a nation built of home owners and farm owners. We want to see their savings protected. We want

Hoover Campaign Poster
This poster effectively illustrates Herbert Hoover's 1928 campaign message: Republican administrations in the 1920s had produced middle-class prosperity, complete with a house in the suburbs and the latest automobile. To remind voters that Hoover as secretary of commerce had promoted industry that made the suburban dream possible, the poster portrays smoking chimneys at a discreet distance. The poster gives no hint that this positive message would give way to outright religious bigotry in the campaign against Democrat (and Catholic) Al Smith.
Collection of Janice L. and David J. Frent.

to see them in steady jobs. We want to see more and more of them insured against death and accident, unemployment and old age. We want them all secure."

But Hoover also had ideological and political liabilities. Principles that appeared strengths in the prosperous 1920s—individual self-reliance, industrial self-management, and a limited federal government—became straitjackets when economic catastrophe struck. Moreover, Hoover had never held an elected public office, had a poor political touch, and was too thin-skinned to be an effective politician. Even so, most Americans considered him "a sort of superman" able to solve any problem. Prophetically, he confided to a friend his fear that "if some unprecedented calamity should come upon the nation . . . I would be sacrificed to the unreasoning disappointment of a people who expected too much." The distorted national economy set the stage for the calamity Hoover so feared.

The Distorted Economy

In the spring of 1929, the United States enjoyed a fragile prosperity. Although America had become the world's leading economy, it had done little to help rebuild Europe's shattered economy after World War I. Instead, the Republican administrations demanded that Allied nations repay their war loans. To repay, Allied governments insisted on large reparation payments from Germany. This tangled web of debts and reparations sapped Europe's economic vitality. Moreover, to boost American business, the United States enacted tariffs that prevented other nations from selling their goods to Americans. Fewer sales meant that foreign nations had less money to buy American goods, which were pouring out in record abundance. American banks propped up the nation's export trade by extending credit to foreign customers, and fresh debt piled onto existing debt in an absurd pyramid. By the end of the decade, the United States had acquired most of the world's gold in return for its exports.

The domestic economy was also in trouble. Wealth was badly distributed. Farmers continued to suffer from low prices and chronic indebtedness; the average income of families working the land amounted to only $240 per year. The wages of industrial workers, though rising during the decade, failed to keep up with productivity and corporate profits. Overall, nearly two-thirds of all American families lived on less than the $2,000 per year that economists estimated would "supply only basic necessities." In sharp contrast, the top 1 percent received 15 percent of the nation's income, an amount equal to that received by the bottom 42 percent of the population. The Coolidge administration worsened the deepening inequality by cutting taxes on the wealthy.

By 1929, the inequality of wealth produced a serious problem in consumption. The rich, brilliantly portrayed in F. Scott Fitzgerald's novel *The Great Gatsby* (1925), gilded the era with their lavish spending; but they could absorb only a tiny fraction of the nation's output. Ordinary folk, on whom the system ultimately depended, were unable to take up the slack. For a time, the new device of installment buying—buying on credit— kept consumer demand up. By the end of the decade, four out of five cars and two out of three radios were bought on credit. Personal indebtedness rose to an all-time high that could not be sustained.

> Prophetically, Hoover confided to a friend his fear that "if some unprecedented calamity should come upon the nation . . . I would be sacrificed to the unreasoning disappointment of a people who expected too much."

Signs of economic trouble began to appear at mid-decade. New construction slowed down. Automobile sales faltered. With nearly thirty million cars on the road, demand had been met, and companies began cutting back production and laying off workers. Banks followed suit. Between 1921 and 1928, as investment and loan opportunities faded, five thousand banks failed, wiping out the life savings of thousands. Still, the boom seemed to roar on, muffling the sounds of economic distress just beneath the surface.

The Crash of 1929

Even as the economy faltered, America's faith in it remained unshaken. Hoping for even bigger slices of the economic pie, Americans speculated wildly in the stock market on Wall Street. Between 1924 and 1929, the values of stocks listed on the New York Stock Exchange increased by more than 400 percent. Buying stocks on margin—that is, putting up only part of the money at the time of purchase—grew rampant. Many people got rich this way, but those who bought on credit could finance their loans only if their stocks increased in value. Speculators could not imagine that the market might fall and they would be forced to meet their margin loans with cash they did not have.

Finally, in the autumn of 1929, the market hesitated. Sniffing danger, investors nervously began to sell their overvalued stocks. The dip quickly became a panic on October 24, the day that came to be known as Black Thursday. Brokers jammed the stock exchange desperately trying to unload shares. Stirred by the cries of "Sell! Sell!" outside their windows, the giants of finance gathered in the offices of J. P. Morgan Jr., son of the nineteenth-century Wall Street lion, to plot ways of restoring confidence. They injected $100 million of their assets to bolster the market and issued brave declarations of faith. But more panic selling came on Black Tuesday, October 29, the day the market suffered a greater fall than ever before. In the next six months, the stock market lost six-sevenths of its total value.

It was once thought that the crash alone caused the Great Depression. It did not. In 1929, the national and international economies were already riddled with severe problems. But the dramatic losses in the stock market crash, the sudden collapse of the mood of irrational exuberance, and the fear of risking what was left acted as a great brake on economic activity. The collapse on Wall Street shattered the New Era's aggressive confidence that America would enjoy perpetually expanding prosperity.

Hoover and the Limits of Individualism

At first, Americans expressed relief that Herbert Hoover resided in the White House when the bubble broke. Unlike some conservatives who believed that the government should do nothing during economic downturns, Hoover believed that "we should use the powers of government to cushion the situation" by preventing future financial panics and mitigating the hardships of

Black Tuesday
Panicked investors crowd the sidewalks outside the New York Stock Exchange on October 29, 1929, the day the market crashed. Wall Street remained jammed all day as worried individuals tried to learn the extent of their losses. A few years later, stock exchange president Richard Whitney went to prison for stealing from other people's accounts to cover his own losses.
© Bettmann/Corbis.

farmers and the unemployed. Hoover was no do-nothing president, but there were limits to his activism.

In November 1929, to keep the stock market collapse from ravaging the entire economy, Hoover called a White House conference of business and labor leaders and urged them to join in a voluntary plan for recovery: Businesses would maintain production and keep their workers on the job; labor would accept existing wages, hours, and conditions. Within a few months, however, the bargain fell apart. As demand for their products declined, industrialists cut production, sliced wages, and laid off workers. Poorly paid or unemployed workers could not buy much, and their decreased spending led to further cuts in production and further loss of jobs. Thus began the terrible spiral of economic decline.

To deal with the problems of rural America, Hoover got Congress to pass the Agricultural Marketing Act in 1929. The act created the Farm Board, which used its budget of $500 million to buy up agricultural surpluses and thus, it was hoped, raise prices. But prices declined. To help end the decline, Hoover joined conservatives in urging protective tariffs on agricultural goods, and the Hawley-Smoot tariff of 1930 established the highest rates in history. The same year, Congress also authorized $420 million for public works projects to give the unemployed jobs and create more purchasing power. In three years, the Hoover administration nearly doubled federal public works expenditures.

But with each year of Hoover's term, the economy weakened. Tariffs did not end the suffering of farmers because foreign nations retaliated with increased tariffs of their own that crippled American farmers' ability to sell abroad. In 1932, Hoover hoped to help hard-pressed industry with the Reconstruction Finance Corporation (RFC), a federal agency empowered to lend government funds to endangered banks and corporations. The theory was **trickle-down economics**: Pump money into the economy at the top, and in the long run, the people at the bottom would benefit. Or as one wag put it, "Feed the sparrows by feeding the horses." In the end, very little of what critics of the RFC called a "millionaires' dole" trickled down to the poor.

And the poor multiplied. Hundreds of thousands of workers lost their jobs each month. By 1932, an astounding one-quarter of the American workforce—more than twelve million people— were unemployed. There was no direct federal assistance, and state services and private charities were swamped. The depression that began in 1929 devastated much of the world, but no other modern nation provided such feeble support to the jobless. Cries grew louder for the federal government to give hurting people relief.

In responding, Hoover revealed the limits of his conception of government's proper role. He compared direct federal aid to the needy to the "dole" in Britain, which he thought destroyed the moral fiber of the chronically unemployed. In 1931, he allowed the Red Cross to distribute government-owned agricultural surpluses to the hungry. In 1932, he relaxed his principles further to offer small federal loans, not gifts, to the states to help them in their relief efforts. But these concessions were no more than Band-Aids on deep wounds. Hoover's circumscribed notions of legitimate government action proved vastly inadequate to address the problems of restarting the economy and ending human suffering.

> The theory was trickle-down economics: Pump money into the economy at the top, and in the long run, the people at the bottom would benefit. Or as one wag put it, "Feed the sparrows by feeding the horses."

REVIEW   Why did the American economy collapse in 1929?

Life in the Depression

In 1930, suffering on a massive scale set in. Despair settled over the land. Men and women hollow-eyed with hunger grew increasingly bewildered and angry in the face of cruel contradictions. They saw agricultural surpluses pile up in the countryside and knew that their children were going to bed hungry. They saw factories standing idle and knew that they and millions of others were willing to work. The gap between the American people and leaders who failed to resolve these contradictions widened as the depression deepened. By 1932, America's economic problems had created a dangerous social and political crisis.

The Human Toll

Statistics only hint at the human tragedy of the Great Depression. When Herbert Hoover took office in 1929, the American economy stood at its peak. When he left in 1933, it had reached its twentieth-century low (Figure 23.3, page 854). In 1929, national income was $88 billion. By 1933, it

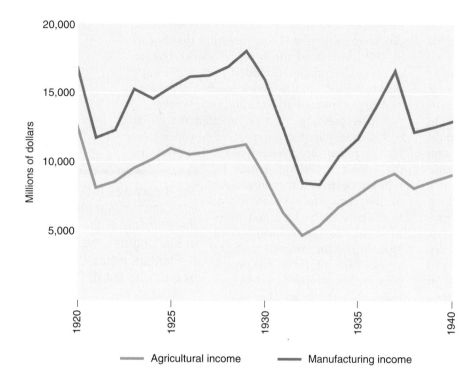

FIGURE 23.3 Manufacturing and Agricultural Income, 1920–1940
After economic collapse, recovery in the 1930s began under New Deal auspices. The sharp declines in 1937–1938, when federal spending was reduced, indicated that New Deal stimuli were still needed to restore manufacturing and agricultural income.

had declined to $40 billion. In 1929, unemployment was 3.1 percent, or 1.5 million workers. By 1933, unemployment stood at 25 percent, or 12.5 million workers. By 1932, more than 9,000 banks had shut their doors, and depositors had lost more than $2.5 billion. The nation's steel industry operated at only 12 percent of capacity.

Jobless, homeless victims wandered in search of work, and the tramp, or hobo, became one of the most visible figures of the decade. Riding the rails or hitchhiking, a million vagabonds tended to move southward and westward, toward the sun and opportunities, they hoped, for seasonal agricultural work. Other unemployed men and women, sick or less hopeful, huddled in doorways, overcome, one man remembered, by "helpless despair and submission." Scavengers haunted alleys behind restaurants and picked over garbage dumps in search of food. One writer told of an elderly woman who always took off her glasses to avoid seeing the maggots crawling over the garbage she ate. Starvation claimed its victims, but enervating malnutrition posed the greater threat. The Children's Bureau announced that one in five schoolchildren did not get enough to eat. "I don't want to steal," a Pennsylvania man wrote to the governor in 1931, "but I won't let my wife and boy cry for something to eat. . . . How long is this going to keep up? I cannot stand it any longer."

An Unemployed Youth
Joblessness was frightening and humiliating. Brought up to believe that if you worked hard, you got ahead, the unemployed had difficulty seeing failure to find work as anything other than personal failure. Many slipped into despair and depression. We can only imagine this young man's story. Utterly alone, sitting on a bench that might be his bed, his hat on the ground and his head in his hands, he looks emotionally battered and perhaps defeated. Whether he found work, joined the throngs of beggars and panhandlers on the streets, or cast his lot with the army of hoboes who rode the rails looking for something better is unknown. Library of Congress.

Deportation to Mexico
In 1931, a crowd gathered at the train yard in Los Angeles to say good-bye to friends and family who were being deported to Mexico. Los Angeles County chartered trains to carry Mexicans and Mexican Americans south, arguing that the $15,000 expense "would be recovered within six weeks in saving on charity." But contrary to popular belief, immigrants did not put undue pressure on social services. Moreover, some of the deportees were American citizens who had never been south of the border.
La Opinión.

Rural poverty was most acute. Tenant farmers and sharecroppers, mainly in the South, came to symbolize how poverty crushed the human spirit. Eight and a half million people, three million of them black, crowded into two- and three-room cabins lacking screens or even doors, without plumbing, electricity, running water, or sanitary wells. They subsisted—just barely—on salt pork, cornmeal, molasses, beans, peas, and whatever they could hunt or fish. All the diseases of dietary and vitamin deficiencies wracked them. When economist John Maynard Keynes was asked whether anything like this degradation had existed before, he replied, "Yes, it was called the Dark Ages and it lasted four hundred years."

There was no federal assistance to meet this human catastrophe, only a patchwork of strapped charities and destitute state and local agencies. For a family of four without any income, the best the city of Philadelphia could do was provide $5.50 per week. That was not enough to live on but was still comparatively generous. New York City, where the greatest number of welfare cases gathered, provided only $2.39 per week; and Detroit, devastated by the auto industry's failure, allotted 60 cents a week before the city ran out of money altogether.

The deepening crisis roused old fears and caused some Americans to look for scapegoats. Among the most thoroughly scapegoated were Mexican Americans. During the 1920s, cheap agricultural labor from Mexico flowed legally across the U.S. border, welcomed by the large farmers. In the 1930s, however, public opinion turned on the newcomers, denouncing them as dangerous aliens who took jobs from Americans. Government officials, most prominently those in Los Angeles County, targeted Mexican residents for deportation regardless of citizenship status. As many as half a million Mexicans and Mexican Americans were deported or fled to Mexico.

The depression deeply affected the American family. Young people postponed marriage. When they did marry, they produced few children. White women, who generally worked in low-paying service areas, did not lose their jobs as often as men who worked in steel, automobile, and other heavy industries. After a decade of rising consumption and conflating consumption with self-worth, idle men suffered a loss of self-esteem. "Before the depression," one unemployed father reported, "I wore the pants in this family, and rightly so." Jobless, he lost "self-respect" and also "the respect of my children, and I am afraid that I am losing my wife." Both government and private employers discriminated against married women workers, but necessity continued to drive women into the marketplace. As a result, by 1940 some 25 percent more women were employed for wages than in 1930.

Denial and Escape

To express his optimism about economic recovery, President Hoover maintained formal dress and manners in the White House, and at dinner, with or without guests, a retinue of valets and waiters attended him. No one was starving, he calmly assured the American people. Contradicting the president's message were makeshift shantytowns, called "Hoovervilles," that sprang up on the edges of America's cities. Newspapers used as cover by those sleeping on the streets were "Hoover blankets." An empty pocket turned inside out was a "Hoover flag," and jackrabbits caught for food were "Hoover hogs." Innumerable bitter jokes circulated about the increasingly unpopular president. One told of Hoover asking for a nickel to telephone a friend. Flipping him a dime, an aide said, "Here, call them both."

While Hoover practiced denial, other Americans sought refuge from reality at the movies. Throughout the depression, between 60 million and 75 million people (nearly two-thirds of the nation) managed to scrape together enough  change to fill the movie palaces every week. Box office hits such as *Forty-second Street* and *Gold Diggers of 1933* capitalized on the hope that prosperity lay just around the corner. But a few filmmakers grappled with hard realities rather than escape them. *Our Daily Bread* (1932) expressed compassion for the down-and-out, while *The Public Enemy* (1931) taught hard lessons about gangsters' ill-gotten gains. Indeed, under the new production code of 1930, designed to protect public morals, all movies had to find some way to show that crime did not pay.

Despite Hollywood's efforts to keep Americans on the right side of the law, crime increased. Away from the movie palaces, out in the countryside, the plight of people who had lost their farms to bank foreclosures led to the romantic idea that bank robbers were only getting back what banks had stolen from the poor. Woody Guthrie, the populist folksinger from Oklahoma, captured the public's tolerance for outlaws in his widely admired tribute to a murderous bank robber with a choirboy face, "The Ballad of Pretty Boy Floyd":

> Yes, as through this world I ramble,
> I see lots of funny men,

> Some will rob you with a six-gun,
> Some will rob you with a pen.
> But as through your life you'll travel,
> Wherever you may roam,
> You won't never see an outlaw drive
> A family from their home.

Working-Class Militancy

Members of the nation's working class bore the brunt of the economic collapse. In Chicago, workingwomen received less than twenty-five cents an hour. Sawmill workers in the West got a nickel. Still, the labor movement, including the dominant American Federation of Labor (AFL), was slow to respond. By 1931, William Green, head of the AFL, had turned militant. "I warn the people who are exploiting the workers," he shouted, "that they can drive them only so far before they will turn on them and destroy them. They are taking no account of the history of nations in which governments have been overturned. Revolutions grow out of the depths of hunger."

Like labor leaders, the American people were slow to anger, then strong in protest. On the morning of March 7, 1932, several thousand unemployed autoworkers massed at the gates of Henry Ford's River Rouge factory in Dearborn, Michigan, to demand work. Ford sent out his private security forces, and when the workers began throwing rocks, Ford's army responded with gunfire, killing four demonstrators and wounding dozens more. An outraged public—forty thousand strong—turned out for the unemployed men's funerals, while editorials and protest rallies across the country denounced Ford's callous resort to violence.

Farmers mounted uprisings of their own. When Congress refused to guarantee farm prices that would at least equal the cost of production, several thousand farmers created the National Farmers' Holiday Association in 1932, so named because its members planned to take a "holiday" from shipping crops to market. When some farmers persisted, militants barricaded roads and dumped thousands of gallons of milk in ditches. Farm militants also resorted to what they called "penny sales." When banks foreclosed and put farms up for auction, neighbors warned others not to bid, bought the foreclosed property for a few pennies, and returned it to the bankrupt owners. Under this kind of pressure, some states suspended debts or reduced mortgages. In California in 1933, when landowners cut their laborers' already substandard wages,

"Scottsboro Boys"
Nine black youths, ranging in age from thirteen to twenty-one, stand in front of rifle-bearing National Guard troops called up by Alabama governor B. M. Miller, who feared a mob lynching after two white women accused the nine of rape in March 1931. In less than two weeks, an all-white jury heard flimsy evidence, convicted the nine of rape, and sentenced them to death. Although none was executed, all nine spent years in jail. Eventually, the state dropped the charges against the youngest four and granted paroles to the others. The last "Scottsboro Boy" left jail in 1950.
© Bettmann/Corbis.

more than 50,000 farmworkers, most of them Mexicans, went on strike. Militancy won farmers little in the way of long-term solutions, but one individual observed that "the biggest and finest crop of revolutions you ever saw is sprouting all over the country right now."

The Great Depression—the massive failure of Western capitalism—propelled the international Communist movement to new heights. In the United States, it brought **socialism** back to life and catapulted the **Communist Party** to its greatest size and influence in American history. Some 100,000 Americans—workers, intellectuals, college students—joined the Communist Party in the belief that only an overthrow of the capitalist system could save the victims of depression. In 1931, the party, through its National Miners Union, carried its convictions into Harlan County, Kentucky, to support a strike by brutalized coal miners. Newspapers and newsreels provided graphic portrayals of the violence unleashed by mine owners' thugs against the strikers. Eventually, the owners beat the miners down, but the Communist Party emerged from the coalfields with a reputation as the most dedicated and fearless champion of the union cause.

Harlan County Coal Strike, 1931

The left also led the fight against racism. Whereas both major parties refused to challenge segregation in the South, the Socialist Party, led by Norman Thomas, attacked the system of sharecropping that left many African Americans in near servitude. The Communist Party also took action. When nine young black men in Scottsboro, Alabama (the "Scottsboro Boys"), were arrested on trumped-up rape charges in 1931, a team of lawyers sent by the party saved the defendants from the electric chair. The party also opposed the efforts of Alabama plantation owners to evict their black tenants. Although Communists were unable to force much change in the deeply entrenched southern way of life, their efforts briefly attracted new recruits to the party. From only about 50 black members in 1930, party totals rose to 10,000 by the end of the decade.

Radicals on the left often sparked action, but protests by moderate workers and farmers occurred on a far greater scale. Breadlines, soup kitchens, foreclosures, unemployment, and cold despair drove patriotic men and women to question American capitalism. "I am as conservative as any man could be," a Wisconsin farmer explained, "but any economic system that has in its power to set me and my wife in the streets, at my age—what can I see but red?"

> REVIEW How did the depression reshape American politics?

Conclusion: Dazzle and Despair

In the aftermath of World War I, America turned its back on progressive crusades and embraced conservative Republican politics, the growing influence of corporate leaders, and business values. Changes in the nation's economy—Henry Ford's automobile revolution, advertising, mass production—propelled fundamental change throughout society. Living standards rose, economic opportunity increased, and Americans threw themselves into private pleasures—gobbling up the latest household goods and fashions, attending baseball and football games and boxing matches, gathering around the radio, and going to the movies. As big cities came to dominate American life, the culture of youth and flappers became the leading edge of what one observer called a "revolution in manners and morals." At home in Harlem and abroad in Paris, American literature, art, and music flourished.

For many Americans, however, none of the glamour and vitality had much meaning. Instead of seeking thrills at speakeasies, plunging into speculation on Wall Street, or escaping abroad, the vast majority struggled just to earn a decent living. Blue-collar America did not participate fully in white-collar prosperity. Rural America was almost entirely left out of the Roaring Twenties. Country folk, deeply suspicious and profoundly discontented, championed prohibition, revived the Klan, attacked immigration, and defended old-time Protestant religion.

Just as the dazzle of the Roaring Twenties hid deep divisions in society, extravagant prosperity masked structural flaws in the economy. The crash of 1929 and the depression that followed starkly revealed the economy's crises of international trade and consumption. Hard times swept high living off the front pages of the nation's newspapers. Different images emerged: hoboes hopping freight trains, strikers confronting police, malnourished sharecroppers staring blankly into the distance, empty apartment buildings alongside cardboard shanty-towns, and mountains of food rotting in the sun while guards with shotguns chased away the hungry.

The depression hurt everyone, but the poor were hurt most. As farmers and workers sank into aching hardship, businessmen rallied around Herbert Hoover to proclaim that private enterprise would get the country moving again. But things fell apart, and Hoover faced increasingly more radical opposition. Membership in the Socialist and Communist parties surged, and more and more Americans contemplated desperate measures. By 1932, the depression had nearly brought the nation to its knees. America faced its greatest crisis since the Civil War, and citizens demanded new leaders who would save them from the "Hoover Depression."

Selected Bibliography

General Works

William E. Leuchtenburg, *The Perils of Prosperity, 1914–1932* (1958).

Michael Parrish, *Anxious Decades: America in Prosperity and Depression, 1920–1941* (1992).

Politics and Economy

Kristi Anderson, *After Suffrage: Women in Partisan and Electoral Politics before the New Deal* (1996).

William J. Barber, *From New Era to New Deal: Herbert Hoover, the Economists, and American Economic Policy, 1921–1933* (1985).

Douglas Brinkley, *Wheels for the World: Henry Ford, His Company, and a Century of Progress, 1903–2003* (2003).

Kendrick A. Clements, *Hoover, Conservation, and Consumerism: Engineering the Good Life* (2000).

Warren I. Cohen, *Empire without Tears: America's Foreign Relations, 1921–1933* (1987).

Paula Elder, *Governor Alfred E. Smith: The Politician as Reformer* (1983).

Steve Fraser, *Every Man a Speculator: A History of Wall Street* (2005).

Colin Gordon, *New Deals: Business, Labor, and Politics in America, 1920–1935* (1994).

Owen Gutfreund, *Twentieth-Century Sprawl: Highways and the Reshaping of the American Landscape* (2004).

Jill Jonnes, *Empires of Light: Edison, Tesla, and Westinghouse, and the Race to Electrify the World* (2003).

Martha L. Olney, *Buy Now, Pay Later: Advertising, Credit, and Consumer Durables in the 1920s* (1991).

Emily S. Rosenberg, *Spreading the American Dream: American Economic and Cultural Expansion, 1890–1945* (1982).

Steven Watts, *People's Tycoon: Henry Ford and the American Century* (2005).

Society and Culture

Douglas Carl Abrams, *Selling the Old-Time Religion: American Fundamentalists and Mass Culture, 1920–1940* (2001).

Francisco E. Balderrama and Raymond Rodriguez, *Decade of Betrayal: Mexican Repatriation in the 1930s* (1995).

Kevin Boyle, *Arc of Justice: A Saga of Race, Civil Rights, and Murder in the Jazz Age* (2004).

Liz Conor, *Spectacular Modern Woman: Feminine Visibility in the 1920s* (2004).

Ruth Schwartz Cowan, *More Work for Mother: The Ironies of Household Technology from the Open Hearth to the Microwave* (1983).

Roger Daniels, *Guarding the Golden Door: American Immigration Policy and Immigrants since 1882* (2004).

Paula S. Fass, *The Damned and the Beautiful: American Youth in the 1920s* (1977).

Caroline Goeser, *Picturing the New Negro: Harlem Renaissance, Print Culture, and Modern Black Identity* (2006).

David J. Goldberg, *Discontented America: The United States in the 1920s* (1999).

David M. Kennedy, *Birth Control in America: The Career of Margaret Sanger* (1970).

Edward J. Larson, *Summer of the Gods: The Scopes Trial and America's Continuing Debate over Science and Religion* (1997).

David Levering Lewis, *W. E. B. Du Bois: The Fight for Equality and the American Century, 1919–1963* (2000).

Nancy MacLean, *Behind the Mask of Chivalry: The Making of the Second Ku Klux Klan* (1994).

David E. Nye, *Electrifying America: Social Meanings of a New Technology, 1880–1940* (1990).

David M. Reimers, *Unwelcome Strangers: American Identity and the Turn against Immigration* (1998).

Susan Smulyan, *Selling Radio: The Commercialization of American Broadcasting, 1920–1934* (1994).

Judith Stein, *The World of Marcus Garvey* (1986).

Studs Terkel, *Hard Times: An Oral History of the Great Depression* (1979, 1986).

Andrew Wiese, *Places of Their Own: African American Suburbanization in the Twentieth Century* (2004).

Nancy Woloch, *Women and the American Experience* (1984).

▶ **For more books about topics in this chapter,** see the Online Bibliography at bedfordstmartins.com/roark.

▶ **For additional firsthand accounts of this period,** see Chapter 23 in Michael Johnson, ed., *Reading the American Past,* Fourth Edition.

▶ **For Web sites, images, and documents related to topics and places in this chapter,** visit bedfordstmartins.com/makehistory.

REVIEWING THE CHAPTER

Follow these steps to review and strengthen your understanding of the chapter.
STEP 1: *Study the* **Key Terms** *and* **Timeline** *to identify the significance of each item listed.*
STEP 2: *Answer the* **Review Questions**, *drawing on key terms and dates to support your answers.*
STEP 3: *Drawing on the Key Terms, Timeline, and Review Questions, answer the broader* **Making Connections** *questions.*

KEY TERMS

Who

Henry Ford (p. 825)
Warren Gamaliel Harding (p. 827)
Calvin Coolidge (p. 827)
Sigmund Freud (p. 835)
Alphonse "Big Al" Capone (p. 836)
Margaret Sanger (p. 837)
W. E. B. Du Bois (p. 840)
Marcus Garvey (p. 840)
Langston Hughes (p. 841)
James Weldon Johnson (p. 841)
Zora Neale Hurston (p. 841)
Aaron Douglas (p. 841)
Charles Lindbergh (p. 844)
Ernest Hemingway (p. 845)
F. Scott Fitzgerald (p. 845)
Nicola Sacco (p. 847)
Bartolomeo Vanzetti (p. 847)
John Scopes (p. 848)
Clarence Darrow (p. 848)
William Jennings Bryan (p. 848)
H. L. Mencken (p. 848)
Herbert Hoover (p. 849)
Alfred E. Smith (p. 849)

Norman Thomas (p. 857)
"Scottsboro Boys" (p. 857)

What

Model T (p. 825)
New Era (p. 826)
Teapot Dome (p. 827)
Five-Power Naval Treaty of 1922 (p. 829)
Kellogg-Briand pact (p. 829)
Dawes Plan (p. 829)
mass production (p. 830)
welfare capitalism (p. 830)
Middletown (p. 830)
installment buying (p. 834)
prohibition (p. 835)
"new woman" (p. 836)
Sheppard-Towner Act (p. 836)
National Woman's Party (p. 837)
Equal Rights Amendment (p. 837)
League of Women Voters (p. 837)
flapper (p. 837)
New Negro (p. 840)

National Association for the Advancement of Colored People (NAACP) (p. 840)
Universal Negro Improvement Association (UNIA) (p. 840)
Black Star Line (p. 840)
Harlem Renaissance (p. 840)
Lost Generation (p. 845)
Johnson-Reid Act (p. 846)
Ku Klux Klan (p. 847)
Scopes trial (p. 848)
crash of 1929 (p. 852)
Farm Board (p. 853)
Hawley-Smoot tariff (p. 853)
Reconstruction Finance Corporation (RFC) (p. 853)
American Federation of Labor (AFL) (p. 856)
National Farmers' Holiday Association (p. 856)
Communist Party (p. 857)
National Miners Union (p. 857)
Socialist Party (p. 857)

TIMELINE

1920 • Eighteenth Amendment goes into effect.
• Nineteenth Amendment ratified.
• Republican Warren G. Harding elected president.

    1921 • Sheppard-Towner Act.
      • Congress restricts immigration.

        1922 • Fordney-McCumber tariff.
          • Five-Power Naval Treaty.

           1923 • Equal Rights Amendment defeated in Congress.
             • Harding dies; Vice President Calvin Coolidge becomes president.

                1924 • Dawes Plan.
                  • Coolidge elected president.
                  • Johnson-Reid Act.

                    1925 • Scopes trial.

                          1927 • Charles Lindbergh flies nonstop across the Atlantic.
                              • Nicola Sacco and Bartolomeo Vanzetti executed.

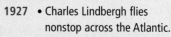

REVIEW QUESTIONS

1. How did the spread of the automobile transform the United States? (pp. 826–34)

2. How did the new freedoms of the 1920s challenge older conceptions of gender and race? (pp. 835–45)

3. Why did the relationship between urban and rural America deteriorate in the 1920s? (pp. 845–49)

4. Why did the American economy collapse in 1929? (pp. 850–53)

5. How did the depression reshape American politics? (pp. 853–58)

MAKING CONNECTIONS

1. In the 1920s, Americans' wariness of the concentration of power in the hands of industrial capitalists gave way to unrestrained confidence in American business. What drove this shift in popular opinion? How did it influence Republicans' approach to governance and the development of the American economy in the 1920s?

2. Americans' encounters with the wealth and increased personal freedom characteristic of the 1920s varied greatly. Discuss the impact such variation had on Americans' responses to new circumstances. Why did some embrace the era's changes, while others resisted them? Ground your answer in a discussion of specific political, legal, or cultural conflicts.

3. How did shifting government policy contribute to both the boom of the 1920s and the bust of 1929? In your answer, consider the part domestic and international policy played in these developments, including taxation, tariffs, and international banking.

4. The Great Depression plunged the nation into a profound crisis with staggering personal and national costs. How did Americans attempt to lessen the impact of these circumstances? In your answer, discuss and compare the responses of individual Americans and the federal government.

▶ FOR PRACTICE QUIZZES, A CUSTOMIZED STUDY PLAN, AND OTHER STUDY TOOLS, see the Online Study Guide at bedfordstmartins.com/roark.

1928 • Kellogg-Briand pact.
   • Republican Herbert Hoover elected president.

   1929 • St. Valentine's Day murders.
       • Farm Board created.
       • Stock market collapses.

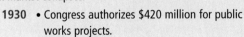

       1930 • Congress authorizes $420 million for public works projects.
           • Hawley-Smoot tariff.

           1931 • "Scottsboro Boys" arrested.
               • Harlan County, Kentucky, coal strike.

               1932 • River Rouge factory demonstration.
                   • Reconstruction Finance Corporation established.
                   • National Farmers' Holiday Association formed.

FRANKLIN ROOSEVELT'S MICROPHONE

President Roosevelt used this microphone to broadcast his famous fireside chats explaining New Deal programs to ordinary Americans. These chats traveled on airwaves into homes throughout the nation, reassuring listeners that Washington cared about the suffering the Great Depression was spreading across the land. Shortly after the first chat in March 1933, a New Yorker, "a citizen of little or no consequence" as he called himself, wrote to the White House in gratitude for "the President's broadcast. I felt that he walked into my home, sat down and in plain and forceful language explained to me how he was tackling the job I and my fellow citizens gave him. . . . Such forceful, direct and honest action commands the respect of all Americans, it is certainly deserving of it."

National Museum of American History, Smithsonian Institution, Behring Center.

24

The New Deal Experiment

1932–1939

I N THE DEPTHS OF THE GREAT DEPRESSION, a Pennsylvania mother with three small children appealed to the Hoover administration for help for her husband, "who is a world war Veteran and saw active service in the trenches, became desperate and applied for Compensation or a pension from the Government and was turned down." With a weekly income of only $15.60, she and her family were suffering. There ought to be enough, she declared, "to pay all world war veterans a pension . . . and there by relieve a lot of suffering, and banish resentment that causes Rebellions and Bolshevism." She asked questions murmured by millions of other desperate Americans: "Oh why is it that it is always a bunch of overley rich, selfish, dumb ignorant money hogs that persist in being Senitors, legislatures, representitives? Where would they and their possessions be if it were not for the Common Soldier, the common laborer that is compelled to work for a starvation wage[?] . . . Right now our good old U.S.A. is sitting on a Seething Volcano."

This mother's plea echoed in the demands of tens of thousands of World War I veterans who gathered in Washington, D.C., during June and July 1932 to lobby for immediate payment of the pension (known as a "bonus"). The veterans came from every state and by nearly every means of transportation. The throng that congregated in a huge camp on the outskirts of Washington appeared "dusty, weary, and melancholy" to a Washington reporter, who noted that the veterans included jobless "truck drivers and blacksmiths, steel workers and coal miners, stenographers and common laborers," in all "a fair cross section" of the nation: immigrants and natives; whites, blacks, and Native Americans. The "one absentee," a black civil rights leader observed, was "James Crow." All the veterans, one journalist wrote, were "down at the heel."

Calling themselves Bonus Marchers or the Bonus Army, the veterans hoped their numbers, solidarity, and poverty would persuade Congress to give them the bonus they had been promised in 1924: $1 for every day they had been in uniform and a bit extra for time served overseas. Instead of cash payments, Congress decided to hand out promissory notes that veterans could not convert to cash until 1945. Bonus Marchers condemned this "tombstone bonus," which would not be paid until many of them were dead. Veterans from Utah and California emblazoned their truck with this message: "We Done a Good Job in France, Now You Do a Good Job in America—We Need the Bonus."

The veterans had supporters in Congress but not in the White House. President Herbert Hoover opposed the payment of an expensive bonus that would require the government to go into debt. Hoover refused to meet with representatives of the Bonus Army, who, his press secretary charged, were "communists or bums." The House of Representatives, controlled by Democrats, voted to pay the promised bonus of $2.4 billion, but the Senate, dominated by Hoover's fellow Republicans, rejected the bonus. Upon hearing of their defeat in the Senate, the Bonus Marchers did not confirm Republican fears of a **Communist** mob

but instead joined in singing "America" before slowly drifting back to their camp.

About twenty thousand veterans remained in Washington, determined, as one of them proclaimed, "to stay here until 1945 if necessary to get our bonus." While the Bonus Army hunkered down in their shanties, Hoover feared that the veterans would riot and spark uprisings throughout the country. He ordered General Douglas MacArthur to evict the Bonus Marchers from the city but not to invade their camp.

On July 28, MacArthur led an attack force of five tanks and five hundred soldiers armed with

Attack on the Bonus Marchers
Washington police, led by five hundred army soldiers commanded by General Douglas MacArthur, participated in the attack on the Bonus Marchers in July 1932. Soldiers lobbed tear gas grenades toward the marchers, quickly breaking up skirmishes like the one shown here, then advanced into the veterans' camp and torched it. At the head of the mounted cavalry attacking the veterans was George S. Patton, who became a famous general in World War II. MacArthur's chief aide was Dwight D. Eisenhower, who subsequently commanded the Allied assault on Nazi Germany and became president. Eisenhower recalled later that he "told that dumb son-of-a-bitch [MacArthur] he had no business going down there" to destroy the Bonus Marchers' camp, in violation of Hoover's orders. Hoover, however, did not discipline MacArthur for his insubordination.
National Archives.

READING THE IMAGE: What does the image reveal about the Bonus March?
CONNECTIONS: How did the Bonus March dramatize the government's ineffective response to the Great Depression?

FOR MORE HELP ANALYZING THIS IMAGE, see the visual activity for this chapter in the Online Study Guide at bedfordstmartins.com/roark.

loaded weapons and fixed bayonets through the streets of Washington. Exceeding Hoover's orders, MacArthur pushed the Bonus Marchers back into their camp, where his soldiers torched the veterans' humble dwellings. While their camp burned, the Bonus Marchers raced away. MacArthur boasted that without his victory over the veterans, "the institutions of our Government would have been severely threatened."

MacArthur's expulsion of the Bonus Army undermined public support for the beleaguered, fearful Hoover. When the Democrats' recently nominated presidential candidate, Franklin Delano Roosevelt, heard about the attack, he correctly predicted that it "will elect me." Voters rejected Hoover, who seemed unsympathetic to the suffering caused by the Great Depression. In Roosevelt's inaugural address in March 1933, barely seven months after the expulsion of the Bonus Army, he proclaimed, "The only thing we have to fear is fear itself." Instead of succumbing to fear and suspicion, Roosevelt said, Americans should roll up their sleeves and find some way out of their present difficulties. Roosevelt's confidence that the government could help citizens energized **New Deal** policies and his presidency, the longest in American history.

When several thousand veterans reassembled in Washington to lobby again for the bonus a few months after Roosevelt's inauguration, the new president's hospitality contrasted with Hoover's hostility. Roosevelt arranged for the veterans to be housed in abandoned military barracks and fed at government expense. He invited a delegation of veterans to the White House, where he chatted casually with them, explaining that he could not support the bonus because he considered it too expensive, although he was determined to help them and other victims of the depression. And, to the veterans' surprise and delight, Eleanor Roosevelt slogged through rain and mud to talk personally with them, to express her sympathy, and to lead them in singing their favorite songs. As the veterans voluntarily left their encampment in Washington, one remarked, "Hoover sent the Army; Roosevelt sent his wife."

Unlike the Bonus Marchers, the tens of millions of other Americans suffering from the Great Depression did not flock to Washington to lobby the government. But like the Bonus Marchers, they appreciated Roosevelt's optimism and expressions of concern. Even more, they welcomed government help from Roosevelt's New Deal initiatives to provide relief for the needy, to speed economic recovery, and to reform basic economic and governmental institutions. Roosevelt's New Deal elicited bitter opposition from critics on the right and left and failed to satisfy fully its own goals of relief, recovery, and reform. But within the Democratic Party, the New Deal energized a powerful political coalition that helped millions of Americans withstand the privations of the Great Depression. In the process, the federal government became a major presence in the daily lives of most American citizens.

Franklin D. Roosevelt: A Patrician in Government

Unlike the millions of Americans in 1932 who had no work, little food, and still less hope, Franklin Roosevelt came from a wealthy and privileged background that contributed to his optimism, self-confidence, and vitality. He constantly drew upon these personal qualities in his political career to bridge the economic, social, and cultural chasm that separated him from the struggles of ordinary Americans. During the twelve years he served as president (1933–1945), many elites came to hate him as a traitor to his class, while millions more Americans, especially the hardworking poor and dispossessed, revered him because he cared about them and their problems.

The Making of a Politician

Born in 1882, Franklin Delano Roosevelt grew up on his father's leafy estate at Hyde Park on the Hudson River, north of New York City. Insulated from the privations experienced by working people, Roosevelt was steeped at home and school in high-minded doctrines of public service and Christian duty to help the poor and weak. He prepared for a career in politics, hoping to follow in the political footsteps of his fifth cousin, Theodore Roosevelt. In 1905, when he married his distant cousin Eleanor Roosevelt, the current president of the United States, Theodore Roosevelt, gave the bride away—a sign of Franklin Roosevelt's gilt-edged political and familial connections.

Unlike cousin Teddy, Franklin Roosevelt sought his political fortune in the Democratic Party. After a two-year stint in the New York legislature, he ascended to national office when Woodrow Wilson appointed him assistant secretary of

Roosevelt's Common Touch

In his reelection as governor of New York in 1930, Franklin Roosevelt boosted his vote total by 700,000 over 1928, and he became the first Democratic candidate for governor to win the vote outside New York City. Sensing that his presentation of himself as a good neighbor was responsible for much of his popularity, Roosevelt arranged to have a friendly chat outside the polls in his hometown of Hyde Park with working-class voter Ruben Appel. In this photograph, Appel seems unaware that Roosevelt's standing was itself a feat of stagecraft. His legs rendered useless by polio, Roosevelt could remain upright only by using the strength he had developed in his arms and shoulders to prop himself up on his cane. Rare photos like this and a taboo against showing Roosevelt in his wheelchair kept the public from thinking of Roosevelt as a "cripple" and unfit for office, or in many cases from even realizing that he was disabled.

Franklin D. Roosevelt Library.

the navy. In 1920, he catapulted to the second spot on the national Democratic ticket, as the vice presidential candidate of presidential nominee James M. Cox. Although Cox lost the election (see chapter 22), Roosevelt's energetic campaigning convinced Democratic leaders that he had a bright future in national politics.

In the summer of 1921, at the age of thirty-nine, his life took a painful detour. He became infected with the polio virus, which paralyzed both his legs. For the rest of his life, he could stand only with his legs encased in heavy steel braces, and he could walk a few awkward steps only by leaning on another person. Tireless physical therapy helped him regain his vitality and intense desire for high political office. But he had to recapture his political momentum mostly from a sitting position, although he studiously avoided being photographed in the wheelchair he used routinely.

After his polio attack, Roosevelt frequently visited a polio therapy facility at Warm Springs, Georgia. There, he combined the health benefits of the soothing waters with political overtures to southern Democrats, which helped make him a rare political creature: a New Yorker from the Democratic Party's urban and immigrant wing with whom whites from the Democratic Party's entrenched southern wing felt comfortable.

Roosevelt's chance to return to political office came in 1928. New York's Democratic governor, Al Smith, urged Roosevelt to succeed him. Smith, the Democrats' presidential nominee, hoped Roosevelt would help secure New York's electoral votes. Although Smith lost in both New York and the nation (see chapter 23), Roosevelt squeaked out a victory. As governor of the nation's most populous state, Roosevelt was poised to showcase his leadership and his suitability for a presidential campaign of his own. His activist policies as governor became a dress rehearsal for his subsequent career as president.

Deeply affected by the cascading woes of the Great Depression, Governor Roosevelt believed that government should intervene to protect citizens from economic hardships rather than do nothing but wait for the law of supply and demand to improve the economy. According to the **laissez-faire** views of many **conservatives**—especially Republicans, but also numerous Democrats—the depression represented the hard hand of the market winnowing the strong survivors from the weak losers. Unlike Roosevelt, conservatives believed that government help for the needy sapped individual initiative and impeded the self-correcting forces of the market by rewarding people for losing the economic struggle to survive. Roosevelt lacked a full-fledged counterargument to these conservative claims, but he sympathized with the plight of poor people. He proclaimed, "To these unfortunate citizens aid must be extended by governments, not as a matter of charity but as a matter of social duty. . . . [No one should go] unfed, unclothed, or unsheltered."

The highlight of Roosevelt's efforts to relieve the economic hardships of New Yorkers was the Temporary Emergency Relief Administration (TERA), created in 1931. It provided an unprecedented $20 million in aid for the poor, earning him the gratitude of needy New Yorkers and the attention of national politicians.

To his supporters, Roosevelt seemed to be a leader determined to attack the economic crisis without deviating from **democracy**—unlike **fascist** parties gaining strength in Europe—or from capitalism—unlike Communists in power in the Soviet Union. (See "Beyond America's Borders," page 870.) Roosevelt's ideas about precisely how to revive the economy were vague. A prominent journalist characterized Roosevelt in 1931 as "a kind of amiable boy scout . . . a pleasant man who, without any important qualifications for the office, would very much like to be president." Such sneering comments did not sway Roosevelt's many supporters, who appreciated his energy, activism, and belief that, as he put it, "the duty of the state towards its citizens is the duty of the servant to its master." Roosevelt's conviction that government could and should do something to help Americans climb out of the economic abyss propelled him into the front ranks of the national Democratic Party.

The Election of 1932

The Democrats who convened in Chicago in July 1932 to nominate their presidential candidate knew that Hoover's unpopularity gave them a historic opportunity to recapture the White House. In fifty-six of the seventy-two years since Abraham Lincoln's election, Republicans had occupied the White House. Now, with the nation gripped by the worst depression in its history, Democrats might reverse generations of Republican rule if they chose the right nominee.

Opposition to Republicans and hunger for office, but little else, united Democrats. Warring factions divided Democrats by region, religion, **culture**, and commitment to the status quo. Southern Democrats chaired powerful committees in Congress thanks to their continual reelection in the one-party South devoted to white supremacy. This southern, native-born, white, rural, **Protestant**, conservative wing of the Democratic Party found little common ground with the northern, immigrant, urban, disproportionately Catholic, **liberal** wing. Rural and native-born *drys* (supporters of prohibition) clashed with urban and foreign-born *wets* (opponents of prohibition). Eastern-establishment Democratic dignitaries shared few goals with angry farmers and factory workers. Still, this unruly coalition of constituencies finally agreed to nominate Franklin Roosevelt as the Democratic presidential candidate.

In his acceptance speech, Roosevelt vowed to help "the forgotten man at the bottom of the pyramid"—such as the Bonus Marchers then in Washington—with "bold, persistent experimentation." Highlighting his differences with Hoover and the Republicans, he proposed to lead the nation with "liberal thought, . . . planned action, . . . [an] enlightened international outlook, and . . . the greatest good to the greatest number of our citizens." He pledged "a new deal for the American people."

Few details about what Roosevelt meant by "a new deal" emerged in the presidential campaign. He declared that "the people of America want more than anything else . . . two things: work . . . with all the moral and spiritual values that go with work . . . and a reasonable measure of security . . . for themselves and for their wives and children." Although Roosevelt never explained exactly how the federal government could provide either work or security, voters decided that whatever his new deal might be, it was better than reelecting Hoover.

Roosevelt won the 1932 presidential election in a historic landslide (Map 24.1, page 868). He received 57 percent of the nation's votes, the first time a Democrat had won a majority of the popular vote since 1852. Roosevelt amassed 472 electoral votes to Hoover's 59, carrying state after state that had voted Republican for years (Map 24.2, page 868). Roosevelt's coattails swept Democrats into control of Congress by large margins. The popular mandate for change was loud and clear.

Roosevelt's victory represented the emergence of what came to be known as the New

> Roosevelt proclaimed, "To these unfortunate citizens aid must be extended by governments, not as a matter of charity but as a matter of social duty. . . . [No one should go] unfed, unclothed, or unsheltered."

would change or whether the changes would re-vive the nation's ailing economy and improve Americans' lives. But Roosevelt and many others knew that the future of American capitalism and democracy was at stake.

> **REVIEW**   Why did Franklin D. Roosevelt win the 1932 presidential election by such a large margin?

Launching the New Deal

At noon on March 4, 1933, Americans gathered around their radios to hear the inaugural address of the newly elected president. Roosevelt began by asserting his "firm belief that the only thing we have to fear is fear itself—nameless, unreasoning, unjustified terror which paralyzes needed efforts to convert retreat into advance." Roosevelt promised "direct, vigorous action" in order "to wage war against the emergency" confronting "a stricken Nation in the midst of a stricken world." The first months of Roosevelt's administration, termed "the Hundred Days," fulfilled that promise in a whirlwind of government initiatives that launched the New Deal.

Roosevelt and his advisers had three interrelated objectives: to provide relief to the destitute, especially the one out of four Americans who were unemployed; to foster the economic recovery of farms and businesses, thereby creating jobs and reducing the need for relief; and to reform the government and economy in ways that would reduce the risk of devastating conse-

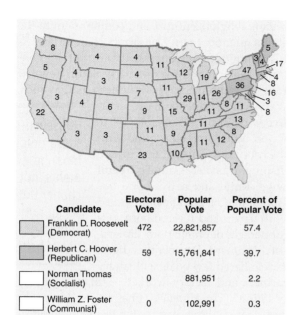

Candidate	Electoral Vote	Popular Vote	Percent of Popular Vote
Franklin D. Roosevelt (Democrat)	472	22,821,857	57.4
Herbert C. Hoover (Republican)	59	15,761,841	39.7
Norman Thomas (Socialist)	0	881,951	2.2
William Z. Foster (Communist)	0	102,991	0.3

MAP 24.1   The Election of 1932

Deal coalition. Attracting support from farmers, factory workers, immigrants, city folk, African Americans, women, and **progressive** intellectuals, Roosevelt launched a realignment of the nation's political loyalties. The New Deal coalition dominated American politics throughout Roosevelt's presidency and remained powerful long after his death in 1945. United less by ideology or support for specific policies, voters in the New Deal coalition instead expressed faith in Roosevelt's promise of a government that would, somehow, change things for the better. Nobody, including Roosevelt, knew exactly what the New Deal

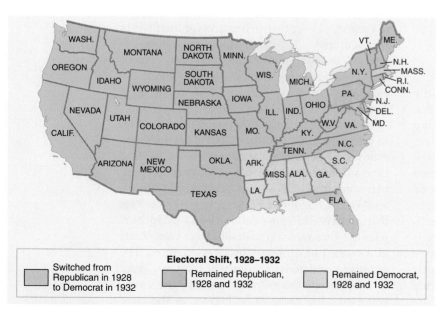

Electoral Shift, 1928–1932

Switched from Republican in 1928 to Democrat in 1932

Remained Republican, 1928 and 1932

Remained Democrat, 1928 and 1932

MAP 24.2   Electoral Shift, 1928–1932
The Democratic victory in 1932 signaled the rise of a New Deal coalition within which women and minorities, many of them new voters, made the Democrats the majority party for the first time in the twentieth century.

READING THE MAP: How many states voted Democratic in 1928? How many states voted Republican in 1932? How many states shifted from Republican to Democratic between 1928 and 1932?
CONNECTIONS: What factions within the Democratic Party opposed Franklin Roosevelt's candidacy in 1932 and why? To what do you attribute his landslide victory?

FOR MORE HELP ANALYZING THIS MAP, see the map activity for this chapter in the Online Study Guide at bedfordstmartins.com/roark.

quences in future economic slumps. The New Deal never fully achieved these goals of relief, recovery, and reform. But by aiming for them, Roosevelt's experimental programs enormously expanded government's role in the nation's economy and society.

The New Dealers

To design and implement the New Deal, Roosevelt needed ideas and people. As governor of New York, he frequently hosted private, informal conversations about social and economic policy with a small group of professors from Columbia University. Dubbed the "Brains Trust," these men and others continued to advise the new president about the problems faced by the nation and how to deal with them.

Hundreds of other reformers rushed to join the Roosevelt administration. Among the most important were two veterans of Roosevelt's New York governorship: Harry Hopkins and Frances Perkins. Hopkins was a tough-talking, softhearted social worker devoted to the **social gospel** of moral and material uplift of the downtrodden. He administered New Deal relief efforts and served as one of the president's loyal confidants. Like Hopkins, Perkins embraced the social gospel tradition, having worked for a time in Jane Addams's Hull House in Chicago. She also had extensive experience trying to improve working conditions in shops and factories. In fact, she had directed New York's investigation of the 1911 Triangle Shirtwaist Factory fire that killed 146 women (see chapter 21). Roosevelt tapped Perkins to serve as secretary of labor, making her the first woman cabinet member in American history—an indication of her expertise and of the growing strength of women in the Democratic Party, which had an active Women's Division.

No New Dealers were more important than the president and his wife, Eleanor. The gregarious president radiated charm and good cheer, giving the New Deal's bureaucratic regulations a benevolent human face. Eleanor Roosevelt became the New Deal's unofficial ambassador. She served, she said, as "the eyes and ears of the New Deal" as she traveled throughout the nation connecting the corridors of power in Washington to Americans of all colors and creeds in church basements, meeting halls, and front parlors. A North Carolina women's rights

Eleanor Roosevelt Serving Unemployed Women
A tireless ambassador of the New Deal, Eleanor Roosevelt used her status as First Lady to highlight New Dealers' sympathy for the plight of poor, unemployed, and neglected working people. Shown here in December 1932, Roosevelt serves soup to jobless women and their children. The carefully posed scene contrasts Roosevelt's broad smile with the somewhat awed concern on the faces of the two women at the end of the table and with the casual, workaday indifference of the kitchen workers in the background. The photo depicts both the value of personal, face-to-face relief efforts and the impossibility of such limited, private gestures to help the millions of Americans in need.
© Bettmann/Corbis.

activist recalled, "One of my great pleasures was meeting Mrs. Roosevelt. . . . [S]he was so free of prejudice . . . [and] she was always willing to take a stand, and there were stands to take about blacks and women."

As Roosevelt's programs swung into action, many Americans benefited directly through jobs and relief or indirectly through economic improvements. In time, the millions of beneficiaries of the New Deal became grassroots New Dealers who expressed their appreciation by voting Democratic on election day. A signal success of the New Deal was to create a durable political coalition of Democrats that would reelect Roosevelt in 1936, 1940, and 1944.

As Roosevelt and his advisers developed plans to meet the economic emergency, their watchwords were *action*, *experiment*, and *improvise*. Without a sharply defined template for how to provide relief, recovery, and reform, they moved

Fascism: Adolf Hitler and National Socialism

The Great Depression paralyzed economies around the globe and seemed to demonstrate that capitalism had failed. Supply and demand, prices and productivity, jobs and wages did not recover simply by waiting for the "invisible hand" of the capitalist marketplace to work its magic. Individual working people and even businesses could do little to restore prosperity. Only governments had the power to kick-start the economy. But many people believed that democracies such as the United States were too weak and divided to take the necessary steps.

President Franklin Roosevelt optimistically declared that the "democratic faith" of Americans in 1933 was "too sturdy" to turn to "alien ideologies like communism and fascism." But authoritarian, antidemocratic Communist and fascist parties battled to seize control of national governments across Europe. In Germany, Adolf Hitler and his fascist National Socialist Party, also known as the Nazis, came to power in 1933 and improved the economy while crushing democracy. Other fascist regimes ruled in Italy, Spain, and elsewhere during the 1920s and 1930s, but no fascist government was more important to the history of the United States and the rest of the world than Nazi Germany.

Hitler rose to power as the leader of a political coalition (composed of Nazis, other conservative parties, and the army) that sought to bring order to the chaotic, violent, and ineffective Weimar democracy that governed Germany in the years following World War I. After Germany's defeat in the war, hyperinflation wiped out the savings of millions of Germans and caused ordinary people to wonder how they would survive. On the eve of World War I, one American dollar had been worth four German marks; by the end of 1923, the same dollar was worth four trillion marks. To buy an egg required a wheelbarrow full of marks.

The Weimar government eventually stabilized the German currency, but it did little to combat unemployment, which ranged between one-third and one-half of the population. Many Germans blamed the terms imposed by the Versailles peace treaty for this economic meltdown. Hitler stoked this discontent, proclaiming his fantasy that an international conspiracy of Communists and financiers—mostly Jews—had caused Germany's defeat and were responsible for its postwar woes. During the 1920s, Hitler's National Socialist Party remained on the extremist margins of German politics, but worsening economic distress and political turmoil increased its support, especially among disgruntled veterans, farmers, small townspeople, shopkeepers, artisans, and other members of the middle and lower-middle classes. The Nazis became the most popular political party by 1932, but they still commanded only one-third of the vote when Hitler became head of the German government in January 1933.

Within a few months, Hitler seized dictatorial power. The Nazis outlawed all political opposition, murdering hundreds and imprisoning more than 100,000 Communists, socialists, union members, and others in the summer of 1933, creating a one-party government. Military officers were required to swear an oath pledging their "unconditional obedience to the Leader of the German Reich and people, Adolph Hitler." To stifle any lingering dissent, the Nazis seized control of every institution in German society, from local governments to choirs and hiking clubs. They created an elaborate system of spies who punished anyone suspected of questioning Nazi rule—for example, by failing to use the Nazi salute and shout "Heil Hitler!" at every opportunity. Hitler boasted that "every person should know for all time that if he raises his hand to strike at the [Nazi] State, certain death will be his lot." The Nazi Gestapo (police) routinely carried out Hitler's threat, making lawless, life-threatening terror a reality throughout German society.

Hitler's obsessive anti-Semitism made Jews a special target of the Nazi police state. The Nazis organized boycotts of Jewish businesses, destroyed and confiscated Jews' property, purged Jews from civilian and military employment, and passed laws prohibiting marriages between Jews and non-Jews. In reality, Jews accounted for only about 1 percent of the German population, and most of them were fully acculturated members of German society. Hitler claimed, however, that Jews and other "enemies of the people"—such as Gypsies, homosexuals, the chronically ill, and the mentally or physically disabled—polluted the purity of Aryan blood. By 1939, the Nazis had rounded up tens of thousands of Jews and other "undesirables" in concentration camps. Tens of thousands more had sought refuge in Europe, the United States, Latin America, and Asia. Hitler and the Nazis relished the persecution of Jews, profited from robbing Jews of their property, and constantly warned about the grave threat Jews posed to Germany—a claim that was completely false.

Hitler's fascist dictatorship had one overriding goal: to rearm Germany and expand German territory—which the Nazis called "living space"—until it encompassed all of Europe and much of the Soviet Union. Hitler grandiosely planned a campaign of conquest that would result in the Nazis' thousand-year dominion over the world. Hitler announced in 1933 that "the rearmament of the German people . . . must always and everywhere stand in the foreground." In consultation with military leaders, the Nazis mobilized German industries to build tanks, ships, aircraft, and weapons as rapidly as possible, all in violation of the terms of the Versailles treaty. Unlike the Communist Soviet Union, fascists in Nazi Germany worked with privately owned industrial firms, which welcomed military production that brought them increased investment, productivity, and profits. The rearmament campaign reduced unemployment from more than 11 million in 1933 to less than 1 million by 1937. Likewise, although the peace treaty limited the size of the German military to 100,000 men, the Nazis had nearly 2.5 million men in uniform by 1939. They financed this

massive militarization by forcing civilians to sacrifice by consuming less and working more and by extortion and robbery of private wealth.

The Nazis barraged Germany with propaganda designed to promote a cult of Hitler worship. The führer (leader) was portrayed as having almost superhuman powers: He embodied the will and destiny of the entire German people, and his genius would lead them to the preeminence in the world they so richly deserved. The famous Nazi film director Leni Riefenstahl echoed this Hitler cult when she wrote to the führer, "You exceed anything

human imagination has the power to conceive, achieving deeds without parallel in the history of mankind."

Hitler welcomed such flattery, which masked the underlying terror, lawlessness, and corruption of his fascist dictatorship. The Nazis reduced unemployment and brought a measure of prosperity to many Germans during the 1930s, by outlawing democracy, suppressing dissent, imprisoning and murdering tens of thousands of people, and preparing for a war that would leave Germany a smoldering ruin twelve years after Hitler seized power.

Germans Salute a Nazi Parade
This photograph depicts the enthusiasm of German men, women, and children who raise their hands in the Nazi salute as fascist officials parade through the streets of Nuremberg in 1938. Although Hitler's police state never won the allegiance of all Germans, most welcomed the economic prosperity and political order imposed by Hitler, and they willingly cooperated with the Nazis' reign of terror, persecution, and rearmament.
United States Holocaust Memorial Museum.

from ideas to policies as quickly as possible, hoping to identify ways to help people and to boost the economy. But underlying New Dealers' experimentation and improvisation were four guiding ideas.

First, Roosevelt and his advisers sought capitalist solutions to the economic crisis. They believed that the depression had resulted from basic imbalances in the nation's capitalist economy—imbalances they wanted to correct. They had no desire to eliminate private property or impose **socialist** programs, such as public ownership of productive resources. Instead, they hoped to save the capitalist economy by remedying its flaws.

Second, Roosevelt's Brains Trust persuaded him that the greatest flaw of America's capitalist economy was underconsumption, the root cause of the current economic paralysis. Underconsumption, New Dealers argued, resulted from the gigantic productive success of capitalism. Factories and farms produced more than they could sell to consumers, causing factories to lay off workers and farmers to lose money on bumper crops. Workers without wages and farmers without profits shrank consumption and choked the economy. Somehow, the balance between consumption and production needed to be restored.

Third, New Dealers believed that the immense size and economic power of American corporations needed to be counterbalanced by government and by organization among workers and small producers. Unlike progressive trustbusters, New Dealers did not seek to splinter big businesses. Huge businesses had developed for good economic reasons and were here to stay. Roosevelt and his advisers hoped to counterbalance big economic institutions and their quest for profits with government programs focused on protecting individuals and the public interest.

Fourth, New Dealers felt that government must somehow moderate the imbalance of wealth created by American capitalism. Wealth concentrated in a few hands reduced consumption by most Americans and thereby contributed to the current economic gridlock. In the long run, government needed to find a way to permit ordinary working people to share more fully in the fruits of the economy. In the short term, New Dealers sought to lend a helping hand to poor people who suffered from the maldistribution of wealth.

Banking and Finance Reform

Roosevelt wasted no time making good on his inaugural pledge for "action now." As he took the oath of office on March 4, the nation's banking system was on the brink of collapse. Since 1930, more than five thousand banks had collapsed. Roosevelt immediately declared a four-day "bank holiday" in order to devise a plan to shore up banks and restore depositors' confidence. Working round the clock, New Dealers drafted the Emergency Banking Act, which gave the secretary of the treasury the power to decide which banks could be safely reopened and to release funds from the Reconstruction Finance Corporation (RFC) to bolster banks' assets. To secure the confidence of depositors, Congress passed the Glass-Steagall Banking Act, setting

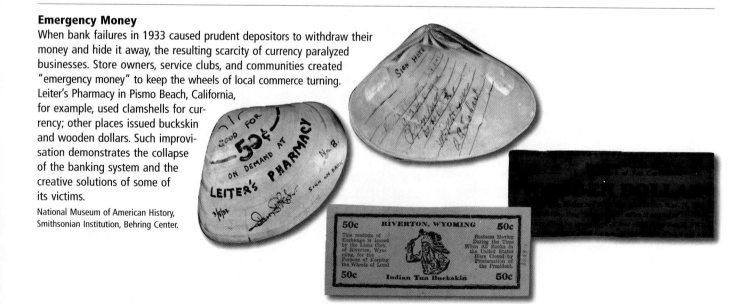

Emergency Money

When bank failures in 1933 caused prudent depositors to withdraw their money and hide it away, the resulting scarcity of currency paralyzed businesses. Store owners, service clubs, and communities created "emergency money" to keep the wheels of local commerce turning. Leiter's Pharmacy in Pismo Beach, California, for example, used clamshells for currency; other places issued buckskin and wooden dollars. Such improvisation demonstrates the collapse of the banking system and the creative solutions of some of its victims.

National Museum of American History, Smithsonian Institution, Behring Center.

up the Federal Deposit Insurance Corporation (FDIC), which guaranteed bank customers that the federal government would reimburse them for deposits if their banks failed.

On Sunday night, March 12, while the banks were still closed, Roosevelt broadcast the first of what became a series of "fireside chats." Speaking in a friendly, informal manner, he addressed the millions of Americans who tuned their radios to hear the president explain these first New Deal initiatives. The new banking legislation, he said, made it "safer to keep your money in a reopened bank than under the mattress." With such plain talk, Roosevelt translated complex matters into common sense. This and subsequent fireside chats forged a direct connection—via radio waves—between Roosevelt and millions of Americans. Evidence of their link to Roosevelt piled up in the White House mail room. Millions shared the views of a man from Paris, Texas, who wrote to Roosevelt, "You are the one & only President that ever helped a Working Class of People. . . . Please help us some way I Pray to God for relief."

The banking legislation and fireside chat worked. Within a few days, most of the nation's major banks reopened, and they remained solvent as reassured depositors switched funds from their mattresses to their bank accounts (Figure 24.1). Some radical critics of the New Deal believed that Roosevelt should have nationalized the banks and made them a cornerstone of economic planning by the federal government. Instead, these first New Deal measures propped up the private banking system with federal funds and subjected banks to federal regulation and oversight. One adviser proclaimed, "Capitalism was saved in eight days," although in reality the rescue operation took much longer to succeed.

In his inaugural address, Roosevelt criticized financiers for their greed and incompetence. To prevent the fraud, corruption, insider trading, and other abuses that had tainted Wall Street and contributed to the crash of 1929, Roosevelt pressed Congress to regulate the stock market. Legislation in 1934 created the Securities and Exchange Commission (SEC) to oversee financial markets by licensing investment dealers, monitoring all stock transactions, and requiring

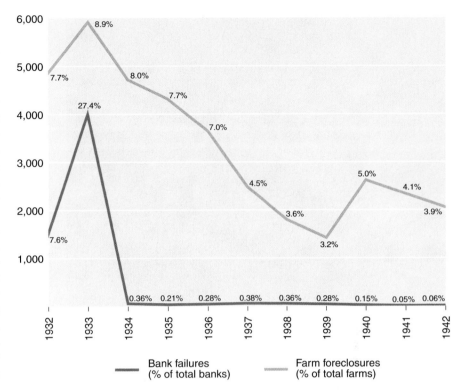

FIGURE 24.1 Bank Failures and Farm Foreclosures, 1932–1942
New Deal legislation to stabilize the economy had its most immediate and striking effect in preventing banks, along with their depositors, from going under and farmers from losing their land.

corporate officers to make full disclosures about their companies. To head the SEC, Roosevelt named an abrasive and ambitious Wall Street financier, Joseph P. Kennedy, who had a somewhat shady reputation for stock manipulation. When critics complained about his selection, Roosevelt replied shrewdly, "Set a thief to catch a thief." Under Kennedy's leadership, the SEC helped a cleaned-up and regulated Wall Street to recover slowly, although the stock market stayed well below its frothy heights of the 1920s.

Relief and Conservation Programs

Patching the nation's financial structure provided little relief for the hungry and unemployed. A poor man from Nebraska asked Eleanor Roosevelt "if the folk who was borned here in America . . . are this Forgotten Man, the President had in mind, [and] if we are this Forgotten Man then we are still Forgotten." Since its founding, the federal government had never assumed responsibility for needy people, except in moments of natural disaster or emergencies such as the Civil War. Instead, churches, private

Civilian Conservation Corps Workers
The Civilian Conservation Corps employed these young men in 1933 to build a truck trail in a remote region of Snoqualmie National Forest in the state of Washington. Instead of using machinery for the heavy construction work, the CCC intentionally used the muscles of working men in order to maximize employment. Although the truck trail provided emergency relief in the form of badly needed jobs, it contributed minimally to the New Deal goals of recovery and reform among the millions of Americans who could not readily leave their families for jobs in the wilderness.
© Bettmann/Corbis.

> Work relief efforts replaced the stigma of welfare with the dignity of jobs. As one woman said about her husband's work relief job, "We aren't on relief anymore. My husband is working for the Government."

charities, county and municipal governments, and occasionally states assumed the burden of poor relief, usually with meager payments. To persuade Americans that the depression necessitated unprecedented federal relief efforts, Harry Hopkins dispatched investigators throughout the nation to describe the plight of impoverished Americans. Reports filtered back to Washington of families surviving on "bull-dog gravy"—a thin paste of lard, flour, and water—along with news that the working hours of tens of thousands of Americans had been cut, reducing their wages to about $1.50 a day. As one New Yorker wrote the government, "We work, ten hours a day for six days. In the grime and dirt of a nation [for] . . . low pay [making us] . . . slaves—slaves of the depression!"

Hopkins's investigators galvanized support for the Federal Emergency Relief Administration (FERA), which provided $500 million to feed the hungry and create jobs. Established in May 1933, FERA supported four million to five million households with $20 or $30 a month. FERA also created jobs for the unemployed on thousands of public works projects, organized by Hopkins into the Civil Works Administration (CWA), which put paychecks worth more than $800 million into the hands of previously jobless workers. Earning wages between forty and sixty cents an hour, laborers renovated schools, dug sewers, and rebuilt roads and bridges. FERA extended the scope of relief to include health and education, providing vaccinations for millions and funding literacy classes.

The most popular work relief program was the Civilian Conservation Corps (CCC), established in March 1933. It offered unemployed young men a chance to earn wages while working to conserve natural resources, a long-standing interest of Roosevelt. Women were excluded from working in the CCC until Eleanor Roosevelt demanded that a token number of young women be hired. One of the three million young men who enlisted in the CCC, Blackie Gold, had been out of work and had to "beg for coal, [and] buy bread that's two, three days old" in order to help support his large family. After he joined the CCC, Gold earned $30 a month and was required to send all but $5 home to his family. By the end of the program in 1942, the three million CCC workers had checked soil erosion, tamed rivers, and planted more than two billion trees. CCC workers left a legacy of vast new recreation areas, along with roads that made those areas accessible to millions of Americans. Just as important, the CCC, CWA, and other work relief efforts replaced the stigma of welfare with the dignity of jobs. As one woman said about her husband's work relief job, "We aren't on relief anymore. My husband is working for the Government."

The New Deal also sought to harness natural resources for hydroelectric power. Continuing a project begun under Hoover, the New Deal completed the colossal Hoover Dam across the Colorado River in Nevada, providing not only electricity but also flood control and irrigation water for Arizona and southern California. In addition, building the dam provided badly needed jobs and wages for thousands of unemployed workers.

The New Deal's most ambitious and controversial natural resources development project was the Tennessee Valley Authority (TVA), created in May 1933 to build dams along the Tennessee River to supply impoverished rural communities with cheap electricity (Map 24.3). The TVA planned model towns for power station workers and new homes for the farmers who would benefit from electricity and flood control. The most ambitious

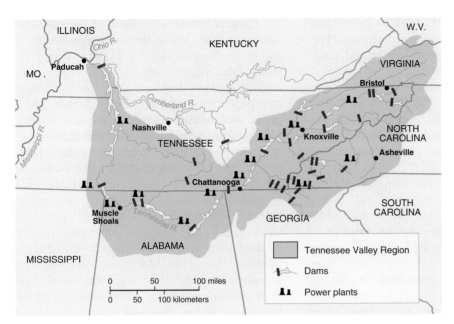

The New Deal created the Tennessee Valley Authority to modernize a vast impoverished region with hydroelectric power dams and, at the same time, to reclaim eroded land and preserve old folkways.

READING THE MAP: How many states were affected by the TVA? How many miles of rivers (approximately) were affected?

CONNECTIONS: What kinds of benefits—economic as well as social and cultural—did TVA programs bring to the region? How might the lives of a poor farming family in Alabama or Tennessee have changed after the mid-1930s owing to these programs?

FOR MORE HELP ANALYZING THIS MAP, see the map activity for this chapter in the Online Study Guide at bedfordstmartins.com/roark.

example of New Deal enthusiasm for planning, the TVA set out to demonstrate that a partnership between the federal government and local residents could overcome the barriers of state governments and private enterprises to make efficient use of abundant natural resources and break the ancient cycle of poverty. The TVA never fully realized these utopian ends, but it improved the lives of millions in the region with electric power, flood protection, soil reclamation, and jobs.

New sources of hydroelectric power helped the New Deal bring the wonders of electricity to country folk, fulfilling an old progressive dream. When Roosevelt became president, 90 percent of rural Americans lacked electricity. Private electric companies refused to build transmission lines into the sparsely settled countryside when they had a profitable market in more accessible and densely populated urban areas. Beginning in 1935, the Rural Electrification Administration (REA) made low-cost loans available to local cooperatives for power plants and transmission lines to serve rural communities. Within ten years, the REA delivered electricity to nine out of ten farms, giving rural Americans access for the first time to modern conveniences that urban people had enjoyed for decades.

Agricultural Initiatives

Farmers had been mired in a depression since the end of World War I. New Dealers diagnosed the farmers' plight as a classic case of overproduction and underconsumption. Following

Rural Electrification and Running Water

New Deal programs brought housing and electricity to rural families like those in this village in east-central Tennessee. The Tennessee Valley Authority provided the houses shown here and the power that flowed through the lines strung from poles along the right side of the road. In this village, the pump operated by the children in the foreground was the only source of water. In addition to providing electric power, the New Deal's Rural Electrification Administration built the necessary infrastructure to bring running water to homes that lacked it. The REA promoted these projects through public outreach campaigns that used posters like this one to increase awareness of the benefits of running water. What difference do you think electricity and running water made in the daily lives of the people in this village?

age-old practices, farmers tried to compensate for low crop prices by growing more crops, hoping to boost their earnings by selling larger quantities. Instead, producing more crops pushed prices lower still. Farm income sank from a disastrously low $6 billion in 1929 to a catastrophically low $2 billion in 1932. The median annual income among farm families plunged to $167, barely one-tenth of the national average.

New Dealers sought to cut agricultural production, thereby raising crop prices and farmers' income. With more money in their pockets, farm families—who made up one-third of all Americans—would then buy more goods and lift consumption in the entire economy. To reduce production, the Agricultural Adjustment Act (AAA) authorized the "domestic allotment plan," which paid farmers *not* to grow crops. Individual farmers who agreed not to plant crops on a portion of their fields (their "allotment") would receive a government payment compensating them for the crops they did not plant. Since crops were already in the ground by the time the act was passed in May 1933, drastic measures were necessary to reduce production immediately. While millions of Americans went to bed hungry, farmers slaughtered millions of cattle, hogs, sheep, and other livestock and destroyed millions of acres of crops in order to qualify for their allotment payments.

With the formation of the Commodity Credit Corporation, the federal government allowed farmers to hold their harvested crops off the market and wait for a higher price. In the meantime, the government stored the crop and gave farmers a "commodity loan" based on a favorable price. If the market price rose above that level, a farmer could sell the crop, repay the loan, and pocket the difference. If the market price never rose above the loan level, the farmer simply took the loan as payment, and the government kept the crop. In effect, commodity loans addressed the problem of underconsumption by making the federal government a major consumer of agricultural goods and reducing farmers' vulnerability to low prices. New Dealers also sponsored the Farm Credit Act (FCA) to provide long-term credit on mortgaged farm property, allowing debt-ridden farmers to avoid foreclosures that were driving thousands off their land (see Figure 24.1).

The president of the Oklahoma Tenant Farmers' Union explained that farmers who got "Triple-A" payments often used the money to buy tractors and then "forced their tenants and [share]croppers off the land."

Crop allotments, commodity loans, and mortgage credit made farmers major beneficiaries of the New Deal. Crop prices rose impressively, farm income jumped 50 percent by 1936, and FCA loans financed 40 percent of farm mortgage debt by the end of the decade. These gains were distributed fairly equally among farmers in the corn, hogs, and wheat region of the Midwest. In the South's cotton belt, however, landlords controlled the distribution of New Deal agricultural benefits and shamelessly rewarded themselves while denying benefits to many sharecroppers and tenant farmers—blacks and whites—by taking the land they had worked out of production and assigning it to the allotment program. Many such tenants and sharecroppers could no longer find work, and their privation worsened. The president of the Oklahoma Tenant Farmers' Union explained that large farmers who got "Triple-A" payments often used the money to buy tractors and then "forced their tenants and [share]croppers off the land," causing these "Americans to be starved and dispossessed of their homes in our land of plenty."

Industrial Recovery

Unlike farmers, industrialists cut production with the onset of the depression. Between 1929 and 1933, industrial production fell more than 40 percent to balance low demand with low supply and thereby maintain prices. But the industrialists' strategy created major economic and social problems for Roosevelt and his advisers, since falling industrial production meant that millions of working people lost their jobs. Unlike farmers, most working people lived in towns and cities and needed jobs to eat. Mass unemployment also reduced consumer demand for industrial products, contributing to a downward spiral in both production and jobs, with no end in sight. Industries responded by reducing wages for employees who still had jobs, further reducing demand—a trend made worse by competition among industrial producers. New Dealers struggled to find a way to break this cycle of unemployment and underconsumption—a way consistent with corporate profits and capitalism.

The New Deal's National Industrial Recovery Act (NIRA) opted for a government-sponsored form of industrial self-government through the National Recovery Administration (NRA), established in June 1933. The NRA en-

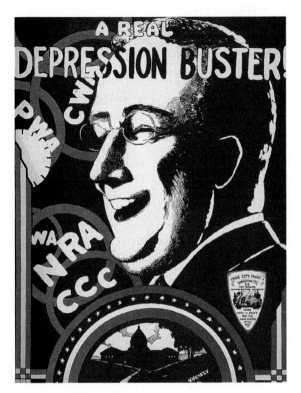

1936 Campaign Poster
This campaign poster calls Roosevelt "A Real Depression Buster" and highlights his alphabet soup of New Deal agencies. Roosevelt's face was so well known that the poster does not even mention his name, the Democratic Party, or the New Deal. It exemplifies the political significance of Roosevelt's confident smile, perhaps the most potent symbol of the New Deal.
Collection of Janice L. and David J. Frent.

couraged industrialists in every part of the economy to agree on rules, known as codes, to define fair working conditions, to set prices, and to minimize competition. The idea behind codes was to stabilize existing industries and maintain their workforces while avoiding what both industrialists and New Dealers termed "destructive competition," which forced employers to cut wages and jobs. Industry after industry wrote elaborate codes addressing detailed features of production, pricing, and competition. In exchange for relaxing federal antitrust regulations that prohibited such business agreements, the NRA received a promise from participating businesses that they would recognize the right of working people to organize and engage in **collective bargaining**. To encourage consumers to patronize businesses participating in NRA codes, the New Deal mounted a public relations campaign that displayed the NRA's Blue Eagle

in shop windows and on billboards throughout the nation.

New Dealers hoped that NRA codes would yield businesses with a social conscience, ensuring fair treatment of workers and consumers and promotion of the general economic welfare. Instead, NRA codes tended to strengthen conventional business practices. Large corporations wrote codes that served primarily their own interests rather than the needs of workers or the welfare of the national economy. (See "Seeking the American Promise," page 878.) The failure of codes to cover agricultural or domestic workers led one woman to complain to Roosevelt that the NRA "never mentioned the robbery of the Housewives" by the privations caused by the depression. Many business leaders criticized NRA codes as heavy-handed government regulation of private enterprise. Some even claimed that the NRA was a homegrown version of Benito Mussolini's corporate fascism taking shape in Italy. In reality, however, compliance with NRA codes was voluntary, and government enforcement efforts were weak to nonexistent. The NRA did little to reduce unemployment, raise consumption, or relieve the depression. In effect, it represented a peace offering to business leaders by Roosevelt and his advisers, conveying the message that the New Deal did not intend to wage war against profits or private enterprise. The peace offering failed, however. Most corporate leaders became active and often bitter opponents of Roosevelt and the New Deal.

> The failure of codes to cover agricultural or domestic workers led one woman to complain to Roosevelt that the NRA "never mentioned the robbery of the Housewives" by the privations caused by the depression.

REVIEW   How did New Dealers try to steer the nation toward recovery from the Great Depression?

Challenges to the New Deal

The first New Deal initiatives engendered fierce criticism and political opposition. From the right, Republicans and business people charged that New Deal programs were too radical, undermining private property, economic stability, and democracy. Critics on the left faulted the New Deal for its failure to allay the human suffering caused by the depression and for its timidity in attacking corporate power and greed.

Textile Workers Strike for Better Wages and Working Conditions

"The 'Stretch-out System' is the cause of the whole trouble," a textile worker declared in 1930, echoing the sentiments of thousands of other mill workers. "There is hundreds of men walking the roads looking for work with wife and kids at home suffering," another mill hand wrote. "The stretch-out is what is wrong."

"The stretch-out" was the term coined by mill workers for the cost-cutting efficiencies implemented by mill owners that led to layoffs and poor working conditions for textile workers during the 1920s and 1930s. Textile manufacturers drastically increased the workload of their employees to cut labor costs and raise productivity. A mill worker who tended thirty looms in 1920 was responsible for ninety to one hundred looms by 1929—if she or he still had a job. "The reason so many people are out of jobs," one mill hand explained in 1933, "is because the mill owners have put two and three men's jobs on one man." A woman who had been working in cotton mills since she was twelve wrote to President Franklin Roosevelt in 1934, "We simply have to fly about our work . . . as if we were putting out a fire or fighting for our life." Layoffs of mill hands in the midst of the Great Depression contributed to further deterioration in wages and working conditions; so many people

were desperate for work, no matter what the wage, that manufacturers were able to cut wages in half. If workers complained, mill owners responded, as one mill hand recalled, "If you don't like it there's a barefoot boy waitin' at the gate for your job." The result, as one textile worker wrote Roosevelt, was that "the ones who are Still at Work are Being Treated as Bad or Worse tha[n] the Slaves were in Slavery times."

Like so many other textile workers who faced the tough choice of working with the stretch-out or not working, Icy Norman was relieved to find work in 1929 at Burlington Mills in Piedmont Heights, North Carolina. Icy's father had worked in cotton mills in Virginia and North Carolina, but when he died in 1928, her mother took Icy and her two brothers from mill to mill to find work. For weeks, the family went "hunting jobs," Icy recalled. "We went everywhere. . . . You just couldn't get a job. Every freight train that you seen pass was loaded down with people going from town to town, hoboing." Icy lucked out at Burlington Mills because the supervisor happened to be a friend of her father's. He hired Icy to wind thread onto bobbins for weaving. At first, she earned only 15 cents a day, but as she became more skilled, her wages rose to $10 a week, a little over 15 cents an hour. "After I got used to being in

there," Icy recalled, "I really loved my work. . . . I got pleasure out of it and it made me happy to do my job." Icy's wages helped support her mother and her siblings. Like thousands of other mill hands, Icy and her family knew that even with the stretch-out, they were lucky to have a job. Still, as one mill worker wrote to Roosevelt, "every textile worker in the South would walk out of the mill today if they were not afraid of starvation."

In September 1934, hundreds of thousands of textile workers throughout the nation overcame their fears and walked out of the mills in the largest strike in American history. Strikers shut down mills from Maine to Alabama. More than half of all textile workers nationwide and about two-thirds of mill hands in the southern heartland of the textile industry walked out, including Icy Norman. Loosely organized by the Textile Workers' Union, the strikers demanded better working conditions and wages through enforcement of the textile code established by the New Deal's National Recovery Administration (NRA).

Like other NRA codes, the textile code was written and administered by the leading textile manufacturers. It provided for a maximum forty-hour workweek, a minimum weekly wage of $12 for southern mill hands and $13 for northern mill workers, and the right of workers to organize unions. Textile workers celebrated the passage of the NRA in June 1933. "It seemed too good to be true," one textile worker observed. A New Deal representative who investigated conditions in mill towns reported, "Every house I visited—mill worker or unemployed—had a picture of the President . . . [in] the place of honor over the mantel." Mill hands told the New Dealer, "We trust in the

Supreme Being and Franklin Roosevelt. . . . [We] know that the President will see that [we] have work and proper wages; and that the stretch-out will be abandoned."

But their faith was misplaced, and the code was widely ignored. When workers complained that mill owners continued the stretch-out, cutting wages and firing any mill hands they suspected of union sympathies, their grievances were heard by their bosses, the textile manufacturers who headed the NRA code authority. In the year before the strike, the textile code authority received nearly 4,000 complaints, investigated 96, and resolved just 1 in favor of a worker. Manufacturers' blatant use of the textile code to bust unions and continue the stretch-out enraged many mill workers who believed they had the support of the New Deal to obtain better wages and working conditions through union organizations.

Boiling with frustration over the failure of the textile code, more than 400,000 mill hands went on strike seeking to realize what they viewed as the unfulfilled promises of the New Deal's NRA by organizing a union to bargain with mill owners to improve wages and working conditions. But after three weeks and numerous violent confrontations with police and National Guardsmen, the combination of the mill owners' intransigence, the Textile Workers' Union's lack of resources, the mill workers' increasingly desperate financial situation, and Roosevelt's focus on the need for industrial peace to achieve economic recovery brought the strike to an end.

The mill hands achieved virtually nothing as a result of the strike. Mill owners continued to flout the textile codes, the stretch-out continued without interruption, and working conditions did not improve. Angry mill owners fired and blacklisted strike leaders, succeeding in their efforts to crush workers' organizations. After the strike, a union leader summarized the bitter lesson he had learned: "Many of us did not understand fully the role of the Government in the struggle between labor and industry . . . that the Government protects the strong, not the weak, and that it operates under pressure and yields to that group which is strong enough to assert itself over the other."

Icy Norman went back to work after the strike ended, and since she was not a union activist, she managed to keep her job until she retired in 1976, after forty-seven years at Burlington Mills. Despite working for the company longer than any other employee, Icy was forced to retire six months before she would have received benefits from a profit-sharing plan. "I begged them to let me work on, but they wouldn't," she recalled. "I give the best part of my life to the Burlington Industries. It kind of hurt me to think that as long as I stayed there and as faithful as I worked, that I didn't get none of that profit." Instead, the company gave her a free visit to a local hairdresser, a tour of the Burlington executive suite, and a farewell handshake.

Striking Mill Workers Jeer Scabs
Textile workers on strike against the Cannon Textile Mills in North Carolina in September 1934 shouted taunts and curses at employees—known as "scabs"—who refused to honor the strikers' picket line. Notice the contrast between the clothing of the strikers and that of the scabs. What might explain this contrast? Although thousands of women like Icy Norman joined the strike, there are no women among the strikers shown here. What might account for the absence of women mill hands in this picket line?
© Bettmann/Corbis.

Resistance to Business Reform

New Deal programs rescued capitalism, but business leaders lambasted Roosevelt, even though their economic prospects improved more than those of most other Americans during the depression. Republicans and business leaders fulminated against New Deal efforts to regulate or reform what they considered their private enterprises. Although concentrated corporate power avoided reform, business leaders still conducted stridently anti–New Deal campaigns that expressed their resentment and fear of regulations, taxes, and unions. One opponent called the president "Stalin Delano Roosevelt" and insisted that the New Deal was really a "Raw Deal."

By 1935, two major business organizations, the National Association of Manufacturers and the Chamber of Commerce, had become openly anti–New Deal. Their critiques were amplified by the American Liberty League, founded in 1934, which blamed the New Deal for betraying basic constitutional guarantees of freedom and individualism. To them, the AAA was a "trend toward fascist control of agriculture," relief programs marked "the end of democracy," and the NRA was a plunge into the "quicksand of visionary experimentation." Although Liberty League membership never exceeded 125,000, its well-financed publicity campaign widened the rift between Roosevelt and business people.

Economic planners who favored rational planning in the public interest and labor leaders who sought to influence wages and working conditions by organizing unions attacked the New Deal from the left. In their view, the NRA stifled enterprise by permitting **monopolistic** practices. They pointed out that industrial trade associations twisted NRA codes to suit their aims, thwarted competition, and engaged in price gouging. Labor leaders especially resented the NRA's willingness to allow businesses to form company-controlled unions while blocking workers from organizing genuine grassroots unions to bargain for themselves.

The Supreme Court stepped into this crossfire of criticisms in May 1935 and declared that the NRA unconstitutionally conferred powers reserved to Congress on an administrative agency staffed by government appointees. The NRA codes soon lost the little authority they had. The failure of the NRA demonstrated the depth of many Americans' resistance to economic planning and the stubborn refusal of business leaders to yield to government regulations or reforms.

Casualties in the Countryside

The AAA weathered critical battering by champions of the old order better than the NRA. Allotment checks for keeping land fallow and crop prices high created loyalty among farmers with enough acreage to participate. As a white farmer in North Carolina declared, "I stand for the New Deal and Roosevelt . . . , the AAA . . . and crop control." Agricultural processors and distributors, however, criticized the AAA. They objected that the program reduced the volume of crop production—the only source of their profits—while they paid a tax on processed crops that funded the very program that disadvantaged them. In 1936, the Supreme Court agreed with their contention that they were victims of an illegal attempt to tax one group (processors and distributors) to enrich another (farmers). Down but not out, the AAA rebounded

Major Legislation of the New Deal's First Hundred Days

	Name of Act	Basic Provisions
March 9, 1933	Emergency Banking Act	Provides for reopening stable banks and authorizing the Reconstruction Finance Corporation (RFC) to supply funds.
March 31, 1933	Civilian Conservation Corps Act	Provides jobs for unemployed young men.
May 12, 1933	Agricultural Adjustment Act	Provides funds to pay farmers for not growing crops.
May 12, 1933	Federal Emergency Relief Act	Provides relief funds for the destitute.
May 18, 1933	Tennessee Valley Authority Act	Creates the TVA to bring electric power and conservation to the area.
June 16, 1933	National Industrial Recovery Act	Specifies cooperation among business, government, and labor in setting fair prices and working conditions.
June 16, 1933	Glass-Steagall Banking Act	Creates the Federal Deposit Insurance Corporation (FDIC) to insure bank deposits.

Evicted Sharecroppers
An unintended consequence of the New Deal's Agricultural Adjustment Administration's plan to maintain farm prices by reducing acreage in production was the eviction of tenant farmers when the land they worked was left idle. These African American sharecroppers were part of a squatters camp that stretched for 150 miles along the western floodplain of the Mississippi River in southeastern Missouri in January 1939. They protested AAA policies that caused cotton farmers to evict them from their homes. Homeless and jobless, camping out with all their earthly belongings, these families were among the many rural laborers whose lives were made worse by New Deal agricultural policies.
© Bettmann/Corbis.

from the Supreme Court ruling by eliminating the offending tax and funding allotment payments from general government revenues.

Protests stirred, however, among those who did not qualify for allotments. The Southern Farm Tenants Union argued passionately that the AAA enriched large farmers and impoverished small farmers who rented rather than owned their land. One black sharecropper explained why only $75 a year from New Deal agricultural subsidies trickled down to her: "De landlord is landlord, de politicians is landlord, de judge is landlord, de shurf [sheriff] is landlord, ever'body is landlord, en we [sharecroppers] ain' got nothin'!" Such testimony showed that the AAA, like the NRA, tended to help most

those who least needed help. Roosevelt's political dependence on southern Democrats caused him to avoid confronting such economic and racial inequities in the South's entrenched order.

Displaced tenants often joined the army of migrant workers who straggled across rural America during the 1930s, some to flee Great Plains dust storms. Many migrants came from Mexico to work Texas cotton, Michigan beans, Idaho sugar beets, and California crops of all kinds. But since the number of people willing to take

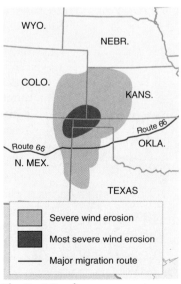

The Dust Bowl

Okie Family
This tenant farmer worked land near Eagleton, Oklahoma, but became sick with pneumonia and lost his farm. The county he had lived in for fifteen years refused to give him Works Progress Administration benefits because he briefly left the county after recovering from his illness. Accompanied by his five children, he carted all his possessions in a toy wagon along a highway while looking for work. Such poor, jobless migrants were common along America's roads during the 1930s.
Library of Congress.

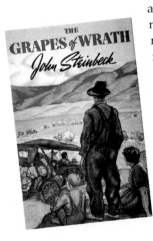

agricultural jobs usually exceeded the number of jobs available, wages fell and native-born white migrants fought to reserve even these low-wage jobs for themselves. Hundreds of thousands of "Okies" streamed out of the Dust Bowl of Oklahoma, Kansas, Texas, and Colorado, where chronic drought and harmful agricultural practices blasted crops and hopes. Parched, poor, and wind-blown, Okies—like the Joad family immortalized in John Steinbeck's novel *The Grapes of Wrath* (1939)—migrated to the lush fields and orchards of Cali-

fornia, congregating in labor camps and hoping to find work and a future. But migrant laborers seldom found steady or secure work. As one Okie said, "When they need us they call us migrants, and when we've picked their crop, we're bums and we got to get out."

Politics on the Fringes

Politically, the New Deal's staunchest opponents were in the Republican Party—organized, well-heeled, mainstream, and determined to challenge Roosevelt at every turn. But the New Deal also faced challenges from the political fringes, fueled by the hardship of the depression and the hope for a cure-all.

Socialists and Communists accused the New Deal of being the handmaiden of business elites and of rescuing capitalism from its self-inflicted crisis. Socialist author Upton Sinclair ran for governor of California in 1934 on a plan he called "End Poverty in California." Sinclair demanded that the state take ownership of idle factories and unused land and give them to cooperatives of working people, a first step toward what he envisioned as a "Cooperative Commonwealth" that would put the needs of people above profits. Sinclair lost the election, ending the most serious socialist electoral challenge to the New Deal.

Many intellectuals and artists sought to advance the cause of more radical change by joining left-wing organizations, including the American Communist Party. At its high point in the 1930s, the party had about thirty thousand members, the large majority of them immigrants, especially Scandinavians in the upper Midwest and eastern European Jews in major eastern and midwestern cities. Individual Communists worked to organize labor unions, protect the civil rights of black people, and help the destitute, but the party preached the overthrow of "bourgeois democracy" and the destruction of capitalism in favor of Soviet-style communism. Party spokesmen termed the NRA a "fascist slave program" and likened Roosevelt and the New Deal to Hitler and the Nazis. Such talk attracted few followers among the nation's millions of poor and unemployed. They wanted jobs and economic security within American capitalism and democracy, not violent revolution to establish a dictatorship of the Communist Party.

More powerful radical challenges to the New Deal sprouted from homegrown roots. Many Americans felt overlooked by New Deal programs that concentrated on finance, agriculture, and industry but did little to produce jobs or aid the poor. The merciless reality of the depression also continued to erode the security of people who still had a job but worried constantly that they, too, might be pushed into the legions of the unemployed and penniless.

A Catholic priest in Detroit named Charles Coughlin spoke to and for many worried Americans in his weekly radio broadcasts, which reached a nationwide audience of 40 million. Father Coughlin expressed outrage at the suffering and inequities that he blamed on Communists, bankers, and "predatory capitalists,"

who, he claimed, were mostly Jews. In 1932, Coughlin applauded Roosevelt's election and declared, "The New Deal is Christ's deal." But Coughlin became frustrated by Roosevelt's refusal to grant him influence, turned against the New Deal, and in 1935 founded the National Union for Social Justice, or Union Party, to challenge Roosevelt in the 1936 presidential election. Tapping the popular appeal of anti-Semitism, Coughlin's Union Party called for an expanded money supply backed by silver so that the poor could be rescued from the "international bankers" responsible for the depression and coddled by Roosevelt.

Among those who answered Father Coughlin's call was Dr. Francis Townsend in Long Beach, California. Angry that many of his retired patients lived in misery, Townsend proposed in 1934 the creation of the Old Age Revolving Pension, which would pay every American over age sixty a pension of $200 a month. To receive the pension, senior citizens had to agree to spend the entire amount within thirty days, thereby stimulating the economy. Townsend organized pension clubs with more than two million paying members and petitioned the federal government to enact his scheme. When the major political parties rebuffed his impractical plan, Townsend merged his forces with Coughlin's Union Party in time for the 1936 election.

A more formidable challenge to the New Deal came from the powerful southern wing of the Democratic Party. Huey Long, son of a back-country Louisiana farmer, was elected governor of the state in 1928 with his slogan "Every man a king, but no one wears a crown." Unlike nearly all other southern white politicians who harped on white supremacy, Long championed the poor over the rich, country people over city folk, and the humble over elites. As governor, "the Kingfish"—as he liked to call himself—delivered on his promises to provide jobs and build roads, schools, and hospitals, but he also behaved ruthlessly to achieve his goals. Journalists routinely referred to him as the "dictator of Louisiana." Swaggering and bullying to get his way, Long delighted his supporters, who elected him to the U.S. Senate in 1932. Senator Long introduced a sweeping "soak the rich" tax bill that would outlaw personal incomes of more than $1 million and inheritances of more than $5 million. When the Senate

> Father Coughlin expressed outrage at the suffering and inequities that he blamed on Communists, bankers, and "predatory capitalists."

Huey Long
Huey Long's ability to adapt his captivating stump-speech style to the radio made him the one rival politician who gave Roosevelt serious concern in the mid-1930s. Long is shown here in 1932 campaigning in Arkansas in support of Hattie Carraway's bid for election to the U.S. Senate. Stigmatized as both a woman and a populist reformer, Carraway seemed a sure loser until Long crossed the border from Louisiana on her behalf. In two weeks of speaking and pressing the flesh, Long brushed aside criticism that he was an interloper and boosted Carraway to victory as part of his crusade to share the wealth.
Corbis.

rejected his proposal, Long decided to run for president, mobilizing more than five million Americans behind his "Share Our Wealth" plan. Like Townsend's scheme, Long's program promised far more than it could deliver. The Share Our Wealth campaign died when Long was assassinated in 1935, but his constituency and the wide appeal of a more equitable distribution of wealth persisted.

The challenges to the New Deal from both Republicans and more radical groups stirred Democrats to solidify their winning coalition. In the midterm congressional elections of 1934— normally a time when a seated president loses support—voters gave New Dealers a landslide victory. Democrats increased their majority in the House of Representatives and gained a two-thirds majority in the Senate.

REVIEW   Why did the New Deal face criticism from both ends of the political spectrum?

Toward a Welfare State

The popular mandate for the New Deal revealed by the congressional elections persuaded Roosevelt to press ahead with bold new efforts to achieve relief, recovery, and reform. Despite the initiatives of the Hundred Days, the depression still strangled the economy. Rumbles of discontent from Father Coughlin, Huey Long, and their supporters showed that New Deal programs had fallen far short of their goals. In 1935, Roosevelt capitalized on his congressional majorities to enact major new programs that signaled the emergence of an American **welfare state**.

Taken together, these New Deal efforts stretched a safety net under the lives of ordinary Americans. Although many citizens remained unprotected, New Deal programs helped millions with jobs, relief, and government support. Knitting together the safety net was the idea that the federal government bore responsibility for the welfare of individual Americans. When individuals suffered because of economic and social forces beyond their control—as in the Great Depression—the federal government had the duty to provide them with a measure of support and protection. The safety net of welfare programs tied the political loyalty of working people to the New Deal and the Democratic Party. As a North Carolina mill worker said, "Mr. Roosevelt is the only man we ever had in the White House who would understand that my boss is a sonofabitch."

Relief for the Unemployed

First and foremost, Americans still needed jobs. Since the private economy left eight million people jobless by 1935, Roosevelt and his advisers launched a massive work relief program. Roosevelt believed that direct government handouts crippled recipients with "spiritual and moral disintegration . . . destructive to the human spirit." Jobs, in contrast, bolstered individuals'

City Activities Mural

During the 1930s, artists—many of them employed by New Deal agencies—painted thousands of murals depicting the variety and vigor of American life. These murals often appeared in public buildings. The mural shown here by Missouri-born artist Thomas Hart Benton illustrates urban life, emphasizing the intoxicating and seductive pleasures of the flesh and the spirit to be found in American cities.

© AXA Financial, Inc. Thomas Hart Benton, *City Activities with Subway,* from *America Today,* 1930. Distemper and egg tempera on gessoed linen with oil glaze 92 x 134½". Collection of AXA Financial, Inc., through its subsidiary, The Equitable Life Assurance Society of the U.S.

READING THE IMAGE: What features of urban experience does Benton emphasize in this mural? What ideas and attitudes, if any, link the people shown here?

CONNECTIONS: To what extent does the mural highlight activities distinct to U.S. cities, compared to urban life in Europe, Africa, or Asia?

FOR MORE HELP ANALYZING THIS IMAGE, see the visual activity for this chapter in the Online Study Guide at bedfordstmartins.com/roark.

"self-respect, . . . self-confidence, . . . courage, and determination." With a congressional appropriation of nearly $5 billion—more than all government revenues in 1934—the New Deal created the Works Progress Administration (WPA) to give unemployed Americans government-funded jobs on public works projects. The WPA put millions of jobless citizens to work on roads, bridges, parks, public buildings, and more. WPA paychecks pumped billions of dollars into the economy, boosting consumption

★★USA★★
WORK
PROGRAM
WPA

along with what Roosevelt termed "the human spirit" of working people. In addition, Congress passed—over Roosevelt's veto—the bonus long sought by the Bonus Marchers, giving veterans an average of $580 and further stimulating the economy.

By 1936, WPA funds provided jobs for 7 percent of the nation's labor force. In effect, the WPA made the federal government the employer of last resort, creating useful jobs when the capitalist economy failed to do so. In hiring, WPA officials tended to discriminate in favor of white men and against women and racial minorities. But by the time the WPA ended in 1943—because mobilization for World War II created full employment—it had made major contributions to both relief and recovery. Overall, WPA jobs put thirteen million men and women to work and gave them paychecks worth $10 billion.

About three out of four WPA jobs involved construction and renovation of the nation's physical infrastructure. WPA workers built 572,000 miles of country roads, 78,000 bridges, 67,000 miles of city streets, 40,000 public buildings, 8,000 parks, 350 airports, and much else. In addition to work with picks, shovels, hammers, nails, bricks, and mortar, the WPA gave jobs to thousands of artists, musicians, actors, journalists, poets, and novelists. The WPA also organized sewing rooms for jobless women, giving them work and wages and allowing them to produce more than 100 million pieces of clothing that were then donated to the needy. One reporter observed that the women "come in [to the sewing rooms] sullen, dejected [and] half starved," but before long, "working in pleasant surroundings [and] having some money and food [do] wonders to restore their health and morale." The WPA reached the most isolated corners of the nation. For example, WPA-funded librarians and nurses on horseback delivered books and health care to remote cabins in Appalachia. Throughout the nation, WPA projects displayed tangible evidence of the New Deal's commitment to public welfare.

Empowering Labor

During the Great Depression, factory workers who managed to keep their jobs worried constantly about being laid off while their wages and working hours were cut. When workers tried to organize labor unions to protect themselves, municipal and state governments usually sided with employers. Since the Gilded Age, the state and federal governments had been far more effective at busting unions than at busting **trusts**. The New Deal dramatically reversed the federal government's stance toward unions. With legislation and political support, the New Deal encouraged an unprecedented wave of union organizing among the nation's working people. When the head of the United Mine Workers, John L. Lewis, told coal miners that "the President wants you to join a union," he exaggerated only a little. New Dealers believed that

unions would counterbalance the organized might of big corporations by defending working people, maintaining wages, and replacing the bloody violence that often accompanied strikes with economic peace and commercial stability.

Violent battles on the nation's streets and docks showed the determination of militant labor leaders to organize unions that would protect jobs as well as wages. In 1934, striking workers in Toledo, Minneapolis, San Francisco, and elsewhere were beaten and shot by police and the National Guard. In Congress, labor leaders lobbied for the National Labor Relations Act (NLRA), a bill sponsored by Senator Robert Wagner of New York that authorized the federal government to intervene in labor disputes and supervise the organization of labor unions. Justly considered a "Magna Carta for labor," the Wagner Act, as it came to be called, guaranteed industrial workers the right to organize unions, putting the might of federal law behind the appeals of labor leaders. The Wagner Act created the National Labor Relations Board (NLRB) to sponsor and oversee elections for union representation. If the majority of workers at a company voted for a union, then the union became the sole bargaining agent for the entire workplace, and the employer was required to negotiate with the elected union leaders. Roosevelt signed the Wagner Act in July 1935, providing for the first time federal support for labor organization—the most important New Deal reform of the industrial order.

The achievements that flowed from the Wagner Act and renewed labor militancy were impressive. When Roosevelt became president in 1933, union membership—almost entirely composed of skilled workers in trade unions affiliated with the American Federation of Labor (AFL)—stood at three million, down by half since the end of World War I. With the support of the Wagner Act, union membership expanded almost fivefold, to fourteen million, by the time of Roosevelt's death in 1945. By then, 30 percent of the workforce was unionized, the highest union representation in American history.

Most of the new union members were factory workers and unskilled laborers, many of them immigrants, women, and African Americans. For decades, established AFL unions had no desire to organize factory and unskilled workers, who struggled along without unions. In 1935, under the aggressive leadership of the mine workers' John L. Lewis and the head of the Amalgamated Clothing Workers, Sidney Hillman, a coalition of unskilled workers formed the Committee for Industrial Organization (CIO; later the Congress of Industrial Organizations). The CIO, helped by the Wagner Act, mobilized organizing drives in major industries. The exceptional courage and organizing skill of labor militants, a few of them Communists, earned the CIO the leadership role in the campaign to organize the bitterly anti-union automobile and steel industries.

The bloody struggle by the CIO-affiliated United Auto Workers (UAW) to organize workers at General Motors climaxed in January 1937. Striking workers occupied the main assembly plant in Flint, Michigan, in a "sit-down" strike that slashed the plant's production of 15,000 cars a week to a mere 150. Stymied, General Motors eventually surrendered and agreed to make the UAW the sole bargaining agent for all

Women's Emergency Brigade Supports Sit-Down Strikers

During the depression, General Motors—the world's largest industrial corporation—cut employment and wages in half. This led to a wave of strikes in thirty-five cities and fourteen states in 1936–1937 that culminated in a sit-down strike in Flint, Michigan. One striking autoworker recalled, "The only benefits we had was to work yourself to death." In February 1937, the wives of the striking autoworkers organized the Women's Emergency Brigade, shown here marching between their husbands inside the Chevrolet plant and the thousands of police and National Guardsmen with fixed bayonets and machine guns surrounding the plant (not shown). The previous day, a fierce battle had taken place between the strikers and General Motors security agents and hired thugs, who attacked strikers with clubs and tear gas, injuring more than twenty autoworkers. Strikers and their supporters smashed the windows of the plant to vent tear gas and allow the sit-down strike to continue. The marching women carried clubs similar to those used to break the windows and to deflect the blows of the General Motors cops. The American flag carried by Mrs. Gerenda Johnson asserted the patriotism of the strikers and their supporters, whom General Motors and other strike opponents labeled "outside agitators, radicals, and Communists."
© Bettmann/Corbis.

the company's workers and to refrain from interfering with union activity. Having subdued the auto industry's leading producer, the UAW expanded its campaign until, after much violence, the entire industry was unionized when the Ford Motor Company capitulated in 1941.

The CIO hoped to ride organizing success in auto plants to victory in the steel mills. But after unionizing the industry giant U.S. Steel, the CIO ran up against fanatic opposition from smaller steel firms. Following a police attack that killed ten strikers at Republic Steel outside Chicago in May 1937, the battered steelworkers halted their organizing campaign. In steel and other major industries, such as the stridently anti-union southern textile mills, organizing efforts stalled until after 1941, when military mobilization created labor shortages that gave workers greater bargaining power.

Social Security and Tax Reform

The single most important feature of the New Deal's emerging welfare state was Social Security. An ambitious, far-reaching, and permanent reform, Social Security was designed to provide a modest income to relieve the poverty of elderly people. Only about 15 percent of older Americans had private pension plans, and during the depression, corporations and banks often failed to pay the meager pensions they had promised. Corporations even fired or demoted employees to avoid or reduce pension payments. Prompted by the popular but impractical panaceas of Dr. Townsend, Father Coughlin, and Huey Long, Roosevelt became the first president to advocate protection for the elderly. He told Congress that "it is our plain duty to provide for that security upon which welfare depends . . . and undertake the great task of furthering the security of the citizen and his family through social insurance."

The political struggle for Social Security highlighted class differences among Americans. Support for the measure came from a coalition of advocacy groups for the elderly and the poor, traditional progressives, leftists, social workers, and labor unions. Arrayed against them were economic conservatives, including the American Liberty League, the National Association of Manufacturers, the Chamber of Commerce, and the

> Roosevelt told Congress that "it is our plain duty to provide for that security upon which welfare depends . . . and undertake the great task of furthering the security of the citizen and his family through social insurance."

American Medical Association. Enact the Social Security system, these conservatives and their representatives in the Republican Party warned, and the government will gain a whip hand over private property, destroy initiative, and reduce proud individuals to spineless loafers.

The large New Deal majority in Congress carried the day in August 1935. The Social Security Act required that pensions for the elderly be funded not by direct government subsidies, but instead by tax contributions from workers and their employers. Although this provision subtracted money from consumption—thus hindering economic recovery—it gave contributing workers a personal stake in the system and made it politically invulnerable. When eligible workers reached retirement age, they were not subject to a means test to prove that they were needy. Instead, they were entitled to receive benefits based on their contributions and years of work. Social Security also created unemployment insurance, paid for by employers' contributions, that provided modest benefits for workers who lost their jobs.

Not all workers benefited from the Social Security Act. It excluded domestic and agricultural workers from receiving benefits, thereby making ineligible about half of all African Americans and more than half of all employed women—about five million people in all. In addition, the law excluded workers employed by religious and nonprofit organizations, such as schools and hospitals, rendering ineligible even more working women and minorities.

In a bow to traditional beliefs about local governments' responsibility for public assistance, Social Security issued multimillion-dollar grants to the states (rather than to individuals) to help support dependent children (a program expanded in 1950 to include Aid to Families with Dependent Children), public health services, and the blind. After the Supreme Court in 1937 upheld the right of Congress to require all citizens to pay for Social Security through federal taxes, the program was expanded to include benefits for dependent survivors of deceased recipients. Although the first Social Security check (for $41.30) was not issued until 1940, the system gave millions of working people the assurance that in the future, when they became too old to work, they would receive a modest income from the federal government. This safety net protected many ordinary working people from fears of a penniless and insecure old age.

Fervent opposition to Social Security struck New Dealers as evidence that the rich had learned little from the depression. Roosevelt had long felt contempt for the moneyed elite who ignored the sufferings of the poor. He looked for a way to redistribute wealth that would weaken conservative opposition, advance the cause of social equity, and defuse political challenges from Huey Long and Father Coughlin. In June 1935, as the Social Security Act was being debated, Roosevelt delivered a message to Congress outlining comprehensive tax reform. Charging that large fortunes put "great and undesirable concentration of control in [the hands of] relatively few individuals," Roosevelt urged a graduated tax on corporations, an inheritance tax, and an increase in maximum personal income taxes. Congress endorsed Roosevelt's basic principle by taxing those with higher incomes at a somewhat higher rate.

Neglected Americans and the New Deal

Although the WPA and other work relief programs aided working people, the average unemployment rate for the 1930s stayed high—17 percent, about one of every six workers. Even many working people remained more or less untouched by New Deal benefits. Workers in industries that resisted unions received little help from the Wagner Act or the WPA. Tens of thousands of women in southern textile mills, for example, commonly received wages of less than ten cents an hour and were fired if they protested. Domestic workers—almost all of them women—and agricultural workers—many of them African, Hispanic, or Asian Americans—were neither unionized nor eligible for Social Security. The patchwork of New Deal reforms erected a two-tier welfare state. In the top tier, organized workers in major industries were the

greatest beneficiaries of New Deal initiatives. In the bottom tier, millions of neglected Americans—women, children, and old folks, along with the unorganized, unskilled, uneducated, and unemployed—often fell through the New Deal safety net.

The New Deal neglected few citizens more than African Americans. About half of black Americans in cities were jobless, more than double the unemployment rate among whites. In the rural South, where the vast majority of African Americans lived, conditions were worse. New Deal agricultural policies such as the AAA favored landowners and often resulted in black sharecroppers and tenants being pushed off the land they farmed. **Disfranchisement** by intimidation and legal subterfuge prevented southern blacks from protesting their plight at the ballot box. Protest risked vicious retaliation from local whites. After years of decline, lynching increased during the 1930s. In Georgia, radical black unionist Angelo Herndon was sentenced to the chain gang for trying to organize black workers. Only 11 of more than 10,000 WPA supervisors in the South were black, even though African Americans accounted for about a third of the region's population. Up north, a 1935 riot that focused on white-owned businesses in Harlem dramatized blacks' resentment and despair. Bitter critics charged that the New Deal's NRA stood for "Negro Run Around" or "Negroes Ruined Again."

Roosevelt responded to such criticisms with great caution, since New Deal reforms required the political support of powerful conservative, segregationist, southern white Democrats, who would be alienated

> Bitter critics charged that the New Deal's NRA stood for "Negro Run Around" or "Negroes Ruined Again."

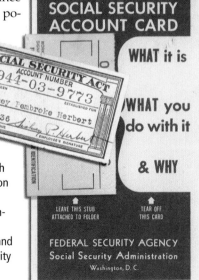

Social Security Card
The Social Security Act required each working American who participated in the system to register with the government and obtain a unique number—the "SSN" familiar to every citizen today—inscribed on an identity card, making benefits portable from one job and one state to another. For the first time in the nation's history, millions of ordinary citizens were numbered, registered, and identified by a government bureaucracy, creating a personal, individualized connection between people and the federal government. Administering the massive agency needed to collect, monitor, and regulate this information and distribute the benefits that flowed from it gave government jobs to tens of thousands, providing security for government workers as well as for Social Security beneficiaries.
Picture Research Consultants & Archives.

by programs that aided blacks. A white Georgia relief worker expressed the common view that "any Nigger who gets over $8 a week is a spoiled Nigger, that's all." Stymied by the political clout of entrenched white racism, New Dealers still tried to attract political support from black leaders. Roosevelt's overtures to African Americans prompted northern black voters in the 1934 congressional elections to shift from the Republican to the Democratic Party, helping elect New Deal Democrats.

Eleanor Roosevelt sponsored the appointment of Mary McLeod Bethune—the energetic cofounder of the National Council on Negro Women—as head of the Division of Negro Affairs in the National Youth Administration. The highest-ranking black official in Roosevelt's administration, Bethune used her position to guide a small number of black professionals and civil rights activists to posts within New Deal agencies. Nicknamed the "Black Cabinet," these men and women composed the first sizable representation of African Americans in white-collar posts in the federal government, and they ultimately helped about one in four African Americans get access to New Deal relief programs.

Despite these gains, by 1940 African Americans still suffered severe handicaps. Most of the thirteen million black workers toiled at low-paying menial jobs, unprotected by the New Deal safety net. Infant mortality was 50 percent greater among blacks than among whites, and life expectancy was twelve years shorter. Making a mockery of the "separate but equal" doctrine, segregated black schools had less money and worse facilities than white schools, and only 1 percent of black students earned college degrees. In southern states, there were no black police officers or judges and hardly any black lawyers, and vigilante violence against blacks went unpunished. For these problems of black Americans, the New Deal offered few remedies.

Hispanic Americans fared no better. About a million Mexican Americans lived in the United States in the 1930s, most of them first- or second-generation immigrants who worked at stoop labor tending crops throughout the West. During the depression, field workers saw their low wages plunge lower still to about a dime an hour. Ten thousand Mexican American pecan shellers in San Antonio, Texas, earned only a nickel an hour. To preserve scarce jobs for U.S. citizens, the federal government choked off immigration from Mexico, while state and local officials prohibited the employment of aliens on work relief projects and deported tens of thousands of Mexican Americans, many with their American-born children. Local white administrators of many New Deal programs throughout the West discriminated against Hispanics and other people of color. When Mexican Americans managed to land jobs on government projects, they often received lower wages than their white counterparts. A New Deal study concluded that

Mary McLeod Bethune
At the urging of Eleanor Roosevelt, Mary McLeod Bethune, a southern educational and civil rights leader, became director of the National Youth Administration's Division of Negro Affairs. The first black woman to head a federal agency, Bethune used her position to promote social change. Here, Bethune takes her mission to the streets to protest the discriminatory hiring practices of the Peoples Drug Store chain in the nation's capital.
Moorland-Spingarn Research Center, Howard University.

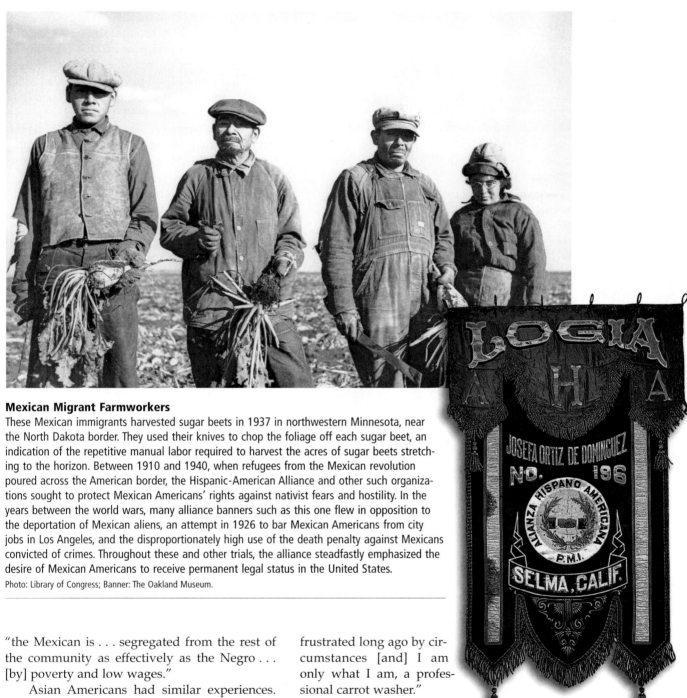

Mexican Migrant Farmworkers

These Mexican immigrants harvested sugar beets in 1937 in northwestern Minnesota, near the North Dakota border. They used their knives to chop the foliage off each sugar beet, an indication of the repetitive manual labor required to harvest the acres of sugar beets stretching to the horizon. Between 1910 and 1940, when refugees from the Mexican revolution poured across the American border, the Hispanic-American Alliance and other such organizations sought to protect Mexican Americans' rights against nativist fears and hostility. In the years between the world wars, many alliance banners such as this one flew in opposition to the deportation of Mexican aliens, an attempt in 1926 to bar Mexican Americans from city jobs in Los Angeles, and the disproportionately high use of the death penalty against Mexicans convicted of crimes. Throughout these and other trials, the alliance steadfastly emphasized the desire of Mexican Americans to receive permanent legal status in the United States.

Photo: Library of Congress; Banner: The Oakland Museum.

"the Mexican is . . . segregated from the rest of the community as effectively as the Negro . . . [by] poverty and low wages."

Asian Americans had similar experiences. Asian immigrants were still excluded from U.S. citizenship and in many states were not permitted to own land. By 1930, more than half of Japanese Americans had been born in the United States, but they were still liable to discrimination. Even college-educated Asian Americans worked in family shops, restaurants, and laundries. One young Asian American expressed the frustration felt by many others: "I am a fruit-stand worker. I would much rather it were doctor or lawyer . . . but my aspirations [were] frustrated long ago by circumstances [and] I am only what I am, a professional carrot washer."

Native Americans also suffered neglect from New Deal agencies. As a group, they remained the poorest of the poor. Since the Dawes Act of 1887 (see chapter 17), the federal government had encouraged Native Americans to assimilate—to abandon their Indian identities and adopt the cultural norms of the majority society. Under the leadership of the New Deal's commissioner of Indian affairs, John Collier, the New Deal's Indian

John Collier Meets with Navajo Representatives
Commissioner of Indian Affairs John Collier receives a Navajo delegation protesting restrictions in the Indian Reorganization Act of 1934. The Navajos display a blanket made from the wool of their own sheep to protest limits on the number of sheep they could raise. Collier had crafted the act to revive Native American society by granting tribes an independent land base and many self-governing powers. However, his attempt to make the reservations economically viable through conservation measures, including restrictions on grass-devouring sheep, roused resistance by Indians who chose traditional ways of using resources. The tension between federal benevolence and Indian views of their own way of life has remained a painful issue.

AP Images.

Reorganization Act (IRA) of 1934 largely reversed that policy. Collier claimed that "the most interesting and important fact about Indians" was that they "do not expect much, often they expect nothing at all; yet they are able to be happy." Given such views, the IRA provided little economic aid to Native Americans, but it did restore their right to own land communally and to have greater control over their own affairs, including a vote on whether they should live under the IRA, as more than two-thirds opted to do in special elections in 1934 and 1935. The IRA brought little immediate benefit to Native Americans and has remained a divisive issue for decades, but it provided an important foundation for Indians' economic, cultural, and political resurgence a generation later (see chapter 28).

The troubadour of working people, singer and songwriter Woody Guthrie, traveled the nation for eight years during the 1930s "by the thumb route . . . no job, no money, no home . . . no nothing." At night, he recalled, other rambling men told him "the story of their life, how it used to be," giving voice to experiences especially common among Americans neglected by the New Deal: "how the home went to pieces, how the young wife died or left, how the mother died in the insane asylum, how Dad tried twice to kill himself, and lay flat on his back for 18 months—and then the crops got to where they wouldn't bring nothing, work in factories would kill a dog . . . and—always, always [you] have to fight and argue and cuss and swear . . . to try to get a nickel more out of the rich bosses."

> **REVIEW**   What features of a welfare state did the New Deal create and why?

The New Deal from Victory to Deadlock

To accelerate the sputtering economic recovery, Roosevelt shifted the emphasis of the New Deal in the mid-1930s. Instead of seeking cooperation from conservative business leaders, he decided to rely on the growing New Deal coalition to enact reforms over the strident opposition of the Supreme Court, Republicans, and corporate interests.

Added to New Deal strength in farm states and big cities were some new allies on the left. Throughout Roosevelt's first term, socialists and Communists denounced the slow pace of change and accused the New Deal of failing to serve the interests of the workers who produced the nation's wealth. But in 1935, the Soviet Union, worried about the threat of fascism in Europe, instructed Communists throughout the world to join hands with non-Communist progressives in a "Popular Front" to advance the fortunes of the working class. With varying degrees of enthusiasm, many radicals switched from opposing the New Deal to supporting its relief programs and encouragement of labor unions.

Roosevelt's conservative opponents reacted to the massing of New Deal force by intensifying their opposition to the welfare state. To Roosevelt, the situation seemed part of a drama that had played out since the nation's beginning, pitting a Hamiltonian faction of wealth and privilege against the heirs of Jefferson, who, like Roosevelt himself, favored a more equitable distribution of wealth and opportunity.

The Election of 1936

Roosevelt believed that the presidential election of 1936 would test his leadership and progressive ideals. The depression still had a stranglehold on the economy. Nearly eight million Americans remained jobless, and millions more were stuck in poverty. Conservative leaders believed that the New Deal's failure to lift the nation out of the depression indicated that Americans were ready for a change. Left-wing critics insisted that the New Deal had missed the opportunity to displace capitalism with a socialist economy and that voters would embrace candidates who recommended more radical remedies.

Republicans turned to the Kansas heartland to select Governor Alfred (Alf) Landon as their presidential nominee. A moderate who had supported some New Deal measures, Landon stressed mainstream Republican proposals to achieve a balanced federal budget and to ease the perils of illness and old age with old-fashioned neighborliness instead of faceless government bureaucracies such as Social Security.

Roosevelt put his faith in the growing coalition of New Deal supporters, who, he believed, shared his conviction that the New Deal was the nation's liberator from a long era of privilege and wealth for a few and "economic slavery" for the rest. At the end of the campaign, Roosevelt assailed his "old enemies . . . business and financial monopoly, speculation, reckless banking, [and] class antagonism," and he proclaimed, "Never before in all our history have these forces been so united against one candidate as they stand today. They are unanimous in their hate for me—and I welcome their hatred."

Roosevelt triumphed spectacularly. He won 60.8 percent of the popular vote—11 million more votes than Landon—making it the widest margin of victory in a presidential election to date. He carried the electoral votes of every state except Maine and Vermont. Third parties—including the Socialist and Communists parties—fell pitifully short of the support they expected and never again mounted a significant challenge to the New Deal. Congressional results were equally lopsided, with Democrats outnumbering Republicans more than three to one in both houses. In northern cities with many immigrant voters, Democrats more than doubled their 1932 tallies.

In his inaugural address, Roosevelt pledged to use his mandate to help all citizens achieve a decent standard of living. He announced, "I see one third of a nation ill-housed, ill-clad, [and] ill-nourished," and he promised to devote his second term to alleviating their hardship.

> Roosevelt announced, "I see one third of a nation ill-housed, ill-clad, [and] ill-nourished," and he promised to devote his second term to alleviating their hardship.

New Deal "Needle-Book"
In the 1936 presidential campaign, Democrats distributed this sewing-needle book to celebrate New Deal achievements during Roosevelt's first term. Evoking Roosevelt's 1932 campaign theme song, "Happy Days Are Here Again," the illustrations on the book emphasize the return of harmony in agriculture, of booming factories providing plenty of jobs, and above all of "happiness restored" at home around the well-appointed dinner table. Notice that the working people in factories are faceless but the white-collar worker and the family are individualized sympathetically. The needle-book signifies Democrats' attempt to mobilize women to vote in gratitude for the happiness supplied by Roosevelt and the New Deal. Like most campaign materials, the needle-book's claims of New Deal success were greatly exaggerated.
Collection of Janice L. and David J. Frent.

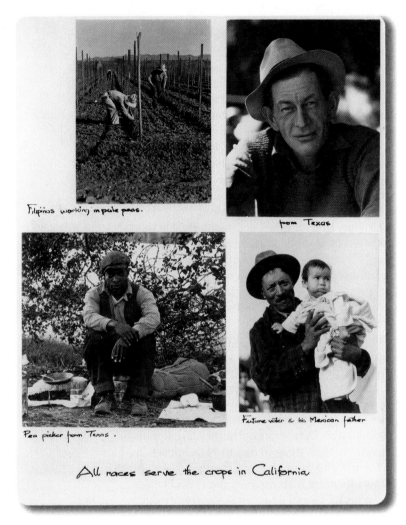

Filipinos working in pole peas.

from Texas

Pea picker from Texas.

Future voter & his Mexican father

All races serve the crops in California

"All Races Serve the Crops in California"
New Deal agencies dispatched dozens of photographers to document the lives of Americans during the 1930s. This page from the 1935 journal of New Deal photographer Dorothea Lange documents migrant workers from the Philippines, Texas, and Mexico whom she encountered in California fields.
Library of Congress.

Court Packing

In the afterglow of his reelection triumph, Roosevelt pondered how to remove the remaining obstacles to New Deal reforms. He decided to target the Supreme Court. Laden with conservative justices appointed by Republican presidents, the Court had invalidated eleven New Deal measures as unconstitutional interferences with free enterprise. Now, Social Security, the Wagner Act, the Securities and Exchange Commission, and other New Deal innovations were moving toward an ominous rendezvous with the justices.

Roosevelt concluded that he must do something to ensure that the Supreme Court's "horse and buggy" notions did not dismantle the New Deal. He proposed that one new justice be added for each existing judge who had served for ten years and was over the age of seventy. In effect, the proposed law would give Roosevelt the power to pack the Court with up to six New Dealers who could outvote the elderly, conservative, Republican justices.

But the president had not reckoned with Americans' deeply rooted deference to the independent authority of the Supreme Court. More than two-thirds of Americans believed that the Court should be free from political interference. Even New Deal supporters were disturbed by the "court-packing" scheme. The suggestion that individuals over age seventy had diminished mental capacity also offended many elderly members of Congress. Roosevelt insisted that the bill was intended to improve the efficiency of an "overworked" Court, but its real purpose was to make room for supporters of New Deal initiatives. A storm of public protest whipped up by conservatives prompted the heavily Democratic Senate to defeat the bill in 1937.

Although Roosevelt's court-packing plan failed, Supreme Court justices got the message. After the furor abated, Chief Justice Charles Evans Hughes and fellow moderate Owen Roberts moderated their views enough to keep the Court from invalidating the Wagner Act and Social Security. Then the most conservative of the elderly justices—the "four horsemen of reaction," one New Dealer called them—retired. Roosevelt eventually named eight justices to the Court—more than any other president. His choice of liberals to fill vacancies on the Court ultimately gave New Deal laws safe passage through the shoals of judicial review.

Reaction and Recession

Emboldened by their defeat of the court-packing plan, Republicans and southern Democrats rallied around their common conservatism to obstruct additional reforms. Former president Herbert Hoover proclaimed that "the New Deal repudiation of Democracy has left the Republican Party alone the guardian of the Ark of the Covenant with its charter of freedom." The New Deal's acts, he continued, were "based upon the coercion and compulsory organization of men" and "born of a Roman despot[,] . . . Karl Marx[,] . . . a British professor[,] . . . American radicals . . . [and] Brain Trusters." Democrats' arguments over whether the New Deal needed to be expanded—and if so, how—undermined the consensus among reformers and sparked antagonism between Congress and the White House. The ominous rise of belligerent regimes in Germany, Italy, Japan, and elsewhere slowed reform as some Americans began to worry more about defending the nation than changing it.

Roosevelt himself favored slowing the pace of the New Deal. He believed that existing New Deal measures had steadily boosted the economy and largely eliminated the depression crisis. In fact, the gross national product in 1937 briefly equaled the 1929 level before dropping lower for the rest of the decade. Unemployment declined to 14 percent in 1937 but quickly spiked upward and stayed higher until 1940. Roosevelt's unwarranted optimism about the economic recovery persuaded him that additional deficit spending by the federal government was no longer necessary. He also worried that pump-priming deficits would cause inflation and reduce the value of hard-earned savings. Accordingly, he moved cautiously toward a balanced budget by cutting funds for relief projects, and he urged the Federal Reserve Board to raise interest rates to tamp down inflation.

Roosevelt's retrenchment soon backfired. The reduction in deficit spending reversed the improving economy. Roosevelt's worries about inflation failed to consider the stubborn realities of unemployment and poverty. Even at the high-water mark of recovery in the summer of 1937, seven million people lacked jobs. In the next few months, national income and production slipped backward so steeply that almost two-thirds of the economic gains since 1933 were lost by June 1938. Farm prices dropped 20 percent, and unemployment rose by more than two million.

This economic reversal hurt the New Deal politically. Conservatives argued that this recession proved that New Deal measures produced only an illusion of progress. The way to weather the recession was to tax and spend less and wait for the natural laws of supply and demand to

Distributing Surplus Food to the Needy
When bountiful harvests produced surplus crops that would depress prices if they were sent to market, the New Deal arranged to distribute some of them to needy Americans. Here, farmworkers near the New Mexico border in east-central Arizona line up to receive a ration of potatoes authorized by the New Deal agent checking the box of index cards. Surplus commodity distribution represented New Dealers' attempt to provide relief for the hungry with crops that otherwise would rot or need to be destroyed in order to limit supply and thereby maintain agricultural prices.
Library of Congress.

restore prosperity. Many New Dealers insisted instead that the continuing depression demanded that Roosevelt revive federal spending and redouble efforts to stimulate the economy. In 1938, Congress heeded such pleas and enacted a massive new program of federal spending.

The New Deal's ad hoc methods received support from the brilliant English economist John Maynard Keynes. In his influential work *The General Theory of Employment, Interest, and Money* (1936), Keynes made a sophisticated, theoretical argument in favor of practices that New Deal relief agencies had developed in a commonsense way. Keynes declared that the depression illustrated that a nation's economic activity could become stalled at a level far short of its true potential. When that happened, only government intervention could pump enough money into the economy to restore prosperity.

Roosevelt never had the inclination or the time to follow his economic advisers into the thicket of **Keynesian** theory. But the recession scare of 1937–1938 taught the president the Keynesian lesson that economic growth had to be carefully nurtured. Escape from the depression required a plan for large-scale spending to alleviate distress and stimulate economic growth. (See "Global Comparison.")

The Last of the New Deal Reforms

From the moment he was sworn in, Roosevelt sought to expand the powers of the presidency. He believed that the president needed more authority to meet emergencies such as the depression and to administer the sprawling federal bureaucracy. In September 1938, Congress passed the Administrative Reorganization Act, which gave Roosevelt (and future presidents) new influence over the bureaucracy. Combined with a Democratic majority in Congress, a now-friendly Supreme Court, and the revival of deficit spending, the newly empowered White House seemed to be in a good position to move ahead with a revitalized New Deal.

Resistance to further reform was also on the rise, however. Conservatives argued that the New Deal had pressed government centralization too far. Even the New Deal's friends became weary of one emergency program after another while economic woes continued to shadow New Deal achievements. By the midpoint of Roosevelt's second term, restive members of Congress balked at new initiatives. Clearly, the

New Deal was losing momentum, but enough support remained for one last burst of reform.

Agriculture still had strong claims on New Deal attention in the face of drought, declining crop prices, and impoverished sharecroppers and tenants. In 1937, the Agriculture Department created the Farm Security Administration (FSA) to provide housing and loans to help tenant farmers become independent. A black tenant farmer in North Carolina who received an FSA loan told a New Deal interviewer, "I wake up in the night sometimes and think I must be half-dead and gone to heaven." But relatively few tenants received loans, because the FSA was starved for funds and ran up against the major farm organizations intent on serving their own interests. For those who owned farms, the New Deal offered renewed prosperity with a second Agricultural Adjustment Act (AAA) in 1938. To moderate price swings by regulating supply, the plan combined production quotas on five staple crops—cotton, tobacco, wheat, corn, and rice—with storage loans through its Commodity Credit Corporation. The most prosperous farmers benefited most, but the act's Federal Surplus Commodities Corporation added an element of charity by issuing food stamps so that the poor could obtain surplus food. The AAA of 1938 brought stability to American agriculture and ample food to most—but not all—tables.

Advocates for the urban poor also made modest gains after decades of neglect. New York senator Robert Wagner convinced Congress to pass the National Housing Act in 1937. By 1941, some 160,000 residences had been made available to poor people at affordable rents. The program did not come close to meeting the need for affordable housing, but for the first time, the federal government took an active role in providing decent urban housing.

The last major piece of New Deal labor legislation, the Fair Labor Standards Act of June 1938, reiterated the New Deal pledge to provide workers with a decent standard of living. After lengthy haggling and compromise that revealed the waning strength of the New Deal, Congress finally agreed to intervene in the long-sacrosanct realm of worker contracts. The new law set wage and hours standards and at long last curbed the use of child labor. The minimum-wage level was modest—twenty-five cents an hour for a maximum of forty-four hours a week. And, in order to attract enough conservative votes, the act exempted merchant seamen, fishermen, domestic help, and farm laborers—relegating most women

GLOBAL COMPARISON

National Populations and Economies, circa 1938

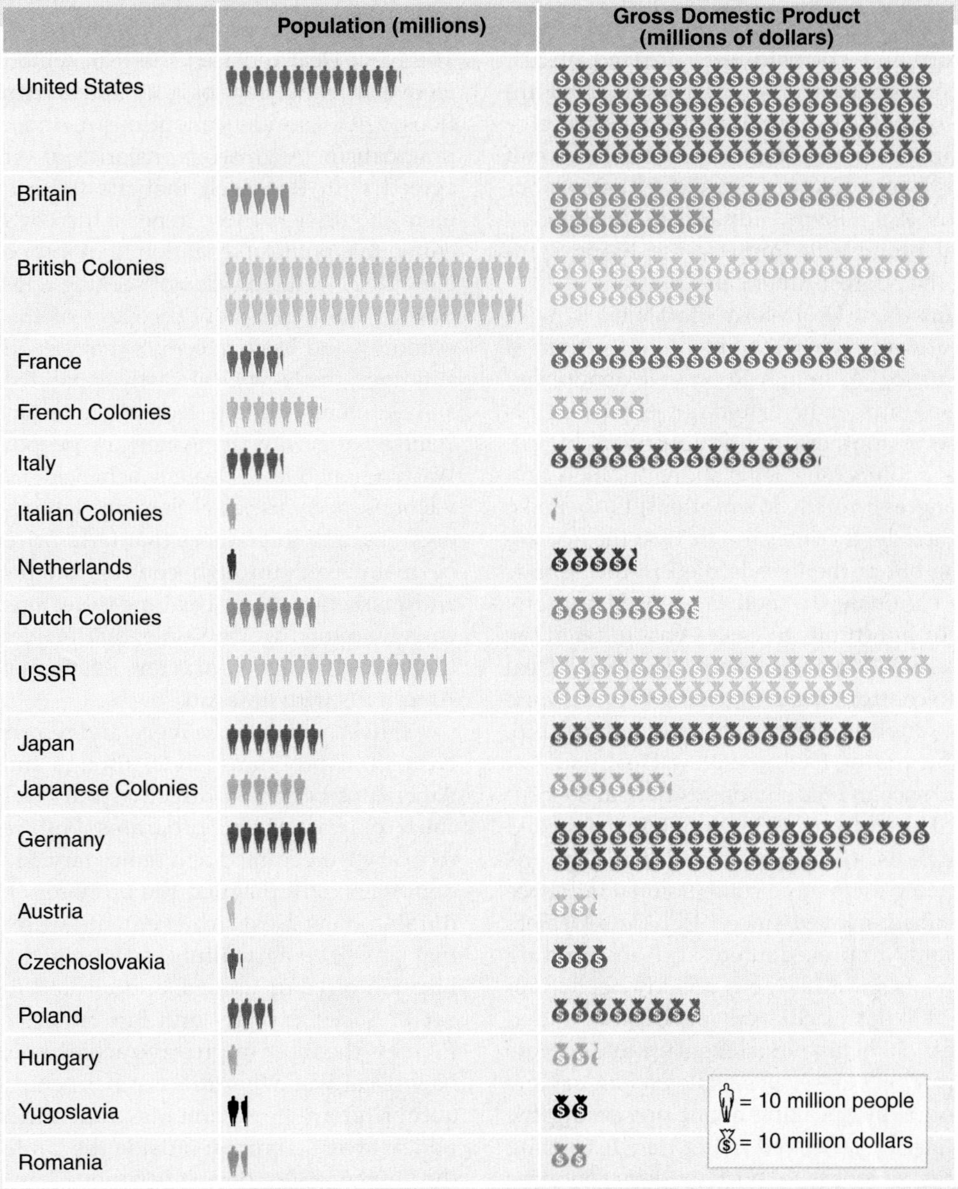

	Population (millions)	Gross Domestic Product (millions of dollars)
United States		
Britain		
British Colonies		
France		
French Colonies		
Italy		
Italian Colonies		
Netherlands		
Dutch Colonies		
USSR		
Japan		
Japanese Colonies		
Germany		
Austria		
Czechoslovakia		
Poland		
Hungary		
Yugoslavia		
Romania		

Key:
= 10 million people
= 10 million dollars

Throughout the Great Depression, the United States remained more productive than any other nation in the world. Despite the lingering effects of the depression, by 1938 the United States produced more than twice as much as Germany and the Soviet Union, nearly three times as much as Britain, more than four times as much as France and Japan, and more than five times as much as Italy. From the viewpoint of Germany, if the European nations listed here could be brought under German control, its economy would be greater than that of the United States and the mightiest in the world. Economically, how important were colonies to the major powers? In general, do these data suggest a relationship between population and gross domestic product?

and African Americans to lower wages. Enforcement of the minimum-wage standards was weak and haphazard. Thousands of workers petitioned the federal government for relief from their substandard wages. Among them were Bill Brown, who worked a forty-four-hour week in a box factory and got paid $8.80 instead of $11, and Minnie Smith, who sewed pockets on clothing for sixty hours a week and did not receive her required sixteen hours of time-and-a-half overtime wages. Nevertheless, the Fair Labor Standards Act slowly advanced Roosevelt's inaugural promise to improve the living standards of the poorest Americans.

The final New Deal reform effort failed to make much headway against the hidebound system of racial injustice. Although Roosevelt denounced lynching as murder, he would not jeopardize his vital base of southern political support by demanding antilynching legislation. In 1934 and 1935, Congress voted down attempts to make lynching a federal crime, and in 1938 the last antilynching bill of the decade died in the Senate. Laws to eliminate the poll tax—used to deny blacks the opportunity to vote—encountered the same overwhelming resistance. The New Deal refused to confront racial injustice with the same vigor it brought to bear on economic hardship.

By the end of 1938, the New Deal had lost steam and encountered stiff opposition. In the congressional elections of 1938, Republicans picked up seven seats in the Senate and eighty in the House, giving them more congressional influence than they had enjoyed since 1932. New Dealers could claim unprecedented and resounding achievements since 1933, but nobody needed reminding that those achievements had not ended the depression. In his annual message to Congress in January 1939, Roosevelt signaled a halt to New Deal reforms by speaking about preserving the progress already achieved rather than extending it. Overseas, nations with much weaker economies than the United States struggled to overcome the woes of the worldwide depression. Germany and Japan resorted to rapid military rearmament to boost their economies and to strengthen their campaigns for territorial conquest. Roosevelt pointed to the ominous threats posed by fascist aggressors in Germany and Japan, and he proposed defense expenditures that surpassed New Deal appropriations for relief and economic recovery.

REVIEW   Why did political support for New Deal reforms decline?

Conclusion: Achievements and Limitations of the New Deal

The New Deal replaced the fear symbolized by Hoover's expulsion of the Bonus Army with Roosevelt's confidence, optimism, and energetic pragmatism. A growing majority of Americans agreed with Roosevelt that the federal government should help those in need, thereby strengthening the political coalition that propelled the New Deal. In the process of seeking relief for victims of the depression, recovery of the general economy, and basic reform of major economic institutions, the New Deal vastly expanded the size and influence of the federal government and changed the way the American people viewed Washington. New Dealers achieved significant victories, such as Social Security, labor's right to organize, and guarantees that farm prices would be maintained through controls on production and marketing. New Deal measures marked the emergence of a welfare state, but the New Deal's limited, two-tier character left many needy Americans with little aid.

Full-scale relief, recovery, and reform eluded New Deal programs. Even though millions of Americans benefited directly from the alphabet soup of agencies and programs, both relief and recovery were limited and temporary. In 1940, the depression still plagued the economy. The most durable New Deal achievements were reforms that stabilized agriculture, encouraged the organization of labor unions, and created the safety net of Social Security and fair labor standards. Perhaps the most impressive achievement of the New Deal was what did not happen. Although authoritarian governments and anticapitalist policies were common outside the United States during the 1930s, they were shunned by the New Deal coalition. The greatest economic crisis the nation had ever faced did not cause Americans to abandon democracy, as happened in Germany, where Adolf Hitler seized dictatorial power. Nor did the nation turn to radical alternatives such as socialism or communism.

Republicans and other conservatives claimed that the New Deal amounted to a form of socialism that threatened democracy and capitalism. But rather than attack capitalism, Franklin Roosevelt sought to save it, and he succeeded. That success also marked the limits of the New Deal's achievements. Like his cousin Teddy,

Franklin Roosevelt understood that a strengthened national government was necessary to curb the destructive tendencies of concentrated economic power. A shift of authority toward the federal government, both Roosevelts believed, would allow capitalist enterprises to be balanced by the nation's democratic tradition. The New Deal stopped far short of challenging capitalism either by undermining private property or by imposing strict national planning.

New Dealers repeatedly described their programs as a kind of warfare against the economic adversities of the 1930s. In the next decade, with the depression only partly vanquished, the Roosevelt administration had to turn from the New Deal's war against economic crisis at home to participate in a worldwide conflagration to defeat the enemies of democracy abroad.

Selected Bibliography

General Works

Gary Dean Best, *The Retreat from Liberalism: Collectivists versus Progressives in the New Deal Years* (2002).

Laura Browder, *Rousing the Nation: Radical Culture in Depression America* (1998).

William H. Chafe, ed., *The Achievement of American Liberalism: The New Deal and Its Legacies* (2003).

Ronald Edsforth, *The New Deal: America's Response to the Great Depression* (2000).

Meg Jacobs, *Pocketbook Politics: Economic Citizenship in Twentieth-Century America* (2004).

David M. Kennedy, *Freedom from Fear: The American People in Depression and War, 1929–1945* (1999).

Alice Kessler-Harris, *In Pursuit of Equity: Women, Men, and the Quest for Economic Citizenship in Twentieth-Century America* (2001).

Alan Lawson, *A Commonwealth of Hope: The New Deal Response to Crisis* (2006).

Suzanne Mettler, *Dividing Citizens: Gender and Federalism in New Deal Public Policy* (1998).

Wolfgang Schivelbusch, *Three New Deals: Reflections on Roosevelt's America, Mussolini's Italy, and Hitler's Germany, 1933–1939* (2006).

Gene Smiley, *Rethinking the Great Depression* (2002).

New Deal Politics

Roger Biles, *The South and the New Deal* (2006).

Blanche Wiesen Cook, *Eleanor Roosevelt*, 2 vols. (1992, 1999).

Paul Dickson and Thomas B. Allen, *The Bonus Army: An American Epic* (2004).

Frank Friedel, *Franklin D. Roosevelt: A Rendezvous with Destiny* (1990).

Alonzo L. Hamby, *For the Survival of Democracy: Franklin Roosevelt and the World Crisis of the 1930s* (2004).

Marian C. McKenna, *Franklin Roosevelt and the Great Constitutional War: The Court-Packing Crisis of 1937* (2002).

Theodore Rosenof, *Economics in the Long Run: New Deal Theorists and Their Legacies, 1933–1993* (1997).

Robert Shogan, *Backlash: The Killing of the New Deal* (2006).

Mary Triece, *On the Picket Line: Strategies of Working-Class Women during the Depression* (2007).

Clyde P. Weed, *The Nemesis of Reform: The Republican Party during the New Deal* (1994).

New Deal Policies

Lizbeth Cohen, *Making a New Deal: Industrial Workers in Chicago, 1919–1939* (1990).

Kathleen G. Donohue, *Freedom from Want: American Liberalism and the Idea of the Consumer* (2004).

Linda Gordon, *Pitied but Not Entitled: Single Mothers and the History of Welfare* (1994).

Michael R. Grey, *New Deal Medicine: The Rural Health Programs of the Farm Security Administration* (1999).

Camille Guerin-Gonzales, *Mexican Workers and the American Dream: Immigration, Repatriation, and California Farm Labor, 1900–1939* (1994).

Janet Irons, *Testing the New Deal: The General Textile Strike of 1934 in the American South* (2000).

Jennifer Klein, *For All These Rights: Business, Labor, and the Shaping of America's Pubic-Private Welfare State* (2003).

Robert C. Lieberman, *Shifting the Color Line: Race and the American Welfare State* (1998).

Julie Novkov, *Constituting Workers, Protecting Women: Gender, Law, and Labor in the Progressive Era and New Deal Years* (2001).

Sarah Phillips, *This Land, This Nation: Conservation, Rural America, and the New Deal* (2007).

Patrick D. Reagan, *Designing a New America: The Origins of New Deal Planning, 1890–1936* (1999).

John A. Salmond, *The General Textile Strike of 1934: From Maine to Alabama* (2002).

Jason Scott Smith, *Building New Deal Liberalism: The Political Economy of Public Works, 1933–1956* (2005).

Landon R. Y. Stors, *Civilizing Capitalism: The National Consumers' League, Women's Activism, and Labor Standards in the New Deal Era* (2000).

▶ For more books about topics in this chapter, see the Online Bibliography at bedfordstmartins.com/roark.

▶ For additional firsthand accounts of this period, see Chapter 24 in Michael Johnson, ed., *Reading the American Past*, Fourth Edition.

▶ For Web sites, images, and documents related to topics and places in this chapter, visit bedfordstmartins.com/makehistory.

REVIEWING THE CHAPTER

Follow these steps to review and strengthen your understanding of the chapter.

STEP 1: *Study the **Key Terms** and **Timeline** to identify the significance of each item listed.*

STEP 2: *Answer the **Review Questions**, drawing on key terms and dates to support your answers.*

STEP 3: *Drawing on the Key Terms, Timeline, and Review Questions, answer the broader **Making Connections** questions.*

KEY TERMS

Who

Bonus Marchers (p. 863)
Herbert Hoover (p. 864)
Douglas MacArthur (p. 864)
Franklin Delano Roosevelt (p. 865)
Harry Hopkins (p. 869)
Frances Perkins (p. 869)
Eleanor Roosevelt (p. 869)
Okies (p. 882)
Upton Sinclair (p. 883)
Charles Coughlin (p. 883)
Francis Townsend (p. 883)
Huey Long (p. 883)
Robert Wagner (p. 886)
Mary McLeod Bethune (p. 890)
John Collier (p. 891)
Alfred (Alf) Landon (p. 893)
John Maynard Keynes (p. 896)

What

Bonus Army (p. 863)
New Deal coalition (p. 868)
Hundred Days (p. 868)
Brains Trust (p. 869)
Emergency Banking Act (p. 872)

Federal Deposit Insurance Corporation (FDIC) (p. 873)
fireside chats (p. 873)
Securities and Exchange Commission (SEC) (p. 873)
Federal Emergency Relief Administration (FERA) (p. 874)
Civil Works Administration (CWA) (p. 874)
Civilian Conservation Corps (CCC) (p. 874)
Tennessee Valley Authority (TVA) (p. 874)
Rural Electrification Administration (REA) (p. 875)
Agricultural Adjustment Act (AAA) (p. 876)
Commodity Credit Corporation (pp. 876, 896)
Farm Credit Act (FCA) (p. 876)
National Recovery Administration (NRA) (p. 876)
American Liberty League (p. 880)
Southern Farm Tenants Union (p. 881)

National Union for Social Justice (Union Party) (p. 883)
Works Progress Administration (WPA) (p. 885)
Wagner Act/National Labor Relations Act (NLRA) (p. 886)
Committee for Industrial Organization (CIO) (p. 887)
sit-down strike (p. 887)
Social Security (p. 888)
unemployment insurance (p. 888)
Division of Negro Affairs (p. 890)
"Black Cabinet" (p. 890)
Indian Reorganization Act (IRA) (p. 892)
"Popular Front" (p. 892)
Administrative Reorganization Act (p. 896)
Farm Security Administration (FSA) (p. 896)
second Agricultural Adjustment Act (AAA) (p. 896)
National Housing Act (p. 896)
Fair Labor Standards Act (p. 896)

TIMELINE

1932 • Bonus Army marches on Washington.

1933 • Democrat Franklin D. Roosevelt becomes president.
• **March–June.** Legislation of the Hundred Days establishes the New Deal.
• Roosevelt closes the nation's banks for a four-day "bank holiday."
• Federal Emergency Relief Administration (FERA) established.

1934 • Securities and Exchange Commission (SEC) created.
• Upton Sinclair loses bid for governorship of California.
• American Liberty League founded.
• Dr. Francis Townsend devises Old Age Revolving Pension scheme.
• Indian Reorganization Act.

REVIEW QUESTIONS

1. Why did Franklin D. Roosevelt win the 1932 presidential election by such a large margin? (pp. 865–68)

2. How did the New Dealers try to steer the nation toward recovery from the Great Depression? (pp. 868–77)

3. Why did groups at both ends of the political spectrum criticize the New Deal? (pp. 877–84)

4. What features of a welfare state did the New Deal create and why? (pp. 884–92)

5. Why did political support for New Deal reforms decline? (pp. 892–98)

MAKING CONNECTIONS

1. Franklin Roosevelt's landslide victory in 1932 changed the political landscape. How did Roosevelt build an effective interregional political coalition for the Democratic Party? How did the challenges of balancing interests within the coalition shape the policies of the New Deal? In your answer, discuss the character of the coalition and specific reforms.

2. New Dealers experimented with varied solutions to the economic disorder of the 1930s. Compare reform efforts targeting rural and industrial America. Were they effective? Why or why not? What do they reveal about how the Roosevelt administration understood the underlying causes of the Great Depression?

3. Although the New Deal enjoyed astonishing popularity, some Americans were consistently critical of Roosevelt's reforms. Why? In your answer, discuss three opponents of the New Deal, being attentive to changes over time in their opinions. Were they able to influence the New Deal? If so, how?

4. Although the New Deal extended help to many Americans, all did not benefit equally from the era's reforms. Who remained outside the reach of New Deal assistance? Why? In your answer, consider how politics shaped the limits of reform, both in constituents' ability to demand assistance and in the federal government's response to their demands.

▶ FOR PRACTICE QUIZZES, A CUSTOMIZED STUDY PLAN, AND OTHER STUDY TOOLS, see the Online Study Guide at bedfordstmartins.com/roark.

1935 • Legislation creates Works Progress Administration (WPA).
 • Wagner Act.
 • Committee for Industrial Organization (CIO) founded.
 • Social Security Act.
 • Father Charles Coughlin begins National Union for Social Justice.

1936 • John Maynard Keynes publishes *The General Theory of Employment, Interest, and Money.*
 • Franklin Roosevelt elected to a second term by a landslide.

1937 • United Auto Workers stages successful sit-down strike at General Motors plant in Flint, Michigan.
 • Roosevelt's court-packing legislation defeated in the Senate.

1937– • Economic recession slows recovery from depression.
1938

1938 • Second Agricultural Adjustment Act and Fair Labor Standards Act.
 • Congress rejects administration's antilynching bill.
 • Administrative Reorganization Act.

NORDEN
BOMBSIGHT

American pilots depended on the Norden bombsight to hit targets in both the European and Pacific theaters throughout World War II. Invented by Carl Norden, a Dutch immigrant raised in Indonesia and educated in Switzerland, the sight combined an analog computer with gyroscopes, gears, and optics to calculate the path of bombs to a target, adjusting for the speed and altitude of the aircraft and the prevailing winds. In ideal conditions, the sight allowed pilots to deliver bombs within a 50-foot radius of a target from an altitude of 20,000 feet, making it possible for American bombers to aim for industrial plants, transportation hubs, bridges, and other high-value enemy targets. In combat, however, the bombsight was less precise. Two-thirds of American bombs unleashed from 20,000 feet actually fell more than 1,000 feet from their targets. Still, the Norden bombsight permitted American bombers to conduct effective high-altitude daytime raids. By contrast, British bombers, which lacked an accurate sighting mechanism, were forced to fly low-altitude, saturation bombing runs at night, when the danger from artillery on the ground was less. To prevent this valuable technology from falling into enemy hands, American bombardiers were trained to destroy the bombsight—by shooting it or by igniting an intense fire that would melt the mechanism into a lump of useless metal—if they were forced down in enemy territory. The Nazis purchased plans for the sight from a disgruntled Norden employee in 1937, but they never used it, focusing instead on dive-bombing tactics in support of ground forces. Paul Tibbets used the Norden bombsight to drop the atomic bomb on Hiroshima, Japan, in August 1945.

Museum of World War II, Natick, MA.

CHAPTER

25

The United States and the Second World War

1939–1945

O N A SUN-DRENCHED FLORIDA AFTERNOON in January 1927, Paul Tibbets took his first airplane ride. Twelve-year-old Tibbets cinched on a leather helmet; clambered into the front seat of the open cockpit of a cloth-covered red, white, and blue biplane; and sailed aloft over Miami. While the barnstorming pilot sitting behind him brought the plane in low over the Hialeah racetrack, Tibbets pitched Baby Ruth candy bars tethered to small paper parachutes to racing fans in the grandstands below. After two more candy-bar drops over the racetrack, the pilot raced to the beach and swooped down to two hundred feet as Tibbets tossed out the remaining candy bars and watched the bathers scramble for chocolate from heaven. After Tibbets and the pilot repeated their stunt for a week, sales of Baby Ruths soared for Tibbets's father's candy business, and Tibbets was hooked on flying.

Born in Quincy, Illinois, in 1915, Tibbets entered the University of Florida in 1933 and took flying lessons at the Gainesville airport. He continued to fly in his spare time and in 1937 decided to join the Army Air Corps to become a military pilot.

Shortly after the Japanese attack on Pearl Harbor in December 1941, Tibbets led a squadron of airplanes flying antisubmarine patrol against German U-boats lurking along the East Coast. When the heavily armored B-17 Flying Fortress bombers began to come off American assembly lines early in 1942, he took a squadron of the new planes from the United States to England. On August 17, 1942, he led the first American daytime bombing raid on German-occupied Europe, releasing 1,100 pounds of bombs from his B-17, nicknamed *Butcher Shop*, on the railroad yards of Rouen in northern France—the first of some 700,000 tons of explosives dropped by American bombers during the air war in Europe.

After numerous raids over Europe, Tibbets was reassigned to the North African campaign, where his duties included ferrying the American commander, General Dwight D. Eisenhower, into the battle zone. After eight months of combat missions, Tibbets returned to the United States and was ordered to test the new B-29 Super Fortress being built in Wichita, Kansas. The B-29 was much bigger than the B-17 and could fly higher and faster, making it ideal for the campaign against Japan. Tibbets's mastery of the B-29 caused him to be singled out in September 1944 to command a top-secret unit training for a special mission.

The mission, officials confided to Tibbets, was to be ready to drop on Japan a bomb that was so powerful it might bring the war to an end. No such

Colonel Paul Tibbets

Before taking off to drop the world's first atomic bomb on Hiroshima, Tibbets posed on the tarmac next to his customized B-29 Super Fortress bomber, named *Enola Gay* in honor of his mother. A crew of eleven hand-picked airmen accompanied Tibbets on the top-secret mission. After the war, President Harry S. Truman invited Tibbets to the White House and told him, "Don't you ever lose any sleep over the fact that you planned and carried out that mission. It was my decision. You had no choice."
© Bettmann/Corbis.

bomb yet existed, but American scientists and engineers were working around the clock to build one. Tibbets kept this secret from his men but took them and his B-29s to Utah to develop a way to drop such a powerful weapon without getting blown up by it. Tibbets trained his pilots to fly at 31,000 feet, then execute a dangerous, sharp, diving turn of 155 degrees that tested the limits of the aircraft but moved it beyond the range of the expected blast.

In May 1945, Tibbets took his B-29s and men to Tinian Island in the Pacific, where they trained for their secret mission by flying raids over Japanese cities and dropping ordinary bombs. The atomic bomb arrived on Tinian on July 26, just ten days after the successful test explosion in the New Mexico desert. Nicknamed "Little Boy,"

the bomb packed the equivalent of 40 million pounds of TNT, or 200,000 of the 200-pound bombs Tibbets and other American airmen had dropped on Europe.

At 2:30 a.m. on August 6, 1945, Tibbets, his crew, and their atomic payload took off in the B-29 bomber *Enola Gay* and headed for Japan. Less than seven hours later, over the city of Hiroshima, Tibbets and his men released Little Boy from the *Enola Gay*'s bomb bay. The plane bucked upward after dropping the 4.5-ton explosive, while Tibbets banked the plane sharply to the right and struggled to maintain control as the shock wave from the explosion blasted past and a purple cloud mushroomed nearly ten miles into the air. For an hour and a half as Tibbets flew back toward Tinian, he could see the mushroom cloud of atomic destruction unleashed by Little Boy. Three days later, Tibbets's men dropped a second atomic bomb on Nagasaki, and within five days, Japan surrendered.

Paul Tibbets's experiences traced an arc followed by millions of Americans during World War II, from the innocence of bombarding Miami with candy bars to the deadly nuclear firestorms that rained down on Japan. Like Tibbets, Americans joined their allies to fight the Axis powers in Europe and Asia. Like his *Enola Gay* crewmen—who hailed from New York, Texas, California, New Jersey, New Mexico, Maryland, North Carolina, Pennsylvania, Michigan, and Nevada—Americans from all regions united to defeat the **fascist** aggressors. American industries mobilized to produce advanced bombers—like the ones Tibbets piloted over Europe, North Africa, and Japan—along with enough other military equipment to supply the American armed forces and their allies. At an enormous cost in human life and suffering, the war brought employment and prosperity to most Americans at home, ending the depression, providing new opportunities for women, and ushering the nation into the postwar world as a triumphant economic and—on the wings of Paul Tibbets's *Enola Gay*—atomic superpower.

Peacetime Dilemmas

The First World War left a dangerous and ultimately deadly legacy. The victors—especially Britain, France, and the United States—sought to avoid future wars at almost any cost. The defeated nations, as well as those who felt humiliated by the Versailles peace settlement—particularly Germany, Italy, and Japan—aspired to reassert their power and avenge their losses by means of renewed warfare. Japan invaded the northern Chinese province of Manchuria in 1931 with ambitions to expand throughout Asia. Italy, led by the fascist Benito Mussolini since 1922, hungered for an empire in Africa. In Germany, National Socialist Adolf Hitler rose to power in 1933 in a quest to dominate Europe and the world. (See chapter 24, "Beyond America's Borders," page 870.) These aggressive, militaristic, antidemocratic regimes seemed a smaller threat to most people in the United States during the 1930s than the economic crisis at home. Shielded from external threats by the Atlantic and Pacific oceans, Americans hoped to avoid entanglement in foreign woes and to concentrate on climbing out of the nation's economic abyss.

Roosevelt and Reluctant Isolation

Like most Americans during the 1930s, Franklin Roosevelt believed that the nation's highest priority was to attack the domestic causes and consequences of the depression. But unlike most Americans, Roosevelt had long advocated an active role for the United States in international affairs. As assistant secretary of the navy in Woodrow Wilson's administration, he championed the significance of naval strength in the global balance of power. After World War I, Roosevelt embraced Wilson's vision that the United States should take the lead in making the world "safe for democracy," and he continued to advocate American membership in the League of Nations during the **isolationist** 1920s. When he ran for governor of New York in 1928, he criticized Republican isolationists for subverting international peace by demanding that battered European nations pay off their wartime loans and reparations in full and on time.

The depression forced Roosevelt to retreat from his previous internationalism. He came to believe that energetic involvement in foreign affairs diverted resources and political support from domestic recovery. During his 1932 presidential campaign, he pulled back from his endorsement of the League of Nations and reversed his previous support for forgiving European war debts. Once in office, Roosevelt sought to combine domestic economic recovery with a low-profile foreign policy that encouraged free trade and disarmament. "Foreign markets must be regained if America's producers are to rebuild a full and domestic prosperity," he explained in 1935. In turn, free trade required international peace, the goal of disarmament.

In pursuit of international amity, Roosevelt was constrained by economic circumstances and American popular opinion. After an opinion poll demonstrated popular support for recognizing the Soviet Union—an international pariah since the Bolshevik Revolution in 1917—Roosevelt established formal diplomatic relations in 1933. But when the League of Nations condemned Japanese and German aggression, Roosevelt did not enlist the nation in the league's attempts to keep the peace because he feared jeopardizing isolationists' support for **New Deal** measures in Congress. America watched from the sidelines when Japan withdrew from the league and ignored the limitations on its navy imposed after World War I. The United States also looked the other way when Hitler rearmed Germany and recalled its representative to the league in 1933, declaring that the international organization sought to thwart Germany's national ambitions. Roosevelt worried that the league's inability to curb German and Japanese violations of league sanctions and the Versailles settlement threatened world peace. But he reassured Americans that the nation would not "use its armed forces for the settlement of any [international] dispute anywhere."

> After World War I, Roosevelt embraced Wilson's vision that the United States should take the lead in making the world "safe for democracy."

The Good Neighbor Policy

In his 1933 inaugural address, Franklin Roosevelt announced that the United States would pursue "the policy of the good neighbor" in international relations. A few weeks later, he emphasized that this policy applied specifically to Latin America, where U.S. military forces had often intervened in local affairs. Now, Roosevelt said, the old policy of arrogant intervention would be replaced by a "helping hand" extended in a desire for friendly cooperation to create "more order in this hemisphere and less dislike." In December 1933 at the Inter-American Conference in Montevideo, Uruguay, Secretary of State Cordell Hull formalized the good neighbor pledge that no nation had the right to intervene in the internal or external affairs of another.

The good neighbor policy did not indicate a U.S. retreat from empire in Latin America. Instead, it declared that the United States would not depend on military force to exercise its influence

Promoting the Good Neighbor Policy
To encourage continuing friendly relations with Latin America during World War II, the Roosevelt administration urged Walt Disney to make the 1942 film *Saludos Amigos* — starring Donald Duck, Goofy, and "the Brazilian Jitterbird," Joe Carioca — largely for distribution south of the border. The good neighbor policy helped prevent Latin American nations from developing meaningful military alliances with the Axis powers during World War II.
© Disney Enterprises, Inc.

in the region. When Mexico nationalized American oil holdings and revolution boiled over in Nicaragua, Guatemala, and Cuba during the 1930s, Roosevelt refrained from sending in the marines to defend the interests of American corporations. In 1934, Roosevelt even withdrew American marines from Haiti, which they had occupied since 1916. Although nonintervention honored the principle of national self-determination, it also permitted the rise of dictators such as Anastasio Somoza in Nicaragua and Fulgencio Batista in Cuba, who exploited and terrorized their nations with private support from U.S. businesses and the hands-off policy of Roosevelt's administration.

Military nonintervention also did not prevent the United States from exerting its economic influence in Latin America. In 1934, Congress passed the Reciprocal Trade Agreements Act, which gave the president the power to reduce tariffs on goods imported into the United States from nations that agreed to lower their own tariffs on U.S. exports. By 1940, twenty-two nations had agreed to reciprocal tariff reductions, helping U.S. exports to Latin America double during Roosevelt's first two terms and contributing to the New Deal's goal of boosting the domestic economy through free trade. Although the economic power of the United States continued to overshadow that of its neighbors, the nonintervention policy planted seeds of friendship and hemispheric solidarity that grew in importance while events in Europe and Asia continued to erode international peace.

The Price of Noninvolvement

In Europe, fascist governments in Italy and Germany threatened military aggression. Italian dictator Benito Mussolini proclaimed, "War is to the man what maternity is to the woman. . . . Peace [is] . . . depressing and a negation of all the fundamental virtues of man." In Germany, Hitler made similar pronouncements and vigorously rebuilt Germany's military strength. German rearmament openly defied the terms of the Versailles peace treaty, but Britain and France only made verbal protests. The overwhelming desire to avoid conflict led Britain in 1935 to permit Germany to begin to rebuild its fleet of surface ships and submarines. Emboldened, Hitler plotted to avenge defeat in World War I by recapturing territories with German inhabitants, all the while accusing Jews of polluting the purity of the Aryan master race. The virulent anti-Semitism of Hitler and his Nazi Party unified non-Jewish Germans and attracted sympathizers among many other Europeans, even in France and Britain, thereby weakening support for opposing Hitler or defending the Jews.

In Japan, a stridently militaristic government planned to follow the invasion of Manchuria in 1931 with conquests extending throughout Southeast Asia. The Manchurian invasion bogged down in a long and vicious war when Chinese Nationalists rallied around their leader Chiang Kai-shek to fight against the Japanese. Preparations for new Japanese conquests continued, however. Early in 1936, Japan openly violated naval limitation treaties it had agreed to and began to build a battle-ready fleet to achieve naval superiority in the Pacific.

In the United States, the hostilities in Asia and Europe reinforced isolationist sentiments. Popular disillusionment with the failure of Woodrow Wilson's idealistic goals caused many Americans to question the nation's participation in World War I. In 1933, Gerald Nye, a Republican from North Dakota, chaired a Senate committee that investigated why the United States had gone to war in 1917. The Nye committee concluded that greedy "merchants of death"—American weapons makers, bankers, and financiers—dragged the nation into the war to line their own pockets. The Nye committee persuaded many Americans that war profiteers might once again push the nation into a world war.

International tensions and the Nye committee report prompted Congress to pass a series of neutrality acts between 1935 and 1937 in order to avoid the circumstances that, they believed, had caused the nation to abandon its isolationism and become a combatant in World War I. The neutrality acts prohibited making loans and selling arms to nations at war and authorized the president to warn Americans about traveling on ships belonging to belligerent countries.

By 1937, as the nation continued to struggle with the depression, the growing conflicts overseas caused some Americans to call for a total embargo on all trade with warring countries. Roosevelt and Congress worried that such an embargo would hurt the nation's economy by reducing production and boosting unemployment. The Neutrality Act of 1937 attempted to reconcile the nation's desire for both peace and foreign trade with a "cash-and-carry" policy that required warring nations to pay cash for nonmilitary goods and to transport them in their own ships. This policy supported foreign trade and thereby benefited the nation's economy, but it also helped foreign aggressors by supplying them with goods and thereby undermining peace.

The desire for peace in France, Britain, and the United States led Germany, Italy, and Japan to launch offensives on the assumption that the Western democracies lacked the will to oppose them. In March 1936, Nazi troops marched into the industry-rich Rhineland on Germany's western border, in blatant violation of the Treaty of Versailles. One month later, Italian armies completed their conquest of Ethiopia, projecting fascist power into Africa. In December 1937, Japanese invaders captured Nanking and celebrated their triumph in the "Rape of Nanking," a deadly rampage of murder, rape, and plunder that killed 200,000 Chinese civilians.

In Spain, a bitter civil war broke out in July 1936 when fascist rebels led by General Francisco Franco attacked the democratically elected Republican government. Both Germany and Italy reinforced Franco with soldiers, weapons, and aircraft, while the Soviet Union provided much less aid to the Republican Loyalists. The Spanish civil war seemed to many observers a dress rehearsal for a coming worldwide conflict, but it did not cause European democracies or the U.S. government to help the Loyalists, despite sympathizing with their cause. More than 3,000 individual Americans enlisted in the Russian-sponsored Abraham Lincoln Brigade to fight for the Loyalists. But, abandoned by the Western nations, the Loyalists and their allies were defeated in 1939, and Franco built a fascist bulwark in southern and western Europe.

Spanish Civil War, 1936–1939

Hostilities in Europe, Africa, and Asia alarmed Roosevelt and other Americans. The president sought to persuade most Americans to moderate their isolationism and find a way to support the victims of fascist aggression. Speaking in Chicago in October 1937, Roosevelt declared that the "epidemic of world lawlessness is spreading" and warned that "mere isolation or neutrality" offered no remedy for the "contagion" of war. Instead, he proposed that the United States "quarantine" aggressor nations and stop the spread of war's contagion.

Roosevelt's speech ignited a storm of protest from isolationists. The *Chicago Tribune* accused the president of seeking to replace "Americanism" with "internationalism." Disappointed by the strength of isolationism and the absence of congressional support for his quarantine policy, Roosevelt remarked, "It's a terrible thing to look over your shoulder when you are trying to lead and find no one there." The popularity of isolationist sentiment convinced Roosevelt that he needed to maneuver carefully if the United States were to help prevent fascist aggressors from conquering Europe and Asia, leaving the United States an isolated and imperiled island of **democracy**.

REVIEW Why did isolationism during the 1930s concern Roosevelt?

The Onset of War

Between 1939 and 1941, fascist victories overseas eventually eroded American isolationism. But initially, fascist anti-Semitism and military conquests in China, Ethiopia, and Spain failed to arouse many Americans, who were still mired in the depression. By 1939, however, continuing German and Japanese aggression caused more and more Americans to believe that it was time for the nation to take a stand. At first, taking a stand was limited to providing material support to the enemies of Germany and Japan, principally Britain, China, and the Soviet Union. But Japan's surprise attack on Pearl Harbor eliminated that restraint, and the nation began to mobilize for an all-out assault on foreign foes.

Nazi Aggression and War in Europe

Under the spell of isolationism, Americans passively watched Hitler's relentless campaign to dominate Europe. Hitler bullied Austria in 1938 into accepting incorporation—*Anschluss*—into the Nazi Third Reich, expanding the territory under Germany's control. Next, Hitler turned

MAP 25.1   Axis Aggression through 1941

For different reasons, Hitler and Mussolini launched a series of surprise military strikes before 1942. Mussolini sought to re-create the Roman empire in the Mediterranean. Hitler struck to reclaim German territories occupied by France after World War I and to annex Austria. When the German dictator began his campaign to rule "inferior" peoples beyond Germany's border by attacking Poland, World War II broke out.

his attention to the German-speaking Sudetenland, granted to Czechoslovakia by the Versailles treaty. The Czechs were prepared to fight rather than surrender their territory, but Britain and France hoped to avoid war by making a deal with Hitler. British prime minister Neville Chamberlain went to Munich, Germany, in September 1938 and offered Hitler terms of "appeasement," as he called it, that would give the Sudetenland to Germany if Hitler agreed to leave the rest of Czechoslovakia alone. Hitler accepted Chamberlain's offer and solemnly promised that he would make no more territorial claims in Europe. Chamberlain returned to England proclaiming that his Munich agreement had achieved "peace in our time." But peace depended on Hitler's keeping a promise he never intended to honor, dooming appeasement from the outset. In March 1939, Hitler boldly marched the German army into Czechoslovakia and conquered it without firing a shot (Map 25.1).

In April 1939, Hitler demanded that Poland return the German territory it had been awarded after World War I. Britain and France finally recognized that appeasement had failed and that Hitler would continue his aggression unless he was defeated by military might. Both Britain and France assured Poland that they would go to war with Germany if Hitler launched an eastward offensive across the Polish border. In turn, Hitler negotiated with his bitter enemy, Soviet premier Joseph Stalin, offering him concessions in order to prevent the Soviet Union from joining Britain and France in opposing a German attack on Poland. Despite the enduring hatred between fascist Germany and the **Communist** Soviet Union, the two powers signed the Nazi-Soviet treaty of nonaggression in August 1939, exposing Poland to an onslaught by the German Wehrmacht (army) and the Soviet Red Army.

At dawn on September 1, 1939, Hitler unleashed his attack on Poland, exhorting his generals to "close your hearts to pity! Act brutally!" German tanks and airplanes led the *blitzkrieg* (literally, "lightning war") that gave lethal mechanized support to the invading infantry. The attack triggered Soviet attacks on eastern Poland and declarations of war from France and Britain two days later, igniting a conflagration that raced around the globe. When it finally ended after Paul Tibbets's historic flight in August 1945, more than 60 million people were dead and untold millions more maimed. But in September 1939, Germany seemed invincible as its

German Invasion of Poland
In 1940, German infantry reserves marched to the eastern front led by two officers on horseback. Although the German blitzkrieg massed thousands of tanks and aircraft at the front, German forces lacked sufficient trucks and other motorized vehicles to move soldiers and military supplies. When Hitler invaded the Soviet Union in June 1941, his armies included some 3,300 tanks and more than 650,000 horses. The Germans' dependence on horse and foot travel limited the mobility of their troops compared to the more thoroughly motorized Allied armies.
© Bettmann/Corbis.

armies sped across Poland, causing many people to wonder if any nation could stop the Nazi war machine. Sooner or later, many people feared, all of Europe would share Poland's fate: defeat, German occupation, and vicious authoritarian government enforced by merciless repression and unblinking terror.

After the Nazis overran Poland, Hitler paused for a few months before launching a westward blitzkrieg. In April 1940, German forces smashed through Denmark and Norway. In May, Germany invaded the Netherlands, Belgium, Luxembourg, and France. The French believed that their Maginot Line, a concrete fortification built after World War I and stretching from the Swiss border to the forested Ardennes region on the edge of Belgium, would halt the German attack (see Map 25.1). But the Maginot Line proved little more than a detour for Hitler's mechanized divisions, which wheeled around the fortification's northern end and raced south toward Paris.

The speed of the German attack trapped more than 300,000 British and

French soldiers, who retreated to the port of Dunkirk, where an improvised armada of British vessels hurriedly ferried them to safety across the English Channel, leaving the Dunkirk beaches strewn with thousands of tons of abandoned military gear. By mid-June 1940, France had surrendered the largest army in the world, signed an armistice that gave Germany control of the entire French coastline and nearly two-thirds of the countryside, and installed a collaborationist government at Vichy in southern France headed by Philippe Pétain. With an empire that stretched across Europe from Poland to France, Hitler seemed poised to vault the English Channel and attack Britain.

The new British prime minister, Winston Churchill, vowed that Britain, unlike France, would never accept a humiliating surrender to Hitler. "We shall fight on the seas and oceans [and] . . . in the air," he proclaimed, "whatever the cost may be, we shall fight on the beaches, . . . and in the fields and in the streets . . . [and] we shall never surrender." Churchill's defiance stiffened British resolve for a last-ditch defense against Hitler's attack, which began in mid-June 1940 when wave after wave of German bombers targeted British military installations and cities, killing tens of thousands of civilians. The undermanned and outgunned Royal Air Force fought as doggedly as Churchill had predicted and finally won the Battle of Britain by November, clearing German bombers from British skies and handing Hitler his first frustrating defeat. Churchill praised the valiant British pilots, declaring that "never . . . was so much owed by so many to so few." Advance knowledge of German plans made possible by British use of the new technology of radar and the ability to decipher Germany's top-secret military codes aided British pilots. Battered and exhausted, Britain could not hold out forever without American help, as Churchill repeatedly wrote Roosevelt in private.

From Neutrality to the Arsenal of Democracy

When the Nazi attack on Poland ignited the war in Europe, Roosevelt issued an official proclamation of American neutrality. Most Americans condemned German aggression and favored Britain and France, but isolationism remained powerful. Roosevelt feared that if Congress did not repeal the arms embargo mandated by the Neutrality Act of 1937, France and Britain would soon succumb to the Nazi onslaught. The president's request for repeal of the embargo provoked isolationists to protest that the United States had no business interfering in a European conflict. After heated debate, Congress voted in November 1939 to revise the neutrality legislation and allow belligerent nations to buy arms, as well as nonmilitary supplies, on a cash-and-carry basis.

In practice, the revised neutrality law permitted Britain and France to purchase American war materiel and carry it across the Atlantic in their own ships, thereby shielding American vessels from attack by German submarines lurking in the Atlantic. Roosevelt feared that such halfhearted support for the antifascist cause threatened the United States. He wrote to a friend, "What worries me is that public opinion . . . is patting itself on the back every morning and thanking God for the Atlantic Ocean (and the Pacific Ocean)" and

Battle of Britain Survivors
During the Battle of Britain, German bombers targeted civilians in British cities. Luftwaffe pilots destroyed the Liverpool home (in the background) of Sarah Manson, the sixty-eight-year-old woman shown here with her daughter and grandchildren. Thousands of other British families suffered similar fates before the Royal Air Force managed to sweep the Luftwaffe from the skies over Britain. Subsequently, the British Bomber Command conducted saturation bombing raids against German cities, causing hundreds of thousands of civilian casualties. During World War II, more civilians were killed in military engagements than in any previous war.
© Bettmann/Corbis.

Enigma Machine

German commanders used the Enigma machine throughout World War II to send top-secret military messages. British intelligence agents broke the Enigma code in late August 1941 and soon began to decipher German messages giving details of military plans and the movements of men and supplies. The decoded intelligence, which the British called "Ultra," was far from perfect, since the Germans made several changes to the Enigma machine during the war, causing temporary Ultra blackouts until the new codes could be decrypted. Still, Allied military planners used Ultra to sink submarines, anticipate German movement, and mount disinformation campaigns that gave German commanders false ideas about Allied goals and tactics. The success of Ultra intelligence remained a closely guarded Allied secret until 1974. One reason for the delay in making this information public was that Allied intelligence agencies gave thousands of Enigma machines to other nations after World War II, permitting the United States and Britain to eavesdrop on the messages sent by the unwitting recipients of these "gifts."

Museum of World War II, Natick, MA.

underestimating "the serious implications" of the European war "for our own future."

Roosevelt searched for a way to aid Britain short of entering a formal alliance or declaring war against Germany. Churchill pleaded for American destroyers, aircraft, and munitions, but he had no money to buy them under the prevailing cash-and-carry neutrality law. In May 1940, Roosevelt asked Congress for almost $1.3 billion in defense spending to expand the navy and multiply the production of airplanes to 50,000 a year. By late summer, as the Battle of Britain raged in the skies over Britain, Roosevelt concocted a scheme to deliver fifty old destroyers to Britain in exchange for American access to British bases in the Western Hemisphere. Claiming the constitutional power to strengthen America's defenses by swapping destroyers for bases, Roosevelt took the first steps toward building a firm Anglo-American alliance against Hitler.

While German Luftwaffe (air force) pilots bombed Britain, Roosevelt decided to run for an unprecedented third term as president in 1940. He hoped to woo voters away from their complacent isolationism to back the nation's international interests as well as New Deal reforms. But the presidential election, which Roosevelt won handily, provided no clear mandate for American involvement in the European war. The Republican candidate, Wendell Willkie, a former Democrat who generally favored New Deal measures and Roosevelt's foreign policy, attacked Roosevelt as a warmonger. Willkie's accusations caused the president to promise voters, "Your boys are not going to be sent into any foreign wars," a pledge counterbalanced by his repeated warnings about the threats to America posed by Nazi aggression.

Empowered by the voters for another presidential term, Roosevelt maneuvered to support Britain in every way short of war. In a fireside chat shortly after Christmas 1940, he proclaimed that it was incumbent on the United States to become "the great arsenal of democracy" and send "every ounce and every ton of munitions and supplies that we can possibly spare to help the defenders who are in the front lines."

In January 1941, Roosevelt proposed the Lend-Lease Act, which allowed the British to obtain arms from the United States without paying cash but with the promise to reimburse the United States when the war ended. The purpose of Lend-Lease, Roosevelt proclaimed, was to defend democracy and human rights throughout the world, specifically the Four Freedoms: "freedom of speech and expression . . . freedom of every person to worship God in his own way . . . freedom from want . . . [and] freedom from fear." Congress passed the Lend-Lease Act in March 1941 and started a flow of support to Britain that totaled more than $50 billion during the war, far more than all federal expenditures combined since Roosevelt had become president in 1933.

Lend-Lease placed the United States on a collision course with Germany. Nazi U-boats (submarines) prowled the Atlantic, preying upon ships laden with supplies for Britain, making it only a matter of time before American citizens and their property would be attacked.

Roosevelt provided naval escorts for Lend-Lease supplies and gave his commanders orders to "shoot on sight" menacing German submarines, thus edging the nation closer to all-out combat.

Stymied in his plans for an invasion of England, Hitler turned his massive army eastward and on June 22, 1941, sprang a surprise attack on the Soviet Union, his erstwhile ally in the 1939 Nazi-Soviet nonaggression pact. Neither Roosevelt nor Churchill had any love for Joseph Stalin or communism, but they both welcomed the Soviet Union to the anti-Nazi cause. Both Western leaders understood that Hitler's attack on Russia would provide relief for the hard-pressed British. Roosevelt quickly persuaded Congress to extend Lend-Lease to the Soviet Union, beginning the shipment of millions of tons of trucks, jeeps, locomotives, and other equipment that, in all, supplied about 10 percent of Russian war materiel.

As Hitler's Wehrmacht raced across the Russian plains and Nazi U-boats tried to choke off supplies to Britain and the Soviet Union, Roosevelt met with Churchill aboard a ship near Newfoundland to cement the Anglo-American alliance. In August 1941, the two leaders issued the Atlantic Charter, pledging the two nations to freedom of the seas and free trade as well as the right of national self-determination. Roosevelt told Churchill privately that the United States would continue to serve as the arsenal of democracy and that he would be watching for some incident that might trigger public support for full-scale American entry into the war against Germany.

Japan Attacks America

Although the likelihood of war with Germany preoccupied Roosevelt, Hitler exercised a measure of restraint in directly provoking America. Japanese ambitions in Asia clashed more openly with American interests and commitments, especially in China and the Philippines. And unlike Hitler, the Japanese high command planned to attack the United States if necessary to pursue their aspirations to rule an Asian empire they termed the Greater East Asia Co-Prosperity Sphere. Appealing to widespread Asian bitterness toward white colonial powers, such as the British in India and Burma, the French in Indochina (now Vietnam), and the Dutch in the East Indies (now Indonesia), the Japanese campaigned to preserve "Asia for the Asians." Japan's invasion of China—which had lasted for ten years by 1941—proved that its true goal was Asia for the Japanese (Map 25.2). Japan coveted the raw materials available from China and Southeast Asia and ignored American demands to stop its campaign of aggression.

In 1940, Japan signaled a new phase of its **imperial** designs by entering a defensive alliance with Germany and Italy—the Tripartite Pact. In 1941, U.S. naval intelligence cracked the Japanese secret code and learned that Tokyo also planned to invade the resource-rich Dutch East Indies. To thwart these plans, in July 1941 Roosevelt announced a trade embargo that denied Japan access to oil, scrap iron, and other goods essential for its war machines. Roosevelt hoped the embargo would strengthen factions within Japan that opposed the militarists and sought to restore relations with the United States.

The American embargo played into the hands of Japanese militarists headed by General Hideki Tojo, who seized control of the government in October 1941 and persuaded other leaders, including Emperor Hirohito, that swift destruction of American naval bases in the Pacific would leave Japan free to follow its destiny. Decoded Japanese messages alerted American officials that an attack on U.S. forces was imminent somewhere in the Pacific, but no American knew where and when the attack would come until it was too late. Early on the morning of December 7, 1941, 183 attack aircraft lifted off six Japanese carriers that had secretly steamed within striking range of the U.S. Pacific Fleet at Pearl Harbor on the Hawaiian island of Oahu. At about eight o'clock, the Japanese planes streaked from the sky, bombing and torpedoing the American fleet riding serenely at anchor in the harbor and destroying hundreds of aircraft parked in neat rows on the runways of Hickam Field. The devastating surprise attack sank or disabled 18 ships, including all of the fleet's battleships; killed more than 2,400 Americans; and wounded more than 1,000, al-

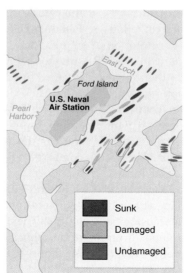

Bombing of Pearl Harbor, December 7, 1941

Ford Island

U.S. Naval Air Station

Pearl Harbor

East Loch

Sunk

Damaged

Undamaged

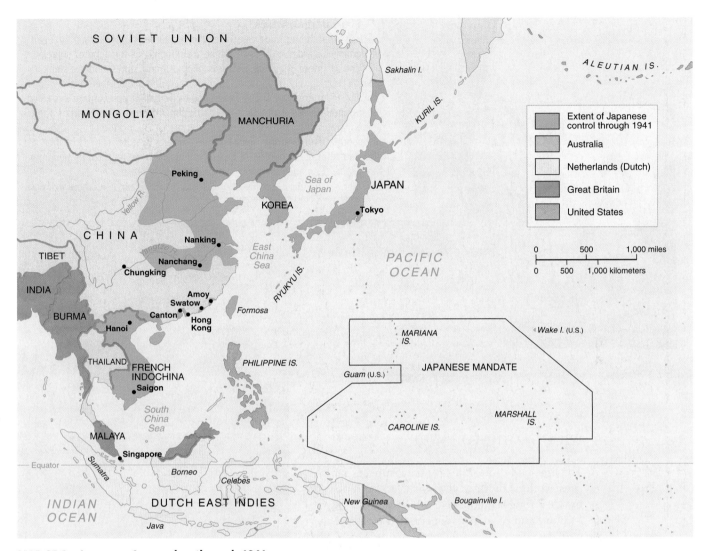

MAP 25.2 Japanese Aggression through 1941
Beginning with the invasion of Manchuria in 1931, Japan sought to extend its imperialist control over most of East Asia. Japanese aggression was driven by the need for raw materials for the country's expanding industries and by the military government's devotion to martial honor.

most crippling U.S. war-making capacity in the Pacific. Luckily for the United States, Japanese pilots failed to destroy the vital machine shops and oil storage facilities at Pearl Harbor, and none of the nation's aircraft carriers happened to be in port at the time of the attack.

The Japanese scored a stunning tactical victory at Pearl Harbor, but in the long run, the attack proved a colossal blunder. The victory made many Japanese commanders overconfident about their military prowess. Worse for the Japanese, Americans instantly united in their desire to fight and avenge the attack, which Roosevelt termed "dastardly and unprovoked." The president vowed that "this form of treachery shall never endanger us again." On December 8,

Congress almost unanimously endorsed the president's call for a declaration of war. The only holdout was the pacifist Republican congresswoman Jeannette Rankin of Montana, who had also opposed U.S. entry into World War I. Neither Hitler nor Mussolini knew about the Japanese attack in advance, but they both declared war against America on December 11, bringing the United States into all-out war with the Axis powers in both Europe and Asia.

REVIEW How did Roosevelt attempt to balance American isolationism with the increasingly ominous international scene of the late 1930s?

Pearl Harbor Attack

This Japanese postcard celebrates the successful surprise attack on Pearl Harbor on December 7, 1941. The postcard highlights the airborne supremacy of the Japanese, the weak defenses of the United States, and the smoking destruction caused by Japanese carrier-based aircraft. Brothers Wesley and Edward Heidt from Los Angeles were one of thirty-four pairs of brothers killed when Japanese warplanes sank the battleship *Arizona* at Pearl Harbor. This pennant was salvaged from the ship's wreckage. Also included here is the official telegram informing the Heidt brothers' mother that her sons "lost their life in the service of their country," a heartbreaking message received by hundreds of thousands of American families over the next four years.

Photo, pennant, and telegram: U.S.S. *Arizona* Memorial, Hawaii, National Park Service/photos by Douglas Peebles; Postcard: www.museumofworldwarii.com.

Mobilizing for War

The time had come, Roosevelt announced, for the prescriptions of "Dr. New Deal" to be replaced by the stronger medicines of "Dr. Win-the-War." Military and civilian leaders rushed to secure the nation against possible attacks, causing Americans of Japanese descent to be stigmatized and sent to internment camps. Roosevelt and his advisers lost no time enlisting millions of Americans in the armed forces to bring the isolationist-era military to fighting strength for a two-front war. The war emergency also required economic mobilization unparalleled in the nation's history. As Dr. Win-the-War, Roosevelt set aside the New Deal goal of reform and plunged headlong into transforming the American economy into the world's greatest military machine, thereby achieving full employment and economic recovery, goals that had eluded the New Deal.

Home-Front Security

Shortly after declaring war against the United States, Hitler dispatched German submarines to hunt American ships along the Atlantic coast from Maine to Florida, where Paul Tibbets and other American pilots tried to destroy them. But the U-boats had devastating success for about

eight months, sinking hundreds of U.S. ships and threatening to disrupt the Lend-Lease lifeline to Britain and the Soviet Union. The submarines benefited from the failure of port cities such as New York and Miami to observe the rules requiring blackouts, allowing U-boats to spot vulnerable ships against the lighted horizon.

Hulks of destroyed vessels littered Atlantic beaches, but by mid-1942, the U.S. navy had chased German submarines away from the East Coast and into the mid-Atlantic, reducing the direct threat to the nation. Naval ships patrolled the nation's coasts, and fortifications were built to defend against seaborne assaults. These and other security measures raised popular awareness of the possibility of an attack on the U.S. mainland, but no such attack occurred.

Within the continental United States, Americans remained sheltered from the chaos and destruction the war was bringing to hundreds of millions in Europe and Asia. Nevertheless, the government worried constantly about espionage and internal subversion. Billboards and posters warned Americans that "Loose lips sink ships" and "Enemy agents are always near; if you don't talk, they won't hear." The campaign for patriotic vigilance focused on German and Japanese foes, but Americans of Japanese descent became targets of official and popular persecution because of Pearl Harbor and long-standing racial prejudice against people of Asian descent.

About 320,000 people of Japanese descent lived in the United States in 1941, two-thirds of them in Hawaii, where they largely escaped wartime persecution because they were essential and valued members of society. On the mainland, however, Japanese Americans were a tiny minority—even along the West Coast, where most of them worked on farms and in small businesses—subject to frenzied wartime suspicions and persecution. A prominent newspaper columnist echoed the widespread sentiment that "the Japanese . . . should be under armed guard to the last man and woman right now and to hell with habeas corpus until the danger is over." Although an official military survey concluded that Japanese Americans posed no danger, popular hostility fueled a campaign to round up all mainland Japanese Americans—two-thirds of them U.S. citizens. "A Jap's a Jap. . . . It makes no difference whether he is an American citizen or not," one official declared.

On February 19, 1942, Roosevelt issued Executive Order 9066, which authorized sending all Americans of Japanese descent to ten make-shift prison (or internment) camps—euphemistically termed "relocation centers"—located in remote areas of the West (Map 25.3). Allowed little time to secure or sell their property, Japanese Americans lost homes and businesses worth about $400 million and lived out the war penned in by barbed wire and armed guards. (See "Documenting the American Promise," page 916.) Although several thousand Japanese Americans served with distinction in the U.S. armed forces and no case of subversion by a Japanese American was ever uncovered, the Supreme Court, in its 1944 *Korematsu* decision, upheld Executive Order 9066's blatant violation of constitutional rights as justified by "military necessity."

MAP 25.3 Western Relocation Authority Centers
Responding to prejudice and fear of sabotage, President Roosevelt authorized the roundup and relocation of all Americans of Japanese descent in 1942. Taken from their homes in the cities and fertile farmland of the far West, Japanese Americans were confined in desolate camps scattered as far east as the Mississippi River.

Japanese Internment Camp at Manzanar, California
Japanese American families line up to enter the mess hall at the Manzanar, California, internment camp in May 1943. The camp was located on the barren, wind-swept eastern slope of the Sierra Nevada. The artist, Kango Takamura, was incarcerated first at Manzanar and later at another camp near Santa Fe, New Mexico. Takamura immigrated to the United States in 1921. Like other internees, he was utterly loyal to the United States, and he tried to make the best of a bad situation. He recalled that the people at Manzanar "had plenty of food . . . not gourmet stuff, but good enough for health." At Santa Fe, he and other internees often organized impromptu games of America's national pastime, baseball. After the war, Takamura returned to Los Angeles and his work with movie studios.
Gift of Kango Takamura, Department of Special Collections, Charles E. Young Research Library, UCLA.

Japanese Internment

D*etermined that the bombing of Pearl Harbor would not be followed by more sneak attacks, military and political leaders on the West Coast targeted persons of Japanese descent—aliens and citizens alike—as potential saboteurs.*

DOCUMENT 1
Final Recommendations of the Commanding General, Western Defense Command and Fourth Army, Submitted to the Secretary of War

Early in 1942, General John DeWitt, commander of the Western Defense Command, persuaded President Franklin Roosevelt to issue an executive order authorizing the removal of Japanese living in the United States. Subsequently, 110,000 Japanese Americans were confined to relocation camps for the duration of the war. DeWitt's recommendation expressed concern for military security by appealing to racist conceptions long used to curb Asian immigration. Japanese Americans and their supporters fought the internment order in the courts as a violation of fundamental constitutional rights, an argument rejected during the war by the U.S. Supreme Court. Long after the war ended, the U.S. government officially apologized for Japanese American internment and issued modest monetary payments to survivors.

February 14, 1942
Memorandum for
the Secretary of War.
Subject: Evacuation of Japanese and Other Subversive Persons from the Pacific Coast.

1. In presenting a recommendation for the evacuation of Japanese and other subversive persons from the Pacific Coast, the following facts have been considered:
a. Mission of the Western Defense Command and Fourth Army.
1) Defense of the Pacific Coast of the Western Defense Command, as extended, against attacks by sea, land, or air;
2) Local protection of establishment and communications vital to the National Defense for which adequate defense cannot be provided by local civilian authorities.
b. Brief Estimate of the Situation.
1) . . . The following are possible and probable enemy activities: . . .
(a) Naval attack on shipping on coastal waters;
(b) Naval attack on coastal cities and vital installations;
(c) Air raids on vital installations, particularly within two hundred miles of the coast;
(d) Sabotage of vital installations throughout the Western Defense Command.

Hostile Naval and air raids will be assisted by enemy agents signaling from the coastline and the vicinity thereof; and by supplying and otherwise assisting enemy vessels and by sabotage.

In the war in which we are now engaged racial affinities are severed by migration. The Japanese race is an enemy race and while many second and third generation Japanese born on United States soil, possessed of United States citizenship, have become "Americanized," the racial strains are undiluted. To conclude otherwise is to expect that children born of white parents on Japanese soil sever all racial affinity and become loyal Japanese subjects, ready to fight and, if necessary, to die for Japan in a war against the nation of their parents. . . .

It, therefore, follows that along the vital Pacific Coast over 112,000 potential enemies, of Japanese extraction, are at large today. There are indications that these are organized and ready for concerted action at a favorable opportunity. The very fact that no sabotage has taken place to date is a disturbing and confirming indication that such action will be taken.

SOURCE: *Final Recommendations*, report by General John Lesesne DeWitt to the United States Secretary of War, February 14, 1942.

DOCUMENT 2
An Oral History of Life in the Japanese American Detention Camps

Imprisoned in bleak surroundings far from home, Japanese American internees sometimes succumbed to despair and bitterness. Looking back after forty years, Kazue Yamane recalled her confinement as a disturbing and baffling experience.

In April 1942, my husband and I and our two children left for camp, and my mother-in-law and father-in-law came about a month later. I wasn't afraid, but I kept asking in my mind, how could they? This is impossible. Even today I still think it was a nightmarish thing. I cannot reconcile myself to the fact that I had to go, that I was interned, that I was segregated, that I was taken away, even though it goes back forty years. . . .

I was separated from my husband; he went to the Santa Fe, New Mexico, camp. All our letters were censored;

all our letters were cut in parts and all that. So we were not too sure what messages was getting through and not getting through, but I do know that I informed him many times of his mother's condition. He should have been allowed to come back to see her, because I thought she wouldn't live too long, but they never did allow him to come back, even for her funeral. They did not allow that. I learned that a lot of the messages didn't get to him; they were crossed out. I now have those letters with me.

In 1944 I was left with his parents and our kids. But I had no time to think of what was going to happen because my child was always sick and I had been quite sick. . . .

My son knew what was going on, and he too had many times asked me why . . . you know, why? why? Of course, I had no explanation why this was happening to us.

Source: Excerpt from *And Justice for All*, by John Tateishi. Copyright © 1999 by John Tateishi. Reprinted by permission of the University of Washington Press.

DOCUMENT 3
The Kikuchi Diary

Charles Kikuchi, a student at the University of California at Berkeley, sought in his prison camp diary to make sense of the internment and to judge where it would lead.

December 7, 1941,
Berkeley, California
Pearl Harbor. We are at war! Jesus Christ, the Japs bombed Hawaii and the entire fleet has been sunk. I just can't believe it. I don't know what in the hell is going to happen to us, but we will all be called into the Army right away.

. . . The next five years will determine the future of the Nisei [Japanese

American citizens]. They are now at the crossroads. Will they be able to take it or will they go under? If we are ever going to prove our Americanism, this is the time. The Anti-Jap feeling is bound to rise to hysterical heights, and it is most likely that the Nisei will be included as Japs. I wanted to go to San Francisco tonight, but Pierre says I am crazy. He says it's best we stick on campus. In any event, we can't remain on the fence, and a positive approach must be taken if we are to have a place in fulfilling the Promise of America. I think the U.S. is in danger of going Fascist too, or maybe Socialist. . . .

I don't know what to think or do. Everybody is in a daze.

April 30, 1942, Berkeley
Today is the day that we are going to get kicked out of Berkeley. It certainly is degrading. . . .

I'm supposed to see my family at Tanforan as Jack told me to give the same family number. I wonder how it is going to be living with them as I haven't done this for years and years? I should have gone over to San Francisco and evacuated with them, but I had a last final to take. I understand that we are going to live in the horse stalls. I hope that the Army has the courtesy to remove the manure first. . . .

July 14, 1942
Marie, Ann, Mitch, Jimmy, Jack, and myself got into a long discussion about how much democracy meant to us as individuals. Mitch says that he would even go in the army and die for it, in spite of the fact that he knew he would be kept down. Marie said that although democracy was not perfect, it was the only system that offered any hope for a future, if we could fulfill its destinies. Jack was a little more skeptical. He even suggested that we [could] be in such

grave danger that we would then realize that we were losing something. Where this point was he could not say. I said that this was what happened in France and they lost all. Jimmy suggested that the colored races of the world had reason to feel despair and mistrust the white man because of the past experiences. . . .

In reviewing the four months here, the chief value I got out of this forced evacuation was the strengthening of the family bonds. I never knew my family before this and this was the first chance that I have had to really get acquainted.

Source: Excerpts (pp. 43, 51, 183, 252) from *The Kikuchi Diary: Chronicle from an American Concentration Camp*, edited by John Modell. Copyright © 1973 by the Board of Trustees of the University of Illinois. Used with the permission of the University of Illinois Press and the author.

QUESTIONS FOR ANALYSIS AND DEBATE

1. What explains General DeWitt's insistence on evacuating the Japanese after he received the report of military investigators that no acts of sabotage had occurred?

2. How do the Kikuchi diary and the oral histories of life in the camps describe the meaning of internment for the detainees?

3. Despite the internment of their families and friends in concentration camps, the Japanese American army unit in Italy earned a larger number of citations for combat heroism than any comparable army group. What hints in the documents here might help explain this combat record?

4. How did the internment camp experience influence the detainees' attitudes about their identity as Americans of Japanese descent?

Building a Citizen Army

In 1940, Roosevelt encouraged Congress to pass the Selective Service Act to register men of military age who would be subject to a **draft** if the need arose. More than 6,000 local draft boards registered more than 30 million men and, when war came, rapidly inducted them into military service. In all, more than 16 million men and women served in uniform during the war, two-thirds of them draftees, mostly young men between the ages of eighteen and twenty-six. Although only about one family in five had a family member in the military, nearly everybody had friends and neighbors who had gone off to war. By the time the war ended, more than 10 million Americans had served in the army, nearly 4 million in the navy, 600,000 in the marines, and 240,000 in the coast guard. In addition, 350,000 women joined the Nurse's Corps and women's military units in the army, navy, and Marine Corps. Though barred from combat duty, these

African American Machine Gunners

These African American soldiers prepare their machine gun for action on the side of a road near Pisa, Italy, in September 1944. These and other black soldiers who served in combat in segregated units repeatedly earned praise from their commanders for gallantry and courage under fire. As a Mississippi-born African American veteran of the Pacific theater recalled, "We had two wars to fight: prejudice . . . and those Japs."

© Bettmann/Corbis.

women worked at nearly every noncombatant assignment, eroding traditional barriers to women's military service.

The Selective Service Act prohibited discrimination "on account of race or color," and almost a million African American men and women donned uniforms, as did half a million Mexican Americans, 25,000 Native Americans, and 13,000 Chinese Americans. The racial insults and discrimination suffered by all people of color made some soldiers ask, as a Mexican American GI did on his way to the European front, "Why fight for America when you have not been treated as an American?" Only black Americans were trained in segregated camps, confined in segregated barracks, and assigned to segregated units. The Red Cross even segregated the blood it used to treat casualties, supposedly protecting wounded whites from contamination by black blood—needless to say, a practice with no scientific merit. Secretary of War Henry Stimson opposed any change in the segregation of blacks, declaring that the military should not serve as a "sociological laboratory." Accordingly, most black Americans were consigned to manual labor, and relatively few served in combat until late in 1944, when the need for military manpower in Europe intensified. Then, as General George Patton told black soldiers in a tank unit in Normandy, "I don't care what color you are, so long as you go up there and kill those Kraut sonsabitches."

Homosexuals also served in the armed forces, although in much smaller numbers than black Americans. Allowed to serve as long as their sexual preferences remained covert, gay Americans, like other minorities, sought to demonstrate their worth under fire. "I was superpatriotic," a gay combat veteran recalled. Another gay GI remarked, "Who in the hell is going to worry about [homosexuality]" in the midst of the life-or-death realities of war?

Conversion to a War Economy

In 1940, the American economy remained mired in the depression. Nearly one worker in seven was still without a job, factories operated far below their productive capacity, and the total federal budget was under $10 billion. Shortly after the attack on Pearl Harbor, Roosevelt announced the goal of converting the economy to produce "overwhelming . . . , crushing superiority of equipment in any theater of the world war." In a rush to produce military supplies, factories were converted from making passenger cars to assembling tanks and airplanes, and production was ramped up to record levels. By the end of the war, there were more jobs than workers, plants were operating at full capacity, and the federal budget topped $100 billion.

To organize and oversee this tidal wave of military production, Roosevelt called upon business leaders to come to Washington and, for the token payment of a dollar a year, head new government agencies such as the War Production Board, which, among other things, set production priorities and pushed for maximum output. Contracts flowed to large corporations such as General Electric, Ford, and U.S. Steel, often on a basis that guaranteed their profits. During the first half of 1942, the government issued contracts worth more than $100 billion, a sum greater than the entire gross national product in 1941.

Booming wartime employment swelled union membership. To speed production, the government asked unions to pledge not to strike. Despite the relentless pace of work, union members kept their no-strike pledge, with the important exception of members of the United Mine Workers, who walked out of the coal mines in 1943, demanding a pay hike and earning the enmity of many Americans.

Overall, conversion to war production achieved Roosevelt's ambitious goal of "overwhelming . . . , crushing superiority" in military goods. At a total cost of $304 billion during the

The Road to War: The United States and World War II

1931	Japan invades Manchuria.
1933	Franklin D. Roosevelt becomes U.S. president.
	Adolf Hitler becomes German chancellor.
1935–1937	Congress passes series of neutrality acts to protect United States from involvement in world conflicts.
1936	**March.** Nazi troops invade Rhineland, violating Treaty of Versailles.
	July. Civil war breaks out in Spain.
	Mussolini's fascist Italian regime conquers Ethiopia.
	November. Roosevelt reelected president.
1937	**December.** Japanese troops capture Nanking, China.
1938	Hitler annexes Austria.
	September 29. Hitler accepts offer of "appeasement" in Munich from British prime minister Neville Chamberlain.
1939	**March.** Hitler invades Czechoslovakia.
	August. Hitler and Stalin sign Nazi-Soviet nonaggression pact.
	September 1. Germany invades Poland, beginning World War II.
	United States and Britain conclude cash-and-carry agreement for arms sales.
1940	**Spring.** German blitzkrieg smashes through Denmark, Norway, Belgium, Luxembourg, Netherlands, and northern France.
	Japan signs Tripartite Pact with Germany and Italy.
	May–June. German armies flank Maginot Line. British and French evacuated from Dunkirk. France surrenders to Germany.
	Summer/Fall. Germany conducts bombing campaign against England.
	November. Roosevelt wins third term as president. Royal Air Force wins Battle of Britain.
1941	**March.** Congress approves Lend-Lease Act, making arms available to Britain.
	June 22. Hitler invades Soviet Union.
	August. Roosevelt and Churchill issue Atlantic Charter.
	October. Militarists led by Hideki Tojo take over Japan.
	December 7. Japanese bomb Pearl Harbor. United States declares war on Japan.
	December 11. Germany and Italy declare war on United States.

Tank Production Line
The General Motors plant shown here assembled automobiles until Roosevelt called for American factories to convert to wartime production as rapidly as possible. This and other plants built tens of thousands of armored vehicles destined principally for Allied soldiers in the European theater, where they dueled with Hitler's panzers.
General Motors Corp. Used with permission, GM Media Archives.

GLOBAL COMPARISON

Weapons Production by the Axis and Allied Powers during World War II

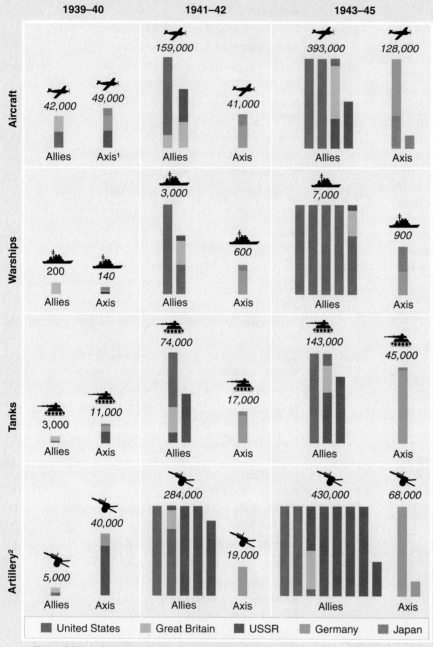

	1939–40	1941–42	1943–45
Aircraft	Allies 42,000 / Axis¹ 49,000	Allies 159,000 / Axis 41,000	Allies 393,000 / Axis 128,000
Warships	Allies 200 / Axis 140	Allies 3,000 / Axis 600	Allies 7,000 / Axis 900
Tanks	Allies 3,000 / Axis 11,000	Allies 74,000 / Axis 17,000	Allies 143,000 / Axis 45,000
Artillery²	Allies 5,000 / Axis 40,000	Allies 284,000 / Axis 19,000	Allies 430,000 / Axis 68,000

Legend: ■ United States ■ Great Britain ■ USSR ■ Germany ■ Japan

¹ The USSR was allied with Germany 1939–40.
² No reliable data exist for Japan.

This chart demonstrates the massive contribution of the United States to Allied weapons production during World War II. In the air and on the sea, U.S. weapons predominated, after 1940 accounting for more aircraft and many more warships than Britain and the Soviet Union combined. Together, the three Allied powers produced about three times as many aircraft and five to eight times as many warships as the two Axis powers. On the ground, the Soviet Union led the other Allies in the production of tanks and artillery, an outgrowth of the colossal battles on the eastern front. Overall, the Allies produced almost three times as many tanks as the Axis powers and more than seven times as many artillery pieces as Germany (no figures are available for Japan). What do these data suggest about the significance of America's entry into the war in December 1941? What do they suggest about the kind of warfare emphasized by each of the belligerents? What do they suggest about the chronology of weapons production during the war?

war, the nation produced an avalanche of military equipment, including 300,000 airplanes, 88,000 tanks, 7,000 ships, 3 million vehicles, billions of bullets, and much more—in all, more than double the combined production of Germany, Japan, and Italy. (See "Global Comparison.") In the last eighteen months of the war, for example, every American in the Pacific theater could draw upon 8,000 pounds of military supplies, in stark contrast with each Japanese soldier's access to only

2 pounds. Giving tangible meaning to the term "arsenal of democracy," this outpouring of military goods supplied not only U.S. forces but also America's allies.

> **REVIEW** How did the Roosevelt administration mobilize the human and industrial resources necessary to fight a two-front war?

Fighting Back

The United States confronted a daunting military challenge in December 1941. The attack on Pearl Harbor destroyed much of its Pacific Fleet, crippling the nation's ability to defend against Japan's massive offensive throughout the southern Pacific. In the Atlantic, Hitler's U-boats sank American ships, while German armies occupied most of western Europe and relentlessly advanced eastward into the Soviet Union. Roosevelt and his military advisers believed that defeating Germany took top priority. To achieve that victory required preventing Hitler from defeating America's allies, Britain and the Soviet Union. If they fell, Hitler would command all the resources of Europe in a probable assault on the United States. To fight back effectively against Germany and Japan, the United States had to coordinate military and political strategy with its allies and muster all its human and economic assets. But in 1941, nobody knew whether that would be enough.

Turning the Tide in the Pacific

In the Pacific theater, Japan's leading military strategist, Admiral Isoroku Yamamoto, ordered an all-out offensive throughout the southern Pacific. He believed that if his forces did not quickly conquer and secure the territories they targeted, Japan would eventually lose the war as a result of America's far greater resources. Swiftly, the Japanese assaulted American airfields in the Philippines and captured U.S. outposts on Guam and Wake Island. Singapore, the great British naval base in Malaya, surrendered to the Japanese in February 1942, and most of Burma had fallen by March. All that stood in the way of Japan's domination of the southern Pacific was the American stronghold in the Philippines.

The Japanese unleashed a withering assault against the Philippines in January 1942 (see

Japanese Pilot's Flag
Japanese pilots often carried small flags covered with admonitions to fight hard and well. This flag belonged to a pilot named Imano, whose relatives sent him aloft with an inscription that read, "Let your divine plane soar in the sky. We who are left behind pray only for your certain success in sinking an enemy ship." Notably, the inscription emphasized harming Japan's enemies rather than returning home safely.
U.S. Naval Academy Museum/photo by Richard D. Bond Jr.

Map 25.5, page 938). The American commander, General Douglas MacArthur, retreated to Australia in March, leaving General Jonathan Wainwright to hold out as long as possible. Wainwright surrendered to the Japanese in May, and the Japanese victors marched the weak and malnourished survivors sixty-five miles to a concentration camp. Thousands of captured American and Filipino soldiers died during the Bataan Death March, and 16,000 more perished in the camps. By the summer of 1942, the Japanese war machine had conquered the oil-rich Dutch East Indies and was poised to strike Australia and New Zealand.

The Japanese had larger, faster, and more heavily armed ships than the United States, and their airplanes outperformed anything the Americans could send up against them. But a daring raid on Tokyo in April 1942 by a squadron of carrier-based B-25 bombers led by Lieutenant Colonel

Flamethrower in Combat in the Solomon Islands
American soldiers used flamethrowers in both the Pacific and European theaters. They were especially effective against enemy soldiers dug into bunkers that were difficult to penetrate by rifle or machine-gun fire. The marine shown here, fighting on New Georgia in the Solomon Islands in 1943, carried on his back canisters of jellied gasoline and compressed air that were combined and projected through the gunlike weapon. The weapon ignited the mixture and spouted an intensely hot flame toward the enemy position. Flamethrowers were dangerous, deadly weapons for both the enemy and the Americans who operated them. Carrying a flamethrower often made one a high-priority target for enemy sharpshooters, and a stray piece of hot shrapnel could explode the flamethrower on the back of a soldier who toted it.
National Museum of American History, Smithsonian Institution, Behring Center.

James Doolittle boosted American morale and demonstrated that even the Japanese imperial capital lay within reach (barely) of American might.

In the spring of 1942, U.S. forces launched a major two-pronged counteroffensive that military officials hoped would reverse the Japanese advance. Forces led by General MacArthur moved north from Australia and attacked the Japanese in the Philippines. Far more decisively, Admiral Chester W. Nimitz sailed his battle fleet west from Hawaii to retake Japanese-held islands in the mid-Pacific. On May 7–8, 1942, in the Coral Sea just north of Australia, the American fleet and carrier-based warplanes defeated a Japanese armada that was sailing around the coast of New Guinea.

Nimitz then learned from an intelligence intercept that the Japanese were massing an invasion force aimed at Midway Island, an outpost guarding the Hawaiian Islands. Nimitz maneuvered his carriers and cruisers into the Central Pacific to surprise the Japanese. In a furious battle that raged June 3–6, American ships and planes delivered a devastating blow to the Japanese navy, sinking a heavy cruiser, two destroyers, and four of Japan's six aircraft carriers. The American fleet lost only one carrier and one destroyer in the fight. The Battle of Midway reversed the balance of naval power in the Pacific and put the Japanese at a disadvantage for the rest of the war. Japan managed to build only six more large carriers during the war, while the United States launched dozens, proving the wisdom of Yamamoto's prediction. The Battle of Midway turned the tide of Japanese advances in the Pacific but did little to dislodge the Japanese from the many places they had conquered and now stoutly defended.

The Campaign in Europe

In the dark months after Pearl Harbor, Hitler's eastern-front armies marched ever deeper into the Soviet Union while his western-front forces prepared to invade Britain. As in World War I, the Germans attempted to starve the British into submission by destroying their seaborne lifeline. Technological advances made German U-boats much more effective than they had been in World War I. In 1941 and 1942, they sank Allied ships faster than new ones could be built. Overall, the U-boat campaign sank 4,700 merchant vessels and nearly 200 warships and killed 40,000 Allied seamen.

Until mid-1943, the outcome of the war in the Atlantic remained in doubt. Then, newly invented radar detectors and production of sufficient destroyer escorts for merchant vessels allowed the Allies to prey upon the lurking U-boats. After suffering a 75 percent casualty rate among U-boat crews, Hitler withdrew German submarines from the North Atlantic in late May 1943. In the next four months, more than 3,500 American supply ships crossed the Atlantic without a single loss. Winning the battle of the Atlantic allowed the United States to continue to supply its British and Soviet allies for the duration of the war and to reduce the imminent threat of a German invasion of Britain.

The most important strategic question confronting the United States and its allies was when and where to open a second front against the Nazis. Stalin demanded that America and Britain mount an immediate and massive assault across the English Channel into western France. A cross-Channel invasion would force Hitler to divert his armies from the eastern front and relieve the pressure on the Soviet Union, which was fighting alone against the full strength of the German Wehrmacht. Churchill and Roosevelt instead delayed opening a second front, allowing the Germans and the Soviets to slug it out. This weakened both the Nazis and the Communists and made an eventual Allied attack on western

France more likely to succeed. Churchill and Roosevelt promised Stalin that they would open a second front, but they decided to strike first in southern Europe and the Mediterranean, which Churchill termed Europe's "soft under-belly."

The plan targeted a region of long-standing British influence in the eastern Mediterranean. In October and November 1942, British forces at El-Alamein in Egypt halted German general Erwin Rommel's drive to capture the Suez Canal, Britain's lifeline to the oil of the Middle East and to British colonies in India and South Asia (see Map 25.4, page 933). In November, an American army under General Dwight D. Eisenhower landed far to the west, in French Morocco. Propelled by American tank units commanded by General George Patton, the Allied armies had defeated the Germans in North Africa by May 1943. The North African campaign killed and captured 350,000 Axis soldiers, pushed the Germans out of Africa, made the Mediterranean safe for Allied shipping, and opened the door for an Allied invasion of Italy.

In January 1943, while the North African campaign was still under way, Roosevelt traveled to the Moroccan city of Casablanca to confer with Churchill and other Allied leaders. Stalin did not attend but urged his allies to keep their promise of opening a major second front in western Europe. Roosevelt and Churchill announced that they would accept nothing less than the "unconditional surrender" of the Axis powers, ruling out peace negotiations. But Churchill and Roosevelt concluded that they needed more time to amass sufficient forces for the cross-Channel invasion of France that Stalin demanded. In the meantime, they planned to capitalize on their success in North Africa and strike against Italy, consigning the Soviet Union to bear the brunt of the Nazi war machine for another year.

> Roosevelt and Churchill announced that they would accept nothing less than the "unconditional surrender" of the Axis powers, ruling out peace negotiations.

On July 10, 1943, combined American and British amphibious forces landed 160,000 troops in Sicily. The badly equipped Italian defenders quickly withdrew to the mainland. Soon afterward, Mussolini was deposed in Italy, ending the reign of Italian fascism. Quickly, the Allies invaded the mainland, and the Italian government surrendered unconditionally. The Germans responded by rushing reinforcements to Italy and seizing control of Rome, turning the Allies' Italian campaign into a series of battles to liberate Italy from German occupation.

German troops dug into strong fortifications and fought to defend every inch of Italy's rugged terrain. Only after a long, deadly, and frustrating campaign up the Italian peninsula did the Allies finally liberate Rome in June 1944. Allied forces continued to push into northern Italy against stubborn German defenses for the remainder of the war, making the Italian campaign the war's deadliest for American infantrymen. One soldier wrote that his buddies "died like butchered swine."

The Italian campaign occupied numerous German divisions that Hitler might otherwise have deployed on the Russian front, but no German forces were actually taken away from the ongoing attack against the Soviet Union. Stalin denounced the Allies' Italian campaign because it left "the Soviet Army, which is fighting not only for its country, but also for its Allies, to do the job alone, almost single-handed." The

Italian campaign exacted a high cost from the Americans and British, bringing the Nazis no closer to surrender and consuming men and materiel that might have been reserved for a second front in France.

REVIEW   How did the United States seek to counter the Japanese in the Pacific and the Germans in Europe?

The Wartime Home Front

The war effort mobilized Americans as never before. Factories strained to churn out ever more bombs, bullets, tanks, ships, and airplanes, which workers rushed to assemble, leaving farms and small towns to congregate in cities. Women took

Relief Column, Tunisia, North Africa

This eyewitness painting depicts a column of American soldiers moving toward the front lines to relieve exhausted and wounded comrades returning from battle in Tunisia in 1943. The artist, Peter Sanfilippo, a twenty-three-year-old private from Brooklyn, New York, served in an artillery unit that fought in North Africa, Sicily, and Italy. Sanfilippo wrote that the "arrival of a relief column of fresh soldiers . . . reassures a battered man's faith in his fellow comrades. The unnerved and wounded are resurrected in spirit to thrive, and thus persevere into a new day." While Sanfilippo was in London awaiting deployment to North Africa, he bought the watercolors he used to make this and other paintings. He said that painting allowed him to "maintain a mental toughness that would defy the savagery of war's violence. When creating, a peaceful and serene mind prevails. The horrors of war shall not overtake me."

Peter Sanfilippo/Veterans History Project, Library of Congress, Institute on World War II and the Human Experience, Florida State University, Tallahassee, FL.

jobs with wrenches and welding torches, boosting the nation's workforce and fraying traditional notions that a woman's place was in the home rather than on the assembly line. Despite rationing and shortages, unprecedented government expenditures for war production brought prosperity to many Americans after years of depression-era poverty (Figure 25.1). Although Americans in uniform risked their lives on battlefields in Europe and Asia, Americans on the U.S. mainland enjoyed complete immunity from foreign attack—in sharp contrast to their Soviet and British allies. The wartime ideology of human rights provided justification for the many sacrifices Americans were required to make in support of the military effort. It also established a standard of basic human equality that became a potent weapon in the campaign for equal rights at home and against the horrifying atrocities of the Holocaust perpetrated by the Nazis.

Women and Families, Guns and Butter

Millions of American women gladly left home toting a lunch pail and changed into overalls and work gloves to take their places on assembly

Female Defense Worker
The war effort brought people and activities together in unlikely ways, leading to unexpected outcomes. This photo appearing in the army magazine *Yank* sought to boost morale by presenting a defense worker as pinup girl. No one could know that the young propeller technician, nineteen-year-old Norma Jean Baker Dougherty, would later remake herself as the glamorous movie star Marilyn Monroe.
David Conover Images; © Norma Jean Enterprises, a division of 733548 Ontario Limited.

FIGURE 25.1   World War II and the Economy, 1942–1945
War mobilization sent employment and union membership soaring. Women found employment in all sectors of the economy, including heavy industry. Although they lost many jobs in heavy industry after the war, they continued to participate in the workforce in increased numbers.

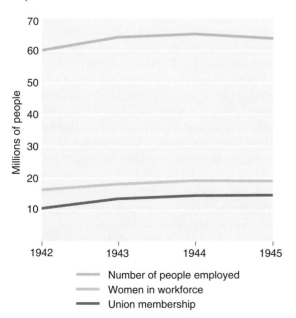

lines in defense industries. At the start of the war, about a quarter of adult women worked outside the home, most as teachers, nurses, social workers, or domestic servants. Few women worked in factories, except for textile mills and sewing industries, because employers and male workers often discriminated against them. But wartime mobilization of the economy and the siphoning of millions of men into the armed forces left factories begging for women workers.

Government advertisements urged women to take industrial jobs by assuring them that their household chores had prepared them for work on the "Victory Line." One billboard proclaimed, "If you've sewed on buttons, or made buttonholes, on a [sewing] machine, you can learn to do spot welding on airplane parts. . . . If you've followed recipes exactly in making cakes, you can learn to load a shell." Millions of women responded, and by the end of the war, women working outside the home numbered 18 million, 50 percent more than in 1939. Contributing to the war effort also paid off in wages that averaged

Patriotic Women on the Home Front

In this cover from the *Saturday Evening Post*, illustrator Norman Rockwell depicts the many contributions to the war effort made by American women. Overburdened with old and new responsibilities, the woman rolls up her sleeves, leans forward, and strides into the fray with determination.

READING THE IMAGE: According to the illustration, what jobs does this patriotic woman have? To what degree has the woman compromised her femininity, if at all? **CONNECTIONS:** What important contributions of women to the war effort did Rockwell fail to capture in this illustration? How might American women have responded to this cover in September 1943?

FOR MORE HELP ANALYZING THIS IMAGE, see the visual activity for this chapter in the Online Study Guide at bedfordstmartins.com/roark.

$31 for a forty-eight-hour week, more than the typical steelworker earned in 1941. A Kentucky woman remembered her job at a munitions plant, where she earned "the fabulous sum of $32 a week. To us it was an absolute miracle. Before that, we made nothing." Although men got paid an average of $54 for comparable wartime work, women accepted the pay differential and welcomed their chance to earn wages and help win the war at the same time.

The majority of married women remained at home, occupied with domestic chores and child care. But they, too, supported the war effort, planting Victory Gardens to provide homegrown vegetables, saving tin cans and newspapers for recycling into war materials, and hoarding pennies and nickels to buy war bonds. Many families scrimped to cope with the 30 percent inflation during the war, but families supported by men and women in manufacturing industries enjoyed wages that grew twice as fast as inflation.

The war influenced how all families spent their earnings. Buying a new washing machine or car was out of the question, since factories that used to build them now made military goods. Many other consumer goods—such as tires, gasoline, shoes, and meat—were rationed at home to meet military needs overseas. But most Americans had more money in their pockets than ever before, and they readily found things to spend it on, including movie tickets, cosmetics, and music recordings. Spending for personal consumption rose by 12 percent during the war.

The wartime prosperity and abundance enjoyed by most Americans contrasted with the experiences of their hard-pressed allies. Personal consumption fell by 22 percent in Britain, and food output plummeted to just one-third of prewar levels in the Soviet Union, creating widespread hunger and even starvation. Few went hungry in the United States. New Deal restraints on agricultural production were lifted, and farm output grew by 25 percent each year during the war, providing an astonishing cornucopia of food to be exported to the Allies.

The Double V Campaign

Fighting against Nazi Germany and its ideology of Aryan racial supremacy, Americans were confronted with the extensive racial prejudice in their own country. Roosevelt declared that black Americans were in the war "not only to defend America but . . . to establish a universal freedom under which a new basis of security and prosperity can be established for all—regardless of station, race, or creed." The *Pittsburgh Courier*, a leading black newspaper, asserted that the wartime emergency called for a "Double V" campaign seeking "victory over our enemies at home and victory over our enemies on the battlefields abroad." It was time, the *Courier* proclaimed, "to persuade, embarrass, compel and shame our government and our nation . . . into a more enlightened attitude."

In 1941, black organizations demanded that the federal government require companies receiving defense contracts to integrate their workforces. A. Philip Randolph, head of the Brotherhood of Sleeping Car Porters, promised that 100,000 African American marchers would descend on Washington if the president did not eliminate discrimination in defense industries. Roosevelt decided to risk offending his white allies in the South and in unions and issued Executive Order 8802 in mid-1941. It authorized the Committee on Fair Employment Practices to investigate and prevent racial discrimination in employment. Civil rights champions hailed the act, and Randolph triumphantly called off the march.

Progress came slowly, however. In 1940, nine out of ten black Americans lived below the federal poverty line, and those who worked earned an average of 39 percent of whites' wages. In search of better jobs and living conditions, 5.5 million black Americans migrated from the South to centers of industrial production in the North and West, making a majority of African Americans city dwellers for the first time in U.S. history. Many discovered that unskilled jobs were available but that unions and employers often barred blacks from skilled trades. At least eighteen major unions—including the machinists, ironworkers, shipbuilders, and railway workers—explicitly prohibited black members. Severe labor shortages and government fair employment standards opened assembly-line jobs in defense plants to African Americans, causing black unemployment to drop by 80 percent during the war. But more jobs did not mean equal pay for blacks. The average income of black families rose during the war, but by the end of the conflict, it still stood at only half of what white families earned.

Blacks' migration to defense jobs intensified racial antagonisms, which boiled over in the hot summer of 1943, when 242 race riots erupted in 47 cities. In the "zoot suit riots" in Los Angeles, hundreds of white servicemen, claiming they were punishing draft dodgers, chased and beat young Mexican American men who dressed in distinctive broad-shouldered, peg-legged zoot suits. The worst mayhem occurred in Detroit, where a long-simmering conflict between whites and blacks over racially segregated housing ignited into a race war. Whites with clubs smashed through black neighborhoods, and blacks retaliated by destroying and looting white-owned businesses. In two days of violence, twenty-five blacks and nine whites were killed, and scores more were injured.

Racial violence created the impetus for the Double V campaign, officially supported by the National Association for the Advancement of Colored People (NAACP), which asserted black Americans' demands for the rights and privileges enjoyed by all other Americans—demands reinforced by the Allies' wartime ideology of freedom and democracy. While the NAACP focused on court challenges to segregation, a new organization founded in 1942, the Congress of Racial Equality (CORE), organized picketing and sit-ins against **Jim Crow** restaurants and theaters. The Double V campaign greatly expanded membership in the NAACP but achieved only limited success against racial discrimination during the war.

> It was time, the *Pittsburgh Courier*, a leading black newspaper, proclaimed, "to persuade, embarrass, compel and shame our government and our nation . . . into a more enlightened attitude."

Wartime Politics and the 1944 Election

Americans rallied around the war effort in unprecedented unity. Despite the consensus on war aims, the strains and stresses of the nation's massive wartime mobilization made it difficult for Roosevelt to maintain his political coalition. Whites often resented blacks who migrated to northern cities, took jobs, and made themselves at home. Many Americans complained about government price controls and the rationing of scarce goods while the war dragged on. Military service overseas kept many Democratic voters from casting ballots in the 1942 congressional elections, and the low turnout helped Republicans make gains in Congress.

Republicans seized the opportunity to roll back New Deal reforms. A **conservative** coalition of Republicans and southern Democrats succeeded in abolishing several New Deal agencies in 1942 and 1943, including the Work Projects Administration and the Civilian Conservation Corps. But the Roosevelt administration fought back. Congress guaranteed absentee ballots for service members, strengthening Democrats at the polls in 1944.

In June 1944, Congress unanimously approved the landmark GI Bill of Rights, promising to give veterans government funds for education, housing, and health care and to provide loans to help them start businesses and buy homes. The GI Bill put the financial resources of the federal government behind the abstract goals of freedom and democracy for which veterans were fighting, and it empowered millions of GIs to better themselves and their families after the war. (See chapter 26, "Seeking the American Promise," page 966.)

After twelve turbulent years in the White House, Roosevelt was exhausted and gravely ill with heart disease, but he was determined to remain president until the war ended. "All that is within me cries out to go back to my home on the Hudson River," he declared. "But as a good soldier . . . I will accept and serve" if reelected president. Roosevelt's poor health made the selection of a vice presidential candidate unusually important. Convinced that many Americans had soured on **liberal** reform, Roosevelt chose Senator Harry S. Truman of Missouri as his running mate. A reliable party man from a southern border state, Truman satisfied urban Democratic leaders while not worrying white southerners who were nervous about challenges to racial segregation.

> "All that is within me cries out to go back to my home on the Hudson River," Roosevelt declared. "But as a good soldier . . . I will accept and serve" if re-elected president.

The Republicans, confident of a strong conservative upsurge in the nation, nominated as their presidential candidate the governor of New York, Thomas E. Dewey, who had made his reputation as a tough crime fighter. In the 1944 presidential campaign, Roosevelt's failing health alarmed many observers, but his frailty was outweighed by Americans' unwillingness to change presidents in the midst of the war and by Dewey's failure to persuade most voters that the New Deal was a creeping **socialist** menace. Voters gave Roosevelt a 53.5 percent majority, his narrowest presidential victory, ensuring his continued leadership as Dr. Win-the-War.

Reaction to the Holocaust

The political crosscurrents in the United States were tame in comparison with the Holocaust, Hitler's vicious campaign to exterminate the Jews. Since the 1930s, the Nazis had persecuted the Jews in Germany and every German-occupied territory, causing many Jews to seek asylum beyond Hitler's reach. (See "Beyond America's Borders," page 930.) Millions of Jews from southern and eastern Europe had arrived in the United States during the late nineteenth and early twentieth centuries. But America's immigration restriction laws of the 1920s had slammed the door shut, allowing in only a small number of immigrants from each nation. Some Americans sought to make exceptions to the quotas for Jews fleeing Nazi persecution, but many Americans resisted. Roosevelt sympathized with the refugees' pleas for help, but he did not want to jeopardize his foreign policy or offend American voters. After Hitler's Anschluss in 1938, thousands of Austrian Jews sought to immigrate to the United States, but 82 percent of Americans opposed admitting them, and they were turned away. Roosevelt tried to persuade countries in Latin America and Africa to accept Jewish refugees, but none would do so. In 1939, friends of the refugees introduced legislation that would have granted asylum to 20,000 German refugee children, most of them Jewish. The bill was defeated in Congress, in large measure because of American anti-Semitism. In 1940, refugee British children—few of whom were Jewish—were welcomed into the United States without delay.

In 1942, numerous reports that Hitler was implementing a "final solution" filtered out of German-occupied Europe. Jews and other "undesirables"—such as Gypsies, religious and political dissenters, and homosexuals—were being sent to concentration camps. Old people, children, and others deemed too weak to work were systematically slaughtered and cremated, while the able-bodied were put to work at slave labor until they died of starvation and abuse. Despite such reports, skeptical U.S. State Department officials refused to grant asylum to Jewish refugees. The U.S. Office of War Information worried that charging Germans with crimes against humanity might incite them to greater resistance and prolong the war. Most Americans, including top officials, believed that reports of the killing camps were exaggerated. Only 152,000 of Europe's millions of Jews managed to gain refuge in the United States prior to America's entry into the war. Afterward, the number of refugees admitted dropped steadily, to just 2,400 by 1944. Those still trapped in Europe could only hope for rescue by the Allied armies.

Desperate to stem the killing, the World Jewish Congress appealed to the Allies to bomb the death camps and the railroad tracks leading to them in order to hamper the killing and block further shipments of victims. The proposals to bomb the camps got no farther than the desks of Assistant Secretary of War John J. McCloy in

The Holocaust, 1933–1945

SWEDEN
DENMARK
LITH.
East Prussia
GERMANY
POLAND
CZECHOSLOVAKIA
SWITZ.   AUSTRIA   HUNGARY
ITALY
YUGOSLAVIA

• Principal German concentration and extermination camp

Washington and Foreign Secretary Anthony Eden in London. Intent on achieving military victory as soon as possible, they repeatedly turned down bombing requests, arguing that the air forces could not spare resources from their military missions. There was an element of moral indifference as well. An eloquent plea from Jewish leader Chaim Weizmann elicited a rejection letter from Eden's Foreign Office that ended with a tragic understatement: "I understand that this decision will be a disappointment to you, but be sure that the matter was considered exhaustively."

The nightmare of the Holocaust was all too real. When Russian troops arrived at Auschwitz in Poland in February 1945, they found emaciated prisoners, skeletal corpses, gas chambers, pits filled with human ashes, and loot the Nazis had stripped from the dead, including hair, gold fillings, and false teeth. At last, the truth about the Holocaust began to be known beyond the Germans who had perpetrated and tolerated these atrocities and the men, women, and children who had succumbed to the genocide. By then, it was too late for the 9 million victims—mostly Jews—of the Nazis' crimes against humanity.

REVIEW How did the war influence American society?

Mass Execution of Jewish Women and Children
On October 14, 1942, Jewish women and children from the village of Mizocz in present-day Ukraine were herded into a ravine, forced to undress and lie facedown, and then shot at point-blank range by German police. This rare photograph, taken by one of the authorities at the scene, shows German officers killing the women who survived the initial gunfire. Throughout the war, Germans routinely murdered defenseless people they considered subhuman, especially on the eastern front. To centralize such executions, the Nazis built death camps, where they systematically slaughtered millions of Jews and other "undesirables." Taken together, such atrocities amounted to genocide, which became known as the Holocaust.
United States Holocaust Memorial Museum.

Toward Unconditional Surrender

By February 1943, Soviet defenders had finally defeated the massive German offensive against Stalingrad, turning the tide of the war in Europe. After gargantuan sacrifices in fighting that had lasted for eighteen months and killed more than 95 percent of the Russian soldiers and noncommissioned officers engaged at Stalingrad, the Red Army forced Hitler's Wehrmacht to turn back toward the west. Now the Soviets and their Western allies faced the task of driving the Nazis out of eastern and western Europe and forcing them to surrender. It was long past time, Stalin proclaimed, for Britain and the United States to open a second front in France, but that offensive was postponed for more than a year after the Red Army's victory at Stalingrad. In the Pacific, the Allies had halted the expansion of the Japanese empire but now had the deadly task of dislodging Japanese

defenders from the far-flung outposts they still occupied. Allied military planners devised a strategy to annihilate Axis resistance by taking advantage of America's industrial superiority.

From Bombing Raids to Berlin

While the Allied campaigns in North Africa and Italy were under way, British and American pilots flew bombing missions from England to the continent as an airborne substitute for the delayed second front on the ground. During night raids, British bombers targeted general areas, hoping to hit civilians, create terror, and undermine morale. Beginning with Paul Tibbets's flight in August 1942, American pilots flew heavily armored B-17s from English airfields in daytime raids on industrial targets vital for the German war machine, especially oil refineries and ball bearing factories.

German air defenses took a fearsome toll on Allied pilots and aircraft. In 1943, two-thirds of American airmen did not survive to complete

Nazi Anti-Semitism and the Atomic Bomb

During the 1930s, Jewish physicists fled Adolf Hitler's fanatical anti-Semitic persecutions and came to the United States, where they played a leading role in the research and development of the atomic bomb. In this way, Nazi anti-Semitism contributed to making the United States the first atomic power.

One of Germany's greatest scientists, Albert Einstein, won the Nobel Prize for physics in 1921. Among other things, Einstein's work demonstrated that the nuclei of atoms of physical matter stored almost inconceivable quantities of energy. A fellow scientist praised Einstein's discoveries as "the greatest achievements in the history of human thought."

Einstein was born in Germany in 1879, grew up in Munich, and by 1914 headed the Kaiser Wilhelm Institute for Physics in Berlin. But he was a Jew, and his ideas were ridiculed by German anti-Semites. A German physicist who had won the Nobel Prize in 1905 attacked Einstein for his "Jewish nonsense," which was "hostile to the German spirit." Einstein wrote to a friend, "Anti-Semitism is strong here [in Berlin] and political reaction is violent." In

1922, anti-Semitic extremists assassinated the German foreign minister, Walter Rathenau, a Jewish chemist and friend of Einstein's. Einstein's associates warned him that he, too, was targeted for assassination.

By 1921, when Einstein won the Nobel Prize, Adolf Hitler, a former corporal in the German infantry, had already organized the Nazi Party and recruited a large private army to intimidate his opponents—Jews foremost among them. Jailed in 1923 for attempting to overthrow the German government, Hitler wrote his Nazi manifesto, *Mein Kampf*, which proclaimed that Jews and Communists had betrayed Germany in the First World War and needed to be eliminated. Jews, Hitler insisted, were "a foreign people," "inferior beings," the "personification of the devil," "a race of dialectical liars," "parasites," and "eternal bloodsuckers," who had the "clear aim of ruining the . . . white race." Hitler's rantings attracted a huge audience in Germany, and his personal Nazi army, which numbered 400,000 by 1933, terrorized and murdered anyone who got in the way.

In January 1933, just weeks before Franklin Roosevelt's inaugura-

tion as president of the United States, Hitler became chancellor of Germany on a tidal wave of popular support for his Nazi Party. Within months, he abolished freedom of speech and assembly, outlawed all political opposition, and exercised absolute dictatorial power. On April 7, Hitler announced the Law for the Restoration of the Professional Civil Service, which stipulated that "civil servants of non-Aryan descent must retire." A non-Aryan was defined as any person "descended from non-Aryan, especially Jewish, parents or grandparents." The law meant that scientists of Jewish descent who worked for state institutions, including universities, no longer had jobs. About 1,600 intellectuals in Germany immediately lost their livelihood and their future in Hitler's Reich. Among them were about a quarter of the physicists in Germany, including Einstein and ten other Nobel Prize winners. The Nazis' anti-Semitism laws forced many leading scientists to leave Germany. Between 1933 and 1941, Einstein and about 100 other Jewish physicists joined hundreds of Jewish intellectuals in an exodus from Nazi Germany to the safety of the United States.

The refugee physicists scrambled to find positions at American universities and research institutes that would allow them to continue their studies. The accelerating pace of research in physics during the 1930s raised the possibility that a way might

their twenty-five-mission tours of duty. In all, 85,000 American airmen were killed in the skies over Europe. Many others were shot down and held as prisoners of war. B-17 copilot Corbin B. Willis Jr. was shot down over Germany in 1944, and four of his five crew members who survived the crash were murdered by German civilians

outraged by repeated Allied bombings. Willis, who spent the remainder of the war in prisoner of war camps, recalled, "you wouldn't really expect them to greet you with roses—so I understood their feeling—I'm sure my own family would be out there swinging and hitting in like circumstances." In February 1944, the arrival of exist to release the phenomenal energy bottled up in atomic nuclei, perhaps even to create a superbomb. Einstein and other scientists considered that possibility remote. But many worried that if scientists loyal to Germany discovered a way to harness nuclear energy, Hitler would have the power to spread Nazi terror throughout the world.

The refugee physicists asked Einstein to write a letter to President Roosevelt explaining the military and political threats posed by the latest research in nuclear physics. In early October 1939, as Hitler's blitzkreig swept through Poland, Roosevelt received Einstein's letter and immediately grasped the central point, exclaiming, "What you are after is to see that the Nazis don't blow us up." Roosevelt quickly convened a small group of distinguished American scientists, who convinced the president to authorize an all-out effort to learn whether an atomic bomb could be built and, if so, to build it. Only weeks before the Japanese attack on Pearl Harbor, Roosevelt decided to launch the Manhattan Project, the top-secret atomic bomb program.

Leading scientists from the United States and Britain responded to the government's appeal: "No matter what you do with the rest of your life, nothing will be as important to the future of the World as your work on this Project right now." Many of the most creative, productive, and irreplaceable scientists involved in the Manhattan Project were physicists who had fled Nazi Germany. Their efforts had brought the possibility of an atomic bomb to Roosevelt's attention. Having personally experienced Nazi anti-Semitism, they understood what was at stake— a world in which either Hitler had the atomic bomb or his enemies did.

In the end, Hitler's scientists failed to develop an atomic bomb, and Germany surrendered before the American bomb was ready to go. But the Manhattan Project succeeded, as Paul Tibbets proved over Hiroshima, Japan, on August 6, 1945. After the war, Leo Szilard, a leader among the refugee physicists, remarked, "If Congress knew the true history of the atomic energy project . . . it would create a special medal to be given to meddling foreigners for distinguished services."

Einstein Becomes a U.S. Citizen

Nazi anti-Semitism caused Albert Einstein to renounce his German citizenship, immigrate to the United States, and—in the 1940 naturalization ceremony recorded in this photo—officially become an American citizen. He is joined here by his secretary, Helen Dukas (right), and his stepdaughter, Margot Einstein (left).

Courtesy, American Institute of Physics Emilio Segré Visual Archives/Brown Brothers.

America's durable and deadly P-51 Mustang fighter gave Allied bombers superior protection. The Mustangs slowly began to sweep the Luftwaffe from the skies, allowing bombers to penetrate deep into Germany and pound civilian and military targets around the clock. In April 1944, the Allies began to target bridges and railroads in northwestern Europe in preparation for their cross-Channel invasion.

In November 1943, Churchill, Roosevelt, and Stalin met in Teheran to discuss wartime strategy and the second front. Roosevelt conceded to Stalin that the Soviet Union would exercise de facto control of the eastern European countries that the Red

D Day Invasion
"Taxi to Hell—and Back" is what Robert Sargent called his photograph of the D Day invasion of Normandy on June 6, 1944. Amid a dense fleet of landing craft, men lucky enough to have made it through rough seas and enemy fire struggle onto the beach to open a second front in Europe. Most of the soldiers in this first wave were cut down by enemy fire from the cliffs beyond the beach.
Library of Congress.

Army occupied as it rolled back the still-potent German Wehrmacht. Stalin agreed to enter the war against Japan once Germany finally surrendered, in effect promising to open a second front in the Pacific theater. Roosevelt and Churchill promised that they would at last launch a massive second-front assault in northern France. Code-named Overlord, the offensive was scheduled to begin in May 1944 with the combined manpower of 4 million Americans massed in England, along with fourteen divisions from Britain, three from Canada, and one each from Poland and France.

General Eisenhower was assigned overall command of Allied forces and stockpiled mountains of military supplies in England. German defenders, directed by General Erwin Rommel, fortified the cliffs and mined the beaches of north-western France. But the huge deployment of Hitler's armies in the east, which were trying to halt the Red Army's westward offensive, left too few German troops to stop the millions of Allied soldiers waiting to attack. More decisive, years of Allied air raids had decimated the German Luftwaffe, which could send aloft only 300 fighter planes against 12,000 Allied aircraft.

Diversionary bombing and false radio messages about armies that did not exist encouraged the Germans to expect an Allied invasion where the English Channel is narrowest. The actual invasion site was three hundred miles away, on the beaches of Normandy (Map 25.4). After frustrating delays caused by stormy weather, Eisenhower launched the largest amphibious assault in world history on D Day, June 6, 1944.

MAP 25.4 The European Theater of World War II, 1942–1945
The Russian reversal of the German offensive at Stalingrad and Leningrad, combined with Allied landings in North Africa and Normandy, trapped Germany in a closing vise of Allied armies on all sides.

READING THE MAP: By November 1942, which nations or parts of nations in the European theater were under Axis control? Which had been absorbed by the Axis powers before the war? Which nations remained neutral? Which ones were affiliated with the Allies?

CONNECTIONS: What were the three fronts in the European theater? When did the Allies initiate actions on each front, and why did Churchill, Stalin, and Roosevelt disagree on the timing of the opening of these fronts?

FOR MORE HELP ANALYZING THIS MAP, see the map activity for this chapter in the Online Study Guide at
bedfordstmartins.com/roark.

Rough seas and deadly fire from German machine guns slowed the assault, but Allied soldiers finally succeeded in securing the beachhead. As naval officer Tracy Sugarman recalled, "What I thought were piles of cordwood [on the beach] I later learned were the bodies of 2,500 men killed by withering fire from the Nazi gun emplacements." Sugarman reported that he and the other GIs who made the landing "were exhausted and we were exultant. We had survived D-Day!"

Within a week, a flood of soldiers, tanks, and other military equipment swamped the Normandy beaches and propelled Allied forces toward Germany. On August 25, the Allies liberated Paris from four years of Nazi occupation. As the giant pincers of the Allied and Soviet armies closed on Germany in December 1944, Hitler ordered a counterattack to capture the Allies' essential supply port at Antwerp, Belgium. In the Battle of the Bulge (December 16, 1944, to January 31, 1945), as the Allies termed it, German forces drove fifty-five miles into Allied lines before being stopped at Bastogne. More than 70,000 Allied soldiers were killed, including

> Naval officer Tracy Sugarman recalled, "What I thought were piles of cordwood [on the beach] I later learned were the bodies of 2,500 men killed by withering fire from the Nazi gun emplacements."

Yalta Conference

In February 1945, U.S. president Franklin Roosevelt (middle) and British prime minister Winston Churchill (left) met with Russian leader Joseph Stalin (right) at the Black Sea resort of Yalta to plan the postwar reconstruction of Europe. Roosevelt, near the end of his life, and Churchill, soon to suffer a reelection defeat, look weary next to the resolute "Man of Steel." Controversy would later arise over whether a stronger stand by the American and British leaders could have prevented the Soviet Union from imposing Communist rule on eastern Europe.

U.S. Army.

more Americans than in any other battle of the war. The Nazis lost more than 100,000 men and hundreds of tanks, fatally depleting Hitler's reserves. Army lieutenant Alvin Dickson observed the macabre scene of "all the bodies . . . frozen stiff. . . . Many dead Americans and Germans are lying beneath the snow now . . . [many with] the ring finger . . . cut off in order to get the ring."

In February 1945, while Allied armies relentlessly pushed German forces backward, Churchill, Stalin, and Roosevelt met secretly at Yalta, a Russian resort town on the Black Sea, to discuss their plans for the postwar world. Seriously ill and noticeably frail, Roosevelt managed to secure Stalin's promise to permit votes of self-determination in the eastern European countries occupied by the Red Army. The Allies pledged to support Chiang Kai-shek as the leader of China. The Soviet Union obtained a role in the postwar governments of Korea and Manchuria in exchange for entering the war against Japan after the defeat of Germany.

The "Big Three" also agreed on the creation of a new international peacekeeping organization, the United Nations (UN). All nations would have a place in the UN General Assembly, but the Security Council would wield decisive power, and its permanent representatives from the Allied powers—China, France, Great Britain, the Soviet Union, and the United States—would possess a veto over UN actions. The American response to the creation of the UN reflected the triumph of internationalism during the nation's mobilization for war. The Senate ratified the United Nations Charter in July 1945 by a vote of 89 to 2.

While Allied armies sped toward Berlin, Allied warplanes dropped more bombs after D Day than in all the previous European bombing raids combined. In February 1945, Allied bombers rained a firestorm of death and destruction on Berlin and Dresden, killing 60,000 civilians. By April 11, Allied armies sweeping in from the west reached the banks of the Elbe River, the agreed-upon rendezvous with the Red Army, and paused while the Soviets smashed into Berlin. In three weeks of vicious house-to-house fighting, the Red Army captured Berlin on May 2. Hitler had committed suicide on April 30, and the provisional German government surrendered unconditionally on May 7. The war in Europe was finally over, with the sacrifice of 135,576 American soldiers, nearly 250,000 British troops, and 9 million Russian combatants. (See "Historical Question," page 936.)

Roosevelt did not live to witness the end of the war. On April 12, while resting in Warm Springs, Georgia, the president suffered a fatal stroke. Americans grieved for the man who had led them through years of depression and world war, and they worried aloud about his successor, Vice President Harry Truman, who would have to steer the nation to victory over Japan and protect American interests in the postwar world.

The Defeat of Japan

After the punishing defeats in the Coral Sea and at Midway, Japan had to quell renewed resistance on the Asian mainland and to fend off Allied naval and air attacks. In 1943, British and American forces, along with Indian and Chinese allies, launched an offensive against Japanese outposts in southern Asia, pushing through Burma and into China, where the armies of Chiang Kai-shek continued to resist conquest. In the Pacific, Americans and their allies attacked Japanese strongholds by sea, air, and land, moving island by island toward the Japanese homeland (Map 25.5, page 938).

The island-hopping campaign began in August 1942, when American marines landed on Guadalcanal in the southern Pacific. For the next six months, a savage battle raged for control of the strategic area. Finally, during the night of February 8, 1943, Japanese forces withdrew. The terrible losses on both sides indicated to the marines how costly it would be to defeat Japan. After the battle, Joseph Steinbacher, a twenty-one-year-old from Alabama, sailed from San Francisco to New Guinea, where, he recalled, "all the cannon fodder waited to be assigned" to replace the killed and wounded.

In mid-1943, American, Australian, and New Zealand forces launched offensives in New Guinea and the Solomon Islands that gradually secured the South Pacific. In the Central Pacific, amphibious forces conquered the Gilbert and Marshall islands, which served as forward bases for decisive air assaults on the Japanese home islands. As the Allies attacked island after island, Japanese soldiers were ordered to refuse to surrender no matter how hopeless their plight. At Tarawa, a barren coral island of less than three square miles, 3,000 Japanese defenders battled American marines for three days, killing 1,000 Americans and wounding 2,000 until the 17 Japanese survivors finally succumbed. Such fierce Japanese resistance spurred remorseless

Why Did the Allies Win World War II?

Tens of millions of people around the globe contributed to the outcome of World War II. Battlefield and home-front sacrifices, determination, perseverance, resilience, mistakes, and luck combined with brains, courage, leadership, and material resources to bring about the Allied victory. One indispensable factor in the Allied victory was the alliance among the major powers: the United States, Great Britain, and the Soviet Union. Fighting alone, none of the Allies could have prevailed against Nazi Germany. Together, they were able to defeat what had been the strongest military power in the world.

The major Axis nations—Germany and Japan—did almost nothing to help each other. In the Pacific, Japan fought alone against the United States and its other allies, especially Australia and China. Britain and the Soviet Union contributed relatively little to Allied efforts in the Pacific. In Europe, Germany enjoyed the support of Hungary, Romania, Bulgaria, and Italy, but none of these nations had the resources and industrial might to field a fully modern army. As late as August 1942, for example, Italian cavalry on horseback brandished sabers and charged Russian lines bristling with tanks. Germany conscripted tens of thousands of men from the territories they occupied as their armies swept east, but such coerced recruits made poorly motivated soldiers.

In contrast, the Allies had a single galvanizing purpose: to defeat Hitler. That goal focused their atten-

tion on the European theater. The United States devoted only about 15 percent of its effort to the war against Japan; the remaining 85 percent was directed against Germany. Little else united the Allies. Political and ideological differences between the capitalist democracies and a Communist dictatorship produced suspicion and mistrust, fed by Joseph Stalin's alliance with Adolf Hitler between 1939 and 1941. Nonetheless, the Allies collaborated to force the unconditional surrender of Germany.

Three militarily significant consequences of the wartime alliance stand out as decisive ingredients of Allied victory: American material support for Britain and the Soviet Union; American and British bombing campaigns and the D Day invasion of Europe; and the Red Army's success in stopping the eastward advance of the German army at Stalingrad, then relentlessly driving it back to Berlin.

The flood of military supplies that poured out of American factories during the war made Allied victory possible. In total, the United States produced two-thirds of all Allied military equipment. The American auto industry, for example, rapidly converted to war production. By 1944, one Ford plant could assemble the 1.5 million parts of a B-24 bomber in just over an hour and repeat the feat hour after hour, month after month. In addition to shipping hundreds of millions of tons of supplies to Britain and stockpiling equipment for the D Day invasion, the United States sent more than half a million

military vehicles to the Soviet Union, accounting for the bulk of the Red Army's motorized transportation. By 1944, American refineries supplied 90 percent of the Allies' high-octane gasoline, prompting Stalin to raise a toast at the Teheran conference "to the American auto industry and the American oil industry," which met the needs of "this . . . war of engines and octanes." American food shipments provided the equivalent of one meal a day for each Russian soldier. The American canned meat Spam was distributed so widely that Soviet troops called it "The Second Front," a sarcastic reference to the Americans' delay in opening a second front in western Europe.

The British and American bombing campaign against German targets in western Europe served as a crucial second-front surrogate until D Day, and it eventually allowed Allied pilots to rule the skies. The bombing campaign reduced the production of tanks, airplanes, and trucks by more than a third and diverted two-thirds of Germany's aircraft and three-quarters of its antiaircraft weapons from supporting the infantry on the eastern front to protecting German cities from Allied air attacks. In addition, improvements in Allied fighter planes allowed British and American pilots to decimate the Luftwaffe. By D Day, the Allies in the west sent aloft more than 12,000 aircraft against only 300 Nazi warplanes. Similarly, 13,000 Soviet aircraft confronted just 500 German fighter planes in the east. Although both the German civilian population and Allied air crews suffered huge casualties as a result of the air campaign, it decisively aided the Soviets' battle against the Germans on the eastern front.

But neither the bombing campaign nor the mountains of American supplies would have won the war if

МЫ ЗЛОМУ ВРАГУ ВСЕ ОТРЕЖЕМ ПУТИ,
ИЗ ПЕТЛИ, ИЗ ЭТОЙ ЕМУ НЕ УЙТИ!

The Eastern Front and the Allied War Effort

The Red Army captured tens of thousands of German soldiers in the battle of Stalingrad, including those shown here making their way through the ruins of the city in the frigid winter of 1942–43. Conditions in the German army were dire. One German soldier wrote in his diary shortly before his surrender, "The horses have already been eaten. I would eat a cat, they say its meat is tasty. The soldiers look like corpses or lunatics. . . . They no longer take cover from Russian shells; they haven't the strength to walk, run away and hide." The Russian poster shown here illustrates the combined efforts of the Allies, declaring, "We won't let the evil enemy escape the noose. He will not evade it."

Photo: © Bettmann/Corbis; Poster: Museum of World War II, Natick, MA.

READING THE IMAGE: What does the depiction of Hitler on the Russian poster suggest about his leadership and character?
CONNECTIONS: What does the poster suggest about the importance of the alliance between the major Allied powers?

FOR MORE HELP ANALYZING THIS IMAGE, see the visual activity for this chapter in the Online Study Guide at
bedfordstmartins.com/roark.

the Soviet Union had not stopped the seemingly unstoppable advance of the German Wehrmacht in the east. Within six months of Hitler's surprise attack on the Soviet Union in June 1941, Stalin's army had lost 4 million soldiers and nearly all its tanks and airplanes, and German armies threatened Moscow. President Franklin Roosevelt's military advisers expected Stalin to capitulate within two or three months. Instead, the Red Army regrouped and managed to halt the Germans' eastward advance by early 1943.

This amazing turn of events required colossal sacrifices by the people of the Soviet Union. As the German army swept east during 1941, Russians frantically dismantled more than 1,500 major industrial plants about to be captured by the Nazis, shipped them east of the Ural Mountains, and reassembled them there. They also built new plants and soon began producing thousands of new tanks, aircraft, and artillery to rearm the Soviet military. Through sheer hard work, the productivity of Soviet war industries more than doubled during the war (see "Global Comparison," page 920). Meanwhile, food production plummeted, allowing the average Russian only one-fourth the amount of food available to the average German. Nearly every able-bodied man not working in a vital war industry was conscripted into the Red Army, which finally crushed the German attackers in the long, merciless battle of Stalingrad and forced the Nazis to begin their retreat west. By the end of the war, about 20 million Soviet civilians and soldiers had been killed, casualties that dwarfed the losses of the other Allies. For every American killed during the war, 45 Soviets died. No contribution to Allied victory was more important than the monumental success of the Soviet Union on the eastern front.

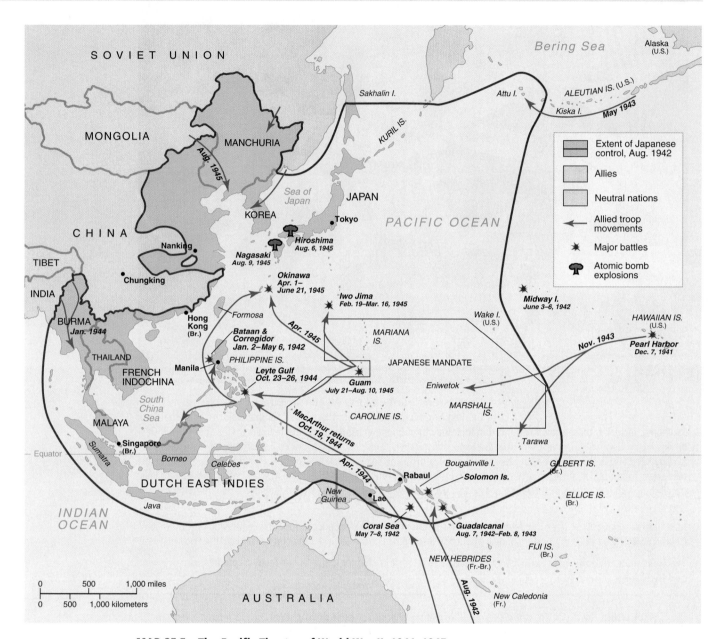

MAP 25.5   The Pacific Theater of World War II, 1941–1945

To drive the Japanese from their far-flung empire, the Allies launched two combined naval and military offensives—one to recapture the Philippines and then attack Japanese forces in China, the other to hop from island to island in the Central Pacific toward the Japanese mainland.

READING THE MAP: What was the extent of Japanese control up until August 1942? Which nations in the Pacific theater sided with the Allies? Which nations remained neutral?

CONNECTIONS: Describe the economic and military motivations behind Japanese domination of the region. How and when did they achieve this dominance? Judging from this map, what strategic and geographic concerns might immediately have prompted Truman and his advisers to consider using the atomic bomb against Japan?

FOR MORE HELP ANALYZING THIS MAP, see the map activity for this chapter in the Online Study Guide at bedfordstmartins.com/roark.

Allied attacks on Japanese-occupied islands, usually begun with air and naval bombardment, followed by amphibious landings by marines and grinding, inch-by-inch combat to root Japanese fighters out of bunkers and caves with grenades, flamethrowers, and anything else at hand.

While the island-hopping campaign kept pressure on Japanese forces, the Allies invaded the Philippines in the fall of 1944. In the four-day Battle of Leyte Gulf, the greatest naval encounter in world history, the American fleet crushed the Japanese armada, clearing the way for Allied victory in the Philippines. While the Philippine campaign was under way, American forces captured two crucial islands—Iwo Jima and Okinawa—from which they planned to launch an attack on the Japanese homeland. To defend Okinawa and prevent the American invaders from getting within close bombing range of their home islands, Japanese leaders ordered thousands of suicide pilots, known as *kamikaze*, to crash their bomb-laden planes into Allied ships. Like airborne torpedoes, kamikaze caused fearsome destruction. But instead of destroying the American fleet, they demolished the last vestige of the Japanese air force. By June 1945, the Japanese were nearly defenseless on the sea and in the air. Still, their leaders prepared to fight to the death for their homeland.

Joseph Steinbacher, now a sergeant, and other troops who had suffered "horrendous" casualties in the Philippines were told by their commanding

Marine Pinned Down on Saipan
More than 100,000 American GIs assaulted the Japanese garrison of 32,000 on Saipan in the Mariana Islands in mid-June 1944. The Japanese fought to the death against overwhelming odds, prolonging the battle for nearly a month and inflicting 14,000 casualties on the Americans. The intensity of the fighting is visible on the face of this marine. More than a thousand Japanese civilians, mostly women and children, rushed to the edge of a 200-foot cliff and committed suicide by leaping onto the rocks below to avoid surrendering. The Japanese defense of Saipan persuaded American military planners that the final assault on the Japanese homeland would cause hundreds of thousands of American casualties.
Marine Corps Photo, National Archives.

Major Campaigns and Battles of World War II, 1939–1945

September 1, 1939	Germany attacks Poland.
September 3, 1939	Britain and France declare war on Germany.
April 1940	Germany attacks Denmark and Norway.
May 1940	Germany invades Netherlands, Belgium, Luxembourg, and France.
June 1940	Italy joins Germany in war against Allies.
June–November 1940	Battle of Britain.
June 22, 1941	Germany invades Soviet Union.
December 7, 1941	Japan attacks Pearl Harbor.
December 8, 1941	U.S. Congress declares war on Japan.
December 11, 1941	Germany and Italy declare war on United States.
January 2–May 6, 1942	Battles of Bataan and Corregidor.
May 7–8, 1942	Battle of the Coral Sea.
June 3–6, 1942	Battle of Midway.
August 1942–February 1943	Battle of Guadalcanal.
August 21, 1942–January 31, 1943	Battle of Stalingrad.
October 23–November 5, 1942	British halt Germans at Battle of El-Alamein.
November 1942–May 1943	Allies mount North African campaign.
July 10, 1943	Allies begin Italian invasion through Sicily.
June 4, 1944	Allies liberate Rome from German occupation.
June 6, 1944	D Day—Allied forces invade Normandy.
August 25, 1944	Allies liberate Paris.
September 12, 1944	Allies enter Germany.
October 23–26, 1944	Battle of Leyte Gulf.
December 16, 1944–January 31, 1945	Battle of the Bulge.
February 19–March 16, 1945	Battle of Iwo Jima.
April 1–June 21, 1945	Battle of Okinawa.
May 2, 1945	Soviet forces capture Berlin.
August 6, 1945	United States drops atomic bomb on Hiroshima.
August 9, 1945	United States drops atomic bomb on Nagasaki.

officer, "Men, in a few short months we are going to invade the island of Kyushu, the southernmost Japanese island. We will be going in on the first wave and are expecting ninety percent casualties the first day. . . . For the few of us left alive [after reinforcements arrive] the war will be over." Steinbacher later recalled his "mental attitude at that moment. I know that I am now a walking dead man and will not have a snowball's chance in hell of making it through the last great battle to conquer the home islands of Japan."

Atomic Warfare

In mid-July 1945, as Allied forces prepared for the final assault on Japan, American scientists tested a secret weapon at an isolated desert site near Los Alamos, New Mexico. In 1942, Roosevelt had authorized the top-secret Manhattan Project to find a way to convert nuclear energy into a superbomb before the Germans added such a weapon to their arsenal. More than 100,000 Americans, led by scientists, engineers, and military officers at Los Alamos, worked frantically to win the fateful race for an atomic bomb. Germany surrendered two and a half months before the test on July 16, 1945, when scientists first witnessed an awesome explosion that sent a mushroom cloud of debris eight miles into the atmosphere.

A delegation of scientists and officials, troubled by the bomb's destructive force, secretly proposed that the United States give a public demonstration of the bomb's cataclysmic power, hoping to persuade Japan's leaders to surrender. With the Japanese incapable of offensive action and blockaded by the Allied fleet, proponents of a demonstration were encouraged because Japanese emissaries were already putting out feelers about peace negotiations. But U.S. government officials quickly rejected such a demonstration: Americans had enough nuclear material for only three bombs, the demonstration bomb might fail to explode, and the Japanese might not surrender even if it did. Also, despite numerous defeats, Japan still had more than 6 million reserves at home, fortified by more than 5,000 kamikaze aircraft stockpiled for a last-ditch defense against the anticipated Allied assault, which U.S. military advisers estimated would cost the lives of at least 250,000 Americans.

President Truman heard about the successful bomb test when he was in Potsdam, Germany,

Hiroshima Bombing
This rare shot taken by a news photographer in Hiroshima immediately after the atomic bomb exploded on August 6, 1945, suggests the shock and incomprehension that survivors later described as their first reactions. On August 9, another atomic bomb created similar devastation in Nagasaki.
UN photo.

negotiating with Stalin about postwar issues. Truman realized that the atomic bomb could hasten the end of the war with Japan, perhaps before the Russians could attack the Japanese in Korea and Manchuria, as Stalin had pledged at Yalta. Within a few months after the defeat of Germany, Truman also recognized that the bomb gave the United States a devastating atomic **monopoly** that could be used to counter Soviet ambitions and advance American interests in the postwar world.

Truman, who had been a commander of combat troops in World War I, saw no reason not to use the atomic bomb against Japan if doing so would save American lives. But first he issued an ultimatum: Japan must surrender unconditionally or face utter ruin. When the Japanese failed to respond by the deadline given, Truman ordered that a bomb be dropped on a Japanese city not already heavily damaged by American raids. On August 6, Colonel Paul Tibbets piloted the *Enola Gay* over Hiroshima and released an atomic bomb, leveling the city and incinerating 78,000 people. Three days later, after the Japanese government still refused to surrender, Tibbets-trained airmen dropped a second atomic bomb on Nagasaki, killing more than 100,000 civilians.

At last, a peace faction took control of the Japanese government, and with American assurance that the emperor could retain his throne after the Allies took over, Japan surrendered on August 14. On a troop ship departing from Europe for what would have been the final assault on Japan, an American soldier spoke for millions of others when he heard the wonderful news that the killing was over: "We are going to grow to adulthood after all."

REVIEW Why did Truman elect to use the atomic bomb against Japan?

Conclusion: Allied Victory and America's Emergence as a Superpower

Shortly after Pearl Harbor, Hitler pronounced America "a decayed country" without "much future"; a country "half Judaized, and the other half Negrified"; a country "where everything is built on the dollar" and bound to fall apart. American mobilization for World War II disproved Hitler's arrogant prophecy, as Paul Tibbets's historic flight dramatized. At a cost of 405,399 American lives, the nation united with its allies to battle Axis aggressors in Europe and Asia and eventually to crush them into unconditional surrender. Almost all Americans believed they had won a "good war" against totalitarian evil. The Allies saved Asia and Europe from enslavement and finally halted the Nazis' genocidal campaign against the Jews and others whom the Nazis considered inferior. To secure human rights and protect the world against future wars, the Roosevelt administration took the lead in creating the United Nations.

Wartime production lifted the nation out of the Great Depression. The gross national product soared to four times what it had been when Roosevelt became president in 1933. Jobs in defense industries eliminated chronic unemployment, provided wages for millions of women workers and African American migrants from southern farms, and boosted Americans' prosperity. Ahead stretched the challenge of maintaining that prosperity while reintegrating millions of uniformed men and women.

By the end of the war, the United States had emerged as a global superpower. Wartime mobilization made the American economy the

strongest in the world, buttressed by the military clout of the nation's nuclear monopoly. Although the war left much of the world a rubble-strewn wasteland, the American mainland had enjoyed immunity from attack. The Japanese occupation of China had left 50 million people without homes and millions more dead, maimed, and orphaned. The German offensive against the Soviet Union had killed more than 20 million Russian soldiers and civilians. Germany and Japan lay in ruins, their economies as shattered as their military forces. The Allies had killed more than 4 million Nazi soldiers and more than 1.2 million Japanese combatants, as well as hundreds of thousands of civilians. But in the gruesome balance sheet of war, the Axis powers had inflicted far more grief, misery, and destruction upon the global victims of their aggression than they had suffered in return.

As the dominant Western nation in the postwar world, the United States asserted its leadership in the reconstruction of Europe while occupying Japan and overseeing its economic and political recovery. America soon confronted new challenges in the tense aftermath of the war, as the Soviets seized political control of eastern Europe, a Communist revolution swept China, and national liberation movements emerged in the colonial empires of Britain and France. The surrender of the Axis powers ended the battles of World War II, but the forces unleashed by the war would shape the United States and the rest of the world for decades to come.

Selected Bibliography

General Works

Max Arthur, ed., *Forgotten Voices of the Second World War: A New History of World War Two in the Words of the Men and Women Who Were There* (2004).

Michael Beschloss, *The Conquerors: Roosevelt, Truman, and the Destruction of Hitler's Germany, 1941–1945* (2002).

Richard Evans, *The Third Reich in Power* (2005).

Niall Ferguson, *The War of the World: Twentieth-Century Conflict and the Descent of the West* (2006).

Thomas Fleming, *The New Dealers' War: Franklin D. Roosevelt and the War within World War II* (2001).

Martin Folly, *The U.S. and World War II: The Awakening Giant* (2002).

Akira Iriye, *The Globalizing of America, 1913–1945* (1995).

David M. Kennedy, *Freedom from Fear: The American People in Depression and War, 1929–1945* (1999).

Paul W. Tibbets Jr., *The Tibbets Story* (1978).

John Toland, *The Rising Sun: The Decline and Fall of the Japanese Empire, 1936–1945* (2001).

Adam Tooze, *The Wages of Destruction: The Making and Breaking of the Nazi Economy* (2006).

Foreign Policy

Tokomo Akami, *Internationalizing the Pacific: The U.S., Japan, and the Institute of Pacific Relations in War and Peace, 1919–1945* (2002).

Elizabeth Borgwardt, *A New Deal for the World: America's Vision for Human Rights* (2005).

Max Paul Friedman, *Nazis and Good Neighbors: The U.S. Campaign against the Germans of Latin America in World War II* (2003).

Tsuyoshi Hasegawa, *Racing the Enemy: Stalin, Truman and the Surrender of Japan* (2005).

J. Robert Moskin, *Mr. Truman's War: The Final Victories of World War II and the Birth of the Postwar World* (2002).

David Reynolds, *From Munich to Pearl Harbor: Roosevelt's America and the Origins of the Second World War* (2001).

Gaddis Smith, *American Diplomacy during the Second World War, 1941–1945* (1985).

Mobilization and the Home Front

Karen Anderson, *Wartime Women: Sex Roles, Family Relations, and the Status of Women during World War II* (1981).

Gerald Astor, *The Right to Fight: A History of African Americans in the Military* (1998).

Jeffrey F. Burton et al., *Confinement and Ethnicity: An Overview of World War II Japanese American Relocation Sites* (2002).

Stephanie A. Carpenter, *On the Farm Front: The Women's Land Army in World War II* (2003).

Roger Daniels, *Concentration Camps: North American Japanese in the United States and Canada during World War II* (1971, 1989).

Daniel R. Ernst and Victor Jew, *Total War and the Law: The American Home Front in World War II* (2002).

Mark Jonathan Harris, Franklin D. Mitchell, and Steve J. Schechter, *The Home Front: America during World War II* (1985).

Susan Hartmann, *The Home Front and Beyond: American Women in the 1940s* (1982).

John W. Jeffries, *Wartime America: The World War II Home Front* (1996).

Wendy Ng, *Japanese American Internment during World War II* (2002).

Military Events

Christopher Browning, *The Origins of the Final Solution: The Evolution of Nazi Jewish Policy* (2004).

John Dower, *War without Mercy: Race and Power in the Pacific War* (1986).

Gerald F. Linderman, *The World within War: America's Combat Experience in World War II* (1997).

Peter Novick, *The Holocaust in American Life* (1999).

Richard Overy, *Why the Allies Won* (1996).

Peter Schrijvers, *The GI War against Japan: American Soldiers in Asia and the Pacific during World War II* (2002).

Thomas W. Zeiler, *Unconditional Defeat: Japan, America and the End of World War II* (2004).

▶ FOR MORE BOOKS ABOUT TOPICS IN THIS CHAPTER, see the Online Bibliography at bedfordstmartins.com/roark.

▶ FOR ADDITIONAL FIRSTHAND ACCOUNTS OF THIS PERIOD, see Chapter 25 in Michael Johnson, ed., *Reading the American Past*, Fourth Edition.

▶ FOR WEB SITES, IMAGES, AND DOCUMENTS RELATED TO TOPICS AND PLACES IN THIS CHAPTER, visit bedfordstmartins.com/makehistory.

REVIEWING THE CHAPTER

Follow these steps to review and strengthen your understanding of the chapter.

STEP 1: *Study the **Key Terms** and **Timeline** to identify the significance of each item listed.*

STEP 2: *Answer the **Review Questions**, drawing on key terms and dates to support your answers.*

STEP 3: *Drawing on the Key Terms, Timeline, and Review Questions, answer the broader **Making Connections** questions.*

KEY TERMS

Who

Paul Tibbets (pp. 903, 929)
Benito Mussolini (pp. 905, 923)
Adolf Hitler (pp. 905, 908)
Chiang Kai-shek (p. 906)
Gerald Nye (p. 907)
Francisco Franco (p. 907)
Neville Chamberlain (p. 909)
Joseph Stalin (p. 909)
Philippe Pétain (p. 910)
Winston Churchill (p. 910)
Wendell Willkie (p. 911)
Hideki Tojo (p. 912)
Emperor Hirohito (p. 912)
Isoroku Yamamoto (p. 921)
Douglas MacArthur (p. 921)
James Doolittle (p. 922)
Chester W. Nimitz (p. 922)
Erwin Rommel (pp. 923, 932)
Dwight D. Eisenhower (pp. 923, 932)
George Patton (p. 923)
A. Philip Randolph (p. 927)

Harry S. Truman (p. 928)
Thomas E. Dewey (p. 928)

What

Enola Gay (pp. 904, 941)
Hiroshima and Nagasaki (pp. 904, 941)
good neighbor policy (p. 905)
Reciprocal Trade Agreements Act (p. 906)
Neutrality Act of 1937 (p. 907)
"Rape of Nanking" (p. 907)
Spanish civil war (p. 907)
Anschluss (p. 908)
Third Reich (p. 908)
Munich agreement (p. 909)
Nazi-Soviet treaty of nonaggression (p. 909)
Maginot Line (p. 909)
Battle of Britain (p. 910)
Lend-Lease Act (p. 911)
Atlantic Charter (p. 912)
Tripartite Pact (p. 912)
Pearl Harbor (p. 912)

U-boats (pp. 914, 923)
internment camps (p. 915)
Korematsu decision (p. 915)
Selective Service Act (p. 918)
War Production Board (p. 919)
Bataan Death March (p. 921)
Battle of Midway (p. 922)
Double V campaign (p. 926)
Committee on Fair Employment Practices (p. 927)
Congress of Racial Equality (CORE) (p. 927)
GI Bill of Rights (p. 927)
Holocaust (p. 928)
Overlord (p. 932)
D Day (p. 932)
Battle of the Bulge (p. 934)
Yalta Conference (p. 934)
United Nations (UN) (p. 935)
Battle of Leyte Gulf (p. 939)
kamikaze (p. 939)
Manhattan Project (p. 940)

TIMELINE

◀**1935–1937** • Congress passes neutrality acts.

1936 • Nazi Germany occupies Rhineland.
• Mussolini conquers Ethiopia.
• Spanish civil war begins.

1937 • Japanese troops capture Nanking.
• Roosevelt introduces his quarantine policy.

1938 • Hitler annexes Austria.
• Munich agreement.

1939 • German troops occupy Czechoslovakia.
• Nazi-Soviet nonaggression pact.
• **September 1.** Germany's attack on Poland begins World War II.

1940 • Germany invades Denmark, Norway, France, Belgium, Luxembourg, and the Netherlands.
• British and French evacuation from Dunkirk.
• Vichy government installed in France.
• Battle of Britain.
• Tripartite Pact signed by Japan, Germany, and Italy.

1941 • Lend-Lease Act.
• **June.** Germany invades Soviet Union.
• **August.** Atlantic Charter issued.
• **December 7.** Japanese attack Pearl Harbor.

REVIEW QUESTIONS

1. Why did isolationism during the 1930s concern Roosevelt? (pp. 904–7)

2. How did Roosevelt attempt to balance American isolationism with the increasingly ominous international scene of the late 1930s? (pp. 908–13)

3. How did the Roosevelt administration mobilize the human and industrial resources necessary to fight a two-front war? (pp. 914–21)

4. How did the United States seek to counter the Japanese in the Pacific and the Germans in Europe? (pp. 921–24)

5. How did the war influence American society? (pp. 924–29)

6. Why did Truman elect to use the atomic bomb against Japan? (pp. 929–42)

MAKING CONNECTIONS

1. Does isolationism bolster or undermine national security and national economic interests? Discuss Roosevelt's evolving answer to this question as revealed in his administration's policies toward Europe. In your answer, consider how other constraints (such as politics, history, and ethics) affected administration policies.

2. World War II brought new prosperity to many Americans. Why did war succeed in creating the full economic recovery that the New Deal had pursued with more limited success? In your answer, discuss both the objectives of specific New Deal economic reforms and the needs of the wartime economy.

3. Japan's attack on Pearl Harbor plunged the United States into war with the Axis powers. How did the United States recover from this attack to play a decisive role in the Allies' victory? Discuss three American military or diplomatic actions and their contribution to the defeat of the Axis powers.

4. As the United States battled racist regimes abroad, the realities of discrimination at home came sharply into focus. How did minorities' contributions to the war effort as soldiers and laborers draw attention to these problems? What were the political implications of these developments? In your answer, consider both grassroots political action and federal policy.

▶ For practice quizzes, a customized study plan, and other study tools, see the Online Study Guide at bedfordstmartins.com/roark.

1942 • Roosevelt authorizes internment of Japanese Americans.
• Japan captures Philippines.
• Congress of Racial Equality (CORE) founded.
• Battles of Coral Sea and Midway.
• Roosevelt authorizes Manhattan Project.
• **November.** U.S. forces invade North Africa.

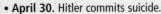

    1943 • Allied leaders demand unconditional surrender of Axis powers.
• Zoot suit riots.
• U.S. and British forces invade Sicily.

        1944 • **June 6.** D Day.

          1945 • **February.** Yalta Conference.
• **April 12.** Roosevelt dies; Vice President Harry Truman becomes president.
• **April 30.** Hitler commits suicide.
• **May 7.** Germany surrenders.
• **July.** United States joins United Nations.
• **August 6.** United States drops atomic bomb on Hiroshima.
• **August 9.** United States drops atomic bomb on Nagasaki.
• **August 14.** Japan surrenders, ending World War II.

COLD WAR COMIC BOOK
Americans barely had time to celebrate the Allied victory in World War II when they perceived a new threat, posed by the Soviet Union. Fear of communism dominated much of postwar American life and politics, even invading popular culture. Four million copies of this comic book, published by a religious organization in 1947, painted a terrifying picture of what would happen to Americans if the Soviets took over the country. Such takeover stories appeared in movies, cartoons, and magazines as well as in other comic books.

Collection of Charles H. Christensen.

26

Cold War Politics in the Truman Years

1945–1953

HEADS TURNED WHEN Congresswoman Helen Gahagan Douglas walked through the U.S. Capitol. From 1945 to 1951, when she represented California's Fourteenth Congressional District in Los Angeles, she had no more than 10 female colleagues at any one time in the 435-member House of Representatives. Not only did she stand out as a woman in a thoroughly masculine institution, but she also drew attention as a tall and strikingly attractive woman, a former Broadway star and opera singer of the 1920s and 1930s. She served in Congress when the fate of the **New Deal** was up for grabs and the nation charted a dramatic new course in foreign policy.

Born in 1900 to affluent parents, Helen Gahagan grew up in Brooklyn, New York. She was drawn to the theater as a child and defied her father to leave Barnard College for the stage after her sophomore year. She quickly won fame on Broadway, where she starred in show after show until she fell in love with one of her leading men, Melvyn Douglas. They married in 1931, and she followed him to Hollywood, where he hoped to advance his movie career. During the 1930s, she bore two children. She continued to appear in theater productions and concerts as well as in one movie, but her career was on the wane.

In contrast to her husband, who held liberal political views from his youth, Douglas abandoned the staunch Republicanism of her parents during the depression, when Franklin D. Roosevelt's leadership captured her admiration. As Hollywood became a hotbed of liberal and radical politics, the Douglases were drawn in. Both were shaken by the anti-Semitism and militarism that they witnessed on a visit to Germany in 1937. "I was overwhelmed by horror and a premonition of disaster," Helen later recalled, vowing never to perform there again and subsequently joining the Anti-Nazi League in California. But migrant workers aroused her greatest passion. Upon hearing of the desperate conditions of tenant farmers moving to California from Oklahoma and other states, she "took [her] first step into politics." Visiting migrant camps, she saw "faces stamped with poverty and despair." "Haunted" by this "human calamity," she agreed to become chair of the John Steinbeck Committee to Aid Migratory Workers.

Douglas's research, speaking, and organizing on behalf of migrant farmworkers brought her to President Roosevelt's attention. She testified before Congress and became a guest at the White House, a friend of Eleanor Roosevelt's, and a campaigner for the president in 1940. In California, she rose fast in party politics, becoming vice chairman of the state Democratic Party and head of the Women's Division. All of these experiences contributed to her

Helen Gahagan Douglas at the Democratic National Convention
Long accustomed as an actress to appearing before an audience, the congress-woman from California was a popular campaigner for the Democrats and a featured speaker at the Democratic National Conventions of 1944 and 1948. Her appeal, shown in this photo from the 1948 convention, sparked interest in her for higher office. The *Washington Post* called it the "first genuine boom in history for a woman for vice-president," but she made it clear that she was not in the running.
© Bettmann/Corbis.

well as revolts from within his own party. The new president confronted domestic problems that the New Deal had not solved—how to sustain economic growth and avoid another depression without the war to fuel the economy—and international challenges that threatened to undermine the nation's security and called for bold international initiatives.

As early as 1946, Truman and his advisers became convinced that the Soviet Union posed a major threat to the United States. The president gradually shaped a policy designed to contain and thwart Soviet power wherever it threatened to spread. By 1947, a new term had been coined to describe the intense rivalry between the superpowers—**cold war**. As a member of the House Foreign Affairs Committee, Douglas urged the administration to find ways to cooperate with the Soviet Union, and she voted against aid to Greece and Turkey, the first step in a new policy to contain the spread of **communism**. Thereafter, she was Truman's loyal ally, supporting the Marshall Plan, the creation of the **North Atlantic Treaty Organization (NATO)**, and the war in Korea. The **containment** policy achieved its goals in Europe, but communism spread in Asia, and at home a wave of anti-Communist hysteria—a second Red scare—harmed many Americans and stifled dissent and debate about U.S. policies.

Douglas's earlier links with leftist and liberal groups; her advocacy of civil rights, women's rights, and federal health, housing, and education programs; and her defense of civil liberties threatened by the crusade against supposed subversives made her and many other liberals easy targets for conservative politicians seeking to capitalize on the anti-Communist fervor. When she decided to run for the U.S. Senate in 1950, she faced Republican Richard M. Nixon. Her opponent had gained national attention as a member of the House Un-American Activities Committee, which sought to expose Communists in government and whose funding Douglas had voted to cut. Nixon's campaign put her on the defensive, labeling her as "pink right down to her underwear" and telephoning thousands of homes on election eve with the anonymous message, "I think you should know Helen Douglas is a Communist." Nixon won a decisive victory but carried throughout his life the appellation Douglas gave him, "Tricky Dick." Douglas's political career ended in defeat, just as much of Truman's domestic agenda fell victim to the Red scare.

decision to run for Congress in 1944 and helped secure her election. She represented not the posh Hollywood district where she lived, but the Fourteenth Congressional District in downtown Los Angeles, with its multiethnic, multiracial population, which helped shape her progressive politics.

Like many other liberals who were devoted to Roosevelt, Douglas was devastated by his death and unsure of his successor, Harry S. Truman. "Who was Harry Truman anyway?" she said. "None of us knew much about him." A compromise choice for the vice presidency, this "accidental president" lacked the charisma, experience, and political skills with which Roosevelt had transformed both foreign and domestic policy, won four presidential elections, and forged a Democratic Party coalition that dominated national politics. Initially criticized and abandoned by many Roosevelt loyalists, Truman faced a resurgent Republican Party, which had gained strength in Congress during World War II, as

From the Grand Alliance to Containment

With Japan's surrender in August 1945, Americans besieged the government for the return of their loved ones. Baby booties arrived at the White House with a note, "Please send my daddy home." Americans looked forward to the dismantling of the large military establishment and expected the Allies, led by the United States and working within the United Nations, to cooperate in the management of international peace. Postwar realities quickly dashed these expectations. A dangerous new threat seemed to arise as the wartime alliance forged by the United States, Great Britain, and the Soviet Union crumbled, and the United States began to develop the means to contain the spread of Soviet power around the globe.

The Cold War Begins

"The guys who came out of World War II were idealistic," reported Harold Russell, a young paratrooper who had lost both hands in a training accident. "We felt the day had come when the wars were all over." Public opinion polls echoed the veterans' confidence in the promise of peace. But political leaders were less optimistic. Once the Allies had overcome a common enemy, the prewar mistrust and antagonism between the Soviet Union and the West resurfaced over their very different visions of the postwar world.

The Western Allies' delay in opening a second front in Western Europe aroused Soviet suspicions during the war. The Soviet Union made supreme wartime sacrifices, losing more than twenty million citizens and vast portions of its agricultural and industrial capacity. At the war's end, Soviet leader Joseph Stalin wanted to make Germany pay for the rebuilding of the Soviet economy and to expand Soviet influence in the world. Above all, he wanted friendly governments on the Soviet Union's borders in Eastern Europe, especially in Poland, through which Germany had attacked Russia twice within twenty-five years. A ruthless dictator, he also wanted to maintain his own power.

In contrast to the Soviet devastation, enemy fire had never touched the mainland of the United States, and its 405,000 dead amounted to just 2 percent of the Soviet loss. With a vastly expanded economy and a monopoly on atomic weapons, the United States was the most powerful nation on the planet. That sheer power, along with U.S. economic interests, policymakers' views about how the recent war might have been avoided, and a belief in the superiority of American institutions and intentions, all affected how American leaders approached the Soviet Union after the war.

Fearing a return of the depression, U.S. officials believed that a healthy economy depended on opportunities abroad. American companies needed access to raw materials, markets for their goods, and security for their investments overseas. These needs could be met best in countries with similar economic and political systems, not in those where government controls interfered with the free flow of products and dollars. As Truman put it in 1947, "The American system can survive in America only if it becomes a world system."

Yet both leaders and citizens regarded their foreign policy not as a self-interested campaign to guarantee economic interests, but as the means to preserve national security and bring freedom, **democracy**, and capitalism to the rest of the world. Laura Briggs spoke for many Americans who believed "it was our destiny to prove that we were the children of God and that our way was right for the world."

Recent history also shaped postwar foreign policy. Americans believed that Britain and France might have prevented World War II had they resisted rather than appeased Hitler's initial aggression. Navy Secretary James V. Forrestal, for example, argued against trying to "buy [the Soviets'] understanding and sympathy. We tried that once with Hitler." This "appeasement" analogy would be invoked repeatedly when the United States faced challenges to the international status quo.

The man with ultimate responsibility for U.S. policy was a keen student of history but came to the White House with little international experience. When Germany attacked the Soviet Union in 1941, then-Senator Truman expressed his hope that the two would kill each other off. As president, he envisioned Soviet-American cooperation, as long as the Soviet Union conformed to U.S. plans for the postwar world and restrained its expansionist impulses. Proud of his ability to make quick decisions, Truman determined to be firm with the Soviets, knowing well that America's nuclear monopoly gave him the upper hand.

Soviet and American interests clashed first in Eastern Europe. Stalin insisted that the Allies'

Joseph Stalin: From Ally to Enemy
These two portrayals of the Soviet leader indicate how quickly the World
War II alliance disintegrated into the cold war. On the left, in a photograph
from a 1944 issue of the popular magazine *Look*, Stalin is shown with two adoring schoolchildren.
The accompanying article depicted him as both an effective leader and a sensitive man who wrote
poetry and loved literature. Only four years later, in 1948, *Look* published Stalin's life story. The photo
on the right frames his face with communism's emblem, the hammer and sickle, symbolizing the alliance
of workers and peasants. The 1944 piece called Stalin a "man of trenchant speech, indomitable will and
extraordinary mental capacity [and a] lover of literature." The 1948 article emphasized his "rise to
absolute power over millions of lives" and depicted him as a "small man with drooping shoulders [who]
tyrannizes one-fifth of the world." What do these two items suggest about the role of the press in
American society?
The Michael Barson Collection/Past Perfect.

wartime agreements gave him a free hand in the countries defeated or liberated by the Red Army, just as the United States was unilaterally reconstructing governments in Italy and Japan. The Soviet dictator used harsh methods to install Communist governments in neighboring Poland and Bulgaria. Elsewhere, the Soviets initially tolerated non-Communist governments in Hungary and Czechoslovakia. And in the spring of 1946, Stalin responded to pressure from the West and removed troops from Iran on the Soviet Union's southwest border, allowing U.S. access to the rich oil fields there.

Stalin considered U.S. officials hypocritical in demanding democratic elections in Eastern Europe while supporting dictatorships friendly to U.S. interests in Latin America. The United States clung to its sphere of influence while opposing Soviet efforts to create its own. But the Western Allies were unwilling to match tough words with military force against the largest army in the world. Under intense domestic pressure to demobilize their own troops, they issued sharp protests but failed to prevent the Soviet

Union from establishing satellite countries in most of Eastern Europe.

In 1946, the wartime Allies contended over Germany's future. American policymakers wanted to demilitarize Germany, but they also sought rapid industrial revival there to foster European economic recovery and thus America's own long-term prosperity. By contrast, the Soviet Union wanted Germany weak militarily and economically, and Stalin demanded heavy reparations to help rebuild the devastated Soviet economy. Unable to settle their differences, the Allies divided Germany. The Soviet Union installed a puppet Communist government in the eastern section, and in December 1946, Britain, France, and the United States unified their occupation zones, beginning the process that established the Federal Republic of Germany—West Germany—in 1949 (Map 26.1).

The war of words escalated early in 1946. Boasting of the superiority of the Soviet system, Stalin told a Moscow audience in February that capitalism inevitably produced war. One month later, Truman traveled with Winston Churchill to Fulton, Missouri, where the former prime minister denounced Soviet suppression of the popular will in Eastern and central Europe. "From Stettin in the Baltic to Trieste in the Adriatic, an **iron curtain** has descended across the Continent," Churchill said. (See "Documenting the American Promise," page 952.) Although Truman did not officially endorse Churchill's iron curtain speech, his presence implied agreement with the idea of joint British-American action to combat Soviet aggression. Stalin regarded the speech as "a call to war against the USSR."

In February 1946, George F. Kennan, a career diplomat with experience in Eastern Europe and Moscow, wrote a comprehensive rationale for hard-line foreign policy. Downplaying the influence of Communist ideology in Soviet policy, he instead stressed the Soviets' insecurity and Stalin's need to maintain authority at home, which he believed prompted Stalin to exaggerate threats from abroad and to expand Soviet power. These circumstances, Kennan argued, made it impossible to negotiate with Stalin. Secretary of State James F. Byrnes and other key Truman advisers agreed with him.

MAP 26.1 The Division of Europe after World War II

The "iron curtain," a term coined by Winston Churchill to refer to the Soviet grip on Eastern and central Europe, divided the continent for nearly fifty years. Communist governments controlled the countries along the Soviet Union's western border. The only exception was Finland, which remained neutral.

READING THE MAP: Is the division of Europe between NATO, Communist, and neutral countries about equal? Why would the location of Berlin pose a problem for the Western allies?

CONNECTIONS: When was NATO founded, and what was its purpose? How did the postwar division of Europe compare with the wartime alliances?

FOR MORE HELP ANALYZING THIS MAP, see the map activity for this chapter in the Online Study Guide at bedfordstmartins.com/roark.

The Emerging Cold War

Although antagonism between the Soviet Union and the West stretched back to the Russian Revolution of 1917, the United States, the Soviet Union, Britain, and other powers had cooperated to win World War II. Early in 1946, however, Soviet and Western leaders publicly expressed distrust and attributed hostile motivations to each other. Within the United States, disagreement arose about how to deal with the Soviet Union.

DOCUMENT 1
Joseph Stalin Addresses a Rally in Moscow, February 9, 1946

In early 1946, Premier Joseph Stalin called on the Soviet people to support his program for economic development. Although Stalin did not address cold war issues, leaders in the West viewed his comments about communism and capitalism and his boasts about the strength of the Red Army as a threat to peace.

The [Second World War] arose as the inevitable result of the development of the world economic and political forces on the basis of monopoly capitalism. . . .

. . . The uneven development of the capitalist countries leads in time to sharp disturbances in their relations, and the group of countries which consider themselves inadequately provided with raw materials and export markets try usually to change this situation and to change the position in their favor by means of armed force. As a result of these factors, the capitalist world is split into two hostile camps and war follows. . . . The Soviet social system has proved to be more capable of life and more stable than a non-Soviet social system. . . .

. . . The Red Army heroically withstood all the adversities of the war, routed completely the armies of our enemies and emerged victoriously from the war. This is recognized by everybody—friend and foe.

[Stalin talks about his new Five-Year Plan.] Apart from the fact that in the very near future the rationing system will be abolished, special attention will be focused on expanding the production of goods for mass consumption, on raising the standard of life of the working people by consistent and systematic reduction of the costs of all goods, and on wide-scale construction of all kinds of scientific research institutes to enable science to develop its forces. I have no doubt that if we render the necessary assistance to our scientists they will be able not only to overtake but also in the very near future to surpass the achievements of science outside the boundaries of our country.

SOURCE: Excerpts from Joseph Stalin, *Vital Speeches of the Day*, February 9, 1946. Reprinted with permission.

DOCUMENT 2
Winston Churchill Delivers His "Iron Curtain" Speech at Westminster College in Fulton, Missouri, March 5, 1946

With Truman sitting on the podium, Winston Churchill, former prime minister of Great Britain, assessed Soviet actions in harsh terms. In response, Stalin equated Churchill with Hitler, as a "firebrand of war."

The United States stands at this time at the pinnacle of world power. It is a solemn moment for the American democracy. With primacy in power is also joined an awe-inspiring accountability to the future. [Churchill then speaks of the need to support the United Nations.]

It would nevertheless be wrong and imprudent to intrust the secret knowledge or experience of the atomic bomb, which the United States, Great Britain and Canada now share, to the world organization [the United Nations], while it is still in its infancy. It would be criminal madness to cast it adrift in this still agitated and ununited world. . . .

. . . I have a strong admiration and regard for the valiant Russian people and for my war-time comrade, Marshal Stalin. . . . We understand the Russians need to be secure on her western frontiers from all renewal of German aggression. . . . It is my duty, however, to place before you certain facts. . . .

From Stettin in the Baltic to Trieste in the Adriatic, an iron curtain has descended across the Continent. Behind that line lie all the capitals of the ancient states of central and eastern Europe. Warsaw, Berlin, Prague, Vienna, Budapest, Belgrade, Bucharest and Sofia, all these famous cities and the populations around them lie in the Soviet sphere and all are subject in one form or another, not only to Soviet influence but to a very high and increasing measure of control from Moscow. . . . The Communist parties, which were very small in all these eastern states of Europe, have been raised to preeminence and power far beyond their numbers and are seeking everywhere to obtain totalitarian control. Police governments are prevailing in nearly every case. . . .

. . . In a great number of countries, far from the Russian frontiers and throughout the world, Communist fifth columns are established and work in complete unity and absolute obedience to the directions they receive from the Communist center.

I do not believe that Soviet Russia desires war. What they desire is the fruits of war and the indefinite expansion of their power and doctrines. . . . Our difficulties and dangers will not be removed by . . . mere waiting to see what happens; nor will they be relieved by a policy of appeasement. . . . I am convinced that there is nothing [the Russians] admire so much as strength, and there is nothing for which they have less respect than for military weakness.

SOURCE: Excerpts from Winston Churchill, *Vital Speeches of the Day*, March 5, 1946. Reprinted with permission.

DOCUMENT 3
Henry A. Wallace Addresses an Election Rally at Madison Square Garden, New York, September 12, 1946

Throughout 1946, Henry A. Wallace, Truman's secretary of commerce, urged the president to take a more conciliatory approach toward the Soviet Union, a position reflected in a speech Wallace gave to a rally of leftist and liberal groups in New York City. Truman believed that Wallace's words undermined his foreign policy and asked for Wallace's resignation.

We cannot rest in the assurance that we invented the atom bomb—and therefore that this agent of destruction will work best for us. He who trusts in the atom bomb will sooner or later perish by the atom bomb— or something worse. . . .

To achieve lasting peace, we must study in detail just how the Russian character was formed— by invasions of Tartars, Mongols, Germans, Poles, Swedes, and French; by the czarist rule based on ignorance, fear and force; by the intervention of the British, French and Americans in Russian affairs from 1919 to 1921; by the geography of the huge Russian land mass situated strategically between Europe and Asia; and by the vitality derived from the rich Russian soil and the strenuous Russian climate. Add to all this the tremendous emotional power which Marxism and Leninism gives to the Russian leaders—and then we can realize that we are reckoning with a force which cannot be handled successfully by a "Get tough with Russia" policy. "Getting tough" never bought anything real and lasting— whether for schoolyard bullies or businessmen or world powers. The tougher we get, the tougher the Russians will get. . . .

. . . We want cooperation. And I believe that we can get cooperation once Russia understands that our primary objective is neither saving the British Empire nor purchasing oil in the Near East with the lives of American soldiers. . . .

On our part we should recognize that we have no more business in the political affairs of Eastern Europe than Russia has in the political affairs of Latin America, Western Europe and the United States. . . . We have to recognize that the Balkans are closer to Russia than to us—and that Russia cannot permit either England or the United States to dominate the politics of that area. . . .

. . . Under friendly peaceful competition the Russian world and the American world will gradually become more alike. The Russians will be forced to grant more and more of the personal freedoms; and we shall become more and more absorbed with the problems of social-economic justice.

SOURCE: Excerpts from Henry A. Wallace, *Vital Speeches of the Day*, September 12, 1946. Reprinted with permission.

QUESTIONS FOR ANALYSIS AND DEBATE

1. What lessons did these three leaders draw from World War II? What did they see as the most critical steps to preventing another war?

2. What differences did these men see between the political and economic systems of the Soviet Union on the one hand and the United States and Western Europe on the other? How do their predictions about these systems differ?

3. What motives did these three men ascribe to Soviet actions? How do Churchill's and Wallace's proposals for the Western response to the Soviet Union differ?

4. Which leader do you think was most optimistic about the prospects for good relationships between Russia and the West? Which was most correct? Why?

Kennan predicted that the Soviet Union would retreat from its expansionist efforts "in the face of superior force," and he recommended that the United States respond with "unalterable counterforce"—the approach that came to be called containment. Kennan ex-pected that containment would eventually end in "either the breakup or the gradual mellowing of Soviet power." This message reached a larger audience when Kennan's views were published in *Foreign Affairs* magazine in July 1947. Kennan later expressed dis-may when his ideas were used to justify what he considered an in-discriminate American response wherever communism seemed likely to arise. Nonetheless, his analysis marked a critical turn-ing point in the development of the cold war, providing a compelling rationale for wielding U.S. power throughout the world.

> According to the Truman Doctrine, the United States would not only resist Soviet military power but also "support free peoples who are resisting attempted sub-jugation by armed minorities or by outside pressures."

Not all public figures accepted the toughen-ing line. In September 1946, Secretary of Com-merce Henry A. Wallace, Truman's predecessor as vice president, urged greater understanding of the Soviets' concerns about their nation's security, in-sisting that "we have no more business in the po-litical affairs of Eastern Europe than Russia has in the political affairs of Latin America." (See "Documenting the American Promise," page 952.) State Department officials were furious, and when Wallace refused to be muzzled on foreign policy topics, Truman fired him.

The Truman Doctrine and the Marshall Plan

In 1947, the United States began to implement the doctrine of containment that would guide foreign policy for the next four decades. It was not an easy transition; Americans approved tak-ing a hard line against the Soviet Union, but they wanted to keep their soldiers and tax dollars at home. In addition to selling containment to the public, Truman had to gain the support of a Republican-controlled Congress, which included a forceful bloc, led by Ohio senator Robert A. Taft, opposed to a strong U.S. presence in Europe.

Crises in two Mediterranean countries trig-gered the implementation of containment. In February 1947, Britain informed the United States that its crippled economy could no longer sustain military assistance either to Greece, where the autocratic government faced a leftist

uprising, or to Turkey, which was trying to resist Soviet pressures. Truman promptly sought con-gressional authority to send military and eco-nomic missions, along with $400 million in aid, to the two countries. Meeting with congressional leaders, Undersecretary of State Dean Acheson predicted that if Greece and Turkey fell, commu-nism would soon consume three-fourths of the world. After a stunned silence, Michigan senator Arthur Vandenberg, the Republican foreign pol-icy leader and a recent convert from **isolationism**, warned that to get approval, Truman would have to "scare hell out of the country."

Truman did just that. Outlining what would later be called the **domino theory**, he warned that if Greece fell to the rebels, "confusion and disorder might well spread throughout the en-tire Middle East" and then create instability in Europe. Failure to act, he said, "may endanger the peace of the world—and shall surely endan-ger the welfare of the nation." According to what came to be called the **Truman Doctrine**, the United States would not only resist Soviet mili-tary power but also "support free peoples who are resisting attempted subjugation by armed minorities or by outside pressures."

The president failed to convince Helen Gahagan Douglas and some of her colleagues in Congress, who wanted the United States to try first to resolve the crises in Greece and Turkey through the United Nations before acting unilat-erally and who opposed propping up the authoritarian Greek government. But the admin-istration won the day, setting a standard for cold war interventions that would aid any kind of government if the only alternative appeared to be communism. Congress did not formally ac-cept the Truman Doctrine when it approved aid for Greece and Turkey. Yet the assumption that national security depended on rescuing any anti-Communist government from internal rebels or outside pressure became the cornerstone of U.S. foreign policy until the end of the 1980s.

A much larger assistance program for Europe followed aid to Greece and Turkey. In May 1947, Acheson described a war-ravaged Western Europe, with "factories destroyed, fields impoverished, transportation systems wrecked, populations scattered and on the borderline of starvation." American citizens were sending generous amounts of private aid, but Europe needed large-scale assistance. It was "a matter of national self-interest," Acheson argued, for the United States to provide aid. Only economic recovery could halt the growth of **socialist** and Communist

Marshall Plan Bread for Greek Children
Greece was one of sixteen European nations that participated in the European Recovery Program.
In this photograph taken in 1949, Greek children receive loaves of bread made from the first ship-
ment of Marshall Plan flour from the United States.
© Bettmann/Corbis.

parties in France and Italy and confine Soviet influence to Eastern Europe.

In March 1948, Congress approved the
European Recovery Program—known as the
Marshall Plan, after retired general George C.
Marshall, who as secretary of state proposed the
plan—and over the next five years, the United
States spent $13 billion to restore the economies
of sixteen Western European nations. Marshall
invited all European nations and the Soviet
Union to cooperate in a request for aid, but as
administration officials expected, the Soviets
objected to the American terms of free trade and
financial disclosure and ordered their Eastern
European satellites likewise to reject the offer.

The Marshall Plan marked the first step toward the European Union. Humanitarian desires
to help destitute Europeans, as well as the strategic
goal of keeping Western Europe free of communism, drove the adoption of this enormous aid pro-

gram. In addition, the assistance program helped
boost the U.S. economy, because the European
nations spent most of the dollars to buy American
products, and Europe's economic recovery created new opportunities for American investment.

In February 1948, while Congress debated
the Marshall Plan, the Soviets
staged a brutal coup and installed
a Communist regime in Czechoslovakia, the last democracy left
in Eastern Europe. Next, Stalin
threatened Western access to Berlin. That former capital of Germany lay within Soviet-controlled
East Germany, but all four Allies
jointly occupied Berlin, dividing it
into separate administrative units.
As the Western Allies moved to
organize West Germany as a separate nation, the Soviets retaliated

Berlin Divided, 1948

by blocking roads and rail lines between West Germany and the Western-held sections of Berlin, cutting off food, fuel, and other essentials to two million inhabitants.

"We stay in Berlin, period," Truman vowed. Yet he wanted to avoid a confrontation with Soviet troops. So for nearly a year, U.S. and British pilots airlifted 2.3 million tons of goods to sustain the West Berliners. Stalin hesitated to shoot down these cargo planes, and in 1949 he lifted the blockade. The city was then divided into East Berlin, under Soviet control, and West Berlin, which became part of West Germany. For many Americans, the Berlin airlift confirmed the wisdom of containment: When challenged, the Russians backed down, as Kennan had predicted. Moreover, the airlift changed the image of the United States in German eyes from an occupying force to a savior.

Building a National Security State

During the Truman years, advocates of the new containment policy fashioned a six-pronged defense strategy: (1) development of atomic weapons, (2) strengthening traditional military power, (3) military alliances with other nations, (4) military and economic aid to friendly nations, (5) an espionage network and secret means to subvert Communist expansion, and (6) a propaganda offensive to win popular admiration for the United States around the world.

In September 1949, the United States lost its nuclear monopoly when officials confirmed that the Soviets had detonated an atomic bomb. In an effort to keep the United States ahead, in January 1950 Truman approved the development of a hydrogen bomb, equivalent to five hundred atomic bombs, rejecting the arguments of several scientists who had worked on the atomic bomb and of George Kennan, who warned of an endless arms race. The "super bomb" was ready by 1954, but the U.S. advantage was brief. In November 1955, the Soviets exploded their own hydrogen bomb.

From the 1950s through the 1980s, **deterrence** formed the basis of American nuclear strategy. To deter the Soviet Union from attacking, the United States strove to maintain a nuclear force more powerful than the Soviets'. Because the Russians pursued a similar policy, the superpowers became locked in an ever-escalating nuclear weapons race, as Kennan had predicted. Albert Einstein, whose mathematical discoveries had laid the foundations for nuclear weapons, commented grimly on the enormous destructive force now possessed by the superpowers. The war that came after World War III, he warned, would "be fought with sticks and stones."

To implement the second component of its containment strategy, the United States beefed up its conventional military power to deter Soviet threats that might not warrant nuclear retaliation. The National Security Act of 1947 streamlined defense planning by uniting the military branches under a single secretary of defense and creating the National Security Council (NSC) to advise the president. With this legislation, the Department of War became the

The Berlin Airlift

Germans living in West Berlin greet a U.S. plane carrying food, fuel, and other necessities during the Soviet blockade that began in June 1948. Truman and his advisers were "prepared to use any means that may be necessary to stay in Berlin," and the president confided in his diary that "we are very close to war." To reduce that risk, Truman chose to supply the city with an airlift rather than send ground convoys to shoot their way through Soviet lines. Apparently impressed with American resolve and resources, Stalin backed down and lifted the blockade in May 1949. The vulnerability of Germans like these helped to ease hostile feelings that other Europeans felt toward their former enemies.
© Bettmann/Corbis.

Department of Defense, a name change emphasizing the nation's growing militarization. "War" denoted a limited time of engagement, "Defense" a permanent, ongoing, and substantial undertaking.

During the Berlin crisis, Congress hiked military appropriations and enacted a peacetime **draft**. In addition, Congress granted permanent status to the women's military branches, though it limited their numbers and rank and banned them from combat. One of military women's staunchest supporters, General Dwight D. Eisenhower, had assured Congress "that after an enlistment or two women will ordinarily—and thank God—they will get married." With 1.5 million men and women in uniform in 1950, the military strength of the United States had quadrupled since the 1930s, and defense expenditures claimed one-third of the federal budget.

Collective security, the third prong of postwar military strategy, also developed during the Berlin showdown. In June 1948, the Senate approved the general principle of regional military alliances. One year later, the United States joined Canada and Western European nations in its first peacetime military alliance, the North Atlantic Treaty Organization (NATO), designed to counter a Soviet threat to Western Europe (see Map 26.1). For the first time in its history, the United States pledged to go to war if one of its allies were attacked.

The fourth element of defense strategy involved foreign assistance programs to strengthen friendly countries, such as aid to Greece and Turkey and the Marshall Plan. In addition, in 1949 Congress approved $1 billion of military aid to its NATO allies, and the government began economic assistance to nations in other parts of the world.

The fifth ingredient of containment improved the government's espionage capacities and ability to deter communism through covert activities. The National Security Act of 1947 created the Central Intelligence Agency (CIA) not only to gather information but also to perform any "functions and duties related to intelligence affecting the national security" that the NSC might authorize. Such activities included propaganda, sabotage, economic warfare, and support for "anti-communist elements in threatened countries of the free world." Secret operations by the CIA helped defeat Italy's Communist Party in the 1948 election there. Subsequently, CIA agents would help topple legitimate foreign governments and violate the rights of U.S. citizens.

Cold War Spying

"Intelligence," the gathering of information to determine the capabilities and intentions of the enemy, is as old as human warfare, but it took on new importance with the onset of the cold war. Created by the National Security Act of 1947, the Central Intelligence Agency (CIA) became one of the most important tools for obtaining Soviet secrets, deceiving the enemy about U.S. plans, countering subversive activities by Communists, and assisting local forces against leaders whom the United States wanted to oust. While much of the CIA's intelligence work took place in Washington, where analysts combed through Communist newspapers, official reports, and leaders' speeches, secret agents operating behind the iron curtain gathered information with bugs and devices such as these cameras hidden in cigarette packs. Spying soon gained a prominent place in popular culture, most notably in more than a dozen movies featuring James Bond, British agent 007. The character first appeared in the 1952 novel *Casino Royale* by former British naval intelligence agent Ian Fleming. Bond made his screen debut in 1962 in the movie *Dr. No.* Jack Naylor Collection.

In many respects, the CIA was virtually unaccountable to Congress or the public.

Finally, the U.S. government sought, through cultural exchanges and propaganda, to win "hearts and minds" throughout the world. As the cold war intensified, the government expanded the Voice of America, created during World War II to broadcast U.S. propaganda abroad. In addition, the State Department sent books, exhibits, and performers to foreign countries. Jazz musicians were especially popular as "cultural ambassadors," tapping into the excitement in many foreign countries about this recognizably American creation.

Louis Armstrong in Düsseldorf
As one of its cold war weapons, the United States sent representatives of American culture abroad. Because jazz was enormously popular around the world, the State Department sponsored tours by black jazz artists. The government also hoped that these unofficial ambassadors would counter the image of the United States as a racist nation. Louis Armstrong, the great trumpet player, singer, and jazz innovator, is shown here playing a child's trumpet amid an admiring crowd in Germany in 1952. Later in the 1950s, when Armstrong became disillusioned with President Eisenhower's failure to act vigorously on civil rights, he canceled a tour of the Soviet Union. Asked by reporters about his refusal to go, he responded, "The people over there ask me what's wrong with my country, what am I supposed to say?"
AP Images.

By 1950, the United States had abandoned age-old tenets of foreign policy. Isolationism and neutrality had given way to a peacetime military alliance and efforts to control events far beyond U.S. borders. Short of war, the United States could not stop the descent of the iron curtain, but it aggressively and successfully promoted economic recovery and a military shield for the rest of Europe.

Superpower Rivalry around the Globe

Efforts to implement containment moved beyond Europe. In Africa, Asia, and the Middle East, World War II accelerated a tide of national liberation movements against war-weakened **imperial** powers. By 1960, forty countries, with more than a quarter of the world's people, had won their independence. These nations came to be referred to collectively, along with Latin America, as the **third world**, a term denoting countries outside the Western (first world) and Soviet (second world) orbits that had not yet developed industrial economies.

Like Woodrow Wilson during World War I, Roosevelt and Truman promoted the ideal of self-determination. The United States granted independence to the Philippines in 1946, applauded the British withdrawal from India, and encouraged France to relinquish its empire in Indochina. At the same time, both the United States and the Soviet Union cultivated in emerging nations governments that were friendly to their own interests.

Leaders of many liberation movements, impressed with the rapid economic growth of Russia, adopted socialist or Communist ideas. Although few had formal ties with the Soviet Union, American leaders saw these movements as a threatening extension of Soviet power. Seeking to hold communism at bay by fostering economic development and political stability, the Truman administration initiated the Point IV

Mao Zedong on the Way to Victory
During World War II, Mao Zedong, leader of China's Communist Party, mobilized peasants around his revolution by implementing land reform where the Communists had control and by fighting valiantly against the Japanese. By the end of 1944, when this photo of Mao addressing his followers was taken, the Communists had a military force of more than half a million and control of more than eighty million Chinese.
© Bettmann/Corbis.

Program in 1949, providing technical aid to developing nations. These modest amounts of aid contrasted sharply with the huge sums provided to Europe, where the administration's priorities lay.

In Asia, civil war raged in China, where the Communists, led by Mao Zedong (Mao Tse-tung), fought the official Nationalist government under Chiang Kai-shek. While the Communists gained support among the peasants for their land reforms and valiant stand against the Japanese, Chiang's corrupt and incompetent government alienated much of the population. Failing in its efforts to promote negotiations between Chiang and Mao, the United States provided almost $3 billion in aid to the Nationalists during the civil war. Yet Truman and his advisers believed that to divert further resources from Europe to China would be futile, given the ineptness of Chiang's government.

In October 1949, Mao established the People's Republic of China (PRC), and the Nationalists fled to the island of Taiwan. Fearing a U.S.-supported invasion to recapture China for the Nationalists, Mao signed a treaty with the Soviet Union in which each nation pledged to defend the other in case of attack. The United States refused to recognize the PRC, blocked its admission to the United Nations, and supported the Nationalist government in Taiwan. Only a massive U.S. military commitment could have stopped the Chinese Communists, yet some Republicans cried that Truman and "the pro-Communists in the State Department" had "lost" China. China became a political albatross for the Democrats, who resolved never again to be vulnerable to charges of being soft on communism.

With China in turmoil, the administration reconsidered its plans for postwar Japan. Initially, the U.S. military occupation had aimed to reform the Japanese government, purge militarists from official positions, and decentralize the economy. But by 1948, U.S. policy had shifted to helping Japan rapidly reindustrialize and secure access to food, markets, and natural resources in Asia. In a short time, the Japanese economy was flourishing. American soldiers remained on military bases in Japan, but the official occupation ended when the two nations signed a peace treaty and a mutual security pact in September 1951. Like West Germany, Japan now sat squarely within the American orbit, ready to serve as an economic hub in a vital area.

The one place where cold war considerations did not control American policy was Palestine. In 1943, then-Senator Harry Truman spoke passionately about Nazi Germany's an-

nihilation of the Jews, asserting, "This is not a Jewish problem, it is an American problem—and we must . . . face it squarely and honorably." As president, he had the opportunity to make good on his words. Jews had been migrating to Palestine, their biblical homeland, since the nineteenth century, resulting in tension and hostilities with the Palestinian Arabs. After World War II, as hundreds of thousands of European Jews sought refuge and the creation of a national homeland in Palestine, fighting devolved into brutal terrorism on both sides.

Haganah Troops Mobilize in Palestine
Haganah originated in the 1910s as a paramilitary group to defend Jewish settlers in Palestine against Arabs who opposed the Zionists' expressed desire to build a Jewish state there. After World War I, Palestine was governed by the British under a League of Nations mandate. During that time, Haganah was an illegal, underground organization, but by the end of World War II, it had gathered a substantial number of members and weapons. After Israel declared itself a nation in 1948, Haganah became the core of the Israel Defense Forces, Israel's main military organization. In this photo, Haganah troops are mobilizing in July 1948 to defend the new state from the armies of the surrounding nations of Syria, Jordan, Egypt, Lebanon, and Iraq. The Israelis won the war, but the declaration of the state of Israel created 700,000 Arab refugees and an issue that would fuel turmoil in the area for decades to come.
© Bettmann/Corbis.

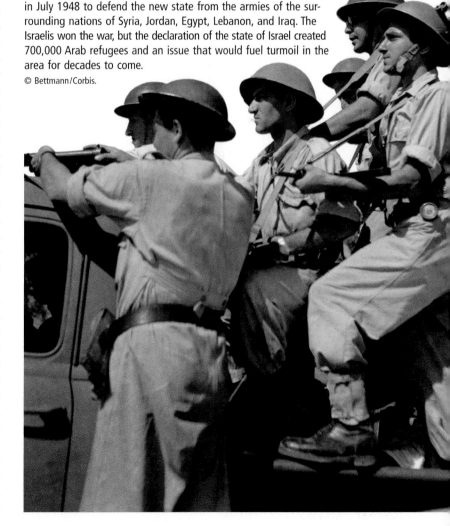

Israel, 1948

Truman's foreign policy experts sought American-Arab friendship as a critical barrier against Soviet influence in the Middle East and as a means to secure access to Arabian oil. Uncharacteristically defying his advisers, the president responded instead to pleas from Jewish organizations, his moral commitment to Holocaust survivors, and his interest in the American Jewish vote for the 1948 election. When Jews in Palestine declared the state of Israel in May 1948, Truman quickly recognized the new country and made its defense the cornerstone of U.S. policy in the Middle East.

REVIEW Why did relations between the United States and the Soviet Union deteriorate after World War II?

Truman and the Fair Deal at Home

Referring to the Civil War general who coined the phrase "War is hell," Truman said in December 1945, "Sherman was wrong. I'm telling you I find peace is hell." Challenged by crises abroad, Truman also faced shortages, strikes, inflation, and other problems attending the reconversion of the economy to peacetime production. At the same time, he tried to expand New Deal reform with his own "Fair Deal" agenda of initiatives in civil rights, housing, education, and health care—efforts hindered by the wave of anti-Communist hysteria sweeping the country. In sharp contrast to his success with Congress in foreign policy, Truman achieved but a modest slice of his domestic agenda.

Reconverting to a Peacetime Economy

Despite scarcities and deprivations during World War II, most Americans had enjoyed a higher standard of living than ever before. Economic experts as well as ordinary citizens worried about sustaining that standard and providing jobs for millions of returning soldiers. Truman wasted no time unveiling his plan, ask-

ing Congress to enact a twenty-one-point program of social and economic reforms. He wanted to maintain the government's power to regulate the economy while it adjusted to peacetime production, and he sought government programs to provide basic essentials such as housing and health care to those in need, programs that had been on the drawing board during the New

---

Women's Role in Peacetime

Like many manufacturers forced to convert to war production during World War II, Proctor Electric Company, which had switched from making appliances to producing bomb fuses, cartridges, and airplane wing flaps, hoped to profit after the war from pent-up consumer demand. Even before the company had fully reconverted its plants, ads tempted consumers with products soon to come and asked them to be patient until Proctor could meet their needs, as this 1946 ad indicates. Picture Research Consultants & Archives.

READING THE IMAGE: This advertisement promotes a toaster, an iron, a waffle maker, and a roaster. Which of these are not in widespread use today? Why do you think this is so? **CONNECTIONS:** Why do you think a woman was featured in this ad? What message about women's employment during and after the war is conveyed here?

FOR MORE HELP ANALYZING THIS IMAGE, see the visual activity for this chapter in the Online Study Guide at bedfordstmartins.com/roark.

Deal. "Not even President Roosevelt ever asked for as much at one sitting," exploded Republican leader Joseph W. Martin Jr.

Congress approved only one of Truman's key proposals—full-employment legislation—and even that was watered down. The Employment Act of 1946 invested the federal government with the responsibility "to promote maximum employment, production, and purchasing power," thereby formalizing what had been implicit in Roosevelt's actions to counter the depression—government's responsibility for maintaining a healthy economy. The law created the Council of Economic Advisors to assist the president, but it authorized no new powers to translate the government's obligation into effective action.

Inflation, not unemployment, turned out to be the most severe problem in the early postwar years. Unable to buy civilian goods during the war, consumers now had $30 billion in savings that they were itching to spend. But shortages of meat, automobiles, housing, and a host of other items persisted. Housing was so scarce that some veterans lived in basements and garages, and one newspaper ran the headline SLOGAN FOR 1946: TWO FAMILIES IN EVERY GARAGE. Until industry could convert fully to civilian production and make more goods available, consumer demand would continue to drive up prices. With a basket of groceries on her arm to dramatize rising costs, Helen Gahagan Douglas urged Congress to support Truman's efforts to maintain price and rent controls. Those efforts fell, however, to pressures from business groups and others determined to curb the growth of government powers.

Labor relations were another thorn in Truman's side. Organized labor survived the war stronger than ever, its 14.5 million members making up 35 percent of the civilian workforce. Yet union members feared the erosion of wartime gains. With wages frozen during the war, the rising incomes of working-class families had come from the availability of higher-paying jobs and the chance to work longer hours. The end of overtime meant a 30 percent cut in take-home pay for most workers.

Women also saw their earnings decline. Polls indicated that as many as 68 to 85 percent wanted to keep their wartime jobs, but most who remained in the workforce had to settle for relatively low-paying jobs in light industry or the service sector (Figure 26.1). Displaced from her shipyard work, Marie Schreiber took a cashier's job, lamenting, "You were back to women's wages, you know . . . practically in half." (See "Historical Question,"

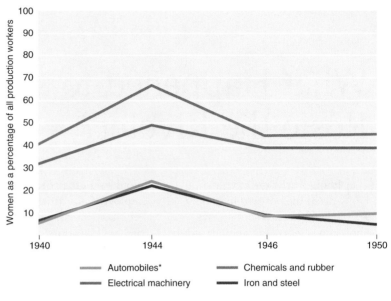

FIGURE 26.1   Women Workers in Selected Industries, 1940–1950
Women demolished the idea that some jobs were "men's work" during World War II, but they failed to maintain their gains in the manufacturing sector after the war.

page 962.) Congresswoman Douglas sponsored bills to require equal pay for equal work, to provide child care for employed mothers, and to create a government commission to study the status of women, goals supported by a number of women's organizations and women in labor unions. Nonetheless, at a time when women were viewed primarily as wives and mothers and when a strong current of opinion resisted further expansion of federal powers, these initiatives got nowhere.

Nor could women expect much from most unions, although they supported equal pay legislation. Organized labor was now engaged in an intense struggle to preserve workers' wartime gains. They turned to the weapon they had set aside during the war as five million workers went out on strike in 1946, more than at any other time in U.S. history, affecting nearly every major industry. Workers saw corporate executives profiting at their expense. Shortly before voting to strike, a former marine and the men he carpooled with calculated that a lavish party given by a company executive had cost more than they would earn in a whole year at the steel mill. "That sort of stuff made us realize, hell we had to bite the bullet . . . the bosses sure didn't give a damn for us."

Although most Americans approved of unions in principle, they became fed up with strikes,

What Happened to Rosie the Riveter?

Although scholars have scrutinized the postwar lives of World War II soldiers, we know much less about another group of veterans—the women who helped fight the war on the domestic front and who were recognized in the popular song "Rosie the Riveter." Statistics show that women's employment fell by more than two million between 1945 and 1947. But gross statistics do not reveal which women left the labor force and why, and they obscure the experiences of women who continued to work but in different jobs.

We do know what public officials and business and labor leaders expected of women who had taken up men's work during the war. With the shadow of the depression still hovering, Americans doubted that the economy could accommodate the six million new women workers along with millions of returning veterans once wartime production had ceased. A nearly universal response to anxieties about unemployment pushed a big part of the responsibility onto women: Their wartime duty had been to produce the goods needed for victory; their postwar obligation was to withdraw from the labor force.

The message that they should quit their jobs "for the sake of their homes as well as the labor situation" overwhelmed women. The company newspaper at Kaiser shipyards in the Pacific Northwest proclaimed in May 1945, "The Kitchen—Women's Big Post-War Goal." Putting words into the mouths of Kaiser's female employees, the article asserted, "Brothers, the tin hat and welder's torch will be yours! . . . The thing we want to do is take off these unfeminine garments and button ourselves into something starched and pretty." A General Electric ad predicted that women would welcome a return to "their old housekeeping routine" because GE intended to transform housework with new appliances. Some experts connected married women's employment to their obligations to help their husbands readjust to civilian life. A psychiatrist warned that women's economic independence might "raise problems in the future," urging women to realize that "reunion means relinquishing [independence]—to some extent at any rate."

Many women gave up their wartime jobs eagerly. Skyrocketing marriage rates and birthrates from that period reveal the attraction of home and family life to people compelled to postpone marriage and childbearing. Thanks to the accumulation of wartime savings, veterans' benefits, and favorable opportunities for men in the postwar economy, most families found it possible to rely on a single wage earner.

The double burdens placed on married women who took wartime jobs provided another reason for women's voluntary withdrawal from the workforce. The wartime scarcity of goods had made housekeeping much more difficult, especially for women who typically worked forty-eight hours a week with one day off. Shopping became a problem: Stores often sold out of goods early in the day, and few shops kept evening or Sunday hours. Washing machines, refrigerators, vacuum cleaners, and other laborsaving appliances were not produced at all during the war. Child care centers accommodated only about 10 percent of the children of employed mothers. Employed women with families to care for were simply worn-out.

Yet surveys reported that 75 percent of women in wartime jobs wanted—and usually needed—to keep working. As two women employed at a Ford plant in Memphis put it, "Women didn't stop eating when the war stopped." Those who struggled to remain in the workforce experienced the most wrenching changes. The vast majority were able to find jobs; in fact, women's workforce participation began growing again in 1947 and equaled the wartime peak by 1950. But women lost the traditionally male, higher-paying jobs in durable goods industries (such as iron and steel, automobile, and machinery production) and were pushed back into the lower-paying light manufacturing and service industries that had customarily welcomed them. In the words of one historian, "Rosie the Riveter had become a file clerk."

Statistics tell part of the story of this displacement. Women virtually disappeared from shipbuilding, and their share of jobs in the auto industry fell from 25 percent in 1944 to 10 percent in 1950. In the burgeoning Los Angeles aircraft industry, the proportion of women plunged from 40 percent at its wartime high to 12 percent in 1948, rising to just 25 percent in the 1950s. Even in light manufacturing, such as the electrical goods industry, where women had claimed one-third of the prewar jobs, women maintained their numbers but were bumped down to lower-paying work. During the war, women had narrowed the wage gap between men and women, but in 1950 women earned only 53 percent of what men did.

How women reacted to their displacement can be pieced together to some extent from what they were willing to say to reporters and oral history interviewers and what they wrote to government agencies and labor unions. "Women do not expect or want to hold jobs at the expense of returning soldiers," proclaimed a resolution passed by the Women's Trade Union League, expressing its members' overwhelming support for veterans' claims to jobs based on seniority awarded for the years of their wartime service. Tina Hill, a black worker at North American Aircraft in Los Angeles, said, "[Being laid off] didn't bother me much. I was just glad that the war was over . . . [and] my husband had a job." Nonetheless, after doing domestic work, she accepted readily when North American called her back: "Was I a happy soul!"

When management violated women's seniority rights by hiring non-veterans, some women protested bitterly. According to one automobile worker, "We have women laid off with seniority . . . and every day they hire in new men off the street. They hire men, they say, to do the heavy work. . . . During the war they didn't care what kind of work we did." When Ford laid off women with as much as twenty-seven years' seniority, 150 women picketed with signs that read, "The Hand That Rocks the Cradle Can Build Tractors, Too." A worker infuriated by her union's failure to protect women's seniority rights told a reporter, "We are making the bullets now, and we will give the [union executive] board members a blast that will blow them out of their shoes."

Protests from a minority of women workers could not save the jobs that the "Rosies" had held during the war. Despite women's often exemplary performance, most employers still saw women and men as different species fit for different roles and deserving of different rewards. Most labor unions paid lip service to representing all their members, but even the most progressive unions gave low priority to protecting women's seniority rights. In the absence of a feminist movement that could have given both visibility and credibility to their claims for equal treatment, most Rosie the Riveters resigned themselves to "women's work."

Women's Postwar Future

This photograph headed a *New York Times Magazine* article in June 1946. Written by the director of the Women's Division of the Department of Labor, the article discussed the needs of women workers, stressing their right to work and to receive equal pay, but it also assumed that women would all but vanish from heavy manufacturing.

Ellen Kaiper Collection, Oakland.

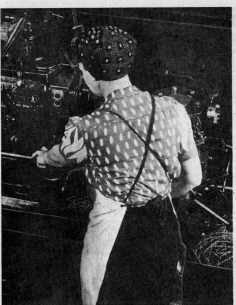

Sisters under the apron—Yesterday's war worker becomes today's housewife.

What's Become of Rosie the Riveter?

blamed unions for rising prices and shortages of consumer goods, and called for government restrictions on organized labor. Truman, too, was dismayed that wartime unity had crumbled, but he spread the blame around, writing to his mother in October 1945: "The Congress [is] balking, labor has gone crazy, and management isn't far from insane in selfishness." When the massive wave of strikes subsided at the end of 1946, workers had won wage increases of about 20 percent, but the loss of overtime along with rising prices left their purchasing power only slightly higher than in 1942.

By 1947, the nation had survived the strains associated with the reconversion of the economy from wartime to peacetime. A number of factors enabled the country to elude the postwar depression that so many had feared. Wartime profits enabled businesses to invest in new plants and equipment. Consumers could now spend their wartime savings on houses, cars, and appliances that had lain beyond their reach during the depression and war. Defense spending and the $38 billion in aid that enabled war-stricken countries to purchase American products also stimulated the economy. A soaring birthrate further sustained consumer demand. Although prosperity was far from universal, the United States entered into a remarkable economic boom that lasted through the 1960s and led to a flood of new consumer goods. (See chapter 27.)

Another economic boost came from the only large welfare measure passed after the New Deal. The Servicemen's Readjustment Act (GI Bill), enacted in 1944, offered 16 million veterans job training and education; unemployment compensation while they looked for jobs; and low-interest loans to purchase homes, farms, and small businesses. (See "Seeking the American Promise," page 966.) By 1948, some 1.3 million veterans had bought houses with government loans. Helping 2.2 million ex-soldiers attend college, the subsidies sparked a boom in higher education. A drugstore clerk before his military service, Don Condren was able to get an engineering degree and buy his first house. "I think the GI Bill gave the whole country an upward boost economically," he said.

Condren overlooked the disparate ways in which the GI Bill operated. Both African Americans and women found themselves unwelcome in veterans groups that provided information about the new benefits. Like key New Deal programs such as unemployment insurance and aid to mothers with dependent children, GI programs were administered at the state and local levels, which especially in the South routinely discriminated against African Americans. Black veterans who sought jobs for which the military had trained them were shuttled into menial labor. One decorated veteran pointed out that the GI Bill "draws no color line," yet "my color bars me from most decent jobs, and if, instead of accepting menial work, I collect my $20 a week readjustment allowance, I am classified as a 'lazy nigger.'" Throughout the country, African Americans were denied Veterans Administration and Federal Housing Administration loans when they sought to buy houses in poorer neighborhoods, because government agencies had designated homes in these areas as risky investments. Thousands of black veterans did benefit from the GI Bill, but it did not help all ex-soldiers equally.

Blacks and Mexican Americans Push for Their Civil Rights

"I spent four years in the army to free a bunch of Frenchmen and Dutchmen," an African American corporal declared, "and I'm hanged if I'm going to let the Alabama version of the Germans kick me around when I get home." Black veterans as well as civilians resolved that the return to peace would not be a return to the racial injustices of prewar America. Their political clout had grown with the migration of two million African Americans to northern and western cities, where they could vote and their ballots could make a difference. Even in the South, the proportion of blacks who could vote inched up from 2 percent to 12 percent in the 1940s. Pursuing civil rights through the courts and Congress, the National Association for the Advancement of Colored People (NAACP) counted half a million members.

In the postwar years, individual African Americans broke through the color barrier, achieving several "firsts." Jackie Robinson integrated major league baseball when he played for the Brooklyn Dodgers in 1947, braving abuse from fans and players to win the Rookie of the Year Award. In 1950, Ralph J. Bunche

received the Nobel Peace Prize for his United Nations work, and Gwendolyn Brooks was awarded the Pulitzer Prize for poetry. Charlie "Bird" Parker, Ella Fitzgerald, and a host of other black musicians were hugely popular across racial lines.

Still, for most African Americans, little had changed, especially in the South, where violence greeted their attempts to assert their rights. Armed white men turned back Medgar Evers (who would become a key civil rights leader in the 1960s) and four other veterans trying to vote in Mississippi. A mob lynched Isaac Nixon for voting in Georgia, and an all-white jury acquitted the men accused of his murder. In the South, governors, U.S. senators, other politicians, and local vigilantes routinely intimidated potential black voters with threats of economic retaliation and violence.

The cold war heightened American leaders' sensitivity to racial issues, as the United States and Soviet Union vied for the allegiance of newly independent nations with nonwhite populations. Soviet propaganda pointed to racial injustice in the United States, and African Americans themselves petitioned the United Nations to pressure the government on their behalf. Republican senator Henry Cabot Lodge called race relations "our Achilles' heel before the world," while Secretary of State Dean Acheson noted that "hostile reaction to [segregation and discrimination] . . . is growing in alarming proportions," endangering "our moral leadership of the free and democratic nations of the world."

"My very stomach turned over when I learned that Negro soldiers just back from overseas were being dumped out of army trucks in Mississippi and beaten," wrote Truman, shaken by the violence and under pressure to act by civil rights leaders and **liberals**. Wrestling with the Democrats' need for northern black and liberal votes as well as southern white votes, Truman acted more boldly on civil rights than any previous president. In 1946, he created the President's Committee on Civil Rights, and in February 1948 he asked Congress to enact the committee's recommendations. The first president to address the NAACP, in June 1947, Truman asserted that all Americans should have equal rights to housing, education, employment, and the ballot.

As with much of his domestic program, the president failed to act aggressively on his bold words. Congress rebuffed Truman's proposals for civil rights legislation, but eleven states outlawed discrimination in employment, and eighteen banned discrimination in public accommodations. Running for reelection in 1948 and pressured by civil rights activists, Truman issued an executive order to desegregate the armed services, but it lay unimplemented until the Korean War. A large gap loomed between what Truman said about civil rights and what his government accomplished, yet desegregation of the military and the administration's support of civil rights cases in the Supreme Court contributed to far-reaching changes, while his Committee on Civil Rights set an agenda for years to come. Breaking with the past, Truman used his office to set a moral agenda for the nation's longest unfulfilled promise.

Although discussion of race and civil rights usually focused on African Americans, Mexican Americans endured similar injustices. In 1929, they had formed the League of United Latin-American Citizens (LULAC) to combat discrimination and segregation in the Southwest. Like black soldiers after World War II, Mexican American veterans believed, as one of them insisted,

> "I spent four years in the army to free a bunch of Frenchmen and Dutchmen," an African American corporal declared, "and I'm hanged if I'm going to let the Alabama version of the Germans kick me around when I get home."

Segregation

The segregation visible on this bus was a feature of life in the South from the late nineteenth century until the 1960s. State and local laws mandated separation from the cradle to the grave. African Americans could not use white hospitals, cemeteries, schools, libraries, swimming pools, restrooms, or drinking fountains. They were relegated to balconies in movie theaters and kept apart from whites in all public meetings. Segregated buses would become the target of the first large-scale civil rights protest, in Montgomery, Alabama, in 1955–1956.
Stan Wayman/Time Life Pictures/Getty Images.

The GI Bill Transforms Higher Education

For Dick Koch, a bombardier who flew B-24s in the Army Air Corps during World War II, the future looked uncertain as the war ground to a close. What would the country do with Koch and the other 16 million military men and women who had served their country?

The generation that fought in World War II had grown up in the Great Depression, when more than 15 million Americans experienced unemployment. Most of the returning veterans had only limited education. Many had never held a job before they entered the service. Haunted by the ghost of the depression, President Franklin Roosevelt warned, "Veterans must not be demobilized into an environment of inflation and unemployment, to a place on a bread line or on a corner selling apples."

The American Legion, a veterans advocacy group formed in 1919, hammered out a plan that called for "a bill of rights for GI Joe and GI Jane." (GI, an abbreviation for "government issue," originally referred to standard military equipment but came to be used for anyone enlisted in any branch of the service.) Introduced in Congress in January 1944, the Servicemen's Readjustment Act, or GI Bill, called for unemployment insurance, loans to veterans for businesses and housing, and, most significantly, payment for higher education, including college, graduate studies, and professional and vocational training. Congress passed the legislation, and on June 22, 1944, just weeks after the D Day invasion of Europe, President Roosevelt signed into law the Servicemen's Readjustment Act, popularly known as the GI Bill.

Not all Americans supported the GI Bill. Some grumbled that unemployment insurance would "coddle loafers." Southern segregationists balked at granting black GIs equal benefits. The president of the University of Chicago predicted that the GI Bill would turn elite campuses into "educational hobo jungles." In the past, college and university education had been the exclusive preserve of the privileged. The GI Bill would change all that. As Senator Bob Dole of Kansas marveled, "It didn't make any difference what my parents' income was or the fact that my dad wore his overalls everyday to work, I still got the benefit."

Dick Koch had been shot down over Germany and spent months as a prisoner of war. Among the few books in the German prison camp was a copy of *The Doctors Mayo*, the story of the family of doctors who founded the prestigious Mayo Clinic. Koch read and reread the book, vowing to become a doctor. But as the son of Russian and German immigrants, his chances seemed slim. When the war ended, Koch returned to California, where he was reunited with his wife, Jean. As soon as he learned of the GI Bill's education benefit, he rushed to enroll in the premed program at the University of California, Berkeley.

Koch was one of more than 2.2 million veterans who headed off to college on the GI Bill. The Veterans Administration paid schools for tuition, fees, and books and issued a monthly stipend to each veteran and his dependents. Dick and Jean Koch scraped by on $90 a month. To make extra money, Jean raised chickens and sold the eggs.

The veterans transformed higher education. Older, more serious, and more diverse in race, class, and ethnicity, they soon crowded college classrooms. By 1947, more than 49 percent of the student body nationwide consisted of veterans. Eager to get ahead, the ex-GIs had little time for fraternities and pep rallies. Koch and his wife started a family that would grow to five children. Colleges that had once expelled students for marrying now rushed to accommodate married students and their children, providing housing in Quonset huts and trailers.

When Koch graduated from Berkeley, he packed his family into an army surplus jeep and drove east to the University of Rochester in New York for medical school. The GI Bill covered graduate and professional school. Koch and his growing family got a stipend of $120 a month.

As it turned out, the government had badly miscalculated how many veterans would take advantage of the GI Bill to get an education. Fewer veterans than anticipated collected the unemployment insurance the bill provided, but many more than expected took advantage of the educational provisions. Instead of the estimated 150,000 a year, by 1947 there were 1,164,000 veterans registered for school on the GI Bill.

The returning GIs changed the country's notion of who merited a college education. Men whose fathers had stood in breadlines during the depression went to school with scions of wealthy families. Black veterans sat in classrooms alongside whites. The children of Catholic and Jewish immigrants, once largely excluded from higher education, flocked to colleges and universities. More than a million ex-GIs, including Dick Koch, became the first members of their families to attend college. These diverse students turned out to be as competent and smart as traditional college students. Even President James B. Conant of Harvard had to concede that the veterans were "the most mature and promising students Harvard has ever had."

The democratization and diversity of higher education did have some significant limits. Southern state universities and colleges remained segregated, barring black veterans from enrolling. As a result, some 20,000 to 60,000 eligible black veterans were turned away because the small historically black colleges in the South had no room for them. Women also found themselves severely disadvantaged by the GI Bill. Although it was designed for GI Jane as well as GI Joe, only 3 percent of the veterans attending college on the GI Bill came from among the 350,000 women who had served in the military. Many servicewomen were not even aware that they qualified for the benefit. As a result of the GI Bill, a gap widened between college-educated men and women, with the percentage of women attending colleges and universities stagnating while the percentage of men climbed.

Nearly 8 million veterans took advantage of the GI Bill's education provision. Among those, a third

Veterans Go to College
So many World War II veterans wanted to use their GI benefits for higher education that colleges were overwhelmed. Many institutions had to turn away students, and they frequently limited the enrollments of women so that they could accommodate veterans. At the University of Iowa, where this photo was taken, veterans like these men comprised 60 percent of the student body.
Margaret Bourke-White/Time Life Pictures/Getty Images.

attended college, just under half enrolled in other types of trade and specialty schools, and the remainder split between farm training and subsidized "on the job" training. Thanks to the GI Bill, 67,000 doctors, 238,000 teachers, 91,000 scientists, 450,000 engineers, and 240,000 accountants received an education. Numbered among those who went to college courtesy of the GI Bill were fourteen Nobel Prize winners, three Supreme Court justices, and three presidents.

The money spent on veterans' education benefits proved to be a good investment. By encouraging veterans to get more education, the GI Bill kept them from flooding the

job market and meant that when they did look for work, they had more skills and commanded higher salaries. Economists estimated that for every dollar spent on GI Bill education benefits, the country got back as much as eight dollars in income taxes.

Dick Koch realized his dream of becoming a doctor, working as a specialist in child development at Childrens Hospital Los Angeles. "We owe everything to the GI Bill," Koch observed. "Four of my five brothers got out of the service and went to school on the GI Bill as well. My whole family owes it a very big debt of gratitude."

that "we had earned our credentials as American citizens. We had paid our dues. . . . We were not about to take any crap." When Mexican Americans encountered difficulties in getting their veterans' benefits, in 1948 a group in Corpus Christi, Texas, led by Dr. Héctor Peréz García, a combat surgeon who had earned the Bronze Star, formed the American GI Forum. The organization took off when the wife of Felix Longoria, who had given his life in the Philippines, was refused the use of a white funeral chapel in Three Rivers, Texas, and was told that her husband would be buried in the Mexican section of the cemetery. With the help of Senator Lyndon Johnson, the GI Forum arranged for burial in Arlington National Cemetery. It went on to become a key national organization battling discrimination against Latinos and electing sympathetic officials.

Women Stand Up for the Empire Zinc Strike

In 1950, Mexican American miners belonging to Local 890 of the International Union of Mine, Mill and Smelter Workers (Mine-Mill) in southern New Mexico went on strike against their employer, Empire Zinc. In 1951, Empire Zinc tried to reopen the mine and got a court order preventing strikers from blocking access. Over the objections of their husbands, the wives of union members took to the picket line so that their husbands would not be subject to fines and jail sentences. As a result, the company was forced to settle the strike in 1952. The Empire Zinc strike was immortalized in the 1954 movie *Salt of the Earth*, which explores the working conditions of, racism against, and gender relations among Mexican Americans at that time.

Archives, University of Colorado at Boulder Libraries/International Union of Mine, Mill and Smelter Workers Papers, Box 557.

"Education is our freedom," read the GI Forum's motto, signifying the importance of learning to Mexican Americans and indirectly their dismay at the routine segregation of children in the public schools. Parents filed a class action suit in Orange County, California, winning a federal court decision in 1947 that outlawed the practice of separating Mexican American and white children in the schools. In 1948, LULAC and the GI Forum persuaded a federal court to outlaw Texas school districts' practice of segregating Mexican American students in separate schools or classes. Such projects paralleled the efforts of the NAACP on behalf of African Americans that would culminate in the *Brown* decision in 1954 (see chapter 27). These efforts, along with challenges to discrimination in employment and efforts for political representation, demonstrated a growing mobilization of Mexican Americans in the Southwest.

The Fair Deal Flounders

Republicans capitalized on public frustrations with economic reconversion in the 1946 congressional election, accusing the administration of "confusion, corruption, and communism." Helen Gahagan Douglas hung on to her seat, but the Republicans captured control of Congress for the first time in fourteen years. Many had campaigned against New Deal "bureaucracy" and "radicalism" in 1946, and they succeeded in the Eightieth Congress to weaken some reform programs and enact tax cuts favoring higher-income groups.

Organized labor took the most severe attack when Congress passed the Taft-Hartley Act over Truman's veto in 1947. Called "Tuff-Heartless" by unions, the law reduced the power of organized labor and made it more difficult to organize workers. For example, states could now pass "right-to-work" laws, which banned the practice of requiring all workers to join a union once a majority had voted for it. Many states, especially in the South and West, rushed to enact such laws, encouraging industries to relocate there. Taft-Hartley maintained the New Deal principle of government protection for **collective bargaining**, but it put the government more squarely between labor and management.

As the 1948 elections approached, Truman faced not only a resurgent Republican Party headed by its nominee, Thomas E. Dewey, but also two revolts within his own party. On the left, Henry A. Wallace, whose foreign policy views had cost him his cabinet seat, led the new

Truman's Whistle-Stop Campaign

Harry Truman rallies a crowd from his campaign train at a stop in Bridgeport, Pennsylvania, in October 1948. His campaign theme song, "I'm Just Wild about Harry," was borrowed, with the words slightly changed, from the 1921 musical *Shuffle Along*. This was the last presidential election in which pollsters predicted the wrong winner. They stopped taking polls in mid-October, after which many voters apparently changed their minds. One commentator praised the American citizenry, who "couldn't be ticketed by the polls, knew its own mind and had picked the rather unlikely but courageous figure of Truman to carry on its banner."

Photo: Truman Library; Sheet music: Collection of Janice L. and David J. Frent.

READING THE IMAGE: This photo was taken one month before the election. Do you think Thomas E. Dewey had second thoughts on seeing such large crowds gather in support of Truman?

CONNECTIONS: President Truman was under attack by the Republicans and could not enact the Fair Deal. Almost everyone thought he would lose the election. Why do you think the American people responded so well to his campaign? In what ways have presidential campaigns changed since Harry Truman's time?

FOR MORE HELP ANALYZING THIS IMAGE, see the visual activity for this chapter in the Online Study Guide at bedfordstmartins.com/roark.

Progressive Party. On the right, South Carolina governor J. Strom Thurmond headed the States' Rights Party—the Dixiecrats—formed by southern Democrats who had walked out of the 1948 Democratic Party convention when it passed a liberal civil rights plank.

Almost alone in believing he could win, Truman crisscrossed the country by train, answering supporters' cries of "Give 'em hell, Harry." So bleak were Truman's prospects that the confi-

dent Dewey ran a low-key campaign, and on election night, the *Chicago Daily Tribune* printed its next day's issue with the headline DEWEY DEFEATS TRUMAN. But Truman took 303 electoral votes to Dewey's 189, and his party regained control of Congress (Map 26.2, page 970). His unexpected victory attested to his skills as a campaigner, broad support for his foreign policy, the enduring popularity of New Deal reform, and appreciation of the booming economy.

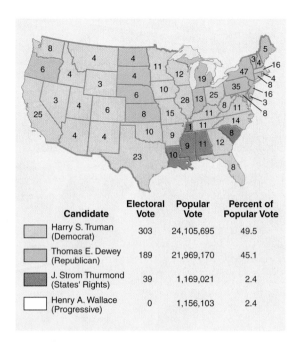

Candidate	Electoral Vote	Popular Vote	Percent of Popular Vote
Harry S. Truman (Democrat)	303	24,105,695	49.5
Thomas E. Dewey (Republican)	189	21,969,170	45.1
J. Strom Thurmond (States' Rights)	39	1,169,021	2.4
Henry A. Wallace (Progressive)	0	1,156,103	2.4

MAP 26.2   The Election of 1948

Truman failed to turn his victory into success for his Fair Deal agenda. Congress made modest improvements in Social Security and raised the minimum wage, but it passed only one significant reform measure. Housing was a top priority for Congresswoman Douglas, who deplored the lack of adequate shelter, especially for veterans reduced to living in "hand-me-down houses for heroes." She was a passionate advocate for the Housing Act of 1949, which authorized 810,000 units of government-constructed housing over the next six years and represented a landmark commitment by the government to address the housing needs of the poor. Yet it fell far short of actual need—just 61,000 units had been built when Truman left office—and slum clearance frequently displaced the poor without providing decent alternatives.

With southern Democrats often joining the Republicans, Congress rejected Truman's civil rights measures and proposals for a federal health care program, aid to education, and a new agriculture program to benefit small farmers and consumers. His efforts to revise immigration policy produced the McCarran-Walter Act of 1952, ending the outright ban on immigration and citizenship for Japanese and other Asians. But the law also authorized the government to bar suspected Communists and homosexuals and maintained the discriminatory quota system established in the 1920s. Truman denounced that provision as

"unworthy of our traditions and our ideals," but Congress overrode his veto.

Although he blamed political opponents for defeating his Fair Deal, Truman in fact devoted much more energy to foreign policy than to his domestic proposals. Moreover, by late 1950, the Korean War embroiled the president in controversy, diverted his attention from domestic affairs, and depleted his power as a legislative leader. His failure to make good on his domestic proposals set the United States apart from most European nations, which by the 1950s had in place comprehensive health, housing, and employment security programs to underwrite the material well-being of their populations.

The Domestic Chill: McCarthyism

Truman's domestic program also suffered from a wave of anti-Communist hysteria that weakened liberal and leftist forces. Both "Red-baiting" (attempts to discredit individuals or ideas by associating them with communism) and official retaliation against leftist critics of the government had flourished during the Red scare at the end of World War I (see chapter 22). A second Red scare convulsed the nation after World War II, born of partisan political maneuvering, collapse of the Soviet-American alliance, setbacks in U.S. foreign policy, and disclosures of Soviet espionage.

Republicans who had attacked the New Deal as a plot of radicals now jumped on cold war events, such as the Soviet takeover of Eastern Europe and the Communist triumph in China, to accuse Democrats of fostering internal subversion. Wisconsin senator Joseph R. McCarthy avowed that "the Communists within our borders have been more responsible for the success of Communism abroad than Soviet Russia." McCarthy's charges—such as the allegation that retired general George C. Marshall belonged to a Communist conspiracy—were reckless and often ludicrous, but the press covered him avidly, and **McCarthyism** became a term synonymous with the anti-Communist crusade.

Revelations of Soviet espionage gave some credibility to fears of internal communism. In 1945, for example, Igor Gouzenko defected from the Soviet Embassy in Ottawa and disclosed a Soviet spy ring. In the United States, a number of ex-Communists, including Whittaker Chambers and Elizabeth Bentley, testified that they and others had provided secret documents to the Soviets. Most alarming of all, in 1950 Klaus Fuchs, a British physicist working on the atomic bomb project, confessed that he was a spy and implicated several Americans, including Ethel and Julius Rosenberg. The Rosenbergs pleaded innocent but were convicted of conspiracy to commit espionage and electrocuted in 1953.

Records opened in the 1990s showed that the Soviet Union did receive secret documents from Americans that probably hastened its development of nuclear weapons by a year or two. Yet membership in the U.S. Communist Party had declined. At the peak of the hysteria, it had only about twenty thousand members, some of them undercover FBI agents. The vast majority of individuals hunted down in the Red scare had simply at one time joined the Communist Party, associated with Communists, or supported radical causes. And most of those activities had taken place long before the cold war had made the Soviet Union an enemy. Investigators often cared little for such distinctions, however.

In Washington, investigations went on in both Congress and the executive branch. Stung by charges of communism in the 1946 midterm elections, Truman issued Executive Order 9835 in March 1947, establishing loyalty review boards throughout the government to investigate every federal employee. "A nightmare from which there [was] no awakening" was how State Department employee Esther Brunauer described it when she and her husband, a chemist in the navy, both lost their jobs because he had joined a Communist youth organization in the 1920s and associated with suspected radicals. After he left office, Truman insisted to a friend, "I wanted security with the rights of individuals protected," but government investigators violated the **Bill of Rights** by allowing anonymous informers to make charges and placing the burden of proof on the accused. More than two thousand civil service employees lost their jobs, and another ten thousand resigned as the program continued into the mid-1950s.

At a time when homosexuality was widely considered to be abnormal and shameful, gay men and lesbians were particularly vulnerable to charges of disloyalty. In the first four years of the loyalty program, more than four hundred suspected homosexuals were fired or resigned over charges of "sexual perversion," and this number grew as the Red scare intensified in the 1950s. Years later, Truman admitted that the loyalty program had been a mistake.

Congressional committees, such as the House Un-American Activities Committee (HUAC), often pushed executive branch officials to go after suspicious employees even more avidly, and these committees also conducted their own investigations of individuals' past and present political associations. When those under scrutiny refused to name names, investigators charged that silence was tantamount to confession, and these "unfriendly witnesses" lost their jobs and suffered public ostracism. In 1947, HUAC investigated radical activity in Hollywood. Frank Sinatra protested, wondering if someone called for "a square deal for the underdog, will they call you a Commie? . . . Are they going to scare us into silence?" Some actors and directors cooperated, but ten refused, citing their First Amendment rights. The "Hollywood Ten" served jail sentences for contempt of Congress, a punishment that Helen Gahagan Douglas

---

Senator Joseph R. McCarthy
Although the Wisconsin senator made his reputation on anticommunism, he seized that issue more from the need to have a platform for his 1950 reelection campaign than from genuine concern grounded in real evidence. McCarthy had loved politics since his high school days in Appleton, Wisconsin, and easily distorted the truth to promote his political ambitions. The 1946 campaign poster in this photograph highlights his service in World War II, which he presented as involving dangerous combat missions as a tail gunner. In fact, he spent his time as an intelligence officer debriefing combat pilots. His only missions were flights over islands no longer controlled by the Japanese.
© Bettmann/Corbis.

fought, and found themselves blacklisted in the movie industry.

The Truman administration also went directly after the Communist Party, prosecuting its leaders under the Smith Act, passed in 1940, which made it a crime to "advocate the overthrow and destruction of the Government of the United States by force and violence." Although civil libertarians argued that the guilty verdicts violated First Amendment rights to freedom of speech, press, and association, the Supreme Court ruled in 1951 (*Dennis v. United States*) that the Communist threat overrode constitutional guarantees.

The domestic cold war spread beyond the nation's capital. State and local governments investigated citizens, demanded loyalty oaths, fired

individuals suspected of disloyalty, banned books from public libraries, and more. Universities dismissed professors, and public school teachers lost their jobs in New York, Los Angeles, and elsewhere. Because the Communist Party had helped organize unions and championed racial justice, labor and civil rights activists fell prey to McCarthyism as well. As African American activist Jack O'Dell remembered, "The segregationists defended segregation by saying they weren't against . . . equal rights for blacks— they were against communism. But their interpretation of Communist was anybody who supported the right of blacks to have civil rights."

McCarthyism caused untold economic and psychological harm to individuals innocent of breaking any law. Thousands of people were humiliated and discredited, hounded from their jobs, even in some cases imprisoned. The anti-Communist crusade violated fundamental constitutional rights of freedom of speech and association, stifled expression of dissenting ideas, and removed unpopular causes from public contemplation.

> **REVIEW** Why did Truman have limited success in implementing his domestic agenda?

The Cold War Becomes Hot: Korea

The cold war erupted into a shooting war in June 1950, when troops from Communist North Korea invaded South Korea. For the first time, Americans went into battle to implement containment. Confirming the global reach of the Truman Doctrine, U.S. involvement in Korea also marked the militarization of American foreign policy. The United States, in concert with the United Nations, ultimately held the line in Korea, but at a great cost in lives, dollars, and domestic unity.

Korea and the Military Implementation of Containment

The war grew out of the artificial division of Korea after World War II as well as long-standing divisions among the Korean people. Having expelled the Japanese, who had controlled Korea since 1904, the United States and the Soviet Union created two occupation zones separated

The Red Scare in Popular Culture
In 1949, producer Howard Hughes provided fodder for the Red scare with his movie *I Married a Communist*. Featuring an all-star cast, the movie tells the story of a dockworker who rose to become a shipping executive and then was used by the Communists, who threatened to expose his left-wing associations in the 1930s.
The Michael Barson Collection/Past Perfect.

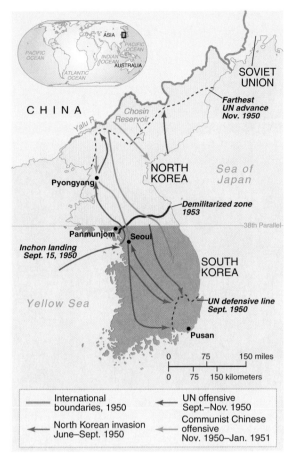

MAP 26.3   The Korean War, 1950–1953
Although each side had plunged deep into enemy territory, the war ended in 1953 with the dividing line between North and South Korea nearly where it had been before the fighting began.

READING THE MAP: How far south did the North Korean forces progress at the height of their invasion? How far north did the UN forces get? What countries border Korea? **CONNECTIONS:** What dangers did the forays of MacArthur's forces to within forty miles of the Korean-Chinese border pose? Why did Truman forbid MacArthur to approach that border? What political considerations on the home front influenced Truman's policy and military strategy regarding Korea?

FOR MORE HELP ANALYZING THIS MAP, see the map activity for this chapter in the Online Study Guide at bedfordstmartins.com/roark.

American-favored candidate, Korean nationalist Syngman Rhee, was elected president, and the United States withdrew most of its troops. In the fall of 1948, the Soviets established the People's Republic of North Korea under Kim Il-sung and also withdrew. Although doubting that Rhee's repressive government could sustain popular support, U.S. officials appreciated his staunch anticommunism and provided small amounts of economic and military aid to South Korea.

Insurgencies of workers and peasants against factory owners, landlords, and the Rhee government claimed 100,000 lives between 1946 and mid-1950, and skirmishes between North and South Korean troops at the thirty-eighth parallel occurred beginning in 1948. In June 1950, however, the civil war turned into an international war when 90,000 North Koreans swept into South Korea. Truman's advisers immediately assumed that the Soviet Union, China, or both had instigated the attack. Revelations decades later indicated that the Russians and the Chinese had acquiesced, but with little enthusiasm. Instead, Kim Il-sung had been the main instigator. Kim wanted to bolster his position by championing Korean unification, and the substantial opposition to Rhee suggested that many South Koreans would support the North Korean army.

> Six days after learning of the North Korean attack, Truman decided to intervene, viewing Korea as "the Greece of the Far East."

On June 30, six days after learning of the attack, Truman decided to intervene, viewing Korea as "the Greece of the Far East." With the Soviet Union boycotting the UN Security Council to protest its refusal to seat a representative from the People's Republic of China, the United States obtained UN sponsorship of a collective effort to repel the attack. Authorized to appoint a commander for the UN force, Truman named General Douglas MacArthur, World War II hero and head of the postwar occupation of Japan.

Sixteen nations, including many NATO allies, sent troops to Korea, but the United States furnished most of the personnel and weapons, deploying almost 1.8 million troops and dictating military strategy. By failing to ask Congress for a declaration of war, Truman violated the spirit if not the letter of the Constitution. Moreover, although Congress authorized the mobilization of troops and appropriated funds to fight the war, the president's political opponents called it "Truman's war" when the military situation worsened.

by the thirty-eighth parallel (Map 26.3). The Soviets supported the Korean Communist Party in the north, while the United States backed the Korean Democratic Party in the south. With Moscow and Washington unable to agree on a unification plan, in July 1948 the United Nations sponsored elections in South Korea. The

POWs in Korea
These demoralized U.S. soldiers reflect the grim situation for U.S. forces during the early months of
the Korean War. Their North Korean captors forced them to march through Seoul in July 1950 carrying
a banner proclaiming the righteousness of the Communist cause and attacking U.S. intervention.
AP Images.

The first American soldiers rushed to Korea unprepared and ill equipped, enduring severe defeats in the first three months of the war. The North Koreans took the capital of Seoul and drove deep into South Korea, forcing UN troops to retreat to Pusan by September. General MacArthur launched a bold counteroffensive at Inchon, 180 miles behind North Korean lines. By mid-October, UN forces had pushed the North Koreans back to the thirty-eighth parallel. Then came the momentous decision of whether to invade North Korea and seek to unify the country.

From Containment to Rollback to Containment

"Troops could not be expected . . . to march up to a surveyor's line and stop," remarked Secretary of State Dean Acheson, reflecting popular and official support for transforming the military objective from containment to elimination of the enemy and unification of Korea. Thus, for the only time during the cold war, the United States tried to roll back communism. With UN approval, on September 27, 1950, Truman authorized MacArthur to cross the thirty-eighth parallel. Concerned about possible intervention by China or the Soviet Union, the president directed the general to keep UN troops away from the Korean-Chinese border. Disregarding the order, MacArthur sent UN forces to within forty miles of China. When the troops approached the Yalu River separating China from Korea, one U.S. army officer recalled, "I thought we had won the war." But 300,000 Chinese soldiers waited on the other side. They stormed across the border, helping the North Koreans recapture Seoul by December.

Under the leadership of General Matthew B. Ridgway, the Eighth Army turned the tide again. During three months of grueling battle, UN forces fought their way back to the thirty-eighth parallel. At that point, Truman decided to seek a negotiated settlement. MacArthur was furious when the goal of the war reverted to containment, which to him represented defeat. Truman and his advisers, however, adamantly opposed a wider war in Asia. According to General Omar Bradley, chairman of the Joint Chiefs of Staff, MacArthur wanted to wage "the wrong war, at the wrong place, at the wrong time, with the wrong enemy."

MacArthur took his case to the public, in effect challenging both the president's authority to conduct foreign policy and the principle of civilian control of the military. Fed up with MacArthur's insubordination, Truman fired him in April 1951. Many Americans, however, sided with MacArthur. "Quite an explosion. . . . Letters of abuse by the dozens," Truman recorded in his diary. The general came home to a hero's welcome, while baseball fans booed the president when he appeared at Washington, D.C.'s Griffith Stadium on opening day.

The adulation for MacArthur reflected American frustrations with containment. Why should Americans die simply to preserve the status quo rather than destroy the enemy once and for all? Siding with MacArthur enabled Americans to hold on to their belief that the United States was all-powerful and to pin the Korean stalemate on the government's ineptitude or willingness to shelter subversives. Moreover, Truman's earlier success in "scaring the hell" out of the country over the threat of communism in Greece and Turkey came back to haunt him. If communism was so evil, why not stamp it out as MacArthur wanted? When Congress investigated MacArthur's firing, all of the top military leaders supported the president, yet Truman never recovered from the political fallout. Nor was he able to end the war. Cease-fire negotiations began in July 1951, but peace talks dragged on for two more years while twelve thousand more U.S. soldiers died.

Korea, Communism, and the 1952 Election

Popular discontent with President Truman's war boosted Republican candidates in the 1952 election. The Republicans' presidential nominee, General Dwight D. Eisenhower, had emerged from World War II with immense popularity. Reared in modest circumstances in Abilene, Kansas, Eisenhower attended West Point and rose steadily through the army ranks. As supreme commander in Europe, he won widespread acclaim for leading the Allied armies to victory over Germany. After the war, he served as army chief of staff and then as president of Columbia University. In 1950, Truman appointed Eisenhower the first supreme commander of NATO forces.

Both Republicans and Democrats had courted Eisenhower for the presidency in 1948. Although the general believed that professional soldiers should stay out of politics, he found compelling reasons to run in 1952. Eisenhower generally agreed with Democratic foreign policy, but he deplored the Democrats' propensity to solve domestic problems with costly new federal programs. He equally disliked the foreign policy views of the leading Republican presidential contender, Senator Robert A. Taft, who attacked containment and sought to cut defense spending. Eisenhower decided to run both to stop Taft and the **conservative** wing of the Republican Party and to turn the Democrats out of the White House.

> "Troops could not be expected . . . to march up to a surveyor's line and stop," remarked Secretary of State Dean Acheson.

Eisenhower defeated Taft for the nomination, but the old guard prevailed on the party platform. It excoriated containment as "negative, futile, and immoral" and charged the Truman administration with shielding "traitors to the Nation in high places." By choosing thirty-nine-year-old Senator Richard M. Nixon for his running mate, Eisenhower helped to appease the right wing of the party and ensured that anticommunism would be a major theme of the campaign.

Richard Milhous Nixon grew up in southern California, worked his way through college and law school, served in the navy, and briefly practiced law. In 1946, he entered politics, helping the Republicans recapture Congress by defeating a liberal incumbent for a seat in the House of Representatives. Nixon quickly made a name for himself as a member of HUAC and a key anti-Communist, moving to the Senate with his victory over Helen Gahagan Douglas in 1950.

With his public approval ratings sinking, Truman decided not to run for reelection. The Democrats nominated Adlai E. Stevenson, the popular governor of Illinois, who was acceptable to both liberals and southerners. Stevenson could not escape the domestic fallout from the Korean

The 1952 Republican Ticket
At the Republican convention in 1952, presidential nominee Dwight D. Eisenhower stands with his wife, Mamie (right); his running mate, Richard Nixon; and Nixon's wife, Patricia (left), at the start of their campaign. The campaign poster refers to scandals involving Truman associates and his failure to end the Korean War.
Photo: © Bettmann/Corbis; Poster: Collection of Janice L. and David J. Frent.

War, however, nor could he match the widespread appeal of Eisenhower. While Eisenhower refrained from Red-baiting, Nixon reprised the anti-Communist tactics of his Senate campaign, calling Stevenson "Adlai the Appeaser" and saying that his opponent had a degree from the "cowardly college of Communist Containment."

The Republican campaign stumbled just once, over the last item of its "Korea, Communism, and Corruption" policy. When the press reported that Nixon had accepted money from a private political fund supported by wealthy Californians, Democrats jumped to the attack, even though such gifts were common and legal. While Eisenhower deliberated about whether to dump Nixon from the ticket, Nixon saved himself by making an emotional nationwide appeal on the new medium of television. He disclosed his finances and documented his modest standard of living. Conceding that the family pet, Checkers,

could be considered an illegal gift (he had received the dog from a Texas salesman), Nixon refused to break his daughters' hearts by returning the cocker spaniel. The overwhelmingly positive response to the "Checkers speech" kept Nixon on the ticket.

Shortly before the election, Eisenhower announced dramatically, "I shall go to Korea," and voters registered their confidence in his ability to end the war. Cutting sharply into traditional Democratic territory, Eisenhower won several southern states and garnered 55 percent of the popular vote overall. His coattails carried a narrow Republican majority to Congress.

An Armistice and the War's Costs

Eisenhower made good on his pledge to end the Korean War. In July 1953, the two sides reached an armistice that left Korea divided, again roughly at the thirty-eighth parallel, with North and South separated by a two-and-one-half-mile wide demilitarized zone (see Map 26.3). The war took the lives of 36,000 Americans and wounded more than 100,000.

Nick Tosques, among thousands of U.S. soldiers who were taken prisoner, spent two and a half years in a prisoner of war camp. "They interrogated us every day," he recalled. "You never knew when they were coming for you. . . . Pretty soon I was telling them anything, just to keep from getting hit." South Korea lost more than 1 million people to war-related causes, and more than 1.8 million North Koreans and Chinese were killed or wounded.

The Truman administration judged the war a success for containment, since the United States had backed up its promise to help nations that were resisting communism. Both Truman and Eisenhower managed to contain what amounted to a world war—involving twenty nations altogether—within a single country. Moreover, despite both presidents' threats to use nuclear weapons, they authorized only conventional weapons in Korea.

The Korean War had an enormous effect on defense policy and spending. In April 1950, two months before the war began, the National Security Council completed a top-secret report on the United States' military strength. The document, known as NSC 68, warned that the survival of the nation required a massive military buildup and the tripling of the defense budget. Truman took no immediate action on these recommendations, but the Korean War brought about nearly all of the military expansion called for in NSC 68, vastly increasing U.S. capacity to act as a global power. Using the Korean crisis to expand American clout elsewhere, Truman won congressional approval to rearm West Germany and commit troops to NATO. Military spending shot up from $14 billion in 1950 to $50 billion in 1953 and remained above $40 billion thereafter. By 1953, defense spending claimed 60 percent of the federal budget, and the size of the armed forces had tripled.

To General Matthew Ridgway, MacArthur's successor as commander of the UN forces, Korea taught the lesson that U.S. forces should never again fight a land war in Asia. Eisenhower concurred. Nevertheless, the Korean War induced the Truman administration to expand its role in Asia by increasing aid to the French, who were fighting to hang on to their colonial empire in Indochina. As U.S. marines retreated from a battle against Chinese soldiers in 1950, they sang, prophetically, "We're Harry's police force on call, / So put back your pack on, / The next step is Saigon, / Cheer up, me lads, bless 'em all."

REVIEW   How did the Korean War shape American foreign policy in the 1950s?

Conclusion: The Cold War's Costs and Consequences

Helen Gahagan Douglas initially resisted designating the Soviet Union as an enemy and opposed the implementation of containment with aid to Greece and Turkey in 1947. By 1948, however, she had gotten behind Truman's decision to fight communism throughout the world, which marked the most momentous foreign policy initiative in the nation's history. More than any development in the postwar world, the cold war defined American politics and society for decades to come. It transformed the federal government, shifting its priorities from domestic to external affairs, greatly expanding its budget, and substantially increasing the power of the president. Military spending helped transform the nation itself, as defense contracts encouraged economic and population booms in the West and Southwest. The nuclear arms race put the people of the world at risk, consumed resources that might have been used to improve living standards, and skewed the economy toward dependence on military projects. While debate persisted about who was responsible for the cold war and whether it could have been avoided, no one could doubt its impact on American society or the world.

> By 1953, defense spending claimed 60 percent of the federal budget, and the size of the armed forces had tripled.

In sharp contrast to foreign policy, the domestic policies of the postwar years reflected continuity with the past. Most of the New Deal reforms remained in place despite Republicans' promises to turn back the clock. Helen Gahagan Douglas came to Congress hoping to expand the New Deal, to help find "a way by which all people can live out their lives in dignity and decency." She avidly supported Truman's proposals for new programs in education, health, agriculture, and civil rights, but a majority of her colleagues did not. Consequently, the poor and minorities suffered even while a majority of Americans enjoyed a higher standard of living in an economy boosted by cold war spending and the reconstruction of Western Europe and Japan.

Many Americans, not accustomed to paying sustained attention to the rest of the world or to fighting wars without total defeat of the enemy, had difficulty accepting the terms of the cold war. Consequently, another high cost of the cold war was the anti-Communist hysteria that swept the nation, costing Douglas a Senate seat and more generally stifling debate and narrowing the range of ideas acceptable for political discussion. Partisan politics and Truman's warnings about the Communist menace fueled McCarthyism, but the obsession with subversion also fed on popular frustrations over the failure of containment to produce clear-cut victories. Convulsing the nation in bitter disunity, McCarthyism reflected a loss of confidence in American power. And that frustration grew with the Korean war, which ended in stalemate rather than the defeat of communism. It would be a major challenge of the next administration to restore national unity and confidence.

Selected Bibliography

General Works

Rodolfo Acuña, *Occupied America: A History of Chicanos* (5th ed., 2004).

Carol Anderson, *Eyes off the Prize: The United Nations and the African American Struggle for Human Rights, 1944–1955* (2003).

Peter L. Hahn, *Caught in the Middle East: U.S. Policy toward the Arab-Israeli Conflict, 1945–1961* (2004).

Alonzo L. Hamby, *Man of the People: A Life of Harry S. Truman* (1995).

Ira Katznelson, *When Affirmative Action Was White: An Untold History of Racial Inequality in Twentieth-Century America* (2005).

James T. Patterson, *Grand Expectations: The United States, 1945–1974* (1996).

Brenda Gayle Plummer, *Rising Wind: Black Americans and U.S. Foreign Affairs, 1935–1960* (1996).

Ingrid Winther Scobie, *Center Stage: Helen Gahagan Douglas: A Life* (1992).

Michael S. Sherry, *In the Shadow of War* (1995).

Domestic Politics and Policies

Jonathan Bell, *The Liberal State on Trial: The Cold War and American Politics in the Truman Years* (2004).

Kevin Boyle, *The UAW and the Heyday of American Liberalism, 1945–1968* (1995).

Griffin Fariello, *Red Scare: Memories of the American Inquisition* (1995).

Kari Frederickson, *The Dixiecrat Revolt and the End of the Solid South, 1932–1968* (2001).

Edward Humes, *Over Here: How the GI Bill Transformed the American Dream* (2006).

David K. Johnson, *The Lavender Scare: The Cold War Persecution of Gays and Lesbians in the Federal Government* (2004).

Suzanne Mettler, *Soldiers to Citizens: The G.I. Bill and the Making of the Greatest Generation* (2005).

Richard Gid Powers, *Not without Honor: The History of American Anticommunism* (1995).

Henry A. J. Ramos, *The American GI Forum: In Pursuit of the Dream, 1948–1983* (1998).

Ellen W. Schrecker, *Many Are the Crimes: McCarthyism in America* (1998).

The Cold War

Robert L. Beisner, *Dean Acheson: A Life in the Cold War* (2006).

Paul Boyer, *By the Dawn's Early Light: American Thought and Culture at the Dawn of the Atomic Age* (1985).

Carolyn Eisenberg, *Drawing the Line: The American Decision to Divide Germany, 1944–1949* (1996).

John Fousek, *To Lead the Free World: American Nationalism and the Cultural Roots of the Cold War* (2000).

John L. Gaddis, *The Cold War: A New History* (2005).

Michael Hogan, *A Cross of Iron: Harry S. Truman and the Origins of the National Security State* (1998).

Melvyn Leffler, *A Preponderance of Power: National Security, the Truman Administration, and the Cold War* (1992).

Ernest R. May, ed., *American Cold War Strategy: Interpreting NSC 68* (1993).

Arnold A. Offner, *Another Such Victory: President Truman and the Cold War, 1945–1953* (2002).

Richard Rhodes, *Dark Sun: The Making of the Hydrogen Bomb* (1995).

Katherine A. S. Sibley, *Red Spies in America: Stolen Secrets and the Dawn of the Cold War* (2004).

Asia and the Korean War

Gordon H. Chang, *Friends and Enemies: The United States, China, and the Soviet Union, 1948–1972* (1990).

Bruce Cumings, *The Origins of the Korean War*, 2 vols. (1981, 1990).

Allen R. Millett, *The War for Korea, 1945–1950: A House Burning* (2005).

Paul J. Pierpaoli Jr., *Truman and Korea: The Political Culture of the Early Cold War* (1999).

Michael Schaller, *Altered States: The United States and Japan since the Occupation* (1997).

William Stueck, *Rethinking the Korean War: A New Diplomatic and Strategic History* (2002).

Stanley Weintraub, *MacArthur's War: Korea and the Undoing of an American Hero* (2000).

▶ **FOR MORE BOOKS ABOUT TOPICS IN THIS CHAPTER,** see the Online Bibliography at bedfordstmartins.com/roark.

▶ **FOR ADDITIONAL FIRSTHAND ACCOUNTS OF THIS PERIOD,** see Chapter 26 in Michael Johnson, ed., *Reading the American Past*, Fourth Edition.

▶ **FOR WEB SITES, IMAGES, AND DOCUMENTS RELATED TO TOPICS AND PLACES IN THIS CHAPTER,** visit bedfordstmartins.com/makehistory.

REVIEWING THE CHAPTER

Follow these steps to review and strengthen your understanding of the chapter.

STEP 1: *Study the **Key Terms** and **Timeline** to identify the significance of each item listed.*

STEP 2: *Answer the **Review Questions**, drawing on key terms and dates to support your answers.*

STEP 3: *Drawing on the Key Terms, Timeline, and Review Questions, answer the broader **Making Connections** questions.*

KEY TERMS

Who

Helen Gahagan Douglas (p. 947)
Harry S. Truman (p. 948)
Joseph Stalin (p. 949)
George F. Kennan (p. 951)
Dean Acheson (p. 954)
Henry A. Wallace (p. 954)
Robert A. Taft (p. 954)
George C. Marshall (p. 955)
Mao Zedong (p. 959)
Chiang Kai-shek (p. 959)
Jackie Robinson (p. 964)
J. Strom Thurmond (p. 969)
Joseph R. McCarthy (p. 971)
Ethel and Julius Rosenberg (p. 971)
Syngman Rhee (p. 973)
Kim Il-sung (p. 973)
Douglas MacArthur (p. 973)

Dwight D. Eisenhower (p. 975)
Richard M. Nixon (p. 975)

What

iron curtain (p. 951)
containment (p. 954)
Truman Doctrine (p. 954)
Marshall Plan (European Recovery Program) (p. 955)
Berlin airlift (p. 956)
hydrogen bomb (p. 956)
National Security Act of 1947 (p. 956)
collective security (p. 957)
North Atlantic Treaty Organization (NATO) (p. 957)
Central Intelligence Agency (CIA) (p. 957)
third world (p. 958)

Fair Deal (p. 960)
Employment Act of 1946 (p. 961)
Servicemen's Readjustment Act (GI Bill) (p. 964)
President's Committee on Civil Rights (p. 965)
League of United Latin-American Citizens (LULAC) (p. 965)
American GI Forum (p. 968)
Taft-Hartley Act (p. 968)
Housing Act of 1949 (p. 970)
McCarran-Walter Act of 1952 (p. 970)
McCarthyism (p. 970)
Truman's loyalty program (p. 971)
House Un-American Activities Committee (HUAC) (p. 971)
NSC 68 (p. 977)

TIMELINE

1945 • Roosevelt dies; Vice President Harry S. Truman becomes president.

    1946 • Postwar labor unrest.
- President's Committee on Civil Rights created.
- United States grants independence to Philippines.
- Employment Act.
- Republicans gain control of Congress.

        1947 • George F. Kennan's article on containment policy published.

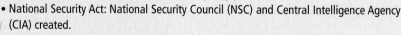

- National Security Act: National Security Council (NSC) and Central Intelligence Agency (CIA) created.
- Truman asks for aid to Greece and Turkey and announces Truman Doctrine.
- Truman establishes loyalty program.

            1948 • Congress approves Marshall Plan.

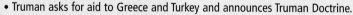

- Women become permanent part of armed services.
- Truman orders desegregation of armed services.
- American GI Forum founded.
- United States recognizes state of Israel.
- Truman elected president.

            1948–
            1949 • Berlin crisis and airlift.

REVIEW QUESTIONS

1. Why did relations between the United States and the Soviet Union deteriorate after World War II? (pp. 949–60)

2. Why did Truman have limited success in implementing his domestic agenda? (pp. 960–72)

3. How did the Korean War shape American foreign policy in the 1950s? (pp. 972–77)

MAKING CONNECTIONS

1. Containment shaped American actions abroad for almost half a century. Why did it become the dominant feature of American foreign policy after World War II? In your answer, discuss both proponents and opponents of the policy.

2. How did returning American servicemen change postwar domestic life in the areas of education and civil rights? In your answer, discuss how wartime experiences influenced their demands.

3. Why did anti-Communist hysteria sweep the country in the early 1950s? How did it shape domestic politics? In your answer, be sure to consider the influence of developments abroad and at home.

▶ For practice quizzes, a customized study plan, and other study tools, see the Online Study Guide at bedfordstmartins.com/roark.

1949 • Communists take over mainland China; Nationalists retreat to Taiwan.
  • North Atlantic Treaty Organization (NATO) formed.
  • Point IV technical aid program begins.
  • Soviet Union explodes atomic bomb.

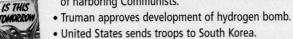

1950 • Senator Joseph McCarthy begins to accuse the U.S. government of harboring Communists.
  • Truman approves development of hydrogen bomb.
  • United States sends troops to South Korea.

1951 • Truman relieves General Douglas MacArthur of command in Korea.
  • United States ends occupation of Japan and signs peace treaty and mutual security pact.

1952 • Republican Dwight D. Eisenhower elected president.

1953 • Armistice halts Korean War.

1956 CADILLAC CONVERTIBLE
The automobile reflected both corporate and family prosperity in the 1950s. By the end of the decade, three out of every four households had a car, and the automotive industry generated one out of every six jobs. This car was manufactured by General Motors, the biggest and richest corporation in the world and the first to sell a billion dollars' worth of products. Costing about $5,000, the Cadillac was GM's top-of-the-line car, one of the first purchases the McDonald brothers made when they struck it rich with their hamburger stand in California. Even the cheaper models that average Americans bought by the millions featured the gas-guzzling size and the space-age design of this Cadillac. A massive interstate highway system begun in 1956 boosted automobile travel, and widespread car ownership went hand in hand with Americans' move to the suburbs and their devotion to consumption.

Ron Kimball Photography.

CHAPTER

27

The Politics and Culture of Abundance

1952–1960

T RAILED BY REPORTERS, U.S. vice president Richard M. Nixon led Soviet premier Nikita Khrushchev through the American National Exhibition in Moscow in July 1959. The display of American consumer goods followed an exhibition of Soviet products in New York, part of a cultural exchange between the two superpowers that reflected a slight thaw in the **cold war** after Khrushchev replaced Stalin. Both Khrushchev and Nixon seized on the propaganda potential of the moment. As they made their way through the display, their verbal sparring turned into a slugfest of words and gestures that reporters dubbed the "kitchen debate."

Showing off a new color television set, Nixon said the Soviet Union "may be ahead of us . . . in the thrust of your rockets for . . . outer space," but he assured Khrushchev that the United States outstripped the Soviets in consumer goods. Nixon linked capitalism with democracy, asserting that the array of products represented "what freedom means to us . . . our right to choose." Moreover, "any steelworker could buy this house," Nixon boasted, as they walked through a six-room ranch-style model. Khrushchev retorted that in the Soviet Union, "you are entitled to housing," whereas in the United States the poor were reduced to sleeping on the pavement.

While the two men inspected appliances in the model kitchen, Nixon declared, "These are designed to make things easier for our women." Khrushchev responded that his country did not have "the capitalist attitude toward women" and appreciated women's contributions to the economy, not their domesticity. The Soviet leader found many of the items on display interesting, he said, but added that "they are not needed in life. . . . They are merely gadgets." In reply, Nixon insisted, "Isn't it far better to be talking about washing machines than machines of war?" Khrushchev agreed, yet he affirmed the persistence of cold war tensions when he later blustered, "We too are giants. You want to threaten—we will answer threats with threats."

The Eisenhower administration (1953–1961) in fact had begun with threats to the Soviet Union. During the 1952 campaign, Republicans had vowed to roll back **communism** and liberate "enslaved" peoples under Soviet rule. In practice, however, President Dwight D. Eisenhower settled for a **containment** policy much like that of his predecessor, Harry S. Truman, though Eisenhower relied more on nuclear weapons and on secret actions by the Central Intelligence Agency (CIA) against left-leaning governments. Yet, as Nixon's visit to Moscow demonstrated, Eisenhower seized on political changes in the Soviet Union to reduce tensions in Soviet-American relations.

The Kitchen Debate
Soviet premier Nikita Khrushchev (left) and Vice President Richard M. Nixon (center) debate the relative merits of their nations' economies at the American National Exhibition held in Moscow in 1959. "You are a lawyer for capitalism and I am a lawyer for communism," Khrushchev told Nixon as each tried to outdo one another.
Howard Sochurek/TimePix/Getty.

culture that also celebrated marriage, family, and traditional gender roles, even as more and more married women took jobs outside the home. Also challenging dominant norms were an emerging youth culture and dissenting writers known as the Beats.

The cold war and the economic boom helped African Americans mount the most dramatic movement of the 1950s, a struggle against the system of segregation and **disfranchisement** that had replaced slavery. Large numbers of African Americans took direct action against the institutions of injustice, developing the organizations, leadership, and strategies to mount a civil rights movement of unprecedented size and power.

Eisenhower and the Politics of the "Middle Way"

Moderation was the guiding principle of Eisenhower's domestic agenda and leadership style. In 1953, he pledged a "middle way between untrammeled freedom of the individual and the demands for the welfare of the whole Nation" and promised that his administration would "avoid government by bureaucracy as carefully as it avoids neglect of the helpless." Eisenhower generally resisted expanding the federal government's activities, he tried to stay on the sidelines when the Supreme Court ordered schools to desegregate, and his administration terminated the federal trusteeship of dozens of Indian tribes.

As an advocate of moderation, however, Eisenhower supported the continuation, and in some cases the expansion, of New Deal programs. He signed key legislation establishing a national highway system and enlarged the federal bureaucracy with a new Department of Health, Education, and Welfare. Nicknamed "Ike" by his friends and the public, the confident war hero remained popular throughout his presidency, but he was not able to lift the Republican Party to national dominance.

Modern Republicanism

In contrast to the old guard conservatives in his party who wanted to repeal much of the New Deal and preferred a unilateral approach to foreign policy, Eisenhower preached "modern Republicanism." This meant resisting additional federal intervention in economic and social life,

Continuity with the Truman administration also characterized domestic policy. Although Eisenhower favored the business community with tax cuts and opposed strong federal efforts in health care, education, and race relations, he did not propose to roll back **New Deal** programs. He even extended the federal government with a massive highway program, and he remained immensely popular through his two terms in office. Most political leaders and experts believed that the stunning economic growth would enable the nation to overcome poverty without cost to the "haves," yet deprivation clung stubbornly to some 20 percent of the population, invisible amid the economic abundance.

The Moscow display testified to the unheard-of material gains savored by most Americans in the postwar era. Cold war weapons production spurred the economy, whose vitality stimulated suburban development, contributed to the burgeoning population and enterprise in the West and Southwest (the **Sun Belt**), and enabled millions of Americans to buy a host of new products. As new homes, television sets, and household appliances transformed their patterns of living, Americans took part in a **consumer** but it did not mean turning the clock back to the 1920s. Democratic control of Congress after the elections of 1954 further contributed to the moderate approach of the Eisenhower administration, whose record overall maintained the course charted by Roosevelt and Truman.

The new president attempted to distance himself from the anti-Communist fervor that had plagued the Truman administration. Yet Eisenhower intensified Truman's loyalty program, allowing the head of any federal agency to dismiss an employee on grounds of loyalty, security, or "suitability." Thousands of civil servants charged with disloyalty lost their jobs. Reflecting his disinclination to involve himself in controversial issues, Eisenhower refused to denounce Senator Joseph McCarthy publicly. Instead, it was left to the senator to destroy himself.

In 1954, McCarthy tightened his own noose when he went after the army. As he hurled reckless charges of communism against military personnel during weeks of televised hearings, public opinion turned against him. When the army's lawyer demanded of McCarthy, "Have you left no sense of decency?" those in the hearing room applauded. A Senate vote to condemn McCarthy in December 1954 marked the end of his influence, but Eisenhower's inaction had allowed the senator to spread his poison longer than he might otherwise have done.

Eisenhower sometimes echoed the **conservative** Republicans' conviction that government was best left in the hands of state officials and that economic decisions were best left to private business. "If all Americans want is security, they can go to prison," Eisenhower commented about social welfare in 1949. Although **liberals** scorned the president's conservatism by calling him "Eisenhoover," the **welfare state** grew somewhat during his administration, and the federal government took on new projects. Eisenhower signed laws bringing ten million more workers into Social Security, increasing the minimum wage, and continuing the federal government's modest role in financing public housing. He enlarged the government with a new Department of Health, Education, and Welfare, naming former Women's Army Corps commander Oveta Culp Hobby to head it. (Hobby was only the second woman ever appointed to a U.S. cabinet post.) And when the spread of polio neared epidemic proportions and terrified parents, Eisenhower obtained funds from Congress to distribute a vaccine, even though conservatives preferred that states assume that responsibility.

Polio Vaccine Distribution in the South
In 1954, American children lined up to be inoculated with the new vaccine to prevent polio. But as this scene from Blytheville, Arkansas, shows, children waiting to receive the vaccine stood in strictly segregated lines.
Charles Bell, *Memphis Commercial Appeal.*

Eisenhower's greatest domestic initiative was the Interstate Highway and Defense System Act of 1956 (Map 27.1, page 986). Promoted as essential to national defense and an impetus to economic growth, the act authorized the construction of a national highway system, with the federal government paying most of the costs through increased fuel and vehicle taxes. Road trips to new places became easier for Americans, and goods moved more quickly around the nation. The new highways also spurred suburban expansion and growth in the fast-food and motel industries. And substantial gains went to the trucking, construction, and automobile industries, which had lobbied hard for the law. The monumental highway project eventually exacted unforeseen costs in the form of air pollution, energy consumption, declining railroads and mass transportation in general, and decay of central cities.

In other areas, Eisenhower restrained federal activity in favor of state governments and private enterprise. His large tax cuts directed most benefits to business and the wealthy, and he stubbornly resisted national health insurance,

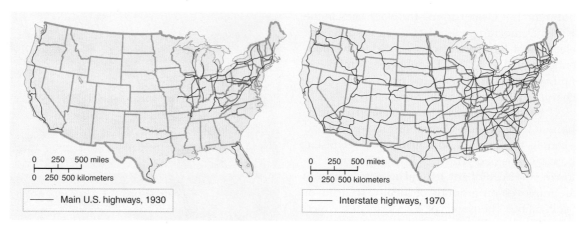

MAP 27.1   The Interstate Highway System, 1930 and 1970
Built with federal funds authorized in the Interstate Highway and Defense System Act of 1956, super-
highways soon crisscrossed the nation. Trucking, construction, gasoline, and travel were among the
industries that prospered, but railroads suffered from the subsidized competition.

READING THE MAP: What regions of the United States had main highways in 1930? What regions did
not? How had the situation changed by 1970?
CONNECTIONS: What impact did the growth of the interstate highway system have on migration patterns in the United States? What benefits did the new interstate highways bring to Americans and
at what costs?

FOR MORE HELP ANALYZING THIS MAP, see the map activity for this chapter in the Online Study Guide at
bedfordstmartins.com/roark.

federal aid to primary and secondary education, and White House leadership on behalf of civil rights. Moreover, whereas Democrats sought to keep nuclear power in government hands, Eisenhower signed legislation authorizing the private manufacture and sale of nuclear energy. Workers began building the first commercial nuclear power plant in Pennsylvania in 1954.

Termination and Relocation of Native Americans

Eisenhower's efforts to limit the activities of the federal government were consistent with a new direction in Indian policy, which reversed the emphasis on strengthening tribal governments and preserving Indian **culture** that had been established in the Indian Reorganization Act of 1934 (see chapter 24). After World War II, when some 25,000 Indians had left their homes for military service and another 40,000 for work in defense industries, policymakers began to favor assimilating Native Americans and ending their special relationships with the government.

To some officials, who reflected the cold war emphasis on conformity to dominant American values, the communal practices of Indians re-

sembled socialism and stifled individual initiative. Eisenhower's commissioner of Indian affairs, Glenn Emmons, expressed the pragmatic view that tribal lands could not produce income sufficient to lift Indians from poverty, but he also revealed the ethnocentrism of policymakers when he insisted that Indians wanted to "work and live like Americans."

By 1960, the government had implemented a three-part program of compensation, termination, and relocation. In 1946, Congress established the Indian Claims Commission to discharge outstanding claims by Native Americans for land taken by the government. When it closed in 1978, the commission had settled 285 cases, with compensation exceeding $800 million. Yet the awards were based on land values at the time the land was taken and did not include interest.

The second policy, termination, also originated in the Truman administration, where Commissioner Dillon S. Myer asserted that his Bureau of Indian Affairs should "not do anything which others can do as well or better" and "nothing for Indians which Indians can do for themselves." Beginning in 1953, Eisenhower signed bills transferring jurisdiction over tribal land to state and local governments and ending the trusteeship relationship between Indians and the federal government. The loss of federal hospitals, schools, and other special arrangements devastated Indian tribes. As had happened after passage of the Dawes Act in 1887 (see chapter 17), some corporate interests and individuals took

Indian Relocation

As part of its new emphasis on assimilation in the late 1940s and 1950s, the Bureau of Indian Affairs distributed this leaflet to entice Native Americans to move from their reservations to cities. Either with government assistance or on their own, thousands of Indians relocated in the years after World War II. In 1950, just 13.4 percent of Indians lived in urban areas. By 1970, 44 percent did so, and by 1990 the figure had reached 63 percent.

National Archives.

READING THE IMAGE: Which of the features shown in this leaflet do you think would have been the most appealing to Native Americans living on reservations? Which might have evoked little interest?

CONNECTIONS: In what ways did the government's plan to assimilate Native Americans succeed? In what ways did it fail?

FOR MORE HELP ANALYZING THIS IMAGE, see the visual activity for this chapter in the Online Study Guide at bedfordstmartins.com/roark.

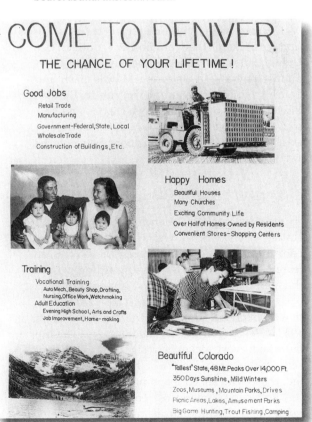

COME TO DENVER

THE CHANCE OF YOUR LIFETIME!

Good Jobs
Retail Trade
Manufacturing
Government-Federal, State, Local
Wholesale Trade
Construction of Buildings, Etc.

Happy Homes
Beautiful Houses
Many Churches
Exciting Community Life
Over Half of Homes Owned by Residents
Convenient Stores-Shopping Centers

Training
Vocational Training
Auto Mech., Beauty Shop, Drafting,
Nursing, Office Work, Watchmaking
Adult Education
Evening High School, Arts and Crafts
Job Improvement, Home-making

Beautiful Colorado
"Tallest" State, 48 Mt. Peaks Over 14,000 Ft.
350 Days Sunshine, Mild Winters
Zoos, Museums, Mountain Parks, Drives
Picnic Areas, Lakes, Amusement Parks
Big Game Hunting, Trout Fishing, Camping

advantage of the opportunity to purchase Indian land cheaply. An Indian leader reported that some of his people saw termination as the "severing of ties already loose and ineffective," but to the great majority, it was "like the strike of doom." The government abandoned termination in the 1960s after some 13,000 Indians and more than one million acres of their land had been affected. Decades later, the Menominee and Klamath tribes fought to reverse termination and secured restoration of their tribal status. Ada Deer led the Menominee restoration movement and later became the first Native American woman to head the Bureau of Indian Affairs.

Relocation, the third piece of Native American policy, began with a pilot program in 1948 and involved more than 100,000 Native Americans by 1973. The government encouraged Indians to move to cities and provided one-way bus tickets there. At the Indians' destinations, relocation centers were supposed to help with housing, job training, and medical care. To make it difficult to return home, government officials sent Indians far away from their reservations—South Dakota Sioux to California, for example, and Alaskan natives to Chicago. Still, about one-third of those who relocated went back to the reservation. Most who stayed in cities faced great difficulties: racism, lack of adequately paying jobs for which they had skills, poor housing in what became Indian ghettos, and the loss of their traditional culture. "I wish we had never left home," one woman said. "It's dirty and noisy, and people all around, crowded. . . . It seems like I never see the sky or trees." Her sons were headed for reform school, and her husband was out of work and drinking.

Reflecting long-standing disagreements among Indians themselves, some who overcame these obstacles applauded the program. One man did not mind that his grandchildren did not consider themselves Indians; he contrasted the urban jobs and educational opportunities with the reservations, where "I see no jobs, nothing to do, everyone just drinks." But most urban Indians remained in or near poverty, and even many who had welcomed relocation eventually determined that they must resist "assimilation to the degree that we would lose our

Major Indian Relocations, 1950–1970

CANADA

Alaskan natives

Chicago

Sioux

Navajo

Los Angeles

Albuquerque

MEXICO

■ Indian reservation, 1970
← Relocations

identity as Indian people, lose our culture and our [way] of living." Within two decades, a national pan-Indian movement emerged to do just that and demand much more for Indians. The new militancy and connections across tribal lines that arose was a by-product of the urbanization of Native Americans (see chapter 28).

The 1956 Election and the Second Term

Not all citizens were living the American dream, but with the nation at peace and the economy booming, Eisenhower easily defeated Adlai Stevenson in 1956, doubling his margin of 1952. Yet Democrats kept control of Congress, and in the midterm elections two years later, they all but wiped out the Republican Party, gaining a 64–34 majority in the Senate and a 282–135 advantage in the House. Although Ike captured voters' hearts, a majority of Americans remained wedded to the programs and policies of the Democrats.

Eisenhower faced more serious leadership challenges in his second term. The economy plunged into a recession in late 1957, and unemployment rose to 7 percent. Eisenhower fought with Congress over the budget and vetoed bills to expand housing, urban development, and public works projects. The president and Congress did reach agreement in two key areas: enacting the first, though largely symbolic, civil rights legislation in a century and establishing a new role for the government in education.

In the end, the first Republican administration after the New Deal left the size and functions of the federal government intact, though it tipped policy somewhat more in favor of corporate interests. Unparalleled prosperity graced the Eisenhower years, and inflation was kept low. The economy weathered two recessions without putting to the test the president's aversion to substantial federal intervention.

Eisenhower celebrated what he called the "wide diffusion of wealth and incomes" across the United States. Yet neglected amid the remarkable abundance were some forty million Americans who lived below the income level designated by the government as the minimum necessary to provide a decent standard of living. Rural poverty was particularly pronounced, as was poverty among African Americans and other minorities. The widespread belief among

> Eisenhower celebrated what he called the "wide diffusion of wealth and incomes" across the United States.

liberals as well as conservatives that an expanding economy would end poverty was unfounded, yet it persisted because the one in five Americans who lived in deprivation were largely voiceless.

> **REVIEW** How did Eisenhower's domestic policies reflect his moderate political vision?

Liberation Rhetoric and the Practice of Containment

At his 1953 inauguration, Eisenhower warned that "forces of good and evil are massed and armed and opposed as rarely before in history." Like Truman, he saw communism as a threat to the nation's security and economic interests. Eisenhower's foreign policy differed from Truman's, however, in three areas: its rhetoric, its means, and—after Stalin's death in 1953—its movement toward accommodation with the Soviet Union.

Republican rhetoric, voiced most prominently by Secretary of State John Foster Dulles, deplored containment as "negative, futile, and immoral" because it accepted the existing Soviet sphere of control. Yet despite promises to roll back Soviet power, the Eisenhower administration continued the containment policy. The United States intervened at the margins of Communist power—in Asia, the Middle East, and Latin America—but not at its core in Europe. Eisenhower assigned nuclear weapons and CIA secret operations larger roles in defense strategy, and he took steps to ease tensions between the two superpowers.

The "New Look" in Foreign Policy

To meet his goals of balancing the budget and cutting taxes, Eisenhower was determined to control military expenditures. Moreover, he feared that massive defense spending would threaten the nation's economic strength. A state based on warfare could destroy the very society it was intended to protect. As he declared in 1953, "Every gun that is made, every warship launched, every rocket fired signifies, in the final sense, a theft from those who hunger and are not fed, those who are cold and not clothed."

Reflecting Americans' confidence in technology and opposition to a large peacetime army,

The Nuclear Arms Race
This *Newsweek* cover showing Soviet leader Nikita Khrushchev (left) and President Dwight D. Eisenhower (right) balanced on the head of a nuclear missile suggests the precarious world created by the nuclear arms race. The table on which the two men sit refers to the arms limitation negotiations under way when the magazine came off the press in 1959.

Eisenhower's defense strategy concentrated U.S. military strength in nuclear weapons, along with the planes and missiles to deliver them. Instead of spending huge amounts for large ground forces of its own, the United States would give friendly nations American weapons and back them up with an ominous nuclear arsenal. This was Eisenhower's "New Look" in foreign policy. Airpower and nuclear weapons provided, in Defense Secretary Charles Wilson's words, a "bigger bang for the buck." Secretary of State Dulles believed that America's willingness to "go to the brink" of war with its intimidating nuclear weapons—a strategy called **brinksmanship**—would block any Soviet efforts to expand.

Nuclear weapons could not stop a Soviet nuclear attack, but in response to one, they could inflict enormous destruction on the USSR. This certainty of "massive retaliation" was meant to deter the Soviets from launching an attack.

Because the Soviet Union could respond similarly to an American first strike, this nuclear standoff became known as mutually assured destruction, or MAD. Winston Churchill called it a "mutual balance of terror." Yet leaders of each nation sought not just balance but nuclear superiority, and they pursued an ever-escalating arms race.

Nuclear weapons were useless, however, in rolling back the **iron curtain**, because they would destroy the very peoples whom the United States promised to liberate. When a revolt against the Soviet-controlled government began in Hungary in 1956, Dulles's liberation rhetoric proved to be empty. A radio plea from Hungarian freedom fighters cried, "SOS! They just brought us a rumor that the American troops will be here within one or two hours." But help did not come. Eisenhower was unwilling to risk U.S. soldiers and possible nuclear war, and Soviet troops soon suppressed the insurrection, killing thirty thousand Hungarians.

Applying Containment to Vietnam

A major challenge to the containment policy came in Southeast Asia. During World War II, a Vietnamese **nationalist** named Ho Chi Minh had founded a coalition called the Vietminh to fight both the occupying Japanese forces and the French colonial rulers. In 1945, the Vietminh declared Vietnam's independence from France, and when France fought to maintain its colony, the area plunged into war (see Map 29.2, page 1071). Because Ho declared himself a Communist, the Truman administration quietly began to provide aid to the French. American principles of national self-determination took a backseat to the battle against communism.

Eisenhower viewed communism in Vietnam much as Truman had regarded it in Greece and Turkey, a view that became known as the **domino theory**. "You have a row of dominoes," Eisenhower explained, and "you knock over the first one, and what will happen to the last one is the certainty that it will go over very quickly." A Communist victory in Southeast Asia, he warned, could trigger the fall of Japan, Taiwan, and the Philippines. By 1954, the United States was contributing 75 percent of the cost of France's war, but Eisenhower resisted a larger role. When the French asked for troops and airplanes from the United States to avert almost certain defeat at Dien Bien Phu, Eisenhower firmly said no. Conscious of U.S. losses in the Korean War, he

Geneva Accords, 1954

would not commit troops to another ground war in Asia.

Dien Bien Phu fell in May 1954 and with it the French colony of Vietnam. Two months later in Geneva, France signed a truce. The Geneva accords temporarily partitioned Vietnam at the seventeenth parallel, separating the Vietminh in the north from the puppet government established by the French in the south. Within two years, the Vietnamese people were to vote in elections for a unified government. The United States did not sign the accords but promised to support free elections.

Some officials warned against U.S. involvement in Vietnam. Defense Secretary Wilson could "see nothing but grief in store for us if we remained in that area." Eisenhower and Dulles nonetheless moved to prop up the dominoes with a new alliance. In September 1954, the United States joined with Britain, France, Australia, New Zealand, Thailand, Pakistan, and the Philippines in the Southeast Asia Treaty Organization (SEATO), committed to the defense of Cambodia, Laos, and South Vietnam. Shortly thereafter, the United States began to send weapons and military advisers to South Vietnam and put the CIA to work infiltrating and destabilizing North Vietnam. Fearing a Communist victory in the elections mandated by the Geneva accords, the United States supported South Vietnamese prime minister Ngo Dinh Diem's refusal to hold the vote.

Between 1955 and 1961, the United States provided $800 million to the South Vietnamese army (the Army of the Republic of Vietnam, or ARVN). Yet the ARVN proved grossly unprepared for the **guerrilla warfare** that began in the late 1950s. With military assistance from Ho Chi Minh's government in Hanoi, Vietminh rebels in the south stepped up their guerrilla attacks on the Diem government. The insurgents gained control over villages in part because the largely Buddhist peasants were outraged by the repressive regime of the Catholic, Westernized Diem. Unwilling to abandon containment, Eisenhower left his successor with the deteriorating situation and a firm commitment to defend South Vietnam against communism.

Interventions in Latin America and the Middle East

While trying to buttress friendly governments in Asia, the Eisenhower administration worked secretly to topple unfriendly ones in Latin America and the Middle East. Increasingly, officials saw internal civil wars in terms of the cold war conflict between the superpowers and tended to view nationalist uprisings as Communist threats to democracy. They acted against governments that not only seemed too leftist but also threatened U.S. economic interests. The Eisenhower administration took this course of action out of sight of Congress and the public, making the CIA an important arm of foreign policy in the 1950s.

The government of Guatemala, under the popularly elected reformist president Jacobo Arbenz, was not Communist or Soviet controlled, but it accepted support from the local Communist Party (see Map 29.1, page 1066). In 1953, Arbenz moved to help landless, poverty-stricken peasants by nationalizing land owned but not cultivated by the United Fruit Company, a U.S. corporation whose annual profits were twice the size of the Guatemalan government's budget. United Fruit refused Arbenz's offer to compensate it at the value of the land the company had declared for tax purposes. Then, in response to the nationalization program, the CIA organized and supported an opposition army that overthrew the elected government and installed a military dictatorship in 1954. United Fruit kept its land, and Guatemala succumbed to a series of destructive civil wars that lasted through the 1990s.

When Cubans' desire for political and economic autonomy erupted in 1959, a CIA agent promised "to take care of Castro just like we took care of Arbenz." American companies had long controlled major Cuban resources—especially sugar, tobacco, and mines—and decisions made in Washington directly influenced the lives of the Cuban people. An uprising in 1959 led by Fidel Castro drove out the U.S.-supported dictator Fulgencio Batista and led the CIA to warn Eisenhower that "Communists and other extreme radicals appear to have penetrated the Castro movement." When the United States denied Castro's requests for loans, he turned to the Soviet Union. And when U.S. companies refused Castro's offer to purchase them at their assessed value, he began to nationalize their property. Many anti-Castro Cubans fled to the United States and reported his atrocities, including the execution of hundreds of Batista's supporters. (See "Seeking the American Promise," page 992.) Before leaving office, Eisenhower broke off diplomatic relations with Cuba and authorized the CIA to train Cuban exiles for an invasion.

In the Middle East, as in Guatemala, the CIA intervened to oust an elected government, support an unpopular dictatorship, and help American corporations (see Map 30.3, page 1118). In 1951, the left-leaning prime minister of Iran, Mohammed Mossadegh, had nationalized oil fields and refineries, thereby threatening Western oil interests. While accepting support

The CIA Helps Restore the Shah of Iran

Kermit Roosevelt, grandson of Theodore Roosevelt and head of CIA operations in the Middle East, organized the coup that ousted Iranian premier Mohammed Mossadegh. In 1952, *Time* magazine called Mossadegh, who was passionately committed to nationalism and democracy, "the Iranian George Washington." But Secretary of State John Foster Dulles believed that restoration of the shah's power would produce a more stable ally and persuaded Eisenhower to approve the coup. This photo shows an Iranian army tank patrolling Teheran, with supporters holding an image of the shah. Just before Roosevelt left Teheran, the shah told him, "I owe my throne to God, my people, my army—and to you."

© Bettmann/Corbis.

from the Iranian Communist Party, Mossadegh also challenged the power of Shah Mohammad Reza Pahlavi, Iran's hereditary leader, who favored foreign oil interests and the Iranian wealthy classes.

Eisenhower noted in his diary how important it was to keep oil-rich areas "under the control of people who are friendly . . . [or] suffer the most disastrous and doleful consequences." He authorized CIA agents to instigate a coup against Mossadegh by bribing army officers and paying Iranians to demonstrate against the government. In August 1953, Iranian army officers captured Mossadegh and reestablished the shah's power, whereupon Iran renegotiated its oil concessions, giving U.S. companies a 40 percent share.

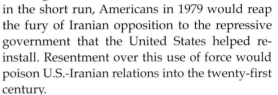

The Suez Crisis, 1956

Although the intervention worked in the short run, Americans in 1979 would reap the fury of Iranian opposition to the repressive government that the United States helped reinstall. Resentment over this use of force would poison U.S.-Iranian relations into the twenty-first century.

Elsewhere in the Middle East, the Eisenhower administration continued Truman's support of Israel but also sought to foster friendships with Arab nations to secure access to oil and build a bulwark against communism. Hindering such efforts were U.S. demands that smaller nations take the American side in the cold war, even when those nations preferred neutrality and the opportunity for assistance from both Western and Communist nations. In 1955, as part of the U.S. effort to win Arab allies, Secretary of State Dulles began talks with Egypt about American support to build the Aswan Dam on the Nile River. The following year, Egypt's leader, Gamal Abdel Nasser, sought arms from Communist Czechoslovakia, formed a military alliance with other Arab nations, and recognized the People's Republic of China. Unwilling to tolerate such independence, Dulles called off the deal for the dam.

On July 26, 1956, Nasser responded by seizing the Suez Canal, then owned by Britain and France. Taking the canal advanced Nasser's prestige and power in the region because it coincided with nationalist aspirations in the Arab world and

Operation Pedro Pan: Young Political Refugees Take Flight

Six-year-old María was awakened before dawn one summer day in Cuba in 1962. Her parents drove her to the Havana airport, with one suitcase and her favorite doll. A paper pinned to her gingham dress gave her name and the phone number of the family friends in Miami who planned to meet her. She traveled with a six-year-old boy whose father in Miami had obtained the visa waivers the children would need to enter the United States. María, excited but anxious, had never been away from her parents before; she would not see them for four months.

On a different flight that summer, a ten-year-old boy named Carlos flew to Miami with his older brother, leaving behind a father they would never see again. Because of their age difference, the boys were separated on arrival and sent to different refugee camps in rural Florida. Through the help of a family acquaintance—a Cuban lawyer working as a janitor in Miami—both boys soon gained temporary placement with foster families just ten blocks apart. A few months later, they were transferred to a juvenile delinquent facility that provided only one meal a day. Finally, a Cuban uncle arrived and took them with him to a small midwestern town where no one spoke Spanish. After three years of traumatic separation, their mother fled Cuba and joined them.

María and Carlos were just two of the more than fourteen thousand unaccompanied children, ages six to eighteen, who left Cuba as part of a special U.S. government–facilitated program called Operation Pedro Pan, functioning for twenty-two months from December 1960 to October 1962. With little money, no knowledge of English, and often no friends or relatives to receive them, the children faced at the minimum daunting loneliness and possibly neglect. What drove the parents of these children to take such an extraordinary step?

The U.S. government had already made unusual accommodation for the large exodus of adult refugees who fled Cuba after Fidel Castro came to power in 1959. No U.S. law yet defined political asylum, but the government relaxed immigration restrictions for Cubans, allowing indefinite entry on tourist visas. Most of the refugees came with little money: Just $5 and thirty pounds of luggage per person were all the Cuban government allowed. Those with U.S. bank accounts had resources to draw on, but the rest needed income, so visa restrictions were relaxed to enable the refugees to work. Additionally, in late 1960, President Dwight D. Eisenhower authorized $1 million in relief and resettlement funds under a little-known provision of the Mutual Security Act, which authorized aid for people "subjected to the captivity of Communist despotism." Shortly thereafter, the new president, John F. Kennedy, released $4 million more and established the Cuban Refugee Program in the Department of Health, Education, and Welfare, which provided job training, health services, and food distribution along with monthly relief checks.

Government assistance was based on several grounds. First, the refugees considered themselves exiles, not immigrants. They intended to return to Cuba as soon as Castro's government fell. The U.S. government shared that expectation (and was taking active steps to help it happen) and thus did not anticipate that the exiles would become permanent residents. Second, the U.S. government felt an obligation to shelter Cubans who had worked in the government or military of deposed dictator Fulgencio Batista, a close U.S. ally. In addition, many Cubans fleeing in the first two years after the revolution had worked for U.S.-owned businesses. Others were wealthy merchants and professionals—doctors, lawyers, university professors. In December 1960, well over a thousand of these upper- and middle-class exiles were arriving each week. By the fall of 1962, 248,000 Cubans had chosen to flee communism, furnishing the United States with a powerful symbolic statement of cold war politics.

An even more potent symbol was Operation Pedro Pan, with its implication that Castro's Cuba had to be truly terrible for parents to part with their children. It recalled the dramatic *kindertransport* of ten thousand Jewish children sent out of Germany and Austria to Britain in

1938 and 1939. But mass death was not impending; Cuban parents fully expected to see their children soon, either in Florida or in Cuba after Castro's regime collapsed. Even so, no one could be sure that it would be possible for parents to follow their children to America. Exit permits and transport were not easy to arrange, and after the U.S.-Soviet showdown in the Cuban missile crisis of October 1962 (see chapter 29), air travel was completely suspended, blocking parental exits for several years.

Cuban parents who opposed Castro feared not for their children's lives, but for their mental well-being. Public schools in Cuba reportedly taught an escalating rhetoric of revolution, while private schools were shut down. Compulsory military service for boys and summer programs

relocating teenagers to jobs teaching literacy in the rural countryside threatened parental rights to determine their children's activities. Relatively prosperous Cuban families did not benefit from Castro's reforms, which focused on improving health and education for the impoverished masses. Their fears of socialized child rearing were reinforced by a program of disinformation allegedly broadcast from a CIA radio station located on the U.S. mainland, which warned parents that "the Revolutionary Government will take [your children] away from you when they turn five and will keep them until they are eighteen." Rumors of Communist indoctrination ran rampant.

Fear of communism gripped the United States in the 1950s, and the Pedro Pan exodus both demonstrated and heightened that fear. The belief

that Communists brainwashed children and turned them against their parents led some Cuban parents to try to save their children by sending them to a country that celebrated freedom. This positive view of Operation Pedro Pan is still held by some people today. In a 2002 speech, President George W. Bush praised Cuban parents of the early 1960s who "were willing to give up their children so they could grow up in a free society." But some of the children themselves, as adults, have questioned whether coming to America was worth the trauma they endured and have speculated that cold war politics might have shaped the operation more than humanitarian concerns.

María de los Angeles Torres and Carlos Eire, two among the thousands, grew up to become university professors in the United States. Like the majority of Pedro Pan children, they are now glad they came here, but they also wonder about the choices their families made. Professor Torres's research for her scholarly study of the children's exodus, *The Lost Apple*, led her to archives in Cuba and Washington, D.C., and to interviews with parents, children, and clandestine workers involved in the program. She realized that she had long avoided discussing the subject with her mother because of their different political outlooks, but she came to understand her mother's perspective. Professor Eire produced a different type of book— a memoir of his childhood titled *Waiting for Snow in Havana: Confessions of a Cuban Boy*. Unlike Torres, he has refused to return to Cuba while Castro remains in power, and he writes, "The world that exists in my memory is so vivid perhaps because I have given up on the idea of ever reclaiming it."

Leaving Havana
A family camera captures María de los Angeles Torres (far left) at the airport in Havana, before her flight to Miami in July 1961.
AP Images.

revenue from the canal could provide capital for constructing the dam. In response to the seizure, Israel, whose forces had been skirmishing with Egyptian troops along their common border since 1948, attacked Egypt with military help from Britain and France. Eisenhower opposed the intervention, recognizing that the Egyptians had claimed their own territory and that Nasser "embodie[d] the emotional demands of the people . . . for independence." He put economic pressure on Britain and France while calling on the United Nations to arrange a truce. The French and British soon pulled back, forcing Israel to retreat.

Despite staying out of the Suez crisis, Eisenhower made it clear that the United States would actively combat communism in the Middle East. In March 1957, Congress passed a joint resolution approving economic and military aid to any Middle Eastern nation "requesting assistance against armed aggression from any country controlled by international communism." The president invoked this "Eisenhower Doctrine" to send aid to Jordan in 1957 and troops to Lebanon in 1958 to counter anti-Western pressures on those governments.

The Nuclear Arms Race

While the Eisenhower administration moved against perceived Communist inroads abroad, a number of events encouraged the president to seek a reduction of superpower tensions. After Stalin's death in 1953, a more moderate leadership under Nikita Khrushchev emerged. The Soviet Union signed a peace treaty with Austria and removed its troops. Like Eisenhower, who remarked privately that the arms race would lead "at worst to atomic warfare, at best to robbing every people and nation on earth of the fruits of their own toil," Khrushchev wanted to reduce defense spending and the threat of nuclear devastation. Eisenhower and Khrushchev met in Geneva in 1955 at the first summit conference since the end of World War II. The meeting symbolized what Eisenhower called "a new spirit of conciliation and cooperation," but it produced no new agreements, and cold war competition persisted.

In August 1957, the Soviets test-fired their first intercontinental ballistic missile (ICBM) and

> Eisenhower remarked privately that the arms race would lead "at worst to atomic warfare, at best to robbing every people and nation on earth of the fruits of their own toil."

two months later beat the United States into space by launching *Sputnik*, the first artificial satellite to circle the earth. After the first American satellite exploded—news headlines called it a "Flopnik"—the United States caught up, launching a successful satellite in January 1958. Nonetheless, *Sputnik* raised fears that the United States lagged behind the USSR not only in missile development and space exploration but also in science and education. Eisenhower insisted that the United States possessed nuclear superiority and tried to diminish public panic. He established the National Aeronautics and Space Administration (NASA) in July 1958, approved a gigantic budget increase for space research and development, and signed the National Defense Education Act, providing loans and scholarships for students in math, foreign languages, and science.

Yet even if the United States did possess nuclear superiority, it could not guarantee security, because both superpowers possessed sufficient nuclear weapons to devastate each other. Most Americans did not follow Civil Defense Administration recommendations to construct home bomb shelters, but they did realize how precarious nuclear weapons had made their lives. The Committee for a Sane Nuclear Policy, an organization founded to oppose the nuclear arms race, had 130 chapters by 1958. It ran one ad that was headlined FACING A DANGER UNLIKE ANY DANGER THAT HAS EVER EXISTED.

Even as the superpowers competed for nuclear dominance, they continued to talk. In 1959, Khrushchev visited the United States, and Nixon went to the Soviet Union, where he engaged in the famous kitchen debate. By 1960, the two sides were within reach of a ban on nuclear testing, and Khrushchev and Eisenhower agreed to meet again in Paris in May.

To avoid jeopardizing the summit, Eisenhower canceled espionage flights over the Soviet Union, but his order came one day too late. On May 1, 1960, a Soviet missile shot down a U-2 spy plane over Soviet territory. The State Department first denied that U.S. planes had been violating Soviet airspace, but the Soviets produced the pilot and the photos taken on his flight. Eisenhower and Khrushchev met briefly in Paris, but the U-2 incident dashed all prospects for a nuclear arms agreement.

Eisenhower's "more bang for the buck" defense budget enormously increased the U.S.

The Age of Nuclear Anxiety

Within just five years after World War II, state and local governments were educating the American people about the nuclear threat. As schools routinely held drills to prepare for possible Soviet attacks, children experienced directly the anxiety and insecurity of the 1950s nuclear arms race. This pamphlet about how to protect oneself from an atomic attack was published by the federal government and distributed to the general public.

Photo: Archive Photos/Getty Images; Pamphlet: Lynn Historical Society.

READING THE IMAGE: What does the image of schoolchildren preparing for a nuclear attack and the pamphlet from the Massachusetts Civil Defense Agency tell you about cold war propaganda?

CONNECTIONS: Is there any irony in the fact that civilians learned how to get ready for a nuclear attack? How effective do you think the strategy pictured here would have been in the event of a nuclear attack?

FOR MORE HELP ANALYZING THIS IMAGE, see the visual activity for this chapter in the Online Study Guide at bedfordstmartins.com/roark.

nuclear capacity, more than quadrupling the stockpile of nuclear weapons. By the time he left office in 1961, the United States had installed ICBMs in the United States and Britain and was prepared to deploy more in Italy and Turkey. The first Polaris submarine carrying nuclear missiles was launched in November 1960.

As Eisenhower left office, he warned about the growing influence of the **military-industrial complex** in American government and life. To contain the defense budget, Eisenhower had struggled against persistent pressures from defense contractors, who, in tandem with the

military, sought more dollars for newer, more powerful weapons systems. In his farewell address, he warned that the "conjunction of an immense military establishment and a large arms industry . . . exercised a total influence . . . in every city, every state house, every office of the federal government." The cold war had created a warfare state.

> **REVIEW** Where and how did Eisenhower practice containment?

New Work and Living Patterns in an Economy of Abundance

Stimulated in part by American military spending, economic productivity increased enormously in the 1950s. A multitude of new items came on the market, and consumption became the order of the day. Millions of Americans enjoyed new homes in the suburbs, and higher education became the norm for the middle class. Although every section of the nation enjoyed the new abundance, the West and Southwest especially boomed in production, commerce, and population.

Work itself changed. Fewer people labored on farms, service sector employment overtook manufacturing jobs, and women's employment grew. These economic shifts disadvantaged some Americans, and they did little to help the forty million who lived in poverty. Most Americans, however, enjoyed a higher standard of living, leading economist John Kenneth Galbraith to call the United States "the affluent society."

Technology Transforms Agriculture and Industry

Between 1940 and 1960, agricultural output mushroomed while the number of farmworkers declined by almost one-third. Farmers achieved nearly miraculous productivity through greater crop specialization, more intensive use of fertilizers, and, above all, mechanization. Tractors, mechanical pickers, and other machines increasingly substituted for human and animal power. A single mechanical cotton picker replaced fifty people and cut the cost of harvesting a bale of cotton from $40 to $5.

Technology Transforms Agriculture
The years from 1945 to 1970 saw a second agricultural revolution in the United States. In 1954, tractors outnumbered mules and horses on farms for the first time. In 1940, it took 1 farmer to feed 10.7 people. By 1960, 1 farmer could supply 25.8 people, and in 1970 that ratio was 1 to 75.8. Threshing machines sweeping across a midwestern wheat field in 1960 exemplify the onslaught of agribusiness. The advertisement shows how one person could plant several rows of corn by barely lifting a finger.
Threshing machine: © Bettmann/Corbis; Advertisement: International Harvester Company.

Poverty in an Era of Abundance
The Whiteheads, a coal-mining family in Kentucky, represented the hidden side of the affluent postwar era. Mrs. John Whitehead, shown here, lived with her husband, their six children, and their six grand-children in this three-room house. It had neither running water nor electricity, and the only access to the house was over a mountain trail. Notice Mrs. Whitehead's hand. What does it tell you about her access to such conveniences as washing machines that Khrushchev dismissed as unnecessary gadgets?
National Archives.

The decline of family farms and the growth of large commercial farming, or **agribusiness**, were both causes and consequences of mechanization. Benefiting handsomely from federal price supports begun in the New Deal, larger farmers could afford technological improvements, whereas smaller producers lacked capital to invest in the machinery necessary to compete. Consequently, average farm size more than doubled between 1940 and 1964, and the number of farms fell by more than 40 percent.

Many small farmers who hung on constituted a core of rural poverty often overlooked in the celebration of affluence. Southern landowners replaced sharecroppers with machines, forcing them off the land. Hundreds of thousands of African Americans joined an exodus to cities, where racial discrimination and a lack of jobs for which they could qualify mired many in urban poverty. A Mississippi woman whose family had worked on a plantation since slavery reported that most of her relatives headed for Chicago when they heard that "it was going to be ma-chines now that harvest the crops." Worrying that "it might be worse up there," she agonized, "I'm afraid to leave and I'm afraid to stay, and whichever I do, I think it might be real bad for my boys and girls."

New technology also increased industrial production. Between 1945 and 1960, for example, the automobile industry cut in half the number of labor-hours needed to manufacture a car. Technology also transformed industries such as electronics, chemicals, and air transportation and promoted the growth of television, plastics, computers, and other newer industries. American businesses enjoyed access to cheap oil, ample markets abroad, and little foreign competition. Moreover, even with Eisenhower's conservative fiscal policies, government spending reached $80 billion annually and created new jobs.

Labor unions enjoyed their greatest success during the 1950s, and real earnings for production workers shot up 40 percent. The merger in 1955 of the American Federation of Labor (AFL) and the Congress of Industrial Organizations

(CIO) improved labor's bargaining position. As one worker put it, "We saw continual improvement in wages, fringe benefits like holidays, vacation, medical plans . . . all sorts of things that provided more security for people." In most industrial nations, governments provided most of the benefits that underwrote workers' security, but the United States developed a mixed system in which company-funded programs won by unions through **collective bargaining** played a much larger role. This system resulted in wide disparities among workers, severely disadvantaging those not represented by unions.

While the absolute number of organized workers continued to grow, union membership peaked at 27.1 percent of the labor force in 1957. Technological advances chipped away at jobs in heavy industry, reducing the number of workers in the steel, copper, and aluminum industries by 17 percent. "You are going to have trouble collecting union dues from all of these machines," commented a Ford manager at a newly automated engine plant to union leader Walter Reuther. Moreover, the economy as a whole was shifting from production to service. Instead of making products, more workers distributed goods, performed services, kept

records, provided education, or carried out government work. Unions made some headway in these fields, especially among government employees, but most service industries resisted unionization.

The growing clerical and service occupations swelled the demand for female workers. By the end of the 1950s, 35 percent of all women over age sixteen worked outside the home—twice as many as in 1940—and women held nearly one-third of all jobs. Women entered a sharply segregated workplace. The vast majority worked in clerical jobs, light manufacturing, domestic service, teaching, and nursing, and because these were female occupations, wages were relatively low. In 1960, the average full-time female worker earned just 60 percent of the average male worker's wages. At the bottom of the employment ladder, black women took home only 42 percent of what white men earned.

Burgeoning Suburbs and Declining Cities

Although suburbs had existed since the nineteenth century, nothing symbolized the affluent society more than their tremendous expansion in the 1950s. Eleven million of the thirteen million new homes built during that decade went up in the suburbs, and by 1960 one in four Americans lived there. As Nixon boasted to Khrushchev during the kitchen debate, the suburbs were accessible to families with modest incomes. Builder William J. Levitt modified the factory assembly-line process, planning nearly identical units so that individual construction workers could move from house to house and perform the same single operation in each one. In 1949, families could purchase these mass-produced houses in his 17,000-home development called Levittown, on Long Island, New York, for just under $8,000 each. Developments similar to Levittown, as well as more luxurious ones, quickly went up throughout the country.

The government underwrote home ownership with low-interest mortgage guarantees through the Federal Housing Administration and the Veterans Administration and by making interest on mortgages tax deductible. Thousands of miles of interstate highway running through urban areas indirectly subsidized

The New Suburbs

A family surveys Levittown as it appeared in 1956. Levitt & Sons provided each family with a nineteen-page brochure explaining all the features of their new home. The brochure included several pages of "those special restrictions" about when and where to hang laundry, the location and size of shrubbery, and how often to mow the lawn. Fences were prohibited, to preserve a "maximum of openness and park-like appearance."

State Museum of PA, PA Historical and Museum Commission.

suburban development. Without the automobile and the freeway, the suburban expansion could not have occurred.

The growing suburbs helped polarize society, especially along racial lines. Each Levittown homeowner signed a contract pledging not to rent or sell to a non-Caucasian. The Supreme Court declared such covenants unenforceable in 1948, but suburban America remained dramatically segregated. Levitt commented, "We can solve a housing problem, or we can try and solve a racial problem, but we cannot combine the two." Contemporary commentators pointed to other flaws of the suburbs. Social critic Lewis Mumford blasted the suburbs as "a multitude of uniform, unidentifiable houses, lined up inflexibly, at uniform distances, on uniform roads, in a treeless communal wasteland, inhabited by people of the same class, the same income, the same age group." By the 1960s, suburbs came under attack for bulldozing the natural environment, creating groundwater contamination, and disrupting wildlife patterns.

An African American Suburb
The pioneer of mass-produced suburban housing, William J. Levitt, reflected the racism that kept blacks out of suburbia when he said, "We can solve a housing problem, or we can try and solve a racial problem, but we cannot combine the two." These African Americans developed their own suburb, a planned community for middle-class blacks in Richmond, California, which welcomed the first families in 1950.
Richmond Public Library.

As white residents joined the suburban migration, blacks moved to cities in search of economic opportunity, increasing their numbers in most cities by 50 percent during the 1950s. Black migrants, however, came to cities that were already in decline, losing not only population but also commerce and industry to the suburbs or to southern and western states. "Detroit is in the doldrums," commented a social welfare worker, as the city lost 100,000 manufacturing jobs in the 1950s. New business facilities began to ring central cities, and shoppers gradually chose suburban malls over downtown department stores. Many of the new jobs lay beyond the reach of the recent black arrivals to the inner cities.

The Rise of the Sun Belt

Americans were on the move westward as well as to the suburbs. Architect Frank Lloyd Wright quipped, "Everything loose will land in Los Angeles." No regions experienced the postwar economic and population booms more intensely than the West and Southwest. After World War II,

California's inhabitants more than doubled, and California overtook New York as the most populous state. Sports franchises followed fans: In 1958, the Brooklyn Dodgers moved to Los Angeles, joined by the Minneapolis Lakers three years later.

A pleasant natural environment drew new residents to the West and Southwest, but no magnet proved stronger than the promise of economic opportunity (Map 27.2, page 1000). As railroads had fueled western growth in the nineteenth century, the automobile and airplane spurred the post–World War II surge. The technology of air-conditioning made possible industrial development and by 1960 cooled nearly eight million homes in the so-called Sun Belt, which stretched from Florida to California. (See "The Promise of Technology," page 1001.)

So important was the defense industry to the South and West that it was later referred to as the "Gun Belt." The aerospace industry boomed in Seattle–Tacoma, Los Angeles, Tucson, and Dallas–Fort Worth, and military bases helped underwrite prosperity in cities such as San Diego and San

Antonio. Although defense dollars benefited other regions, the Sun Belt captured the lion's share of cold war spending for the research and production of bombers and missiles, other weapons, and satellites. By the 1960s, nearly one of every three California workers held a defense-related job.

The surging populations and industries soon raised environmental concerns. Providing sufficient water and power to cities and to agribusiness meant replacing free-flowing rivers in the West with a series of dams and reservoirs. Native Americans lost salmon fishing sites on the Columbia River, and dams on the Upper Missouri displaced nine hundred Indian families. Sprawling urban and suburban settlement without efficient public transportation contributed to blankets of smog over cities such as Los Angeles.

Development began to degrade the very environment that people had come to the area to enjoy.

The high-technology basis of postwar economic development drew well-educated, highly skilled workers to the West. But the economic promise also attracted the poor. "We see opportunity all around us here. . . . We smell freedom here, and maybe soon we can taste it," commented a black mother in California. Between 1945 and 1960, more than one-third of the African Americans who left the South moved west, and more blacks moved to California than to any other state.

The Mexican American population also grew, especially in California and Texas. To supply California's vast agribusiness industry, the government continued the *bracero* **program** begun during World War II (see chapter 25). Until the program

MAP 27.2   The Rise of the Sun Belt, 1940–1980

The growth of defense industries, a non-unionized labor force, and the spread of air-conditioning all helped spur economic development and population growth, which made the Sun Belt the fastest-growing region of the country between 1940 and 1980.

READING THE MAP: What states experienced population growth of more than 20 percent? What states experienced the largest population growth?

CONNECTIONS: What stimulated the population boom in the Southwest? What role did the cold war play in this boom? What role did African Americans play in the western population boom?

FOR MORE HELP ANALYZING THIS MAP, see the map activity for this chapter in the Online Study Guide at bedfordstmartins.com/roark.

Air-Conditioning

Combining two technological advances of the late nineteenth century, refrigeration and electricity, air-conditioning developed primarily in response to the needs of industry. In 1902, Willis Haviland Carrier, a twenty-six-year-old American engineer who formulated basic theories of air-conditioning, designed the first system to control temperature and humidity and installed it in a Brooklyn printing plant. In 1915, he founded the Carrier Corporation to manufacture air-conditioning equipment.

Because fibers are sensitive to moisture, the textile industry provided an early and important market for air-conditioning. The process also helped popularize movie theaters by making them a cool as well as an entertaining retreat during the hot summer months. Room air conditioners began to appear in the 1930s. The 1955 Hotpoint ad shown here promoted the clean air that would come with the purchase of a room air conditioner. Fewer than a million homes had room air conditioners in 1950, but nearly eight million did in 1960, and more than half of all homes had some form of air-conditioning by 1975, as its status changed from a luxury to a necessity. By the end of the twentieth century, more than 80 percent of households had air-conditioning, and it had become standard equipment on automobiles.

Air-conditioning was a mixed blessing. On the one hand, companies no longer had to shut down and send workers home when heat and humidity became unbearable, and air quality inside businesses, homes, and cars improved. On the other hand, air conditioners consumed large amounts of energy and contributed to outdoor air pollution. Like other technologies such as television and, more recently, the Internet, air-conditioning had an isolating effect as people deserted front porches and backyards for closed-up houses and thus reduced their opportunities to interact with neighbors. Perhaps its greatest impact on the nation was to make possible the industrial and population explosion in the Sun Belt. By facilitating the movement of commerce, industry, and tourism to the South and Southwest, air-conditioning made that region more like the rest of the nation. One historian of the South, referring disparagingly to the transformation worked by air-conditioning on that region, proclaimed that "[General Electric] has proved a more devastating invader than even General Sherman."

Advertising Home Air-Conditioning
This Hotpoint ad from 1955 promised consumers clean as well as cool air.
Hotpoint/General Electric Company.

---

ended in 1964, more than 100,000 Mexicans entered the United States each year to labor in the fields—and many of them stayed, legally or illegally. But permanent Mexican immigration was not as welcome as Mexicans' low-wage labor. The government launched a series of raids in 1954 called "Operation Wetback." More than one million Mexicans without documentation were deported, and the operation made U.S. citizens of Mexican descent feel unwelcome and threatened them with incidents of mistaken identity.

At the same time, Mexican American citizens gained a small victory in their ongoing struggle for civil rights in *Hernandez v. Texas*. When a Texas jury convicted Pete Hernandez of murder, lawyers from the American GI Forum and the League of United Latin-American Citizens (see chapter 26) appealed on the grounds that persons

Rounding Up Undocumented Migrants
Not all Mexican Americans who wanted to work in the United States were accommodated by the *bracero* program. In 1953, Los Angeles police arrested these men who did not have legal documents and were hiding in a freight train. Some Americans used the crude term "wetback" to refer to illegal Mexican immigrants because many of them swam across the Rio Grande, which forms part of the border between the United States and Mexico.
© Bettmann/Corbis.

of Mexican origin had been routinely excluded from jury service. In 1954, the Supreme Court decided the first Mexican American civil rights case of the post–World War II era, ruling unanimously that Mexican Americans constituted a distinct group and that their systematic exclusion from juries violated the constitutional guarantee of equal protection.

Free of the discrimination faced by minorities, white Americans reaped the fullest fruits of prosperity in the West. In April 1950, when California developers advertised the opening of Lakewood, a large housing development in Los Angeles County, thirty thousand people lined up to purchase tract houses for $8,000 to $10,000 ($68,000 to $85,000 in 2007 dollars). Many of the new homeowners were veterans, blue-collar and lower-level white-collar workers whose defense-based jobs at McDonnell Douglas and other aerospace corporations enabled them to fulfill the American dream of the 1950s. A huge shopping mall, Lakewood Center, offered myriad products of the consumer culture. The workers' children also had access to community colleges and six state universities— all within easy reach of Lakewood.

The Democratization of Higher Education

California's university system was the most dramatic example of a spectacular transformation of higher education. Between 1940 and 1960, college enrollments in the United States leaped from 1.5 million to 3.6 million. More than 40 percent of young Americans attended college by the mid-1960s, up from 15 percent in the 1940s. More families could afford to keep their children in school longer, and the federal government subsidized the education of more than two million veterans. The cold war also sent millions of federal dollars to universities for defense-related research. Tax dollars spent on higher education more than doubled from 1950 to 1960, as state governments vastly expanded the number of public colleges and universities, and municipalities began to build two-year community colleges.

All Americans did not benefit equally from the democratization of higher education. Although the college enrollments of blacks surged from 37,000 in 1941 to 90,000 in 1961, African Americans constituted only about 5 percent of all college students, less than half their percentage of the population. Black men and women attended college in nearly equal numbers, but for a time, the educational gap between white men and women grew. Although the number of college women increased, it did not keep pace with the number of men. In 1940, women had earned 40 percent of undergraduate degrees, but as veterans flocked to college campuses, women's proportion fell to 25 percent in 1950 and rebounded to only 33 percent by 1960.

The large veteran enrollments did make the traditional student body more diverse along lines of class, age, and marital status. Colleges relaxed rules that had forbidden students to marry in order to accommodate the mature, war-tempered population. Unlike men, however, women tended to drop out of college after marriage and to take jobs so their husbands could stay in school. Reflecting gender norms of the 1950s, most college women responding to a survey agreed that "it is natural for a woman to be satisfied with her husband's success and not crave personal achievement." A decade later, many of these same women would resent their second-class status and become **feminists**.

> **REVIEW** How did technology contribute to changes in the economy, suburbanization, and the growth of the Sun Belt?

The Culture of Abundance

The unprecedented prosperity of the 1950s intensified the transformation of the nation into a consumer society, changing the way Americans lived and converting the traditional work ethic into an ethic of consumption. Rising incomes enabled more people to marry earlier, the birthrate soared, and dominant values celebrated family life and traditional gender roles. Religious observance expanded even as Americans sought satisfaction in material possessions. Television, entering the homes of most Americans, both reflected and helped promote a consumer culture. Undercurrents of rebellion, especially among young people, and women's increasing employment defied some of the dominant norms but did not greatly disrupt the complacency of the 1950s.

Consumption Rules the Day

"If you grew up in the 1950s," journalist Robert Samuelson remembered, "you were a daily witness to the marvels of affluence . . . [to] a seemingly endless array of new gadgets and machines." Scorned by Khrushchev during the kitchen debate as unnecessary gadgets, consumer items flooded American society in the 1950s. Although the purchase and display of consumer goods had always been part of American life (see chapter 23), by the 1950s consumption had become a reigning value, vital for economic prosperity and essential to individuals' identity and status. In place of the traditional emphasis on work and savings, the consumer culture encouraged satisfaction and happiness through the purchase and use of new products.

The consumer culture rested on a firm material base (Figure 27.1). Between 1950 and 1960, both the gross national product (the value of all goods and services produced during a year) and median family income grew by 25 percent in constant dollars. Economists claimed that 60 percent of Americans enjoyed middle-class incomes in 1960. Referring to the popular ranch-style houses in the new suburbs, *House Beautiful* magazine boasted, "Our houses are all on one level, like our class structure." Though ignoring the one in five Americans who still lived in poverty, the statement did reflect the increasing

ability of people to consume products that made class differences less visible. By 1960, four out of every five families owned a television set, nearly all had a refrigerator, and most owned at least one car. The number of shopping centers quadrupled between 1957 and 1963.

Several forces spurred this unparalleled abundance. A population surge—from 152 million in 1950 to 180 million in 1960—expanded the demand for products and boosted industries ranging from housing to baby goods. Consumer borrowing also fueled the economic boom, as people increasingly made purchases on installment plans. Diner's Club issued the first credit card in 1951, and private debt more than doubled during the decade. In 1955, *Life* magazine noted a "revolution in consumer purchasing." Instead of saving their money for future purchases, Americans now bought on credit and enjoyed their possessions while they paid for them.

Although the sheer need to support themselves and their families explained most women's employment, a desire to secure some of the new abundance pulled growing numbers of women out of the home. In fact, married women's employment rose more than any other group in the 1950s. As one remarked, "My Joe can't put five

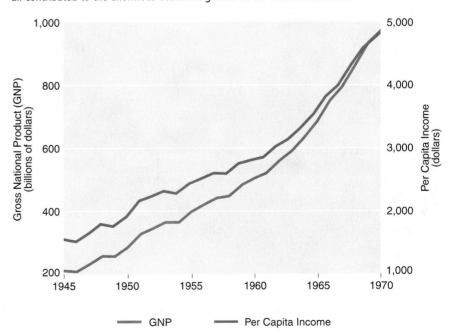

FIGURE 27.1   The Postwar Economic Boom: GNP and Per Capita Income, 1945–1970

American dominance of the worldwide market, innovative technologies that led to new industries such as computers and plastics, population growth, and increases in worker productivity all contributed to the enormous economic growth of the United States after World War II.

kids through college . . . and the washer had to be replaced, and Ann was ashamed to bring friends home because the living room furniture was such a mess, so I went to work." The standards for family happiness imposed by the consumer culture increasingly required a second income.

The Revival of Domesticity and Religion

Even as married women took jobs in unprecedented numbers, a dominant ideology celebrated traditional family life and conventional gender roles. Both popular culture and public figures defined the ideal family as a male breadwinner, a full-time homemaker, and three or four children in a new suburban home. The emphasis on home and family life reflected to some extent the desire for security amid anxieties about the cold war and nuclear menace. Like Nixon in the kitchen debate, one government official saw women's role in cold war terms, charging that

the Soviet Union viewed women "first as a source of manpower, second as a mother," and insisting that "the highest calling of a woman's sex is the home."

Writer and feminist Betty Friedan gave a name to the idealization of women's domestic roles in the 1950s in her book *The Feminine Mystique*, published in 1963. Friedan criticized advertisers, social scientists, educators, women's magazines, and public officials for pressuring women to seek fulfillment in serving others. According to the feminine mystique that they promulgated, biological differences dictated entirely different roles for men and women. The ideal woman kept a spotless house, raised perfect children, served her husband's career, and provided him with emotional and sexual satisfaction. Not many women directly challenged the feminine mystique, but Edith Stern, a college-educated writer, maintained that "many arguments about the joys of housewifery have been advanced, largely by those who have never had to work at it."

Although the glorification of domesticity clashed with women's increasing employment, many Americans' lives did embody the family ideal. Postwar prosperity enabled people to marry earlier and to have more children. The American birthrate, in decline since the nineteenth century, soared between 1945 and 1965, peaking in 1957 with 4.3 million births and producing the "baby boom" generation. (See "Global Comparison" and appendix II, page A-49.) Experts such as the best-selling author Dr. Benjamin Spock encouraged mothers to devote even more attention to child rearing, while they also urged fathers to cultivate family "togetherness" by spending more time with their children.

Along with a renewed emphasis on family life, the 1950s witnessed a surge of interest in religion. By 1960, about 63 percent of Americans belonged to a church or synagogue, up from 50 percent in 1940. Polls reported that 95 percent of all Americans believed in God. Roman Catholic archbishop Fulton J. Sheen was so popular due to his books and TV shows that in 1952, he won an Emmy Award for "Most Outstanding Television Personality." Evangelism took on new life, most notably in the nationwide crusades of Baptist minister Billy Graham, whose powerful oratory moved mass audiences to accept Christ. Congress linked religion more closely to the state

Evangelist Billy Graham Preaches in Detroit
Billy Graham, a young Baptist minister from North Carolina, electrified mass audiences across the country, exhorting them to find salvation in Jesus Christ and to uphold Christian moral standards. Perhaps reflecting their ambivalence about their avid participation in a consumer society, Americans flocked to hear him speak, even as he condemned their sinfulness in being "materialistic, worldly, secular, greedy, and covetous." Here he preaches to an overflow crowd at the Detroit State Fairgrounds in 1953.
Archives of the Billy Graham Center, Wheaton, Illinois.

GLOBAL COMPARISON

The Baby Boom in International Perspective

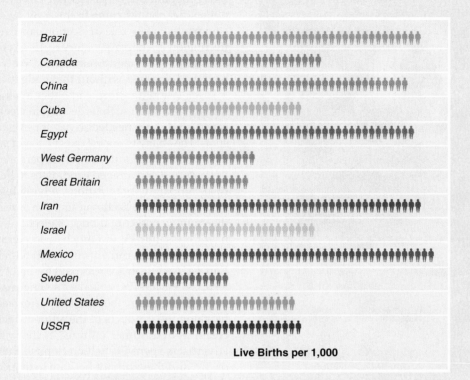

Brazil	
Canada	
China	
Cuba	
Egypt	
West Germany	
Great Britain	
Iran	
Israel	
Mexico	
Sweden	
United States	
USSR	

Live Births per 1,000

The United States was not alone in welcoming bumper crops of babies in the 1950s. High fertility continued in nonindustrialized countries, while in Europe, as in the United States, birthrates rebounded from low levels during the Great Depression and World War II. Which countries had birthrates comparable to those of the United States? What might explain why countries such as Brazil, China, Iran, and Mexico had birthrates so much higher than those in the United States? What might explain why birthrates in Europe were significantly lower than those in the United States?

by adding "under God" to the pledge of allegiance in 1954 and by requiring in 1955 that "In God We Trust" be printed on all currency.

Eisenhower's pastor attributed the renewed interest in religion to the prosperous economy, which "provided the leisure, the energy, and the means for a level of human and spiritual values never before reached." Religion also calmed anxieties in the nuclear age, while ministers such as Graham made the cold war a holy war, labeling communism "a great sinister anti-Christian movement masterminded by Satan." Some critics questioned the depth of the religious revival, attributing the growth in church membership to a desire for conformity and a need for social outlets. One commentator, for example, noted that 53 percent of Americans could not name any book of the Christian Bible's New Testament.

Television Transforms Culture and Politics

Just as family life and religion offered a respite from cold war anxieties, so too did the new medium of television. In 1950, fewer than 10 percent of American homes boasted a television set, but by 1960 about 87 percent of all households owned one. On average, Americans spent more than five hours each day in front of the screen.

Viewers were especially attracted to situation comedies, which projected the family ideal and the feminine mystique into millions of homes. On TV, married women did not have paying jobs, and they deferred to their husbands, though they often got the upper hand through subtle manipulation. In the most popular television show of the early 1950s, *I Love Lucy*, the

The Made-for-TV Family
The Adventures of Ozzie and Harriet began as a radio
program in the 1940s and ran on television from 1952 to 1966.
Along with other family sitcoms, it idealized white family life,
in which no one got divorced or became gravely ill, no one took drugs or
seriously misbehaved, fathers held white-collar jobs, mothers did not work
outside the home, and husbands and wives slept in twin beds. Following
the 1950s norm, Ozzie sought to fulfill his role as head of the household,
but the impeccably dressed and high-heeled Harriet more often appeared
as the wise and sensible one, who rescued Ozzie and the teenage boys,
David and Ricky, from their misadventures. In what ways do today's sitcoms
differ from those of the 1950s?
Picture Research Consultants & Archives.

husband-and-wife team of Lucille Ball and Desi
Arnaz played the couple Lucy and Ricky
Ricardo. In step with the trends, they had a child
and moved from an apartment in the city to a
house in suburbia. Ricky would not let Lucy get
a job, and many plots depicted her zany attempts
to thwart his objections.

Television began to affect politics in the 1950s.
Senator Joseph McCarthy's reckless attacks on
army members were televised nationwide in 1954

and contributed to his downfall. Eisenhower's
1952 presidential campaign used TV ads for the
first time, although he was not happy that "an
old soldier should come to this." By 1960, television played a key role in election campaigns. Reflecting on his narrow victory in 1960, president-
elect John F. Kennedy remarked, "We wouldn't
have had a prayer without that gadget."

Television transformed politics in other ways.
Money played a much larger role in elections because candidates needed to pay for expensive TV
spots. The ability to appeal directly to voters in their
living rooms put a premium on personal attrac-
tiveness and encouraged candidates to build their
own campaign organizations, relying less on political parties. The declining strength of parties and
the growing power of money in elections were not
new trends, but TV did much to accelerate them.

Unlike government-financed television in
Europe, American TV was paid for by private enterprise. What NBC called a "selling machine in
every living room" became the major vehicle for
hawking the products of the affluent society and
creating a consumer culture. In the mid-1950s,
advertisers spent $10 billion to push their goods
on TV, and they did not hesitate to interfere with
shows that might jeopardize the sale of their
products. The cigarette company that sponsored
the *Camel News Caravan* banned any news film
clips showing "No Smoking" signs. Television
programs themselves, not just commercials, tan-
talized viewers with things to buy. On *Queen for
a Day*, for example, the women with the most
pitiful personal stories won fur coats, vacuum
cleaners, and other merchandise prominently displaying sponsors' names.

In 1961, Newton Minow, chairman of the
Federal Communications Commission, called television a "vast wasteland." While acknowledging
some of TV's great achievements, particularly
documentaries and drama, Minow depicted it
as "a procession of game shows, . . . formula
comedies about totally unbelievable families,
blood and thunder, mayhem, violence, sadism,
murder . . . and cartoons." But viewers kept
tuning in. In little more than a decade, television
came to dominate Americans' leisure time, influence their consumption patterns, and shape their
perceptions of the nation's leadership.

Countercurrents

Pockets of dissent underlay the complacency of
the 1950s. Some intellectuals took exception to
the materialism and conformity of the era. In *The*

Lonely Crowd (1950), sociologist David Riesman lamented a shift from the "inner-directed" to the "other-directed" individual. In contrast to the independent thinking that had characterized earlier Americans, Riesman found a regrettable eagerness to adapt to external standards of behavior and belief. Sharing that distaste for the importance of "belonging," William H. Whyte Jr., in his popular book *The Organization Man* (1956), blamed the modern corporation for making employees tailor themselves to the group, thus sacrificing risk taking and independence for dull conformity. Vance Packard's 1959 best seller, *The Status Seekers*, decried "the vigorous merchandising of goods as status-symbols" and argued that "class lines . . . appear to be hardening."

Implicit in much of the critique of consumer culture was concern about the loss of traditional masculinity. Consumption itself was associated with women and their presumed greater susceptibility to manipulation. Men, required to conform and get along in order to get ahead, moved farther away from the individualism and aggressiveness that had been associated with masculinity in the nineteenth century. Moreover, the increase in married women's employment compromised the male ideal of breadwinner, and experts were calling on men to spend more time with their families and practice togetherness in the domestic sphere.

Into this gender confusion came *Playboy*, which began publication in 1953 and quickly gained a circulation of one million. The new magazine idealized masculine independence in the form of bachelorhood, pitying men who were "trapped" in marriages and assaulting the reigning middle-class norms of domesticity and respectability. By associating the sophisticated bachelor with good wine, music, furnishings, and the like, the magazine made consumption more masculine. With photographs of naked young women, *Playboy* promoted sexual freedom, at least for men.

In fact, new research on Americans' sexual behavior disclosed that it often departed from the family ideal of the postwar era. Two books published by Alfred Kinsey and other researchers at Indiana University—*Sexual Behavior in the Human Male* (1948) and *Sexual Behavior in the Human Female* (1953)—uncovered a surprising range of sexual conduct. Surveying more than sixteen thousand individuals, Kinsey found that 85 percent of the men and 50 percent of the women had had sex before marriage, half of the

husbands and a quarter of the wives had engaged in adultery, and one-third of the men and one-seventh of the women reported homosexual experiences.

Although Kinsey's sampling procedures later cast doubt on his ability to generalize across the population, the books became best sellers. They also drew a firestorm of outrage, especially because Kinsey insisted on the natural variability of human sexuality and refused to make moral judgments. Evangelist Billy Graham protested "the damage this book will do to the already deteriorating morals of America," and the Rockefeller Foundation stopped funding Kinsey's work.

Less direct challenges to mainstream standards appeared in the everyday behavior of young Americans. "Roll over Beethoven and tell Tchaikovsky the news!" belted out Chuck Berry in his 1956 hit record celebrating a new form of music that combined country sounds and black rhythm and blues—rock and roll. White teenagers lionized Elvis Presley, who shocked their parents with his tight pants, hip-rolling gestures, and sensuous rock-and-roll music. "Before there was Elvis . . . I started going crazy for 'race music,'" recalled a white man of his teenage years. "It had a beat. I loved it. . . . That got me into trouble with my parents and the schools." His recollection underscored African Americans' contributions to rock and roll, as well as the rebellion expressed by white youths' attraction to black music.

The most blatant revolt against conventionality came from the self-proclaimed Beat generation, a small group of primarily male literary figures based in New York City's Greenwich Village and in San Francisco. Rejecting nearly everything in mainstream culture—patriotism, consumerism, technology, conventional family life, discipline—the Beats celebrated spontaneity and absolute personal freedom, including drug consumption and freewheeling sex. In his landmark poem *Howl* (1956), Allen Ginsberg inveighed against "Robot apartments! invisible suburbs! skeleton treasuries! blind capitals! demonic industries! . . . monstrous bombs!" and denounced the social forces that "frightened me out of my natural ecstasy!" Jack Kerouac, who gave the Beat generation its name, published the best-selling novel *On the Road* (1957), whose energetic,

> Vance Packard's 1959 best seller, *The Status Seekers*, decried "the vigorous merchandising of goods as status-symbols" and argued that "class lines . . . appear to be hardening."

stream-of-consciousness, bebop-style prose narrated the impetuous cross-country travels of two young men. "The only people for me," he wrote, "are the mad ones . . . desirous of everything at the same time, the ones who never yawn or say a commonplace thing, but burn, burn, burn like fabulous yellow roman candles exploding like spiders across the stars." The Beats' shocking lifestyles affronted "square" Americans, but their rebelliousness would provide a model for a much larger movement of youthful dissidents in the 1960s.

Bold new styles in the visual arts also showed the 1950s to be more than a decade of bland conventionality. An artistic revolution that flowered in New York City, known as "action painting" or "abstract expressionism," rejected the idea that painting should represent recognizable forms. Jackson Pollock and other abstract expressionists, emphasizing spontaneity, poured,

Elvis Presley

Young people seeking escape from white middle-class conformity thrilled to Elvis Presley's pulsating music, long sideburns and ducktail haircut, colorful clothing, and suggestive movements. His gyrating hips, illustrated in these 1957 photographs, led to the appellation "Elvis the Pelvis." Adult viewers complained about his "grunt and groin antics" and "unnecessary bump and grind routine."

© Bettmann/Corbis.

Jackson Pollock

Jackson Pollock, the leading artist of the post–World War II revolution in painting, illustrates his technique in this 1949 photograph, which became a U.S. postage stamp in 1999 (with the cigarette airbrushed out). Pollock dripped paint onto the canvas with sticks, turkey basters, and hard brushes. He worked with the canvas on the floor because, he said, "I feel nearer, more a part of the painting. . . . I can walk around it, work from the four sides and be literally 'in' the painting." Married to the artist Lee Krasner, Pollock died in a car crash in 1956 while speeding down a road near his Long Island home.

Jackson Pollock: Martha Holmes/Time Life Pictures/Getty Images; Paint cans and brushes: Pollock-Krasner House.

dripped, and threw paint on canvases or substituted sticks and other implements for brushes. The new form of painting so captivated and redirected the Western art world that New York replaced Paris as its center.

REVIEW   Why did American consumption expand so dramatically in the 1950s, and what aspects of society and culture did it influence?

Emergence of a Civil Rights Movement

Building on the civil rights initiatives begun during World War II and its aftermath, African Americans posed the most dramatic challenge to the status quo of the 1950s as they sought to overcome the political and social barriers that had replaced the literal bonds of slavery. Every southern state mandated rigid segregation in public settings ranging from hospitals and schools to drinking fountains and restrooms. Voting laws and practices in the South disfranchised the vast majority of African Americans in that region; employment discrimination kept them at the bottom of the economic ladder throughout the country.

Although black protest was as old as American racism, in the 1950s a grassroots movement arose that attracted national attention and the support of white liberals. Pressed by civil rights groups, the Supreme Court delivered significant institutional reforms, but the most important changes of all occurred among blacks themselves. Ordinary African Americans in substantial numbers sought their own liberation, building a movement that would transform race relations in the United States.

African Americans Challenge the Supreme Court and the President

Several factors spurred black protest in the 1950s. Between 1940 and 1960, more than three million African Americans moved from the South into areas where they could vote and exert political pressure. Black leaders made sure that foreign policy officials realized how racist practices at home handicapped the United States in its competition with the Soviet Union for allies among newly independent nations. In the South, the very system of segregation meant that African Americans controlled certain organizational resources, such as churches and colleges, where leadership skills could be honed and networks developed.

The legal strategy of the major civil rights organization, the National Association for the Advancement of Colored People (NAACP), reached its crowning achievement with the Supreme Court decision in *Brown v. Board of Education* in 1954. *Brown* consolidated five separate suits that reflected the growing determination of black Americans to fight for their rights. Oliver Brown, a World War II veteran and welder in Topeka, Kansas, filed suit because his eight-year-old daughter had to pass by a white school just seven blocks from their home to attend a black school more than a mile away. In Virginia, sixteen-year-old Barbara Johns, angered at the wretched conditions in her black high school, came home one day and announced, "I walked out of school this morning and carried 450 students with me." The walkout Johns initiated resulted in another of the suits joined in *Brown*. The NAACP's lead lawyer, future Supreme Court justice Thurgood Marshall, urged the Court to overturn the "separate but equal" precedent established in *Plessy v. Ferguson* in 1896 (see chapter 21). A unanimous Court, headed by Chief Justice Earl Warren, declared, "Separate educational facilities are inherently unequal" and thus violated the Fourteenth Amendment.

Ultimate responsibility for enforcement of the decision lay with President Eisenhower, but he refused to endorse *Brown*. He also kept silent in 1955 when whites murdered Emmett Till, a fourteen-year-old black boy who had allegedly whistled at a white woman in Mississippi. Reflecting his own racial prejudice, his preference for limited federal intervention in the states, and a leadership style that favored consensus and gradual progress, Eisenhower kept his distance from civil rights issues. Such inaction fortified southern resistance to school desegregation and contributed to the gravest constitutional crisis since the Civil War.

The crisis came in Little Rock, Arkansas, in September 1957. Local officials dutifully prepared for the integration of Central High School, but Governor Orval Faubus sent Arkansas National Guard troops to block the enrollment of nine black students, claiming that their presence would cause public disorder. Later, he agreed to allow them to enter but withdrew the National Guard, leaving the students to face an angry white mob. "During those years when we desperately needed approval from our peers," Melba Patillo Beals remembered, "we were victims of the most harsh rejection imaginable." As television cameras transmitted the ugly scene across the nation, Eisenhower was forced to send regular army troops to Little Rock, the first federal military intervention in the South since Reconstruction. Even though he took pains to explain that he had acted to preserve the law, not promote integration, southern leaders were outraged. To Georgia senator Richard Russell, the soldiers were like "Hitler's storm troops." Escorted by paratroopers, the black students stayed in school, and Eisenhower withdrew the army in November. Other southern cities avoided integration by closing public schools and using tax dollars to support private white-only schools. Seven years after *Brown*, only

Sixteen-year-old Barbara Johns, angered at the wretched conditions in her black high school, came home one day and announced, "I walked out of school this morning and carried 450 students with me."

School Integration in Little Rock, Arkansas
The nine African American teenagers who integrated Central High School in Little Rock, Arkansas, endured nearly three weeks of threats and hateful taunts before they even got through the doors. Here Elizabeth Eckford tries to ignore angry students and adults as she approaches the entrance to the school, only to be blocked by Arkansas National Guardsmen. Even after President Eisenhower intervened to enable the "Little Rock Nine" to attend school, they were called names, tripped, spat upon, and otherwise harassed by some white students. When Minnijean Brown, one of the black students, could take no more, she dumped a bowl of chili on a white boy who had taunted her. After she was expelled for that act, cards circulated among white students reading, "One Down . . . Eight to Go."
Francis Miller / TimePix / Getty.

6.4 percent of southern black students attended integrated schools. (See "Documenting the American Promise," page 1012.)

Eisenhower did order the integration of public facilities in Washington, D.C., and on military bases, and he supported the first federal civil rights legislation since Reconstruction. Yet the Civil Rights Acts of 1957 and 1960 lacked effective enforcement mechanisms, a compromise to avoid a filibuster by southern senators, leaving southern blacks still unprotected in their basic rights. Baseball star Jackie Robinson spoke for many African Americans when he wired Eisenhower in 1957, "We disagree that half a loaf is better than none. Have waited this long for a bill with meaning—can wait a little longer." Eisenhower appointed the first black professional

to the White House staff, E. Frederick Morrow, but Morrow confided in his diary, "I feel ridiculous . . . trying to defend the administration's record on civil rights."

Montgomery and Mass Protest

From slave revolts and individual acts of defiance through the legal and lobbying efforts of the NAACP, black protest had a long tradition. What set the civil rights movement of the 1950s and 1960s apart was the large number of people involved, their willingness to confront white institutions directly, and the use of nonviolent protest and **civil disobedience** to bring about change. The Congress of Racial Equality (CORE) and other groups had experimented with these

The *Brown* Decision

Brown v. Board of Education
of Topeka *was the principal
Supreme Court decision in the
transformation of African Americans'
legal and political status during the
1950s and 1960s. Responding to lawsuits argued by NAACP lawyers,
Brown was the culmination of a series
of Supreme Court rulings between 1938
and 1950 that chipped away at an earlier
Court's decision in* Plessy v. Ferguson
*(1896) permitting "separate but equal"
public facilities.*

DOCUMENT 1
*Brown v. Board of Education
of Topeka*, May 1954

*In 1954, Chief Justice Earl Warren
delivered the unanimous opinion of
the Supreme Court in* Brown v. Board
of Education of Topeka, *declaring
racial segregation in public education
unconstitutional and explaining why.*

In these days, it is doubtful that any
child may reasonably be expected
to succeed in life if he is denied the
opportunity of an education. Such
an opportunity, if the state has undertaken to provide it, is a right that must
be made available to all on equal
terms. . . .

We come then to the question
presented: Does segregation of children in public schools solely on the
basis of race, even though the physical facilities and other "tangible"
factors may be equal, deprive the
children of the minority group of
equal educational opportunities?
We believe that it does. . . .

In *McLaurin* [a 1950 case], the
Court, in requiring that a Negro
admitted to a white graduate school

be treated like all other students,
again resorted to intangible considerations: ". . . his ability to study, to
engage in discussions and exchange
views with other students, and,
in general, to learn his profession."
Such considerations apply with
added force to children in grade
and high schools. To separate them
from others of similar age and qualifications solely because of their
race generates a feeling of inferiority
as to their status in the community
that may affect their hearts and
minds in a way unlikely ever to be
undone.

We conclude that in the field
of public education the doctrine of
"separate but equal" has no place.
Separate educational facilities are
inherently unequal.

SOURCE: *Brown*, 347 U.S. 483 (1954).

DOCUMENT 2
Southern Manifesto
on Integration, March 1956

The Brown *decision, along with a
second Supreme Court ruling in 1955
about implementing desegregation,
outraged many southern whites. In
1956, more than one hundred members
of Congress signed a manifesto pledging resistance to the rulings.*

We regard the decision of the
Supreme Court in the school cases
as a clear abuse of judicial power.
It climaxes a trend in the Federal
judiciary undertaking to legislate . . . and to encroach upon the
reserved rights of the states and the
people.

The original Constitution does
not mention education. Neither does

the Fourteenth Amendment nor any
amendment. . . . The Supreme Court
of the United States, with no legal
basis for such action, undertook to
exercise their naked judicial power
and substituted their personal political
and social ideas for the established
law of the land.

This unwarranted exercise of
power by the court, contrary to the
Constitution, is creating chaos and
confusion in the states principally
affected. It is destroying the ami-
cable relations between the white
and negro races that have been
created through ninety years of
patient effort by the good people
of both races. It has planted hatred
and suspicion where there has been
heretofore friendship and understanding. . . .

We pledge ourselves to use all
lawful means to bring about a reversal
of this decision which is contrary to
the Constitution and to prevent the
use of force in its implementation.

SOURCE: "Southern Manifesto on
Integration" (1956).

*In the face of white hostility, black
children carried the burden of implementing the* Brown *decision. The
following accounts by black students
reflect varied experiences, but even
those who entered white schools fairly
easily found obstacles to their full participation in school activities.
Nonetheless, they cherished the new
opportunities, favoring integration for
reasons different from those given by
the Supreme Court.*

DOCUMENT 3
A High School Boy
in Oak Ridge, Tennessee, 1957

I like it a whole lot better than the
colored school. You have a chance
to learn more and you have more

sports. I play forward or guard on the basketball team, only I don't get to participate in all games. Some teams don't mind my playing. Some teams object not because of the fellows on the team, but because of the people in their community. Mostly it's the fans or the board of education that decides against me. . . . The same situation occurs in baseball. I'm catcher, but the first game I didn't get to participate in. A farm club of the major league wrote the coach that they were interested in seeing me play so maybe I'll get to play the next time.

SOURCE: Dorothy Sterling, *Tender Warriors* (New York: Hill and Wang, 1958), 83. Copyright © 1958 by Hill and Wang. Reprinted with permission.

DOCUMENT 4
A High School Girl in Louisville, Kentucky, 1957

I'm accepted now as an individual rather than as a person belonging to the Negro race. People say to me, "I'm glad I met you because if I met someone else I might not have liked them." I don't think it's fair, this individual acceptance. I feel like I was some ambassador from some foreign country.

I couldn't go out for any extracurricular activities. Cheerleading, band, drum majorettes, the people who are members of these organizations, they go to camps in the summer which are segregated. Well, what can you do? It just leaves me out. It's not the school, it's the community.

SOURCE: Dorothy Sterling, *Tender Warriors* (New York: Hill and Wang, 1958), 83. Copyright © 1958 by Hill and Wang. Reprinted with permission.

DOCUMENT 5
A High School Girl in the Deep South, May 1966

The first day a news reporter rode the bus with us. All around us were state troopers. In front of them were federal marshals. When we got to town there were lines of people and cars all along the road. A man without a badge or anything got on the bus and started beating up the newspaper reporter. . . . He was crying and bleeding. When we got to the school the students were all around looking through the windows. The mayor said we couldn't come there because the school was already filled to capacity [and] if six of us came in it would be a fire hazard. He told us to turn around and go back. We turned around and the students started yelling and clapping. When we went back [after obtaining a court order] there were no students there at all. There were only two teachers left so they had to bring a couple of teachers from other places. [The white students did not return, so the six black students finished the year by themselves.] The shocking thing was during the graduation ceremonies. All six of the students got together to make a speech. After we finished, I looked around and saw three teachers crying. The principal had tears in his eyes and he got up to make a little speech about us. He said at first he didn't think he would enjoy being around us. You could see in his face that he was really touched. We said something like we really enjoyed school together and that we were glad they stuck it out and all that kind of stuff.

SOURCE: *In Their Own Words: A Student Appraisal of What Happened after School Desegregation* (Washington, D.C.: Department of Health, Education, and Welfare, Office of Education, 1966), 17–18.

DOCUMENT 6
A High School Girl in the Deep South, May 1966

I chose to go because I felt that I could get a better education here. I knew that the [black] school that I was then attending wasn't giving me exactly what I should have had. As far as the Science Department was concerned, it just didn't have the chemicals we needed and I just decided to change. When I went over the students there weren't very friendly and when I graduated they still weren't. They didn't want us there and they made that plain, but we went there anyway and we stuck it out. The lessons there were harder, lots harder, but I studied and I managed to pass all my subjects.

SOURCE: *In Their Own Words: A Student Appraisal of What Happened after School Desegregation* (Washington, D.C.: Department of Health, Education, and Welfare, Office of Education, 1966), 44.

QUESTIONS FOR ANALYSIS AND DEBATE

1. What reasons did the Supreme Court give in favor of desegregation? What reasons did black students give for wanting to attend integrated schools? How do these reasons differ?

2. What arguments did the southern legislators make against the Supreme Court decision? Did they question its power to make the decision or the content of the decision itself?

3. What obstacles remained for African American students to confront once they had been admitted to integrated schools?

4. What conditions do you feel would be worth enduring to obtain a better education?

Montgomery Civil Rights Leaders
During the Montgomery bus boycott, local white officials sought to intimidate African Americans with arrests and lawsuits. Here Rosa Parks, one of ninety-two defendants, ascends the steps of the Montgomery County courthouse in March 1956, accompanied by longtime civil rights leader E. D. Nixon. He felt that Parks would be a perfect plaintiff in a suit against segregation, and Parks agreed. "The white people couldn't say that there was anything I had done to deserve such treatment except to be born black."
AP Images.

tactics in the 1940s, and African Americans had boycotted the segregated bus system in Baton Rouge, Louisiana, in 1953, but the first sustained protest to claim national attention began in Montgomery, Alabama, on December 1, 1955.

On that day, police arrested Rosa Parks for violating a local segregation ordinance. Riding a crowded bus home from her job as a seamstress in a department store, she refused to give up her seat so that a white man could sit down. "People always say that I didn't give up my seat because I was tired, but that isn't true," Parks recalled. "I was not tired physically. . . . I was not old. . . . I was forty-two. No, the only tired I was, was tired of giving in." The bus driver called the police, who promptly arrested her.

> "People always say that I didn't give up my seat because I was tired, but that isn't true," Rosa Parks recalled. "I was not tired physically. . . . I was . . . tired of giving in."

Parks had long been active in the local NAACP, headed by E. D. Nixon. They had already talked about challenging bus segregation. So had the Women's Political Council (WPC), composed of black professional women and led by Jo Ann Robinson, an English professor at Alabama State College who had been humiliated by a bus driver when she had inadvertently sat in the white section of the bus. Such local individuals and organizations, long committed to improving conditions for African Americans, laid critical foundations for the black freedom struggle throughout the South.

When word came of Parks's arrest and decision to fight the case, WPC leaders immediately mobilized teachers and students to distribute fliers calling for Montgomery blacks to stay off the buses. E. D. Nixon called a mass meeting at the Holt Street Baptist Church, where a crowd of supporters stretched for blocks outside. Those

Martin Luther King Jr.
In February 1957, *Time* magazine featured the leader of the Montgomery bus boycott, Martin Luther King Jr., on its cover. Seven years later, in 1964, he appeared on the cover again, this time as the magazine's "Man of the Year." That year, at the age of thirty-five, King was awarded the Nobel Peace Prize. He was the youngest person ever to be so honored.
Time Life Pictures/Getty Images.

Montgomery blacks summoned their courage and determination in abundance. They walked miles to get to work, contributed their meager financial resources, and stood up with dignity to intimidation and police harassment. An older woman insisted, "I'm not walking for myself, I'm walking for my children and my grandchildren." Jo Ann Robinson, a cautious driver, got seventeen traffic tickets in the space of two months. Authorities arrested several leaders, and whites firebombed King's house. Yet the movement persisted until November 1956, when the Supreme Court declared unconstitutional Alabama's laws requiring bus segregation. Blacks had demonstrated that they could sustain a lengthy protest and would not be intimidated.

King's face on the cover of *Time* magazine in February 1957 marked the start of his rapid rise to national and international fame. In January, black clergy from across the South had chosen King to head the Southern Christian Leadership Conference (SCLC), newly established to coordinate local protests against segregation and disfranchisement. The prominence of King and other ministers obscured the substantial numbers and critical importance of black women in the movement. In fact, the SCLC owed much of its success to Ella Baker, a seasoned activist who came from New York to set up and run its office in Atlanta. Meanwhile, the SCLC, the NAACP, and CORE developed centers in several southern cities, paving the way for a mass movement that would revolutionize the racial system of the South.

assembled founded the Montgomery Improvement Association (MIA) to organize a bus boycott. The MIA arranged volunteer car pools and marshaled more than 90 percent of the black community to sustain the yearlong boycott.

Elected to head the MIA was twenty-six-year-old Martin Luther King Jr., the new pastor at the Dexter Avenue Baptist Church, who had a doctorate in theology from Boston University. A captivating speaker, King spoke to mass meetings at churches throughout the boycott, inspiring blacks' courage and commitment by linking racial justice to the redeeming power of Christian love. He promised, "If you will protest courageously and yet with dignity and Christian love . . . historians will have to pause and say, 'There lived a great people—a black people— who injected a new meaning and dignity into the veins of civilization.'"

> **REVIEW** What were the goals and strategies of civil rights activists in the 1950s?

Conclusion: Peace and Prosperity Mask Unmet Challenges

At the American National Exhibition in Moscow in 1959, the consumer goods that Nixon proudly displayed to Khrushchev and the cold war competition that crackled through their dialogue reflected two dominant themes of the 1950s: the prosperity of the U.S. economy and the superpowers' success in keeping cold war competition within the bounds of peace. The tremendous economic growth of the 1950s, which raised the standard of living for most Americans, resulted in part from the cold war: One of every ten American jobs depended directly on defense spending.

Affluence changed the very landscape of the United States. Suburban housing developments sprang up, interstate highways began to divide cities and connect the country, farms declined in number but grew in size, and population and industry moved south and west. Daily habits and even values of ordinary people shifted as the economy became more service oriented and the opportunity to buy a host of new products intensified the growth of a consumer culture.

The general prosperity and seeming conformity, however, masked a number of developments and problems that Americans would face head-on in later years: rising resistance to an unjust racial system, a 20 percent poverty rate, the movement of married women into the labor force, and the emergence of a self-conscious youth generation. Although the federal government's defense spending and housing, highway, and education subsidies played a large role in the economic boom, in general Eisenhower tried to curb domestic programs and let private enterprise have its way. His administration maintained the welfare state inherited from the Democrats but resisted substantial further reforms.

In global affairs, Eisenhower exercised restraint on large issues, recognizing the limits of U.S. power. In the name of **deterrence**, he promoted the development of more destructive atomic weapons, but he withstood pressures for even larger defense budgets. Still, Eisenhower took from Truman the assumption that the United States must fight communism everywhere, and when movements in Iran, Guatemala, Cuba, and Vietnam seemed too radical, too friendly to communism, or too inimical to American economic interests, he tried to undermine them, often with secret operations and severe consequences for native populations.

Although Eisenhower presided over eight years of peace and prosperity, his foreign policy inspired anti-Americanism, established dangerous precedents for the expansion of executive power, and forged commitments and interventions that future generations would deem unwise. As Eisenhower's successors took on the struggle against communism and grappled with the domestic challenges of race, poverty, and urban decay that he had avoided, the tranquility and consensus of the 1950s would give way to the turbulence and conflict of the 1960s.

Selected Bibliography

Eisenhower's Administration

Steven Z. Freiberger, *Dawn over Suez: The Rise of American Power in the Middle East, 1953–1957* (1992).

David Halberstam, *The Fifties* (1993).

George C. Herring, *America's Longest War: The United States and Vietnam, 1950–1975* (2nd rev. ed., 1986).

Stephen Kinzer, *All the Shah's Men: An American Coup and the Roots of Middle East Terror* (2003).

Chester J. Pach Jr. and Elmo Richardson, *The Presidency of Dwight D. Eisenhower* (rev. ed., 1991).

Stephen G. Rabe, *Eisenhower and Latin America: The Foreign Policy of Anticommunism* (1988).

Economic and Social Developments

Rosalyn Baxandall and Elizabeth Ewen, *Picture Windows: How the Suburbs Happened* (2000).

Lizabeth Cohen, *A Consumers' Republic: The Politics of Mass Consumption in Postwar America* (2003).

Gail Cooper, *Air-Conditioning America: Engineers and the Controlled Environment, 1900–1960* (1998).

Kenneth T. Jackson, *Crabgrass Frontier: The Suburbanization of the United States* (1985).

Tom Lewis, *Divided Highways: Building the Interstate Highways, Transforming American Life* (1999).

David Oshinsky, *Polio: An American Story* (2005).

Adam Rome, *The Bulldozer in the Countryside: Suburban Sprawl and the Rise of American Environmentalism* (2001).

Bruce J. Schulman, *From Cotton Belt to Sunbelt: Federal Policy, Economic Development, and the Transformation of the South, 1938–1980* (1994).

Gender, the Family, and Culture

Erik Barnouw, *Tube of Plenty: The Evolution of American Television* (rev. ed., 1982).

Stephanie Coontz, *The Way We Never Were: American Families and the Nostalgia Trip* (1992).

Robert Ellwood, *The Fifties Spiritual Marketplace: American Religion in a Decade of Conflict* (1997).

James Gilbert, *Men in the Middle: Searching for Masculinity in the 1950s* (2005).

Peter Guralnick, *Last Train to Memphis: The Rise of Elvis Presley* (1994).

James Howard Jones, *Alfred C. Kinsey: A Public/Private Life* (1998).

Elaine Tyler May, *Homeward Bound: American Families in the Cold War Era* (1988).

Joanne Meyerowitz, ed., *Not June Cleaver: Women and Gender in Postwar America, 1945–1960* (1994).

James Miller, *Flowers in the Dustbin: The Rise of Rock and Roll, 1947–1977* (1999).

Lynn Spigel, *Make Room for TV: Television and the Family Ideal in Postwar America* (1992).

Steven Watson, *The Birth of the Beat Generation: Visionaries, Rebels, and Hipsters, 1944–1960* (1995).

Minorities and Civil Rights

Melba Patillo Beals, *Warriors Don't Cry: A Searing Memoir of the Battle to Integrate Little Rock's Central High* (1994).

Taylor Branch, *Parting the Waters: America in the King Years, 1954–1963* (1988).

Mary L. Dudziak, *Cold War Civil Rights: Race and the Image of American Democracy* (2000).

Donald L. Fixico, *Termination and Relocation: Federal Indian Policy, 1945–1960* (1986).

David J. Garrow, ed., *The Montgomery Boycott and the Women Who Started It: The Memoir of Jo Ann Gibson Robinson* (1987).

Richard Kluger, *Simple Justice: The History of* Brown v. Board of Education *and Black America's Struggle for Equality* (1976).

Mae Ngai, *Impossible Subjects: Illegal Aliens and the Making of Modern America* (2005).

James T. Patterson, *Brown v. Board of Education: A Civil Rights Milestone and Its Troubled Legacy* (2001).

Barbara Ransby, *Ella Baker and the Black Freedom Movement* (2003).

Thomas J. Sugrue, *The Origins of the Urban Crisis: Race and Inequality in Postwar Detroit* (1996).

Juan Williams, *Thurgood Marshall: American Revolutionary* (1998).

▶ **For more books about topics in this chapter,** see the Online Bibliography at bedfordstmartins.com/roark.

▶ **For additional firsthand accounts of this period,** see Chapter 27 in Michael Johnson, ed., *Reading the American Past,* Fourth Edition.

▶ **For Web sites, images, and documents related to topics and places in this chapter,** visit bedfordstmartins.com/makehistory.

REVIEWING THE CHAPTER

Follow these steps to review and strengthen your understanding of the chapter.
STEP 1: *Study the* **Key Terms** *and* **Timeline** *to identify the significance of each item listed.*
STEP 2: *Answer the* **Review Questions**, *drawing on key terms and dates to support your answers.*
STEP 3: *Drawing on the Key Terms, Timeline, and Review Questions, answer the broader* **Making Connections** *questions.*

KEY TERMS

Who
Richard M. Nixon (p. 983)
Nikita Khrushchev (pp. 983, 994)
Dwight D. Eisenhower (pp. 983, 988)
John Foster Dulles (p. 988)
Ho Chi Minh (p. 989)
Ngo Dinh Diem (p. 990)
Jacobo Arbenz (p. 990)
Fidel Castro (p. 990)
Mohammed Mossadegh (p. 991)
Gamal Abdel Nasser (p. 991)
William J. Levitt (p. 998)
Betty Friedan (p. 1004)
Billy Graham (p. 1004)
Alfred Kinsey (p. 1007)
Thurgood Marshall (p. 1010)
Earl Warren (p. 1010)
Emmett Till (p. 1010)
Rosa Parks (p. 1014)
E. D. Nixon (p. 1014)
Jo Ann Robinson (p. 1014)
Martin Luther King Jr. (p. 1015)
Ella Baker (p. 1015)

What
kitchen debate (p. 983)
Interstate Highway and Defense System Act of 1956 (p. 985)
Indian Claims Commission (p. 986)
"New Look" (p. 989)
brinksmanship (p. 989)
mutually assured destruction (MAD) (p. 989)
domino theory (p. 989)
Geneva accords (p. 990)
Southeast Asia Treaty Organization (SEATO) (p. 990)
United Fruit Company (p. 990)
Suez crisis (p. 994)
Eisenhower Doctrine (p. 994)
Sputnik (p. 994)
National Aeronautics and Space Administration (NASA) (p. 994)
National Defense Education Act (p. 994)
U-2 incident (p. 994)
military-industrial complex (p. 995)
affluent society (p. 996)

Levittown (p. 998)
Sun Belt (p. 999)
Operation Wetback (p. 1001)
Hernandez v. Texas (p. 1001)
baby boom (p. 1004)
Beat generation (p. 1007)
National Association for the Advancement of Colored People (NAACP) (p. 1010)
Brown v. Board of Education (p. 1010)
Central High School, Little Rock, Arkansas (p. 1010)
Civil Rights Acts of 1957 and 1960 (p. 1011)
Montgomery, Alabama, Women's Political Council (WPC) (p. 1014)
Montgomery bus boycott (p. 1015)
Southern Christian Leadership Conference (SCLC) (p. 1015)

TIMELINE

1952 • Republican Dwight D. Eisenhower elected president.

           1953 • Termination of special status of American Indians and relocation of thousands off reservations.
                 • CIA engineers coup against government of Iran.

                      1954 • CIA stages coup against government of Guatemala.
                             • France signs Geneva accords, withdrawing from Vietnam.
                             • United States organizes Southeast Asia Treaty Organization (SEATO) and begins aid to South Vietnam.
                             • Government launches Operation Wetback.
                             • Building of first commercial nuclear power plant begins.
                             • *Hernandez v. Texas.*
                             • *Brown v. Board of Education.*
                             • Senate condemns Senator Joseph McCarthy.

                                    1955 • Eisenhower and Khrushchev meet in Geneva.
                                    1955– • Montgomery, Alabama, bus boycott.
                                    1956

REVIEW QUESTIONS

1. How did Eisenhower's domestic policies reflect his moderate political vision? (pp. 984–88)

2. Where and how did Eisenhower practice containment? (pp. 988–95)

3. How did technology contribute to changes in the economy, suburbanization, and the growth of the Sun Belt? (pp. 996–1002)

4. Why did American consumption expand so dramatically in the 1950s, and what aspects of society and culture did it influence? (pp. 1003–9)

5. What were the goals and strategies of civil rights activists in the 1950s? (pp. 1009–15)

MAKING CONNECTIONS

1. Both President Truman and President Eisenhower perceived a grave threat in the Soviet Union and the spread of communism around the world. How did these two presidents approach foreign policy during the cold war? In your answer, consider their similarities and differences.

2. The 1950s brought significant changes to the everyday lives of many Americans. Discuss the economic and demographic changes that contributed to the growth of suburbs and the Sun Belt. How did these trends shape the culture of abundance? In your answer, consider both Americans who participated in these trends and those who did not.

3. During the 1950s, actions by the federal government and the courts had a significant impact on African Americans, Native Americans, and Mexican Americans. Discuss how new policies and court actions came about and how laws affected these groups for better and for worse.

4. Eisenhower was the first Republican president since the New Deal had transformed the federal government. How did his "modern Republicanism" address Roosevelt's legacy? How did the shape and character of government change or not change during Eisenhower's administration?

▶ FOR PRACTICE QUIZZES, A CUSTOMIZED STUDY PLAN, AND OTHER STUDY TOOLS, see the Online Study Guide at bedfordstmartins.com/roark.

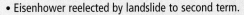

1956 • Interstate Highway and Defense System Act.
      • Eisenhower reelected by landslide to second term.
      • *Howl* published.

    1957 • Southern Christian Leadership Conference (SCLC) founded.
            • Soviets launch *Sputnik*.
            • Labor union membership peaks at 27.1 percent of labor force.
            • *On the Road* published.

      1958 • National Aeronautics and Space Administration (NASA) established.

        1959 • Kitchen debate between Nixon and Khrushchev.

          1960 • Soviets shoot down U.S. U-2 spy plane.
               • Thirty-five percent of women work outside the home.
               • One-quarter of Americans live in suburbs.

"COUNTRY JOE" McDONALD'S GUITAR

Music was an indispensable element of protest movements in the 1960s. Civil rights demonstrators sang "We Shall Overcome," antiwar rallies featured folk and rock singers, and hippies turned on to acid rock. The guitar was the central musical instrument for each kind of music: traditional African American, folk, and rock. This wooden acoustic guitar, adorned with a peace symbol, belonged to "Country Joe" McDonald, who started his band, Country Joe and the Fish, at a draft protest in Oakland, California, in 1965. The band was one of many that originated in the San Francisco Bay area, but its popularity soon spread across the country.

The Oakland Museum of California.

Reform, Rebellion, and Reaction

1960–1974

O N AUGUST 31, 1962, Fannie Lou Hamer boarded a bus carrying eighteen African Americans from Ruleville, Mississippi, to the county seat in Indianola, where they intended to register to vote. Blacks accounted for more than 60 percent of Sunflower County's population but only 1.2 percent of registered voters. Before young civil rights activists arrived in Ruleville to start a voter registration drive, Hamer recalled, "I didn't know that a Negro could register and vote." Her forty-five years of poverty, exploitation, and political **disfranchisement** typified the lives of most blacks in the rural South. The daughter of sharecroppers, Hamer began work in the cotton fields at age six, attending school in a one-room shack from December to March and only until she was twelve. She later married Perry Hamer and moved onto a plantation, where both she and her husband worked in the fields and she did domestic work for the owner and recorded the cotton that sharecroppers harvested.

At the Indianola County courthouse, Hamer and her companions had to pass through a hostile, white, gun-carrying crowd. Using a common practice to deny blacks the vote, the registrar tested Hamer on an obscure section of the state constitution, which had not been part of her schooling. She failed the test but resolved to try again. When the plantation owner ordered Hamer to withdraw her registration application or get off his land, she left the plantation. Ten days later, bullets flew into the home of friends who had taken her in. Refusing to be intimidated, she registered to vote on her third attempt, attended a civil rights leadership training conference, and began to mobilize others to vote. In 1963, she and other activists were arrested in Winona, Mississippi, and brutally beaten. Hamer went from jail to the hospital, where her sister could not recognize her battered face.

Fannie Lou Hamer's courage and determination made her a prominent figure in the black freedom struggle. Such activists shook the nation's conscience, provided a protest model for other groups, and pushed the government to enact not only civil rights legislation but also a host of other **liberal** policies. Although the federal government often tried to curb civil rights protest, the two Democratic presidents of the 1960s favored using government to ameliorate social and economic problems. After John F. Kennedy was assassinated in November 1963, Lyndon B. Johnson launched the **Great Society**—a multitude of efforts to promote racial justice, education, medical care, urban development, environmental and economic health, and more.

Mississippi Freedom Democratic Party Rally
Fannie Lou Hamer (left foreground) and other activists sing at a rally outside the Democratic National Convention hall in 1964, supporting the Mississippi Freedom Democratic Party (MFDP) in its challenge to the all-white delegation sent by the regular Mississippi Democratic Party. Next to Hamer is Eleanor Holmes Norton, a civil rights lawyer, and Ella Baker (far right), who helped organize the Southern Christian Leadership Conference and later managed MFDP headquarters in Washington, D.C.
Matt Herron/Take Stock.

Those who struggled for racial justice lost property and sometimes their lives, but by the end of the decade, American law had caught up with the American ideal of equality.

Yet legal change did not go far enough. Strong civil rights legislation and pathbreaking Supreme Court decisions did little to mitigate the deplorable economic conditions of African Americans nationwide, on which Hamer and others increasingly focused after 1965. Nor were liberal politicians consistently reliable supporters, as Hamer found out in 1964 when President Johnson and his allies rebuffed black Mississippi Democrats' efforts to be represented at the Democratic National Convention. "We followed all the laws that the white people themselves made," she said, only to find that "the white man is not going to give up his power to us. . . . We have to take [it] for ourselves." By 1966, a minority of African American activists were demand-ing black power; the movement soon splintered, and white support sharply declined. The war in Vietnam stifled liberal reform, while a growing number of **conservatives** protested that the Great Society went too far and condemned the challenge to American values and institutions mounted by blacks, students, and others.

Though disillusioned and often frustrated, Fannie Lou Hamer remained an activist until her death in 1977, participating in new social movements stimulated by the black freedom struggle. In 1969, she supported students at Mississippi Valley State College who demanded black studies courses and a voice in campus decisions. In 1972, she attended the first conference of the National Women's Political Caucus, established to achieve greater representation for women in government. The caucus was part of a diverse **feminist** movement that transformed women's legal status as well as the everyday relationships between women and men.

Feminists and other groups, including ethnic minorities, environmentalists, and gays and lesbians, carried the tide of reform into the 1970s. They pushed the Republican administration of Richard M. Nixon to sustain the liberalism of the 1960s, with its emphasis on a strong government role in regulating the economy, guaranteeing the welfare and rights of all individuals, and improving the quality of life. Despite its conservative rhetoric, the Nixon administration implemented school desegregation and **affirmative action** and adopted pathbreaking measures in environmental regulation, equality for women, and justice for Native Americans. The years between 1960 and 1974 contained the greatest efforts to reconcile America's promise with reality since the **New Deal**.

Liberalism at High Tide

At the Democratic National Convention in 1960, John F. Kennedy announced "a New Frontier" that would confront "unsolved problems of peace and war, unconquered pockets of ignorance and prejudice, unanswered questions of poverty and surplus." Four years later, Lyndon B. Johnson invoked the ideal of a "Great Society, [which] rests on abundance and liberty for all [and] demands an end to poverty and racial injustice."

Acting under the liberal faith that government should use its power to solve social and economic problems, end injustice, and promote the welfare of all citizens, the Democratic administrations of the 1960s won legislation on civil rights, poverty, education, medical care, housing, consumer protection, and environmental protection. These measures took up the unfulfilled agendas of the New Deal and Fair Deal, responded to new demands for rights from African Americans and other groups, and addressed new concerns growing out of the maturation of a consumer society and rapid economic growth.

The Unrealized Promise of Kennedy's New Frontier

John F. Kennedy grew up in privilege, the child of an Irish Catholic businessman who served in Franklin D. Roosevelt's administration and nourished political ambitions for his sons. Helped by a distinguished World War II navy record, Kennedy won election to the House of Representatives in 1946 and the Senate in

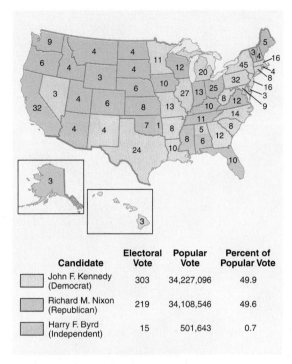

Candidate	Electoral Vote	Popular Vote	Percent of Popular Vote
John F. Kennedy (Democrat)	303	34,227,096	49.9
Richard M. Nixon (Republican)	219	34,108,546	49.6
Harry F. Byrd (Independent)	15	501,643	0.7

MAP 28.1   The Election of 1960

1952. His record in Congress was unremarkable, but with a powerful political machine, his family's fortune, and a dynamic personal appeal, Kennedy won the Democratic presidential nomination in 1960. He stunned many Democrats by choosing as his running mate Lyndon B. Johnson of Texas, a rival for the presidential nomination whom liberals disparaged as a typical southern conservative.

Kennedy defeated his Republican opponent, Vice President Richard M. Nixon, in an excruciatingly close election (Map 28.1). African American voters contributed to his victory, helping to offset the 52 percent of the white vote cast for Nixon and contributing to Kennedy's 118,550-vote margin overall. Lyndon Johnson helped the ticket carry most of the South, and a rise in unemployment in 1960 also favored the Democrats. Finally, Kennedy benefited from the nation's first televised presidential debates, during which he appeared cool, confident, and handsome beside a nervous, sweaty, and pale Nixon.

The Kennedy administration projected energy, idealism, and glamour, although in fact Kennedy was in most ways a cautious, pragmatic politician. The first president to hold live televised press conferences, Kennedy charmed the audience with his grace, vigor, and self-mocking wit. He kept hidden from the public serious health problems

The Kennedy Appeal
The youth and glamour of the Kennedy administration are apparent in this photo of the president and his wife attired for his inauguration gala. The gown that Jacqueline Kennedy had designed by Oleg Cassini for the occasion bore a cockade at the waist, indicating her French ancestry and keen interest in history and culture. This interest was reflected in White House social events that elevated Washington's cultural scene by featuring artists, writers, scholars, and musicians. Well aware of the First Lady's appeal to the public, the president asked the driver taking them to the gala to "turn on the lights so they can see Jackie."
© Bettmann/Corbis.

and affairs with several women, making himself vulnerable to blackmail and risking the dignity of his office. Journalists turned a blind eye, instead projecting warm images of an energetic, youthful president with his chic and cultured wife, Jacqueline.

At his inauguration, the forty-three-year-old Kennedy declared that a "new generation" was assuming leadership, and he called on Americans to cast off complacency and self-indulgence and serve the common good. "Ask not what your country can do for you," he implored, "ask what you can do for your country." Although Kennedy's idealism inspired many, especially the young, he failed to redeem campaign promises to expand the **welfare state**. Two central items on the Democratic agenda since the Truman administration, federal aid for education and health care for the elderly, got nowhere. Moreover, he declined to assume leadership on behalf of racial justice until late in his term, when civil rights activists gave him no choice. But he did sign legislation making it illegal to pay women less than men for the same work (see page 1049).

Moved by the desperate conditions he observed when he campaigned in Appalachia in 1960, Kennedy responded to a number of reformers concerned about rising rates of juvenile delinquency and seeking to push poverty onto the national agenda. For instance, in 1962, he read Michael Harrington's *The Other America*, which described the poverty that left more than one in five Americans "maimed in body and spirit, existing at levels beneath those necessary for human decency." By 1962, Kennedy had won support for a $2 billion urban renewal program; area redevelopment legislation that offered incentives to businesses to locate, and thereby provide jobs, in economically depressed areas; and a training program for the unemployed. In the summer of 1963, Kennedy asked aides to plan a full-scale attack on poverty, and he issued a dramatic call for a comprehensive civil rights bill, marking a turning point in his domestic agenda.

Kennedy had promised to make economic growth a key objective. "A rising tide lifts all boats" expressed his belief that economic growth could eradicate poverty and solve most social problems, as well as make the nation more competitive with the Soviet Union. Kennedy's economic advisers argued that reducing taxes would infuse money into the economy and thus increase demand, boost production, and decrease unemployment. To that end, he asked Congress to pass an enormous tax cut in 1963. This use of fiscal policy to stimulate the economy even when there was no recession was called the "new economics."

Kennedy did not live to see approval of his tax bill. Passed in February 1964, the law contributed to the greatest economic boom since World War II. Unemployment dropped to 4.1 percent, and the gross national product shot up by 7 to 9 percent annually between 1964 and 1966. Some liberal critics of the tax cut, however, pointed out that it favored those who were well-off and that economic growth alone would not eliminate poverty. They argued instead for increased spending on social programs.

Kennedy's economic efforts were in their infancy when he fell victim to an assassin's bullet on November 22, 1963. That event touched Americans as had no other since the end of World War II. Within minutes of the shooting—which occurred as Kennedy's motorcade passed through Dallas, Texas—radio and television broadcast the unfolding horror to the nation. Millions watched the return of *Air Force One* to Washington, bearing the president's coffin, his widow in her bloodstained suit, and the new president, Lyndon Baines Johnson.

Stunned Americans struggled with what had happened and why. Soon after the assassination, police arrested Lee Harvey Oswald and concluded that he had fired the shots from a nearby building. Two days later, as a television audience watched Oswald being transferred from one jail to another, a local nightclub operator, Jack Ruby, killed him. Suspicions arose that Ruby murdered Oswald to cover up a conspiracy by ultraconservative Texans who hated Kennedy, or by Communists who supported Castro's Cuba. To get at the truth, President Johnson appointed a commission headed by Chief Justice Earl Warren, which concluded in September 1964 that both Oswald and Ruby had acted alone. Although several experts pointed to errors and omissions in the report, and some contested the lone-killer explanation, most scholars agreed that no conspiracy had existed.

Debate continued over how to assess Kennedy's domestic record. It had been unremarkable in his first two years, but his proposals on taxes, civil rights, and poverty in 1963 suggested an important shift. Whether Kennedy could have persuaded Congress to enact his initiatives remained in

The "Johnson Treatment"
Abe Fortas, a distinguished lawyer who had argued a major criminal rights case, *Gideon v. Wainwright* (1963), before the Supreme Court, was a close friend and adviser of President Johnson. This photograph of the president and Fortas taken in July 1965 illustrates how Johnson used his body as well as his voice to bend people to his will.
Yoichi R. Okamoto/LBJ Library Collection.

question. In the words of journalist James Reston, "What was killed was not only the president but the promise. . . . He never reached his meridian: We saw him only as a rising sun."

Johnson Fulfills the Kennedy Promise

Lyndon B. Johnson assumed the presidency with a wealth of political experience. A self-made man from the Texas Hill Country, he had won election to the House of Representatives in 1937 and to the Senate in 1948. Although his Texas base required caution on civil rights and attention to the interests of oil and other big businesses, Johnson's growing desire for national leadership had led him to take more liberal stands. After 1955, he used his post as Senate majority leader brilliantly to force a consensus on civil rights legislation in 1957 and 1960. His own modest upbringing in an impoverished area, his admiration for Franklin Roosevelt, and his fierce ambition to outdo the New Deal president all spurred his commitment to reform. Equally compelling were external pressures generated by the black freedom struggle and the host of movements it helped inspire.

Johnson's coarse wit, extreme vanity, and Texas accent repulsed those who preferred the sophisticated Kennedy style. Lacking his predecessor's eloquence, Johnson excelled behind the scenes, where he could entice, maneuver, or threaten legislators to support his objectives. The famous "Johnson treatment" became legendary. In his ability to achieve consensus around his goals, he had few peers in American history.

"I had to take the dead man's program and turn it into a martyr's cause," Johnson declared, entreating Congress to act so that "John Fitzgerald Kennedy did not live or die in vain." He won over fiscal conservatives and signed Kennedy's tax cut bill in February 1964. Still more revolutionary was the passage of the Civil Rights Act in 1964, which Kennedy had proposed in response to the black freedom struggle. It was the strongest such measure since Reconstruction, and its passage required every ounce of Johnson's political skill to pry sufficient votes from Republicans to balance the "nays" of southern Democrats. Senate Republican leader Everett Dirksen's aide reported that Johnson "never left him alone for thirty minutes."

Antipoverty legislation followed fast on the heels of the Civil Rights Act. Johnson urged aides to "push ahead full tilt" on a poverty program that was still in an embryonic state when Kennedy died. Just two months after the president called for "an unconditional war on poverty" in his January 1964 State of the Union message, the administration rushed a draft bill to Congress, which responded with equal haste in August. The Economic Opportunity Act of 1964 authorized ten programs under the new Office of Economic Opportunity and allocated $800 million for the first year (about 1 percent of the federal budget). Many provisions targeted youths, including Head Start for preschoolers, work-study grants for college students, and the Job Corps for unemployed young people. There were also loans to businesses willing to hire the long-term unemployed; aid to small farmers; and the Volunteers in Service to America (VISTA) program, which paid modest wages to volunteers working with the disadvantaged. A legal services program provided lawyers for the poor, leading to lawsuits that enforced their rights to welfare programs.

> Johnson urged aides to "push ahead full tilt" on a poverty program that was still in an embryonic state when Kennedy died.

The most novel and controversial part of the law, the Community Action Program (CAP), required "maximum feasible participation" of the poor themselves in antipoverty programs. This approach resembled the "participatory democracy" of young white and black activists and members of other social movements of the 1960s, encouraging ordinary people to challenge established leaders and institutions. Poor people began to organize local community action programs to take control of their neighborhoods and make welfare agencies, school boards, police departments, and housing authorities more accountable to the people they served.

When mayors complained that activists were causing trouble for local governments and "fostering class struggle," Johnson backed off from pushing genuine representation for the poor. Nonetheless, CAP gave people usually excluded from government an opportunity to act on their own behalf and to develop leadership skills. To a Mississippi sharecropper forced by poverty to leave school to work before he learned to read and write, a local CAP literacy program provided basic skills and self-respect. "It has meant more to me than I can express," he said. "I can now write my name and I will be able to help my younger children when they start school."

Policymaking for a Great Society

Having steered the nation through the assassination trauma and established his capacity for national leadership, Johnson projected stability and security in the midst of a booming economy. Few voters wanted to risk the dramatic change promised by his Republican opponent in the 1964 election, Arizona senator Barry M. Goldwater, who attacked the welfare state and suggested using nuclear weapons if necessary to crush **communism** in Vietnam. Although Goldwater captured five southern states, Johnson achieved a record-breaking landslide of 61 percent of the popular vote. Democrats won resounding majorities in the House (295–140) and Senate (68–32), yet, as we shall see in chapter 30, Goldwater's campaign aroused considerable grassroots support. A movement on the right grew alongside the more noticeable left and liberal movements, eventually attaining conservative ascendancy in national politics.

"I want to see a whole bunch of coonskins on the wall," Johnson told his aides, using a hunting analogy to stress his ambitious legislative goals that would usher in what he called the "Great Society." The large Democratic majorities in Congress and the political capital drawn from his landslide victory enabled Johnson to succeed mightily. He persuaded Congress to act on discrimination, poverty, education, medical care, housing, consumer and environmental protection, and more. Reporters called the legislation of the Eighty-ninth Congress (1965–1966) "a political miracle."

The Economic Opportunity Act of 1964 was the opening shot in the War on Poverty. Congress doubled the program's funding in 1965 and passed new initiatives to promote economic development. Targeting depressed regions that the general economic boom had bypassed, these measures—like the tax cut of 1964—sought to help the poor indirectly by stimulating economic growth and providing jobs through road building and other public works projects. In addition, the Model Cities Act of 1965 authorized more than $1 billion to improve conditions in the nation's slums.

Other antipoverty efforts provided direct aid. A new food stamp program largely replaced the distribution of surplus commodities, giving poor people greater choice in obtaining food. Rent supplements also allowed more options, enabling some poor families to avoid public housing projects. Moreover, a movement of welfare mothers, the National Welfare Rights Organization, assisted by antipoverty lawyers, pushed administrators of Aid to Families with Dependent Children (ADFC) to ease restrictions on welfare recipients. The number of families receiving assistance jumped from less than one million in 1960 to three million by 1972, benefiting 90 percent of those eligible.

Central to Johnson's War on Poverty were efforts to equip the poor with the skills necessary to find jobs. A former schoolteacher, Johnson saw federal support for public education as a natural extension of the New Deal; it had been on the Democratic Party agenda for two decades. To Roosevelt's Four Freedoms (see chapter 25), Johnson added a fifth: "freedom from ignorance." His Elementary and Secondary Education Act of 1965 marked a turning point by involving the federal government in K–12 education. Combating poverty with federal funds, the measure sent dollars to local school districts based on the number of poor children educated therein, and it provided equipment and supplies to private and parochial schools to be used for poor children. That same year, Congress passed the Higher Education Act, vastly expanding federal assistance to colleges and universities for buildings, programs, scholarships, and low-interest student loans.

The federal government's responsibility for health care marked an even more significant watershed. Faced with a powerful medical lobby that opposed national health insurance as "socialized medicine," Johnson pared back Truman's proposed plan for government-sponsored universal care. Instead, he focused on the elderly, who constituted a large portion of the nation's poor. Congress responded with the Medicare program, providing the elderly with universal compulsory medical insurance financed largely through Social Security taxes. A separate program, Medicaid, authorized federal grants to supplement state-paid medical care for poor people.

Whereas federal aid to education, Medicare, and Medicaid fulfilled New Deal and Fair Deal promises, the Great Society's civil rights legislation represented a break with tradition and an expansion of liberalism. Racial minorities were neglected or discriminated against in such New Deal programs as old-age assistance and unemployment insurance. Moreover, Truman's call for measures to end racial discrimination bore few results. By contrast, the Civil Rights Act of 1964 made discrimination in employment, education, and public accommodations illegal. The Voting Rights Act of 1965 banned literacy tests like the one that stymied Fannie Lou Hamer and authorized federal intervention to ensure access to the voting booth.

Another form of discrimination fell with the Immigration and Nationality Act of 1965, which abolished fifty-year-old quotas based on national origins that were biased against immigrants from areas outside northern and western Europe. Signing the bill at the Statue of Liberty, Johnson proclaimed the end of "a cruel and enduring harm." The law maintained caps on the total number of immigrants and for the first time limited those from the Western Hemisphere; preference was now given to immediate relatives of U.S. citizens and to those with desirable skills. Senator Edward Kennedy predicted that "our cities will not be flooded with a million citizens annually," but the measure's unanticipated consequences did nearly that, triggering a surge of immigration near the end of the century (see chapter 31).

Great Society benefits reached well beyond victims of discrimination and the poor. Medicare, for example, covered the elderly, regardless of income. A surge of consumer activism

A Tribute to Johnson for Medicare
George Niedermeyer, who lived in Hollywood, Florida, and received a Social Security pension, painted pieces of wood and glued them together to create this thank-you to President Johnson for establishing Medicare. Niedermeyer entrusted his congressional representative, Claude Pepper, known for his support of the interests of the elderly, to deliver the four-foot-tall tribute to Johnson in 1967.
LBJ Library, photo by Henry Groskinsky.

President Johnson Signs the Immigration and Nationality Act
Signing the Immigration and Nationality Act of 1965 at the Statue of Liberty in New York
harbor, Johnson celebrated the end of "the harsh injustice of the national origins quota
system." To Johnson's right are Lady Bird Johnson and Vice President Hubert H. Humphrey.
Muriel Humphrey is behind the president; to her left are Senator Edward Kennedy and
Senator Robert Kennedy. The law had passed by huge majorities in the House and Senate
and was not expected to change significantly the number of immigrants or the ethnic
composition of the population. In a classic case of unintended consequences, both assumptions were proved wrong by the 1980s.
Lyndon B. Johnson Presidential Library.

ernment programs arose. Some Americans expressed their opposition with buttons reading "I fight poverty—I work." The Vietnam War dealt the largest blow to Johnson's ambitions, diverting his attention from domestic affairs, spawning an antiwar movement that crippled his leadership, and devouring tax dollars that might have been used for reform (see chapter 29).

Against these odds, in 1968 Johnson pried out of Congress one more civil rights law, which banned discrimination in housing and jury service. He also signed the National Housing Act of 1968, which authorized an enormous increase in the construction of low-income housing—1.7 million units over three years—and, by leaving construction and ownership in private hands, a new way of providing it. Government-guaranteed low-interest loans spurred developers to build houses and enabled poor people to purchase those homes.

Assessing the Great Society

Measured by statistics, the reduction in poverty in the 1960s was considerable. The number of impoverished Americans fell from more than 20 percent of the population in 1959 to around 13 percent in 1968 (Figure 28.1). Those who Johnson had said "lived on the outskirts of hope" gained more control of their circumstances and a sense of their right to a fairer share of America's bounty. Assessing what turned her family of longtime welfare recipients into tax-paying workers, Rosemary Bray concluded, "What fueled our dreams and fired our belief that our lives could change for the better was the promise of the civil rights movement and the war on poverty." A Mexican American beneficiary of a jobs program that trained him to be a sheet metal worker reported that his children "will finish high school and maybe go to college. . . . I see my family and I know the chains are broken."

Certain groups fared much better than others, however. Large numbers of the aged and male-headed families rose out of poverty, while the plight of female-headed families actually worsened. Whites escaped poverty at a faster rate than racial and ethnic minorities. Great Society programs contributed to a burgeoning black middle class, and the proportion of African Americans who were poor fell by 10 percentage

fueled by Ralph Nader's exposé of the auto industry, *Unsafe at Any Speed* (1965), won legislation making cars safer and raising standards for the food, drug, and cosmetics industries.

Johnson himself insisted that the Great Society meet "not just the needs of the body but the desire for beauty and hunger for community" and that it enable Americans "to live the good life." In 1965, he became the first president to send Congress a special message on the environment, obtaining measures to control water and air pollution and to preserve the natural beauty of the American landscape. First Lady "Lady Bird" Johnson made beautification of the environment her primary public project. In addition, the National Arts and Humanities Act of 1965 funded artists, musicians, writers, and scholars and brought their work to public audiences.

The flood of reform legislation dwindled after 1966, when Democratic majorities in Congress diminished and a backlash against gov-

> Johnson insisted that the Great Society meet "not just the needs of the body but the desire for beauty and hunger for community" and that it enable Americans "to live the good life."

points between 1966 and 1974. Still, one-third of them remained impoverished (see Figure 28.1).

Conservative critics charged that Great Society programs discouraged initiative by giving the poor "handouts." Liberal critics claimed that the emphasis on training and education unjustly placed the responsibility for poverty on the poor themselves rather than on an economic system that could not provide enough adequately paying jobs. Most government training programs prepared graduates for low-skilled labor and could not guarantee employment. In contrast to the New Deal, the Great Society avoided structural reform of the economy and spurned public works projects as a means of providing jobs for the disadvantaged.

Who reaped the greatest advantages from Great Society programs? Programs such as Medicare and those addressing consumer safety and environmental reform benefited Americans across the board. Most of the funds for economically depressed areas built highways and thus helped the construction industry. Real estate developers, investors, and moderate-income families benefited most from the National Housing Act of 1968. Commercial development and high-income housing often relied on slum clearance programs, which displaced the poor and caused blacks to refer to urban renewal as "Negro removal." Physicians' fees and hospital costs soared after the enactment of Medicare and Medicaid, resulting in advantages for both health care providers and the elderly and poor.

Some critics argued that ending poverty required a redistribution of income—raising taxes and using those funds to create jobs, overhaul welfare systems, and rebuild slums. Great Society programs did invest more heavily in the public sector, but Johnson's efforts relied on economic growth for funding rather than on new taxes on the rich or middle class. There was no significant redistribution of income, despite large increases in subsidies for food stamps, housing, medical care, and AFDC. The poorest 20 percent of the population received 5.1 percent of total national income in 1964 and 5.4 percent in 1974. Economic prosperity allowed spending for the poor to rise and significantly improved

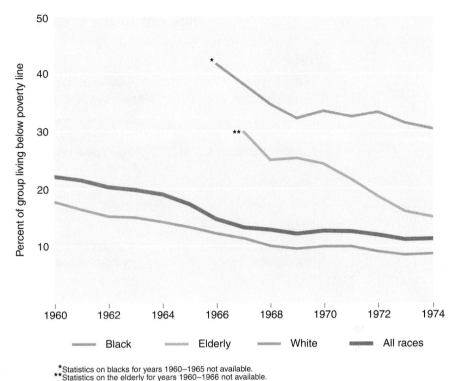

FIGURE 28.1 Poverty in the United States, 1960–1974
The short-term effects of economic growth and the Great Society's attack on poverty are seen here. Which groups experienced the sharpest decline in poverty, and what might account for the differences?

the lives of millions, but that spending never approached the amounts necessary to claim victory in the War on Poverty.

The Judicial Revolution

A key element of liberalism's ascendancy emerged in the Supreme Court under Chief Justice Earl Warren (1953–1969). In contrast to the Progressive Era and the New Deal, when federal courts blocked reform, the Supreme Court in the 1960s proved a strong ally, often moving out in front of Congress and public opinion. Expanding the Constitution's promise of equality and individual rights, the Court's decisions supported an activist government to prevent injustice and provided new protections to disadvantaged groups and accused criminals.

Following the pathbreaking *Brown v. Board of Education* school desegregation decision of 1954 (see chapter 27), the Court ruled against all-white public facilities and struck down educational plans devised by southern states to avoid integration. In cases upholding the rights

Reforms of the Great Society, 1964–1968

1964

Twenty-fourth Amendment	Abolishes poll tax as prerequisite for voting.
Tax Reduction Act	Provides $10 billion in tax cuts in 1964 and 1965.
Civil Rights Act	Bans discrimination in public accommodations, public education, and employment and extends protections to American Indians on reservations.
Economic Opportunity Act	Creates programs for the disadvantaged, including Head Start, VISTA, the Job Corps, and CAP.
Wilderness Preservation Act	Sets aside 9.1 million acres of national forest for protection.

1965

Elementary and Secondary Education Act	Provides $1.3 billion in aid to elementary and secondary schools.
Medical Care Act	Provides health insurance (Medicare) for all citizens age sixty-five and over. Extends federal health benefits to welfare recipients (Medicaid).
Voting Rights Act	Bans literacy tests and other voting tests and authorizes the federal government to act directly to enable African Americans to both register and vote.
Executive Order 11246	Bans discrimination on the basis of race, religion, and national origin by employers awarded government contracts and requires them to "take affirmative action to ensure equal opportunity."
Department of Housing and Urban Development (HUD)	Created to provide programs to address housing and community issues.
National Arts and Humanities Act	Creates National Endowment for the Arts (NEA) and humanities (NEH) to support the work of artists, musicians, writers, and scholars.
Water Quality Act	Requires states to set and enforce water quality standards.
Immigration and Nationality Act	Abolishes fifty-year-old quotas based on national origins, increasing the number of non-Western and southern and eastern European immigrants.
Air Quality Act	Imposes air pollution standards for motor vehicles.
Higher Education Act	Expands federal assistance to colleges and universities.

1966

National Traffic and Motor Vehicle Safety Act	Establishes federal safety standards.
Highway Safety Act	Requires federally approved safety programs at the state level.
Department of Transportation	Created to administer transportation programs and policies.
Model Cities Act	Authorizes more than $1 billion to ameliorate the nation's slums.

1967

Executive Order 11375	Extends an earlier executive order banning discrimination and requiring affirmative action by federal contractors to cover women.

1968

Civil Rights Act of 1968	Bans discrimination in housing and jury service.
National Housing Act	Subsidizes the private construction of 1.7 million units of low-income housing.

of freedom of assembly and speech, it enabled the black freedom struggle to continue sit-ins, marches, and other tactics crucial to its success. In addition, a unanimous Court in *Loving v. Virginia* (1967) struck down state laws banning interracial marriage. The justices' declaration that marriage was one of the "basic civil rights of man," a "fundamental freedom," would later be repeated by gay men and lesbians seeking the right to marry.

Chief Justice Warren considered *Baker v. Carr* (1963) his most important decision. The case grew out of a complaint that Tennessee electoral districts were drawn so inequitably that sparsely populated rural districts had far more representatives than densely populated urban areas. Using the Fourteenth Amendment guarantee of "equal protection of the laws," *Baker* established the principle of "one person, one vote" for both state legislatures and the House of Representatives. Most states had to redraw electoral districts, thus making state legislatures more responsive to metropolitan interests.

The egalitarian thrust of the Warren Court also reformed the criminal justice system as the justices used the Fourteenth Amendment to overturn a series of convictions on the grounds that the accused had been deprived of "life, liberty, or property, without due process of law." In decisions that dramatically altered law enforcement practices and the treatment of individuals accused of a crime, the Court declared that states, as well as the federal government, were subject to the **Bill of Rights**. For example, in *Gideon v. Wainwright* (1963), the Court ruled that when accused criminals could not afford to hire a lawyer, states must provide a lawyer without charge. In 1966, *Miranda v. Arizona* required police officers to inform suspects of their rights upon arrest. It also overturned convictions based on evidence obtained by unlawful arrest, by electronic surveillance, or without a search warrant.

As Supreme Court decisions overturned judicial precedents and often moved ahead of public opinion, critics accused the justices of obstructing law enforcement and letting criminals go free. The mayor of Los Angeles, for example, equated *Miranda* with "handcuffing the police." Liberals, however, argued that these rulings promoted equal treatment in the criminal justice system: The wealthy always had access to legal counsel, and practiced criminals were well aware of their right to remain silent. The beneficiaries of the decisions were the poor and the ignorant, as well as the general population, whose right to privacy was strengthened by the stricter guidelines for admissible evidence.

The Court's decisions on prayer and Bible reading in public schools provoked even greater outrage. *Abington School District v. Schempp* (1963) ruled that a Pennsylvania law requiring Bible reading and prayer in the schools violated the First Amendment principle of separation of church and state. Later decisions ruled against official prayer in public schools even if students were not required to participate. These decisions left students free to pray on their own, but an infuriated Alabama legislator complained, "They put Negroes in the schools and now they've driven God out." The Court's supporters, however, declared that the religion cases protected the rights of non-Christians and atheists.

Two or three justices who believed that the Court was overstepping its authority often issued sharp dissents. Outside the Court, opponents worked to pass laws or constitutional amendments that would upset despised decisions, and billboards demanded, "Impeach Earl Warren." Critics of the Court were part of a larger backlash mounting against Great Society liberalism. Nonetheless, the Court's major decisions withstood the test of time.

REVIEW How did the Kennedy and Johnson administrations exemplify a liberal vision of the federal government?

The Second Reconstruction

As much as Supreme Court decisions, the black freedom struggle distinguished the liberalism of the 1960s from that of the New Deal. Before the Great Society reforms—and, in fact, contributing to them—African Americans had mobilized a movement that struck down legal separation and discrimination in the South. Whereas the first Reconstruction reflected the power of northern Republicans in the aftermath of the Civil War, the second Reconstruction depended heavily on the courage and determination of black people themselves. Sheyann Webb, one of the thousands of marchers in the 1965 Selma, Alabama, campaign for voting rights, recalled, "We were just people, ordinary people, and we did it."

Lunch Counter Sit-in

John Salter Jr., a professor at Tougaloo College, and students Joan Trumpauer and Anne Moody take part in a 1963 sit-in at the Woolworth's lunch counter in Jackson, Mississippi. Shortly before this photograph was taken, whites had thrown two students to the floor, and police had arrested one student. Salter was spattered with mustard and ketchup. In 1968, Moody published *Coming of Age in Mississippi*, a popular book about her experiences in the black freedom struggle.
State Historical Society of Wisconsin.

READING THE IMAGE: What does the photograph tell you about black civil rights activity of the early 1960s?

CONNECTIONS: How would you describe the changes in race relations between African Americans and whites in the United States in the first half of the 1960s?

FOR MORE HELP ANALYZING THIS IMAGE, see the visual activity for this chapter in the Online Study Guide at bedfordstmartins.com/roark.

The early black freedom struggle focused on legal rights in the South and won widespread acceptance. But when African Americans began to attack racial injustice in the rest of the country and to challenge the deplorable economic conditions that equal rights left untouched, a strong backlash developed as the movement itself lost cohesion.

The Flowering of the Black Freedom Struggle

The Montgomery bus boycott of 1955–1956 gave racial issues national visibility, produced a leader in Martin Luther King Jr., and demon-

strated the effectiveness of mass organization. In the 1960s, protest expanded dramatically, mobilizing blacks into direct confrontation with the people and institutions that segregated and discriminated against them: retail establishments, public parks and libraries, buses and depots, voting registrars, and police forces.

Massive direct action began in February 1960, when four African American college students in Greensboro, North Carolina, requested service at the whites-only Woolworth's lunch counter. Within days, hundreds of young people joined them, and others launched sit-ins in thirty-one southern cities. At Southern Christian

Leadership Conference (SCLC) headquarters, Ella Baker picked up the phone and challenged her young contacts at various colleges: "What are you going to do? It's time to move."

Baker organized a meeting of student activists in April 1960 and supported their decision to form a new organization, independent from the older generation. They founded the Student Nonviolent Coordinating Committee (SNCC, pronounced "snick") and initially embraced **civil disobedience** and the nonviolence principles of Martin Luther King Jr. Activists would directly confront their oppressors and stand up for their rights, but they would not respond if attacked. In the words of SNCC leader James Lawson, "Nonviolence nurtures the atmosphere in which reconciliation and justice become actual possibilities." Instead of the top-down leadership of King and established civil rights organizations, however, SNCC adopted a decentralized, nonhierarchical structure that fostered decision making and the development of leadership at the grassroots level.

The activists' optimism and commitment to nonviolence soon underwent severe testing. Although some cities quietly met student demands, more typically activists encountered violence. Hostile whites poured food over demonstrators, burned them with cigarettes, called them "niggers," and pelted them with rocks. Local police attacked protesters with dogs, clubs, fire hoses, and tear gas; they arrested more than 3,600 demonstrators in the year following the Greensboro sit-in.

Another wave of protest occurred in May 1961, when the Congress of Racial Equality (CORE) organized Freedom Rides to integrate interstate transportation in the South. When a group of six whites and seven blacks traveling from Washington, D.C., to New Orleans reached Alabama, whites bombed their bus and beat the riders with baseball bats so fiercely that an observer "couldn't see their faces through the blood." CORE rebuffed President Kennedy's pleas to call off the rides. But after a huge mob attacked the riders in Montgomery, Alabama, and injured a government observer, Attorney General Robert Kennedy dispatched federal marshals to restore order. Although violence against the riders abated, Freedom Riders arriving in Jackson, Mississippi, were promptly arrested, and several hundred spent part of the summer in jail. All told, more than four hundred blacks and whites participated in the Freedom Rides, which manifested the typical elements of the black freedom struggle: administration

efforts to stop the protests, officials' reluctance to step in to protect demonstrators, and the steely courage of African Americans in the face of tremendous violence against them.

Encouraged by Kennedy administration officials who preferred voter registration to civil disobedience (it was more likely to benefit the Democratic Party), SNCC and other groups began the Voter Education Project in the summer of 1961. Seeking to register voters in the South, they, too, met violence. Whites bombed black churches, threw tenant farmers out of their homes, and beat and jailed activists such as Fannie Lou Hamer. In June 1963, a white man gunned down Mississippi NAACP leader Medgar Evers in front of his house in Jackson; the murderer eluded conviction until

Civil Rights Freedom Rides, May 1961

Freedom Riders Attacked

Although Martin Luther King Jr. praised the courage of the Freedom Riders, he predicted that they would "never make it through Alabama." On May 14, 1961, a mob of some two hundred white men surrounded a Greyhound bus in Anniston, Alabama, pounding on it and slashing the tires. The driver sped away, pursued by about fifty cars, until the flat tires brought the bus to a halt outside the town. The mob renewed their assault, hurling a firebomb into the bus. As the choking passengers disembarked, they were beaten with clubs until Alabama state troopers arrived, subdued the crowd, and took the injured riders to the hospital. Photos of the flaming bus made news around the world.

© Bettmann/Corbis.

the 1990s. Similar violence met King's 1963 campaign in Birmingham, Alabama, to integrate public facilities and open jobs to blacks. The police attacked demonstrators with dogs, cattle prods, and fire hoses—brutalities that television broadcast around the world. Bombs exploded at the motel where King was staying and at his brother's house. Four months later, a bomb killed four black girls at a Birmingham Sunday school.

The largest demonstration drew 250,000 blacks and whites to the nation's capital in August 1963 in the March on Washington for Jobs and Freedom, inspired by the strategy of A. Philip Randolph in 1941 (see chapter 25). Speaking from the Lincoln Memorial, King put his indelible stamp on the day. He invoked the Bible, Negro spirituals, and patriotic anthems, drawing on all the passion and skills that made him the greatest orator of his day. "I have a dream," he repeated again and again, that "the sons of former slaves and the sons of former slave owners will be able to sit down together at the table of brotherhood." With the crowd roaring in support, he imagined the day "when all of God's children . . . will be able to join hands and sing . . . 'Free at last, free at last; thank God Almighty, we are free at last.'"

The euphoria of the March on Washington quickly faded as activists returned to continued violence in the South. In 1964, the Mississippi Freedom Summer Project mobilized more than a thousand northern black and white college students to conduct a voter registration drive. Resistance was fierce, inflamed by the sight of white activist women working alongside black men. By the end of the summer, only twelve hundred new voters had been allowed to register. Southern whites had killed several activists, beaten eighty, arrested more than a thousand, and burned thirty-five black churches. Hidden resistance came from the federal government itself, as the FBI spied on King and other leaders and expanded its activities to "expose, disrupt, misdirect, discredit, or otherwise neutralize" black protest.

Still, the movement persisted. In March 1965, Alabama state troopers used such fierce force to turn back a voting rights march from Selma to the state capitol in Montgomery that

John Lewis, chairman of SNCC, counted the Selma campaign as one of his most meaningful experiences: "In October of that year the Voting Rights bill was passed and we all felt we'd had a part in it."

the incident earned the name "Bloody Sunday" and compelled President Johnson to call up the Alabama National Guard to protect the marchers. Before the Selma campaign was over, whites had killed three demonstrators. Battered and hospitalized on Bloody Sunday, John Lewis, chairman of SNCC (and later a congressman), managed to make the final march to the capitol, which he counted as one of his most meaningful experiences: "In October of that year the Voting Rights bill was passed and we all felt we'd had a part in it."

The Response in Washington

Civil rights leaders would have to wear sneakers, Lyndon Johnson said, if they were going to keep up with him. But both Kennedy and Johnson, reluctant to alienate crucial Democratic voters in the South and their representatives in Congress, acted less on their own initiative than in response to the black freedom struggle, moving only when events gave them little choice.

Kennedy sent federal marshals to Montgomery to protect the Freedom Riders, dispatched troops to enable air force veteran James H. Meredith to enroll in the all-white University of Mississippi in 1962, and called up the Alabama National Guard during the Birmingham demonstrations. But, aware of the political costs of deploying federal force, he told activists pleading for more federal protection that law enforcement was a local matter.

In June 1963, Kennedy finally made good on his promise to seek strong antidiscrimination legislation. Pointing to the injustice suffered by blacks, Kennedy asked white Americans, "Who among us would then be content with the counsels of patience and delay?" Johnson took up Kennedy's commitment with passion, assisted by a number of factors. Scenes of violence against peaceful demonstrators appalled many television viewers across the nation. The resulting public support, the "Johnson treatment," and the president's appeal to memories of the martyred Kennedy all produced the most important civil rights law since Reconstruction.

The Civil Rights Act of 1964 guaranteed access for all Americans to public accommodations, public education, employment, and voting, thus sounding the death knell for the South's system of segregation and discrimination. The law also extended constitutional protections to Indians on reservations. Title VII of the measure,

The Selma March for Voting Rights
In 1963, the Student Nonviolent Coordinating Committee (SNCC) began a campaign for voting rights in Selma, Alabama, where white officials had registered only 335 of the 15,000 African Americans of voting age. As often happened, after younger activists got things started, Martin Luther King Jr. came to Selma in January 1965. He planned a fifty-four-mile march from Selma to Montgomery, the state capital, to insist that blacks be registered to vote. Warned of a serious threat on his life, however, he did not lead the march. In this photo, young African Americans carrying the flag march with nuns, priests, and other supporters. During the march, Juanita Williams wore out her shoes (shown here), which are now displayed at the National Museum of History in Washington, D.C. What do you think motivated the marchers to carry the American flag?
Photo: Steve Shapiro/TimePix/Getty; Shoes: Smithsonian Institution, Washington, D.C.

banning discrimination in employment, not only attacked racial discrimination outside the South but also outlawed job discrimination against women. Because Title VII applied to every aspect of employment, including wages, hiring, and promotion, it represented a giant step toward equal employment opportunity for white women as well as racial minorities.

Responding to black voter registration drives in the South, Johnson soon demanded legislation to remove "every remaining obstacle to the right and the opportunity to vote." In August 1965, he signed the Voting Rights Act, which empowered the federal government to intervene directly to enable African Americans to both register and vote, thereby launching a major transformation in southern politics. Implementation of the act depended on the efforts of blacks themselves, whose voting rates shot up dramatically (Map 28.2, page 1036). In turn, the number of African Americans holding political office in the South increased from a handful in 1964 to more than a thousand by 1972. Gains at the local level translated into tangible benefits as black officials upgraded public facilities, police protection, roads, and other basic services for their constituents.

Johnson had also declared the need "to move beyond opportunity to achievement," to realize "not just equality as a right and theory, but equality as fact and result." To this end, he issued an executive order in 1965 to require employers holding government contracts (affecting about one-third of the labor force) to take affirmative action to ensure equal opportunity. Extended to cover women in 1967, the controversial affirmative action program was called "reverse discrimination" by people who incorrectly thought that it required quotas and the hiring of unqualified candidates. In fact, it required employers to counter the effects of centuries of oppression by acting forcefully to align their labor force with the available pool of qualified candidates. Most corporations came to see affirmative action as a good employment practice.

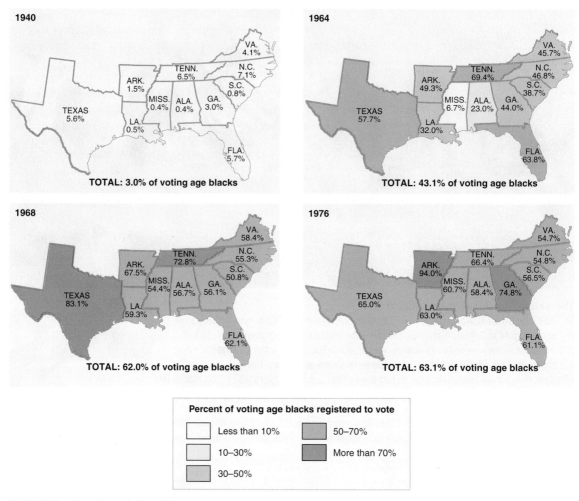

Percent of voting age blacks registered to vote

Less than 10%

10–30%

30–50%

50–70%

More than 70%

MAP 28.2   The Rise of the African American Vote, 1940–1976
Voting rates of southern blacks increased gradually in the 1940s and 1950s but shot up dramatically in the deep South after the Voting Rights Act of 1965 provided for federal agents to enforce African Americans' right to vote.

READING THE MAP: When did the biggest change in African American voter registration occur in the South? Which states had the highest and which had the lowest voter registration rates in 1968? **CONNECTIONS:** What role did African American voters play in the 1960 election? What were the targets of three major voting drives in the 1960s?

FOR MORE HELP ANALYZING THIS MAP, see the map activity for this chapter in the Online Study Guide at bedfordstmartins.com/roark.

In 1968, Johnson pried one final bill from a Congress increasingly resistant to calls for liberal reform. Opposition to civil rights outside the South had already appeared in 1963, when the California legislature passed a law banning discrimination in housing. Realtors led a repeal movement, which overturned the law in a statewide initiative and indicated that a majority of voters were more concerned with keeping the government out of their decisions to do as they pleased with their property than with the rights of mi-

norities to be free of discrimination. And when Martin Luther King Jr. launched a campaign against de facto segregation in Chicago in 1966, demonstrators were met by jeers and stones thrown by thousands of whites. Johnson tried for two years to get a federal open-housing law, succeeding only in 1968 in the wake of King's assassination. The Civil Rights Act of 1968 banned racial discrimination in housing and jury selection and authorized federal intervention when states failed to protect civil rights workers from violence.

Black Power and Urban Rebellions

By 1966, civil rights activism had undergone dramatic changes. Black protest extended to the entire nation, demanding not just legal equality but also economic justice and no longer holding nonviolence as its basic principle. None of these developments was entirely new. Some African Americans had always armed themselves in self-defense, and even in the early 1960s, many activists doubted that demonstrators' passive suffering would change the hearts of racists. Still, the black freedom struggle began to appear more threatening to the white majority.

In part, the new emphases resulted from a combination of heightened activism and unrealized promise. Integration and legal equality did little to improve quickly the material conditions of blacks, and black rage at oppressive conditions erupted in waves of urban uprisings (Map 28.3)

MAP 28.3   Urban Uprisings, 1965–1968

As black residents of the Watts district of Los Angeles watched a white police officer strike a twenty-one-year-old African American, whom he had just pulled over for driving drunk, one of the onlookers shouted, "We've got no rights at all—it's just like Selma." The altercation escalated into a full-scale five-day uprising, during which young blacks set fires, looted, and attacked police and firefighters. When thousands of National Guardsmen and police finally quelled the riot, 34 people were dead, 900 blacks had been injured and 4,000 arrested, hundreds of families had lost their homes, and scores of businesses had been wiped out. Similar violence, though usually not on such a large scale, erupted in dozens of cities across the nation during the next three summers, as this map indicates. The urban violence provoked an intense backlash among whites against black aspirations, yet rioting and looting seemed to many young blacks the only means available to protest the poverty, lack of opportunity, and official insensitivity that they experienced daily. As one government worker commented when parts of Washington, D.C., went up in flames after Martin Luther King's death in 1968, "The black people in this city were really happy for three days. They have been kicked so long, and this is the one high spot in their life."

READING THE MAP: In what regions and cities of the United States were the 1960s uprisings concentrated? What years saw the greatest unrest?

CONNECTIONS: What were some of the causes of racial unrest in America's cities during this period? Whom did whites generally hold responsible for the violence and why?

FOR MORE HELP ANALYZING THIS MAP, see the map activity for this chapter in the Online Study Guide at bedfordstmartins.com/roark.

Uprisings in urban ghettos
● 1965–1966   ■ 1967–1968

from 1965 to 1968. The Watts district of Los Angeles in August 1965, Newark and Detroit in July 1967, and the nation's capital in April 1968 saw the most looting and destruction of property, but violence visited hundreds of cities, usually after an incident between white police and local blacks. The Detroit riots ended in 43 deaths (30 at the hands of law enforcement officers, with most of the victims black), 7,000 arrests, and 1,300 destroyed buildings.

> Stokely Carmichael called integration "a subterfuge for the maintenance of white supremacy" and rejected assimilation because it implied white superiority.

In the North, Malcolm X posed a powerful new challenge to the ethos of nonviolence. In 1952, he went to work for the Nation of Islam, which drew on the long tradition of **black nationalism** and whose adherents called themselves Black Muslims. Calling for black pride and autonomy, separation from the "corrupt [white] society," and self-defense against white violence, Malcolm X attracted a large following, especially in urban ghettos. In 1964, he left the Nation of Islam, began to cultivate a wider constituency, and expressed an openness to working with black integrationists and with whites. At a Harlem rally in February 1965, three Black Muslims shot and killed him.

The ideas espoused by Malcolm X resonated with younger activists. At a June 1966 rally in Greenwood, Mississippi, SNCC chairman Stokely Carmichael gave those principles a new name when he shouted, "We want black power." Those words quickly became the rallying cry in SNCC and CORE, and the black power movement riveted national attention in the late 1960s. A young autoworker in Detroit enthused, "I dig what Stokely Carmichael said. . . . Whites appear to be friendly by passing a few laws, but my basic situation gets worse and worse." Young black activists shared Fannie Lou Hamer's disillusion with white liberals, remembering how Democratic Party officials had sold out the Mississippi Freedom Democratic Party at the 1964 convention.

Carmichael called integration "a subterfuge for the maintenance of white supremacy" and rejected assimilation because it implied white superiority. African Americans were encouraged to develop independent businesses, control their own schools and communities, and form all-black political organizations. The phrase "Black is beautiful" emphasized pride in African American **culture** and connections to dark-skinned people around the world. According to black power advocates, nonviolence brought only more beatings and killings. After police killed an unarmed black teenager in San Francisco in 1966, Huey Newton and Bobby Seale organized the Black Panther Party for Self-Defense and armed its members to defend themselves against police brutality.

The press paid inordinate attention to black radicals, and the civil rights movement encountered a severe white backlash. Although the urban riots of the mid-1960s erupted spontaneously, triggered by specific incidents of police mistreatment, horrified whites blamed the riots on black power militants. By 1966, a full 85 percent of the white population—up from 34 percent two years earlier—thought that African Americans were pressing for too much too quickly. White autoworkers in St. Louis expressed their anxiety about equal opportunity for African Americans by setting a can of shoe polish next to a sign reading, "Paint your face black and you can get anything."

Malcolm X in Egypt

Malcolm X stands in front of the pyramids in Egypt during a trip to Africa and the Middle East in 1964. Partly as a result of meeting Muslims of all colors, as well as other whites who were committed to ending racism, he no longer equated whites with the devil. "The white man is not inherently evil," he concluded, "but America's racist society influences him to act evilly."

John Launois / Black Star / Stockphoto.com.

Afro Rake

In a movement that paralleled the white counterculture in the 1960s and 1970s, young African Americans began to reject middle-class blacks' tendency to fashion their appearance after that of whites. They adopted African styles of dress and let their hair grow into a natural Afro style. In her poem "Homage to My Hair," Lucille Clifton celebrated the expression of authentic black identity: "when I feel her jump up and dance / i hear the music! my God / i'm talking about my nappy hair!" African Americans used combs like this Afro rake, or pick, which makes further political statements with its clenched fist and peace symbol.

Salamandu, courtesy National Afro-American Museum and Cultural Center; Courtesy Antonio's Manufacturing Inc., Cresson, PA.

Agreeing with black power advocates about the need for "a radical reconstruction of society," Martin Luther King Jr. expanded the scope of the struggle. In 1965, he mounted a drive for better jobs, schools, and housing in Chicago, and in 1968 he planned a Poor People's March to Washington to seek greater antipoverty efforts. Yet he clung to nonviolence and integration as the means to this end. In April 1968, the thirty-nine-year-old leader went to Memphis to support striking municipal sanitation workers. There, on April 4, he was murdered by an escaped white convict.

Although black power organizations made most of the headlines, they failed to capture the massive support from African Americans that King and other earlier leaders had attracted. Nor could they alleviate the poverty and racism entrenched in the urban North and West. Black militants were harassed by the FBI and jailed; some encounters left both black militants and police dead. Yet black power's emphasis on racial pride and its critique of American institutions resonated loudly and helped shape the protest activities of other groups.

REVIEW How did the civil rights movement change in the mid-1960s?

A Multitude of Movements

The civil rights movement's undeniable moral claims helped make protest more respectable, while its impact on public opinion and government policy encouraged other groups with grievances. Native Americans, Latinos, college students, women, gay men and lesbians, environmentalists, and others drew on the black freedom struggle for inspiration and models of activism. These groups engaged in direct-action protests, expressed their own cultural nationalism, and challenged dominant institutions and values. Like participants in the black freedom struggle, they met strong resistance, and their accomplishments fell far below their aims. Still, their grievances gained attention in the political arena, and they expanded justice and opportunity for many of their constituents.

Native American Protest

Native American activism took on fresh militancy and goals in the 1960s. The termination and relocation programs of the 1940s and 1950s, contrary to their intent, stirred Indian resistance, a sense of Indian identity across tribal lines, and a determination to preserve traditional culture. In 1961, a more militant generation of Native Americans expressed growing discontent with the government and with the older Indian leadership by forming the National Indian Youth Council (NIYC). The cry "red power" reflected the influence of black radicalism on Native Americans who rejected assimilation and sought the freedom to control their own circumstances.

Native Americans demonstrated and occupied land and public buildings, claiming rights to natural resources and territory they had owned collectively before European settlement.

For example, beginning in 1963, Northwest Indians mounted "fish-ins" to enforce century-old treaty rights. In 1969, Native American militants captured world attention when several dozen seized Alcatraz Island, an abandoned federal prison in San Francisco Bay, claiming their right of "first discovery" of this land. They remained on the island for nineteen months, using the occupation to publicize injustices against Indians, promote pan-Indian cooperation, celebrate traditional cultures, and inspire other activists. One of the organizers, Dr. LaNada Boyer, a Shoshoni-Bannock Indian and the first Native American to attend the University of California, Berkeley, said of Alcatraz, "We were able to raise, not only the consciousness of other American people, but our own people as well, to reestablish our identity as Indian people, as a culture, as political entities."

In Minneapolis in 1968, two Chippewa Indians, Dennis Banks and George Mitchell, founded the American Indian Movement (AIM) to attack problems in cities, where about 300,000 Indians lived. AIM sought to protect Indians from police harassment, secure antipoverty funds, and establish "survival schools" to teach Indian history and values. The new movement's appeal quickly spread beyond urban areas and filled many Indians, especially young people, with a sense of purpose. AIM members did not have "that hangdog reservation look I was used to," Lakota activist and author Mary Crow Dog wrote, and their visit to her South Dakota reservation "loosened a sort of earthquake inside me."

Occupation of the Bureau of Indian Affairs

Native American activists despised the Bureau of Indian Affairs (BIA), an agency of the Department of the Interior that supervised and provided services to recognized tribes. The bureau was a symbol of all the injustices they endured. Although President Nixon nearly tripled the BIA's budget, his administration spent little on off-reservation Indians. Representing these urban Indians, the American Indian Movement (AIM) organized the "Trail of Broken Treaties" caravan to Washington, D.C., in 1972, and on November 2, hundreds of Indians occupied the BIA. Pressured by the Nixon administration and fearful that riot police would attack them, the occupiers agreed to leave after six days based on promises that the government would create a task force to study their grievances, that it would not prosecute them, and that it would finance their travels home. As in the much longer seizure of Alcatraz Island in 1969, the demonstrators failed to win their demands but gained attention for their cause. What is the significance of the flag in this photo?
© Bettmann/Corbis.

AIM leaders helped organize the "Trail of Broken Treaties" caravan to the nation's capital in 1972, when some of the activists took over the Bureau of Indian Affairs to express their outrage at the bureau's paternalism, policies, and bureaucratic interference in Indians' lives. In 1973, a much longer siege occurred on the Lakota Sioux reservation in South Dakota. Conflicts there between AIM militants and older tribal leaders led AIM to take over for seventy-two days the village of Wounded Knee, where U.S. troops had massacred more than one hundred Sioux Indians in 1890.

Although these dramatic occupations failed to achieve their specific goals, Indians won the end of relocation and termination policies; greater tribal sovereignty and control over community services; enhanced health, education, and other services; and protection of Indian religious practices. A number of laws and court decisions restored rights to ancestral lands or compensated tribes for land seized in violation of treaties. Native Americans recovered a measure of respect and pride. In a special message on the "Forgotten American" in 1968, President Johnson recognized their assertion of "the right of the First Americans to remain Indians while exercising their rights as Americans."

Latino Struggles for Justice

The fastest-growing minority group in the 1960s was Latinos, or Hispanic Americans, an extraordinarily varied population encompassing people of Mexican, Puerto Rican, Caribbean, and other Latin American origins. (The term *Latino* stresses their common bonds as a minority group in the United States. The older, less political term *Hispanic* also includes those with origins in Spain.) People of Puerto Rican and Caribbean descent flocked to East Coast cities, but more than half of the nation's Latino population—including some six million Mexican Americans—lived in California, Texas, Arizona, New Mexico, and Colorado. In addition, thousands illegally crossed the two-thousand-mile border between Mexico and the United States in search of economic opportunity.

Political organization of Mexican Americans dated back to the League of United Latin-American Citizens (LULAC) in 1929, which aided newer immigrants and fought segregation and discrimination through litigation (see chapter 26). In the 1960s, however, young Mexican

Americans, like African Americans and Native Americans, increasingly rejected traditional politics in favor of direct action. One symbol of this generational challenge was young activists' adoption of the term *Chicano* (from *mejicano*, the Spanish word for "Mexican").

Chicano protest drew national attention to California, where Cesar Chavez and Dolores Huerta organized a movement to improve the wretched conditions of migrant agricultural workers. As a child moving from farm to farm with his family, living in soggy tents, and exploited by labor contractors, Chavez changed schools frequently and encountered indifference and discrimination from teachers. One, he recalled, "hung a sign on me that said, 'I am a clown, I speak Spanish.'" After serving in World War II, Chavez began to organize voter registration drives among Mexican Americans. He also began to study labor history and the ideas of Catholic reformers and India's independence leader Mahatma Gandhi.

In contrast to Chavez, Dolores Huerta grew up in an integrated urban neighborhood where she avoided the farmworkers' grinding poverty but witnessed subtle forms of discrimination. Once, a high school teacher challenged her authorship of an essay because it was so well written. After completing community college and starting a family, she met Chavez. Believing that a labor union was the key to progress, they founded the United Farm Workers (UFW) in 1962. Although Chavez headed the union until his death in 1993, Huerta was indispensable to its vitality. One UFW leader described her as "a thirty-five-year-old firebrand in 1965 . . . commanding crusty macho *campesinos* twenty years her senior."

To gain leverage for striking workers, the UFW capitalized on consumer consciousness and mounted a nationwide boycott of California grapes. An estimated seventeen million Americans observed the boycott and helped win a wage increase for the workers in 1970. Although the UFW struggled and lost membership during the 1970s, it helped politicize Mexican Americans and improved farmworkers' lives.

Other Chicanos mobilized to force the Equal Employment Opportunity Commission (EEOC), the enforcement agency of Title VII of the Civil Rights Act of 1964, to act against job discrimination against Mexican Americans. LULAC, the American GI Forum (see chapter 26), and other groups picketed government offices. President Johnson

Cesar Chavez and Dolores Huerta
Chavez and Huerta confer in Delano, California, in early 1968 during the United Farm Workers' five-year struggle with grape growers for better wages and working conditions and union recognition. The symbols surrounding them reflect the UFW's origins and connections. Chavez was a devout Catholic, as were many of the farmworkers, and his commitment to reform was nourished by liberal Catholics. Reading about Mahatma Gandhi's leadership in the movement for India's independence also had a profound impact on him. He adopted Gandhi's ideas about civil disobedience and nonviolence, and, like Gandhi, he undertook fasting to demonstrate his determination to obtain social justice. People from across the country supported the UFW's strike and grape boycott, including Senator Robert Kennedy, before his assassination in June 1968. Huerta left her teaching job to organize workers, saying, "I thought I could do more by organizing farm workers than by trying to teach their hungry children." She raised eleven children of her own while leading the UFW.
Arthur Schatz/TimePix/Getty Images.

responded in 1967 by appointing Vicente T. Ximenes as the first Mexican American to serve on the commission and by creating a special committee on Mexican American affairs.

Claiming "brown power," Chicanos organized to end discrimination in education, gain political power, and combat police brutality. In 1968, high school students in southwestern cities launched a wave of strikes called "Blow Outs" to protest racism in the public schools. In Denver, Rodolfo "Corky" Gonzales set up "freedom schools" where Chicano children studied the Spanish language and Mexican American history. The nationalist strains of Chicano protest were evident in La Raza Unida (the United Race), a political party founded in 1970 by José Angel Gutierrez in Texas and based on cultural pride and brotherhood. Along with blacks and Native Americans, Chicanos continued to be disproportionately represented among the poor, but they gradually won more political offices, more effective enforcement of antidiscrimination legislation, and greater respect for their culture.

Student Rebellion, the New Left, and the Counterculture

Although materially and legally more secure than their African American, Indian, and Latino counterparts, white youths also expressed dissent, supporting the black freedom struggle and launching student protests, the antiwar movement, and the new feminist and environmental movements. Challenging establishment institutions and traditional values, young activists helped change higher education, the family, the national government, and other key institutions. Young Americans were part of a larger, international phenomenon, as student movements arose in Mexico, Germany, Turkey, Czechoslovakia, Japan, and other nations around the globe. (See chapter 29, "Beyond America's Borders," page 1084.)

The central organization of white student protest was Students for a Democratic Society (SDS), formed in 1960 from an older **socialist**-oriented organization. In 1962, the organizers wrote in their statement of purpose, "We are people of this generation, bred in at least modest comfort, housed now in universities, looking uncomfortably at the world we inherit." The idealistic students criticized the complacency of their elders, the remoteness of decision makers, and the powerlessness and alienation generated by a bureaucratic society. Their goal of "participatory democracy" echoed the antihierarchical and grassroots leadership style of Ella Baker and SNCC. SDS aimed to mobilize a "New Left" around the goals of civil rights, peace, and universal economic security. Other forms of student activism soon followed.

The first large-scale white student protest arose at the University of California, Berkeley, in 1964, when university officials banned students from setting up tables to recruit support for various causes. Led by whites back from civil rights work in the South, the students claimed the right to freedom of expression and political action. The "free speech" movement occupied the administration building, and more than seven hundred students were arrested before the California Board of Regents overturned the new restrictions.

Hundreds of student rallies and building occupations followed on campuses across the country, especially after 1965, when opposition to the Vietnam War mounted and students protested against universities' links to the military (see chapter 29). Students also changed the collegiate environment. Women at the University of Chicago, for example, charged in 1969 that all universities "discriminate against women, impede their full intellectual development, deny them places on the faculty, exploit talented women and mistreat women students." At Howard University, African American students called for a "Black Awareness Research Institute" and demanded that academic departments "place more emphasis on how these disciplines may be used to effect the liberation of black people." Across the country, students won curricular reforms such as black studies and women's studies programs, more financial aid for minority and poor students, independence from paternalistic rules, and a larger voice in campus decision making. (See "Documenting the American Promise," page 1044.)

Student rebels came from the "baby boom" generation that swelled college enrollments in the 1960s and gave young people a sense of power and generational solidarity. Most white student activists came from middle-class families; with no immediate need to support themselves, they had the luxury of attacking the very system that made their rebellion possible. Such conduct bewildered and angered older Americans, even more so when it blended into a cultural revolution against nearly every conventional standard of behavior.

Drawing on the ideas of the Beats of the 1950s, the counterculture often overlapped the New Left and student movements. Cultural radicals, or "hippies," as they were called, rejected mainstream values such as the work ethic, materialism, rationality, order, and sexual control. Seeking personal rather than political change, they advocated "Do your own thing" and drew attention with their long hair and wildly colorful clothing. They sought to discard inhibitions and elevate their senses with illegal drugs such as marijuana and LSD. The Haight-Ashbury district of San Francisco harbored the most famous hippie community, but thousands of radicals established communes in cities or on farms, where they renounced private property and shared everything, often including sexual partners.

> SDS organizers wrote in their statement of purpose, "We are people of this generation, bred in at least modest comfort, housed now in universities, looking uncomfortably at the world we inherit."

Rock and folk music defined both the counterculture and the political left. English groups such as the Beatles and the Rolling Stones and homegrown performers such as Bob Dylan, Janis Joplin, Jefferson Airplane, and Jerry Garcia's Grateful Dead took American youth by storm. Music during the 1960s often carried insurgent political and social messages that reflected radical youth culture. Despairing of the violence around the world and the threat of nuclear annihilation, "Eve of Destruction," a top hit of 1965, reminded young men, "You're old enough to kill but not for votin'." The Woodstock Music

Festival, which featured the greatest rock and folk musicians of the era and drew 400,000 young people to a farm in Bethel, New York, in 1969, epitomized the centrality of music to the youth rebellion.

The hippies faded away in the 1970s, but many elements of the counterculture—rock music, jeans, and long hair, as well as new social attitudes—filtered into the mainstream. More tolerant approaches to sexual behaviors spawned what came to be called the "sexual revolution," with help from the birth control pill, which

Student Protest

The waves of student protest that rolled across college campuses in the 1960s were all the more surprising because observers had found the "silent generation" of the 1950s so complacent and conformist. Although the majority of college students did not participate in the rebellions, a sizable number of students at all kinds of colleges and universities challenged traditional authority, criticized established institutions, and demanded a voice for themselves in the decisions that affected their lives.

DOCUMENT 1
Edward Schwartz on Student Power, October 1967

Student activist Edward Schwartz wrote this statement to represent the views of the National Student Association, the largest college student organization in the 1960s. Ironically, this association, which contributed to the student upheaval of the sixties, had been founded a decade earlier, with secret funding from the CIA, as a liberal group to counter communism.

The educational premise behind demands for student power reflects the notion that people learn through living, through the process of integrating their thoughts with their actions, through testing their values against those of a community, through a capacity to act. College presidents who invoke legal authority to prove educational theory assume that growth is the ability to accept what the past has created. Student power is a medium through which people integrate their own experience with a slice of the past which seems appro-

priate, with their efforts to intensify the relationships between the community within the university.

Let this principle apply—he who must obey the rule should make it.

Students should make the rules governing dormitory hours, boy-girl visitation, student unions, student fees, clubs, newspapers, and the like. Faculty and administrators should advise—attempt to persuade, even. Yet the student should bear the burden of choice.

Students and faculty should co-decide curricular policy.

Students, faculty, and administration should co-decide admissions policy, overall college policy affecting the community, even areas like university investment. . . . Student power should not be argued on legal grounds. It is not a legal principle. It is an educational principle.

Student power is threatening to those who wield power now, but this is understandable. A student should threaten his administrators outside of class, just as bright students threaten professors inside of class. Student power ultimately challenges everyone in the university—the students who must decide; the faculty and administrators who must rethink their own view of community relations in order to persuade.

People who say that student power means anarchy imply really that students are rabble who have no ability to form community and to adhere to decisions made by community. Student power is not the negation of rules—it is the creation of a new process for the enactment of rules. Student power is not the elimination of authority, it is the

development of a democratic standard of authority.

SOURCE: Excerpt from "He Who Must Obey the Rule Should Make It," from *The University Crisis Reader*, vol. 1, *The Liberal University under Attack* by Immanuel Wallerstein and Paul Starr, eds., pp. 482–84. Copyright © 1971 by Random House, Inc. Reprinted with permission.

DOCUMENT 2
SDS Explanation of the Columbia Strike, September 1968

One of the longest and most violent student protests occurred in New York City at Columbia University in April and May 1968, when white and black students occupied five buildings for a week. A subsequent student strike closed the university for the rest of the academic year. One of the key issues arose from the university's practice of expanding by buying up land in neighboring Harlem and evicting black tenants. The members of the Columbia chapter of Students for a Democratic Society (SDS), one of various factions among the protesters, rationalized their actions in the following statement.

When we seized five buildings at Columbia University, we engaged the force of wealth, privilege, property—and the force of state violence that always accompanies them—with little more than our own ideals, our fears, and a vague sense of outrage at the injustices of our society. Martin Luther King had just been shot, his name demeaned by Columbia officials who refused to grant a decent wage to Puerto Rican workers, and who had recently grabbed part of Harlem for a student gym. . . .

For years Columbia Trustees had evicted tenants from their homes, taken land through city deals, and fired workers for trying to form a union. For years they had trained officers for Vietnam who, as ROTC literature indicates, killed Vietnamese peasants in their own country. In secret work for the IDA [Institute for Defense Analysis] and the CIA, in chemical-biological war research for the Department of War, the Trustees implicated their own University in genocide. They had consistently . . . lied to their own constituents and published CIA books under the guise of independent scholarship. . . . We lived in an institution that channeled us, marked us, ranked us, failed us, used us, and treated masses of humanity with class contempt. . . .

Columbia, standing at the top of a hill, looked down on Harlem. . . . People who survived in Harlem had been evicted by the Trustees from Morningside or still paid rent to Columbia. . . . We walked to our classrooms across land that had been privatized; we studied in buildings that had once been homes in a city that is underhoused; and we listened to the apologies for Cold War and capital in our classes.

Columbia professors often claim that the University is a neutral institution. . . . Many professors pursue all sides of a question as an end in itself. They find a certain refuge in the difficulty of defining good and evil. The result is a clogging of their moral sense, their capacity for collective justice. . . . What liberals call neutrality is really one of the ways by which the faculty protects its special status in society.

A University could not, even if it wanted, choose to be really value-free. It can choose good values; it can choose bad values; or it can remain ignorant of the values on which it acts. . . . A social institution should at least articulate its own perspec-

tive, so that its own values may be consciously applied or modified. It is a typical fallacy of American teaching, that to remain silent on crucial issues is to be objective with your own constituents. Actually a "neutral" institution is far more manipulative than a University committed to avowed goals and tasks.

SOURCE: Excerpt from "The Columbia Statement," Columbia SDS, from *The University Crisis Reader*, vol. 1, *The Liberal University under Attack* by Immanuel Wallerstein and Paul Starr, eds., pp. 23–47. Copyright © 1971 by Random House, Inc. Reprinted with permission.

DOCUMENT 3
Counterthrust on Student Power, Spring 1967

While the majority of students simply avoided involvement in campus rebellions, some students actively criticized the protesters. The largest conservative student organization was Young Americans for Freedom, which more than doubled in size during the 1960s. The following selection, from a leaflet titled "Student Power Is a Farce," reflected the views of Counterthrust, a conservative group at Wayne State University in Michigan.

Our University is being treated to the insanity of Left-Wing students demanding the run of the University. . . . Wayne students are told by the Left that "student power" merely means more democracy on campus. This is an outright lie! Student power is a Left-Wing catchword symbolizing campus militancy and radicalism. In actuality, the Left-Wing, spearheaded by the SDS [Students for a Democratic Society] want to radically alter the university community. . . .

The Leftists charge a sinister plot by private enterprise to train students for jobs at taxpayers' expense. Evidently it never occurred to the

SDS that private enterprise is also the biggest single taxpayer for schools. But, of course, that would require a little thought on the part of the SDS which they have already demonstrated they are incapable of. . . .

The byword of student power-union advocates is Radicalism. . . . Fraternities and student Governments will have no place in student power-unions since both are considered allies of the status quo and thus useless. . . . As responsible Wayne students, we cannot allow our University to be used by Leftists for their narrow purposes. We were invited to this campus by the Michigan Taxpayer to receive an education. Let us honor that invitation.

SOURCE: "Student Power Is a Farce," Counterthrust, from *The University Crisis Reader*, vol. 1, *The Liberal University under Attack* by Immanuel Wallerstein and Paul Starr, eds., pp. 487–88. Copyright © 1971 by Random House, Inc. Reprinted with permission.

QUESTIONS FOR ANALYSIS AND DEBATE

1. How do the statements by Edward Schwartz and the Columbia SDS chapter differ in the issues they address?
2. What did Counterthrust see as the biggest problem with student protesters?
3. Do you agree or disagree with the Columbia SDS chapter's assertion that it is impossible for a university to be neutral or value-free? Why or why not?
4. To what extent do your own campus policies and practices suggest that student protest during the 1960s and 1970s made a difference? What changes that the protesters demanded are not evident at your college or university? Should they be?

The Pill

"Modern woman is at last free as man is free, to dispose of her own body," declared Clare Boothe Luce, playwright and former congresswoman, describing the impact of the birth control pill. Barrier methods of contraception, such as condoms and diaphragms, had been available for decades, but they required action at the time of sexual relations and were subject to failure. By contrast, the Pill separated contraception from the act of sexual intercourse, and it was nearly 100 percent effective in preventing pregnancy. "Gone are the days when women live in terror of the sexual embrace because it means still another pregnancy, still another year of sickness, another child to care for," one woman exulted. The Pill gave women freedom and control, the opportunity to enjoy sex just as men did.

The work of countless individuals contributed to the Pill, but two reform-minded women and three male scientists played especially prominent roles. Margaret Sanger had fought for women's control over reproduction since the 1910s. By the 1940s, Sanger, the founder of Planned Parenthood, had made development of an oral contraceptive her main priority, and she turned to her friend and longtime supporter of the birth control movement Katharine Dexter McCormick for help. McCormick, the second woman to graduate from the Massachusetts Institute of Technology (MIT), had supported women's rights since the suffrage movement, and her husband's illness, which she feared could be passed on to any children they might have, gave her a personal interest in birth control. When her husband died, she inherited an enormous fortune, and in 1952 Sanger persuaded her to bankroll research on the Pill, to which she gave $2 million over the years.

McCormick's fortune supported biologist Gregory Goodwin Pincus, who at Sanger's urging had begun work on an oral contraceptive in 1951, and his collaborators, biologist Min-Chueh Chang and physician John Rock, the latter of whom conducted trials on progesterone with his patients. After discovering that progesterone could suppress ovulation, the researchers relied on the critical work of chemists to synthesize the hormone. In 1956, Pincus began a large-scale clinical trial of a pill called Enovid on women in Puerto Rico, and in 1960 the Food and Drug Administration (FDA) approved Enovid. Women rushed to their doctors for prescriptions. Within three years, more than two million women were using it, and the number continued to increase.

In 1962, reports of fatal blood clots in Enovid users raised concerns about the safety of the Pill. These concerns were confirmed in 1969 by an FDA report. Publication of feminist journalist Barbara Seaman's *The Doctors' Case against the Pill* in 1969 and congressional hearings in 1970 increased opposition to the Pill. Unaware of Sanger's role and motivations in the invention of the Pill, some feminists objected to "unsafe contraceptives foisted on uninformed women for the profit of the drug and medical industries and for the convenience of men." Contro-

became available in the 1960s. (See "The Promise of Technology" above.) Self-fulfillment became a dominant concern of many Americans, and questioning of authority became more widespread.

Gay Men and Lesbians Organize

More permissive sexual norms did not stretch easily to include tolerance of homosexuality. Gay men and lesbians avoided the discrimination and segregation suffered by racial and ethnic minorities only by concealing their essential identities. Those who couldn't or wouldn't found themselves fired from jobs, arrested for their sexual activities, deprived of their children, denied admission to the United States as immigrants, or accused of being "perverted." While most kept their sexuality hidden, in the 1950s, some gays and lesbians began to organize.

Some of the first gay associations were founded in response to the government's aggressive efforts to keep homosexuals out of the civil service. Several gay men filed lawsuits against the government, and in October 1965, a picket line formed outside the White House with signs calling discrimination against homosexuals "as immoral as discrimination against Negroes and Jews." Not until ten years later, however, did the versy about the Pill's safety spurred consumer health activism among women and encouraged them to question medical experts.

Manufacturers reduced dramatically the amounts of estrogen and progesterone in oral contraceptives, thereby decreasing the incidence of nausea, headache, stomach pain, and other side effects, but the Pill continued to put women at somewhat greater risk for stroke, cancer, and other ailments. Moreover, the Pill required visits to the doctor, was not covered by most group health insurance plans, and did not protect against sexually transmitted diseases.

Nonetheless, for American women the Pill remained the leading form of contraception, used by more than eleven million women in 2002. The Pill itself did not cause the mass movement of women into the workplace, the declining birthrate, or the relaxation of traditional sexual norms, but it was one of the factors contributing to these sweeping changes in the second half of the twentieth century. Its invention marked a watershed in the history of birth control, which Margaret Sanger believed was "for women the key to liberty."

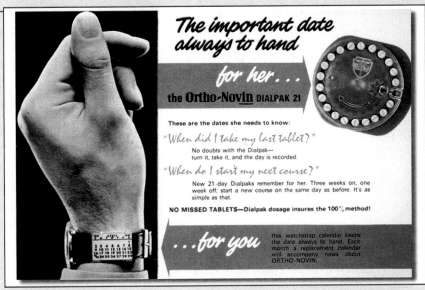

Advertising the Pill

The pharmaceutical company G. D. Searle first brought the Pill to market, but two years later, Johnson & Johnson put out its own version, Ortho-Novin brand through its subsidiary Ortho Pharmaceutical. Early prescriptions came simply as a bottle of pills, but in 1963 Ortho Pharmaceutical introduced the Dialpak, to help women remember to take the daily tablet. At that time, federal law prohibited direct advertising of prescription drugs to consumers, so the companies competing for the lucrative contraceptive business advertised to doctors. This 1965 ad shows doctors how the Ortho-Novin Dialpak will tell "her" when she has taken her last pill and when to take the next one. And, typical of the way drugs are marketed in the United States, it promises "for you," the doctor, a gift—in this case, a calendar that can be attached to a watchband.

National Museum of American History, Smithsonian Institution, Behring Center.

READING THE IMAGE: What are two clues to determining the audience to which this ad is directed? What assumptions does it make about women and about physicians?
CONNECTIONS: How important was control of reproduction to the women's movement that arose in the mid-1960s? How might the Pill have been connected to changes in sexual practices and attitudes? The Pill worked by interfering with women's fertility rather than men's. How was this both an advantage and a disadvantage to women?

FOR MORE HELP ANALYZING THIS IMAGE, see the visual activity for this chapter in the Online Study Guide at bedfordstmartins.com/roark.

Civil Service Commission formally announce the end of its antigay policy.

The spark that ignited a larger movement was struck in 1969 when police raided a gay bar, the Stonewall Inn, in New York City's Greenwich Village, and gay men and lesbians fought back. "Suddenly, they were not submissive anymore," a police officer remarked. Energized by the defiance shown at the Stonewall riots, gay men and lesbians founded a host of new groups, often demonstrating the influence of other 1960s movements by choosing names such as Gay Liberation Front and slogans such as "Gay is good" and by showing up on college campuses. A more

reformist organization, the National Gay and Lesbian Task Force, was founded in 1973 to ensure that sustained, national attention was given to gay issues.

The gay rights movement struggled much longer and harder to win recognition than did other social movements. In 1972, a gay man and a lesbian addressed the Democratic National Convention for the first time, but they took the podium at 2 a.m. Gay rights did not get into the party's platform until 1980. Also in 1972, Ann Arbor, Michigan, passed the first antidiscrimination ordinance, and two years later, Elaine Noble's election to the Massachusetts legislature marked the first time an openly gay candidate won state office. In 1973, gay activists persuaded the American Psychiatric Association to remove its designation of homosexuality as a mental disease. It would take decades for these initial gains to improve conditions for most homosexuals,

Gay Rights Protests

Protests attacking discrimination against homosexuals began in the 1950s with lawsuits to stop the federal government from routinely dismissing gay men and lesbians from civil service jobs. In the 1960s, inspired by the black freedom struggle, gay rights groups began to demonstrate at the White House and at government offices. This photo, published on the cover of the *Ladder*, a magazine launched by the lesbian rights group Daughters of Bilitis in October 1956, shows Lilli Vincenz leading a group of twenty-three protesters in front of the Civil Service Commission. The protesters agreed to look "conservative and conventional" in their dress and appearance. Even so, one *Washington Post* reporter remembered, "I thought they must be totally reckless or weird." Although the gay rights movement won significant support in the courts, it was not until 1975 that the Civil Service Commission completely abandoned its discriminatory regulations.

Courtesy of Department of Special Collections, Stanford University Libraries.

THE LADDER Adults Only Oct. 1965
a LESBIAN review

HOMOPHILE GROUPS PICKET IN NATION'S CAPITAL

but by the mid-1970s, gay men and lesbians had established a movement through which they could claim equal rights and express pride in their sexual identities.

A New Movement to Save the Environment

Although environmentalism differed from other social movements in that it was organized around a cause rather than the particular identity of its members, it exhibited the influence of other movements and like them contributed to a redefinition of liberalism in the 1960s and beyond. One aspect of the new environmental movement resembled the conservation movement born in the **Progressive** Era to preserve portions of nature for recreational and aesthetic purposes and conserve it for future use (see chapter 21). Especially in the West, the post–World War II explosion of economic growth and mushrooming population, with the resulting demands for electricity and water, made such efforts seem even more critical. Environmental groups began mobilizing in the 1950s to stop the construction of dams that would disrupt national parks and wilderness areas.

The new environmentalists, however, went beyond conservationism to attack the ravaging effects of industrial development on human life and health. The polluted air and water and the spread of deadly chemicals attending economic growth threatened wildlife, plants, and the delicate ecological balance that sustained human life. To the leaders of a new organization, Friends of the Earth, unlimited economic growth was "no longer healthy, but a cancer."

Biologist Rachel Carson drew national attention to environmental concerns in 1962 with her best seller *Silent Spring*, which described the harmful effects of toxic chemicals such as the pesticide DDT. The Sierra Club and other older conservation organizations expanded their agendas, and a host of new groups arose. Millions of Americans expressed environmental concerns on the first observation of Earth Day in April 1970. Students distributed fliers encouraging recycling, Girl Scouts removed garbage from the Potomac River, African Americans in St. Louis demonstrated the effects of poisons in lead paint, and people across the country planted trees.

Responding to these concerns, the federal government staked out a broad role in environmental regulation. Lyndon Johnson sent the first presidential message on the environment to Congress and signed laws controlling air and water pollution and preserving the American landscape. Richard Nixon's 1970 State of the Union message called "clean air, clean water, open spaces . . . the birthright of every American," and that year he created the Environmental Protection Agency (EPA) to enforce clean air and water policies and regulate pesticides. Congress also passed the Occupational Safety and Health Act (OSHA), protecting workers against workplace accidents and disease, and the Clean Air Act of 1970, setting national standards for air quality and restricting factory and automobile emissions of carbon dioxide and other pollutants. Even with lenient enforcement and substantial population and economic growth, air pollutants in major cities had decreased by one-third by 1990.

Nevertheless, the dominant value of economic growth often trumped environmental concerns, especially by the late 1970s, when antigovernment sentiment rose and the economy slumped. Corporations seeking to expand, apply new technologies, or exploit natural resources resisted restrictions. "If you're hungry and out of work, eat an environmentalist," read a union bumper sticker reflecting fears that regulations threatened jobs. Many Americans who wanted to protect the environment also valued economic expansion, personal acquisition, and convenience. Despite these conflicts, the environmental movement achieved cleaner air and water, a reduction in toxic wastes, and some preservation of endangered species and wilderness. And Americans now recognized that human beings had developed the power to destroy life on earth.

> **REVIEW** How did the black freedom struggle influence other reform movements of the 1960s and 1970s?

The New Wave of Feminism

On August 26, 1970, fifty years after women won the right to vote, tens of thousands of women across the country took to the streets—radical women in jeans and conservatively dressed suburbanites, peace activists and politicians, and a sprinkling of women of color. They carried signs reading "Sisterhood Is Powerful" and "Don't Cook Dinner—Starve a Rat Today." Some of

Earth Day in the Nation's Capital
Building on the success of the teach-ins about the Vietnam War, Democratic senator Gaylord Nelson of Wisconsin came up with the idea of Earth Day "to shake up the political establishment and force this issue [environmentalism] onto the national agenda." As a result, on April 22, 1970, some twenty million people participated in grassroots demonstrations all over the country. This banner displayed on the Mall in Washington, D.C., focused on clean air. Other activists dramatized oil spills, toxic dumps, pesticides, polluted rivers and lakes, the loss of wilderness, and the extinction of wildlife.
Dennis Brack / Black Star / Stockphoto.com.

the banners opposed the war in Vietnam, others demanded racial justice, but women's own liberation stood at the forefront.

Becoming visible by the late 1960s, the women's movement reached its high tide in the 1970s and persisted in various forms into the twenty-first century. By that time, despite a powerful countermovement, women had experienced tremendous transformations in their legal status, public opportunities, and personal and sexual relationships, and popular expectations about appropriate gender roles had shifted dramatically.

> Richard Nixon's 1970 State of the Union message called "clean air, clean water, open spaces . . . the birthright of every American."

A Multifaceted Movement Emerges

Beginning in the 1940s, large demographic changes laid the preconditions for a resurgence of feminism. As ever larger numbers of women took jobs, the importance of their paid work to the economy and to their families belied the idea of women as dependent, domestic beings and awakened many women in the labor force, especially labor union women, to the inferior conditions of their employment. The democratization of higher education brought more women to college campuses, where their aspirations exceeded the confines of domesticity and of routine, subordinate jobs.

Policy initiatives in the early 1960s reflected both these larger transformations and the efforts of small bands of women's rights activists. In 1961, Assistant Secretary of Labor Esther Peterson persuaded President Kennedy to create the President's Commission on the Status of Women (PCSW). Chaired by Eleanor Roosevelt, the com-

mission reported its findings in October 1963, eight months after Betty Friedan attacked sex discrimination in *The Feminine Mystique* (see chapter 27). Though not challenging women's domestic roles, the commission reported widespread discrimination against women and recommended remedies. Counterparts of the PCSW sprang up in every state, filled with women eager for action.

The PCSW highlighted a practice that women's organizations and labor unions had sought to eliminate for two decades: the age-old custom of paying women less than men for the same work. Their efforts were rewarded when Kennedy signed the Equal Pay Act in June 1963,

Founding the National Women's Political Caucus

In 1971, feminists created the National Women's Political Caucus, an organization with the goal of electing women to office and increasing their voice in political party affairs. The founders are shown here: from left to right, *Ms.* editor Gloria Steinem, Congresswoman Bella Abzug, Congresswoman Shirley Chisholm, and *The Feminine Mystique* author Betty Friedan. The caucus filled its bipartisan governing board with diverse women, representing Native Americans, Chicanas, union leaders, welfare rights activists, and religious women. Dedicated to combating sexism, racism, institutional violence, and poverty, this political arm of the women's movement supported feminist candidates of both parties and both sexes.

AP Images.

making wage disparities based on gender illegal. Within a few years, women began to win pay increases and back pay worth millions of dollars, although four decades later, women still had not closed the income gap.

Like other movements, the rise of feminism owed much to the black freedom struggle, which created a moral climate sensitive to injustice and provided precedents and strategies that feminists followed. Women gained the ban against sex discrimination in Title VII of the Civil Rights Act of 1964 and the extension of affirmative action to women by piggybacking onto civil rights measures. They soon grew impatient when the government failed to take these new policies seriously and moved slowly to enforce them. The head of Title VII's enforcement agency called the sex discrimination provision "a fluke . . . conceived out of wedlock" and told reporters that men were entitled to have female secretaries. Outraged and deciding they needed a "civil rights organization for women," Betty Friedan, civil rights activist Pauli Murray, several union women, and others founded the National Organization for Women (NOW) in 1966.

Simultaneously, a more radical feminism grew among civil rights and New Left activists. In 1965, two white women, Mary King and Casey Hayden, wrote that their work in SNCC had taught them "to think radically about the personal worth and abilities of people whose role in society had gone unchallenged before" and that "a lot of women in the movement have begun trying to apply those lessons to their own relations with men." Although most black women did not consider themselves to be marginalized in the movement, and in fact often led local groups, King and Hayden presented their ideas to white male radicals in the New Left, who responded with indifference or ridicule. By contrast, their message invigorated other white women who shared their frustration with subordinate roles. Many women walked out of New Left organizations, and by 1967 they had created an independent women's liberation movement composed of small groups across the nation.

Women's liberation began to gain public attention, especially when dozens of women picketed the Miss America beauty pageant in 1968, protesting against being forced "to compete for male approval [and] enslaved by ludicrous 'beauty' standards." They crowned a sheep Miss America and invited women to throw away their "bras, girdles, curlers, false eyelashes, wigs," and other "objects of female torture." Women began

to speak publicly about personal experiences that had always been shrouded in secrecy, such as rape and abortion. Throughout the country, women joined consciousness-raising groups, where they discovered that what they had considered "personal" problems reflected an entrenched system of discrimination against and devaluation of women.

Radical feminists, who called their movement "women's liberation," differed from feminists in NOW and other more mainstream groups in several ways. NOW focused on equal treatment for women in the public sphere; women's liberation emphasized ending women's subordination in the family and in other personal relationships. Groups such as NOW wanted to integrate women into existing institutions; radical groups insisted that women's liberation required a total transformation of economic, political, and social institutions. Differences between these two strands of feminism blurred in the 1970s, as NOW and other mainstream groups embraced many of the issues raised by radicals.

> Dozens of women picketed the Miss America beauty pageant in 1968, protesting against being forced "to compete for male approval [and] enslaved by ludicrous 'beauty' standards."

Although NOW elected a black president, Aileen Hernandez, in 1970, the new feminism's leadership and constituency were predominantly white and middle-class. Women of color criticized white women's organizations for their frequent indifference to the disproportionate poverty experienced by minority women and their vulnerability to additional layers of discrimination based on race or ethnicity. One black woman said, "My mother took care of rich white kids. I didn't think they were oppressed." To black women, much more frequently compelled to work in the lowest-paying jobs for their families' survival, employment did not necessarily look like liberation. Cellestine Ware, an African American writer and a founder of New York Radical Feminists, insisted that black and white women could work together "only if the movement changes its priorities to work on issues that affect the lives of minority group women."

In addition to struggling with vast differences among women, feminism also contended with the refusal of the mass media to take women's grievances seriously. The press neglected or misreported on other movements, but it reserved its ridicule for feminism. When the Associated Press distributed a story on the marches and demonstrations of August 1970, for example, it used the headline IT'S WOMEN'S DAY TODAY—WATCH IT, BUB! The *Chicago Defender* titled its story on a local event "No Bra Burning in Rally," and when the House of Representatives passed an equal rights amendment to the U.S. Constitution in 1970, the *New York Times* criticized it in an editorial titled "The Henpecked House." After Gloria Steinem founded *Ms: The New Magazine for Women* in 1972, feminists had their own mass-circulation periodical controlled by women. *Ms.* ignored the recipes and fashion tips of typical women's magazines and featured literature by women writers and articles on a broad range of feminist issues.

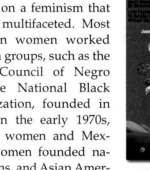

Ms. reported on a feminism that was exceedingly multifaceted. Most African American women worked through their own groups, such as the older National Council of Negro Women and the National Black Feminist Organization, founded in 1973. Similarly, in the early 1970s, American Indian women and Mexican American women founded national organizations, and Asian American women formed local movements. Labor union women had been fighting for workplace gender justice since the 1940s, and blue-collar women organized the National Coalition of Labor Union Women in 1974. Lesbians established collectives throughout the country, as well as their own caucuses in organizations such as NOW. Welfare mothers formed the National Welfare Rights Organization, and religious women mobilized in the National Council of Churches of Christ to "place the question of women's liberation in the main stream of the church's concern." Women founded a host of other groups that focused on single issues such as health, abortion rights, education, and violence against women. In addition, U.S. feminists interacted with women abroad, joining a movement that crossed national boundaries. (See "Beyond America's Borders," page 1054.)

Common threads underlay the great diversity of organizations, issues, and activities. Above all, feminism represented the belief that women were barred from, unequally treated in, or poorly served by the male-dominated public arena, encompassing politics, medicine, law, education, and religion. Many feminists also sought equality in the private sphere, challenging traditional norms that identified women primarily as wives and mothers or sex objects, subservient to men.

Feminist Gains Spark a Countermovement

Although more an effect than a cause of women's rising employment, feminism lifted female aspirations and helped lower barriers to posts monopolized by men. Women made some inroads into skilled crafts and management positions. Between 1970 and 2000, their share of law degrees shot up from 5 percent to nearly 50 percent, and their proportion of medical degrees from less than 10 percent to more than 35 percent. Women gained political offices very slowly; yet by 2006, they constituted about 15 percent of Congress and more than 20 percent of all state executives and legislators.

Feminists also encountered frustrations along with achievements. Despite some inroads into male-dominated occupations, most women still worked in low-paying, traditionally female jobs. Employed women continued to bear primary responsibility for their homes and families, thereby working a "double day." Congress attempted to ease this burden with a comprehensive child care bill in 1971, but President Nixon vetoed it.

Despite this setback, during the 1970s women gained the most sweeping changes in laws and policies since they won the right to vote in 1920. In 1972, Congress passed the Equal Rights Amendment (ERA), which would outlaw differential treatment of men and women under all state and federal laws.

Although public opinion polls registered support for most feminist goals, by the mid-1970s a strong countermovement focused on preventing ratification of the ERA arose. Phyllis Schlafly, a conservative activist in the Republican Party, mobilized thousands of women at the grassroots level who believed that traditional gender roles were God given and feared that feminism would devalue their own roles as wives and mothers. These women, marching on state capitols, persuaded some male legislators to block ratification. When the time limit ran out in 1982, only thirty-five states had ratified the

"Without the full capacity to limit her own reproduction," abortion rights activist Lucinda Cisler insisted, "a woman's other 'freedoms' are tantalizing mockeries that cannot be exercised."

amendment, three short of the necessary three-fourths majority. (See chapter 30, "Historical Question," page 1122, and the map on page 1128.)

Along with groups of doctors and lawyers who had sought abortion law reform since the 1950s, feminists pressured state legislatures to end restrictions on abortion. "Without the full capacity to limit her own reproduction," abortion rights activist Lucinda Cisler insisted, "a woman's other 'freedoms' are tantalizing mockeries that cannot be exercised." In 1973, the Supreme Court issued the landmark *Roe v. Wade* decision, ruling that the Constitution protects the right to abortion, which states cannot prohibit in the early stages of pregnancy.

This decision spurred even more intense opposition than the ERA. Many Americans believed that human life begins with conception and equated abortion with murder. The Catholic Church and other religious organizations provided institutional support for their protest; conservative politicians and their supporters constituted another segment of the right-to-life movement. Like ERA opponents with whom they often overlapped, the right-to-life movement mobilized thousands of women who believed that abortion disparaged motherhood and that feminism threatened their traditional roles. Beginning in 1977, abortion foes got Congress to restrict the right to abortion by denying coverage under Medicaid and other government-financed health programs, and the Supreme Court allowed states to impose other obstacles. These restraints especially disadvantaged poor and rural women.

Despite resistance, feminists won other lasting gains. Title IX of the Education Amendments Act of 1972 banned sex discrimination in all aspects of education, such as admissions, athletics, and faculty hiring. Congress also outlawed sex discrimination in credit in 1974, opened U.S. military academies to women in 1976, and prohibited discrimination against pregnant workers in 1978. Moreover, the Supreme Court struck down laws that treated men and women differently in Social Security, welfare and military benefits, and workers' compensation.

At the state and local levels, women saw reforms in areas that radical feminists had first brought attention to. They won laws forcing police departments and the legal system to treat rape victims more justly and humanely. No longer did a woman have to prove that she had put up a fight against a rapist or see her sexual history paraded before the courtroom; rape was now a crime even when it was committed by a husband against his wife. Activists also pushed domestic violence onto the public agenda. They obtained government financing for shelters for battered women and laws ensuring both greater protection for victims of domestic violence and more effective prosecution of abusers.

REVIEW Why did a strong countermovement emerge to oppose feminist reform?

Liberal Reform in the Nixon Administration

Feminism was not the only movement to arouse strong antagonism. Opposition to civil rights measures, Great Society reforms, and protest groups—along with frustrations surrounding the war in Vietnam (see chapter 29)—delivered the White House to Republican Richard M. Nixon in 1968. As presidential candidate, Nixon attacked the Great Society for "pouring billions of dollars into programs that have failed," and he promised to represent the "forgotten Americans, the non-shouters, the non-demonstrators."

Yet despite Nixon's desire to attract southern whites and other Democrats disaffected by Johnson's reforms and by protesters, liberal policies persisted into the early 1970s. The Nixon administration either promoted or accepted substantially greater federal assistance to the poor; new protections for African Americans, Native Americans, women, and other groups; major environmental regulations; and financial policies deviating sharply from traditional Republican economics.

Extending the Welfare State and Regulating the Economy

A number of factors shaped the liberal policies of the Nixon administration. Not only did the Democrats continue to control Congress, but Nixon also wanted to preserve support from moderates in his party and increase Republican ranks by attracting some traditional Democrats. He could not entirely ignore grassroots movements, and several of his advisers were sympathetic to particular concerns, such as environmentalism

Transnational Feminisms

When American women began to protest sex discrimination in the 1960s, most were unaware that they belonged to a movement stretching back more than a century and across oceans. In 1850, Polish-born Ernestine Rose told a women's rights convention in Massachusetts, "We are not contending here for the rights of the women of New England, or of old England, but of the world." Her statement affirmed the connections among women from European countries and the United States, who wrote and visited each other and exchanged ideas and inspiration in the first international women's movement.

By the early twentieth century, women had formalized such connections. For example, the International Alliance of Women, founded in 1904 to promote global woman **suffrage**, expanded its agenda to include equal pay and employment, peace, married women's citizenship, and more. By 1929, the alliance claimed national organizations in fifty-one countries, including the United States and most of Europe, China, Egypt, India, Japan, Palestine, and several Latin American nations.

Alliance women struggled to create a "universal sisterhood." White Christian women from the United States and Europe dominated the organization and blithely assumed that they could speak for all women. But oppression and discrimination looked quite different to women in other parts of the world.

In **colonized** countries such as India and Egypt, feminism arose alongside movements for independence from the very **imperial** nations that were home to most alliance leaders. Egyptian feminist and nationalist Huda Sha'arawi was the only Muslim among the international leadership. She worked closely with the alliance on many issues, but she realized the need to address the particular interests of Arab women overlooked or opposed by Euro-American feminists, and she established the Arab Feminist Union in 1945.

Global connections among women increased dramatically in 1945 with the creation of the United Nations. Its charter affirmed "the equal rights of men and women" and "fundamental freedoms for all without distinction as to race, sex, language, or religion." Two years later, the UN established the Commission on the Status of Women, creating a forum for women from around the globe to meet and be heard. In 1948, it adopted the Universal Declaration of Human Rights, which enumerated an extensive set of rights and explicitly rejected sex discrimination. These and other international commitments to justice for women went far beyond any rights guaranteed to women by the U.S. legal system or by the laws of most other nations, thereby setting standards and raising expectations. The UN, for example, asserted women's right to equal pay in 1951, twelve years before the U.S. Congress did so, and the international body attacked discrimination in education a decade before Congress passed Title IX.

The UN helped launch a global feminist movement of unparalleled size and diversity when it declared 1975 International Women's Year and sponsored a conference in Mexico City. Six thousand women came to Mexico City on their own; official delegates from 125 nations approved the World Plan of Action for Women and prompted the UN to declare 1976 to 1985 the UN Decade for Women.

In response to the call for action in individual countries, the U.S. government funded the National Women's Conference in Houston, Texas, in 1977. More than two thousand state delegates attended, representing a cross section of American womanhood. They adopted the National Plan of Action, not only supporting ratification of the ERA and reproductive freedom but also addressing the needs of specific groups of women, including the elderly, lesbians, racial minorities, rural women, and homemakers. For the first time, the U.S. women's movement had a comprehensive national agenda setting goals for decades to come.

The three themes of the UN Decade for Women—equality, development, and peace—reflected an effort to address the enormously diverse needs of women throughout the world. Feminists from Western nations who focused on equal rights met criticism from women who represented impoverished **third world** countries and insisted that women's issues must include economic development and anticolonialism. Ever larger UN-sponsored meetings followed Mexico City—Copenhagen in 1980, Nairobi in 1985, and Beijing in 1995, where twenty thousand women gathered. These global exchanges taught American feminists that to participate in a truly international movement, they would have to revise their Western-centered perspective on women's needs.

American feminists also learned that theirs was not always the most advanced nation when it came to women's welfare and status. Most industrialized countries provided paid maternity leave and public child care. By 2000, women had headed governments in more than thirty countries, including India, Israel, and Britain. Many nations, such as Argentina, Egypt, India, and the European Union, had some form of affirmative action to increase the numbers of women in government. And whereas American women held 13.8 percent of the seats in the House of Representatives, women constituted 20 percent of the lower house in South Korea, 30 percent in Germany, and more than 35 percent in Norway, Denmark, and Sweden.

Despite enormous differences among women around the world, internationally minded feminists continued to seek common ground. As Gertrude Mongella, secretary-general of the Beijing conference, insisted in 1995, "A revolution has begun and there is no going back. . . . This revolution is too just, too important, and too long overdue."

International Women's Year Tribune

A majority of delegates at the UN International Women's Year Conference in Mexico City in July 1975 were women, but men provided the leadership, and delegates frequently took positions mandated by their governments but not necessarily reflecting the interests of women. In contrast, nongovernmental organizations associated with the UN sponsored a Tribune on the other side of the city, where six thousand women attended workshops that they or their organizations designed. There participants expressed the conflicting priorities of Western women and women from developing countries, and they argued over whether issues such as apartheid in South Africa and self-government for Palestinians were women's issues. Despite their disagreements, most women left Mexico City enlightened and energized. © Bettye Lane.

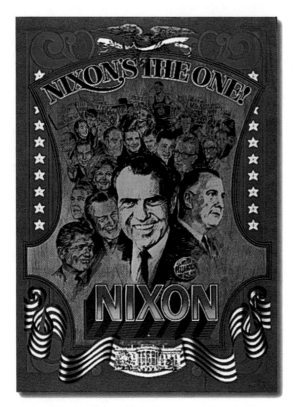

Nixon's 1968 Campaign
Seeking the presidency in 1968—a turbulent year of protests, riots, and assassinations—Richard Nixon tried to appeal to a broad spectrum of voters, reflected in this campaign poster. Prominent Republicans of all stripes appear in the poster, including the liberal Nelson Rockefeller and the conservative Barry Goldwater. While his slogan "Champion of Forgotten America" spoke to white Americans alienated by the Great Society's programs for minorities and the poor, the appearance on the poster of the black Republican senator Edward Brooke and basketball player Wilt Chamberlain of the Los Angeles Lakers gave a nod to African Americans. Nixon also appealed to youths by supporting the vote for eighteen-year-olds and promising to end the draft.
Collection of Janice L. and David J. Frent.

and Native American rights. Serious economic problems also compelled new approaches, and although Nixon's real passion lay in foreign policy, he knew that history's approving gaze would depend in part on how he handled problems at home.

Under Nixon, government assistance programs grew. Congress resisted his attempts to eliminate the Office of Economic Opportunity. Key programs such as Medicaid, Head Start, Legal Services, and job training remained intact. Social Security benefits—now required to rise with the cost of living—increased; subsidies

for low-income housing tripled; and a new billion-dollar program provided Pell grants for low-income students to attend college. In response to growing public concern about undernourishment, Nixon supported a huge expansion of the food stamp program, which benefited 12.5 million recipients. Noting the disparity between Nixon's political speeches and his practice as president, one of his speechwriters, the archconservative Pat Buchanan, grumbled, "Vigorously did we inveigh against the Great Society, enthusiastically did we fund it."

Nixon also acted contrary to his antigovernment rhetoric when economic crises and energy shortages induced him to increase the federal government's power in the marketplace. By 1970, both inflation and unemployment had surpassed 6 percent. This unprecedented combination of a stagnant economy and inflation was dubbed "stagflation." Domestic troubles were compounded by the decline of American dominance in the international economy. Fully recovered from World War II, the economies of Japan and Western Europe grew faster than the U.S. economy in the 1970s. Foreign cars, electronic equipment, and other products competed favorably with American goods throughout the world. In 1971, for the first time in decades, the United States imported more than it exported. Because the amount of dollars in foreign hands exceeded U.S. gold reserves, the nation could no longer back up its currency with gold.

With an eye to the 1972 election, Nixon abandoned the convertibility of dollars into gold and devalued the dollar to increase exports by making American goods cheaper in foreign markets. To protect domestic manufacturers, he imposed a 10 percent surcharge on most imports, and he froze wages and prices, thus enabling the government to stimulate the economy without fueling inflation. In the short run, these policies worked, and Nixon was resoundingly reelected in 1972. Yet by 1974, unemployment had crept back up and inflation soared, leaving to Nixon's successor the most severe economic crisis since the depression of the 1930s.

Soaring energy prices intensified stagflation. Throughout the post–World War II economic boom, the nation's abundant oil deposits and access to cheap Middle Eastern oil had encouraged the building of large cars and glass-enclosed skyscrapers with no concern for fuel efficiency. By the 1970s, the United States, with just 6 percent of the world's population, was consuming one-third of its fuel resources.

In the fall of 1973, the United States faced its first energy crisis. Arab nations, furious at the administration's support of Israel during the Yom Kippur War (see chapter 29), cut off oil shipments to the United States. As oil supplies fell in the winter of 1973–74, long lines formed at gas stations, where prices had nearly doubled, and many homes were cold. In response, Nixon authorized temporary emergency measures allocating petroleum and establishing a national 55-mile-per-hour speed limit to save gasoline. The energy crisis eased, but the nation had yet to come to grips with its seemingly unquenchable demand for fuel and dependence on foreign oil.

More permanently, Nixon expanded the government's regulatory role with a host of environmental protection measures. He proclaimed in 1970 that the nation must make "reparations for the damage we have done to our air, to our land and to our water" and urged Congress to "end the plunder of America's natural heritage." In addition to establishing the Environmental Protection Agency, he signed strong clean air legislation and measures to regulate noise pollution, oil spill cleanup, and the dumping of pesticides into the oceans. Environmentalists claimed that Nixon failed to do enough, pointing particularly to his veto—for budgetary reasons—of the Clean Water Act of 1972, which Congress overrode. Yet Nixon's environmental initiatives surpassed those of previous administrations.

Responding to Demands for Social Justice

To woo white southerners and northern workers away from the Democratic Party, Nixon's 1968 campaign had exploited hostility to black protest and new civil rights policies, but his administration had to answer to the courts and to Congress. In 1968, fourteen years after the *Brown* decision, school desegregation had barely touched the South: Two-thirds of African American children did not have a single white schoolmate. Like Eisenhower, Nixon was reluctant to use federal power to compel integration, but the Supreme Court overruled administration efforts to delay court-ordered desegregation and compelled it to enforce the law. By the time Nixon left office, fewer than one in ten southern black children attended totally segregated schools.

Nixon also began to implement affirmative action among federal contractors and unions and awarded more government contracts and loans to minority businesses. Congress took the initiative in other areas. In 1970, it extended the Voting Rights Act of 1965 by five years, and in 1972 it strengthened the Civil Rights Act of 1964 by enlarging the powers of the Equal Employment Opportunity Commission and authorizing the commission to initiate lawsuits against employers suspected of discrimination.

Women as well as minority groups benefited from the implementation of affirmative action and the strengthened EEOC, but several measures of the Nixon administration also specifically attacked sex discrimination. The president privately expressed patronizing attitudes about women, who he thought were more "erratic" and "emotional" than men. "Thank God we don't have any in the Cabinet," he told aides. Yet again, he confronted a growing popular movement and listened to more open-minded advisers and Republican feminists. Nixon vetoed a child care bill and publicly opposed abortion, but he signed the pathbreaking Title IX, guaranteeing equality in all aspects of education, and allowed his Labor Department to push affirmative action.

President Nixon gave more public support for justice to Native Americans than to any other protest group. While not bowing to radical demands, the administration dealt cautiously with extreme protests, such as the occupation of the Bureau of Indian Affairs in Washington, D.C., and the village of Wounded Knee, South Dakota. Nixon signed measures recognizing claims of Alaskan and New Mexican Indians and restoring tribal status to the Menominee, whose status had been terminated in 1961. He also set in motion legislation restoring additional tribal lands and granting Indians more control over their schools and other service institutions.

> **REVIEW** Why and how did Republican president Richard Nixon expand the liberal reforms of previous administrations?

Conclusion: Achievements and Limitations of Liberalism

Senate majority leader Mike Mansfield was not alone in concluding that Lyndon Johnson "has done more than FDR ever did, or ever thought of doing." The Great Society had expanded the New Deal's focus on economic security, refashioning liberalism to embrace individual rights and to extend material well-being to groups neglected by or discriminated against in New Deal programs. Yet opposition to Johnson's leadership grew so strong by 1968 that he abandoned hopes for reelection. As his liberal vision lay in ruins, he asked, "How was it possible that all these people could be so ungrateful to me after I have given them so much?"

Fannie Lou Hamer could have provided a number of reasons. Support from the federal government was minimal when her efforts and those of others to help southern blacks obtain their rights met with violence. Moreover, her attempts to use Johnson's antipoverty programs to help poor blacks in Mississippi eventually ended in failure. Internal problems hampered her projects, but they also reflected some of the more general shortcomings of the War on Poverty. Hastily planned and inadequately funded, many antipoverty programs significantly benefited industry and the nonpoor. The War on Poverty focused more on remediating individual shortcomings than on economic and political reforms that would ensure adequately paying jobs for all. Because Johnson launched an all-out war in Vietnam and refused to ask for sacrifices from prosperous Americans, the Great Society never commanded the resources necessary for victory over poverty.

Furthermore, black aspirations exceeded white Americans' commitment to genuine equality. When the civil rights movement moved to attack racial barriers long entrenched throughout the nation and sought equality in fact as well as in law, it faced a powerful backlash. By the end of the 1960s, the revolution in the legal status of African Americans was complete, but the black freedom struggle had lost much of its momentum, and African Americans remained, with Native Americans and Chicanos, at the bottom of the economic ladder.

Critics of Johnson's Great Society overlooked its more successful and lasting elements. Medicare and Medicaid provided access to health care for the elderly and the poor and contributed to a sharp decline in poverty among aged Americans. Federal aid for education and housing became permanent elements of national policy. Moreover, Richard Nixon's otherwise conservative administration implemented school desegregation in the South and affirmative action, expanded government assistance to the disadvantaged, initiated substantial environ-

mental regulations, and secured new rights for Native Americans and women. Women especially benefited from the decline of discrimination, and significant numbers of African Americans and other minority groups began to enter the middle class.

Yet the perceived shortcomings of government programs contributed to social turmoil and fueled the resurgence of conservative politics. Young radicals launched direct confrontations with the government and universities that, together with racial conflict, escalated into political discord and social disorder. The war in Vietnam polarized American society as much as did racial issues or the behavior of young people, and it devoured resources that might have been used for social reform and undermined faith in presidential leadership.

Selected Bibliography

The Black Freedom Struggle

Raymond Arsenault, *Freedom Riders: 1961 and the Struggle for Racial Justice* (2006).
Taylor Branch, *America in the King Years*, 3 vols. (1988, 1998, 2006).
Michael Eric Dyson, *Making Malcolm: The Myth and Meaning of Malcolm X* (1995).
Chana Kai Lee, *For Freedom's Sake: The Life of Fannie Lou Hamer* (1999).
Charles Payne, *I've Got the Light of Freedom: The Organizing Tradition and the Mississippi Freedom Struggle* (1995).
Barbara Ransby, *Ella Baker and the Black Freedom Movement: A Radical Democratic Vision* (2003).
Timothy Tyson, *Radio Free Dixie: Robert F. Williams and the Roots of Black Power* (1999).

Politics, Policies, and Court Decisions

Robert Dallek, *An Unfinished Life: John F. Kennedy, 1917–1963* (2003).
Maurice Isserman and Michael Kazin, *America Divided: The Civil War of the 1960s* (2000).
Michael B. Katz, *The Undeserving Poor: From the War on Poverty to the War on Welfare* (1989).
Nancy MacLean, *Freedom Is Not Enough: The Opening of the American Workplace* (2006).
Rick Perlstein, *Before the Storm: Barry Goldwater and the Unmaking of the American Consensus* (2001).
Gerald Posner, *Case Closed: Lee Harvey Oswald and the Assassination of JFK* (1993).
Lucas A. Powe Jr., *The Warren Court and American Politics* (2000).
John D. Skrentny, *The Minority Rights Revolution* (2002).

Irwin Unger, *The Best of Intentions: The Triumph and Failure of the Great Society* (1996).

Tom Wicker, *One of Us: Richard Nixon and the American Dream* (1991).

Randall B. Woods, *LBJ: Architect of American Ambition* (2006).

Protest Movements

Terry H. Anderson, *The Movement and the Sixties* (1995).

John D'Emilio, William B. Turner, and Urvashi Vaid, *Creating Change: Sexuality, Public Policy, and Civil Rights* (2000).

Manuel G. Gonzales, *Mexicanos: A History of Mexicans in the United States* (1999).

James Miller, *"Democracy Is in the Streets": From Port Huron to the Siege of Chicago* (1987).

F. Arturo Rosales, *Chicano! The History of the Mexican American Civil Rights Movement* (2nd rev. ed., 1997).

Peter Chaat Smith and Robert Allen Warrior, *Like a Hurricane: The Indian Movement from Alcatraz to Wounded Knee* (1996).

William Wei, *The Asian American Movement* (1993).

Cultural Change, Sexual Revolution, and Feminism

David Allyn, *Make Love, Not War: The Sexual Revolution, an Unfettered History* (2000).

Sara Evans, *Tidal Wave: How Women Changed America at Century's End* (2003).

David Garrow, *Liberty and Sexuality: The Right to Privacy and the Making of* Roe v. Wade (1994).

Susan M. Hartmann, *The Other Feminists: Activists in the Liberal Establishment* (1998).

Laura Marks, *Sexual Chemistry: A History of the Contraceptive Pill* (2001).

James Miller, *Flowers in the Dustbin: The Rise of Rock and Roll, 1947–1977* (1999).

Benita Roth, *Separate Roads to Feminism: Black, Chicana, and White Feminist Movements in America's Second Wave* (2004).

William L. Van Deburg, *New Days in Babylon: The Black Power Movement and American Culture, 1965–1975* (1993).

▶ FOR MORE BOOKS ABOUT TOPICS IN THIS CHAPTER, see the Online Bibliography at bedfordstmartins.com/roark.

▶ FOR ADDITIONAL FIRSTHAND ACCOUNTS OF THIS PERIOD, see Chapter 28 in Michael Johnson, ed., *Reading the American Past*, Fourth Edition.

▶ FOR WEB SITES, IMAGES, AND DOCUMENTS RELATED TO TOPICS AND PLACES IN THIS CHAPTER, visit bedfordstmartins.com/makehistory.

REVIEWING THE CHAPTER

Follow these steps to review and strengthen your understanding of the chapter.

STEP 1: *Study the **Key Terms** and **Timeline** to identify the significance of each item listed.*

STEP 2: *Answer the **Review Questions**, drawing on key terms and dates to support your answers.*

STEP 3: *Drawing on the Key Terms, Timeline, and Review Questions, answer the broader **Making Connections** questions.*

KEY TERMS

Who

Fannie Lou Hamer (p. 1021)
John F. Kennedy (p. 1021)
Lyndon B. Johnson (p. 1023)
Lee Harvey Oswald (p. 1025)
Earl Warren (p. 1025)
Barry M. Goldwater (p. 1026)
Martin Luther King Jr. (p. 1032)
Medgar Evers (p. 1033)
Malcolm X (p. 1038)
Stokely Carmichael (p. 1038)
Cesar Chavez (p. 1041)
Dolores Huerta (p. 1041)
Elaine Noble (p. 1047)
Rachel Carson (p. 1048)
Betty Friedan (p. 1050)
Gloria Steinem (p. 1052)
Phyllis Schlafly (p. 1052)
Richard M. Nixon (p. 1053)

What

Great Society (pp. 1021, 1028)
Economic Opportunity Act of 1964 (p. 1026)

Elementary and Secondary Education Act of 1965 (p. 1027)
Medicare (p. 1027)
Medicaid (p. 1027)
Voting Rights Act of 1965 (p. 1027)
Immigration and Nationality Act of 1965 (p. 1027)
Loving v. Virginia (p. 1031)
Baker v. Carr (p. 1031)
Gideon v. Wainwright (p. 1031)
Miranda v. Arizona (p. 1031)
Abington School District v. Schempp (p. 1031)
Student Nonviolent Coordinating Committee (SNCC) (p. 1033)
Congress of Racial Equality (CORE) (p. 1033)
Freedom Rides (p. 1033)
Voter Education Project (p. 1033)
March on Washington (p. 1034)
Mississippi Freedom Summer Project (p. 1034)
Selma march (p. 1034)
Civil Rights Acts of 1964 and 1968 (pp. 1025, 1036)

Black Panther Party for Self-Defense (p. 1038)
American Indian Movement (AIM) (p. 1040)
United Farm Workers (UFW) (p. 1041)
La Raza Unida (p. 1042)
Students for a Democratic Society (SDS) (p. 1042)
Stonewall riots (p. 1047)
Environmental Protection Agency (EPA) (p. 1049)
Occupational Safety and Health Act (OSHA) (p. 1049)
Clean Air Act of 1970 (p. 1049)
President's Commission on the Status of Women (PCSW) (p. 1050)
Equal Pay Act (p. 1050)
National Organization for Women (NOW) (p. 1051)
Equal Rights Amendment (ERA) (p. 1052)
Roe v. Wade (p. 1053)
Title IX (p. 1053)

TIMELINE

1960 • Lunch counter sit-ins.
• Democrat John F. Kennedy elected president.
• Student Nonviolent Coordinating Committee (SNCC) established.
• Students for a Democratic Society (SDS) founded.
• FDA approves birth control pill.

1961 • Congress of Racial Equality (CORE) sponsors Freedom Rides.

1962 • United Farm Workers (UFW) founded.

1963 • *The Feminine Mystique* published.
• President's Commission on the Status of Women issues report.
• Equal Pay Act.
• *Baker v. Carr.*
• *Abington School District v. Schempp.*
• March on Washington.
• President Kennedy assassinated; Lyndon B. Johnson becomes president.

1964 • Civil Rights Act.
• Economic Opportunity Act.
• Tax cuts enacted.

1965 • Selma-to-Montgomery march.
• Voting Rights Act.

1965– • Congress passes most of Johnson's Great Society
1966 domestic programs.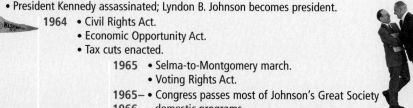

REVIEW QUESTIONS

1. How did the Kennedy and Johnson administrations exemplify a liberal vision of the federal government? (pp. 1023–31)

2. How did the civil rights movement change in the mid-1960s? (pp. 1031–39)

3. How did the black freedom struggle influence other reform movements of the 1960s and 1970s? (pp. 1039–49)

4. Why did a strong countermovement emerge to oppose feminist reform? (pp. 1049–53)

5. Why and how did Republican president Richard Nixon expand the liberal reforms of previous administrations? (pp. 1053–57)

MAKING CONNECTIONS

1. Both Franklin Roosevelt's New Deal and Lyndon Johnson's Great Society attacked poverty. How was Johnson's approach different from Roosevelt's? Which was more successful, and what contributed to the relative successes and failures of each approach?

2. During the 1960s, African Americans made substantial gains in asserting their freedoms and rights. Discuss how the civil rights movement produced significant social change. Were there limits to its success? What part did government play in this process?

3. Women participated in various ways in the feminism that emerged in the 1960s. How can we explain the rise of this movement? What assumptions and goals were held in common in this diverse movement?

4. Most of the reform movements of the 1960s sought equality as one of their key priorities, but significant differences existed among Americans in general about what equality meant. Should equality be limited to equal treatment under the law, or should it extend to economic welfare, education, sexual relations, and other aspects of life? Examining two reform movements, discuss how different ideas of equality contributed to the accomplishments and disappointments of each movement.

▶ FOR PRACTICE QUIZZES, A CUSTOMIZED STUDY PLAN, AND OTHER STUDY TOOLS, see the Online Study Guide at bedfordstmartins.com/roark.

1966 • Black Panther Party for Self-Defense founded.
- *Miranda v. Arizona.*
- National Organization for Women (NOW) founded.
 1967 • Detroit riots.
  - *Loving v. Virginia.*
  1968 • Martin Luther King Jr. assassinated.
   - American Indian Movement (AIM) founded.
   - Republican Richard M. Nixon elected president.
   1969 • Stonewall riots.
    1970 • First Earth Day celebrated.
     - Occupational Safety and Health Act.
     - Environmental Protection Agency established.
     - Clean Air Act.
     1971 • Nixon takes the United States off the gold standard and freezes prices and wages.
      1972 • Title IX of Education Amendments Act.
       - Congress passes Equal Rights Amendment; sends it to states for ratification.
       - American Indians' "Trail of Broken Treaties" caravan to Washington, D.C.
        1973 • AIM members occupy Wounded Knee, South Dakota.
         - *Roe v. Wade.*

FATIGUE HAT WITH BUTTONS
The button on this fatigue hat belonging
to a veteran who served two tours of duty in
Vietnam demonstrates veterans' response to the many
Americans who just wanted to forget the war that the United
States failed to win. Because their war was so different from other American wars,
Vietnam veterans often returned home to hostility or indifference. The POW-MIA pin refers to prisoners of war and
those missing in action. This man was unusual in serving two tours of duty; most soldiers served only one year. Why
might he have gone back for a second tour? How might his experiences have differed in the two periods, which were
separated by five years?

Nancy Gewitz/Antique Textile Resource/Picture Research Consultants & Archives.

CHAPTER 29

Vietnam and the Limits of Power

1961–1975

A S A PLANELOAD OF SOLDIERS prepared to land, the pilot announced, "Gentlemen, we'll be touching down in Da Nang, Vietnam, in about ten minutes. . . . On behalf of the entire crew and staff, I'd like to say we've enjoyed having you with us . . . and we hope to see all of you again next year on your way home. Goodbye and good luck." As the number of U.S. soldiers fighting in Vietnam soared, after 1966 most went to war on commercial airliners, complete with stewardesses (as they were called then) in miniskirts.

The picture of military personnel traveling to battle like business executives or tourists only hints at how different the Vietnam War was from America's previous wars. Marine infantry officer Philip Caputo landed at Da Nang in March 1965 confident, as were many soldiers in previous wars, that the enemy "would be quickly beaten and that we were doing something altogether noble and good." But in just a few months, "what had begun as an adventurous expedition had turned into an exhausting, indecisive war of attrition in which we fought for no other cause than our own survival."

Another soldier discovered even more quickly that "something was wrong." Wondering about the wire mesh that wrapped the military bus he boarded just after landing, he was told, "The gooks will throw grenades through the windows." Soldiers in Vietnam initially used the racist word *gook* to refer to the enemy—the North Vietnamese or their supporters in the South—but it soon became a term used for any Vietnamese. One American reported on the "changes coming over guys on our side—decent fellows, who wouldn't dream of calling an Oriental a 'gook' back home." The problem was that "they couldn't tell who was their friend and who wasn't. Day after day, out on patrol we'd come to . . . a shabby village, and the elders would welcome us and the children come running with smiles on their faces, waiting for the candy we'd give them. But . . . just as we were leaving the village behind, the enemy would open up on us, and there was bitterness among us that the villagers hadn't given us warning."

Americans' horrifying and bewildering experiences in Vietnam grew out of **cold war** commitments made in the 1940s and 1950s by Presidents Harry S. Truman and Dwight D. Eisenhower. John F. Kennedy wholeheartedly took on those commitments, promising more flexible and vigorous efforts to thwart **communism**. The most memorable words of his 1961 inaugural address declared that the United States would "pay any price, bear any burden, meet any hardship, support any friend, oppose any foe to assure the survival and the success of liberty." Philip Caputo joined the Marine Corps to gain independence and adventure, but he also reported being "seduced into uniform by Kennedy's challenge . . . and by the missionary idealism he had awakened in us."

Vietnam became the foremost test of John F. Kennedy's anticommunism. He sent increasing amounts of American arms and personnel to sustain the South Vietnamese government, but it

American Soldiers Confront the South Vietnamese
The unconventional nature of the Vietnam War often resulted in U.S. soldiers harming the very people they were sent to save. There were no fixed battle lines, soldiers could not tell which South Vietnamese civilians were supporting the North Vietnamese, and U.S. troops destroyed villages and farmland in an effort to seek out and eliminate North Vietnamese soldiers and their civilian allies. In this photo, a trooper of the U.S. First Cavalry stands guard while a medic treats South Vietnamese civilians who had been wounded during a search-and-destroy mission near Da Nang in October 1967. The mission destroyed their hamlet.
© Bettmann/Corbis.

was Lyndon B. Johnson who dramatically escalated that commitment in 1965 and turned a civil war among the Vietnamese into America's war. At peak strength in 1968, 543,000 U.S. military personnel served in Vietnam; all told, some 2.6 million saw duty there throughout the war. Yet this massive intervention not only failed to defeat North Vietnam but also created intense discord at home. It cost President Johnson another term in office and contributed to the political demise of his Republican successor, Richard M. Nixon. Some Americans lauded the government's goal in Vietnam and decried only its failure to pursue it effectively. Others believed that preserving a non-Communist South Vietnam was neither in the best interests of the United States nor within its capacity or moral right to achieve.

But none could deny the war's enormous costs. Lieutenant Caputo lamented that "our idealism was lost, our morals corrupted, and the purpose forgotten." Martin Luther King Jr. mourned "the promises of the Great Society . . . shot down on the battlefield of Vietnam." In addition to derailing domestic reform, the war exacted a heavy toll in American lives and dollars, disrupted the economy, kindled internal conflict, and led to the violation of protesters' rights, leaving a deep and lasting mark on the nation.

As the United States fought communism in Vietnam and, on a much smaller scale, in other **third world** countries, American leaders moved to ease cold war tensions with the major Communist powers. After a dramatic standoff with the Soviet Union during the Cuban missile crisis, the United States began to cooperate with its cold war enemy to limit nuclear testing and the spread of nuclear weapons. In 1972, the two superpowers agreed for the first time to restrict the development of new nuclear weapons. In addition, Nixon's historic visit to China in 1972 marked the abandonment of the policy of isolating China and paved the way for normal diplomatic relations by the end of the 1970s.

New Frontiers in Foreign Policy

John F. Kennedy moved quickly to fulfill his promise to pursue **containment** more aggressively and with more flexible means. In contrast to the Eisenhower administration's emphasis on nuclear weapons, Kennedy was determined to expand not only the nation's nuclear capacity but also its ability to fight conventional battles and to engage in **guerrilla warfare**. To ensure U.S. superiority over the Soviet Union in every domain, Kennedy accelerated the nation's space exploration program and increased attention to the third world. To deny the Soviets a nuclear outpost in the Western Hemisphere, he took the United States to the brink of nuclear war during the 1962 Cuban missile crisis. Less dramatically but no less tenaciously, Kennedy sent increasing amounts of American arms and personnel to South Vietnam in an effort to save the government from Communist insurgents.

Meeting the "Hour of Maximum Danger"

Underlying Kennedy's foreign policy was an assumption that the United States had "gone soft—physically, mentally, spiritually soft," as he put it in 1960. He called the Eisenhower era "years of drift and impotency," and he associated that administration with femininity when he mocked Nixon's kitchen debate with Soviet premier Nikita Khrushchev as well as Nixon's celebration of American consumer goods. "I would rather take my television black and white and have the largest rockets in the world," Kennedy declared. Often photographed engaging in vigorous sports, he and his closest advisers projected a masculine style that was tough, competitive, and hard-driving.

Having campaigned against the Eisenhower administration for relying too heavily on nuclear weapons, Kennedy moved to build up conventional ground forces, to provide a **flexible response** to Communist expansion. He also charged that limits on defense spending had caused the United States to fall behind even in nuclear capability. In January 1961, Kennedy warned that the nation faced a grave peril: "Each day the crises multiply. . . . Each day we draw nearer the hour of maximum danger."

Although the president exaggerated the threat to national security, several developments in 1961 heightened the sense of crisis and provided a rationalization for his military buildup. Shortly before Kennedy's inauguration, Khrushchev publicly encouraged "wars of national liberation," thereby aligning the Soviet Union with independence movements in the third world that were often anti-Western. His statement reflected in part the Soviet competition with China for the allegiance of emerging nations, but U.S.

officials saw in his words a threat to the status quo of containment.

Cuba, just ninety miles off the Florida coast, posed the most immediate threat to the United States. Fidel Castro's revolution had already moved Cuba into the Soviet orbit, and Eisenhower's CIA had been planning an invasion of the island by Cuban exiles living in the United States. Kennedy ordered the invasion to proceed even though his military advisers gave it only a fair chance of success. To do otherwise, the president believed, would create an appearance of weakness.

On April 17, 1961, about 1,400 anti-Castro exiles trained and armed by the CIA landed at the Bay of Pigs on the south shore of Cuba (Map 29.1, page 1066). Contrary to U.S. expectations, no popular uprising materialized to support the anti-Castro brigade. Kennedy refused to provide direct military support, and the invaders quickly fell to Castro's forces. The disaster humiliated Kennedy and the United States, posing a stark contrast to the president's inaugural promise of a new, more effective foreign policy. The attempted armed interference evoked memories of **Yankee imperialism** among Latin Americans, aligned Cuba even more closely with the Soviet Union, and helped Castro consolidate his power.

> "I would rather take my television black and white and have the largest rockets in the world," Kennedy declared.

Days before the Bay of Pigs invasion, the Soviet Union delivered a psychological blow when a Soviet astronaut became the first human being to orbit the earth. In May 1961, Kennedy called for a huge new commitment to the space program, with the goal of sending a man to the moon by 1970. Responding to his call to "win the battle that is now going on around the world between freedom and tyranny," Congress authorized the Apollo program and boosted appropriations for space exploration. John H. Glenn orbited the earth in 1962, and seven years later, in July 1969, two U.S. astronauts landed on the moon.

Early in his presidency, Kennedy sought a meeting with Khrushchev to show him "that we can be as tough as he is." But when the two met in June 1961 in Vienna, Austria, Khrushchev was belligerent and shook the president's confidence. The stunned Kennedy reported privately, "He just beat [the] hell out of me. . . . If he thinks I'm inexperienced and have no guts . . . we won't get anywhere with him." Khrushchev demanded an agreement recognizing the existence of two Germanys. Otherwise, he warned, the

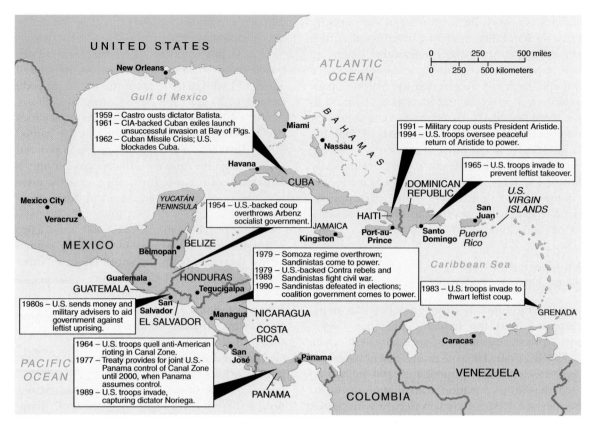

MAP 29.1   U.S. Involvement in Latin America and the Caribbean, 1954–1994
During the cold war, the United States frequently intervened in Central American and Caribbean countries to suppress Communist or leftist movements.

READING THE MAP: How many and which Latin American countries did the United States invade directly? What was the extent of U.S. indirect involvement in other upheavals in the region?
CONNECTIONS: What role did geographic proximity play in U.S. policy toward the region? What was the significance of the Cuban missile crisis for U.S. foreign policy? Did the political party of the intervening administration make a difference? Why or why not?

FOR MORE HELP ANALYZING THIS MAP, see the map activity for this chapter in the Online Study Guide at
bedfordstmartins.com/roark.

Soviets would sign a separate treaty with East Germany, a move that would threaten America's occupation rights in and access to West Berlin, which lay some one hundred miles within East Germany.

Khrushchev was concerned about the massive exodus of East Germans into West Berlin, a major embarrassment for the Communists. To stop this flow of escapees from behind the **iron curtain,** in August 1961 East Germany shocked the world by erecting a wall between East and West Berlin. With the Berlin Wall stemming the tide of migration and Kennedy insisting that West Berlin was "the great testing place of Western courage and will," Khrushchev backed

off from his threats. But not until 1972 did the superpowers recognize East and West Germany as separate nations and guarantee Western access to West Berlin.

Kennedy used the Berlin crisis to add $3.2 billion to the defense budget. He increased draft calls and mobilized the reserves and National Guard, adding 300,000 troops to the military. By providing for a "flexible response" strategy, this buildup of conventional forces met his demand for "a wider choice than humiliation or all-out nuclear action." Nonetheless, Kennedy also pushed for the development of new nuclear weapons and delivery systems, more than doubling the nation's nuclear force within three years.

Humans Reach the Moon
In July 1969, less than a decade after President John F. Kennedy announced the goal of "landing a man on the moon and returning him safely to the earth," the space capsule *Apollo 11* carried astronauts Edwin E. ("Buzz") Aldrin Jr. and Neil A. Armstrong to the moon. Other missions soon followed. In this 1971 photograph of the *Apollo 15* mission, astronaut James B. Irwin salutes the flag near the lunar module and lunar roving vehicle. Because the moon is windless, the flag had to be stretched on supports.
NASA/Johnson Space Center.

New Approaches to the Third World

Complementing Kennedy's hard-line policy toward the Soviet Union were fresh approaches to the **nationalist** movements that had convulsed the world since the end of World War II. In 1960 alone, seventeen African nations gained their independence. Much more than his predecessors, the president publicly supported third world aspirations, believing that the United States could win the hearts and minds of people in developing nations by helping to fulfill hopes for autonomy and **democracy**.

To that end, in 1961 Kennedy created the Alliance for Progress, promising $20 billion in aid for Latin America over the next decade. Like the Marshall Plan (see chapter 26), the Alliance for Progress was designed to thwart communism and hold nations within the American sphere by fostering economic development. Likewise, the new Agency for International Development (AID) emphasized economic over military aid in foreign assistance programs.

Also in 1961, Kennedy launched his most dramatic third world initiative with an idea borrowed from Senator Hubert H. Humphrey: the Peace Corps. The program recruited young men and women to work in developing countries, many of them responding to Kennedy's appeal for idealism and sacrifice in his inaugural address.

Peace Corps Volunteers in Bolivia
The majority of Peace Corps volunteers worked on educational projects in developing countries. Others helped increase food production, build public works, and curb diseases, as did these volunteers, Rita Helmkamp and Ed Dennison, vaccinating a young Bolivian girl. President John F. Kennedy saw the Peace Corps volunteers, with their dedication to freedom, "overcoming the efforts of Mr. Khrushchev's missionaries who are dedicated to undermining that freedom." In the course of their missions, however, some volunteers came to question the United States' single-minded focus on stopping the spread of communism.
David S. Boyer © National Geographic Society.

One volunteer spoke of his service as a way to ease his guilt at having been "born between clean sheets when others were issued into the dust with a birthright of hunger." After studying a country's language and **culture**, Peace Corps volunteers went to work directly with its people, opening schools, providing basic health care, and assisting with agriculture, nutrition, and small economic enterprises. By the mid-1970s, more than 60,000 volunteers had served two-year stints in Latin America, Africa, and Asia.

> One Peace Corps volunteer spoke of his service as a way to ease his guilt at having been "born between clean sheets when others were issued into the dust with a birthright of hunger."

Nevertheless, Kennedy's foreign aid initiatives fell far short of their objectives. Though generally welcomed, Peace Corps projects did not address the receiving countries' larger eco-nomic and political structures, and they numbered too few to make a dent in the poverty and suffering in third world countries. By 1969, the United States had provided only half of the $20 billion promised to the Alliance for Progress, much of which went to military projects or into the pockets of corrupt ruling elites. In addition, a soaring birthrate in Latin America counteracted economic gains, and these nations increasingly bore heavy foreign debt.

Kennedy also used direct military means to bring political stability to the third world. He rapidly expanded the "special forces" corps that had been established under Eisenhower to aid groups sympathetic to the United States and fighting against Communist-leaning national liberation movements. These counterinsurgency forces, including the army's Green Berets and the navy SEALs, constituted elite military corps trained to wage guerrilla warfare and equipped with the latest technology. They would get their first test in Vietnam.

The Arms Race and the Nuclear Brink

The final piece of Kennedy's defense strategy was to strengthen American nuclear dominance. The president realized quickly that the "missile gap" he had decried during the 1960 campaign was a myth, but that did not lessen his determination to make the United States even stronger. He upped the number of nuclear weapons based in Europe from 2,500 to 7,200 and multiplied fivefold the supply of intercontinental ballistic missiles (ICBMs). Concerned that this buildup would enable the United States to launch a first strike and wipe out Soviet missile sites before they could respond, the Soviet Union stepped up its own ICBM program. Thus began the most intense arms race in history.

The superpowers came perilously close to using their weapons of terror in 1962, when Khrushchev decided to install nuclear missiles in Cuba, while insisting to Kennedy that he had no intention to do so. Khrushchev wanted to protect Cuba from further U.S. attempts at intervention, and he sought to balance the U.S. missiles aimed at the Soviet Union from Britain, Italy, and Turkey. On October 16, the CIA showed Kennedy aerial photographs of missile launching sites under construction in Cuba. Considering this an intolerable threat to the United States, the president met daily in secret with a small group of advisers to manage the ensuing thirteen-day Cuban missile crisis. Rather than conducting quiet negotiations with the Soviets, Kennedy launched a public showdown. On October 22, he announced to a television audience that the military was on full alert and that the navy would turn back any Soviet vessel suspected of carrying offensive missiles to Cuba. (Only later did the United States find out that offensive missiles were already there.) Kennedy warned Khrushchev that any attack launched from Cuba would trigger a full nuclear assault against the Soviet Union.

Projecting the appearance of toughness was paramount to President Kennedy. Although the missiles did not "alter the strategic balance in fact," according to one of his aides, "that balance would have been substantially altered in appearance; and in matters of national will and world leadership such appearances contribute to reality." Kennedy feared that Soviet missiles in Cuba would intimidate other Latin American governments. "Communism and Castroism are going to be spread . . . as governments frightened by this new evidence of power [fall]."

But if Kennedy was willing to risk nuclear war for appearances, he also exercised caution, refusing advice from the military to bomb the missile sites. On October 24, Russian ships carrying nuclear warheads toward Cuba suddenly turned back. When one ship crossed the blockade line, Kennedy matched Khrushchev's restraint, ordering the navy to follow the ship rather than attempt to stop it.

While Americans experienced the cold war's most fearful days, Kennedy and Khrushchev negotiated an agreement. Ultimately, the Soviets removed the missiles and pledged not to introduce new offensive weapons into Cuba. The United States promised not to invade the island. Secretly, Kennedy also agreed to remove the U.S. missiles from Turkey. The Cuban crisis led to Khrushchev's fall from power two years later, and Kennedy emerged triumphant. "I cut his balls off," Kennedy rejoiced in private, reflecting considerations of manhood that helped shape his foreign policy. The image of an inexperienced president fumbling the Bay of Pigs invasion gave way to that of a brilliant

Cuban Missile Crisis, 1962

leader combining firmness with restraint, bearing the United States through its "hour of maximum danger."

Having proved his toughness, Kennedy worked with Khrushchev to prevent future confrontations by installing a special "hot line" to speed top-level communication at critical moments. In a major speech at American University in June 1963, Kennedy called for a reexamination of cold war assumptions, asking Americans "not to see conflict as inevitable." Acknowledging the superpowers' immense differences, Kennedy stressed what they had in common: "We all breathe the same air. We all cherish our children's future and we are all mortal." Kennedy also called for an end to "a vicious cycle" in which "new weapons beget counterweapons." In August 1963, the United States, the Soviet Union, and Great Britain signed a limited test ban treaty, reducing the threat of radioactive fallout from nuclear testing and raising hopes for further superpower accord.

Preparing for the Worst during the Cuban Missile Crisis
Waiting out the tense days after President Kennedy issued the ultimatum to the Soviet Union to halt shipments of missile materials to Cuba, many Americans tried to prepare for the worst possible outcome. Owners of Chalet Suzanne, a hotel in Lake Wales, Florida, canned several thousand cases of well water, labeled "NASK" for Nuclear Attack Survival Kit.
Courtesy Chalet Suzanne Foods, Inc., Lake Wales, Florida. Photo by David Woods.

U.S. Involvement in Vietnam

1954   **May**   French colonial presence ends with Vietnamese victory at Dien Bien Phu.

July   Geneva accords establish temporary division of North and South Vietnam at seventeenth parallel and provide for free elections.

September   United States joins with European, East Asian, and other nations to form Southeast Asia Treaty Organization (SEATO).

Eisenhower administration begins to send weapons and military advisers to South Vietnam to bolster Diem government.

1955–1961   United States sends $800 million in aid to South Vietnamese army (ARVN) to support its struggle with North Vietnamese government.

1961–1963   Under Kennedy administration, military aid to South Vietnam doubles, and number of military advisers reaches 9,000.

1963   South Vietnamese military overthrows Diem's government.

1964   President Johnson uses Gulf of Tonkin incident to escalate war.

1965   Johnson administration initiates Operation Rolling Thunder, intensifying bombing of North Vietnam.

1965–1967   Number of U.S. troops in Vietnam increases, reaching 543,000 in 1968, but U.S. and ARVN forces make only limited progress against the guerrilla forces, resulting in a stalemate.

1968   **January 30**   Tet Offensive causes widespread destruction and heavy casualties.

March 31   Johnson announces reduction in bombing of North Vietnam, plans for peace talks, and his decision not to run for another presidential term.

1969   Nixon administration initiates secret bombing of Cambodia, increases bombing of North Vietnam while reducing U.S. troops in the South, and pursues peace talks.

1970   Nixon orders joint U.S.-ARVN invasion of Cambodia.

1970–1971   U.S. troops in Vietnam decrease from 334,600 to 140,000.

1972   With peace talks stalled in December, Nixon administration orders most devastating bombing of North Vietnam of war.

1973   **January 27**   United States, North Vietnam, and South Vietnam sign formal accord in Paris marking end of U.S. involvement.

1975   North Vietnam launches new offensive in South Vietnam, defeating ARVN. Vietcong troops occupy Saigon, renaming it Ho Chi Minh City.

A Growing War in Vietnam

In his speech at American University, Kennedy criticized the idea of "a Pax Americana enforced on the world by American weapons of war," but he increased the flow of those weapons into South Vietnam. The foreign policy setbacks during his early months in office suggested the need to make a stand somewhere. "There are just so many con-cessions that one can make to the Communists in one year and survive politically," he said, recognizing the blows to the Democratic Party when China was "lost" to communism in 1949.

Kennedy's strong anticommunism and attachment to a vigorous foreign policy prepared him to expand the commitment in Vietnam that he had inherited from Eisenhower. Foreign policy experts of Kennedy's generation took from the Munich agreement in 1938—when Britain and France acceded to Germany's annexation of part of Czechoslovakia—the lesson that appeasement didn't work. Convinced that China and the Soviet Union were behind Ho Chi Minh's efforts to unify Vietnam under his leadership, Kennedy's key military adviser, General Maxwell Taylor, argued that holding firm in Vietnam would show the Soviets and Chinese that wars of national liberation were not "cheap, safe, and disavowable [but] costly, dangerous, and doomed to failure." The new counterinsurgency program could provide the means to do just that.

By the time Kennedy took office, more than $1 billion in aid and seven hundred U.S. military advisers had failed to stabilize South Vietnam. Two major obstacles stood in the way of this objective. First, the South Vietnamese insurgents—whom Americans called Vietcong, short for *Vietnam Cong-san* ("Vietnamese Communists")—were an indigenous force whose initiative came from within, not from the Soviet Union or China. Because the Saigon government refused to hold the elections promised in the 1954 Geneva accords, the rebels saw no choice but to take up arms. Increasingly, Ho Chi Minh's Communist government in North Vietnam supplied them with weapons and soldiers.

Second, the South Vietnamese government and army (the Army of the Republic of Vietnam, or ARVN) refused to satisfy the demands of the insurgents but could not defeat them militarily. Ngo Dinh Diem, South Vietnamese premier from 1954 to 1963, chose self-serving military leaders for their personal loyalty rather than for their effectiveness. Many South Vietnamese, the majority of whom were Buddhists, saw the Catholic Diem as a tool of the West. His government's corruption and brutal repression of opponents alienated many South Vietnamese, not just the Communists. Even Secretary of State Dean Rusk called him "an oriental despot."

The growing intervention by North Vietnam made matters worse. In 1960, the Hanoi government established the National Liberation Front

(NLF), composed of South Vietnamese rebels but directed by the northern army. In addition, Hanoi constructed a network of infiltration routes (called the "Ho Chi Minh Trail") in neighboring Laos and Cambodia, through which it sent people and supplies to help liberate the South (Map 29.2). Violence escalated between 1960 and 1963, bringing the Saigon government close to collapse.

Kennedy responded to the deteriorating situation with measured steps. Some advisers called for an all-out effort, using any force necessary to save South Vietnam from communism. Others questioned whether such a victory was either necessary or possible. Undersecretary of State Chester Bowles, for example, warned that the American effort was "headed full blast up a dead end street," while W. Averell Harriman, foreign policy adviser to Roosevelt and Truman, warned that the United States should not "stake its prestige" on a government that he deemed unsalvageable.

Taking the middle ground, Kennedy gradually escalated the U.S. commitment, nonetheless worrying that each step was "like taking a drink. . . . The effect wears off, and you have to take another." By the spring of 1963, military aid had doubled, and the 9,000 Americans serving in Vietnam as military advisers occasionally participated in actual combat. Although the United States extracted new promises of reform from Diem, the South Vietnamese government never made good on them.

Reflecting racist attitudes of American superiority over nonwhite populations, officials assumed that the U.S. military's technology and sheer power could win in Vietnam. Soldiers such

as Philip Caputo carried to Vietnam "the pride and overpowering self-assurance" that victory was inevitable. Yet advanced weapons were ill suited to the guerrilla warfare practiced by the enemy, whose surprise attacks were designed to weaken support for the South Vietnamese government. In addition, U.S. weapons and strategy harmed the very people they were intended to save. Thousands of peasants were uprooted

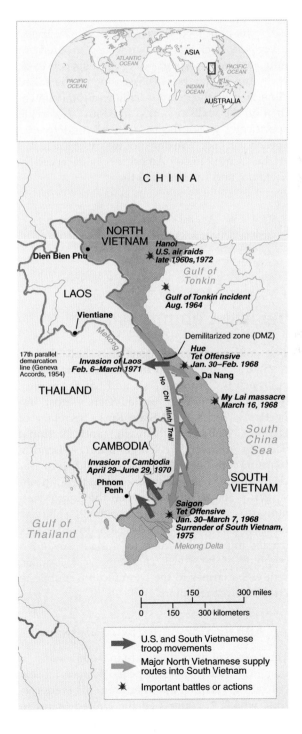

MAP 29.2   The Vietnam War, 1964–1975
The United States sent 2.6 million soldiers to Vietnam and spent more than $150 billion on the longest war in American history, but it was unable to prevent the unification of Vietnam under a Communist government.

READING THE MAP: What accords divided Vietnam into two nations? When were these accords signed, and where was the line of division drawn? Through what countries did the Ho Chi Minh Trail go?

CONNECTIONS: What was the Gulf of Tonkin incident, and how did the United States respond? What was the Tet Offensive, and how did it affect the war?

FOR MORE HELP ANALYZING THIS MAP, see the map activity for this chapter in the Online Study Guide at bedfordstmartins.com/roark.

and resettled in "strategic hamlets," supposedly secure from the Communists. Those left in the countryside fell victim to bombs—containing the highly flammable substance napalm—dropped by the U.S.-backed ARVN to quell the Vietcong. In January 1962, U.S. planes began to spray herbicides such as Agent Orange to destroy the Vietcong's jungle hideouts and food supply.

With tacit permission from Washington, South Vietnamese military leaders executed a coup against Diem and his brother, who headed the secret police, on November 2, 1963. Kennedy expressed shock that the two were murdered but indicated no change in policy. In a speech to be given on the day he was assassinated, he called Americans to their responsibilities as "the watchmen on the walls of world freedom." Referring specifically to Southeast Asia, his undelivered speech warned, "We dare not weary of the task." At his death, 16,000 Americans had served in Vietnam, and 100 had died there.

> **REVIEW**   Why did Kennedy believe that engagement in Vietnam was crucial to his foreign policy?

Lyndon Johnson's War against Communism

The cold war assumptions that had shaped Kennedy's foreign policy underlay his successor's approach to Southeast Asia and Latin America. Retaining Kennedy's key advisers—most importantly, Secretary of State Rusk, Secretary of Defense Robert McNamara, and National Security Adviser McGeorge Bundy—Lyndon Johnson continued the massive buildup of nuclear weapons and conventional and counterinsurgency forces. In 1965, when the South Vietnamese government approached collapse, Johnson made the fateful decisions to order U.S. troops into combat and to initiate sustained bombing of the North. That same year, Johnson sent U.S. marines to the Dominican Republic to crush a leftist rebellion.

An All-Out Commitment in Vietnam

The president who wanted to make his mark on domestic policy was compelled to face the excruciating dilemma inherited from his predecessors, who had committed the United States to stopping communism in Vietnam. Early in his administration, the general public paid little attention to Vietnam and seemed willing to follow the administration's lead. Yet some advisers, politicians, and international leaders raised questions about the wisdom of a greater commitment in Vietnam, viewing the situation there as a civil war rather than Communist aggression. Only French president Charles de Gaulle openly challenged U.S. policy, but most international leaders did not consider Vietnam crucial to containing communism and were not prepared to share the military burden in more than token ways. Several leading Democrats, including Senate majority leader Mike Mansfield, privately argued that a stable South Vietnam was unlikely. Mansfield wondered whether Vietnam could be won with a "limited expenditure of American lives and resources somewhere commensurate with our national interests." Senate Armed Services Committee member Richard Russell warned, "It'd take a half million men. They'd be bogged down there for ten years." Although critics expressed their own ambivalence and did not offer any clear-cut solutions, they urged the administration to pursue a face-saving way out, such as reconvening the Geneva conference that had partitioned Vietnam in 1954.

Johnson ignored the opportunity for disengagement that these critics saw in 1964 and expanded the United States' military involvement. Along with most of his advisers, he believed that the long-standing commitment to South Vietnam put American credibility on the line. Moreover, the president's own credibility also came into play. Like Kennedy, he feared the domestic political repercussions and especially what disengagement without victory might do to his ability to achieve his Great Society (see chapter 28). His own insecurities, fear of being compared unfavorably with Kennedy, and concern for his "manliness" precluded a course that might make him appear soft or cowardly. Mansfield's views, he said, were those of a "milquetoast."

Johnson understood the ineffectiveness of his South Vietnamese allies and agonized over sending young men into combat. Yet he continued to dispatch more military advisers, weapons, and economic aid, and in August 1964, he seized an opportunity to increase the pressure on North Vietnam. During a routine espionage mission in the Gulf of Tonkin, off the coast of North Vietnam, two U.S. destroyers reported that North Vietnamese gunboats had fired on them on August 2 and 4 (see Map 29.2). Johnson quickly ordered air strikes on North Vietnamese torpedo bases and oil storage facilities, and he sought authority from Congress to take "all necessary measures to repel any armed attacks against the forces of the United States and to prevent further aggression." By covering up uncertainty about whether the second attack had even occurred and the provocative U.S. actions of staging covert raids and operating close to the North Vietnamese coast, he misled Congress and the public about the situation. As a result, Congress supported Johnson's strategy with the Gulf of Tonkin Resolution on August 7, 1964, with just two senators voting against it.

The president's tough stance only two months before the 1964 election helped counter the charges made by his opponent, Arizona senator Barry Goldwater, that he was "soft on communism." Yet Johnson also presented himself as the peace candidate. When Goldwater proposed massive bombing of North Vietnam, Johnson assured Americans that "we are not going to send American boys nine or ten thousand miles away from home to do what Asian boys ought to be doing for themselves."

Soon after winning reelection, however, Johnson did widen the war. He rejected peace overtures from North Vietnam, which insisted on American withdrawal and a coalition government in South Vietnam as steps toward ultimate unification of the country. Instead, he accepted the advice of McNamara and other aides to begin a bombing campaign against the North. Operation Rolling Thunder, a strategy of gradually intensified bombing of North Vietnam, began in February 1965. Less than a month later, Johnson ordered the first U.S. combat troops to South Vietnam, and in July he shifted U.S. troops from defensive to offensive operations, dispatching 50,000 more soldiers (Figure 29.1). Although the administration downplayed the import of these decisions in order to maintain public and congressional support, they marked a critical turning point. Now it was genuinely America's war.

> Senate Armed Services Committee member Richard Russell warned, "It'd take a half million men [to win Vietnam]. They'd be bogged down there for ten years."

Preventing Another Castro in Latin America

Closer to home, Johnson faced persistent problems in Latin America despite the efforts of the Alliance for Progress. Thirteen times during the 1960s, military coups toppled Latin American governments, and local insurgencies grew apace. The administration's response varied from case to case but centered on the determination to prevent any more Castro-type revolutions.

In 1964, riots erupted in the Panama Canal Zone, which the United States had seized and made a U.S. territory early in the century (see chapter 21). Instigated by Panamanians who viewed the United States as a colonial power, the riots left four U.S. soldiers and more than twenty Panamanians dead. Johnson sent troops to quell

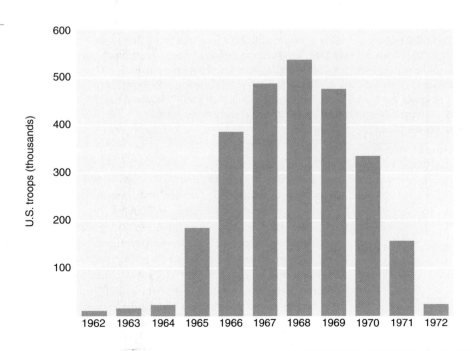

FIGURE 29.1 U.S. Troops in Vietnam, 1962–1972
The steepest increases in the American military presence in Vietnam came in 1965 and 1966. Although troop levels declined significantly in 1971 and 1972, the United States continued massive bombing attacks.

U.S. Troops in the Dominican Republic
These U.S. paratroopers were among the 20,000 troops sent to the Dominican Republic in April and May 1965. The American invasion helped restore peace but kept the popularly elected government of Juan Bosch from regaining office. Dominicans expressed their outrage in anti-American slogans that greeted troops throughout the capital, Santo Domingo. Bosch himself said, "This was a democratic revolution smashed by the leading democracy in the world."
© Bettmann/Corbis.

launched an uprising against the military government, Johnson sent more than 20,000 soldiers to quell what he perceived to be a leftist revolt and take control of the island. A truce was arranged, and in 1966 Dominicans voted in a constitutional government under a moderate rightist.

This first outright show of Yankee force in Latin America in four decades damaged the administration at home and abroad. Although it had justified intervention on the grounds that Communists were among the rebels, it quickly became clear that they had played no significant role, and U.S. actions kept the reform-oriented Boschists from returning to power. Moreover, the president had not consulted the Dominicans or the Organization of American States (OAS), to which the United States had pledged that it would respect national sovereignty in Latin America. Only after the troops had already landed in the Dominican Republic did Johnson ask for approval from the OAS. Several nations, including Mexico, Chile, and Venezuela, refused to grant it.

The Americanized War

The military success in the Dominican Republic no doubt encouraged the president to press on in Vietnam. During Operation Rolling Thunder from 1965 to early 1968, the United States gradually escalated attacks against the North Vietnamese and their Vietcong allies, endeavoring to break their will without provoking intervention by the Chinese, as they had done in Korea. Johnson himself scrutinized military plans, boasting, "They can't even bomb an outhouse without my approval."

Over the course of the war, U.S. pilots dropped 3.2 million tons of explosives, more than the United States had dropped in all of World War II. Claiming monthly death tolls of more than 2,000 North Vietnamese, the intensive bombing nonetheless failed to dampen the Hanoi government's commitment. (See "Historical Question," page 1076.) In the South, the United States rained down more than twice the tonnage of bombs dropped on North Vietnam.

General William Westmoreland's strategy of attrition was designed to search out and kill the Vietcong and North Vietnamese regular army. The military used helicopters extensively to conduct offensives all over South Vietnam. (See "The Promise of Technology," page 1080.) Because there was no battlefront as in previous wars,

the disturbance, but he also initiated negotiations that eventually led to the transfer of the canal to Panamanian authority in 2000.

Elsewhere, Johnson's Latin American policy generated new cries of "Yankee imperialism." In 1961, voters in the Dominican Republic ousted a long-standing dictator and elected a constitutional government headed by reformist Juan Bosch, who was overthrown by a military coup two years later. In 1965, when Bosch supporters officials calculated progress not in territory seized but in "body counts" and "kill ratios"— the number of enemies killed relative to the cost in American and ARVN lives. According to U.S. army officer Colin Powell, who served two tours in Vietnam and later served as U.S. secretary of state under George W. Bush, "The Army desperately needed something to measure. What military objectives could we claim in this week's report? A hill? A valley? A hamlet? Rarely. Consequently, bodies became the measure." In this situation, American soldiers did not always distinguish between military combatants and civilians; according to Lieutenant Philip Caputo, the operating rule was "If it's dead and Vietnamese, it's VC [Vietcong]."

Teenagers fought the Vietnam War, in contrast to World War II, where the average soldier was twenty-six years old. Until the voting age dropped from twenty-one to eighteen in 1971, most soldiers, whose average age was nineteen, could not even vote for the officials who sent them to war. Men of all classes had fought in World War II, but Vietnam was the war of the poor and working class, who constituted about 80 percent of the troops. More privileged youths avoided the **draft** by using college deferments or family connections to get into the National Guard. Sent from Plainville, Kansas, to Vietnam in 1965, Mike Clodfelter could not recall "a single middle-class son of the town's businessmen, lawyers, doctors, or ranchers from my high school graduating class who experienced the Armageddon of our generation."

Much more than World War II, Vietnam was a men's war. Because the United States did not undergo full mobilization for Vietnam, officials did not seek women's sacrifices for the war effort. In response to a reporter who said that some military women were distressed at not being called to serve in Vietnam, Johnson joked, "Well there is always a chance of anything taking place when our women are sufficiently distressed." Still, between 7,500 and 10,000 women served in Vietnam, the vast majority of them nurses. Although women were not allowed to carry weapons, they did come under enemy fire, and eight lost their lives. Many more struggled with their helplessness in the face of the dead and maimed bodies they tended. "When you finally saved a life," said Peggy DuVall, "you wondered what kind of life you had saved."

Early in the war, African Americans constituted 31 percent of combat troops, often choosing the military over the meager opportunities in the civilian economy. Special forces ranger Arthur E. Woodley Jr. recalled, "I was just what my country needed. A black patriot. . . . The only way I could possibly make it out of the ghetto was to be the best soldier I possibly could." Death rates among black soldiers were disproportionately high until 1966, when the military adjusted personnel assignments to achieve a better racial balance.

The young troops faced extremely difficult conditions. Soldiers fought in thick jungles and swamps filled with leeches, in oppressive heat, rain, and humidity. Lieutenant Caputo remembered "weeks of expectant waiting and, at random intervals, conducting vicious manhunts through jungles and swamps where snipers harassed us constantly and booby traps cut us down one by

> Soldier Mike Clodfelter could not recall "a single middle-class son of the town's businessmen, lawyers, doctors, or ranchers from my high school graduating class who experienced the Armageddon of our generation."

Vietnam: The War of the Young

The anguished face of this soldier, marine corpsman Vernon Wike, who is giving first aid to a wounded comrade, reflects the youth of the soldiers who fought in the Vietnam War. The average age of the soldiers was nineteen. When one young marine received his supplies, he wondered, "What did I need with shaving equipment? I was only seventeen. I didn't have hair under my *arms* let alone my face." This photo was taken in 1967 by twenty-two-year-old Frenchwoman Catherine Leroy, who risked her life as a freelance photographer to document the war. She was wounded by mortar fire and captured by the North Vietnamese during the Tet Offensive.

© Catherine Leroy/(Contact Press Images).

Why Couldn't the United States Bomb Its Way to Victory in Vietnam?

World War II demonstrated the critical importance of airpower in modern war. According to the official U.S. study of strategic bombing during World War II, "No nation can long survive the free exploitation of air weapons over its homeland." In the Vietnam War, U.S. planes delivered even more explosives than they had in World War II. Why, then, did strategic bombing not bring victory in Vietnam?

"Our airpower did not fail us; it was the decision makers," asserted Admiral U. S. Grant Sharp, World War II veteran and commander in chief of the Pacific Command during the Vietnam War. Military officials welcomed President Johnson's order to begin bombing North Vietnam in February 1965 as a means to destroy the North's capacity and will to support the Communist insurgents in South Vietnam. But they chafed at Johnson's strategy of gradual escalation and the restrictions he imposed on Operation Rolling Thunder, the three-and-a-half-year bombing campaign. Military officials believed that the United States should have begun Operation Rolling Thunder with all-out massive bombing and continued until the devastation brought North Vietnam to its knees. Instead, they charged, civilian decision makers

compelled the military to fight with one hand tied behind its back. Their arguments echoed General Douglas MacArthur's criticism of Truman's policy during the Korean War—although these officials did not repeat MacArthur's insubordination.

Unlike military officials, who could single-mindedly focus on defeating the enemy, the president needed to balance military objectives against political considerations, and he found compelling reasons to limit the application of airpower. Recalling the Korean War, Johnson noted that "China is there on the [North Vietnamese] border with 700 million men," and he studiously avoided action that might provoke intervention by the Chinese, who now possessed nuclear weapons. Johnson's strategy also aimed to keep the Soviet Union out of the war, to contain antiwar sentiment at home, and to avert international criticism of the United States.

Consequently, the president forbade bombing of areas where high civilian casualties might result and areas near the Chinese border. He banned strikes on airfields and missile sites that were under construction and thus likely to contain Chinese or Soviet advisers, and he refused to mine North Vietnam's harbors, through which Soviet

ships brought goods to North Vietnam. But Johnson did escalate the pressure, increasing the intensity of the bombing fourfold by 1968. In all, Operation Rolling Thunder rained 643,000 tons of bombs on North Vietnam between 1965 and 1968.

Military leaders agreed with Johnson's desire to spare civilians. The Joint Chiefs of Staff never proposed, for example, strikes against a system of dikes and dams that could have disrupted food production and flooded Hanoi under twenty feet of water. Rather, they focused on destroying North Vietnam's industry and transportation system. Noncombatant casualties in North Vietnam contrasted sharply with those in World War II, when Anglo-American bombing of Dresden, Germany, alone took more than 35,000 civilian lives and the firebombing of Japan caused 330,000 civilian deaths. In three and a half years, Operation Rolling Thunder claimed an estimated 52,000 civilian lives.

North Vietnam's relatively low level of economic development and its government's ability to mobilize citizens counteracted the military superiority of the United States. Sheer human-power compensated for the demolition of transportation sources, industry sites, and electric power plants. When bombs struck a rail line, civilians rushed in with bicycles to unload a train's cargo, carry it beyond the break, and load it onto a second train. Three hundred thousand full-time workers and 200,000 farmers labored in their spare time to keep the Ho Chi Minh Trail usable in spite of heavy bombing. When bridges were destroyed, the North Vietnamese resorted to ferries and bamboo pontoons, and they rebuilt bridges slightly underwater to make them harder to detect from the air. They scattered oil storage facilities and production centers throughout the countryside, and when bombs knocked out electric power plants, the Vietnamese used portable generators and lit oil lamps and candles in their homes.

North Vietnam's military needs were relatively small, and officials found ample means to meet them. In 1967, North Vietnam had only about 55,000 soldiers in South Vietnam, and because they waged a guerrilla war with only sporadic fighting, the insurgents in the South did not require huge amounts of supplies. Even after Communist forces in the South increased, the total non-food needs of these soldiers were estimated at just one-fifth of what a single U.S. division required. What U.S. bombs destroyed, the North Vietnamese replaced with Chinese and Soviet imports. China provided 600,000 tons of rice in 1967 alone, and it supplied small arms and ammunition, vehicles, and other goods throughout the war. Competing with China for influence in North Vietnam and favor in the third world, the Soviets contributed tanks, fighter planes, surface-to-air missiles, and other sophisticated weapons. An estimated $2 billion of foreign aid

substantially curtailed the effect of Operation Rolling Thunder, and the Soviet-installed modern defense systems made the bombing more difficult and dangerous for U.S. pilots.

Short of decimating the civilian population, it is questionable whether more intense bombing could have completely halted North Vietnamese support for the Vietcong, given the nature of the North Vietnamese economy, the determination and ingenuity of the North Vietnamese people, and the plentiful assistance from China and the Soviet Union. Whether the strategic bombing that worked so well in a world war against major industrial powers could be effective in a third world guerrilla war remained in doubt after the Vietnam War.

The B-52 Bomber
After 1965, B-52 bombers constantly filled the skies over Vietnam, and at times over Laos and Cambodia. Designed originally to deliver nuclear bombs, a single B-52 carried thirty tons of explosives. A mission of six planes could destroy an area one-half mile wide by three miles long. The B-52 flew too high to be heard on the ground, but its bombs hit with such force that they could kill people in underground shelters.
Co Rentmeester, *Life* magazine / TimePix / Getty.

one." Soldiers in previous wars had served "for the duration," but each Vietnam warrior served a one-year tour of duty. A commander called it "the worst personnel policy in history," because men had less incentive to fight near the end of their tours, wanting merely to stay alive and whole. The U.S. military inflicted great losses on the enemy, yet the war remained a stalemate. As infantryman Tim O'Brien reported, "We slay one of them, hit a mine, kill another, hit another mine. . . . And each piece of ground left behind is his [the enemy's] from the moment we are gone on our next hunt."

The South Vietnamese government was an enormous obstacle to victory, even though in 1965 it settled into a period of stability led by Air Marshal Nguyen Cao Ky and General Nguyen Van Thieu. Graft and corruption continued to flourish, and Ky and Thieu failed to rally popular support. In the intensified fighting and inability to distinguish friend from foe, ARVN and American troops killed and wounded thousands of South Vietnamese civilians and destroyed their villages. By 1968, five million people, nearly 30 percent of the population, had become refugees. Huge infusions of American dollars and goods to the South Vietnamese government produced prostitution and rampant inflation, hurt local industries, and increased dependence on foreign aid. The failure to stabilize South Vietnam even as the U.S. military presence expanded enormously created grave challenges for the administration at home.

> **REVIEW** How did American troops serving in Vietnam differ from those who served in World War II, and how were their experiences different?

Chemical Weapons
The U.S. military began to use the tear gas CS (o-chlorobenzylidenemalononitrile) in grenades in Vietnam in 1964 and was discharging more than two million pounds of CS a year by 1969. It was used in operations such as the one shown here. The marine has just thrown a CS gas grenade into a tunnel to flush out the enemy and make the tunnel unusable for several months. Military planes also dropped or sprayed CS from the air to rid large areas of land of enemy forces. CS is usually not lethal but has incapacitating effects. Nonetheless, its use evoked criticism both at home and abroad. The *New York Times* noted that "no other country has employed such a weapon in recent warfare." The Political Committee of the UN General Assembly maintained that generally recognized rules of warfare prohibited the use of any chemical agents.
Marine: James H. Pickerell/Stock Connection; Gas: Ordinance Museum/Aberdeen Proving Grounds.

A Nation Polarized

Soon President Johnson was fighting a war on two fronts. Domestic opposition to the war in Southeast Asia grew significantly after 1965 as daily television broadcasts of the carnage of Vietnam made it the first "living-room war." In March 1968, torn between his domestic critics and the military's clamor for more troops, Johnson announced restrictions on the bombing, a new effort at negotiations, and his decision not to pursue reelection. Throughout 1968, demonstrations, violence, and assassinations convulsed the nation. Vietnam took center stage in the election, and voters narrowly favored the Republican candidate, former vice president Richard Nixon, who promised to achieve "peace with honor."

The Widening War at Home

Johnson's authorization of Operation Rolling Thunder swelled the previously quiet doubts and criticism into a mass movement against the war. In April 1965, Students for a Democratic Society (SDS) recruited 20,000 people for a demonstration in Washington, D.C., and SDS chapters sprang up on more than 300 college campuses. Thousands of students joined campus protests against Reserve Officers Training Corps (ROTC) programs, CIA recruiters, manufacturers of war materials, and university research for the Department of Defense. Martin Luther King Jr. deployed his moral authority against the war, rebuking the U.S. government in 1967 as "the greatest purveyor of violence in the world today" and calling opposition to the war "the privilege and burden of all of us who deem ourselves bound by allegiances and loyalties which are broader and deeper than nationalism." Environmentalists attacked the use of chemical weapons, such as the deadly dioxin-product Agent Orange, which the military used to destroy foliage where the enemy might hide. A new draft policy in 1967 ended deferments for postgraduate education and upped male students' stake in ending the war. In the spring of 1968, as many as one million college and high school students participated in a nationwide strike.

Antiwar sentiment also entered society's mainstream. The *New York Times* began questioning administration policy in 1965, and by 1968 media critics included the *Wall Street Journal, Life* magazine, and popular TV anchorman Walter Cronkite. Clergy, business people, scientists, and physicians formed their own groups to pressure Johnson to stop the bombing and start negotiations. An increasing number of prominent Democratic senators, including J. William Fulbright, George McGovern, and majority leader Mike Mansfield, urged Johnson to substitute negotiation for force. Fulbright's book *The Arrogance of Power* warned against the "tendency of great nations to equate power with virtue" and urged American leaders not to think of the country as "God's chosen savior of mankind."

Opposition to the war took diverse forms: letter-writing campaigns to officials, teach-ins on college campuses, mass marches, student strikes, withholding of federal taxes, draft card and flag burnings, **civil disobedience** against military centers and producers of war materials, and attempts to stop trains carrying troops. Although the peace movement never claimed a majority of the population, it focused media attention on the war and severely limited the administration's options. The twenty-year-old consensus around cold war foreign policy had broken down.

Many would not fight in the war. The World Boxing Association stripped Muhammad Ali of his world heavyweight title when he refused to serve in what he called a "white man's war." More than 170,000 men who opposed the war on moral or religious grounds gained conscientious objector status and performed nonmilitary duties at home or in Vietnam. About 60,000 fled the country to escape the draft, and more than 200,000 were accused of failing to register or of committing other draft offenses.

Mothers against the War
Women played an active role in the opposition to the Vietnam War—and not just college students or radicals. In 1961, years before Vietnam became an issue, Women Strike for Peace (WSP) was founded to work for nuclear disarmament. Identifying themselves as "concerned housewives" and mothers, an estimated 50,000 women throughout the country staged a one-day protest, calling on President Kennedy to "end the arms race—not the human race." As early as 1963, WSP began to "alert the public to the dangers and horrors of the war in Vietnam," and throughout the war, it played a vigorous role in the antiwar movement, mobilizing around the slogan "Not Our Sons, Not Your Sons, Not Their Sons." In February 1967, WSP became the first group to take an antiwar protest to the Pentagon. The women in this photograph were among more than 2,000 women who gathered at the Pentagon, using their shoes to bang on the doors, which were locked as they approached. What characteristics of the war did these women focus on? In what ways were their objections to the war similar to and different from those of other protesters?
© Bettmann/Corbis.

When he got his induction notice in 1968, Tim O'Brien agonized over what to do. He opposed the war, but avoiding the draft would subject his family to criticism and embarrassment in his small Minnesota town, where young men were expected to serve their country. In addition, he said, "I owed the prairie something. For twenty-

The Military Helicopter

Reflecting on how the Vietnam War would have been fought without helicopters, General William C. Westmoreland concluded, "We would have been fighting a different war, for a smaller area, at a greater cost, with less effectiveness." Waging war in Vietnam without helicopters, he maintained, would have been like fighting Hitler's army in Europe without tanks.

It took more than three decades after the first successful airplane flight in 1903 for engineers to develop an aircraft that could take off and land vertically, move in any direction, and remain stationary in the air. The man frequently identified as the inventor of the helicopter in the United States, Russian engineer Igor Sikorsky, developed two helicopters in 1909 and 1910, but neither succeeded. After the Russian Revolution of 1917, Sikorsky immigrated to the United States and organized a company that produced airplanes while he continued to work on the helicopter. German engineers produced the first practical helicopter in 1936, but the United States was not far behind.

As was true of much new technology in the twentieth century, the federal government supported research and development. Congress first appropriated funds to develop the helicopter in 1938, and Sikorsky and his associates produced the first helicopter for the Army Air Corps in 1942. During World War II, the United States used helicopters for some rescue operations in the Pacific theater, and Germany used them for artillery spotting and reconnaissance. The U.S. military employed helicopters for medical evacuations in Korea, but not until manufacturers replaced piston engines with smaller, lighter gas-turbine engines did helicopters play a central role in military operations.

Although the army developed its plans for the use of helicopters in the 1950s within the context of nuclear war, once the United States began to assist the South Vietnamese in military operations, the helicopter became a central feature of the war. The particular nature of the conflict in Vietnam—the guerrilla tactics of the enemy, the conduct of fighting all over South Vietnam rather than across a fixed battlefront, and the mountains and dense jungles, with limited landing areas—put a premium on the helicopter's mobility and maneuverability. Already in December 1961, long before U.S. troops actually saw combat in Vietnam, the army used thirty-two of its helicopters to transfer some 1,000 South Vietnamese paratroopers for an attack on suspected Vietcong headquarters. To U.S. army captain Colin Powell, serving as an adviser to a South Vietnamese army battalion in a remote spot near the Laotian border in 1962, the helicopter "became my closest link to the world I had left." A U.S. marine pilot flew in a helicopter every two weeks, and at those times, Powell remembered, "my anticipation was almost sexual. This flier brought my latest batch of paperbacks, my carton of Salems, and my mail."

The UH-1 Iroquois (known as the "Huey") was the most widely used helicopter; thousands of them carried infantry units all over South Vietnam. One marine commented that "we commuted to and from the war," although it was hardly an ordinary commute when helicopters had to land in the midst of enemy fire. Choppers also transported artillery and ammunition, performed reconnaissance, picked up downed pilots, and evacuated the dead and wounded. Mounted with machine guns and grenade launchers, heli-

one years I'd lived under its laws, accepted its education . . . wallowed in its luxuries, played on its Little League teams." In the end, he could not bring himself to desert his country. Although he held to his belief that "the war was wrong," O'Brien went to Vietnam with the army.

Opponents of the war held far from unanimous views. Those who saw the conflict in moral terms wanted total withdrawal, insisting that their country had no right to interfere in a civil war in another country and stressing the suffering of the Vietnamese people. A larger segment of antiwar sentiment reflected practical considerations—the belief that the war could not be won at a bearable cost. Not demanding total withdrawal, those activists wanted Johnson to stop bombing North Vietnam and seek negotiations.

Working-class people were no more antiwar than other groups, but they recognized the class dimensions of the war and the public opposition to it. A firefighter whose son had died in Vietnam said bitterly, "It's people like us who give up our sons for the country. The businesspeople, they run the country and make money from it.

Helicopters in Vietnam
Men of the First Squadron, Ninth Cavalry, First Cavalry Division leap from a Bell UH-1 Iroquois helicopter near Chu Lai, South Vietnam, during Operation Oregon in 1967 as they begin a reconnaissance mission.
© Bettmann/Corbis.

central were helicopters to a soldier's experience that, one noted, "when the helicopters flew off, a feeling of abandonment came over us."

Journalists hitched rides on helicopters "like taxis" to see the war firsthand. Michael Herr, who wrote for *Esquire* and other magazines, flew on hundreds of them. He remembered "choppers rising straight out of small cleared jungle spaces, wobbling down onto city rooftops, cartons of rations and ammunition thrown off, dead and wounded loaded on. Sometimes they were so plentiful and loose that you could touch down at five or six places a day."

The massive use of helicopters, of course, failed to defeat the enemy in Vietnam. Although air mobility played a key role in the successes of the U.S. and South Vietnamese armies, it alone could not win the war. In the words of one military adviser, "After all, when you come to think of it, the use of helicopters is a tacit admission that we don't control the ground. And in the long run, it's control of the ground that wins or loses the war." Helicopters remained important to the very end of the U.S. presence in Vietnam. As Saigon fell to the Communists in 1975, choppers carried the remaining Americans and some of their South Vietnamese allies out of danger.

copters served as attack vehicles. The largest, the CH-47 ("Chinook"), could carry thirty-three soldiers or considerable amounts of cargo and even rescue smaller downed aircraft. Chinooks also dropped two and a half tons of napalm on the enemy in just one delivery.

Helicopters enabled military personnel to receive unprecedented support. In Vietnam, it was not unusual for American soldiers in the field to be provided with hot meals rather than cold C rations. More important was the medical evacuation helicopter, called the "Dust-off," which could hoist injured soldiers to safety without touching land. Most of those wounded in Vietnam were promptly evacuated to hospitals, and those with grave injuries were sped to base facilities in the Pacific region or the United States. These improvements in medical evacuation, combined with advances in medicine, helped raise the ratio of surviving wounded to dead to 6:1, in contrast to a World War II ratio of 2.6:1. So

The college types . . . go to Washington and tell the government what to do. . . . But their sons don't end up in the swamps over there, in Vietnam."

The antiwar movement outraged millions of Americans who supported the war. Some members of the generation who had fought against Hitler could not understand younger men's refusal to support their government. "How can Americans take sides against their own young men sent to Vietnam to fight and perhaps to die?" asked supporters of government policy. They expressed their anger at war protesters with bumper stickers that read "America: Love It or Leave It."

By 1967, the administration realized that "discontent with the war is now wide and deep," as McGeorge Bundy put it. Recognizing public opinion as a critical weapon in the war effort, President Johnson used various means to silence critics. He equated opposition to the war with communism and assistance to the enemy. To avoid focusing attention on the war's costs, he eschewed price and wage controls to control inflation and delayed asking for a tax increase to pay for the war. Not until June 1968 did Congress pass a 10 percent income tax surcharge, after Johnson promised to cut domestic spending.

The Tet Attack on the U.S. Embassy
Launched by the North Vietnamese in January 1968, the Tet Offensive took the war to major cities for the first time, breaching even the U.S. Embassy in Saigon, where they killed two American soldiers and held the compound for six hours. Here U.S. ambassador Ellsworth Bunker, with reporters and military police, inspects damage after the attack, including two enemy bodies.
Dick Swanson/Time Life Pictures/Getty Images.

Great Society programs suffered, but the surcharge failed to reverse the inflationary surge.

The administration also deceived the public by making optimistic statements about the war's progress and concealing ever-graver doubts within the administration about the possibility of success in Vietnam. Johnson tried to discredit war critics, calling them "Nervous Nellies" or Communists, and he ordered the CIA to spy on peace advocates, resulting in CIA files on more than 7,000 citizens. Without the president's specific authorization, the FBI infiltrated the peace movement, disrupted its work, and spread false information about activists. Even the resort to illegal measures failed to subdue the opposition.

1968: Year of Upheaval

The year 1968 was a year of violent confrontations around the world. Protests against governments erupted from Mexico City to Paris to Tokyo, usually led by students in collaboration with workers. (See "Beyond America's Borders," page 1084.) American society also became increasingly po-

larized. On one side were the so-called **hawks**, who charged that the United States was fighting with one hand tied behind its back and called for intensification of the war. The **doves** wanted de-escalation or withdrawal. As U.S. troop strength neared half a million and military deaths approached 20,000 by the end of 1967, most people were torn between weariness with the war and worry about reneging on the Americans' commitment. As one woman said to a pollster, "I want to get out but I don't want to give up."

Grave doubts penetrated the administration itself in 1967. Secretary of Defense Robert McNamara, a principal architect of U.S. involvement, now believed that the North Vietnamese "won't quit no matter how much bombing we do." And he feared for the image of the United States, "the world's greatest superpower, killing or seriously injuring 1,000 noncombatants a week, while trying to pound a tiny, backward nation into submission on an issue whose merits are hotly disputed." McNamara did not publicly oppose the war, but in early 1968 he left the administration.

A critical turning point came with the Tet Offensive, which began on January 30, 1968. Just a few weeks after General Westmoreland reported that "the enemy has been driven away from the population centers [and] compelled to disperse," the North Vietnamese and Vietcong attacked key cities and every major American base in South Vietnam. This was the biggest surprise of the war, and not simply because both sides had customarily observed a truce during the Vietnamese New Year holiday (called Tet). The offensive displayed the Communists' vitality and refusal to be intimidated by the presence of half a million American soldiers. Militarily, the enemy suffered a defeat, losing more than 30,000 men, ten times as many as ARVN and U.S. forces. Psychologically, however, Tet was devastating to the United States.

African American Antiwar Protest

The first expression of African American opposition to the war in Vietnam occurred in Mississippi in July 1965 when a group of civil rights workers called for draft resistance. Blacks should not fight for freedom in Vietnam "until all the Negro People are free in Mississippi," the activists said, and they should not risk their lives "and kill other Colored People in Santo Domingo and Viet Nam." This protester on the West Coast expresses similar sentiments in April 1967.

Joe Flowers/Black Star/Stockphoto.com.

The Tet Offensive underscored the credibility gap between official statements and the war's actual progress. TV anchorman Walter Cronkite wondered, "What the hell is going on? I thought we were winning the war." The attacks created a million more South Vietnamese refugees as well as widespread destruction. Explaining how he had defended a village, a U.S. army official said, "We had to destroy the town to save it." The statement epitomized for more and more Americans the brutality and senselessness of the war. Public approval of Johnson's handling of it dropped to 26 percent.

In the aftermath of Tet, Johnson considered a request from Westmoreland for 200,000 more troops. He conferred with advisers in the Defense Department and an unofficial group of foreign policy experts who had been key architects of cold war policies for two decades. Dean Acheson, Truman's secretary of state, summarized their conclusion: "We can no longer do the job we set out to do in the time we have left and we must begin to take steps to disengage."

On March 31, 1968, Lyndon Johnson announced in a televised speech that the United States would reduce its bombing of North Vietnam and that he was prepared to begin peace talks. Then he made the stunning declaration that he would not run for reelection. The gradual escalation of the war was over, and military strategy shifted from "Americanization" to "Vietnamization" of the war. But this was not a shift in policy. The goal remained a non-Communist South Vietnam; the United States would simply rely more heavily on the South Vietnamese to achieve it.

Negotiations began in Paris in May 1968. The United States would not agree to recognition of the Hanoi government's National Liberation Front, to a coalition government, or to American withdrawal. The North Vietnamese would agree to nothing less. Although the talks continued, so did the fighting.

Meanwhile, violence escalated at home. Some two hundred protests on college campuses occurred in the spring of 1968. In the bloodiest action, students occupied buildings at Columbia University in New York City, with demands related to the university's war-related research and to its treatment of African Americans. (See chapter 28, "Documenting the American Promise," page 1044.) When negotiations failed, university officials called in the city police, who cleared the buildings, injuring scores of demonstrators and arresting more than seven hundred. An ensuing student strike prematurely ended the academic year.

1968: A Year of Protest

To many people living through it, 1968 looked like the start of a worldwide political revolution. Sporadic and largely unrelated protests occurring in a few European and U.S. cities in 1967 took on an urgency the following year, sparked by growing dismay over the U.S. war in Vietnam. A surge of enthusiasm for greater democracy jumped over borders and challenged authorities in many countries around the world. Such global chain-reaction moments are rare. The democratic revolutions on both sides of the Atlantic in the late eighteenth century offer one example. The failed multiple revolutions of 1848 prompted by food shortages and unemployment across Europe are another. Although local grievances ignited many of the protests in 1968, a common and defining feature of them all was the central role played by university students.

In nearly every country affected, accelerated birthrates following World War II and a vast expansion of higher education in the 1960s had created an unprecedented group of young people free of family or job obligations. Campuses provided both the loci for political organizing and the initial grievances that made students ripe for activism.

A key catalyst for the transnational protests of 1968 was the Vietnam War. As the conflict entered its fourth year, half a million U.S. troops occupied the country; 20,000 American soldiers had died, as well as five to ten times as many Vietnamese soldiers and civilians. Angered by the war and hungry for reform in their own countries, youths around the world took

inspiration from the Tet Offensive of late January 1968, when North Vietnam's National Liberation Front gained the upper hand in the war. Superpower states were not invincible; they could be challenged, the protesters reasoned.

The protests of 1968 unfolded with rapidity, giving rise to excitement and apprehension. From February to December, demonstrations swept through the United States, West Germany, France, Czechoslovakia, Mexico, Japan, Britain, Poland, Italy, Spain, Yugoslavia, Pakistan, Northern Ireland, Brazil, and China. Many demonstrators expressed transnational solidarity by carrying the flag of the National Liberation Front or placards bearing the image of Ernesto "Che" Guevara, a Latin American radical killed by the Bolivian military in 1967. In Europe, students connected under the rallying cry, "We Shall Fight, We Will Win—Paris London Rome Berlin." And yet there was in fact little international coordination of events or any shared plan for remaking the world among the radicals.

One of the first large-scale protests occurred in February at West Berlin's Free University, where student leaders sponsored the Vietnam Congress calling for "an international manifestation of solidarity" with the people of Vietnam. The event drew 10,000 participants from ten countries. Protests continued throughout the spring, prompting the West German government to pass emergency laws to stifle disorder. In February and March, demonstrations flared up in Madrid, Warsaw, Rome, São Paulo, and London, met by police with clubs and at least one death (in Brazil). As

with the protesters, police also took their cues from worldwide events, reacting more forcefully and quickly to demonstrations in light of commotions in other countries. Charges of police brutality, disseminated in television and newspaper reports, fed the cycle of protest further.

In April and May, violence erupted in the United States. Martin Luther King Jr.'s assassination on April 4 ignited riots in many U.S. cities. Less than a month later, students at Columbia University in New York seized buildings and shut down the campus, leading to a bloody showdown between police and protesters.

In May, rebellion paralyzed France. The initial provocation occurred at a university north of Paris when students complained about student services. Disturbances then spread to the Sorbonne in the capital city. Police teargassed a small rally, only to face tens of thousands of students streaming into Paris over the next few days. Violence escalated as protesters barricaded streets on the Left Bank. Independent radio stations broadcast live interviews with demonstrators, bypassing the official radio news, and soon a million people were in the streets. Workers joined the rebellion, shutting down factories across France. Students proclaimed that "exceptional domestic and international conditions" had brought powerless students and workers together around the world. By late May, France was in deep crisis. Banks, railroads, and shipyards had shut down, and a promise of generous wage hikes had done nothing to end the nationwide strike. President Charles de Gaulle attempted to gain control by calling up French troops, scheduling a general election in late June, criminalizing demonstrations, and evicting striking workers from factories.

Czech Students Greet the Soviets
In August 1968, Soviet soldiers arriving in Prague to suppress rebellion were met by crowds of youths. Here students waving the Czechoslovak flag stand on a toppled Volkswagen van while others surround the Soviet tank.
© Bettmann/Corbis.

Prague, the capital of Communist Czechoslovakia, was also stirring in May. A liberal president, Alexander Dubček, pushed for reforms against heavy-handed Soviet control, giving rise to hopes for greater freedom. Students demonstrated; manifestos were signed by thousands. But this "Prague Spring" was cut short in August when Soviet tanks rumbled into the country and Dubček was arrested. When some 5,000 students staged a sit-down strike in Prague to protest, Soviet authorities exercised restraint to avoid a bloody confrontation. Throughout Europe, students marched on Soviet embassies to protest the crackdown. At the same moment in the United States, television brought riots between youth protesters and Chicago police outside the Democratic National Convention into American living rooms.

A government backlash against protests in Mexico began in earnest in July, when marchers carrying posters of Fidel Castro and Che Guevara were attacked by police with clubs. When thousands rallied to protest the violence, police fired into the crowd, killing several students. A key complaint of the protesters was the cost to host the upcoming Olympic Games. Protesters believed that the money should have been used to alleviate the country's widespread poverty. The games, slated for October in Mexico City, created pressure for the authorities to clear the city of dissidents. August and September brought increasingly violent clashes. One frequent chant was, "We don't want Olympic Games; we want revolution." On October 2, some 10,000 students assembled for a rally in the Plaza de las Tres Culturas. After dark, jeeps with machine guns arrived. At least 100 to 200 protesters were killed, and another several hundred were wounded. The Olympic Games went on as scheduled ten days later.

In the wake of the massacre, protesters staged demonstrations and attacks on Mexican embassies in Chile, Nicaragua, the Netherlands, Italy, France, and Britain. By December, more episodes of violence against protesters occurred in Spain, Pakistan, and Northern Ireland. In the United States, violence diminished generally, but not in urban ghettos, where the Black Panther Party was gaining strength.

By year's end, a kind of stunned exhaustion set in. The Prague Spring had been shut down by the Soviets, the student-led protests in France and Germany had reached a stalemate, and Republican Richard Nixon had won the U.S. presidential election with promises to maintain law and order at home and to end the war in Vietnam, the latter a political concession driven by the year of protests. The year of global protest ended with despair and fear on all sides. Student protest did not disappear in 1969, but the excitement of worldwide revolutionary solidarity was blunted by the very real threat of fatal consequences faced by protesters.

In June, two months after the murder of Martin Luther King Jr. and the riots that followed, another assassination shook the nation. Senator Robert F. Kennedy, campaigning in California for the Democratic Party's presidential nomination, was shot by a Palestinian Arab refugee who was outraged by Kennedy's support for Israel.

In August, protesters battled the police in Chicago, where the Democratic Party had convened to nominate its presidential ticket. Several thousand demonstrators came to the city, some to support the peace candidate Senator Eugene McCarthy, others to act more aggressively. Many of the latter had been mobilized by the Youth International Party (Yippies), a splinter group of SDS. Its leaders, Abbie Hoffman and Jerry Rubin, urged protesters to demonstrate their hatred of the establishment by provoking the police and creating chaos. They expressed their disdain

for the Democratic Party and liberal politics by bringing a live pig as their candidate.

Chicago's Democratic mayor Richard J. Daley issued a ban on rallies and marches, ordered a curfew, and mobilized thousands of police. On August 25, demonstrators responded to police orders to disperse with insults and jeers, whereupon police attacked protesters with tear gas and clubs. Street battles continued for three days, culminating in a police riot on the night of August 28. Taunted by the crowd, the police used mace and nightsticks, clubbing not only those who had come to provoke violence but also reporters, peaceful demonstrators, and convention delegates.

Although the bloodshed in Chicago horrified those who saw it on television, it had little effect on the outcome of either major party's convention. An assassin had ended Robert Kennedy's promising campaign in June, and Vice President Hubert H. Humphrey trounced the remaining antiwar candidate, Eugene McCarthy, by nearly three to one for the Democratic nomination. McCarthy's refusal to share the podium with Humphrey as the convention ended underscored the bitter split within the party. In contrast, the Republican convention nominated former vice president Richard Nixon on the first ballot. For his running mate, Nixon chose Maryland governor Spiro T. Agnew, hoping to gather southern support.

For the first time in nearly fifty years, a strong third party also entered the electoral scene. Former Alabama governor George C. Wallace, a staunch segregationist, ran on the ticket of the American Independent Party. Wallace appealed to Americans nationwide who were disenchanted with the reforms and rebellions of the 1960s and outraged by assaults on traditional values. Nixon guardedly played on resentments that fueled the Wallace campaign, calling for "law and order" and attacking liberal Supreme Court decisions, busing for school desegregation, and protesters of all sorts.

The two major-party candidates differed little on the central issue of Vietnam. Nixon promised to "bring an honorable end" to the war but did not indicate how he would do it. Humphrey had strong reservations about U.S. policy in Vietnam, yet as vice president he wanted to avoid a break with Johnson. The president boosted Humphrey's campaign at the end of October when he announced a halt to the bombing of North Vietnam, but it was not

Protest in Chicago

The worst violence surrounding the 1968 Democratic National Convention in Chicago came on August 28 when protesters decided to assemble in Grant Park and march to the convention site. Near the Hilton Hotel, where most of the delegates stayed, some 3,000 protesters came up against a line of police. The police attacked not only the demonstrators but also reporters, hotel guests, and bystanders with nightsticks and mace, driving a crowd through the plate-glass window of the hotel and injuring hundreds. Here a policeman sprays Mace on the crowd.

AP Images/Michael Boyer.

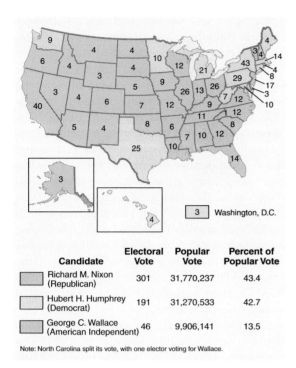

Candidate	Electoral Vote	Popular Vote	Percent of Popular Vote
Richard M. Nixon (Republican)	301	31,770,237	43.4
Hubert H. Humphrey (Democrat)	191	31,270,533	42.7
George C. Wallace (American Independent)	46	9,906,141	13.5

Note: North Carolina split its vote, with one elector voting for Wallace.

MAP 29.3 The Election of 1968

enough. With nearly ten million votes (13 percent of the total), the American Independent Party produced the strongest third-party finish since 1924. Nixon edged out Humphrey by just half a million popular votes but garnered 301 electoral college votes to Humphrey's 191 and Wallace's 46 (Map 29.3). The Democrats lost a few seats in Congress but kept control of both houses.

The 1968 election revealed deep cracks in the coalition that had kept the Democrats in power for most of the previous thirty years. Johnson's liberal policies on race shattered a century of Democratic Party dominance in the South, which delivered all its electoral votes to Wallace or Nixon. Elsewhere, large numbers of blue-collar workers broke union ranks to vote for Wallace or Nixon, along with other groups that associated the Democrats with racial turmoil, poverty programs, inflation, changing sexual mores, and failure to turn the tide in Vietnam. These resentments would soon be mobilized into a resurging right in American politics (see chapter 30).

> **REVIEW** How did the Vietnam War shape the election of 1968?

Nixon, Détente, and the Search for Peace in Vietnam

Nixon assumed the presidency with ambitious foreign policy goals, hoping to make his mark on history by applying his broad understanding of international relations to a changing world. Diverging from Republican orthodoxy, his dramatic overtures to the Soviet Union and China reduced decades-old hostilities. Yet anticommunism remained central to U.S. policy. In Latin America, Africa, and the Middle East, Nixon backed repressive regimes when the alternatives suggested victories for the left. Relying on public deception, secrecy, and silencing of opponents even more than his predecessor, Nixon aggressively pursued the war in Vietnam, expanding the conflict into Cambodia and Laos and ferociously bombing North Vietnam. Yet in the end, he was forced to settle for peace without victory.

Moving toward Détente with the Soviet Union and China

In Nixon's view, the "rigid and bipolar world of the 1940s and 1950s" was giving way to "the fluidity of a new era of multilateral diplomacy." Well aware of the increasing conflict between the Soviet Union and China that escalated into military skirmishes along their common border in 1969, he worked with National Security Adviser Henry A. Kissinger, his key foreign policy adviser, to exploit the situation. Nixon and Kissinger believed that if these two nations checked each other's power, their threat to the United States would lessen. According to Nixon, Soviet-Chinese hostility "served our purpose best if we maintained closer relations with each side than they did with each other." In addition, these two nations might be used to help the United States extricate itself from Vietnam.

> According to Nixon, Soviet-Chinese hostility "served our purpose best if we maintained closer relations with each side than they did with each other."

Following two years of secret negotiations, in February 1972 Nixon became the nation's first president to set foot on Chinese soil—an astonishing act by a man who had climbed the political ladder as a fervent anti-Communist. Recognizing that his anti-Communist credentials were what enabled him to conduct this shift in U.S.-Chinese relations with no significant domestic repercussions, Nixon remarked to Chinese leader Mao Zedong, "Those on the right can do what those on the left only talk about." Although the act was largely symbolic, cultural and scientific exchanges followed, and American manufacturers began to find markets in China—small steps in the process of **globalization** that would take giant strides in the 1990s (see chapter 31).

As Nixon and Kissinger had hoped, the warming of U.S.-Chinese relations increased Soviet responsiveness to their strategy of **détente**, their term for easing conflict with the Soviet Union. Détente meant not abandoning containment but instead focusing on issues of common concern, such as arms control and trade. Containment would be achieved not only by military threat but also by ensuring that Soviet and Chinese stakes in a stable international order would restrain the leaders of those countries from precipitating crises. Nixon's goal was "a stronger healthy United States, Europe, Soviet Union, China, Japan, each balancing the other."

Arms control, trade, and stability in Europe were three areas where the United States and the Soviet Union had common interests. In May 1972, three months after his return from China, Nixon visited Moscow, signing several agreements on trade and cooperation in science and space. Most significantly, Soviet and U.S. leaders concluded arms limitation treaties that had grown out of the Strategic Arms Limitation Talks (SALT) begun in 1969. Both sides agreed to limit antiballistic missiles (ABMs) to two each. Giving up pursuit of a defense against nuclear weapons was a move of crucial importance, because it prevented either nation from building so secure an ABM defense against a nuclear attack that it would risk a first strike.

Gerald Ford, who became president when Nixon resigned in 1974 (see chapter 30), failed to sustain détente. The secrecy of the Nixon-Kissinger initiatives had alienated legislators, and some Democrats charged that détente ignored Soviet violations of human rights. Members of both parties worried that Soviet strength was overtaking that of the United States. In response, Congress derailed trade agreements with the Soviet Union, refusing economic favors unless the Soviets stopped their harsh treatment of internal dissidents and Jews.

Nonetheless, U.S., Soviet, and European leaders signed a historic agreement in 1975 in Helsinki, Finland, formally recognizing the post–World War II boundaries in Europe. Members of both major American political parties objected to the Helsinki accords because they acknowledged Soviet domination over Eastern Europe—a condition that had triggered the cold war thirty years earlier. To get Western consent to the accords, the Soviets had to accept a clause stating that the signing countries recognized "the universal significance of human rights and fundamental freedoms." Dissidents in the Soviet Union and its Eastern European satellites soon used this official promise of rights to mount challenges to the Soviet dictatorship that would culminate in its overthrow fifteen years later.

Shoring Up Anticommunism in the Third World

Nixon promised in 1973, "The time has passed when America will make every other nation's conflict our own . . . or presume to tell the

Nixon in China

"This was the week that changed the world," proclaimed President Nixon in February 1972, emphasizing the stunning turnaround in relations with America's former enemy, the People's Republic of China. Nixon's trip was meticulously planned to dramatize the event on television and, aside from criticism from some conservatives, won overwhelming support from Americans. The Great Wall of China forms the setting for this photograph of Nixon and his wife, Pat.

Nixon Presidential Materials Project, National Archives and Record Administration.

people of other nations how to manage their own affairs." Yet in Vietnam and elsewhere, Nixon and Kissinger continued to equate Marxism with a threat to U.S. interests and actively resisted social revolutions that might lead to communism.

Consequently, the Nixon administration helped to overthrow Salvador Allende, a self-proclaimed Marxist who was elected president of Chile in 1970. Since 1964, the Central Intelligence Agency (CIA) and U.S. corporations concerned about nationalization of their Chilean properties had assisted Allende's opponents. After Allende became president, Nixon ordered the CIA director to make the Chilean economy "scream" and thus destabilize his government. In 1973, with the help of the CIA, the Chilean military engineered a coup, killed Allende, and established a brutal dictatorship under General Augusto Pinochet, ending decades of democracy in Chile. Representative government was re-established in 1990, and in 2006 a Chilean court charged Pinochet with torture, kidnapping, and murder.

In other parts of the world, too, the Nixon administration stood by repressive regimes. In southern Africa, it eased pressures on white minority governments that tyrannized blacks. The National Security Council assumed that the "whites are here to stay. . . . There is no hope for the blacks to gain the political rights they seek through violence, which will lead only to chaos and increased opportunities for Communists." In the Middle East, the United States sent secret, massive arms shipments to support the shah of Iran's harsh regime because Iran had enormous petroleum

Chile

Israeli Territorial Gains in the Six-Day War, 1967

reserves and seemed a stable anti-Communist ally. Unnoticed by most Americans, the administration cemented a relationship that turned many Iranians against the United States and would ignite a new crisis when the shah was overthrown in 1979 (see chapter 30).

Like his predecessors, Nixon pursued a delicate balance between defending Israel's security and seeking the goodwill of Arab nations strategically and economically important to the United States. Conflict between Israel and the Arab nations had escalated into the Six-Day War in 1967, when Israel attacked Egypt after that nation had massed troops on its border and cut off the sea passage to Israel's southern port. Although Syria and Jordan joined the war on Egypt's side, Israel won a stunning victory, seizing territory that amounted to twice its original size. Israeli forces took control of the Sinai Peninsula and Gaza Strip from Egypt, the Golan Heights from Syria, and the West Bank (which included the Arab sector of Jerusalem, a city sacred to Jews, Christians, and Muslims alike) from Jordan.

That decisive victory did not quell Middle Eastern turmoil. In October 1973, on the Jewish holiday Yom Kippur, Egypt and Syria surprised Israel with a full-scale attack. When the Nixon administration sided with Israel in the Yom Kippur War, Arab nations retaliated with an oil embargo that created severe shortages in the United States. After Israel repulsed the attack, Kissinger attempted to mediate between Israel and the Arab nations, efforts that continued for more than three decades with only limited success. The Arab countries refused to recognize Israel's right to exist, Israel began to settle its citizens in territories occupied during the Six-Day War, and no solution could be found for the Palestinian refugees who had been displaced by the creation of Israel in the late 1940s. The simmering conflict contributed to anti-American sentiment among Arabs who viewed the United States as Israel's supporter.

Vietnam Becomes Nixon's War

"I'm not going to end up like LBJ, holed up in the White House afraid to show my face on the street," the new president asserted. "I'm going to stop that war. Fast." Nixon gradually withdrew U.S. ground troops, but he was no more willing than Eisenhower, Kennedy, or Johnson to be the president who allowed South Vietnam to fall to the Communists. To Nixon and Kissinger, that

Pro-War Demonstrators

Advocates as well as opponents of the war in Vietnam took to the streets, as these New Yorkers did in support of the U.S. invasion of Cambodia in May 1970. Construction workers—called "hard hats"—and other union members marched with American flags and posters championing President Nixon's policies and blasting New York mayor John Lindsay for his antiwar position. Following the demonstration, sympathetic union leaders presented Nixon with an honorary hard hat. Paul Fusco/Magnum Photos, Inc.

READING THE IMAGE: What do the hard hats in the photograph symbolize in terms of identity and politics?
CONNECTIONS: What, if anything, was the relationship between President Nixon being presented with a hard hat after a pro-war demonstration and the unraveling of the Democratic Party coalition?

FOR MORE HELP ANALYZING THIS IMAGE, see the visual activity for this chapter in the Online Study Guide at bedfordstmartins.com/roark.

goal was tied to the larger objective of maintaining American credibility. Regardless of the wisdom of the initial intervention, Kissinger asserted, "the commitment of 500,000 Americans has settled the importance of Vietnam. For what is involved now is confidence in American promises."

From 1969 to 1972, Nixon and Kissinger pursued a four-pronged approach. First, they tried to strengthen the South Vietnamese military and government. Second, to disarm the antiwar movement at home, Nixon gradually replaced U.S. forces with South Vietnamese soldiers and American technology and bombs. Third, Nixon and Kissinger negotiated with both North Vietnam and the Soviet Union. Fourth, the military applied intensive bombing to persuade Hanoi to accept American terms at the bargaining table.

As part of the Vietnamization of the war, ARVN forces grew to more than a million, and the South Vietnamese air force became the fourth largest in the world. U.S. advisers and funds also promoted land reform, village elections, and the building of schools, hospitals, and transportation facilities. Meanwhile, U.S. forces withdrew, decreasing from 543,000 in 1968 to 140,000 by the end of 1971, a move that critics called merely "changing the color of the corpses." Despite reduced draft calls and a decrease in the number of American deaths from nearly 800 a month in 1969 to 352 in 1970, more than 20,000 Americans perished in Vietnam during the last four years of the war.

In the spring of 1969, Nixon began a ferocious air war in Cambodia, carefully hiding it from Congress and the public for more than a year. Seeking to knock out North Vietnamese sanctuaries in Cambodia, Americans dropped more than 100,000 tons of bombs but succeeded only in sending the North Vietnamese to other hiding places. Echoing Johnson, Kissinger believed that a "fourth-rate power like North Vietnam" had to have a "breaking point," but the hundreds of thousands of tons of bombs delivered by U.S. pilots failed to find it. (See "Historical Question," page 1076.)

To support a new, pro-Western Cambodian government installed through a military coup in 1970 and "to show the enemy that we were still serious about our commitment in Vietnam," Nixon ordered a joint U.S.-ARVN invasion of Cambodia in April 1970. That order made Vietnam "Nixon's war" and provoked outrage at home. Nixon made a belligerent speech defending his move and emphasizing the importance of U.S. credibility: "If when the chips are down, the world's most powerful nation acts like a pitiful helpless giant, the forces of totalitarianism and anarchy will threaten free nations" everywhere. Upon reading a draft of the speech, a cabinet member predicted, "This will make the students puke."

They did more. In response, more than 100,000 people protested in Washington, D.C., and students boycotted classes on hundreds of campuses. At Kent State University in Ohio, National Guard troops were dispatched after protesting students burned an old ROTC building. Then, at a rally there on May 4, when some students threw rocks at the troops, they fired at the students, killing four and wounding ten others. "They're starting to treat their own children like they treat us," commented a black woman in Harlem. In a confrontation at Jackson State College in Mississippi on May 14, police shot into a dormitory, killing two black students. And in August, police in Los Angeles used tear gas and clubs against Chicano antiwar protesters.

Congressional reaction to the invasion of Cambodia revealed increasing concern about abuses of presidential power. In the name of national security, presidents since Franklin Roosevelt had conducted foreign policy without the consent or sometimes even the knowledge of Congress—for example, Eisenhower in Iran and Johnson in the Dominican Republic. But in their determination to win the war in Vietnam, Johnson and Nixon had taken extreme measures to deceive the public and silence their critics. The bombing and invasion of Cambodia infuriated enough legislators that the Senate voted to terminate the Gulf of Tonkin Resolution, which had given the president virtually a blank check in Vietnam, and to cut off funds for the Cambodian operation. The House refused to go along, but by the end of June, Nixon had pulled all U.S. troops out of Cambodia.

U.S. Invasion of Cambodia, 1970

Students Killed at Kent State

On May 4, 1970, John Filo, a photojournalism student at Kent State University in Ohio, decided to take pictures of students demonstrating against President Nixon's recently announced decision to invade Cambodia. He observed several hundred protesters, some of whom threw rocks at National Guardsmen, who in turn sprayed tear gas toward the students. Suddenly, some guardsmen opened fire, killing four students and wounding ten. Filo took this photograph of fourteen-year-old runaway Mary Ann Vecchio sobbing over the dead body of Kent State student Jeffrey Miller. He sent his photographs to the Associated Press; this one was published around the world and won Filo a Pulitzer Prize.

John Filo.

READING THE IMAGE: What responses do you think this photograph might have evoked from those who opposed the war in Vietnam? How might those who supported the war have reacted to it?
CONNECTIONS: What effect did Nixon's order to invade Cambodia have on the antiwar movement?

FOR MORE HELP ANALYZING THIS IMAGE, see the visual activity for this chapter in the Online Study Guide at bedfordstmartins.com/roark.

The Cambodian invasion failed to break the will of North Vietnam, but it set in motion a terrible tragedy for the Cambodian people. The North Vietnamese moved further into Cambodia and strengthened the Khmer Rouge, Communist insurgents attempting to overthrow the U.S.-supported government of Lon Nol. A brutal civil war raged until 1975, when the Khmer Rouge triumphed and imposed a savage rule, slaughtering millions of Cambodians and giving the name "killing fields" to the land of a historically peaceful people.

In 1971, Vietnam veterans themselves became a visible part of the peace movement, the first men in U.S. history to protest a war in which they had fought. Veterans held a public investigation of "war crimes" in Vietnam, rallied in front of the Capitol, and cast away their war medals. In May 1971, veterans numbered among the 40,000 protesters who engaged in civil disobedience in an effort to shut down Washington. Officials made more than 12,000 arrests, which courts later ruled violations of protesters' rights.

After the spring of 1971, there were fewer massive antiwar demonstrations, but protest continued. Public attention focused on the court-martial of Lieutenant William Calley, which began in November 1970 and resulted in his conviction. During the trial, Americans learned that in March 1968, Calley's company had systematically killed every inhabitant of the hamlet of My Lai, nearly all of whom were old men, women, and children. Estimates put the death toll at more than 400 villagers. The Americans had encountered no enemy forces there. The military covered up the atrocity for more than a year before a journalist exposed it. Eventually, twelve officers and enlisted men were charged with murder or assault to commit murder, but only Calley was convicted.

Administration policy suffered another blow in June 1971 with the publication of the *Pentagon Papers*, secret government documents consisting mostly of a study that Defense Secretary Robert McNamara had ordered in 1967. The *New York Times* got the material from Daniel Ellsberg, who had worked on the study and whose attempts to persuade officials of the war's futility had been unsuccessful. Even though the study did not cover the Nixon administration, government lawyers went to court to stop further publication, in part out of fear that other information would be leaked. The

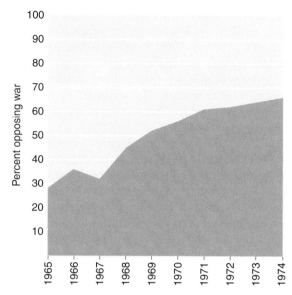

FIGURE 29.2   Public Opinion about the Vietnam War, 1965–1974
This chart reflects the percentage of people answering "yes" to a Gallup poll question: "In view of the developments since we entered the fighting in Vietnam, do you think the United States made a mistake in sending troops to fight in Vietnam?"

Supreme Court, however, was more concerned about freedom of the press, arguing that the attempt to stop publication was a "flagrant, indefensible" violation of the First Amendment. Subsequent circulation of the *Pentagon Papers*, which revealed considerable pessimism among officials during the early years of the war even as they made rosy promises, heightened disillusionment with the war by casting doubts on the government's credibility. More than 60 percent of Americans polled in 1971 considered it a mistake to have sent American troops to Vietnam (Figure 29.2); 58 percent believed the war to be immoral.

Military morale sank in the last years of the war. Having been exposed to the antiwar movement at home, many of the remaining soldiers had less faith in the war than their predecessors had had. Racial tensions among soldiers mounted, many soldiers sought escape in illegal drugs, and they committed hundreds of "fraggings," attacks on officers by enlisted men. In a 1971 report, "The Collapse of the Armed Forces," a retired Marine Corps colonel described the lack of discipline: "Our army that now remains in Vietnam [is] near mutinous."

The Peace Accords and the Legacy of Defeat

Nixon and Kissinger continued to believe that intensive firepower could bring the North Vietnamese to their knees, and they combined that force with negotiation. In March 1972, responding to a strong North Vietnamese offensive, the United States resumed sustained bombing of the North, mined Haiphong and other harbors for the first time, and announced a naval blockade. With peace talks stalled, in December Nixon ordered the most devastating bombing of North Vietnam yet.

The intense bombing, called "jugular diplomacy" by Kissinger, was costly to both sides, but it brought renewed negotiations. On January 27, 1973, representatives of the United States, North Vietnam, South Vietnam, and the Vietcong (now called the People's Revolutionary Government) signed a formal accord in Paris. The agreement required removal of all U.S. troops and military advisers but allowed North Vietnamese forces to remain. Both sides agreed to return prisoners of war. Nixon called the agreement "peace with honor," but it in fact allowed only a face-saving withdrawal for the United States.

Fighting resumed immediately among the Vietnamese. Nixon's efforts to support the South Vietnamese government, and indeed his ability to govern at all, were increasingly eroded by what came to be known as the Watergate scandal (see chapter 30). Nixon had been forced to give up his office by 1975, when North Vietnam launched a new offensive. On May 1, it occupied Saigon and renamed it Ho Chi Minh City to honor the Communist leader. The Americans hastily evacuated, along with 150,000 of their South Vietnamese allies.

Confusion, humiliation, and tragedy marked the rushed departure. The United States lacked sufficient transportation capabilities and time to evacuate all those South Vietnamese who wanted to leave. U.S. marines beat back desperate Vietnamese trying to escape through the U.S. Embassy. Former lieutenant Philip Caputo, who had returned to South Vietnam as a journalist and got out at the last minute, felt "like a deserter." His helicopter "took some ground fire from South Vietnamese soldiers who probably felt that the Americans had betrayed them."

During the four years it took Nixon to end the war, he had expanded the conflict into Cambodia and Laos and had launched massive bombing campaigns in Vietnam. Although increasing numbers of legislators criticized the war, Congress never denied the president the funds to fight it and never rescinded the Gulf of Tonkin Resolution. Only after the peace accords did the legislative branch stiffen its constitutional authority in the making of war, passing the War Powers Act in November 1973. The law required the president to report to Congress within forty-eight hours of deploying military forces abroad. If Congress failed to endorse the president's action within sixty days, the troops

Evacuating South Vietnam

As Communist troops rolled south toward Saigon in the spring of 1975, desperate South Vietnamese attempted to flee along with the departing Americans. These South Vietnamese, carrying little or nothing, attempt to scale the wall of the U.S. Embassy to reach evacuation helicopters. Thousands of Vietnamese who wanted to be evacuated were left behind. Even though space for evacuees was desperately limited, South Vietnamese president Nguyen Van Thieu fled to Taiwan on a U.S. plane, taking with him fifteen tons of baggage.

AP Images.

would have to be withdrawn. The new law, however, did little to dispel the distrust of and disillusionment with the government that had swelled with Americans' realization that their leaders had not told the truth about Vietnam.

The disorder that had accompanied antiwar protests and bitter divisions among Americans were other legacies of the war. Even children of Nixon administration officials protested the war that their fathers were waging. Vietnam diverted money from domestic programs and sounded the death knell of Johnson's Great Society. It created federal budget deficits and triggered inflation that contributed to ongoing economic crises throughout the 1970s (see chapter 30).

Four presidents had declared that the survival of South Vietnam was essential for the United States to prevail in the cold war, but their dire predictions that a Communist victory in South Vietnam would set the dominoes cascading did not materialize. Although Vietnam, Laos, and Cambodia all fell within the Communist camp in the spring of 1975, Thailand, Burma, Malaysia, and the rest of Southeast Asia did not. When China and Vietnam reverted to their historically hostile relationship, the myth of a monolithic Communist power overrunning Asia evaporated.

The long pursuit of victory in Vietnam complicated the United States' relations with other nations, as even its staunchest ally, Britain, doubted the wisdom of the war. The spectacle of terrifying American power used against a small Asian country alienated many in the third world and compromised efforts to win the hearts and minds of people in developing nations through initiatives such as the Peace Corps and the Alliance for Progress.

The cruelest legacy of Vietnam fell on those who had served. "We would not return to cheering crowds, parades, and the pealing of great cathedral bells," wrote Philip Caputo. The failure of the United States to win the war, its unpopularity at home, and its character as a guerrilla war denied veterans the traditional homecoming of returning soldiers. Veterans themselves expressed two kinds of reactions to the defeat. Many believed in the war's purposes and felt betrayed by the government for not letting them and their now-dead comrades win it. Other veterans blamed the government for sacrificing the nation's youth in an immoral, unnecessary,

The cruelest legacy of Vietnam fell on those who had served. "We would not return to cheering crowds, parades, and the pealing of great cathedral bells," wrote Philip Caputo.

TABLE 29.1	VIETNAM WAR CASUALTIES
United States	
Battle deaths	47,415
Other deaths	10,785
Wounded	103,284
South Vietnam	
Killed in action	110,357
Military wounded	499,026
Civilians killed	415,000
Civilians wounded	913,000
Communist Regulars and Guerrillas	
Killed in action	66,000

SOURCE: U.S. Department of Defense.

or useless war, expressing their sense of the war's futility by referring to their dead comrades as having been "wasted." Sometimes identifying with the Vietnamese more than with their white comrades, veterans belonging to minority groups had more reason to doubt the nobility of their purpose. A Native American soldier assigned to resettle Vietnamese civilians found it to be "just like when they moved us to the rez [reservation]. We shouldn't have done that."

Because the Vietnam War was a civil, guerrilla war, combat was especially brutal (Table 29.1). The terrors of conventional warfare were multiplied, and so were the motivations to commit atrocities. The massacre at My Lai was only the most widely publicized war crime. To demonstrate the immorality of the war, peace advocates stressed the atrocities, contributing to a distorted image of the Vietnam veteran as dehumanized and violent.

Most veterans came home to public neglect; some faced harassment from antiwar activists who failed to distinguish the war from the warriors. A veteran remembered the "feelings of rejection and scorn that a bunch of depressed and confused young men experienced when they returned home from doing what their country told them to do." Government benefits were less generous to Vietnam veterans than they had been to those of the past two wars. Yet two-thirds of Vietnam veterans said that they would serve again, and most veterans readjusted well to civilian life.

Nonetheless, some suffered long after the war ended. The Veterans Administration (VA)

The Vietnam Veterans Memorial
In 1979, a group of Vietnam veterans formed the Vietnam Veterans Memorial Fund to raise a memorial in commemoration of those who had served in the war. Nearly 1,500 artists submitted designs in a national competition, and eight experts unanimously selected the plan of twenty-one-year-old Maya Lin, whose parents had fled China in 1948. Her five-hundred-foot, sloping, V-shaped wall of polished black granite was inscribed with the names of every service member who perished in Vietnam, in the order in which they died. To appease critics who wanted a more heroic, lifelike monument, a traditional sculpture of three servicemen was added to the site, and yet another statue, depicting three uniformed women tending a fallen soldier, was added in 1993. Located near the Lincoln Memorial on the Washington Mall, the memorial attracts millions of visitors each year, especially veterans. As one explained at the memorial's dedication in 1982, veterans come "to find the names of those we lost in the war, as if by tracing the letters into the granite we could find what was left of ourselves."
© Bettmann/Corbis; National Archives.

estimated that nearly one-sixth of the veterans suffered from post-traumatic stress disorder, with its symptoms of fear, recurring nightmares, feelings of guilt and shame, violence, drug and alcohol abuse, and suicidal tendencies. Thirty years after performing army intelligence work in Saigon, Doris Allen "still hit the floor sometimes when [she heard] loud bangs." In the late 1970s, many of those who had served in Vietnam began to produce deformed children and fell ill themselves with cancer, severe skin disorders, and other ailments. Veterans claimed a link between those illnesses and Agent Orange, an herbicide that contained the deadly poison dioxin, which the military had sprayed by the millions of gallons over Vietnam. Not until 1991 did Congress provide assistance to veterans with diseases linked to the poison.

By then, the climate had changed. The war began to enter the realm of popular culture, with novels, TV shows, and hit movies depicting a broad range of military experience—from soldiers reduced to brutality to men and women serving with courage and integrity. The incorporation of the Vietnam War into the collective experience was symbolized most dramatically in the Vietnam Veterans Memorial unveiled in Washington, D.C., in November 1982. Designed by Yale architecture student Maya Lin, the black, V-shaped wall inscribed with the names of 58,200 men and women lost in the war became one of the most popular sites in the nation's capital. In an article describing the memorial's dedication, a Vietnam combat veteran spoke to and for his former comrades: "Welcome home. The war is over."

REVIEW How did Nixon try to bring American involvement in Vietnam to a close?

Conclusion:
An Unwinnable War

Vietnam was America's longest war. The United States spent more than $150 billion (nearly $600 billion in 2007 dollars) and sent 2.6 million young men and women to Vietnam. Of those, 58,200 never returned, and 150,000 suffered serious injury. The war shattered consensus at home, increased presidential power at the expense of congressional authority and public accountability, weakened the economy and domestic reform, and contributed to the downfall of two presidents.

Even as Nixon and Kissinger took steps to ease cold war tensions with the major Communist powers—the Soviet Union and China, which were also the main suppliers of the North Vietnamese—they also acted vigorously throughout the third world to install or prop up anti-Communist governments. They embraced their predecessors' commitment to South Vietnam as a necessary cold war engagement because they believed that to do otherwise would threaten American credibility and make the United States appear weak. Defeat in Vietnam did not make the United States the "pitiful helpless giant" predicted by Nixon, but it did mark the relative decline of U.S. power and the impossibility of containment on a global scale.

One of the constraints on U.S. power was the tenacity of revolutionary movements determined to achieve national independence. Marine lieutenant Philip Caputo recalled his surprise at discovering "that the men we had scorned as peasant guerrillas were, in fact, a lethal, determined enemy." Overestimating the effectiveness of American technological superiority, U.S. officials badly underestimated the sacrifices that the enemy was willing to make and failed to realize how easily the United States could be perceived as a colonial intruder.

A second constraint on Eisenhower, Kennedy, Johnson, and Nixon was their resolve to avoid a major confrontation with the Soviet Union or China. For Johnson, who conducted the largest escalation of the war, caution was especially critical so as not to provoke direct intervention by the Communist superpowers. After China exploded its first atomic bomb in 1964, the potential heightened for the Vietnam conflict to escalate into worldwide disaster.

Third, in Vietnam the United States sought to prop up an extremely weak ally engaged in a civil war. The South Vietnamese government never won the support of its people, and the intense devastation the war brought to civilians only made things worse. Short of taking over the South Vietnamese government and military, the United States could do little to strengthen South Vietnam's ability to resist communism.

Finally, domestic opposition to the war, which by 1968 included significant portions of mainstream America, constrained the options of Johnson and Nixon. As the war dragged on, with increasing American casualties and growing evidence of the damage being inflicted on innocent Vietnamese, more and more civilians wearied of the conflict. Even some who had fought in the war joined the movement, including Philip Caputo, who sent his campaign ribbons and a bitter letter of protest to the White House. In 1973, Nixon and Kissinger bowed to the resolution of the enemy and the limitations of U.S. power. As the war wound down, passions surrounding it contributed to a rising conservative movement that would substantially alter the post–World War II political order.

Selected Bibliography

Foreign Policy under Kennedy, Johnson, and Nixon

H. W. Brands, *The Wages of Globalism: Lyndon Johnson and the Limits of American Power* (1995).

Robert Dallek, *Nixon and Kissinger: Partners in Power* (2007).

Lawrence Freedman, *Kennedy's Wars: Berlin, Cuba, Laos, and Vietnam* (2000).

Aleksandr Fursenko and Timothy J. Naftali, *One Hell of a Gamble: The Secret History of the Cuban Missile Crisis* (1998).

Elizabeth Cobbs Hoffman, *All You Need Is Love: The Peace Corps and the Spirit of the 1960s* (1998).

Walter Isaacson, *Kissinger: A Biography* (1992).

Lester D. Langley, *America and the Americans: The United States in the Western Hemisphere* (1989).

Margaret Macmillan, *Nixon and Mao: The Week That Changed the World* (2007).

Walter A. McDougall, *The Heavens and the Earth: A Political History of the Space Age* (1985).

Keith L. Nelson, *The Making of Détente: Soviet-American Relations in the Shadow of Vietnam* (1995).

Stephen G. Rabe, *The Most Dangerous Area in the World: John F. Kennedy Confronts Communist Revolution in Latin America* (1999).

Jeremi Suri, *Power and Protest: Global Revolution and the Rise of Détente* (2003).

The War in Vietnam

Robert Buzzanco, *Masters of War: Military Dissent and Politics in the Vietnam Era* (1996).

Mark Clodfelter, *The Limits of Air Power: The American Bombing of North Vietnam* (1989).

George C. Herring, *America's Longest War: The United States and Vietnam, 1950–1975* (1986).

Arnold R. Isaacs, *Vietnam Shadows: The War, Its Ghosts, and Its Legacy* (1997).

David Kaiser, *American Tragedy: Kennedy, Johnson, and the Origins of the Vietnam War* (2000).

Jeffrey P. Kimball, *Nixon's Vietnam War* (1998).

A. J. Langguth, *Our Vietnam/Nuoc Viet Ta: A History of the War, 1954–1975* (2000).

Fredrik Logevall, *Choosing War: The Lost Chance for Peace and the Escalation of the War in Vietnam* (1999).

David F. Schmitz, *The Tet Offensive: Politics, War, and Public Opinion* (2005).

Marilyn B. Young, *The Vietnam Wars, 1945–1990* (1991).

Those Who Served

Christian G. Appy, *Working-Class War: American Combat Soldiers in Vietnam* (1993).

Philip Caputo, *A Rumor of War* (1977).

David Donovan, *Once a Warrior King: Memories of an Officer in Vietnam* (1985).

Kathryn Marshall, *In the Combat Zone: Vivid Personal Recollections of the Vietnam War from the Women Who Served There* (1987).

Harry Maurer, *Strange Ground: Americans in Vietnam, 1945–1975, an Oral History* (1998).

Al Santoli, *Everything We Had: An Oral History of the Vietnam War* (1981).

James E. Westheider, *Fighting on Two Fronts: African Americans and the Vietnam War* (1997).

Politics and the Antiwar Movement

Tariq Ali and Susan Watkins, *1968: Marching in the Streets* (1998).

Dan T. Carter, *The Politics of Race: George Wallace, the Origins of the New Conservatism, and the Transformation of American Politics* (1995).

Charles DeBenedetti, with Charles Chatfield, *An American Ordeal: The Antiwar Movement in the Vietnam Era* (1990).

Michael S. Foley, *Confronting the War Machine: Draft Resistance during the Vietnam War* (2003).

Andrew E. Hunt, *The Turning: A History of Vietnam Veterans against the War* (1999).

Rhodri Jeffreys-Jones, *Peace Now! American Society and the Ending of the Vietnam War* (1999).

Kim McQuaid, *The Anxious Years: America in the Vietnam and Watergate Era* (1989).

David Rudenstine, *The Day the Presses Stopped: A History of the Pentagon Papers Case* (1996).

Amy Swerdlow, *Women Strike for Peace: Traditional Motherhood and Radical Politics in the 1960s* (1993).

▶ FOR MORE BOOKS ABOUT TOPICS IN THIS CHAPTER, see the Online Bibliography at bedfordstmartins.com/roark.

▶ FOR ADDITIONAL FIRSTHAND ACCOUNTS OF THIS PERIOD, see Chapter 29 in Michael Johnson, ed., *Reading the American Past*, Fourth Edition.

▶ FOR WEB SITES, IMAGES, AND DOCUMENTS RELATED TO TOPICS AND PLACES IN THIS CHAPTER, visit bedfordstmartins.com/makehistory.

REVIEWING THE CHAPTER

Follow these steps to review and strengthen your understanding of the chapter.

STEP 1: *Study the* **Key Terms** *and* **Timeline** *to identify the significance of each item listed.*

STEP 2: *Answer the* **Review Questions***, drawing on key terms and dates to support your answers.*

STEP 3: *Drawing on the Key Terms, Timeline, and Review Questions, answer the broader* **Making Connections** *questions.*

KEY TERMS

Who

John F. Kennedy (p. 1064)
Nikita Khrushchev (p. 1065)
Fidel Castro (p. 1065)
Ho Chi Minh (p. 1070)
Ngo Dinh Diem (p. 1072)
Lyndon B. Johnson (p. 1072)
Mike Mansfield (p. 1074)
Juan Bosch (p. 1074)
William Westmoreland
    (p. 1074)
Martin Luther King Jr. (p. 1078)
Robert McNamara (p. 1082)
Robert F. Kennedy (p. 1086)
Eugene McCarthy (p. 1086)
Hubert H. Humphrey (p. 1086)
Richard M. Nixon (p. 1086)
George C. Wallace (p. 1086)
Henry A. Kissinger (p. 1087)
Mao Zedong (p. 1088)
Gerald Ford (p. 1088)

Salvador Allende (p. 1089)
Augusto Pinochet (p. 1089)

What

Bay of Pigs (p. 1065)
Apollo program (p. 1065)
Berlin Wall (p. 1066)
Alliance for Progress (p. 1067)
Agency for International Development
    (AID) (p. 1067)
Peace Corps (p. 1067)
intercontinental ballistic missiles
    (ICBMs) (p. 1068)
Cuban missile crisis (p. 1069)
Vietcong (p. 1070)
Army of the Republic of Vietnam
    (ARVN) (p. 1070)
National Liberation Front (NLF)
    (p. 1070)
Ho Chi Minh Trail (p. 1071)
Agent Orange (p. 1072)

Gulf of Tonkin Resolution (p. 1073)
Operation Rolling Thunder (p. 1073)
Organization of American States (OAS)
    (p. 1074)
Students for a Democratic Society (SDS)
    (p. 1078)
Tet Offensive (p. 1082)
Youth International Party (Yippies)
    (p. 1086)
American Independent Party (p. 1086)
Strategic Arms Limitation Talks (SALT)
    (p. 1088)
antiballistic missiles (ABMs) (p. 1088)
Helsinki accords (p. 1088)
Six-Day War (p. 1089)
Yom Kippur War (p. 1089)
Kent State University (p. 1091)
Jackson State College (p. 1091)
My Lai massacre (p. 1092)
Pentagon Papers (p. 1092)
War Powers Act (p. 1093)

TIMELINE

1961 • Bay of Pigs invasion.
• Berlin Wall erected.
• Kennedy administration increases military aid to South Vietnam.
• Alliance for Progress established.
• Peace Corps created.

    1962 • Cuban missile crisis.

        1963 • Limited nuclear test ban treaty signed.
• President Kennedy assassinated; Lyndon B. Johnson becomes president.

           1964 • Anti-American rioting in Panama Canal Zone.
• Gulf of Tonkin Resolution.

                1965 • First major demonstration against Vietnam War.
• Operation Rolling Thunder begins.
• Johnson orders the first combat troops to Vietnam.
• U.S. troops invade Dominican Republic.

                    1967 • Arab-Israeli Six-Day War.

                        1968 • Hundreds of thousands of Americans demonstrate against Vietnam War.
• Tet Offensive.
• Johnson decides not to seek second term.
• Police and protesters clash near Democratic convention in Chicago.
• Republican Richard Nixon elected president.

REVIEW QUESTIONS

1. Why did Kennedy believe that engagement in Vietnam was crucial to his foreign policy? (pp. 1064–72)

2. How did American troops serving in Vietnam differ from those who served in World War II, and how were their experiences different? (pp. 1072–78)

3. How did the Vietnam War shape the election of 1968? (pp. 1078–87)

4. How did Nixon try to bring American involvement in Vietnam to a close? (pp. 1087–95)

MAKING CONNECTIONS

1. Cuba featured prominently in the most dramatic foreign policy actions of the Kennedy administration. Citing specific events, discuss why Cuba was an area of great concern to the administration. How did Cuba figure into Kennedy's cold war policies? Were his actions in regard to Cuba effective?

2. Explain the Gulf of Tonkin incident and its significance to American foreign policy. How did President Lyndon Johnson respond to the incident? What considerations, domestic and international, contributed to his course of action?

3. The United States' engagement in Vietnam divided the nation. Discuss the range of American responses to the war. How did they change over time? How did domestic political concerns shape the country's response to the war? How did the war shape domestic politics in the 1960s and early 1970s?

4. What was détente, and how did it affect the United States' cold war foreign policy? What were its achievements and limitations? In your answer, discuss how Nixon's approach to communism built on and departed from the previous two administrations' approaches.

▶ FOR PRACTICE QUIZZES, A CUSTOMIZED STUDY PLAN, AND OTHER STUDY TOOLS, see the Online Study Guide at bedfordstmartins.com/roark.

1969 • American astronauts land on moon.
• Nixon orders secret bombing of Cambodia.

1970 • Nixon orders invasion of Cambodia.
• Students killed during protests at Kent State and Jackson State.

1971 • *New York Times* publishes *Pentagon Papers.*

1972 • Nixon becomes first U.S. president to visit China.
• Nixon visits Moscow to sign arms limitation treaties with Soviets.

1973 • Paris Peace Accords.
• War Powers Act.
• CIA-backed military coup in Chile.
• Arab oil embargo following Yom Kippur War.

1975 • North Vietnam takes over South Vietnam, ending the war.
• Helsinki accords.

MAKING AMERICA "REAGAN COUNTRY"

This delegate badge from the 1980 Republican National Convention
played on themes that would characterize Ronald Reagan's presidential campaigns and the
politics and policies of the 1980s. Just as the badge appealed to patriotic sentiments with the flag, the
Statue of Liberty, and the space program, Reagan encouraged Americans to take pride in their nation and
celebrate its achievements instead of focusing on its shortcomings. His image as a cowboy brought to
mind some of the movies he had acted in and his favorite recreation—working on his ranch in California—
as well as the independence and rugged individualism of the West, where he had made his home since the
1940s. The West housed key elements in the surge of conservatism that ensured Reagan's victory in 1980;
shaped his administration's antigovernment, anti-Communist agenda; and helped reverse the liberal direction that national politics had taken in the 1960s.

National Museum of American History, Smithsonian Institution, Behring Center.

CHAPTER

30

America Moves to the Right

1969–1989

P HYLLIS SCHLAFLY experienced "one of the most exciting days of my life" when she heard **conservative** Republican Barry Goldwater address the National Federation of Republican Women in 1963. Like Goldwater, she opposed the moderate stance of the Eisenhower administration and current Republican leadership. Both Schlafly and Goldwater wanted the United States to go beyond merely containing **communism** and to eliminate that threat entirely. They also wanted to cut back the government in Washington, especially its role in providing social welfare and enforcing civil rights. Disappointed by Goldwater's loss to Lyndon Johnson in 1964, Schlafly nevertheless took heart in the conservatives' ability to engineer his nomination. She assailed the policy innovations and turmoil of the 1960s, adding new issues to the conservative agenda and helping to build a grassroots movement that would redefine the Republican Party and American politics into the twenty-first century.

Phyllis Stewart was born in St. Louis in 1924, attended Catholic schools, and worked her way through Washington University testing ammunition at a World War II defense plant. She earned an M.A. in government from Radcliffe College in 1945 and went to work at the American Enterprise Institute, where she imbibed the think tank's conservatism. Returning to the Midwest, she married Fred Schlafly, an Alton, Illinois, attorney whose anticommunism and antigovernment passions equaled hers. The mother of six children, Schlafly claimed, "I don't think there's anything as much fun as taking care of a baby," and she asserted that she would "rather scrub bathroom floors" than write political articles.

Yet while insisting that caring for home and family was women's most important career, Schlafly spent much of her time on the road—writing, speaking, leading Republican women's organizations, and testifying before legislative committees. She lost two bids for Congress in her heavily Democratic district in Illinois, in 1952 and again in 1970. Her book, *A Choice Not an Echo*, which she self-published in 1964, pushed Barry Goldwater for president and sold more than a million copies. In 1967, she began publishing *The Phyllis Schlafly Report*, a monthly newsletter about current political issues. Throughout the 1950s and 1960s, Schlafly called for stronger efforts to combat communism at home and abroad, a more powerful military, and a less active government in domestic affairs—all traditional conservative goals.

In the 1970s, Schlafly began to address new issues, including **feminism** and the Equal Rights Amendment, abortion, gay rights, busing for racial integration, and religion in the schools. Her positions resonated with many

VOL. 5, NO. 10, SECTION 2   Box 618, ALTON, ILLINOIS 62002   MAY, 1972

The Fraud Called The Equal Rights Amendment

If there ever was an example of how a tiny minority can cram its views down the throats of the majority, it is the Equal Rights Amendment, called ERA. A noisy claque of women's lib agitators rammed ERA through Congress, intimidating the men into voting for it so they would not be labeled "anti-woman."

The ERA passed Congress with big majorities on March 22, 1972 and was sent to the states for ratification. When it is ratified by 38 states, it will become the law of the land. Within two hours of Senate passage, Hawaii ratified it. New Hampshire and Nebraska, both anxious to be second, rushed their approval the next day. Then in steady succession came Iowa, Idaho, Delaware, Kansas, Texas, Maryland, Tennessee, Alaska, Rhode Island, and New Jersey. As this goes to press, 13 states have ratified it and others are on the verge of doing so.

Three states have rejected it: Oklahoma, Vermont and Connecticut.

What is ERA? The Amendment reads: "Equality of rights under the law shall not be denied or abridged by the United States or by any state on account of sex."

Does that sound good? Don't kid yourself. This innocuous-sounding amendment will take away far more important rights than it will ever give. This was made abundantly clear by the debate in Congress. Senator Sam Ervin (D., N.C.) called it "the most drastic measure in Senate history." He proved this by putting into the *Congressional Record* an article from the *Yale Law Journal* of April 1971.

The importance of this *Yale Law Journal* article is that both the proponents and the opponents of ERA agree that it is an accurate analysis of the consequences of ERA. Congresswoman Martha Griffiths, a leading proponent of ERA, sent a copy of this article to every member of Congress, stating that "It will ... very understand the purposes and effe ... Rights Amendment.... The arti ... ERA will work in ...

the most important of all women's rights.

"In all states husbands are primarily liable for the support of their wives and children.... The child support sections of the criminal nonsupport laws ... could not be sustained where only the male is liable for support." (YLJ, pp. 944-945)

"The Equal Rights Amendment would bar a state from imposing greater liability for support on a husband than on a wife merely because of his sex." (YLJ, p. 945)

"Like the duty of support during marriage and the obligation to pay alimony in the case of separation or divorce, nonsupport would have to be eliminated as a ground for divorce against husbands only...." (YLJ, p. 951)

"The Equal Rights Amendment would not require that alimony be abolished but only that it be available equally to men and women." (YLJ, p. 952)

2. ERA will wipe out the laws which protect only women against sex crimes such as rape.

"Courts faced with criminal laws which do not apply equally to men and women would be likely to invalidate the laws rather than extending or rewriting them to apply to women and men alike." (YLJ, p. 966)

"Seduction laws, statutory rape laws, laws prohibiting obscene language in the presence of women, prostitution and 'manifest danger' laws ... The Equal Rights Amendment would not permit such laws, which base their sex discriminatory classification on social stereotypes." (YLJ, p. 954)

"The statutory rape laws, which punish men for having sexual intercourse with any wom ... under an age specified by law ... suffer from a ... fect under the ... ual Rights Amendme ...

"To ... ngling out ...

The Phyllis Schlafly Report

Phyllis Schlafly's monthly newsletter for members of her conservative Eagle Forum began in 1967 with articles attacking federal social programs and calling for stronger measures and weapons to fight communism. When Congress passed the Equal Rights Amendment in 1972, the *Report* began to add antifeminism and other concerns of the New Right to its agenda, including opposition to abortion rights, to sex education in the schools, and to protections for gays and lesbians. Schlafly's attacks on feminism appealed to many people; subscribers to her newsletter numbered more than 35,000 in the mid-1970s. Feminist leader Betty Friedan told Schlafly, "I consider you a traitor to your sex. I consider you an Aunt Tom." Courtesy of Phyllis Schlafly.

Americans fed up with the protest movements, expansion of government, challenges to authority, and loosening of moral standards that seemed to define the 1960s. And the votes of those Americans began to reshape American politics—in Richard Nixon's victories in the presidential elections of 1968 and 1972; in the presidency of Jimmy Carter, whose policies stood substantially to the right of his Democratic predecessors; and in conservative Ronald Reagan's capture of the Republican Party, the presidency, and the political agenda in 1980.

Although Richard Nixon did not embrace the entire conservative agenda, he sought to make

the Republicans the dominant party by appealing to disaffected blue-collar and southern white Democrats. The Watergate revelations forced Nixon to leave the presidency in disgrace in 1974, and his Republican successor, Gerald Ford, occupied the Oval Office for little more than two years; but the shift of the political spectrum to the right continued even when Democrat Jimmy Carter captured the White House in 1976. Anti-government sentiment grew out of the deceptions of the Johnson administration, Nixon's abuse of presidential powers, and the inability of Presidents Ford and Carter to resolve domestic and foreign crises. As Americans saw surging unemployment and inflation—an unprecedented combination called stagflation—shrink their incomes, their confidence in government and willingness to pay taxes eroded.

In 1980, Phyllis Schlafly's call for "a choice not an echo" was realized when Ronald Reagan won the presidency. Cutting taxes and government regulations, attacking social programs, expanding the nation's military capacity, and pressuring the Soviet Union and communism in the **third world**, Reagan addressed the hopes of traditional conservatives. Like Schlafly, he also championed the concerns of the **New Right**, opposing abortion and sexual permissiveness and supporting a larger role for religion in public life. Reagan's goals encountered resistance from feminists, civil rights groups, environmentalists, and others who fought to keep what they had won in the 1960s and 1970s. Although his administration failed to enact the entire conservative agenda, enormously increased the national debt, and engaged in illegal activities to thwart communism in Latin America, Reagan's popularity helped send his vice president, George H. W. Bush, to the White House at the end of his second term. And Reagan's determined optimism and spirited leadership contributed to a revival in national pride and confidence.

Nixon and the Rise of Postwar Conservatism

As we saw in chapter 28, Nixon acquiesced in the continuation of most **Great Society** programs and even approved pathbreaking environmental and minority and women's rights measures. Yet his public rhetoric and certain of his actions signaled the country's rightward move in both politics and sentiment. Whereas Kennedy had appealed to Americans to contribute to the common good, Nixon invited Americans to "let each of us ask—not just what will government do for me, but what can I do for myself?" His words invoked individualism and reliance on the market and private enterprise rather than on government, preferences that would grow stronger in the nation during the 1970s and beyond.

During Nixon's presidency, a new strand of conservatism joined the older movement that focused on anticommunism, a strong national defense, and a limited federal role in domestic affairs. New conservatives, whom Phyllis Schlafly helped mobilize, wanted to restore what they considered traditional moral values by increasing the presence of Christianity in public life and opposing sex education, feminism, abortion, homosexuality, and sexual permissiveness.

Emergence of a Grassroots Movement

Although Lyndon Johnson's landslide victory over Barry Goldwater in 1964 seemed to mark the triumph of **liberalism**, the election results actually concealed a rising conservative movement. Defining his purpose as "enlarging freedom at home and safeguarding it from the forces of tyranny abroad," Goldwater, an Arizona senator, echoed the ideas of conservative intellectuals who argued that government intrusions into economic life hindered prosperity, stifled personal responsibility, and interfered with individuals' rights to determine their own values. Conservatives assailed big government in domestic affairs but demanded a strong military to eradicate "Godless communism."

Behind Goldwater's nomination was a growing grassroots movement. Vigorous especially in the South and West, it included middle-class suburban women and men, members of the rabidly anti-Communist John Birch Society, and college students in the new Young Americans for Freedom (YAF). They did not give up when he lost the election. Margaret Minek, a community organizer for Goldwater, insisted, "We have a . . . flame . . . burning and the energy it gives off needs to be utilized." In California, newly energized conservatives like Minek helped Ronald Reagan defeat the incumbent liberal governor, Edmund Brown, in 1966, another

sign of the right's rising strength. Reagan linked Brown with the Watts riot and student disruptions at the University of California at Berkeley, exploiting popular fears about rising taxes, student rebellion, and black demands for justice.

Grassroots conservatism was not limited to the West and South, but a number of **Sun Belt** characteristics made it especially strong in places such as Orange County, California; Dallas, Texas; Scottsdale, Arizona; and Jefferson Parish, Louisiana. Such predominantly white areas contained relatively homogeneous, skilled, and economically comfortable populations, as well as military bases and defense production facilities. The West harbored a long-standing tradition of **Protestant** morality, individualism, and opposition to interference by a remote federal government. That tradition continued with the emergence of the New Right, even though it was hardly consistent with the Sun Belt's economic dependence on defense spending and on huge federal projects that provided water and power for the burgeoning population and its economy.

The South, which also benefited from military bases, the space program, and other federal projects, shared the West's antipathy toward the federal government. Hostility to racial change, however, was much more central to the South's conservatism. After signing the Civil Rights Act of 1964, President Lyndon Johnson remarked privately, "I think we just delivered the South to the Republican Party." Indeed, Barry Goldwater carried five southern states in 1964. Even though Goldwater had voted against the law because he saw it as an unwarranted expansion of federal power, not because he favored segregation and discrimination, a southern White Citizens' Council leader said, "He voted against the Civil Rights Act, and we just showed our appreciation."

Grassroots movements emerged around what conservatives believed marked the "moral decline" of their nation. In 1962, Mel and Norma Gabler began scrutinizing school textbooks under consideration by the Texas board of education. They were able to torpedo many of the books that they found not in conformity with "the Christian-Judeo morals, values, and standards as given to us by God through . . . the Bible," and they lent their expertise to like-minded citizens throughout the country. (See "Seeking the American Promise," page 1104.) Sex education roused the ire of Eleanor Howe in Anaheim, California, who felt that "nothing [in the sex education curriculum] depicted my values. . . . It wasn't so much the information. It was the shift in values." The Supreme

A Mother Campaigns for a Say in Her Children's Education

Although historians usually trace the rise of conservatism through national elections and the capture of the presidency and Congress, the most intense political battles of the 1970s and 1980s were often fought at the local level. None were more impassioned than those mounted by parents who wanted a say in what their children should be taught in the public schools. In the 1920s, school curriculum seized national attention during the *Scopes* trial over the teaching of evolution. In the 1970s, the introduction of sex education and new textbooks in the Kanawha County, West Virginia, school district prompted Alice Moore to challenge the teaching of material she deemed harmful to her children. As a result, she organized a movement to gain parents' control over their children's education.

Kanawha County encompasses the state capital of Charleston as well as surrounding towns and rural areas containing chemical plants, coal mines, small hamlets, and fundamentalist churches. Although in the 1970s, 90 percent of the district was white, class and cultural lines separated the relatively well-educated and cosmopolitan Charleston urbanites from families in the surrounding areas bound more tightly to traditional Appalachian culture. Alice Moore, a native of Mississippi, lived in a small town on the outskirts of Charleston with her husband, a fundamentalist minister, and their four young children, who attended local schools. While getting her hair done in 1969,

Moore picked up a magazine that reported on a battle in Anaheim, California, over the teaching of sex education in the schools. She never thought that the Anaheim controversy could occur in West Virginia, but she soon learned that sex education was coming to the Kanawha County school district. Examining the program, she found it to be a "humanistic, atheistic attack on God," which interfered with "our relationship with our children, what we wanted to teach them, what we wanted them to believe, how we wanted them to behave." Rallying like-minded citizens, she won a seat on the five-person Kanawha County school board by defeating an incumbent. Taking office in 1970, she failed to terminate the sex education program but managed to dilute the curriculum.

The school district's adoption of a new English language arts curriculum in 1974 provoked even greater controversy. The new program, similar to those sweeping school districts across the country, was largely a byproduct of 1960s reform movements. In an effort to teach children about the larger world, new textbooks incorporated writings by African Americans and other minority groups; provided materials to help teachers address various student needs, interests, and skills; and encouraged students to think critically and independently.

Objecting to both the philosophy and the content of the new curriculum, Alice Moore began to mobilize opposition, calling on fundamentalist ministers and holding meetings in churches. In June 1974, at a meeting

before an impassioned crowd of more than a thousand, she persuaded the school board to eliminate 8 of the 325 books but failed to prevent adoption of the curriculum by a vote of three to two. Opponents then redoubled their efforts, and the textbook war was on, echoing concerns that were energizing the Christian Right across the country.

Protesters condemned what they considered disrespect for authority, American patriotism, and the free-enterprise system in the new materials. Moore attacked a short story by the black activist and writer Eldridge Cleaver for its "un-American and highly political views." One of her allies, a conservative chemical company owner, vilified the curriculum as "liberal, socialist, even communist-inspired."

While textbook opponents claimed that the new materials condoned disrespect of authority, they themselves challenged the authority of distant "experts" to decide what was best for their children. When the National Education Association, a professional organization of educators, came to Charleston to investigate the controversy, Moore refused to cooperate. "Who gave the NEA the right to come into Kanawha County to judge the mentality and intelligence of Kanawha County parents?" she asked. To Appalachian people who had long endured exploitation by timber, mining, and other outside interests, the new curriculum seemed yet another infringement on their lives by outsiders.

Moore and her supporters also objected to the curriculum's multicultural materials, designed to illustrate the diversity of American society. Believing that such content promoted disunity, Moore wanted the schools to get "off this ethnic kick." Moreover, antitextbook forces disliked the nonstandard English that appeared in some of the literature, as well as what they considered the "trashy"

Alice Moore Campaigns for the School Board

Alice Moore's campaign for re-election to the Kanawha County Board of Education in 1976 emphasized the moral issues that triggered her first bid for a seat on the board in 1970 and the grassroots movement she led against the introduction of the new curriculum in 1974. Her appeal also included the antigovernment sentiments of the older right, railing against "Washington Bureaucrats" and government expenditures. Moore ran her first campaign for the board with the slogan "We need a mother on the board of education." She bore her fifth child while serving on the board, but one of the policies she championed prohibited pregnant girls from attending high school because she considered them "disruptive." Moore left Charleston in 1980 when her husband moved to a new church in Ohio.

WV Division of Culture & History.

RE-ELECT

ALICE MOORE

FOR

BOARD of EDUCATION

Dear Friends,

The schools belong to the people who pay for them, not Washington Bureaucrats, not School Administrators, not National Education Organizations.

Nationally, education is costing us more than 61 billion dollars a year, more than is spent on education by all the rest of the world combined. This is a 1000 percent increase in 20 years while enrollment has barely doubled. Yet, almost one third of our high school graduates cannot pass college placement exams and this number increases annually.

Are your children getting the education you want for them? I am convinced most parents expect the schools, for which we pay and for which we provide the children, to:

- Offer the best academic education possible with emphasis on basic skills.

- Respect family privacy and our right as parents to rear our children according to our own moral, ethical and religious beliefs without interference.

- Provide a disciplined and morally up-lifting educational climate for the safety and peace of mind for both students and teachers. Stop coddling the class trouble-makers at the expense of serious minded students.

- Operate the schools as efficiently as private enterprise.

As a board member, I have tried to represent the public interest, not an Educational Bureaucracy. This is the kind of education I want for my five children. If this is what you want, please give me your vote and contact your friends on my behalf.

Sincerely yours,
(Mrs.) Alice Moore

The final board vote is at the May 11 primary. Democrats, Republicans and Independents can vote for me, for this non-partisan position.

through April 1975, when one of the ministers who led the crusade was sentenced to prison for conspiracy to plant bombs.

The school board ended up keeping most of the new curriculum, but parents were allowed to check off from a list those books they did not want their children to read, and many teachers avoided hassles by not using any of the new books. The board also set new guidelines for choosing textbooks, which included banning profanity, material that might encourage "sedition or revolution against our government," books that suggested a different form of government was better, and material that "intrude[d] into the privacy of students' homes by asking personal questions about the inner feelings or behavior of themselves or their parents."

Conflicts over public school curriculum continued to strike communities throughout the nation into the twenty-first century, although none equaled the war in Kanawha County. Some conservative parents retreated from the public schools entirely. By 2000, parents were homeschooling more than one million children, and the number of private Christian schools soared, accommodating parents who, in Moore's words, "can't put their children in public schools and allow them to have their beliefs torn away." Those who believed that students should be exposed to a diversity of ideas in order to form their own beliefs were in the majority, but Christian conservatives such as Moore continued to fight for control over what their children were taught.

aspects of urban ghetto life. "Why the hell do we have to indoctrinate our children out here in semi-rural communities with the problems of the inner city?" a protester asked. One sign carried by a demonstrator— "Even Hillbillies Have Constitutional Rights"—spoke to the resentment that poorer whites often felt at the attention given to racial and ethnic minorities.

The new sexual permissiveness emerging in the 1960s also aroused antitextbook forces horrified at the open-mindedness reflected in the new curriculum. Moore condemned a poem by e. e. cummings because "it was dealing with sexual intercourse and pretty explicitly." The sexual realism in some of the materials inflamed fundamentalist protesters above all because it defied their belief in the system of right and wrong

laid out in the Bible, which they interpreted literally. To Moore, morality was not a relative issue: "God's law is absolute."

Such deeply held beliefs inspired opponents to keep their children home when school opened in September, achieving an absentee rate of around 20 percent. Defying their union leadership, thousands of miners went out on a sympathy strike, and Charleston bus drivers observed the boycott, while protesters set up picket lines and staged demonstrations. Three schools were bombed, district headquarters were dynamited, and guns were fired on both sides. Antitextbook supporters streamed into Charleston, including representatives from the conservative think tank the Heritage Foundation, the John Birch Society, and the Ku Klux Klan. The violence gradually subsided, but protests went on

Court's liberal decisions on issues such as school prayer, obscenity, and birth control also galvanized conservatives to restore "traditional values" to the nation.

In the 1970s, grassroots protests against taxes grew alongside concerns about morality. As inflation and unemployment threatened Americans' economic security, many also found themselves paying higher taxes, especially in the form of property taxes as the value of their homes increased. In 1978, Californians revolted in a popular referendum reducing property taxes by more than one-half and limiting the state legislature's ability to raise taxes. What a newspaper called a "primal scream by the People against Big Government" spread to similar antitax crusades in other states.

The Tax Revolt

Neighbors gather on the lawn of Los Angeles homeowner Mark Slade to rally for Proposition 13, an initiative campaign launched by conservative activist Howard Jarvis in 1978. Jarvis opposed the New Deal and an active government generally, but many homeowners rallied to his antitax cause because rising land values and new assessments had increased their property taxes sharply, as their signs indicate. After the passage of Proposition 13 by a large majority, tax revolts spread across the nation. Some thirty-seven states cut property taxes, and twenty-eight reduced income taxes. The tax issue helped the Republican Party end nearly half a century of Democratic dominance.

Tony Korody/Getty Images.

Nixon Courts the Right

In his 1968 presidential campaign, Richard Nixon exploited hostility to black protest and new civil rights policies, wooing white southerners and a considerable number of northern voters away from the Democratic Party. As president, he used this "southern strategy" to make further inroads into traditional Democratic strongholds in the 1972 election.

The Nixon administration reluctantly enforced court orders to achieve high degrees of integration in southern schools, but it resisted efforts to deal with segregation outside the South. In northern and western cities, where segregation resulted from residential patterns as well as decisions by school district officials, half of all African American children attended nearly all-black schools. After courts began to order the transfer of students between schools in white and black neighborhoods to achieve desegregation and the Supreme Court assented in *Swann v. Charlotte-Mecklenburg Board of Education* in 1971, busing became "political dynamite," according to a Gallup poll. "We've had all we can take of judicial interference with local schools," Phyllis Schlafly railed in 1972.

Children had been riding buses to school for decades, but busing for racial integration provoked fury. Violence erupted in Boston in 1974 when a district judge ruled for the National Association for the Advancement of Colored People (NAACP) in its suit against the Boston school committee. The judge found that school officials had maintained what amounted to a dual system and ordered busing "if necessary to achieve a unitary school system." When black students began to attend the formerly all-white South Boston High School, white students boycotted classes and angry whites threw rocks at black students disembarking from buses. White parents blasted the judge as a privileged liberal residing in the suburbs, where residents would not be touched by busing. As was true elsewhere, the whites most affected came from working-class families who remained in cities abandoned by the more affluent and whose children often rode buses to predominantly black, overcrowded schools with deficient facilities. Clarence McDonough decried the liberal officials who bused his "kid half way around Boston so that a bunch of politicians can end up their careers with a clear conscience."

African Americans themselves were conflicted about sending their children on long rides to schools where teachers might not welcome or respect them. Democratic congresswoman Shirley Chisholm saw busing as an artificial solution to residential segregation and inadequate school financing. Still, she knew that when white children were bused into black schools, "the school board would suddenly see the wisdom of improving those schools and giving them a fair share of the annual budget."

White parents and students eventually became more accepting of integration, especially after the creation of magnet schools and other new mechanisms for desegregation offered more choice. Nonetheless, integration propelled white flight to the suburbs. The number of white students in Boston public schools by 1987 was just one-third of what it had been in 1974.

Nixon failed to persuade Congress to end court-ordered busing, but after he had appointed four new justices, the Supreme Court moved in

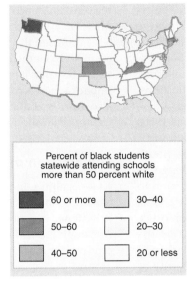

Percent of black students
statewide attending schools
more than 50 percent white

■	60 or more	▫	30–40
▨	50–60	□	20–30
▨	40–50	□	20 or less

Integration of Public Schools, 1968

his direction in the 1974 case *Milliken v. Bradley*, imposing strict limits on the use of busing to achieve racial balance. Nixon's judicial appointments also reflected the southern strategy. He criticized the Supreme Court under Chief Justice Earl Warren as being "unprecedentedly politically active . . . using their interpretation of the law to remake American society according to their own social, political, and ideological precepts." When Warren resigned in 1969, Nixon replaced him with Warren E. Burger, a federal appeals court judge who was a **strict constructionist**—someone inclined to interpret the Constitution narrowly and to limit government intervention on behalf of individual rights.

Unions and civil rights groups, however, mounted strong campaigns against Nixon's next two nominees, both conservative southern judges, and the Senate forced him to settle on more moderate candidates. The Burger Court proved more sympathetic than the Warren Court to the president's agenda, restricting somewhat the protections of individual rights established by the previous Court, but continuing to uphold

School Busing

Controversy over busing as a means to integrate public schools erupted in Boston when the 1974–1975 school year started. Opposition was especially high in white ethnic neighborhoods such as South Boston. Residents there resented liberal judges from the suburbs assigning them the burden of integration. Clashes between blacks and whites in South Boston, such as this one in February 1975 outside Boston's Hyde Park High School, prompted authorities to dispatch police to protect black students.
AP Images.

many of the liberal programs of the 1960s. For example, the Court limited the range of **affirmative action** in *Regents of the University of California v. Bakke* (1978), but it allowed affirmative action programs to attack the results of past discrimination if they avoided strict quotas or racial classifications.

Nixon's southern strategy and other repercussions of the civil rights revolution of the 1960s ended the Democratic hold on the "solid South." In 1964, Senator Strom Thurmond of South Carolina, leader of the Dixiecrat challenge to Truman in 1948, changed his party affiliation to Republican. North Carolina senator Jesse Helms followed suit in 1971, and aspirants for office throughout the South began to realize that the future for Democratic candidates had darkened there. By 2005, Republicans held the majority of southern seats in both houses of Congress and governorships in seven southern states.

In addition to capitalizing on racial issues, Nixon aligned himself with those fearful about women's changing roles and new demands. In 1971, he vetoed a bill providing federal funds for day care centers with a message that combined the old and new conservatism. Parents should purchase child care services "in the private, open market," he insisted, not through government programs. He played to concerns of social conservatives by warning about the measure's "family-weakening implications." In response to the movement to liberalize abortion laws, Nixon sided with "defenders of the right to life of the unborn." He did not comment publicly on *Roe v. Wade* (1973), but his earlier stance against abortion anticipated the Republican Party's eventual embrace of this as a key issue for the New Right.

> **REVIEW** How did Nixon's policies reflect the increasing influence of conservatives on the Republican Party?

Constitutional Crisis and Restoration

Nixon's ability to attract Democrats resulted in his resounding victory in the 1972 election. Two years later, however, the so-called Watergate scandal caused him to abandon his office. Nixon's abuse of power and efforts to cover up crimes committed by subordinates betrayed the public trust and forced the first presidential resignation in history. His handpicked successor, Gerald Ford, helped restore confidence in the presidency, but the aftermath of Watergate and severe economic problems returned the White House to the Democrats in 1976. Nonetheless, so robust was the conservative tide that it not only survived the temporary setback when Nixon resigned the presidency but also quickly challenged the Democratic administration that followed.

The Election of 1972

Nixon's ability to appeal to concerns about Vietnam, race, law and order, and traditional morality heightened his prospects for reelection in 1972. Although the war in Vietnam continued, antiwar protests diminished with the decrease in American ground forces and casualties. Nixon's economic initiatives had temporarily checked inflation and unemployment, and his attacks on busing and antiwar protesters had appealed to the right, positioning him favorably for the 1972 election.

A large field of contenders vied for the Democratic nomination, including New York representative Shirley Chisholm, the first African American to make a serious bid for the presidency. On the right, Governor George Wallace of Alabama resurfaced to capture a series of southern primaries as well as those of Michigan and Maryland, but his campaign was cut short when a shot fired by a deranged man left him paralyzed below the waist. South Dakota senator George S. McGovern came to the Democratic convention as the clear leader, and the composition of the convention delegates made his position even stronger.

After the bitter 1968 convention, the Democrats had reformed their rules, requiring delegations to represent the proportions of minorities, women, and youths in their states. These newcomers displaced many regular Democrats—officeholders, labor leaders, and representatives of entrenched ethnic groups. One labor leader thought that "the Democratic party was taken over by the kooks," referring to the considerable numbers of young people and women among these newcomers who were to the left of party regulars. Though easily nominated, McGovern struggled against Nixon from the outset. Republicans portrayed him as a left extremist, and his support for busing, a generous welfare program, immediate withdrawal from Vietnam, and deep cuts in the Pentagon's budget alienated conservative Democrats.

Seeing a parallel with Goldwater in 1964, a Nixon speechwriter called McGovern "Nixon's gift from the gods." Indeed, Nixon achieved a landslide victory second only to Johnson's, winning 60.7 percent of the popular vote and every state except Massachusetts. Although the Democrats maintained control of Congress, Nixon won majorities among traditional Democrats—southerners, Catholics, urbanites, and blue-collar workers. The president, however, had little time to savor his triumph, as revelations began to emerge about crimes committed to ensure the victory.

Watergate

During the early-morning hours of June 17, 1972, five men working for Nixon's reelection campaign crept into Democratic Party headquarters in the Watergate complex in Washington, D.C. Intending to repair a bugging device installed in an earlier break-in, they were discovered and arrested on the scene. Nixon and his aides then tried to cover up the intruders' connection to administration officials, setting in motion the most serious constitutional crisis since the Civil War. Reporters dubbed the scandal "Watergate."

Over the next two years, Americans learned that Nixon and his associates had engaged in other abuses, such as accepting illegal campaign contributions, using so-called dirty tricks to sabotage Democratic candidates, and unlawfully attempting to silence critics of the Vietnam War. Nixon was not the first president to lie to the public or to misuse power. Every president since Franklin D. Roosevelt had enlarged the powers of his office, justifying his actions as necessary to protect national security. This expansion of executive powers, often called the "imperial presidency," weakened the traditional **checks and balances** on the executive branch and opened the door to abuses.

No president, however, had dared to go as far as Nixon, who saw opposition to his policies as a personal attack and was willing to violate the Constitution to stop it. The Watergate scandal began when White House adviser Charles Colson established a secret unit nicknamed the "plumbers" to stop the kinds of "leaks" that had led to publication of the *Pentagon Papers* in 1971 (see chapter 29). These men soon turned to projects to disrupt and discredit Democrats, and in 1972 they broke into Watergate to bug the Democratic Party's phones.

Upon the arrest of the Watergate burglars, Nixon plotted to conceal links between the burglars and the White House while publicly denying any connection. In April 1973, after investigations by a grand jury and the Senate suggested that White House aides had been involved, Nixon accepted official responsibility for Watergate but denied any knowledge of the break-in or cover-up. He also announced the resignations of three White House aides and the attorney general. In May, he authorized the appointment of an independent special prosecutor, Archibald Cox, to conduct an investigation.

Meanwhile, sensational revelations exploded in the Senate investigating committee, headed by Democrat Samuel J. Ervin of North Carolina. White House counsel John Dean described projects to harass "enemies" through tax audits and other illegal means and implicated the president in efforts to cover up the Watergate break-in. The most damaging blow struck when a White House aide disclosed that all conversations in the Oval Office were taped. Both Cox and the Ervin committee immediately asked for the tapes related to Watergate. When Nixon refused, citing executive privilege and separation of powers, Cox and Ervin took their case to court.

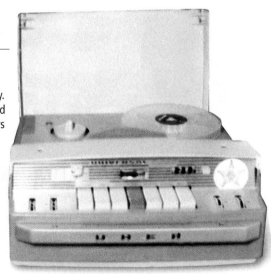

The Gap in the Watergate Tapes

Franklin Roosevelt installed the first recording apparatus in the White House under his desk in 1940, but neither he, Truman, nor Eisenhower recorded conversations extensively. John F. Kennedy was the first president to put in a complete taping network, and Richard Nixon was the first to use a voice-activated system. This system taped about 2,800 hours of conversations, which most participants did not know were being recorded. When Nixon was compelled to turn over the tapes during the Watergate investigation, an eighteen-and-a-half-minute gap was discovered in a conversation between Nixon and his chief of staff, H. R. Haldeman, just three days after the Watergate break-in. Nixon's secretary, Rose Mary Woods, said that her foot must have slipped on the controls while she was transcribing the tape, using the transcription machine pictured here. Others, noting that the gap contained several separate erasings, suggested that the clumsiness of the deed linked it to Nixon.

Nixon Presidential Materials Project, National Archives and Records Administration.

Additional disclosures exposed Nixon's misuse of federal funds and tax evasion. In August 1973, Vice President Spiro Agnew resigned after an investigation revealed that he had taken bribes while governor of Maryland. Although Nixon's choice of House minority leader Gerald Ford of Michigan to succeed Agnew won widespread approval, Agnew's resignation further tarnished the administration.

On October 19, 1973, Nixon ordered special prosecutor Cox to stop trying to obtain the Oval Office tapes. When Cox refused, Nixon directed Attorney General Elliot Richardson to fire Cox. Richardson instead resigned, as did the next man in line at the Justice Department. Finally, the solicitor general, Robert Bork, agreed to carry out the president's order and fire Cox. The press called the series of dismissals and resignations the "Saturday night massacre." Soon 250,000 telegrams condemning Nixon's action flooded the White House, and his popular support plummeted to 27 percent.

In a famous televised speech, Nixon insisted, "I am not a crook," but in February 1974, the House of Representatives voted to begin an **impeachment** investigation. In April, Nixon began to release edited transcripts of the tapes. As the public read passages sprinkled with "expletive deleted," House Republican leader Hugh Scott of Pennsylvania abandoned his support of

> As the public read passages sprinkled with "expletive deleted," House Republican leader Hugh Scott of Pennsylvania abandoned his support of the president, calling the Watergate transcripts a "deplorable, shabby, disgusting, and immoral performance by all."

the president, calling the transcripts a "deplorable, shabby, disgusting, and immoral performance by all." The transcripts revealed Nixon's orders to aides in March 1973: "I don't give a shit what happens. I want you all to stonewall it, let them plead the Fifth Amendment, cover up or anything else, if it'll save it—save the plan."

In July 1974, the House Judiciary Committee began debate over specific charges for impeachment: (1) obstruction of justice, (2) abuse of power, (3) contempt of Congress, (4) unconstitutional waging of war by the secret bombing of Cambodia, and (5) tax evasion and the selling of political favors. The committee voted to take the first three charges to the House, where a vote of impeachment seemed certain. Ordered by a unanimous Supreme Court to hand over the remaining tapes, Nixon released transcripts on August 5 that contained his conversations about how to use the CIA to hinder the FBI's investigation of the break-in. This was sufficient evidence to seal his fate.

Nixon announced his resignation to a national television audience on August 8, 1974. Acknowledging some incorrect judgments, he insisted that he had always tried to do what was best for the nation. The next morning, Nixon ended a rambling, emotional farewell to his staff with some advice: "Always give your best, never get discouraged, never get petty; always remember, others may hate you, but those who hate you don't win unless you hate them, and then you destroy yourself." Had he practiced that advice, he might have saved his presidency.

Nixon Resigns
The first president in U.S. history to resign his office, Nixon refused to admit guilt, even though tapes of his conversations indicated that he had obstructed justice, abused his power, and lied. In the decades after his resignation, he gradually rehabilitated his reputation and became an elder statesman and foreign policy adviser. All the living presidents attended his funeral in 1994. Here, he and his wife, Pat, are escorted by his successor, Gerald Ford, and his wife, Betty, as they leave the White House.
© Bettmann/Corbis.

The Ford Presidency and the 1976 Election

Gerald R. Ford, who had represented Michigan in the House of Representatives since 1948, had built a reputation as a conservative party loyalist. Not a brilliant thinker, he was known for his integrity, humility, and dedication to public office. "I'm a Ford, not a Lincoln," he acknowledged. Most of official Washington and the American public looked favorably on his succession as president.

Upon taking office, Ford announced, "Our long nightmare is over," but he shocked many Americans one month later when he ended the particular nightmare of the former president. On September 8, 1974, he granted Nixon a pardon "for all offenses against the United States which he . . . has committed or may have committed or taken part in" during his presidency. This most generous presidential pardon ever issued saved Nixon from nearly certain indictment and trial. The pardon provoked a tremendous outcry from Congress and the public. Democratic senator Mike Mansfield declared, "All men are created equal," and "that includes presidents and plumbers." Democrats made impressive gains in the November congressional elections, while Ford's action gave Nixon a new political life. Having gained a pardon without having to admit that he had broken the law, violated his oath of office, and betrayed the public trust, he rebuilt his image over the next two decades into that of an elder statesman. Thirty of his associates ultimately pleaded guilty to or were convicted of crimes related to Watergate.

Congress moved to guard against the types of abuses revealed in the Watergate investigations. The Federal Election Campaign Act of 1974, for example, established public financing of presidential campaigns and imposed some restrictions on contributions to help prevent the selling of political favors. Yet politicians found other ways of raising money, for example through political action committees (PACs) of interest groups, to which individuals could contribute more than they could to individual candidates. Moreover, in the 1976 case *Buckley v. Valeo*, the Supreme Court struck down limitations on campaign spending by equating such spending with freedom of speech, guaranteed by the First Amendment. Ever-larger campaign donations flowed to candidates from interest groups, corporations, labor unions, and wealthy individuals. In 1978, Congress established a nonpartisan procedure for appointing special prosecutors.

The law was used to investigate possible criminal actions by Presidents Reagan and Clinton (see chapter 31), as well as several lesser officials, before it expired in 1998.

Special investigating committees in Congress discovered a host of illegal FBI and CIA activities stretching back to the 1950s, including harassment of political dissenters and plots to assassinate Fidel Castro and other foreign leaders. In response to these revelations, President Ford established new controls on covert operations, and Congress created permanent committees to oversee the intelligence agencies. Yet these measures did little to diminish the public's cynicism and lack of trust in government that had been developing since the 1960s.

Disillusionment with government grew as the Ford administration seemed unable to resolve serious economic problems: a low growth rate, high unemployment, a foreign trade deficit, and soaring energy prices tied to dependence on oil from abroad. Ford carried these burdens into the election campaign of 1976, while contending with a major challenge from the Republican right. Blasting Nixon's and Ford's foreign policy of **détente** for causing the "loss of U.S. military supremacy," California governor Ronald Reagan came close to capturing the nomination.

The Democrats nominated James Earl "Jimmy" Carter Jr., former governor of Georgia. A graduate of the U.S. Naval Academy, Carter spent seven years as a nuclear engineer in the navy before returning to Plains, Georgia, to run the family peanut farming business. Carefully prepared on policy issues, the soft-spoken candidate appealed to the rise of **evangelical** religion and alienation from government by stressing his profound faith as a "born-again Christian" and his distance from the government in Washington. Although he selected liberal senator Walter F. Mondale of Minnesota as his running mate and accepted a platform compatible with traditional Democratic principles, Carter's nomination nonetheless marked a decided rightward turn in the party.

In light of the revelations of corruption in the Nixon administration, Carter had considerable appeal as a candidate who carried his own bags, lived modestly, and taught a Bible class at his Baptist church. He also benefited from Ford's failure to solve the country's economic problems, which helped him win the traditional Democratic coalition of blacks, organized labor,

> Not a brilliant thinker, Ford was known for his integrity, humility, and dedication to public office. "I'm a Ford, not a Lincoln," he acknowledged.

and ethnic groups, and even recapture some of the white southerners who had voted for Nixon in 1972. Yet although Democrats retained substantial margins in Congress, Carter received just 50 percent of the popular vote to Ford's 48 percent (Map 30.1).

> **REVIEW**　Why did Nixon resign the presidency in August 1974?

The "Outsider" Presidency of Jimmy Carter

Carter promised a government that was "competent" as well as "honest, decent, open, fair, and compassionate." He also warned Americans "that even our great Nation has its recognized limits, and that we can neither answer all questions nor solve all problems." Carter's humility, personal honesty, and decency helped revive trust in the presidency but did not inspire confidence in his ability to lead the nation through domestic and foreign crises.

Energy shortages and stagflation worsened, exposing Carter's deficiencies in working with Congress and rallying the public to his objectives. His administration achieved notable advances in environmental and energy policies, and he oversaw foreign policy successes concerning the Panama Canal, China, and the Middle East. Yet near the end of his term, Soviet-American relations deteriorated, new crises emerged in the Middle East, and the economy plummeted, all costing him a second term.

Retreat from Liberalism

Jimmy Carter vowed "to help the poor and aged, to improve education, and to provide jobs," but at the same time "not to waste money." When his desire to help conflicted with his goal to limit spending, Carter's commitment to reform took second place. Increasing numbers of Americans unhappy about their tax dollars being used to benefit the disadvantaged while stagflation eroded their own material status welcomed Carter's approach. But his fiscal stringency frustrated liberal Democrats pushing for major welfare reform and a national health insurance program. They accused him of deserting the Democratic reform tradition stretching back to Franklin D. Roosevelt.

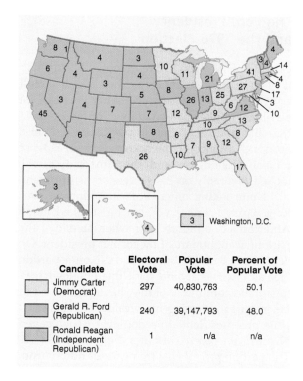

Candidate	Electoral Vote	Popular Vote	Percent of Popular Vote
Jimmy Carter (Democrat)	297	40,830,763	50.1
Gerald R. Ford (Republican)	240	39,147,793	48.0
Ronald Reagan (Independent Republican)	1	n/a	n/a

MAP 30.1　The Election of 1976

A number of factors hindered Carter's ability to lead. His outsider status had helped him win office but left him without strong ties to party leaders in Congress, who often found him self-righteous, overly self-confident, and not inclined to compromise. Democrats complained of inadequate consultation and Carter's tendency to flood them with comprehensive proposals when they were more accustomed to incremental reforms. In addition, Carter refused to offer simple solutions to the American people, who had a short attention span and were impatient for quick action against the forces that were squeezing their pocketbooks. Moreover, even though the Democrats continued to control Congress, party leaders were hard-pressed to deliver a united front. Reforms in response to highly publicized scandals that had touched congressional leaders in the 1960s had reduced the power of committee chairs and decentralized the decision-making process.

Even an expert in the art of persuasion might not have done much better than Carter. The economic problems he inherited from the Nixon and Ford administrations—unemployment, inflation, and sluggish economic growth—confounded economic doctrine, which assumed that when unemployment was high, inflation would be low,

Jimmy Carter's Inauguration
After his inauguration in January 1977, Jimmy Carter eschewed the customary presidential limousine and instead walked with his wife, daughter, and two sons and their wives down Pennsylvania Avenue from the Capitol to the White House. He wanted to emphasize his opposition to some of the trappings of office that separated government from the people. Ordering cabinet heads to drive their own cars, he told the American people, "Government officials can't be sensitive to your problems if we are living like royalty here."
Jimmy Carter Presidential Library.

and vice versa. Usually, rising prices accompanied a humming economy with a strong demand for labor. Now, however, the nation faced steep inflation and high unemployment at the same time.

Carter first targeted unemployment. Although liberals complained that his programs did not do enough, Carter signed bills pumping $14 billion into the economy through public works and public service jobs programs and cutting taxes by $34 billion over a three-year period. Unemployment, which had hovered near 8 percent in late 1976, fell below 6 percent in 1978. But then inflation surged. Working people, wrote one journalist, "winced and ached. . . . Promises had been made to all of them over the two decades; but now the promises were being redeemed in money which might become as worthless as Confederate dollars." To curb inflation, Carter curtailed federal spending, and the Federal Reserve Board tightened the money supply. Not only did these measures fail to halt inflation, which surpassed 13

percent in 1980, but they also contributed to rising unemployment, reversing the gains made in Carter's first two years.

Long-standing liberal objectives made little headway under Carter. His commitment to holding down the federal budget frustrated Democrats pushing for comprehensive welfare reform, national health insurance, and a wide-ranging program to create jobs for all by making the government the employer of last resort. Carter did sign legislation to ensure solvency in the Social Security system, but the measure increased both employer and employee contributions, thereby increasing the tax burden of lower- and middle-income Americans.

By contrast, corporations and wealthy individuals gained from new legislation, such as a sharp cut in the capital gains tax. When the

> When inflation surged, working people, wrote one journalist, "winced and ached. . . . Promises had been made to all of them . . . ; but now the promises were being redeemed in money which might become as worthless as Confederate dollars."

Chrysler Corporation approached bankruptcy in 1979, Congress provided $1.5 billion in loan guarantees to ensure the survival of the tenth-largest corporation in the country. Congress also acted on Carter's proposals to give greater rein to free enterprise, deregulating airlines in 1978 and the banking, trucking, and railroad industries in 1980. Carter's successor would move much further, implementing conservatives' attachment to a free market and unfettered private enterprise.

Energy and Environmental Reform

Complicating the government's efforts to deal with stagflation was the nation's enormous consumption of energy and its dependence on foreign nations to fill one-third of its energy demands. Fuel shortages and skyrocketing oil prices threatened the entire economy, just as they had during the energy crisis of 1973. Consequently,

Carter proposed a comprehensive program to conserve energy, and he elevated its importance by establishing the Department of Energy. Beset with competing demands among energy producers and consumers, Congress picked Carter's program apart. The National Energy Act of 1978 penalized manufacturers of gas-guzzling automobiles and provided other incentives for conservation and development of alternative fuels, but the act fell far short of a long-term, comprehensive program.

In 1979, a new upheaval in the Middle East, the Iranian revolution, created the most severe energy crisis yet. In midsummer, 60 percent of gasoline stations closed down because of shortages; frustrated drivers sat in long lines at stations that were open, where they paid unprecedentedly high prices for gas. "We are struggling with a profound transition from a time of abundance to a time of growing scarcity in energy," Carter told the nation, and he asked Congress for additional measures to address this problem. Congress reduced controls on oil and gas to stimulate American production and imposed a windfall profits tax on producers to redistribute some of the profits that would accrue to them as a result of deregulation.

All of Carter's energy measures failed to reduce American dependence on foreign oil. European nations shared that dependence but more successfully controlled consumption. They levied high taxes on gasoline, causing people to rely more on public transportation and manufacturers to produce more energy-efficient cars, in the process also limiting the release of carbon gases into the atmosphere. In the automobile-dependent United States, however, where public transit was poor, people were accustomed to driving long distances, and many were seething over what they considered high taxes, politicians dismissed that approach. By the end of the century, the United States, with 6 percent of the world's population, would consume more than 25 percent of global oil production. (See "Global Comparison," page 1115, and Map 30.2, page 1116.)

One source of alternative fuel, nuclear energy, aroused opposition from a vigorous environmental movement. Activists warned of radiation leakage, potential accidents, and the hazards of radioactive wastes from nuclear power plants, which provided about 10 percent of the nation's electricity in the 1970s. In 1976, hundreds of members of the Clamshell Alliance went to jail for attempting to block construction of a nuclear power plant in Seabrook, New Hampshire. Groups such as the Abalone Alliance in Cali-

The Fuel Shortage

This billboard was sponsored by the Outdoor Advertising Association of America in 1980, while Iran held Americans hostage in Teheran (see page 1119) and gasoline shortages and rising gas prices vexed motorists all over the country. The shortages and high prices were sparked by the Iranian revolution, which brought to power Ayatollah Ruholla Khomeini, pictured on the billboard. The ad appeals to drivers to observe the 55-mile-per-hour national speed limit imposed in 1974 during the first oil crisis.

John W. Hartman Center/Duke University Special Collections Library.

READING THE IMAGE: What assumptions does the billboard make about Americans' reactions to the Iran hostage crisis? What reasons does the ad give for drivers to respect the speed limit? What reasons are omitted?

CONNECTIONS: What impact did the hostage and oil crises have on American politics?

FOR MORE HELP ANALYZING THIS IMAGE, see the visual activity for this chapter in the Online Study Guide at bedfordstmartins.com/roark.

GLOBAL COMPARISON

Energy Consumption per Capita, 1980

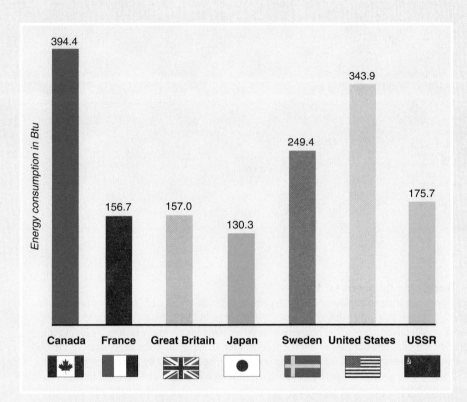

Energy consumption in Btu

Canada	France	Great Britain	Japan	Sweden	United States	USSR
394.4	156.7	157.0	130.3	249.4	343.9	175.7

Relative to most other industrialized nations, the United States consumed energy voraciously, with a per capita rate of consumption in 1980 that was more than twice as high as that of Britain, France, and Japan and nearly twice as high as that of the Soviet Union. A number of factors influence a nation's energy consumption (shown here in British thermal units, or Btu), including standard of living, climate, size of landmass and dispersal of population, availability and price of energy, and government policies such as support for public transportation. What country had a per capita rate of consumption even higher than that of the United States?

fornia and SHAD (Sound and Hudson against Atomic Development) on Long Island, New York, sprang up across the United States to demand an environment safe from nuclear radiation and waste.

The perils of nuclear energy claimed international attention in March 1979, when an accident occurred at the Three Mile Island nuclear facility near Harrisburg, Pennsylvania. Technicians worked for days to prevent a meltdown of the reactor core. Popular opposition and the great expense of building nuclear power plants stalled further development of the industry. The explosion of a nuclear reactor and the spread of deadly radiation in

Chernobyl, Ukraine, in 1986 further solidified antinuclear concerns as part of the environmental movement.

A disaster at Love Canal in Niagara Falls, New York, advanced other environmental goals by underscoring the human costs of unregulated development. Residents there suffering high rates of serious illness noted that their homes sat amid highly toxic waste products from a nearby chemical company. One Love Canal resident, Lois Gibbs, who eventually headed a national movement against toxic wastes, explained how she and many other women were galvanized to become environmentalists: "I never thought of myself as an activist or organizer. I was

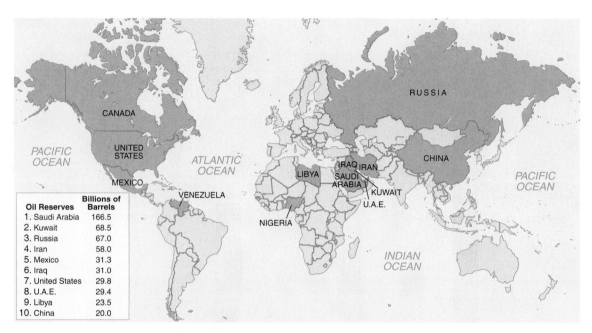

MAP 30.2 Worldwide Oil Reserves, 1980
Data produced by geologists and engineers enable experts to estimate the size of "proved oil reserves," quantities that are recoverable with existing technology and prices. In 1980, the total worldwide reserves were estimated at 645 billion barrels. The recovery of reserves depends on many factors, including the precise location of the oil. Large portions of the U.S. reserves, for example, lie under deep water in the Gulf of Mexico, where it is expensive to drill and where operations can be disrupted by hurricanes. But the U.S. government is much more generous than most nations in allowing oil companies to take oil from public land, imposing relatively low taxes and royalty payments.

READING THE MAP: Where did the United States rank in 1980 in the possession of oil reserves? About what portion of the total oil reserves are located in the Middle East?
CONNECTIONS: At what points during the 1970s did the United States experience oil shortages? What caused these shortages?

FOR MORE HELP ANALYZING THIS MAP, see the map activity for this chapter in the Online Study Guide at
bedfordstmartins.com/roark.

a housewife, a mother, but all of a sudden it was my family, my children, and my neighbors." Finally responding to the activists in 1978, the State of New York agreed to help families relocate, and the Carter administration sponsored legislation in 1980 that created the so-called Superfund, $1.6 billion for cleanup of hazardous wastes left by the chemical industry.

Carter's environmental legislation did not stop there. He signed bills to improve clean air and water programs; to expand the Arctic National Wildlife Refuge preserve (ANWR) in Alaska; and to control strip-mining, which left destructive scars on the land. During the 1979 gasoline crisis, Carter attempted to balance the development of domestic fuel sources with environmental concerns. Acknowledging that "some of the new technologies we will need to develop pose environmental risks," he upset some envi-

ronmental activists. But he also won legislation to conserve energy and to provide incentives for the development of environmentally friendly alternative fuels, such as solar energy.

Promoting Human Rights Abroad

Campaigning in 1976, Jimmy Carter charged that his predecessors' foreign policy violated the nation's principles of freedom and human dignity. "We're ashamed of what our government is as we deal with other nations around the world," he said. Carter promised to reverse the cynical support of dictators, secret diplomacy, interference in the internal affairs of other countries, and excessive reliance on military solutions.

Human rights formed the cornerstone of his approach. Carter administration officials chastised governments that denied their citizens basic rights, and they applied economic pressure, denying aid or trading privileges to nations such as Argentina, Chile, and El Salvador, as well as to the white minority governments of Rhodesia and South Africa, which brutally violated the rights of their black majorities. Yet in other instances, Carter sacrificed human rights ideals in favor of strategic and security considerations. He invoked no sanctions against repressive governments in Iran, South Korea, and the Philippines, for example, and he established formal diplomatic relations with the People's Republic of China in 1979, even though the Chinese government blatantly refused to grant its people **democratic** rights.

Carter's human rights principles faced another test when a popular movement overthrew an oppressive dictatorship in Nicaragua. U.S. officials were uneasy about the leftist Sandinistas who led the rebellion and had ties to Cuba. Once they assumed power in 1979, however, Carter recognized the new government and sent economic aid, signaling that the way a government treated its citizens was as important as how anti-Communist and friendly to American interests it was.

Applying moral principles to relations with Panama, Carter sped up negotiations over control of the Panama Canal and in 1977 obtained a treaty providing for joint control of the canal until 2000, when Panama would take over. Supporters viewed the treaty as recompense for the blatant use of U.S. power to obtain the canal in 1903. Opponents insisted on retaining the vital waterway. "We bought it, we paid for it, it's ours," claimed Ronald Reagan during the presidential primaries of 1976. It took a massive effort by the administration to get Senate ratification of the treaty.

Seeking to promote peace in the Middle East, Carter seized on the courage of Egyptian president Anwar Sadat, the first Arab leader to risk his political career by talking directly with Israeli officials. Carter invited Sadat and Israeli prime minister Menachem Begin to the presidential retreat at Camp David, Maryland, where he applied his tenacious diplomacy, mediating between the two for thirteen days. These talks led to an agreement—the Camp David accords— that Begin and Sadat signed at the White House in March 1979. Egypt became the first Arab state to recognize Israel, and Israel agreed to gradual withdrawal from the Sinai Peninsula, which it had seized in the 1967 Six-Day War (Map 30.3, page 1118). Although the issues of Palestinian self-determination in other Israeli-occupied territories (the West Bank and Gaza) and the plight of Palestinian refugees remained unresolved, Carter had facilitated the first meaningful steps toward peace in the Middle East.

The Cold War Intensifies

Consistent with his human rights approach, Carter preferred to pursue national security through nonmilitary means and initially sought accommodation with the Soviet Union. But in 1979, he abandoned efforts to obtain Senate ratification of a new strategic arms limitation treaty and began development of an enormous new missile system and intermediate-range missiles to be deployed in Western Europe.

Carter's decision to pursue a military buildup came in 1979 when the Soviet Union invaded neighboring Afghanistan, whose recently installed Communist government was threatened by Muslim opposition (see Map 30.3). Insisting that the Soviet aggression "could pose the greatest threat to peace since the Second World War," Carter also imposed economic sanctions on the Soviet Union, barred U.S. participation in the 1980 Summer Olympic Games in Moscow, and obtained legislation requiring all nineteen-year-old men to register for the **draft**.

Claiming that Soviet actions jeopardized oil supplies from the Middle East, the president announced the "Carter Doctrine," threatening the use of any means necessary to prevent an outside force from gaining control of the Persian Gulf. His human rights policy fell by the wayside as the United States stepped up aid to the military dictatorship in Afghanistan's neighbor, Pakistan. Carter authorized the CIA to provide aid secretly to the Afghan rebels, which it funneled through Pakistan. Finally, Carter called for hefty increases in defense spending.

Events in Iran also encouraged this reversion to a hard-line, militaristic approach. All the U.S. arms and aid had not enabled the shah to crush Iranian dissidents who still resented the CIA's role in the overthrow of the Mossadegh government in 1953 (see chapter 27), condemned the shah's savage attempts to silence opposition, and detested his adoption of Western **culture** and values. These grievances erupted into a revolution in 1979 that forced the shah out of Iran. Just two years earlier, Carter had pronounced the shah's government "an island of stability," and the revolution shocked U.S. officials who failed to detect the

> Carter insisted that Soviet aggression in Afghanistan "could pose the greatest threat to peace since the Second World War."

growing hostility toward American support for dictators in the Middle East. The new provisional government began talks with the United States, but it soon gave way to Shiite Islamic **fundamentalists** led by Ayatollah Ruholla Khomeini, whom the shah had exiled in 1964.

Carter's decision to allow the shah into the United States for medical treatment intensified anti-Americanism among Iranians, who believed that the United States would put the shah back in power as it had done in 1953. Demonstrations against the United States escalated in the capital city of Teheran. On November 4, 1979, a crowd broke into the U.S. Embassy and seized sixty-six U.S. diplomats, CIA officers, citizens, and military attachés (who were ordered not to fire). Refusing their demands that the shah be returned to Iran for trial, Carter froze Iranian assets in U.S. banks and placed an embargo on Iranian oil. In April 1980, he sent a small military operation into Iran, but the rescue mission failed.

The disastrous rescue attempt and scenes of blindfolded and cuffed U.S. citizens paraded before TV cameras fed Americans' feelings of impotence, simmering since the defeat in Vietnam. These frustrations in turn increased support for a more militaristic foreign policy. Opposition to Soviet-American détente, combined with the Soviet invasion of Afghanistan, nullified the thaw in relations that had begun in the 1960s.

MAP 30.3   The Middle East, 1948–1989

Determination to preserve access to the rich oil reserves of the Middle East and commitment to the security of Israel were the fundamental—and often conflicting—principles of U.S. foreign policy in that region.

Reading the map: Where did the United States become involved diplomatically or militarily in the Middle East between 1948 and 1989? Which countries are members of OPEC?

Connections: What role did U.S. foreign policy regarding the Middle East and events in Israel play in provoking the 1973 Arab oil embargo against the United States? What precipitated the taking of U.S. hostages in Iran in 1979? Was U.S. intervention in the country a factor? If so, why?

For more help analyzing this map, see the map activity for this chapter in the Online Study Guide at bedfordstmartins.com/roark.

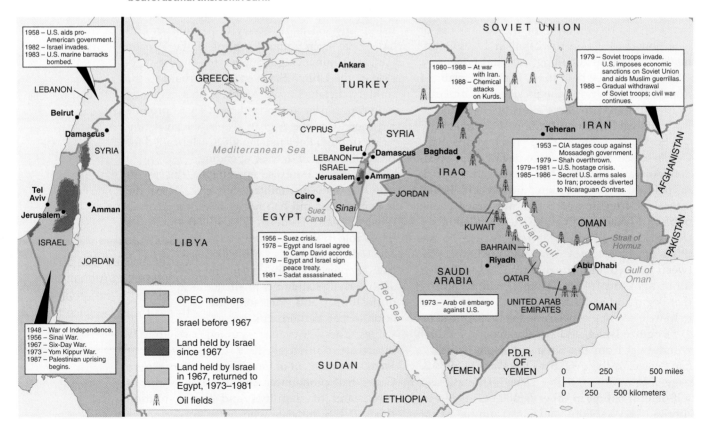

1958 – U.S. aids pro-American government.
1982 – Israel invades.
1983 – U.S. marine barracks bombed.

1980–1988 – At war with Iran.
1988 – Chemical attacks on Kurds.

1979 – Soviet troops invade. U.S. imposes economic sanctions on Soviet Union and aids Muslim guerrillas.
1988 – Gradual withdrawal of Soviet troops; civil war continues.

1953 – CIA stages coup against Mossadegh government.
1979 – Shah overthrown.
1979–1981 – U.S. hostage crisis.
1985–1986 – Secret U.S. arms sales to Iran; proceeds diverted to Nicaraguan Contras.

1956 – Suez crisis.
1978 – Egypt and Israel agree to Camp David accords.
1979 – Egypt and Israel sign peace treaty.
1981 – Sadat assassinated.

1973 – Arab oil embargo against U.S.

1948 – War of Independence.
1956 – Sinai War.
1967 – Six-Day War.
1973 – Yom Kippur War.
1987 – Palestinian uprising begins.

OPEC members
Israel before 1967
Land held by Israel since 1967
Land held by Israel in 1967, returned to Egypt, 1973–1981
Oil fields

American Hostages in Iran
For more than a year—from November 4, 1979, to January 20, 1981—Americans regularly saw TV images of the hostages taken by Iranian militants when they occupied the U.S. Embassy in Teheran. Many Americans donned yellow ribbons or tied them around trees and car antennas to demonstrate their concern for the hostages. Early in the crisis, Ayatollah Khomeini ordered the release of thirteen of the sixty-six hostages, all women or African Americans, because he believed they were not spies and had already endured "the oppression of American society." Here the thirteen are presented to the press shortly before their release.
Hostages: © Sygma/Corbis; Ribbon: Collection of Janice L. and David J. Frent.

The American hostages in Iran filled the news during the 1980 presidential campaign and contributed to Carter's defeat. Iran freed the hostages the day he left office, but relations with the United States remained tense.

> **REVIEW** How did Carter attempt to balance his commitment to human rights and anticommunism in his foreign policy?

Ronald Reagan and the Conservative Ascendancy

Ronald Reagan's election in 1980 marked the most important turning point in politics since Franklin D. Roosevelt won the presidency in 1932. Eisenhower and Nixon were middle-of-the-road Republicans, but Reagan's victory established conservatism's dominance in the Republican Party. Since the 1930s, the Democrats had defined the major issues. In the 1980s, the Republicans assumed that initiative, while Democrats searched for voter support by moving toward the right. The United States was not alone in this political shift. Conservatives rose to power in Britain with Prime Minister Margaret Thatcher, and they led governments in Germany, Canada, and Sweden, while socialist and social democratic governments in France and elsewhere trimmed their welfare states.

On the domestic front, the Reagan administration embraced the conservative Christian values of the New Right, but it left its most important mark on the economy: victory over inflation, deregulation of industry, a moratorium on social spending, enormous tax cuts, and a staggering

Ronald Reagan Nominated for President
Nancy and Ronald Reagan respond to cheers at the 1980 Republican National Convention, where he was nominated for president. Reagan became one of the most popular presidents of the twentieth century.
Lester Sloan/Woodfin Camp & Associates.

federal budget deficit. Economic expansion, which took off after 1983, helped the middle class and brought great wealth to some, but the percentage of poor Americans increased, and income distribution became more unequal. Although the Reagan era did not see a policy revolution comparable to that of the **New Deal**, it dealt a sharp blow to the liberalism that had informed American politics since that time.

Appealing to the New Right and Beyond

The oldest candidate ever nominated for the presidency, Ronald Reagan was born in Tampico, Illinois, in 1911. After attending a small religious college, he worked as a sportscaster before becoming a movie actor. He initially shared the politics of his staunchly Democratic father but moved to the right in the 1940s and 1950s and campaigned for Goldwater in 1964.

Reagan's political career took off when he was elected governor of California in 1966. He ran as a conservative, but in office he displayed considerable flexibility, approving a major tax increase, a strong water pollution bill, and a liberal abortion law. Displaying similar agility in the 1980 presidential campaign, he softened earlier attacks on programs such as Social Security and chose the moderate George H. W. Bush as his running mate.

Despite his move to the center, some Republicans balked at his nomination and at the party platform, which reflected the concerns of the party's right wing. For example, after Phyllis Schlafly persuaded the party to reverse its forty-year support for the Equal Rights Amendment, moderate and liberal Republican women protested outside the convention hall. (See "Historical Question," page 1122.) Some Republicans found a more acceptable presidential candidate in Illinois representative John B. Anderson, who deserted his party to run as an independent.

Reagan's campaign capitalized on the economic recession and the international challenges symbolized by the Americans held hostage in Iran. Repeatedly, Reagan asked voters, "Are you better off now than you were four years ago?" He promised to "take government off the backs of the people" and to restore Americans' morale and other nations' respect. A narrow majority of voters, 51 percent, responded to Reagan's upbeat message. Carter won 41 percent of the vote, and 7 percent went to Anderson. The 1980 election also delivered control of the Senate to the Republicans for the first time since the 1950s.

While the economy and Iran sealed Reagan's victory, he also benefited from the burgeoning grassroots conservative movements. An extraordinarily adept politician, Reagan appealed to a wide spectrum of groups and sentiments: free-market advocates, militant anti-Communists, fundamentalist Christians, white southerners, and white working-class Democrats—the so-called "Reagan Democrats," disenchanted with the Great Society and suffering from the high inflation and unemployment rates of the 1970s.

A critical bloc of Reagan's support came from religious conservatives, predominantly Protestants, who constituted a relatively new phenomenon in politics known as the New Right or New Christian Right. During the 1970s, evangelical and fundamentalist Christianity claimed thousands of new adherents, making adept use of sophisticated mass-mailing techniques and the "electronic ministry." Evangelical ministers such as Pat Robertson preached to huge television audiences, attacking feminism, abortion, and homosexuality and calling for the restoration of old-fashioned "family values." They wanted prayer back in the schools and sex education out of them. A considerable number of Catholics, such as Phyllis Schlafly, shared the fundamentalists' goal of a return to their version of "Christian values."

Conservatives created a raft of political organizations, such as the Moral Majority, founded by minister Jerry Falwell in 1979 to fight "left-wing, social-welfare bills, . . . pornography, homosexuality, [and] the advocacy of immorality in school textbooks." The Christian Coalition, created by Pat Robertson in 1989, claimed 1.6 million members and control of the  Republican Party in more than a dozen states. The instruments of more traditional conservatives, who advocated limited government at home and militant anticommunism abroad, likewise flourished. These included publications such as the *National Review*, founded in the 1950s and edited by William F. Buckley Jr., and conservative think tanks such as the American Enterprise Institute. The monthly *Phyllis Schlafly Report* merged the sentiments of the old and new right, which were also manifest in its publisher's organization, Eagle Forum.

Reagan embraced the full spectrum of conservatism, including its inconsistencies. For example, the New Right's demand for government intervention into private matters to stop abortion and homosexuality conflicted with the traditional conservative attachment to **laissez faire**. Reagan avowed agreement on abortion, school prayer, and other New Right issues, but he did not push hard for so-called moral or social policies. Instead, his major achievements lay in areas most important to the older right—strengthening the nation's anti-Communist posture and reducing taxes and government restraints on free enterprise. "In the present crisis," Reagan declared, "government is not the solution to our problem, government is the problem."

Reagan's admirers stretched far beyond conservatives. The extraordinarily popular president was liked even by Americans who opposed his policies and even when he made glaring mistakes. At one meeting, he failed to recognize his secretary of housing and urban development, the only African American in his cabinet. On another occasion, he proclaimed that vegetation caused 90 percent of all air pollution, prompting student environmentalists to adorn a tree with a sign read-

ing, "Chop me down before I kill again." Reagan made so many misstatements that aides tried to keep him away from reporters, and they carefully scripted the former actor's public appearances.

Reagan's optimism, confidence, and easygoing humor formed a large part of his appeal. Ignoring the darker moments of the American past, he presented a version of history that Americans could feel good about. Listeners understood his declaration that it was "morning in America" as a promise that the best was yet to come. Reagan also gained public sympathy after being shot by a would-be assassin in March 1981. Just before surgery to remove the bullet, Reagan joked to physicians, "I hope you're Republicans." His tremendous popularity helped him withstand serious charges of executive branch misconduct in his second term.

Unleashing Free Enterprise

Reagan's first domestic objective was a massive tax cut. Although tax reduction in the face of a large budget deficit contradicted traditional Republican economic doctrine, Reagan relied on a new theory called **supply-side economics**, which held that cutting taxes would actually increase revenue. Supply-siders insisted that lower taxes would enable businesses to expand, encourage individuals to work harder because they could keep more of their earnings, and increase the production of goods and services—the supply—which in turn would boost demand. Reagan promised that the economy would grow so much that the government would recoup the lost taxes, but instead it incurred a galloping deficit.

In the summer of 1981, Congress passed the Economic Recovery Tax Act, the largest tax reduction in U.S. history. Rates of individuals with the lowest incomes fell from 14 percent to 11 percent, while those of individuals with the highest incomes dropped from 70 percent to 50 percent. The law gave corporations tax breaks and cut taxes on capital gains, gifts, and inheritances. A second measure, the Tax Reform Act of 1986, reduced taxes even more, lowering the maximum rate on individual income to 28 percent and on business income to 35 percent. Although the 1986 law narrowed loopholes used primarily by the wealthy, affluent Americans saved far more on their tax bills than did average taxpayers, and the distribution of wealth tipped further in favor of the rich.

> "In the present crisis," Reagan declared, "government is not the solution to our problem, government is the problem."

Why Did the ERA Fail?

The proposed Equal Rights Amendment to the U.S. Constitution guaranteed simply that women and men would be treated equally under the law: "Equality of rights under the law shall not be denied or abridged by the United States or by any State on account of sex." Two more short sections gave Congress enforcement powers and provided that the ERA would take effect two years after ratification. By the 1970s, it had become the symbol of the late-twentieth-century women's movement.

Members of a small, militant feminist organization, the National Woman's Party, first proposed an equal rights amendment to the Constitution in 1923, but it won little support either in Congress or among the public before the resurgence of feminism in the mid-1960s. In 1968, the National Organization for Women (NOW) made it a key objective and, armed with support from traditional women's organizations and liberal groups, began to pressure Congress. The pressure took many forms, including **civil disobedience**. In early 1970, for example, NOW members disrupted a Senate subcommittee hearing on extending the vote to eighteen-year-olds, demanding Senate hearings on the ERA. Feminists and their allies, including women in both political parties, lobbied Congress and flooded some congressional offices with fifteen hundred letters a month.

Despite opposition in committee hearings, both houses of the Democratic-controlled Congress passed the amendment by overwhelming margins, 354 to 23 in the House and 84 to 8 in the Senate. Within three hours of Senate passage in March

1972, Hawaii rushed to become the first state to ratify. By the end of 1972, twenty-three states had done so. Public opinion heavily favored ratification, peaking at 74 percent in favor in 1974 and never falling below 52 percent, while the opposition never topped 31 percent. Yet even after Congress extended the time period for ratification until 1982, the ERA failed. The Constitution requires approval of amendments by three-fourths of the states, and only thirty-five states ratified, three short of the minimum needed (see the map on page 1128). Why did a measure with so much congressional and popular support fail?

The ERA encountered well-organized and passionate opposition linked to the growing conservative forces in the 1970s. Opponents ranged from religious organizations, such as the National Council of Catholic Women, to local groups such as HOTDOGS (Humanitarians Opposed to the Degradation of Our Girls), sponsored by the John Birch Society in Utah. Leading the resistance was Phyllis Schlafly.

Conservatives' opposition to the ERA reflected in part their distaste for big government and their demand for a strong defense system to counter communism. Schlafly predicted that the amendment would transfer power from state legislatures and even from families to the federal government. The ERA would put women in fox-holes alongside men, she warned, weakening the military and making the nation more vulnerable to communism. To these arguments, the New Right added claims that the ERA would destroy the American family.

ERA opponents raised fears about the amendment by suggesting

extravagant ways in which courts might interpret it. Senator Samuel J. Ervin Jr., nationally known for his chairing of the Watergate hearings, claimed that the ERA would eliminate laws against rape, require male and female prisoners to be housed together, and deprive women of alimony and child support. Others claimed that it would legalize homosexual marriage. Overall, the anti-ERA forces emphasized sex differences. By destroying the distinct sex roles on which the family was based, Ervin claimed, the ERA would destroy the family and produce "increased rates of alcoholism, suicide, and possible sexual deviation."

Anti-ERA arguments spoke to many women's religious beliefs and understandings of their own self-interest. In contrast to feminists who viewed traditional sex roles as constructed by society, anti-ERA men and women believed that they were God given. Evangelical minister and politician Jerry Falwell declared the ERA "a definite violation of holy Scripture [and its] mandate that 'the husband is the head of the wife.'" Many ERA opponents were full-time housewives who had no stake in equal treatment in the marketplace and who feared that the amendment would eliminate the duty of men to support their families. Women in both camps recognized the precariousness of economic security, but whereas feminists wanted to render women self-sustaining, antifeminists wanted men to bear responsibility for their support.

Schlafly and other conservative leaders skillfully mobilized women who saw their traditional roles threatened. In October 1972, she established a national movement called STOP (Stop Taking Our Privileges) ERA, which was so highly organized that it could respond immediately when action was necessary.

For instance, when a state legislature began to consider ratification, STOP ERA members deluged legislators with letters and lobbied them personally in state capitols. In Illinois, they gave lawmakers apple pies with notes attached that read, "My heart and my hand went into this dough / For the sake of the family please vote 'no.'" Opponents also brought baby girls to the legislature wearing signs that pleaded, "Please don't draft me." Another opposition group, Happiness of Womanhood (HOW), presented California legislators with mice bearing the message, "Do you want to be a man or a mouse?"

ERA opponents had an easier task than supporters, because the framers of the Constitution had stacked the odds against revision. All opponents had to do was to convince a minority of legislators in a minority of states to preserve the status quo. Supporters, by contrast, had to persuade a majority of lawmakers in three-quarters of the states that the need to guarantee women equal rights was urgent and could not be accomplished without a constitutional amendment. In addition, ERA forces had concentrated on winning Congress and were not prepared for the state campaigns. The intensity of the opposition took them by surprise.

Feminists had to overcome the tendency of men to trivialize women's rights. For example, when the House initially passed the ERA in 1970, the *New York Times* printed a critical editorial under the title "The Henpecked House." The conservative columnist James J. Kilpatrick called the ERA "the contrivance of a gang of professional harpies" that congressmen had voted for simply to "get these furies off their backs." The very gains feminists made in the 1960s and 1970s also worked against approval of the ERA. Congress had already banned

Phyllis Schlafly Derails the ERA in Illinois
Illinois was one of the most hotly contested states in the battle over ratification of the Equal Rights Amendment. Here Schlafly rallies ERA opponents in the state capitol in 1975. Schlafly's STOP ERA movement succeeded in Illinois, her home state and the only northern state that failed to ratify. Despite time-consuming and energetic political activities that involved traveling and speaking across the country, Schlafly insisted on calling herself a housewife.
© Bettmann/Corbis.

sex discrimination in employment, education, credit, and other areas, and the Supreme Court had struck down several state and federal laws that treated men and women differently. Even though the Court did not ban all distinctions based on sex, its decisions made it harder for ERA advocates to demonstrate the urgency of constitutional revision.

So why did the ERA fail? It failed because a handful of men in a handful of state legislatures voted against it. The shift of only a few votes in states such as Illinois and North Carolina would have meant ratification. Phyllis Schlafly's forces played a key role in the defeat, because men could vote "no" and take cover behind the many women who opposed it. And those women

proved willing to commit time, energy, and money to block ratification because conservative leaders convinced them that the ERA threatened their very way of life.

Feminists did not leave the ERA battle empty-handed, however. The National Organization for Women grew enormously during the struggle for ratification. Thousands of women were mobilized across the political spectrum and participated in the political arena for the first time. Fourteen states passed their own equal rights amendments after 1970. And feminists continued to struggle in the legislative and judicial arenas for the expansion of women's rights, struggles that continue to bear fruit in the twenty-first century.

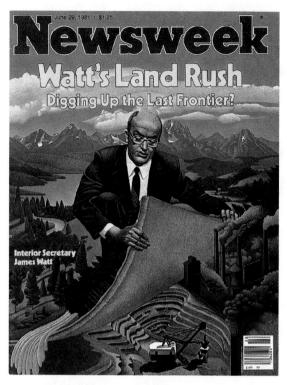

June 29, 1981 / $1.25

Newsweek

Watt's Land Rush

Digging Up the Last Frontier?

Interior Secretary
James Watt

Controversy over the Environment

Secretary of the Interior James Watt joined the Reagan cabinet committed to dismantling many of the environmental regulations of the previous two decades. His efforts drew considerable opposition, and he failed to turn back the clock substantially. In 1983, President Reagan appointed a more moderate replacement. What exactly does this *Newsweek* cover suggest that Watt wants to do to the environment?

Illustration by Wilson McLean. Reprinted with permission of the artist and *Newsweek* magazine.

READING THE IMAGE: Is the *Newsweek* cover critical of Reagan's environmental policies?
CONNECTIONS: What were Reagan's environmental policies? How did these policies reflect his conservative political ideology?

FOR MORE HELP ANALYZING THIS IMAGE, see the visual activity for this chapter in the Online Study Guide at bedfordstmartins.com/roark.

"Hack, chop, crunch!" were *Time* magazine's words for Reagan's efforts to free private enterprise from government restraints. Carter had confined deregulation to particular industries, such as air transportation and banking, while increasing health, safety, and environmental regulations. The Reagan administration, by contrast, pursued across-the-board deregulation. It declined to enforce the Sherman Antitrust Act (see chapter 18), which was designed to limit

monopoly, against an unprecedented number of business mergers and takeovers. Reagan also loosened regulations protecting employee health and safety, and he weakened labor unions. When thousands of members of the Professional Air Traffic Controllers Organization (PATCO) struck in 1981, Reagan fired them, destroying their union (which had supported his election) and intimidating organized labor.

Ronald Reagan loved the outdoors and his remote ranch in southern California, where all told he spent nearly a year of his two-term presidency. Yet he blamed environmental laws for the nation's sluggish economic growth and targeted them for deregulation. His first secretary of the interior, James Watt, declared, "We will mine more, drill more, cut more timber," and he released federal lands to private exploitation. Meanwhile, the head of the Environmental Protection Agency relaxed enforcement of air and water pollution standards. Of environmentalists, Reagan wisecracked, "I don't think they'll be happy until the White House looks like a bird's nest," but their numbers grew in opposition to his administration's policies. Popular support for environmental protection forced several environmental officials to resign and blocked full realization of Reagan's deregulatory goals.

Deregulation of the banking industry, begun under Carter with bipartisan support, created a crisis in the savings and loan industry. Some of the newly deregulated savings and loan institutions (S&Ls) extended enormous loans to real estate developers and invested in other high-yield but risky ventures. S&L owners reaped lavish profits, and their depositors enjoyed high interest rates. But when real estate values began to plunge, hundreds of S&Ls went bankrupt. After Congress voted to bail out the S&L industry in 1989, the burden of the largest financial scandal in U.S. history, estimated at more than $100 billion, fell on American taxpayers.

The S&L crisis deepened the federal deficit, which soared despite Reagan's pledge to pare federal spending. When the administration cut funds for food stamps, job training, aid to low-income students, and other social welfare programs, hundreds of thousands of people lost benefits. Increases in defense spending, however, far exceeded the budget cuts, and the deficit continued to climb: from $74 billion in 1981 to a high of $220 billion in 1986. Under Reagan, the nation's debt tripled to $2.3 trillion, and interest on the debt consumed one-seventh of all federal expenditures. And despite all of his antigovernment rhetoric, the number of federal employees actually grew from 2.9 million to 3.1 million during his presidency.

It took the severest recession since the 1930s to squeeze inflation out of the U.S. economy. Unemployment approached 11 percent late in 1982, and record numbers of banks and businesses closed. The threat of unemployment further undermined organized labor, forcing unions to make concessions that management insisted were necessary for industry's survival. In 1983, the economy recovered and entered a period of unprecedented growth.

That economic upswing and Reagan's own popularity posed a formidable challenge to the Democrats in the 1984 election. They nominated Carter's vice president, Walter F. Mondale, to head the ticket, but even his precedent-breaking move in choosing a woman as his running mate (New York representative Geraldine A. Ferraro) did not save the Democrats from a humiliating defeat. Reagan charged his opponents with concentrating on America's failures, while he emphasized success and possibility. Democrats, he claimed, "see an America where every day is April 15th [the due date for income tax returns] . . . we see an America where every day is the Fourth of July."

Voters responded to the president's sunny vision and the economic comeback, giving him a landslide victory with 59 percent of the popular vote and a 523-to-13 margin in the electoral college. Winning only Mondale's home state of Minnesota, the Democrats pondered how to stem the exodus of longtime loyalists—particularly southern white males—to the Republican Party. Stung by Republican charges that the Democratic Party was captive to "special interests" such as labor, women, and minorities, some Democratic leaders, including the young Arkansas governor, Bill Clinton, urged a further party shift toward the right.

Winners and Losers in a Flourishing Economy

After the economy took off in 1983, some Americans won great fortunes as popular culture celebrated making money and displaying wealth. Books by business wizards topped best seller lists, the press described lavish million-dollar parties, and a new television show, *Life-*

styles of the Rich and Famous, drew large audiences. College students listed making money as their primary ambition.

Participating conspicuously in the new affluence were members of the baby boom generation, known popularly as "yuppies," short for "young urban professionals." These mostly white, well-educated young men and women lived in urban condominiums and pursued fast-track careers. They also consumed lavishly—fancy cars, health clubs, expensive vacations, and electronic gadgets. Though definitely a minority, they established consumption standards that many tried to emulate. And, in fact, millions of Americans enjoyed larger houses that they filled with such new products as VCRs, microwave ovens, and personal computers.

Many of the newly wealthy got rich from moving assets around rather than from producing goods. Notable exceptions included Steven Jobs, who invented the Apple computer in his garage; Bill Gates, who transformed the software industry; and Liz Claiborne, who turned a $250,000 investment into a billion-dollar fashion enterprise. But many others made money by manipulating debt and restructuring corporations through mergers and takeovers. Most financial wizards operated within the law, but occasionally greed led to criminal convictions. Michael Milken took home well over $50 million a year before he landed in jail for using insider information to maximize his financial manipulations.

> "Hack, chop, crunch!" were *Time* magazine's words for Reagan's efforts to free private enterprise from government restraints.

Other economic problems remained. The U.S. steel, automobile, and electronics industries were surpassed by those of Germany and Japan. Americans bought more Volkswagens and Hondas and fewer Fords and Chevrolets. With Americans purchasing more foreign-made goods than domestic producers were able to sell abroad, the nation's trade deficit (the difference between imports and exports) soared.

International competition forced the collapse of some older companies. Others moved factories and jobs abroad to be closer to foreign markets or to benefit from the low wages in countries such as Mexico and Korea. Service industries expanded during this process of **de-industrialization** and created new jobs at home, but these jobs paid substantially lower wages. When David Ramos was laid off in 1982 from his $12.75-an-hour job in a steel plant, his wages fell to $5 an hour as a security guard, forcing his family to rely on food stamps. The number of full-time workers earning wages below the poverty level ($12,195 for a family of four in 1990) rose from 12 percent to 18 percent of all workers in the 1980s.

The weakening of organized labor combined with the decline in manufacturing to erode the position of blue-collar workers. Chicago steelworker Ike Mazo, who contemplated the $6-an-hour jobs available to him, fumed, "It's an attack on the living standards of workers." Increasingly, a second income was needed to stave off economic decline. By 1990, nearly 60 percent of married women with young children worked outside the home. Yet even with two incomes, fewer young families could afford a home or provide a good life for their children. "I worry about their future every day," Mazo's wife confessed. "Will we be able to put them through college? . . . Will they be out in the workforce working for four dollars an hour?" The average $10,000 disparity between men's and women's annual earnings made things even harder for the nearly 20 percent of families headed by women.

In keeping with conservative philosophy, Reagan adhered to **trickle-down economics**, insisting that a booming economy would benefit everyone. Average personal income did rise during his tenure, but the trend toward greater economic inequality that had begun in the 1970s intensified in the 1980s, encouraged in part by his tax policies. The rich got richer, a portion of the middle class did well, and the poor got poorer. Personal income shot up sharply for the wealthiest 20 percent of Americans, while it fell for the poorest by 9.8 percent between 1979 and 1987.

Poverty statistics, too, revealed a reversal of the trend toward greater equality. Between 1980 and 1988, poor people increased from 11.7 percent to 13.5 percent of the total U.S. population—the highest poverty rate in the industrialized world. Social Security and Medicare helped keep the poverty rate among the elderly relatively low. Less fortunate were other groups that the economic boom had bypassed: racial minorities, female-headed families, and children. One child in five lived in poverty. Although overall unemployment fell below 6 percent after 1983, more than 10 percent of black men could not find a job.

Even as the economy boomed, affluent urbanites walked past men and women sleeping in subway stations and on park benches. Experts debated the total number of homeless Americans—estimates ranged from 350,000 upward—but no one doubted that homelessness had increased. Those without shelter included the victims of long-term unemployment, the erosion of welfare benefits, and slum clearance, as well as Vietnam veterans and individuals suffering from mental illness, drug addiction, and alcoholism.

REVIEW Why did economic inequality increase during the Reagan administration?

Continuing Struggles over Rights

The rise of conservatism put liberal social movements on the defensive, as the Reagan administration moved away from the national commitment to equal opportunity undertaken in the 1960s and the president's federal court appointments reflected that shift. Feminists and minority groups fought to defend protections they had recently won, and they achieved some limited gains. The gay and lesbian rights movement actually grew in numbers, edging attitudes toward greater tolerance and winning important protections at the state and local levels.

Battles in the Courts and Congress

President Reagan agreed with conservatives that the nation had moved too far in guaranteeing rights to minority groups. Crying "reverse discrimination," they maintained that affirmative action unfairly hurt whites. Instead they called for "color-blind" policies, ignoring statistics showing that minorities and white women still lagged far behind white men in opportunities and income. Intense mobilization by civil rights groups, educational leaders, and even corporate America prevented the administration from abandoning affirmative action, and the Supreme Court upheld important antidiscrimination policies. Moreover, although Reagan wanted to allow the Voting Rights Act to expire, Congress voted to extend it with veto-proof majorities. The administration did, however, put the brakes on civil rights enforcement by appointing con-

Homelessness
The increased presence of homeless people in cities across the nation challenged the view of the 1980s as a decade of prosperity. Hundreds of homeless people could be found on the sidewalks of the nation's capital every night. In November 1987, during the first snowfall of the season, a homeless man sleeps in Washington, D.C.'s Lafayette Square, across from the White House. What might the location of this homeless man suggest to viewers of the photograph?
© Bettmann/Corbis.

servatives to the Justice Department, the Civil Rights Commission, and other agencies and by slashing their budgets.

Congress stepped in to defend antidiscrimination programs after the Justice Department persuaded the Supreme Court to severely weaken Title IX of the Education Amendments Act of 1972, a key law promoting equal opportunity in education. *Grove City v. Bell* (1984) allowed the Justice Department to abandon dozens of civil rights cases against schools and colleges, which in turn galvanized a coalition of civil rights organizations and groups representing women, the aged, and the disabled, along with their allies. In 1988, Congress passed the Civil Rights Restoration Act, which reversed the administration's victory in *Grove City* and banned any organization that practiced discrimination on the basis of race, color, national origin, sex, disability, or age from receiving government funds.

The *Grove City* decision reflected a rightward movement in the federal judiciary, upon which liberals had counted as a powerful ally in their struggles for civil rights and social justice. President Reagan encouraged this trend by taking advantage of the opportunity to appoint half of the 761 federal court judges and three new Supreme Court justices. By carefully selecting conservative candidates, he turned the tide in favor of strict construction—the literal interpretation of the Constitution that narrowly adheres to the words of its authors, thereby limiting judicial power to protect individual rights.

Reagan's first Supreme Court appointment was Sandra Day O'Connor, a moderate conservative. Liberals defeated his nomination of ultra-conservative Robert Bork in a bitter contest, but the appointments of Antonin Scalia and Anthony M. Kennedy gave strict constructionists a slim majority. The full impact of these appointments became clear after Reagan left office, as the Court allowed states to impose restrictions that weakened access to abortion for poor and uneducated women, reduced protections against employment discrimination, and whittled down legal safeguards against the death penalty.

Feminism on the Defensive

One of the signal achievements of the New Right was capturing the Republican Party's position on women's rights. For the first time in its history, the Republican Party took an explicitly antifeminist tone, opposing both the Equal Rights Amendment (ERA) and a woman's right to abortion, key goals of women's rights activists. When the time limit for ratification of the ERA ran out in 1982, Phyllis Schlafly celebrated victory on the issue that had first galvanized her antifeminist campaign, while amendment supporters looked for the silver lining. Sonia Johnson, who was excommunicated by the Mormon Church for her feminism in 1979, exaggerated only somewhat when she called the ratification struggle "the greatest political training ground for women in the history of the world." (See chapter 28 and "Historical Question," page 1122.)

Cast on the defensive, feminists began to focus even more on women's economic and family problems, where they found some common ground with the Reagan administration. The Child Support Enforcement Amendments Act helped single and divorced mothers to collect court-ordered child support payments from absent fathers. The Retirement Equity Act of 1984 benefited divorced and older women by strengthening their claims to their husbands' pensions and enabling women to qualify more easily for private retirement pensions.

The Reagan administration had its own concerns about women, specifically about the **gender gap**—women's tendency to vote for liberal and Democratic candidates in larger numbers than men did. (Party leaders welcomed the opposite element of that trend: white men's movement into Republican ranks.) Reagan eventually appointed three women to cabinet posts and, in 1981, selected the first woman, Sandra Day O'Connor, for the Supreme Court, despite the

The Fight for the Equal Rights Amendment

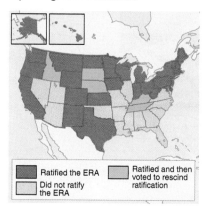

Ratified the ERA
Did not ratify the ERA
Ratified and then voted to rescind ratification

Christian Right's objection to her support of abortion. But these actions accompanied a general decline in the number of women and minorities in high-level government positions. And with higher poverty rates than men, women suffered most from Reagan's cuts in social programs.

Although court decisions placed restrictions on women's ability to obtain abortions, feminists fought successfully to retain the basic principles of *Roe v. Wade*. Moreover, they won a key decision from the Supreme Court ruling that sexual harassment in the workplace constituted sex dis-

Confrontations over Abortion
Failing to win a constitutional amendment banning abortion, some groups in the right-to-life movement adopted more militant tactics in the late 1970s and 1980s, picketing abortion clinics, yelling at patients and employees, and trying to block entrance into clinics. Here police outside a clinic in Silver Spring, Maryland, remove protesters, arresting more than twenty of them. Although the courts and law enforcement agencies defended women's access to abortion clinics, the harassment, negative publicity, and fear for their own safety caused many clinic operators to shut down their facilities.
© Bettmann/Corbis.

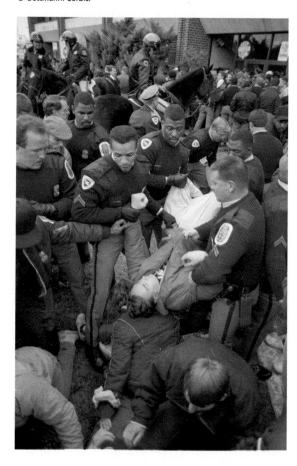

crimination. However, the women's movement hit a stone wall in efforts to improve day care services and promote pay equity—equal pay for traditionally female jobs that were comparable in worth to jobs held primarily by men. The women's movement pursued locally what it failed to achieve at the federal level. The pay equity movement took hold in several states, and many states strengthened their laws against rape. States also increased funding for domestic violence programs and stepped up efforts to protect victims and prosecute abusers.

Gay Pride Parades

In June 1970, gays and lesbians marched in New York City to commemorate the first anniversary of the Stonewall riot (see chapter 28). Since then, gay pride parades have taken place throughout the United States and in other countries every year in June. A history professor, Robert Dawidoff, pointed out that the parades are not about "flaunting private things in public," as some people charged, but a way for gay men and lesbians to express "pride in our history . . . in having survived the thousand petty harassments and reminders of a special status we neither seek nor merit." Increasingly, friends, supporters, and families of homosexuals participate in the parades, as this sign from a parade in Los Angeles indicates.

© Bettmann/Corbis.

The Gay and Lesbian Rights Movement

In contrast to feminism and other social movements, gay and lesbian rights activism grew during the 1980s, galvanized in part by the discovery in 1981 of a devastating new disease, acquired immune deficiency syndrome (AIDS). Because initially the disease disproportionately affected male homosexuals, as the epidemic swept through communities of gay men in New York and San Francisco, activists mobilized to promote public funding for AIDS education, prevention, and treatment.

The gay and lesbian rights movement helped closeted homosexuals experience the relief of "coming out." Their visibility increased awareness, if not always acceptance, of homosexuality among the larger population. Beginning with the election of Elaine Noble to the Massachusetts legislature in 1974, several openly gay politicians won offices from mayor to member of Congress, and the Democrats began to include gay rights in their party platforms. Activists organized gay rights marches throughout the country, turning out half a million people in New York City in 1987.

Popular attitudes about homosexuality moved toward greater tolerance but remained complex, leading to uneven changes in policies. (See "Documenting the American Promise," page 1130.) Dozens of cities banned job discrimination against homosexuals, and beginning with Wisconsin in 1982, eleven states made sexual orientation a protected category under civil rights laws. Local governments and large corporations began to offer health insurance and other benefits to same-sex domestic partners.

Yet a strong countermovement challenged the drive for recognition of gay rights. The Christian Right targeted gays and lesbians as symbols of national immorality and succeeded in overturning some homosexual rights measures, which already lagged far behind antidiscrimination guarantees for minorities and women. Many states removed antisodomy laws from the books, but the conservative position won out in a 1986 Supreme Court decision that upheld the constitutionality of such laws. Until the Court reversed that opinion in 2003, more

Antidiscrimination Laws for Gays and Lesbians, 1982–2000

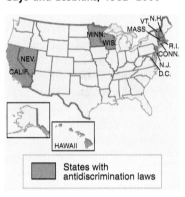

States with antidiscrimination laws

Protecting Gay and Lesbian Rights

Since the 1970s, the gay and lesbian rights movement has worked for passage of laws and ordinances to protect homosexuals from discrimination. In 1982, Wisconsin became the first state to ban discrimination on the basis of sexual orientation, following the lead of several cities throughout the United States that passed gay rights ordinances in the 1970s. By the mid-1990s, nine states and more than eighty cities had such legislation on the books. These measures ignited controversy that surrounded the issue into the twenty-first century.

DOCUMENT 1
Ordinance of the City of Minneapolis, 1974

In 1974, the city council of Minneapolis amended its civil rights ordinance to cover discrimination based on sexual preference. The law provided a rationale for banning discrimination and, unlike some laws focusing exclusively on employment, encompassed a broad range of activities.

It is determined that discriminatory practices based on race, color, creed, religion, national origin, sex, or affectional or sexual preference, with respect to employment, labor union membership, housing accommodations, property rights, education, public accommodations, and public services, or any of them, tend to create and intensify conditions of poverty, ill health, unrest, civil disobedience, lawlessness, and vice and adversely affect the public health, safety, order, convenience, and general welfare; such discriminatory practices threaten the rights, privileges, and opportunities of all inhabitants of the city and such rights, privileges, and opportunities are hereby to be declared civil rights, and the adoption of this Chapter is deemed to be an exercise of the policy power of the City to protect such rights.

SOURCE: Excerpt from *The Rights of Gay People: The Basic ACLU Guide to a Gay Person's Rights* by Norman Dorsen and Aryeh Neier, eds., p. 251.

DOCUMENT 2
Letter to the Editor of the *New York Times* from Paul Moore, November 23, 1981

Paul Moore, Episcopal bishop of New York, made a religious argument for gay rights in his letter to the editor of the New York Times.

I quote our diocesan resolution: "Whereas this Convention, without making any judgment on the morality of homosexuality, agrees that homosexuals are entitled to full civil rights. Now therefore be it resolved this Convention supports laws guaranteeing homosexuals all civil rights guaranteed to other citizens."

The Bible stands for justice and compassion for all of God's children. To deny civil rights to anyone for something he or she cannot help is against the clear commandment of justice and love, which is the message of the word of God.

As a New Yorker I find it incredible that this great city, populated by more gay persons than any other city in the world, still denies them basic human rights. They make an enormous contribution to the commercial, artistic, and religious life of our city.

SOURCE: Paul Moore, reprinted with permission.

DOCUMENT 3
Vatican Congregation for the Doctrine of the Faith, August 6, 1992

The following statement from the Roman Catholic Church reflects the views of many religious groups that take positions against gay rights.

"Sexual orientation" does not constitute a quality comparable to race, ethnic background, etc., in respect to nondiscrimination. Unlike these, homosexual orientation is an objective disorder and evokes moral concern.

There are areas in which it is not unjust discrimination to take sexual orientation into account, for example, in the placement of children for adoption or foster care, in employment of teachers or athletic coaches, and in military recruitment.

SOURCE: Vatican Congregation for the Doctrine of the Faith, *Origins*, August 6, 1992. Reprinted with permission.

DOCUMENT 4
Testimony of Charles Cochrane Jr. before the House Subcommittee on Employment Opportunities of the Committee on Education and Labor, January 27, 1982

Although the U.S. Congress has never enacted legislation banning discrimination on the basis of sexual orientation, it has considered a number of bills for that purpose. Charles Cochrane Jr., an army veteran and police sergeant, testified on behalf of such a bill in 1982.

I am very proud of being a New York City policeman. And I am equally proud of being gay. I have always been gay.

I have been out of the closet for 4 years. November 6 was my anniversary. It took me 34 years to muster enough courage to declare myself openly.

We gays are loathed by some, pitied by others, and misunderstood by most. We are not cruel, wicked, cursed, sick, or possessed by demons. We are artists, business people, police officers, and clergymen. We are scientists, truck drivers, politicians; we work in every field. We are loving human beings who are in some ways different. . . .

During the early years of my association with the New York City Police Department a great deal of energy did go into guarding and concealing my innermost feelings. I believed that I would be subjected to ridicule and harassment were my colleagues to learn of my sexual orientation. Happily, when I actually began to integrate the various aspects of my total self, those who knew me did not reject me.

Then what need is there for such legislation as H.R. 1454? The crying need of others, still trapped in their closets, who must be protected, who must be reassured that honesty about themselves and their lives will not cost them their homes or their jobs. . . .

The bill before you will not act as a proselytizing agent in matters of sexual orientation or preference. It will not include affirmative action provisions. Passage of this bill will protect the inherent human rights of all people of the United States, while in no way diminishing the rights of those who do not see the need for such legislation. Finally, it will signify, quite clearly, recognition and compassion for a group which is often maligned without justification.

SOURCE: U.S. House Subcommittee on Employment Opportunities of the Committee on Education and Labor, Hearing on H.R. 1454, 97th Cong., 2nd sess., 1982, 54–56.

DOCUMENT 5
Carl F. Horowitz, "Homosexuality's Legal Revolution," May 1991

Carl Horowitz, a policy analyst at a conservative think tank, the Heritage Foundation, expresses some of the arguments of those opposed to government protection of homosexual rights.

Homosexual activists have all but completed their campaign to persuade the nation's educational establishment that homosexuality is normal "alternative" behavior, and thus any adverse reaction to it is akin to a phobia, such as fear of heights, or an ethnic prejudice, such as anti-Semitism.

The movement now stands on the verge of fully realizing its use of law to . . . intimidate heterosexuals uncomfortable about coming into contact with it. . . .

The movement seeks to win sinecures through the state, and over any objections by "homophobic" opposition. With a cloud of a heavy fine or even a jail sentence hanging over a mortgage lender, a rental agent, or a job interviewer who might be discomforted by them, homosexuals under these laws can win employment, credit, housing, and other economic entitlements. Heterosexuals would have no right to discriminate against homosexuals, but apparently, not vice versa. . . .

These laws will create market bottlenecks. Heterosexuals and even "closeted" homosexuals will be at a competitive disadvantage for jobs and housing. . . .

The new legalism will increase heterosexual anger—and even violence—toward homosexuals.

SOURCE: Carl F. Horowitz, "Homosexuality's Legal Revolution," *Freeman*, May 1991.

QUESTIONS FOR ANALYSIS AND DEBATE

1. According to these documents, how would heterosexuals be affected by laws protecting gay and lesbian rights?
2. Which of these documents suggest that the civil rights movement influenced the authors' views on homosexual rights?
3. What do you think is the strongest argument for government protection of homosexual rights? What do you think is the strongest argument against government protection?

than a dozen states retained laws that left homosexuals vulnerable to criminal charges for private consensual behavior.

REVIEW   What gains and setbacks did minorities, feminists, and gays and lesbians experience during the Reagan years?

Ronald Reagan Confronts an "Evil Empire"

Running for president in the wake of the Soviet invasion of Afghanistan and the Iranian hostage crisis, Reagan accused Carter of weakening the military and losing the confidence of the nation's allies and the respect of its enemies. As president, he accelerated the arms buildup begun by Carter and harshly censured the Soviet Union, calling it "an evil empire." Yet despite the new

aggressiveness—or, as some argued, because of it—Reagan presided over the most impressive thaw in superpower conflict since the **cold war** had begun. On the periphery of the cold war, however, Reagan practiced militant anticommunism, authorizing aid to antileftist movements in Asia, Africa, and Central America and dispatching troops to the Middle East and the Caribbean. When Congress blocked Reagan's efforts to assist opponents of the leftist government in Nicaragua, administration officials resorted to secret and illegal means to effect their agenda.

Militarization and Interventions Abroad

Reagan expanded the military with new bombers and missiles, an enhanced nuclear force in Europe, a larger navy, and a rapid-deployment force. Despite the growing budget deficit, Congress approved most of these programs, and military expenditures shot up by one-third in the first half of the 1980s. Throughout Reagan's

Attack on the Marine Barracks in Beirut
On October 23, 1983, members of Islamic Jihad, an anti-Israel, anti-Western terrorist group sponsored by Iran, demonstrated their hostility toward the U.S. troops stationed in Lebanon by exploding a car bomb outside the U.S. marine compound near the Beirut airport and killing 241 Americans. In the aftermath of the attack, army colonel Colin Powell, assistant to the secretary of defense, approved the decision to withdraw from Lebanon, believing that "America [was] sticking its hand into a thousand-year-old hornet's nest" in the Middle East. The question of whether and when to risk American lives abroad for peacekeeping or humanitarian purposes would vex policymakers in the ensuing decades. Shown here are military personnel searching for and removing bodies of their dead comrades.
© Bettmann/Corbis.

presidency, defense spending averaged $216 billion a year, up from $158 billion in the Carter years and higher even than in the Vietnam era.

Reagan justified the military buildup as a means to negotiate with the Soviets from a position of strength, but it provoked an outburst of pleas to halt the arms race. A rally demanding a freeze on additional nuclear weapons drew 700,000 people in New York City in 1982. Hundreds of thousands demonstrated across Europe, stimulated by fears of new U.S. missiles scheduled for deployment in **North Atlantic Treaty Organization (NATO)** countries in 1983.

Reagan startled many of his own advisers in March 1983 by announcing plans for research on the Strategic Defense Initiative (SDI). Immediately dubbed "Star Wars" by critics who doubted its feasibility, the project would deploy lasers in space to destroy enemy missiles before they could reach their targets. Reagan conceded that SDI could appear as "an aggressive policy" allowing the United States to strike first and not fear retaliation. The Soviets reacted angrily because SDI violated the 1972 Antiballistic Missile Treaty and would require huge investments to develop their own Star Wars technology. Future administrations continued to spend billions on SDI research, but without producing a working system.

The U.S. military buildup could not extinguish a newer threat to international stability—force or violence initiated by nonstate organizations and designed to gain political objectives by frightening civilian populations. Such terrorism had a long history throughout the world, but in the 1970s and 1980s, Americans saw it escalate in the Middle East, used by Palestinians after the Israeli occupation of the West Bank and by other groups hostile to Western policies. A new terrorist organization, Hezbollah, composed of Shiite Muslims and backed by Iran and Syria, was founded in Lebanon in 1982 after Israeli forces invaded that country to stop the Palestine Liberation Organization (PLO) from using sanctuaries in Lebanon to launch attacks on Israel.

Reagan's effort to stabilize Lebanon by sending 2,000 marines to join an international peacekeeping mission failed. In April 1983, a suicide attack on the U.S. Embassy in Beirut killed 63 people, and in October a Hezbollah fighter drove a bomb-filled truck into a U.S. marine barracks there, killing 241 marines (see Map 30.3). The attack prompted the withdrawal of U.S. troops,

and Lebanon remained in chaos, while incidents of murder, kidnapping, and hijacking by various Middle Eastern extremist groups continued. Reagan adamantly proclaimed his refusal to negotiate, insisting that to bargain with terrorists would only encourage more assaults.

Following a cold war pattern begun under Eisenhower, the Reagan administration sought to contain leftist movements close to home and across the globe. In October 1983, 5,000 U.S. troops invaded Grenada, a small island nation in the Caribbean that had succumbed to a left-wing, Marxist coup. In Asia, the United States moved more quietly, aiding the Afghan rebels' war against Afghanistan's Soviet-backed government. In the African nation of Angola, the United States armed rebel forces against the government supported by both the Soviet Union and Cuba. Reagan also sided with the South African government, which was brutally suppressing black protest against apartheid, forcing Congress to override his veto in order to impose economic sanctions against South Africa.

Administration officials were most fearful of left-wing movements in Central America, which Reagan claimed could "destabilize the entire region from the Panama Canal to Mexico." When a leftist uprising occurred in El Salvador in 1981, the United States sent money and military advisers to prop up the authoritarian government even though it had committed murderous human rights violations. In neighboring Nicaragua, where Reagan aimed to unseat the left-wing Sandinistas, who had toppled a long-standing dictatorship, the administration aided the Contras (literally, "opposers"), a coalition of armed opposition to the Sandinistas.

El Salvador and Nicaragua

The Iran-Contra Scandal

The Reagan administration's commitment to the Contras revealed that the War Powers Act had not settled the question of presidential versus congressional authority in using force abroad. Fearing another Vietnam, many Americans opposed aligning the United States with reactionary forces not supported by the majority of Nicaraguans. Congress strongly and repeatedly instructed the president to stop aid to the Contras, but the administration continued to secretly provide them weapons and training. Through legal and illegal means, the Reagan administration sustained the Contras and helped wreck the Nicaraguan economy, thereby undermining support for the Sandinista government. After nine years of civil war, Nicaragua's president, Daniel Ortega, agreed to a political settlement, and when he was defeated by a coalition of all the opposition groups, he stepped aside.

Secret aid to the Contras was part of a larger project that came to be known as the Iran-Contra scandal. It began in 1985, when leaders of the National Security Council, NSC aide marine lieutenant colonel Oliver North, and CIA director William Casey arranged to sell arms to Iran, then in the midst of an eight-year war with neighboring Iraq. They did so, even while the United States supplied Iraq with funds and weapons, to get Iran to pressure Hezbollah to release seven American hostages being held in Lebanon (see Map 30.3). Funds from the arms sales were then channeled through Swiss bank accounts to aid the Nicaraguan Contras. Over the objections of his secretary of state, who called it "a very bad idea," and his secretary of defense, Reagan approved the arms sales, but the three subsequently denied knowing that the proceeds were diverted to the Contras.

> The independent prosecutor's final report on the Iran-Contra affair concluded that Reagan had "knowingly participated or at least acquiesced" in covering up the scandal.

When news of the affair surfaced in November 1986, the Reagan administration faced serious charges. The president's aides had bargained with terrorists, which Reagan had vowed never to do, and, more seriously, had defied Congress's express ban on military aid for the Contras. Investigations by an independent prosecutor appointed by Reagan led to a trial that aired live on the relatively new medium of cable television. Seven individuals pleaded guilty or were convicted of lying to Congress and destroying evidence. North's felony conviction was later overturned on a technicality, and President George H. W. Bush pardoned the other six officials in December 1992. The independent prosecutor's final report found no evidence that Reagan had broken the law, but it concluded that both Reagan and Vice President Bush had known about the diversion of funds to the Contras and that Reagan had "knowingly par-

ticipated or at least acquiesced" in covering up the scandal—the most serious case of executive branch misconduct since Watergate.

A Thaw in Soviet-American Relations

A momentous reduction in cold war tensions soon overshadowed the Iran-Contra scandal. The new Soviet-American accord depended both on Reagan's flexibility and on an innovative Soviet head of state who recognized that his country's domestic problems demanded an easing of cold war antagonism. Mikhail Gorbachev assumed power in 1985 determined to revitalize an inefficient Soviet economy incapable of delivering basic consumer goods. Hoping to stimulate production and streamline distribution, Gorbachev introduced some elements of free enterprise and proclaimed a new era of *glasnost* (greater freedom of expression), eventually allow-

Nuclear Freeze Campaign
Sixteen-year-old Justin Martino made this mask to wear in a 1985 march on the Pentagon in support of disarmament and world peace. Martino wanted to express his belief that "the arms race has no end except the end of life," and he later donated the mask to the Smithsonian Museum of American History. Worldwide demonstrations for nuclear disarmament achieved limited success when the United States and Soviet Union signed arms limitation agreements in 1987.
Smithsonian Institution, Washington, D.C.

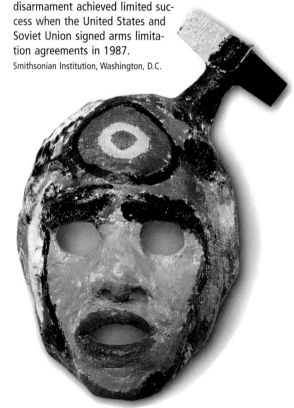

The Cold War Thaws
U.S. president Ronald Reagan and Soviet premier Mikhail Gorbachev shake hands as they meet
in June 1988 for a round of Strategic Arms Reduction Talks (START). Moving beyond the Strategic
Arms Limitation Talks (SALT) of the 1970s, these negotiations aimed to reduce rather than limit
nuclear warheads and the bombers that carried them. The talks culminated with a comprehensive
treaty signed by Reagan's successor, George H. W. Bush, and Gorbachev in July 1991.
Kenneth Jarecke/Contact Press Images.

ing new political parties, contested elections, and
challenges to Communist rule.

Concerns about immense defense budgets
moved both Reagan and Gorbachev to the negotiating table. Enormous military expenditures
stood between the Soviet premier and his goal of
economic revival. With growing popular support for arms reductions, along with a push from
his wife, Nancy, Reagan made disarmament a
major goal in his last years in office and readily
responded when Gorbachev took the initiative.
A positive personal chemistry developed between them, and they met four times between
1985 and 1988. Although Reagan's insistence on
proceeding with SDI nearly killed the talks, by
December 1987 the superpowers had completed an intermediate-range nuclear forces
(INF) agreement. The treaty eliminated all
short- and medium-range missiles from Europe
and provided for on-site inspection for the first

time. This was also the first time either nation
had pledged to eliminate weapons already in
place.

In 1988, Gorbachev further reduced tensions
by announcing a gradual withdrawal from
Afghanistan, which had become the Soviet
equivalent of America's Vietnam. In addition,
the Soviet Union, the United States, and Cuba
agreed on a political settlement for the civil war
in the African nation of Angola. And in the
Middle East, both superpowers supported a
cease-fire and peace talks in the eight-year war
between Iran and Iraq. Within three years, the
cold war that had defined the world for nearly
half a century would be history.

REVIEW   How did anticommunism shape
Reagan's foreign policy?

Conclusion: Reversing the Course of Government

"Ours was the first revolution in the history of mankind that truly reversed the course of government," boasted Ronald Reagan in his farewell address in 1989. The word *revolution* exaggerated the change, but his administration did mark the slowdown or reversal of expanding federal budgets, programs, and regulations that had taken off in the 1930s. Although he did not deliver on the social or moral issues dear to the heart of the New Right, Reagan represented the "choice not an echo" that Phyllis Schlafly had called for in 1964, as he used his skills as "the Great Communicator" to cultivate antigovernment sentiment and undo the liberal assumptions of the New Deal.

Distrust of the federal government grew along with the backlash against the reforms of the 1960s and the conduct of the Vietnam War. Watergate and other misdeeds of the Nixon administration further disillusioned Americans. Presidents Ford and Carter restored morality to the White House, but neither could solve the gravest economic problems since the Great Depression—a low rate of economic growth, stagflation, and an increasing trade deficit. Even the Democrat Carter gave higher priority to fiscal austerity than to social reform, and he began the government's retreat from regulation of key industries.

A new conservative movement helped Reagan win the presidency and flourished during his administration. Reagan's tax cuts, combined with hefty increases in defense spending, created a federal deficit crisis that justified cuts in social welfare spending and made new federal initiatives unthinkable. Many Americans continued to support specific federal programs—especially those, such as Social Security and Medicare, that reached beyond the poor—but public sentiment about the government in general had taken a U-turn from the Roosevelt era. Instead of seeing the government as a helpful and problem-solving institution, many believed that not only was it ineffective at solving national problems, but it often made things worse. As Reagan appointed new Supreme Court justices, the Court retreated from liberalism, restricting the government's authority to protect individual rights and regulate the economy.

With the economic recovery that set in after 1982 and his optimistic rhetoric, Reagan lifted the confidence of Americans about their nation and its promise—confidence that had eroded with the economic and foreign policy blows of the 1970s. Beginning his presidency with harsh rhetoric against the Soviet Union and a huge military buildup, Reagan helped move the two superpowers to the highest level of cooperation since the cold war began. Although that accord was not welcome to strong anti-Communist conservatives like Phyllis Schlafly, it signaled developments that would transform American-Soviet relations—and the world—in the next decade.

Selected Bibliography

General Works

Edward D. Berkowitz, *Something Happened: A Political and Cultural Overview of the Seventies* (2006).
John Ehrman, *The Eighties: America in the Age of Reagan* (2005).
Burton I. Kaufmann, *The Presidency of James Earl Carter* (1993).
Robert Mason, *Richard Nixon and the Quest for a New Majority* (2004).
Keith W. Olson, *Watergate: The Presidential Scandal That Shook America* (2003).
James T. Patterson, *Restless Giant: The United States from Watergate to* Bush v. Gore (2005).
Richard Reeves, *President Reagan: The Triumph of Imagination* (2005).
Bruce J. Schulman, *The Seventies: The Great Shift in American Culture, Society, and Politics* (2001).
Gil Troy, *Morning in America: How Ronald Reagan Invented the 1980s* (2005).

Foreign Policy

David Farber, *Taken Hostage: The Iran Hostage Crisis and America's First Encounter with Radical Islam* (2004).
Beth A. Fischer, *The Reagan Reversal: Foreign Policy and the End of the Cold War* (1997).
Frances FitzGerald, *Way Out There in the Blue: Reagan, Star Wars, and the End of the Cold War* (2000).
William M. LeoGrande, *Our Own Backyard: The United States in Central America, 1977–1992* (1998).
Paul Lettow, *Ronald Reagan and His Quest to Abolish Nuclear Weapons* (2005).
Douglas Little, *American Orientalism: The United States and the Middle East since 1945* (2002).
Gaddis Smith, *Morality, Reason, and Power: American Diplomacy in the Carter Years* (1986).

The Economy, Energy, and the Environment

W. Carl Biven, *Jimmy Carter's Economy: Policy in an Age of Limits* (2003).

Jefferson Cowie, *Capital Moves: RCA's Seventy-Year Quest for Cheap Labor* (1999).

Samuel P. Hays, *A History of Environmental Politics since 1945* (2000).

Christopher Jencks, *The Homeless* (1994).

Hal K. Rothman, *The Greening of a Nation? Environmentalism in the United States since 1945* (1998).

Robert J. Samuelson, *The American Dream in the Age of Entitlement, 1945–1995* (1996).

John W. Sloan, *The Reagan Effect: Economics and Presidential Leadership* (1999).

Social Movements and Contests over Rights

Terry H. Anderson, *The Pursuit of Fairness: A History of Affirmative Action* (2004).

John A. Andrew, *The Other Side of the Sixties: Young Americans for Freedom and the Rise of Conservative Politics* (1997).

Elizabeth A. Armstrong, *Forging Gay Identities: Organizing Sexuality in San Francisco, 1950–1994* (2003).

Donald T. Critchlow, *Phyllis Schlafly and Grassroots Conservatism: A Woman's Crusade* (2005).

Godfrey Hodgson, *The World Turned Right Side Up: A History of the Conservative Ascendancy in America* (1996).

J. Anthony Lukas, *Common Ground: A Turbulent Decade in the Lives of Three American Families* (1986).

William Martin, *With God on Our Side: The Rise of the Religious Right in America* (1996).

Donald G. Mathews and Jane Sherron De Hart, *Sex, Gender, and the Politics of the ERA* (1990).

Lisa McGirr, *Suburban Warriors: The Origins of the New American Right* (2001).

James F. Simon, *The Center Holds: The Power Struggle inside the Rehnquist Court* (1995).

▶ **For more books about topics in this chapter,** see the Online Bibliography at bedfordstmartins.com/roark.

▶ **For additional firsthand accounts of this period,** see Chapter 30 in Michael Johnson, ed., *Reading the American Past*, Fourth Edition.

▶ **For Web sites, images, and documents related to topics and places in this chapter,** visit bedfordstmartins.com/makehistory.

REVIEWING THE CHAPTER

Follow these steps to review and strengthen your understanding of the chapter.

STEP 1: *Study the **Key Terms** and **Timeline** to identify the significance of each item listed.*

STEP 2: *Answer the **Review Questions**, drawing on key terms and dates to support your answers.*

STEP 3: *Drawing on the Key Terms, Timeline, and Review Questions, answer the broader **Making Connections** questions.*

KEY TERMS

Who

Phyllis Schlafly (p. 1101)
Barry Goldwater (p. 1101)
Richard Nixon (p. 1102)
Shirley Chisholm (p. 1107)
Warren E. Burger (p. 1107)
George S. McGovern (p. 1108)
Archibald Cox (p. 1109)
Samuel J. Ervin (p. 1109)
Spiro Agnew (p. 1110)
Gerald R. Ford (p. 1110)
James Earl "Jimmy" Carter Jr. (p. 1111)
Walter F. Mondale (p. 1111)
Anwar Sadat (p. 1117)
Menachem Begin (p. 1117)
Ronald Reagan (p. 1119)
George H. W. Bush (p. 1120)
Jerry Falwell (p. 1121)
Pat Robertson (p. 1121)
Geraldine A. Ferraro (p. 1125)
Sandra Day O'Connor (p. 1127)

Oliver North (p. 1134)
Mikhail Gorbachev (p. 1134)

What

South Boston High School (p. 1106)
Milliken v. Bradley (p. 1107)
Regents of the University of California v. Bakke (p. 1108)
Roe v. Wade (p. 1108)
Watergate (p. 1108)
"Saturday night massacre" (p. 1110)
Federal Election Campaign Act of 1974 (p. 1111)
National Energy Act of 1978 (p. 1114)
Three Mile Island (p. 1115)
Love Canal (p. 1115)
Superfund (p. 1116)
Panama Canal Treaty (p. 1117)
Camp David accords (p. 1117)
Carter Doctrine (p. 1117)
Iran hostage crisis (p. 1119)

Christian Right (p. 1119)
supply-side economics (p. 1121)
Economic Recovery Tax Act (p. 1121)
PATCO strike (p. 1124)
S&L crisis (p. 1124)
Grove City v. Bell (p. 1127)
Equal Rights Amendment (ERA) (p. 1128)
Child Support Enforcement Amendments Act (p. 1128)
Retirement Equity Act of 1984 (p. 1128)
acquired immune deficiency syndrome (AIDS) (p. 1129)
Strategic Defense Initiative (SDI) (p. 1129)
bombing of U.S. marine barracks in Lebanon (p. 1133)
Iran-Contra scandal (p. 1134)
glasnost (p. 1134)
intermediate-range nuclear forces (INF) agreement (p. 1135)

TIMELINE

◄ **1966** • Republican Ronald Reagan elected governor of California.

1968 • Republican Richard Nixon elected president.

1969 • Warren E. Burger appointed chief justice of U.S. Supreme Court.

1971 • Nixon vetoes comprehensive child care bill.

1972 • Nixon campaign aides arrested at Watergate complex.

1974 • Nixon resigns; Gerald Ford becomes president.
• Ford pardons Nixon of any crimes he may have committed while president.
• *Milliken v. Bradley.*

1976 • Democrat Jimmy Carter elected president.

1977 • United States signs Panama Canal Treaty.

1978 • *Regents of University of California v. Bakke.*
• Congress deregulates airlines.

REVIEW QUESTIONS

1. How did Nixon's policies reflect the increasing influence of conservatives on the Republican Party? (pp. 1102–8)

2. Why did Nixon resign the presidency in August 1974? (pp. 1108–12)

3. How did Carter attempt to balance his commitment to human rights and anticommunism in his foreign policy? (pp. 1112–19)

4. Why did economic inequality increase during the Reagan administration? (pp. 1119–26)

5. What gains and setbacks did minorities, feminists, and gays and lesbians experience during the Reagan years? (pp. 1126–32)

6. How did anticommunism shape Reagan's foreign policy? (pp. 1132–35)

MAKING CONNECTIONS

1. What was Watergate's legacy for American politics in the following decade? In your answer, explain what led to Nixon's resignation. How did Congress try to prevent such abuses of power in the future?

2. Both ends of the American political spectrum changed significantly in the 1970s and 1980s. Describe these changes and discuss how they shaped contemporary American politics. In your answer, be sure to cite specific political developments.

3. Recent experiences in Vietnam hung over the foreign policy decisions of Presidents Carter and Reagan. How

did each president try to reconcile the lessons of that conflict and the ongoing cold war? In your answer, be sure to discuss the legacy of the Vietnam War on the United States in the 1970s and 1980s.

4. American regional politics shifted in significant ways during the 1970s and 1980s. Why was grassroots conservatism particularly strong in the Sun Belt? What was its relationship to the civil rights and equal opportunity developments of the 1960s?

▶ FOR PRACTICE QUIZZES, A CUSTOMIZED STUDY PLAN, AND OTHER STUDY TOOLS, see the Online Study Guide at bedfordstmartins.com/roark.

1979 • Camp David accords signed.
  • Carter establishes formal diplomatic relations with China.
  • Soviet Union invades Afghanistan.
  • Hostage crisis in Iran begins.
  • Moral Majority founded.

  1980 • Congress deregulates banking, trucking, and railroad industries.
    • Congress passes Superfund legislation.
    • Republican Ronald Reagan elected president.

    1981 • Researchers identify AIDS virus.
      • Economic Recovery Tax Act.

       1982 • Large demonstrations against nuclear weapons.

        1983 • Terrorist bomb kills 241 U.S. marines in Beirut, Lebanon.
          • Reagan announces plans for Strategic Defense Initiative ("Star Wars").

            1986 • Iran-Contra scandal.

            1987 • INF agreement signed.

            1988 • Civil Rights Restoration Act.

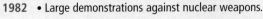

A SHRINKING WORLD

The cellular telephone was one of the new technologies contributing to the intensifying globalization that occurred with the end of the cold war in 1990. Connecting users to conventional telephone networks through microwave radio frequencies, wireless phones began to be used in Tokyo in 1979, and the first American system began in 1983. Cellular systems have improved communication for people in countries that lack good wire-based telephone systems, facilitating commerce as well as connecting far-flung family members and other individuals. The terrorists who struck the World Trade Center towers and the Pentagon on September 11, 2001, used mobile devices to coordinate the attacks, and many victims of the terror spoke their last words to loved ones on cell phones. By 2006, there were more than 200 million wireless subscribers in the United States and 2 billion around the world. Rapid development of cell phone technology has enabled people not only to call friends and business associates but also to connect to the Internet, take photographs, download music and movies, and send and receive e-mail.

The End of the Cold War and the Challenges of Globalization

Since 1989

I N HIS MOSCOW HOTEL ROOM on April 22, 1988, Ronald Reagan's national security adviser, army general Colin L. Powell, contemplated the plans that Premier Mikhail Gorbachev had just announced, which would dramatically alter the Soviet Union's government and economy. "Lying there in bed," Powell recalled, "I realized that one phase of my life had ended, and another was about to begin. Up until now, as a soldier, my mission had been to confront, contain, and if necessary, combat **communism**. Now I had to think about a world without a **Cold War**." For the next sixteen years, Powell would have a central place in redefining his country's role in a world transformed.

Colin Powell was born in Harlem in 1937 and grew up in the Bronx, the son of parents who had emigrated from Jamaica in 1920. His father headed the shipping department in a garment factory, where his mother worked as a seamstress. After attending public schools, Powell enrolled in City College of New York, where he joined the army's Reserve Officers Training Corps (ROTC) program, the defining experience of his college years. "The discipline, the structure, the camaraderie, the sense of belonging," he said, "were what I craved." Commissioned as a lieutenant when he graduated in 1958, Powell began a lifelong career in military and public service, rising to the highest rank of four-star general. He chose to stay in the army primarily because "I loved what I was doing." But he also recognized that "for a black, no other avenue in American society offered so much opportunity."

Powell's two tours of duty in Vietnam taught him that "you do not squander courage and lives without clear purpose, without the country's backing, and without full commitment." In his subsequent capacities as national security adviser to Ronald Reagan, chairman of the Joint Chiefs of Staff in the George H. W. Bush and Bill Clinton administrations, and secretary of state under George W. Bush, Powell endeavored to keep his country out of "halfhearted warfare for half-baked reasons that the American people could not understand or support."

Powell's sense that Gorbachev's reforms would bring about the end of the cold war became a reality more quickly than anyone anticipated. Eastern Europe broke free from Communist control in 1989, and the Soviet Union disintegrated in 1991. As the lone superpower, the United States deployed both

Secretary of State Colin Powell
Among the many characteristics that helped Colin Powell rise through the ranks of the army and serve in four presidential administrations were his loyalty and discretion. The decision by George W. Bush to invade Iraq in March 2003 ran counter to Powell's commitment to acting through the international community and sacrificing American lives only when a vital interest was at stake and a plan for ending the intervention had been established. Although Secretary of State Powell's position lost out to that of the more hawkish Vice President Dick Cheney and Secretary of Defense Donald Rumsfeld, Powell stayed in his job until 2005 and defended administration policy. In this photo taken at the White House in February 2003, he listens to Rumsfeld. National Security Adviser Condoleezza Rice stands behind them.
Charles Ommanney/Contact Press Images for Newsweek.

military and diplomatic power throughout the 1990s during episodes of instability in Latin America, the Middle East, eastern Europe, and Asia, almost always in concert with the major nations of Europe and Asia. In 1991, in its first full-fledged war since Vietnam, the United States led a United Nations–authorized force of twenty-eight nations to repel Iraq's invasion of Kuwait.

During his temporary retirement from public service in the 1990s, Powell remarked that "neither of the two major parties fits me comfortably." Many Americans seemed to agree: They turned Republican George H. W. Bush out of office in 1992 but elected Republican Congresses during Democrat Bill Clinton's adminis-

tration. When Republican George W. Bush (son of George H. W. Bush) entered the White House in 2001, he faced a nearly evenly divided Congress. Between 1989 and 2000, domestic policies reflected a slight retreat from the **conservatism** of the Reagan years. The first Bush administration approved tighter environmental protections and new rights for people with disabilities, and President Clinton signed measures strengthening gun control and aiding low-wage earners. But the pendulum swung back to the right in the second Bush presidency.

All three presidents shared a commitment to hastening the **globalization** processes that were linking nations together in an increasingly connected economy. As capital, products, information, and people crossed national boundaries at greater speed, the United States experienced a surge of immigration rivaling that of a century earlier, which had brought Powell's parents to the United States. Powell cheered globalization, predicting that the world would become "defined by trade relations, by the flow of information, capital, technology, and goods, rather than by armies glaring at each other across borders."

He was not so naive as to anticipate a world "without war or conflict," recognizing challenges such as nuclear proliferation, **nationalist** passions in areas of former Soviet dominance, civil wars in Africa, and Islamic **fundamentalism**. But he shared other Americans' shock when in September 2001 deadly terrorist attacks in New York City and Washington, D.C., exposed American vulnerability to new and horrifying threats. The administration's response to terrorism overwhelmed Secretary of State Powell's commitments to internationalism, multilateralism, and military restraint as George W. Bush began a second war against Iraq, implementing a distinct shift to a foreign policy based on preemptive attacks against presumed threats and going it alone if necessary.

Domestic Stalemate and Global Upheaval: The Presidency of George H. W. Bush

Vice President George H. W. Bush announced his bid for the presidency in the 1988 election, declaring, "We don't need radical new directions." Generally satisfied with the agenda set by Ronald Reagan and facing a Democratic-controlled Congress, Bush proposed few domestic initiatives. His dispatch of troops to oust the corrupt dictator of Panama, Manuel Noriega, represented a much longer continuity, following a century of U.S. intervention in Latin America.

Yet as the most dramatic changes since the 1940s swept through the world, Bush confronted situations that did not fit the simpler free world versus communism framework that had guided foreign policy since World War II. Most Americans approved of Bush's handling of two challenges to U.S. foreign policy and military capacity: the disintegration of the Soviet Union and its

hold over Eastern Europe, and Iraq's invasion of neighboring Kuwait. But voters' concern over a sluggish economy and other domestic problems limited Bush to one term in the White House.

Gridlock in Government

The son of a wealthy New England senator, George Herbert Walker Bush fought in World War II, earned a degree from Yale, and then settled in Texas to make his own way in the oil industry and politics. He served in Congress during the 1960s and headed the CIA during the Nixon and Ford years. When Ronald Reagan achieved a commanding lead in the 1980 presidential primaries, Bush put his own ambitions on hold, adjusted his more moderate policy positions to fit Reagan's conservative agenda, and accepted second place on the Republican ticket. At the end of Reagan's second term, Republicans rewarded him with the presidential nomination.

Several candidates competed for the Democratic nomination in 1988. The Reverend Jesse Jackson—whose Rainbow Coalition campaign centered on the needs of minorities, women, the working class, and the poor—made an impressive bid, winning several primaries and seven million votes. But a more centrist candidate, Massachusetts governor Michael Dukakis, won the nomination. On election day, half the eligible voters stayed home, indicating their disgust with the negative campaigning or their satisfaction with the Republican record on peace and prosperity. Divided government would remain, however, as 54 percent of the voters chose Bush but the Democrats gained seats in the House and Senate.

Although President Bush saw himself primarily as guardian and beneficiary of the Reagan legacy, he promised "a kinder, gentler nation" and was more inclined than Reagan to approve government activity in the private sphere. For example, he signed the Clean Air Act of 1990, the strongest, most comprehensive environmental law in history. It required power plants to cut sulfur dioxide emissions by more than half in ten years and oil companies to develop cleaner-burning gasoline.

Some forty million Americans reaped the benefits of a second regulatory measure, the Americans with Disabilities Act (1990). Job discrimination against people with disabilities was

Suing for Access: Disability and the Courts

When the Americans with Disabilities Act (ADA) passed in 1990, Beverly Jones was elated. "For me, the passage of the ADA was like opening a door that had been closed to me for so long," she said. The ADA promised to protect people with disabilities from discrimination by private employers, public agencies, and state and local governments in employment, public services, public transportation, public accommodations, and telecommunications. A civil rights act, the ADA aimed to provide equal opportunity and access for people with disabilities and followed in a long tradition of Americans fighting for their rights.

Jones, a single mother with two children, joined the ranks of the 2.2 million Americans who use a wheelchair after an automobile accident in 1984 resulted in paraplegia. Determined not to "allow what I wanted in life to be denied because of . . . physical limitations," she trained as a court reporter and in 1990, the year the ADA passed, went to work to support herself and her kids. But Jones found that despite the ADA's promise to make facilities accessible for disabled people, she was not always able to do her job, because in Tennessee, where she worked, seven out of ten

courthouses were not wheelchair accessible. "I could not even get in the front door or the side or back door," Jones recalled. "I was often forced to ask complete strangers to carry me up the stairs." She found the experiences "humiliating and frightening."

Motivated by her anger, Jones became a national adult representative for Easter Seals Disability Services in 1997 and worked tirelessly to promote rights for the disabled. "I spoke to local, state, and federal officials. I talked to anyone who would listen. But I could not get anyone's attention," she stated. "The door that I thought had been opened was still closed and my freedom to live my dream was still a dream, and turning into a nightmare."

So in 1998, Jones filed a lawsuit against the State of Tennessee, joining five other plaintiffs who alleged that the state was in violation of Title II of the ADA, which prohibits governmental entities from denying public services, programs, and activities to individuals because of a disability. George Lane, another plaintiff in the suit, had injured his hip and pelvis in a car accident. Cited for reckless driving, he went to court in a wheelchair, and when he found the second-floor courtroom inaccessible, he

crawled up the stairs. When the court adjourned for lunch, he crawled back down. That afternoon, he refused to crawl upstairs again and was arrested and jailed for failing to appear in court. Lane said that he would never forget the humiliation of having to drag his body up the thirty tile steps of the Polk County Courthouse. For Beverly Jones, the decision to file the suit came after she had to ask a judge to carry her to a restroom. "I was forced to turn down jobs, or face humiliating experiences," she testified. Lane, Jones, and the four other plaintiffs sought legal redress and damages of $250,000 each.

The case dragged on for six years without a ruling on the substance of their claims. Tennessee immediately countersued, challenging the constitutionality of the ADA's requirement that states make public facilities accessible to people with disabilities. Finally, in 2004, the case of *Tennessee v. Lane* reached the Supreme Court.

In the fourteen years since the passage of the ADA, the legal landscape in America had changed markedly. Conservatives on the bench showed a revived interest in **states' rights**, espousing a "new federalism" that challenged the right of Congress to tell the states what to do. Citing *sovereign immunity* (protection from lawsuits), granted to states by the Eleventh Amendment to the Constitution, courts began to question the right of Congress to make federal laws binding on the states. In 2001, in a dramatic example of the trend to limit

now illegal, and private businesses, public accommodations, and transportation facilities had to be made handicapped accessible. Cynthia Jones, publisher of a magazine on disability politics, noticed a breeze that stirred over the White House lawn at the signing of the bill. She said, "It was kind of like a new breath of air was sweeping across America. . . . People knew they had

rights. That was wonderful." (See "Seeking the American Promise," above.)

Yet Bush also needed to satisfy party conservatives. His most famous campaign pledge had been "Read my lips: No new taxes," and he opposed most proposals requiring additional federal funds. "If you're looking for George Bush's domestic program, and many people are, this is it:

Congress's power, the Supreme Court held that Congress lacked a constitutional basis for permitting states to be sued under Title I of the ADA, which applies to state employment.

In *Tennessee v. Lane*, the state cited this decision, claiming sovereign immunity and challenging the constitutionality of the ADA. The state's solicitor general argued that the law "imposes obligations on the states that go far beyond what the Constitution itself requires." Carol Westlake, executive director of the Tennessee Disability Coalition, pointed out that Tennessee's claim of states' rights was the same argument used to deny civil rights to African Americans in the 1950s and 1960s. In January 2004, as the Supreme Court heard arguments in the case, activists demonstrated outside the Court, chanting, "Justice for all; we won't crawl."

At stake was not only the right of people with disabilities to sue a state when denied access to public facilities but also the right of Congress to make federal laws binding on the states. In May 2004, in a five-to-four decision, the Supreme Court ruled that states that failed to make their courthouses accessible to people with disabilities could be sued for damages under federal disability law. But rather than validate, or even address, Congress's attempt to force states to make public services and programs accessible to the disabled, the Court confined its ruling to the specific context presented in the case: access to courts. By the narrowest possible

margin, with the crucial fifth vote cast by Justice Sandra Day O'Connor, the Court focused on one narrow application of the ADA and upheld it in the face of Tennessee's claim of constitutional immunity.

"My case is over," Jones acknowledged. "We have accomplished what we wanted to be achieved." But she worried that the Court's fragile majority might be at risk with the appointment of Justice John Roberts to replace retiring Justice O'Connor

in 2005. "Without the protections that Congress guaranteed in the Americans with Disabilities Act," Jones testified at Roberts's confirmation hearing in the Senate, "my life and the lives of millions of other people with disabilities would be a lot harder."

At present, her fears have not been borne out. In a 2006 decision involving the ADA, the new Roberts Court ruled unanimously that a Georgia prisoner could sue the state for failing to accommodate his disability.

Beverly Jones

Beverly Jones is shown here in her wheelchair next to one of the Tennessee courthouse stairways that made her job as a court reporter so difficult. "As a single mom supporting myself and two kids," she said, "I could not afford to quit my job or strictly limit my work to accessible courthouses." In 1998, Jones filed suit under the Americans with Disabilities Act. Six years later, in 2004, the Supreme Court upheld her right to enforce the protections the ADA granted to the disabled.

AP Images.

the veto pen," charged Democratic House majority leader Richard Gephardt. Bush vetoed thirty-six bills, including those that would have lifted abortion restrictions, extended unemployment benefits, raised taxes, mandated family and medical leave for workers, and reformed campaign financing. Press reports increasingly used the words *stalemate, gridlock,* and *divided government.*

Continuing a trend begun during the Reagan years, states tried to compensate for this paralysis, becoming more innovative than Washington. "Our federal politics are gridlocked, and governors have become the ones who have to have the courage to put their necks out," said a spokesperson for the governors. States passed bills to block corporate takeovers, establish parental

Bush and Taxes

When George H. W. Bush accepted the Republican nomination for president in 1988, he addressed an issue central to conservative politics. "Read my lips," he told convention delegates: "No new taxes." Yet the federal budget deficit he had inherited from Ronald Reagan grew even larger, and Bush decided that fiscal responsibility required him to curb the accelerating debt with a package of both budget and tax cuts. Many Republicans were outraged, and Bush had to depend on Democrats' votes in Congress to pass the measure. Editorial cartoonists had a field day with the controversy. Here, conservative cartoonist Scott Stantis, then at the *Arizona Republic* in Phoenix, likened Bush to Pinocchio, whose nose grew when he lied. Scott Stantis/Copley News Service.

READING THE IMAGE: What does the artist assume about newspaper readers' knowledge of Bush's politics? What other explanations for Bush's turnaround on the tax issue does the editorial neglect?

CONNECTIONS: Why were taxes such a central element of conservative politics in the 1980s? To what extent did Bush's tax increases alleviate the budget deficit?

FOR MORE HELP ANALYZING THIS IMAGE, see the visual activity for this chapter in the Online Study Guide at bedfordstmartins.com/roark.

president in 1990 to abandon his "no new taxes" pledge, a move that outraged advocates of **supply-side economics** and other conservatives. The new law, which Bush depended on Democrats to pass, authorized modest tax increases for high-income Americans and higher taxes on gasoline, cigarettes, alcohol, and luxury items. Despite criticism from many Republicans, the taxes had little effect on the massive tax reductions of the early 1980s, leaving intact a key element of Reagan's legacy. Neither the new revenues nor controls on spending curbed the deficit, which was boosted by rising costs for Social Security and Medicare/Medicaid, as well as by spending on war and natural disasters.

Bush also continued Reagan's efforts to create a more conservative Supreme Court. His first nominee, federal appeals court judge David Souter, won easy confirmation by the Senate. But in 1991, when the only African American on the Court, Justice Thurgood Marshall, retired, Bush set off a national controversy. He nominated Clarence Thomas, a conservative black appeals court judge, who had opposed **affirmative action** as head of the Equal Employment Opportunity Commission (EEOC) under Reagan. Charging that Thomas would not protect minority rights, the National Association for the Advancement of Colored People (NAACP) and other **liberal** organizations fought the nomination. Then Anita Hill, a black law professor and former EEOC employee, shook the confirmation process by accusing Thomas of sexual harassment.

Before the Senate Judiciary Committee, Thomas angrily denied the charges, claiming that he was the victim of a "high-tech lynching for uppity blacks." Hill's testimony failed to sway the Senate, which voted narrowly to confirm him. The hearings angered many women, who noted that only two women sat in the Senate and none on the Judiciary Committee and denounced the male senators for failing to take sexual harassment seriously. **Feminists** complained that men "still don't get it" and redoubled their efforts to get more women into office, making 1992 a banner year for women elected to office. Thomas's confirmation solidified the Supreme Court's shift to the right.

leave policies, require equal pay for jobs of equal worth, improve food labeling, and protect the environment. Beginning in the 1980s, a few states began to pass measures guaranteeing gay and lesbian rights. In the 1990s, dozens of cities passed ordinances requiring businesses receiving tax abatements or other city benefits to pay wages well above the federal minimum wage. And in 1999, California passed a gun control bill with much tougher restrictions on assault weapons than reformers had been able to get through Congress.

A huge **federal budget deficit** inherited from the Reagan administration impelled the

Going to War in Central America and the Persian Gulf

President Bush won greater support for his actions abroad, and he twice sent U.S. soldiers into battle. Nearly every cold war president before him had dispatched aid or troops to Central America and the Caribbean in the name of suppressing communism, but Bush intervened in Panama for different reasons. The United States had tolerated and, in fact, paid Panamanian dictator Manuel Noriega when he had helped the Contras in Nicaragua and served as a CIA informer about Communist activities in the region. But in 1989, after Noriega was indicted for drug trafficking by a grand jury in Miami, Florida, and after his troops killed an American marine, President Bush ordered 25,000 military personnel into Panama. In an invasion labeled "Operation Just Cause," U.S. forces quickly overcame Noriega's troops, sustaining 23 deaths, while hundreds of Panamanians died, many of them civilians. Chairman of the Joint Chiefs of Staff Colin Powell noted that "our euphoria over our victory in Just Cause was not universal." Both the United Nations and the Organization of American States censured the unilateral action by the United States.

If the invasion of Panama fit within the century-old tradition of **Yankee imperialism**, Bush's second military engagement rested solidly on international approval. Considering Iran America's major enemy in the Middle East, U.S. officials had quietly assisted the Iraqi dictator Saddam Hussein in his war against neighboring Iran, which he began in 1980 and which ended inconclusively in 1988 with heavy losses on both sides. In August 1990, Hussein sent troops into the small, oil-rich country of Kuwait to the south (Map 31.1, page 1148), and within days the invasion neared the Saudi Arabian border, threatening the world's largest oil reserves. President Bush reacted quickly, ordering a massive mobilization of American forces and assembling an international coalition to stand up to Iraq. He invoked principles of national self-determination and international law, but long-standing interests in Middle Eastern oil also drove the U.S. response. As the largest importer of oil, the United States consumed one-fourth of the world's supply, 20 percent of which came from Iraq and Kuwait.

Reflecting the easing of cold war tensions, the Soviet Union joined the United States in condemning Hussein and cut off arms shipments to Iraq. The UN declared an embargo on Iraqi oil and authorized the use of force if Iraq did not withdraw from Kuwait by January 15, 1991. By then the United States had deployed 400,000 soldiers to Saudi Arabia; they were joined by 265,000 troops from some two dozen other nations, including Egypt, Syria, and several other Arab states. "The community of nations has resolutely gathered to condemn and repel lawless aggression," Bush announced. "With few exceptions, the world now stands as one."

With Iraqi forces still in Kuwait, in January 1991 Bush asked Congress to approve war. Considerable sentiment favored waiting to see if the embargo and other means would force Hussein to back down, a position quietly urged within the administration by Colin Powell. Linking the crisis to the failure of U.S. energy conservation,

The Gulf War
These soldiers arriving in Dhahran, Saudi Arabia, were part of the massive military buildup in the Persian Gulf area before the U.S.-led coalition drove Iraq out of Kuwait. For the first time, women served in combat-support positions. More than 33,000 women were stationed throughout the area; eleven died, and two were held as prisoners. Among their duties were piloting planes and helicopters, directing artillery, and fighting fires.
© Bettmann/Corbis.

Democratic senator Edward M. Kennedy insisted, "Not a single American life should be sacrificed in a war for the price of oil." Congress debated for three days and then authorized war by a margin of five votes in the Senate and sixty-seven in the House. On January 17, 1991, the U.S.-led coalition launched Operation Desert Storm, a forty-day air war against Iraq that entailed bombing military targets, power plants, oil refineries, and transportation networks. Having severely crippled Iraq by air, the coalition then stormed into Kuwait with

massive ground forces on February 23. Within one hundred hours, Hussein announced that he would withdraw from Kuwait (see Map 31.1).

"By God, we've kicked the Vietnam syndrome once and for all," President Bush exulted on March 1. Most Americans found no moral ambiguity in the Persian Gulf War and took pride in the display of military competence. In contrast to the loss of 58,000 American lives in Vietnam, 270 U.S. service members perished in Desert Storm. The United States stood at the apex of global

MAP 31.1 Events in the Middle East, 1989–2007

During the Persian Gulf War of 1991, Egypt, Syria, and other Middle Eastern nations joined the coalition against Iraq, and the twenty-two-member Arab League supported the war as a means to liberate Kuwait. After September 11, 2001, the Arab League approved of U.S. military operations in Afghanistan because the attacks "were an attack on the common values of the world, not just on the United States." Yet, except for the countries where the United States had military bases—Bahrain, Kuwait, Qatar, and Saudi Arabia—no Arab country supported the American invasion and occupation of Iraq in 2003. Arab hostility toward the United States also reflected the deterioration of Israeli-Palestinian relations after 1999, as Arabs charged that the United States allowed Israel to deny Palestinians land and liberty.

READING THE MAP: In what countries are the sources of oil located? In what countries does the United States have military bases?

CONNECTIONS: What conditions prompted the U.S. military interventions in Iraq and Afghanistan in 1991, 2001, and 2003? What were the U.S. goals in each of these interventions? To what extent were those goals realized?

FOR MORE HELP ANALYZING THIS MAP, see the map activity for this chapter in the Online Study Guide at bedfordstmartins.com/roark.

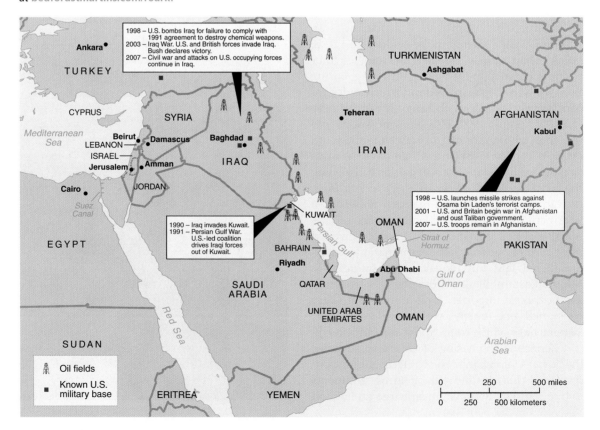

Fall of the Berlin Wall

After 1961, the Berlin Wall stood as the prime symbol of the cold war and the iron grip of communism over Eastern Europe and the Soviet Union. More than four hundred Eastern Europeans were killed trying to flee to the West. After Communist authorities opened the wall on November 9, 1989, permitting free travel between East and West Germany, Berliners from both sides gathered at the wall to celebrate.
Eric Bouvet/Gamma Press Images.

READING THE IMAGE: What does the image tell you about the revolutions in Eastern Europe in 1989?
CONNECTIONS: What were the major factors that made possible the dismantling of the Berlin Wall, the major symbol of the cold war in Europe?

FOR MORE HELP ANALYZING THIS IMAGE, see the visual activity for this chapter in the Online Study Guide at bedfordstmartins.com/roark.

leadership, steering a coalition in which Arab nations fought beside their former colonial rulers.

Some Americans criticized the Bush administration for ending the war without deposing Hussein. But Bush pointed out that the UN mandate limited the mission to driving Iraqi forces out of Kuwait, and he recognized the fear among Middle Eastern leaders that an effort to oust Hussein would destabilize the region. His secretary of defense Richard Cheney questioned the ability of coalition forces to secure a stable government to replace Hussein and considered the price of a long occupation too high. Administration officials believed that the war had crippled Iraq's military power and that economic sanctions and Hussein's pledges not to rearm or develop weapons of mass destruction, secured by a system of UN inspections, would contain the dictator.

Yet Middle Eastern stability remained elusive. Israel, which had endured Iraqi missile attacks, was more secure, but the Israeli-Palestinian conflict remained intractable. Despite military losses,

Saddam Hussein remained in power and turned his war machine on Iraqi Kurds and Shiite Muslims whom the United States had encouraged to rebel. Iraqi citizens suffered malnutrition, disease, and death caused by the continuing embargo and the destruction of the nation's infrastructure. And Hussein found ways to conceal arms from UN weapons inspectors before he threw them out in 1998.

The End of the Cold War

Soviet support in the war to turn back Iraqi aggression marked how greatly relations between the United States and the USSR had changed in just a few years. The forces of change that Gorbachev had encouraged in the Communist world (see chapter 30) swept through Eastern Europe in 1989, where popular uprisings demanded an end to state repression, official corruption, and economic bureaucracies unable to deliver an acceptable standard of living. Communist governments toppled

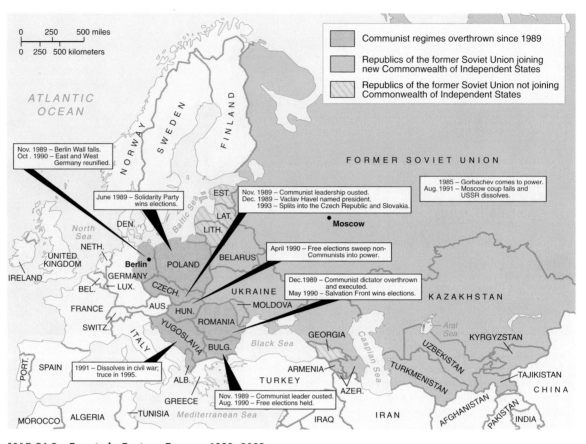

MAP 31.2   Events in Eastern Europe, 1989–2002
The overthrow of Communist governments throughout Eastern Europe and the splintering of the Soviet Union into more than a dozen separate nations were the most momentous changes in world history since World War II.

READING THE MAP: Which country was the first to overthrow its Communist government? Which was the last? In which nations did elections usher in a change in government?
CONNECTIONS: What problems did Mikhail Gorbachev try to solve, and how did he try to solve them? What policy launched by Ronald Reagan contributed to Soviet dilemmas? (See chapter 30.) Did it create any problems in the United States?

FOR MORE HELP ANALYZING THIS MAP, see the map activity for this chapter in the Online Study Guide at
bedfordstmartins.com/roark.

like dominoes (Map 31.2), virtually without bloodshed, because Gorbachev refused to prop them up with Soviet armies, a stand that won him the Nobel Peace Prize in 1990. East Germany opened its border with West Germany, and in November 1989, ecstatic Germans danced on the Berlin Wall, which had separated East and West since 1961, using whatever was at hand to demolish that dominant symbol of the cold war. An amazed East Berliner crossed over the line exclaiming, "They just let us go. I can't believe it."

Promoted by President Bush, unification of East and West Germany sped to completion in 1990, and former **iron curtain** countries such as the Czech Republic, Hungary, and Poland were

lining up to join **NATO**. Although U.S. military forces remained in Europe as part of NATO, Europe no longer depended on the United States for its security. Its economic clout also grew as Western Europe, including unified Germany, formed a common economic market in 1992. The destiny of Europe, to which the United States and the Soviet Union had held the key for forty-five years, now lay in European hands.

Inspired by the liberation of Eastern Europe, republics within the Soviet Union soon sought their own independence, while Gorbachev's efforts at economic change brought widespread destitution. According to one Muscovite, "Gorbachev knew how to bring us freedom but he did not know how to make sausage." In December 1991, Boris Yeltsin, president of the Russian Republic, announced that Russia and eleven other republics had formed a new entity, the Commonwealth of Independent States (CIS), and other former Soviet states declared their independence. With nothing left to govern, Gorbachev resigned. The Soviet Union had dissolved, and with it the cold war tensions that had defined U.S. foreign policy for decades.

China and North Korea resisted the liberalizing tides sweeping the world. In 1989, Chinese soldiers killed hundreds of pro-**democracy** demonstrators in Tiananmen Square in Beijing, and the Communist government cracked down on advocates of reform, arresting some ten thousand citizens. North Korea remained under a Communist dictatorship committed to developing nuclear weapons.

"The post–cold war world is decidedly not postnuclear," declared one U.S. official. In 1990, the United States and Soviet Union had signed the Strategic Arms Reduction Talks (START) treaty, which cut about 30 percent of each superpower's nuclear arsenal. And in 1996, the UN General Assembly overwhelmingly approved a total nuclear test ban treaty. Yet India and Pakistan, hostile neighbors, refused to sign the treaty, and both exploded atomic devices in 1998, increasing the nuclear risk in South Asia. Moreover, in a highly partisan vote, the Republican-controlled Senate defeated U.S. ratification of the test ban treaty in October 1999, halting a decade of progress on nuclear weapons control. In 2006, North Korea exploded a nuclear device, a reminder that the potential for rogue nations and terrorist groups to develop nuclear weapons threatened international peace and security.

The 1992 Election

Despite ongoing instability in the Middle East, in March 1991 Bush's chances for reelection in 1992 looked golden. The Gulf War victory catapulted his approval rating to 88 percent, causing the most prominent Democrats to opt out of the presidential race. But that did not deter William Jefferson "Bill" Clinton, who at age forty-five had served as governor of Arkansas for twelve years. Like Jimmy Carter in 1976 and Michael Dukakis in 1988, Clinton and his running mate, Tennessee senator

Albert Gore Jr., presented themselves as "New Democrats." Both belonged to the Democratic Leadership Council, which Clinton had helped found in 1985 to rid the party of its liberal image.

In an approach reminiscent of Richard Nixon's appeal to "forgotten Americans" in 1968, Clinton promised to work for the "forgotten middle class," who "do the work, pay the taxes, raise the kids, and play by the rules." Disavowing the "tax and spend" label that Republicans pinned on his party, he promised a tax cut for the middle class and pledged to reinvigorate government and the economy. Moreover, Clinton claimed, "we're going to put an end to welfare as we know it."

> Clinton promised to work for the "forgotten middle class," who "do the work, pay the taxes, raise the kids, and play by the rules."

With no new crises to display his foreign policy talents, Bush was vulnerable to voters' concerns about the ailing economy and to the Clinton campaign's emphasis on bread-and-butter issues. As foreign competition drove businesses to trim budgets, victims of corporate downsizing and outsourcing worried about finding new jobs, while other workers worried about keeping theirs. Unemployment edged over 7 percent in 1992.

Clinton and Gore on Tour
The gregarious Bill Clinton excelled at political campaigning, and the youth of the first baby boomer candidates appealed to many. During the 1992 presidential campaign, Clinton and his wife, Hillary—accompanied by running mate Al Gore and his wife, Tipper—went out on several bus tours as a way of demonstrating the Democrats' connection to ordinary people. Not far from this campaign stop in Sylvester, Georgia, the bus caravan passed by a hand-made sign that read "Bubbas for Clinton/Gore."
© Ira Wyman/Sygma/Corbis.

The popularity of a third candidate, self-made Texas billionaire H. Ross Perot, revealed Americans' frustrations with government and the major parties. Although Perot gave no press conferences, he used television extensively and attracted a sizable grassroots movement with his down-to-earth personality and appeals to voters' disgust with Washington. Perot's candidacy hurt the president more than it hurt Clinton, and it established the federal budget deficit as a key campaign issue.

Fifty-five percent of those eligible showed up at the polls, just barely reversing the thirty-year decline in voter turnout. Clinton won 43 percent of the popular vote, Bush 38 percent, and Perot 19 percent—the strongest third-party finish in eighty years. By casting two-thirds of their votes against Bush, voters suggested a mandate for change but not the direction that change should take.

> **REVIEW**   Why did George H. W. Bush lose the presidency in 1992?

The Clinton Administration's Search for the Middle Ground

The president who asserted that "the era of big government is over" was not Ronald Reagan but Bill Clinton, reflecting the Democratic Party's move to the right that had begun with Jimmy Carter in the 1970s. Clinton did not completely abandon liberal principles. He signed important measures benefiting the working poor; delivered incremental reforms to feminists, environmentalists, and other groups; and spoke out in favor of affirmative action and gay rights. Yet his administration attended more to the concerns of middle-class Americans than to the needs of the poor, and it restrained federal programs and appropriations for the disadvantaged.

Clinton's eight-year presidency witnessed the longest economic boom in history and ended with a budget surplus. Although various factors generated the prosperity, many Americans identified Clinton with the buoyant economy, elected him to a second term, and continued to support him even when his reckless sexual behavior resulted in **impeachment**. The Senate did not find sufficient cause to remove him from office, but the scandal crippled Clinton's leadership in his last years in office.

Clinton's Promise of Change

Clinton wanted to restore confidence in government as a force for good but also to avoid alienating antigovernment voters. The huge budget deficit that he inherited—$4.4 trillion in 1993—further precluded substantial federal initiatives. Moreover, just as Clinton was short on cash, he also lacked political capital. Perot's challenges denied Clinton a majority of the popular vote in both 1992 and 1996, and the Republicans controlled Congress for all but his first two years in office. Throughout most of his presidency, he was burdened by investigations into past financial activities and private indiscretions. While the president had an extraordinary knack for appealing to voters, making them feel that he liked and understood them, he could not translate that attraction into gains for his party.

Despite these obstacles, Clinton achieved a number of incremental reforms. Using his executive authority, he eased restrictions on abortion and signed several bills that Republicans had previously blocked. In 1993, Congress enacted gun control legislation and the Family and Medical Leave Act, which entitled workers in larger companies to unpaid leave for childbirth, adoption, and family medical emergencies. Another goal of the women's movement, the Violence against Women Act of 1994, authorized $1.6 billion and new remedies for combating sexual assault and domestic violence. Clinton won stricter air pollution controls and greater protection for wilderness areas and national forests and parks. Other liberal measures of the Clinton administration included an increase in the minimum wage, expansion of aid to low- and moderate-income college students, and the creation of AmeriCorps, a program enabling students to pay for their education with community service. Most significantly, Clinton pushed through a substantial increase in the Earned Income Tax Credit (EITC) for low-wage earners, a program begun under Ford in 1975. The EITC gave tax cuts to people who worked full-time at meager wages or, if they paid no taxes, a subsidy to lift their family income above the poverty line. By 2003, some fifteen million low-income families were benefiting from the EITC, almost half of them minorities. One expert called it "the largest antipoverty program since the **Great Society**."

Clinton's Appointments
President Clinton not only appointed more women to high government posts than any previous president, but he also broke new ground by appointing them to offices traditionally considered to be male territory. During his presidency, Janet Reno served as attorney general, Laura Tyson as chair of the President's Council of Economic Advisers, Sheila Widnall as secretary of the air force, and Madeleine Albright first as ambassador to the United Nations and then as secretary of state. Here, Albright (left) and Reno (second from right) applaud Clinton's 1999 State of the Union address with other cabinet members.
AP Images/Doug Mills.

Shortly before Clinton took office, the economy had begun to rebound, and the boom that followed helped boost his popularity through the 1990s. Economic expansion, along with budget cuts, tax increases, and declining unemployment, produced in 1998 the first budget surplus since 1969. Despite the biggest tax cut since 1981—a 1997 law reducing taxes on estates and capital gains and providing tax credits for families with children and for higher education—the surplus grew. The seemingly inexorable growth of government debt had turned around.

Clinton stumbled badly, however, in his efforts to provide universal health insurance and curb skyrocketing medical costs. Under the direction of First Lady Hillary Rodham Clinton and with very little congressional consultation, the administration proposed an ambitious, complicated plan that much of the health care industry charged would mean higher taxes and government interference in medical decisions. Congress enacted piecemeal reform enabling workers who changed jobs to retain health insurance and underwriting health care for five

million uninsured children, but affordable health care for all remained elusive.

Along with efforts to promote government as a positive force, Clinton used his appointing powers to change its face to one that "looked like America," building on the gradual progress women and minorities had made during the previous decades. For example, African Americans and women had become mayors in major cities from New York to San Francisco. Virginia had elected the first black governor since Reconstruction, and Florida the first Latino. In the executive branch, Clinton appointed the most diverse group of department heads ever assembled, including six women, three African Americans, and two Latinos. Secretary of Commerce Norman Y. Mineta became the first Asian American to hold a cabinet post. Janet Reno became the first female attorney general and Madeleine K. Albright the first female secretary of state. Clinton's judicial appointments had a similar cast. Of his first 129 appointments to federal courts, nearly one-third were women, 31 were black, and 11 were Latino. In 1993, he named the second woman to the

Supreme Court, Ruth Bader Ginsburg, whose arguments had won key women's rights rulings from the Supreme Court before she became an appeals court judge in 1980.

The Clinton Administration Moves Right

Although parts of Clinton's agenda fell within the liberal tradition, his presidency overall moved the Democratic Party to the right. The $4.4 trillion deficit he inherited precluded significant federal spending, and the 1994 elections swept away the Democratic majorities in both houses of Congress, encouraging Clinton to embrace more strongly Republican issues such as reforming welfare and downsizing government. Led by Representative Newt Gingrich of Georgia, Republicans claimed the 1994 election as a mandate for their "contract with America," a conservative platform to end "government that is too big, too intrusive, and too easy with the public's money" and to elect "a Congress that respects the values and shares the faith of the American family." Most voters did not know the details of the "contract," and opposition from Democrats and moderate Republicans blocked passage of most of the pledges, but Gingrich succeeded in moving the debate to the right.

The most extreme antigovernment sentiment developed far from Washington in the form of grassroots armed militias. Their stance celebrated white Christian supremacy and reflected conservatives' hostility to such diverse things as taxes and the United Nations. Claiming the need to defend themselves from government tyranny, they stockpiled weapons and anticipated government repression. Their ranks grew with passage of gun control legislation and after government agents stormed the headquarters of an armed religious cult in Waco, Texas, in April 1993, resulting in more than 80 deaths. On the second anniversary of that event, a bomb leveled a federal building in Oklahoma City, taking 169 lives in the worst terrorist attack in the nation's history up to that point. Authorities quickly arrested two militia members, who were tried and convicted in 1997.

Clinton bowed to conservative views on gay and lesbian rights, backing away from a campaign promise to lift the ban on gays in the military. Homosexuals served in the military in many other nations, including France and Israel, but U.S. military leaders and key legislators ob-

jected. Instead, in 1993 he announced the "don't ask, don't tell" policy, forbidding officials from asking military personnel about their sexuality but allowing the dismissal of men and women who said they were gay or engaged in homosexual behavior. Eventually, more than ten thousand homosexuals were discharged, one of whom was army Arabic linguist Cathleen Glover. "The military preaches integrity, integrity, integrity," she said, "but asks you to lie to everyone around you." In 1996, Clinton also signed the Defense of Marriage Act, prohibiting the federal government from recognizing state-licensed marriages between same-sex couples.

Nonetheless, gays and lesbians continued to make strides as attitudes about homosexuality became more tolerant. By 2006, more than half of the five hundred largest companies provided health benefits to same-sex domestic partners and included sexual orientation in their nondiscrimination policies. More than twenty-five states banned discrimination in public employment, and many of those laws extended to private employment, housing, and education. In 2000, the Vermont legislature created a category called "civil unions" for same-sex couples, which entitled them to rights available to married couples in legal matters such as inheritance, taxation, and medical decisions. Most states banned gay marriage, but by 2006 five states offered gays the opportunity to legalize their relationships with civil unions.

Clinton's efforts to cast himself as a centrist were apparent in his handling of the **New Deal** program Aid to Families with Dependent Children (AFDC), which most people called welfare. Public sentiment about poverty had been shifting since the 1960s. Instead of blaming poverty on the lack of adequate jobs or other external circumstances, more people blamed the poor themselves and believed that welfare programs trapped the poor in cycles of dependency. Many questioned why they should be subsidizing poor mothers now that so many women had joined the labor force. Nearly everyone considered work better than welfare, but supporters of AFDC doubted that the economy could provide sufficient jobs at decent wages. Moreover, most estimates showed that welfare cost less than government job training, child care, and other assistance poor people needed for the transition from welfare to work.

By vetoing two measures on welfare reform, Clinton forced a less punitive bill, which he signed as the 1996 election approached. The Personal Responsibility and Work Opportunity Reconciliation Act abolished AFDC and with it the nation's fifty-year pledge to provide a minimum level of subsistence for all children. The law provided grants to the states in a program called Temporary Assistance for Needy Families (TANF), but it limited welfare payments to two years, regardless of whether the recipient could find a job, and it set a lifetime limit of aid at five years. Reflecting growing controversy over immigration, TANF also barred legal immigrants who had not become citizens from obtaining food stamps and other benefits and allowed states to stop Medicaid for legal immigrants.

Marian Wright Edelman, president of the Children's Defense Fund, called Clinton's signing of the bill a "moment of shame." In its first decade, the law produced neither the horrors predicted by its critics nor the successes promised by its advocates. As intended, it did force single mothers to seek employment, cutting welfare rolls from 12.5 million to 4.5 million between 1996 and 2006. Yet not all former welfare recipients became self-supporting. Forty percent of former welfare mothers were not working regularly after being cut from the rolls, and those who did find jobs earned on average only about $12,000 a year. More than one-third of children living in female-headed families still lived in poverty.

Clinton's signature on the new law denied Republicans a partisan issue in the 1996 presidential campaign. The president ran as a moderate who would save the country from extremist Republicans, while the Republican Party also moved to the center, passing over conservatives to nominate Kansan Robert Dole, a World War II hero and former Senate majority leader. Clinton won 49 percent of the votes; 41 percent went to Dole and 9 percent to third-party candidate Ross Perot. In the largest **gender gap** to date, women gave 54 percent of their votes to Clinton and 38 percent to Dole, while men split their votes nearly evenly. Although Clinton won reelection with room to spare, voters sent a Republican majority back to Congress.

Impeaching the President

Clinton's genial and articulate style, his ability to capture the middle ground of the electorate, and the nation's economic resurgence enabled the self-proclaimed "comeback kid" to survive scan-

The End of Welfare
When Congress ended Aid to Families with Dependent Children (AFDC), the welfare system established during the New Deal, and replaced it with Temporary Assistance for Needy Families (TANF), LuAnne St. Clair wondered how she and her five children would fare when her welfare payments ended. American Indian mothers had to overcome, with other welfare recipients, the problems of acquiring job training and child care so they could find employment. But Indian women also faced the lack of sufficient jobs on reservations, to which they had strong family, cultural, and religious ties. In 1997, a year after the passage of TANF, St. Clair worried that she would have to leave the White Earth Reservation in Mahnomen, Minnesota, to find work.
AP Images/Dawn Villella.

dals and an impeachment trial in 1998. Early in his presidency, charges of illegal activities related to firings of White House staff, political use of FBI records, and "Whitewater"—the nickname for real estate dealings that the Clintons had conducted in Arkansas—led to an official investigation by an independent prosecutor. The president also faced a sexual harassment lawsuit filed in 1994 by a state employee claiming that Clinton had made unwanted sexual advances while he was governor. A federal court threw out the case in 1998, but another sexual scandal more seriously threatened Clinton's presidency.

In January 1998, Kenneth Starr, independent prosecutor for Whitewater, began to investigate the charge that Clinton had had sexual relations with a twenty-one-year-old White House intern, Monica Lewinsky, and then lied about it to a federal grand jury. At first, Clinton vehemently denied the charge, but subsequently he bowed to the mounting evidence against him. Starr took his case for impeachment to the House of Representatives, which in December 1998 voted, mostly along party lines, to impeach the president on two counts: perjury and obstruction of justice. Clinton became the second president (the first was Andrew Johnson, in 1868) to be impeached by the House and tried by the Senate.

> A majority of senators, including some Republicans, seemed to agree with a Clinton advocate that the president's behavior in regard to Monica Lewinsky, though "indefensible, outrageous, unforgivable, shameless," did not warrant his removal from office.

Most Americans condemned the president's private behavior but approved of the job he was doing and thus opposed impeachment. Some saw Starr as a fanatic invading individuals' privacy. One man said, "Let him get a divorce from his wife. Don't take him out of office and disrupt the country." Those favoring impeachment insisted that the president must set a high moral standard for the nation and that lying to a grand jury, even over a private matter, was a serious offense.

The Senate trial, held in early 1999, was less partisan. A number of senators believed Clinton to be guilty of perjury and obstruction of justice but did not believe that those actions constituted the high crimes and misdemeanors required by the Constitution for removal from office. With a two-thirds majority needed for that result, the Senate voted 45 to 55 on the perjury count and 50

to 50 on the obstruction of justice count. A majority, including some Republicans, seemed to agree with a Clinton advocate that the president's behavior, though "indefensible, outrageous, unforgivable, shameless," did not warrant his removal from office.

The investigation that triggered events leading up to impeachment ended in 2000 when the independent prosecutor reported insufficient evidence of illegalities related to the Whitewater land deals. The probe had cost taxpayers almost $60 million. In the face of widespread dissatisfaction with Whitewater and other investigations by special prosecutors, Congress let the independent counsel act expire in 1998. Although more than 60 percent of Americans gave Clinton high marks on his job performance throughout the scandal, it distracted him from domestic and international problems and precluded significant policy advances in his last years in office.

The Booming Economy of the 1990s

Clinton's ability to weather the impeachment crisis owed much to the prosperous economy, which in 1991 began its longest period of expansion in U.S. history. During the 1990s, the gross domestic product grew by more than one-third, thirteen million new jobs were created, inflation remained in check, unemployment reached 4 percent (its lowest point in twenty-five years), and the stock market soared.

The president eagerly took credit for the thriving economy, and his policies did contribute to the boom. He made deficit reduction a priority, and in exchange the Federal Reserve Board and bond market traders lowered interest rates, which in turn encouraged economic expansion by making money easier to borrow. Businesses also prospered because they had squeezed down their costs through restructuring and laying off workers. Economic problems in Europe and Asia helped American firms become more competitive in the international market. And the computer revolution and the application of information technology boosted productivity.

People at all income levels benefited from the economic boom, but it had uneven effects. Gaps between rich and poor, as well as between the wealthy and the middle class, which had been growing since the 1970s, failed to narrow (Figure 31.1). This persistence of inequality in a rising economy was linked in part to the growing use of information technology, which in-

FIGURE 31.1 The Growth of Inequality: Changes in Family Income, 1969–1998
For most of the post–World War II period, income increased for all groups on the economic ladder. But after 1979, the income of the poorest families actually declined, while the income of the richest 20 percent of the population grew substantially.

Adapted from the *New York Times*, 1989.

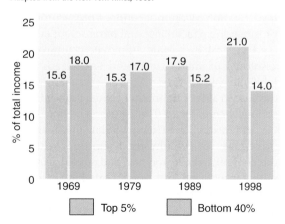

% of total income

	1969	1979	1989	1998
Top 5%	15.6	15.3	17.9	21.0
Bottom 40%	18.0	17.0	15.2	14.0

☐ Top 5%   ☐ Bottom 40%

creased demand for highly skilled workers, while the movement of manufacturing jobs abroad lessened opportunities and wages for the less skilled. In addition, deregulation and the continuing decline of unions hurt lower-skilled workers, and the national minimum wage failed to keep up with inflation.

Although more minorities than ever attained middle-class status, in general people of color remained lowest on the economic ladder, reflecting Colin Powell's observation that "race still casts a shadow over our society." For instance, in 2005 the median income for white households surpassed $50,000, but it stood at only $31,000 and $36,000 for African American and Latino households, respectively. Median family income for Asian Americans exceeded that of whites, primarily because Asian families had more education and more wage earners. That year, poverty afflicted about 25 percent of blacks, 22 percent of Latinos, and 11.1 percent of Asian Americans, in contrast to 8.3 percent of whites.

REVIEW What policies of the Clinton administration reflect the president's efforts to move his party to the right?

The United States in a Globalizing World

America's economic success in the 1990s was linked to its dominance in the world economy. From that position, President Clinton tried to shape the tremendous transformations occurring in a process that came to be called globalization—the growing integration and interdependence of national citizens and economies. Building on the initiatives of the Bush administration, Clinton lowered a number of barriers to trade across national borders, despite stiff opposition from critics who emphasized the economic deprivation and environmental devastation that often resulted. Debates likewise arose over the large numbers of immigrants entering the United States.

Clinton agreed with Bush that the United States must retain its economic and military dominance over all other nations. The president took military action in Somalia, Haiti, the Middle East, and eastern Europe, and he pushed hard to ease the conflict between Israel and the Palestinians.

Yet no new global strategy emerged to replace the **containment** of communism as the decisive factor in the exercise of American power abroad.

Defining America's Place in a New World Order

In 1991, President George H. W. Bush declared a "new world order" emerging from the ashes of the cold war. As the sole superpower, the United States was determined to let no nation challenge its military superiority or global leadership. (See "Global Comparison," page 1158.) Bush and Clinton alike pushed for an open world, with the United States at the apex serving as a model of capitalism, freedom, and democracy. Yet policymakers struggled to define guiding principles for deciding when and how to use the nation's military and diplomatic power in a post–cold war world of some 190 nations. Combating Saddam Hussein's naked aggression and threat to vital oil reserves seemed the obvious course to Bush and his advisers in 1991. Determining the appropriate action in other areas of instability, however, proved much more difficult, and the United States under Clinton applied its force inconsistently throughout the 1990s.

Africa was a case in point, where civil wars, famine, and extreme human suffering rarely evoked a strong American response. In 1991, President Bush ended economic sanctions against South Africa as it began to recognize the rights of its black majority. In 1992, guided largely by humanitarian concern, Bush had attached U.S. forces to a UN operation in the small northern African country of Somalia, where famine and civil war raged. In 1993, President Clinton allowed the humanitarian mission in Somalia to turn into "nation building"—an effort to establish a stable government—and eighteen U.S. soldiers were killed. The outcry at home, after Americans saw film of Somalis dragging a soldier's corpse through the streets, suggested that most citizens were unwilling to sacrifice lives when no vital economic or political interest seemed threatened. Indeed, both the United States and the United Nations stood by in 1994 when more than half a million people were massacred in a brutal civil war in the central African nation of Rwanda.

As always, the United States was more inclined to use force nearer its borders, but in the case of the Caribbean country of Haiti, it gained international support for intervention. In 1991, after a military coup overthrew Jean-Bertrand

GLOBAL COMPARISON

Countries with the Highest Military Expenditures, 2005

United States
$478.2 billion

United Kingdom
$48.3 billion

France
$46.2 billion

Japan
$42.1 billion

China
$41.0 billion

Germany
$33.2 billion

Italy
$27.2 billion

Saudi Arabia
$25.2 billion

Russia
$21.0 billion

India
$20.4 billion

During the cold war, the military budgets of the United States and the Soviet Union were relatively even. For example, in 1983 U.S. military expenditures stood at $217 billion compared to $213 billion for the USSR. Even before the Iraq War, which began in 2003, the U.S. military budget constituted 47 percent of total world military expenditures. That proportion rose to 48 percent in 2005, with the United States spending nearly ten times as much as its nearest competitor. The U.S. defense budget reflects the determination of Democratic and Republican administrations alike to maintain dominance in the world, even while the capacities of its traditional enemies have been greatly diminished.

as Haiti faced grave economic challenges and a new rebellion in 2004.

In eastern Europe, the collapse of communism ignited the most severe crisis on the continent since the 1940s. During the cold war, the Communist government of Yugoslavia, a federation of six republics, had held ethnic tensions in check, and many Muslims, Croats, and Serbs had grown accustomed to living and working together. After the Communists were swept out in 1989, Yugoslavia splintered into separate states and fell into civil war as ruthless leaders exploited ethnic differences to bolster their power.

The Serbs' aggression under President Slobodan Milosevic against Bosnian Muslims in particular horrified much of the world, but both European and U.S. leaders hesitated to use military force. As reports of terror, rape, and torture in Bosnia increased, American leaders worried about the image of the world's strongest nation unwilling to use its power to stop the violence.

Finally, in 1995, Clinton ordered U.S. fliers to join NATO forces in intensive bombing of Serbian military concentrations. That effort and successful offensives by the Croatian and Bosnian armies forced Milosevic to the bargaining table. In November 1995, the United States brought representatives from Serbia, Croatia, and Bosnia to Dayton, Ohio, where they hammered out a peace treaty. President Clinton then agreed to send twenty thousand American troops to Bosnia as part of a NATO peacekeeping mission.

In 1998, new fighting broke out in the southern Serbian province of Kosovo, where ethnic

Breakup of Yugoslavia

Yugoslavia 1945–1991
Yugoslavia since 1992

Aristide, the democratically elected president of Haiti, thousands of Haitians tried to escape political violence and poverty, many on flimsy boats heading for Florida. In 1994, Clinton got the United Nations to impose economic sanctions on Haiti and to authorize intervention by U.S. troops. Hours before twenty thousand troops were to invade Haiti, the military leaders promised to step down. U.S. forces peacefully landed and began disarming Haitian soldiers, and Aristide was restored to power. Initially a huge success, U.S. policy continued to be tested

Albanians, who constituted 90 percent of the population, were making a bid for independence. The Serbian army brutally retaliated, driving out one-third of Kosovo's 1.8 million Albanian Muslims. In 1999, NATO launched a U.S.-led bombing attack on Serbian military and government targets that, after three months, forced Milosevic to agree to a peace settlement. Serbians voted Milosevic out of office in October 2000, and he died in 2006 while on trial for genocide by a UN war crimes tribunal.

Elsewhere, Clinton remained willing to deploy U.S. power when he could send missiles rather than soldiers, and he was prepared to act without international support or UN sanction. In August 1998, bombs exploded at the U.S. embassies in Kenya and Tanzania, killing 12 Americans and more than 250 Africans. Clinton retaliated with missile attacks on terrorist training camps in Afghanistan and facilities in Sudan controlled by Osama bin Laden, a Saudi-born millionaire who financed the Islamic-extremist terrorist network linked to the embassy attacks.

Clinton also launched air strikes against Iraq in 1993 when a plot to assassinate former president Bush was uncovered; in 1996 after Saddam Hussein attacked the Kurds in northern Iraq; and repeatedly between 1998 and 2000 after Hussein expelled UN weapons inspectors. The attacks, from bases in Turkey, Kuwait, and Saudi Arabia, sent thousands of bombs and missiles against Iraqi military installations and research facilities but failed to make Hussein more compliant. Whereas Bush had acted in the Gulf War with the support of an international force that included Arab states, Clinton acted unilaterally and in the face of Arab opposition.

To ameliorate the Israeli-Palestinian conflict, a major source of Arab hostility toward the West, Clinton used diplomatic rather than military power. In 1993, due largely to the efforts of the Norwegian government, Yasir Arafat, head of the Palestine Liberation Organization (PLO), and Yitzhak Rabin, Israeli prime minister, recognized the existence of each other's states for the first time and agreed to Israeli withdrawal from the Gaza Strip and Jericho, allowing for Palestinian

U.S. Troops in Kosovo
In 1999, American troops joined a NATO peacekeeping unit in the former Yugoslav province of Kosovo after a U.S.-led NATO bombing campaign forced the Serbian army to withdraw. The NATO soldiers were dispatched to monitor the departure of Serbian troops, assist the return of ethnic Albanians who had fled the Serb army, and reestablish civil governments. Here, an ethnic Albanian boy walks beside Specialist Brent Baldwin from Jonesville, Michigan, as he patrols the town of Gnjilane in southeast Kosovo in May 2000.
AP Images.

1993 – Israel and PLO sign accords.
1994 – Israel and Jordan sign peace treaty.
2000 – Progress of Israeli-Palestinian negotiations halts and violence escalates.
2005 – Israel withdraws from Gaza.
2006 – Israel at war with Hezbollah in Lebanon.

Events in Israel since 1989

self-government there. In July 1994, Clinton presided over another turning point as Rabin and King Hussein of Jordan signed a declaration of peace. Yet difficult issues remained to be settled: control of Jerusalem, with sites sacred to Christians, Jews, and Muslims alike; the fate of Palestinian refugees; and the more than 200,000 Israeli settlers living in the West Bank, the land seized by Israel in 1967, where 3 million Palestinians were determined to establish their own state. Clinton's last effort to broker negotiations between the PLO and Israel failed in 2000, and violence between Israelis and Palestinians consumed the area, strengthening anti-American sentiment among Arabs, who saw the United States as Israel's ally.

Debates over Globalization

The Clinton administration moved energetically on the economic side to speed up the growth of a "global marketplace." The process of globalization had begun in the fifteenth century, when Europeans began to trade with and populate other parts of the world. Between the U.S. Civil War and World War I, products, capital, and labor crossed national boundaries in ever-larger numbers. In that era, globalization was based on **imperialism**, as Western nations took direct control of foreign territories, extracted their natural resources, and restricted manufacturing. Late-twentieth-century globalization, in contrast, advanced among sovereign nations and involved the industrialization of less developed areas, such as Korea and China. Other distinguishing marks of the more recent globalization were its scope and intensity: New communications technologies such as the Internet and cell phones connected nations, corporations, and individuals—nearly the entire planet—at much greater speed and much less cost than ever before. (See "The Promise of Technology," page 1162.)

Building on efforts by Presidents Reagan and Bush, Clinton sought to speed up globalization,

> "International trade and global financial markets are very good at generating wealth," conceded an American businessman, "but they cannot take care of other social needs, such as the preservation of peace, alleviation of poverty, [and] protection of the environment."

seeking new measures to ease restrictions on international commerce. In November 1993, he won congressional approval of the North American Free Trade Agreement (NAFTA). Organized labor and others fearing loss of jobs and industries to Mexico lobbied vigorously against NAFTA, and a majority of Democrats opposed it, but Republican support ensured approval. The agreement eliminated all tariffs and trade barriers among the United States, Canada, and Mexico, making the NAFTA trio the second-largest trading bloc in the world after the European Union. In 1994, the Senate ratified the General Agreement on Tariffs and Trade (GATT), establishing the World Trade Organization (WTO) to enforce among some 135 member nations substantial tariff reductions, the elimination of import quotas, and other provisions of the GATT treaty. And in 2005, Clinton's successor, George W. Bush, got Congress to lower more trade barriers with the passage of the Central American–Dominican Republic Free Trade Agreement (CAFTA-DR).

As Clinton worked to ease restrictions on the free flow of products and capital across national borders, debates about globalization raged. Much of corporate America welcomed the elimination of trade barriers. "Ideally, you'd have every plant you own on a barge," remarked Jack Welch, CEO of General Electric. Critics linked globalization to the weakening of unions, the erosion of the social safety net provided for workers since the 1930s, and the growing gap between rich and poor. Demanding "fair trade" rather than simply free trade, they wanted trade treaties requiring other countries to enforce decent wage and labor standards. Environmentalists similarly wanted countries seeking increased commerce with the United States to adopt measures that would eliminate or reduce pollution and prevent the destruction of endangered species.

In November 1999, tens of thousands of activists dramatized the globalization debate when they gathered in Seattle, Washington, to protest a meeting of the WTO. Protesters charged the WTO with promoting a global economy that destroyed the environment, devastated poorer developing nations, and undercut living standards and wages for workers. At the Seattle demonstrations and elsewhere, U.S. labor unions emphasized the flight of factory jobs to developing nations as corporate executives sought cheaper labor to lower production costs. (See "Beyond America's Borders," page 1164.) Tico Almeida, fresh out of college, was thrilled to hear "workers and unions from rich and poor countries alike stand together and say, 'We want rules for workers' rights to be integrated into the global economy.'"

Globalization controversies often centered on relationships between the United States, which dominated the world's industrial core, and the developing nations on the periphery, whose cheap labor and lax environmental standards caught the eye of investors. United Students against Sweatshops, for example, attacked the international conglomerate Nike, which paid Chinese workers $1.50 to produce a pair of shoes selling for more than $100 in the United States. Yet many leaders of developing nations actively sought foreign investment, insisting that wages deemed pitiful by Americans offered people in poor nations a much better living than they could otherwise obtain. At the same time, developing countries often pointed to the hypocrisy of the United States in advocating free trade in industry while heavily subsidizing its own agricultural sector. "When countries like America, Britain and France subsidize their farmers," complained John Nagenda, a grower in Uganda, "we get hurt."

The demonstrations in Seattle and protests that followed in Washington, D.C., and other parts of the world also targeted international financial institutions such as the World Bank and International Monetary Fund (IMF). Activists charged that the IMF forced devastating regulations on developing nations, which had little voice in trade policy decisions. For example, the IMF often required poor nations to privatize state industries, deregulate their economies, and cut social welfare spending in order to obtain loans. Whereas globalization's cheerleaders argued that in the long run, everyone would benefit, critics focused on the short-term victims. "International trade and global financial markets are very good at generating wealth," conceded American businessman George Soros, "but they cannot take care of other social needs, such as the preservation of peace, alleviation of poverty, protection of the environment, labor conditions, or human rights."

Critics of globalization enjoyed a few successes. In 2000, President Clinton signed an executive order requiring an environmental impact review before the signing of any trade agreement. Beyond the United States, officials from the World Bank and the IMF, along with representatives from wealthy economies, promised in 2000 to provide poor nations more debt relief and a greater voice in decisions about loans and grants. According to World Bank president James D. Wolfensohn, "Our challenge is to make globalization an instrument of opportunity and inclusion—not fear."

The Internationalization of the United States

Globalization was typically associated with the expansion of American enterprise and **culture** to other countries, yet the United States experienced within its own borders the dynamic forces of globalization. Already in the 1980s, Japanese, European, and Middle Eastern investors had purchased American stocks and bonds, real estate, and corporations such as Firestone, Brooks Brothers, and

Protests against the WTO
Environmentalists and animal protection advocates were among the diverse array of groups demonstrating against the World Trade Organization when it attempted to meet in Seattle, Washington, in November 1999. These activists dressed as sea turtles to protest WTO agreements permitting economic actions that they believed threatened the survival of the animals.
AP Images.

The Internet

The network that links millions of computers throughout the world began to alter the lives of millions of Americans in the 1990s. Just 313,000 computers were linked to the Internet in 1990; six years later, 10 million were connected. By the year 2000, a majority of Americans logged on to the Internet at home or at work to send and receive e-mail, shop, chat, download music, read the news, play games, trade stocks, conduct research, and more.

Like many technological innovations of the post–World War II era, the Internet began as a product of government funding inspired by the cold war. Shortly after the Soviets launched *Sputnik*, in 1958 President Eisenhower created the Advanced Research Projects Agency (ARPA) to push research on technology. In 1969, the U.S. Department of Defense established ARPANET, which developed a system called packet switching, a technology first invented by MIT graduate student Leonard Kleinrock to route digitized messages between computers. Not only would such a system be able to handle vast amounts of information—allowing many users to share computers and communication lines—but it would provide security for military secrets and enable communication to continue even if some computers were damaged by an enemy attack. By 1971, ARPANET linked twenty-three computers, most of them at research universities.

New networks soon developed as universities and research centers rushed to join ARPANET. In 1982, the military created its own separate network for security reasons. Mean-while, the National Science Foundation (NSF) took over much of the technology and sponsored development of a civilian "backbone network" called NSFNET, which allowed disparate networks to connect with one another. In 1980, fewer than 200 networks were connected, but by 1988 what had come to be called the Internet linked more than 50,000 host computers.

Electronic mail had not been on the minds of defense officials when they developed packet switching, but it quickly surpassed all other forms of traffic on the young Internet. It was much faster than "snail mail," the scornful term computer users applied to mail sent via the postal service, and it was much cheaper than long-distance telephone conversations. Moreover, two people could communicate on the same day without having to be at their phones at the same time, and they could do so easily across different time zones.

As ownership of personal computers spread, people not only exchanged e-mail but also began to put entire documents on the Net. Two key inventions helped users find and retrieve such material. In 1991, researchers at the University of Minnesota launched a retrieval system called "gopher," a slang term for one who fetches things and also the university's mascot. Then came the World Wide Web, first proposed in 1989 by researchers at a physics institute in Geneva, Switzerland. In the mid-1990s, browsers such as Netscape greatly simplified access to a seemingly infinite supply of interconnected documents on the Web, and the "information superhighway" was born.

Commercialization quickly followed, as Wall Street's fervor over the new medium swelled to a near frenzy in the late 1990s. The "dot-com boom" saw the rise of today's most well-known Internet companies, such as Amazon.com, eBay, and Google, but a glut of followers, even with generous investments from speculative venture capitalists, were doomed to failure. Due in large part to the collapse of the dot-com boom, the stock market crashed in 2000, leading the country into a recession.

Despite the dot-com bust, the Internet tremendously enhanced the capabilities of both the workplace and the marketplace, facilitating the growth of a global economy. It quickly distributed capital, made it easier for companies to manage operations abroad, and even enabled employees to work together across thousands of miles. In 1997, for example, computer programmers in Beijing developing a project for IBM sent their work at the end of the day via the Internet to IBM workers in Seattle, who built on it and then passed it on to programmers in Belarus and Latvia, who did the same and relayed it on to counterparts in India, who passed it on to the Beijing group, who started the process all over again until the project was finished. According to IBM executive John Patrick, "It's like we've created a forty-eight-hour day."

The Internet was central to what journalist Thomas L. Friedman called "the democratization of information." Dictatorships could no longer keep their subjects ignorant of what was going on in the rest of the world or restrain dissidents from communicating with one another. The Internet carried the potential to empower people even in democratic nations.

The Internet Links the World
By the end of the twentieth century, even the poorest countries had some access to the Internet. President Bill Clinton displayed his fervent faith in the promise of technology to encourage democracy, claiming that "when over 100 million people in China can get on the Net, it will be impossible to maintain a closed political and economic society." In Iran, where the theocratic government tightly restricted women, young girls turned to the Internet for discussions about sex and marriage. As one seventeen-year-old declared, "What else can we do when we cannot have a normal social life?" Here, Buddhist monks stand outside an Internet café in the Cambodian capital of Phnom Penh in December 2000.
Phillip Lopez/AFP/Getty Images.

Antiglobalization protesters mobilized much of their support via the Internet, online "distance learning" began to breach geographical and financial barriers to formal education, and the Internet became a popular recruitment and campaign tool during the 2004 presidential race.

Although this great leveling of information access had its benefits, the Internet also served as an important haven for terrorists, pornographers, and members of hate groups who wished to remain anonymous, and it provided a means for hackers to steal information or disrupt productivity with sophisticated electronic viruses. In addition, some social critics worry that the Internet is taking the place of human relationships. A 2000 survey found that 20 percent of the people who went online five or more hours a week spent less time with family and friends or at social events than they had before gaining access to the Net.

Other critics have pointed to the disparate access to information technology, a "digital divide" across class and racial lines. As costs of hardware and software plummeted during the 1990s, computers and access to the Internet grew dramatically but unevenly. By 2006, 74 percent of white Americans logged on to the Internet, but just 61 percent of African Americans did so. Even so, the Internet is well on its way to becoming as ubiquitous as television, but with a much greater and varied impact. A computer software engineer who helped develop the Internet remarked, "It has already changed everything we do."

Jobs in a Globalizing Era

In November 2001, Paul Sufronko, a supervisor at Rocky Shoes and Boots in the small town of Nelsonville, Ohio, handed out final paychecks to the company's last sixty-seven employees in the United States, ending a process of outsourcing jobs that had begun in the 1980s. Before his own job ended, Sufronko traveled to Rocky plants in Puerto Rico and the Dominican Republic to complete the transfer of production and to train a local worker to replace him. Asked about his job loss, the thirty-six-year-old said, "I had other plans. Things just didn't work out."

Many Americans did not take the loss of their jobs to foreign workers so philosophically. One, a son of Mexican American sharecroppers, who was laid off when Chrysler shut down Jeep production in Kenosha, Wisconsin, in 1988, mourned the loss of "pride in being an autoworker." A coworker believed that "corporations are looking for a disposable workforce. . . . No commitment to community; no commitment to country."

In 1960, American workers made 96 percent of all shoes bought in the United States; by 2000, nearly all shoes came from abroad. The globalizing process was not a new experience for Julio Lopez, a tempo-rary beneficiary of Rocky's outsourcing of labor. Born in Puerto Rico, he first worked in a New York toy factory, until it moved its operations overseas. Returning to Puerto Rico, he spent twenty-three years making shoes for another company, until it sought cheaper labor elsewhere. In 2001, he found work at Rocky's Puerto Rico plant at the minimum wage of $5.15 an hour, less than half of what Nelsonville workers had earned. Lopez hoped that the factory would stay in Puerto Rico for eight more years. "Then I will be sixty-two, and I can retire." His hopes were not unusual, and his concerns were not unfounded. Lillian Chaparro, the plant manager, spoke about the perpetual motion of jobs: "It's like a chain, you know? The jobs leave the U.S. They come here. Then they go to the Dominican, to China. That's why I push people— we have to be able to compete."

The athletic shoe manufacturer Nike was one of the first companies to exploit the advantages of production abroad, turning to Japan in the 1960s. When labor costs there began to rise, Nike shifted production to South Korea. When Korean workers demanded better wages and working conditions, Nike moved production to China, Indonesia, and Thailand. Local contractors in Indonesia paid workers as little as fifteen cents an hour as they churned out seventy million pairs of shoes in 1996.

Charles Seitz, who lost his job at Eastman Kodak in Rochester, New York, when the company moved some operations to China and Mexico, was not entirely wrong when he said, "There's nothing made here anymore." In the 1950s, one-third of all American workers were employed in manufacturing; by the twenty-first century, just 10 percent of them produced goods. Of course, not all the job losses resulted from the transfer of work overseas. At Kodak, for example, a machine took the place of fourteen workers who previously had mixed film-making ingredients. In the 1980s and 1990s, American corporations sought intensely to increase production so that they could downsize their work-forces and reduce labor costs. Moreover, some companies built plants abroad in order to be close to burgeoning markets there, as foreign automakers did when they began operations in the United States. Because so many companies contracted out production to foreign companies rather than employing foreign workers directly, the number of U.S. jobs lost through outsourcing is difficult to calculate.

The outsourcing of work did not end with manufacturing jobs. By 2003, corporations were relying on workers abroad, especially in India, for a wide range of service and professional work. For example, 1,700

20th Century Fox. Local communities welcomed foreign capital, and states competed to recruit foreign automakers to establish plants within their boundaries. American non-union workers began to produce Hondas in Marysville, Ohio, and BMWs in Spartanburg, South Carolina. By 2002, the paychecks of nearly 4 million American workers came from European-owned companies.

Globalization was transforming not just the economy but American society as well, as the United States experienced a tremendous surge of immigration in the late twentieth century. (See engineers and scientists conducted research for General Electric in Bangalore, India, which became the South Asian equivalent of California's Silicon Valley. East Indians managed Avis's online car rentals, while technology experts in Bangalore provided telephone help for Dell computer users. And American schoolchildren received online tutoring from teachers in Cochin, India.

A research firm executive pointed to the power of technology to overcome distance and noted, "You can get crackerjack Java programmers in India right out of college for $5,000 a year versus $60,000." Some critics not only worried about the immediate loss of jobs at home but also feared the long-term consequences for the American economy. "If we continue losing these jobs," argued a computer software executive, "our schools will stop producing the computer engineers and programmers we need for the future."

The flight of jobs has not been entirely one-way. Seeking to move production closer to its market, Honda in 1982 became the first Japanese company to manufacture cars in the United States, hiring more than 150,000 American workers by 2003. Other automakers followed. In all, about 5 percent of all American workers in 2003 received their paychecks from foreign companies operating in the United States.

The vast majority of jobs, however, moved in the opposite direction.

In 2003, one of the most distinctive American products rolled off a U.S. production line for the last time. The blue jeans company founded in 1853 by Levi Strauss closed its last plants in the United States, contracting out its work to suppliers in fifty other countries from Latin America to Asia. The company's president refused to see any significance in the move. "Consumers are used to buying products from all over the world," he said. "The issue is not where they're made." But Clara Flores, who had sewn hems for Levi Strauss for

twenty-four years in San Antonio, Texas, wondered, "Where are we ever going to find something like this?" Marivel Gutierez, a side-seam operator, acknowledged that workers in Mexico and elsewhere would benefit, suggesting the globalization of the American dream. "But what happens to our American dream?" Workers like these stood as stark reminders that as the benefits of the free flow of economic enterprise across national borders reached many, globalization left multitudes of victims in its wake.

U.S. Products Made Abroad

Eastman Kodak workers assemble disposable cameras at the U.S. company's factory in Xiamen, China, in 2004. Since the 1980s, cheap labor has attracted U.S. manufacturing to China, where it has contributed to China's astonishing economic growth, averaging around 8 percent annually over the past two decades.

AP Images.

appendix II, page A-51.) By 2006, the nation housed 35.7 million immigrants, who constituted 12.4 percent of the population. The 20 million who arrived between 1980 and 2005 surpassed the previous peak immigration of the first two decades of the twentieth century and exhibited a striking difference in country of origin. Eighty-five percent of the earlier immigrants had come from Europe; by the 1980s, almost half of the new arrivals were Asians, and nearly 40 percent came from Latin America and the Caribbean. Consequently, immigration changed the racial and ethnic composition of the nation. By 2004, the Asian and Pacific Islander population had grown to 13 million, and the number of Latinos had increased to more than 41 million, becoming—at 14 percent—the largest minority group in the nation.

The promise of economic opportunity, as always, lured immigrants to America, and the Immigration and Nationality Act of 1965 enabled them to come. Although the law set an annual ceiling of 270,000 immigrants, it allowed close relatives of U.S. citizens to enter above the ceiling, thus creating migration chains by which once newcomers became citizens, their spouses, children, and parents also gained entry. In addition, the cold war had sent U.S. military and other personnel around the world, enabling foreigners to learn about the nation and make personal contacts with citizens. And during the cold war, U.S. immigration policy was generous to people who wished to escape communism, welcoming more than 800,000 Cubans after Castro's revolution in 1959 and more than 600,000 Vietnamese, Laotians, and Cambodians in the years following the Vietnam War.

The racial composition of the new immigration heightened the century-old wariness of native-born Americans toward recent arrivals. Pressure for more restrictive policies stemmed from beliefs that immigrants took jobs from the native-born, suppressed wages by accepting low-paying employment, or eroded the dominant culture and language. Americans expressed particular hostility toward the millions of immigrants who entered the country illegally—an estimated 4.4 million between 2000 and 2005—even though the economy depended on their cheap labor. The Immigration Reform and Control Act of 1986, which penalized employers who hired undocumented aliens but also granted amnesty to some 2 million illegal immigrants who had been in the country before 1982, did little to stem the tide.

The new immigration was once again making America an international, interracial society. The largest numbers of immigrants flocked to California, New York, Texas, Florida, New Jersey, and Illinois, but new immigrants dispersed much more throughout the country than did those of the early twentieth century. Taquerias, sushi bars, and Vietnamese restaurants appeared in southeastern and midwestern towns; cable TV companies added Spanish-language stations; and the international sport of soccer soared in popularity. Mixed marriages also displayed the growing fusion of cultures, recognized by the Census Bureau in 2000 when it let Americans check more than one racial category on their forms. Only half-joking, the famous golfer Tiger Woods called himself a "Cablinasian" to reflect his mixed heritage of Caucasian, black, American Indian, and Asian. Demographers predicted that by 2050, the U.S. population would be just over 50 percent white, 16 percent black, 24 percent Latino, and 9 percent Asian.

Like their predecessors a hundred years earlier, the majority of post-1965 immigrants were unskilled and poor. They took the lowest-paying jobs, including farm and yard work, child and elder care, and cleaning services—work that employers insisted they could not get enough native-born Americans to perform. Yet a significant number of immigrants were highly skilled workers, sought after by burgeoning high-tech industries. For example, in 1999 about one-third of the scientists and engineers who worked in

Immigrant Labor

Large commercial farms depended on Latino workers, who constituted more than 45 percent of agricultural labor in 2002. A majority of these workers were citizens, and not all were immigrants, but growers insisted that they could not supply Americans with fresh produce without the labor of immigrants, legal and illegal. The dependence of agriculture and service industries on immigrant labor helped block movements for greater immigration restrictions. The workers here are harvesting strawberries near Carlsbad, California. In 2002, the median weekly pay for migrant farmworkers was $300.

Sandy Huffaker/Getty Images.

California's Silicon Valley had been born abroad. A majority of the thirty-one employees of UroGenesys, a California biotech company, were immigrants from countries such as Vietnam, Poland, Lebanon, China, India, Israel, Scotland, and Peru. The company's owner boasted, "I cannot think of another country in the world where you could so easily put such a team together."

> **REVIEW** Who criticized free trade agreements and why?

President George W. Bush: Conservatism at Home and Radical Initiatives Abroad

The second son of a former president to gain the White House, George W. Bush pushed an agenda that was closer to Ronald Reagan's than that of his father, George H. W. Bush. The younger Bush signed key legislation to improve public school education and to subsidize prescription drugs for elderly citizens. But he also persuaded Congress to pass enormous tax cuts that favored the wealthy, reduced environmental protections, and tipped the balance on the Supreme Court with two conservative appointments. The tax cuts, along with spending on new international and domestic crises, turned the substantial budget surplus that Bush had inherited into the largest deficit in the nation's history.

As Islamist terrorism replaced communism as the primary threat to U.S. security, the Bush administration launched a war in Afghanistan in 2001 and expanded the federal government's powers to investigate and detain individuals. In distinct contrast to his father's multilateral and cautious approach to foreign policy, George W. Bush adopted a policy of unilateralism and preemption by going to war against Iraq in 2003. The president was reelected by a majority of voters in 2004, but even at huge costs, the Iraq War failed to secure American objectives, and Bush confronted serious foreign and domestic crises in his second term.

The Disputed Election of 2000

Even though Clinton's presidency ended with a flourishing economy, Albert Gore, his vice president, failed to retain the White House for the Democrats in the election of 2000. Gore's running mate, Connecticut senator Joseph Lieberman, was the first Jewish American to run on a major-party ticket, and public opinion polls indicated that a majority of Americans agreed with the Democratic nominees on most issues. Yet many voters found Gore's style stiff and pompous and considered him too willing to change his positions for political advantage. He was further burdened with the taint of Clinton administration scandals.

George W. Bush emerged as the Republican nominee from a series of bountifully funded, hard-fought primaries. The oldest son of former president George H. W. Bush, he had attended Yale and Harvard, worked in the oil industry and as managing partner of the Texas Rangers

The Disputed Election

While attorneys representing presidential candidates George W. Bush and Al Gore pursued lawsuits over the counting of ballots that would determine who won Florida's twenty-five electoral college votes, partisan supporters took to the streets. Here, backers of both sides rally outside the Supreme Court in Washington, D.C., on Monday, December 11, 2000, the day before the Court issued its five-to-four ruling that ended the hand-recounts of ballots and consequently secured the presidency for Bush. Critics charged that the five justices who voted to stop the recounts had applied partisanship rather than objectivity to the case, pointing out that if those justices had followed their custom of favoring state over federal authority, they would have allowed Florida to continue the recounts.

AP Images.

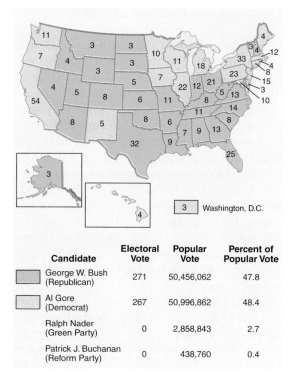

Candidate	Electoral Vote	Popular Vote	Percent of Popular Vote
George W. Bush (Republican)	271	50,456,062	47.8
Al Gore (Democrat)	267	50,996,862	48.4
Ralph Nader (Green Party)	0	2,858,843	2.7
Patrick J. Buchanan (Reform Party)	0	438,760	0.4

MAP 31.3   The Election of 2000

baseball team, and served as governor of Texas since 1994. Inexperienced in national and international affairs, Bush chose for his running mate a seasoned official, Richard B. Cheney, who had served in the Nixon, Ford, and first Bush administrations.

Both candidates ran cautious campaigns, accommodating their positions to what polls indicated voters wanted. Bush's strategy mirrored Clinton's in 1992. Calling himself a "compassionate conservative," Bush separated himself from the extreme right wing of his party and tried to co-opt Democratic issues such as education. Like Republicans before him, he promised substantial cuts in taxes and federal spending.

Many observers predicted that the amazingly strong economy would give Gore the edge, and he did surpass Bush by more than half a million votes. Once the polls closed, however, it became clear that Florida's 25 electoral college votes would decide the presidency. Bush's margin was so tiny in Florida, where his brother served as governor, that it prompted an automatic recount of the votes, which eventually gave Bush an edge of 537 votes.

> For the first time since 1888, a president who failed to win the popular vote took office in 2001.

Meanwhile, the Democrats asked for hand-counting of Florida ballots in several heavily Democratic counties where voting machine errors and confusing ballots may have left thousands of Gore votes unrecorded. The Republicans, in turn, went to court to try to stop the hand-counts. The outcome of the 2000 election hung in the balance for more than a month as cases went all the way to the Supreme Court. Finally, a bitterly divided Supreme Court ruled five to four against further recounts, and Gore conceded the presidency to Bush on December 13, 2000. For the first time since 1888, a president who failed to win the popular vote took office (Map 31.3). Despite the lack of a popular mandate, the Bush administration set out to make dramatic policy changes.

The Domestic Policies of a "Compassionate Conservative"

As was the case with his predecessor, Bush's appointments brought significant diversity to the executive branch. He chose African Americans Colin Powell as secretary of state and Condoleezza Rice first as national security adviser and subsequently as secretary of state, when Powell left that office in January 2005. Five of Bush's top-level appointees were women, including Secretary of Labor Elaine L. Chao, the first Asian American woman to serve in the cabinet. In 2005, Alberto R. Gonzales, a Latino, became attorney general.

Bush moved quickly on his domestic agenda, building on his campaign promise to govern as a "compassionate conservative." A devout born-again Christian, he immediately established the White House Office of Faith-Based and Community Initiatives to encourage religious and community groups to participate in government programs aimed at prison inmates, drug addicts, the unemployed, and other groups. The religious right praised the initiatives, but others charged that they violated the constitutional separation of church and state, and federal courts ruled in more than a dozen cases that faith ministries were using government funds to indoctrinate the people they served.

Bush's fiscal policies were more conservative and more compassionate toward the rich than toward average Americans. In 2001, he signed a bill reducing taxes over the next ten years by $1.35 trillion. A 2003 tax law slashed another $320 billion. The laws heavily favored the rich by reducing income taxes, phasing out estate taxes, and cutting tax rates on capital gains and dividends. They also provided benefits for married couples and families with children, offered tax deductions for college expenses, and gave an immediate rebate of up to $300 to each taxpayer.

The administration insisted that the tax cuts would promote economic growth and jolt the economy out of the recession that had begun in 2000, when the dot-com stock bubble burst. Opponents stressed inequities in the tax cuts and pointed to a mushrooming federal deficit—the highest in U.S. history—that surpassed $400 billion in 2004. Senator Joseph Lieberman charged that Bush's tax cuts were "giving the most to those who need it least, piling more debt on the backs of our children and robbing Social Security and Medicare to pay for it." Republicans had traditionally railed against budget deficits, but now they saw them as a way to limit the size of the federal government. "Anything that will help us stop spending money, I'm in favor of," declared Representative Sue Myrick from North Carolina. "And if there's a deficit, that may help us." The economy did recover, and the deficit dropped to $250 billion in 2006; but the national debt had grown from $5.7 trillion in 2000 to $8.3 trillion in 2006, costing the government $406 billion in interest payments that year. The United States became increasingly dependent on China and other foreign investors, who held more than half of the debt.

As Clinton had done, Bush altered environmental policy by issuing regulations that did not require congressional approval. But whereas Clinton had imposed greater controls, Bush weakened environmental protection to benefit his larger goals of reducing government regulation, promoting economic growth, and increasing energy production. The Senate blocked Bush's efforts to allow drilling for oil in the Arctic National Wildlife Refuge, but elsewhere the administration opened millions of wilderness acres of public land to the mining, oil, and timber industries. Bush imposed new restrictions on diesel pollutants and relaxed environmental requirements under the Clean Air Act and Clean Water Act. To worldwide dismay, the administration withdrew from the Kyoto Protocol on global warming, signed in 1997 by 178 nations to reduce greenhouse gas emissions. "Shame on Bush," chanted protesters when Secretary of State Powell addressed the Earth Summit in 2002.

While environmentalists pushed for measures to limit American energy consumption, the administration called for more rapid development of energy resources. During his second term, as gasoline prices reached all-time highs in 2005, Bush signed the Energy Policy Act, a compromise bill providing $14 billion in subsidies to producers of oil, coal, nuclear power, and alternative sources of energy. After Hurricanes Katrina and Rita ravaged oil and natural gas production in the Gulf of Mexico in 2005, Bush asked Americans to conserve energy but proposed no new regulations.

Conservatives hailed Bush's appointment of two new Supreme Court justices. In 2005, John Roberts, who had served in the Reagan and George H. W. Bush administrations, was named chief justice. The president faced a stiffer challenge in finding a successor to the moderate Sandra Day O'Connor, who retired shortly thereafter. His first choice, Harriet Miers, had questionable credentials—she had never served as a judge—and drew opposition from both the right and the left before eventually stepping aside. Bush then nominated Samuel A. Alito, a staunch conservative who won confirmation by a narrow and mostly partisan margin of 58 to 42.

> Senator Joseph Lieberman charged that George W. Bush's tax cuts were "giving the most to those who need it least, piling more debt on the backs of our children and robbing Social Security and Medicare to pay for it."

In contrast to the partisan conflict that attended judicial appointments and tax and environmental policy, Bush mobilized bipartisan support behind the No Child Left Behind (NCLB) Act of 2002. The law marked the greatest change in federal education policy since the 1960s, substantially extending the role of the federal government in public education, a realm historically left to the state and local governments. Promising to end, in Bush's words, "the story of children being just shuffled through the system," the law required every school to meet annual testing standards, provided penalties for failing schools, and allowed parents to transfer their children out of such schools. It authorized an increase in federal aid aimed primarily at the poorest districts, but not enough for Senator Paul Wellstone of Minnesota, one of the few critics of the education bill, who asked, "How can you reach the goal of leaving no child behind on a tin cup budget?" This query anticipated problems that states would face in implementing the legislation, because only 7 percent of their education budgets came from the federal government. By 2004, most states were straining to meet the demands of the new education standards as they struggled with severe budget crises.

The Bush administration's second major effort to co-opt Democratic Party issues constituted what the president hailed as "the greatest advance in health care coverage for America's seniors" since the start of Medicare in 1965. In

Hurricane Katrina
Residents of the poverty-stricken Lower Ninth Ward of New Orleans cry for help after floods submerged 80 percent of the city in the wake of Hurricane Katrina in August 2005. The boat was useless to these people because it had lost its motor. Some residents waited as long as five days to be rescued. A historian of the disaster wrote, "Americans were not used to seeing their country in ruins, their people in want."
AP Images/David J. Phillip.

December 2003, the president signed a bill authorizing prescription drug benefits for the elderly and at the same time expanding the role of private insurers in the Medicare system. Most Democrats opposed the legislation, charging that it left big gaps in coverage, subsidized private insurers with federal funds to compete with Medicare, banned imports of low-priced drugs, and prohibited the government from negotiating with drug companies to reduce prices. Legislators of both parties worried about the cost of the new drug benefit, estimated to surpass $500 billion after it took effect in 2006. Although the law's requirement that beneficiaries choose from dozens of private insurance plans made the program confusing, more than 80 percent of the elderly who signed up for the benefit were at least "somewhat satisfied" with the program. Medical costs overall continued to soar, and the number of uninsured Americans reached 46.6 million in 2006.

One domestic undertaking of the Bush administration found little approval anywhere: its handling of Hurricane Katrina, which in August 2005 devastated the coasts of Alabama, Louisiana, and Mississippi and ultimately resulted in some fifteen hundred deaths. Dodging the worst of the storm itself, residents of New Orleans suffered catastrophe when some of the levees broke, flooding 80 percent of the city. What happened next shook a deeply rooted assumption held by Americans, even conservatives who were devoted to limited government: that government owed its citizens protection from natural disasters. Federal, state, and local officials failed the citizens of New Orleans in two ways: They had not built the levees to withstand such a deluge, and they failed to rescue citizens when the levees broke and flooded their homes.

Although most New Orleans residents left the city before the hurricane hit, some decided to ride it out, and others were too old, too poor, or too sick to flee. More than one-fourth of all households did not own a car, and others could not afford alternative housing. One man responsible for thirteen relatives later said, "I'd like to ask the mayor how you take fourteen people with no finances and book them in a hotel. It's not that we didn't leave. It's that we couldn't leave." Thousands abandoned in the city spent anguished days waiting on rooftops for help; wading in filthy, toxic water; and enduring the heat, stench, disorder, and lack of basic necessities at the convention center and Superdome, where they had been told to go for safety and protection.

"How can we save the world if we can't save our own people?" wondered a Louisianan whose home escaped damage. He was one of hundreds of people with small boats who rushed to rescue people from their rooftops. Thousands of other volunteers helped evacuees in distant cities and a year later were still traveling to the Gulf Coast to assist with reconstruction. Millions more opened their pocketbooks to aid the victims. Yet the immense private generosity and the superb response of a few groups, such as the U.S. coast guard and the Louisiana Department of Wildlife and Fisheries, could not make up for the feeling that the nation had failed some of its citizens when they needed it most. A year later, only 40 percent of the population had returned home, and restoration of the city lay years in the future. Moreover, since so many of Katrina's hardest-hit victims were poor and black (the poverty rate among children in New Orleans exceeded 40 percent before the storm), the disaster highlighted the severe injustices and deprivations remaining in American society.

The Globalization of Terrorism

The response to Hurricane Katrina contrasted sharply with the Bush administration's decisive reaction to the horror that had unfolded four years earlier on the morning of September 11, 2001. In the most deadly attack ever launched on American soil, nineteen terrorists hijacked four planes and flew three of them into the twin towers of New York City's World Trade Center and the Pentagon in Washington, D.C.; the fourth crashed in a field in Pennsylvania. The attacks took nearly 2,800 lives, including U.S. citizens and people from ninety countries. The nation, indeed the world, was stunned.

The hijackers were members of Osama bin Laden's Al Qaeda international terrorist network, some of whom had been living in the United States for several years. Organized from bin Laden's sanctuaries in Afghanistan, where the radical Muslim Taliban government had taken control, the attacks reflected several elements of globalization. The technological advances and increased mobility accompanying globalization facilitated bin Laden's worldwide coordination of Al Qaeda and aided the hijackers' activities. Moreover, Islamic extremists were enraged by the spread of Western goods, culture, and values into the Muslim world, as well as by the 1991 Persian Gulf War against Iraq and the stationing of American troops in Saudi Arabia, bin Laden's homeland. Acting on a dis-

The "Tribute in Light"
Twin pillars of light, projected by eighty-eight searchlights in the place where the World Trade Center's twin towers had stood, soared as a monument to the victims of the terrorist attacks of September 11, 2001. Sharon Weicman, who worked as a volunteer for a month on the site, was drawn by the illumination, remarking, "The closer I got, the more at peace I felt." Turned on at the six-month anniversary of the attack, the "Tribute in Light" was dimmed one month later and has been illuminated every year since on September 11.
AP Images/Daniel Derella.

torted interpretation of one of the world's great religions, bin Laden sought to rid the Middle East of Western influence and install puritanical Muslim control. Whether poor or middle-class, living in Middle Eastern homelands governed by undemocratic and corrupt governments or in Western cities where they felt alienated and despised, the 9/11 terrorists and others who came

Afghanistan

after them saw the West, and especially the United States, as the evil source of their humiliation and the supporter of Israel's oppression of Palestinian Muslims.

In the wake of the September 11 attacks, President Bush's public approval rating skyrocketed as he sought a global alliance against terrorism and won at least verbal support from most governments. On October 11, the United States and Britain began bombing Afghanistan, and American special forces aided the Northern Alliance, the Taliban government's main opposition. By December, the Taliban government was destroyed, but bin Laden had not been captured, and numerous Al Qaeda forces had escaped or remained in hiding throughout the world. Afghans elected a new national government, but although the United States still had 27,000 troops in Afghanistan seven years later, economic stability and physical security remained out of reach.

At home, the balance between **liberty** and security tilted. Throughout the country, anti-immigrant sentiment revived, and anyone appearing to be Middle Eastern or practicing Islam was likely to arouse suspicion. Authorities arrested more than a thousand Arabs and Muslims, and an internal study by the Justice Department later reported that many people with no connection to terrorism spent months in jail, denied their rights. "I think America overreacted . . . by singling out Arab-named men like myself," said Shanaz Mohammed, who was jailed for eight months for an immigration violation.

"The smoke was still coming out of the rubble in New York City when we passed the law," said C. L. Otter, Republican representative from Idaho, referring to the USA Patriot Act, which Congress approved by huge margins in October 2001. The law gave the government new powers to monitor suspected terrorists and their associates, including the ability to pry personal information about individuals from libraries, universities, and businesses, while allowing more exchange of information between criminal investigators and those investigating foreign threats. It soon provoked calls for revision from both conservatives and liberals. Kathleen MacKenzie, a councilwoman in Ann Arbor, Michigan, explained why the council passed a resolution op-

posing the Patriot Act: "[A]s awful as we feel about September 11 and as concerned as we were about national safety, we felt that giving up [rights] was too high a price to pay." A security official countered, "If you don't violate someone's human rights some of the time, you probably aren't doing your job."

Insisting that presidential powers were virtually limitless in times of national crisis, Bush stretched his powers as commander in chief until he met resistance from the courts and Congress. In 2001, the administration established special military commissions to try prisoners captured in Afghanistan and taken to the U.S. military base at Guantánamo, Cuba. But in 2006, responding to a suit filed by one of the some five hundred detainees who had languished there for years, the Supreme Court ruled five to three that Congress had not authorized such tribunals and that they violated international law. In 2006, congressional leaders became openly critical of the administration for wiretapping phone calls made and received by U.S. residents without obtaining the warrants required by law, and a federal district court ruled that the wiretapping program violated privacy, free speech, and the separation of powers.

The government also sought to protect Americans from future terrorist attacks through the greatest reorganization of the executive branch since 1948. In November 2002, Congress authorized the new Department of Homeland Security (DHS), combining 170,000 federal employees from twenty-two agencies through which responsibilities for different aspects of domestic security had been dispersed. Chief among the department's duties were intelligence analysis; immigration and border security; chemical, biological, and nuclear countermeasures; and emergency preparedness and response. During the new department's first five years, no terrorist attacks were launched in the United States, but doubts were raised about its effectiveness when its subagency, the Federal Emergency Management Agency (FEMA), failed so badly in response to Hurricane Katrina.

Unilateralism, Preemption, and the Iraq War

The Bush administration sought collective action against the Taliban, but on most other international issues, it adopted a go-it-alone approach. In addition to withdrawing from the Kyoto Protocol on global warming and violating international rules about the treatment of military prisoners, it scrapped the 1972 Antiballistic Missile Treaty in order to develop the space-based Strategic Defense Initiative (SDI) first proposed by Ronald Reagan. Bush also withdrew the United States from the UN's International Criminal Court, and he rejected an agreement to enforce bans on the development and possession of biological weapons—an agreement signed by all of America's European allies.

Nowhere was the new policy of unilateralism more striking than in a new war against Iraq, a war pushed by Vice President Dick Cheney and Secretary of Defense Donald H. Rumsfeld, but not Secretary of State Colin Powell. In his State of the Union message in January 2002, Bush identified Iraq, Iran, and North Korea as an "axis of evil." His words alarmed political leaders in both Europe and Asia, who insisted that those three nations posed entirely different challenges. Preferring to emphasize diplomacy rather than confrontation, Bush's opponents in Europe and Asia objected to his unilateral assessment.

Nonetheless, addressing West Point graduates in June, President Bush proclaimed a new policy for American security based not on containment but on preemption: "Traditional concepts of deterrence will not work against a terrorist enemy whose avowed tactics are wanton destruction and the targeting of innocents; whose so-called soldiers seek martyrdom in death and whose most potent protection is statelessness." Because nuclear, chemical, and biological weapons enabled "even weak states and small groups [to] attain a catastrophic power to strike great nations," the United States had to "be ready for preemptive action." For a century, the United States had intervened militarily and unilaterally in the affairs of small nations, but it had not gone to war except to repel aggression against itself or its allies. The president's claim that the United States had the right to start a war was at odds with international law and with many Americans' understanding of their nation's ideals. It distressed most of America's great-power allies.

Nonetheless, the Bush administration moved deliberately to apply the doctrine of preemption to Iraq, whose dic-

tator, Saddam Hussein, appeared to be in violation of UN resolutions from the 1991 Gulf War requiring Iraq to destroy and stop further development of nuclear, chemical, and biological weapons. In November 2002, the United States persuaded the UN Security Council to pass a resolution requiring Iraq to disarm or face "serious consequences." When Iraq failed to comply fully with new UN inspections, the Bush administration decided on war. Making (now widely disputed) claims that Hussein had links to Al Qaeda and harbored terrorists and that Iraq possessed weapons of mass destruction, the president insisted that the threat was immediate and great enough to justify preemptive action. Despite opposition from the Arab world and most major nations—including France, Germany, China, and Russia—which preferred to give the UN inspectors more time, the United States and Britain invaded Iraq on March 19, 2003, supported by some thirty nations (see Map 31.1). This coalition included Australia, Italy, Japan, and Spain but few major powers or traditional allies. The coalition forces won an easy and decisive victory, and Bush declared the end of the war on May 1. Saddam Hussein remained at large until December 2003.

Arabs were glad to see the end of Hussein, but many did not welcome the presence of American troops in Iraq. As the publisher of a Lebanese newspaper put it, "[Iraqis] have to choose between the night of tyranny and the night of humiliation stemming from foreign occupation." Moreover, damage from U.S. bombing and widespread looting resulting from the failure of U.S. troops to secure order and provide basic necessities left Iraqis wondering how much they had gained. "With Saddam there was tyranny, but at least you had a salary to put food on your family's table," said a young father from Hussein's hometown of Tikrit. Tha'ar Abdul Qader, who worked at a children's hospital in Baghdad, complained, "They can take our oil, but at least they should let us have electricity and water." In March 2003, President Bush promised that the lives of Iraqis would

> "I think America overreacted . . . by singling out Arab-named men like myself," said Shanaz Mohammed, who was jailed for eight months for an immigration violation in the wake of September 11.

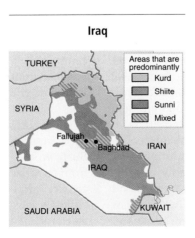

Iraq

TURKEY

SYRIA

Fallujah

Baghdad   IRAN

IRAQ

SAUDI ARABIA   KUWAIT

Areas that are predominantly
- Kurd
- Shiite
- Sunni
- Mixed

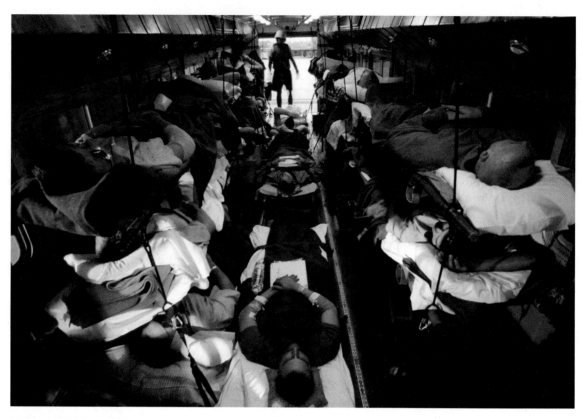

The Iraq War
By September 2007, 3,700 American soldiers had died in Iraq, and more than 25,000 had been wounded. Of those wounded, more than 12,000 were so damaged that they could not return to duty. These soldiers are being transported from a field hospital in Balad, Iraq, to a plane that will take them to Germany for further treatment. They were casualties of the heavy fighting in Fallujah in November 2004.
© Bettmann/Corbis.

"dramatically improve," but four years later Iraqis had less electricity than they had had before the war, and a majority lacked access to clean water. Continuing violence had caused 2 million to flee their country and displaced 1.9 million within Iraq.

The administration had not planned adequately for the occupation and sent far fewer forces to Iraq than it had deployed in 1991 in response to Iraq's invasion of Kuwait. The 140,000 American forces in Iraq came under attack almost daily from remnants of the former Hussein regime, religious extremists, and hundreds of foreign terrorists now entering the chaotic country. Seeking to divide Iraqis and undermine the occupation, terrorists launched deadly assaults on such targets as the UN mission in Baghdad and Red Cross headquarters, as well as on major mosques and Iraqi citizens, resulting in tens of

thousands dead. L. Paul Bremer, who headed the Iraqi occupation for fourteen months, believed that U.S. forces were "spread too thin on the ground. During my morning intelligence briefings, I would sometimes picture an understrength fire crew racing from one blaze to another."

The war became an issue in the presidential campaign of 2004, which registered the highest voter turnout since 1968. Massachusetts senator John Kerry, the Democratic nominee, criticized Bush's unilateralist foreign policy and the administration's conduct of the war. A slim majority of voters, however, indicated their belief that Bush would better protect American security from terrorist threats than Kerry. Once again, the election turned on a single state. This time it was Ohio, which gave Bush a 286 to 252 victory in the electoral college. The president won 50.7 percent of the popular vote to Kerry's 48.3 percent and carried Republican majorities into Congress.

In June 2004, the United States transferred sovereignty to an interim Iraqi government, and in January 2005, about 58 percent of Iraqis eligible to vote risked their safety to elect a national assembly. The daunting challenges facing the national assembly were to write a constitution, satisfy Iraq's sharply divided political blocs, and decide to what extent Islamic religious law would shape the new government. Violence escalated against government officials, Iraqi civilians, and occupation forces. A nineteen-year-old Iraqi, confined to his house by his parents, who feared he could be killed or lured into terrorist activities, said, "If I'm killed, it doesn't even matter because I'm dead right now." Some observers spoke of **guerrilla warfare**, "quagmire," and civil war, evoking comparisons with the U.S. experience in Vietnam. By 2006, when U.S. military deaths approached 3,000 and Iraqi civilian casualties reached tens of thousands, public opinion polls in the United States found that a majority of Americans believed that the Iraq War was a mistake.

The president's father, George H. W. Bush, had refused to invade Iraq at the end of the 1991 Gulf War. He explained that Colin Powell, Dick Cheney, and other advisers agreed that "unilaterally exceeding the United Nations' mandate would have destroyed the precedent of international response to aggression that we hoped to establish." The first Bush administration resisted making the nation "an occupying power in a bitterly hostile land," refusing to incur the "incalculable human and political costs" that such an invasion would produce.

By 2006, his son's very different approach was subject to criticism that crossed party lines and included leading military figures. Critics acknowledged that the U.S. military had felled a brutal dictator, but coalition forces were not sufficiently numerous or prepared for the turmoil that followed the invasion, nor did they find the weapons of mass destruction or links to Osama bin Laden that administration officials had insisted made the war necessary. Rather, in the chaos induced by the invasion of Iraq, more than a thousand terrorists entered Iraq—the place, according to one expert, "for fundamentalists to go . . . to stick it to the West."

The war and occupation exacted a steep price not only in dollars but also in American and Iraqi lives, U.S. relations with the other great powers, and the nation's reputation in the world,

especially among Arab nations. Revelations of prisoner abuse in the Abu Ghraib prison in Iraq and in the Guantánamo detention camp housing captives from the Afghan war further tarnished the U.S. image. Anti-Americanism around the world rose to its highest point in history. The budget deficit swelled, and resources were diverted to Iraq from other national security challenges, including the stabilization of Afghanistan, the elimination of bin Laden and Al Qaeda, and the threats posed by North Korea's and Iran's pursuit of nuclear weapons.

Voters registered their dissatisfaction with the war in the 2006 congressional elections, turning control of both houses over to the Democrats for the first time since 1994. President Bush replaced Secretary of Defense Donald Rumsfeld, and the administration displayed more willingness to work with other nations in dealing with Iraq, Iran, and North Korea. Yet Bush clung to the goal of bringing democracy to the Middle East, even as the situation in Iraq deteriorated. Despite opposition from the Democratic-controlled Congress, who wanted a timetable for withdrawal from Iraq and turning over responsibility for security to the Iraqi government, in 2007 the administration began a troop surge that increased U.S. forces in Iraq to 160,000. Officials made no promises about how long the U.S. military would be needed, and the conflict over the war at home intensified.

REVIEW Why did the United States invade Iraq in March 2003?

Conclusion: Defining the Government's Role at Home and Abroad

On March 21, 2003, some 225 years after the birth of the United States, Colin Powell referred to the unfinished nature of the American promise when he declared that the question of America's role in the world "isn't answered yet." In fact, the end of the cold war, the rise of international terrorism, and the George W. Bush administration's doctrines of preemption and unilateralism sparked new debates over the long-standing question of how the United States should act beyond its borders.

Nor had Americans set to rest questions about the role of government at home. In a population so greatly derived from people fleeing oppressive governments, Americans had debated for more than two centuries what responsibilities the government could or should shoulder and what was best left to private enterprise, families, churches, and other voluntary institutions. Far more than other democracies, the United States had taken the path of private rather than public obligation, individual rather than collective solutions. In the twentieth century, Americans had significantly enlarged the federal government's powers and responsibilities, but the last three decades of the twentieth century had seen a decline of trust in government's ability to improve people's lives, even as a poverty rate of 20 percent among children and a growing gap between rich and poor survived the economic boom of the 1990s.

The shifting of control of the government back and forth between Republicans and Democrats from 1989 to 2006 revealed a dynamic debate over the role of government in domestic affairs. The protections enacted for people with disabilities during the first Bush administration and Bill Clinton's incremental reforms in some social areas built on a deep-rooted tradition that sought to realize the American promise of justice and human well-being. Those who mobilized against the ravages of globalization worked internationally for what **populists**, **progressives**, New Deal reformers, and many activists of the 1960s had sought for the domestic population: protection of individual rights, curbs on **laissez-faire** capitalism, assistance for victims of rapid economic change, and fiscal policies that placed greater responsibility on those best able to pay for the collective good. The second Bush administration, however—with a few exceptions, such as the No Child Left Behind Act and the prescription drug program for the elderly—advocated a more limited role for the federal government.

As the United States entered the twenty-first century, it became ever more deeply embedded in the global economy as products, information, and people crossed borders with amazing speed and frequency. Although the end of the cold war brought about unanticipated cooperation between the United States and its former enemies, globalization also contributed to international instability and the threat of deadly terrorism to a nation unaccustomed to foreign attacks within

its own borders. In response to those dangers, the second Bush administration began to chart a departure from the multilateral approach to foreign policy that had been built up by Republican and Democratic administrations alike since World War II. Yet as the United States became mired in reconstruction efforts in Iraq, Americans continued to debate how the nation could best maintain domestic security while still exercising its economic and military power on a rapidly changing planet.

Selected Bibliography

Domestic Politics, Policies, and Economic Change

Douglas Brinkley, *The Great Deluge: Hurricane Katrina, New Orleans, and the Mississippi Gulf Coast* (2006).
Alfred D. Chandler Jr., *Inventing the Electronic Century: The Epic Story of the Consumer Electronics and Computer Science Industries* (2001).
Colin Gordon, *Dead on Arrival: The Politics of Health Care in Twentieth-Century America* (2003).
John Robert Greene, *The Presidency of George Bush* (2000).
John F. Harris, *The Survivor: Bill Clinton in the White House* (2005).
Bruce D. Meyer and Douglas Holtz-Eakin, *Making Work Pay: The Earned Income Tax Credit and Its Impact on America's Families* (2002).
Richard A. Posner, *Breaking the Deadlock: The 2000 Election, the Constitution, and the Courts* (2001).
Richard K. Scotch, *From Good Will to Civil Rights: Transforming Federal Disability Policy* (rev. ed., 2001).
David K. Shipler, *The Working Poor: Invisible in America* (2004).

Globalization and Immigration

Frank D. Bean and Gillian Stevens, *America's Newcomers and the Dynamics of Diversity* (2003).
George J. Borjas, *Heaven's Door: Immigration Policy and the American Economy* (1999).
Jeremy Brecher, Tim Costello, and Brendan Smith, *Globalization from Below* (2000).
Thomas L. Friedman, *The World Is Flat* (2005).
Otis L. Graham, *Unguarded Gates: A History of America's Immigration Crisis* (2004).
John R. MacArthur, *The Selling of "Free Trade": NAFTA, Washington, and the Subversion of American Democracy* (2000).
David M. Reimers, *Other Immigrants: The Global Origins of the American People* (2005).
Joseph E. Stiglitz, *Globalization and Its Discontents* (2002).

Foreign Policy after the Cold War

Andrew J. Bacevich, *American Empire: The Realities and Consequences of U.S. Diplomacy* (2002).

Ivo H. Daalder and James M. Lindsay, *America Unbound: The Bush Revolution in Foreign Policy* (2003).

Karen DeYoung, *Soldier: The Life of Colin Powell* (2006).

Lawrence Freedman and Efraim Karsh, *The Gulf Conflict, 1990–1991: Diplomacy and War in the New World Order* (1993).

David Halberstam, *War in a Time of Peace: Bush, Clinton, and the Generals* (2001).

Paul Kennedy, *The Parliament of Man: The Past, Present, and Future of the United Nations* (2006).

James Mann, *Rise of the Vulcans: The History of Bush's War Cabinet* (2004).

Joseph S. Nye Jr., *The Paradox of American Power: Why the World's Only Superpower Can't Go It Alone* (2002).

Terrorism and the Iraq War

Peter L. Bergen, *Holy War, Inc.: Inside the Secret World of Osama bin Laden* (2001).

Gilles Kepel, *Jihad: The Trail of Political Islam* (2002).

Daniel Levitas, *The Terrorist Next Door: The Militia Movement and the Radical Right* (2002).

National Commission on Terrorist Attacks, *The 9/11 Commission Report: Final Report of the National Commission on Terrorist Attacks upon the United States* (2004).

George Packer, *The Assassins' Gate: America in Iraq* (2005).

Gary Rosen, ed., *The Right War? The Conservative Debate on Iraq* (2005).

Anthony Shadid, *Night Draws Near: Iraq's People in the Shadow of America's War* (2005).

Ron Suskind, *The One Percent Doctrine: Deep Inside America's Pursuit of Its Enemies since 9/11* (2006).

Lawrence Wright, *The Looming Tower: Al-Qaeda and the Road to 9/11* (2006).

▶ **FOR MORE BOOKS ABOUT TOPICS IN THIS CHAPTER,** see the Online Bibliography at bedfordstmartins.com/roark.

▶ **FOR ADDITIONAL FIRSTHAND ACCOUNTS OF THIS PERIOD,** see Chapter 31 in Michael Johnson, ed., *Reading the American Past*, Fourth Edition.

▶ **FOR WEB SITES, IMAGES, AND DOCUMENTS RELATED TO TOPICS AND PLACES IN THIS CHAPTER,** visit bedfordstmartins.com/makehistory.

REVIEWING THE CHAPTER

Follow these steps to review and strengthen your understanding of the chapter.

STEP 1: *Study the **Key Terms** and **Timeline** to identify the significance of each item listed.*

STEP 2: *Answer the **Review Questions**, drawing on key terms and dates to support your answers.*

STEP 3: *Drawing on the Key Terms, Timeline, and Review Questions, answer the broader **Making Connections** questions.*

KEY TERMS

Who

Colin L. Powell (p. 1141)
George H. W. Bush (p. 1143)
Jesse Jackson (p. 1143)
Clarence Thomas (p. 1146)
Anita Hill (p. 1146)
Manuel Noriega (p. 1147)
Saddam Hussein (p. 1147)
William Jefferson "Bill" Clinton (p. 1151)
Albert Gore Jr. (pp. 1151, 1167)
H. Ross Perot (p. 1152)
Hillary Rodham Clinton (p. 1153)
Kenneth Starr (p. 1155)
Monica Lewinsky (p. 1155)
Osama bin Laden (pp. 1159, 1171)
George W. Bush (p. 1160)
Richard B. Cheney (p. 1168)
Donald H. Rumsfeld (p. 1173)
John Kerry (p. 1174)

What

Clean Air Act of 1990 (p. 1143)
Americans with Disabilities Act (p. 1143)
Operation Just Cause (p. 1147)
Operation Desert Storm (p. 1148)
Family and Medical Leave Act (p. 1152)
Violence against Women Act (p. 1152)
Earned Income Tax Credit (EITC) (p. 1152)
Oklahoma City bombing (p. 1154)
"don't ask, don't tell" policy (p. 1154)
Defense of Marriage Act (p. 1154)
Personal Responsibility and Work Opportunity Reconciliation Act (p. 1155)
Whitewater investigations (p. 1155)
North American Free Trade Agreement (NAFTA) (p. 1160)
General Agreement on Tariffs and Trade (GATT) (p. 1160)
World Trade Organization (WTO) (p. 1160)

Central American–Dominican Republic Free Trade Agreement (CAFTA-DR) (p. 1160)
International Monetary Fund (IMF) (p. 1161)
Immigration Reform and Control Act of 1986 (p. 1166)
Office of Faith-Based and Community Initiatives (p. 1168)
Kyoto Protocol (p. 1168)
No Child Left Behind Act (p. 1169)
Medicare reform (p. 1170)
Hurricane Katrina (p. 1170)
September 11 attacks (p. 1171)
Al Qaeda (p. 1171)
Taliban (p. 1171)
USA Patriot Act (p. 1172)
Department of Homeland Security (p. 1172)
Iraq War (p. 1173)

TIMELINE

◄ **1988** • Republican George H. W. Bush elected president.

    1989 • Communism collapses in Eastern Europe; Berlin Wall falls.
          • United States invades Panama.

      1990 • Americans with Disabilities Act.

        1991 • Persian Gulf War.

          1992 • Democrat William Jefferson "Bill" Clinton elected president.

            1993 • Israel and PLO sign peace accords.
                • North American Free Trade Agreement (NAFTA).
                • Clinton announces policy for gays in military.
                • Family and Medical Leave Act.

              1994 • United States sends troops to Haiti.
                  • General Agreement on Tariffs and Trade (GATT) establishes World Trade Organization (WTO).

                1995 • Bombing of federal building in Oklahoma City.

                  1996 • Personal Responsibility and Work Opportunity Reconciliation Act.
                    • President Clinton reelected.

                    1997 • Tax cut enacted.

                      1998 • United States bombs terrorist sites in Afghanistan and Sudan.
                        • United States bombs Iraq.
                        • President Clinton impeached.

REVIEW QUESTIONS

1. Why did George H. W. Bush lose the presidency in 1992? (pp. 1143–52)

2. What policies of the Clinton administration reflect the president's efforts to move his party to the right? (pp. 1152–57)

3. Who criticized free trade agreements and why? (pp. 1157–67)

4. Why did the United States invade Iraq in March 2003? (pp. 1167–75)

MAKING CONNECTIONS

1. How did George H. W. Bush continue the policies of his predecessor, Ronald Reagan? How did he depart from them?

2. President Bill Clinton called himself a "New Democrat." How did his policies and goals differ from those of Democrats in the past?

3. In the late twentieth century, economic globalization transformed the United States. Explain what globalization is and describe how it affected the U.S. economy and population in the 1990s.

4. The terrorist attacks of September 11, 2001, were unprecedented. What gave rise to the attacks? How did the nation respond?

▶ FOR PRACTICE QUIZZES, A CUSTOMIZED STUDY PLAN, AND OTHER STUDY TOOLS, see the Online Study Guide at bedfordstmartins.com/roark.

1999 • Senate trial fails to approve articles of impeachment.
     • United States, with NATO, bombs Serbia.

  2000 • Republican George W. Bush elected president.

    2001 • **September 11.** Terrorists attack World Trade Center and Pentagon.
         • United States attacks Afghanistan, driving out Taliban government.
         • USA Patriot Act.
         • $1.35 trillion tax cut.

      2002 • No Child Left Behind Act.
           • Department of Homeland Security established.

        2003 • United States attacks Iraq, driving out Saddam Hussein.
             • Prescription drug coverage added to Medicare.

          2004 • George W. Bush reelected president.

            2005 • Hurricane Katrina.

                 • Central American–Dominican Republic Free Trade Agreement (CAFTA-DR).

              2006 • Majority of Americans believe Iraq War was a mistake.

                2007 • Bush begins troop surge in Iraq.

Documents

For additional documents see the DocLinks feature at bedfordstmartins.com/roark.

THE DECLARATION OF INDEPENDENCE

In Congress, July 4, 1776,

THE UNANIMOUS DECLARATION OF THE
THIRTEEN UNITED STATES OF AMERICA

When in the course of human events, it becomes necessary for one people to dissolve the political bands which have connected them with another, and to assume, among the powers of the earth, the separate and equal station to which the laws of nature and of nature's God entitle them, a decent respect to the opinions of mankind requires that they should declare the causes which impel them to the separation.

We hold these truths to be self-evident, that all men are created equal; that they are endowed by their Creator with certain unalienable rights; that among these, are life, liberty, and the pursuit of happiness. That, to secure these rights, governments are instituted among men, deriving their just powers from the consent of the governed; that, whenever any form of government becomes destructive of these ends, it is the right of the people to alter or to abolish it, and to institute a new government, laying its foundation on such principles, and organizing its powers in such form, as to them shall seem most likely to effect their safety and happiness. Prudence, indeed, will dictate that governments long established, should not be changed for light and transient causes; and, accordingly, all experience hath shown, that mankind are more disposed to suffer, while evils are sufferable, than to right themselves by abolishing the forms to which they are accustomed. But, when a long train of abuses and usurpations, pursuing invariably the same object, evinces a design to reduce them under absolute despotism, it is their right, it is their duty, to throw off such government and to provide new guards for their future security. Such has been the patient sufferance of these colonies, and such is now the necessity which constrains them to alter their former systems of government. The history of the present King of Great Britain is a history of repeated injuries and usurpations, all having, in direct object, the establishment of an absolute tyranny over these States. To prove this, let facts be submitted to a candid world:

He has refused his assent to laws the most wholesome and necessary for the public good.

He has forbidden his governors to pass laws of immediate and pressing importance, unless suspended in their operation till his assent should be obtained; and, when so suspended, he has utterly neglected to attend to them.

He has refused to pass other laws for the accommodation of large districts of people, unless those people would relinquish the right of representation in the legislature; a right inestimable to them, and formidable to tyrants only.

He has called together legislative bodies at places unusual, uncomfortable, and distant from the depository of their public records, for the sole purpose of fatiguing them into compliance with his measures.

He has dissolved representative houses repeatedly for opposing, with manly firmness, his invasions on the rights of the people.

He has refused, for a long time after such dissolutions, to cause others to be elected; whereby the legislative powers, incapable of annihilation, have returned to the people at large for their exercise; the state remaining in the mean-time exposed to all the danger of invasion from without, and convulsions within.

He has endeavoured to prevent the population of these States; for that purpose, obstructing the laws for naturalization of foreigners, refusing to pass others to encourage their migration hither, and raising the conditions of new appropriations of lands.

He has obstructed the administration of justice, by refusing his assent to laws for establishing judiciary powers.

He has made judges dependent on his will alone, for the tenure of their offices, and the amount and payment of their salaries.

He has erected a multitude of new offices, and sent hither swarms of officers to harass our people, and eat out their substance.

He has kept among us, in times of peace, standing armies, without the consent of our legislature.

He has affected to render the military independent of, and superior to, the civil power.

He has combined, with others, to subject us to a jurisdiction foreign to our Constitution, and unacknowledged by our laws; giving his assent to their acts of pretended legislation:

For quartering large bodies of armed troops among us:

For protecting them by a mock trial, from punishment, for any murders which they should commit on the inhabitants of these States:

For cutting off our trade with all parts of the world:

For imposing taxes on us without our consent:

For depriving us, in many cases, of the benefit of trial by jury:

For transporting us beyond seas to be tried for pretended offences:

For abolishing the free system of English laws in a neighboring province, establishing therein an arbitrary government, and enlarging its boundaries, so as to render it at once an example and fit instrument for introducing the same absolute rule into these colonies:

For taking away our charters, abolishing our most valuable laws, and altering, fundamentally, the powers of our governments:

For suspending our own legislatures, and declaring themselves invested with power to legislate for us in all cases whatsoever.

He has abdicated government here, by declaring us out of his protection, and waging war against us.

He has plundered our seas, ravaged our coasts, burnt our towns, and destroyed the lives of our people.

He is, at this time, transporting large armies of foreign mercenaries to complete the works of death, desolation, and tyranny, already begun, with circumstances of cruelty and perfidy scarcely paralleled in the most barbarous ages, and totally unworthy the head of a civilized nation.

He has constrained our fellow citizens, taken captive on the high seas, to bear arms against their country, to become the executioners of their friends, and brethren, or to fall themselves by their hands.

He has excited domestic insurrections amongst us, and has endeavored to bring on the inhabitants of our frontiers, the merciless Indian savages, whose known rule of warfare is an undistinguished destruction of all ages, sexes, and conditions.

In every stage of these oppressions, we have petitioned for redress; in the most humble terms; our repeated petitions have been answered only by repeated injury. A prince, whose character is thus marked by every act which may define a tyrant, is unfit to be the ruler of a free people.

Nor have we been wanting in attention to our British brethren. We have warned them, from time to time, of attempts made by their legislature to extend an unwarrantable jurisdiction over us. We have reminded them of the circumstances of our emigration and settlement here. We have appealed to their native justice and magnanimity, and we have conjured them, by the ties of our common kindred, to disavow these usurpations, which would inevitably interrupt our connections and correspondence. They, too, have been deaf to the voice of justice and consanguinity. We must, therefore, acquiesce in the necessity which denounces our separation, and hold them as we hold the rest of mankind, enemies in war, in peace, friends.

We, therefore, the representatives of the United States of America, in general Congress assembled, appealing to the Supreme Judge of the world for the rectitude of our intentions, do, in the name, and by authority of the good people of these colonies, solemnly publish and declare, that these united colonies are, and of right ought to be, free and independent states: that they are absolved from all allegiance to the British Crown, and that all political connection between them and the state of Great Britain is, and ought to be, totally dissolved; and that, as free and independent states, they have full power to levy war, conclude peace, contract alliances, establish commerce, and to do all other acts and things which independent states may of right do. And, for the support of this declaration, with a firm reliance on the protection of Divine Providence, we mutually pledge to each other our lives, our fortunes, and our sacred honor.

The foregoing Declaration was, by order of Congress, engrossed, and signed by the following members:

JOHN HANCOCK

New Hampshire
Josiah Bartlett
William Whipple
Matthew Thornton

Massachusetts Bay
Samuel Adams
John Adams
Robert Treat Paine
Elbridge Gerry

Rhode Island
Stephen Hopkins
William Ellery

Connecticut
Roger Sherman
Samuel Huntington
William Williams
Oliver Wolcott

New York
William Floyd
Phillip Livingston
Francis Lewis
Lewis Morris

New Jersey
Richard Stockton
John Witherspoon
Francis Hopkinson
John Hart
Abraham Clark

Pennsylvania
Robert Morris
Benjamin Rush
Benjamin Franklin
John Morton
George Clymer
James Smith
George Taylor
James Wilson
George Ross

THE ARTICLES OF CONFEDERATION AND PERPETUAL UNION

Delaware	North Carolina	Virginia	Georgia
Caesar Rodney	William Hooper	George Wythe	Button Gwinnett
George Read	Joseph Hewes	Richard Henry Lee	Lyman Hall
Thomas M'Kean	John Penn	Thomas Jefferson	George Walton
		Benjamin Harrison	
Maryland	**South Carolina**	Thomas Nelson, Jr.	
Samuel Chase	Edward Rutledge	Francis Lightfoot Lee	
William Paca	Thomas Heyward, Jr.	Carter Braxton	
Thomas Stone	Thomas Lynch, Jr.		
Charles Carroll,	Arthur Middleton		
of Carrollton			

Resolved, That copies of the Declaration be sent to the several assemblies, conventions, and committees, or councils of safety, and to the several commanding officers of the continental troops; that it be proclaimed in each of the United States, at the head of the army.

THE ARTICLES OF CONFEDERATION AND PERPETUAL UNION

Agreed to in Congress, November 15, 1777.
Ratified March 1781.

BETWEEN THE STATES OF NEW HAMPSHIRE, MASSACHU-SETTS BAY, RHODE ISLAND AND PROVIDENCE PLANTA-TIONS, CONNECTICUT, NEW YORK, NEW JERSEY, PENN-SYLVANIA, DELAWARE, MARYLAND, VIRGINIA, NORTH CAROLINA, SOUTH CAROLINA, GEORGIA.*

Article 1

The stile of this confederacy shall be "The United States of America."

Article 2

Each State retains its sovereignty, freedom and independence, and every power, jurisdiction, and right, which is not by this confederation expressly delegated to the United States, in Congress assembled.

Article 3

The said states hereby severally enter into a firm league of friendship with each other for their common defence, the security of their liberties and their mutual and general welfare; binding themselves to assist each other against all force offered to, or attacks made upon them, or any of them, on account of religion, sovereignty, trade, or any other pretence whatever.

---

*This copy of the final draft of the Articles of Confederation is taken from the *Journals*, 9:907–925, November 15, 1777.

Article 4

The better to secure and perpetuate mutual friendship and intercourse among the people of the different states in this union, the free inhabitants of each of these states, paupers, vagabonds, and fugitives from justice excepted, shall be entitled to all privileges and immunities of free citizens in the several states; and the people of each State shall have free ingress and regress to and from any other State, and shall enjoy therein all the privileges of trade and commerce, subject to the same duties, impositions, and restrictions, as the inhabitants thereof respectively; provided, that such restrictions shall not extend so far as to prevent the removal of property, imported into any State, to any other State of which the owner is an inhabitant; provided also, that no imposition, duties, or restriction, shall be laid by any State on the property of the United States, or either of them.

If any person guilty of, or charged with treason, felony, or other high misdemeanor in any State, shall flee from justice and be found in any of the United States, he shall, upon demand of the governor or executive power of the State from which he fled, be delivered up and removed to the State having jurisdiction of his offence.

Full faith and credit shall be given in each of these states to the records, acts, and judicial proceedings of the courts and magistrates of every other State.

Article 5

For the more convenient management of the general interests of the United States, delegates shall be annually appointed, in such manner as the legislature of each State shall direct, to meet in Congress, on the 1st Monday in November in every year, with a power reserved to each State to recall its delegates, or any of them, at any time within the year, and to send others in their stead for the remainder of the year.

No State shall be represented in Congress by less than two, nor by more than seven members; and no person shall be capable of being a delegate for more than three years in any term of six years; nor shall any person, being a delegate, be capable of holding any office under the United States, for which he, or any other for his benefit, receives any salary, fees, or emolument of any kind.

Each State shall maintain its own delegates in a meeting of the states, and while they act as members of the committee of the states.

In determining questions in the United States, in Congress assembled, each State shall have one vote.

Freedom of speech and debate in Congress shall not be impeached or questioned in any court or place out of Congress: and the members of Congress shall be protected in their persons from arrests and imprisonments, during the time of their going to and from, and attendance on Congress, except for treason, felony, or breach of the peace.

Article 6

No State, without the consent of the United States, in Congress assembled, shall send any embassy to, or receive any embassy from, or enter into any conference, agreement, alliance, or treaty with any king, prince, or state; nor shall any person, holding any office of profit or trust under the United States, or any of them, accept of any present, emolument, office or title, of any kind whatever, from any king, prince, or foreign state; nor shall the United States, in Congress assembled, or any of them, grant any title of nobility.

No two or more states shall enter into any treaty, confederation, or alliance, whatever, between them, without the consent of the United States, in Congress assembled, specifying accurately the purposes for which the same is to be entered into, and how long it shall continue.

No state shall lay any imposts or duties which may interfere with any stipulations in treaties entered into by the United States, in Congress assembled, with any king, prince, or state, in pursuance of any treaties already proposed by Congress to the courts of France and Spain.

No vessels of war shall be kept up in time of peace by any State, except such number only as shall be deemed necessary by the United States, in Congress assembled, for the defence of such State or its trade; nor shall any body of forces be kept up by any State, in time of peace, except such number

only as, in the judgment of the United States, in Congress assembled, shall be deemed requisite to garrison the forts necessary for the defence of such State; but every State shall always keep up a well regulated and disciplined militia, sufficiently armed and accoutred, and shall provide, and constantly have ready for use, in public stores, a due number of field pieces and tents, and a proper quantity of arms, ammunition and camp equipage.

No State shall engage in any war without the consent of the United States, in Congress assembled, unless such State be actually invaded by enemies, or shall have received certain advice of a resolution being formed by some nation of Indians to invade such State, and the danger is so imminent as not to admit of a delay till the United States, in Congress assembled, can be consulted; nor shall any State grant commissions to any ships or vessels of war, nor letters of marque or reprisal, except it be after a declaration of war by the United States, in Congress assembled, and then only against the kingdom or state, and the subjects thereof, against which war has been so declared, and under such regulations as shall be established by the United States, in Congress assembled, unless such State be infested by pirates, in which case vessels of war may be fitted out for that occasion, and kept so long as the danger shall continue, or until the United States, in Congress assembled, shall determine otherwise.

Article 7

When land forces are raised by any State for the common defence, all officers of or under the rank of colonel, shall be appointed by the legislature of each State respectively, by whom such forces shall be raised, or in such manner as such State shall direct; and all vacancies shall be filled up by the State which first made the appointment.

Article 8

All charges of war and all other expences, that shall be incurred for the common defence or general welfare, and allowed by the United States, in Congress assembled, shall be defrayed out of a common treasury, which shall be supplied by the several states, in proportion to the value of all land within each State, granted to or surveyed for any person, as such land and the buildings and improvements thereon shall be estimated according to such mode as the United States, in Congress assembled, shall, from time to time, direct and appoint.

The taxes for paying that proportion shall be laid and levied by the authority and direction of the legislatures of the several states, within the time agreed upon by the United States, in Congress assembled.

THE ARTICLES OF CONFEDERATION AND PERPETUAL UNION

Article 9

The United States, in Congress assembled, shall have the sole and exclusive right and power of determining on peace and war, except in the cases mentioned in the 6th article; of sending and receiving ambassadors; entering into treaties and alliances, provided that no treaty of commerce shall be made, whereby the legislative power of the respective states shall be restrained from imposing such imposts and duties on foreigners as their own people are subjected to, or from prohibiting the exportation or importation of any species of goods or commodities whatsoever; of establishing rules for deciding, in all cases, what captures on land or water shall be legal, and in what manner prizes, taken by land or naval forces in the service of the United States, shall be divided or appropriated; of granting letters of marque and reprisal in times of peace; appointing courts for the trial of piracies and felonies committed on the high seas, and establishing courts for receiving and determining, finally, appeals in all cases of captures; provided, that no member of Congress shall be appointed a judge of any of the said courts.

The United States, in Congress assembled, shall also be the last resort on appeal in all disputes and differences now subsisting, or that hereafter may arise between two or more states concerning boundary, jurisdiction or any other cause whatever; which authority shall always be exercised in the manner following: whenever the legislative or executive authority, or lawful agent of any State, in controversy with another, shall present a petition to Congress, stating the matter in question, and praying for a hearing, notice thereof shall be given, by order of Congress, to the legislative or executive authority of the other State in controversy, and a day assigned for the appearance of the parties by their lawful agents, who shall then be directed to appoint, by joint consent, commissioners or judges to constitute a court for hearing and determining the matter in question; but, if they cannot agree, Congress shall name three persons out of each of the United States, and from the list of such persons each party shall alternately strike out one, the petitioners beginning, until the number shall be reduced to thirteen; and from that number not less than seven, nor more than nine names, as Congress shall direct, shall, in the presence of Congress, be drawn out by lot; and the persons whose names shall be so drawn, or any five of them, shall be commissioners or judges to hear and finally determine the controversy, so always as a major part of the judges who shall hear the cause shall agree in the determination; and if either party shall neglect to attend at the day appointed, without shewing reasons which Congress shall judge sufficient, or, being present, shall refuse to strike, the Congress shall proceed to nominate three persons out of each State, and the secretary of Congress shall strike in behalf of such party absent or refusing; and the judgment and sentence of the court to be appointed, in the manner before prescribed, shall be final and conclusive; and if any of the parties shall refuse to submit to the authority of such court, or to appear or defend their claim or cause, the court shall nevertheless proceed to pronounce sentence or judgment, which shall, in like manner, be final and decisive, the judgment or sentence and other proceedings begin, in either case, transmitted to Congress, and lodged among the acts of Congress for the security of the parties concerned: provided, that every commissioner, before he sits in judgment, shall take an oath, to be administered by one of the judges of the supreme or superior court of the State where the cause shall be tried, "well and truly to hear and determine the matter in question, according to the best of his judgment, without favour, affection, or hope of reward:" provided, also, that no State shall be deprived of territory for the benefit of the United States.

All controversies concerning the private right of soil, claimed under different grants of two or more states, whose jurisdictions, as they may respect such lands and the states which passed such grants, are adjusted, the said grants, or either of them, being at the same time claimed to have originated antecedent to such settlement of jurisdiction, shall, on the petition of either party to the Congress of the United States, be finally determined, as near as may be, in the same manner as is before prescribed for deciding disputes respecting territorial jurisdiction between different states.

The United States, in Congress assembled, shall also have the sole and exclusive right and power of regulating the alloy and value of coin struck by their own authority, or by that of the respective states; fixing the standard of weights and measures throughout the United States; regulating the trade and managing all affairs with the Indians not members of any of the states; provided that the legislative right of any State within its own limits be not infringed or violated; establishing and regulating post offices from one State to another throughout all the United States, and exacting such postage on the papers passing through the same as may be requisite to defray the expences of the said office; appointing all officers of the land forces in the service of the United States, excepting regimental officers; appointing all the officers of the naval forces, and commissioning all officers whatever in the service of the United States; making rules for the government and regulation of the said land and naval forces, and directing their operations.

The United States, in Congress assembled, shall have authority to appoint a committee to sit in the recess of Congress, to be denominated "a Committee of the States," and to consist of one delegate from each State, and to appoint such other committees and civil officers as may be necessary for managing the general affairs of the United States, under their direction; to appoint one of their number to preside; provided that no person be allowed to serve in the office of president more than one year in any term of three years; to ascertain the necessary sums of money to be raised for the service of the United States, and to appropriate and apply the same for defraying the public expences; to borrow money or emit bills on the credit of the United States, transmitting, every half year, to the respective states, an account of the sums of money so borrowed or emitted; to build and equip a navy; to agree upon the number of land forces, and to make requisitions from each State for its quota, in proportion to the number of white inhabitants in such State; which requisitions shall be binding; and thereupon, the legislature of each State shall appoint the regimental officers, raise the men, and cloathe, arm, and equip them in a soldier-like manner, at the expence of the United States; and the officers and men so cloathed, armed, and equipped, shall march to the place appointed and within the time agreed on by the United States, in Congress assembled; but if the United States, in Congress assembled, shall, on consideration of circumstances, judge proper that any State should not raise men, or should raise a smaller number than its quota, and that any other State should raise a greater number of men than the quota thereof, such extra number shall be raised, officered, cloathed, armed, and equipped in the same manner as the quota of such State, unless the legislature of such State shall judge that such extra number cannot be safely spared out of the same, in which case they shall raise, officer, cloathe, arm, and equip as many of such extra number as they judge can be safely spared. And the officers and men so cloathed, armed, and equipped, shall march to the place appointed and within the time agreed on by the United States, in Congress assembled.

The United States, in Congress assembled, shall never engage in a war, nor grant letters of marque and reprisal in time of peace, nor enter into any treaties or alliances, nor coin money, nor regulate the value thereof, nor ascertain the sums and expences necessary for the defence and welfare of the United States, or any of them: nor emit bills, nor borrow money on the credit of the United States, nor appropriate money, nor agree upon the number of vessels of war to be built or purchased, or the number of land or sea forces to be raised, nor appoint a commander in chief of the army or navy, unless nine states assent to the same; nor shall a question on any other point, except for adjourning from day to day, be determined, unless by the votes of a majority of the United States, in Congress assembled.

The Congress of the United States shall have power to adjourn to any time within the year, and to any place within the United States, so that no period of adjournment be for a longer duration than the space of six months, and shall publish the journal of their proceedings monthly, except such parts thereof, relating to treaties, alliances or military operations, as, in their judgment, require secrecy; and the yeas and nays of the delegates of each State on any question shall be entered on the journal, when it is desired by any delegate; and the delegates of a State, or any of them, at his, or their request, shall be furnished with a transcript of the said journal, except such parts as are above excepted, to lay before the legislatures of the several states.

Article 10

The committee of the states, or any nine of them, shall be authorized to execute, in the recess of Congress, such of the powers of Congress as the United States, in Congress assembled, by the consent of nine states, shall, from time to time, think expedient to vest them with; provided, that no power be delegated to the said committee, for the exercise of which, by the articles of confederation, the voice of nine states, in the Congress of the United States assembled, is requisite.

Article 11

Canada acceding to this confederation, and joining in the measures of the United States, shall be admitted into and entitled to all the advantages of this union; but no other colony shall be admitted into the same, unless such admission be agreed to by nine states.

Article 12

All bills of credit emitted, monies borrowed and debts contracted by, or under the authority of Congress before the assembling of the United States, in pursuance of the present confederation, shall be deemed and considered as a charge against the United States, for payment and satisfaction whereof the said United States and the public faith are hereby solemnly pledged.

Article 13

Every State shall abide by the determinations of the United States, in Congress assembled, on all questions which, by this confederation, are submitted to them. And the articles of this confederation shall be inviolably observed by every State, and the union shall be perpetual; nor shall any alteration at any time hereafter be made in any of them, unless such alteration be agreed to in a Congress of the United States, and be afterwards confirmed by the legislatures of every State.

These articles shall be proposed to the legislatures of all the United States, to be considered, and if approved of by them, they are advised to authorize their delegates to ratify the same in the Congress of the United States; which being done, the same shall become conclusive.

THE CONSTITUTION OF THE UNITED STATES*

Agreed to by Philadelphia Convention, September 17, 1787. Implemented March 4, 1789.

Preamble

We the people of the United States, in order to form a more perfect union, establish justice, insure domestic tranquility, provide for the common defense, promote the general welfare, and secure the blessings of liberty to ourselves and our posterity, do ordain and establish this Constitution for the United States of America.

Article I

Section 1 All legislative powers herein granted shall be vested in a Congress of the United States, which shall consist of a Senate and a House of Representatives.

Section 2 The House of Representatives shall be composed of members chosen every second year by the people of the several States, and the electors in each State shall have the qualifications requisite for electors of the most numerous branch of the State Legislature.

No person shall be a Representative who shall not have attained to the age of twenty-five years, and been seven years a citizen of the United States, and who shall not, when elected, be an inhabitant of that State in which he shall be chosen.

Representatives and direct taxes shall be apportioned among the several States which may be included within this Union, according to their respective numbers, *which shall be determined by adding to the whole number of free persons, including those bound to service for a term of years and excluding Indians not taxed, three-fifths of all other persons.* The actual enumeration shall be made within three years after the first meeting of the Congress of the United States, and within every subsequent term of ten years, in such manner as they shall by law direct. The number of Representatives shall not exceed one for every thirty thousand, but each State shall have at least one Representative; *and until such enumeration shall be made, the State of New Hampshire shall be entitled to choose three, Massachusetts eight, Rhode Island and Providence Plantations one, Connecticut five, New York six, New Jersey four, Pennsylvania eight, Delaware one, Maryland six, Virginia ten, North Carolina five, South Carolina five, and Georgia three.*

When vacancies happen in the representation from any State, the Executive authority thereof shall issue writs of election to fill such vacancies.

The House of Representatives shall choose their Speaker and other officers; and shall have the sole power of impeachment.

Section 3 The Senate of the United States shall be composed of two Senators from each State, *chosen by the legislature thereof,* for six years; and each Senator shall have one vote.

Immediately after they shall be assembled in consequence of the first election, they shall be divided as equally as may be into three classes. The seats of the Senators of the first class shall be vacated at the expiration of the second year, of the second class at the expiration of the fourth year, and of the third class at the expiration of the sixth year, so that one-third may be chosen every second year; *and if vacancies happen by resignation or otherwise, during the recess of the legislature of any State, the Executive thereof may make temporary appointments until the next meeting of the legislature, which shall then fill such vacancies.*

No person shall be a Senator who shall not have attained to the age of thirty years, and been nine years a citizen of the United States, and who shall not, when elected, be an inhabitant of that State for which he shall be chosen.

The Vice-President of the United States shall be President of the Senate, but shall have no vote, unless they be equally divided.

The Senate shall choose their other officers, and also a President *pro tempore,* in the absence of the Vice-President, or when he shall exercise the office of President of the United States.

The Senate shall have the sole power to try all impeachments. When sitting for that purpose, they shall be on oath or affirmation. When the President of the United States is tried, the Chief Justice shall preside: and no person shall be convicted without the concurrence of two-thirds of the members present.

Judgment in cases of impeachment shall not extend further than to removal from the office, and disqualification to hold and enjoy any office of honor, trust or profit under the United States: but the party convicted shall nevertheless be liable and subject to indictment, trial, judgment and punishment, according to law.

Section 4 The times, places and manner of holding elections for Senators and Representatives shall be prescribed in each State by the legislature thereof; but the Congress may at any time by law make or alter such regulations, except as to the places of choosing Senators.

The Congress shall assemble at least once in every year, and such meeting *shall be on the first*

---

* Passages no longer in effect are in italic type.

Monday in December, unless they shall by law appoint a different day.

Section 5 Each house shall be the judge of the elections, returns and qualifications of its own members, and a majority of each shall constitute a quorum to do business; but a smaller number may adjourn from day to day, and may be authorized to compel the attendance of absent members, in such manner, and under such penalties, as each house may provide.

Each house may determine the rules of its proceedings, punish its members for disorderly behavior, and with the concurrence of two-thirds, expel a member.

Each house shall keep a journal of its proceedings, and from time to time publish the same, excepting such parts as may in their judgment require secrecy; and the yeas and nays of the members of either house on any question shall, at the desire of one-fifth of those present, be entered on the journal.

Neither house, during the session of Congress, shall, without the consent of the other, adjourn for more than three days, nor to any other place than that in which the two houses shall be sitting.

Section 6 The Senators and Representatives shall receive a compensation for their services, to be ascertained by law and paid out of the treasury of the United States. They shall in all cases except treason, felony and breach of the peace, be privileged from arrest during their attendance at the session of their respective houses, and in going to and returning from the same; and for any speech or debate in either house, they shall not be questioned in any other place.

No Senator or Representative shall, during the time for which he was elected, be appointed to any civil office under the authority of the United States, which shall have been created, or the emoluments whereof shall have been increased, during such time; and no person holding any office under the United States shall be a member of either house during his continuance in office.

Section 7 All bills for raising revenue shall originate in the House of Representatives; but the Senate may propose or concur with amendments as on other bills.

Every bill which shall have passed the House of Representatives and the Senate, shall, before it become a law, be presented to the President of the United States; if he approve he shall sign it, but if not he shall return it with objections to that house in which it shall have originated, who shall enter the objections at large on their journal, and proceed to reconsider it. If after such reconsideration two-thirds of that house shall agree to pass the bill, it shall be sent, together with the objections, to the other house, by which it shall likewise be reconsidered, and, if approved by two-thirds of that house, it shall become a law. But in all such cases the votes of both houses shall be determined by yeas and nays, and the names of the persons voting for and against the bill shall be entered on the journal of each house respectively. If any bill shall not be returned by the President within ten days (Sundays excepted) after it shall have been presented to him, the same shall be a law, in like manner as if he had signed it, unless the Congress by their adjournment prevent its return, in which case it shall not be a law.

Every order, resolution, or vote to which the concurrence of the Senate and House of Representatives may be necessary (except on a question of adjournment) shall be presented to the President of the United States; and before the same shall take effect, shall be approved by him, or being disapproved by him, shall be repassed by two-thirds of the Senate and House of Representatives, according to the rules and limitations prescribed in the case of a bill.

Section 8 The Congress shall have power

To lay and collect taxes, duties, imposts, and excises, to pay the debts and provide for the common defense and general welfare of the United States; but all duties, imposts and excises shall be uniform throughout the United States;

To borrow money on the credit of the United States;

To regulate commerce with foreign nations, and among the several States, and with the Indian tribes;

To establish an uniform rule of naturalization, and uniform laws on the subject of bankruptcies throughout the United States;

To coin money, regulate the value thereof, and of foreign coin, and fix the standard of weights and measures;

To provide for the punishment of counterfeiting the securities and current coin of the United States;

To establish post offices and post roads;

To promote the progress of science and useful arts by securing for limited times to authors and inventors the exclusive right to their respective writings and discoveries;

To constitute tribunals inferior to the Supreme Court;

To define and punish piracies and felonies committed on the high seas and offences against the law of nations;

To declare war, grant letters of marque and reprisal, and make rules concerning captures on land and water;

To raise and support armies, but no appropriation of money to that use shall be for a longer term than two years;

To provide and maintain a navy;

To make rules for the government and regulation of the land and naval forces;

THE CONSTITUTION OF THE UNITED STATES

To provide for calling forth the militia to execute the laws of the Union, suppress insurrections and repel invasions;

To provide for organizing, arming, and disciplining the militia, and for governing such part of them as may be employed in the service of the United States, reserving to the States respectively the appointment of the officers, and the authority of training the militia according to the discipline prescribed by Congress;

To exercise exclusive legislation in all cases whatsoever, over such district (not exceeding ten miles square) as may, by cession of particular States, and the acceptance of Congress, become the seat of the government of the United States, and to exercise like authority over all places purchased by the consent of the legislature of the State, in which the same shall be, for erection of forts, magazines, arsenals, dock-yards, and other needful buildings;—and

To make all laws which shall be necessary and proper for carrying into execution the foregoing powers, and all other powers vested by this Constitution in the government of the United States, or in any department or officer thereof.

Section 9 *The migration or importation of such persons as any of the States now existing shall think proper to admit shall not be prohibited by the Congress prior to the year one thousand eight hundred and eight; but a tax or duty may be imposed on such importation, not exceeding ten dollars for each person.*

The privilege of the writ of habeas corpus shall not be suspended, unless when in cases of rebellion or invasion the public safety may require it.

No bill of attainder or ex post facto law shall be passed.

No capitation, or other direct, tax shall be laid, unless in proportion to the census or enumeration herein before directed to be taken.

No tax or duty shall be laid on articles exported from any State.

No preference shall be given by any regulation of commerce or revenue to the ports of one State over those of another; nor shall vessels bound to, or from, one State be obliged to enter, clear, or pay duties in another.

No money shall be drawn from the treasury, but in consequence of appropriations made by law; and a regular statement and account of the receipts and expenditures of all public money shall be published from time to time.

No title of nobility shall be granted by the United States: and no person holding any office of profit or trust under them, shall, without the consent of the Congress, accept of any present, emolument, office, or title, of any kind whatever, from any king, prince, or foreign state.

Section 10 No State shall enter into any treaty, alliance, or confederation; grant letters of marque

and reprisal; coin money; emit bills of credit; make anything but gold and silver coin a tender in payment of debts; pass any bill of attainder, ex post facto law, or law impairing the obligation of contracts, or grant any title of nobility.

No State shall, without the consent of Congress, lay any imposts or duties on imports or exports, except what may be absolutely necessary for executing its inspection laws: and the net produce of all duties and imposts, laid by any State on imports or exports, shall be for the use of the treasury of the United States; and all such laws shall be subject to the revision and control of the Congress.

No State shall, without the consent of Congress, lay any duty of tonnage, keep troops, or ships of war in time of peace, enter into any agreement or compact with another State, or with a foreign power, or engage in war, unless actually invaded, or in such imminent danger as will not admit of delay.

Article II

Section 1 The executive power shall be vested in a President of the United States of America. He shall hold his office during the term of four years, and, together with the Vice-President, chosen for the same term, be elected as follows:

Each State shall appoint, in such manner as the legislature thereof may direct, a number of electors, equal to the whole number of Senators and Representatives to which the State may be entitled in the Congress; but no Senator or Representative, or person holding an office of trust or profit under the United States, shall be appointed an elector.

The electors shall meet in their respective States, and vote by ballot for two persons, of whom one at least shall not be an inhabitant of the same State with themselves. And they shall make a list of all the persons voted for, and of the number of votes for each; which list they shall sign and certify, and transmit sealed to the seat of government of the United States, directed to the President of the Senate. The President of the Senate shall, in the presence of the Senate and House of Representatives, open all the certificates, and the votes shall then be counted. The person having the greatest number of votes shall be the President, if such number be a majority of the whole number of electors appointed; and if there be more than one who have such majority, and have an equal number of votes, then the House of Representatives shall immediately choose by ballot one of them for President; and if no person have a majority, then from the five highest on the list said house shall in like manner choose the President. But in choosing the President the votes shall be taken by States, the representation from each State having one vote; a quorum for this purpose shall consist of a member or members from two-thirds of the States, and a majority of all the States shall be necessary to a choice. In every case, after the choice of the President, the person having the greatest number of votes of the electors shall be the Vice-President. But if there should remain two or more who have equal votes, the Senate shall choose from them by ballot the Vice-President.

The Congress may determine the time of choosing the electors, and the day on which they shall give their votes; which day shall be the same throughout the United States.

No person except a natural-born citizen, *or a citizen of the United States at the time of the adoption of this Constitution*, shall be eligible to the office of President; neither shall any person be eligible to that office who shall not have attained to the age of thirty-five years, and been fourteen years a resident within the United States.

In cases of the removal of the President from office or of his death, resignation, or inability to discharge the powers and duties of the said office, the same shall devolve on the Vice-President, and the Congress may by law provide for the case of removal, death, resignation, or inability, both of the President and Vice-President, declaring what officer shall then act as President, and such officer shall act accordingly, until the disability be removed, or a President shall be elected.

The President shall, at stated times, receive for his services a compensation, which shall neither be increased nor diminished during the period for which he shall have been elected, and he shall not receive within that period any other emolument from the United States, or any of them.

Before he enter on the execution of his office, he shall take the following oath or affirmation:—"I do solemnly swear (or affirm) that I will faithfully execute the office of the President of the United States, and will to the best of my ability preserve, protect and defend the Constitution of the United States."

Section 2 The President shall be commander in chief of the army and navy of the United States, and of the militia of the several States, when called into the actual service of the United States; he may require the opinion, in writing, of the principal officer in each of the executive departments, upon any subject relating to the duties of their respective offices, and he shall have power to grant reprieves and pardons for offenses against the United States, except in cases of impeachment.

He shall have power, by and with the advice and consent of the Senate, to make treaties, provided two-thirds of the Senators present concur; and he shall nominate, and by and with the advice and consent of the Senate, shall appoint ambassadors, other public ministers and consuls, judges of the Supreme Court, and all other officers of the United States, whose appointments are not herein otherwise provided for, and which shall be established by law: but Congress may by law vest the appointment of such inferior officers, as they think proper, in the President alone, in the courts of law, or in the heads of departments.

The President shall have power to fill up all vacancies that may happen during the recess of the Senate, by granting commissions which shall expire at the end of their next session.

Section 3 He shall from time to time give to the Congress information of the state of the Union, and recommend to their consideration such measures as he shall judge necessary and expedient; he may, on extraordinary occasions, convene both houses, or either of them, and in case of disagreement between them, with respect to the time of adjournment, he may adjourn them to such time as he shall think proper; he shall receive ambassadors and other public ministers; he shall take care that the laws be faithfully executed, and shall commission all the officers of the United States.

Section 4 The President, Vice-President and all civil officers of the United States shall be removed from office on impeachment for, and on conviction of, treason, bribery, or other high crimes and misdemeanors.

Article III

Section 1 The judicial power of the United States shall be vested in one Supreme Court, and in such inferior courts as the Congress may from time to time ordain and establish. The judges, both of the Supreme and inferior courts, shall hold their offices during good behavior, and shall, at stated times, receive for their services a compensation which shall not be diminished during their continuance in office.

Section 2 The judicial power shall extend to all cases, in law and equity, arising under this Constitution, the laws of the United States, and treaties made, or which shall be made, under their authority;—to all cases affecting ambassadors, other public ministers and consuls;—to all cases of admiralty and maritime jurisdiction;—to controversies to which the United States shall be a party;—to controversies between two or more States;—*between a State and citizens of another State;*—between citizens of different States;—between citizens of the same State claiming lands under grants of different States, and between a State, or the citizens thereof, and foreign states, citizens or subjects.

In all cases affecting ambassadors, other public ministers and consuls, and those in which a State shall be party, the Supreme Court shall have original jurisdiction. In all the other cases before mentioned, the Supreme Court shall have appellate jurisdiction, both as to law and fact, with such exceptions, and under such regulations, as the Congress shall make.

THE CONSTITUTION OF THE UNITED STATES

The trial of all crimes, except in cases of impeachment, shall be by jury; and such trial shall be held in the State where said crimes shall have been committed; but when not committed within any State, the trial shall be at such place or places as the Congress may by Law have directed.

Section 3 Treason against the United States shall consist only in levying war against them, or in adhering to their enemies, giving them aid and comfort. No person shall be convicted of treason unless on the testimony of two witnesses to the same overt act, or on confession in open court.

The Congress shall have power to declare the punishment of treason, but no attainder of treason shall work corruption of blood, or forfeiture except during the life of the person attainted.

Article IV

Section 1 Full faith and credit shall be given in each State to the public acts, records, and judicial proceedings of every other State. And the Congress may by general laws prescribe the manner in which such acts, records, and proceedings shall be proved, and the effect thereof.

Section 2 The citizens of each State shall be entitled to all privileges and immunities of citizens in the several States.

A person charged in any State with treason, felony, or other crime, who shall flee from justice, and be found in another State, shall on demand of the executive authority of the State from which he fled, be delivered up, to be removed to the State having jurisdiction of the crime.

No Person held to service or labor in one State, under the laws thereof, escaping into another, shall, in consequence of any law or regulation therein, be discharged from such service or labor, but shall be delivered up on claim of the party to whom such service or labor may be due.

Section 3 New States may be admitted by the Congress into this Union; but no new State shall be formed or erected within the jurisdiction of any other State; nor any State be formed by the junction of two or more States, or parts of States, without the consent of the legislatures of the States concerned as well as of the Congress.

The Congress shall have power to dispose of and make all needful rules and regulations respecting the territory or other property belonging to the United States; and nothing in this Constitution shall be so construed as to prejudice any claims of the United States, or of any particular State.

Section 4 The United States shall guarantee to every State in this Union a republican form of government, and shall protect each of them against invasion; and on application of the legislature, or of the executive (when the legislature cannot be convened), against domestic violence.

Article V

The Congress, whenever two-thirds of both houses shall deem it necessary, shall propose amendments to this Constitution, or, on the application of the legislatures of two-thirds of the several States, shall call a convention for proposing amendments, which, in either case, shall be valid to all intents and purposes, as part of this Constitution, when ratified by the legislatures of three-fourths of the several States, or by conventions in three-fourths thereof, as the one or the other mode of ratification may be proposed by the Congress; provided *that no amendments which may be made prior to the year one thousand eight hundred and eight shall in any manner affect the first and fourth clauses in the ninth section of the first article*; and that no State, without its consent, shall be deprived of its equal suffrage in the Senate.

Article VI

All debts contracted and engagements entered into, before the adoption of this Constitution, shall be as valid against the United States under this Constitution, as under the Confederation.

This Constitution, and the laws of the United States which shall be made in pursuance thereof; and all treaties made, or which shall be made, under the authority of the United States, shall be the supreme law of the land; and the judges in every State shall be bound thereby, anything in the Constitution or laws of any State to the contrary notwithstanding.

The Senators and Representatives before mentioned, and the members of the several State legislatures, and all executive and judicial officers, both of the United States and of the several States, shall be bound by oath or affirmation to support this Constitution; but no religious test shall ever be required as a qualification to any office or public trust under the United States.

Article VII

The ratification of the conventions of nine States shall be sufficient for the establishment of this Constitution between the States so ratifying the same.

Done in convention by the unanimous consent of the States present, the seventeenth day of September in the year of our Lord one thousand seven hundred and eighty-seven and of the Independence of the United States of America the twelfth. In witness whereof we have hereunto subscribed our names.

GEORGE WASHINGTON
PRESIDENT AND DEPUTY FROM VIRGINIA

New Hampshire
John Langdon
Nicholas Gilman

Massachusetts
Nathaniel Gorham
Rufus King

Connecticut
William Samuel
  Johnson
Roger Sherman

New York
Alexander Hamilton

New Jersey
William Livingston
David Brearley
William Paterson
Jonathan Dayton

Pennsylvania
Benjamin Franklin
Thomas Mifflin
Robert Morris
George Clymer
Thomas FitzSimons
Jared Ingersoll
James Wilson
Gouverneur Morris

Delaware
George Read
Gunning Bedford, Jr.
John Dickinson
Richard Bassett
Jacob Broom

Maryland
James McHenry
Daniel of St. Thomas
  Jenifer
Daniel Carroll

Virginia
John Blair
James Madison, Jr.

North Carolina
William Blount
Richard Dobbs Spaight
Hugh Williamson

South Carolina
John Rutledge
Charles Cotesworth
  Pinckney
Charles Pinckney
Pierce Butler

Georgia
William Few
Abraham Baldwin

AMENDMENTS TO THE CONSTITUTION WITH ANNOTATIONS
(including the six unratified amendments)

IN THEIR EFFORT TO GAIN Antifederalists' support for the Constitution, Federalists frequently pointed to the inclusion of Article 5, which provides an orderly method of amending the Constitution. In contrast, the Articles of Confederation, which were universally recognized as seriously flawed, offered no means of amendment. For their part, Antifederalists argued that the amendment process was so "intricate" that one might as easily roll "sixes an hundred times in succession" as change the Constitution.

The system for amendment laid out in the Constitution requires that two-thirds of both houses of Congress agree to a proposed amendment, which must then be ratified by three-quarters of the legislatures of the states. Alternatively, an amendment may be proposed by a convention called by the legislatures of two-thirds of the states. Since 1789, members of Congress have proposed thousands of amendments. Besides the seventeen amendments added since 1789, only the six "unratified" ones included here were approved by two-thirds of both houses and sent to the states for ratification.

Among the many amendments that never made it out of Congress have been proposals to declare dueling, divorce, and interracial marriage unconstitutional as well as proposals to establish a national university, to acknowledge the sovereignty of Jesus Christ, and to prohibit any person from possessing wealth in excess of $10 million.*

Among the issues facing Americans today that might lead to constitutional amendment are efforts to balance the federal budget, to limit the number of terms elected officials may serve, to limit access to or prohibit abortion, to establish English as the official language of the United States, and to prohibit flag burning. None of these proposed amendments has yet garnered enough support in Congress to be sent to the states for ratification.

Although the first ten amendments to the Constitution are commonly known as the Bill of Rights, only Amendments 1–8 actually provide guarantees of individual rights. Amendments 9 and 10 deal with the structure of power within the constitutional system. The Bill of Rights was promised to appease Antifederalists who refused to ratify the Constitution without guarantees of individual liberties and limitations to federal power. After studying more than two hundred amendments recommended by the ratifying conventions of the states, Federalist James Madison presented a list of seventeen to Congress, which used Madison's list as the foundation for the twelve amendments that were sent to the states for ratification. Ten of the twelve were adopted in 1791. The first on the list of twelve,

* Richard B. Bernstein, *Amending America* (New York: Times Books, 1993), 177–81.

known as the Reapportionment Amendment, was never adopted (see page A-15). The second proposed amendment was adopted in 1992 as Amendment 27 (see page A-24).

Amendment I

Congress shall make no law respecting an establishment of religion, or prohibiting the free exercise thereof; or abridging the freedom of speech, or of the press; or the right of the people peaceably to assemble, and to petition the government for a redress of grievances.

♦ ♦ ♦

The First Amendment is a potent symbol for many Americans. Most are well aware of their rights to free speech, freedom of the press, and freedom of religion and their rights to assemble and to petition, even if they cannot cite the exact words of this amendment.

The First Amendment guarantee of freedom of religion has two clauses: the "free exercise clause," which allows individuals to practice or not practice any religion, and the "establishment clause," which prevents the federal government from discriminating against or favoring any particular religion. This clause was designed to create what Thomas Jefferson referred to as "a wall of separation between church and state." In the 1960s, the Supreme Court ruled that the First Amendment prohibits prayer (see Engel v. Vitale, *online) and Bible reading in public schools.*

Although the rights to free speech and freedom of the press are established in the First Amendment, it was not until the twentieth century that the Supreme Court began to explore the full meaning of these guarantees. In 1919, the Court ruled in Schenck v. United States *(online) that the government could suppress free expression only where it could cite a "clear and present danger." In a decision that continues to raise controversies, the Court ruled in 1990, in* Texas v. Johnson, *that flag burning is a form of symbolic speech protected by the First Amendment.*

Amendment II

A well-regulated militia being necessary to the security of a free State, the right of the people to keep and bear arms shall not be infringed.

♦ ♦ ♦

Fear of a standing army under the control of a hostile government made the Second Amendment an important part of the Bill of Rights. Advocates of gun ownership claim that the amendment prevents the government from regulating firearms. Proponents of gun control argue that the amendment is designed only to protect the right of the states to maintain militia units.

In 1939, the Supreme Court ruled in United States v. Miller *that the Second Amendment did not protect the right of an individual to own a sawed-off shotgun, which it argued was not ordinary militia equipment. Since then, the Supreme Court has refused to hear Second Amendment cases, while lower courts have upheld firearms regulations. Several justices currently on the bench seem to favor a narrow interpretation of the Second Amendment, which would allow gun control legislation. The controversy over the impact of the Second Amendment on gun owners and gun control legislation will certainly continue.*

Amendment III

No soldier shall, in time of peace, be quartered in any house without the consent of the owner, nor in time of war, but in a manner to be prescribed by law.

♦ ♦ ♦

The Third Amendment was extremely important to the framers of the Constitution, but today it is nearly forgotten. American colonists were especially outraged that they were forced to quarter British troops in the years before and during the American Revolution. The philosophy of the Third Amendment has been viewed by some justices and scholars as the foundation of the modern constitutional right to privacy. One example of this can be found in Justice William O. Douglas's opinion in Griswold v. Connecticut *(online).*

Amendment IV

The right of the people to be secure in their persons, houses, papers, and effects, against unreasonable searches and seizures, shall not be violated, and no warrants shall issue but upon probable cause, supported by oath or affirmation, and particularly describing the place to be searched, and the persons or things to be seized.

♦ ♦ ♦

In the years before the Revolution, the houses, barns, stores, and warehouses of American colonists were ransacked by British authorities under "writs of assistance" or general warrants. The British, thus empowered, searched for seditious material or smuggled goods that could then be used as evidence against colonists who were charged with a crime only after the items were found.

The first part of the Fourth Amendment protects citizens from "unreasonable" searches and seizures. The Supreme Court has interpreted this protection as well as the words search *and* seizure *in different ways at different times. At one time, the Court did not recognize electronic eavesdropping as a form of search and seizure, though it does today. At times, an "unreasonable" search has been almost any search carried out without a warrant, but in the two decades before 1969, the Court sometimes sanctioned warrantless searches that it considered reasonable based on "the total atmosphere of the case."*

The second part of the Fourth Amendment defines the procedure for issuing a search warrant and states the requirement of "probable cause," which is generally viewed as evidence indicating that a suspect has committed an offense.

The Fourth Amendment has been controversial because the Court has sometimes excluded evidence that has been seized in violation of constitutional standards. The justification is that excluding such evidence deters violations of the amendment, but doing so may allow a guilty person to escape punishment.

Amendment V

No person shall be held to answer for a capital, or otherwise infamous crime, unless on a presentment or indictment of a grand jury, except in cases arising in the land or naval forces, or in the militia, when in actual service in time of war or public danger; nor shall any person be subject for the same offence to be twice put in jeopardy of life or limb; nor shall be compelled in any criminal case to be a witness against himself, nor be deprived of life, liberty, or property, without due process of law; nor shall private property be taken for public use without just compensation.

♦ ♦ ♦

The Fifth Amendment protects people against government authority in the prosecution of criminal offenses. It prohibits the state, first, from charging a person with a serious crime without a grand jury hearing to decide whether there is sufficient evidence to support the charge and, second, from charging a person with the same crime twice. The best-known aspect of the Fifth Amendment is that it prevents a person from being "compelled . . . to be a witness against himself." The last clause, the "takings clause," limits the power of the government to seize property.

Although invoking the Fifth Amendment is popularly viewed as a confession of guilt, a person may be innocent yet still fear prosecution. For example, during the Red-baiting era of the late 1940s and 1950s, many people who had participated in legal activities that were associated with the Communist Party claimed the Fifth Amendment privilege rather than testify before the House Un-American Activities Committee because the mood of the times cast those activities in a negative light. Since "taking the Fifth" was viewed as an admission of guilt, those people often lost their jobs or became unemployable. (See chapter 26.) Nonetheless, the right to protect oneself against self-incrimination plays an important role in guarding against the collective power of the state.

Amendment VI

In all criminal prosecutions, the accused shall enjoy the right to a speedy and public trial, by an impartial jury of the State and district wherein the crime shall have been committed, which district shall have been previously ascertained by law, and to be informed of the nature and cause of the accusation; to be confronted with the witnesses against him; to have compulsory process for obtaining witnesses in his favor, and to have the assistance of counsel for his defence.

♦ ♦ ♦

The original Constitution put few limits on the government's power to investigate, prosecute, and punish crime. This process was of great concern to the early Americans, however, and of the twenty-eight rights specified in the first eight amendments, fifteen have to do with it. Seven rights are specified in the Sixth Amendment. These include the right to a speedy trial, a public trial, a jury trial, a notice of accusation, confrontation by opposing witnesses, testimony by favorable witnesses, and the assistance of counsel.

Although this amendment originally guaranteed these rights only in cases involving the federal government, the adoption of the Fourteenth Amendment began a process of applying the protections of the Bill of Rights to the states through court cases such as Gideon v. Wainwright *(online).*

Amendment VII

In suits at common law, where the value in controversy shall exceed twenty dollars, the right of trial by jury shall be preserved, and no fact tried by a jury shall be otherwise reexamined in any court of the United States, than according to the rules of the common law.

♦ ♦ ♦

This amendment guarantees people the same right to a trial by jury as was guaranteed by English common law in 1791. Under common law, in civil trials (those involving money damages) the role of the judge was to settle questions of law and that of the jury was to settle questions of fact. The amendment does not specify the size of the jury or its role in a trial, however. The Supreme Court has generally held that those issues be determined by English common law of 1791, which stated that a jury consists of twelve people, that a trial must be conducted before a judge who instructs the jury on the law and advises it on facts, and that a verdict must be unanimous.

Amendment VIII

Excessive bail shall not be required, nor excessive fines imposed, nor cruel and unusual punishments inflicted.

♦ ♦ ♦

The language used to guarantee the three rights in this amendment was inspired by the English Bill of Rights of

AMENDMENTS TO THE CONSTITUTION WITH ANNOTATIONS

1689. The Supreme Court has not had a lot to say about "excessive fines." In recent years it has agreed that despite the provision against "excessive bail," persons who are believed to be dangerous to others can be held without bail even before they have been convicted.

Although opponents of the death penalty have not succeeded in using the Eighth Amendment to achieve the end of capital punishment, the clause regarding "cruel and unusual punishments" has been used to prohibit capital punishment in certain cases (see Furman v. Georgia, *online) and to require improved conditions in prisons.*

Amendment IX

The enumeration in the Constitution, of certain rights, shall not be construed to deny or disparage others retained by the people.

♦ ♦ ♦

Some Federalists feared that inclusion of the Bill of Rights in the Constitution would allow later generations of interpreters to claim that the people had surrendered any rights not specifically enumerated there. To guard against this, Madison added language that became the Ninth Amendment. Interest in this heretofore largely ignored amendment revived in 1965 when it was used in a concurring opinion in Griswold v. Connecticut *(online). While Justice William O. Douglas called on the Third Amendment to support the right to privacy in deciding that case, Justice Arthur Goldberg, in the concurring opinion, argued that the right to privacy regarding contraception was an unenumerated right that was protected by the Ninth Amendment.*

In 1980, the Court ruled that the right of the press to attend a public trial was protected by the Ninth Amendment. While some scholars argue that modern judges cannot identify the unenumerated rights that the framers were trying to protect, others argue that the Ninth Amendment should be read as providing a constitutional "presumption of liberty" that allows people to act in any way that does not violate the rights of others.

Amendment X

The powers not delegated to the United States by the Constitution, nor prohibited by it to the States, are reserved to the States respectively, or to the people.

♦ ♦ ♦

The Antifederalists were especially eager to see a "reserved powers clause" explicitly guaranteeing the states control over their internal affairs. Not surprisingly, the Tenth Amendment has been a frequent battleground in the struggle over states' rights and federal supremacy. Prior to the Civil War, the Democratic Republican Party and Jacksonian Democrats invoked the Tenth Amendment to prohibit the federal government from making decisions about whether people in individual states could own slaves. The Tenth Amendment was virtually suspended during Reconstruction following the Civil War. In 1883, however, the Supreme Court declared the Civil Rights Act of 1875 unconstitutional on the grounds that it violated the Tenth Amendment. Business interests also called on the amendment to block efforts at federal regulation.

The Court was inconsistent over the next several decades as it attempted to resolve the tension between the restrictions of the Tenth Amendment and the powers the Constitution granted to Congress to regulate interstate commerce and levy taxes. The Court upheld the Pure Food and Drug Act (1906), the Meat Inspection Acts (1906 and 1907), and the White Slave Traffic Act (1910), all of which affected the states, but struck down an act prohibiting interstate shipment of goods produced through child labor. Between 1934 and 1935, a number of New Deal programs created by Franklin D. Roosevelt were declared unconstitutional on the grounds that they violated the Tenth Amendment. (See chapter 24.) As Roosevelt appointees changed the composition of the Court, the Tenth Amendment was declared to have no substantive meaning. Generally, the amendment is held to protect the rights of states to regulate internal matters such as local government, education, commerce, labor, and business, as well as matters involving families such as marriage, divorce, and inheritance within the state.

Unratified Amendment

Reapportionment Amendment (proposed by Congress September 25, 1789, along with the Bill of Rights)

After the first enumeration required by the first article of the Constitution, there shall be one Representative for every thirty thousand, until the number shall amount to one hundred, after which the proportion shall be so regulated by Congress, that there shall be not less than one hundred Representatives, nor less than one Representative for every forty thousand persons, until the number of Representatives shall amount to two hundred; after which the proportion shall be so regulated by Congress, that there shall not be less than two hundred Representatives, nor more than one Representative for every fifty thousand persons.

♦ ♦ ♦

If the Reapportionment Amendment had passed and remained in effect, the House of Representatives today would have more than 5,000 members rather than 435.

Amendment XI
[Adopted 1798]

The judicial power of the United States shall not be construed to extend to any suit in law or equity, commenced or prosecuted against one of the United States by citizens of another State, or by citizens or subjects of any foreign state.

◆◆◆

In 1793, the Supreme Court ruled in favor of Alexander Chisholm, executor of the estate of a deceased South Carolina merchant. Chisholm was suing the state of Georgia because the merchant had never been paid for provisions he had supplied during the Revolution. Many regarded this Court decision as an error that violated the intent of the Constitution.

Antifederalists had long feared a federal court system with the power to overrule a state court. When the Constitution was being drafted, Federalists had assured worried Antifederalists that section 2 of Article 3, which allows federal courts to hear cases "between a State and citizens of another State," did not mean that the federal courts were authorized to hear suits against a state by citizens of another state or a foreign country. Antifederalists and many other Americans feared a powerful federal court system because they worried that it would become like the British courts of this period, which were accountable only to the monarch. Furthermore, Chisholm v. Georgia *prompted a series of suits against state governments by creditors and suppliers who had made loans during the war.*

In addition, state legislators and Congress feared that the shaky economies of the new states, as well as the country as a whole, would be destroyed, especially if loyalists who had fled to other countries sought reimbursement for land and property that had been seized. The day after the Supreme Court announced its decision, a resolution proposing the Eleventh Amendment, which overturned the decision in Chisholm v. Georgia, *was introduced in the U.S. Senate.*

Amendment XII
[Adopted 1804]

The electors shall meet in their respective States, and vote by ballot for President and Vice-President, one of whom, at least, shall not be an inhabitant of the same State with themselves; they shall name in their ballots the person voted for as President, and in distinct ballots the person voted for as Vice-President, and they shall make distinct lists of all persons voted for as President, and of all persons voted for as Vice-President, and of the number of votes for each, which lists they shall sign and certify, and transmit sealed to the seat of government of the United States, directed to the President of the Senate;—the President of the Senate shall, in the presence of the Senate and House of Representatives, open all the certificates and the votes shall then be counted;—the person having the greatest number of votes for President shall be the President, if such number be a majority of the whole number of electors appointed; and if no person have such majority, then from the persons having the highest numbers not exceeding three on the list of those voted for as President, the House of Representatives shall choose immediately, by ballot, the President. But in choosing the President, the votes shall be taken by States, the representation from each State having one vote; a quorum for this purpose shall consist of a member or members from two-thirds of the States, and a majority of all the States shall be necessary to a choice. And if the House of Representatives shall not choose a President whenever the right of choice shall devolve upon them, before *the fourth day of March* next following, then the Vice-President shall act as President, as in the case of the death or other constitutional disability of the President.

The person having the greatest number of votes as Vice-President shall be the Vice-President, if such number be a majority of the whole number of electors appointed; and if no person have a majority, then from the two highest numbers on the list the Senate shall choose the Vice-President; a quorum for the purpose shall consist of two-thirds of the whole number of Senators, and a majority of the whole number shall be necessary to a choice. But no person constitutionally ineligible to the office of President shall be eligible to that of Vice-President of the United States.

◆◆◆

The framers of the Constitution disliked political parties and assumed that none would ever form. Under the original system, electors chosen by the states would each vote for two candidates. The candidate who won the most votes would become president, while the person who won the second-highest number of votes would become vice president. Rivalries between Federalists and Antifederalists led to the formation of political parties, however, even before George Washington had left office. Though Washington was elected unanimously in 1789 and 1792, the elections of 1796 and 1800 were procedural disasters because of party maneuvering (see chapters 9 and 10). In 1796, Federalist John Adams was chosen as president, and his great rival, the Antifederalist Thomas Jefferson (whose party was called the Republican Party), became his vice president. In 1800, all the electors cast their two votes as one of two party blocs. Jefferson and his fellow Republican nominee, Aaron Burr, were tied with 73 votes each. The contest went to the House of Representatives, which finally elected Jefferson after 36 ballots. The Twelfth Amendment prevents these problems by requiring electors to vote separately for the president and vice president.

Unratified Amendment

Titles of Nobility Amendment (proposed by Congress May 1, 1810)

If any citizen of the United States shall accept, claim, receive or retain any title of nobility or honor or shall, without the consent of Congress, accept and retain any present, pension, office or emolument of any kind whatever, from any emperor, king, prince or foreign power, such person shall cease to be a citizen of the United States, and shall be incapable of holding any office of trust or profit under them or either of them.

◆◆◆

This amendment would have extended Article 1, section 9, clause 8 of the Constitution, which prevents the awarding of titles by the United States and the acceptance of such awards from foreign powers without congressional consent. Historians speculate that general nervousness about the power of the emperor Napoleon, who was at that time extending France's empire throughout Europe, may have prompted the proposal. Though it fell one vote short of ratification, Congress and the American people thought the proposal had been ratified, and it was included in many nineteenth-century editions of the Constitution.

The Civil War and Reconstruction Amendments (Thirteenth, Fourteenth, and Fifteenth Amendments)

In the four months between the election of Abraham Lincoln and his inauguration, more than 200 proposed constitutional amendments were presented to Congress as part of a desperate attempt to hold the rapidly dissolving Union together. Most of these were efforts to appease the southern states by protecting the right to own slaves or by disfranchising African Americans through constitutional amendment. None were able to win the votes required from Congress to send them to the states. The relatively innocuous Corwin Amendment seemed to be the only hope for preserving the Union by amending the Constitution.

The northern victors in the Civil War tried to restructure the Constitution just as the war had restructured the nation. Yet they were often divided in their goals. Some wanted to end slavery; others hoped for social and economic equality regardless of race; others hoped that extending the power of the ballot box to former slaves would help create a new political order. The debates over the Thirteenth, Fourteenth, and Fifteenth Amendments were bitter. Few of those who fought for these changes were satisfied with the amendments themselves; fewer still were satisfied with their interpretation. Although the amendments put an end to the legal status of slavery, it took nearly a hundred years after the amendments' passage before most of the descendants of former slaves could begin to experience the economic, social, and political equality the amendments had been intended to provide.

Unratified Amendment

Corwin Amendment (proposed by Congress March 2, 1861)

No amendment shall be made to the Constitution which will authorize or give to Congress the power to abolish or interfere, within any State, with the domestic institutions thereof, including that of persons held to labor or service by the laws of said State.

◆◆◆

Following the election of Abraham Lincoln, Congress scrambled to try to prevent the secession of the slaveholding states. House member Thomas Corwin of Ohio proposed the "unamendable" amendment in the hope that by protecting slavery where it existed, Congress would keep the southern states in the Union. Lincoln indicated his support for the proposed amendment in his first inaugural address. Only Ohio and Maryland ratified the Corwin Amendment before it was forgotten.

Amendment XIII

[Adopted 1865]

Section 1 Neither slavery nor involuntary servitude, except as a punishment for crime whereof the party shall have been duly convicted, shall exist within the United States, or any place subject to their jurisdiction.

Section 2 Congress shall have power to enforce this article by appropriate legislation.

◆◆◆

Although President Lincoln had abolished slavery in the Confederacy with the Emancipation Proclamation of 1863, abolitionists wanted to rid the entire country of slavery. The Thirteenth Amendment did this in a clear and straightforward manner. In February 1865, when the proposal was approved by the House, the gallery of the House was newly opened to black Americans who had a chance at last to see their government at work. Passage of the proposal was greeted by wild cheers from the gallery as well as tears on the House floor, where congressional representatives openly embraced one another.

The problem of ratification remained, however. The Union position was that the Confederate states were part of the country of thirty-six states. Therefore, twenty-seven states were needed to ratify the amendment. When Kentucky and Delaware rejected it, backers realized that without approval from at least four former Confederate states, the amendment would fail. Lincoln's successor, President Andrew Johnson, made ratification of the Thirteenth Amendment a condition for southern states to rejoin the Union. Under those terms, all the former Confederate states except Mississippi accepted the Thirteenth Amendment, and by the end of 1865 the amendment had become part of the Constitution and slavery had been prohibited in the United States.

Amendment XIV

[Adopted 1868]

Section 1   All persons born or naturalized in the United States, and subject to the jurisdiction thereof, are citizens of the United States and of the State wherein they reside. No State shall make or enforce any law which shall abridge the privileges or immunities of citizens of the United States; nor shall any State deprive any person of life, liberty, or property, without due process of law; nor deny to any person within its jurisdiction the equal protection of the laws.

Section 2   Representatives shall be appointed among the several States according to their respective numbers, counting the whole number of persons in each State, excluding Indians not taxed. But when the right to vote at any election for the choice of Electors for President and Vice-President of the United States, Representatives in Congress, the executive and judicial officers of a State, or the members of the legislature thereof, is denied to any of the male inhabitants of such State, being twenty-one years of age and citizens of the United States, or in any way abridged, except for participation in rebellion, or other crime, the basis of representation therein shall be reduced in the proportion which the number of such male citizens shall bear to the whole number of male citizens twenty-one years of age in such State.

Section 3   No person shall be a Senator or Representative in Congress, or Elector of President and Vice-President, or hold any office, civil or military, under the United States, or under any State, who, having previously taken an oath, as a member of Congress, or as an officer of the United States, or as a member of any State legislature, or as an executive or judicial officer of any State, to support the Constitution of the United States, shall have engaged in insurrection or rebellion against the same, or given aid or comfort to the enemies thereof. Congress may, by a vote of two-thirds of each house, remove such disability.

Section 4   The validity of the public debt of the United States, authorized by law, including debts incurred for payment of pensions and bounties for services in suppressing insurrection or rebellion, shall not be questioned. But neither the United States nor any State shall assume or pay any debt or obligation incurred in aid of insurrection or rebellion against the United States, or any claim for the loss or emancipation of any slave; but all such debts, obligations, and claims shall be held illegal and void.

Section 5   The Congress shall have power to enforce, by appropriate legislation, the provisions of this article.

♦♦♦

Without Lincoln's leadership in the reconstruction of the nation following the Civil War, it soon became clear that the Thirteenth Amendment needed additional constitutional support. Less than a year after Lincoln's assassination, Andrew Johnson was ready to bring the former Confederate states back into the Union with few changes in their governments or politics. Anxious Republicans drafted the Fourteenth Amendment to prevent that from happening. The most important provisions of this complex amendment made all native-born or naturalized persons American citizens and prohibited states from abridging the "privileges or immunities" of citizens; depriving them of "life, liberty, or property, without due process of law"; and denying them "equal protection of the laws." In essence, it made all ex-slaves citizens and protected the rights of all citizens against violation by their own state governments.

As occurred in the case of the Thirteenth Amendment, former Confederate states were forced to ratify the amendment as a condition of representation in the House and the Senate. The intentions of the Fourteenth Amendment, and how those intentions should be enforced, have been the most debated point of constitutional history. The terms due process *and* equal protection *have been especially troublesome. Was the amendment designed to outlaw racial segregation? Or was the goal simply to prevent the leaders of the rebellious South from gaining political power?*

The framers of the Fourteenth Amendment hoped Article 2 would produce black voters who would increase the power of the Republican Party. The federal government, however, never used its power to punish states for denying blacks their right to vote. Although the Fourteenth Amendment had an immediate impact in giving black Americans citizenship, it did nothing to protect blacks from the vengeance of whites once Reconstruction ended. In the late nineteenth and early twentieth centuries, section 1 of the Fourteenth Amendment was often used to protect business interests and strike down laws protecting workers on the grounds that the rights of "persons," that is, corporations, were protected by "due process." More recently, the Fourteenth Amendment has been used to justify school desegregation and affirmative action programs, as well as to dismantle such programs.

Amendment XV

[Adopted 1870]

Section 1   The right of citizens of the United States to vote shall not be denied or abridged by the United States or by any State on account of race, color, or previous condition of servitude.

Section 2   The Congress shall have power to enforce this article by appropriate legislation.

♦ ♦ ♦

The Fifteenth Amendment was the last major piece of Reconstruction legislation. While earlier Reconstruction acts had already required black suffrage in the South, the Fifteenth Amendment extended black voting rights to the entire nation. Some Republicans felt morally obligated to do away with the double standard between North and South since many northern states had stubbornly refused to enfranchise blacks. Others believed that the freedman's ballot required the extra protection of a constitutional amendment to shield it from white counterattack. But partisan advantage also played an important role in the amendment's passage, since Republicans hoped that by giving the ballot to northern blacks, they could lessen their political vulnerability.

Many women's rights advocates had fought for the amendment. They had felt betrayed by the inclusion of the word male *in section 2 of the Fourteenth Amendment and were further angered when the proposed Fifteenth Amendment failed to prohibit denial of the right to vote on the grounds of sex as well as "race, color, or previous condition of servitude." In this amendment, for the first time, the federal government claimed the power to regulate the franchise, or vote. It was also the first time the Constitution placed limits on the power of the states to regulate access to the franchise. Although ratified in 1870, the amendment was not enforced until the twentieth century.*

The Progressive Amendments (Sixteenth–Nineteenth Amendments)

No amendments were added to the Constitution between the Civil War and the Progressive Era. America was changing, however, in fundamental ways. The rapid industrialization of the United States after the Civil War led to many social and economic problems. Hundreds of amendments were proposed, but none received enough support in Congress to be sent to the states. Some scholars believe that regional differences and rivalries were so strong during this period that it was almost impossible to gain a consensus on a constitutional amendment. During the Progressive Era, however, the Constitution was amended four times in seven years.

Amendment XVI

[Adopted 1913]

The Congress shall have power to lay and collect taxes on incomes, from whatever source derived, without apportionment among the several States, and without regard to any census or enumeration.

♦ ♦ ♦

Until passage of the Sixteenth Amendment, most of the money used to run the federal government came from customs duties and taxes on specific items, such as liquor. During the Civil War, the federal government taxed incomes as an emergency measure. Pressure to enact an income tax came from those who were concerned about the growing gap between rich and poor in the United States. The Populist Party began campaigning for a graduated income tax in 1892, and support continued to grow. By 1909, thirty-three proposed income tax amendments had been presented in Congress, but lobbying by corporate and other special interests had defeated them all. In June 1909, the growing pressure for an income tax, which had been endorsed by Presidents Roosevelt and Taft, finally pushed an amendment through the Senate. The required thirty-six states had ratified the amendment by February 1913.

Amendment XVII

[Adopted 1913]

Section 1   The Senate of the United States shall be composed of two Senators from each State, elected by the people thereof, for six years; and each Senator shall have one vote. The electors in each State shall have the qualifications requisite for electors of [voters for] the most numerous branch of the State legislatures.

Section 2   When vacancies happen in the representation of any State in the Senate, the executive authority of such State shall issue writs of election to fill such vacancies: Provided, that the Legislature of any State may empower the executive thereof to make temporary appointments until the people fill the vacancies by election as the Legislature may direct.

Section 3   This amendment shall not be so construed as to affect the election or term of any Senator chosen before it becomes valid as part of the Constitution.

♦ ♦ ♦

The framers of the Constitution saw the members of the House as the representatives of the people and the members of the Senate as the representatives of the states. Originally senators were to be chosen by the state legislators. According to reform advocates, however, the growth of private industry and transportation conglomerates during the Gilded Age had created a network of corruption in which wealth and power were exchanged for influence and votes in the Senate. Senator Nelson Aldrich, who represented Rhode Island in the late nineteenth and early twentieth centuries, for example, was known as "the senator from Standard Oil" because of his open support of special business interests.

Efforts to amend the Constitution to allow direct election of senators had begun in 1826, but since any proposal had to be approved by the Senate, reform seemed impossible. Progressives tried to gain influence in the Senate by instituting party caucuses and primary elections, which gave citizens the chance to express their choice of a senator who could then be officially elected by the state legislature. By 1910, fourteen of the country's thirty senators received popular votes through a state primary before the state legislature made its selection. Despairing of getting a proposal through the Senate, supporters of a direct-election amendment had begun in 1893 to seek a convention of representatives from two-thirds of the states to propose an amendment that could then be ratified. By 1905, thirty-one of forty-five states had endorsed such an amendment. Finally, in 1911, despite extraordinary opposition, a proposed amendment passed the Senate; by 1913, it had been ratified.

Amendment XVIII

[Adopted 1919; repealed 1933 by Amendment XXI]

Section 1   After one year from the ratification of this article the manufacture, sale, or transportation of intoxicating liquors within, the importation thereof into, or the exportation thereof from the United States and all territory subject to the jurisdiction thereof, for beverage purposes, is hereby prohibited.

Section 2   The Congress and the several States shall have concurrent power to enforce this article by appropriate legislation.

Section 3   This article shall be inoperative unless it shall have been ratified as an amendment to the Constitution by the legislatures of the several States, as provided by the Constitution, within seven years from the date of the submission thereof to the States by the Congress.

♦ ♦ ♦

The Prohibition Party, formed in 1869, began calling for a constitutional amendment to outlaw alcoholic beverages in 1872. A prohibition amendment was first proposed in the Senate in 1876 and was revived eighteen times before 1913. Between 1913 and 1919, another thirty-nine attempts were made to prohibit liquor in the United States through a constitutional amendment. Prohibition became a key element of the progressive agenda as reformers linked alcohol and

drunkenness to numerous social problems, including the corruption of immigrant voters. While opponents of such an amendment argued that it was undemocratic, supporters claimed that their efforts had widespread public support. The admission of twelve "dry" western states to the Union in the early twentieth century and the spirit of sacrifice during World War I laid the groundwork for passage and ratification of the Eighteenth Amendment in 1919. Opponents added a time limit to the amendment in the hope that they could thus block ratification, but this effort failed. (See also Amendment XXI.)

Amendment XIX

[Adopted 1920]

Section 1   The right of citizens of the United States to vote shall not be denied or abridged by the United States or by any State on account of sex.

Section 2   Congress shall have the power to enforce this article by appropriate legislation.

♦ ♦ ♦

Advocates of women's rights tried and failed to link woman suffrage to the Fourteenth and Fifteenth Amendments. Nonetheless, the effort for woman suffrage continued. Between 1878 and 1912, at least one and sometimes as many as four proposed amendments were introduced in Congress each year to grant women the right to vote. While over time women won very limited voting rights in some states, at both the state and federal levels opposition to an amendment for woman suffrage remained very strong. President Woodrow Wilson and other officials felt that the federal government should not interfere with the power of the states in this matter. Others worried that granting suffrage to women would encourage ethnic minorities to exercise their own right to vote. And many were concerned that giving women the vote would result in their abandoning traditional gender roles. In 1919, following a protracted and often bitter campaign of protest in which women went on hunger strikes and chained themselves to fences, an amendment was introduced with the backing of President Wilson. It narrowly passed the Senate (after efforts to limit the suffrage to white women failed) and was adopted in 1920 after Tennessee became the thirty-sixth state to ratify it.

Unratified Amendment

Child Labor Amendment (proposed by Congress June 2, 1924)

Section 1   The Congress shall have power to limit, regulate, and prohibit the labor of persons under eighteen years of age.

Section 2   The power of the several States is unimpaired by this article except that the operation of

AMENDMENTS TO THE CONSTITUTION WITH ANNOTATIONS

State laws shall be suspended to the extent necessary to give effect to legislation enacted by Congress.

◆ ◆ ◆

Throughout the late nineteenth and early twentieth centuries, alarm over the condition of child workers grew. Opponents of child labor argued that children worked in dangerous and unhealthy conditions, that they took jobs from adult workers, that they depressed wages in certain industries, and that states that allowed child labor had an economic advantage over those that did not. Defenders of child labor claimed that children provided needed income in many families, that working at a young age developed character, and that the effort to prohibit the practice constituted an invasion of family privacy.

In 1916, Congress passed a law that made it illegal to sell goods made by children through interstate commerce. The Supreme Court, however, ruled that the law violated the limits on the power of Congress to regulate interstate commerce. Congress then tried to penalize industries that used child labor by taxing such goods. This measure was also thrown out by the courts. In response, reformers set out to amend the Constitution. The proposed amendment was ratified by twenty-eight states, but by 1925, thirteen states had rejected it. Passage of the Fair Labor Standards Act in 1938, which was upheld by the Supreme Court in 1941, made the amendment irrelevant.

Amendment XX

[Adopted 1933]

Section 1 The terms of the President and Vice-President shall end at noon on the 20th day of January, and the terms of Senators and Representatives at noon on the 3rd day of January, of the years in which such terms would have ended if this article had not been ratified; and the terms of their successors shall then begin.

Section 2 The Congress shall assemble at least once in every year, and such meeting shall begin at noon on the 3rd day of January, unless they shall by law appoint a different day.

Section 3 If, at the time fixed for the beginning of the term of the President, the President-elect shall have died, the Vice-President-elect shall become President. If a President shall not have been chosen before the time fixed for the beginning of his term, or if the President-elect shall have failed to qualify, then the Vice-President-elect shall act as President until a President shall have qualified; and the Congress may by law provide for the case wherein neither a President-elect nor a Vice-President-elect shall have qualified, declaring who shall then act as President, or the manner in which one who is to act shall be selected, and such person shall act accordingly until a President or Vice-President shall have qualified.

Section 4 The Congress may by law provide for the case of the death of any of the persons from whom the House of Representatives may choose a President whenever the right of choice shall have devolved upon them, and for the case of the death of any of the persons from whom the Senate may choose a Vice-President whenever the right of choice shall have devolved upon them.

Section 5 Sections 1 and 2 shall take effect on the 15th day of October following the ratification of this article.

Section 6 This article shall be inoperative unless it shall have been ratified as an amendment to the Constitution by the Legislatures of three-fourths of the several States within seven years from the date of its submission.

◆ ◆ ◆

Until 1933, presidents took office on March 4. Since elections are held in early November and electoral votes are counted in mid-December, this meant that more than three months passed between the time a new president was elected and when he took office. Moving the inauguration to January shortened the transition period and allowed Congress to begin its term closer to the time of the president's inauguration. Although this seems like a minor change, an amendment was required because the Constitution specifies terms of office. This amendment also deals with questions of succession in the event that a president- or vice president-elect dies before assuming office. Section 3 also clarifies a method for resolving a deadlock in the electoral college.

Amendment XXI

[Adopted 1933]

Section 1 The eighteenth article of amendment to the Constitution of the United States is hereby repealed.

Section 2 The transportation or importation into any State, Territory, or Possession of the United States for delivery or use therein of intoxicating liquors, in violation of the laws thereof, is hereby prohibited.

Section 3 This article shall be inoperative unless it shall have been ratified as an amendment to the Constitution by conventions in the several States, as provided in the Constitution, within seven years from the date of the submission thereof to the States by the Congress.

◆ ◆ ◆

Widespread violation of the Volstead Act, the law enacted to enforce prohibition, made the United States a nation of lawbreakers. Prohibition caused more problems than it solved by encouraging crime, bribery, and corruption. Further, a coalition of liquor and beer manufacturers, personal liberty advocates, and constitutional scholars joined forces to challenge the amendment. By 1929, thirty proposed repeal amendments had been introduced in Congress, and the Democratic Party made repeal part of its platform in the 1932 presidential campaign. The Twenty-first Amendment was proposed in February 1933 and ratified less than a year later. The failure of the effort to enforce prohibition through a constitutional amendment has often been cited by opponents to subsequent efforts to shape public virtue and private morality.

Amendment XXII

[Adopted 1951]

Section 1   No person shall be elected to the office of the President more than twice, and no person who has held the office of President, or acted as President, for more than two years of a term to which some other person was elected President shall be elected to the office of President more than once. But this article shall not apply to any person holding the office of President when this Article was proposed by the Congress, and shall not prevent any person who may be holding the office of President, or acting as President, during the term within which this Article becomes operative from holding the office of President or acting as President during the remainder of such term.

Section 2   This article shall be inoperative unless it shall have been ratified as an amendment to the Constitution by the legislatures of three-fourths of the several States within seven years from the date of its submission to the States by the Congress.

♦ ♦ ♦

George Washington's refusal to seek a third term of office set a precedent that stood until 1912, when former president Theodore Roosevelt sought, without success, another term as an independent candidate. Democrat Franklin Roosevelt was the only president to seek and win a fourth term, though he did so amid great controversy. Roosevelt died in April 1945, a few months after the beginning of his fourth term. In 1946, Republicans won control of the House and the Senate, and early in 1947 a proposal for an amendment to limit future presidents to two four-year terms was offered to the states for ratification. Democratic critics of the Twenty-second Amendment charged that it was a partisan posthumous jab at Roosevelt.

Since the Twenty-second Amendment was adopted, however, the only presidents who might have been able to seek a third term, had it not existed, were Republicans Dwight Eisenhower, Ronald Reagan, and George W. Bush, and Democrat Bill Clinton. Since 1826, Congress has entertained 160 proposed amendments to

limit the president to one six-year term. Such amendments have been backed by fifteen presidents, including Gerald Ford and Jimmy Carter.

Amendment XXIII

[Adopted 1961]

Section 1   The District constituting the seat of Government of the United States shall appoint in such manner as the Congress may direct: A number of electors of President and Vice-President equal to the whole number of Senators and Representatives in Congress to which the District would be entitled if it were a State, but in no event more than the least populous State; they shall be in addition to those appointed by the States, but they shall be considered for the purposes of the election of President and Vice-President, to be electors appointed by a State; and they shall meet in the District and perform such duties as provided by the twelfth article of amendment.

Section 2   The Congress shall have the power to enforce this article by appropriate legislation.

♦ ♦ ♦

When Washington, D.C., was established as a federal district, no one expected that a significant number of people would make it their permanent and primary residence. A proposal to allow citizens of the district to vote in presidential elections was approved by Congress in June 1960 and was ratified on March 29, 1961.

Amendment XXIV

[Adopted 1964]

Section 1   The right of citizens of the United States to vote in any primary or other election for President or Vice-President, for electors for President or Vice-President, or for Senator or Representative in Congress, shall not be denied or abridged by the United States or any State by reason of failure to pay any poll tax or other tax.

Section 2   The Congress shall have the power to enforce this article by appropriate legislation.

♦ ♦ ♦

In the colonial and Revolutionary eras, financial independence was seen as necessary to political independence, and the poll tax was used as a requirement for voting. By the twentieth century, however, the poll tax was used mostly to bar poor people, especially southern blacks, from voting. While conservatives complained that the amendment interfered with states' rights, liberals thought that the amendment did not go far enough because it barred the poll tax only in national elections and not in state or local elections. The amendment was ratified in 1964, however, and two years later, the Supreme Court ruled that poll taxes in state and local elections also violated the equal protection clause of the Fourteenth Amendment.

Amendment XXV

[Adopted 1967]

Section 1   In case of the removal of the President from office or of his death or resignation, the Vice-President shall become President.

Section 2   Whenever there is a vacancy in the office of the Vice-President, the President shall nominate a Vice-President who shall take office upon confirmation by a majority vote of both Houses of Congress.

Section 3   Whenever the President transmits to the President pro tempore of the Senate and the Speaker of the House of Representatives his written declaration that he is unable to discharge the powers and duties of his office, and until he transmits to them a written declaration to the contrary, such powers and duties shall be discharged by the Vice-President as Acting President.

Section 4   Whenever the Vice-President and a majority of either the principal officers of the executive departments or of such other body as Congress may by law provide, transmit to the President pro tempore of the Senate and the Speaker of the House of Representatives their written declaration that the President is unable to discharge the powers and duties of his office, the Vice-President shall immediately assume the powers and duties of the office as Acting President.

Thereafter, when the President transmits to the President pro tempore of the Senate and the Speaker of the House of Representatives his written declaration that no inability exists, he shall resume the powers and duties of his office unless the Vice-President and a majority of either the principal officers of the executive department[s] or of such other body as Congress may by law provide, transmit within four days to the President pro tempore of the Senate and the Speaker of the House of Representatives their written declaration that the President is unable to discharge the powers and duties of his office. Thereupon Congress shall decide the issue, assembling within forty-eight hours for that purpose if not in session. If the Congress, within twenty-one days after receipt of the latter written declaration, or, if Congress is not in session, within twenty-one days after Congress is required to assemble, determines by two-thirds vote of both Houses that the President is unable to discharge the powers and duties of his office, the Vice-President shall continue to discharge

the same as Acting President; otherwise, the President shall resume the powers and duties of his office.

♦ ♦ ♦

The framers of the Constitution established the office of vice president because someone was needed to preside over the Senate. The first president to die in office was William Henry Harrison, in 1841. Vice President John Tyler had himself sworn in as president, setting a precedent that was followed when seven later presidents died in office. The assassination of President James A. Garfield in 1881 posed a new problem, however. After he was shot, the president was incapacitated for two months before he died; he was unable to lead the country, while his vice president, Chester A. Arthur, was unable to assume leadership. Efforts to resolve questions of succession in the event of a presidential disability thus began with the death of Garfield.

In 1963, the assassination of President John F. Kennedy galvanized Congress to action. Vice President Lyndon Johnson was a chain smoker with a history of heart trouble. According to the 1947 Presidential Succession Act, the two men who stood in line to succeed him were the seventy-two-year-old Speaker of the House and the eighty-six-year-old president of the Senate. There were serious concerns that any of these men might become incapacitated while serving as chief executive. The first time the Twenty-fifth Amendment was used, however, was not in the case of presidential death or illness, but during the Watergate crisis. When Vice President Spiro T. Agnew was forced to resign following allegations of bribery and tax violations, President Richard M. Nixon appointed House Minority Leader Gerald R. Ford vice president. Ford became president following Nixon's resignation eight months later and named Nelson A. Rockefeller as his vice president. Thus, for more than two years, the two highest offices in the country were held by people who had not been elected to them.

Amendment XXVI

[Adopted 1971]

Section 1   The right of citizens of the United States, who are eighteen years of age or older, to vote shall not be denied or abridged by the United States or by any State on account of age.

Section 2   The Congress shall have power to enforce this article by appropriate legislation.

♦ ♦ ♦

Efforts to lower the voting age from twenty-one to eighteen began during World War II. Recognizing that those who were old enough to fight a war should have some say in the government policies that involved them in the war, Presidents Eisenhower, Johnson, and Nixon endorsed the idea. In 1970, the combined pressure of the antiwar movement and the demographic pressure of the baby boom generation led to a Voting Rights Act lowering the voting age in federal, state, and local elections.

In Oregon v. Mitchell (1970), the state of Oregon challenged the right of Congress to determine the age at which people could vote in state or local elections. The Supreme Court agreed with Oregon. Since the Voting Rights Act was ruled unconstitutional, the Constitution had to be amended to allow passage of a law that would lower the voting age. The amendment was ratified in a little more than three months, making it the most rapidly ratified amendment in U.S. history.

Unratified Amendment

Equal Rights Amendment (proposed by Congress March 22, 1972; seven-year deadline for ratification extended to June 30, 1982)

Section 1   Equality of rights under the law shall not be denied or abridged by the United States or by any State on account of sex.

Section 2   The Congress shall have the power to enforce, by appropriate legislation, the provisions of this article.

Section 3   This amendment shall take effect two years after the date of ratification.

◆ ◆ ◆

In 1923, soon after women had won the right to vote, Alice Paul, a leading activist in the woman suffrage movement, proposed an amendment requiring equal treatment of men and women. Opponents of the proposal argued that such an amendment would invalidate laws that protected women and would make women subject to the military draft. After the 1964 Civil Rights Act was adopted, protective workplace legislation was removed anyway.

The renewal of the women's movement, as a by-product of the civil rights and antiwar movements, led to a revival of the Equal Rights Amendment (ERA) in Congress. Disagreements over language held up congressional passage of the proposed amendment, but on March 22, 1972, the Senate approved the ERA by a vote of 84 to 8, and it was sent to the states. Six states ratified the amendment within two days, and by the middle of 1973 the amendment seemed well on its way to adoption, with thirty of the needed thirty-eight states having ratified it. In the mid-1970s, however, a powerful "Stop ERA" campaign developed. The campaign portrayed the ERA as a threat to "family values" and traditional relationships between men and women. Although thirty-five states ultimately ratified the ERA, five of those state legislatures voted to rescind ratification, and the amendment was never adopted.

Unratified Amendment

D.C. Statehood Amendment (proposed by Congress August 22, 1978)

Section 1   For purposes of representation in the Congress, election of the President and Vice-President, and article V of this Constitution, the District constituting the seat of government of the United States shall be treated as though it were a State.

Section 2   The exercise of the rights and powers conferred under this article shall be by the people of the District constituting the seat of government, and as shall be provided by Congress.

Section 3   The twenty-third article of amendment to the Constitution of the United States is hereby repealed.

Section 4   This article shall be inoperative, unless it shall have been ratified as an amendment to the Constitution by the legislatures of three-fourths of the several states within seven years from the date of its submission.

◆ ◆ ◆

The 1961 ratification of the Twenty-third Amendment, giving residents of the District of Columbia the right to vote for a president and vice president, inspired an effort to give residents of the district full voting rights. In 1966, President Lyndon Johnson appointed a mayor and city council; in 1971, D.C. residents were allowed to name a nonvoting delegate to the House; and in 1981, residents were allowed to elect the mayor and city council. Congress retained the right to overrule laws that might affect commuters, the height of federal buildings, and selection of judges and prosecutors. The district's nonvoting delegate to Congress, Walter Fauntroy, lobbied fiercely for a congressional amendment granting statehood to the district. In 1978, a proposed amendment was approved and sent to the states. A number of states quickly ratified the amendment, but, like the ERA, the D.C. Statehood Amendment ran into trouble. Opponents argued that section 2 created a separate category of "nominal" statehood. They argued that the federal district should be eliminated and that the territory should be reabsorbed into the state of Maryland. Although these theoretical arguments were strong, some scholars believe that racist attitudes toward the predominantly black population of the city was also a factor leading to the defeat of the amendment.

Amendment XXVII

[Adopted 1992]

No law, varying the compensation for the services of the Senators and Representatives, shall take effect, until an election of Representatives shall have intervened.

♦♦♦

While the Twenty-sixth Amendment was the most rapidly ratified amendment in U.S. history, the Twenty-seventh Amendment had the longest journey to ratification. First proposed by James Madison in 1789 as part of the package that included the Bill of Rights, this amendment had been ratified by only six states by 1791. In 1873, however, it was ratified by Ohio to protest a massive retroactive salary increase by the federal government. Unlike later proposed amend-ments, this one came with no time limit on ratification. In the early 1980s, Gregory D. Watson, a University of Texas economics major, discovered the "lost" amendment and began a single-handed campaign to get state legislators to introduce it for ratification. In 1983, it was accepted by Maine. In 1984, it passed the Colorado legislature. Ratifications trickled in slowly until May 1992, when Michigan and New Jersey became the thirty-eighth and thirty-ninth states, respectively, to ratify. This amendment prevents members of Congress from raising their own salaries without giving voters a chance to vote them out of office before they can benefit from the raises.

THE CONSTITUTION OF THE CONFEDERATE STATES OF AMERICA

In framing the Constitution of the Confederate States, the authors adopted, with numerous small but signifi-cant changes and additions, the language of the Con-stitution of the United States, and followed the same order of arrangement of articles and sections. The revi-sions that they made to the original Constitution are shown here. The parts stricken out are enclosed in brack-ets, and the new matter added in framing the Confed-erate Constitution is printed in italics.

Adopted March 11, 1861

WE, the People of the [United States] *Confederated States, each State acting in its sovereign and independent character,* in order to form a [more perfect Union] *permanent Federal government,* establish Justice, in-sure domestic Tranquillity [provide for the common defense, promote the general Welfare], and secure the Blessings of Liberty to ourselves and our Posterity, *invoking the favor and guidance of Almighty God,* do ordain and establish this Constitution for the [United] *Confederate* States of America.

Article I

Section I All legislative Powers herein [granted] *delegated,* shall be vested in a Congress of the [United] *Confederate* States, which shall consist of a Senate and House of Representatives.

Section II The House of Representatives shall be composed of Members chosen every second Year by the People of the several States, and the Electors in each State shall *be citizens of the Confederate States, and* have the Qualifications requisite for Electors of the most numerous Branch of the State Legislature; *but no person of foreign birth, and not a citizen of the Confederate States, shall be allowed to vote for any offi-cer, civil or political, State or federal.*

No Person shall be a Representative who shall not have attained to the Age of twenty-five Years, and [been seven Years a Citizen of the United] *be a citizen of the Confederate* States, and who shall not, when elected, be an Inhabitant of that State in which he shall be chosen.

Representatives and direct Taxes shall be ap-portioned among the several States which may be included within this [Union] *Confederacy,* according to their respective Numbers, which shall be deter-mined by adding to the whole Number of free Persons, including those bound to Service for a Term of Years, and excluding Indians not taxed, three-fifths of all [other Persons] *slaves.* The actual Enumeration shall be made within three Years after the first Meeting of the Congress of the [United] *Confederate* States, and within every subsequent Term of ten Years, in such Manner as they shall by Law direct. The Number of Representatives shall not exceed one for every [thirty] *fifty* Thousand, but each State shall have at Least one Representative; and until such enumeration shall be made, the State of [New Hampshire shall be entitled to choose three, Massachusetts eight, Rhode Island and Providence Plantations one, Connecticut five, New York six, New Jersey four, Pennsylvania eight, Delaware one, Maryland six, Virginia ten, North Carolina five, South Carolina five, and Georgia three] *South Carolina shall be entitled to choose six, the State of Georgia ten, the State of Alabama nine, the State of Florida two, the State of Mississippi seven, the State of Louisiana six, and the State of Texas six.*

When vacancies happen in the Representation from any State, the Executive Authority thereof shall issue Writs of Election to fill such Vacancies.

The House of Representatives shall choose their Speaker and other Officers; and shall have the sole Power of Impeachment; *except that any judicial or other federal officer resident and acting solely within the limits of any State, may be impeached by a vote of two-thirds of both branches of the Legislature thereof.*

Section III   The Senate of the [United] *Confederate* States shall be composed of two Senators from each State, chosen by the Legislature thereof, for six Years, *at the regular session next immediately preceding the commencement of the term of service;* and each Senator shall have one Vote.

Immediately after they shall be assembled in Consequence of the first Election, they shall be divided as equally as may be into three Classes. The Seats of the Senators of the first Class shall be vacated at the Expiration of the second Year, of the second Class at the Expiration of the fourth Year, and of the third Class at the Expiration of the sixth Year, so that one-third may be chosen every second Year; and if Vacancies happen by Resignation, or otherwise, during the Recess of the Legislature of any State, the Executive thereof may make temporary Appointments until the next Meeting of the Legislature, which shall then fill such Vacancies.

No Person shall be a Senator who shall not have attained to the Age of thirty Years, and [been nine Years a Citizen of the United] *be a citizen of the Confederate* States, and who shall not, when elected, be an Inhabitant of that State for which he shall be chosen.

The Vice President of the [United] *Confederate* States shall be President of the Senate, but shall have no Vote, unless they be equally divided.

The Senate shall choose their other Officers, and also a President *pro tempore,* in the Absence of the Vice President, or when he shall exercise the Office of President of the United States.

The Senate shall have the sole Power to try all Impeachments. When sitting for that Purpose, they shall be on Oath or Affirmation. When the President of the [United] *Confederate* States is tried, the Chief Justice shall preside: And no Person shall be convicted without the Concurrence of two-thirds of the Members present.

Judgment in Cases of Impeachment shall not extend further than to removal from Office, and Disqualification to hold and enjoy any Office of honour, Trust or Profit under the [United] *Confederate* States; but the Party convicted shall nevertheless be liable and subject to Indictment, Trial, Judgment and Punishment, according to Law.

Section IV   The Times, Places and Manner of holding Elections for Senators and Representatives, shall be prescribed in each State by the Legislature thereof, *subject to the provisions of this Constitution;* but the Congress may at any time by Law make or alter such Regulations, except as to the *times and* places of choosing Senators.

The Congress shall assemble at least once in every Year, and such Meeting shall be on the first Monday in December, unless they shall by Law appoint a different Day.

Section V   Each House shall be the Judge of the Elections, Returns and Qualifications of its own Members, and a Majority of each shall constitute a Quorum to do Business; but a smaller Number may adjourn from day to day, and may be authorized to compel the Attendance of absent Members, in such Manner, and under such Penalties as each House may provide.

Each House may determine the Rules of its Proceedings, punish its Members for disorderly Behaviour, and, with the Concurrence of two-thirds *of the whole number* expel a Member.

Each House shall keep a Journal of its Proceedings, and from time to time publish the same, excepting such Parts as may in their Judgment require Secrecy; and the Yeas and Nays of the Members of either House on any question shall, at the Desire of one-fifth of those Present, be entered on the Journal.

Neither House, during the Session of Congress, shall, without the Consent of the other, adjourn for more than three days, nor to any other Place than that in which the two Houses shall be sitting.

Section VI   The Senators and Representatives shall receive a Compensation for their Services, to be ascertained by Law, and paid out of the Treasury of the [United] *Confederate* States. They shall in all Cases, except Treason [Felony] and Breach of the Peace, be privileged from Arrest during their Attendance at the Session of their respective Houses, and in going to and returning from the same; and for any Speech or Debate in either House, they shall not be questioned in any other Place.

No Senator or Representative shall, during the Time for which he was elected, be appointed to any civil Office under the Authority of the [United] *Confederate* States, which shall have been created, or the Emoluments whereof shall have been increased during such time; and no Person holding any Office under the [United] *Confederate* States, shall be a Member of either House during his Continuance in Office. *But Congress may, by law, grant to the principal officers in each of the executive departments a seat upon the floor of either House, with the privilege of discussing any measures appertaining to his department.*

Section VII   All Bills for raising Revenue shall originate in the House of Representatives; but the Senate may propose or concur with Amendments as on other Bills.

Every Bill which shall have passed [the House of Representatives and the Senate] *both Houses,* shall, before it become a Law, be presented to the President of the [United] *Confederate* States; If he approve he shall sign it, but if not he shall return it, with his Objections to that House in which it shall have originated, who shall enter the Objections at

THE CONSTITUTION OF THE CONFEDERATE STATES OF AMERICA

large on their Journal, and proceed to reconsider it. If after such Reconsideration two-thirds of that House shall agree to pass the Bill, it shall be sent, together with the Objections, to the other House, by which it shall likewise be reconsidered, and if approved by two-thirds of that House, it shall become a Law. But in all *such* Cases the Votes of both Houses shall be determined by Yeas and Nays, and the Names of the Persons voting for and against the Bill shall be entered on the Journal of each House respectively. If any Bill shall not be returned by the President within ten Days (Sundays excepted) after it shall have been presented to him, the Same shall be a law, in like Manner as if he had signed it, unless the Congress by their Adjournment prevent its return, in which Case it shall not be a Law. *The President may approve any appropriation and disapprove any other appropriation in the same bill. In such case he shall, in signing the bill, designate the appropriation disapproved, and shall return a copy of such appropriation, with his objections, to the House in which the bill shall have originated; and the same proceedings shall then be had as in case of other bills disapproved by the President.*

Every Order, Resolution, or Vote to which the Concurrence of [the Senate and House of Representatives] *both Houses* may be necessary (except on a question of Adjournment), shall be presented to the President of the [United] *Confederate* States; and before the Same shall take Effect, shall be approved by him, or being disapproved by him, [shall] *may* be repassed by two-thirds of [the Senate and House of Representatives] *both Houses,* according to the Rules and Limitations prescribed in the Case of a Bill.

Section VIII The Congress shall have Power

To lay and collect Taxes, Duties, Imposts and *Excises, for revenue necessary* to pay the Debts [and], provide for the common Defense [and general Welfare of the United States; but], *and carry on the government of the Confederate States; but no bounties shall be granted from the treasury, nor shall any duties, or taxes, or importation from foreign nations be laid to promote or foster any branch of industry; and* all Duties, Imposts and Excises shall be uniform throughout the [United] *Confederate* States;

To borrow Money on the credit of the [United] *Confederate* States;

To regulate Commerce with foreign Nations, and among the several States, and with the Indian Tribes; *but neither this, nor any other clause contained in this Constitution, shall ever be construed to delegate the power to Congress to appropriate money for any internal improvement intended to facilitate commerce; except for the purpose of furnishing lights, beacons, and buoys, and other aids to navigation upon the coasts, and the improvement of harbors, and the removing of obstructions in river navigation; in all such cases such duties shall be laid on the navigation facilitated thereby, as may be necessary to pay the costs and expenses thereof;*

To establish an uniform Rule of Naturalization, and uniform Laws on the subject of Bankruptcies throughout the [United] *Confederate* States; *but no law of Congress shall discharge any debt contracted before the passage of the same;*

To coin Money, regulate the Value thereof, and of foreign Coin, and fix the Standard of Weights and Measures;

To provide for the Punishment of counterfeiting the Securities and current Coin of the [United] *Confederate* States;

To establish Post Offices and post [Roads] *routes; but the expenses of the Postoffice Department, after the first day of March, in the year of our Lord eighteen hundred and sixty-three, shall be paid out of its own revenues;*

To promote the progress of Science and useful Arts, by securing for limited Times to Authors and Inventors the exclusive Right to their respective Writings and Discoveries;

To constitute Tribunals inferior to the supreme Court;

To define and punish Piracies and Felonies committed on the high Seas, and Offences against the Law of Nations;

To declare War, grant Letters of Marque and Reprisal, and make Rules concerning Captures on Land and Water;

To raise and support Armies, but no Appropriation of Money to that Use shall be for a longer Term than two Years;

To provide and maintain a Navy;

To make Rules for the Government and Regulation of the land and naval Forces;

To provide for calling forth the Militia to execute the Laws of the [Union] *Confederate States,* suppress Insurrections and repel Invasions;

To provide for organizing, arming, and disciplining the Militia and for governing such Part of them as may be employed in the Service of the [United] *Confederate* States, reserving to the States respectively, the Appointment of the Officers, and the Authority of training the Militia according to the Discipline prescribed by Congress;

To exercise exclusive Legislation in all Cases whatsoever, over such District (not exceeding ten Miles square) as may, by Cession of particular States, and the Acceptance of Congress, become the Seat of the Government of the [United] *Confederate* States, and to exercise like Authority over all Places purchased by the Consent of the Legislature of the State in which the Same shall be, for the Erection of Forts, Magazines, Arsenals, Dock Yards, and other needful Buildings;—And

To make all Laws which shall be necessary and proper for carrying into Execution the foregoing Powers, and all other Powers vested by this Constitution in the Government of the [United] *Confederate* States or in any Department or Officer thereof.

Section IX   [The Migration or Importation of such Persons as any of the States now existing shall think proper to admit, shall not be prohibited by the Congress prior to the Year one thousand eight hundred and eight, but a Tax or Duty may be imposed on such Importation, not exceeding ten dollars for each Person.] *The importation of negroes of the African race from any foreign country other than the slaveholding States or territories of the United States of America, is hereby forbidden; and Congress is required to pass such laws as shall effectually prevent the same. Congress shall also have power to prohibit the introduction of slaves from any State not a member of, or territory not belonging to, this Confederacy.*

The Privilege of the Writ of Habeas Corpus shall not be suspended, unless when in Cases of Rebellion or Invasion the public Safety may require it. No Bill of Attainder or ex post facto Law, *or law denying or impairing the right of property in negro slaves,* shall be passed.

No Capitation, or other direct, Tax shall be laid, unless in Proportion to the Census or Enumeration herein before directed to be taken.

No Tax or Duty shall be laid on Articles exported from any State, *except by a vote of two-thirds of both Houses.*

No Preference shall be given by any Regulation of Commerce or Revenue to the Ports of one State over those of another; nor shall Vessels bound to, or from, one State, be obliged to enter, clear, or pay Duties in another.

No Money shall be drawn from the Treasury, but in Consequence of Appropriations made by Law; and a regular Statement and Account of the Receipts and Expenditures of all public Money shall be published from time to time.

Congress shall appropriate no money from the Treasury except by a vote of two-thirds of both Houses, taken by yeas and nays, unless it be asked and estimated for by some one of the heads of departments and submitted to Congress by the President; or for the purpose of paying its own expenses and contingencies; or for the payment of claims against the Confederate States, the justice of which shall have been officially declared by a tribunal for the investigation of claims against the Government, which it is hereby made the duty of Congress to establish.

All bills appropriating money shall specify in Federal currency the exact amount of each appropriation and the purposes for which it is made; and Congress shall grant no extra compensation to any public contractor, officer, agent or servant, after such contract shall have been made or such service rendered.

No Title of Nobility shall be granted by the [United] *Confederate* States; and no Person holding any Office of Profit or Trust under them, shall, without the Consent of the Congress, accept of any present, Emolument, Office, or Title, of any kind whatever, from any King, Prince or foreign State.

[Here the framers of the Confederate Constitution insert the U.S. Bill of Rights.]

Congress shall make no law respecting an establishment of religion, or prohibiting the free exercise thereof; or abridging the freedom of speech, or of the press; or the right of the people peaceably to assemble, and to petition the Government for a redress of grievances.

A well-regulated Militia, being necessary to the security of a free State, the right of the people to keep and bear Arms shall not be infringed.

No Soldier shall, in time of peace, be quartered in any house, without the consent of the Owner, nor in time of war, but in a manner to be prescribed by law.

The right of the people to be secure in their persons, houses, papers, and effects, against unreasonable searches and seizures, shall not be violated, and no Warrants shall issue, but upon probable cause, supported by Oath or affirmation, and particularly describing the place to be searched, and the persons or things to be seized.

No person shall be held to answer for a capital, or otherwise infamous crime, unless on a presentment or indictment of a Grand Jury, except in cases arising in the land or naval forces, or in the Militia, when in actual service in time of War or public danger; nor shall any person be subject for the same offence to be twice put in jeopardy of life or limb; nor shall be compelled in any Criminal Case to be a witness against himself, nor be deprived of life, liberty or property without due process of law; nor shall private property be taken for public use, without just compensation.

In all criminal prosecutions, the accused shall enjoy the right to a speedy and public trial, by an impartial jury of the State and district wherein the crime shall have been committed, which district shall have been previously ascertained by law, and to be informed of the nature and cause of the accusation; to be confronted with the witnesses against him; to have Compulsory process for obtaining Witnesses in his favour, and to have the Assistance of Counsel for his defence.

In Suits at common law, where the value in controversy shall exceed twenty dollars, the right of trial by jury shall be preserved, and no fact tried by a jury shall be otherwise reexamined in any Court of the [United] *Confederate* States, than according to the rules of the common law.

Excessive bail shall not be required, nor excessive fines imposed, nor cruel and unusual punishments inflicted.

Every law or resolution having the force of law, shall relate to but one subject, and that shall be expressed in the title.

Section X   No State shall enter into any Treaty, Alliance, or Confederation; grant Letters of Marque and Reprisal; coin Money; [emit Bills of Credit;] make any Thing but gold and silver Coin a Tender in Payment of Debts; pass any Bill of Attainder, *or* ex post facto Law, or Law impairing the Obligation of Contracts, or grant any Title of Nobility.

No State shall, without the consent of the Congress, lay any Imposts or Duties on Imports or Exports, except what may be absolutely necessary for executing its inspection Laws: and the net Produce of all Duties and Imposts, laid by any State on Imports or Exports, shall be for the Use of the Treasury of the [United] *Confederate* States; and all such Laws shall be subject to the Revision and Control of the Congress.

No State shall, without the Consent of Congress, lay any Duty of Tonnage, *except on sea-going vessels, for the improvement of its rivers and harbors navigated by the said vessels; but such duties shall not conflict with any treaties of the Confederate States with foreign nations; and any surplus of revenue thus derived shall, after making such improvement, be paid into the common treasury; nor shall any State* keep Troops, or Ships of War in time of Peace, enter into any Agreement or Compact with another State, or with a foreign Power, or engage in War, unless actually invaded, or in such imminent Danger as will not admit of Delay. *But when any river divides or flows through two or more States, they may enter into compacts with each other to improve the navigation thereof.*

Article II

Section I [The executive Power shall be vested in a President of the United States of America. He shall hold his Office during the Term of four Years, and, together with the Vice President, chosen for the same Term, be elected, as follows:] *The executive power shall be vested in a President of the Confederate States of America. He and the Vice President shall hold their offices for the term of six years; but the President shall not be re-eligible. The President and Vice President shall be elected as follows:*

Each State shall appoint in such Manner as the Legislature thereof may direct, a Number of Electors, equal to the whole Number of Senators and Representatives to which the State may be entitled in the Congress; but no Senator or Representative, or Person holding an Office of Trust or Profit under the [United] *Confederate* States, shall be appointed an Elector.

The Electors shall meet in their respective States, and vote by ballot for President and Vice President, one of whom, at least, shall not be an inhabitant of the same State with themselves; they shall name in their ballots the person voted for as President, and in distinct ballots the person voted for as Vice President, and they shall make distinct lists of all persons voted for as President, and of all persons voted for as Vice President, and of the number of votes for each, which lists they shall sign and certify, and transmit sealed to the seat of the government of the [United] *Confederate* States, directed to the President of the Senate;—The President of the Senate shall, in the presence of the Senate and House of Representatives, open all the certificates and the votes shall then be counted;—The person having the greatest number of votes for President shall be the President, if such number be a majority of the whole number of Electors appointed; and if no person have such majority, then from the persons having the highest numbers not exceeding three on the list of those voted for as President, the House of Representatives shall choose immediately, by ballot, the President. But in choosing the President, the votes shall be taken by States, the representation from each State having one vote; a quorum for this purpose shall consist of a member or members from two-thirds of the States, and a majority of all the States shall be necessary to a choice. And if the House of Representatives shall not choose a President whenever the right of choice shall devolve upon them, before the fourth day of March next following, then the Vice President shall act as President, as in the case of the death or other constitutional disability of the President. The person having the greatest number of votes as Vice President shall be the Vice President, if such number be a majority of the whole number of Electors appointed, and if no person have a majority, then from the two highest numbers on the list the Senate shall choose the Vice President; a quorum for the purpose shall consist of two-thirds of the whole number of Senators, and a majority of the whole number shall be necessary to a choice. But no person constitutionally ineligible to the office of President shall be eligible to that of Vice President of the [United] *Confederate* States.

The Congress may determine the Time of choosing the Electors, and the Day on which they shall give their Votes; which Day shall be the same throughout the [United] *Confederate* States.

No Person except a natural-born Citizen [or a Citizen of the United States] *of the Confederate States, or a citizen thereof,* at the time of the Adoption of this Constitution, *or a citizen thereof born in the United States prior to the 20th of December, 1860,* shall be eligible to the Office of President; neither shall any Person be eligible to that Office who shall not have attained to the Age of thirty-five Years, and been fourteen Years a Resident within the [United States] *limits of the Confederate States, as they may exist at the time of his election.*

In Cases of the Removal of the President from Office, or of his Death, Resignation, or Inability to discharge the Powers and Duties of the said Office, the same shall devolve on the Vice President, and the Congress may by Law provide for the Case of Removal, Death, Resignation, or Inability, both of the President and Vice President, declaring what Officer shall then act as President, and such Officer shall act accordingly, until the Disability be removed, or a President shall be elected.

The President shall, at stated Times, receive for his Services, a Compensation, which shall neither be increased nor diminished during the Period for which he shall have been elected, and he shall not receive within that Period any other Emolument from the [United] *Confederate* States or any of them.

Before he enters on the Execution of his Office, he shall take the following Oath or Affirmation—"I do solemnly swear (or affirm) that I will faithfully execute the Office of President of the [United] *Confederate* States, and will to the best of my Ability, preserve, protect and defend the Constitution [of the United States] *thereof."*

Section II   The President shall be Commander in Chief of the Army and Navy of the [United] *Confederate* States, and of the Militia of the several States, when called into the actual Service of the [United] *Confederate* States; he may require the Opinion, in writing, of the principal Officer in each of the executive Departments, upon any Subject relating to the Duties of their respective Offices, and he shall have Power to grant Reprieves and Pardons for Offenses against the [United] *Confederate* States, except in Cases of Impeachment.

He shall have Power, by and with the Advice and Consent of the Senate, to make Treaties, provided two-thirds of the Senators present concur; and he shall nominate, and by and with the Advice and Consent of the Senate, shall appoint Ambassadors, other public Ministers and Consuls, Judges of the supreme Court, and all other Officers of the [United] *Confederate* States, whose Appointments are not herein otherwise provided for, and which shall be established by Law: but the Congress may by Law vest the Appointment of such inferior Officers, as they think proper, in the President alone, in the Courts of Law, or in the Heads of Departments. *The principal officer in each of the executive departments, and all persons connected with the diplomatic service, may be removed from office at the pleasure of the President. All other civil officers of the executive department may be removed at any time by the President, or other appointing power, when their services are unnecessary, or for dishonesty, incapacity, inefficiency, misconduct, or neglect of duty; and when so removed, the removal shall be reported to the Senate, together with the reasons therefor.*

The President shall have Power to fill [up] all Vacancies that may happen during the Recess of the Senate, by granting Commissions which shall expire at the End of their next Session.

Section III   [He] *The President* shall from time to time give to the Congress Information of the State of the [Union] *Confederacy,* and recommend to their Consideration such Measures as he shall judge necessary and expedient; he may, on extraordinary Occasions, convene both Houses, or either of them, and in Case of Disagreement between them, with Respect to the Time of Adjournment, he may adjourn them to such Time as he shall think proper;

he shall receive Ambassadors and other public Ministers; he shall take Care that the Laws be faithfully executed, and shall Commission all the officers of the [United] *Confederate* States.

Section IV   The President, Vice President and all civil Officers of the [United] *Confederate* States, shall be removed from Office or Impeachment for, and Conviction of, Treason, Bribery, or other high Crimes and Misdemeanors.

Article III

Section I   The judicial Power of the [United] *Confederate* States shall be vested in one [supreme] *Superior* Court, and in such inferior Courts as the Congress may from time to time ordain and establish. The Judges, both of the supreme and inferior Courts, shall hold their Offices during good Behavior, and shall, at stated Times, receive for their Services a Compensation, which shall not be diminished during their Continuance in Office.

Section II   The judicial Power shall extend to all cases [in Law and Equity, arising under this Constitution], *arising under this Constitution, in law and equity,* the Laws of the [United] *Confederate* States, and Treaties made, or which shall be made, under their Authority;—to all Cases affecting Ambassadors, other public Ministers, and Consuls;—to all Cases of admiralty and maritime Jurisdiction;—to Controversies to which the [United] *Confederate* States shall be a Party;—to Controversies between two or more States;—between a State and Citizens of another State *where the State is plaintiff;*—between Citizens *claiming lands under grants* of different States,—[between Citizens of the same State claiming Lands under Grants of different States,] and between a State, or the Citizens thereof, and foreign States, Citizens or Subjects; *but no State shall be sued by a citizen or subject of any foreign State.*

In all Cases affecting Ambassadors, other public Ministers and Consuls, and those in which a State shall be Party, the supreme Court shall have original Jurisdiction. In all the other Cases before mentioned, the supreme Court shall have appellate Jurisdiction, both as to Law and Fact, with such Exceptions, and under such Regulations as the Congress shall make.

The Trial of all Crimes, except in Cases of Impeachment, shall be by Jury; and such Trial shall be held in the State where the said Crime[s] shall have been committed; but when not committed within any State, the Trial shall be at such Place or Places as the Congress may by Law have directed.

Section III   Treason against the [United] *Confederate* States shall consist only in levying War against them, or in adhering to their Enemies, giving them Aid and Comfort. No Person shall be convicted of Treason unless on the Testimony of two Witnesses to the same overt Act, or on Confession in open Court.

The Congress shall have Power to declare the Punishment of Treason, but no Attainder of Treason shall work Corruption of Blood, or Forfeiture except during the Life of the Person attainted.

Article IV

Section I Full Faith and Credit shall be given in each State to the public Acts, Records, and judicial Proceedings of every other State. And the Congress may by general Laws prescribe the Manner in which such Acts, Records and Proceedings shall be proved, and the Effect thereof.

Section II The Citizens of each State shall be entitled to all Privileges and Immunities of Citizens in the several States, *and shall have the right of transit and sojourn in any State of this Confederacy, with their slaves and other property; and the right of property in such slaves shall not be impaired.*

A Person charged in any State with Treason, Felony, or other Crime, who shall flee from Justice, and be found in another State, shall on Demand of the executive Authority of the State from which he fled, be delivered up, to be removed to the State having Jurisdiction of the Crime.

No *slave or* Person held to Service or Labor in [one State] *any State or Territory of the Confederate States* under the Laws thereof, escaping *or unlawfully carried* into another, shall, in Consequence of any Law or Regulation therein, be discharged from such Service or Labor, but shall be delivered up on Claim of the Party to whom such *slave belongs, or to whom such* Service or Labor may be due.

Section III [New States may be admitted by the Congress into this Union;] *Other States may be admitted into this Confederacy by a vote of two-thirds of the whole House of Representatives and two-thirds of the Senate, the Senate voting by States;* but no new State shall be formed or erected within the Jurisdiction of any other State; nor any State be formed by the Junction of two or more States, or Parts of States, without the Consent of the Legislatures of the States concerned as well as of the Congress.

The Congress shall have Power to dispose of and make all needful Rules and Regulations [respecting the Territory or other Property belonging to the United States; and nothing in this Constitution shall be so construed as to Prejudice any Claims of the United States, or of any particular State] *concerning the property of the Confederate States, including the lands thereof.*

The Confederate States may acquire new territory, and Congress shall have power to legislate and provide governments for the inhabitants of all territory belonging to the Confederate States lying without the limits of the several States, and may permit them, at such times and in such manner as it may by law provide, to form States to be admitted into the Confederacy. In all such territory the institution of negro slavery as it now exists in the Confederate States shall be recognized and protected by Congress and by the territorial government, and the inhabitants of the several Confederate States and territories shall have the right to take to such territory any slaves lawfully held by them in any of the States or Territories of the Confederate States.

[Section IV] The [United] *Confederate* States shall guarantee to every State [in this Union] *that now is, or hereafter may become, a member of this Confederacy*, a Republican Form of Government, and shall protect each of them against Invasion; and on Application of the Legislature, or of the Executive (when the Legislature [cannot be convened] *is not in session*) against domestic Violence.

Article V

[The Congress, whenever two-thirds of both Houses shall deem it necessary, shall propose Amendments to this Constitution, or on the Application of the Legislatures of two-thirds of the several States, shall call a Convention for proposing Amendments, which, in either Case, shall be valid to all Intents and Purposes, as Part of this Constitution, when ratified by the Legislatures of three-fourths of the several States, or by Conventions in three-fourths thereof, as the one or the other Mode of Ratification may be proposed by the Congress; Provided that no Amendment which may be made prior to the Year one thousand eight hundred and eight shall in any Manner affect the first and fourth Clauses in the Ninth Section of the first Article; and that no State, without its Consent, shall be deprived of its equal Suffrage in the Senate.]

Upon the demand of any three States, legally assembled in their several Conventions, the Congress shall summon a Convention of all the States, to take into consideration such amendments to the Constitution as the said States shall concur in suggesting at the time when the said demand is made; and should any of the proposed amendments to the Constitution be agreed on by the said Convention—voting by States—and the same be ratified by the Legislatures of two-thirds of the several States, or by Conventions in two-thirds thereof—as the one or the other mode of ratification may be proposed by the general Convention—they shall henceforward form a part of this Constitution. But no State shall, without its consent, be deprived of its equal representation in the Senate.

Article VI

The Government established by this Constitution is the successor of the Provisional Government of the

THE CONSTITUTION OF THE CONFEDERATE STATES OF AMERICA

Confederate States of America, and all laws passed by the latter shall continue in force until the same shall be repealed or modified; and all the officers appointed by the same shall remain in office until their successors are appointed and qualified or the offices abolished.

All Debts contracted and Engagements entered into, before the Adoption of this Constitution, shall be as valid against the [United] *Confederate* States under this Constitution, as under the [Confederation] *Provisional Government.*

This Constitution and the Laws of the [United] *Confederate* States [which shall be] made in Pursuance thereof; and all Treaties made, or which shall be made, under the authority of the [United] *Confederate* States, shall be the supreme Law of the Land; and the Judges in every State shall be bound thereby, any Thing in the Constitution or Laws of any State to the Contrary notwithstanding.

The Senators and Representatives before mentioned, and the Members of the several State Legislatures, and all executive and judicial Officers, both of the [United] *Confederate* States and of the several States, shall be bound by Oath or Affirmation, to support this Constitution; but no religious Test shall ever be required as a Qualification to any Office or public Trust under the [United] *Confederate* States.

The enumeration in the Constitution, of certain rights, shall not be construed to deny or disparage others retained by the people *of the several States.*

The powers not delegated to the [United] *Confederate* States by the Constitution, nor prohibited by it to the States, are reserved to the States respectively, or to the people.

Article VII

The Ratification of the Conventions of [nine] *five* States shall be sufficient for the Establishment of this Constitution between the States so ratifying the same.

When five States shall have ratified this Constitution, in the manner before specified, the Congress under the Provisional Constitution shall prescribe the time for holding the election of President and Vice President; and for the meeting of the electoral college; and for counting the votes and inaugurating the President. They shall also prescribe the time for holding the first election of members of Congress under this Constitution, and the time for assembling the same. Until the assembling of such Congress, the Congress under the Provisional Constitution shall continue to exercise the legislative powers granted them, not extending beyond the time limited by the Constitution of the Provisional Government.

[Done in Convention by the Unanimous Consent of the States present, the Seventeenth Day of September in the Year of our Lord one thousand seven hundred and eighty-seven and of the Independence of the United States of America the Twelfth.] *Adopted unanimously March 11, 1861.*

Facts and Figures: Government, Economy, and Demographics

U.S. Politics and Government

PRESIDENTIAL ELECTIONS

Year	Candidates	Parties	Popular Vote	Percentage of Popular Vote	Electoral Vote	Percentage of Voter Participation
1789	**GEORGE WASHINGTON (Va.)***				69	
	John Adams				34	
	Others				35	
1792	**GEORGE WASHINGTON (Va.)**				132	
	John Adams				77	
	George Clinton				50	
	Others				5	
1796	**JOHN ADAMS (Mass.)**	Federalist			71	
	Thomas Jefferson	Democratic-Republican			68	
	Thomas Pinckney	Federalist			59	
	Aaron Burr	Dem.-Rep.			30	
	Others				48	
1800	**THOMAS JEFFERSON (Va.)**	Dem.-Rep.			73	
	Aaron Burr	Dem.-Rep.			73	
	John Adams	Federalist			65	
	C. C. Pinckney	Federalist			64	
	John Jay	Federalist			1	
1804	**THOMAS JEFFERSON (Va.)**	Dem.-Rep.			162	
	C. C. Pinckney	Federalist			14	
1808	**JAMES MADISON (Va.)**	Dem.-Rep.			122	
	C. C. Pinckney	Federalist			47	
	George Clinton	Dem.-Rep.			6	
1812	**JAMES MADISON (Va.)**	Dem.-Rep.			128	
	De Witt Clinton	Federalist			89	
1816	**JAMES MONROE (Va.)**	Dem.-Rep.			183	
	Rufus King	Federalist			34	
1820	**JAMES MONROE (Va.)**	Dem.-Rep.			231	
	John Quincy Adams	Dem.-Rep.			1	
1824	**JOHN Q. ADAMS (Mass.)**	Dem.-Rep.	108,740	30.5	84	26.9
	Andrew Jackson	Dem.-Rep.	153,544	43.1	99	
	William H. Crawford	Dem.-Rep.	46,618	13.1	41	
	Henry Clay	Dem.-Rep.	47,136	13.2	37	
1828	**ANDREW JACKSON (Tenn.)**	Democratic	647,286	56.0	178	57.6
	John Quincy Adams	National Republican	508,064	44.0	83	

*State of residence when elected president.

A-33

Year	Candidates	Parties	Popular Vote	Percentage of Popular Vote	Electoral Vote	Percentage of Voter Participation
1832	**ANDREW JACKSON (Tenn.)**	Democratic	687,502	55.0	219	55.4
	Henry Clay	National Republican	530,189	42.4	49	
	John Floyd	Independent			11	
	William Wirt	Anti-Mason	33,108	2.6	7	
1836	**MARTIN VAN BUREN (N.Y.)**	Democratic	765,483	50.9	170	57.8
	W. H. Harrison	Whig			73	
	Hugh L. White	Whig	739,795	49.1	26	
	Daniel Webster	Whig			14	
	W. P. Mangum	Independent			11	
1840	**WILLIAM H. HARRISON (Ohio)**	Whig	1,274,624	53.1	234	78.0
	Martin Van Buren	Democratic	1,127,781	46.9	60	
	J. G. Birney	Liberty	7,069		—	
1844	**JAMES K. POLK (Tenn.)**	Democratic	1,338,464	49.6	170	78.9
	Henry Clay	Whig	1,300,097	48.1	105	
	J. G. Birney	Liberty	62,300	2.3	—	
1848	**ZACHARY TAYLOR (La.)**	Whig	1,360,099	47.4	163	72.7
	Lewis Cass	Democratic	1,220,544	42.5	127	
	Martin Van Buren	Free-Soil	291,263	10.1	—	
1852	**FRANKLIN PIERCE (N.H.)**	Democratic	1,601,117	50.9	254	69.6
	Winfield Scott	Whig	1,385,453	44.1	42	
	John P. Hale	Free-Soil	155,825	5.0	—	
1856	**JAMES BUCHANAN (Pa.)**	Democratic	1,832,995	45.3	174	78.9
	John C. Frémont	Republican	1,339,932	33.1	114	
	Millard Fillmore	American	871,731	21.6	8	
1860	**ABRAHAM LINCOLN (Ill.)**	Republican	1,866,452	39.8	180	81.2
	Stephen A. Douglas	Democratic	1,375,157	29.4	12	
	John C. Breckinridge	Democratic	847,953	18.1	72	
	John Bell	Union	590,631	12.6	39	
1864	**ABRAHAM LINCOLN (Ill.)**	Republican	2,213,665	55.1	212	73.8
	George B. McClellan	Democratic	1,805,237	44.9	21	
1868	**ULYSSES S. GRANT (Ill.)**	Republican	3,012,833	52.7	214	78.1
	Horatio Seymour	Democratic	2,703,249	47.3	80	
1872	**ULYSSES S. GRANT (Ill.)**	Republican	3,597,132	55.6	286	71.3
	Horace Greeley	Democratic; Liberal Republican	2,834,125	43.9	66	
1876	**RUTHERFORD B. HAYES (Ohio)**	Republican	4,036,298	48.0	185	81.8
	Samuel J. Tilden	Democratic	4,288,590	51.0	184	
1880	**JAMES A. GARFIELD (Ohio)**	Republican	4,454,416	48.5	214	79.4
	Winfield S. Hancock	Democratic	4,444,952	48.1	155	
1884	**GROVER CLEVELAND (N.Y.)**	Democratic	4,874,986	48.5	219	77.5
	James G. Blaine	Republican	4,851,981	48.3	182	
1888	**BENJAMIN HARRISON (Ind.)**	Republican	5,439,853	47.9	233	79.3
	Grover Cleveland	Democratic	5,540,309	48.6	168	
1892	**GROVER CLEVELAND (N.Y.)**	Democratic	5,555,426	46.1	277	74.7
	Benjamin Harrison	Republican	5,182,690	43.0	145	
	James B. Weaver	People's	1,029,846	8.5	22	
1896	**WILLIAM McKINLEY (Ohio)**	Republican	7,104,779	51.1	271	79.3
	William J. Bryan	Democratic-People's	6,502,925	47.7	176	
1900	**WILLIAM McKINLEY (Ohio)**	Republican	7,207,923	51.7	292	73.2
	William J. Bryan	Dem.-Populist	6,358,133	45.5	155	
1904	**THEODORE ROOSEVELT (N.Y.)**	Republican	7,623,486	57.9	336	65.2
	Alton B. Parker	Democratic	5,077,911	37.6	140	
	Eugene V. Debs	Socialist	402,283	3.0	—	

Year	Candidates	Parties	Popular Vote	Percentage of Popular Vote	Electoral Vote	Percentage of Voter Participation
1908	**WILLIAM H. TAFT (Ohio)**	Republican	7,678,908	51.6	321	65.4
	William J. Bryan	Democratic	6,409,104	43.1	162	
	Eugene V. Debs	Socialist	420,793	2.8	—	
1912	**WOODROW WILSON (N.J.)**	Democratic	6,293,454	41.9	435	58.8
	Theodore Roosevelt	Progressive	4,119,538	27.4	88	
	William H. Taft	Republican	3,484,980	23.2	8	
	Eugene V. Debs	Socialist	900,672	6.1	—	
1916	**WOODROW WILSON (N.J.)**	Democratic	9,129,606	49.4	277	61.6
	Charles E. Hughes	Republican	8,538,221	46.2	254	
	A. L. Benson	Socialist	585,113	3.2	—	
1920	**WARREN G. HARDING (Ohio)**	Republican	16,143,407	60.5	404	49.2
	James M. Cox	Democratic	9,130,328	34.2	127	
	Eugene V. Debs	Socialist	919,799	3.4	—	
1924	**CALVIN COOLIDGE (Mass.)**	Republican	15,725,016	54.0	382	48.9
	John W. Davis	Democratic	8,386,503	28.8	136	
	Robert M. La Follette	Progressive	4,822,856	16.6	13	
1928	**HERBERT HOOVER (Calif.)**	Republican	21,391,381	57.4	444	56.9
	Alfred E. Smith	Democratic	15,016,443	40.3	87	
	Norman Thomas	Socialist	881,951	2.3	—	
	William Z. Foster	Communist	102,991	0.3	—	
1932	**FRANKLIN D. ROOSEVELT (N.Y.)**	Democratic	22,821,857	57.4	472	56.9
	Herbert Hoover	Republican	15,761,841	39.7	59	
	Norman Thomas	Socialist	881,951	2.2	—	
1936	**FRANKLIN D. ROOSEVELT (N.Y.)**	Democratic	27,751,597	60.8	523	61.0
	Alfred M. Landon	Republican	16,679,583	36.5	8	
	William Lemke	Union	882,479	1.9	—	
1940	**FRANKLIN D. ROOSEVELT (N.Y.)**	Democratic	27,244,160	54.8	449	62.5
	Wendell Willkie	Republican	22,305,198	44.8	82	
1944	**FRANKLIN D. ROOSEVELT (N.Y.)**	Democratic	25,602,504	53.5	432	55.9
	Thomas E. Dewey	Republican	22,006,285	46.0	99	
1948	**HARRY S. TRUMAN (Mo.)**	Democratic	24,105,695	49.5	303	53.0
	Thomas E. Dewey	Republican	21,969,170	45.1	189	
	J. Strom Thurmond	States'-Rights Democratic	1,169,021	2.4	38	
	Henry A. Wallace	Progressive	1,156,103	2.4	—	
1952	**DWIGHT D. EISENHOWER (N.Y.)**	Republican	33,936,252	55.1	442	63.3
	Adlai Stevenson	Democratic	27,314,992	44.4	89	
1956	**DWIGHT D. EISENHOWER (N.Y.)**	Republican	35,575,420	57.6	457	60.6
	Adlai Stevenson	Democratic	26,033,066	42.1	73	
	Other	—	—		1	
1960	**JOHN F. KENNEDY (Mass.)**	Democratic	34,227,096	49.9	303	62.8
	Richard M. Nixon	Republican	34,108,546	49.6	219	
	Other	—	—		15	
1964	**LYNDON B. JOHNSON (Texas)**	Democratic	43,126,506	61.1	486	61.7
	Barry M. Goldwater	Republican	27,176,799	38.5	52	
1968	**RICHARD M. NIXON (N.Y.)**	Republican	31,770,237	43.4	301	60.9
	Hubert H. Humphrey	Democratic	31,270,533	42.7	191	
	George Wallace	American Indep.	9,906,141	13.5	46	
1972	**RICHARD M. NIXON (N.Y.)**	Republican	47,169,911	60.7	520	55.2
	George S. McGovern	Democratic	29,170,383	37.5	17	
	Other	—	—		1	
1976	**JIMMY CARTER (Ga.)**	Democratic	40,830,763	50.0	297	53.5
	Gerald R. Ford	Republican	39,147,793	48.0	240	
	Other	—	1,575,459	2.1	—	

Year	Candidates	Parties	Popular Vote	Percentage of Popular Vote	Electoral Vote	Percentage of Voter Participation
1980	**RONALD REAGAN (Calif.)**	Republican	43,901,812	51.0	489	54.0
	Jimmy Carter	Democratic	35,483,820	41.0	49	
	John B. Anderson	Independent	5,719,722	7.0	—	
	Ed Clark	Libertarian	921,188	1.1	—	
1984	**RONALD REAGAN (Calif.)**	Republican	54,455,075	59.0	525	53.1
	Walter Mondale	Democratic	37,577,185	41.0	13	
1988	**GEORGE H. W. BUSH (Texas)**	Republican	47,946,422	54.0	426	50.2
	Michael S. Dukakis	Democratic	41,016,429	46.0	112	
1992	**WILLIAM J. CLINTON (Ark.)**	Democratic	44,908,254	43.0	370	55.9
	George H. W. Bush	Republican	39,102,282	38.0	168	
	H. Ross Perot	Independent	19,721,433	19.0	—	
1996	**WILLIAM J. CLINTON (Ark.)**	Democratic	47,401,185	49.2	379	49.0
	Robert Dole	Republican	39,197,469	40.7	159	
	H. Ross Perot	Independent	8,085,294	8.4	—	
2000	**GEORGE W. BUSH (Texas)**	Republican	50,456,062	47.8	271	51.2
	Al Gore	Democratic	50,996,862	48.4	267	
	Ralph Nader	Green Party	2,858,843	2.7	—	
	Patrick J. Buchanan	—	438,760	0.4	—	
2004	**GEORGE W. BUSH (Texas)**	Republican	61,872,711	50.7	286	60.3
	John F. Kerry	Democratic	58,894,584	48.3	252	
	Other	—	1,582,185	1.3	—	

PRESIDENTS, VICE PRESIDENTS, AND SECRETARIES OF STATE

The Washington Administration (1789–1797)
Vice President	John Adams	1789–1797
Secretary of State	Thomas Jefferson	1789–1793
	Edmund Randolph	1794–1795
	Timothy Pickering	1795–1797

The John Adams Administration (1797–1801)
Vice President	Thomas Jefferson	1797–1801
Secretary of State	Timothy Pickering	1797–1800
	John Marshall	1800–1801

The Jefferson Administration (1801–1809)
Vice President	Aaron Burr	1801–1805
	George Clinton	1805–1809
Secretary of State	James Madison	1801–1809

The Madison Administration (1809–1817)
Vice President	George Clinton	1809–1813
	Elbridge Gerry	1813–1817
Secretary of State	Robert Smith	1809–1811
	James Monroe	1811–1817

The Monroe Administration (1817–1825)
Vice President	Daniel Tompkins	1817–1825
Secretary of State	John Quincy Adams	1817–1825

The John Quincy Adams Administration (1825–1829)
Vice President	John C. Calhoun	1825–1829
Secretary of State	Henry Clay	1825–1829

The Jackson Administration (1829–1837)
Vice President	John C. Calhoun	1829–1833
	Martin Van Buren	1833–1837
Secretary of State	Martin Van Buren	1829–1831
	Edward Livingston	1831–1833
	Louis McLane	1833–1834
	John Forsyth	1834–1837

The Van Buren Administration (1837–1841)
Vice President	Richard M. Johnson	1837–1841
Secretary of State	John Forsyth	1837–1841

The William Harrison Administration (1841)
Vice President	John Tyler	1841
Secretary of State	Daniel Webster	1841

The Tyler Administration (1841–1845)
Vice President	None	
Secretary of State	Daniel Webster	1841–1843
	Hugh S. Legaré	1843
	Abel P. Upshur	1843–1844
	John C. Calhoun	1844–1845

U.S. POLITICS AND GOVERNMENT

The Polk Administration (1845–1849)

Vice President	George M. Dallas	1845–1849
Secretary of State	James Buchanan	1845–1849

The Taylor Administration (1849–1850)

Vice President	Millard Fillmore	1849–1850
Secretary of State	John M. Clayton	1849–1850

The Fillmore Administration (1850–1853)

Vice President	None	
Secretary of State	Daniel Webster	1850–1852
	Edward Everett	1852–1853

The Pierce Administration (1853–1857)

Vice President	William R. King	1853–1857
Secretary of State	William L. Marcy	1853–1857

The Buchanan Administration (1857–1861)

Vice President	John C. Breckinridge	1857–1861
Secretary of State	Lewis Cass	1857–1860
	Jeremiah S. Black	1860–1861

The Lincoln Administration (1861–1865)

Vice President	Hannibal Hamlin	1861–1865
	Andrew Johnson	1865
Secretary of State	William H. Seward	1861–1865

The Andrew Johnson Administration (1865–1869)

Vice President	None	
Secretary of State	William H. Seward	1865–1869

The Grant Administration (1869–1877)

Vice President	Schuyler Colfax	1869–1873
	Henry Wilson	1873–1877
Secretary of State	Elihu B. Washburne	1869
	Hamilton Fish	1869–1877

The Hayes Administration (1877–1881)

Vice President	William A. Wheeler	1877–1881
Secretary of State	William M. Evarts	1877–1881

The Garfield Administration (1881)

Vice President	Chester A. Arthur	1881
Secretary of State	James G. Blaine	1881

The Arthur Administration (1881–1885)

Vice President	None	
Secretary of State	F. T. Frelinghuysen	1881–1885

The Cleveland Administration (1885–1889)

Vice President	Thomas A. Hendricks	1885–1889
Secretary of State	Thomas F. Bayard	1885–1889

The Benjamin Harrison Administration (1889–1893)

Vice President	Levi P. Morton	1889–1893
Secretary of State	James G. Blaine	1889–1892
	John W. Foster	1892–1893

The Cleveland Administration (1893–1897)

Vice President	Adlai E. Stevenson	1893–1897
Secretary of State	Walter Q. Gresham	1893–1895
	Richard Olney	1895–1897

The McKinley Administration (1897–1901)

Vice President	Garret A. Hobart	1897–1901
	Theodore Roosevelt	1901
Secretary of State	John Sherman	1897–1898
	William R. Day	1898
	John Hay	1898–1901

The Theodore Roosevelt Administration (1901–1909)

Vice President	Charles Fairbanks	1905–1909
Secretary of State	John Hay	1901–1905
	Elihu Root	1905–1909
	Robert Bacon	1909

The Taft Administration (1909–1913)

Vice President	James S. Sherman	1909–1913
Secretary of State	Philander C. Knox	1909–1913

The Wilson Administration (1913–1921)

Vice President	Thomas R. Marshall	1913–1921
Secretary of State	William J. Bryan	1913–1915
	Robert Lansing	1915–1920
	Bainbridge Colby	1920–1921

The Harding Administration (1921–1923)

Vice President	Calvin Coolidge	1921–1923
Secretary of State	Charles E. Hughes	1921–1923

The Coolidge Administration (1923–1929)

Vice President	Charles G. Dawes	1925–1929
Secretary of State	Charles E. Hughes	1923–1925
	Frank B. Kellogg	1925–1929

The Hoover Administration (1929–1933)

Vice President	Charles Curtis	1929–1933
Secretary of State	Henry L. Stimson	1929–1933

The Franklin D. Roosevelt Administration (1933–1945)

Vice President	John Nance Garner	1933–1941
	Henry A. Wallace	1941–1945
	Harry S. Truman	1945
Secretary of State	Cordell Hull	1933–1944
	Edward R. Stettinius Jr.	1944–1945

The Truman Administration (1945–1953)

Vice President	Alben W. Barkley	1949–1953
Secretary of State	Edward R. Stettinius Jr.	1945
	James F. Byrnes	1945–1947
	George C. Marshall	1947–1949
	Dean G. Acheson	1949–1953

The Eisenhower Administration (1953–1961)

Vice President	Richard M. Nixon	1953–1961
Secretary of State	John Foster Dulles	1953–1959
	Christian A. Herter	1959–1961

The Kennedy Administration (1961–1963)

Vice President	Lyndon B. Johnson	1961–1963
Secretary of State	Dean Rusk	1961–1963

The Lyndon Johnson Administration (1963–1969)

Vice President	Hubert H. Humphrey	1965–1969
Secretary of State	Dean Rusk	1963–1969

The Nixon Administration (1969–1974)

Vice President	Spiro T. Agnew	1969–1973
	Gerald R. Ford	1973–1974
Secretary of State	William P. Rogers	1969–1973
	Henry A. Kissinger	1973–1974

The Ford Administration (1974–1977)

Vice President	Nelson A. Rockefeller	1974–1977
Secretary of State	Henry A. Kissinger	1974–1977

The Carter Administration (1977–1981)

Vice President	Walter F. Mondale	1977–1981
Secretary of State	Cyrus R. Vance	1977–1980
	Edmund Muskie	1980–1981

The Reagan Administration (1981–1989)

Vice President	George H. W. Bush	1981–1989
Secretary of State	Alexander M. Haig	1981–1982
	George P. Shultz	1982–1989

The George H. W. Bush Administration (1989–1993)

Vice President	J. Danforth Quayle	1989–1993
Secretary of State	James A. Baker III	1989–1992
	Lawrence S. Eagleburger	1992–1993

The Clinton Administration (1993–2001)

Vice President	Albert Gore	1993–2001
Secretary of State	Warren M. Christopher	1993–1997
	Madeleine K. Albright	1997–2001

The George W. Bush Administration (2001–)

Vice President	Richard Cheney	2001–
Secretary of State	Colin Powell	2001–2005
	Condoleezza Rice	2005–

ADMISSION OF STATES TO THE UNION

State	Date of Admission	State	Date of Admission
Delaware	December 7, 1787	Rhode Island	May 29, 1790
Pennsylvania	December 12, 1787	Vermont	March 4, 1791
New Jersey	December 18, 1787	Kentucky	June 1, 1792
Georgia	January 2, 1788	Tennessee	June 1, 1796
Connecticut	January 9, 1788	Ohio	March 1, 1803
Massachusetts	February 6, 1788	Louisiana	April 30, 1812
Maryland	April 28, 1788	Indiana	December 11, 1816
South Carolina	May 23, 1788	Mississippi	December 10, 1817
New Hampshire	June 21, 1788	Illinois	December 3, 1818
Virginia	June 25, 1788	Alabama	December 14, 1819
New York	July 26, 1788	Maine	March 15, 1820
North Carolina	November 21, 1789	Missouri	August 10, 1821

ADMISSION OF STATES TO THE UNION

State	Date of Admission	State	Date of Admission
Arkansas	June 15, 1836	Colorado	August 1, 1876
Michigan	January 16, 1837	North Dakota	November 2, 1889
Florida	March 3, 1845	South Dakota	November 2, 1889
Texas	December 29, 1845	Montana	November 8, 1889
Iowa	December 28, 1846	Washington	November 11, 1889
Wisconsin	May 29, 1848	Idaho	July 3, 1890
California	September 9, 1850	Wyoming	July 10, 1890
Minnesota	May 11, 1858	Utah	January 4, 1896
Oregon	February 14, 1859	Oklahoma	November 16, 1907
Kansas	January 29, 1861	New Mexico	January 6, 1912
West Virginia	June 19, 1863	Arizona	February 14, 1912
Nevada	October 31, 1864	Alaska	January 3, 1959
Nebraska	March 1, 1867	Hawaii	August 21, 1959

SUPREME COURT JUSTICES

Name	Service	Appointed by	Name	Service	Appointed by
John Jay*	1789–1795	Washington	Philip P. Barbour	1836–1841	Jackson
James Wilson	1789–1798	Washington	John Catron	1837–1865	Van Buren
John Blair	1789–1796	Washington	John McKinley	1837–1852	Van Buren
John Rutledge	1790–1791	Washington	Peter V. Daniel	1841–1860	Van Buren
William Cushing	1790–1810	Washington	Samuel Nelson	1845–1872	Tyler
James Iredell	1790–1799	Washington	Levi Woodbury	1845–1851	Polk
Thomas Johnson	1791–1793	Washington	Robert C. Grier	1846–1870	Polk
William Paterson	1793–1806	Washington	Benjamin R. Curtis	1851–1857	Fillmore
John Rutledge†	1795	Washington	John A. Campbell	1853–1861	Pierce
Samuel Chase	1796–1811	Washington	Nathan Clifford	1858–1881	Buchanan
Oliver Ellsworth	1796–1799	Washington	Noah H. Swayne	1862–1881	Lincoln
Bushrod Washington	1798–1829	J. Adams	Samuel F. Miller	1862–1890	Lincoln
			David Davis	1862–1877	Lincoln
Alfred Moore	1799–1804	J. Adams	Stephen J. Field	1863–1897	Lincoln
John Marshall	1801–1835	J. Adams	**Salmon P. Chase**	1864–1873	Lincoln
William Johnson	1804–1834	Jefferson	William Strong	1870–1880	Grant
Henry B. Livingston	1806–1823	Jefferson	Joseph P. Bradley	1870–1892	Grant
Thomas Todd	1807–1826	Jefferson	Ward Hunt	1873–1882	Grant
Gabriel Duval	1811–1836	Madison	**Morrison R. Waite**	1874–1888	Grant
Joseph Story	1811–1845	Madison	John M. Harlan	1877–1911	Hayes
Smith Thompson	1823–1843	Monroe	William B. Woods	1880–1887	Hayes
Robert Trimble	1826–1828	J. Q. Adams	Stanley Matthews	1881–1889	Garfield
John McLean	1829–1861	Jackson	Horace Gray	1882–1902	Arthur
Henry Baldwin	1830–1844	Jackson	Samuel Blatchford	1882–1893	Arthur
James M. Wayne	1835–1867	Jackson	Lucius Q. C. Lamar	1888–1893	Cleveland
Roger B. Taney	1836–1864	Jackson	**Melville W. Fuller**	1888–1910	Cleveland
			David J. Brewer	1889–1910	B. Harrison
			Henry B. Brown	1890–1906	B. Harrison
			George Shiras	1892–1903	B. Harrison
			Howell E. Jackson	1893–1895	B. Harrison

*Chief Justices appear in bold type.
†Acting Chief Justice; Senate refused to confirm appointment.

Name	Service	Appointed by	Name	Service	Appointed by
Edward D. White	1894–1910	Cleveland	Harold H. Burton	1945–1958	Truman
Rufus W. Peckham	1896–1909	Cleveland	**Frederick M. Vinson**	1946–1953	Truman
Joseph McKenna	1898–1925	McKinley	Tom C. Clark	1949–1967	Truman
Oliver W. Holmes	1902–1932	T. Roosevelt	Sherman Minton	1949–1956	Truman
William R. Day	1903–1922	T. Roosevelt	**Earl Warren**	1953–1969	Eisenhower
William H. Moody	1906–1910	T. Roosevelt	John Marshall Harlan	1955–1971	Eisenhower
Horace H. Lurton	1910–1914	Taft	William J. Brennan Jr.	1956–1990	Eisenhower
Charles E. Hughes	1910–1916	Taft	Charles E. Whittaker	1957–1962	Eisenhower
Willis Van Devanter	1910–1937	Taft	Potter Stewart	1958–1981	Eisenhower
Edward D. White	1910–1921	Taft	Byron R. White	1962–1993	Kennedy
Joseph R. Lamar	1911–1916	Taft	Arthur J. Goldberg	1962–1965	Kennedy
Mahlon Pitney	1912–1922	Taft	Abe Fortas	1965–1969	L. Johnson
James C. McReynolds	1914–1941	Wilson	Thurgood Marshall	1967–1991	L. Johnson
Louis D. Brandeis	1916–1939	Wilson	**Warren E. Burger**	1969–1986	Nixon
John H. Clarke	1916–1922	Wilson	Harry A. Blackmun	1970–1994	Nixon
William H. Taft	1921–1930	Harding	Lewis F. Powell Jr.	1972–1988	Nixon
George Sutherland	1922–1938	Harding	William H. Rehnquist	1972–1986	Nixon
Pierce Butler	1923–1939	Harding	John Paul Stevens	1975–	Ford
Edward T. Sanford	1923–1930	Harding	Sandra Day O'Connor	1981–2006	Reagan
Harlan F. Stone	1925–1941	Coolidge	**William H. Rehnquist**	1986–2005	Reagan
Charles E. Hughes	1930–1941	Hoover	Antonin Scalia	1986–	Reagan
Owen J. Roberts	1930–1945	Hoover	Anthony M. Kennedy	1988–	Reagan
Benjamin N. Cardozo	1932–1938	Hoover	David H. Souter	1990–	G. H. W. Bush
Hugo L. Black	1937–1971	F. Roosevelt	Clarence Thomas	1991–	G. H. W. Bush
Stanley F. Reed	1938–1957	F. Roosevelt	Ruth Bader Ginsburg	1993–	Clinton
Felix Frankfurter	1939–1962	F. Roosevelt	Stephen Breyer	1994–	Clinton
William O. Douglas	1939–1975	F. Roosevelt	**John G. Roberts Jr.**	2005–	G. W. Bush
Frank Murphy	1940–1949	F. Roosevelt	Samuel Anthony Alito Jr.	2006–	G. W. Bush
Harlan F. Stone	1941–1946	F. Roosevelt			
James F. Byrnes	1941–1942	F. Roosevelt			
Robert H. Jackson	1941–1954	F. Roosevelt			
Wiley B. Rutledge	1943–1949	F. Roosevelt			

SIGNIFICANT SUPREME COURT CASES

Marbury v. Madison (1803)

This case established the right of the Supreme Court to review the constitutionality of laws. The decision involved judicial appointments made during the last hours of the administration of President John Adams. Some commissions, including that of William Marbury, had not yet been delivered when President Thomas Jefferson took office. Infuriated by the last-minute nature of Adams's Federalist appointments, Jefferson refused to send the undelivered commissions out, and Marbury decided to sue. The Supreme Court, presided over by John Marshall, a Federalist who had assisted Adams in the judicial appointments, ruled that although Marbury's commission was valid and the new president should have delivered it, the Court could not compel him to do so. The Court based its reasoning on a finding that the grounds of Marbury's suit, resting in the Judiciary Act of 1789, were in conflict with the Constitution.

For the first time, the Court had overturned a national law on the grounds that it was unconstitutional. John Marshall had quietly established the concept of judicial review: The Supreme Court had given itself the authority to nullify acts of the other branches of the federal government. Although the Constitution provides for judicial review, the Court had not exercised this power before and did not use it again until 1857. It seems likely that if the Court had waited until 1857 to use this power, it would have been difficult to establish.

McCulloch v. Maryland (1819)

In 1816, Congress authorized the creation of a national bank. To protect its own banks from competition with a branch of the national bank in Baltimore, the state legislature of Maryland placed a tax of 2 percent on all notes issued by any bank operating in Maryland that was not chartered by the state. McCulloch, cashier of the Baltimore branch of the Bank of the United States, was convicted for refusing to pay the tax. Under the leadership of Chief Justice John Marshall, the Court ruled that the federal government had the power to establish a bank, even though that specific authority was not mentioned in the Constitution.

Marshall maintained that the authority could be reasonably implied from Article 1, section 8, which gives Congress the power to make all laws that are necessary and proper to execute the enumerated powers. Marshall also held that Maryland could not tax the national bank because in a conflict between federal and state laws, the federal law must take precedence. Thus he established the principles of implied powers and federal supremacy, both of which set a precedent for subsequent expansion of federal power at the expense of the states.

Scott v. Sandford (1857)

Dred Scott was a slave who sued for his own and his family's freedom on the grounds that, with his master, he had traveled to and lived in free territory that did not allow slavery. When his case reached the Supreme Court, the justices saw an opportunity to settle once and for all the vexing question of slavery in the territories. The Court's decision in this case proved that it enjoyed no special immunity from the sectional and partisan passions of the time. Five of the nine justices were from the South and seven were Democrats.

Chief Justice Roger B. Taney hated Republicans and detested racial equality; his decision reflects those prejudices. He wrote an opinion not only declaring that Scott was still a slave but also claiming that the Constitution denied citizenship or rights to blacks, that Congress had no right to exclude slavery from the territories, and that the Missouri Compromise was unconstitutional. While southern Democrats gloated over this seven-to-two decision, sectional tensions were further inflamed, and the young Republican Party's claim that a hostile "slave power" was conspiring to destroy northern liberties was given further credence. The decision brought the nation closer to civil war and is generally regarded as the worst decision ever rendered by the Supreme Court.

Butchers' Benevolent Association of New Orleans v. Crescent City Livestock Landing and Slaughterhouse Co. (1873)

The Slaughterhouse cases, as the cases docketed under the Butchers' title were known, were the first legal test of the Fourteenth Amendment. To cut down on cases of cholera believed to be caused by contaminated water, the state of Louisiana prohibited the slaughter of livestock in New Orleans except in one slaughterhouse, effectively giving that slaughterhouse a monopoly. Other New Orleans butchers claimed that the state had deprived them of their occupation without due process of law, thus violating the Fourteenth Amendment.

In a five-to-four decision, the Court upheld the Louisiana law, declaring that the Fourteenth Amendment protected only the rights of federal citizenship, like voting in federal elections and interstate travel. The federal government thus was not obliged to protect basic civil rights from violation by state governments. This decision would have significant implications for African Americans and their struggle for civil rights in the twentieth century.

United States v. E. C. Knight Co. (1895)

Also known as the Sugar Trust case, this was among the first cases to reveal the weakness of the Sherman Antitrust Act in the hands of a pro-business Supreme Court. In 1895, American Sugar Refining Company purchased four other sugar producers, including the E. C. Knight Company, and thus took control of more than 98 percent of the sugar refining in the United States. In an effort to limit monopoly, the government brought suit against all five of the companies for violating the Sherman Antitrust Act, which outlawed trusts and other business combinations in restraint of trade. The Court dismissed the suit, however, arguing that the law applied only to commerce and not to manufacturing, defining the latter as a local concern and not part of the interstate commerce that the government could regulate.

Plessy v. Ferguson (1896)

African American Homer Plessy challenged a Louisiana law that required segregation on trains passing through the state. After ensuring that the railroad and the conductor knew that he was of mixed race (Plessy appeared to be white but under the racial code of Louisiana was classified as "colored" because he was one-eighth black), he refused to move to the "colored only" section of the coach. The Court ruled against Plessy by a vote of seven to one, declaring that "separate but equal" facilities were permissible according to section 1 of the Fourteenth Amendment, which calls upon the states to provide "equal protection of the laws" to anyone within their jurisdiction. Although the case was viewed as relatively insignificant at the time, it cast a long shadow over several decades.

Initially, the decision was viewed as a victory for segregationists, but in the 1930s and 1940s civil rights advocates referred to the doctrine of "separate but equal" in their efforts to end segregation. They argued that segregated institutions and accommodations were often *not* equal to those available to whites, and finally succeeded in overturning *Plessy* in *Brown v. Board of Education* in 1954 (see below).

Lochner v. New York (1905)

In this case, the Court ruled against a New York state law that prohibited employees from working in bakeries more than ten hours a day or sixty hours a week. The purpose of the law was to protect the health of workers, but the Court ruled that it was unconstitutional because it violated "freedom of contract" implicitly protected by the due process clause of the Fourteenth Amendment. Most of the justices believed strongly in a laissez-faire economic system that favored survival of the fittest. They felt that government protection of workers interfered with this system. In a dissenting opinion, Justice Oliver Wendell Holmes accused the majority of distorting the Constitution and of deciding the case on "an economic theory which a large part of the country does not entertain."

Muller v. Oregon (1908)

In 1905, Curt Muller, owner of a Portland, Oregon, laundry, demanded that one of his employees, Mrs. Elmer Gotcher, work more than the ten hours allowed as a maximum workday for women under Oregon law. Muller argued that the law violated his "freedom of contract" as established in prior Supreme Court decisions.

Progressive lawyer Louis D. Brandeis defended the Oregon law by arguing that a state could be justified in abridging freedom of contract when the health, safety, and welfare of workers was at issue. His innovative strategy drew on ninety-five pages of excerpts from factory and medical reports to substantiate his argument that there was a direct connection between long hours and the health of women and thus the health of the nation. In a unanimous decision, the Court upheld the Oregon law, but later generations of women fighting for equality would question the strategy of arguing that women's reproductive role entitled them to special treatment.

Schenck v. United States (1919)

During World War I, Charles Schenck and other members of the Socialist Party printed and mailed out flyers urging young men who were subject to the draft to oppose the war in Europe. In upholding the conviction of Schenck for publishing a pamphlet urging draft resistance, Justice Oliver Wendell Holmes established the "clear and present danger" test for freedom of speech. Such utterances as Schenck's during a time of national peril, Holmes wrote, could be considered the equivalent of shouting "Fire!" in a crowded theater. Congress had the right to protect the public against such an incitement to panic, the Court ruled in a unanimous decision. But the analogy was a false one. Schenck's pamphlet had little power to provoke a public firmly opposed to its message. Although Holmes later modified his position to state that the danger must relate to an immediate evil and a specific action, the "clear and present danger" test laid the groundwork for those who later sought to limit First Amendment freedoms.

Schechter Poultry Corp. v. United States (1935)

During the Great Depression, the National Industrial Recovery Act (NIRA), which was passed under President Franklin D. Roosevelt, established fair competition codes that were designed to help businesses. The Schechter brothers of New York City, who sold chickens, were convicted of violating the codes. The Supreme Court ruled that the NIRA unconstitutionally conferred legislative power on an administrative agency and overstepped the limits of federal power to regulate interstate commerce. The decision was a significant blow to the New Deal recovery program, demonstrating both historic American resistance to economic planning and the refusal of the business community to yield its autonomy unless it was forced to do so.

Brown v. Board of Education (1954)

In 1950, the families of eight Topeka, Kansas, children sued the Topeka Board of Education. The children were blacks who lived within walking distance of a whites-only school. The segregated school system required them to take a time-consuming, inconvenient, and dangerous route to get to a black school, and their parents argued that there was no reason their children should not be allowed to attend the nearest school. By the time the case reached the Supreme Court, it had been joined with similar cases regarding segregated schools in other states and the District of Columbia. A team of lawyers from the National Association for the Advancement of Colored People (NAACP), led by Thurgood Marshall (who would later be appointed to the Supreme Court), urged the Court to overturn the fifty-eight-year-old precedent established in *Plessy v. Ferguson*, which had enshrined "separate but equal" as the law of the land. A unanimous Court, led by Chief Justice Earl Warren, declared that "separate educational facilities are inherently unequal" and thus violate the Fourteenth Amendment. In 1955, the Court called for desegregation "with all deliberate speed" but established no deadline.

Roth v. United States (1957)

In 1957, New Yorker Samuel Roth was convicted of sending obscene materials through the mail in a case that ultimately reached the Supreme Court. With a six-to-three vote, the Court reaffirmed the historical view that obscenity is not protected by the First Amendment. Yet it broke new ground by declaring that a work could be judged obscene only if, "taken as a whole," it appealed to the "prurient interest" of "the average person."

Prior to this case, work could be judged obscene if portions were thought able to "deprave and corrupt" the most susceptible part of an audience (such as children). Thus, serious works of literature such as Theodore Dreiser's *An American Tragedy*, which was banned in Boston when first published, had received no protection. Although this decision continued to pose problems of definition, it did help to protect most works that attempt to convey ideas, even if those ideas have to do with sex, from the threat of obscenity laws.

Engel v. Vitale (1962)

In 1959, five parents with ten children in the New Hyde Park, New York, school system sued the school board. The parents argued that the so-called Regents' Prayer that public school students in New York recited at the start of every school day violated the doctrine of separation of church and state outlined in the First Amendment. In 1962, the Supreme Court voted six to one in favor of banning the Regents' Prayer.

The decision threw the religious community into an uproar. Many religious leaders expressed dismay and even shock; others welcomed the decision. Several efforts to introduce an amendment allowing school prayer have failed. Subsequent Supreme Court decisions have banned reading of the Bible in public schools. The Court has also declared mandatory flag saluting to be an infringement of religious and personal freedoms.

Gideon v. Wainwright (1963)

When Clarence Earl Gideon was tried for breaking into a poolroom, the state of Florida rejected his demand for a court-appointed lawyer as guaranteed by the Sixth Amendment. In 1963, the Court upheld his demand in a unanimous decision that established the obligation of states to provide attorneys for indigent defendants in felony cases. Prior to this decision, the right to an attorney had applied only to federal cases, not state cases. In its ruling in *Gideon v. Wainwright*, the Supreme Court applied the Sixth through the Fourteenth Amendments to the states. In 1972, the Supreme Court extended the right to legal representation to all cases, not just felony cases, in its decision in *Argersinger v. Hamlin*.

Griswold v. Connecticut (1965)

With a vote of seven to two, the Supreme Court reversed an "uncommonly silly law" (in the words of Justice Potter Stewart) that made it a crime for anyone in the state of Connecticut to use any drug, article, or instrument to prevent conception. *Griswold* became a landmark case because here, for the first time, the Court explicitly invested with full constitutional status "fundamental personal rights," such as the right to privacy, that were not expressly enumerated in the Bill of Rights. The majority opinion in the case held that the law infringed on the constitutionally protected right to privacy of married persons.

Although the Court had previously recognized fundamental rights not expressly enumerated in the Bill of Rights (such as the right to procreate in *Skinner v. Oklahoma* in 1942), *Griswold* was the first time the Court had justified, at length, the practice of investing such unenumerated rights with full constitutional status. Writing for the majority, Justice William O. Douglas explained that the First, Third, Fourth, Fifth, and Ninth Amendments imply "zones of privacy" that are the foundation for the general right to privacy affirmed in this case.

Miranda v. Arizona (1966)

In 1966, the Supreme Court, by a vote of five to four, upheld the case of Ernesto Miranda, who appealed a murder conviction on the grounds that police had gotten him to confess without giving him access to an attorney. The *Miranda* case was the culmination of the Court's efforts to find a meaningful way of determining whether police had used due process in extracting confessions from people accused of crimes. The *Miranda* decision upholds the Fifth Amendment protection against self-incrimination outside the courtroom and requires that suspects be given what came to be known as the "Miranda warning," which advises them of their right to remain silent and warns them that anything they say might be used against them in a court of law. Suspects must also be told that they have a right to counsel.

New York Times Co. v. United States (1971)

With a six-to-three vote, the Court upheld the right of the *New York Times* and the *Washington Post* to print materials from the so-called *Pentagon Papers*, a secret government study of U.S. policy in Vietnam, leaked by dissident Pentagon official Daniel Ellsberg. Since the papers revealed deception and secrecy in the conduct of the Vietnam War, the Nixon administration had quickly obtained a court injunction against their further publication, claiming that suppression was in the interests of national security. The Supreme Court's decision overturning the injunction strengthened the First Amendment protection of freedom of the press.

Furman v. Georgia (1972)

In this case, the Supreme Court ruled five to four that the death penalty for murder or rape violated the cruel and unusual punishment clause of the Eighth Amendment because the manner in which the death penalty was meted out was irregular, "arbitrary," and "cruel." In response, most states enacted new statutes that allow the death penalty to be imposed only after a postconviction hearing at which evidence must be presented to show that "aggravating" or "mitigating" circumstances were factors in the crime. If the postconviction hearing hands down a death sentence, the case is automatically reviewed by an appellate court.

In 1976, the Court ruled in *Gregg v. Georgia* that these statutes were not unconstitutional. In 1977, the Court ruled in *Coker v. Georgia* that the death penalty for rape was "disproportionate and excessive," thus allowing the death penalty only in murder cases. Between 1977 and 1991, some 150 people were executed in the United States. Public opinion polls indicate that about 70 percent of Americans favor the death penalty for murder. Capital punishment continues to generate controversy, however, as opponents argue that there is no evidence that the death penalty deters crime and that its use reflects racial and economic bias.

Roe v. Wade (1973)

In 1973, the Court found, by a vote of seven to two, that state laws restricting access to abortion violated a woman's right to privacy guaranteed by the due process clause of the Fourteenth Amendment. The decision was based on the cases of two women living in Texas and Georgia, both states with stringent antiabortion laws. Upholding the individual rights of both women and physicians, the Court ruled that the Constitution protects the right to abortion and that states cannot prohibit abortions in the early stages of pregnancy.

The decision stimulated great debate among legal scholars as well as the public. Critics argued that since abortion was never addressed in the Constitution, the Court could not claim that legislation violated fundamental values of the Constitution. They also argued that since abortion was a medical procedure with an acknowledged impact on a fetus, it was inappropriate to invoke the kind of "privacy" argument that was used in *Griswold v. Connecticut* (see page A-43), which was about contraception. Defenders suggested that the case should be argued as a case of gender discrimination, which did violate the equal protection clause of the Fourteenth Amendment. Others said that the right to privacy in sexual matters was indeed a fundamental right.

Regents of the University of California v. Bakke (1978)

When Allan Bakke, a white man, was not accepted by the University of California Medical School at Davis, he filed a lawsuit alleging that the admissions program, which set up different standards for test scores and grades for members of certain minority groups, violated the Civil Rights Act of 1964, which outlawed racial or ethnic preferences in programs supported by federal funds. Bakke further argued that the university's practice of setting aside spaces for minority applicants denied him equal protection as guaranteed by the Fourteenth Amendment. In a five-to-four decision, the Court ordered that Bakke be admitted to the medical school, yet it sanctioned affirmative action programs to attack the results of past discrimination as long as strict quotas or racial classifications were not involved.

Webster v. Reproductive Health Services (1989)

By a vote of five to four, the Court upheld several restrictions on the availability of abortions as imposed by Missouri state law. It upheld restrictions on the use of state property, including public hospitals, for abortions. It also upheld a provision requiring physicians to perform tests to determine the viability of a fetus that a doctor judged to be twenty weeks of age or older. Although the justices did not go so far as to overturn the decision in *Roe v. Wade* (see at left), the ruling galvanized interest groups on both sides of the abortion issue. Opponents of abortion pressured state legislatures to place greater restrictions on abortions; those who favored availability of abortion tried to mobilize public action by presenting the decision as a major threat to the right to choose abortion.

Cipollone v. Liggett (1992)

In a seven-to-two decision, the Court ruled in favor of the family of Rose Cipollone, a woman who died of lung cancer after smoking for forty-two years. The Court rejected arguments that health warnings on cigarette packages protected tobacco manufacturers from personal injury suits filed by smokers who contract cancer and other serious illnesses.

Miller v. Johnson (1995)

In a five-to-four decision, the Supreme Court ruled that voting districts created to increase the voting power of racial minorities were unconstitutional. The decision threatens dozens of congressional, state, and local voting districts that were drawn to give minorities more representation as had been required by the Justice Department under the Voting Rights Act. If states are required to redraw voting districts, the number of black members of Congress could be sharply reduced.

Romer v. Evans (1996)

In a six-to-three decision, the Court struck down a Colorado amendment that forbade local governments from banning discrimination against homosexuals.

Writing for the majority, Justice Anthony Kennedy said that forbidding communities from taking action to protect the rights of homosexuals and not of other groups unlawfully deprived gays and lesbians of opportunities that were available to others. Kennedy based the decision on the guarantee of equal protection under the law as provided by the Fourteenth Amendment.

Bush v. Palm Beach County Canvassing Board (2000)

In a bitterly argued five-to-four decision, the Court reversed the Florida Supreme Court's previous order for a hand recount of contested presidential election ballots in several counties of that battleground state, effectively securing the presidency for Texas Republican governor George W. Bush. The ruling ended a protracted legal dispute between presidential candidates Bush and Vice President Al Gore while inflaming public opinion: For the first time since 1888, a president who failed to win the popular vote took office. Critics charged that the Supreme Court had applied partisanship rather than objectivity to the case, pointing out that the decision went against this Court's customary interpretation of the Constitution to favor state over federal authority.

The American Economy

THESE FIVE "SNAPSHOTS" of the U.S. economy show significant changes over the past century and a half. In 1849, the agricultural sector was by far the largest contributor to the economy. By the turn of the century, with advances in technology and an abundance of cheap labor and raw materials, the country had experienced remarkable industrial expansion, and the manufacturing industries dominated. By 1950, the service sector had increased significantly, fueled by the consumerism of the 1920s and the post–World War II years, and the economy was becoming more diversified. Note that by 1990, the government's share in the economy had grown to more than 10 percent and activity in both the trade and manufacturing sectors had declined, partly as a result of competition from Western Europe and Asia. Manufacturing continued to decline, and by 2001 the service and finance, real estate, and insurance sectors had all grown steadily to eclipse it.

Main Sectors of the U.S. Economy: 1849, 1899, 1950, 1990, 2001

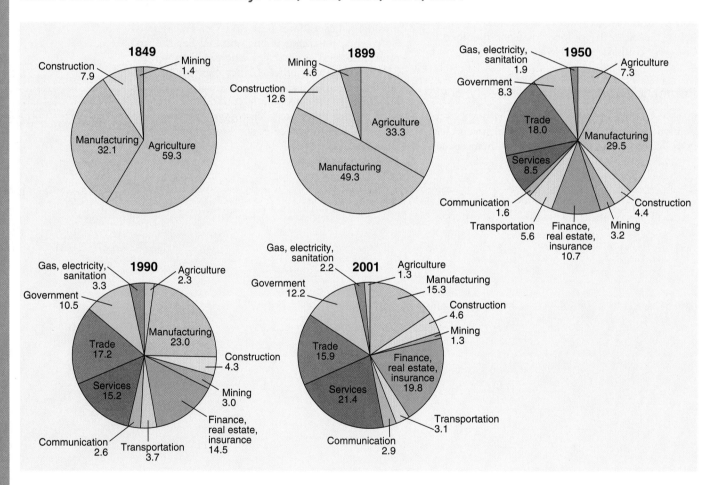

SOURCE: Data from *Historical Statistics of the United States, Colonial Times to 1970* (1975); *Statistical Abstract of the United States, 1998;* U.S. Bureau of Economic Analysis, *Industry Accounts Data, 2001.*

THE AMERICAN ECONOMY

FEDERAL SPENDING AND THE ECONOMY, 1790–2005

Year	Gross National Product (in billions)	Foreign Trade (in millions)		Federal Budget (in billions)	Federal Surplus/Deficit (in billions)	Federal Debt (in billions)
		Exports	Imports			
1790	NA	20	23	0.004	0.00015	0.076
1800	NA	71	91	0.011	0.0006	0.083
1810	NA	67	85	0.008	0.0012	0.053
1820	NA	70	74	0.018	−0.0004	0.091
1830	NA	74	71	0.015	0.100	0.049
1840	NA	132	107	0.024	−0.005	0.004
1850	NA	152	178	0.040	0.004	0.064
1860	NA	400	362	0.063	−0.01	0.065
1870	7.4	451	462	0.310	0.10	2.4
1880	11.2	853	761	0.268	0.07	2.1
1890	13.1	910	823	0.318	0.09	1.2
1900	18.7	1,499	930	0.521	0.05	1.2
1910	35.3	1,919	1,646	0.694	−0.02	1.1
1920	91.5	8,664	5,784	6.357	0.3	24.3
1930	90.4	4,013	3,500	3.320	0.7	16.3
1940	99.7	4,030	7,433	9.6	−2.7	43.0
1950	284.8	10,816	9,125	43.1	−2.2	257.4
1960	503.7	19,600	15,046	92.2	0.3	286.3
1970	977.1	42,700	40,189	195.6	−2.8	371.0
1980	2,631.7	220,600	244,871	590.9	−73.8	907.7
1990	5,832.2	393,600	495,300	1,253.2	−221.2	3,266.1
2000	9,848.0	1,070,054	1,445,438	1,788.8	236.4	5,701.9
2002	10,436.7	974,107	1,392,145	2,011.0	−157.8	6,255.4
2005	12,487.1	1,275,245	1,991,975	2,472.2	−423.2	7,905.3

SOURCE: *Historical Statistics of the U.S., Colonial Times to 1970* (1975), *Statistical Abstract of the U.S., 1996* (1996), *Statistical Abstract of the U.S., 1999* (1999), and *Statistical Abstract of the U.S., 2007* (2007).

A Demographic Profile of the United States and Its People

Population

FROM AN ESTIMATED 4,600 white inhabitants in 1630, the country's population grew to a total of more than 280 million in 2000. It is important to note that the U.S. census, first conducted in 1790 and the source of these figures, counted blacks, both free and slave, but did not include American Indians until 1860. The years 1790 to 1900 saw the most rapid population growth, with an average increase of 25 to 35 percent per decade. In addition to "natural" growth—birthrate exceeding death rate—immigration was also a factor in that rise, especially between 1840 and 1860, 1880 and 1890, and 1900 and 1910 (see table on page A-51). The twentieth century witnessed slower growth, partly a result of 1920s immigration restrictions and a decline in the birthrate, especially during the depression era and the 1960s and 1970s. The U.S. population is expected to reach almost 300 million by the year 2010.

POPULATION GROWTH, 1630–2000

Year	Population	Percent Increase	Year	Population	Percent Increase
1630	4,600	—	1820	9,638,453	33.1
1640	26,600	473.3	1830	12,866,020	33.5
1650	50,400	89.1	1840	17,069,453	32.7
1660	75,100	49.0	1850	23,191,876	35.9
1670	111,900	49.1	1860	31,443,321	35.6
1680	151,500	35.4	1870	39,818,449	26.6
1690	210,400	38.9	1880	50,155,783	26.0
1700	250,900	19.3	1890	62,947,714	25.5
1710	331,700	32.2	1900	75,994,575	20.7
1720	466,200	40.5	1910	91,972,266	21.0
1730	629,400	35.0	1920	105,710,620	14.9
1740	905,600	43.9	1930	122,775,046	16.1
1750	1,170,800	30.0	1940	131,669,275	7.2
1760	1,593,600	36.1	1950	150,697,361	14.5
1770	2,148,100	34.8	1960	179,323,175	19.0
1780	2,780,400	29.4	1970	203,302,031	13.4
1790	3,929,214	41.3	1980	226,542,199	11.4
1800	5,308,483	35.1	1990	248,718,302	9.8
1810	7,239,881	36.4	2000	281,422,509	13.1

SOURCE: *Historical Statistics of the U.S.* (1960), *Historical Statistics of the U.S., Colonial Times to 1970* (1975), *Statistical Abstract of the U.S., 1996* (1996), and *Statistical Abstract of the U.S., 2003* (2003).

A DEMOGRAPHIC PROFILE OF THE UNITED STATES AND ITS PEOPLE

Birthrate, 1820–2000

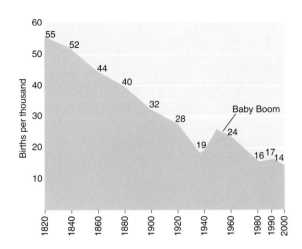

SOURCE: Data from *Historical Statistics of the U.S., Colonial Times to 1970* (1975) and *Statistical Abstract of the U.S., 2003* (2003).

Death Rate, 1900–2000

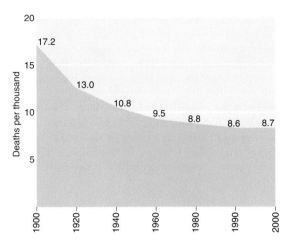

SOURCE: Data from *Historical Statistics of the U.S., Colonial Times to 1970* (1975) and *Statistical Abstract of the U.S., 2003* (2003).

Life Expectancy, 1900–2000

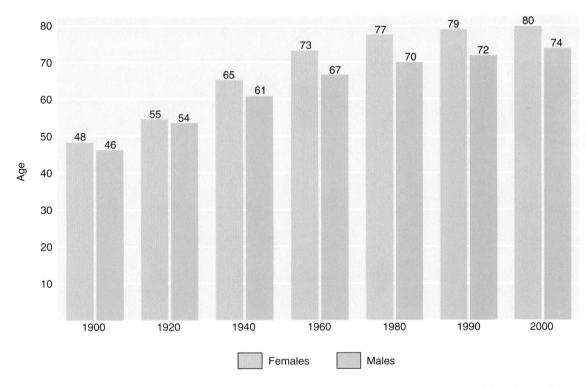

SOURCE: Data from *Historical Statistics of the U.S., Colonial Times to 1970* (1975) and *Statistical Abstract of the U.S., 2003* (2003).

MIGRATION AND IMMIGRATION

WE TEND TO ASSOCIATE INTERNAL MIGRATION with movement westward, yet equally significant has been the movement of the nation's population from the country to the city. In 1790, the first U.S. census recorded that approximately 95 percent of the population lived in rural areas. By 1990, that figure had fallen to less than 25 percent. The decline of the agricultural way of life, late-nineteenth-century industrialization, and immigration have all contributed to increased urbanization. A more recent trend has been the migration, especially since the 1970s, of people to the Sun Belt states of the South and West, lured by factors as various as economic opportunities in the defense and high-tech industries and good weather. This migration has swelled the size of cities like Houston, Dallas, Tucson, Phoenix, and San Diego, all of which in recent years ranked among the top ten most populous U.S. cities.

Rural and Urban Population, 1750–2000

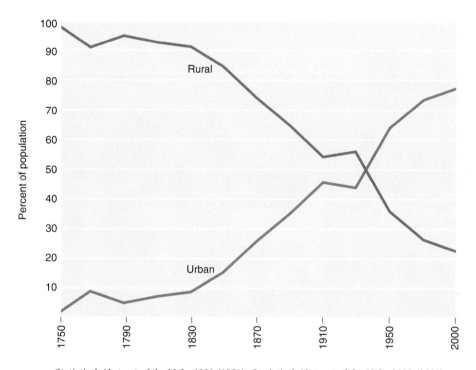

SOURCE: *Statistical Abstract of the U.S., 1991* (1991), *Statistical Abstract of the U.S., 2002* (2002).

MIGRATION AND IMMIGRATION

THE QUANTITY AND CHARACTER OF IMMIGRATION to the United States has varied greatly over time. During the first major influx, between 1840 and 1860, newcomers hailed primarily from northern and western Europe. From 1880 to 1915, when rates soared even more dramatically, the profile changed, with 80 percent of the "new immigration" coming from central, eastern, and southern Europe. Following World War I, strict quotas reduced the flow considerably. Note also the significant falloff during the years of the Great Depression and World War II. The sources of immigration during the last half century have changed significantly, with the majority of people coming from Latin America, the Caribbean, and Asia. The latest surge during the 1980s and 1990s brought more immigrants to the United States than in any decade except 1901–1910.

RATES OF IMMIGRATION, 1821–2005

Year	Number	Rate per Thousand of Total Resident Population
1821–1830	151,824	1.6
1831–1840	599,125	4.6
1841–1850	1,713,521	10.0
1851–1860	2,598,214	11.2
1861–1870	2,314,824	7.4
1871–1880	2,812,191	7.1
1881–1890	5,246,613	10.5
1891–1900	3,687,546	5.8
1901–1910	8,795,386	11.6
1911–1920	5,735,811	6.2
1921–1930	4,107,209	3.9
1931–1940	528,431	0.4
1941–1950	1,035,039	0.7
1951–1960	2,515,479	1.6
1961–1970	3,321,677	1.8
1971–1980	4,493,300	2.2
1981–1990	7,338,100	3.0
1991	1,827,167	7.2
1992	973,977	3.8
1993	904,292	3.5
1994	804,416	3.1
1995	720,461	2.7
1996	915,900	3.4
1997	798,378	2.9
1998	654,451	2.4
1999	646,568	2.3
2000	849,807	3.0
2001	1,064,318	3.7
2002	1,063,732	3.7
2003	704,000	2.4
2004	958,000	3.3
2005	1,122,000	3.8

SOURCE: *Historical Statistics of the U.S., Colonial Times to 1970* (1975), *2002 Yearbook of Immigration Statistics* (2002), and *Statistical Abstract of the U.S., 1996, 1999, 2003, and 2005* (1996, 1999, 2003, 2005).

Major Trends in Immigration, 1820–2000

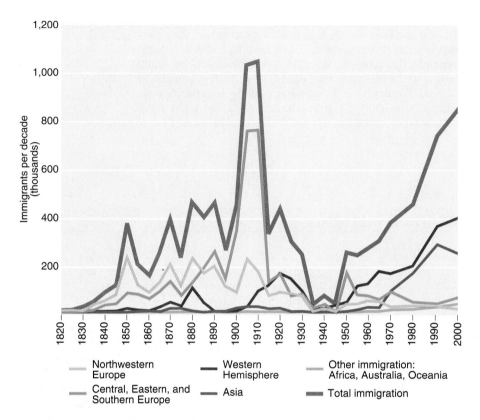

SOURCE: Data from *Historical Statistics of the U.S., Colonial Times to 1970* (1975), *Statistical Abstract of the U.S., 1999* (1999), and *Statistical Abstract of the U.S., 2003* (2003).

Research Resources in U.S. History

For help refining your research skills, finding what you need on the Web, and using it effectively, see "Online Research and Reference Aids" at bedfordstmartins.com/roark.

WHILE DOING RESEARCH IN HISTORY, you will use the library to track down primary and secondary sources and to answer questions that arise as you learn more about your topic. This appendix suggests helpful indexes, references, periodicals, and sources of primary documents. It also offers an overview of electronic resources available through the Internet. The materials listed here are not carried at all libraries, but they will give you an idea of the range of sources available. Remember, too, that librarians are an extremely helpful resource. They can direct you to useful materials throughout your research process.

Bibliographies and Indexes

American Historical Association Guide to Historical Literature. 3rd ed. New York: Oxford University Press, 1995. Offers 27,000 citations to important historical literature, arranged in forty-eight sections covering theory, international history, and regional history. An indispensable guide recently updated to include current trends in historical research.

American History and Life. Santa Barbara: ABC-Clio, 1964–. Covers publications of all sorts on U.S. and Canadian history and culture in a chronological/regional format, with abstracts and alphabetical indexes. Available in computerized format. The most complete ongoing bibliography for American history.

Freidel, Frank Burt. *Harvard Guide to American History.* Cambridge: Harvard University Press, Belknap Press, 1974. Provides citations to books and articles on American history published before 1970. The first volume is arranged topically, the second chronologically. Though it does not cover current scholarship, it is a classic and remains useful for tracing older publications.

Prucha, Francis Paul. *Handbook for Research in American History: A Guide to Bibliographies and Other Reference Works.* 2nd rev. ed. Lincoln: University of Nebraska Press, 1994. Introduces a variety of research tools, including electronic

ones. A good source to consult when planning an in-depth research project.

General Overviews

Dictionary of American Biography. New York: Scribner's, 1928–1937, with supplements. Gives substantial biographies of prominent Americans in history.

Dictionary of American History. New York: Scribner's, 1976. An encyclopedia of terms, places, and concepts in U.S. history; other more specialized sets include the *Encyclopedia of North American Colonies* and the *Encyclopedia of the Confederacy.*

Encyclopedia of American Social History. New York: Scribner's, 1993. Surveys topics such as religion, class, gender, race, popular culture, regionalism, and everyday life from pre-Columbian to modern times.

Encyclopedia of the United States in the Twentieth Century. New York: Scribner's, 1996. An overview of American cultural, social, and intellectual history in articles arranged topically with useful bibliographies for further research.

Specialized Information

Black Women in America: An Historical Encyclopedia. Brooklyn: Carlson, 1993. A scholarly compilation of biographical and topical articles that constitute a definitive history of African American women.

Carruth, Gordon. *The Encyclopedia of American Facts and Dates.* 10th ed. New York: HarperCollins, 1997. Covers American history chronologically from 1986 to the present, offering information on treaties, battles, explorations, popular culture, philosophy, literature, and so on, mixing significant events with telling trivia. Tables allow for reviewing a year from a variety of angles. A thorough index helps pinpoint specific facts in time.

Cook, Chris. *Dictionary of Historical Terms.* 2nd ed. New York: Peter Bendrick, 1990. Covers a wide variety of terms—events, places, institutions, and topics—in history for all periods and places in a remarkably small package. A good place for quick identification of terms in the field.

Dictionary of Afro-American Slavery. New York: Greenwood, 1985. Surveys important people, events, and topics, with useful bibliographies; similar works include *Dictionary of the Vietnam War, Historical Dictionary of the New Deal*, and *Historical Dictionary of the Progressive Era*.

Knappman-Frost, Elizabeth. *The ABC-Clio Companion to Women's Progress in America*. Santa Barbara: ABC-Clio, 1994. Covers American women who were notable for their time as well as topics and organizations that have been significant in women's quest for equality. Each article is brief; there are a chronology and a bibliography at the back of the book.

United States Bureau of the Census. *Historical Statistics of the United States, Colonial Times to 1970*. Washington, D.C.: Government Printing Office, 1975. Offers vital statistics, economic figures, and social data for the United States. An index at the back helps locate tables by subject. For statistics since 1970, consult the annual *Statistical Abstract of the United States*.

Primary Resources

There are many routes to finding contemporary material for historical research. You may search your library catalog using the name of a prominent historical figure as an author; you may also find anthologies covering particular themes or periods in history. Consider also the following special materials for your research.

THE PRESS

American Periodical Series, 1741–1900. Ann Arbor: University Microfilms, 1946–1979. Microfilm collection of periodicals from the colonial period to 1900. An index identifies periodicals that focused on particular topics.

Herstory Microfilm Collection. Berkeley: Women's History Research Center, 1973. A microfilm collection of alternative feminist periodicals published between 1960 and 1980. Offers an interesting documentary history of the women's movement.

New York Times. New York: New York Times, 1851–. Many libraries have this newspaper on microfilm going back to its beginning in 1851. An index is available to locate specific dates and pages of news stories; it also provides detailed chronologies of events as they were reported in the news.

Readers' Guide to Periodical Literature. New York: Wilson, 1900–. This index to popular magazines started in 1900; an earlier index, *Poole's Index to Periodical Literature*, covers 1802–1906, though it does not provide such thorough indexing.

DIARIES, PAMPHLETS, BOOKS

The American Culture Series. Ann Arbor: University Microfilms, 1941–1974. A microfilm set, with a useful index, featuring books and pamphlets published between 1493 and 1875.

American Women's Diaries. New Canaan: Readex, 1984–. A collection of reproductions of women's diaries. There are different series for different regions of the country.

The March of America Facsimile Series. Ann Arbor: University Microfilms, 1966. A collection of more than ninety facsimiles of travel accounts to the New World published in English or English translation from the fifteenth through the nineteenth century.

Women in America from Colonial Times to the Twentieth Century. New York: Arno, 1974. A collection of reprints of dozens of books written by women describing women's lives and experiences in their own words.

GOVERNMENT DOCUMENTS

Congressional Record. Washington, D.C.: Government Printing Office, 1874–. Covers daily debates and proceedings of Congress. Earlier series were called *Debates and Proceedings in the Congress of the United States* and *The Congressional Globe*.

Foreign Relations of the United States. Washington, D.C.: Department of State, 1861–. A collection of documents from 1861, including diplomatic papers, correspondence, and memoranda, that provides a documentary record of U.S. foreign policy.

Public Papers of the Presidents. Washington, D.C.: Office of the Federal Register, 1957–. Includes major documents issued by the executive branch from the Hoover administration to the present.

Serial Set. Washington, D.C.: Government Printing Office, 1789–1969. A huge collection of congressional documents, available in many libraries on microfiche, with a useful index.

LOCAL HISTORY COLLECTIONS

State and county historical societies often house a wealth of historical documents; consider their resources when planning your research—you may find yourself working with material that no one else has analyzed before.

Internet Resources

The Internet is a useful place for scholars to communicate and publish information. Electronic discussion lists, electronic journals, and primary texts are among the resources available to historians. The following sources are good places to find historical information. You can also search the Web using any of a number of search engines. However, bear in

INTERNET RESOURCES

mind that there is no board of editors screening Internet sites for accuracy or usefulness. Be critical of all of your sources, particularly those found on the Internet. Note that when this book went to press, the sites listed below were active and maintained.

The American Civil War Homepage. <http://sunsite.utk.edu/civil-war/warweb.html> A comprehensive resource bank on the American Civil War. Maintained by George Hoemann of the University of Tennessee, the site contains letters, documents, photographs, information about battles, links to other sites, and regiment rosters.

American Memory: Historical Collections for the National Digital Library. <http://memory.loc.gov/ammem/index.html> A Web site that features digitized primary source materials from the Library of Congress, among them African American pamphlets, Civil War photographs, documents from the Constitutional Convention of 1774–1790, materials on woman suffrage, and oral histories.

Historical Text Archive. <http://historicaltextarchive.com/> One of the oldest and largest Internet archives of historical documents, articles, photographs, and more. Includes sections on Native American, African American, and U.S. history, in which can be found texts of the Declaration of Independence, the Constitution of Iroquois Nations, World War II surrender documents, and a great deal more.

Index of Native American Resources on the Internet. <http://www.hanksville.org/NAresources> A vast index of Native American resources organized by category. Within the history category, links are organized under subcategories: oral history, written history, geographical areas, timelines, and photographs and photographic archives. A central place to come in the search for information on Native American history.

Internet Resources for Students of Afro-American History and Culture. <http://www.libraries.rutgers.edu/rul/rr_gateway/research_guides/history/afrores.shtml> A good place to begin research on topics in African American history. The site is indexed and linked to a wide variety of sources, including primary documents, text collections, and archival sources on African American history. Individual documents such as slave narratives and petitions, and speeches by W. E. B. Du Bois and Martin Luther King Jr. are categorized by century.

Make History. <http://www.bedfordstmartins.com/makehistory> Comprising the content of five online libraries—Map Central, the Bedford Image Library, DocLinks, HistoryLinks, and PlaceLinks—Make History provides access to relevant digital content including maps, documents, and Web links. Searchable by keyword, topic, date, or specific chapter of *The American Promise.*

NativeWeb. <http://www.nativeweb.org> One of the best organized and most accessible sites available on Native American issues, *NativeWeb* combines an events calendar and message board with history, statistics, a list of news sources, archives, new and updated related sites each week, and documents.

Perry-Castañeda Library Map Collection. <http://www.lib.utexas.edu/maps/> The University of Texas at Austin library has put over seven hundred United States maps on the Web along with hundreds of other maps from around the world. The collection includes both historical and contemporary maps.

Smithsonian Institution. <http://www.si.edu> Organized by subject, such as military history or Hispanic/Latino American resources, this site offers selected links to sites hosted by Smithsonian museums and organizations. Content includes graphics of museum pieces and relevant textual information, book suggestions, maps, and links.

Supreme Court Collection. <http://www.law.cornell.edu/supct/> This database can be used to search for information on various Supreme Court cases. Although the site primarily covers cases that occurred after 1990, there is information on some earlier historic cases. The justices' opinions, as originally written, are also included.

United States Holocaust Memorial Museum. <http://www.ushmm.org> This site contains information about the Holocaust Museum in Washington, D.C., in particular and the Holocaust in general, and it lists links to related sites.

Women's History Resources. <http://www.mcps.k12.md.us/curriculum/socialstd/Women_Bookmarks.html> An extensive listing of women's history sources available on the Internet. The site indexes resources on subjects as diverse as woman suffrage, women in the workplace, and celebrated women writers. Some of the links are to equally vast indexes, providing an overwhelming wealth of information.

WWW-VL History Index. <http://vlib.iue.it/history/> A vast list of more than 1,700 links to sites of interest to historians, arranged by general topic and by continent and country. The United States history page includes links to online research tools as well as links arranged by topic and historical period.

GLOSSARY OF HISTORICAL VOCABULARY

A Note to Students: This list of terms is provided to help you with historical and economic vocabulary. Many of these terms refer to broad, enduring concepts that you may encounter not only in further studies of history but also when following current events. The terms appear in bold at their first use in each chapter. In the glossary, the page numbers of those chapter-by-chapter appearances are provided so you can look up the terms' uses in various periods and contexts. For definitions and discussions of words not included here, consult a dictionary and the book's index, which will point you to topics covered at greater length in the book.

affirmative action Policies established in the 1960s and 1970s by governments, businesses, universities, and other institutions to overcome the effects of past discrimination against specific groups such as racial and ethnic minorities and women. Measures to ensure equal opportunity include setting goals for admission, hiring, and promotion; considering minority status when allocating resources; and actively encouraging victims of past discrimination to apply for jobs and other resources. (pp. 1023, 1108, 1146)

agribusiness Farming on a large scale, using the production, processing, and distribution methods of modern business. Farming became a big business, not just a way to feed a family and make a living, in the late nineteenth century as farms got larger and more mechanized. In the 1940s and 1950s, specialized commercial farms replaced many family-run operations and grew to an enormous scale. (pp. 619, 997)

alliance system The military and diplomatic system formulated in an effort to create a balance of power in pre–World War I Europe. Nations were bound together by rigid and comprehensive treaties that promised mutual aid in the case of attack by specific nations. The system swung into action after the Austrian archduke Franz Ferdinand was assassinated in Sarajevo on June 28, 1914, dragging most of Europe into war. (p. 791)

anarchist A person who rebels against established order and authority. An anarchist is someone who believes that government of any kind is unnecessary and undesirable and should be replaced with voluntary cooperation and free association. Anarchists became increasingly visible in the United States in the late nineteenth and early twentieth centuries. They advocated revolution and grew in numbers through appeals to discontented laborers. Anarchists frequently employed violence in an attempt to achieve their goals. In 1901, anarchist Leon Czolgosz assassinated President William McKinley. (pp. 683, 716, 756, 847)

antebellum A term that means "before a war" and commonly refers to the period prior to the Civil War. (p. 557)

artisan A term commonly used prior to 1900 to describe a skilled craftsman, such as a cabinetmaker. (p. 677)

Bill of Rights The commonly used term for the first ten amendments to the U.S. Constitution. The Bill of Rights (the last of which was ratified in 1791) guarantees individual liberties and defines limitations to federal power. Many states made the promise of the prompt addition of a bill of rights a precondition for their ratification of the Constitution. (pp. 674, 971, 1031)

black nationalism A term linked to several African American movements emphasizing racial pride, separation from whites and white institutions, and black autonomy. Black nationalism gained in popularity with the rise of Marcus Garvey and the Universal Negro Improvement Association (1917–1927) and later with the Black Panther Party, Malcolm X, and other participants of the black power movements of the 1960s. (pp. 840, 1038)

bloody shirt A refrain used by Republicans in the late nineteenth century to remind the voting public that the Democratic Party, dominated by the South, was largely responsible for the Civil War and that the Republican Party had led the victory to preserve the Union. Republicans urged their constituents to "vote the way you shot." (pp. 580, 648)

***bracero* program** A policy begun during World War II to help with wartime agriculture in which Mexican laborers (*braceros*) were permitted to enter the United States and work for a limited period of time but not to gain citizenship or permanent residence. The program officially ended in 1964. (p. 1000)

brinksmanship A cold war practice of appearing willing and able to resort to nuclear war in order to make an enemy back down. Secretary of State John Foster Dulles was the foremost proponent of this policy. (p. 989)

checks and balances A system in which the executive, legislative, and judicial branches of the government curb each other's power. Checks and balances were written into the U.S. Constitution during the Constitutional Convention of 1787. (p. 1109)

civil disobedience The public and peaceful violation of certain laws or government orders on the part of individuals or groups who act out of a profound conviction that the law or directive is unjust or immoral and who are prepared to accept the consequences of their actions. Civil disobedience was practiced most famously in U.S. history in the black freedom struggle of the 1960s. (pp. 779, 1011, 1033, 1079, 1122)

civil service The administrative service of a government. This term often applies to reforms following the passage of the Pendleton Act in 1883, which set qualifications for U.S. government jobs and sought to remove such jobs from political influence. (pp. 581, 653) *See also* spoils system.

closed shop An establishment in which every employee is required to join a union in order to obtain a job. (p. 828)

cold war The hostile and tense relationship that existed between the Soviet Union on the one hand and the United States and other Western nations on the other from 1947 to 1989. This war was said to be "cold" because the hostility stopped short of armed (hot) conflict, which was warded off by the strategy of nuclear deterrence. (pp. 948, 983, 1063, 1132, 1141) *See also* deterrence.

collective bargaining Negotiation by a group of workers (usually through a union) and their employer concerning rates of pay and working conditions. (pp. 802, 877, 968, 998)

collective security An association of independent nations that agree to accept and implement decisions made by the group, including going to war in defense of one or more members. The United States resolutely avoided such alliances until after World War II, when it created the North Atlantic Treaty Organization (NATO) in response to the threat posed by the Soviet Union. (pp. 810, 828, 957) *See also* North Atlantic Treaty Organization.

colonization The process by which a country or society gains control over another, primarily through settlement. (pp. 727, 789, 1054)

communism (Communist Party) A system of government and political organization, based on Marxist-Leninist ideals, in which a single authoritarian party controls the economy through state ownership of production, as a means toward reaching the final stage of Marxist theory in which the state dissolves and economic goods are distributed evenly for the common good. Communists around the globe encouraged the spread of communism in other nations in hopes of fomenting worldwide revolution. At its peak in the 1930s, the Communist Party of the United States worked closely with labor unions and insisted that only the overthrow of the capitalist system by its workers could save the victims of the Great Depression. After World War II, the Communist power and aspirations of the Soviet Union were held to be a direct threat to American democracy, prompting the cold war. (pp. 813, 857, 864, 909, 948, 983, 1026, 1063, 1101, 1141) *See also* cold war.

conscription Compulsory military service. Americans were first subject to conscription during the Civil War. The Selective Service Act of 1940 marked the first peacetime use of conscription. (pp. 670, 794) *See also* draft.

conservatism A political and moral outlook dating back to Alexander Hamilton's belief in a strong central government resting on a solid banking foundation. Currently associated with the Republican Party, conservatism today places a high premium on military preparedness, free market economics, low taxes, and strong sexual morality. (pp. 563, 641, 711, 760, 827, 866, 927, 975, 985, 1022, 1101, 1142)

consumer culture (consumerism) A society that places high value on, and devotes substantial resources to, the purchase and display of material goods. Elements of American consumerism were evident in the nineteenth century but really took hold in the twentieth century with installment buying and advertising in the 1920s and again with the postwar prosperity of the 1950s. (pp. 629, 682, 837, 984)

containment The U.S. foreign policy developed after World War II to hold in check the power and influence of the Soviet Union and other groups or nations espousing communism. The strategy was first fully articulated by diplomat George F. Kennan in 1946–1947. (pp. 948, 983, 1064, 1157)

cult of domesticity The nineteenth-century belief that women's place was in the home, where they should create a haven for harried men working in the outside world. This ideal was made possible by the separation of the workplace and the home and was used to sentimentalize the home and women's role in it. (pp. 688, 721) *See also* separate spheres.

culture A term used here to connote what is commonly called "way of life." It refers not only to how a group of people supplied themselves with food and shelter but also to their family relationships, social groupings, religious ideas, and other features of their lives. (pp. 592, 629, 791, 834, 867, 984, 1038, 1068, 1117, 1164)

de-industrialization A long period of decline in the industrial sector. The term often refers specifically to the decline of manufacturing and the growth of the service sector of the economy in post–World War II America. This shift and the loss of manufacturing resulting from it were caused by more efficient and automated production techniques at home, increased competition from foreign-made goods, and the use of cheap labor abroad by U.S. manufacturers. (p. 1125)

democracy A system of government in which the people have the power to rule, either directly or indirectly, through their elected representatives. Believing that direct democracy was dangerous, the framers of the Constitution created a government that gave direct voice to the people only in the House of Representatives and that placed a check on that voice in the Senate by offering unlimited six-year terms to senators, elected by the state legislatures to protect them from the whims of democratic majorities. The framers further curbed the perceived dangers of democracy by giving each of the three branches of government (legislative, executive, and judicial) the ability to check the power of the other two.

(pp. 570, 627, 686, 706, 756, 788, 867, 907, 949, 1067, 1117, 1151) *See also* checks and balances.

détente French for "loosening." The term refers to the easing of tensions between the United States and the Soviet Union during the Nixon administration. (pp. 1088, 1111)

deterrence The linchpin of U.S. military strategy during the cold war. The strategy of deterrence dictated that the United States would maintain a nuclear arsenal so substantial that the Soviet Union would refrain from attacking the United States and its allies out of fear that the United States would retaliate in devastating proportions. The Soviets pursued a similar strategy. (pp. 956, 1016)

disfranchisement The denial of suffrage to a group or individual through legal or other means. Beginning in 1890, southern progressives preached the disfranchisement of black voters as a "reform" of the electoral system. The most common means of eliminating black voters were poll taxes and literacy tests. (pp. 569, 779, 815, 889, 984, 1021)

domino theory The assumption underlying U.S. foreign policy from the early cold war until the end of the Vietnam War. The theory was that if one country fell to communism, neighboring countries also would fall under Communist control. (pp. 954, 989)

doves Peace advocates, particularly during the Vietnam War. (p. 1082)

draft (draftee) A system for selecting individuals for compulsory military service. A draftee is an individual selected through this process. (pp. 794, 918, 957, 1075, 1117) *See also* conscription.

emancipation The act of freeing from slavery or bondage. The emancipation of American slaves, a goal shared by slaves and abolitionists alike, occurred with the passage of the Thirteenth Amendment in 1865. (pp. 555, 815)

evangelicalism The trend in Protestant Christianity stressing salvation through conversion, repentance of sin, adherence to Scripture, and the importance of preaching over ritual. During the Second Great Awakening in the 1830s, evangelicals worshipped at camp meetings and religious revivals led by exuberant preachers. (pp. 652, 1111) *See also* Second Great Awakening.

fascism An authoritarian system of government characterized by dictatorial rule, disdain for international stability, and a conviction that warfare is the only means by which a nation can attain greatness. Nazi Germany and Mussolini's Italy are the prime examples of fascism. (pp. 867, 904)

federal budget deficit The situation resulting when the government spends more money than it takes in. (pp. 1120, 1146)

feminism The belief that men and women have the inherent right to equal social, political, and economic opportunities. The suffrage movement and second-wave feminism of the 1960s and 1970s were the most visible and successful manifestations of feminism, but feminist ideas were expressed in a variety of statements and movements as early as the late eighteenth century and continue to be expressed in the twenty-first. (pp. 572, 778, 836, 1002, 1022, 1101, 1146)

finance capitalism Refers to investment sponsored by banks and bankers and the profits garnered from the sale of financial assets such as stocks and bonds. The decades at the end of the twentieth century are known as a period of finance capitalism because banks and financiers increasingly took on the role of stabilizing markets and reorganizing industries. (p. 641)

flexible response Military strategy employed by the Kennedy and Johnson administrations designed to match a wide range of military threats by complementing nuclear weapons with the buildup of conventional and special forces and using them all in a gradual and calibrated way as needed. Flexible response was a departure from the strategy of massive retaliation used by the Eisenhower administration. (p. 1065)

franchise The right to vote. The franchise was gradually widened in the United States to include groups such as women and African Americans, who had no vote when the Constitution was ratified. (pp. 572, 720) *See also* suffrage.

free labor Work conducted free from constraint and in accordance with the laborer's personal inclinations and will. Prior to the Civil War, free labor became an ideal championed by Republicans (who were primarily Northerners) to articulate individuals' right to work how and where they wished and to accumulate property in their own name. The ideal of free labor lay at the heart of the North's argument that slavery should not be extended into the western territories. (p. 556)

free silver The late-nineteenth-century call by silver barons and poor American farmers for the widespread coinage of silver and for silver to be used as a base upon which to expand the paper money supply. The coinage of silver created a more inflationary monetary system that benefited debtors. (pp. 656, 711) *See also* gold standard.

frontier A borderland area. In U.S. history, this refers to the borderland between the areas primarily inhabited by Europeans or their descendants and the areas solely inhabited by Native Americans. (p. 593)

fundamentalism Strict adherence to core, often religious beliefs. The term has varying meanings for different religious groups. Protestant fundamentalists adhere to a literal interpretation of the Bible and thus deny the possibility of evolution. Muslim fundamentalists believe that traditional Islamic law should govern nations and that Western influences should be banned. (pp. 848, 1118, 1143)

gender gap An electoral phenomenon that became apparent in the 1980s when men and women began to display different preferences in voting. Women tended to favor liberal candidates, and men tended to support conservatives. The key voter groups contributing to the gender gap were single women and women who worked outside the home. (pp. 1128, 1155)

globalization The spread of political, cultural, and economic influences and connections among countries, businesses, and individuals around the world through trade, immigration, communication, and other means. In the late twentieth century, globalization was intensified by new communications technology that connected individuals, corporations, and nations with greater speed at low prices. This led to an increase in political and economic interdependence and mutual influence among nations. (pp. 1088, 1142)

gold standard A monetary system in which any circulating currency was exchangeable for a specific amount of gold. Advocates for the gold standard believed that gold alone should be used for coinage and that the total value of paper banknotes should never exceed the government's supply of gold. The triumph of gold standard supporter William McKinley in the 1896 presidential election was a big victory for supporters of this policy. (pp. 659, 707) *See also* free silver.

gospel of wealth The idea that wealth garnered from earthly success should be used for good works. Andrew Carnegie promoted this view in an 1889 essay in which he maintained that the wealthy should serve as stewards and act in the best interests of society as a whole. (pp. 645, 748)

Great Society President Lyndon Johnson's domestic program, which included civil rights legislation, antipoverty programs, government subsidy of medical care, federal aid to education, consumer protection, and aid to the arts and humanities. (pp. 1021, 1102, 1152)

guerrilla warfare Fighting carried out by an irregular military force usually organized into small, highly mobile groups. Guerrilla combat was common in the Vietnam War and during the American Revolution. Guerrilla warfare is often effective against opponents who have greater material resources. (pp. 574, 601, 733, 990, 1065, 1175)

hawks Advocates of aggressive military action or all-out war, particularly during the Vietnam War. (p. 1082)

holding company A system of business organization whereby competing companies are combined under one central administration in order to curb competition and ensure profit. Pioneered in the late 1880s by John D. Rockefeller, holding companies, such as Standard Oil, exercised monopoly control even as the government threatened to outlaw trusts as a violation of free trade. (p. 636) *See also* monopoly; trust.

horizontal integration A system in which a single person or corporation creates several subsidiary businesses to sell a product in different markets. John D. Rockefeller pioneered the use of horizontal integration in the 1880s to control the refining process, giving him a virtual monopoly on the oil-refining business. (p. 635) *See also* vertical integration; monopoly.

impeachment The process by which formal charges of wrongdoing are brought against a president, a governor, or a federal judge. (pp. 571, 1110, 1152)

imperialism The system by which great powers gain control of overseas territories. The United States became an imperialist power by gaining control of Puerto Rico, Guam, the Philippines, and Cuba as a result of the Spanish-American War. (pp. 582, 706, 790, 912, 958, 1054, 1160)

iron curtain A metaphor coined by Winston Churchill during his commencement address at Westminster College in Fulton, Missouri, in 1946, to refer to the political, ideological, and military barriers that separated Soviet-controlled Eastern Europe from the rest of Europe and the West following World War II. (pp. 951, 989, 1066, 1150)

isolationism A foreign policy perspective characterized by a desire to have the United States withdraw from the conflicts of the world and enjoy the protection of two vast oceans. (pp. 727, 810, 828, 905, 954)

Jim Crow The system of racial segregation that developed in the post–Civil War South and extended well into the twentieth century; it replaced slavery as the chief instrument of white supremacy. Jim Crow laws segregated African Americans in public facilities such as trains and streetcars and denied them basic civil rights, including the right to vote. It was also at this time that the doctrine of "separate but equal" became institutionalized. (pp. 578, 673, 779, 927)

Keynesian economics A theory developed by economist John Maynard Keynes that guided U.S. economic policy from the New Deal to the 1970s. According to Keynesians, the federal government has a duty to stimulate and manage the economy by spending money on public works projects and by making general tax cuts in order to put more money into the hands of ordinary people, thus creating demand. (p. 896)

laissez-faire The doctrine, based on economic theory, that government should not interfere in business or the economy. Laissez-faire ideas guided American government policy in the late nineteenth century and conservative politics in the twentieth century. Business interests that supported laissez-faire in the late nineteenth century accepted government interference when it took the form of tariffs or subsidies that worked to their benefit. A broader use of the term refers to the simple philosophy of abstaining from interference. (pp. 645, 706, 746, 850, 866, 1121, 1176)

land grant A gift of land from a government, usually intended to encourage settlement or development. The British government issued several land grants to encourage development in the American colonies. In the mid-nineteenth century, the U.S. government issued land grants to encourage railroad development and, through the passage of the Land-Grant College Act (also known as the Morrill Act) in 1862, set aside public land to support universities. (pp. 609, 629)

liberalism The political doctrine that government rests on the consent of the governed and is duty-bound to protect the freedom and property of the individual. In the twentieth century, liberalism became associated with the idea that government should regulate the economy and ensure the material well-being and individual rights of all people. (pp. 714, 746, 820, 867, 928, 965, 985, 1021, 1103, 1146)

liberty The condition of being free or enjoying freedom from control. This term also refers to the possession of certain social, political, or economic rights, such as the right to own and control property. Eighteenth-century American colonists invoked the principle to argue for strict limitations on government's ability to tax its subjects. (pp. 561, 791, 1172)

manifest destiny A term coined by journalist John O'Sullivan in 1845 to express the popular nineteenth-century belief that the United States was destined to expand westward to the Pacific Ocean and had an irrefutable right and God-given responsibility to do so. This idea provided an ideological shield for westward expansion and masked the economic and political motivations of many of those who championed it. (p. 727)

McCarthyism The practice of searching out suspected Communists and others outside mainstream American society, discrediting them, and hounding them from government and other employment. The term derives from Senator Joseph McCarthy, who gained notoriety for leading such repressive activities from 1950 to 1954. (p. 970)

military-industrial complex A term first used by President Dwight D. Eisenhower to refer to the aggregate power and influence of the armed forces in conjunction with the aerospace, munitions, and other industries that produced supplies for the military in the post–World War II era. (p. 995)

miscegenation The sexual mixing of races. In slave states, despite the social stigma and legal restrictions on interracial sex, masters' almost unlimited power over their female slaves meant that liaisons inevitably occurred. Many states maintained laws against miscegenation into the 1950s. (pp. 650, 840)

monopoly Exclusive control and domination by a single business entity over an entire industry through ownership, command of supply, or other means. Gilded Age businesses monopolized their industries quite profitably, often organizing holding companies and trusts to do so. (pp. 586, 618, 636, 706, 757, 880, 941, 1124) *See also* holding company; trust.

Monroe Doctrine President James Monroe's 1823 declaration that the Western Hemisphere was closed to any further colonization or interference by European powers. In exchange, Monroe pledged that the United States would not become involved in European struggles. Although Monroe could not back his policy with action, it was an important formulation of national goals. (pp. 727, 768, 789)

nationalism A strong feeling of devotion and loyalty toward one nation over others. Nationalism encourages the promotion of the nation's common culture, language, and customs. (pp. 788, 989)

nativism Bias against immigrants and in favor of native-born inhabitants. American nativists especially favor persons who come from white, Anglo-Saxon, Protestant lines over those from other racial, ethnic, and religious heritages. Nativists may include former immigrants who view new immigrants as incapable of assimilation. Many nativists, such as members of the Know-Nothing Party in the nineteenth century and the Ku Klux Klan through the contemporary period, voice anti-immigrant, anti-Catholic, and anti-Semitic sentiments. (pp. 611, 748, 845)

New Deal The group of social and economic programs that President Franklin Roosevelt developed to provide relief for the needy, speed economic recovery, and reform economic and government institutions. The New Deal was a massive effort to bring the United States out of the Great Depression and ensure its future prosperity. (pp. 711, 865, 905, 947, 984, 1023, 1120, 1154)

New Right Politically active religious conservatives who became particularly vocal in the 1980s. The New Right criticized feminism, opposed abortion and homosexuality, and promoted "family values" and military preparedness. (p. 1102)

New South A vision of the South, promoted after the Civil War by Henry Grady, editor of the *Atlanta Constitution*, that urged the South to abandon its dependence on agriculture and use its cheap labor and natural resources to compete with northern industry. Many Southerners migrated from farms to cities in the late nineteenth century, and Northerners and foreigners invested a significant amount of capital in railroads, cotton and textiles, mining, lumber, iron, steel, and tobacco in the region. (pp. 555, 649)

North Atlantic Treaty Organization (NATO) A post–World War II alliance that joined the United States, Canada, and Western European nations into a military coalition designed to counter the Soviet Union's efforts to expand. Each NATO member pledged to go to war if any member was attacked. Since the end of the cold war, NATO has been expanding to include the formerly Communist countries of Eastern Europe. (pp. 948, 1133, 1150)

oligopoly A competitive system in which several large corporations dominate an industry by dividing the market so each business has a share of it. More prevalent than outright monopolies during the late 1800s, the oligopolies of the Gilded Age successfully muted competition and benefited the corporations that participated in this type of arrangement. (pp. 606, 644)

planters Owners of large farms (or, more specifically, plantations) that were worked by twenty or more slaves. By 1860, planters had accrued a great deal of local, statewide, and national political power in the South despite the fact that they represented a minority of the white electorate. Planters' dominance of southern politics demonstrated both the power of tradition and stability among southern voters and the planters' success at convincing white voters that the slave system benefited all whites, even those without slaves. (pp. 557, 649)

plutocracy A society ruled by the richest members. The excesses of the Gilded Age and the fact that just 1 percent of the population owned more than half the real and personal property in the country led many to question whether the United States was indeed a plutocracy. (p. 677)

pogrom An organized and often officially encouraged massacre of an ethnic minority; usually used in reference to attacks on Jews. (p. 672)

Populism A political movement that led to the creation of the People's Party, primarily comprising southern and western farmers who railed against big business and advocated business and economic reforms, including government ownership of the railroads. The movement peaked in the late nineteenth century. The Populist ticket won more than 1 million votes in the presidential election of 1892 and 1.5 million in the congressional elections of 1894. The term *populism* has come to mean any political movement that advocates on behalf of the common person, particularly for government intervention against big business. (pp. 706, 754, 1176)

pragmatism A philosophical movement whose American proponents, William James and John Dewey, stated that there were no eternal truths and that the real worth of any idea lay in its consequences. Dewey tested his theories in the classroom, pioneering in American education the role of process over content and encouraging students to learn by doing. American pragmatists championed social experimentation, providing an important impetus for progressive reform in the early part of the twentieth century. (p. 754)

progressivism (progressive movement) A wide-ranging twentieth-century reform movement that advocated government activism to mitigate the problems created by urban industrialism. Progressivism reached its peak in 1912 with the creation of the Progressive Party, which ran Theodore Roosevelt for president. The term *progressivism* has come to mean any general effort advocating for social welfare programs. (pp. 677, 711, 746, 788, 825, 868, 1048, 1176)

Protestantism A powerful Christian reform movement that began in the sixteenth century with Martin Luther's critiques of the Roman Catholic Church. Over the centuries, Protestantism has taken many different forms, branching into numerous denominations with differing systems of worship. (pp. 648, 748, 845, 876, 1103)

reform Darwinism A social theory, based on Charles Darwin's theory of evolution, that emphasized activism, arguing that humans could speed up evolution by altering the environment. A challenge to social Darwinism, reform Darwinism condemned laissez-faire and demanded that the government take a more active approach to solving social problems. It became the ideological basis for progressive reform in the late nineteenth and early twentieth centuries. (p. 754) *See also* laissez-faire; social Darwinism.

scientific management A system of organizing work, developed by Frederick Winslow Taylor in the late nineteenth century, to increase efficiency and productivity by breaking tasks into their component parts and training workers to perform specific parts. Labor resisted this effort because it de-skilled workers and led to the speedup of production lines. Taylor's ideas were most popular at the height of the Progressive Era. (p. 754)

separate spheres A concept of gender relations that developed in the Jacksonian era and continued well into the twentieth century, holding that women's proper place was in the world of hearth and home (the private sphere) and men's was in the world of commerce and politics (the public sphere). The doctrine of separate spheres eroded slowly over the nineteenth and twentieth centuries as women became more and more involved in public activities. (pp. 650, 688, 837) *See also* cult of domesticity.

social Darwinism A social theory, based on Charles Darwin's theory of evolution, that argued that all progress in human society came as the result of competition and natural selection. Gilded Age proponents such as William Graham Sumner and Herbert Spencer claimed that reform was useless because the rich and poor were precisely where nature intended them to be and intervention would retard the progress of humanity. (pp. 644, 672, 722, 748) *See also* reform Darwinism.

social gospel movement A religious movement in the late nineteenth and early twentieth centuries founded on the idea that Christians have a responsibility to reform society as well as individuals. Social gospel adherents encouraged people to put Christ's teachings to work in their daily lives by actively promoting social justice. (pp. 747, 869)

socialism A governing system in which the state owns and operates the largest and most important parts of the economy. (pp. 686, 711, 750, 804, 857, 872, 928, 954, 1042)

social purity movement A movement to end prostitution and eradicate venereal disease, often accompanied by the censorship of materials deemed "obscene." (p. 747)

spoils system An arrangement in which party leaders reward party loyalists with government jobs. This slang term for *patronage* comes from the saying "To the victor go the spoils." Widespread government corruption during the Gilded Age spurred reformers to curb the spoils system through the passage of the Pendleton Act in 1883, which created the Civil Service Commission to award government jobs on the basis of merit. (pp. 581, 648) *See also* civil service.

states' rights A strict interpretation of the Constitution that holds that federal power over the states is limited and that the states hold ultimate sovereignty. First expressed in 1798 through the passage of the Virginia and

Kentucky Resolutions, which were based on the assumption that the states have the right to judge the constitutionality of federal laws, the states' rights philosophy became a cornerstone of the South's resistance to federal control of slavery. (pp. 562, 737, 1144)

strict constructionism An approach to constitutional law that attempts to adhere to the original intent of the writers of the Constitution. Strict construction often produces Supreme Court decisions that defer to the legislative branch and to the states and restrict the power of the federal government. Opponents of strict construction argue that the Constitution is an organic document that must be interpreted to meet conditions unimagined when it was written. (p. 1107)

suffrage The right to vote. The term *suffrage* is most often associated with the efforts of American women to secure voting rights. (pp. 556, 650, 705, 746, 788) *See also* franchise.

Sun Belt The southern and southwestern regions of the United States, which grew tremendously in industry, population, and influence after World War II. (pp. 984, 1103)

supply-side economics An economic theory based on the premise that tax cuts for the wealthy and for corporations encourage investment and production (supply), which in turn stimulate consumption. Embraced by the Reagan administration and other conservative Republicans, this theory reversed Keynesian economic policy, which assumes that the way to stimulate the economy is to create demand through federal spending on public works and general tax cuts that put more money into the hands of ordinary people. (pp. 1121, 1146) *See also* Keynesian economics.

temperance movement The reform movement to end drunkenness by urging people to abstain from the consumption of alcohol. Begun in the 1820s, this movement achieved its greatest political victory with the passage of a constitutional amendment in 1919 that prohibited the manufacture, sale, and transportation of alcohol. That amendment was repealed in 1933. (pp. 651, 720, 748)

third world Originally a cold war term linked to decolonization, *third world* was first used in the late 1950s to describe newly independent countries in Africa and Asia that were not aligned with either Communist nations (the second world) or non-Communist nations (the first world). Later, the term was applied to all poor, nonindustrialized countries, in Latin America as well as in Africa and Asia. Many international experts see *third world* as a problematic category when applied to such a large and disparate group of nations, and they criticize the discriminatory hierarchy suggested by the term. (pp. 958, 1054, 1102)

trickle-down economics The theory that financial benefits and incentives given to big businesses in the top tier of the economy will flow down to smaller businesses and individuals and thus benefit the entire nation. President Herbert Hoover unsuccessfully used the trickle-down strategy in his attempt to pull the nation out of the Great Depression, stimulating the economy through government investment in large economic enterprises and public works such as construction of the Hoover Dam. In the late twentieth century, conservatives used this economic theory to justify large tax cuts and other financial benefits for corporations and the wealthy. (pp. 853, 1126)

Truman Doctrine President Harry S. Truman's assertion that American security depended on stopping any Communist government from taking over any non-Communist government—even nondemocratic and repressive dictatorships—anywhere in the world. Beginning in 1947 with American aid to help Greece and Turkey stave off Communist pressures, this approach became a cornerstone of American foreign policy during the cold war. (p. 954)

trust A corporate system in which corporations give shares of their stock to trustees, who coordinate the industry to ensure profits to the participating corporations and curb competition. Pioneered by Standard Oil, such business practices were deemed unfair, were moderated by the Sherman Antitrust Act (1890), and were finally abolished by the combined efforts of Presidents Theodore Roosevelt and William Howard Taft and the sponsors of the 1914 Clayton Antitrust Act. The term *trust* is also loosely applied to all large business combinations. (pp. 635, 746, 886) *See also* holding company.

vertical integration A system in which a single person or corporation controls all processes of an industry from start to finished product. Andrew Carnegie first used vertical integration in the 1870s, controlling every aspect of steel production from the mining of iron ore to the manufacturing of the final product, thereby maximizing profits by eliminating the use of outside suppliers or services. (p. 633)

welfare capitalism The idea that a capitalistic, industrial society can operate benevolently to improve the lives of workers. The notion of welfare capitalism became popular in the 1920s as industries extended the benefits of scientific management to improve safety and sanitation in the workplace as well as institute paid vacations and pension plans. (p. 830) *See also* scientific management.

welfare state A nation or state in which the government assumes responsibility for some or all of the individual and social welfare of its citizens. Welfare states commonly provide education, health care, food programs for the poor, unemployment compensation, and other social benefits. The United States dramatically expanded its role as a welfare state with the provisions of the New Deal in the 1930s. (pp. 884, 985, 1024)

Yankee imperialism A cry raised in Latin American countries against the United States when it intervened militarily in the region without invitation or consent from those countries. (pp. 1065, 1147)

yeoman A farmer who owned a small plot of land that was sufficient to support a family and was tilled by family members and perhaps a few servants. (pp. 573, 620)

Spot Artifact Credits

p. 560 (Bible) Anacostia Museum, Smithsonian Institution, Washington, D.C.; p. 571 (ticket) Collection of Janice L. and David J. Frent; p. 579 (plow) Courtesy Deere & Company; p. 580 (election artifact) Collection of Janice L. and David J. Frent; p. 601 (decorative shirt) Image courtesy of National Park Service, Nez Percé National Historical Park. Catalogue #BIHO1256; p. 602 (moccasins) Photo Addison Doty, Santa Fe, NM; p. 604 (silver bar) The Oakland Museum; p. 613 (bucket) Kansas State Historical Society; p. 634 (lamp) Picture Research Consultants & Archives; p. 640 (telephone) Smithsonian Institution, Washington, D.C.; p. 649 (cigarettes) Courtesy of Duke Homestead and Tobacco Museum; p. 679 (sewing machine) National Museum of American History, Smithsonian Institution, Washington, D.C.; p. 683 (typewriter) National Museum of American History, Smithsonian Institution, Washington, D.C.; p. 690 (baseball, card, and glove) Smithsonian Institution, Washington, D.C.; p. 693 (faucet) Picture Research Consultants & Archives; p. 716 (dagger) Library & Archives Division, Historical Society of Western Pennsylvania; p. 718 (paycheck) Chicago Historical Society, Archives and Manuscript Department; p. 725 (button) Collection of Janice L. and David J. Frent; p. 729 (magazine cover) Granger Collection; p. 755 (token) The Western Reserve Historical Society, Cleveland, Ohio; p. 777 (IWW poster) Library of Congress; p. 779 (flag) National Museum of American History, Smithsonian Institution; p. 794 (machine gun) National Museum of American History, Smithsonian Institution, Behring Center; p. 801 ("Save Wheat" poster) Herbert Hoover Presidential Library; p. 804 (suffrage bird) Collection of Janice L. and David J. Frent; p. 811 (IWW poster) Picture Research Consultants & Archives; p. 830 (refrigerator) From the Collection of The Henry Ford; p. 841 (Hughes book) Picture Research Consultants & Archives; p. 844 (button) Private Collection; p. 845 (*This Side of Paradise*) Matthew J. & Arlyn Bruccoli Collection of F. Scott Fitzgerald, University of South Carolina; p. 856 (movie poster) Collection of Hershenson-Allen Archives; p. 866 (wheelchair) FDR Library/photo by Hudson Valley Photo Studio; p. 867 (1932 buttons) Collection of Janice L. and David J. Frent; p. 882 (*Grapes of Wrath*) Granger Collection; p. 885 (WPA poster) Picture Research Consultants & Archives; p. 909 (panzer) U.S. Army Ordnance Museum Foundation, Inc.; p. 911 (Good Neighbor button) Collection of Colonel Stuart S. Corning, Jr./Picture Research Consultants, Inc.; p. 926 (Double V button) Private Collection; p. 941 (atomic bomb) National Archives; p. 951 (Truman and Churchill button) Collection of Janice L. and David J. Frent; p. 964 (baseball card) The Michael Barson Collection/Past Perfect; p. 968 (banner) Dr. Hector P. Garcia Papers, Special Collections & Archives, Texas A & M University, Corpus Christi, Bell Library; p. 977 (Korean DMZ sign) Diana Walker/Time Life Pictures/Getty Images; p. 985 (sign) NEW Traffic Safety; p. 1004 (*The Feminine Mystique*) W. W. Norton & Company, Inc. N.Y.C. © 1963; p. 1007 (album cover) Chess Records; p. 1010 (NAACP button) Collection of Janice L. and David J. Frent; p. 1027 (food stamps) Getty Images; p. 1034 (pennant) Private Collection; p. 1040 (Indian resistance button) Collection of Janice L. and David J. Frent; p. 1043 (ticket) Picture Research Consultants & Archives; p. 1052 (magazine) Young Americans for Freedom; p. 1068 (beret) West Point Museum, United States Military Academy, West Point, N.Y.; p. 1078 (Vietnam button) Picture Research Consultants & Archives; p. 1080 (antiwar button) Collection of Janice L. and David J. Frent; p. 1103 (magazine) Young Americans for Freedom; p. 1115 (*Time* cover) Time Life Pictures/Getty Images; p. 1121 (bumper sticker) Courtesy, Christian Coalition; p. 1125 (Yuppie handbook) Book cover from *The Yuppies Handbook: The State-of-the-Art Manual for Young Urban Professionals* by Marissa Piesman and Marilee Hartley. Copyright © 1984 Marissa Piesman and Marilee Hartley; p. 1143 (poster) National Museum of American History, Smithsonian Institution, Behring Center; p. 1152 (logo) Americorps; p. 1166 (documents) Nolo.

A note about the index:

Names of individuals appear in boldface; biographical dates are included for major historical figures.

Letters in parentheses following pages refer to:
(i)   illustrations, including photographs and artifacts, as well as information in picture captions
(f)   figures, including charts and graphs
(m)   maps
(b)   boxed features (such as "Historical Question")
(t)   tables

Antitrust laws, 636, 657, 658, 757, 771, 773, 774, 1124(b)
Antwerp, Belgium, 934
Apartment living, 692–693
Apollo program, 1067(i)
Appel, Ruben, 866(i)
Apprenticeship laws, 562–563
Arab allies, cultivation of, 991, 994
Arab Feminist Union, 1054(b)
Arafat, Yasir, 1159
Arapaho tribe, 597, 603(i)
Arbenz, Jacobo, 990
Arbitration, 686, 718, 765(i), 768
Arctic National Wildlife Refuge (ANWR), 1116, 1169
Argentina, 669, 670(f)
Arikara Indians, 600
Aristide, Jean-Bertrand, 1157–1158
Arizona
  buffalo soldiers in, 609
  gold rush in, 603
  guerrilla warfare in, 601
  Mescalero Apache Agency in, 592
  reservation in, 601
  statehood for, 612(f)
  territorial government of, 608
Arizona (battleship), 914(i)
Arkansas
  Farmers' Alliance in, 708
  polio vaccine distribution in, 985(i)
  during Reconstruction, 585
  school desegregation in, 1010–1011, 1011(i)
  statehood for, 612(f)
Arlington, National Cemetery, 968
Armistice, 799
Armour, Philip, 637
Arms limitation agreement (1987), 1134(i)
Arms race, during cold war, 994–995, 995(i), 1016, 1064, 1066, 1068–1069, 1069(m), 1079(i), 1088, 1134(i), 1135
Armstrong, Louis, 841, 958(i)
Armstrong, Neil A. (1930–), 1067(i)
Army of the Republic of Vietnam (ARVN), 990, 1070(t), 1072, 1075, 1078, 1090. See also Vietnam War (1964–1975)
ARPANET, 1162(b)
Arrogance of Power, The (Fulbright), 1079
Art
  African American, 840(i), 841
  of 1950s, 1008–1009, 1009(i)
Arthur, Chester A. (1829–1886), 654
Artificial limbs, 566–567(b), 567(i)
Artificial satellites, 994
Artisans, in labor force, 677
Asia. See also specific countries
  communism in, 948
  Open Door policy in, 727, 729, 732–733, 732(i), 768–769
  restrictions on immigrants from, 846
  Taft administration policy on, 771
  trade with, 728(i)
Asian Americans
  income of, 1157
  New Deal and, 891
  progressivism and, 779
  in World War II, 918
Asian immigrants
  in agriculture, 619
  in California gold rush, 610, 673
  citizenship for, 611

  laws barring, 611, 619, 673, 818, 846–847, 970
  in mines, 606, 610
  railroads and, 610–611, 611(i), 673
Assassinations
  of James Garfield, 654
  of John F. Kennedy, 1021, 1025
  of Robert F. Kennedy, 1042(i), 1086
  of Martin Luther King Jr., 1037(i), 1039, 1084(b), 1086
  of Abraham Lincoln, 561
  of William McKinley, 654
Assembly lines, 825–826, 830
Assimilation, of Native Americans, 591–592, 592(i), 596, 599(b), 986–988
Aswan Dam, 991
Atchison, Topeka, and Santa Fe Railroad, 630(m)
Atlanta, Georgia, race riot in (1906), 781, 782
Atlanta Compromise, 780
Atlanta Constitution, 649
Atlantic and Pacific Railroad, 630(m)
Atlantic Charter (1941), 919(t)
Atlantic magazine, 838(b)
Atlantic Monthly, 638(b)
Atomic bomb, 1016
  deterrence and, 956–957, 1016
  invention of, 930(b), 931(b), 940–941
  Nazi anti-Semitism and, 930–931(b)
  Norden bombsight and, 902(i)
  Soviet Union and, 956, 994–995, 995(i)
  use of, in Japan, 903–904, 904(i), 940–942, 940(t), 941(i), 1076(b)
Auschwitz concentration camp, 929
Austin, Raymond, 796(b)
Australia, 921, 922, 935
Austria, 809, 908, 919(t)
Austria-Hungary, 791, 791(m), 809
Automobile industry
  in Detroit, 818, 825, 826, 829–830, 830(m), 842(b), 856, 887–888
  energy crisis and, 1114
  foreign-made cars and, 1125
  globalization and, 1164, 1164(b), 1165(b)
  growth of, 982(i)
  invention of automobile, 824(i), 825–826, 826(i)
  labor movement and, 856
  need for gas stations in, 831(i)
  technology in, 824(i), 825–826, 826(i), 997
  wages in, 834
"Axis of evil," 1173
Axis powers (World War II), 906, 908(m), 912, 913, 920(f), 936(b). See also Germany; Italy; Japan

Babbitt (Lewis), 845
"Baby boom," 1004, 1005(f), 1043, 1125
Baer, George, 758–759
Baghdad, Iraq, 1173
Baker, Ella, 1015, 1022(i), 1033, 1043
Baker, Newton D., 794
Baker v. Carr (1963), 1031
Bakke, Regents of the University of California v. (1978), 1108
Balch, Emily Greene, 804
Baldwin, Brent, 1159(i)
Baldwin, Mary, 802(i)
Balkans, 809
"Ballad of Pretty Boy Floyd, The," 856
Baltimore and Ohio (B&O) Railroad, 683

Bandana, campaign souvenir, 744(i)
Bank(s) and banking
  consolidation and, 641, 644–647
  failure of, 872, 872(i), 873(f)
  during Great Depression, 854
  law on, 774, 872–873, 880(t)
  reforms involving, 774, 872–873
  Tammany Bank, 695(i)
Bank holiday, 872
Banks, Dennis, 1040
Baptist and Commoner, 849
Barboncito (Navajo leader), 594
Barcelona, Spain, 667
Barr, Elizabeth, 709
Barry, Leonora, 685–686
Baruch, Bernard, 801
Baseball, 690, 828(i), 841(f), 844, 964, 1011
Bataan, Battle of (1942), 940(t)
Bataan Death March, 921
Batista, Fulgencio, 906, 990–991
Battle(s). See War(s); *names of specific battles*
Bavaria, 816(b)
Baxter Street courtyard (New York City), 763(i)
Bay of Pigs (Cuba), 1065, 1066(m), 1069
Bayonet Constitution (Hawaii), 730(b)
"Bayonet rule," 583, 585
Beals, Melba Patillo, 1010
Beat generation, 1007–1008, 1043
Beaufort, South Carolina, 556(i)
Beer garden, German, 690
Begin, Menachem, 1117
Beijing (Peking), China, 729, 1151
Beirut, Lebanon, 1132(i), 1133
Belgium, 753(b), 909, 919(t), 934, 940(t)
Bell, Alexander Graham (1847–1922), 640
Belleau Wood, France, 799
"Belonging," importance of, 1007
"Bends," 665, 666
Bentley, Elizabeth, 970
Benton, Thomas Hart (1889–1975), 885(i)
Berger, Victor, 814
Berlin, Germany
  crisis in, 956, 956(i), 1066
  division of, 955–956, 955(m), 956(i), 1065–1066
  end of cold war in, 1149(i), 1150
  industry in, 667
  Treaty of (1899), 733
  in World War II, 935, 940(t)
Berlin airlift, 956, 956(i)
Berlin Wall, 1066, 1149(i), 1150
Berliner, Emile, 698(b)
Berry, Chuck, 1007
Berryman, Clifford, 758(i)
Bessemer, Henry (1813–1898), 633
Bessemer process, 633
Bethel, New York, 1043
Bethlehem Steel, 644, 813
Bethune, Mary McLeod (1875–1955), 890, 890(i)
"Big stick" policy (T. Roosevelt), 765, 765(i), 768–769, 789
Bill of Rights
  federal, 674(b), 971, 1031
  GI, 927–928, 964, 966–967, 967(i)
"Billion Dollar Congress," 657
bin Laden, Osama, 1159, 1171–1172, 1175
Biological weapons, 1173
Birmingham, Alabama, 649, 1034

Birth control, 777–778, 777(i), 837, 838(b), 1043, 1046–1047(b), 1047(i)
Birth of a Nation (film), 847
Birthrate, post–World War II, 1004, 1005(f)
Bisno, Abraham, 674–675(b), 675(i)
Bison, 596–597, 596(i), 600, 704(i)
Black(s). *See* African Americans (blacks); Freedmen
Black Awareness Research Institute, 1043
"Black Cabinet," 890
Black codes, 562–564, 563(i)
Black Elk (Oglala holy man), 600
Black freedom struggle, 1032–1039, 1032(i), 1033(i), 1033(m), 1035(i), 1036(m), 1037(m), 1038(i), 1039(i)
"Black gold," 634. *See also* Oil industry
Black Hills, conflict over, 597, 600
Black Kettle (Cheyenne leader), 595
Black Muslims, 1038, 1038(i)
Black nationalism, 840, 1038–1039
Black Panther Party, 1038, 1085(b)
Black power, 1037–1039, 1037(m)
Black Star Line, 840
Black Thursday (1929), 852
Black Tuesday (1929), 852, 852(i)
Blackouts, 914
Blaine, James G. (1830–1893), 626(i), 653, 655–656, 657, 729, 730(b)
Blair, Francis P., 583(i)
Blitzkrieg, 909, 909(i), 919(t), 931(b)
"Bloody shirt, waving the," 580, 585, 648, 657
"Bloody Sunday" (1965), 1034
Blytheville, Arkansas, 985(i)
Board of Indian Commissioners, 592
Boarding schools, 591
Boats and ships
  aircraft carriers, 912–913
  battleships, 912–913, 914(i)
  Great White Fleet, 769
  Lusitania, sinking of, 792, 792(i), 792(m), 793
  Maine, sinking of, 734, 734(i), 736–737(b), 737(i)
  steamships, 670, 675(b), 793
  submarines. *See* Submarines
  Sussex (British steamer), sinking of, 793
  U-boats. *See* Submarines
Boers, 598–599(b)
Bogotá, 768
Bolivia, 1068(i), 1084(b)
Bolshevism, 813–814, 814(i), 815, 816–817(b)
Bomb(s). *See also* Atomic bomb; Hydrogen bomb
  hydrogen, 956
  in Vietnam War, 1070–1078, 1077(i), 1093
  in World War II, 902(i), 903–904, 910, 910(i), 919(t), 921–922, 929–931, 935, 936(b), 1076(b)
Bomb shelters, 994
Bombers, 903–904, 904(i), 910, 921–922, 929–931, 935, 936(b), 941
Bond, James, 957(i)
Bonfield, John "Blackjack," 687
Bonus Army (1932), 863–864, 864(i)
Bootblacks, 679, 680(i)
Booth, John Wilkes, 561
Bootlegging, 835–836, 836(i)
Borah, William (1865–1940), 810, 816(b)
Bork, Robert, 1110, 1127
Bosch, Juan, 1074, 1074(i)

Bosnia, 791, 1158
Bosque Redondo Reservation (New Mexico), 594
Bossism, 694–697, 695(i), 746, 757
Boston (American ship), 731(b)
Boston, Massachusetts
  immigrants in, 671
  police strike of 1919 in, 812
  school busing in, 1106, 1107(i)
  subways in, 693, 694
Boston Public Library, 633, 634, 634(i), 694
Bow, Clara, 844
Bowles, Chester, 1071
Boxer uprising (China), 728–729
Boxing, 844
Boycotts, 686, 718, 719, 1041. *See also* Bus boycott
Boyer, LaNada, 1040
Bracero program, 1000–1002, 1002(i)
Bradley, Omar (1893–1991), 975
Brains Trust, 869, 872, 894
Brandeis, Louis (1856–1941), 753(b), 775
Bray, Rosemary, 1028
Breaker boys, 759(i)
Bremer, L. Paul, 1174
Brest-Litovsk Treaty (1918), 798
Briand, Aristide, 829
Bridges, 664(i), 665–666, 666(i), 691–692, 697
Briggs, Laura, 949
Brinksmanship, 989
Britain. *See* Great Britain
Britain, Battle of (1940), 910, 911, 919(t), 940(t)
British Bomber Command, 910(i)
British Guiana, 729
British immigrants, 669, 670(f), 671(f)
Brody, Galicia, 675(b)
Brooke, Edward, 1056(i)
Brooklyn, New York, birth control clinic in, 777(i)
Brooks, Gwendolyn, 965
Brooks, John Graham, 752(b)
Brotherhood of Sleeping Car Porters, 927
Brown, Edmund, 1103
Brown, Harold, 642(b)
Brown, Minnijean, 1011(i)
Brown, Oliver, 1010
Brown v. Board of Education (1954), 968, 1010–1011, 1011(i), 1012–1013(b), 1029, 1057
Browner, Ken, 767(b)
Brownsville, New York, birth control clinic in, 777(i)
Brunauer, Esther, 971
Bryan, William Jennings (1860–1925)
  as political candidate, 725–726, 725(i), 738–739, 760, 769
  in Scopes trial, 848–849
  in Wilson administration, 789, 792, 793
Bryce, James, 695
Buchanan, Pat, 1056
Buckley, William F., Jr., 1121
Buckley v. Valeo (1976), 1111
"Buckwheats," 668
Buffalo, New York, 714, 756
Buffalo banner, 704(i)
Buffalo hunting, 596–597, 596(i), 600
Buffalo Telegraph, 655
Bulge, Battle of the (1944–1945), 934–935, 940(t)
Bull Hill, Colorado, 716

Bull Moose Party, 772, 773, 773(i), 775
"Bully pulpit," 757, 757(i)
Bunche, Ralph J., 964–965
Bundy, McGeorge, 1072, 1080
Bunker, Ellsworth, 1082(i)
Bureau of Refugees, Freedmen, and Abandoned Lands, 557
Burger, Warren E., 1107–1108
Burleson, Albert, 805
Burlington Mills (North Carolina), 878(b), 879(b)
Burnham, Daniel, 696(i), 697
Bus boycott, 1011, 1014–1015, 1014(i), 1015(i), 1032
Bush, George H. W. (1924–)
  background of, 1143
  conservatism of, 1143, 1144
  economic sanctions against South Africa and, 1157
  in election of 1988, 1143
  in election of 1992, 1151–1152
  foreign policy of, 1143, 1147–1151, 1147(i), 1148(m), 1149(i), 1150(m)
  Gulf War and, 1143, 1147–1149, 1148(m), 1175
  on new world order, 1157
  pardons for Iran-Contra scandal and, 1134
  presidency of, 1134, 1135(i), 1142, 1143–1152
  treaty with Soviet Union signed by, 1135(i)
  as vice president, 1102, 1120
Bush, George W. (1946–), 993(b), 1075, 1141
  on "axis of evil," 1173
  background of, 1167–1168
  conservatism and, 1168–1171
  domestic policies of, 1168–1171
  on education, 1169–1170
  in election of 2000, 1167–1168, 1167(i), 1168(m)
  in election of 2004, 1174–1175
  on environment, 1169
  fiscal policies of, 1168–1169
  foreign policy of, 1171–1175
  Iraq War and, 1173–1175, 1174(i)
  preemption strategy of, 1173
  presidency of, 993(b), 1075, 1141, 1142, 1142(i), 1167–1175
  Supreme Court and, 1167
  on terrorism, 1171–1172
  on trade barriers, 1160
  on unilateralism, 1173
Business. *See also* Corporations; Industrialism; Industries
  closed shops in, 828
  collusion with government, 761
  government and, 827–828
  holding companies in, 636, 658
  horizontal integration in, 635–636
  vertical integration in, 633–634, 637
Busing, 1106–1107, 1107(i)
Busts, economic, 628. *See also* Depression; Great Depression (1930s)
Butler, Nicholas Murray, 804
Byington, Margaret, 689
Byrnes, James F., 951

Cable cars, 693
Cadillac, 982(i)
Cady, Elizabeth. *See* Stanton, Elizabeth Cady

Mining
  Asian immigrants in, 606, 610
  children in, 759(i)
  "cooling-off rooms" in, 606, 607(i)
  dangers of, 606–607
  hydraulic, 604–605(b), 605(i)
  of iron, 633
  in Pennsylvania, 633
  placer, 604(b)
  of silver, 606, 606(m)
  strikes in, 714, 716–717, 758–760,
    759(i), 857, 968(i)
  in West, 597, 603–611, 605(i), 606(m),
    607(i)
Minneapolis, 1130(b)
Minnesota
  migrant farmworkers in, 891(i)
  Native Americans in, 595
  statehood for, 612(f)
Minow, Newton, 1006
Miranda v. Arizona (1966), 1031
Miscegenation (amalgamation), 650, 840
Miss America beauty pageant, 1051
Missiles
  antiballistic (ABMs), 1088, 1133, 1173
  in Cuban missile crisis, 1064, 1065,
    1068–1069, 1069(m)
  intercontinental ballistic missiles
    (ICBMs), 994, 995, 1068–1069,
    1069(m)
  strategic arms limitation treaty on,
    1117, 1135
Missionaries
  in China, 728–729, 728(i)
  in Hawaii, 730(b)
  at turn of twentieth century, 728–729,
    728(i)
  women, 728(i), 729, 730(b)
Mississippi
  activism in, 1021–1023, 1022(i), 1091
  African American opposition to
    Vietnam War in, 1083(i)
  discrimination against African
    Americans in, 562, 780, 1032(i),
    1033, 1034
  during Reconstruction, 562, 564, 577,
    584, 585
  during second Reconstruction, 1032(i),
    1033, 1034, 1038
  segregation in, 780
Mississippi Freedom Democratic Party
  (MFDP), 1022(i), 1038
Mississippi Freedom Summer Project,
  1034
Mississippi River, 592, 593
Missouri
  agriculture in, 881(i)
  People's (Populist) Party conventions
    in (1892 and 1896), 705–706, 706(i),
    710, 715, 722, 724, 725–726
  statehood for, 612(f)
Mitchell, George (Native American
  leader), 1040
Mizocz, Ukraine, 929(i)
Mobilization
  during Berlin crisis, 1066
  of Israeli troops, 959(i)
  for World War I, 792(i), 794, 795(i), 800,
    801
  for World War II, 914–921, 915(i),
    915(m), 918(i), 919(i), 919(t), 942
Model Cities Act (1965), 1026, 1030(t)
Model T Ford, 824(i), 825, 826(i)

Mohammed, Shanaz, 1172, 1173
Mondale, Walter F. (1928–), 1111, 1125
Money
  emergency, 872(i)
  gold standard for, 658(i), 659–660, 707,
    724, 725, 1056
  "In God We Trust" on, 1005
  paper, 659, 711
  silver, 658–659, 658(i)
"Money trust," 641, 774
Mongella, Gertrude, 1055
Monongahela River, 633, 689, 714
Monopoly
  atomic bomb and, 941, 942, 956
  curbing, 704(i), 706, 757
  on land, 618–619
  New Deal and, 880
  in oil industry, 636
  political, 586
  in telegraph industry, 629(i), 711
Monroe, Alabama, 572–573
Monroe, James (1758–1831), foreign
  policy of, 729. *See also* Monroe
  Doctrine (1823)
Monroe, Marilyn, 925(i)
Monroe Doctrine (1823), 727, 729,
  732–733, 732(i), 765(i), 768, 789
Montana
  buffalo soldiers in, 609(i)
  gold rush in, 603
  statehood for, 612(f)
  territorial government of, 608
Montevideo, Uruguay, 905
Montgomery, Alabama, 965(i)
  bus boycott in, 1011, 1014–1015,
    1014(i), 1015(i), 1032
  Freedom Riders in, 1033, 1034
  voting rights march to, 1034, 1035(i)
Montgomery (Alabama) Improvement
  Association (MIA), 1015
Moody, Anne, 1032(i)
Moon landing, 1067(i)
Moore, Alice, 1104–1105(b), 1105(i)
Moore, Paul, 1130(b)
Moral Majority, 1121
Morgan, J. P. (1837–1913), 644(i)
  in financial industry, 659, 758, 761,
    774
  industrialism and, 628, 660
  Roosevelt (T.) and, 758, 771
  in steel industry, 641, 644, 645(i)
  wealth of, 642(b), 645
Morgan, J. P., Jr., 852
Mormon(s), 610, 1128
Morocco, 768, 923
Morrow, E. Frederick, 1011
Morse, Samuel F. B. (1791–1872), 630
Mortgages, 998
Morton, Jelly Roll, 841
Moscow, Russia, 983, 984, 984(i), 1015,
  1088, 1150–1151
Mosher, Clelia Duel, 838–839(b)
Mossadegh, Mohammed, 991, 991(i),
  1117
Motion picture camera, 640
Mount Zion Baptist Church (San
  Antonio, Texas), 561(i)
Movies, 805(i), 839(i), 841, 841(f), 844,
  856
Ms.: The New Magazine for Women, 1052,
  1052(i)
Muckraking, 760
Mugwumps, 653–654, 655

Muir, John (1838–1914), 764, 766–767(b),
  767(i)
Muller v. Oregon (1908), 750–751, 753(b)
Mumford, Lewis, 999
Muncie, Indiana, 830
Munich agreement (1938), 909, 1070
Municipal government, 693–697, 695(i),
  696(i), 700
Munn v. Illinois (1877), 657
Murray, Pauli, 1051
Music
  African American, 837, 841, 844, 957,
    958(i), 1007
  during cold war, 957
  folk, 1043
  jazz, 837, 841, 844, 957, 958(i)
  during protest movement (1960s),
    1020(i), 1043
  rock and roll, 1007, 1008(i), 1043
Muslims
  in Afghanistan, 1117, 1118
  Beirut bombing by, 1132(i)
  Beirut bombings and, 1132(i), 1133
  Black, 1038, 1038(i)
  in Eastern Europe, 1158–1159, 1159(i)
  feminist, 1054(b)
  Reagan administration and, 1133
  terrorist acts of, 1143, 1171–1172,
    1171(i)
Mussolini, Benito (1883–1945), 877, 905
  aggression of, 908, 908(m)
  on war, 906
  in World War II, 919(t), 923
Mutual Security Act, 992(b)
Mutually assured destruction (MAD),
  989
My Lai massacre, 1092, 1094
Myer, Dillon S., 986
Myrick, Sue, 1169

NAACP (National Association for the
    Advancement of Colored People)
  antilynching law and, 651(i), 840
  black protest and, 1011
  Boston schools and, 1106
  on civil rights of African Americans,
    964, 968, 1010, 1011, 1012(b), 1014,
    1015
  founding of, 651(i), 782
  on racial violence, 842(b), 927
  on Supreme Court nominee Clarence
    Thomas, 1146
Nader, Ralph, 1028
Nagasaki, Japan, 904, 940(t), 941
Nagenda, John, 1161
Nanking, China, 907, 919(t)
NASA (National Aeronautics and Space
    Administration), 994
Nasser, Gamal Abdel, 991, 994
Nast, Thomas, 581(i), 695
Nathan, Maud, 753(b)
National American Woman Suffrage
    Association (NAWSA), 722,
    778–779, 803, 806(b), 807(b)
National Arts and Humanities Act (1965),
    1028, 1030(t)
National Association of Colored Women
    (NACW), 651, 651(i)
National Association of Manufacturers,
    880, 888
National Black Feminist Organization, 1052
National Coalition of Labor Union
    Women, 1052

ATLAS OF THE TERRITORIAL GROWTH OF THE UNITED STATES

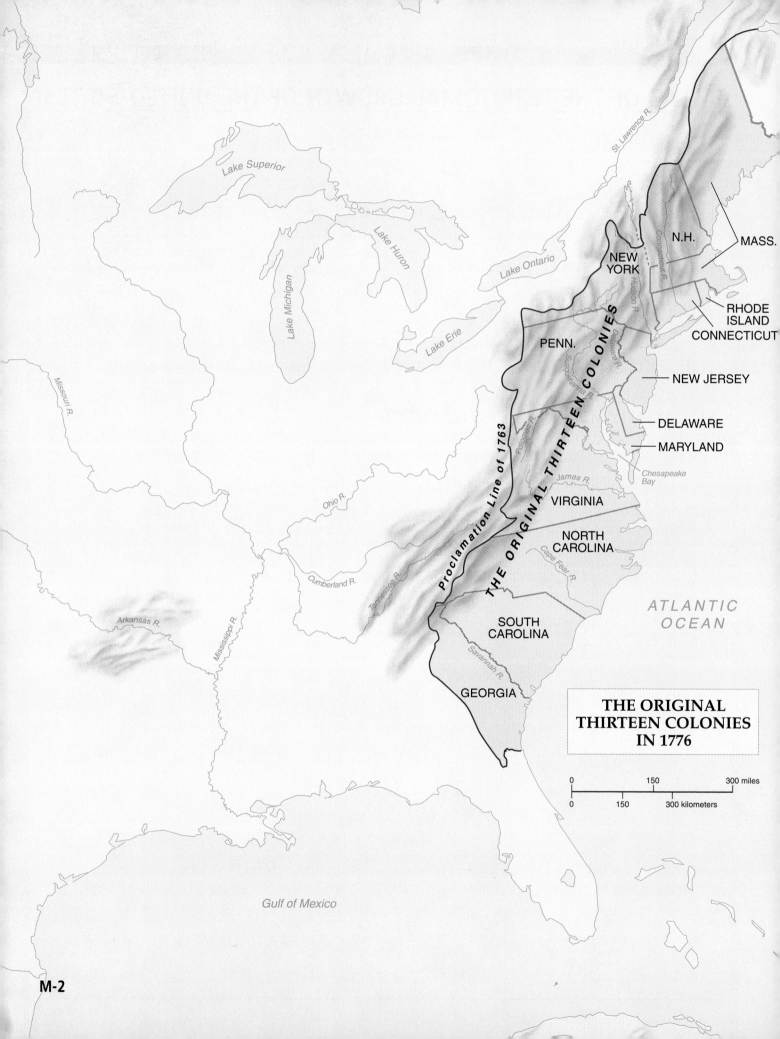

Lake Superior

Lake Huron

Lake Michigan

Lake Ontario

Lake Erie

St. Lawrence R.

Missouri R.

Ohio R.

Cumberland R.

Tennessee R.

Mississippi R.

Arkansas R.

Proclamation Line of 1763

THE ORIGINAL THIRTEEN COLONIES

NEW YORK

PENN.

N.H.

MASS.

RHODE ISLAND

CONNECTICUT

NEW JERSEY

DELAWARE

MARYLAND

Connecticut R.

Hudson R.

Delaware R.

Susquehanna R.

Potomac R.

James R.

Chesapeake Bay

VIRGINIA

NORTH CAROLINA

Cape Fear R.

SOUTH CAROLINA

Savannah R.

GEORGIA

ATLANTIC OCEAN

Gulf of Mexico

THE ORIGINAL THIRTEEN COLONIES IN 1776

0   150   300 miles

0   150   300 kilometers

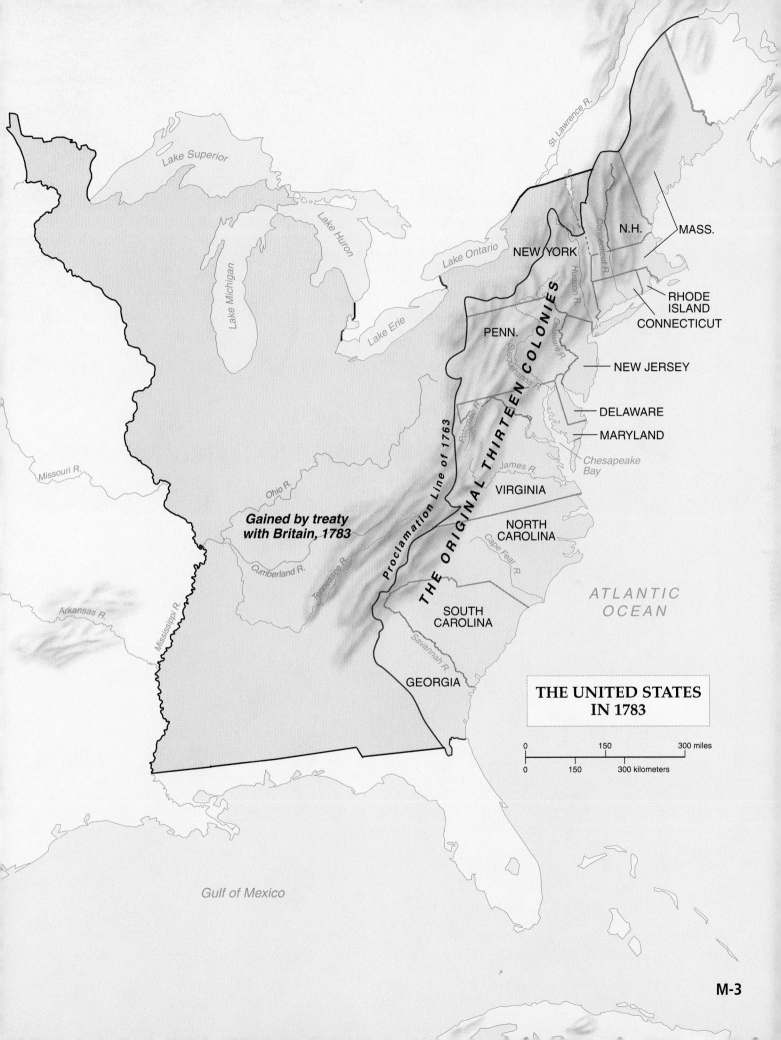

Lake Superior

Lake Michigan

Lake Huron

Lake Ontario

Lake Erie

St. Lawrence R.

Missouri R.

Arkansas R.

Mississippi R.

Ohio R.

Cumberland R.

Tennessee R.

**Gained by treaty
with Britain, 1783**

Proclamation Line of 1763

THE ORIGINAL THIRTEEN COLONIES

N.H.

MASS.

NEW YORK

Hudson R.

Connecticut R.

RHODE
ISLAND

CONNECTICUT

PENN.

Susquehanna R.

Delaware R.

NEW JERSEY

DELAWARE

MARYLAND

Potomac R.

James R.

Chesapeake
Bay

VIRGINIA

NORTH
CAROLINA

Cape Fear R.

SOUTH
CAROLINA

Savannah R.

GEORGIA

ATLANTIC
OCEAN

Gulf of Mexico

| THE UNITED STATES IN 1783 |

0   150   300 miles

0   150   300 kilometers

M-3

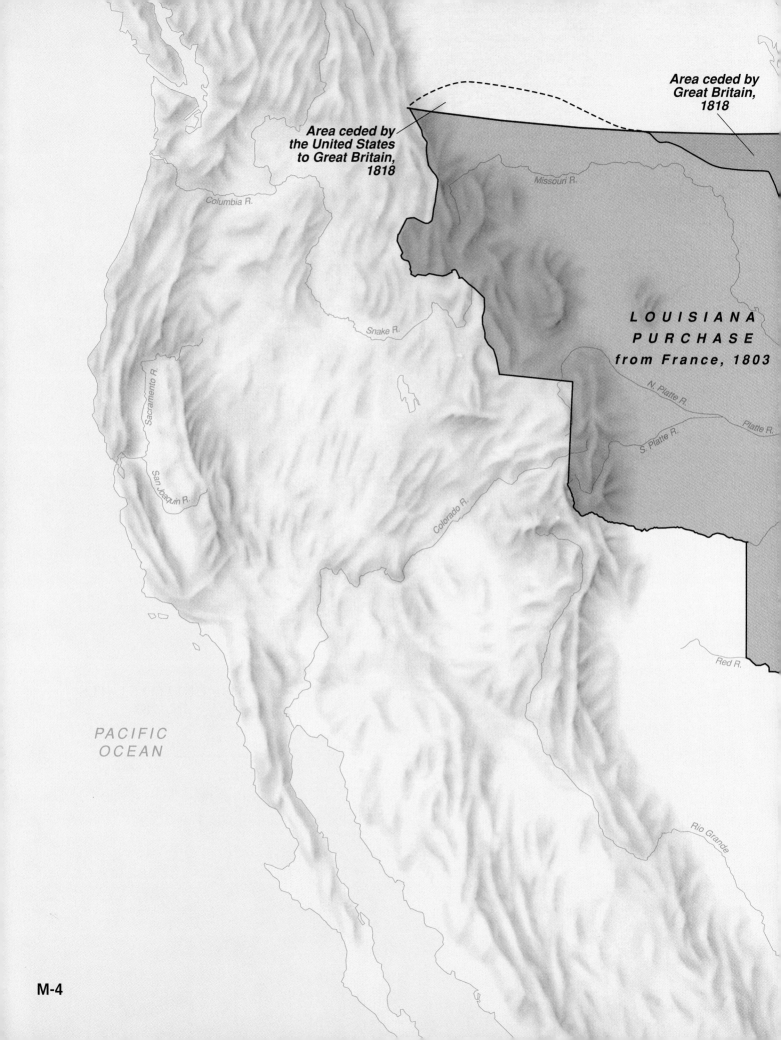

Area ceded by
Great Britain,
1818

Area ceded by
the United States
to Great Britain,
1818

Columbia R.

Missouri R.

Snake R.

LOUISIANA
PURCHASE
from France, 1803

N. Platte R.

Platte R.

S. Platte R.

Sacramento R.

San Joaquin R.

Colorado R.

Red R.

PACIFIC
OCEAN

Rio Grande

M-4

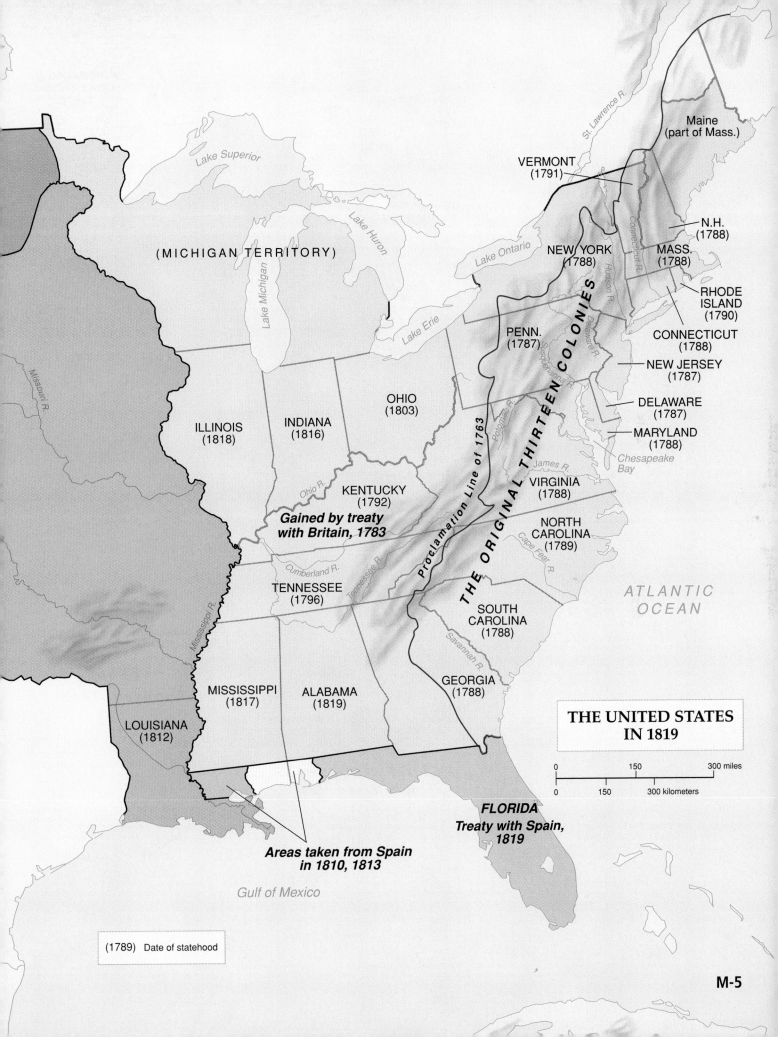

Maine
(part of Mass.)

VERMONT
(1791)

(MICHIGAN TERRITORY)

Lake Superior

Lake Michigan

Lake Huron

Lake Ontario

Lake Erie

St. Lawrence R.

Connecticut R.

NEW YORK
(1788)

N.H.
(1788)

MASS.
(1788)

Hudson R.

RHODE
ISLAND
(1790)

PENN.
(1787)

CONNECTICUT
(1788)

Delaware R.

NEW JERSEY
(1787)

Susquehanna R.

DELAWARE
(1787)

OHIO
(1803)

MARYLAND
(1788)

Potomac R.

Chesapeake
Bay

ILLINOIS
(1818)

INDIANA
(1816)

James R.

VIRGINIA
(1788)

Missouri R.

KENTUCKY
(1792)

Ohio R.

**Gained by treaty
with Britain, 1783**

Proclamation Line of 1763

THE ORIGINAL THIRTEEN COLONIES

NORTH
CAROLINA
(1789)

Cape Fear R.

Cumberland R.

Mississippi R.

TENNESSEE
(1796)

Tennessee R.

SOUTH
CAROLINA
(1788)

ATLANTIC
OCEAN

MISSISSIPPI
(1817)

ALABAMA
(1819)

GEORGIA
(1788)

Savannah R.

LOUISIANA
(1812)

**THE UNITED STATES
IN 1819**

| 0 | 150 | 300 miles |
| 0 | 150 | 300 kilometers |

**Areas taken from Spain
in 1810, 1813**

FLORIDA
**Treaty with Spain,
1819**

Gulf of Mexico

(1789)   Date of statehood

M-5

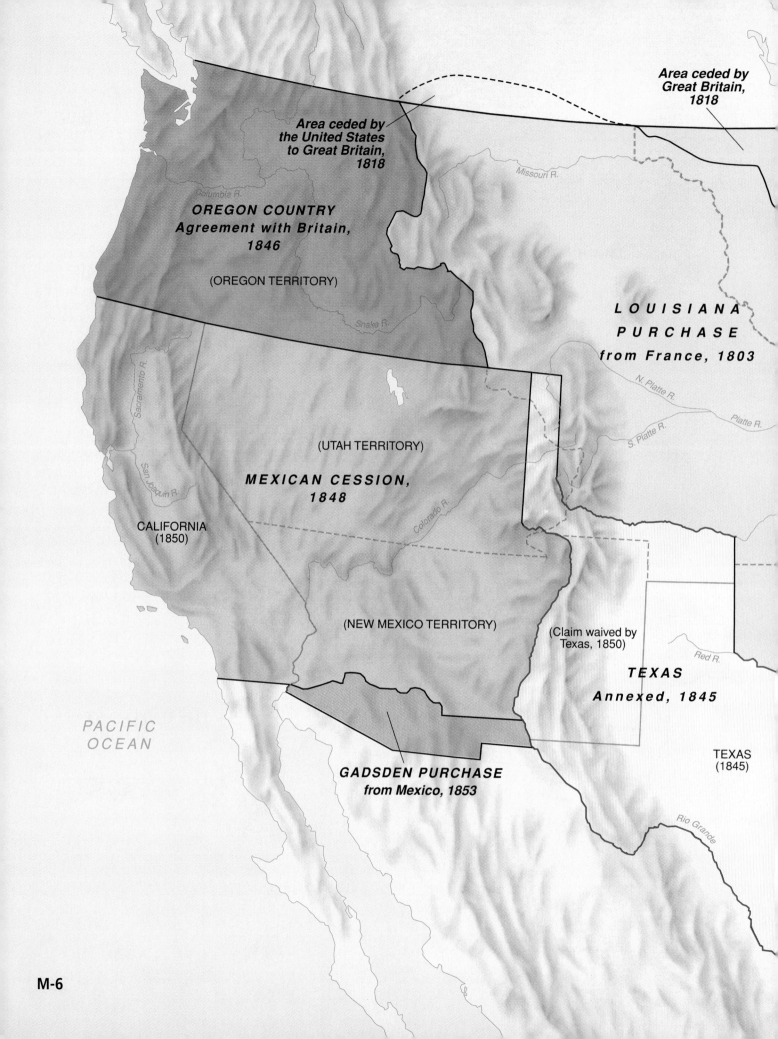

Area ceded by
Great Britain,
1818

Area ceded by
the United States
to Great Britain,
1818

Columbia R.

Missouri R.

OREGON COUNTRY
Agreement with Britain,
1846

(OREGON TERRITORY)

Snake R.

L O U I S I A N A
P U R C H A S E
from France, 1803

N. Platte R.

S. Platte R.

Platte R.

Sacramento R.

(UTAH TERRITORY)

MEXICAN CESSION,
1848

CALIFORNIA
(1850)

San Joaquin R.

Colorado R.

(NEW MEXICO TERRITORY)

(Claim waived by
Texas, 1850)

Red R.

TEXAS
Annexed, 1845

TEXAS
(1845)

PACIFIC
OCEAN

GADSDEN PURCHASE
from Mexico, 1853

Rio Grande

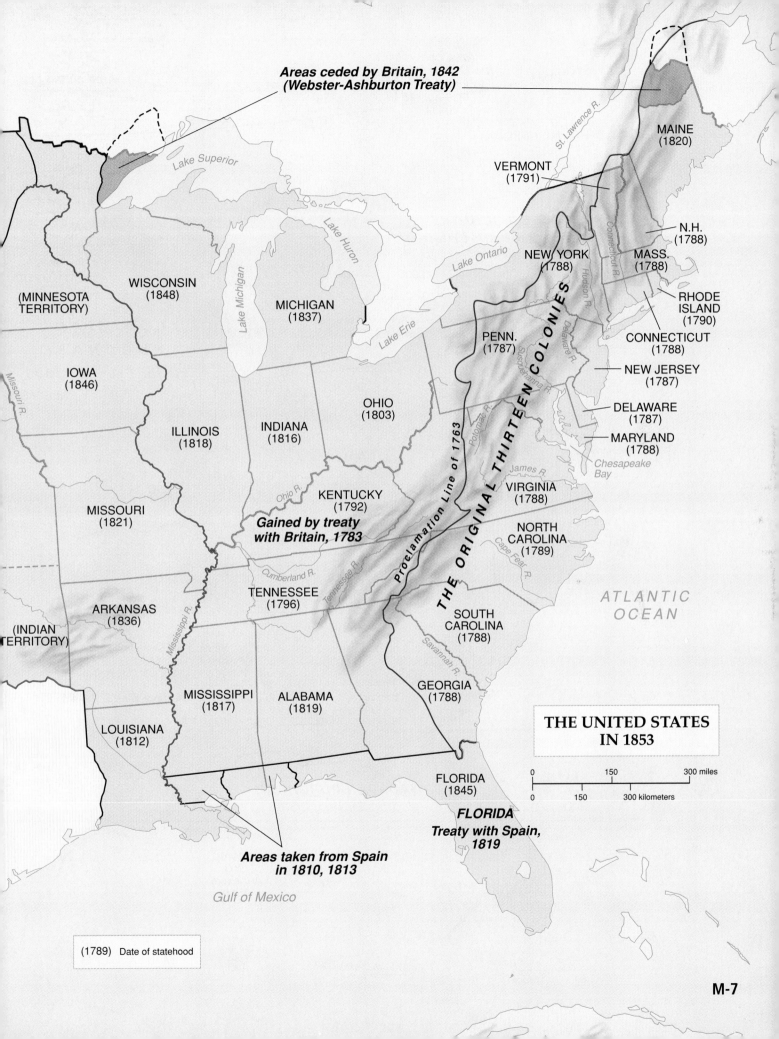

Areas ceded by Britain, 1842
(Webster-Ashburton Treaty)

MAINE
(1820)

VERMONT
(1791)

St. Lawrence R.

Lake Superior

N.H.
(1788)

NEW YORK
(1788)

MASS.
(1788)

Connecticut R.

RHODE
ISLAND
(1790)

CONNECTICUT
(1788)

Lake Ontario

Hudson R.

(MINNESOTA
TERRITORY)

WISCONSIN
(1848)

MICHIGAN
(1837)

Lake Huron

Lake Michigan

Lake Erie

PENN.
(1787)

Susquehanna R.

Delaware R.

NEW JERSEY
(1787)

DELAWARE
(1787)

MARYLAND
(1788)

Chesapeake
Bay

IOWA
(1846)

Missouri R.

OHIO
(1803)

ILLINOIS
(1818)

INDIANA
(1816)

Potomac R.

Proclamation Line of 1763

THE ORIGINAL THIRTEEN COLONIES

James R.

VIRGINIA
(1788)

KENTUCKY
(1792)

Ohio R.

Gained by treaty
with Britain, 1783

MISSOURI
(1821)

NORTH
CAROLINA
(1789)

Cape Fear R.

Cumberland R.

TENNESSEE
(1796)

Tennessee R.

ARKANSAS
(1836)

SOUTH
CAROLINA
(1788)

Savannah R.

(INDIAN
TERRITORY)

ATLANTIC
OCEAN

MISSISSIPPI
(1817)

ALABAMA
(1819)

GEORGIA
(1788)

Mississippi R.

LOUISIANA
(1812)

THE UNITED STATES
IN 1853

0   150   300 miles

0   150   300 kilometers

FLORIDA
(1845)

Areas taken from Spain
in 1810, 1813

FLORIDA
Treaty with Spain,
1819

Gulf of Mexico

(1789)   Date of statehood

M-7

Area ceded by
the United States
to Great Britain,
1818

Area ceded by
Great Britain,
1818

★ Olympia   WASHINGTON
(1889)

Missouri R.

NORTH DAKOTA
(1889)

Bismarck ★

Columbia R.

★ Salem   OREGON COUNTRY
Agreement with Britain,
1846

OREGON
(1859)

IDAHO
(1890)

★ Boise

★ Helena   MONTANA
(1889)

Snake R.

SOUTH DAKOTA
(1889)

Pierre ★

WYOMING
(1890)

LOUISIANA
PURCHASE
from France, 1803

N. Platte R.

NEBRASKA
(1867)

Sacramento R.

★ Salt Lake
City

Cheyenne ★

S. Platte R.

Platte R.

★ Carson City

NEVADA
(1864)

★ Sacramento

UTAH
(1896)

★ Denver

MEXICAN CESSION
1848

San Joaquin R.

Colorado R.

COLORADO
(1876)

KANSAS
(1861)

CALIFORNIA
(1850)

PACIFIC
OCEAN

ARIZONA
(1912)

★ Phoenix

★ Santa Fe

NEW
MEXICO
(1912)

TEXAS
Annexed, 1845

Red R.

GADSDEN PURCHASE
from Mexico, 1853

TEXAS
(1845)

Rio Grande

ARCTIC OCEAN

RUSSIA

ALASKA
(1959)
**Purchased from
Russia, 1867**

CANADA

Yukon R.

Bering
Sea

Gulf of
Alaska

Juneau ★

HAWAII
(1959)
*Annexed,
1898*

★ Honolulu

PACIFIC
OCEAN

0   250   500 miles

0   250   500 kilometers

0   50   100 miles

0   50   100 kilometers

MEXICO

M-8

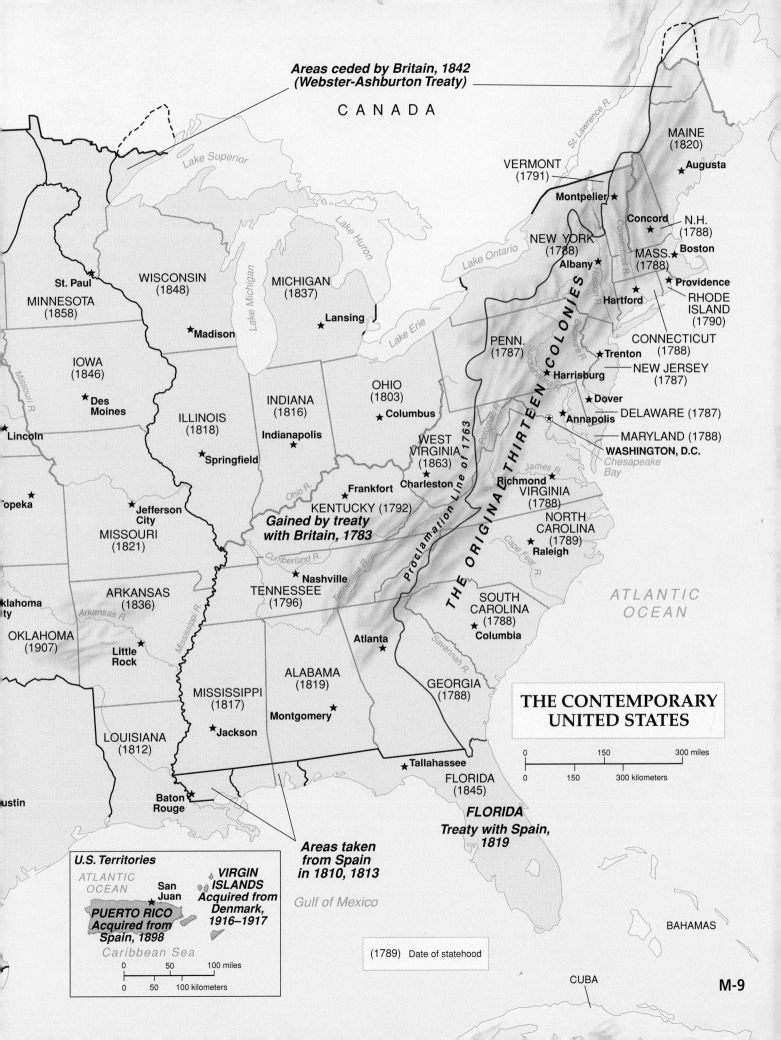

Areas ceded by Britain, 1842
(Webster-Ashburton Treaty)

CANADA

Lake Superior

Lake Huron

Lake Michigan

Lake Ontario

Lake Erie

St. Lawrence R.

MAINE
(1820)

★ Augusta

VERMONT
(1791)

Montpelier ★

Concord
★

N.H.
(1788)

NEW YORK
(1788)

Albany ★

MASS.
(1788)

★ Boston

Hudson R.

Connecticut R.

Hartford
★

★ Providence

RHODE
ISLAND
(1790)

MINNESOTA
(1858)

St. Paul ★

WISCONSIN
(1848)

MICHIGAN
(1837)

Lansing ★

IOWA
(1846)

★ Madison

★ Des
Moines

Missouri R.

ILLINOIS
(1818)

INDIANA
(1816)

OHIO
(1803)

Columbus ★

PENN.
(1787)

Delaware R.

★ Trenton

Harrisburg ★

CONNECTICUT
(1788)

NEW JERSEY
(1787)

★ Dover

DELAWARE (1787)

Lincoln ★

Indianapolis ★

Ohio R.

WEST
VIRGINIA
(1863)

Potomac R.

⊛ Annapolis

Annapolis

MARYLAND (1788)

WASHINGTON, D.C.

*Chesapeake
Bay*

★ Springfield

Frankfort ★

Charleston ★

Richmond ★

James R.

VIRGINIA
(1788)

Topeka ★

Jefferson
City ★

MISSOURI
(1821)

KENTUCKY (1792)

Cumberland R.

**Gained by treaty
with Britain, 1783**

Proclamation Line of 1763

THE ORIGINAL THIRTEEN COLONIES

NORTH
CAROLINA
(1789)

★ Raleigh

Cape Fear R.

ATLANTIC
OCEAN

klahoma
ty

OKLAHOMA
(1907)

Arkansas R.

ARKANSAS
(1836)

★ Little
Rock

TENNESSEE
(1796)

★ Nashville

Tennessee R.

Atlanta ★

SOUTH
CAROLINA
(1788)

Columbia ★

Savannah R.

Mississippi R.

MISSISSIPPI
(1817)

ALABAMA
(1819)

Montgomery ★

GEORGIA
(1788)

**THE CONTEMPORARY
UNITED STATES**

0   150   300 miles

0   150   300 kilometers

ustin

LOUISIANA
(1812)

★ Jackson

Baton
Rouge ★

**Areas taken
from Spain
in 1810, 1813**

★ Tallahassee

FLORIDA
(1845)

FLORIDA
**Treaty with Spain,
1819**

Gulf of Mexico

BAHAMAS

U.S. Territories

*ATLANTIC
OCEAN*

San
Juan ★

PUERTO RICO
**Acquired from
Spain, 1898**

♪ **VIRGIN
ISLANDS**
**Acquired
from
Denmark,
1916–1917**

Caribbean Sea

0   50   100 miles

0   50   100 kilometers

(1789)   Date of statehood

CUBA

M-9

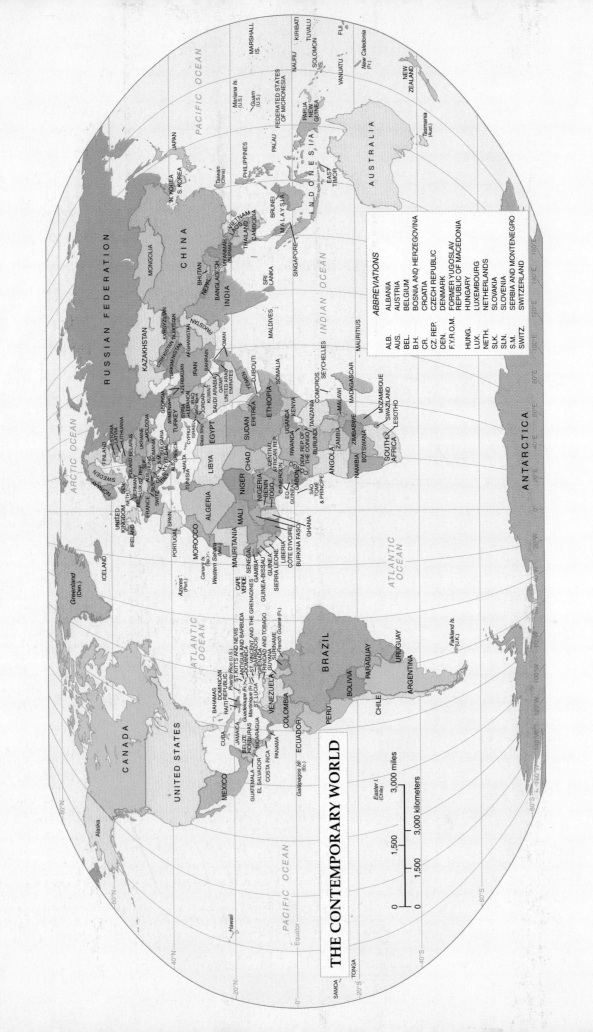

THE CONTEMPORARY WORLD